CASES AND MATERIALS
ON
INTERNATIONAL LAW

SEVENTH EDITION

By

DAVID HARRIS, LL.M., PH.D., C.M.G.
Emeritus Professor in Residence and Co-Director
Human Rights Law Centre, University of Nottingham

SWEET & MAXWELL

THOMSON REUTERS

First Edition (1973)
Second Impression (1976)
Second Edition (1979)
Third Edition (1983)
Second Impression (1986)
Third Impression (1987)
Fourth Impression (1989)
Fifth Impression (1990)
Fourth Edition (1991)
Second Impression (1992)
Third Impression (1993)
Fourth Impression (1995)
Fifth Impression (1996)
Fifth Edition (1998)
Sixth Edition (2004)
Seventh Edition (2010)

Published in 2010 by Thomson Reuters (Legal) Limited
(Registered in England & Wales, Company No 1679046.
Registered office and address for service: 100 Avenue Road, London, NW3 3PF)
trading as Sweet & Maxwell.

Typeset by YHT Ltd, London
Printed and bound in Great Britain by Ashford Colour Printers

For further information on our products and services, visit:
www.sweetandmaxwell.co.uk

ISBN 9781847032782

No natural forests were destroyed to make this product,
only naturally farmed timber was used and re-planted

British Library Cataloguing in Publication Data
A CIP catalogue record for this book
is available from the British Library

ACKNOWLEDGEMENTS

Grateful acknowledgement is made to the following authors and publishers for permission to quote from their works:

"A More Secure World: Our Shared Responsibility", Report of the Secretary General's High Level Panel on Threats, Challenges and Change (2004). Reprinted by permission of the United Nations.

"Nato Intervention in Kosovo", Security Council, 3988th Meeting. UN Doc S/PV.3988. March, 24 1999. Reprinted by permission of the United Nations.

A/RES/ES-10/15. Reprinted by permission of the United Nations.

Acheson, Dean, "Remarks" (1963) 57 A.S.I.L. Proc. 14. Reprinted with permission of the American Society of International Law.

American Journal of International Law 72(1978). Reprinted with permission of the American Society of International Law.

Aumeeruddy-Cziffra v Mauritius (the *Mauritian Women* case) (1981) 1 Selected Decisions H.R.C. 67. Reprinted by permission of the United Nations.

Barrett and Sutcliffe v Jamaica HRC Report, G.A.O.R., 47th Sess., Supp.40. Reprinted by permission of the United Nations.

Bleier v Uraguay (1982) 1 Selected Decisions H.R.C. 109 at 112. Reprinted by permission of the United Nations.

Boyle, Kevin, *New Institutions for Human Rights Protection* (2009) pp.12–46. Reprinted by permission of Oxford University Press.

Brierly, J. L.: *The Law of Nations: An Introduction to the International Law of Peace* (6th edn 1963). Reprinted by permission of Oxford University Press.

Broeks v Netherlands Human Rights Committee (1987) 2 Selected Decisions H.R.C. 196. Reprinted by permission of the United Nations.

Brownlie, Ian and Bowett, Derek: *British Yearbook of International law* (1981) cols 277–279/1121–1122 and cols 1097–1098. Reprinted by permission of Oxford University Press.

Brownlie, Ian and Bowett, Derek, *British Yearbook of International law* (1986) pp.27–28. Reprinted by permission of Oxford University Press.

Brownlie, Ian and Bowett, Derek, *British Yearbook of International law* (1991) p.559. Reprinted by permission of Oxford University Press.

Brownlie, Ian and Bowett, Derek: *British Yearbook of International law* (1992) pp.85, 92. Reprinted by permission of Oxford University Press.

Brownlie, Ian: *International Law and the use of force by states* (1991). Reprinted by permission of Oxford University Press.

Caglar v Billingham [1996] S.T.C. 150 at 171. Reproduced by permission of permission of Reed Elsevier (UK) Limited, trading as LexisNexis.

Carballal v Uruguay (1981) 1 Selected Decisions H.R.C. 63 at 64–65. Reprinted by permission of the United Nations.

Cassese, Antonio: *International Law* (2nd edn 2005) pp.165–166. Reprinted by permission of Oxford University Press.

Charter of the United Nations (3rd edn 1969), p.49. Reprinted by permission of the United Nations.

Craven, Matthew "The European Community Arbitration Commission on Yugoslavia", *British Yearbook of International Law* (1996). pp.370–371. Reprinted by permission on Oxford University Press.

Crawford, James: *The Creation of States in International Law* (1979) p.118. Reprinted by permission of Oxford University Press.

Danning v Netherlands (1987) 2 Selected Decisions H.R.C. 205. Reprinted by permission of the United Nations.

De Becker case (1958–59) 2 Y.B.E.C.H.R. 214. Reprinted by permission of Koninklijke BRILL NV.

Declaration on the Granting of Independence to Colonial Territories and Peoples 75 G.A. Resolution 1514 (XV). December 14, 1960. G.A.O.R. 15th Sess., Supp. 16, p.66. Reprinted by permission of the United Nations.

Estrella v Uruguay Human Rights Committee. (1983) 2 Selected Decisions H.R.C. 93. Reprinted by permission of the United Nations.

Evans, Malcolm: *International Law* (2nd edn 2006) pp.602–604. Reprinted by permission of Oxford University Press.

Fillastre and Bizouarn v Bolivia HRC Report, G.A.O.R., 48th Sess., Supp.40, (1992) p.294. Reprinted by permission of the United Nations.

Fitzmaurice, Gerald "Some Problems Regarding the Formal Sources of International Law", *Symbolae Verzijl* (1958) p.153. Reprinted by permission of Koninklijke BRILL NV.

Fitzmaurice, Gerald "The General Principles of International Law Considered from the Standpoint of the Rule of Law", *Recueil des Cours*, Collected Courses, Volume 92 (1957-II). Reprinted by permission of Koninklijke BRILL NV.

Fitzmaurice, Gerald: "The Foundations of the Authority of International law and the Problem of Enforcement", *Modern Law Review* (1956). Reprinted by permission of Wiley-Blackwell.

Fitzmaurice, Gerald: "The Law and Procedure of the International Court of Justice: Treaty Interpretation and Certain Other Treaty Points" (1951) 28 B.Y.I.L. 1. Reprinted by permission of Chatham House (The Royal Institute of International Affairs).

Galloway, L. Thomas: *Recognizing foreign governments: the practice of the United States* (1978). Reprinted by permission of the American Enterprise Institute.

General Assembly Declaration on Principles of International Law concerning Friendly Relations and Co-operation among States in accordance with the Charter of the United Nations 1970. Reprinted by permission of the United Nations.

Gray, Christine: *International Law and the Use of Force* (2nd edn 2004) pp.722–726. Reprinted by permission of Oxford University Press.

Gross, Leo: *Future of the International Court of Justice* (1972) pp.61–64. Reprinted by permission of Oxford University Press.

Guerrero v Colombia (1982) 1 Selected Decisions H.R.C. 112. Reprinted by permission of the United Nations.

Guiding Principles Applicable to Unilateral Declarations of States Capable of Creating Legal Obligations 2006, UN Doc.A/61/10 p.367. Reprinted by permission of the United Nations.

Henkin, Louis: *How Nations Behave* (1979), pp.121–127. Reproduced with permission of Colombia University Press.

Higgins, Rosalyn, "Respecting Sovereign States and running a tight Courtroom" from *International Comparative Law Quarterly* 121 at 122–123 (2001). Reprinted by permission of Cambridge University Press.

Higgins, Rosalyn, *Problems and Process: International Law and How We Use It* (1995) pp.96–97. Reprinted by permission of Oxford University Press.

Iron Rhine Railway Arbitration, 2005. Reprinted by permission of Permanent Court of Arbitration.

Jennings, Robert and Watts, Arthur: *Oppenheim's International Law* (9th edn 1992), Vol.I. Reprinted by permission of Oxford University Press.

Jessup, Philip C., *A Modern Law of Nations* (1948) pp.6–8. Reprinted with the permission of Scribner, a Division of Simon & Schuster, Inc., from A MODERN LAW OF NATIONS by Philip C. Jessup. Copyright © 1946, 1947, 1948 by Macmillan Publishing Company; copyright renewed © 1973, 1974, 1975 by Philip C. Jessup. All rights reserved.

Higgins, Rosalyn, "The Anglo Norwegian Fishing Case" from *International Comparative Law Quarterly* 145 (1952). Reprinted by permission of Cambridge University Press.

Johnson, D. H. N.: "The Anglo Norwegian Fishing Case" from *International Comparative Law Quarterly* 145 (1952). Reprinted by permission of Cambridge University Press.

Kuwait v American Independent Oil Co (1982) International Legal Materials. Reprinted by permission of the American Society of International Law.

Lantsova v Russian Federation CCPR/C/74/D/763/1997. Reprinted by permission of the United Nations.

Lauterpacht, Hersch: "Survey Of International Law In Relation To The Work Of Codification Of The International Law Commission", Memorandum prepared for the UN Secretariat, UN Doc.A/CN.4/1/ Rev.1 (February 10, 1949) pp.19–20. Reprinted by permission of the United Nations.

Mbenge v Zaire (1983) 2 Selected Decisions H.R.C. 76 at 79. Reprinted by permission of the United Nations.

McGoldrick, Dominic: *From 9–11 to the Iraq War 2003: International Law in an Age of Complexity*. Reprinted by permission of Hart Publishing Ltd.

McMahon, J.F.: "Legal Aspects of Outer Space" (1962) 38 B.Y.I.L. 339. Reprinted by permission of Chatham House (The Royal Institute of International Affairs).

McNair, A. D.: "The Functions and Differing Legal Character of Treaties" (1930) 11 B.Y.I.L. 100. Reprinted by permission of Chatham House (The Royal Institute of International Affairs).

Mcrae, Donald: "The Legal Effect of Interpretive Declarations", *British Yearbook of International Law* Vol.49 (1979) pp.172–173. Reprinted by permission of Oxford University Press.

Meeker, L.: "Defensive Quarantine and the Law" from *American Journal of International Law* (1963). Reprinted by permission of the American Society of International Law.

Meron, Theodor: *Human Rights and Humanitarian Norms as Customary Law* (1989) pp.95–98. Reprinted by permission of Oxford University Press.

Minister of Health v Treatment Action Campaign (2002) Butterworths' Human Rights Cases 1. Reproduced by permission of Reed Elsevier (UK) Limited, trading as LexisNexis.

Morgenthau, Hans J.: *Politics Among nations* (6th edn 1985), pp.312–313. Reprinted by permission of McGraw-Hill.

Pratt and Morgan v Jamaica HRC Report, G.A.O.R., 44th Sess., Supp.40, p.222 at 230 (1989). Reprinted by permission of the United Nations.

Report of the Study Group on the International Court of Justice established by the British Institute of International and Comparative Law, *International Comparative Law Quarterly* (1996) pp.24–25. Published by permission of Cambridge University Press.

Restatement (Third) Foreign Relations Law of the United States, copyright 1987 by The American Law Institute. Reprinted with permission. All rights reserved.

Rosenne, Shabtai: *The Law and Practice of the International Court, 1920–2005* (2006). Reprinted by permission of Koninklijke BRILL NV.

Rosenstock, Robert, "The ILC and State Responsibility" from *American Journal of International Law* (2002). Reprinted by permission of the American Society of International Law.

Security Council, S/PV.3988, p.4, March 26, 1999. Reprinted by permission of the United Nations.

Shirer, William L.: *The Rise and Fall of the Third Reich* (N.Y.: Simon and Schuster, Inc., 1959).

Sieghart, Paul: *Lawful Rights of Mankind* (1986) p.151. Reprinted with permission of Oxford University Press.

Sierra Leone Telecommunications Co Ltd v Barclays Bank Plc, [1998] All. E.R. 821, QB. Reproduced by permission of permission of Reed Elsevier (UK) Limited, trading as LexisNexis.

Silva v Uruguay Human Rights Committee. (1981) 1 Selected Decisions H.R.C. 65. Reprinted by permission of the United Nations.

Simma, Bruno: *Charter of the United Nations* (2nd edn 2002) Vol.1, pp.722–726. Reprinted by permission of Oxford University Press.

Sloan, Blaine, *United Nations General Assembly Resolutions in our Changing World* (1991) pp.71–75. Reprinted by permission of Koninklijke BRILL NV.

Sztucki, Jerzy: "Reflections on International Soft Law", *Festskrift till Lars Hjerner* (1961). Reprinted by permission of Norstedts Juridik.

The Entebbe Incident UN Doc. S/PV. 1939, pp.27, 51–59, 92 and UN Doc. S/PV.

Thürer, Daniel: 'The "failed State" and International Law', in: *International Review of the Red Cross*, No. 836, 1999, pp.731-761. Reprinted by permission of International Committee of the Red Cross.

UN Doc. CCPR/CO/70/GAB. Reprinted by permission of the United Nations.

UN Doc. S/PV. 3245. Reprinted by permission of the United Nations.

UN Doc. 5/PV 2360, p.38. Reprinted by permission of the United Nations.

UN Doc. S/1466; S.C.O.R., 5th Year, Supp. for Jan/May 1950, p.19. Reprinted by permission of the United Nations.

UN Doc. ST/LEG/SER./A/105, November 1955, Prefatory Note. Reprinted by permission of the United Nations.

United Kingdom Declaration accepting the Compulsory Jurisdiction of the Court. Reprinted by permission of the United Nations.

Universal Declaration of Human Rights 1948 G.A. Resolution 217A (III), G.A.O.R., 3rd Sess., Part I, p.71. Reprinted by permission of the United Nations.

van Hoof, G. J. H.: *Rethinking the Sources of International Law* (1983), pp.187–189. Reprinted by permission of Kluwer Publishing.

Vienna Convention on the Law of Treaties (1969). Reprinted by permission of the United Nations.

Vuolanne v Finland HRC Report, G.A.O.R., 44th Sess., Supp.40, p.249 (1989). Reprinted by permission of the United Nations.

Waldock, "General Course on Public International Law" (1962), *Recueil des Cours*, Collected Courses, Volume 106 (1962-II). Reprinted by permission of Koninklijke BRILL NV.

Wolfke, Karol: *Custom in Present International Law* (1993). Reprinted by permission of Koninklijke BRILL NV.

Y.B.I.L.C., 1966, II. Reprinted by permission of the United Nations.

PREFACE TO THE SEVENTH EDITION

There have been many important developments in international law since the last edition of this casebook. The credit for many of these goes to the International Court of Justice. The Court's *Wall* advisory opinion is notable for its further clarification of the inter-relationship of international humanitarian law and international human rights law and its confirmation of the extra-territorial effect of UN human rights treaties, as well as for its ruling that the wall could not be justified on grounds of self defence. Self defence was also in issue in the *Armed Activities* case, in which the Court gave an important judgment on various aspects of the prohibition of the use of armed force, in one of the very few cases in which this crucial area of international law has been squarely addressed by it. When the same litigants returned to The Hague in the *Armed Activities (New Application)* case, the Court, disappointingly, rejected an argument that a reservation to the Genocide Convention was invalid as contrary to *ius cogens*; but at least it did recognise, for the first time in its history, that *ius cogens* is a concept known to customary international law. Similarly, its findings in the *Genocide* case on claims of genocide in the Balkan conflict have met with a mixed response. Very welcome were the Court's clarifications of the law on diplomatic protection of individuals and companies in the *Diallo* case. In other judgments there were more rulings on maritime boundaries and territorial title, which have long been the Court's staple diet. In one of these judgments, in the *Pedra Branca* case, the Court pronounced helpfully on prescription as a basis for title. Finally, the doctrine of *forum prorogatum* came alive again, with the Court's ruling that it had jurisdiction on this basis in the *Certain Questions of Mutual Assistance* case. At the time of writing, the Court had yet to give its eagerly anticipated response to the General Assembly's request for an advisory opinion on the *Kosovo* case.

But the International Court of Justice has had no monopoly as a source of recent developments in international law. ICSID arbitration awards, such as the *CMS Gas* case, have applied the law concerning necessity as a ground precluding wrongfulness and the Eritrea-Ethiopia Claims Commission has given a controversial ruling on the legality of obtaining title by the use of force (*Partial Award: Ius Ad Bellum: Ethiopia's Claims 1-8 Claims*). The International Law Commission has produced new texts, including its Draft Articles on Diplomatic Protection, which contain some challenging proposals for progressive development, and its Guiding Principles applicable to Unilateral Declarations of States. A decision on the question whether the Commission's Draft Articles on State Responsibility for Internationally Wrongful Acts will be translated into a treaty was further postponed. Elsewhere, the Security Council was unexpectedly called upon to "legislate" in an unfamiliar area, empowering states to act against the seizure of ships off Somalia.

An important institutional change took place in the UN human rights system, with the replacement of the UN Commission on Human Rights by the UN Human Rights Council. Although the Council is proving to be no less influenced by politics than its predecessor, its new Universal Periodic Review procedure may become a significant innovation. New UN human rights instruments have also been adopted, particularly the Convention on the Rights of Persons with Disabilities, the Convention for the

Protection of All Persons from Enforced Disappearance and the Declaration on the Rights of Indigenous Peoples. The HRC and CAT have given important rulings on extraordinary rendition (Agiza , Alzery) and abortion (Llantoy Huamain).

In responding to these and other developments, I have been greatly assisted in bringing the casebook up to date by Chris Henderson, a former PhD student in the University of Nottingham School of Law, and Claire Balding, an intern on the University of Nottingham Talent Builder programme in the Human Rights Law Centre of the School of Law. I would like to thank them for their excellent work as research assistants in the preparation of this new edition.

The book generally takes account of developments as far as January 2010. Where possible, more recent developments have been noted.

D.J. Harris
Human Rights Law Centre
School of Law
University of Nottingham
April 2010

CONTENTS

TABLE OF CASES
(UK AND INTERNATIONAL)

*[Page references in **bold** type indicate extracts of the case.]*

TABLE OF NATIONAL STATUTES, ETC.

*[Page references in **bold** type indicate extracts of the statute.]*

TABLE OF STATUTORY INSTRUMENTS, ETC.

TABLE OF TREATIES

*[Page references in **bold** type indicate extracts of the treaty.]*

TABLE OF OTHER DOCUMENTS

[*Page references in* **bold** *type indicate extracted material.*]

Security Council Resolutions

Miscellaneous

TABLE OF ABBREVIATIONS

Af.J.I.C.L	African Journal of International and Comparative Law
A.J.I.L	American Journal of International Law
A.S.I.L Proc	American Society of International Law Proceedings
A.J.H.R	Australian Journal of Human Rights
A.Y.I.L	Australian Yearbook of International Law
O.Z.O.R.V	Austrian Journal of Public and International Law
B.J.I.L	Berkeley Journal of International Law
B.U.I.L.J	Boston University International Law Journal
Brierly	Brierly, *The Law of Nations*, 6th edn 1963
B.D.I.L	British Digest of International Law
B.F.S.P	British and Foreign State Papers 1812/1814-1939
B.J.I.S	British Journal of International Studies
B.P.I.L	British Practice in International Law
B.Y.I.L	British Yearbook of International Law
Brownlie	Brownlie, *Principles of Public International Law*, 7th edn 2008
Calif. L.R	California Law Review
C.W.I.L.J	California Western International Law Journal
C.W.R.J.I.L.	Case Western Reserve Journal of International Law
C.L.J	Cambridge Law Journal
C.Y.I.L	Canadian Yearbook of International Law
Cardozo L.R	Cardozo Law Review
Chi. J.I.L	Chicago Journal of International Law
C.J.T.L	Columbia Journal of Transnational Law
Col. L.R	Columbia Law Review
C.P.U.K.I.L	Contemporary Practice of the United Kingdom in the Field of International Law–Survey and Comment
Crim. L.R	Criminal Law Review
C.L.P	Current Legal Problems
Denver J.I.L.P	Denver Journal of International Law and Policy
Duke J.C.I.L	Duke Journal of Comparative and International Law
E.C.O.W.A.S	Economic Community of West African States
E.C.O.S.O.C	Economic and Social Council, UN
E.C.H.R	European Convention on Human Rights
E.C.R	European Court of Justice Reports
E.C.S.C	European Coal and Steel Community
E.Ct.H.R.R	European Court of Human Rights Reports

E.E.C	European Economic Community
E.H.R.L.R	European Human Rights Law Review
E.H.R.R	European Human Rights Reports
E.J.I.L	European Journal of International Law
E.J.M.L	European Journal of Migration and Law
E.L.R	European Law Review
Emory I.L.R	Emory International Law Review
E.T.S	European Treaty Series
Ethics and Int. Affairs	Ethics and International Affairs
E.W.C.A	England and Wales Court of Appeal
E.W.H.C	England and Wales High Court
F.L.R	Family Law Reports
Flor. J.I.L	Florida Journal of International Law
Fla.St.U.J. Trans.L.P	Florida State University Journal of Transitional Law and Policy
F.C.O	Foreign and Commonwealth Office, United Kingdom
For. Invest. L.J	Foreign Investment Law Journal
G.A.O.R	General Assembly Official Records
Georgetown. Im. L.J	Georgetown Immigration Law Journal
Geo. Wash. J.I.L.E	George Washington Journal of Law and Economics
G.W.L.R	George Washington Law Review
Ga. J.I.C.L	Georgia Journal of International and Comparative Law
G.Y.I.L	German Yearbook of International Law
Hackworth	Hackworth, *Digest of International Law* 8 vols, 1940-1944
Harv. H.R.J	Harvard Human Rights Journal
H.H.R.Y	Harvard Human Rights Yearbook
H.I.L.J	Harvard International Law Journal
Houston L.R	Houston Law Review
H.R.L.J	Human Rights Law Journal
H.R.L.R	Human Rights Law Review
H.R.Q	Human Rights Quarterly
Ind. J.I.L	Indian Journal of International Law
Int. Affairs	International Affairs
Int. Am. Com H.R.	Inter-American Commission on Human Rights
Inter-Am.Ct.H.R	Inter-American Court of Human Rights
Int.Arb	International Arbitration
I.A.E.A	International Atomic Energy Agency
I.B.R.D	International Bank for Reconstruction and Development
I.C.S.I.D	International Centre for Settlement of Investment Disputes
I.C.S.I.D. Rev.-F.I.L.J	International Centre for Settlement of Investment Disputes Review – Foreign Investment Law Journal
I.C.A.O	International Civil Aviation Organization
I.C.J Rev	Review of the International Commission of Jurists
I.C.L.Q	International and Comparative Law Quarterly
Int. Conc	International Conciliation
I.C.T.Y	International Criminal Tribunal for Former Yugoslavia
I.C.C	International Criminal Court
I.C.J Rep	International Court of Justice Reports

I.H.R.R	International Human Rights Reports
I.J.C.L	International Journal of Constitutional Law
I.J.L.F	International Journal of Law and Family
I.L.O	International Labour Organization
I.L.A	International Law Association
I.L.C	International Law Commission
I.L.R	International Law Reports
Int. Lawyer	International Lawyer
I.L.M	International Legal Materials
I.M.F	International Monetary Fund
Int.Org	International Organisation
I.R.R.C	International Review of the Red Cross
Iowa L.R	Iowa Law Review
Iran-U.S.C.T.R	Iran-US Claims Tribunal Reports
Is. Y.H.R	Israel Yearbook on Human Rights
J. African L	Journal of African Law
J.C.S.L	Journal of Conflict and Security Law
J.H.R	Journal of Human Rights
J. Int. Arb.	Journal of International Arbitration
Jo. Int. Crim. J	Journal of International Criminal Justice
Jo. Int. Studies	Journal of International Studies
J. World Investment and Trade	Journal of World Investment and Trade
J.W.T.L	Journal of World Trade Law
L.Q.R	Law Quarterly Review
L.N.O.J	League of Nations Official Journal
L.N.T.S	League of Nations Treaty Series
L.J.I.L	Leiden Journal of International Law
L.D.G.J	Librairie Générale de Droit et de Jurisprudence
L.L.A. I.C. L.R	Loyola of Los Angeles International and Comparative Law Review
McNair	McNair. *International Law Opinions*, 3 vols, 1956
McNair, *Treaties*	McNair, *The Law of Treaties*, 2nd edn 1961
Maine L.R	Maine Law Review
Max Planck Ybk	Max Planck Yearbook of UN Law
M.J.I.L	Melbourne Journal of International Law
Mel.U.L.R	Melbourne University Law Review
Mich. J.I.L	Michigan Journal of International Law
Mich. L.R	Michigan Law Review
M.L.R	Modern Law Review
N.A.F.T.A	North American Free Trade Agreement
N.A.T.O	North Atlantic Treaty Organization
N.I.L.Q	Northern Ireland Legal Quarterly
N.I.L.R	Netherlands International Law Review
Nordic J.I.L	Nordic Journal of International Law
N.T.I.R	Nordisk Tidsskrift for International Ret
N.Q.H.R	Netherlands Quarterly of Human Rights
N.Y.I.L	Netherlands Yearbook of International Law

N.Y.U.J.I.L & P.	New York University Journal of International Law and Politics
N.Y.U.J.I.P	New York University Journal of Legislation and Public Policy
N.Z.T.S	New Zealand Treaty Series
O.A.S	Organisation of American States
O.A.U	Organisation of African Unity
O.E.C.D	Organisation for Economic Co-operation and Development
O.J.E.C	Official Journal of the European Communities
O.S.C.E	Organisation for Security and Co-operation in Europe
P.A.U.T.S	Pan American Union Treaty Series
P.C.A	Permanent Court of Arbitration
P.C.I.J Rep	Permanent Court of International Justice Reports
Penn State L.R	Penn State Law Review
Phil.L.J	Philippine Law Journal
Pol. Perspectives	Political Perspectives
Pol. Studies	Political Studies
Pol. Y.I.L	Polish Yearbook of International Law
P.L	Public Law
R.B.D.I	Revue Belge de Droit International
Rec. Acad	Recueil des cours (Hague Academy)
R.G.D.I.P	Revue Generale de Droit International Public
R.I.A.A	Reports of International Arbitral Awards
Rutgers L.R	Rutgers Law Review
S.A.J.H.R	South African Journal on Human Rights
S.A.J.L	South African Law Journal
S.A.L.R	South African Law Reports
S.C.O.R	Security Council Official Records
S.C.R	Supreme Court of Canada Reports
Sing. J.I.C.L	Singapore Journal of International and Comparative Law
S.J.I.L.C	Syracuse Journal of International Law and Commerce
Stanford J.I.L	Stanford Journal of International Law
Sydney L.R	Sydney Law Review
Texas I.L.J	Texas International Law Journal
Texas L.R	Texas Law Review
T.E.U	Treaty on European Union
Trans. Grot. Soc	Transactions of the Grotius Society
Tul. L.R	Tulane Law Review
U.K.M.I.L	United Kingdom Materials in International Law
U.K.T.S	United Kingdom Treaty Series
U.N.C.I.O	United Nations Conference on International Organisation
U.N.C.L.O.S	United Nations Conference on the Law of the Sea
U.N.C.T.A.D	United Nations Conference on Trade and Development
U.N.D.P	United Nations Development Programme
U.N.E.S.C.O	United Nations Educational, Scientific and Cultural Organization
U.N.I.C.E.F	United Nations Children's Fund
U.N.I.D.O	United Nations Industrial Development Organization
U.N.R.I.A.A	United Nations Reports of International Arbitral Awards
U.N.T.A.C	United Nations Transitional Authority in Cambodia

U.N.T.A.E.T	United Nations Transitional Authority for East Timor
U.N.T.S	United Nations Treaty Series
U.S.D.I.L	Digest of United States Practice in International Law
U.S. For. Rel.	United States Foreign Relations
U.S.T.S	United States Treaty Series
U.Tas.L.R	University of Tasmania Law Review
Vand. J.T.L	Vanderbilt Journal of Transnational Law
Virg. J.I.L	Virginia Journal of International Law
Virg. L.R	Virginia Law Review
Wash. L.R	Washington Law Review
Whiteman	Whiteman, *Digest of International Law*, 14 vols, 1963–1970
W.H.O	World Health Organisation
W.I.P.O.	World Intellectual Property Organisation
Yale J.I.L	Yale Journal of International Law
Yale L.J	Yale Law Journal
Y.B.E.C.H.R	Yearbook of the European Convention on Human Rights
Y.B.I.L.C	Yearbook of the International Law Commission
Y.I.H.L	Yearbook of International Humanitarian Law
Z.A.O.R.V	Zeitschrift fur Auslandisches Offentliches Recht und Volkerrecht

1 INTRODUCTION[1]

1. INTERNATIONAL LAW AS "LAW"

BRIERLY, THE LAW OF NATIONS

Waldock (6th edn, 1963), pp.41–42, 68–76

Law can only exist in a society, and there can be no society without a system of law to regulate the relations of its members with one another. If then we speak of the "law of nations", we are assuming that a "society" of nations exists, and the assumption that the whole of the civilized world constitutes in any real sense a single society or community is one which we are not justified in making without examination. In any case the character of the law of nations is necessarily determined by that of the society within which it operates, and neither can be understood without the other.

The law of nations had its origin among a few kindred nations of western Europe which, despite their frequent quarrels and even despite the religious schism of the sixteenth century, all had and were all conscious of having a common background in the Christian religion and the civilization of Greece and Rome. They were in a real sense a society of nations. But the rise of the modern state system undermined the tradition of the unity of Christendom, and eventually gave rise to those sentiments of exclusive nationalism which are rife in the world today. It is true that side by side with this development there has been an immense growth of the factors that make states mutually dependent on one another. Modern science has given us vastly increased facilities and speed of communications, and modern commerce has created demands for the commodities of other nations which even the extravagances of modern economic nationalism are not able to stifle. If human affairs were more wisely ordered, and if men were clearer-sighted than they are in seeing their own interests, it might be that this interdependence of the nations would lead to a strengthening of their feelings of community. But their interdependence is mainly in material things, and though material bonds are necessary, they are not enough without a common social consciousness; without that they are as likely to lead to friction as to friendship. Some sentiment of shared responsibility for the conduct of a common life is a necessary element in any society, and the necessary force behind any system of law; and the strength of any legal system is proportionate to the strength of such a sentiment.

It has often been said that international law ought to be classified as a branch of ethics rather than of law. The question is partly one of words, because its solution will clearly depend on the definition of law which we choose to adopt; in any case it does not affect the value of the subject one way or the other, though those who deny the legal character of international law often speak as though "ethical" were a depreciatory epithet. But in fact it is both practically inconvenient and also contrary to the best juristic thought to deny its legal character. It is

---

[1] Allott, *The Health of Nations* (2002); Brownlie, *The Rule of Law in International Affairs* (1998); Byers, ed., *The Role of International Law in International Politics* (2000); Cassese, *International Law in a Divided World* (1986); Charlesworth and Chinkin, *The Boundaries of International Law: A Feminist Analysis* (2000); Franck, *The Power of Legitimacy Among Nations* (1990); Higgins, *Problems and Process* (1994); Jennings (1958) 34 B.Y.I.L. 334; Koskenniemi, *From Apology to Utopia: The Structure of International Legal Argument* (1989); Koskenniemi, *The Gentle Civilizer of Nations* (2001); Mosler, *The International Society as a Legal Community* (1980); Müllerson, *Ordering Amnesty: International Law in International Society* (2000); Rosenne, *The Perplexities of Modern International Law* (2004); Schachter, *International Law in Theory and Practice* (1991); Scobbie in Evans, ed., *International Law* (2nd edn 2006), Ch.5; Slaughter, *A New World Order* (2004); Symposium: The European Tradition in International Law (2003) 14 E.J.I.L. 653.

inconvenient because if international law is nothing but international morality, it is certainly not the whole of international morality, and it is difficult to see how we are to distinguish it from those other admittedly moral standards which we apply in forming our judgments on the conduct of states.[2] Ordinary usage certainly uses two tests in judging the "rightness" of a state's act, a moral test and one which is somehow felt to be independent of morality. Every state habitually commits acts of selfishness which are often gravely injurious to other states, and yet are not contrary to international law; but we do not on that account necessarily judge them to have been "right". It is confusing and pedantic to say that both these tests are moral. Moreover, it is the pedantry of the theorist and not of the practical man; for questions of international law are invariably treated as legal questions by the foreign offices which conduct our international business, and in the courts, national or international, before which they are brought; legal forms and methods are used in diplomatic controversies and in judicial and arbitral proceedings, and authorities and precedents are cited in argument as a matter of course. It is significant too that when a breach of international law is alleged by one party to a controversy, the act impugned is practically never defended by claiming the right of private judgment, which would be the natural defence if the issue concerned the morality of the act, but always by attempting to prove that no rule has been violated. . . .[3]

If, as Sir Frederick Pollock[4] writes, and as probably most competent jurists would today agree, the only essential conditions for the existence of law are the existence of a political community, and the recognition by its members of settled rules binding upon them in that capacity, international law seems on the whole to satisfy these conditions. . . .[5]

The best view is that international law is in fact just a system of customary law, upon which has been erected, almost entirely within the last two generations, a superstructure of "conventional" or treaty-made law, and some of its chief defects are precisely those that the history of law teaches us to expect in a customary system. It is a common mistake to suppose that of these the most conspicuous is the frequency of its violation. Violations of law are rare in all customary systems, and they are so in international law. . . . For the law is normally observed because, as we shall see, the demands that it makes on states are generally not exacting, and on the whole states find it convenient to observe it. . . . But the weakness of international law lies deeper than any mere question of sanctions. It is not the existence of a police force that makes a system of law strong and respected, but the strength of the law that makes it possible for a police force to be effectively organized. The imperative character of law is felt so strongly and obedience to it has become so much a matter of habit within a highly civilized state that national law has developed a machinery of enforcement which generally works smoothly, though never so smoothly as to make breaches impossible. If the imperative character of international law were equally strongly felt, the institution of definite international sanctions would easily follow.

A customary system of law can never be adequate to the needs of any but a primitive society, and the paradox of the international society is that, whilst on the material side it is far from primitive, and therefore needs a strong and fairly elaborate system of law for the regulation of the clashes to which the material interdependence of different states is constantly giving rise, its spiritual cohesion is, as we have already seen, weak, and as long as that is so the weakness will inevitably be reflected in a weak and primitive system of law.[6]

Among the most serious shortcomings of the present system are the rudimentary character of the institutions which exist for the making and the application of the law, and the narrow restrictions on its range. . . . There is no legislature to keep the law abreast of new needs in the international society; no executive power to enforce the law; and although certain administrative bodies have been created, these, though important in themselves, are

---

[2]   Ed., e.g. the legality and morality of refusing economic aid to poor countries (see below, p.476), or asylum to refugees (see below, p.471), is to be judged by different standards. And the use of nuclear weapons, which may be thought generally to be immoral, may be lawful in some extreme cases of self defence: *Legality of Nuclear Weapons* case, below, p.788.

[3]   Ed. See, e.g. the British justification for the invasion of Suez: the Lord Chancellor (Lord Kilmuir), *Hansard*, HL Vol.199, col.1348 (November 1, 1956), and the Argentinian justification for the invasion of the Falkland Islands, below, p.750.

[4]   *First Book of Jurisprudence*, p.28.

[5]   Ed. In *The Outlook for International Law* (1944), p.5, Brierly writes: "The best evidence for the existence of international law is that every actual state recognises that it does exist and that it is itself under obligation to observe it. States may often violate international law, just as individuals often violate municipal law, but no more than individuals do states defend their violations by claiming that they are above the law."

[6]   Ed. cf. Corbett, *Law in Diplomacy* (1959), pp.273–274: "What is principally missing is the measure of agreement on supreme common values, the sense of community, loyalty, and mutual tolerance which within the State make compulsory institutions bearable. The reserved domain and the whole legal concept of sovereignty correspond to the fact that the State remains in the hearts and minds of men the highest center of human authority and chief guardian of the most treasured values . . . the State continues to be for practical purposes the chief end of man. So long as this is so, whatever their covenants or declarations, governments will not assume in practice a position of general subjection to a law of nations."

far from being adequate for the mass of business which ought to be treated today as of international concern. There exist also convenient machinery for the arbitration of disputes and a standing court of justice, but the range of action of these is limited because resort to them is not compulsory.[7]

The restricted range of international law is merely the counterpart of the wide freedom of independent action which states claim in virtue of their sovereignty. ... Law will never play a really effective part in international relations until it can annex to its own sphere some of the matters which at present lie within the "domestic jurisdictions" of the several states. ...[8]

It is a natural consequence of the absence of authoritative law-declaring machinery that many of the principles of international law, and even more the detailed application of accepted principles, are uncertain. But on the whole the layman tends to exaggerate this defect. It is not in the nature of any law to provide mathematically certain solutions of problems which may be presented to it; for uncertainty cannot be eliminated from law so long as the possible conjunctions of facts remain infinitely various. Although therefore the difference between international law and the law of a state in this respect is important it is one of degree and not of kind, and it tends to be reduced as the practice of resorting to international courts, which are able to work out the detailed practical implication of general principles, becomes more common.[9] The difficulty of formulating the rules of international law with precision is a necessary consequence of the kinds of evidence upon which we have to rely in order to establish them. ...

Brierly then discusses the international law attitude to the legality of war.[10]

Whether from a review of all these shortcomings we ought to conclude that international law is a failure depends upon what we assume to be its aim. It has not failed to serve the purposes for which states have chosen to use it; in fact it serves these purposes reasonably well ... the practice of international law proceeds on much the same lines as that of any other kind of law, with the foreign offices taking the place of the private legal adviser[11] and exchanging arguments about the facts and the law, and later, more often than is sometimes supposed, with a hearing before some form of international tribunal. The volume of this work is considerable,[12] but most of it is not sensational. ... That does not mean that the matters to which it does relate are unimportant in themselves; often they are very important to particular interests or individuals. But it means that international law is performing a useful and indeed a necessary function in international life in enabling states to carry on their day-to-day intercourse along orderly and predictable lines. That is the role for which states have chosen to use it and for that it has proved a serviceable instrument.

Notes

1. *Ubi societas ibi ius*. Is there an international society with a sufficient sense of community to permit one realistically to expect a more than fragmentary system of international law? Or are

---

[7] Ed. See below, Ch.12.
[8] Ed. Matters within the "domestic jurisdiction" of a state are matters not regulated by international law so that a state is free to act in its discretion. They are numerous and varied, ranging from the admission of aliens to the regulation of cruelty of cats. Other examples are listed in the *Nicaragua (Merits)* case, para.205, below, p.727. The extent of a state's domestic jurisdiction changes with the development of custom and with the treaty obligations it undertakes. For example, the post-1945 international law of human rights—both customary and treaty—greatly limit a state's former freedom to ill-treat their nationals: see Ch.9. For the concept in the UN Charter, see below, p.826.
[9] Ed. This is optimistic. Although the World Court's docket is now fuller than it has generally been, see below, p.836, and there are now more international courts and tribunals than formerly, the lack of many cases interpreting the increasing number of "law-making" treaties (see below, p.35) presents a problem. In municipal law, a new statute that raises questions of interpretation is soon taken to court for a ruling. This is unlikely to happen in international law, e.g. it took over 40 years for the ICJ to construe art.2(4), UN Charter: see the *Nicaragua (Merits)* case, below, p.727. An outstanding exception is the European Convention on Human Rights, the meaning of which has been established by the jurisprudence of the European Court of Human Rights.
[10] See below, Ch.11.
[11] Ed. On the role of the Foreign Office legal adviser, see Berman in Wickremasinghe, ed., *The International Lawyer as Practitioner* (2000), p.3; Merillat, ed., *Legal Advisers and Foreign Affairs* (1964); Vallat, *International Law and the Practitioner* (1966); and Wood in Evans, ed., *International Law* (2003), p.25.
[12] Ed. The UK, for example, enters into over 100 treaties each year and requires legal advice and representation in the UN and other international fora.

the attitudes and interests of the world's different geo-political groupings of states too diverse to allow this?[13] An important positive development in this regard has been the end of the Cold War and of the influence of the Soviet theory of international law, with its emphasis upon state sovereignty and rejection of bourgeois law.[14] Although some communist states (e.g. China,[15] Cuba, North Korea, Vietnam) remain, the most significant divisions among states are those between developing and developed states, whose economic and other interests differ greatly, and, in some respects, between Islamic states and the West.[16]

A problem of a different kind, namely the continuing reluctance of all states to surrender sovereign powers, is pointed out by De Visscher[17]:

"It is therefore pure illusion to expect from the mere arrangement of inter-State relations the establishment of a community order; this can find a solid foundation only in the development of the true international spirit in men. . . . There will be no international community so long as the political ends of the State overshadow the human ends of power."

Reflecting upon recent developments, Simma and Paulus[18] are more positive:

"To sum up, the world of the famous 'Lotus principle',[19] according to which states are only bound by their express consent, seems to be gradually giving way to a more communitarian, more highly institutionalized international law, in which states 'channel' the pursuit of most of their individual interests through multilateral institutions. Even if private actors, whether groups or individuals, have not yet become regular subjects of general international law, the system as a whole increasingly permeates state boundaries for the sake of protection of individual and group rights. Therefore, we suggest adopting a 'Grotian' view, but to mix it, as it were, with elements of both 'Vattelianism' and 'Kantianism', and with an increasing pull toward institutionalization. In any case, the concept of an 'international community' contains as much aspiration as reality. To quote the former President of the International Court of Justice, Mohammed Bedjaoui, in his Declaration appended to the 1996 *Advisory Opinion on Nuclear Weapons*,[20] an opinion which perfectly demonstrates the contradictory elements inherent in contemporary international society[21]:

'Despite the still modest breakthrough of "supra-nationalism", the progress made in terms of the institutionalization, not to say integration and "globalization" of international society

---

[13] See Simma and Paulus (1998) 9 E.J.I.L. 266.
[14] On the Soviet theory, see Tunkin, *Theory of International Law* (1970), English translation by Butler (1974); and Kartashkin in Macdonald and Johnston, eds, *The Structure and Process of International Law* (1983), p.79. On international law after the Cold War, see Damrosch, Danilenko and Müllerson, eds, *Beyond Confrontation: International Law for the Post Cold War Era* (1995); Macdonald in Wellens, ed., *International Law: Theory and Practice* (1998), p.61; Müllerson, *International Law, Rights and Politics* (1994); Reisman (1993) 87 A.J.I.L. 83; Vereshchetin and Müllerson (1990) 28 C.J.T.L. 291.
[15] For the Chinese approach, see Delisle (2000) 94 A.S.I.L. Proc. 207; Kent, *Beyond Compliance: China, International Organisations and Global Security* (2007); Keyuan Zou, *China's Legal Reform: Towards the Rule of Law* (2007), Ch.10; Wang Tieya (1990-II) 221 Hague Recueil 199; Wang Tieya, ed., *International Law* (1995).
[16] See Bahar (1992) 33 H.I.L.J. 145. On the problems that sharia law presents for human rights, see below, p.538.
[17] De Visscher, *Theory and Reality in Public International Law* (trans. by Corbett, rev. ed. 1968), p.94. See also Mosler, above, p.1, n.1, pp.17–47.
[18] Simma and Paulus (1998) 9 E.J.I.L. 266 at 276–277.
[19] Ed. See the *Lotus* case, below, p.230.
[20] *Legality of the Threat or Use of Nuclear Weapons*, Advisory Opinion, Declaration of President Bedjaoui, para.12, I.C.J. Rep. (1996) 226, at 270, 271 (para.13).
[21] Official English translation.

is undeniable. ... The resolutely positivist, voluntarist approach of international law still current at the beginning of the century ... has been replaced by an objective conception of international law, a law more readily seeking to reflect a collective juridical conscience and respond to the social necessities of States organized as a community.'"

2.   *The Austinian Handicap.* "Is international law 'law?'" is a standard sherry party question. Its sometimes irritating persistence is very largely the responsibility of John Austin, an English jurist of the first part of the nineteenth century and a familiar friend of any student who has taken a course in jurisprudence. He defined laws "properly so-called" as commands and "positive law", which he regarded as the "appropriate matter of jurisprudence", as the commands of a sovereign.[22] A sovereign he defined as a person who received the habitual obedience of the members of an independent political society and who, in turn, did not owe such obedience to any other person. Rules of international law did not qualify as rules of "positive law" by this test and, not being commands of any sort, were placed by Austin in the category of "laws improperly so-called". This uncompromising and unhappily phrased rejection of international law's claim to be law of the same order as municipal law[23] has, to this day, upset international lawyers and placed them on the defensive. Although international law is still not "law" according to Austin's test, most international lawyers would at least dispute that that test is more helpful than certain others (e.g. that of Pollock, quoted by Brierly) by which international law could be said to be "law".[24]

3.   *The "Law Habit".* No writer would seem to dissent from the view expressed by Brierly that, in terms of the number, as opposed to the political importance, of the occasions on which international law is complied with, it is more honoured in the observance than in the breach. Jessup,[25] for example, takes Brierly's view:

"Wars, breaches of treaties, oppression of the weak by the strong, are the headlines of the daily press and of the history textbooks. The superficial observer has not noted the steady observance of such treaties as that under which letters are carried all over the world at rates fixed by the Universal Postal Union. He ignores the fact that there is scarcely an instance in two hundred years in which an ambassador has been subjected to suit in courts of the country where he is stationed.... The superficial observer has not read the hundreds of decisions handed down by international courts called Mixed Claims Commissions, which have awarded money damages duly paid by the defendant states.... He may be unfamiliar with the extent to which international law has been incorporated in national law and has thus secured an enforcement agency through the ordinary governmental machinery of the national states.... One of the wisest and most experienced of them all, John Bassett Moore, has recorded his observation that on the whole international law is as well observed as national law. The Director of the Yale Institute of International Studies has recently remarked that those 'who make light of treaty commitments in general seem to ignore the fact that the vast majority of such engagements are continuously, honestly, and regularly observed even under adverse

---

[22]   See *The Province of Jurisprudence Determined* (1832), Lectures I, V and VI. A recent edition is that edited by Rumble in 1995.
[23]   This is the term used in international law to refer to the law of a state.
[24]   For the view that the question whether international law is "law" is a verbal one not worth bothering with: see Glanville Williams (1945) 22 B.Y.I.L. 146 at 163. See also Hart, *The Concept of Law* (2nd edn 1994), pp.214–215.
[25]   *A Modern Law of Nations* (1948), pp.6–8. Reprinted with the permission of Scribner, a Division of Simon & Schuster, Inc., from A MODERN LAW OF NATIONS by Philip C. Jessup. Copyright © 1947, 1948 by Macmillan Publishing Company; copyright renewed © 1973, 1974, 1975 by Philip C. Jessup. All rights reserved.

conditions and at considerable inconvenience to the parties.'... The record proves that there is a 'law habit' in international relations. It is not immaterial to add that the instances in which judgments of international tribunals have been flouted are so rare that the headline-reader may well place them in the man-bites-dog category."[26]

Although there is clearly some merit to the "law habit" view, might it not, to some extent, be misleading? What has to be emphasised as strongly is that a state can usually flout international law if it wants to and get away with it. How relevant also is a comparison of the number or percentage of violations of municipal and international law? The point about a train robber is that if there is a good case against him and if his whereabouts are known he will be punished. The USSR and the US were not arraigned for intervening unlawfully in Afghanistan in 1979[27] and Grenada in 1983[28] respectively and Israel, though condemned by the UN, has not been brought to book for its violations of its obligations as an occupying power in the Middle East.[29] Political and economic considerations may be crucial to the decision of the international community to act. Iraq's invasion of Kuwait, which affected Western oil interests, was rapidly dealt with, but there was no such physical retaliation against Indonesia's invasion of East Timor, see below, p.109.

But are we asking too much of international law? Are we expecting it to be effective often in disputes in which we would not imagine law to apply, or at least not to be in the forefront, within a state because of the political importance of the problem?

MORGENTHAU, POLITICS AMONG NATIONS[30]

(6th edn, 1985), pp.312–313

The great majority of the rules of international law are generally observed by all nations without actual compulsion, for it is generally in the interest of all nations concerned to honor their obligations under international law. A nation will hesitate to infringe upon the rights of foreign diplomats residing in its capital; for it has an interest, identical with the interests of all other nations, in the universal observance of the rules of international law which extend their protection to its own diplomatic representatives in foreign capitals as well as to the foreign diplomats in its own capital.[31] A nation will likewise be reluctant to disregard its obligations under a commercial treaty, since the benefits that it expects from the execution of the treaty by the other contracting

---

[26]   Nantwi, *The Enforcement of International Judicial Decisions and Arbitral Awards in Public International Law* (1966), Ch.IV, records only a few cases, constituting but a very small proportion of the whole, in which the losing state has not complied with the decision or award. All of the decisions and opinions of the P.C.I.J. were followed; those of the ICJ have been less effective: see below, p.836. World Court jurisdiction is voluntary so that the parties are predisposed (although this is not necessarily true of cases brought under the "optional clause": see below, p.846) to accept the ruling made. Note that one of the rulings of the ICJ not complied with was that against Albania in the *Corfu Channel* case which had initially been brought before the Court very much against Albania's will: see below, p.844. Note also that the percentage of disputes between states referred to the Court is minute.

[27]   See below, p.744.

[28]   See below, p.745.

[29]   See below, p.194.

[30]   See also on sanctions and the enforcement of international law, Damrosch (1994) 8 Ethics and Int. Affairs 59; Doxey (1983) 15 C.W.R.J.I.L. 273; Gowlland-Debbas, ed., *United Nations Sanctions and International Law* (2001); Hufbauer, Schott and Elliott, *Economic Sanctions Reconsidered* (2nd edn 1990); Joyner (1995) 16 A.Y.I.L. 241; Leyton-Brown, ed., *The Utility of International Economic Sanctions* (1987); Renwick, *Economic Sanctions* (1981); Rubin (1993) 34 H.I.L.J. 149; Schwebel, ed., *The Effectiveness of International Decisions* (1971); White and Abass, in Evans, ed., *International Law* (2nd edn, 2006), Ch.17; and the Heidelberg Colloquium on the Enforcement of International Obligations, papers printed in (1987) 47 Z.A.O.R.V. 3.

[31]   Ed. See, e.g. the 1965 US Moscow embassy incident, below, p.307.

parties are complementary to those anticipated by the latter. It may thus stand to lose more than it would gain by not fulfilling its part of the bargain. This is particularly so in the long run, since a nation that has the reputation of reneging on its commercial obligations will find it hard to conclude commercial treaties beneficial to itself.

Most rules of international law formulate in legal terms such identical or complementary interests. It is for this reason that they generally enforce themselves, as it were, and that there is generally no need for a specific enforcement action. In most cases in which such rules of international law are actually violated despite the underlying community of interests, satisfaction is given to the wronged party either voluntarily or in consequence of adjudication. . . .

Thus the great majority of rules of international law are generally unaffected by the weakness of its system of enforcement, for voluntary compliance prevents the problem of enforcement from arising altogether. The problem of enforcement becomes acute, however, in that minority of important and generally spectacular cases, particularly important in the context of our discussion, in which compliance with international law and its enforcement have a direct bearing upon the relative power of the nations concerned. In those cases . . . considerations of power rather than of law determine compliance and enforcement.

FITZMAURICE, THE FOUNDATIONS OF THE AUTHORITY OF INTERNATIONAL LAW AND THE PROBLEM OF ENFORCEMENT

(1956) 19 M.L.R. 1

With regard to the actual position concerning the enforceability of the international legal system, there has always been a respectable body of international lawyers that has both considered enforceability to be a necessary characteristic of any system of law, properly so called, and has also believed that international law possessed this characteristic, even if only in a rough and rudimentary form. Oppenheim, for instance, whose treatise may be cited because it constitutes so very much the practitioner's Bible, so to speak, . . . defines law as

> a body of rules for human conduct within a community which, by common consent of this community, shall be enforced by external power [8th edn p.10, para.5].

. . . so great a modernist as Kelsen seems, in one of his latest works, *Principles of International Law*, published in 1952, to incline towards a similar view. He says, on page 5 of this work, that

> . . . law is a coercive order. It provides for socially organised sanctions, and these can be clearly distinguished from a religious order on the one hand and a merely moral order on the other hand. As a coercive order, the law is that specific social technique which consists in the attempt to bring about the desired social conduct of men through the threat of a measure of coercion which is to be taken in case of . . . legally wrong conduct.

Later, on page 14 of the same work, Kelsen points out that in decentralised societies (and the international society is such a society), enforcement of the law is accomplished through the application of the principle of self-help. The legal order leaves the enforcement function to the individuals injured by a delict or illegality. . . .

Eventually—see particularly pages 18–39 of the book—Kelsen appears to reach the conclusion that, judged by these tests, international law is true law because, broadly speaking, it provides sanctions, such as the adoption of reprisals, war, and the use of force generally, and makes the employment of these sanctions lawful as a counter-measure against a legal wrong, but unlawful in all other cases. . . .

Without necessarily subscribing fully to all these views, it can fairly be said that up to a comparatively recent date, war, and the use of force generally, did constitute in some sense a recognised method of enforcing international law; or, more accurately, a means whereby in the last resort a dispute between States as to their rights could be settled. It was a means of settlement or enforcement analogous in the international field to the "blood feud" or "ordeal by battle" or single combat, by which, in a more primitive stage of national societies, disputes between individuals or groups were settled—and it has always been the case, and still is, that the international society tends to reflect national society at an earlier stage of development. . . .

. . . There is no need to retail the steps by which, in the period following on the first world war, up to date, war has, by a series of measures, been divested of its former basic legitimacy. . . .

Now this is, of course, very well, and greatly to be welcomed: no one would wish it otherwise. But it has given rise to one curious and perhaps unforeseen consequence—for in so far as war, or the use of force, was a means, however crude, by which an injured State could assert or defend its legal rights, as the case might be—then the position now is that international law is less enforceable today then it ever has been in the whole of its history—for nothing definite or certain has been put in the place of force as a means of settlement....

It must be concluded that although the international order may have made [through Chapter VII of the UN Charter[32]] some attempt at progress in repressing or countering that particular type of illegality that consists in armed aggression or breach of the peace, it has not yet made much progress in the enforcement of international rights and obligations generally, or of international law as such. It now frowns on self-help, without, however, as yet having put anything in its place. It is obvious that such a situation is unsatisfactory. Fortunately, there can be set against it not only the fact that international law has never, in practice, been more than partly dependent for its authority[33] on the possibility of its physical enforcement, but also the principle that no system of law depends, or can, in the last resort, depend for its authority solely on the chances of enforcement. If it did, it could never in practice be enforced. The assumed certainty of enforcement in the national society masks the fact that, in general, the law does not have to be enforced, not so much because it is taken for granted that it would be, but because it commands in practice the general assent or tolerance of the community.

The real foundation of the authority of international law resides similarly in the fact that the States making up the international society recognise it as binding upon them, and, moreover, as a system that *ipso facto* binds them *as* members of the society, irrespective of their individual wills.

Notes

1.   The general absence of compulsory judicial or arbitral remedies and the decentralised nature of the international community inevitably mean that *self-help* is the option that is most likely to be available to a state when faced with a breach of an international obligation owed to it by another state. Self-help may take the form of countermeasures or acts of retorsion. A *countermeasure* is an act not involving the use of armed force[34] that is contrary to international law but that is rendered lawful as a proportionate response to a prior illegal act by another state and that is intended to induce compliance with its international law obligations by that state.[35] *Acts of retorsion* are acts which, although unfriendly, are, unlike countermeasures, not illegal under international law. They are unfriendly acts in response to both unlawful acts and lawful but unfriendly acts.

2.   So far as sanctions organised through the international community are concerned, the main ones are those within the power of the United Nations.[36] They are of limited scope and, insofar as they are exercisable by the Security Council, are subject to the "veto". Friedmann[37] argues that in the "international law of co-operation", which operates in areas in which states participate in activities furthering common state interests through international organisations or otherwise, a sanction of exclusion from the benefits of such activities is available. He gives as an example the power of the World Bank to grant or withhold development funds:

"... if a borrowing state were to confiscate without compensation and in a discriminatory

[32]   Ed. See below, Ch.11.

[33]   Ed. The author states elsewhere in the article that "authority" is "a term here used in the sense of prestige."

[34]   The unilateral use of armed force is now generally prohibited by art.2(4) of the UN Charter: see below, p.723.

[35]   The term "countermeasure" is now used in place of "reprisal", except in international humanitarian law following its use in the *Air Services Agreement* case (1978) 18 R.I.A.A. 416. The rules on countermeasures are covered by the ILC's Articles on State Responsibility: see below, pp.455 et seq. Cf. the *Gabčíkovo-Nagymaros Project* case, paras 83–87, below, p.870.

[36]   E.g. in 1994, the UK impounded a Montenegrin owned ship (the *MV Playa*) in the enforcement of UN Security Council sanctions against the former Yugoslavia: see U.K.M.I.L. (1993); (1994) B.Y.I.L. 680. See further on collective UN sanctions, below, Ch.11.

[37]   *The Changing Structure of International Law* (1964), p.88.

manner, the property of foreign investors ... it would find itself excluded from participation in further development aid."[38]

As Friedmann suggests, the national interest of the defaulting state in continued participation must be at least as great as that in the course of action that caused it to default for such a sanction to be effective. When Indonesia withdrew from the United Nations in 1965 it left those United Nations specialised agencies from which it "did not have much benefit" but remained a member of the World Health Organisation which was conducting a malaria campaign in Indonesia at the time.[39] Political pressures, such as those at work in the *Certain Expenses* case in the United Nations,[40] may also prevent the application of such sanctions in some cases.

3. An effective way of enforcing international law is through national courts, whose judgments are backed by the power of the state. But not all rules of international law can readily be made the subject of national litigation. For example, the rules of diplomatic and sovereign immunity are commonly applied in national courts, but those prohibiting the use of force are not. Another factor is the extent to which customary international law and self-executing treaties are a part of the law of the land and hence enforceable in the local courts.[41]

4. Of considerable importance in the enforcement of some kinds of international law is the activity of non-governmental organisations (NGOs), such as Greenpeace and Amnesty International. As well as assisting in the development of international law through their participation in international meetings and conferences at which issues are discussed and treaties drafted,[42] NGOs play a role in making information available to the many committees or commissions that enforce treaty obligations (e.g. those under environmental or human rights treaties) and in generally bringing pressure to bear upon states to comply with international law.

5. How do the sanctions available in international law differ from those in any developed system of municipal law? What improvements in the former are (i) desirable; (ii) reasonable to expect?[43]

----

2. THE DEVELOPMENT OF INTERNATIONAL LAW

A. *Generally*

Modern international law has its origins in the Europe of the sixteenth and seventeenth centuries. Although communities of states regulated by law had previously existed in Europe (e.g. in Greece) and elsewhere (e.g. in India) it is, for reasons apparent from subsequent world history, the law created to govern the diplomatic, commercial, military and other relations of the society of Christian states forming the Europe of that time that provides the basis for the present law. Although the writers[44]

---

[38] *The Changing Structure of International Law* (1964), p.91. Note that the UK Government managed in 1972 to postpone at least consideration of Tanzanian loan proposals by the World Bank on the ground that Tanzania had not paid adequate compensation for British property it had nationalised: *The Times*, January 28, 1972, p.21.

[39] *The Times*, January 19, 1965, p.8. This, of course, was a case of voluntary withdrawal, but the attitude might well be adopted in cases of expulsion too.

[40] See below, p.831.

[41] See below, pp.65 et seq.

[42] E.g. the Coalition (of NGOs) for the International Criminal Court played an important role in the establishment of the International Criminal Court.

[43] See Fisher, *Improving Compliance with International Law* (1981).

[44] See below, p.44.

who recorded (and, to a large extent, invented) this early "Law of Nations"[45] may have regarded it as having universal application, it was for many generations really no more than the Public Law of Europe. International law was first extended beyond Europe at the end of the eighteenth and at the beginning of the nineteenth centuries to the states that succeeded the rebel European colonies of North and South America respectively. By the mid- nineteenth century, Turkey had been accepted as the first non-Christian subject of international law. By 1914, increasing European penetration into Asia had led to the "admission", though scarcely on terms of equality,[46] of other such subjects, including Persia, China and Japan. It was the advent in 1920 of the League of Nations, membership of which was open to "any" state (art.1, Covenant), that, as much as any other single event, marked the beginning of the present situation in which international law applies automatically to all states whatever their location or character. Since that time, the community of states has increased dramatically in number to close to 200.

Other changes of great importance too have occurred in the present century. Resort to war has been made illegal and a system of collective enforcement of peace and security has been initiated—though not very successfully[47]—through the United Nations in place of self-help. The change in the balance of interests and values in the world community resulting from the independence since 1945 of colonial and similar territories has had an effect in shaping or reshaping some international law rules.[48] The demise of Oppenheim's doctrine that "States solely and exclusively are the subject of International Law"[49] is also evident. The growth of public international organisations in particular bears witness to this. If other claimants still have very limited personality,[50] it is nonetheless the case that inter-state treaties are increasingly concerned with the "trans-national" affairs, to use Jessup's terminology,[51] of private individuals and companies.

Of great importance too is the increase in the subject-matter of international law to cover what Friedmann has called "the international law of co-operation."[52] The development of the international law of human rights and international environmental law are notable examples of this more positive, community-minded kind of law. Science too has had considerable effect. It has added two new territorial areas—outer space and the deep sea-bed—for which international law rules are required, and it has produced nuclear weapons, which have revised thinking about some existing rules and caused the introduction of new ones.

---

[45] The term "international law" would appear to have been coined later by Bentham (1748–1832).

[46] A system of capitulations, which in some cases lasted well into the present century, commonly applied by which European nationals present in the territory of the capitulating state were subject not to its local law or courts, but were subject instead to their national law administered in the territory of the capitulating state by their national consular courts.

[47] But see the Security Council action against Iraq in the first, although not the second, Iraq War, below pp.809 and 814.

[48] On the comparable impact of communist states during the Soviet period, see above, p.4.

[49] Oppenheim (1st edn 1905), Vol.I, para.13. Oppenheim, p.956, now reads, in its 9th edn Vol.I, p.16, "States are the principal subjects of international law."

[50] A significant recent development has been the re-emergence of individual international criminal responsibility for heinous crimes, coupled with international bodies to enforce it: see below, p.537.

[51] See Jessup, *Transnational Law* (1956), pp.15–16.

[52] See above, p.8, n.37, pp.60 et seq. On Friedmann's distinction between the older "law of coexistence" and the development of the "law of cooperation", see Abi-Saab (1998) 9 E.J.I.L. 248.

B. The Impact of Developing States[53]

HENKIN, HOW NATIONS BEHAVE

(2nd edn, 1979), pp.121–127. Some footnotes omitted

We are frequently reminded that international law was the product of European civilization. ... One might expect, then, that this law would not survive the decline of Europe's dominance, surely would not govern a society of nations most of which were not European, not Christian, not imperialist, not capitalist, which did not participate in the development of the law, and whose interests were different from those of the nations that shaped the law. In fact, however, international law has survived and would not be unrecognizable to our parents and teachers in the law and in diplomacy. The new nations raised the theoretical difficulties which have long troubled jurists as to why newborn nations should be bound by pre-existing law.[54] Some of those nations spoke and speak suspiciously of white, colonial law and have proclaimed the need for revolutionary transformations. Many indeed have challenged particular principles. But all were eager to enter international society and to accept its law.

The reasons why new nations accepted international law are not difficult to perceive. They came into an established system accepted by all nations, including the revolutionary governments and the many small powers which had supported their struggle for self-determination. Acceptance into that society as an independent equal was the proof and crown of their successful struggle, and international law provided the indispensable framework for living in that society. They adopted traditional forms in international trade and the growing co-operation for welfare of which they have been the principal beneficiaries, and early in their young history they have had to invoke international law in their disputes, among themselves or with others—on the Indus River and in Kashmir, between India and Bangladesh, on the definition of the continental shelf....

The explosion of new states ... has made it yet more difficult to make new law. It has been long established that law of universal applicability can be made only by universal agreement or acquiescence; the likelihood of general agreement decreases, of course, as the number of nations who must agree increases. New universal customary law, then, may become a rarity.... The multilateral convention, then, has become the principal form of general law-making, but already experience suggests that universality (or general acceptance) will be hard to come by.... General agreement may be possible only to codify accepted basic principles and practices, or perhaps to adopt some general, imprecise, and ambiguous standards to which time and experience may give some agreed content....

The reluctance to make new law and the difficulties of making it do not apply equally to unmaking or remaking old law. Whatever the theory, new nations can in fact have a sharp impact on the law by collective "massive resistance", especially where older states are reluctant to insist on the old law.... Customary law cannot long retain validity if a substantial number of states reject it....

In several particular respects, however, the new nations, especially as they joined with other developing states and emerged as the Third World, have created new law in their image and interest. The Third World has succeeded where it was united and determined, had the full support of the Communist World, and had some support or sympathy, at least not resistance, among Western powers. They have succeeded in making that new law in the face of the principle of unanimity, by reinterpreting universal agreements (e.g. the UN Charter), by overwhelming or silencing or even disregarding remaining opposition, especially through the use of UN resolutions. To date, the changes they have achieved in international law have been limited and special....

The success of Third World countries in virtually ending colonialism and racism, their solidarity on economic issues and their ability to extend that solidarity to other issues, on which enough of them feel strongly, have stirred dreams or fears that they might try to eliminate or erode the principle of unanimity in favor of more law-making by majority. Increasingly, they have been encouraged to seek new institutions based essentially on "one state-one vote" and majority rule (e.g. the International Sea-bed Authority (see below, p.413)); to eliminate special voting rights (like the veto in the UN Security Council); to increase the matters subject to majority vote, e.g. in UN General Assembly resolutions. They have effectively exploited other procedures, for example, decision

---

[53] See also Anand, ed., *Asian States and the Development of Universal International Law* (1972); Elias, *New Horizons in International Law* (2nd edn by Ssekandi, 1992); Hague Academy Workshop, *The Future of International Law in a Multicultural World* (1984); Higgins, *Conflict of Interests: International Law in a Divided World* (1965); Kilson, ed., *New States in the Modern World* (1975); Makonnen, *International Law and the New States of Africa* (1983).

[54] Ed. See below, p.96.

by "consensus."[55] The developed majority perhaps originally saw in that change protection against being overwhelmed by top-sided majority votes, but in time the drives for consensus, where the Third World largely agreed, began to weigh heavily on would-be dissenters not to dissent. And resolutions in the United Nations and other multilateral bodies have begun to weigh more heavily in the law-making process.

Note

For instances of the impact of the "new nations" upon international law, see the General Assembly Declaration on the Granting of Independence to Colonial Countries and Peoples,[56] the Vienna Convention on the Law of Treaties[57] (which was the first of the "law-making" treaties prepared by the International Law Commission in the drafting of which the "new nations" participated fully) and the 1982 Convention on the Law of the Sea.[58] Note also the impact they have had in the debate over the rules on the treatment of aliens,[59] and the rules concerning the use of force.[60]

C. The End of the Cold War

HENKIN, INTERNATIONAL LAW: POLITICS AND VALUES

(1995), pp.280–283

The international system is substantially changed from what it was a half-century ago. Sixty states have become near-200, most of them new states. ... For a quarter-century they grouped in three "worlds," two of them defined by ideology, the third by non-alignment—by a spirit of "a plague on both your worlds" and by bonds of common colonial history, resentment, poverty. Towards the end of the twentieth century, that configuration of three worlds has vanished: there is no Second World, therefore no Third World. But surely we are not one world. The political system is fluid and its configuration difficult to describe and to characterize; surely, it is too early for confident prognostications as to what will emerge. ...

   The demise of Communism, the disintegration of the Soviet empire, and the fragmentation of the Soviet Union changed the world order fundamentally. Immediately, dramatically, importantly, it revived the Security Council [which] ... acted, almost as originally intended, to defeat aggression and restore international peace in the Persian Gulf. It took a broad view of the demands of international peace and security to support humanitarian intervention by various means (including economic sanctions) in the former Yugoslavia, Haiti, Libya and Cambodia, and by a measure of military intervention to bring food and order in Somalia.[61] ...

   Despite revolution in East and Central Europe, and the resulting changed world order, one ought not anticipate radical change in the law in the decades ahead. The inter-state system will be long with us and therefore inter-state politics and inter-state (international) law ... But the international political system is no longer characterized by intense bipolarism and we have moved into a field of more fluid political forces.

   By some measures, the United States is the only super-Power, but others may claim super-Power status by virtue of other indicia, and all are exploring hesitatingly, uncertainly, their place and their posture. The former U.S.S.R., now fragmented and in financial difficulties, in search of internal stability and new international roles, is not to be discounted. The Third World will still have the solidarity forged by a common colonial history and common problems of underdevelopment, and its numbers will count, but the significance of being "Third," unaligned, will lessen, and perhaps too its political weight and influence. The system, I expect, will be characterized by divisions that are pragmatic rather than ideological, economic rather than political, and even the

---

[55] Ed. On the attempt at "consensus" in the drafting of the 1982 Convention on the Law of the Sea, see below, p.323.
[56] Below, p.112.
[57] Below, Ch.10.
[58] Below, Ch.7.
[59] Below, Ch.8.
[60] Below, Ch.11.
[61] Ed. Sadly, these promising developments in the early post-Cold War period have proved a false dawn: there is now much less optimism about the role that the Security Council can continue to play: see further, below, Ch.11.

common gross distinction between developed and less-developed states will blur and we will recognize a fluid spectrum of degrees of development as some state economies flourish and others falter.

The new array of forces in the system will surely have effect on the content of international law and on compliance with that law. The former U.S.S.R. is not a super-Power, but cooperation rather than confrontation between it and the United States promises new law[62] and better compliance from both of them and in the system at large. Surely, global cold war will not be the obstacle to the development of new law and institutions, for peace and security, human rights,[63] the environment, or to the use and growth and modernization of the International Court of Justice. No other state—China—or groups of states will succeed to the U.S.S.R. role, though China may continue norms and institutions—in human rights, in collective economic-social action, in Security Council intervention.

---

[62] Ed. E.g. the common position of the US and the Russian Federation on the innocent passage of warships, below, p.352.
[63] Ed. E.g. see the beneficial effect of the end of the Cold War on the working of the UN Human Rights Committee, below, p.561.

2 THE SOURCES OF INTERNATIONAL LAW

1. GENERALLY[1]

ARTICLE 38 (1) STATUTE OF THE INTERNATIONAL COURT OF JUSTICE

1. The Court, whose function is to decide in accordance with international law such disputes as are submitted to it, shall apply:

a. international conventions, whether general or particular, establishing rules expressly recognised by the contesting states;

b. international custom, as evidence of a general practice accepted as law;

c. the general principles of law recognised by civilised nations;

d. subject to the provisions of Article 59, judicial decisions and the teachings of the most highly qualified publicists of the various nations, as subsidiary means for the determination of rules of law.

SCHWARZENBERGER, INTERNATIONAL LAW

(3rd edn, 1957), Vol.1, pp.26–27. Footnote omitted

This paragraph [art.38(1)] deals with two different issues. Sub-paragraphs (a)–(c) are concerned with the pedigree of the rules of international law. In sub-paragraph (d), some of the means for the determination of alleged rules of international law are enumerated.

In order to enable the World Court to apply any asserted rule of international law, it must be shown that it is the product of one, or more, of three law-creating processes: treaties, international customary law or the general principles of law recognised by civilised nations. The significance of this enumeration lies in its exclusiveness. It rules out other potential law-creating processes such as natural law, moral postulates or the doctrine[2] of international law. Conversely, the court is bound to take into consideration any asserted rule which bears the hall-mark of one of these three law-creating processes. It is immaterial whether such a rule is also claimed as their own by any of the various brands of natural law, has its origin in considerations of humanity, or is postulated by the standards of civilisation.

This interpretation of paragraph 1 of Article 38 is further strengthened by the following paragraph.[3] The power of the Court to decide a case *ex aequo et bono*, that is to say, to ignore rules which are the product of any of the above three law-creating agencies and to substitute itself as a law-creating agency, depends on agreement of

---

[1] See Boyle and Chinkin, *The Making of International Law* (2007); Danilenko, *Law Making in the International Community* (1993); Degan, *Sources of International Law* (1997); Fitzmaurice, *Symbolae Verzijl* (1958), p.153; Jennings, *Cambridge–Tilburg Lectures: 3rd Series* (1983), pp.3–32; Mendelson, in Lowe and Fitzmaurice, eds., *Fifty Years of the International Court of Justice* (1996); Parry, *The Sources and Evidences of International Law* (1965); Szasz, in Schachter and Joyner, eds., *United Nations Legal Order* (1995), Vol.1, Ch.1; Thirlway in Evans, ed., *International Law* (2nd edn, 2006) Ch.4; Van Hoof, *Rethinking the Sources of International Law* (1983).

[2] Ed. By "doctrine" is meant the views of writers.

[3] Ed. art.38(2).

the parties to a dispute. In other words, such power must itself rest on a rule created by one of the three normal law-creating processes, in this case, a treaty.

In terms of a more conventional terminology, sub-paragraphs (*a*)–(*c*) of paragraph 1 of Article 38 of the Statute of the World Court deal with the three formal sources of international law to which the Court may resort and exclude material sources as such.[4] ...

By way of contrast to the law-creating processes, sub-paragraph (*d*) of paragraph 1 of Article 38 refers to decisions of judicial institutions and the teachings of the most highly qualified publicists as "subsidiary means for the determination of rules of law." It follows that principal means for the determination of rules of law must exist. In close leaning on this text, these principal and subsidiary means of evidence are called law-determining agencies. Each of these is composed of more or less fallible human beings, and these cannot be taken to be passive agents who merely reflect true international law as it were in a faithful mirror. This term, therefore, is also meant to bring out the unavoidable subjective and formative element which all these agencies have in common. Whereas, in the case of the law-creating processes, the emphasis lies on the forms by which any particular rule of international law is created, in the case of the law-determining agencies it is on how an alleged rule is to be verified.

Notes

1. Article 38 follows the wording of the same Article in the Statute of the Permanent Court of International Justice (which preceded the International Court of Justice as the primary court of the international community[5]), except that the words "whose function is to decide in accordance with international law such disputes as are submitted to it" are inserted in para.1. The original text was drafted in 1920 by an Advisory Committee of Jurists appointed by the League of Nations.[6] Although they were concerned to draft a text relating directly only to the functioning of the P.C.I.J., art.38 is generally accepted as a correct statement of the sources of international law.

2. *Classification of sources.* The distinction between "formal" and "material" sources to which Schwarzenberger refers was explained by Salmond[7] in the following terms:

    "A formal source is that from which a rule of law derives its force and validity. ... The material sources, on the other hand, are those from which is derived the matter, not the validity of the law. The material source supplies the substance of the rule to which the formal source gives the force and nature of law."

    For example, a rule will be legally binding if it meets the requirements of a custom, which is a formal source of international law, and its substance will be indicated by state practice, which is the material source of custom. The term *evidence* is then used in the sense that diplomatic correspondence, for example, is evidence of state practice.

3. *Order of application.*[8] When drafting the original text of art.38, the Advisory Committee of Jurists considered a proposal that it should state that the sources listed should be considered by the Court "in the undermentioned order"[9] (i.e. the order (a) to (d) in which they now appear). Opposing the proposal, M. Ricci-Busatti (Italy) is reported as saying:

---

4   Ed. For the view that treaties are not a formal source of law, see Fitzmaurice, below, p.34.
5   The term World Court is commonly used to refer to each of these Courts. See below, p.838.
6   For a record of the Committee's work, see Permanent Court of International Justice, Advisory Committee of Jurists, *Procés verbaux of the Proceedings of the Committee* (June 16–July 24, 1920, L.N. Publication, 1920).
7   *Jurisprudence* (7th edn 1924), para.44.
8   See Akehurst (1974–75) 47 B.Y.I.L. 273; Czaplinski and Danilenko (1990) 21 N.Y.I.L. 3; Koskenniemi (1997) 8 E.J.I.L. 566; Shelton (2006) 100 A.J.I.L. 291.
9   See above, n.6, p.344.

"These words were not only superfluous, but they might also suggest the idea that the judge was not authorised to draw upon a certain source, for instance point 3,[10] before having applied conventions and customs mentioned respectively in points 1 and 2. That would be a mis-interpretation of the Committee's intentions."[11]

In response, the President of the Committee, Baron Descamps (Belgium), remarked, however, that:

"there was a natural classification. If two States concluded a treaty in which the solution of the dispute could be found, the Court must not apply international custom and neglect the treaty.[12] If a well-known custom exists, there is no occasion to resort to a general principle of law. We shall indicate an order of natural *précellence*, without requiring in a given case the agreement of several sources."[13]

M. Ricci-Busatti held to his opinion. He said:

"if the expression *'ordre successif'* [undermentioned order] only meant that a convention should be considered before, for instance, customary law, it is unnecessary. It is a fundamental principle of law that a special rule goes before general law. This expression also seems to fail to recognise that these various sources may be applied simultaneously, and also that the nature of each source differs."[14]

Agreement with M. Ricci-Busatti was expressed by other members and the statement was omitted.[15]

----

2. Custom[16]

See the *Lotus* case, below, p.230, the *Anglo-Norwegian Fisheries* case, below, p.327, the *Nicaragua (Merits)* case, below, p.727, and the *Legality of Nuclear Weapons* case, below, p.788. These cases are important to an understanding of the nature of custom and the extracts printed later in this book should be read at the same time as those from the cases extracted in this chapter.

---

[10]   Ed. General principles of law.
[11]   See above, n.6, p.337.
[12]   Ed. This must now be read subject to the rules concerning ius cogens: see below, p.694.
[13]   See above, n.6, p.337.
[14]   ibid.
[15]   ibid., p.338.
[16]   See Akehurst (1974–75) 47 B.Y.I.L. 1; Byers, *Custom, Power and the Power of Rules* (1999); D'Amato, *The Concept of Custom in International Law* (1971); Guzman (2005) 26 Mich. M.J.I.L. 115; Kammerhofer (2004) 15 E.J.I.L. 523; Lauterpacht, *The Development of International Law by the International Court* (1958), pp.368–393; Lowe (1983) 9 Rev. Int. Studies 207; Mendelson (1998) 272 Hague Recueil 155; Müllerson, in Wellens, ed., *International Law: Theory and Practice* (1998), p.161; Roberts (2001) 95 A.J.I.L. 757; Thirlway, *International Customary Law and Codification* (1972); Wolfke, *Custom in Present International Law* (2nd edn 1993); Final Report of the Committee on the Formation of Customary International Law, *I.L.A. 69th Conference Report* (2000), p.712.

ASYLUM CASE[17]

Colombia v Peru

I.C.J. Reports 1950, p.266

After an unsuccessful rebellion in Peru in 1948, a warrant was issued for the arrest on a criminal charge arising out of the rebellion of one of its leaders, Haya de la Torre, a Peruvian national. He was granted asylum by Colombia in its Peruvian Embassy in Lima. Colombia sought, and Peru refused, a safe conduct to allow Haya de la Torre out of the country. Colombia brought this case against Peru, asking the Court to rule, inter alia, that:

"Colombia, as the state granting asylum, is competent to qualify the offence[18] for the purposes of the said asylum."[19]

It argued for such a ruling on the basis of both treaty provisions and "American international law in general". In the following extract, the Court considered the latter basis for the Colombian argument.

Judgment of the Court

The Colombian Government has finally invoked "American international law in general." In addition to the rules arising from agreements which have already been considered, it has relied on an alleged regional or local custom peculiar to Latin-American States.

   The Party which relies on a custom of this kind must prove that this custom is established in such a manner that it has become binding on the other Party. The Colombian Government must prove that the rule invoked by it is in accordance with a constant and uniform usage practised by the States in question, and that this usage is the expression of a right appertaining to the State granting asylum and a duty incumbent on the territorial State. This follows from Article 38 of the Statute of the Court, which refers to international custom "as evidence of a general practice accepted as law."

   ... the Colombian Government has referred to a large number of cases in which diplomatic asylum was in fact granted and respected. But it has not shown that the alleged rule of unilateral and definitive qualification was invoked or ... that it was, apart from conventional stipulations, exercised by the States granting asylum as a right appertaining to them and respected by the territorial State as a duty incumbent on them and not merely for reasons of political expediency. The facts brought to the knowledge of the Court disclose so much uncertainty and contradiction, so much fluctuation and discrepancy in the exercise of diplomatic asylum and in the official views expressed on various occasions, there has been so much inconsistency in the rapid succession of conventions on asylum, ratified by some States and rejected by others, and the practice has been so much influenced by considerations of political expediency in the various cases, that it is not possible to discern in all this any constant and uniform usage, accepted as law, with regard to the alleged rule of unilateral and definitive qualification of the offence.

   The Court cannot therefore find that the Colombian Government has proved the existence of such a custom. But even if it could be supposed that such a custom existed between certain Latin-American States only, it could not be invoked against Peru which, far from having by its attitude adhered to it, has, on the contrary, repudiated it by refraining from ratifying the Montevideo Conventions of 1933 and 1939, which were the first to include a rule concerning the qualification of the offence in matters of diplomatic asylum.

---

[17]   See Briggs (1951) 45 A.J.I.L. 728.
[18]   i.e. to characterise the offence—in this case to say whether it was a political offence or not.
[19]   I.C.J. Rep. 1950, p.273.

Notes

1.   The Court's description of custom as a "constant and uniform usage, accepted as law" has long been quoted as a convenient and accurate formula. In other terms, in the *Legality of Nuclear Weapons* case,[20] the Court confirmed that the substance of customary rules is to be found "primarily in the actual practice and *opinio juris* of states." These two are sometimes referred to as the objective and subjective elements of custom respectively.

2.   *General and Local Customs.* As the Court recognised in this case, although art.38(1)(b) refers to "a general" practice, it allows for local (or regional) customs amongst a group of states or just two states[21] in their relations inter se as well as for general customs binding upon the international community as a whole. Local customs may supplement or derogate from general customary international law (subject to rules of ius cogens[22]). A leading Soviet writer, Tunkin,[23] identified socialist international law as a form of local international law which was "coming to replace contemporary general international law" in the relations between socialist states. An example of such law was the Brezhnev Doctrine, which justified intervention by socialist states in the affairs of any one of them to preserve socialism.[24] The Brezhnev Doctrine no longer applies and it is not clear that any other rules of socialist international law remain in the post-USSR era.

      Although local customs exist, general customs are by far the more numerous and important.

3.   *State Practice.* By "usage" the Court means a usage that is to be found in the practice of states.[25] The International Law Commission included the following in a non-exhaustive list[26] of the forms that state practice may take: treaties, decisions of international and national courts, national legislation, diplomatic correspondence, opinions of national legal advisers and the practice of international organisations.[27] Other categories listed by Brownlie[28] include policy statements, press releases, official manuals on legal questions, e.g. manuals of military law, executive decisions and practices, orders to naval forces etc. and comments by governments on drafts produced by the International Law Commission."[29]

      In his opinion in the *Anglo-Norwegian Fisheries* case[30] Judge Read said in respect of state practice and with particular reference to the facts of the case before him:

      "This cannot be established by citing cases where coastal States have made extensive claims, but have not maintained their claims by the actual assertion of sovereignty over trespassing foreign ships. Such claims may be important as starting points, which, if not challenged, may ripen into historic title in the course of time. The only convincing evidence of State practice is to be found in seizures, where the coastal State asserts its sovereignty over the water in

---

[20] For the full passage from the opinion, see below, p.790.
[21] Such a custom was found to exist between India and Portugal in the *Right of Passage* case, below, p.220.
[22] On ius cogens, see below, p.694.
[23] *Theory of International Law, op. cit.,* p.4, n.14, above, p.444.
[24] *Theory of International Law,* p.433.
[25] On the question whether the practice of other international persons may contribute to the development of custom, see below, p.129.
[26] (1950) II Y.B.I.L.C., 368–372.
[27] "Records of the cumulating practice of international organisations may be regarded as evidence of customary international law with reference to States relations to the organisations": (1950) II Y.B.I.L.C. p.372.
[28] Brownlie, p.6.
[29] cf. Government reaction to the practice of such bodies as the Human Rights Committee: see below, p.665.
[30] I.C.J. Rep. 1951, p.191.

question by arresting a foreign ship and by maintaining its position in the course of diplomatic negotiation and international arbitration."

How far should Judge Read's emphasis upon "action rather than words" be carried? Although acts in support of a claim may be "the only convincing evidence" where the claim is challenged by the acts of another state, abstract statements of a legal position have been recognised as being of value in other cases, as the extract from the *North Sea Continental Shelf* cases below shows. As to the relevance of General Assembly resolutions, see below, p.52.

On the need to take care in assessing the significance of a state's acts or pronouncements, Brierly[31] states:

"There are multifarious occasions on which persons who act or speak in the name of a state do acts or make declarations which either express or imply some view on a matter of international law. Any such act or declaration may, so far as it goes, be some evidence that a custom, and therefore that a rule of international law, does or does not exist; but of course its value as evidence will be altogether determined by the occasion and the circumstances. States, like individuals, often put forward contentions for the purpose of supporting a particular case which do not necessarily represent their settled or impartial opinion."

Unfortunately,[32] the evidence of state practice is not as available as it should be to permit considered opinions on many questions of customary international law.

At present, only the practice of the United States is available in a comprehensive form.[33] There are also very useful, but less extensive, digests of British, French, Italian and Swiss practice.[34] The practice of other states is less generally available, although the increasing number of national *Yearbooks* and law reviews on international law with national state practice sections is making recent practice more readily accessible. A lot of evidence of state practice is available to the public at the time that it comes into being in such sources as parliamentary papers, law reports and newspapers. Much of it (e.g. diplomatic correspondence and other confidential government papers), is, however, subject to rules such as that in the United Kingdom under which government records are not available to the public until 30 years have elapsed.[35]

---

[31] Brierly, p.4.

[32] Anyone who has spent time sifting through records of state practice may not agree with the use of this word.

[33] See the *Digests of International Law*, edited successively by Wharton (3 vols, 1887), Moore (8 vols, 1906), Hackworth (8 vols, 1940–44) and Whiteman (14 vols, 1963–70); the *Digest of United States Practice in International Law* (1973–80); the *Cumulative Digest of United States Practice in International Law 1981–88*. Annual or other volumes of the *Digest* coveer 1989 onwards. There is also the *U.S. Foreign Relations* and *Official Opinions of the Attorney-General of the U.S.* series of documents and the A.J.I.L. *Contemporary Practice* sections.

[34] With regard to the UK see Parry, ed., *British Digest of International Law* (only Vols 2b, 5, 6, 7 and 8 of Phase I (1860–1914) published); Smith, *Great Britain and the Law of Nations* (2 vols, 1932, 1935); McNair, *International Law Opinions* (3 vols, 1956); and E. Lauterpacht, *British Practice in International Law* (B.P.I.L.) (1963–67). The last of these was preceded by *Contemporary Practice of the United Kingdom in the Field of International Law*, which was first published as a series of occasional articles in the I.C.L.Q. covering the years 1956–59 and then published separately in 1962. *United Kingdom Materials in International Law* (U.K.M.I.L.), published annually (1978–) in the B.Y.I.L. and the *Current Legal Developments* sections in the I.C.L.Q. (1987–) are valuable current sources. The *Digest of the Diplomatic Correspondence of the European States* in the *Fontes Juris Gentium* series includes that of Great Britain for the years 1856–78. There is also the *British and Foreign State Papers* series of documents (terminated 1968). As to France and Switzerland, see *Répertoire de la pratique française en matière de droit international public* (7 vols, 1962–72) and *Répertoire suisse de droit international 1914–1939*, 4 vols. There are also annual yearbooks, such as the A.Y.I.L., C.Y.I.L.. N.Y.I.L. and the Italian Y.I.L. that have national practice sections.

[35] Public Records Act 1967.

NORTH SEA CONTINENTAL SHELF CASES[36]

Federal Republic of Germany v Denmark and The Netherlands

I.C.J. Reports 1969, p.3

A number of bilateral agreements had been made drawing lateral or median lines delimiting the North Sea continental shelves[37] of adjacent and opposite states, including two lateral line agreements between the Netherlands and the Federal Republic of Germany (1964) and Denmark and the Federal Republic of Germany (1965). Each of these last two agreements, however, did no more than draw a dividing line for a short distance from the coast beginning at the point at which the land boundary of the two states concerned was located. Further agreement had proved impossible. Special agreements were concluded between the Netherlands and the Federal Republic of Germany and between Denmark and the Federal Republic of Germany referring the problem to the ICJ. In each special agreement the question put to the Court was:

"What principles and rules of international law are applicable to the delimitation as between the Parties of the areas of the continental shelf in the North Sea which appertain to each of them beyond the partial boundary [already] determined ...?"

The two cases were joined by the Court. Denmark and the Netherlands argued that the "equidistance-special circumstances principle" in art.6(2) of the 1958 Geneva Convention on the Continental Shelf[38] applied. The Federal Republic of Germany denied this and proposed "the doctrine of the just and equitable share". The reason for the Federal Republic's opposition to the "equidistance-special circumstances principle" was that the principle has the effect, as the Court pointed out,[39] on a concave coastline such as that shared by the three states concerned of giving the state in the middle—in this case West Germany—a smaller continental shelf than it might otherwise obtain.

The Court rejected the West German proposal. After rejecting also the Danish and Dutch argument that art.6(2) stated or crystallised customary international law at the time of its adoption, it continued:

Judgment of the Court

70. ... Denmark and the Netherlands ... [argue] that even if there was at the date of the Geneva Convention no rule of customary international law in favour of the equidistance principle, and no such rule was crystallised in Article 6 of the Convention, nevertheless such a rule has come into being since the Convention, partly because of its own impact, partly on the basis of subsequent State practice, and that this rule, being now a rule of customary international law binding on all States, including therefore the Federal Republic, should be declared applicable to the delimitation of the boundaries between the Parties' respective continental shelf areas in the North Sea.

71. In so far as this contention is based on the view that Article 6 of the Convention has had the influence, and has produced the effect described, it clearly involves treating that Article as a norm-creating provision which has constituted the foundation of, or has generated a rule which, while only conventional or contractual in its origin,

---

[36]   See D'Amato (1970) 64 A.J.I.L. 892; Friedmann (1970) 64 A.J.I.L. 229; and Nelson (1972) 35 M.L.R. 52.

[37]   On the law of the continental shelf, see below, p.399.

[38]   art.6(2) reads: "... In the absence of agreement, and unless another boundary line is justified by special circumstances, the boundary shall be determined by application of the principle of equidistance from the nearest points of the baselines from which the breadth of the territorial sea of each state is measured."

[39]   I.C.J. Rep. 1969, p.17.

has since passed into the general *corpus* of international law, and is now accepted as such by the *opinio juris*, so as to have become binding even for countries which have never, and do not, become parties to the Convention. There is no doubt that this process is a perfectly possible one and does from time to time occur: it constitutes indeed one of the recognised methods by which new rules of customary international law may be formed. At the same time this result is not lightly to be regarded as having been attained.

72. It would in the first place be necessary that the provision concerned should, at all events potentially, be of a fundamentally norm-creating character such as could be regarded as forming the basis of a general rule of law. Considered *in abstracto* the equidistance principle might be said to fulfil this requirement. Yet in the particular form in which it is embodied in Article 6 of the Geneva Convention, and having regard to the relationship of that Article to other provisions of the Convention, this must be open to some doubt. In the first place, Article 6 is so framed as to put second the obligation to make use of the equidistance method, causing it to come after a primary obligation to effect delimitation by agreement. Such a primary obligation constitutes an unusual preface to what is claimed to be a potential general rule of law. Without attempting to enter into, still less pronounce upon any question of *jus cogens*,[40] it is well understood that, in practice, rules of international law can, by agreement, be derogated from in particular cases, or as between particular parties—but this is not normally the subject of any express provision, as it is in Article 6 of the Geneva Convention. Secondly the part played by the notion of special circumstances relative to the principle of equidistance as embodied in Article 6, and the very considerable, still unresolved controversies as to the exact meaning and scope of this notion, must raise further doubts as to the potentially norm-creating character of the rule. Finally, the faculty of making reservations to Article 6, while it might not of itself prevent the equidistance principle being eventually received as general law, does add considerably to the difficulty of regarding this result as having been brought about (or being potentially possible) on the basis of the Convention: for so long as this faculty continues to exist, and is not the subject of any revision brought about in consequence of a request made under Article 13 of the Convention—of which there is at present no official indication—it is the Convention itself which would, for the reasons already indicated, seem to deny to the provisions of Article 6 the same norm-creating character as, for instance, Articles 1 and 2 possess.

73. With respect to the other elements usually regarded as necessary before a conventional rule can be considered to have become a general rule of international law, it might be that, even without the passage of any considerable period of time, a very widespread and representative participation in the Convention might suffice of itself, provided it included that of States whose interests were specially affected. In the present case however, the Court notes that, even if allowance is made for the existence of a number of States to whom participation in the Geneva Convention is not open, or which, by reason for instance of being land-locked States, would have no interest in becoming parties to it, the number of ratifications and accessions so far secured is, though respectable, hardly sufficient. That non-ratification may sometimes be due to factors other than active dis-approval of the Convention concerned can hardly constitute a basis on which positive acceptance of its principles can be implied. The reasons are speculative, but the facts remain.

74. As regards the time element, the Court notes that it is over ten years since the Convention was signed, but that it is even now less than five since it came into force in June 1964, and that when the present proceedings were brought it was less than three years, while less than one had elapsed at the time when the respective negotiations between the Federal Republic and the other two Parties for a complete delimitation broke down on the question of the application of the equidistance principle. Although the passage of only a short period of time is not necessarily, or of itself, a bar to the formation of a new rule of customary international law on the basis of what was originally a purely conventional rule, an indispensable requirement would be that within the period in question, short though it might be, State practice, including that of States whose interests are specially affected, should have been both extensive and virtually uniform in the sense of the provision invoked—and should moreover have occurred in such a way as to show a general recognition that a rule of law or legal obligation is involved.

75. The Court must now consider whether State practice in the matter of continental shelf delimitation has, subsequent to the Geneva Convention, been of such a kind as to satisfy this requirement.... Some fifteen cases have been cited in the course of the present proceedings, occurring mostly since the signature of the 1958 Geneva Convention, in which continental shelf boundaries have been delimited according to the equidistance principle—in the majority of the cases by agreement, in a few others, unilaterally—or else the delimitation was foreshadowed but has not yet been carried out.... even if these various cases constituted more than a very small proportion of those potentially calling for delimitation in the world as a whole, the Court would not think it

---

[40] Ed. See below, p.694.

necessary to enumerate or evaluate them separately, since there are, *a priori*, several grounds which deprive them of weight as precedents in the present context.

76. ... Over half the States concerned, whether acting unilaterally or conjointly, were or shortly became parties to the Geneva Convention, and were therefore presumably, so far as they were concerned, acting actually or potentially in the application of the Convention. From their action no inference could legitimately be drawn as to the existence of a rule of customary international law in favour of the equidistance principle. As regards those States, on the other hand, which were not, and have not become parties to the Convention, the basis of their action can only be problematical and must remain entirely speculative. Clearly, they were not applying the Convention. But from that no inference could justifiably be drawn that they believed themselves to be applying a mandatory rule of customary international law. There is not a shred of evidence that they did and ... there is no lack of other reasons for using the equidistance method, so that acting, or agreeing to act in a certain way, does not of itself demonstrate anything of a juridical nature.

77. The essential point in this connection—and it seems necessary to stress it—is that even if these instances of action by non-parties to the Convention were much more numerous than they in fact are, they would not, even in the aggregate, suffice in themselves to constitute the *opinio juris*—for, in order to achieve this result, two conditions must be fulfilled. Not only must the acts concerned amount to a settled practice, but they must also be such, or be carried out in such a way, as to be evidence of a belief that this practice is rendered obligatory by the existence of a rule of law requiring it. The need for such a belief, i.e. the existence of a subjective element, is implicit in the very notion of the *opinio juris sive necessitatis*. The States concerned must therefore feel that they are conforming to what amounts to a legal obligation. The frequency, or even habitual character of the acts is not in itself enough. There are many international acts, e.g. in the field of ceremonial and protocol, which are performed almost invariably, but which are motivated only by considerations of courtesy, convenience or tradition, and not by any sense of legal duty.

78. In this respect the Court follows the view adopted by the Permanent Court of International Justice in the *Lotus* case,[41] as stated in the following passage, the principle of which is, by analogy, applicable almost word for word, *mutatis mutandis*, to the present case (P.C.I.J., Series A, No.10, 1927, at p.28):

> Even if the rarity of the judicial decisions to be found ... were sufficient to prove ... the circumstance alleged ... it would merely show that States had often, in practice, abstained from instituting criminal proceedings, and not that they recognised themselves as being obliged to do so; for only if such abstention were based on their being conscious of having a duty to abstain would it be possible to speak of an international custom. The alleged fact does not allow one to infer that States have been conscious of having such a duty; on the other hand ... there are other circumstances calculated to show that the contrary is true.

Applying this dictum to the present case, the position is simply that in certain cases—not a great number—the States concerned agreed to draw or did draw the boundaries concerned according to the principle of equidistance. There is no evidence that they so acted because they felt legally compelled to draw them in this way by reason of a rule of customary law obliging them to do so—especially considering that they might have been motivated by other obvious factors. ...

81. The Court accordingly concludes that if the Geneva Convention was not in its origins or inception declaratory of a mandatory rule of customary international law enjoining the use of the equidistance principle for the delimitation of continental shelf areas between adjacent States neither has its subsequent effect been constitutive of such a rule; and that State practice up-to-date has equally been insufficient for the purpose. ...

Having thus found that neither of the approaches argued for by the parties was a part of international law, the Court then proceeded to spell out the customary international law principles and rules that did apply "as between States faced with an issue concerning the lateral delimitation of adjacent continental shelves." ...

85. It emerges from the history of the development of the legal régime of the continental shelf. ... that the essential reason why the equidistance method is not to be regarded as a rule of law is that, if it were to be compulsorily applied in all situations, this would not be consonant with certain basic legal notions which. ... have

---

[41] Ed. See below, p.230.

from the beginning reflected the *opinio juris* in the matter of delimitation; those principles being that delimitation must be the object of agreement between the States concerned, and that such agreement must be arrived at in accordance with equitable principles. . . .

88. . . . Whatever the legal reasoning of a court of justice, its decisions must by definition be just, and therefore in that sense equitable. Nevertheless, when mention is made of a court dispensing justice or declaring the law, what is meant is that the decision finds its objective justification in considerations lying not outside but within the rules, and in this field it is precisely a rule of law that calls for the application of equitable principles. . . . There is consequently no question in this case of any decision *ex aequo et bono*, such as would not be possible under the conditions prescribed by Article 38, paragraph 2, of the Court's Statute. . . .

91. Equity does not necessarily imply equality. There can never be any question of completely refashioning nature, and equity does not require that a State without access to the sea should be allotted an area of continental shelf, any more than there could be a question of rendering the situation of a State with an extensive coastline similar to that of a State with a restricted coastline. Equality is to be reckoned within the same plane, and it is not such natural inequalities as these that equity could remedy. But in the present case there are three States whose North Sea coastlines are in fact comparable in length and which, therefore, have been given broadly equal treatment by nature except that the configuration of one of the coastlines would, if the equidistance method is used, deny to one of these States treatment equal or comparable to that given the other two. Here indeed is a case where, in a theoretical situation of equality within the same order, an inequality is created.

92. It has however been maintained that no one method of delimitation can prevent such results and that all can lead to relative injustices. This argument. . . can only strengthen the view that it is necessary to seek not one method of delimitation but one goal. . . . As the operation of delimiting is a matter of determining areas appertaining to different jurisdictions, it is a truism to say that the determination must be equitable; rather is the problem above all one of defining the means whereby the delimitation can be carried out in such a way as to be recognized as equitable. . . .

101. For these reasons, THE COURT, by eleven votes to six,[42] finds that, in each case,

(A)   the use of the equidistance method of delimitation not being obligatory as between the Parties; and

(B)   there being no other single method of delimitation the use of which is in all circumstances obligatory;

(C)   the principles and rules of international law applicable to the delimitation as between the Parties . . . are as follows:

(1)   delimitation is to be effected by agreement in accordance with equitable principles, and taking account of all the relevant circumstances, in such a way as to leave as much as possible to each Party all those parts of the continental shelf that constitute a natural prolongation of its land territory into and under the sea, without encroachment on the natural prolongation of the land territory of the other;

(2)   if, in the application of the preceding sub-paragraph, the delimitation leaves to the Parties areas that overlap, these are to be divided between them in agreed proportions or, failing agreement, equally, unless they decide on a régime of joint jurisdiction, user, or exploitation for the zones of overlap or any part of them;

(D)   in the course of the negotiations, the factors to be taken into account are to include:

(1)   the general configuration of the coasts of the Parties, as well as the presence of any special or unusual features;

(2)   so far as known or readily ascertainable, the physical and geological structure, and natural resources, of the continental shelf areas involved;

(3)   the element of a reasonable degree of proportionality, which a delimitation carried out in accordance with equitable principles ought to bring about between the extent of the continental shelf areas appertaining to the coastal State and the length of its coast measured in the general direction of the coastline, account being taken for this purpose of the effects, actual or prospective, of any other continental shelf delimitations between adjacent States in the same region.[43]

---

[42]   The judges in the majority were President Bustamente y Rivero; Judges Sir Gerald Fitzmaurice, Jessup, Sir Muhammad Zafrulla Khan, Padilla Nervo, Forster, Gros, Ammoun, Petrén and Onyeama; Judge ad hoc Mosler. Vice-President Koretsky; Judges Tanaka, Morelli, Bengzon and Lachs; Judge ad hoc Sørensen dissented.

[43]   Ed. The parties agreed upon the delimitation of their continental shelves inter se on the basis of the Court's judgment by treaties made in 1971: for texts, see *Yearbook of the ICJ* 1970–71, pp.118 et seq.

DISSENTING OPINION OF JUDGE TANAKA

To decide whether these two factors [usage and *opinio juris*] in the formative process of a customary law exist or not, is a delicate and difficult matter. The repetition, the number of examples of State practice, the duration of time required for the generation of customary law cannot be mathematically and uniformly decided. Each fact requires to be evaluated relatively according to the different occasions and circumstances.... what is important in the matter at issue is not the number or figure of ratifications of and accessions to the Convention or of examples of subsequent State practice, but the meaning which they would imply in the particular circumstances. We cannot evaluate the ratification of the Convention by a large maritime country or the State practice represented by its concluding an agreement on the basis of the equidistance principle, as having exactly the same importance as similar acts by a land-locked country which possesses no particular interest in the delimitation of the continental shelf.

Next, so far as ... *opinio juris sive necessitatis* is concerned, it is extremely difficult to get evidence of its existence in concrete cases. This factor, relating to international motivation and being of a psychological nature, cannot be ascertained very easily, particularly when diverse legislative and executive organs of a government participate in an internal process of decision-making in respect of ratification or other State acts. There is no other way than to ascertain the existence of *opinio juris* from the fact of the external existence of a certain custom and its necessity felt in the international community, rather than to seek evidence as to the subjective motives for each example of State practice, which is something which is impossible of achievement....

DISSENTING OPINION OF JUDGE LACHS

Delay in the ratification of and accession to multilateral treaties is a well-known phenomenon in contemporary treaty practice ... experience indicates that in most cases [it is] caused by factors extraneous to the substance and objective of the instrument in question.

... [This] indicates that the number of ratifications and accessions cannot, in itself, be considered conclusive with regard to the general acceptance of a given instrument.

In the case of the Convention on the Continental Shelf, there are other elements that must be given their due weight. In particular, thirty-one States came into existence during the period between its signature (June 28, 1958) and its entry into force (June 10, 1964), while thirteen other nations have since acceded to independence. Thus the time during which these forty-four States could have completed the necessary procedure enabling them to become parties to the Convention has been rather limited, in some cases very limited. Taking into account the great and urgent problems each of them had to face, one cannot be surprised that many of them did not consider it a matter of priority. This notwithstanding, nine of those States have acceded to the Convention. Twenty-six of the total number of States in existence are moreover land-locked and cannot be considered as having a special and immediate interest in speedy accession to the Convention (only five of them have in fact acceded).

Finally, it is noteworthy that about seventy States are at present engaged in the exploration and exploitation of continental shelf areas.

It is the above analysis which is relevant, not the straight comparison between the total number of States in existence and the number of parties to the Convention. It reveals in fact that the number of parties to the Convention on the Continental Shelf is very impressive, including as it does the majority of States actively engaged in the exploration of continental shelves.

... in the world today an essential factor in the formation of a new rule of general international law is to be taken into account: namely that States with different political, economic and legal systems, States of all continents, participate in the process. No more can a general rule of international law be established by the fiat of one or of a few, or—as it was once claimed—by the consensus of European States only....

All this leads to the conclusion that the principles and rules enshrined in the Convention, and in particular the equidistance rule, have been accepted not only by those States which are parties to the Convention on the Continental Shelf, but also by those which have subsequently followed it in agreements, or in their legislation, or have acquiesced in it when faced with legislative acts of other States affecting them. This can be viewed as evidence of a practice widespread enough to satisfy the criteria for a general rule of law.

For to become binding, a rule or principle of international law need not pass the test of universal acceptance. This is reflected in several statements of the Court, e.g.: "generally ... adopted in the practice of States" (*Fisheries, Judgment*, I.C.J. Reports 1951, p.128). Not all States have ... an opportunity or possibility of applying a given rule. The evidence should be sought in the behaviour of a great number of States, possibly the majority of States, in any case the great majority of the interested States....

DISSENTING OPINION OF JUDGE AD HOC SØRENSEN

I agree, of course, that one should not lightly reach the conclusion that a convention is binding upon a non-contracting State. But I find it necessary to take account of the fact—to which the Court does not give specific weight—that the Geneva Convention belongs to a particular category of multilateral conventions, namely those which result from the work of the United Nations in the field of codification and progressive development of international law, under Article 13 of the Charter....

According to classic doctrine ... [the] practice [necessary to establish a rule of customary international law] must have been pursued over a certain length of time. There have even been those who have maintained the necessity of "immemorial usage". In its previous jurisprudence, however, the Court does not seem to have laid down strict requirements as to the duration of the usage or practice which may be accepted as law. In particular, it does not seem to have drawn any conclusion in this respect from the ordinary meaning of the word "custom" when used in other contexts.... The possibility has thus been reserved of recognising the rapid emergence of a new rule of customary law based on the recent practice of States. This is particularly important in view of the extremely dynamic process of evolution in which the international community is engaged at the present stage of history.[44] Whether the mainspring of this evolution is to be found in the development of ideas, in social and economic factors, or in new technology, it is characteristic of our time that new problems and circumstances incessantly arise and imperatively call for legal regulation. In situations of this nature, a convention adopted as part of the combined process of codification and progressive development of international law may well constitute, or come to constitute the decisive evidence of generally accepted new rules of international law. The fact that it does not purport simply to be declaratory of existing customary law is immaterial in this context. The convention may serve as an authoritative guide for the practice of States faced with the relevant new legal problems, and its provisions thus become the nucleus around which a new set of generally recognised legal rules may crystallise. The word "custom," with its traditional time connotation, may not even be an adequate expression for the purpose of describing this particular source of law.

... The adoption of the Geneva Convention on the Continental Shelf was a very significant element in the process of creating new rules of international law in a field which urgently required legal regulation.... No State which has exercised sovereign rights over its continental shelf in conformity with the provisions of the Convention has been met with protests by other States....

I do not find it necessary to go into the question of the *opinio juris*. This is a problem of legal doctrine which may cause great difficulties in international adjudication. In view of the manner in which international relations are conducted, there may be numerous cases in which it is practically impossible for one government to produce conclusive evidence of the motives which have prompted the action and policy of other governments. Without going into all aspects of the doctrinal debate on this issue, I wish only to cite the following passage by one of the most qualified commentators on the jurisprudence of the Court. Examining the conditions of the *opinio necessitatis juris* Sir Hersch Lauterpacht writes:

> Unless judicial activity is to result in reducing the legal significance of the most potent source of rules of international law, namely, the conduct of States, it would appear that the accurate principle on the subject consists in regarding all uniform conduct of Governments (or, in appropriate cases, abstention therefrom) as evidencing the *opinio necessitatis juris* except when it is shown that the conduct in question was not accompanied by any such intention. (Sir Hersch Lauterpacht: *The Development of International Law by the International Court*, London, 1958, p.380.)

Applying these considerations to the circumstances of the present cases, I think that the practice of States referred to above may be taken as sufficient evidence of the existence of any necessary *opinio juris*.

In my opinion, the conclusion may therefore safely be drawn that as a result of a continuous process over a

---

[44]   Ed. Judge Lachs took the same view in his Opinion. He gave the following example of the "rapid emergence" of a customary rule: "... the first instruments that man sent into outer space traversed the airspace of States and circled above them in outer space, yet the launching States sought no permission nor did the other States protest. This is how the freedom of movement into outer space, and in it, came to be established and recognised as law within a remarkably short period of time" (p.230). Cf. the "Instant" emergence of the right of "pre-emptive self defence", post 9/11, see Gray, below p.772. On "instant custom", see Cheng in Macdonald and Johnston, eds., *The Structure and Process of International Law* (1983), p.513 at p.532 and Guzman (2005) 27 M.J.I.L. 115. See further below, p.56, n.181.

quarter of a century, the rules embodied in the Geneva Convention on the Continental Shelf have now attained the status of generally accepted rules of international law.

That being so, it is nevertheless necessary to examine in particular the attitude of the Federal Republic of Germany with regard to the Convention. In the *Fisheries Case* the Court said that the ten-mile rule would in any event "appear to be inapplicable as against Norway inasmuch as she has always opposed any attempt to apply it to the Norwegian coast" (I.C.J. Reports 1951, p.131). Similarly, it might be argued in the present cases that the Convention on the Continental Shelf would be inapplicable as against the Federal Republic, if she had consistently refused to recognise it as an expression of generally accepted rules of international law and had objected to its applicability as against her. But far from adopting such an attitude, the Federal Republic has gone quite a long way towards recognising the Convention. It is part of the whole picture, though not decisive in itself, that the Federal Republic signed the Convention in 1958, immediately before the time-limit for signature under Article 8. More significant is the fact that the Federal Republic has relied on the Convention for the purpose of asserting her own rights in the continental shelf.... This attitude is relevant, not so much in the context of the traditional legal concepts of recognition, acquiescence or estoppel, as in the context of the general process of creating international legal rules of universal applicability. At a decisive stage of this formative process, an interested State, which was not a party to the Convention, formally recorded its view that the Convention was an expression of generally applicable international law. This view being perfectly well founded, that State is not now in a position to escape the authority of the Convention.

It has been asserted that the possibility, made available by Article 12, of entering reservations to certain articles of the Convention, makes it difficult to understand the articles in question as embodying generally accepted rules of international law.... In my view, the faculty of making reservations to a treaty provision has no necessary connection with the question whether or not the provision can be considered as expressing a generally recognised rule of law. To substantiate this opinion it may be sufficient to point out that a number of reservations have been made to provisions of the Convention on the High Seas, although this Convention, according to its preamble, is "generally declaratory of established principles of international law." Some of these reservations have been objected to by other contracting States, while other reservations have been tacitly accepted. The acceptance, whether tacit or express, of a reservation made by a contracting party does not have the effect of depriving the Convention as a whole, or the relevant article in particular, of its declaratory character. It only has the effect of establishing a special contractual relationship between the parties concerned within the general framework of the customary law embodied in the Convention. Provided the customary rule does not belong to the category of *jus cogens*, a special contractual relationship of this nature is not invalid as such. Consequently, there is no incompatibility between the faculty of making reservations to certain articles of the Convention on the Continental Shelf and the recognition of that Convention or the particular articles as an expression of generally accepted rules of international law.

Notes

1. *Treaties as a material source of custom. The North Sea Continental Shelf* cases, which are among the relatively few cases in which the World Court has discussed in any detail the requirements for the existence of a rule of customary international law, were concerned with a question of increasing importance as the process of codifying and developing international law by multi-lateral treaties continues, namely the role of such treaties as state practice and hence as a material source of customary international law binding upon parties and non-parties alike.[45]

    In the Court's opinion, a treaty provision[46] may relate to custom in one of three ways. It may be declaratory of custom at the time that the provision is adopted[47]; it may crystallise custom, as

---

[45] Examples recognised by the ICJ are the Fourth Hague Convention on Land Warfare 1907 and its Regulations, 100 BFSP 338; 1 Bevans 631; the *Wall* case, I.C.J. Rep. 2004, p.172, and some articles of the Vienna Convention on the Law of Treaties 1969: see below p.638. See on this question Baxter (1970–I) 129 Hague Recueil 25; Charney (1986) 61 Wash. L.R. 971; Czaplinski (1989) 38 I.C.L.Q. 151; D'Amato, n.36, above, Ch.5; Jennings, in Wilner, ed., *Jus et Societas: Essays in Tribute to Wolfgang Friedmann* (1979), p.159; Villiger, *Customary International Law and Treaties* (1985); Weisburd (1988) 21 Vand. J.T.L. 1.

[46] This includes a provision in a treaty that is not yet in force, or even a draft treaty text.

[47] As Judge ad hoc Sørenson points out, the preamble to the High Seas Convention 1958, states that it is "generally declaratory of established principles of international law".

states agree on the provision to be adopted during the treaty drafting process; or the provision may come to be accepted and followed by states as custom in their practice after the treaty's adoption.[48] On the facts of the case, the third possibility was the one most closely examined by the Court. Why, in the opinion of the Court, would Denmark's and the Netherlands' task have been easier if they had been arguing that the rules in arts 1 or 2 of the Continental Shelf Convention (instead of that in art.6) had become a part of customary international law? Since states may contract out of a rule of customary international law in their relations inter se, should, as the Court suggests (para.72), it matter whether a treaty rule which is claimed to be a custom is one to which reservations are permitted? Does the Court's judgment indicate whether bilateral (as well as multilateral) treaties may be evidence of state practice? Is it possible that in some cases it may be precisely because the rights and duties set out in a treaty are not a part of customary international law that the parties feel the need to make it?[49]

2.   Whereas the question in the *North Sea Continental Shelf* cases was whether a treaty rule was binding as custom upon a non-party to the treaty, the question in the *Nicaragua (Merits)* case[50] was whether customary rules applied in the relations between two states when rules covering the same ground also existed in treaties to which those states were parties. In that case, Nicaragua claimed that the US had used armed force and intervened in its affairs contrary to international law. The Court accepted that it could not consider US liability under the UN Charter and other multilateral treaties to which the US and Nicaragua were parties. This was because of a US reservation to its acceptance of the Court's jurisdiction that excluded "disputes arising under a multilateral treaty". The question for the Court therefore was whether the customary rules on armed force and intervention continued to bind the parties in parallel with the obligations under the UN Charter and other treaties they had accepted, so that the Court could apply them despite the US reservation. Holding that they did, the Court stated:

"177 . . . The existence of identical rules in international treaty law and customary law has been clearly recognized by the Court in the *North Sea Continental Shelf* cases. To a large extent, those cases turned on the question whether a rule enshrined in a treaty also existed as a customary rule, either because the treaty had merely codified the custom, or caused it to "crystallize", or because it had influenced its subsequent adoption. The Court found that this identity of content in treaty law and in customary international law did not exist in the case of the rule invoked, which appeared in one article of the treaty, but did not suggest that such identity was debarred as a matter of principle: on the contrary, it considered it to be clear that certain other articles of the treaty in question "were . . . regarded as reflecting, or as crystal-lizing, received or at least emergent rules of customary international law" (I.C.J. Reports 1969, p.39, para.63). More generally, there are no grounds for holding that when customary international law is comprised of rules identical to those of treaty law, the latter "supervenes" the former, so that the customary international law has no further existence of its own.

178.   There are a number of reasons for [this conclusion] . . . In a legal dispute affecting two States, one of them may argue that the applicability of a treaty rule to its own conduct depends on the other State's conduct in respect of the application of other rules, on other subjects, also included in the same treaty. For example, if a State exercises its right to

---

[48]   The position is similar to that concerning General Assembly resolutions (see below, p.52): statements made by states during the drafting process, the agreed treaty text, and later state reaction to the treaty, may be state practice indicative to custom.

[49]   See, on the questions in these last two sentences, the *Lotus* case, below, p.727.

[50]   I.C.J. Rep. 1986, p.14 at 94. For further extracts from the Court's judgment, see below, p.230.

terminate or suspend the operation of a treaty on the ground of the violation by the other party of a "provision essential to the accomplishment of the object or purpose of the treaty" (in the words of art.60, para.3(*b*), of the Vienna Convention on the Law of Treaties), it is exempted, vis-à-vis the other State, from a rule of treaty-law because of the breach by that other State of a different rule of treaty-law. But if the two rules in question also exist as rules of customary international law, the failure of the one State to apply the one rule does not justify the other State in declining to apply the other rule. Rules which are identical in treaty law and in customary international law are also distinguishable by reference to the methods of interpretation and application. A State may accept a rule contained in a treaty not simply because it favours the application of the rule itself, but also because the treaty establishes what that State regards as desirable institutions or mechanisms to ensure implementation of the rule. Thus, if that rule parallels a rule of customary international law, two rules of the same content are subject to separate treatment as regards the organs competent to verify their implementation, depending on whether they are customary rules or treaty rules. The present dispute illustrates this point."[51]

The situation where the treaty and customary rules are *not* identical, but merely apply in the same field, is an *a fortiori* case for the application of the Court's approach. This was the situation in the *Nicaragua (Merits)* case in respect of the UN Charter and customary rules on self defence: see judgment para.176, below, p.727.

3. As well as stating rules on the particular question of the role of treaties as a material source of custom, the Court's judgment in the *North Sea* cases, and those of several of the judges who gave separate opinions (see Judge Sørensen, above, at n.44), throws light on the nature of customary international law in other respects also. For example, it recognises that there is no precise length of time during which a practice must exist; the position is simply that it must be followed long enough to show that the other requirements of a custom are met.

The Court's approach to the question of the number and kind of states whose practice has to be established is also instructive. It demonstrates that a practice does not have to be followed by all states for it to be the basis of a general custom and that the practice of states with a particular interest in the subject matter is the most relevant (para.73).[52] As to the practice of the most influential states, in the course of considering whether there was sufficient evidence of state practice to justify the conclusion that the doctrine of the continental shelf was a part of general customary international law, Lauterpacht[53] states:

"... assuming here that we are confronted with the creation of new international law by custom, what matters is not so much the number of states participating in its creation and the length of the period within which that change takes place, as the relative importance, in any particular sphere, of states inaugurating the change. In a matter closely related to the principle of the freedom of the seas the conduct of the two principal maritime Powers—such as Great Britain and the United States—is of special importance. With regard to the continental

---

[51] Writers are divided on the merits of the Court's approach, with some arguing that the custom is abrogated or suspended while the treaty is in force: see Czaplinski (1989) 38 I.C.L.Q. 151 at 164.

[52] cf. the *Legality of Nuclear Weapons* case, para.96, below, p.788, in which the ICJ paid special attention to the practice of states with nuclear weapons when considering whether their use was lawful.

[53] (1950) 27 B.Y.I.L. 376 at 394.

shelf and submarine areas generally these two states inaugurated the development and their initiative was treated as authoritative almost as a matter of course from the outset."

Which states' practice, if any, should be given particular weight when considering (a) the general customary international law concerning outer space and (b) whether the rule concerning the making of reservations to multilateral treaties has been changed?

In the *Nicaragua (Merits)* case, the ICJ confirmed that when deciding a case on the basis of *general* customary international law, it must discover that law from the practice of states as a whole: it is not sufficient that the states parties to the case have a common view of what that law is.[54]

4. *Opinio juris sive necessitatis*.[55] As the Court indicates in its judgment in the *North Sea* cases (para.77), the second requirement of a custom[56]—acceptance that it is binding in law—is necessary to distinguish it from a rule of international comity,[57] which is a rule based upon a consistent practice in the relations of states which is not accompanied by a feeling of legal obligation. The saluting by a ship at sea of another ship flying a different flag is an example. Another example—which may now have been translated into a rule of customary international law[58]—is the rule by which the goods of a diplomatic agent and his family are immune from customs duty.

As the opinions of Judges Tanaka and Sørensen stress, it is often difficult to discover the necessary *opinio juris* because the reason underlying a state's adoption or acceptance of a particular practice is not clear. In this connection, Judge Sørensen (following Lauterpacht) suggested that *opinio juris* may be presumed to exist if a uniform practice is proven. The judgment of the Court (para.78), however, adopts a stricter approach. Accordingly, in the *Legality of Nuclear Weapons* case,[59] the Court declined to find a rule prohibiting the use of nuclear weapons from the fact that no recourse had been had to them for 50 years. It was necessary also to show that this "constant and uniform" non-use resulted from a feeling of obligation on the part of states generally, which was not the case: many states reserved the right to use them as a part of a policy of deterrence.

Another difficulty with *opinio juris* is that the first states to adopt a new practice are supposed to be acting on the basis that it is binding even as they do so. It was this that Lauterpacht[60] had in mind when he referred to:

---

54 *Nicaragua (Merits)* case, judgment para.184, below, p.727. In the *Maritime Delimitation and Territorial Questions Between Qatar and Bahrain (Merits)* case (I.C.J. Rep. 2001, p.40), the Court noted that "the parties agree that the provisions of art.15 of the 1982 Convention on the Law of the Sea [on maritime boundaries] . . . are part of customary law", but then went on to state and apply the Court's own conclusion that art.15 "is to be regarded as having a customary character." The Court did not refer to its *Nicaragua* judgment. The situation considered above is different from the situation in which the states parties to the case agree (or one of them asserts to the Court's satisfaction) that there is a *local* custom binding on them, in which case there is no need to look to the practice of states generally.

55 See Cheng in Yee and Wang, eds, *International Law in the Post-Cold War Period* (2001) p.56; Elias (1995) 44 I.C.L.Q. 501; Maluwa (1994) 6 Af.J.I.C.L. 387; Mendelson (1995) 66 B.Y.I.L. 177; Yee (2000) 43 G.Y.I.L. 227.

56 There is an overlap between the two requirements in the sense that *opinio juris* is to be found in state practice, e.g. where a state protests at the conduct of another state on the basis that it is illegal.

57 Note that national courts sometimes use the term "international comity" as a synonym for international law: see Akehurst (1972–1973) 46 B.Y.I.L. 145 at 214–216.

58 See arts 36 and 37, Vienna Convention on Diplomatic Relations 1961, below, p.299.

59 Judgment, paras 64–67, below, p.788.

60 (1950) 27 B.Y.I.L. 376 at 395.

"the mysterious phenomenon of customary international law which is deemed to be a source of law only on condition that it is in accordance with law."

Would it be correct to say that in the early days of the formation of a new rule the state or states adopting the practice either do not think about whether it is binding or, if they are thinking about its significance in the development of international law, put it forward more as an "offer", which other states can accept or reject, rather than as something which they are convinced is already binding? On this view, the feeling of obligation, if it arises at all, arises only later when there has been general adoption or acceptance of the practice or "offer".

The above discussion supposes that the *opinio juris* required for a customary rule is accompanied by "constant and uniform" state practice in the subject area of the rule. In a new departure, in the *Nicaragua* (*Merits*) case, below, p.727, the ICJ relied upon evidence of *opinio juris* found in General Assembly resolutions to establish the customary rule on the use of force by states, without referring also to any extra-General Assembly state practice involving the use of force. Although referring in its judgment to the need for both "actual practice and opinio juris" (para.183), the Court would, in the particular context of General Assembly resolutions, seem to have found proof of *opinio juris* by itself to be sufficient.[61]

5.   What if one state, or just a few states, protest at a practice? Can it, or they, prevent it from establishing a custom? Judge Tanaka, in his dissenting opinion in the *South West Africa* cases, (*Second Phase*),[62] stated:

"the answer must be in the negative for the reason that Article 38, paragraph 1(*b*), of the Statute does not exclude the possibility of a few dissidents for the purpose of the creation of a customary international law and that the contrary view of a particular State or States would result in the permission of obstruction by veto, which could not have been expected by the legislator who drafted the said Article."

Does the *Anglo-Norwegian Fisheries* case[63] indicate, as Judge Sørensen suggests, that although a dissenting state may not by itself prevent a rule from coming into being, a state will not be bound by the rule if it maintains its dissent throughout the rule's formative period? Would any state, for example, that were to have protested consistently from 1957 (when the first satellite was launched) onwards against the passage of satellites through its airspace, now be bound by any change in the law affecting the upper limit of a state's airspace that may have resulted from the general acquiescence by states in the passage of satellites over their territory? And what was the effect of the consistent opposition by France to any rule prohibiting nuclear tests on the high seas during the 1960s and early 1970s? Is France bound by any such rule that developed?[64] On this question of the "persistent objector", the US *Restatement*[65] reads:

"... in principle a state that indicates its dissent from a practice while the law is still in the

---

[61]   See further the discussion of General Assembly resolutions, below, p.52.

[62]   I.C.J. Rep. 1966, p.291.

[63]   Below, p.327. See also the final paragraph of the extract from the *Asylum* case quoted above, p.18.

[64]   See below, p.365. See also the position of developed states in respect of the majority view within the UN on expropriation: see below, pp.474 et seq.; and deep sea bed mining, see below, p.411.

[65]   *Restatement of the Foreign Relations Law of the U.S., Third* (1987), Vol.I, para.102, comment, p.26. On the persistent objector, see also Charney (1985) 56 B.Y.I.L. 1; Colson (1986) 61 Wash. L.R. 957; Lau (2005) 6 Chi. J.I.L. 495; Stein (1985) 26 H.I.L.J. 457.

process of development is not bound by that rule even after it matures. Historically, such dissent and consequent exemption from a principle that became general customary law has been rare."

In the view of some writers[66] a persistent objector cannot escape being bound by a new rule of customary international law that has the character of ius cogens: see note 8 below.

6.   What is the effect of dissent by a state *after* a custom has been established? Can this by itself affect the application of the custom to the dissenting state? In answering this question, does it matter whether the dissenting state was in existence or not at the time that the custom came into being?[67] Can the dissent of one state bring down a custom if it is coupled with that of others? If so, there is clearly a stage when states leading an assault upon a custom are, although participating in an accepted law-changing process, delinquents.[68] Another intrinsic weakness in the customary international law-making process is that, in some cases, e.g. that concerning the breadth of the territorial sea,[69] the change from one rule of customary international law to another is unacceptably slow with an interim period of considerable uncertainty.[70]

7.   For the purpose of the formation of rules of customary international law, consent is commonly indicated by state practice not in the form of positive statements or other action approving or following the practice in question, but of acquiescence. This MacGibbon[71] describes as "silence or absence of protest in circumstances which generally call for a positive reaction signifying an objection." For example, if the law concerning airspace has been changed as a result of the use of satellites, the practice of all but the states participating in satellite launching has consisted mostly of acquiescence in this sense. As the *Anglo- Norwegian Fisheries* case[72] shows, acquiescence cannot be established unless a state has actual or constructive knowledge of the claim being made. How strict a standard did the Court apply in that case in finding that the United Kingdom did have knowledge of the Norwegian claims? Would you agree with Johnson's comment that:

> "under the Court's formulation, it would seem that ignorance as to another State's legislation on territorial waters, however excusable, can be fatal, and that States may neglect at their own risk, to study each other's statute-books?"[73]

8.   *Ius cogens.* Some rules of customary international law are rules of ius cogens, or peremptory norms. The concept of ius cogens originated in the law of treaties, in which there is a rule prohibiting states from making a treaty contrary to a rule of ius cogens that proscribes conduct

---

[66]   See, e.g. Henkin, *International Law: Politics and Values* (1995), p.39. For a full discussion of the issues, see Charney (1993) 87 A.J.I.L. 529 at 541 and Danilenko, above, p.16, n.1, Ch.8.

[67]   See below, p.96.

[68]   What, for example, was the legal position of Iceland in the late 1950s when it insisted upon a 12-mile exclusive fishing zone off its coast—something that was questionable then but clearly lawful now (partly because of Iceland's efforts)? What was Iceland's position in the 1970s when it claimed, again to the tune of protest by other states, an exclusive fishing zone of 50 miles (also now clearly lawful)? On the US claim to a right of pre-emptive self defence, see below, p.775.

[69]   See below, p.326.

[70]   See Friedmann, p.8, n.37, above, pp.121–123.

[71]   (1954) 31 B.Y.I.L. 143. See also MacGibbon (1957) 33 B.Y.I.L. 115 and Sinclair, in Lowe and Fitzmaurice, eds, *Fifty Years of the International Court of Justice* (1996), p.104. And see the definition in the *Gulf of Maine* case, I.C.J. Rep. 1984, p.246 at 305.

[72]   See below, p.327.

[73]   (1952) 1 I.C.L.Q. 145 at 166.

that is fundamentally unacceptable to the international community.[74] As noted above, for some writers, the concept also has significance in the formation of customary rules of international law. For those writers, a persistent objector cannot escape being bound by a new customary rule that has the character of ius cogens. For example, Henkins,[75] citing state practice, states that South Africa's objection to including *apartheid* as a violation of customary international law and of ius cogens has been generally disregarded. The status of a customary rule as ius cogens may have other consequences too, outside of the law of treaties. States may clearly not derogate by local custom from existing general custom that is ius cogens. The International Law Commission's Draft Articles on Responsibility of States[76] also propose that states must co-operate to bring to an end a serious breach of ius cogens and must not recognise as lawful a situation created thereby. However, courts have rejected arguments that state actors who commit torture are not protected by the law of state immunity[77] or that reservations to the ICJ's jurisdiction under the Genocide Convention are invalid even though torture and genocide are contrary to ius cogens.[78]

9.   Some rules of customary international law are often broken. For example, it is not uncommon for states illegally to resort to armed force or to intervene in the affairs of other states[79] and more than one government has tortured its opponents.[80] In such cases, the question must be whether the delinquent and other states continue to recognise breaches of the rule as illegal. In this connection, note that in the *Nicaragua (Merits)* case, para.186, below, p.727, the ICJ acknowledged that a practice does not always have to be followed for it to indicate a custom: it is sufficient that any departure from the practice is recognised as illegal.

10.   The above materials concerning custom are based upon the voluntarist or consensual theory of the nature of international law, by which states are bound only by that to which they consent. Although this is a theory that presents certain theoretical problems,[81] it remains the one to which the ICJ adheres and one from which, not surprisingly, states do not appear to dissent in their practice. If the theory may involve an element of fiction, it is not easy to find a substitute that is both more intellectually defensible and as serviceable as a working hypothesis.

---

[74] On ius cogens in the law of treaties, see below, p.694. Examples of ius cogens rules are the prohibitions on the use of armed force and genocide. For other rules, see below, p.698.

[75] See Henkin, above, n.66. On the prohibition of apartheid and UN sanctions against South Africa, see below, p.824. For different views as to whether South Africa was a "persistent objector", see Chaney, above n.66.

[76] Article 41, below, p.452.

[77] *Al Adsani v UK*, E.Ct.H.R.R. 2001-IX; (2002) 34 E.H.R.R. 11; and *Jones v Saudi Arabia* [2006] UKHL 26. But see *Ferrini v GRF* (2004) Cass. sez un 5044/04, Italian Ct of Cass. See Bates (2007) 7 H.R.L.R. 651; McGregor (2008) 18 E.J.I.L. 913; and Shelton, above, p.16, n.8.

[78] *Armed Activities (New Application: 2002)* case, below, p.655. See also the separate opinion of Judge ad hoc Dugard, in that case, below, p.696.

[79] See below, Ch.11.

[80] See below, p.630.

[81] See, e.g. Charney (1993) 87 A.J.I.L. 529 and Lobo de Souza (1995) 44 I.C.L.Q. 521. Problems commonly pointed to concern (i) the reason why new states are bound by existing customary law; (ii) the question of a ius cogens exception to the "persistent objector" rule; and (iii) the "mysterious phenomenon" identified by Lauterpacht, above, p.31. The voluntarist theory has far fewer problems with treaties as sources than with custom.

CASSESE, INTERNATIONAL LAW

(2nd edn, 2005) pp.165–166. Footnote omitted

8.4 THE PRESENT ROLE OF CUSTOM

After the Second World War custom increasingly lost ground in two respects: existing customary rules were eroded more and more by fresh practice, and resort to custom to regulate new matters became relatively rare. These developments were largely due to the growing assertiveness of socialist countries and the massive presence of Third World States in the international arena. Both groups insisted on the need radically to revise old customary rules, which appeared to them to be the distillation of traditional Western values, the quintessence of the outlook they opposed. They demanded legal change. Custom is not the most suitable instrument for achieving such change. The insecurity inherent in its unwritten character and its protracted process of development rendered it disadvantageous to the Third World. ... The majority of States accordingly turned to the codification and progressive development of international law through treaties.

Another general reason for the demotion of custom is that the membership of the world community is far larger than in the heyday of international customary law (in the space of one hundred years the number of States has risen from about 40 to nearly 200). Even more important, members of the world community are deeply divided economically and politically. It has, therefore, become extremely difficult for general rules to receive the support of the bulk of such a large number of very diverse States. By the same token, it is nowadays exceedingly difficult to ascertain whether a new rule has emerged, for it is not always possible to get hold of the huge body of evidence required.

Nevertheless, the existence today of so many international organizations to a great extent facilitates and speeds up the custom-creating process, at least in those areas where States are prepared to bring general rules into being. In particular, the UN makes a major contribution as it offers a forum where States are able to exchange and, where possible, harmonize their views to arrive at some form of compromise with other groups. Within UN representative bodies, chiefly the GA, as well as in other international fora, general consent on the least common denominator often evolves: the majority of States eventually succeed in overcoming opposition by individual States, and in achieving general standards of behaviour. The latter come to constitute the normative core of subsequent practice and the basis for the drafting of treaties (or the evolution of customary rules). In other words, those general standards of behaviour represent a sort of bridge between the previous normative vacuum and the future detailed regulation afforded by treaty making or customary law. They provide basic guidelines; the treaty provisions (or customary rules) which usually follow in time provide the nuts and bolts, as it were—the technicalities calculated to bind international standards together and make them more detailed— besides, in the case of treaties, setting up the necessary techniques of supervision.

It follows that custom is by no means on the wane eveywhere. ...

3. TREATIES[82]

FITZMAURICE, SOME PROBLEMS REGARDING THE FORMAL SOURCES OF INTERNATIONAL LAW

(1958) Symbolae Verzijl, p.153. Some footnotes omitted

Considered in themselves, and particularly in their inception, treaties are, formally, a source of obligation rather than a source of law. In their contractual aspect,[83] they are no more a source of law than an ordinary private law contract; which simply creates rights and obligations. ... In this connexion, the attempts which have been made

---

[82] See Jenks, *The Prospects of International Adjudication* (1964); Jennings, in Wilner, ed., *Jus et Societas: Essays in Tribute to Wolfgang Friedmann* (1979), pp.159–168; McNair, *Treaties*, App.I; Starke (1946) 23 B.Y.I.L. 341.

[83] It may be recalled that in the *Reservations to the Genocide Convention* case, the jointly dissenting Judges (Guerrero, McNair, Read and Hsu Mo), speaking of the so-called "law-making" general multilateral convention, pointed out that the circumstance "that this activity is often described as 'legislative' or 'quasi-legislative', must not obscure the fact that the legal basis of these conventions, and the essential thing that brings them into force, is the common consent of the parties"— (I.C.J. Rep. 1951, p.32).

to ascribe a law-making character to *all* treaties irrespective of the character of their content or the number of the parties to them, by postulating that some treaties create "particular" international law and others "general", is of extremely dubious validity. There is really no such thing as "particular" international treaty law, though there are particular international treaty rights and obligations. The only "law" that enters into these is derived, not from the treaty creating them—or from any treaty—but from the principle *pacta sunt servanda*—an antecedent general principle of law. The law is that the obligation must be carried out, but the obligation is not, in itself, law.... A statute is always, *from its inception*, law: a treaty may reflect, or lead to, law but, *particularly* in its inception, is not, as such, "law".... True, where it reflects (e.g. codifies) existing law, non-parties may conform to the same rules, but they do so by virtue of the rules of general law thus reflected in the treaty, not by virtue of the treaty itself. In that sense, the treaty may be an instrument in which the law is conveniently stated, and evidence of what it is, but it is still not itself the law—it is still formally not a source of law but only evidence of it. Where a treaty is, or rather becomes, a *material* source of law, because the rules it contains come to be generally regarded as representing rules of universal applicability, it will nevertheless be the case that when non-parties apply or conform to these rules, this will be because the rules are or have become rules of general law....

This position is equally true, strictly speaking, of *parties* to the treaty also. If the treaty reflects (codifies) existing law, then, in applying it, the parties merely conform to general law obligations already valid for them....

The position is the same, even as regards parties to a treaty, in those cases where the treaty does not reflect existing law but leads to the emergence of a new general rule of law. Before that occurs, the parties apply the treaty, not as law, but as an obligation inter se which antecedent general law respecting treaties compels them to carry out because they have undertaken to do so. If the treaty rule does eventually pass into general law, its formal source *as law* ... is clearly custom or practice—i.e. its adoption into general customary law. The parties, in applying it, are no doubt also (or still) applying the treaty: but, as they would now be bound to apply it even if there were no treaty (or if the treaty, *quâ instrument*, had lapsed or the party concerned had formally "denounced," or given notice of withdrawal from it), its legal basis as *law* is clearly not the treaty, although it retains a treaty basis of *obligation* so far as the parties inter se are concerned....

Notes

1. There are now many multilateral treaties to which a large number of states are parties which lay down general rules of conduct for the parties to them. The Vienna Convention on Diplomatic Relations 1961[84] is a good example. They are sometimes referred to as "law-making treaties" or "international legislation." Such terms are probably sufficiently useful to justify their retention even though they are strictly inaccurate. Note also that, in the past at least, the Great Powers have, in effect, legislated for other states by treaty on a number of occasions. Thus the Final Act of the Congress of Vienna 1815, inter alia, made Switzerland a neutral state and provided for free navigation on certain international rivers.[85]

2. It scarcely needs adding that whatever dignity treaties may lose by not being "a formal source of law", in practice they are a very, and increasingly, important source of a state's rights and duties.

3. Imagine that State A agrees with State B by treaty that it will hand over to B certain war criminals, including X, if they should enter A. X, a national of State C, enters A as the ambassador of C to A. A hands him over to B. C claims that A has thereby violated a customary international law rule concerning the treatment of diplomatic representatives. Assuming that there is a customary rule concerning the treatment of diplomatic representatives that C can rely on, would A be able to rely on its treaty obligation towards B as a defence to any claim by C? If A had not handed X over, could B have claimed successfully against A for the breach of a treaty

---

[84] Below, p.296. The 1949 Red Cross (Geneva) Conventions (194 parties), 75 UNTS 31, and the UN Charter (in respect of its law-making provisions, e.g. art.2(4), see below, p.723), are other examples. So are some UN human rights treaties: e.g. the 1989 Convention on the Rights of the Child has 191 parties.

[85] On the juridical nature of such treaties, and of treaties such as the 1959 Antarctic Treaty and also of boundary treaties, see below, p.687.

obligation? Should a treaty be interpreted as being consistent with customary international law in the absence of clear wording to the contrary?

----

4. GENERAL PRINCIPLES OF LAW[86]

WALDOCK, GENERAL COURSE ON PUBLIC INTERNATIONAL LAW

(1962–II) 106 Hague Recueil 54. Some footnotes omitted

On one side there are jurists like Verdross,[87] who say that Article 38 has the effect of incorporating "natural law" in international law and even claim that positive rules of international law are invalid if they conflict with natural law. At the other extreme are jurists like Guggenheim,[88] and Tunkin,[89] who maintain that paragraph (c) adds nothing to what is already covered by treaties and custom; for these authorities hold that general principles of national law are part of international law only to the extent that they have been adopted by States in treaties or recognised in State practice. In between stand the majority of jurists.... They take the line that general principles recognised in national law constitute a reservoir of principles which an international judge is authorised by Article 38 to apply in an international dispute, if their application appears relevant and appropriate in the different context of inter-State relations.

The *travaux préparatoires* of Article 38 and the decisions of international tribunals support the position taken by the majority. ...

The Court, it must be admitted, has shown restraint in its recourse to "general principles of national law" as authority for its own pronouncements, although individual judges have been less reluctant to invoke them as support for their opinions.[90] Even when apparently relying on this source of law, the Court has not infrequently either referred also to customary law or left it ambiguous as to whether it was speaking of a general principle of national or international law.

... The main spheres in which these principles have been held to apply have been either the general principles of legal liability and of reparation for breaches of international obligations or the administration of international justice.... For example, in the *Chorzow Factory Case*[91] the Permanent Court described the principle, that a party cannot take advantage of its own wrong, as a principle "generally accepted in the jurisprudence of international arbitration, as well as by municipal courts"; and at a later stage of the same case[92] the Court said that "it is a general conception of law that every violation of an engagement involves an obligation to make reparation," and it went on to speak of restitution and damages. ...

As to the administration of justice, there are a number of references to "general principles of law" in connection with questions of jurisdiction, procedure, evidence or other aspects of the judicial process. Thus, speaking in the *Corfu Channel Case*[93] of circumstantial evidence, the International Court said: "this indirect evidence is admitted in all systems of law, and its use is recognised by international decisions...."

In inter-State relations, however, the Court has shown little disposition to transport into international law substantive doctrines or institutions of national law; as distinct from principles of legal liability and reparation. ...

The correct conclusion, it seems to me, to draw from the practice of the Court may well be that it treats the "common law" which it is authorised to apply under Article 38, paragraphs (b) and (c), very much as a single corpus of law. In this corpus customary law enormously predominates and most of the law applied by the Court falls within it. But paragraph (c) adds to this corpus—very much in the way actually intended by its authors—a

------

[86]   See Cheng, *General Principles of Law: as Applied by International Courts and Tribunals* (1953); Fitzmaurice (1953) 30 B.Y.I.L. 1; Friedmann, above, p.8, n.37, Ch.12; H. C. Gutteridge (1953) 38 Trans. Grot. Soc. 125; Jenks, above, n.82, Ch.6.
[87]   See Rec. Acad. 1935, II, pp.204–206; and R.G.D.I.P., 1938, pp.44–52.
[88]   *Traité de droit international public,* I, p.152.
[89]   Rec. Acad. 1958, III, pp.25–26.
[90]   Ed. See, e.g. Judge Lauterpacht's opinion in the *Norwegian Loans* case, below, p.856.
[91]   (1927) A/9 at 31.
[92]   (1928) A/17 at 29.
[93]   I.C.J. Rep. 1949, p.18. Ed. Note also the Court's reliance upon "elementary considerations of humanity" in that case: p.22. Cf. *Legality of Nuclear Weapons* case, I.C.J. Rep. 1996, p.226 at p.262.

flexible element which enables the Court to give greater completeness to customary law and in some limited degree to extend it.

... as Lord McNair pointed out in the *South-West Africa Case*,[94] it is never a question of importing into international law private law institutions "lock, stock and barrel", ready made and fully equipped with a set of rules. It is rather a question of finding in the private law institutions indications of legal policy and principles appropriate to the solution of the international problem in hand. It is not the concrete manifestations of a principle in different national systems—which are anyhow likely to vary—but the general concept of law underlying them that the international judge is entitled to apply under paragraph (c).

Accordingly, the question arises as to what basic conditions must be satisfied before a principle qualifies to be considered "a general principle of law recognised by civilised nations". The phrase "civilised nations" now has an antiquated look. The intention in using it, clearly, was to leave out of account undeveloped legal systems so that a general principle present in the principal legal systems of the world would not be disqualified from application in international law merely by reason of its absence from, for example, the tribal law of a backward people.... Accordingly, we are quite safe in construing "the general principles of law recognised by civilised nations" as meaning to-day simply the general principles recognised in the legal systems of independent States.

The number of independent States, we know, has doubled since 1920, and is now over one hundred. Does this mean that today a principle has to pass the test of a hundred legal systems and that in this legal tower of Babel no principle will ever be able to qualify for application under paragraph (c)? Two considerations, it is thought, permit us to be reassured on this point.

First, by the accidents of history, some of the principal European systems of law have penetrated over large areas of the globe, mixing in greater or less degree with the indigenous law and often displacing it in just those spheres of law in which we have seen that international law has most readily borrowed from domestic law. In consequence, there is a much larger unity in the fundamental concepts of the legal systems of the world today than there might otherwise have been....

Secondly, it was never intended under paragraph (c) that proof should be furnished of the manifestation of a principle in every known legal system considered to be civilised; and certainly it has never been the practice of the Court or of arbitral tribunals to insist upon proof of the widespread manifestations of a principle or to indulge in elaborate comparative studies of the legal systems of the world. Truth to tell, arbitral tribunals, which usually consist of one, three or five judges, have probably done no more in most cases than take into account their own knowledge of the principles of the systems in which the arbitrators were themselves trained, and these would usually have been Roman law, Common law, or Germanic systems.

Notes

1. In the course of discussion by the Advisory Committee of Jurists on art.38(1)(c), Lord Phillimore (Great Britain), who, with Mr Root (US), was the author of that provision, pointed out that:

    "the general principles referred to ... were those which were accepted by all nations *in foro domestico*, such as certain principles of procedure, the principle of good faith, and the principle of *res judicata, etc.*"[95]

    He later said that by "general principles" he meant "Maxims of law."[96] In the same discussion the President of the Committee, Baron Descamps (Belgium), stated that the draft that became art.38(1)(c) "was necessary to meet the possibility of a *non liquet*."[97]

---

[94] I.C.J. Rep. 1950, p.148.

[95] See above, p.16, n.6, p.335. Res judicata was applied as a "generally recognised principle of law" in the UN *Administrative Tribunal* case, 1954 I.C.J. Rep. p.47 at 53.

[96] ibid.

[97] ibid. p.336. i.e. the possibility that a court or tribunal could not decide a case because of a "gap" in the law. Remarkably, the ICJ applied the doctrine of *non liquet* in the *Legality of Nuclear Weapons* case, below, p.788. See Weil (1998) 36 Col. J.T.L. 109.

2. Fitzmaurice[98] suggests that a "rule answers the question "what": a principle in effect answers the question "why". Has the World Court followed this distinction in its practice?

3. General principles continue to be identified by international tribunals. For example, in *Sea-Land Service Inc v Iran*,[99] it was stated that the concept of unjust enrichment is "widely accepted as having been assimilated into the catalogue of general principles of law available to be applied by international tribunals." In the *Barcelona Traction* case,[100] the ICJ relied upon the "lifting the veil" principle, which it found "admitted by municipal law" generally, when deciding that, in exceptional circumstances, the national state of the shareholders of a company could act to protect them in place of the national state of the company. In the *Gabčíkovo-Nagymaros Project* case,[101] the same court relied upon the principle *ex injuria jus non oritur*. Cassese[102] notes that ad hoc international criminal tribunals, such as the Yugoslav Tribunal ("ICTY"):

> "have frequently resorted to general principles of criminal law recognised in the principal legal systems of the world—common law systems and civil law system"

and that

> "Article 21 of ICC Statute envisages the possibility that the Court might resort to such a subsidiary source".

4. Not all claims to the title of "general principle" have been accepted. In the *South West Africa* cases (*Second Phase*),[103] the ICJ found that the *actio popularis* was known only to certain legal systems and hence was not a general principle. Similarly, the French law of administrative contracts was held in the *Texaco* case[104] to lack sufficient acceptance in other families of legal systems. In the *Abu Dhabi Arbitration*[105] the English law principle of interpretation *expressio unius est exclusio alterius* was held to be a principle "rooted in the good sense and common practice of the generality of civilised nations," but the English rule that grants by a sovereign should be construed against the grantee (which was thought peculiarly English) was not.

5. Consider when reading the cases in these materials whether the Court has taken much advantage of the scope that art.38(1)(c) gives for judicial legislation.[106] Would it be true to say that the Court has used such "straws" of state practice as it has been able to find to build a custom at least as often as it has relied upon general principles?

6. *General principles of international law.* It should be noted that there are also principles of *international* law, serving important and diverse purposes, that are a part of customary international law and hence are rooted in art.38(1)(a), not (c). Nonetheless, the state practice underlying some of these principles consists of national legislation or case law that could equally be seen as generating a "general principle of law recognised by civilised nations" in the sense of

---

[98] (1957–II) 92 Hague Recueil 1 at 7.
[99] 6 Iran—U.S.C.T.R. 149 at 168–169 (1984).
[100] I.C.J. Rep. 1970, p.6 at 39.
[101] I.C.J. Rep. 1997, p.7 at 76.
[102] *International Law* (2nd edn 2005) p.163. He cites the definition of rape adopted by the ICTY in the *Furundzija* case (case No.IT-95-17/1-T, T Ch II 10 Dec 1998).
[103] I.C.J. Rep. 1966, p.6.
[104] Below, p.494.
[105] (1952) 1 I.C.L.Q. 247. See also *Seaco v Iran* (1992) 28 Iran—U.S.C.T.R. 198 at 209 (promissory estoppel not a general principle).
[106] For examples of the greater use to which general principles might be put, see Friedmann, above, p.8, n.37, Ch.12.

art.38(1)(c). Examples of general principles of international law are the principles of the sovereign equality of states[107] and estoppel[108] and, in international environmental law, the precautionary principle[109] and the principle that there is a duty to mitigate harm to the environment caused by development, which has been stated to be a "principle of general international law".[110]

THE DIVERSION OF WATER FROM THE MEUSE CASE

Netherlands v Belgium (1937)

P.C.I.J. Reports, Series A/B, No.70, pp.76–77

INDIVIDUAL OPINION OF JUDGE HUDSON

What are widely known as principles of equity have long been considered to constitute a part of international law, and as such they have often been applied by international tribunals....

The Court has not been expressly authorised by its Statute to apply equity as distinguished from law.... Article 38 of the Statute expressly directs the application of "general principles of law recognised by civilised nations," and in more than one nation principles of equity have an established place in the legal system. The Court's recognition of equity as a part of international law is in no way restricted by the special power conferred upon it "to decide a case *ex aequo et bono*, if the parties agree thereto." ... It must be concluded, therefore, that under Article 38 of the Statute, if not independently of that Article, the Court has some freedom to consider principles of equity as part of the international law which it must apply.

It would seem to be an important principle of equity that where two parties have assumed an identical or a reciprocal obligation, one party which is engaged in a continuing non-performance of that obligation should not be permitted to take advantage of a similar non-performance of that obligation by the other party. The principle finds expression in the so-called maxims of equity which exercised great influence in the creative period of the development of the Anglo-American law. Some of these maxims are, "Equality is equity"; "He who seeks equity must do equity." It is in line with such maxims that "a court of equity refuses relief to a plaintiff whose conduct in regard to the subject-matter of the litigation has been improper." ... A very similar principle was received into Roman Law.... This conception was the basis of Articles 320 and 322 of the German Civil Code, and even where a code is silent on the point Planiol states the general principle that *"dans tout rapport synallagmatique, chacune des deux parties ne peut exiger la prestation qui lui est due que si elle offre elle-même d'exécuter son obligation."* ...

Notes[111]

1. In the *River Meuse* case, the Netherlands claimed that Belgium had infringed a treaty obligation by building canals that altered the flow of water in the River Meuse. In the above passage, Judge Hudson was responding to an argument that the Netherlands had lost the right to bring its claim because of similar earlier conduct on its part. Clearly, he understood "principles of equity" as being principles common to national legal systems generally that were a part of international law by virtue of art.38(1)(c).

---

[107] See UN Charter art.2(1).
[108] See the *Pedra Branca* case, 2008 I.C.J. Rep. para.228.
[109] *OSPAR Arbitration*, 2003 P.C.A. p.86 (www.pca.opa.org)
[110] *Iron Rhine Railway Arbitration*, 2005 P.C.A. p.29 (www.pca.opa.org).
[111] On equity in international law, see Janis (1983) 9 Brooklyn J.I.L. 7; Jennings (1986) 42 Annuaire Suisse 27; Lapidoth (1987) 22 Israel L.R. 161; E. Lauterpacht, *Aspects of the Administration of International Justice* (1991), Ch.7; Lowe (1992) 12 A.Y.I.L. 54; Rossi, *Equity and International Law* (1993); Van Dijk, in Heere, ed., *International Law and its Sources* (1989), p.1.

2. The ICJ has increasingly referred to "equity" in its judgments in recent years. For example, in the *Gulf of Maine* case,[112] it stated that the concepts of acquiescence and estoppel in international law "follow from the fundamental principles of good faith and equity." Note also its reference to "considerations of equity" when seeking to apply the law of diplomatic protection "reasonably" in the *Barcelona Traction* case[113]; its incorporation of "equitable principles" into its statement of a rule for the determination of continental shelf boundaries in the *North Sea Continental Shelf* cases[114]; its emphasis on the need to achieve an "equitable result" in that and later maritime and land boundary cases[115]; and its search for an "equitable solution derived from the applicable law" in the *Fisheries Jurisdiction* cases.[116] In what different ways was the Court using "equity" when applying the sources of law in these cases? As a "general principle of law?" As a concept found in state practice and hence a part of custom? Or in the way that judges often use it, namely to achieve a fair result on the facts when applying a legal rule? Note that maritime boundary cases referred to have been criticised for introducing, through their reliance upon equity, an unduly subjective and uncertain element into international law. Thus in his dissenting opinion in the *Gulf of Maine* case, Judge Gros stated[117]:

    "... equity left, without any objective elements of control, to the wisdom of the judge reminds us that equity was once measured by 'the Chancellor's foot'; I doubt that international justice can long survive an equity measured by the judge's eye. When equity is simply a reflection of the judge's perception, the Courts which judge in this way part company from those which apply the law."

3. In the United Nations, equity has been referred to in General Assembly resolutions and other documents concerning the New International Economic Order[118] as a part of a "distributive justice" argument favouring the establishment of a new economic order that is more sympathetic to the needs of developing countries. Law-making treaties also now commonly rely upon equity, with the 1982 Law of the Sea Convention[119] being a striking example.[120]

4. *Natural Law* played an important part in the development of international law in its early years. According to the positivist approach, however, it is at best a material source of international law

---

[112] I.C.J. Rep. 1984, p.246 at 305.
[113] Below, p.519.
[114] Above, p.21.
[115] See below, p.408. In this context, the ICJ explained the role of "equity" in international law in the *Continental Shelf* (*Tunisia v Libya*) case, I.C.J. Rep. 1982, p.18 at 60, as follows: "the legal concept of equity is a general principle directly applicable as law. ... The task of the Court ... is ... to apply equitable principles as part of international law, and to balance up the various considerations which it regards as relevant in order to produce an equitable result. While it is clear that no rigid rules exist as to the exact weight to be attached to each element in the case, this is very far from being an exercise of discretion or conciliation; nor is it an operation of distributive justice." Inequality of natural resources is not relevant: see, e.g. the *Land, Island and Maritime Frontier Dispute* case, I.C.J. Rep. 1992, p.376. See Miyoshi, *Considerations of Equity in the Settlement of Territorial and Boundary Disputes* (1993).
[116] I.C.J. Rep. 1974, p.3 at 33. In the *Frontier Dispute* case, I.C.J. Rep. 1986, p.540 at 567–568, when determining a land boundary, the ICJ had "regard to equity *infra legem*, that is that form of equity which constitutes a method of interpretation of the law in force". cf. the *Land, Island and Maritime Frontier Dispute* case, ICJ 1992, p.351.
[117] I.C.J. Rep. 1984, p.386. cf. Brownlie (1979–II) 162 Hague Recueil 245 at 287.
[118] See, e.g. the preamble to the 1974 Charter of Economic Rights and Duties of States, below p.475, ("mindful of the need to establish a just and equitable economic and social order.")
[119] See, e.g. arts 59, 74, 140, below, pp.393, 394, 409.
[120] See also the 1997 Convention on Non-Navigational Uses of International Watercourses art.5 (1997) 36 I.L.M. 700.

today. The following passage from the *North American Dredging Company* case[121] is a forceful statement of the positivist point of view:

"The law of nature may have been helpful, some three centuries ago, to build up a new law of nations, and the conception of inalienable rights of men and nations may have exercised a salutary influence, some one hundred and fifty years ago, on the development of modern democracy on both sides of the ocean; but they have failed as a durable foundation of either municipal or international law and cannot be used in the present day as substitutes for positive municipal law, on the one hand, and for positive international law, as recognised by nations and governments through their acts and statements, on the other hand."

Fitzmaurice, however, argues that some general principles of law in the sense of art.38(1)(c),

"involving inherently necessary principles of natural law, are such as to cause natural law, at any rate in that aspect of it that relates to these principles, to be a formal, not merely a material, source of law."[122]

He gives a number of examples, including the rule *pacta sunt servanda*, and the

"rule that a State or government cannot plead the provisions or deficiencies of its own internal laws or constitution as a ground or excuse for non-compliance with its international obligations."[123]

----

5. JUDICIAL DECISIONS

SCHWARZENBERGER, INTERNATIONAL LAW

(3rd edn 1957), Vol.I pp.30 et seq. Some footnotes omitted

It may be asked why the views expressed by international judges in their official capacity should carry greater weight than if contained in private studies. The answer certainly cannot be derived in the international field from the principle of *stare decisis*. Nevertheless, it appears advisable not to overestimate the difference between the binding and persuasive authority of judgments. A perusal of the practice of the World Court will reveal remarkable consistency in its judgments. It certainly did not hesitate to refer to, and to quote from, its previous judgments and advisory opinions. Yet the true answer lies first in the greater degree of responsibility and care that the average lawyer shows when he deals in a judicial capacity with real issues as compared with private comments on such issues or the discussion of hypothetical cases. There is a world of difference between practising shooting with dummy ammunition at a wooden target and firing in earnest with live ammunition at a living target. In addition, where a case is argued by experienced counsel from two or more angles, and where the court is composed of members with widely differing legal training and experience, it is more likely that an all-round view of the matter will be taken than where the same topic is turned over by a writer in the isolation of his study or even discussed with colleagues. . . .

Nevertheless, even the World Court is but an element of a law-determining agency[124]—and, be it recalled, of a subsidiary law-determining agency—and, therefore, should not be sacrosanct against sympathetic, but searching

---

[121] *U.S. v Mexico* (1926) 4. R.I.A.A. 26.
[122] See above, p.15, n.1, p.174.
[123] ibid. pp.164–165.
[124] Ed. For the meaning of this term, see above, p.16.

criticism. The persuasive character of its judgments and advisory opinions depends on the fullness and cogency of the reasoning offered. It is probably not accidental that the least convincing statements on international law made by the International Court of Justice excel by a remarkable economy of argument. In view of the element of compromise that is the price of any majority decision, this is not surprising. Exactly for this reason, the minority opinions of judges who could not square it with their judicial conscience to join the "compact majority" are especially precious and, in some cases, may constitute evidence of a kind which has at least the same, or even higher, intrinsic value than any particular majority opinion. At this point, the autonomy of the Doctrine of international law must necessarily assert itself. It then becomes the task of a writer to state without fear or favour why he considers any particular judicial pronouncements appear to err, for instance, on the side of either excessive caution or daring.

Municipal courts are not quite in the same category as international courts and tribunals. In the case of the judgments of the courts of some countries it may be justifiable to praise them in the terms in which Chancellor Kent spoke of the decisions of English courts and, especially, of the decisions of the English High Court of Admiralty:

> In the investigation of the rules of the modern law of nations, particularly with regard to the extensive field of maritime capture, reference is generally and freely made to the decisions of the English courts. ... They contain more intrinsic argument, more full and precise details, more accurate illustrations, and are of more authority than the loose dicta of elementary writers.[125]

Yet there are countries in which the independence of the judiciary from the executive is not so much cherished as in countries in which the rule of law in the Western sense is recognised. Furthermore, the judges of municipal courts are more likely to suffer from subconscious national bias than a body of international judges drawn from all quarters of the globe. It is very much easier for the latter to guard against this most dangerous type of "inarticulate major premise."

Notes

1. For the common lawyer, the most striking feature of the role of international courts and tribunals, and one of which he constantly needs to remind himself, is that cases do not make law. Article 59 of the Statute of the International Court of Justice, for example, provides that "the decision of the Court has no binding force except between the parties and in respect of that particular case."[126] In taking this approach, international law follows the civil law tradition. Yet although judgments do not constitute a formal source of law, those of the World Court at least play a larger part in the development of international law than theory might suggest. State practice seldom points so clearly in one direction as to leave the Court no discretion in its formulation of a custom.[127] Quite often it is non-existent, sparse or contradictory so that the Court is thrust into the speculative realm of general principles and analogy to decide a case. In other words, the World Court, as any other international court or tribunal, is by no means the mechanical recorder of law that might be supposed, a fact which becomes important in assessing the contribution of the Court because of the undoubted influence that its pronouncements have on subsequent state practice. The impact of the judgments and opinions in

---

[125] Kent's *Commentaries on American Law* (1986), Vol.I, pp.69–70.
[126] See Scobbie (1999) 20 A.Y.I.L. 299.
[127] For an extreme case where the Court's law-making role would be patent, note the controversy concerning the standard to apply to the treatment of the property of aliens: see below, Ch.8.

the *Anglo-Norwegian Fisheries*,[128] *Reservations*[129] and *Reparation* cases,[130] for example, bears ample witness to this influence.[131] Note also Judge Azevedo's view in the *Asylum* case[132]:

> "It should be remembered ... that the decision in a particular case has deep repercussions, particularly in international law, because views which have been confirmed by that decision acquire quasi-legislative value, in spite of the legal principle to the effect that the decision has no binding force except between the parties and in respect of that particular case (Statute, art.59)."

2. International courts and tribunals not only do not make law; they are also not bound by their previous decisions as to the law which they apply. But despite this absence of a doctrine of binding precedent, the World Court, as Schwarzenberger makes clear, does tend to follow or feel the need to distinguish its own jurisprudence.[133] It relies very heavily upon this jurisprudence and only occasionally refers to that of other courts or tribunals.[134] Often the Court will cite only its own case law for a proposition and not bother to refer to state practice supporting it.[135] Other international courts[136] and tribunals[137] that decide more than one case tend naturally to build up a consistent jurisprudence too. Although there is no hierarchy of courts, the World Court is indisputably pre-eminent and its judgments and advisory opinions are highly persuasive for other international courts and tribunals.[138] The persuasiveness of the pronouncements of international courts and tribunals apart from the World Court for any other international court or tribunal depends very much, as Schwarzenberger suggests, upon their intrinsic merits.[139]

3. Among the many examples of judicial decisions of municipal courts discussing and applying rules of international law, see the cases below on the recognition of states and governments and on state and diplomatic immunity.[140]

----

[128] Below, p.327.
[129] Below, p.654.
[130] Below, p.120.
[131] One exceptional instance of a ruling by the Court *not* finding general acceptance is that in the *Lotus* case on criminal jurisdiction in respect of collisions at sea: see below, p.241. The Court's doctrine of "preferential fishing rights" for coastal states beyond the 12-mile limits in the *Fisheries Jurisdiction* (*Merits*) cases, I.C.J. Rep. 1974, p.3, also was not adopted in the 1982 Convention on the Law of the Sea.
[132] I.C.J. Rep. 1950, p.332.
[133] See, e.g. the Court's treatment of its earlier jurisprudence in the *Barcelona Traction* case, below, p.515; and in the *Certain Phosphate Lands in Nauru* case, I.C.J. Rep. 1992, p.240 at 259–260. Note in the *Barcelona Traction* case the way in which the Court distinguishes the *Nottebohm* case. Would it in fact be correct to say that the Court was there making use of the distinction between ratio decidendi and obiter dicta, which does not formally exist in international law? See generally, Shahabuddeen, *Precedent in the Woreld Court* (1996).
[134] For references to other tribunals, see the *Land, Island and Maritime Frontier Dispute* case, I.C.J. Rep. 1992, p.351 at 563 (*Island of Palmas* case, below, p.163) and the *Jan Mayen* case, I.C.J. Rep. 1993, p.38 at 67 (*Anglo-French Continental Shelf* case, below, p.408).
[135] See Kearney, in Gross, ed., *The Future of the International Court of Justice* (1976), Vol.II, p.610 at 698.
[136] e.g. the European Court of Human Rights.
[137] e.g. the Mexican Claims Commissions of the 1920s and 1930s and the US-Iranian Claims Tribunal: see the cases below, Ch.8.
[138] Note, however, the restricted reading in the *Flegenheimer* case (1958) 25 I.L.R. 91, of the ICJ's judgment in the *Nottebohm* case.
[139] Thus the European Commission of Human Rights—in a binding decision as to admissibility—felt itself quite free in the *Nielsen* case, 2 Y.B.E.C.H.R. 412, to disagree with the tribunal in the *Salem* case (1932) 2 R.I.AA. 1161.
[140] Below, Chs 4 and 6. National court decisions are state practice for the purposes of custom: see, e.g. the *Arrest Warrant* case, para.58, below, p.293.

6. WRITERS

PARRY, THE SOURCES AND EVIDENCES OF INTERNATIONAL LAW

(1965), pp.103–105

In the Court's Statute "the teachings of the most highly qualified publicists" are assigned the same subsidiary status, whatever that may be, as judicial decisions. Upon a long view, there would seem to be no legal order wherein the publicist—a peculiar term—has played a greater part than international law. Grotius is the father of the law of nations. And ... at the beginning of the last century, all States seemed to rely heavily on Vattel. Indeed both the books and the opinions of the nineteenth century seem often to resemble catalogues of the praises of famous men. "Hear also what Hall sayeth. Hear the comfortable words of Oppenheim" is an incantation which persists even into this century.

The credit is to be given to Judge Jessup[141] for finding a truly devastating example of the opposite point of view, that of the Court of Admiralty, expressed in the case of *The Renard*[142] in 1778.... The question was how long a prize must be in the captor's hands for the original property in her to be divested. Opposing counsel offered opposing opinions of Grotius and Bynkershoek. And the Court "observed that there was something ridiculous in the decisive way each lawyer, as quoted, had given his opinion. Grotius might as well have laid down, for a rule, twelve hours, as twenty-four; or forty-eight, as twelve. A pedantic man in his closet dictates the law of nations; everybody quotes, and nobody minds him. The usage is plainly as arbitrary as it is uncertain; and who shall decide, when doctors disagree? Bynkershoek, as is natural to every writer or speaker who comes after another, is delighted to contradict Grotius...."

It is difficult not to see truth as well as humour in this. And it is also no doubt true that, as the body of judicial decisions increases, the authority of the commentator is diminished.... The literature of international law, to which the majority of the World Court at least pays scant lip-service, possesses evident defects. One of the most frequent charges brought against it is that it displays a great deal of national bias. The charge is probably exaggerated. The fact is that international lawyers are inevitably municipal lawyers first of all. The law, furthermore, is inevitably a somewhat conservative training. The writers of one country thus reflect their national legal tradition and technique rather than any national political viewpoint....

Notes

1. *The current role of writers*. Wolfke,[143] a Polish writer, describes the role of writers today as consisting in the:

   > "analysis of facts and opinions and in drawing conclusions on binding customary rules and on trends of their evolution. Such conclusions, like all generalisations of this kind, involve unrestricted supplementation by introducing elements lacking and hence, a creative factor. Further, by attracting attention to international practice and appraising it, the writers indirectly influence its further evolution, that is the development of customs.
   >
   >   At present, the influence of doctrine on the formation of international law in general is certainly rather behind-the-scenes and anonymous. To disregard it would, however, be, to say the least, unjustified."

2. *Their earlier role*. The contribution of writers was a much more important one in the formative period of international law. They were largely responsible for establishing the basic idea that there was such a thing as law governing the relations between states. In addition, they exercised

---

[141] *Transnational Law* (1956), p.11.
[142] Hay & M. 222.
[143] See above, p.17, n.16, p.77.

a much more creative role in the determination of particular rules of law than would be possible today.[144] Their statements of the law were derived by deduction from natural law principles, by analogy from Roman law, and by generalisation from what state practice they could find, as well as from more bizarre sources such as the writings of Homer. It was after Grotius (1583–1645) that writers became polarised into one of three schools: the "naturalists", of whom Pufendorf (1632–94) is the most well known, who based international law on natural law; the "positivists", such as Bynkershoek (1673–1743), who based it on the consent of states evidenced in state practice; and the "eclectics" or "Grotians", including Vattel (1714–67), who, like Grotius, relied on both. By the nineteenth century, most writers were positivists, reflecting the general change of attitude to natural law thinking. By that time also, as their adoption of positivism ensured, the role of writers had declined to its present state.

3.   For a less charitable view of the objectivity of writers than that of Parry, note the following comment by the Arbitrator (Huber) in the *Spanish Zones of Morocco Claims*[145]:

> "It is true that the great majority of writers show a very marked tendency to restrict the responsibility of States. Their doctrines, however, are frequently politically inspired and represent a natural reaction against unjustified intervention in the affairs of certain nations."

---

7. UNILATERAL ACTS OF STATES

Note

Various kinds of unilateral acts by states may have legal significance or consequences for them. They include acts making claims or renouncing them (e.g. to territory), acts of recognition (e.g. of governments) or protest (e.g. against humanitarian intervention in another state) and the ratification of treaties. In addition to such acts, which may contribute as state practice to the formation of custom or involve the application of international law rules, a state may accept a legal obligation by a public unilateral act made, either orally or in writing, by a person competent to act for the state, vis-à-vis either the international community at large or one or more states.[146] This possibility was recognised in the *Nuclear Tests* cases and is now the subject of *Guiding Principles* adopted by the International Law Commission. In some respects, the rules governing such declarations parallel those applicable to treaties, and, as is shown by the *Legal Status of Eastern Greenland* case, below, it may be difficult to distinguish between a unilateral act giving rise to a legal obligation and a treaty composed of two unilateral statements that do so. As in the case of treaties, Fitzmaurice's distinction (above, p.34), between sources of law and obligations applies.

---

[144] Occasionally, a writer may still make an impact upon state practice, e.g. the "right to development" emerged first in academic literature: see below, p.625, n.292.
[145] *G.B. v Spain* (1925) 2 R.I.A.A. 615 at 640. Translation.
[146] See Suy, in *Droit du pouvoir, pouvoir du droit: mélanges offerts à Jean Salmon* (2007), p.631.

LEGAL STATUS OF EASTERN GREENLAND

Denmark v Norway (1933)

P.C.I.J. Reports, Series A/B, No.53

In addition to claiming sovereignty over Greenland in this case on the basis of occupation (see the summary above, p.173), Denmark also argued that Norway had recognised Danish sovereignty over the island by the "Ihlen Declaration." M.Ihlen was the Norwegian Foreign Minister. In conversations on July 14, 1919, with the Danish Minister accredited to Norway, the latter suggested to M. Ihlen that Denmark would raise no objection to any claim Norway might want to make at the Paris Peace Conference to Spitzbergen if Norway would not oppose the claim that Denmark was to make at the same Conference to the whole of Greenland. On July 22, 1919, M. Ihlen, in the course of further conversations with the Danish Minister, declared that "the Norwegian Government would not make any difficulty" concerning the Danish claim. These were the terms used as they were minuted by M. Ihlen for his Government's own purposes. Denmark argued before the Court that this undertaking was binding upon Norway. Judge Anzilotti agreed with the Court on this point.

Judgment of the Court

This declaration by M.Ihlen has been relied on by Counsel for Denmark as a recognition of an existing Danish sovereignty in Greenland. The Court is unable to accept this point of view. A careful examination of the words used and of the circumstances in which they were used, as well as of the subsequent developments, shows that M. Ihlen cannot have meant to be giving then and there a definitive recognition of Danish sovereignty over Greenland, and shows also that he cannot have been understood by the Danish Government at the time as having done so. In the text of M.Ihlen's minute, submitted by the Norwegian Government, which has not been disputed by the Danish Government, the phrase used by M.Ihlen is couched in the future tense: "ne fera pas de difficultés"; he had been informed that it was at the Peace Conference that the Danish Government intended to bring up the question: and two years later—when assurances had been received from the Principal Allied Powers—the Danish Government made a further application to the Norwegian Government to obtain the recognition which they desired of Danish sovereignty over all Greenland.

Nevertheless, the point which must now be considered is whether the Ihlen declaration—even if not con-stituting a definitive recognition of Danish sovereignty—did not constitute an engagement obliging Norway to refrain from occupying any part of Greenland.

... It is clear from the relevant Danish documents which preceded the Danish Minister's démarche at Christiania on July 14th, 1919, that the Danish attitude in the Spitzbergen question and the Norwegian attitude in the Greenland question were regarded in Denmark as interdependent, and this interdependence appears to be reflected also in M. Ihlen's minute of the interview. Even if this interdependence—which, in view of the affirmative reply of the Norwegian Government, in whose name the Minister for Foreign Affairs was speaking, would have created a bilateral engagement—is not held to have been established, it can hardly be denied that what Denmark was asking of Norway ("not to make any difficulties in the settlement of the [Greenland] question") was equivalent to what she was indicating her readiness to concede in the Spitzbergen question (to refrain from opposing "the wishes of Norway in regard to the settlement of this question"). What Denmark desired to obtain from Norway was that the latter should do nothing to obstruct the Danish plans in regard to Greenland. The declaration which the Minister for Foreign Affairs gave on July 22nd, 1919, on behalf of the Norwegian Gov-ernment, was definitely affirmative: "I told the Danish Minister today that the Norwegian Government would not make any difficulty in the settlement of this question."

The Court considers it beyond all dispute that a reply of this nature given by the Minister of Foreign Affairs on behalf of his Government in response to a request by the diplomatic representative of a foreign Power, in regard to a question falling within his province, is binding upon the country to which the Minister belongs.

... It follows that, as a result of the undertaking involved in the Ihlen declaration of July 22, 1919, Norway is under an obligation to refrain from contesting Danish sovereignty over Greenland as a whole, and *a fortiori* to refrain from occupying a part of Greenland.

Note

Was there an oral treaty in this case, or a unilateral declaration made in the context of diplomatic negotiation that was legally binding?[147]

NUCLEAR TEST CASES

Australia v France; New Zealand v France

I.C.J. Reports 1974, pp.253, 457

For the facts, see below, p.365. The Court found, by nine votes to six,[148] that "the claim of Australia no longer has any object and that the Court is therefore not called upon to given a decision thereon." The Court reached this conclusion because France had indicated its intention not to hold any further tests in the atmosphere in the South Pacific after its 1974 series of tests. It gave this undertaking by way of a series of unilateral public announcements in that year. The Court considered the legal significance of these statements in the following passage in the judgment in the Australian case. The companion case brought by New Zealand against France resulted in a similar ruling.

Judgment of the Court

34. ... The first statement is contained in the Communiqué issued by the Office of the President of the French Republic on June 8, 1974 ...

> The Office of the President of the Republic takes this opportunity of stating that in view of the stage reached in carrying out the French nuclear defence programme France will be in a position to pass on to the stage of underground explosions as soon as the series of tests planned for this summer is completed.

A copy of the Communiqué was transmitted with a Note dated June 11, 1974 from the French Embassy in Canberra to the Australian Department of Foreign Affairs ...

37. The next statement to be considered ... will be that made on July 25, at a press conference given by the President of the Republic, when he said:

> ... on this question of nuclear tests, you know that the Prime Minister has publicly expressed himself in the National Assembly in his speech introducing the Government's programme. He had indicated that French nuclear testing would continue. I had myself made it clear that this round of atmospheric tests would be the last, and so the members of the Government were completely informed of our intentions in this respect ...

39. On September 25, 1974, the French Minister for Foreign Affairs, addressing the United Nations General Assembly, said:

> We have now reached a stage in our nuclear technology that makes it possible for us to continue our programme by underground testing, and we have taken steps to do so as early as next year.

The French Minister of Defence made similar statements on French television and at a press conference. ...

43. It is well recognised that declarations made by way of unilateral acts, concerning legal or factual situations, may have the effect of creating legal obligations. Declarations of this kind may be, and often are, very

---

[147] See Garner (1933) 27 A.J.I.L. 493; Hambro *Festschrift Spiropoulos* (1057), p.227; McNair *Treaties*, p.101.
[148] The judges in the majority were President Lachs; Judges Forster, Gros, Bengzon, Petrén, Ignacio-Pinto, Morozov, Nagendra Singh, and Ruda. The dissenting judges were Judges Onyeama, Dillard, de Castro, Jiménez de Aréchaga, Sir Humphrey Waldock; Judge *ad hoc* Sir Garfield Barwick.

specific. When it is the intention of the State making the declaration that it should become bound according to its terms, that intention confers on the declaration the character of a legal undertaking, the State being thenceforth legally required to follow a course of conduct consistent with the declaration. An undertaking of this kind, if given publicly, and with an intent to be bound, even though not made within the context of international negotiations, is binding. In these circumstances, nothing in the nature of a *quid pro quo* nor any subsequent acceptance of the declaration, nor even any reply or reaction from other States, is required for the declaration to take effect, since such a requirement would be inconsistent with the strictly unilateral nature of the juridical act by which the pronouncement by the State was made.

44. Of course, not all unilateral acts imply obligation; but a State may choose to take up a certain position in relation to a particular matter with the intention of being bound—the intention is to be ascertained by interpretation of the act. When States make statements by which their freedom of action is to be limited, a restrictive interpretation is called for.[149]

45. With regard to the question of form, it should be observed that this is not a domain in which international law imposes any special or strict requirements. Whether a statement is made orally or in writing makes no essential difference, for such statements made in particular circumstances may create commitments in international law, which does not require that they should be couched in written form ...

46. One of the basic principles governing the creation and performance of legal obligations, whatever their source, is the principle of good faith. Trust and confidence are inherent in international co-operation, in particular in an age when this co-operation in many fields is becoming increasingly essential. Just as the very rule of *pacta sunt servanda* in the law of treaties is based on good faith, so also is the binding character of an international obligation assumed by unilateral declaration. Thus interested States may take cognizance of unilateral declarations and place confidence in them, and are entitled to require that the obligation thus created be respected ...

49. Of the statements by the French Government now before the Court, the most essential are clearly those made by the President of the Republic. There can be no doubt, in view of his function, that his public communications or statements, oral or written, as Head of State, are in international relations acts of the French State. His statements, and those of members of the French Government acting under his authority ... constitute a whole. Thus, in whatever form these statements were expressed, they must be held to constitute an engagement of the State, having regard to their intention and to the circumstances in which they were made ...

51. In announcing that the 1974 series of atmospheric tests would be the last, the French Government conveyed to the world at large, including the Applicant, its intention effectively to terminate these tests. It was bound to assume that other States might take note of these statements and rely on their being effective. The validity of these statements and their legal consequences must be considered within the general framework of the security of international intercourse, and the confidence and trust which are so essential in the relations among States. It is from the actual substance of these statements, and from the circumstances attending their making, that the legal implications of the unilateral act must be deduced. The objects of these statements are clear and they were addressed to the international community as a whole, and the Court holds that they constitute an undertaking possessing legal effect.... It is true that the French Government has consistently maintained, for example in a Note dated February 7, 1973 from the French Ambassador in Canberra to the Prime Minister and Minister for Foreign Affairs of Australia, that it "has the conviction that its nuclear experiments have not violated any rule of international law," nor did France recognise that it was bound by any rule of international law to terminate its tests, but this does not affect the legal consequences of the statements examined above. The Court finds that the unilateral undertaking resulting from these statements cannot be interpreted as having been made in implicit reliance on an arbitrary power of reconsideration. The Court finds further that the French Government has undertaken an obligation the precise nature and limits of which must be understood in accordance with the actual terms in which they have been publicly expressed.

DISSENTING OPINION OF JUDGE SIR GARFIELD BARWICK ...

... The Judgment finds an intention to enter into a binding legal obligation after giving the warning that statements limiting a State's freedom of action should receive a restrictive interpretation ... I regret to say that I am unable to do so. There seems to be nothing, either in the language used or in the circumstances of its employment, which in my opinion would warrant, and certainly nothing to compel, the conclusion that those making the statements were intending to enter into a solemn and far-reaching international obligation. ... I

---

[149] Ed. See the *Pedra Blanca* case, I.C.J. Rep. 2008, para.229.

would have thought myself that the more natural conclusion to draw from the various statements was that they were statements of policy. . . .

Notes

1. The undertaking in this case was quite different from that in the *Eastern Greenland* case in being clearly unilateral, made in public, not in the course of negotiations and without a quid pro quo. Although there was at the time little evidence to support it, the rule state by the Court whereby a state may be bound by a unilateral public pronouncement intended by it to be binding without more has now taken root.

2. The *Nuclear Tests* case was applied in the *Armed Activities (New Application: 2002)* case.[150] One argument put by the Democratic Republic of the Congo ("DRC") was that the Rwandan reservation to the Genocide Convention, by which it did not accept art.9 of the Convention, giving the ICJ jurisdiction in disputes arising under it, had been withdrawn, or would be withdrawn, as a result of the following statement made by its Minister of Justice before the UN Commission on Human Rights:

    "Rwanda is one of the countries that has ratified the greatest number of international human rights instruments. In 2004 alone, our Government ratified ten of them, including those concerning the rights of women, the prevention and repression of corruption, the prohibition of weapons of mass destruction, and the environment. The few instruments not yet ratified will shortly be ratified and past reservations not yet withdrawn will shortly be withdrawn."

    Rejecting the DRC's argument, the Court stated in part:

    ". . .the Court observes that, in accordance with its consistent jurisprudence (*Nuclear Tests (Australia* v. *France), Judgment, I.C.J. Reports 1974*), . . . it is a well-established rule of international law that the Head of State, the Head of Government and the Minister for Foreign Affairs are deemed to represent the State merely by virtue of exercising their functions, including for the performance, on behalf of the said State, of unilateral acts having the force of international commitments.[151] The Court moreover recalls that, in the matter of conclusion of treaties, this rule of customary law finds expression in Article 7, paragraph 2, of the Vienna Convention on the Law of Treaties [below, p.646] . . .

    47. The Court notes, however, that with increasing frequency in modern international relations other persons representing a State in specific fields may be authorized by that State to bind it by their statements in respect of matters falling within their purview. . . .

    48. In this case, the Court notes first that Ms Mukabagwiza spoke before the United Nations Commission on Human Rights in her capacity as Minister of Justice of Rwanda and that she indicated *inter alia* that she was making her statement "on behalf of the Rwandan people". The Court further notes that the questions relating to the protection of human rights which were the subject of that statement fall within the purview of a Minister of Justice. It is the Court's view that the possibility cannot be ruled out in principle that a Minister of Justice may, under certain circumstances, bind the State he or she represents by his or her statements. . . .

---

[150] I.C.J. Rep. 2006, p.6.
[151] Ed. On statements by Heads of State, etc. see Watts (1994–II) 247 Hague Recueil 9.

49 In order to determine the legal effect of that statement, the Court must, however, examine its actual content as well as the circumstances in which it was made . . .

50 On the first point, the Court recalls that a statement of this kind can create legal obligations only if it is made in clear and specific terms (see *Nuclear Tests (Australia v. France)*) . . .In this regard the Court observes that in her statement the Minister of Justice of Rwanda indicated that "past reservations not yet withdrawn [would] shortly be withdrawn", without refering explicitly to the reservation made by Rwanda to Article IX of the Genocide Convention. The statement merely raises in general terms the question of Rwandan reservations. As such, the expression "past reservations not yet withdrawn" refers without distinction to any reservation made by Rwanda to any international treaty to which it is a party. Viewed in its context, this expression may, it is true, be interpreted as referring solely to the reservations made by Rwanda to "international human rights instruments", to which reference is made in an earlier passage of the statement. In this connection the Court notes, however, that the international instruments in question must in the circumstances be understood in a broad sense, since, according to the statement itself, they appear to encompass not only instruments "concerning the rights of women" but also those concerning "the prevention and repression of corruption, the prohibition of weapons of mass destruction, and the environment". The Court is therefore bound to note the indeterminate character of the international treaties referred to by the Rwandan Minister of Justice in her statement.

51. The Court further observes that this statement merely indicates that "past reservations not yet withdrawn will shortly be withdrawn", without indicating any precise time-frame for such withdrawals.

52. . . . Given the general nature of its wording, the statement cannot therefore be considered as confirmation by Rwanda of a previous decision to withdraw its reservation to Article IX of the Genocide Convention, or as any sort of unilateral commitment on its part have legal effects in regard to such withdrawal; at most, it can be interpreted as a declaration of intent, very general in scope.

53. This conclusion is corroborated by an examination of the circumstances in which the statement is made. Thus the Court notes that it was in the context of a presentation of general policy on the promotion and protection of human rights that the Minister of Justice of Rwanda made her statement before the United Nations Commission on Human Rights."

3. At a meeting in Sintra of parties to the 1992 OSPAR Convention, the UK Government stated that no new commercial contracts would be accepted for reprocessing spent radioactive fuel at Dounreay, an announcement that was recorded and welcomed in the Sintra Ministerial Statement 1998. Relying on the *Nuclear Tests* case, the tribunal in the *OSPAR Arbitration*,[152] stated that it "was arguable" that this statement "may have created an international obligation on its part and in relation to the other states represented at the ministerial meeting." As this and other cases illustrate, the acceptance of the *Nuclear Tests* rule as customary international law should make government ministers doubly careful in what they say in public and how they say it (so as not to display an intention to be legally bound).

4. The customary international rules concerning the legal effect of unilateral acts, or declarations, developed in the *Nuclear Tests* and *Armed Activities* cases were formulated by the International

---

[152] P.C.A. 2003, para.90 (*www.pca/cpa.org*). The Tribunal found no need to decide the question. For other examples of unilateral acts creating legal obligations, see the Commentary to the ILC Guiding Principles, in UN Doc.A/61/10, and the 8th Report of its Special Rapporteur, UN Doc.A/CN.4/557.

Law Commission in its *Guiding Principles Applicable to Unilateral Declarations of States Capable of Creating Legal Obligations 2006*,[153] as follows:

The International Law Commission ...

Adopts the following Guiding Principles which relate only to unilateral acts *stricto sensu,* i.e. those taking the form of formal declarations formulated by a State with the intent to produce obligations under international law,

1. Declarations publicly made and manifesting the will to be bound may have the effect of creating legal obligations. When the conditions for this are met, the binding character of such declarations is based on good faith; States concerned may then take them into consideration and rely on them; such States are entitled to require that such obligations be respected;

2. Any State possesses capacity to undertake legal obligations through unilateral declarations;

3. To determine the legal effects of such declarations, it is necessary to take account of their content, of all the factual circumstances in which they were made, and of the reactions to which they gave rise;

4. A unilateral declaration binds the State internationally only if it is made by an authority vested with the power to do so. By virtue of their functions, heads of State, heads of Government and ministers for foreign affairs are competent to formulate such declarations. Other persons representing the State in specified areas may be authorized to bind it, through their declarations, in areas falling within their competence;

5. Unilateral declarations may be formulated orally or in writing;

6. Unilateral declarations may be addressed to the international community as a whole, to one or several States or to other entities;

7. A unilateral declaration entails obligations for the formulating State only if it is stated in clear and specific terms. In the case of doubt as to the scope of the obligations resulting from such a declaration, such obligations must be interpreted in a restrictive manner. In interpreting the content of such obligations, weight shall be given first and foremost to the text of the declaration, together with the context and the circumstances in which it was formulated;

8. A unilateral declaration which is in conflict with a peremptory norm of general international law is void;

9. No obligation may result for other States from the unilateral declaration of a State. However, the other State or States concerned may incur obligations in relation to such a unilateral declaration to the extent that they clearly accepted such a declaration;

10. A unilateral declaration that has created legal obligations for the State making the declaration cannot be revoked arbitrarily. In assessing whether a revocation would be arbitrary, consideration should be given to:

(i) Any specific terms of the declaration relating to revocation;
(ii) The extent to which those to whom the obligations are owed have relied on such obligations;
(iii) The extent to which there has been a fundamental change in the circumstances.

---

[153] UN Doc.A/61/10, p.367. The General Assembly took note of the Principles and recommended their dissemination: GA Res 61/14 (2006).

8. GENERAL ASSEMBLY RESOLUTIONS[154]

SLOAN, UNITED NATIONS GENERAL ASSEMBLY RESOLUTIONS IN OUR CHANGING WORLD

(1991), pp.71–75. Some footnotes omitted

General Assembly resolutions may ... be related to customary international law ... as one of the elements required for the validation of a customary rule ... [i.e.] practice or usage and *opinio juris*. ...

Unless one takes the extreme, and untenable, position that only physical acts constitute practice, General Assembly resolutions which are collective pronouncements of States must be considered a part of State practice. Dr. Akehurst defines State practice as "any act or statement by a State from which views about customary law can be inferred; it includes physical acts, claims, declarations *in abstracto* (such as General Assembly resolutions), national laws, national judgments and omissions."[155] ...

State practice may be evidenced either in declarations of general principle or in resolutions dealing with particular cases. The latter, when they involve the application of legal rules and principles, are even more clearly precedents. A condemnatory resolution adopted by 150 States might be compared to 150 diplomatic protests. ...

With respect to declarations of general principles it may be objected that practice, to be constitutive of custom, must relate to a specific claim or dispute. It is doubtful if State practice was ever so narrowly confined. ... Nor ... is such a test supported by a review of the materials which States and tribunals examine in determining a rule of customary international law. ...[156]

It is also suggested [by writers] that resolutions may satisfy the subjective element (*opinio juris*) of customary international law by expressly articulating a belief concerning the existence of principles and rules of international law.[157] Such belief may also be implied either by the terms and context of a resolution or by the circumstances surrounding its adoption, particularly if the resolution is dealing with a specific dispute or situation.

The International Court of Justice in its Judgment of 27 June 1986 in the case of *Nicaragua v. United States*,[158] in considering whether the Charter obligation to refrain from the threat or use of force was also a principle of customary international law, stated:

> The Court has however to be satisfied that there exists in customary international law an *opinio juris* as to the binding character of such abstention. This *opinio juris* may, though with all due caution, be deduced from, inter alia, the attitude of the Parties and the attitude of States towards certain General Assembly resolutions, and particularly resolution 2625 (XXV). ... The effect of consent to the text of such resolutions cannot be understood as merely that of a "reiteration or elucidation" of the treaty commitment undertaken in the Charter. On the contrary, it must be understood as an acceptance of the validity of the rule or set of rules declared by the resolution by themselves ...

---

[154] See Asamoah, *The Legal Significance of the Declarations of the General Assembly of the United Nations* (1966); Bleicher (1969) 63 A.J.I.L. 444; Castaneda, *Legal Effects of UN Resolutions* (1969, English translation by Amoia); Cheng (1965) 5 Ind. J.I.L. 23; Higgins (1970) 64 Proc. A.S.I.L. 37; id., (1987) 24 Coexistence 21; Johnson (1955–6) 32 B.Y.I.L. 97; MacGibbon, in Cheng, ed., *International Law: Teaching and Practice* (1982), Ch.2; Schachter (1982–V) 178 Hague Recueil 114; Schachber., in Mararcyk, ed., *Theory of International Law at the Threshold of the 21ˢᵗ Century* (1996), p.531. Schwebel (1979) 73 Proc. A.S.I.L. 301; Skubiszewski (1986) 15 Pol. Y.I.L. 135; Sloan, *United Nations General Assembly Resolutions in Our Changing World* (1991), Ch.2; Tunkin, *Theory of International Law*, above, p.4, n.14, pp.165, 170, 172; Tunkin, (1987) 24 Coexistence 5; Van Hoof, above, p.15, n.1, Ch.10.

[155] Ed. above, p.17, n.16, p.53.

[156] Ed. As to the latter, see as well as the *Nicaragua* case, below, p.727, the ICJ's use of General Assembly resolutions in the *Western Sahara* case, below, p.106, and the *Legal Consequences* case, I.C.J. Rep. 1971, p.16 at 31, and their use by arbitral tribunals in the *Texaco* and *Aminoil* cases, below, pp.494 and 498.

[157] Ed. The author cites, inter alia, Higgins, above, at n.154, p.42; Jennings, above, at p.15, n.1, p.11–15; and Van Hoof, above, at p.15, n.1, pp.182–183.

[158] Ed. Judgment, para.188, printed in full below, p.727.

This position of the Court on *opinio juris* has met a mixed reception particularly among American scholars.[159] But its seminal importance for the genesis of international law is not to be ignored. . . .

In indicating an *opinio juris* on the part of the States Members, Assembly resolutions may supply the missing element in a line of existing State practice and thus consummate usage into custom . . . or they may inspire practice which will develop into law. But they may do something more.

It is interesting to consider whether the same resolution can contain both the objective and subjective elements—practice and *opinio juris*. Certainly a single act of a State may, and in fact to be significant should, be practice accompanied by the belief that that practice is required by law. Resolutions adopted in a particular case might also be practice accompanied by *opinio juris*, and there seems no logical reason why declaratory resolutions may not also combine the two elements.

These elements need not be of the same quantity and intensity in each case.[160] In some instances a large body of practice with a lesser showing of belief may be sufficient to validate a rule, while in other instances very little practice but intense belief may also suffice. Some observers have considered that in special circumstances the overwhelming weight of one of the elements may be enough. In the case of the General Assembly the element of *opinio juris* may predominate in declaratory resolutions, while the element of practice may be more evident in resolutions dealing with specific incidents. Both elements may, however, be present in either type of resolution. . . .

Ordinarily *opinio juris* either accompanies practice, or appears at a later stage to consummate it into law. It is possible, however, that an *opinio juris* expressed in a resolution of the General Assembly will be itself sufficient, or may stimulate a practice which will eventually be consolidated into customary international law.

Notes

1. United Nations General Assembly resolutions that declare principles or state rules of international law in abstract terms[161] or that apply such rules to particular cases[162] are now an important feature of international relations. Article 38(1), Statute of the ICJ was not drafted with them in mind and there is uncertainty as to their role in relation to the sources of international law. What is clear is that, other than in regard to certain internal matters,[163] General Assembly resolutions are not as such legally binding upon Member or non-Member States in the manner of legislation enacted by national parliaments. In terms of the sources listed in art.38(1),

---

[159] Ed. The author refers, inter alia, to the comments by various authors in (1987) 81 A.J.I.L. 77. See especially D'Amato, id., 101 at 102, who considers that the Court "misunderstands" custom and, by starting with a "disembodied rule", to be followed by state practice in the subject area of the rule, "gets it completely backwards".

[160] Comparing *Nicaragua v. U.S.* to some earlier cases, Dean Kirgis [(1987) 81 A.J.I.L. 149] points out that "[t]he cases can be reconciled . . . if one views the elements of custom not as fixed and mutually exclusive, but as interchangeable along a sliding scale."

[161] Examples are the 1960 Declaration on the Granting of Independence to Colonial Territories and Peoples, below, p.104; the 1962 Resolution on Permanent Sovereignty over Natural Resources, below, p.474; the 1963 Declaration of Legal Principles Governing Activities of States in the Exploration and Use of Outer Space, below, p.212, n.197; the 1965 Declaration on the Inadmissibility of Intervention in the Domestic Affairs of States, below, p.742; the 1970 Declaration on the Principles of International Law Concerning Friendly Relations among States, below, App.III. As to the 1974 Declaration on the Establishment of a New International Economic Order and the 1974 Charter of Economic Rights and Duties of States, see below, p.476. The following notes are limited to resolutions of the UN General Assembly. Insofar as other inter-governmental organisations of universal membership (e.g. ICAO, UNESCO) adopt non-binding resolutions that state international law rules, the same considerations and arguments as are mentioned in this section apply.

[162] See, e.g. the General Assembly resolutions condemning USSR intervention in Afghanistan, below, p.744, or calling for non-recognition of South African homelands below, p.101, which are the collective equivalent of individual state protest. Might Security Council condemnations, (e.g. of Israeli occupation of territory: see below, p.194, and UK border raids in the Yemen: Resolution 188, S.C.O.R., 19th year, 1111th Meeting, April 9, 1964) also be regarded in the same way?

[163] e.g. the determination of the UN budget: art.17(1), UN Charter. As to the Assembly's power to terminate a League of Nations mandate, see the *Legal Consequences* case, I.C.J. Rep. 1971, p.16 at 51.

although some writers[164] have argued that General Assembly resolutions might be seen as informal treaties or as indicating general principles of law, the most common view—which is that examined by Sloan in the above extract—is that they contribute in some way to the formation of custom.[165]

2.   It is generally agreed by writers that General Assembly resolutions may serve as a convenient statement of a custom already established by state practice of a more traditional kind (diplomatic notes, etc.). But, as Sloan suggests, General Assembly resolutions may also contribute to the formation of custom as a kind of "collective" state practice.[166] They are the collective equivalent of unilateral general statements[167] or, in the context of a particular dispute, "150 diplomatic protests." The process by which they are adopted (adopted unanimously, or nearly unanimously, or by consensus or otherwise) establishes whether the practice is a "general" one. Their repetition in later resolutions[168] goes to the "constancy" and "uniformity" of the practice, as does the conduct of states in conformity with the rules stated in them in their practice outside the General Assembly.[169] As to the requirement of *opinio juris*, this will be evidenced, as Sloan indicates, by the wording of the resolution[170]; by statements made in the General Assembly in debate prior to its adoption or later in explanation of a vote[171]; or by statements made elsewhere.

3.   Remarkably, in the *Nicaragua* case,[172] the ICJ relied solely on General Assembly resolutions when spelling out the customary rule prohibiting the use of force: it did not look beyond the General Assembly to state practice in "the real world", in Mac Gibbon's phrase (above). The Court referred to General Assembly resolutions expressly and solely to demonstrate the existence of the necessary *opinio juris*, or subjective element of custom: it did not follow the approach countenanced by Sloan by which General Assembly resolutions that declare principles or rules of international law in the abstract may be seen as state practice satisfying the "material" or objective element as well. In other words, the Court reached its decision on the custom prohibiting the use of force on the basis just of evidence of the required *opinio juris*, which it found in

---

[164] See, e.g., Asamoah, above, n.154, pp.61–62, 70.

[165] Some General Assembly resolutions may be seen as elaborating upon the meaning of treaty provisions in the Charter (e.g. the 1970 Declaration on Principles of International Law, below, App.III, elaborates upon the meaning of art.2(4) and the Universal Declaration of Human Rights below, p.548, amplifies the meaning of "human rights" in the UN Charter). This, however, does not solve the problem of classification where such resolutions are also understood to state rules of international law that are binding upon states independently of their treaty obligations: see the *Nicaragua (Merits)* case, below p.727.

[166] For a different view, see MacGibbon, in Cheng, below, n.169:
"... the kind of State practice which is appropriate to the formation of rules of customary international law is not voting or even making statements in the General Assembly, but what States do and have done 'on the ground' in their relations with other States—not the resolution itself, but actual practice in the sense of the provisions of the resolutions. In other words, it is real State practice in the real world which is required, not the formal conduct of States within the limited and artificial context of the General Assembly."
cf. Thirlway, above, p.17, n.16, p.66.

[167] e.g. the UK statement on humanitarian intervention, below, p.785.

[168] e.g. the many resolutions on self-determination cited in the *Western Sahara* case, below, p.106.

[169] Ed. In his dissenting opinion in the *South West Africa* cases (Second Phase), I.C.J. Rep. 1966, p.292, Judge Tanaka stated: "Of course we cannot admit that individual resolutions, declarations, judgments, decisions, etc. have binding force upon the members of the organization. What is required for customary international law is the repetition of the same practice; accordingly, in this case resolutions, declarations, etc., on the same matter in the same, or diverse, organizations must take place repeatedly. ... This collective, cumulative and organic process of custom-generation can be characterized as the middle way between legislation by convention and the traditional process of custom making, and can be seen to have an important role from the viewpoint of the development of international law."
cf. Higgins, in Cheng, ed., *International Law: Teaching and Practice* (1982), pp.27–29.

[170] e.g. the 1970 Declaration on Principles of International Law, below, App.III. See its title and text.

[171] e.g. Mrs Roosevelt's statement that the Universal Declaration on Human Rights was not legally binding, below, p.552.

[172] See the extracts from the judgment, below, p.727.

General Assembly resolutions. As Sloan indicates, this novel approach has been reconciled with earlier Court jurisprudence by Kirgis by a "sliding scale" explanation. By this, General Assembly resolutions of the abstract, declaratory kind have a special role in establishing custom. Note, however, that the Court did, although in a rather cursory fashion, refer to state practice in the "real world" (as well as *opinio juris* derived from General Assembly resolutions) in the *Nicaragua* case (paras 206–207) when considering the rule on the legality of intervention and, to a greater extent, in the *Legality of Nuclear Weapons* case[173] on the non-use of nuclear weapons.

4. But whatever the opinion of writers and the judgments of courts, the views of states, who by their practice decide the customary rules on the sources of international law, as to the status and impact of General Assembly resolutions remain crucial. In this connection, the following careful pronouncement by the US Department of State[174] is significant:

> "As a broad statement of U.S. policy in this regard, I think it is fair to state that General Assembly resolutions are regarded as recommendations to Member States of the United Nations.
>
>   To the extent, which is exceptional, that such resolutions are meant to be declaratory of international law, are adopted with the support of all members, and are observed by the practice of states, such resolutions are evidence of customary international law on a particular subject matter."

When the question of the role of General Assembly resolutions was considered by states in the General Assembly Sixth Committee in 1974 in the context of a review of the work of the ICJ, there was general agreement that General Assembly resolutions were not to be seen as a new source of international law, additional to those listed in art.38. There was, however, acceptance of the idea that they may be evidence of custom. The representative of Mexico[175] went as far as any:

> ". . . it was not a question of adding another source of international law to those enumerated in that Article but rather of drawing attention to certain elements of legal interpretation to which the Court must inevitably have recourse when deciding in accordance with international law such disputes as were submitted to it—in strict implementation, of course, of Article 38 of its Statute. The Court unquestionably had to take account of international custom as reflected in the many resolutions and declarations adopted year after year by the General Assembly, whose very reiteration was irrefutable proof of the *diuturnitas* [usage] which had traditionally been recognized as one of the constituent elements of international custom. He mentioned by way of example [Resolutions 1514,[176] 2625,[177] and 2749[178]]. . . . Those and many other General Assembly declarations and resolutions of a similar type reflected the desire of Member States to promulgate juridical rules of unquestionable validity to which they all subscribed, in other words, the general *opinio juris*, which was the second traditional element of custom."

---

[173] Opinion, paras 65–67, below, p.788. Cf. the *Wall* case, I.C.J. Rep. 2004, p.136 at p.171.
[174] Letter by Mr Schwebel, Deputy Legal Adviser of the Department of State, 1975 U.S.D.I.L. 85.
[175] G.A.O.R., 29th Sess., A/C.6/SR. 1486, p.133.
[176] Below, p.104.
[177] Below, App.III.
[178] Declaration of Principles Governing the Sea-Bed 1970, (1971) 10 I.L.M. 220.

More cautiously, the representative of the UK[179] stated:

"While it was true that General Assembly resolutions might reflect or be evidence of developments in international law, that was not the same as saying that General Assembly resolutions could themselves develop international law. His delegation could not accept the latter proposition.... Even the evidential value of General Assembly resolutions must depend on their circumstances. Many resolutions were of such a nature and had such a content that they could have no relevance to the development of international law."

When assessing these official statements, note the following comment by Sohn[180]:

"... there is wide consensus that these declarations [e.g. Resolution 2625, App.III, below] actually established new rules of international law binding upon all States. This is not treaty-making but a new method of creating customary international law.

... Thus the United Nations has made possible the creation of "instant international law."[181] Many traditional international lawyers have not reconciled themselves yet to this new approach and some legal advisers of Foreign Offices still like to raise doubts about the true nature and effect of such Declarations. But it is quite obvious that most States have found this new procedure quite useful and are willing to apply it whenever they are confronted with important issues of interpreting the basic rules of the Charter of the United Nations or of developing new law for new areas made accessible by modern science and technology. In a rapidly changing world the United Nations has found a method, albeit restricted by the rule of unanimity or quasi-unanimity, to adapt the principles of its Charter and the rules of customary international law to the changing times with an efficiency which even its most optimistic founders did not anticipate."

----

9. "SOFT LAW"[182]

VAN HOOF, RETHINKING THE SOURCES OF INTERNATIONAL LAW

(1983), pp.187–189. Some footnotes omitted

This brings us to a ... school of thought which ... was to a large extent equally prompted by the questions involved in the legal nature of General Assembly resolutions, but its tenets also apply to other documents whose legal status is unclear.... authors belonging to this ... group do not make a black-and-white distinction between

---

[179] G.A.O.R., 29th Sess., A/C.6/SR. 1492, p.167.

[180] In Bos, ed., *The Present State of International Law and Other Essays* (1973), p.39, pp.52–53.

[181] Ed. See Cheng (1965) 5 Ind. J.I.L. 23. Cheng used the now celebrated phrase "instant customary international law" to describe the process by which, in a series of resolutions in the early 1960s, see below, p.212, the General Assembly had spelt out a new legal regime on outer space. In debate on this new regime, a number of states accepted that General Assembly resolutions had a (not precisely defined) role to play in the development of international law. For example, the US representative stated: "When a General Assembly resolution proclaimed principles of international law ... and was adopted unanimously, it represented the law as generally accepted in the international community." U.N. Doc. A/AC.105/C.2/SR.20, p.11.

[182] See Boyle in Evans, ed., *International Law* (2nd edn 2006), Ch.5; Chinkin (1989) 38 I.C.L.Q. 850; Dupuy (1991) 12 Mich. J.I.L. 420; Hillgenberg (1999) 10 E.J.I.L. 499; Schachter (1977) 71 A.J.I.L. 296; Seidl-Hohenveldern (1979–II) 163 Hague Recueil 164; Shelton, ed., *Commitment and Compliance: the Role of Non-Binding Norms in the International Legal System* (2000); Sztucki, in *Festskrift Hjerner* (1990), p.549.

law and non-law. After testing a new type of instrument on the basis of the criteria of the traditional sources, they conclude that these instruments cannot be considered as "full-fledged" rules of international law. On the other hand, they stress that these instruments fulfil at least some, if not a great number, of the criteria required for rules to be considered rules of international law and cannot therefore be simply put aside as non-law. In other words, they acknowledge that there exists a considerable "grey area" of "soft-law" between the white space of law and the black territory of non-law. Simultaneously, they make the salient point that the "grey area" may greatly affect the white one and explain, sometimes in considerable detail, in what ways "soft-law" can have legal effects. . . .

The "soft-law" approach is an important asset to the doctrine of international law . . . its main contribution . . . is that it has started to map out the legal implications of legally non-binding instruments, in particular also their relation with full-fledged legal rules. This job . . . is extremely useful, as in international law, because of the lack of a formal organizational structure, "soft-law" rules play a more prominent role than in national legal systems and are likely to do so also in the future.

Notes

1. "Soft law" consists of written instruments that spell out rules of conduct that are not intended to be legally binding, so that they are not subject to the law of treaties and do not generate the *opinio juris* required for them to be state practice contributing to custom.[183] Not being legally binding, they cannot be enforced in court. Examples of "soft law" include the Helsinki Final Act 1975,[184] the Bonn Declaration on International Terrorism 1978[185]; and the Rio Declaration on Environmental and Development 1992.[186]

2. While it may be paradoxical and confusing to call something "law" when it is *not* law, the concept is nonetheless useful to describe instruments that clearly have an impact on international relations and that may later harden into custom[187] or become the basis of a treaty.[188] And, as Jennings[189] has stated, "recommendations may not make law, but you would hesitate to advise a government that it may, therefore, ignore them, even in a legal argument." Seidl-Hohenveldern[190] suggests that the main value of international "soft law," which is very important in the field of international economic law, is as a device "to overcome a deadlock in relations between states pursuing conflicting ideological and/or economic aims."

3. The concept has, however, been criticised. Sztucki[191] summarises the criticisms as follows:

   "*Primo*, the term is inadequate and misleading. There are no two levels or "species" of law—something is law or is not law. *Secundo*, the concept is counterproductive or even dangerous. On the one hand, it creates illusory expectations of (perhaps even insistence on) compliance with what no one is obliged to comply; and on the other hand, it exposes binding legal norms for risks of neglect, and international law as a whole for risks of erosion, by blurring the threshold between what is legally binding and what is not."

---

[183] On the related concept of international comity, see above, p.30.

[184] See below, p.536. But see the *Nicaragua (Merits)* case, judgment para.189, below, p.727.

[185] (1978) 17 I.L.M. 1285.

[186] (1992) 31 I.L.M. 874.

[187] e.g. the Universal Declaration on Human Rights 1948 was "soft law" when it was adopted but has since to some extent hardened into custom: see below, p.552.

[188] e.g. the General Assembly Declaration on Torture 1975, G.A. Resn. 3452, G.A.D.R., 30th Sess., Supp.34, p.91 (1975).

[189] See above, p.15, n.1, p.14. Although only discussing General Assembly resolutions, which are a major source of "soft law", this comment applied to "soft law" generally.

[190] See above, n.182, p.193.

[191] See above, n.182, pp.550–551.

10. CODIFICATION AND PROGRESSIVE DEVELOPMENT OF INTERNATIONAL LAW

Note

The codification of international law has been the subject of public and private action at various levels since the late nineteenth century. Before the First World War notable success was achieved by the Hague Conventions of 1899 and 1907, resulting from the Hague Conferences of the same years, on the laws of war and neutrality. Between the two world wars, the League of Nations sponsored a Codification Conference at The Hague in 1930 which was prepared for in optimistic mood and which examined the law of nationality, territorial waters and state responsibility. It was a great disappointment when agreement proved possible only on certain aspects of the law of nationality.

In 1946, with the major part of international law still to be found in the uncollated practice of states, the General Assembly, acting under art.13 of the Charter of the United Nations, established the International Law Commission.[192] The Commission was given the function of promoting the "progressive development" and "codification" of international law. By "progressive development" is meant "the preparation of draft conventions on subjects which have not yet been regulated by international law or in regard to which the law has not yet been sufficiently developed in the practice of States."[193] "Codification" means "the more precise formulation and systematisation of rules of international law in fields where there already has been extensive State practice, precedent and doctrine."[194] Most of the Commission's work now consists of "progressive development" rather than "codification", although the two are closely intertwined.[195]

A number of multilateral conventions now in force are the result of the Commission's work. The procedure is generally for the Commission to prepare, on the basis of reports made by a member appointed as special rapporteur, a set of draft articles which are submitted to states for their comments by the General Assembly Sixth Committee. The United Nations may then decide to call a diplomatic conference for the adoption of a treaty based on the Commission's draft. For example, the four 1958 Geneva Conventions on the Law of the Sea,[196] the 1961 Vienna Convention on Diplomatic Relations,[197] the 1969 Vienna Convention on the Law of Treaties,[198] and the 1998 Statute of the International Criminal Court,[199] all result from the Commission's work in this way. Recently completed Commission work includes Draft Articles on Prevention of Transboundary Harm from Hazardous Activities 2001; Draft Articles on the Responsibility of States for Internationally Wrongful Acts 2991; Draft Articles on Diplomatic Protection 2006; Draft Principles on the Allocation of Loss in the Case of Transboundary Harm Arising out of Hazardous Activities 2006; and Guiding Principles

---

[192] See Anderson, Boyle, Lowe and Wickremasinghe, *The International Law Commission and the Future of International Law* (1998); Boyle and Chinkin, *The Making of International Law* (2007), Ch.4. El Baradei, Franck and Trachtenberg, *The International Law Commission: the Need for a New Direction* (1981); Graefrath (1991) 85 A.J.I.L. 595; McRae (1987) 25 C.Y.I.L. 355; Ramcharan, *The International Law Commission* (1977); Rosenne, 2 Max Planck Ybk. UN Law 1 (1998); Sinclair, *The International Law Commission* (1987); Watts, *The International Law Commission 1949–1998* (1999), 3 vols. A theme in much of this literature is the need to rethink the Commission's role and its working methods. In 1995, the General Assembly requested the ILC to review its working methods: G.A. Res 50/45. For the ILC's response, see ILC 1996 Report, G.A.O.R., 51st Sess., Supp. 10. The future of the ILC was debated at a seminar held to mark its 60th anniversary on 19/20 May, 2008: see *www.un.org/law/ilc*.

[193] Art.15, Statute of the ILC.

[194] ibid.

[195] On their relationship, see the dissenting opinion of Judge ad hoc Sørensen in the *North Sea Continental Shelf* cases I.C.J. Rep. 1969, pp.212–213.

[196] Below, Ch.7.

[197] ibid.

[198] Below, Ch.10.

[199] UN Doc. A/CONF 183/9; (1998) 37 I.L.M. 999; (1999) 6 I.H.R.R. 232.

Applicable to Unilateral Declarations of States Capable of Creating Legal Obligations 2006.[200] These may lead to treaties later. Even if the Commission's work does not result in a treaty text, it may nonetheless prove influential in practice. Thus the Draft Articles on Responsibility of States for Internationally Wrongful Acts have been already cited by both the ICJ[201] and the International Tribunal on the law of the Sea.[202] As Lauterpacht[203] stated, the texts prepared by the Commission are, in terms of the rules about sources of international law in art.38(1)(c), ICJ Statute, "at least in the category of writings of the more qualified publicists".

Projects at present under way within the Commission include reservations to treaties, effects of armed conflicts on treaties, the obligation to extradite or prosecute, the expulsions of aliens, the protection of persons in the event of disasters, the responsibility of international organisations, and shared natural resources.[204]

The Commission, which meets as authorised by the General Assembly for two sessions each year amounting to 10 to 12 weeks, is composed of 34 members, "who shall be persons of recognised competence in international law."[205] Members are elected for five year terms (eligible for re-election)[206] by the "General Assembly from a list of candidates nominated by the Governments of State Members of the United Nations",[207] which "shall bear in mind that the persons to be elected to the Commission should individually possess the qualifications required and that in the Commission as a whole representation of the main forms of civilization and of the principal legal systems of the world should be assured."[208] Members sit as individuals and not as representatives of their Governments.[209] While confirming that "many of its members are high officials in the foreign ministry of their countries and even represent them in the Sixth Committee" of the General Assembly, one former member has stressed that nonetheless the independent status of members "remains the decisive aspect in determining the nature of the Commission".[210]

It is noticeable that the Commission has not been used in the drafting of a number of important UN sponsored law-making treaties. Thus human rights treaties have mostly been within the jurisdiction of the Charter-based UN Commission on Human Rights (now the Human Rights Council)[211]; the Committee on Outer Space[212] has been seized with responsibility for treaties on outer space; the

---

[200] All of these Draft Articles may be found at *www.un.org/law/ilc.*

[201] *Gabičíkovo-Nagymaros* case, I.C.J. Rep. p.7 at 38; and the *Immunity from Legal Process* case, I.C.J. Rep. 1999, p.62 at 87.

[202] *M/V Saiga (No.2)* case, (1999) 38 I.L.M. 1323, paras 98, 133, 171. See also below, p.63, for use of the ILC Draft Declaration on Rights and Duties of States.

[203] "Survey of International Law in Relation to the Work of Codification of the International Law Commission" in E. Lauterpacht, ed., *International Law, Being the Collected Papers of Hersch Lauterpacht* (1970) Vol.1, p.445.

[204] See *www.un.org/law/ilc.*

[205] Statute of the ILC, art.2(1).

[206] art.10.

[207] art.3.

[208] art.8. G.A. Res 36/39, November 18, 1981, para.3, amending arts 2 and 9 of the ILC Statute, also specifies that composition should consist of 8 nationals from African States; 7 nationals from Asian States; 3 nationals from Eastern European States; 6 nationals from Latin American States; 8 nationals from Western European or other States; plus two other members from one African or Eastern European and Asian or Latin American states in rotation.

[209] However, the methods of work of the Commission involve consultation with states and a former Chairman of the Commission has pointed out that while members "generally do not extend undue deference to the views of their own or any other country ... most Commission members do not labor in a vacuum or for abstract ends. Most are sensitive to the fact that the utility of their work requires acceptance by a broad community of states ... States do not give orders, but they are clients without whom the Commission's work comes to little." Rosenstock (2002) 96 A.J.I.L. 792 at 794.

[210] Graefrath, above, n.192, p.600, n.62. The Sixth Committee is the Assembly's legal committee. It debates the Commission's annual reports and is in a position to give guidance to the Commission on the direction that its work should take to have the necessary political backing of states.

[211] See below, p.545.

[212] See below, p.215.

1982 Law of the Sea Convention[213] was the work of UNCLOS III; and recent key environmental and trade law treaties derive from other initiatives.[214] The ILC's non-involvement in some of these activities may be partly because of its own reluctance to move beyond areas of traditional international law in which there is a sizeable amount of non-controversial state practice or international caselaw upon which to draw and partly, more recently, because of the reluctance of states to leave politically contentious issues involving the progressive development of international law to a body which is not composed of representatives of states.[215]

It is noticeable also that while the ILC's work has led to a number of treaties (see those listed above) that are now the recognised source for the rules or developments in important areas of present day international law, some of the ILC's work has not been so successful, with some treaties not being widely ratified[216] or not entering into force at all.[217]

Nonetheless, the ILC continues to play an important role in the codification and progressive development of international law, as evidenced most recently by the strong impact of its Draft Statute of International Criminal Court and of its Draft Articles on Responsibility of States for Internationally Wrongful Acts.

---

[213] See below, p.322.

[214] See e.g. the 1992 Biodiversity Convention, (1992) 31 I.L.M. 882, and the 1994 Agreement on Trade-Related Aspects of Intellectual Property Rights (TRIPS Agreement), (1994) 33 I.L.M. 81.

[215] See further, El Baradei, Franck and Trachtenberg, above, n.192, Ch.2.

[216] e.g. 1978 Vienna Convention on Succession of States in Respect of Treaties: see below, p.116.

[217] e.g. 1986 Vienna Convention on the Law of Treaties between State and International Organisations or Between International Organisations, below, at p.641, and the 1975 Vienna Convention on the Representation of States in Their relations with International Organisations of a Universal Character, A/Conf 67, 16; (1975) 69 A.J.I.L. 730. The UN Convention on Jurisdictional Immunities of States and Their Property 2004 below, p.276, has as yet attracted few ratifications.

3 INTERNATIONAL LAW AND MUNICIPAL LAW

1. MONISM AND DUALISM

FITZMAURICE, THE GENERAL PRINCIPLES OF INTERNATIONAL LAW CONSIDERED FROM THE STANDPOINT OF THE RULE OF LAW

(1957–II) 92 Hague Recueil 1 at 70–80. Some footnotes omitted

This controversy [between monism and dualism] turns on whether international law and internal law are two separate legal orders, existing independently of one another—and, if so, on what basis it can be said that either is superior to or supreme over the other; or whether they are both part of the same order, one or other of them being supreme over the other *within that order*. The first view is the dualist view, the second monist. . . . [A] radical view of the whole subject may be propounded to the effect that the entire monist-dualist controversy is unreal, artificial and strictly beside the point, because it assumes something that has to exist for there to be any controversy at all—and which in fact does not exist—namely a *common field* in which the two legal orders under discussion both simultaneously have their spheres of activity. . . . For instance . . . it would be idle to start a controversy about whether the English legal system was superior to or supreme over the French or *vice-versa*, because these systems do not pretend to have the same field of application. . . . There is indeed no basis on which it is even possible to start an argument because, although these legal systems may in a certain sense come into conflict in particular cases, thus giving rise to problems of what is called Conflict Law, or Private International Law, each country has its own conflict rules whereby it settles such problems arising before its own Courts. Ultimately therefore, there can be no conflict between any two systems *in the domestic field*, for any apparent conflict is automatically settled by the domestic conflict rules of the forum. Any conflict between them in the international field, that is to say on the inter-governmental plane, would fall to be resolved by international law, because in that field international law is not only supreme, but in effect the only system there is. Domestic law does not, as such, apply at all in the international field. But the supremacy of international law in that field exists, not because of any inherent supremacy of international law as a category over national law as a category, but for other reasons. It is, rather, a supremacy of exactly the same order as the supremacy of French law in France, and of English law in England—i.e. a supremacy not arising from *content*, but from the field of operation—not because the law is *French* but because the place, the field, is *France*. The view here suggested is neither dualist nor monist. It is precisely the view put forward in the following passage from Anzilotti,[1] who is often miscalled a dualist in this respect:

> It follows from the same principle that there cannot be conflict between rules belonging to different juridical orders, and, consequently, in particular between international and internal law. To speak of conflict between international law and internal law is as inaccurate as to speak of conflict between the laws of different States: in reality the existence of a conflict between norms belonging to different juridical orders cannot be affirmed except from a standpoint outside both the one and the other.

The logic of this cannot be contravened, and in actual fact, the necessity for a common field of operation as the

---

[1] *Corso di diritto internazionale.* This passage is translated from the French translation by Gidel, p.57.

basis of any discussion as to the relations between two legal orders, is recognised by modern protagonists of the monist-dualist controversy. This can be seen from the following sentence in an article by a writer of the monist school,[2] reading: "Two normative systems with binding force *in the same field* must form part of the same order"—[italics added]. This may be true, or at least it is capable of discussion, if the two orders in question *are* binding in the same field, but not otherwise. Consider again a sentence such as the following one, taken from one of the most eminent and justly celebrated modern exponents of the positivist-monist view[3]: "International law and national law cannot be mutually different and mutually independent systems ... if ... both systems are considered to be valid for the same space and at the same time." Everything here depends of course on the "if"— which surely assumes the very point that has to be proved. What calls for question is precisely the phrase "valid for the same space at the same time." Had this passage said "valid simultaneously for the same class of relations," it would not have been open to question, though only because international and national law do not in fact govern the same set of relations. To say this is not to deny the validity of the monist view, but only its relevance in this particular connexion. Equally, the relevance of the dualist view is denied.[4] Recognising, as they evidently do, that only relations between legal orders that operate in the same field can usefully and mean-ingfully be discussed, the protagonists of the monist-dualist controversy seem to be driven to trying to *create* the necessary common field—though it is more particularly the monists who seek to do this, since the dualists can rest quite content with the existence of two orders, provided they operate in separate fields. The endeavour to create a common field takes the form in effect of denying the existence or reality of the State, or reducing it to the sum total of the individuals composing it. For instance, the same eminent authority, evidently aware of the difficulty that must arise unless there is a common field, has suggested the following solution[5]:

> The mutual independence of international and national law is often substantiated by the alleged fact that the two systems regulate different subject matters. National law, it is said, regulates the behaviour of individuals, international law the behaviour of States. We have already shown that the behaviour of States is reducible to the behaviour of individuals representing the State. Thus the alleged difference in subject matter between international and national law cannot be a difference between the kinds of subjects whose behaviour they regulate. ...

Formally, therefore, international and domestic law as *systems* can never come into conflict. What may occur is something strictly different, namely a conflict of *obligations*, or an inability for the State *on the domestic plane* to act in the manner required by international law. The supremacy of international law in the international field does not in these circumstances entail that the judge in the municipal courts of the State must override local law and apply international law. Whether he does or can do this depends on the local law itself, and on what legislative or administrative steps can be or are taken to deal with the matter. The supremacy of international law in the international field simply means that if nothing can be or is done, the State will, on the international plane, have committed a breach of its international law obligations, for which it will be internationally responsible, and in respect of which it cannot plead the condition of its domestic law by way of absolution. International law does not therefore in any way purport to govern the content of national law in the national field—nor does it need to. It simply says—and this is all it needs to say—that certain things are not valid according to international law, and that if a State in the application of its domestic law acts contrary to international law in these respects, it will commit a breach of its international obligations.

Note

Controversy between monism and dualism has taxed and divided international lawyers over many years. It is most relevant when considering whether a national court should apply a rule of inter-national law. Consider when examining the cases in the remainder of this chapter whether the international and municipal courts and tribunals that decided them show any awareness of the monist-dualist controversy.

---

2   J. G. Starke, "Monism and Dualism in the Theory of International Law" in *British Year Book* (1936), p.74.
3   Professor Kelsen, *The Principles of International Law*, Rinehart (1952), p.404. Ed. Now see 2nd edn 1967, p.553.
4   If either view were relevant, the monist would seem preferable, but only on the basis that there is a legal order, natural law, behind and above both domestic and international law, which affirms the supremacy of international law. ...
5   Kelsen, *op. cit* ... *ibid*. Ed. Now see 2nd edn 1967, p.544.

----

2. MUNICIPAL LAW IN INTERNATIONAL LAW[6]

DRAFT DECLARATION ON RIGHTS AND DUTIES OF STATES 1949

Y.B.I.L.C. 1949, pp.286, 288

The Draft Declaration was prepared by the International Law Commission. The United Nations General Assembly noted it and commended it to members and jurists as a "notable and substantial contribution towards the progressive development of international law and its codification": G.A. Resn. 375 (IV), G.A.O.R., 4th Session, *Resolutions*, p.66 (1949).

Article 13

Every state has the duty to carry out in good faith its obligations arising from treaties and other sources of international law, and it may not invoke provisions in its constitution or its laws as an excuse for failure to perform this duty.

Notes

1. There is ample judicial and arbitral authority for the rule that a state cannot rely upon its municipal law to avoid its international law obligations. For example, in the *Alabama Claims Arbitration*,[7] the Tribunal rejected the British argument that because its constitutional law was not such as to provide it with the power to interfere with the private construction and sailing of the ships concerned, Great Britain had not violated its obligations as a neutral in the United States Civil War by allowing the construction and sailing to occur:

    "... the government of Her Britannic Majesty cannot justify itself for a failure in due diligence on the plea of insufficiency of the legal means of action which it possessed."

2. The 1969 Vienna Convention on the Law of Treaties provides that a state may not invoke its municipal law as a justification for not complying with its treaty obligations (art.27, below, p.671) and that non-compliance with municipal law rules on the competence to make treaties may not generally be invoked to invalidate to its consent to a treaty (art.46, below, p.687).

EXCHANGE OF GREEK AND TURKISH POPULATIONS CASE

Advisory Opinion. P.C.I.J. Reports, Series B, No.10, p.20 (1925)

Referring to art.18 of the Treaty of Lausanne 1923, by which the parties undertook "to introduce in their respective laws such modifications as may be necessary with a view to ensuring the execution of the present Convention," the Court stated:

----

[6]   See Ferrari-Bravo, in McDonald and Johnston, eds, *The Structure and Process of International Law* (1983), pp.715 and 725 and Jenks, *The Prospects of International Adjudication* (1964), Ch.9.

[7]   *U.S. v G.B.*, Moore, (1872) 1 Int.Arb. 495 at 656.

Opinion of the Court

This clause ... merely lays stress on a principle which is self-evident, according to which a State which has contracted valid international obligations is bound to make in its legislation such modifications as may be necessary to ensure the fulfilment of the obligations undertaken.

Notes

1. If State A and State B make a treaty by which each agrees to allow the nationals of the other into its territory on terms better than those required by customary international law, and if State A fails to make the necessary changes in its local law to allow the admission of the nationals of State B on the terms agreed, has State A violated international law if no national of State B has tried to obtain, and been refused, admission under the treaty?[8]

2. If, contrary to customary international law, State A claims jurisdiction to board ships on the high seas flying the flag of another state and gives its navy power under its municipal law so to act, does it *thereby* violate international law?[9]

BRAZILIAN LOANS CASE

France v Brazil (1929)

P.C.I.J. Reports, Series A, No.21, pp.124–125

The question in this case was one of the interpretation of certain Brazilian Government loans, some bonds of which were held by French nationals. The loans were governed by Brazilian law. The Court ruled that it had jurisdiction under art.36 of its Statute to decide cases such as the one before it involving disputes between states which turned not upon international law but the interpretation of municipal law. In the following passage the Court considered how it should go about interpreting municipal law when called upon to do so. The Agreement between the parties referring the case to the Court read in part: "In estimating the weight to be attached to any municipal law of either country which may be applicable to the dispute, the Permanent Court of International Justice shall not be bound by the decisions of the respective courts" (art.VI).

Judgment of the Court

Though bound to apply municipal law when circumstances so require, the Court, which is a tribunal of international law, and which, in this capacity, is deemed itself to know what this law is, is not obliged also to know the municipal law of the various countries. All that can be said in this respect is that the Court may possibly be obliged to obtain knowledge regarding the municipal law which has to be applied. And this it must do, either by means of evidence furnished it by the Parties or by means of any researches which the Court may think fit to undertake or to cause to be undertaken.

Once the Court has arrived at the conclusion that it is necessary to apply the municipal law of a particular country, there seems no doubt that it must seek to apply it as it would be applied in that country. It would not be applying the municipal law of a country if it were to apply it in a manner different from that in which that law would be applied in the country in which it is in force.

It follows that the Court must pay the utmost regard to the decisions of the municipal courts of a country, for it is with the aid of their jurisprudence that it will be enabled to decide what are the rules which, in actual fact, are

---

8   See Fitzmaurice, above, p.61, pp.89–90; McNair, *Treaties*, p.100; Schwarzenberger, p.614.
9   See Fitzmaurice, above, n.8 and the ILC Draft Articles on Responsibility of States, commentary to art.12, below, p.432.

applied in the country the law of which is recognised as applicable in a given case. If the Court were obliged to disregard the decisions of municipal courts, the result would be that it might in certain circumstances apply rules other than those actually applied; this would seem to be contrary to the whole theory on which the application of municipal law is based.

Of course, the Court will endeavour to make a just appreciation of the jurisprudence of municipal courts. If this is uncertain or divided, it will rest with the Court to select the interpretation which it considers most in conformity with the law. … As the Court has already observed in the judgment in the case of Serbian loans,[10] it would be a most delicate matter to do so, in a case concerning public policy—a conception the definition of which in any particular country is largely dependant on the opinion prevailing at any given time in such country itself—and in a case where no relevant provisions directly relate to the question at issue. Such are the reasons according to which the Court considers that it must construe Article VI of the Special Agreement to mean that, while the Court is authorised to depart from the jurisprudence of the municipal courts, it remains entirely free to decide that there is no ground for attributing to the municipal law a meaning other than that attributed to it by that jurisprudence.

Notes

1. If a nationalisation statute enacted by State A were alleged to be contrary to international law by State B before an international court or tribunal and if the dispute turned upon the meaning of the compensation provision in the statute, how would the Court or tribunal go about interpreting that provision (a) if the statute had not been construed by State A's courts; (b) if it had been construed by them but State B alleged that the Court in the case in which this was done had failed to follow a binding precedent that would have led it to a different conclusion?

2. As stated by the P.C.I.J. in the *Certain German Interests in Polish Upper Silesia* case,[11] municipal law, and how it is applied by the administration and courts of a state, is also relevant at the international law level as constituting acts of the state by which its compliance with its international law obligations are to be judged.

----

3. INTERNATIONAL LAW IN MUNICIPAL LAW[12]

A. The United Kingdom[13]

i. Customary International Law

TRIQUET v BATH

(1764) 3 Burr. 1478. Court of King's Bench

In this case, in which the defendant, a domestic servant of the Bavarian Minister to Great Britain, successfully claimed diplomatic immunity, Lord Mansfield discussed the position of international law in English law.

---

[10]   Ed. P.C.I.J. Rep., Series A. No.20, p.46 (1929).

[11]   See the extract from the P.C.I.J.'s judgment quoted and applied in the *Saiga (No.2)* case, para.120, below, p.369.

[12]   See Cassese (1985–III) 192 Hague Recueil 331; Jacobs and Roberts, eds, *The Effects of Treaties in Domestic Law* (1987); Int. Law Assn., 66th Conference Report (1994), p.326; Morgenstern (1950) 27 B.Y.I.L. 42; Seidl-Hohenveldern (1963) 12 I.C.L.Q. 88; Wildhaber and Breitenmoser (1988) 48 Z.A.O.R.V. 163. For a detailed survey of state practice, see Shaw, *International Law* (6th edn 2009), pp.138 et seq.

[13]   See Butler (1987) 24 Coexistence 67; Fawcett, *The British Commonwealth in International Law* (1963), Ch.2; Holdsworth, *Essays in Law and History* (1946), pp.260–272; Jenks, above, n.6, Ch.13; Lauterpacht (1939) 25 Trans. Grot. Soc. 51; Mann, *Foreign Affairs in English Courts* (1986), Chs 5, 6.

LORD MANSFIELD

This privilege of foreign ministers and their domestic servants depends upon the law of nations. The Act of Parliament of 7 Ann. c. 12,[14] is declaratory of it....

I remember in a case before Lord Talbot, of *Buvot v. Barbuit*[15] upon a motion to discharge the defendant (who was in execution for not performing a decree), "because he was agent of commerce, commissioned by the King of Prussia, and received here as such"; the matter was very elaborately argued at the Bar; and a solemn deliberate opinion given to the Court. These questions arose and were discussed.... "What was the rule of decision: the Act of Parliament; or, the law of nations." Lord Talbot declared a clear opinion; "That the law of nations, in its full extent was part of the law of England." ...

I remember, too, Lord Hardwicke's declaring his opinion to the same effect; and denying that Lord Chief Justice Holt ever had any doubt as to the law of nations being part of the law of England, upon the occasion of the arrest of the Russian Ambassador [which had led to the Act of Anne].

Note

Although the discussion in the English cases in this section is in terms of English law, the question in issue is one of the public law of the United Kingdom as a whole. *Triquet v Bath* and *Buvot v Barbuit* are two of the cases commonly cited in support of the view that United Kingdom law adopts the "incorporation" approach to the reception of customary international law as part of common law, by which customary international law is automatically regarded as a part of common law, without the need for a national court decision in each particular case.

R. v KEYN

(1876) 2 Ex.D. 63. Court for Crown Cases Reserved

The *Franconia*, a German ship, collided with the *Strathclyde*, a British ship, at a point in the English Channel within three miles of the English coast. The defendant, the German captain of the *Franconia*, was prosecuted at the Central Criminal Court for the manslaughter of a passenger on board the *Strathclyde* who died as a result of the collision. The defendant was found guilty, but the question whether an English court had jurisdiction to try the case was reserved for the Court for Crown Cases Reserved[16] which decided, by seven votes to six, that it did not. The following is an extract from the judgment of Cockburn C.J. who was one of the judges in the majority.

COCKBURN C.J.

On board a foreign ship on the high seas, the foreigner is liable to the law of the foreign ship only. It is only when a foreign ship comes into the ports or waters of another state that the ship and those on board become subject to the local law. These are the established rules of the law of nations. They have been adopted into our own municipal law, and must be taken to form part of it.

... Unless, therefore, the accused, Keyn, at the time of the offence of which he has been convicted was committed, was on British territory or on board a British ship, he could not be properly brought to trial under English law, in the absence of express legislation.

On the question whether the three mile belt of sea surrounding Great Britain was British territory in

---

[14]   Ed. Diplomatic Privileges Act 1708.
[15]   Ed. (1737) Cases t. Talb. 281.
[16]   The case was argued twice. On the first occasion a court of six judges was equally divided.

English law, Cockburn C.J. ruled first that it was not such according to "the ancient law of England".[17] He then considered whether it had become such because of a rule of customary international law to that effect. After concluding that the opinions of writers on the width of sea over which jurisdiction could be exercised and on the nature of any such jurisdiction was conflicting, Lord Cockburn continued:

> ... even if entire unanimity had existed ... the question would still remain, how far the law as stated by the publicists had received the assent of the civilized nations of the world.... To be binding, the law must have received the assent of the nations who are to be bound by it. This assent may be express, as by treaty or the acknowledged concurrence of governments, or may be implied from established usage.... Nor, in my opinion, would the clearest proof of unanimous assent on the part of other nations be sufficient to authorise the tribunals of this country to apply, without an Act of Parliament, what would practically amount to a new law. In so doing we should be unjustifiably usurping the province of the legislature. The assent of nations is doubtless sufficient to give the power of parliamentary legislation in a matter otherwise within the sphere of international law; but it would be powerless to confer without such legislation a jurisdiction beyond and unknown to the law, such as that now insisted on, a jurisdiction over foreigners in foreign ships on a portion of the high seas.
>
> When I am told that all other nations have assented to such an absolute dominion on the part of the littoral state, over this portion of the sea, as that their ships may be excluded from it, and that, without any open legislation, or notice to them or their subjects, the latter may be held liable to the local law, I ask, first, what proof there is of such assent as here asserted; and, secondly, to what extent has such assent been carried? a question of infinite importance, when, undirected by legislation, we are called upon to apply the law on the strength of such assent....

Cockburn C.J. examined the evidence of treaties and of usage and concluded that in neither case was it clear.

> It may well be, I say again, that—after all that has been said and done in this respect—after the instances which have been mentioned of the adoption of the three-mile distance, and the repeated assertion of this doctrine by the writers on public law, a nation which should now deal with this portion of the sea as its own, so as to make foreigners within it subject to its law, for the prevention and punishment of offences, would not be considered as infringing the rights of other nations. But I apprehend that as the ability so to deal with these waters would result, not from any original or inherent right, but, from the acquiescence of other states, some outward manifestation of the national will, in the shape of open practice or municipal legislation, so as to amount, at least constructively, to an occupation of that which was before unappropriated, would be necessary to render the foreigner, not previously amenable to our general law, subject to its control. That such legislation, whether consistent with the general law of nations or not, would be binding on the tribunals of this country— leaving the question of its consistency with international law to be determined between the governments of the respective nations—can of course admit of no doubt. The question is whether such legislation would not, at all events, be necessary to justify our Courts in applying the law of this country to foreigners under entirely novel circumstances in which it has never been applied before.
>
> It is obviously one thing to say that the legislature of a nation may, from the common assent of other nations, have acquired the full right to legislate over a part of that which was before high sea, and as such common to all the world; another and very different thing to say that the law of the local state becomes thereby at once, without anything more, applicable to foreigners within such part, or that, independently of legislation, the Courts of the local state can *proprio vigore* so apply it. The one position does not follow from the other; and it is essential to keep the two things, the power of Parliament to legislate, and the authority of our Courts, without such legislation, to apply the criminal law where it could not have been applied before, altogether distinct, which, it is evident, is not always done. It is unnecessary to the defence, and equally so to the decision of the case, to determine whether Parliament has the right to treat the three-mile zone as part of the realm consistently with international law. That is a matter on which it is for Parliament itself to decide. It is enough for us that it has, so far as to be binding upon us, the power to do so. The question is whether, acting judicially, we can treat the power of Parliament to legislate as making up for the absence of actual legislation. I am clearly of opinion that

---

[17] 2 Ex.D. 174.

we cannot, and that it is only in the instances in which foreigners on the seas have been made specifically liable to our law by statutory enactment that the law can be applied to them.

Finally, on the question of the location of the offence, Cockburn C.J. ruled that although the defendant's action had had its effect on board the *Strathclyde*, the offence of manslaughter could not be said to have been committed there so as to give an English court jurisdiction over it. [18]

Pollock B. and Field J. concurred in the judgment of Cockburn C.J. Kelly C.B., Bramwell J.A., Lush J., and Sir Robert Phillimore gave concurring judgments. Lord Coleridge C.J., Brett and Amphlett JJ.A., Grove, Denman, and Lindley JJ., gave dissenting judgments.

Notes

1. *R. v Keyn* was reversed by the Territorial Waters Jurisdiction Act 1878, the preamble to which reads:

    "Whereas the rightful jurisdiction of Her Majesty, her heirs and successors, extends *and always has extended* over the open seas adjacent to the coasts of the United Kingdom and of all other parts of Her Majesty's dominions to such a distance as is necessary for the defence and security of such dominions...." [19]

2. Is Cockburn C.J.'s judgment, which is the leading one among those given by the judges in the majority, consistent with the "incorporation" approach to the reception of customary international law? Or does it support the "transformation" approach, according to which only such rules of international law are a part of the municipal law of a state as are actually adopted by a state's courts or legislature in their or its discretion? Did any rule of United Kingdom constitutional law influence Cockburn C.J. in his judgment?[20] Note the following comment on his judgment by Lauterpacht[21]:

    "... it cannot be said that this judgment amounts to a rejection of the rule that international law is a part of the law of England. Writers seem to forget that the main issue of the controversy in the case was not the question whether a rule of international law can be enforced without an Act of Parliament; what *was* in dispute was the existence and the extent of a rule of international law relating to jurisdiction in territorial waters."

3. Which view of the relationship between international and municipal law (monist, dualist) does the "transformation" approach support?

---

[18] See Beckett (1927) 8 B.Y.I.L. 108.
[19] Italics added.
[20] See Brownlie, p.43.
[21] *Private Law Sources and Analogies of International Law* (1927), p.76, footnote. See also *Pianka v The Queen* [1979] A.C. 107 PC.

R. v JONES (MARGARET)

[2006] UKHL 16; [2007] 1 A.C. 136, House of Lords

The appellants had been charged or convicted of criminal damage and other offences at US and UK air-force bases and a military port in the UK aimed at impeding the war in Iraq, which they regarded as constituting the international law crime of aggression. The main issue in this case was whether they could rely upon the defence under s.3 of the Criminal Law Act 1967 of using reasonable force "to prevent crime", leading to the question whether aggression, which Lord Bingham accepted was a crime under customary international law, was a "crime" for the purposes of s.3. The following extract considers in turn the appellants' key arguments (1, 3, 5) addressed to this question. The appeal was dismissed unanimously.

LORD BINGHAM OF CORNHILL

(1) Customary international law is (without the need for any domestic statute or judicial decision) part of the domestic law of England and Wales.

11. The appellants contended that the law of nations in its full extent is part of the law of England and Wales. The Crown did not challenge the general truth of this proposition, for which there is indeed old and high authority: see, for example, *Triquet v Bath* ... I would for my part hesitate, at any rate without much fuller argument, to accept this proposition in quite the unqualified terms in which it has often been stated. There seems to be truth in Brierly's contention ("International Law of England" (1935) 51 LQR 24, 31), also espoused by the appellants, that international law is not a part, but is one of the sources, of English law. There was, however, no issue between the parties on this matter, and I am content to accept the general truth of the proposition for present purposes since the only relevant qualification is the subject of consideration below. ...

(3) Crimes recognised in customary international law are (without the need for any domestic statute or judicial decision) recognised and enforced by the domestic law of England and Wales.

20. In supporting this proposition the appellants were able to rely on the great authority of Blackstone who (in Book IV, chap 5, p 68, of his *Commentaries*) listed the "principal offences against the law of nations, animadverted on as such by the municipal laws of England" as violation of safe conducts, infringement of the rights of ambassadors and piracy. ...

22. While the appellants acknowledged the paucity of authority on the assimilation of customary international law crimes into municipal law, other than those listed by Blackstone, they contended that war crimes earned inclusion in any modern list. ...It would seem to me at least arguable that war crimes, recognised as such in customary international law, would now be triable and punishable under the domestic criminal law of this country irrespective of any domestic statute. But it is not necessary to decide that question, since war crimes are something quite distinct from the crime of aggression.

23. I would accordingly accept that a crime recognised in customary international law may be assimilated into the domestic criminal law of this country. The appellants, however, go further and contend that that result follow automatically. The authorities, as I read them, do not support that proposition. Lord Cockburn CJ rejected it in *R v Keyn* [above at p.66] ...In *R v Bow Street Metropolitan Stipendiary Magistrate, Ex p Pinochet Ugarte (No 3)* [2000] 1 AC 147 the issue was whether British courts had jurisdiction, before section 134 of the Criminal Justice Act 1988 [which made torture a criminal offence] came into force, to try those accused of torture abroad. But I agree with the observation of Buxton LJ in *Hutchinson v Newbury Magistrates' Court* (2000) 122 ILR 499, 506, which a contention similar to the appellants' was advanced:

"It is also in my view impossible to reconcile that contention with the debate in *Pinochet (No 3)* which concluded, illuminatingly subject to the specific dissent on this point of Lord Millett, that although State torture had long been an international crime in the highest sense (to adopt the formulation of Lord Browne-Wilkinson [2000] 1 AC page 198F) and therefore a crime universally in whatsoever territory it occurred, it was only with the passing of Section 134 of the Criminal Justice Act 1988 that the English criminal courts acquired jurisdiction over 'international', that is to say extra territorial, torture."

In the context of genocide, an argument based on automatic assimilation was rejected by a majority of the

Federal Court of Australia in *Nulyarimma v Thompson* (1999) 120 ILR 353. In the context of abduction it was rejected by the Supreme Court of the United States in *Sosa v Alverez-Machain et al* 542 US 692 (2004). It is, I think, true that "customary international law is applicable in the English courts only where the constitution permits": O'Keefe, "Customary International Crimes in English Courts" (2001) BYIL 293, 335. I respectfully agree with the observations of Sir Franklin Berman (*Asserting Jurisdiction: International and European Legal Perspectives,* ed M Evans and S Konstantinidis, 2003, p 11) answering the question whether customary international law is capable of creating a crime directly triable in a national court:

"The first question is open to a myriad of answers, depending on the characteristic features of the particular national legal system in view. Looking at it simply from the point of view of English law, the answer would seem to be no; international law could not create a crime triable directly, without the intervention of Parliament, in an English court. What international law could, however, do is to perform its well-understood validating function, by establishing the legal basis (legal justification) for Parliament to legislate, so far as it purports to exercise control over the conduct of non-nationals abroad. This answer is inevitably tied up with the attitude taken towards the possibility of the creation of new offences under common law. Inasmuch as the reception of customary international law into English law takes place under common law, and inasmuch as the development of new customary international law remains very much the consequence of international behaviour by the Executive, in which neither the Legislature nor the Courts, nor any other branch of the constitution, need have played any part, it would be odd if the Executive could, by means of that kind, acting in concert with other States, amend or modify specifically the *criminal* law, with all the consequences that flow for the liberty of the individual and rights of personal property. There are, besides, powerful reasons of political accountability, regularity and legal certainty for saying that the power to create crimes should now be regarded as reserved exclusively to Parliament, by Statute." ...

(5) ... "crime" in section 3 means a crime in the domestic law of England and Wales, and the crime of aggression is such.

27. I approach this proposition assuming the correctness of the conclusion already reached, that "crime" in section 3 means a crime in the domestic law of England and Wales and that a crime recognised as such in customary international law (such as the crime of aggression) may, but need not, become part of the domestic law of England and Wales without the need for any domestic statute or judicial decision.

28. The lack of any statutory incorporation is not, however, a neutral factor, for two main reasons. The first is that there now exists no power in the courts to create new criminal offences, as decided by a unanimous House in *Knuller (Publishing, Printing and Promotions) Ltd v Director of Public Prosecutions* [1973] AC 435. While old common law offences survive until abolished or superseded by statute, new ones are not created. Statute is now the sole source of new criminal offences. The second reason is that when it is sought to give domestic effect to crimes established in customary international law, the practice is to legislate. Examples may be found in the Geneva Conventions Act 1957 and the Geneva Conventions (Amendment) Act 1995, dealing with breaches of the Geneva Conventions of 1949 and the Additional Protocols of 1977; the Genocide Act 1969, giving effect to the Genocide Convention of 1948; and the Criminal Justice Act 1988, s 134, giving effect to the Torture Convention of 1984; the War Crime Act 1991, giving jurisdiction to try war crimes committed abroad by foreign nationals; the Merchant Shipping and Maritime Security Act 1997, s 26, giving effect to provisions of the United Nations Convention on the Law of the Sea 1982 relating to piracy; and sections 51 and 52 of the International Criminal Court Act 2001, giving effect to the Rome Statute by providing for the trial here of persons accused of genocide, crimes against humanity and war crimes, but not, significantly, the crime of aggression. It would be anomalous if the crime of aggression, excluded (obviously deliberately) from the 2001 Act, were to be treated as a domestic crime, since it would not be subject to the constraints (as to the need for the Attorney General's consent, the mode of trial, the requisite *mens rea,* the liability of secondary parties and maximum penalties) applicable to the crimes which were included.

29. These reasons, taken together, are very strong grounds for rejecting the appellants' contention, since they reflect what has become an important democratic principle in this country: that it is for those representing the people of the country in Parliament, not the executive and not the judges, to decide what conduct should be treated as lying so far outside the bounds of what is acceptable in our society as to attract criminal penalties. One would need very compelling reasons for departing from that principle.

30. In the present case, involving the crime of aggression, there are compelling reasons for not departing. A charge of aggression, if laid against an individual in a domestic court, would involve determination of his responsibility as a leader but would presuppose commission of the crime by his own state or a foreign state. Thus

resolution of the charge would (unless the issue had been decided by the Security Council or some other third party) call for a decision on the culpability in going to war either of Her Majesty's Government or a foreign government, or perhaps both if the states had gone to war as allies. But there are well-established rules that the courts will be very slow to review the exercise of prerogative powers in relation to the conduct of foreign affairs and the deployment of the armed services, and very slow to adjudicate upon rights arising out of transactions entered into between sovereign states on the plane of international law. ...

Lord Bingham also noted that a person acting lawfully to obstruct the war might be committing treason; and that there might be problems with the disclosure of evidence.

I am of the clear opinion that the crime of agression is not a crime in the domestic law of England and Wales within the meaning of section 3.

LORD HOFFMAN delivered a concurring speech. LORDS RODGER, CARSWELL AND MANSE concurred.

Note

This case confirms that general statements to the effect that "the common law incorporates the rule of customary international law"[22] do not mean that a crime that is recognised by customary international law is thereby automatically incorporated into United Kingdom law so as to provide a basis for prosecution in its municipal courts or otherwise amount to a "crime" in that law; constitutional considerations by which only Parliament may create a criminal offence come into play.

WEST RAND CENTRAL GOLD MINING CO. v R.

[1905] 2 K.B. 391. King's Bench Division

The South African Republic seized gold, the property of the suppliant, a British company, in a manner allegedly contrary to the law of the Republic. When Great Britain annexed the Republic in 1900, a petition of right was brought against the Crown to recover the gold or compensation for its loss. Upon the Crown's demur, the Court rejected the suppliant's contention that a conquering state was liable in international law for the financial obligations of its predecessor. It was therefore not required to rule upon the argument that the alleged rule was a part of English law. Nonetheless, Lord Alverstone, delivering the opinion of the Court, made the following comments.

LORD ALVERSTONE C.J.

It is quite true that whatever has received the common consent of civilised nations must have received the assent of our country, and that to which we have assented along with other nations in general may properly be called international law, and as such will be acknowledged and applied by our municipal tribunals when legitimate occasion arises for those tribunals to decide questions to which doctrines of international law may be relevant. But any doctrine so invoked must be one really accepted as binding between nations, and the international law sought to be applied must, like anything else, be proved by satisfactory evidence, which must shew either that the particular proposition put forward has been recognised and acted upon by our own country, or that it is of such a nature, and has been so widely and generally accepted, that it can hardly be supposed that any civilised

---

[22] Per Lord Lloyd in *R. v Bow Street Magistrates Ex p. Pinochet (No.1)* [2001] 1 A.C. 61 at 90. Cf. Lord Slynn at 77; and Lord Millett in *R. v Bow Street Magistrates Ex p. Pinochet (No.3)* [2001] 1 A.C. 147 at 276.

State would repudiate it. . . . *Barbuit's Case*,[23] *Triquet v. Bath*,[24] and *Heathfield v. Chilton*[25] are cases in which the Courts of law have recognised and have given effect to the privilege of ambassadors as established by international law. But the expressions used by Lord Mansfield when dealing with the particular and recognised rule of international law on this subject, that the law of nations forms part of the law of England, ought not to be construed so as to include as part of the law of England opinions of text-writers upon a question as to which there is no evidence that Great Britain has ever assented, and a fortiori if they are contrary to the principles of her laws as declared by her Courts. The cases of *Wolff v. Oxholm*[26] and *Rex v. Keyn*[27] are only illustrations of the same rule—namely, that questions of international law may arise, and may have to be considered in connection with the administration of municipal law.

Notes

1. What explanation of *R. v Keyn* does this case support?[28] If a "proposition put forward has been recognised and acted upon by our own country," is this sufficient to establish it as a rule of customary international law for the purpose of its application by an English court? Would it be sufficient to establish it as such for the purpose of its application by an international court or tribunal?

2. Would Lord Alverstone permit the incorporation of a customary rule that was contrary to existing common law? In *Chung Chi Cheung v The King*,[29] Lord Atkin, delivering the opinion of the Privy Council, stated:

    > "It must always be remembered that, so far, at any rate, as the Courts of this Country are concerned, international law has no validity save in so far as its principles are accepted and adopted by our own domestic law. There is no external power that imposes its rule upon our own code of substantive law or procedure.
    >
    >   The Courts acknowledge the existence of a body of rules which nations accept amongst themselves. On any judicial issue they seek to ascertain what the relevant rule is, and having found it, they will treat it as incorporated into the domestic law, so far as it is not inconsistent with rules enacted by statutes *or finally declared by* their tribunals."

    Lord Atkin then considered and applied the international law rules on state immunity in respect of public ships.

    Lord Denning quoted the first sentence of the above passage from Lord Atkin's speech when following the "transformation" approach in *Thakrar v Secretary of State for the Home Office*.[30] Lord Denning changed his mind in *Trendtex Trading Corp. v Central Bank of Nigeria*[31] where he adopted the "incorporation" approach. The problem in the *Trendtex* case was whether the doctrine of precedent in English law applies to common law rules that incorporate rules of customary international law so that a change in international law can only be recognised by the English courts as a part of common law within the limits of that doctrine.[32] The majority in that

---

[23] Ed., i.e. *Buvot v. Barbuit*, above, p.66.
[24] Ed. Above, p.65.
[25] 4 Burr. 2016.
[26] (1817) 6 M. & S. 92.
[27] Ed. Above, p.66.
[28] See Westlake, (1906) 22 L.Q.R. 14.
[29] [1939] A.C. 160 at 167–168. Italics added.
[30] [1974] Q.B. 684 CA.
[31] [1977] Q.B. 529 CA. For the facts, see the extract below, p.273. cf. Nourse L.J. in *Maclaine Watson v Dept of Trade* [1989] Ch. 72 at 207, CA.
[32] See Morgenstern, above, p.65, n.12, pp.80–82.

case—Lord Denning M.R. and Shaw L.J.—thought that there was an exception to the doctrine of precedent so that, for example, the Court of Appeal could apply a new rule of international law even though there were Court of Appeal decisions to the contrary based upon the rule's predecessor. Stephenson L.J., dissenting, considered that the Court of Appeal's earlier decisions were binding upon it in the usual way. In *Thai-Europe Tapioca Service Ltd v Govt of Pakistan*[33] two other members of the Court of Appeal—Lawton and Scarman L.JJ.—had earlier taken the view later taken by Stephenson L.J. in the *Trendtex* case. Scarman L.J. stated:

"I think that it is important to realise that a rule of international law, once incorporated into our law by decisions of a competent court, is not an inference of fact but a rule of law. It therefore becomes part of our municipal law and the doctrine of *stare decisis* applies as much as to that as to a rule of law with a strictly municipal provenance."[34]

In the *Trendtex*[35] case, Shaw L.J. disagreed:

"It is with diffidence that I venture to suggest that there may be a flaw in the reasoning which led to [the *Thai-Europe* Court of Appeal's] conclusion as to the application of the principle of *stare decisis*. . . . May it not be that the true principle as to the application of international law is that the English courts must at any given time discover what the prevailing international rule is and apply that rule? . . .

What *is* immutable is the principle of English law that the law of nations (not what *was* the law of nations) must be applied in the courts of England. The rule of stare decisis operates to preclude a court from overriding a decision which binds it in regard to a particular rule of (international) law, it does not prevent a court from applying a rule which did not exist when the earlier decision was made if the new rule has had the effect in international law of extinguishing the old rule. . . .

Lawton L.J. [in the *Thai-Europe* case] expressed concern as to the possible prejudice which might result to those engaged in international trade if changes in international law brought about *ipso facto* corresponding changes in the law of England. But even the law of England changes quite apart from what may be happening to international law. Moreover, changes in rules of international law do not come about abruptly; and changes will not be recognised in an English court without convincing support. Those engaged in world commerce will not be insensible to the incidence of such changes over the years. Lastly there must be a greater risk of confusion if precepts discarded outside England by a majority (or perhaps all) of civilised states are preserved as effective in the English courts in a sort of judicial aspic."

3. *Prize courts.* These constitute a special case. In accordance with international law, prize claims arising out of the capture of ships in war are heard before prize courts. These are courts set up by maritime states, such as the United Kingdom. Although municipal courts, they administer the (customary and treaty) international law of prize. In *The Zamora*,[36] the Judicial Committee of the Privy Council held that a British prize court had to apply that law even though it conflicted with an order in council. Such a court would, however, be bound by a British statute.[37]

---

33 [1975] 1 W.L.R. 1485.
34 [1975] 1 W.L.R. 1485 at 1495.
35 [1977] Q.B. 578. cf. Lord Slynn in *R v Bow Street Magistrates Exp. Pinochet (No.1)* [2001] 1 A.C. 61 at 77 HL.
36 [1916] 2 A.C. 77.
37 [1916] 2 A.C. 77 at 93.

MORTENSEN v PETERS

(1906) 8 F. (J.) 93. Court of Justiciary. Scotland

The Fishery Board for Scotland issued a byelaw under the Herring Fishery (Scotland) Act 1889 making it an offence ("no person . . . shall") to fish by beam or otter trawling in the Moray Firth, part of which is more than three miles from the nearest point of land.[38] By the Sea Fisheries Regulation (Scotland) Act 1895, s.10(4), "any person" who fished by beam or otter trawling in contravention of that byelaw was subject to a fine or imprisonment. The appellant was a Dane and the master of a Norwegian ship. He was convicted in a Scottish court of the above offence for otter trawling at a place covered by the byelaw but beyond the three mile limit. His appeal against conviction was dismissed unanimously by a full bench of 12 judges.

LORD JUSTICE-GENERAL (LORD DUNEDIN)

It is not disputed that if the appellant had been a British subject in a British ship he would have been rightly convicted. . . .

I apprehend that the question is one of construction, and of construction only. In this Court we have nothing to do with the question of whether the Legislature has or has not done what foreign powers may consider a usurpation in a question with them. Neither are we a tribunal sitting to decide whether an Act of the Legislature is ultra vires as in contravention of generally acknowledged principles of international law. For us an Act of Parliament duly passed by Lords and Commons and assented to by the King, is supreme, and we are bound to give effect to its terms. The counsel for the appellant advanced the proposition that statutes creating offences must be presumed to apply only (1) to British subjects; and (2) to foreign subjects in British territory; and that short of express enactment their application should not be further extended. The appellant is admittedly not a British subject, which excludes (1); and he further argued that the *locus delicti*, being in the sea beyond the three-mile limit, was not within British territory; and that consequently the appellant was not included in the prohibition of the statute. Viewed as general propositions the two presumptions put forward by the appellant may be taken as correct. This, however, advances the matter but little, for like all presumptions they may be redargued [i.e. rebutted], and the question remains whether they have been redargued on this occasion.

The first thing to be noted is that the prohibition here, a breach of which constitutes the offence, is not an absolute prohibition against doing a certain thing, but against doing it in a certain place. Now, when the Legislature, using words of admitted generality—"It shall not be lawful," *etc.*, "Every person who," *etc.*—conditions an offence by territorial limits, it creates, I think, a very strong inference that it is, for the purposes specified, assuming a right to legislate for that territory against all persons whomsoever. This inference seems to me still further strengthened when it is obvious that the remedy to the mischief sought to be obtained by the prohibition would be either defeated or rendered less effective if all persons whosoever were not affected by the enactment.
. . .

It is said by the appellant that all this must give way to the consideration that International Law has firmly fixed that a *locus* such as this is beyond the limits of territorial sovereignty, and that consequently it is not to be thought that in such a place the Legislature could seek to affect any but the King's subjects.

It is a trite observation that there is no such thing as a standard of international law extraneous to the domestic law of a kingdom, to which appeal may be made. International law, so far as this Court is concerned, is the body of doctrine regarding the international rights and duties of states which has been adopted and made part of the law of Scotland. Now, can it be said to be clear by the law of Scotland that the *locus* here is beyond what the legislature may assert right to affect by legislation against all whomsoever for the purpose of regulating methods of fishing?

I do not think I need say anything about what is known as the three-mile limit. It may be assumed that within the three miles the territorial sovereignty would be sufficient to cover any such legislation as the present. It is enough to say that that is not a proof of the counter proposition that outside the three miles no such result could be looked for. The *locus* although outside the three-mile limit, is within the bay known as the Moray Firth, and the

---

[38] The Firth as defined by statute was a little over 70 miles wide at its mouth.

Moray Firth, says the respondent, is *intra fauces terrae*. Now, I cannot say that there is any definition of what *fauces terrae* exactly are. But there are at least three points which go far to shew that this spot might be considered as lying therein.

1. The dicta of the Scottish institutional writers seem to shew that it would be no usurpation, according to the law of Scotland, so to consider it. . . .

2. The same statute[39] puts forward claims to what are at least analogous places. If attention is paid to the schedule appended to section 6, many places will be found far beyond the three-mile limit—e.g. the Firth of Clyde near its mouth. I am not ignoring that it may be said that this in one sense is proving *idem per idem*, but none the less I do not think the fact can be ignored.

3. There are many instances to be found in decided cases where the right of a nation to legislate for waters more or less landlocked or landembraced, although beyond the three-mile limit, has been admitted. . . .

It seems to me therefore, without laying down the proposition that the Moray Firth is for every purpose within the territorial sovereignty, it can at least be clearly said that the appellant cannot make out his proposition that it is inconceivable that the British Legislature should attempt for fishery regulation to legislate against all and sundry in such a place. And if that is so, then I revert to the considerations already stated which as a matter of construction made me think that it did so legislate. . . .

LORD KYLLACHY

. . . This Court is of course not entitled to canvass the power of the Legislature to make the enactment. The only question open is as to its just construction. . . .

Now dealing, first, with the point of construction—the question as to what the statutory enactment means—it may probably be conceded that there is always a certain presumption against the Legislature of a country asserting or assuming the existence of a territorial jurisdiction going clearly beyond limits established by the common consent of nations—that is to say, by international law. . . . But then it is only a presumption, and as such it must always give way to the language used if it is clear, and also to all counter presumptions which may legitimately be had in view in determining, on ordinary principles, the true meaning and intent of the legislation. Express words will of course be conclusive, and so also will plain implication.

The concurring judgments of Lord Johnston and Lord Salvesen are omitted.

Notes

1. Whereas the earlier cases in this section have concerned custom and common law, *Mortensen v Peters* concerned custom and statutes. In reality the trawler of which the appellant was captain was British financed, controlled and crewed.[40] It had been given a foreign master and registration in the hope of circumventing the Fishery Board's regulations. Shortly after *Mortensen v Peters*, a number of other successful prosecutions of Norwegian masters of foreign ships occurred. In some cases the convicted men went to prison rather than pay a fine. They were released, however, after protests by Norway. In March, 1907, a Foreign Office spokesman stated in the House of Commons: "The Act of Parliament as interpreted by the High Court of Justiciary is in conflict with international law."[41] In 1909, Parliament tried another approach. It enacted the Trawling in Prohibited Areas Prevention Act which prohibited the landing in the United Kingdom of fish caught contrary to the legislation applied in *Mortensen v Peters*.

2. Is it possible that Lord Dunedin might have decided the case differently if there had been no argument at all for saying that the Moray Firth was *intra fauces terrae*? If so, why? Because the statute would then have conflicted with the customary international law on freedom of fishing on the high seas, or because of a presumption that Parliament will not legislate contrary to international law?

---

[39] Ed. Herring Fishery (Scotland) Act 1889.
[40] See Fulton, *The Sovereignty of the Sea* (1911), p.722.
[41] *Hansard*, HC, Vol.170, col.472 (March 4, 1907).

3.   A statute may sometimes incorporate a rule of customary international law by reference. For example, s.7 of the Territorial Waters Jurisdiction Act 1878 defines the "territorial waters of Her Majesty's Dominions" as "such part of the sea . . . as is deemed by international law to be within the territorial sovereignty of Her Majesty."[42]

----

ii. Treaties[43]

THE PARLEMENT BELGE

(1878–79) 4 P.D. 129. Probate, Divorce and Admiralty Division

SIR ROBERT PHILLIMORE

In the month of February, 1878, the owners of the steam-tug *Daring* served a writ on board the steamship *Parlement Belge* against the owners of that vessel and her freight, in which they claimed the sum of £3500 for damage, arising out of a collision which occurred between that vessel and the steam-tug *Daring* on the 14th of February 1878, off Dover.

. . . it is in substance contended that this steamship *Parlement Belge* is not amenable to the process of this Court, first, on the ground that she is the property of the King of the Belgians, and at the time of collision was controlled and employed by him. Secondly, that her Majesty the Queen, by a convention with the King of the Belgians,[44] has placed this packet-boat in the category of a public ship of war. . . .

. . . the plaintiffs in this suit have a statutable right of action against the *Parlement Belge*, unless that vessel be of that privileged class which is not amenable to a court of law. . . .

The *Parlement Belge* is a packet conveying certain mails and carrying a considerable commerce, officered, as I have said, by Belgian officers and flying the Belgian pennon.

Upon the whole, I am of opinion that neither upon principle, precedent, nor analogy of general international law, should I be warranted in considering the *Parlement Belge* as belonging to that category of public vessels which are exempt from process of law and all private claims.

I now approach the consideration of the second question. . . .

It is admitted that this convention has not been confirmed by any statute; but it has been contended on the part of the Crown both that it was competent to her Majesty to make this convention, and also to put its provisions into operation without the confirmation of them by parliament. The plaintiffs admit the former, but deny the latter of these propositions.

The power of the Crown to make treaties with foreign states is indisputable. . . .

Blackstone is quoted on the prerogative power to make treaties

Blackstone must have known very well that there were a class of treaties the provisions of which were inoperative without the confirmation of the legislature; while there were others which operated without such confirmation. The strongest instance of the latter, perhaps, which could be cited is the Declaration of Paris in 1856, by which the Crown in the exercise of its prerogative deprived this country of belligerent rights, which very high authorities in the state and in the law had considered to be of vital importance to it. But this declaration did not affect the private rights of the subject; and the question before me is whether this treaty does affect private rights, and therefore required the sanction of the legislature.

The authority of Chancellor Kent was relied on. That learned writer observes:

Treaties of peace, when made by the competent power, are obligatory upon the whole nation. If the treaty requires the payment of money to carry it into effect, and the money cannot be raised but by an Act of the

---

[42] See also *Post Office v Estuary Radio Ltd* [1968] 2 Q.B. 740 CA.
[43] See Mann (1958–59) 44 Trans. Grot. Soc. 29.
[44] Ed. A Postal Convention of 1876.

legislature, the treaty is morally obligatory upon the legislature to pass the law, and to refuse it would be a breach of public faith. Kent's Comm. Vol.i. p.166 (ed. 1873).

And he further observes:

There can be no doubt that the power competent to bind the nation by treaty may alienate the public domain and property by treaty . . .

If the Crown had power without the authority of parliament by this treaty to order that the *Parlement Belge* should be entitled to all the privileges of a ship of war, then the warrant, which is prayed for against her as a wrong-doer on account of the collision, cannot issue, and the right of the subject, but for this order unquestionable, to recover damages for the injuries done to him by her is extinguished.

This is a use of the treaty-making prerogative of the Crown which I believe to be without precedent, and in principle contrary to the laws of the constitution. Let me consider to what consequences it leads. If the Crown without the authority of parliament, may by process of diplomacy shelter a foreigner from the action of one of her Majesty's subjects who has suffered injury at his hands, I do not see why it might not also give a like privilege of immunity to a number of foreign merchant vessels or to a number of foreign individuals. The law of this country has indeed incorporated those portions of international law which give immunity and privileges to foreign ships of war and foreign ambassadors; but I do not think that it has therefore given the Crown authority to clothe with this immunity foreign vessels, which are really not vessels of war, or foreign persons, who are not really ambassadors.

Let me say one word more in conclusion. Mr. Bowen, in his very able speech, dwelt forcibly upon the wrong which would be done to this packet if, being invited to enter ports of this country with the privileges of a ship of war, she should find them denied to her. I acknowledge the hardship, but the remedy, in my opinion, is not to be found in depriving the British subject without his consent, direct or implied, of his right of action against a wrong-doer, but by the agency of diplomacy, and proper measures of compensation and arrangement, between the Governments of Great Britain and Belgium. I must allow the warrant of arrest to issue.

Notes

1. The decision was reversed by the Court of Appeal[45] on the ground that, contrary to the ruling of Sir Robert Phillimore, the immunity sought was available at customary international law and hence at common law. The ruling at first instance to the effect that a treaty cannot adversely affect private law rights unless it has been made a part of United Kingdom law by Parliament is still good law. On the question whether individuals may rely in the United Kingdom courts upon provisions in treaties concluded by the United Kingdom as the basis for a claim, see *Rustomjee v R.*, below, p.464. The position was explained by Lord Oliver in *Maclaine Watson v Dept. of Trade*[46] as follows:

    "... as a matter of the constitutional law of the United Kingdom, the royal prerogative, whilst it embraces the making of treaties, does not extend to altering the law or conferring rights on individuals or depriving individuals of rights which they enjoy in domestic law without the intervention of Parliament. Treaties, as it is sometimes expressed, are not self-executing. Quite simply, a treaty is not part of English law unless and until it has been incorporated into the law by legislation. So far as individuals are concerned, it is res inter alios acta from which they cannot derive rights and by which they cannot be deprived of rights or subjected to obligations; and it is outside the purview of the Court not only because it is made in the conduct of foreign relations, which are a prerogative of the Crown, but also because, as a source of rights and obligations, it is irrelevant."

---

[45] (1880) 5 P.D. 197.
[46] [1990] 2 A.C. 418 at 500 HL.

2. In *Porter v Freudenberg*,[47] the Court of Appeal had to consider whether "the old rule (not peculiar to English law, though it has been more prominent in England than elsewhere) that an alien enemy's rights of action are suspended during the war"[48] had been abrogated by the 1907 Hague Convention on Land Warfare. The Court ruled, *as a matter of construction of the Convention*, that it had not done so. It is possible to read the judgment as meaning that the Convention *could* have had this effect without statutory implementation as an exercise of the prerogative power if it had been appropriately worded.

ATT.-GEN. FOR CANADA v ATT.-GEN. FOR ONTARIO

[1937] A.C. 326. Judicial Committee of the Privy Council

The Dominion Parliament of Canada legislated to implement certain international labour conventions. On appeal from the Supreme Court of Canada, the Judicial Committee advised that the legislation was ultra vires the Dominion Parliament; that legislative competence on the subject concerned vested in the legislatures of the Provinces. The following statement of principle was made by Lord Atkin in the course of delivering the Committee's opinion.

LORD ATKIN

It will be essential to keep in mind the distinction between (1.) the formation, and (2.) the performance, of the obligations constituted by a treaty, using that word as comprising any agreement between two or more sovereign States. Within the British Empire there is a well-established rule that the making of a treaty is an executive act, while the performance of its obligations, if they entail alteration of the existing domestic law, requires legislative action. Unlike some other countries, the stipulations of a treaty duly ratified do not within the Empire, by virtue of the treaty alone, have the force of law. If the national executive, the government of the day, decide to incur the obligations of a treaty which involve alteration of law they have to run the risk of obtaining the assent of Parliament to the necessary statute or statutes. To make themselves as secure as possible they will often in such cases before final ratification seek to obtain from Parliament an expression of approval. But it has never been suggested, and it is not the law, that such an expression of approval operates as law, or that in law it precludes the assenting Parliament, or any subsequent Parliament, from refusing to give its sanction to any legislative proposals that may subsequently be brought before it. Parliament, no doubt, as the Chief Justice points out, has a constitutional control over the executive: but it cannot be disputed that the creation of the obligations undertaken in treaties and the assent to their form and quality are the function of the executive alone. Once they are created, while they bind the State as against the other contracting parties, Parliament may refuse to perform them and so leave the State in default.

Note

On the treaty-making power within the United Kingdom, see below, p.644.

---

47   [1915] 1 K.B. 857. See McNair (1928) 9 B.Y.I.L. 59.
48   [1915] 1 K.B. 857 at 877.

R. v SECRETARY OF STATE FOR THE HOME DEPARTMENT, EX P. BRIND

[1991] 1 A.C. 696. House of Lords

By s.29(3) of the Broadcasting Act 1981, the Home Secretary could "at any time, by notice in writing require the [Independent Broadcasting Authority (IBA)] ... to refrain from broadcasting any matter or classes of matter specified in the notice." An almost identically worded power was included in cl.13(4) of the 1981 Licence and Agreement between the Home Secretary and the BBC. Acting under these powers, in 1988 the Home Secretary issued directives to the IBA and the BBC requiring them to refrain from broadcasting on television or radio "words spoken" by any person representing or purporting to represent certain organisations. These organisations were organisations proscribed under the Prevention of Terrorism (Temporary Provisions) Act 1984 or the Northern Ireland (Emergency Provisions) Act 1978, and also Sinn Fein, Republican Sinn Fein and the Ulster Defence Association. The prohibition applied only to the direct speech of such persons. It was permissible to report what they said or to have actors broadcasting their words.

In this case, the applicants, who were journalists and a National Union of Journalists employee, sought judicial review by way of (i) a declaration to the effect that the Home Secretary's directives were ultra vires and (ii) certiorari, to quash them. Having failed before the Divisional Court and a unanimous Court of Appeal, the applicants appealed to the House of Lords where they relied mainly on the argument that the Home Secretary's discretionary powers under the 1981 Act and the BBC Licence, were exercisable subject to art.10 of the European Convention on Human Rights (ECHR). The appeal was dismissed unanimously.

LORD BRIDGE

It is accepted, of course, by the appellants that, like any other treaty obligations which have not been embodied in the law by statute, the Convention is not part of the domestic law, that the courts accordingly have no power to enforce Convention rights directly and that, if domestic legislation conflicts with the Convention, the courts must nevertheless enforce it. But it is already well settled that, in construing any provision in domestic legislation which is ambiguous in the sense that it is capable of a meaning which either conforms to or conflicts with the Convention, the courts will presume that Parliament intended to legislate in conformity with the Convention, not in conflict with it. Hence, it is submitted, when a statute confers upon an administrative authority a discretion capable of being exercised in a way which infringes any basic human right protected by the Convention, it may similarly be presumed that the legislative intention was that the discretion should be exercised within the limitations which the Convention imposes. I confess that I found considerable persuasive force in this submission. But in the end I have been convinced that the logic of it is flawed. When confronted with a simple choice between two possible interpretations of some specific statutory provision, the presumption whereby the courts prefer that which avoids conflict between our domestic legislation and our international treaty obligations is a mere canon of construction which involves no importation of international law into the domestic field. But where Parliament has conferred on the executive an administrative discretion without indicating the precise limits within which it must be exercised, to presume that it must be exercised within Convention limits would be to go far beyond the resolution of an ambiguity. It would be to impute to Parliament an intention not only that the executive should exercise the discretion in conformity with the Convention, but also that the domestic courts should enforce that conformity by the importation into domestic administrative law of the text of the Convention and the jurisprudence of the European Court of Human Rights in the interpretation and application of it. If such a presumption is to apply to the statutory discretion exercised by the Secretary of State under section 29(3) of the Act of 1981 in the instant case, it must also apply to any other statutory discretion exercised by the executive which is capable of involving an infringement of Convention rights. When Parliament has been content for so long to leave those who complain that their Convention rights have been infringed to seek their remedy in Strasbourg, it would be surprising suddenly to find that the judiciary had, without Parliament's aid, the means to incorporate the Convention into such an important area of domestic law and I cannot escape the conclusion that this would be a judicial usurpation of the legislative function ...

Lords Ackner, Templeman, Roskill and Lowry delivered concurring speeches.

Notes

1. As stated in the *Brind* case, it is well established in United Kingdom law that a treaty to which the United Kingdom is a party should be referred to and followed in the interpretation of an ambiguous statute, but that, applying a dualist approach, it cannot prevail over a clearly worded statute that contradicts it.

    What the *Brind* case is mainly authority for is that a discretionary executive power, whether under a statute or the prerogative and whether exercisable by a lowly immigration officer or a Secretary of State, is not to be interpreted as limited by United Kingdom treaty obligations, particularly those under the ECHR in the pre-Human Rights Act 1998 period.

2. Before the Human Rights Act, the ECHR gave rise to a number of cases in which the relationship between unincorporated treaties and United Kingdom law was discussed.[49] Although the statements made in these cases are often couched in terms only of the ECHR, there is no logical reason why they should not apply to other unincorporated treaties too and still remain valid for such treaties. It may be, however, that the Convention's key role in the debate about the adoption of a "bill of rights" in the United Kingdom coloured some judicial pronouncements.

3. As to the current status of the ECHR in United Kingdom law, it is not directly incorporated by the Human Rights Act 1998: inconsistent legislation (whether earlier or later than the Act) remains valid. Instead, the rights in the ECHR are indirectly incorporated into United Kingdom law as "Convention rights". The United Kingdom courts are required by the Act to interpret primary legislation compatibly with Convention rights so far as this is possible, taking into account the interpretation that has been given to them at Strasbourg. If, despite all efforts, this is not possible, the courts may make a "declaration of incompatibility". Such a declaration does not render the legislation invalid, but the Government is empowered to remove the incompatibility using a special fast track legislative procedure to do so. In addition, public authorities must not act inconsistently with Convention rights, unless UK legislation leaves them with no choice but to do so.[50]

4. A statute may be intended to incorporate a treaty into United Kingdom law or it may co-incidentally apply in an area to which a treaty applies also. In the former case, it is clear that the statute should be interpreted consistently with the treaty (see the *Salomon* case, below, p.81). The *Brind* case suggests that, in accordance with the presumption that Parliament intends to comply with international law, the same rule applies in a case of co-incidence also—at least where the treaty obligation pre-dates the statute. The same conclusion follows from *Waddington v Miah*,[51] where Lord Reid, speaking for the whole House of Lords, said (when considering whether an offence created under the Immigration Act 1971 was intended to operate retro-spectively) that in view of the Universal Declaration of Human Rights (art.11)[52] and the ECHR (art.7) "it is hardly credible that any government department would promote or that Parliament would pass retrospective criminal legislation."

5. A related question is whether the courts should take into account a treaty to which the United Kingdom is a party when applying the common law. Various dicta concerning the ECHR are

---

49 See Cunningham (1994) 43 I.C.L.Q. 537. On the relationship between EC law and that of Member States, see Lasok, *Law and Institutions of the European Communities* (7th edn 2001), Chs 13–15.

50 See further, Bailey, Harris and Jones, *Civil Liberties: Cases and Materials* (6th edn 2009, by Bailey and Taylor), Ch.1.

51 [1974] 1 W.L.R. 683 at 694.

52 Below, p.549.

clearly to this effect. For example, Scarman L.J. argued in *Ahmad v Inner London Education Authority*[53] for the use of the ECHR in applying "common law principles" and in *Att.-Gen. v BBC*,[54] as Lord Scarman, he stated that "if the issue should ultimately be . . . a question of legal policy," regard must be had to the same Convention. Similarly, in *Cassell v Broome*,[55] Lord Kilbrandon stated:

"... Since all commercial publication is undertaken for profit, one must be watchful against holding the profit motive to be sufficient to justify punitive damages: to do so would be seriously to hamper what must be regarded, at least since the European Convention [on Human Rights] was ratified, as a constitutional right to free speech."

In *Att. Gen. v Guardian Newspapers (No.2)*,[56] Lord Goff, applying the equitable doctrine of breach of confidence, stated that "I conceive it to be my duty, when I am free to do so, to interpret the law in accordance with the obligations of the Crown under this treaty [the ECHR]". However, Sir Robert Megarry, V.C., suggested a limit in *Malone v M.P.C.*[57] After holding that the ECHR could not directly establish a right to privacy in English law because it had not been incorporated by statute as law in the United Kingdom, the Vice-Chancellor rejected an argument to the effect that it could be used to do so indirectly, by taking it into account when developing the common law:

"I readily accept that if the question before me were one of construing a statute enacted with the purpose of giving effect to obligations imposed by the Convention, the Court would readily seek to construe the legislation in a way that would effectuate the Convention rather than frustrate it. However, no relevant legislation of that sort is in existence. It seems to me that where Parliament has abstained from legislating on a point that is plainly suitable for legislation, it is indeed difficult for the Court to lay down new rules of common law or equity that will carry out the Crown's treaty obligations, or to discover for the first time that such rules have always existed."

SALOMON v COMMISSIONERS OF CUSTOMS AND EXCISE

[1967] 2 Q.B. 116. Court of Appeal

The Court was required to interpret an ambiguous provision in the Customs and Excise Act 1952. The Act, drafted in Parliament's own language, was intended to implement the 1950 Convention on the Valuation of Goods for Customs Purposes, a treaty to which a number of European states were parties. The Convention was not included as a Schedule to the Act, or anywhere referred to in it. The question arose whether recourse could be had to the treaty to interpret the statute.

---

[53] [1978] Q.B. 36 at 48 CA.
[54] [1981] A.C. 303 at 354 HL. Lord Fraser suggested the same "where our domestic law is not firmly settled" (at 352). The ECHR was also referred to as a guide when determining public policy in *Blathwayt v Baron Cawley* [1976] A.C. 397 HL.
[55] [1972] A.C. 1027 at 1133.
[56] [1990] 1 A.C. 109 at 283 HL.
[57] [1979] Ch. 344 at 379.

DIPLOCK L.J.

Where, by a treaty, Her Majesty's Government undertakes either to introduce domestic legislation to achieve a specified result in the United Kingdom or to secure a specified result which can only be achieved by legislation, the treaty, since in English law it is not self-operating, remains irrelevant to any issue in the English courts until Her Majesty's Government has taken steps by way of legislation to fulfil its treaty obligations. Once the Government has legislated, which it may do in anticipation of the coming into effect of the treaty, as it did in this case, the court must in the first instance construe the legislation, for that is what the court has to apply. If the terms of the legislation are clear and unambiguous, they must be given effect to, whether or not they carry out Her Majesty's treaty obligations, for the sovereign power of the Queen in Parliament extends to breaking treaties (see *Ellerman Lines v. Murray*[58] ...) and any remedy for such a breach of an international obligation lies in a forum other than Her Majesty's own courts. But if the terms of the legislation are not clear but are reasonably capable of more than one meaning, the treaty itself becomes relevant, for there is a prima facie presumption that Parliament does not intend to act in breach of international law, including therein specific treaty obligations; and if one of the meanings which can reasonably be ascribed to the legislation is consonant with the treaty obligations and another or others are not, the meaning which is consonant is to be preferred ...

It has been argued that the terms of an international convention cannot be consulted to resolve ambiguities or obscurities in a statute unless the statute itself contains either in the enacting part or in the preamble an express reference to the international convention which it is the purpose of the state to implement. The judge seems to have been persuaded that *Ellerman Lines etc. v. Murray etc.* was authority for this proposition. But, with respect, it is not. The statute with which that case was concerned did not refer to the convention. The case is authority only for the proposition for which I have already cited it. ... I can see no reason in comity or common sense for imposing such a limitation upon the right and duty of the court to consult an international convention to resolve ambiguities and obscurities in a statutory enactment. If from extrinsic evidence it is plain that the enactment was intended to fulfil Her Majesty's Government's obligations under a particular convention, it matters not that there is no express reference to the convention in the statute. One must not presume that Parliament intends to break an international convention merely because it does not say expressly that it is intending to observe it. Of course the court must not merely guess that the statute was intended to give effect to a particular international convention. The extrinsic evidence of the connection must be cogent.

Lord Denning L.J. and Russell L.J. delivered concurring judgments.

Notes

1. On the duty to interpret a statute or order in council that is intended to implement a treaty so as to give effect to the treaty if the language of the statute or order allows, see also *Post Office v Estuary Radio Ltd*,[59] *Benin v Whimster*[60] and *The Jade*.[61]

2. In *Buchanan v Babco*,[62] the Carriage of Goods by Road Act 1965, s.1, provided that the English (but not the other, French) authentic text of the multilateral 1956 Convention on the Contract for the International Carriage of Goods by Road, which text was included as a Schedule to the Act, should have the force of law in the United Kingdom. Indicating the rules of interpretation that should apply in the interpretation of the English text of the Convention as a part of English law, Lord Wilberforce[63] stated:

    "I think that the correct approach is to interpret the English text, which after all is likely to be used by many others than British businessmen, in a normal manner, appropriate for the

---

[58] [1931] A.C. 126 HL.
[59] [1968] 2 Q.B. 740 CA.
[60] [1976] Q.B. 297 CA.
[61] [1976] 1 W.L.R. 430 at 436 HL.
[62] [1978] A.C. 141 HL.
[63] [1978] A.C. 141 at 152.

interpretation of an international convention, unconstrained by technical rules of English law, or by English legal precedent, but on broad principles of general acceptation ... Moreover, it is perfectly legitimate ... to look for assistance, if assistance is needed, to the French text. ... There is no need to impose a preliminary test of ambiguity [before doing so]."

3.   In *Fothergill v Monarch Airlines*,[64] Lord Diplock stated that the rules on the interpretation of treaties in the Vienna Convention on the Law of Treaties 1969, which emphasise the purpose of a treaty and permit recourse to its *travaux préparatoires*, should be followed by United Kingdom courts when interpreting a treaty that has been incorporated into United Kingdom law:

> "Indeed, in the case of Acts of Parliament giving effect to international conventions concluded after the coming into force of the Vienna Convention on the Law of Treaties (Cmnd. 4140), I think an English court might well be under a constitutional obligation to do so. By ratifying that Convention, Her Majesty's Government has undertaken an international obligation on behalf of the United Kingdom to interpret future treaties in this manner and since under our constitution the function of interpreting the written law is an exercise of judicial power and rests with the courts of justice, that obligation assumed by the United Kingdom falls to be performed by those courts."

Lord Diplock's emphasis upon the purpose of a treaty was repeated by Lord Hope in *Sidhu v British Airways*.[65] Referring to the *Fothergill* case, he stated: "It is now well established that a purposive approach should be taken to the interpretation of international conventions which have the force of law in this country."

4.   The rules governing the use of *travaux préparatoires* in the interpretation of a treaty that is made a part of United Kingdom law were also considered in the *Fothergill* case. In that case, the Carriage by Air Act 1961, s.1, enacted that the 1929 Warsaw Convention for the Unification of Certain Rules regarding Air Transport should have the force of law in the United Kingdom.[66] The two (French and English) authentic texts were scheduled to the Act. Interpreting the word "damage" (*avarie*) in the Convention to include loss of, as well as injury to, goods, the House of Lords held that recourse could be had to the *travaux préparatoires* of the Convention to interpret it. Lord Wilberforce[67] stated:

> "These cases [of recourse to *travaux préparatoires*] should be rare, and only where two conditions are fulfilled, first, that the material involved is public and accessible, and, secondly, that the *travaux préparatoires* clearly and indisputably point to a definite legislative intention."

Lord Scarman[68] agreed with Lord Wilberforce and, emphasising the need for uniformity of interpretation, pointed out that the courts of most other states would look to the *travaux*

---

[64]   [1981] A.C. 251 at 283 HL. For criticism of the UK courts' use of the Vienna Convention for interpretation, see Gardiner (1995) 44 I.C.L.Q. 620.

[65]   [1997] A.C. 430 at 442 HL. For a case in which a treaty's text, rather than its purpose, was decisive, see *Semco Salvage and Marine Pte Ltd v Lancer Navigation* [1997] A.C. 455 HL. See Lord Mustill at 467–468.

[66]   cf. the Child Abduction and Custody Act 1985, which gives the 1980 Hague Convention on International Child Abduction the force of law. The 1980 Convention is to be interpreted purposively: *Re F. (Minor; abduction)* [1995] 3 All E.R. 641 at 645 CA.

[67]   [1981] A.C. 251 at 278. Lord Fraser considered that recourse could not be had to the *travaux* in this case because they had not been sufficiently well published to the persons whose rights were affected: at 287.

[68]   [1981] A.C. 251 at 283.

préparatoires. Lord Wilberforce's approach was adopted as *ratio* in *Gatoil International Inc. v Arkwright-Boston Manufacturers Mutual Insurance Co.*[69]

In *R. v Secretary of State for the Home Dept Ex p. Sivakumaran*,[70] recourse was had to the *travaux préparatoires* of the 1951 Convention on the Status of Refugees when interpreting a part of the British Immigration Rules that was taken word for word from the Convention. Although not formally incorporated by statute, the Convention had "for all practical purposes," (per Lord Keith) been incorporated into United Kingdom law.

B. *The United States*[71]

HEAD MONEY CASES: EDYE v ROBERTSON

112 U.S. 580 (1884). US Supreme Court

It was argued in this case that an Act of Congress conflicted with earlier US treaties and that therefore it was invalid. The Court, which was unanimous, found no such conflict on the facts of the case but nonetheless made the following statement of principle.

MR JUSTICE MILLER (FOR THE COURT)

A treaty is primarily a compact between independent Nations. . . . But a treaty may also contain provisions which confer certain rights upon the citizens or subjects of one of the Nations residing in the territorial limits of the other, which partake of the nature of municipal law, and which are capable of enforcement as between private parties in the courts of the country. . . . The Constitution of the United States [art.VI] places such provisions as these in the same category as other laws of Congress by its declaration that "This Constitution and the laws made in pursuance thereof, and all treaties made or which shall be made under authority of the United States, shall be the supreme law of the land." A treaty, then, is a law of the land as an Act of Congress is, whenever its provisions prescribe a rule by which the rights of the private citizen or subject may be determined. And when such rights are of a nature to be enforced in a court of justice, that court resorts to the treaty for a rule of decision for the case before it, as it would to a statute.

But even in this aspect of the case, there is nothing in this law which makes it irrepealable or unchangeable. The Constitution gives it no superiority over an Act of Congress in this respect, which may be repealed or modified by an Act of a later date. . . .

In short, we are of opinion that, so far as a treaty is made by the United States with any foreign Nation can become the subject of judicial cognisance in the courts of this country, it is subject to such Acts as Congress may pass for its enforcement, modification or repeal.

SEI FUJII v CALIFORNIA

242 P. 2d 617; 19 I.L.R. 312 (1952). Supreme Court of California

GIBSON C.J.

Plaintiff, an alien Japanese . . . appeals from a judgment declaring that certain land purchased by him in 1948 had escheated to the state. There is no treaty between this country and Japan which confers upon plaintiff the right to own land, and the sole question presented on this appeal is the validity of the California alien land law.

---

69 [1985] A.C. 255 HL.
70 [1988] 2 A.C. 958 HL.
71 See *Restatement of the Foreign Relations Law of the U.S., Third* (1987), Vol.1, Pt I, Ch.2; Henkin (1984) 82 Mich. L.R. 1555; ibid. (1986–7) 100 H.L.R. 853; Paust, *International Law as Law of the United States* (1996); Vagts (2001) 95 A.J.I.L. 313.

It is first contended that the land law has been invalidated and superseded by the provisions of the United Nations Charter pledging the member nations to promote the observance of human rights and fundamental freedoms without distinction as to race. Plaintiff relies on statements in the preamble and in Articles 1, 55 and 56 of the Charter....[72]

It is not disputed that the Charter is a treaty, and our federal Constitution provides that treaties made under the authority of the United States are part of the supreme law of the land and that the judges in every state are bound thereby. U.S.Const., art. VI. A treaty, however, does not automatically supersede local laws which are inconsistent with it unless the treaty provisions are self-executing. In the words of Chief Justice Marshall: A treaty is "to be regarded in courts of justice as equivalent to an act of the Legislature, whenever it operates of itself, without the aid of any legislative provision. But when the terms of the stipulation import a contract—when either of the parties engages to perform a particular act, the treaty addresses itself to the political, not the judicial department; and the Legislature must execute the contract, before it can become a rule for the court." *Foster v. Neilson*, 1829, 2 Pet. 253, 314, 7 L.Ed. 415.

In determining whether a treaty is self-executing courts look to the intent of the signatory parties as manifested by the language of the instrument, and if the instrument is uncertain, recourse may be had to the circumstances surrounding its execution. See *Foster v. Neilson.* ... In order for a treaty provision to be operative without the aid of implementing legislation and to have the force and effect of a statute, it must appear that the framers of the treaty intended to prescribe a rule that, standing alone, would be enforceable in the courts. See Head Money Cases [*Edye v Robertson*]. ...[73]

It is clear that the provisions of the preamble and of Article 1 of the Charter which are claimed to be in conflict with the alien land law are not self-executing. They state general purposes and objectives of the United Nations Organisation and do not purport to impose legal obligations on the individual member nations or to create rights in private persons. ... Although the member-nations have obligated themselves [in arts 55 and 56] to co-operate with the international organisation in promoting respect for, and observance of, human rights, it is plain that it was contemplated that future legislative action by the several nations would be required to accomplish the declared objectives, and there is nothing to indicate that these provisions were intended to become rules of law for the courts of this country upon the ratification of the Charter.

The language used in Articles 55 and 56 is not the type customarily employed in treaties which have been held to be self-executing and to create rights and duties in individuals. For example, the treaty involved in *Clark v. Allen*, 331 U.S. 503, 507–508 ... relating to the rights of a national of one country to inherit real property located in another country, specifically provided that "such national shall be allowed a term of three years in which to sell the [property] ... and withdraw the proceeds ..." free from any discriminatory taxation. ... In other instances treaty provisions were enforced without implementing legislation where they prescribed in detail the rules governing rights and obligations of individuals or specifically provided that citizens of one nation shall have the same rights while in the other country as are enjoyed by that country's own citizens. *Bacardi Corp. v. Domenech*, 311 U.S. 150, *Asakura v. City of Seattle*, 265 U.S. 332, 340.

It is significant to note that when the framers of the Charter intended to make certain provisions effective without the aid of implementing legislation they employed language which is clear and definite and manifests that intention. [The Court referred to arts 104 and 105.[74]] ... In *Curran v. City of New York*, 191 Misc. 229, 77 N.Y.S. 2d 206, 212, these articles were treated as being self-executory.

We are satisfied, however, that the Charter provisions relied on by plaintiff were not intended to supersede existing domestic legislation, and we cannot hold that they operate to invalidate the alien land law.[75]

---

[72] Ed. Below, App.l.
[73] Ed. Above, p.91.
[74] Ed. Below, App.l.
[75] Ed. This ruling by the Court, which reversed that of the California Court of Appeals, was unanimous. The Court, nonetheless, decided the case in favour of the plaintiff on another ground.

Notes

1.   The result of these cases is that "self executing"[76] treaties, or particular treaty provisions, will be treated by American courts as a part of American law and as having the status of a federal statute, so that they are replaced by later, contradictory federal legislation.[77] As to the relationship between "self executing" treaty provisions and later state law, in *Asakura v City of Seattle*,[78] in which a conflict was alleged (but not found) between a 1911 treaty and a 1921 city ordinance, the US Supreme Court stated: "The rule established by it [the treaty] cannot be rendered nugatory in any part of the United States by municipal ordinances or state laws." In *Johnson v Browne*,[79] the US Supreme Court, in holding that certain federal statutory provisions had not been repealed by treaty, stated: "Repeals by implication are never favoured, and a later treaty will not be regarded as repealing an earlier statute by implication unless the two are absolutely incompatible and the statute cannot be enforced without antagonising the treaty." In *Cook v U.S.*,[80] the US Supreme Court noted that "a treaty will not be abrogated or modified by a later [federal] statute unless such purpose on the part of the Congress has been clearly expressed."

     In addition to "treaties", which are made by the President with the advice and consent of the Senate,[81] the US may also enter into "executive agreements" which are made by the President acting alone.[82] Both types of agreements are treaties for the purposes of international law. In *U.S. v Pink*[83] the Supreme Court stated: "A treaty is a Law of the Land under the supremacy clause (art.VI, cl.2) of the Constitution. Such international compacts and agreements as the Litvinoff Assignment [an executive agreement] have a similar dignity." Whereas subsequent federal legislation will override an executive agreement, it is not clear whether an executive agreement will supersede prior federal legislation.[84] An executive agreement may override existing state law.[85]

2.   The question whether the US courts must follow rulings of the ICJ was in issue in a series of cases brought against the US[86] before the ICJ arising our of non-compliance by the US with its obligations under art.36 of the Vienna Convention on Consular Relations 1963, to inform foreign nationals of the right to consular access.[87] The US Supreme Count held that the ICJ's interpretation of a treaty to which the US was a party (in this cases the 1963 Convention), while deserving "respectful consideration", was not legally binding upon it:

---

[76]   The decision whether a treaty provision is "self executing" is one for a state's national courts: the criteria relied upon in the *Head Money* cases are comparable to those used by national courts in the many other states that make use of the concept of "self executing" treaties. See Buergenthal (1992–IV) 235 Hague Recueil 303; and Jackson (1992) 86 A.J.I.L. 310. On the US approach, see Paust (1988) 82 A.J.I.L. 760; and Vasquez (1995) 89 A.J.I.L. 695.

[77]   See, e.g. *Breard v Greene*, 523 U.S. 371 (1998).

[78]   265 U.S. 332 at 341 (1924).

[79]   205 U.S. 309 at 321 (1907).

[80]   288 U.S. 102 at 119–120 (1933).

[81]   US Constitution, art.II, s.2.

[82]   See below, p.645.

[83]   315 U.S. 203 at 230 (1942).

[84]   See Clark (2007) 93 Virg L.R. 1574.

[85]   *American Insurance Association v Garamendi* 539 US 396 (2003).

[86]   The *Vienna Convention on Consular Relations* case (*Paraguay v US*) I.C.J. Rep. 1998, p.248; the *LaGrand* case (*Germany v US*) see below, p.870; and the *Avena* case (*Mexico v US*) I.C.J. Rep. 2004, p.12.

[87]   See Shany, *Regulating Jurisdictional Relations between National and International Courts* (2007) p.45.

"If treaties are to be given effect as federal law under our legal system, determining their meaning as a matter of federal law is emphatically the province and duty of the judicial department, headed by the "one Supreme Court" established under the Constitution."[88]

Although not ruling expressly upon the point, the Supreme Court also clearly took the view that it was not bound by provisional measures ordered by the ICJ[89] indicating that a person sentenced to the death penalty should not be executed while the question of US compliance with art.36 in his case was pending before the ICJ, even though provisional measures are legally-binding in international law.[90]

3.   As far as customary international law is concerned, the following general statement by Gray J. in *The Paquete Habana*[91] applies:

"International law is part of our law, and must be ascertained and administered by the Courts of Justice of appropriate jurisdiction, as often as questions of right depending upon it are duly presented for their determination. For this purpose, where there is no treaty and no controlling executive or legislative act or judicial decision, resort must be had to the customs and usages of civilised nations ..."

In that case, the US Supreme Court found and applied a customary rule of international law exempting coastal fishing vessels from capture as prize of war. However, in *Garcia-Mir v Meese*[92] it was held that although the lengthy detention of illegal Cuban immigrants was contrary to customary international law, their detention was not contrary to US law because the Attorney–General's decision to detain them was, in terms of *The Paquete Habana* judgment, a "controlling executive act."

The "modern view is that customary international law in the United States is federal law and its determination by the federal courts is binding on the State courts".[93] However, it does not prevail over an earlier (or later) federal statute.[94]

On the use of customary international law in tort claims in American courts alleging that conduct is in violation of the "law of nations", see the *Filartiga* case, below, p.630.

----

[88]   *Sanchex-Llamas v Oregon*, 548 U.S. 557 at 581.
[89]   See the orders in the *Vienna Convention on Consular Relations* case, above at n.86; the *La Grand* case, I.C.J. Rep. 1999, p.9; and the *Avema* case, I.C.J. Rep. 2003, p.77. On the *LaGrand* case, see further below, p.870.
[90]   See, e.g. *Breard v Greene*, 523 U.S. 371 (1998) and *Medellin v Texas*, 170 L. Ed.2d. 190 (2008). In these cases the appellants were executed after the Supreme Court denied certiorari and while the cases were still pending before the ICJ.
[91]   175 U.S. 677 at 700 (1900).
[92]   788 F.2d 1446 (1986). For criticism of the decision, see Henkin (1986) 80 A.J.I.L. 930.
[93]   Restatement, above, at n.71.
[94]   *Committee of US Citizens Living in Nicaragua v Reagan*, 859 F 2d. 929 (1988).

4. THE EXECUTIVE CERTIFICATE

Notes

1. *British practice.*[95] Oppenheim[96] states:

    "At common law it is the practice of English courts to accept as conclusive statements by or on behalf of the Secretary of State for Foreign and Commonwealth Affairs relating to certain categories of questions of fact in the field of international affairs. In such cases the statement is conclusive even in the face of contrary evidence. ... The categories of cases on which prerogative statements by the Foreign and Commonwealth Office (or its predecessors) have, at common law, been treated as conclusive include: (a) whether a foreign state or government has been recognised by the United Kingdom either *de facto* or *de jure*[97]; (b) whether recognition has been granted to conquest by another State or to other changes of territorial title, and generally, whether certain territory is under the sovereignty of one foreign State or another; (c) the sovereign status of a foreign State or its monarch; (d) the commencement and termination of a state of war against another country; (e) whether a state of war exists with a foreign country or between two foreign countries; (f) the existence of a case for reprisals in maritime war; (g) whether a person is entitled to diplomatic status; (h) the existence or extent of British jurisdiction in a foreign country."

    However, Foreign Office certificates are not regarded as conclusive in the interpretation of statutes or the construction of documents: see *Re Al-Fin Corporation's Patent*, below, p.161.

    The "practice" of the courts, which has only become established in the present century,[98] has been confirmed by statute in a number of areas of foreign affairs. Thus a Foreign Office certificate is "conclusive evidence" on matters of diplomatic and state immunity under the Diplomatic Privileges Act 1964, s.4, below, p.316, and the State Immunity Act 1978, s.21.[99] In *R. v Secretary of State for Foreign and Commonwealth Affairs Ex p. Trawnik*,[100] it was held that a certificate issued under the State Immunity Act 1978, s.21, is not subject to judicial review on *Wednesbury* principles; it is reviewable only if it constitutes a nullity.

2. In *The Fagernes*,[101] in which the Court of Appeal asked for and received from the Attorney-General a statement on the question whether a point in the Bristol Channel was regarded by the Crown as British territory, Atkin L.J. stated:

    "What is the territory of the Crown is a matter of judicial notice. The Court has, therefore, to inform itself from the best material available. ... Any definite statement from the proper representative of the Crown as to the territory of the Crown must be treated as conclusive."

    Lawrence L.J. took the same position. Bankes L.J. was of the opinion that a statement by the

---

[95] See Lyons (1946) 23 B.Y.I.L. 240; (1952) 29 B.Y.I.L. 227; (1957) 33 B.Y.I.L. 302; Mann, above, p.72, n.13, Chs 2, 3; Warbrick (1986) 35 I.C.L.Q. 138; Wilmshurst (1986) 35 I.C.L.Q. 157.
[96] Oppenheim, Vol.I., p.1046. Footnotes omitted.
[97] On certificates concerning the recognition of states and governments, see below, p.148.
[98] See Lyons (1946) 23 B.Y.I.L. 240.
[99] See also s.1(7) of the Deep Sea Mining (Temporary Provisions) Act 1981. For a fuller list, see Wilmshurst, above, n.95, p.165.
[100] *The Times*, April 18, 1985 (Q.B.D.). See Warbrick, above, n.95.
[101] [1927] P. 311 at 324. See Edeson (1973) 89 L.Q.R. 364.

Crown was persuasive but not binding. In *Post Office v Estuary Radio Ltd*,[102] the Court of Appeal followed the approach of Atkin and Lawrence L.JJ.

3. In *Duff Development Co v Govt of Kelantan*[103] Lord Sumner based the conclusive nature of certificates upon the "best evidence" rule and, to a lesser degree, the "one voice" doctrine, i.e. the doctrine that the courts and the executive should follow the same approach on matters of foreign affairs. The following statement by Sir Francis Vallat,[104] Legal Adviser to the Foreign Office, suggests another reason why the courts should accept a certificate:

> "It is believed that the test of a true certificate is not whether the facts are peculiarly within the knowledge of the Foreign Office or such as the Foreign Office may reasonably be expected to know or which the Foreign Office ought to know in the conduct of its business, but the presence of some element of recognition by Her Majesty's Government.[105] The logic of this position is sound. On matters of pure fact the view of the Foreign Office must be based on the type of evidence normally used to prove facts before a Court, and it is such evidence rather than the certificate that ought in general to be produced before the Court. When, however, it comes to a matter of recognition, there is no source which can state with equal authority what is or is not recognised by the Government."

---

[102] [1968] 2 Q.B. 740.
[103] [1924] A.C. 797 HL. The *Duff Development Co* case was cited as authority for the conclusive nature of Foreign Office certificates in the *Carl Zeiss* case, below, p.173.
[104] *International Law and the Practitioner* (1966), p.54.
[105] cf. *Spinney v Royal Ins. Co.* [1980] 1 Lloyd's Rep. 406 QB.

4 PERSONALITY

1. GENERALLY

O'CONNELL, INTERNATIONAL LAW

(2nd edn 1970), Vol.I, pp.80–82

IT is clear that the word "person" is used to refer to one who is a legal actor, but that it is of no assistance in ascertaining who or what is competent to act. Only the rules of law can determine this, and they may select different entities and endow them with different legal functions, so that it is a mistake to suppose that merely by describing an entity as a "person" one is formulating its capacities in law....

The correct questions should be: (a) Do the rules of international law establish that this claimant to capacity has the capacity which it claims? (b) What exactly is the capacity which it claims and which is allowed to it, or in other words, just what sorts of legal relations may this entity enter into? If the claimant to capacity is a novelty there will be, of course, no rule of international law on the subject at all until it appears and asserts itself, whereupon there arises question (c), should the entity be recognised as having the capacity which it claims to have? Recognition here means acquiescence in the claim by the other parties to international actions....

Capacity implies personality, but always it is capacity *to do those particular acts*. Therefore "personality" as a term is only short-hand for the proposition that an entity is endowed by international law with legal capacity. But entity A may have capacity to perform acts X and Y, but not act Z, entity B to perform acts Y and Z but not act X, and entity C to perform all three.

2. STATES[1]

A. *Generally*

MONTEVIDEO CONVENTION ON RIGHTS AND DUTIES OF STATES 1933

(1934) 165 L.N.T.S. 19; U.S.T.S. 881; 4 Malloy 4807; 28 A.J.I.L., Supp., 75

Article I

The State as a person of international law should possess the following qualifications: (a) a permanent population; (b) a defined territory; (c) government; and (d) capacity to enter into relations with other States.

---

[1] See Crawford, *The Creation of States in International Law* (2nd edn 2006); and Marek, *Identity and Continuity of States in Public International Law* (2nd edn 1968).

Notes

1. For a list of most of the states in the international community, who now total over 190, see the list of members of the United Nations, below App.II.[2] The Vatican City is the only state that is generally recognised by the international community that is not a member of the United Nations.[3] State numbers increased greatly with the dissolution of the USSR and the SFRY in the 1990s.[4]

2. The Montevideo Convention was adopted by the 7th International Conference of American States. Fifteen Latin American states and the United States are parties to it. The Convention is commonly accepted as reflecting, in general terms, the requirements of statehood at customary international law. There is some evidence, however, to suggest that these requirements, which are concerned solely with the effectiveness of the entity claiming the rights and duties of a state, have recently been supplemented by others—independence achieved: (i) in accordance with the principle of self-determination;[5] and (ii) not in the pursuance of racist policies[6]—of a political or moral character.[7] The term "state" may be given a different meaning for the purposes of a particular treaty.[8] The role of recognition by other states in the attainment of international personality by a state is considered below, p.130.

3. *Population and territory.* There is no lower limit to the size of a state's population and territory. Nauru, for example, has only 9,000 inhabitants and is only eight square miles in area. The Vatican City has even fewer permanent residents and, whatever domain it may have elsewhere, has less than 100 acres on earth.[9]

    There is ample evidence in state practice and in judicial and arbitral decisions to show that to be a state it is not necessary for an entity to have exactly defined or undisputed boundaries, either at the time that it comes into being or subsequently. Israel, for example, is undoubtedly a state although its borders have never been settled.[10] In *Deutsche Continental Gas-Gesellschaft v Polish State*[11] the German-Polish Mixed Arbitral Tribunal said:

    > "In order to say that a State exists and can be recognised as such . . . it is enough that . . . [its]

---

[2] The European mini-states of Andorra, Liechtenstein, Monaco and San Marino joined the UN in the early 1990s. Andorra was formerly a "fief" under the joint suzerainty of its two co-princes, the President of the French Republic and the Bishop of Urgel (Spain), who were responsible for its international relations. In 1993, it became a state, with the consent of the two co-princes, who remain its head of state. Monaco and San Marino have close treaty relations with France and Italy respectively: see O'Connell, *International Law* (2nd edn 1970), Vol.I, pp.290–291. As to Liechtenstein, see below, p.99. The South Pacific mini-states of Kiribati, Nauru, Tonga and Tuvalu became UN members in 1999 or 2000.

[3] The Vatican City has never applied for UN membership. It has observer status within the UN system. On its classification as a state, see below, p.129. Other controversial candidates include Kosovo, Palestine and Taiwan.

[4] See below, p.133.

[5] See the *Southern Rhodesia* case, below, p.101.

[6] See the *Transkei* case, below, p.101.

[7] See Crawford, above, p.91, n.1, pp.106 and 226. Crawford also suggests that independence obtained by the use of force contrary to art.2(4) of the UN Charter may in some cases not give rise to statehood: Crawford, p.118; see also, below, p.110. See also Grant (1999) 37 C.J.T.L. 403.

[8] On its meaning in the UN Charter, see Higgins, *The Development of International Law through the Political Organs of The United Nations* (1963), pp.11–57 and Dugard, *Recognition and the United Nations* (1987), pp.51–111.

[9] On "mini" states generally, see Duursma, *Fragmentation and the International Relations of Micro-States* (1996); Harden, ed., *Small is Dangerous: Micro States in a Macro World* (1985); and Rapaport, Muteba and Therattil, *Small States and Territories: Status and Problems* (1971).

[10] See below, pp.192 et seq.

[11] (1929) 5 A.D. 11 at 15.

territory has a sufficient consistency, even though its boundaries have not yet been accurately delimited."

4. *Government*. One of the preliminary questions which arose in the *Aaland Islands* case was the date on which Finland became a state. Finland had been a part of the Russian Empire until the Russian Revolution. When the new Soviet Government issued a manifesto proclaiming the right of all peoples within the Russian Empire to self-determination, the Finnish Diet, or Parliament, declared Finland's independence on December 4, 1917. This was recognised by the Soviet Government but there was opposition within Finland by those, including a section of the army, who continued to support the old Russian régime and to reject the idea of independence. As a result, violence broke out and for a time the Government of the new state was able to maintain order only with the help of Soviet troops. The Report of the International Committee of Jurists appointed to consider the case reads (in a passage which bears upon "independence" as well as "government" as requirements of statehood):

> "In the midst of revolution and anarchy, certain elements essential to the existence of a State, even some elements of fact, were lacking for a fairly considerable period. Political and social life was disorganised; the authorities were not strong enough to assert themselves; civil war was rife; further, the Diet, the legality of which had been disputed by a large section of the people, had been dispersed by the revolutionary party, and the Government had been chased from the capital and forcibly prevented from carrying out its duties; the armed camps and the police were divided into two opposing forces, and Russian troops, and after a time Germans also, took part in the civil war between the inhabitants and between the Red and White Finnish troops. It is, therefore, difficult to say at what exact date the Finnish Republic, in the legal sense of the term, actually became a definitely constituted sovereign State. This certainly did not take place until a stable political organisation had been created, and until the public authorities had become strong enough to assert themselves throughout the territories of the State without the assistance of foreign troops. It would appear that it was in May 1918, that the civil war ended and that the foreign troops began to leave the country, so that from that time onwards it was possible to re-establish order and normal political and social life, little by little."[12]

State practice suggests that the requirement of a "stable political organisation" in control of the territory does not apply during a civil war or where there is a collapse of law and order in a state that already exists.

A state that currently has problems of effective government is *Somalia*. Since President Barre's Government was overthrown in a civil war in 1991, fighting has persisted between rival militias with different territorial bases. A separate state of Somaliland declared its independence in the north west of Somalia in 1991, but, although having a stable and effective Government in control of its territory, has not gained international recognition by any state.[13] The 1991 Djibouti Conference of interested states and parties led to the establishment of an interim Government, but this did not have effective control of Mogadishu, the capital, or the country at large.[14] UN forces

---

[12] L.N.O.J., Special Supp. No.3, p.3 (1920).
[13] The UK, for example, does "not recognise Somaliland as an independent state", Minister of State, FCO, *Hansard*, HC Vol.450, col.1770 WA October 24, 2006. See Schoiswohl, *Status and (Human Rights) Obligations of Non-Recognised De Facto Regimes in International Law: The Case of Somaliland* (2004).
[14] See *Republic of Somalia v Woodhouse Drake & Carey Suisse S.A.*, below, p.145.

were sent into Somalia between 1992 and 1995, but failed to bring the situation under control.[15] After several more years in which Somalia lacked an effective central government, in 2004 Somalia warlords and political leaders signed a peace agreement in Nairobi, which led to the establishment of a Transitional Federal Government ("TFG"). In 2006, the Islamic Courts Union ("ICU"), which has an Islamic state agenda, took control of Mogadishi by force. Ethiopian troops then entered the country in support of the TFG and to "protect Ethiopian sovereignty", and the ICU was forced to retreat. When Ethiopian troops left Somalia in 2009, fighting continued between the ICU and forces backing the TFG, with the former recovering control of much territory by mid-2009. During the whole of the period from 1991 onwards, Somalia has remained a UN member and continued to be recognised as a state by the international community.[16]

5.   *Failed states.* Somalia in the 1990s is an example of what are sometimes known as failed states. These are characterised by Thürer[17] as follows:

> "Three elements can be said to characterize the phenomenon of the 'failed State' from the political and legal point of view.
>
>   — Firstly, there is the geographical and territorial aspect, namely the fact that 'failed States' are essentially associated with internal and endogenous problems, even though these may incidentally have cross-border impacts. The situation confronting us then is one of an implosion rather than an explosion of the structures of power and authority, the disintegration and destructuring of States rather than their dismemberment.
>   — Secondly, there is the political aspect, namely the internal collapse of law and order. The emphasis here is on the total or near total breakdown of structures guaranteeing law and order rather than the kind of fragmentation of State authority seen in civil wars, where clearly identified military or paramilitary rebels fight either to strengthen their own position within the State or to break away from it.
>   — Thirdly, there is the functional aspect, namely the absence of bodies capable, on the one hand, of representing the State at the international level and, on the other, of being influenced by the outside world.
>
> From a legal point of view, it could be said that the 'failed State' is one which, though retaining legal capacity, has for all practical purposes lost the ability to exercise it. A key element in this respect is the fact that there is no body which can commit the State in an effective and legally binding way, for example, by concluding an agreement."

Other examples given by Thürer of failed states at different times in the past 30 years are Afghanistan, Bosnia-Herzegovina, Cambodia, Lebanon, Liberia, Sierra Leone and the Democratic Republic of Congo. What is noticeable is that all of these states, like Somalia, have continued to be recognised as states during their time of failure.

---

[15]   See below, pp.781, 830.

[16]   The UK recognises the "Republic of Somalia" as a state: Minister of State, FCO, *Hansard*, HC Vol.325, col.739 (February 16, 1999). As its government, "Somalia does not have diplomatic representation in the UK and the security situation in Somalia does not allow us to have a diplomatic mission in Mogadishu. However, we acknowledge the Transitional Federal Government as the current Government in power in Somalia and deal with them on that basis": FCO spokesman, *Hansard*, HL, WA 149 (June 10, 2009).

[17]   (1999) No.836 International Review of the Red Cross 731.

6. *International territories*.[18] Several territories in existing states that have experienced serious armed conflict have in recent years been placed under UN organised administration on an interim basis pending a final settlement. Cambodia[19] and East Timor[20] were such internationalised territories in the 1990s, and Kosovo[21] was one later.[22]

7. *Kosovo*. Kosovo was formerly a province of Serbia within the SFRY that was allowed considerable governmental autonomy because of its large ethnic Albanian majority. In 1991, following cur-tailment of its autonomy by the Milosevic Government, Kosovo unsuccessfully declared itself an independent state. In the late 1990s, Kosovo resistance to Milosevic policies led to an escalation of fighting between the Kosovo Liberation Army (KLA) and FRY forces. In 1999, the Rambouillet Conference proposed a settlement plan involving an interim period of autonomy for Kosovo within the FRY, secured by the presence of NATO troops. In March 1999, when this plan was rejected by the FRY, NATO began aerial bombing of the FRY, including Belgrade.[23] In June 1999, the FRY "surrendered" and agreed to the withdrawal of FRY security forces from Kosovo and their replacement by a NATO-led military force. Thereupon, the Security Council, acting under Chapter VII, authorised the Secretary General to "establish an international civil presence in Kosovo in order to provide an interim administration for Kosovo under which the people of Kosovo can enjoy substantial autonomy within the Federal Republic of Yugoslavia which will provide transitional administration while establishing and overseeing the development of pro-visional democratic self-governing institutions."[24] The resulting Interim Administration Mission in Kosovo ("UNMIK") governed Kosovo. All legislative and executive jurisdiction in Kosovo were vested in UNMIK and exercised by the Secretary-General's Special Representative.[25] There was also a NATO-led military peace keeping presence ("KFOR"). In 2007, a plan prepared by Mr Ahtissari, the UN Special Envoy, proposed that Kosovo be given autonomy, with full powers of self-government under EU supervision; although Belgrade was given no governmental powers, Kosovo was to remain a part of Serbian territory. The plan was rejected by Serbia, leading the Assembly of Kosovo, with the Serbian minority representatives abstaining, to declare the inde-pendence of the state of the Republic of Kosovo in February 2008. Serbia continues to regard Kosovo as Serbian territory. Although the Republic of Kosovo claims the status of an indepen-dent state, UNMIK remains in place providing assistance, although, as of December 2008, the European Union Rule of Law Mission in Kosovo ("EULEX"), acting also under SC Resolution 1244, has taken over most of UNMIK's support role, providing the Kosovo government with police, judicial and customs assistance. In addition, KFOR, the Nato-led peace keeping force, continues to operate in the Republic of Kosovo.

By January 2010, 65 states had recognised the Republic of Kosovo as a state, including the UK

---

18 See Wilde *International Territorial Administration* (2008); Strohmeyer (2001) 95 A.J.I.L. 46; and Ydit, *Internationalised Territories* (1961). An earlier example before World War II was the Free City of Danzig (Gdansk).

19 The UN Transitional Authority in Cambodia (UNTAC) was established by the 1991 Agreement on the Comprehensive Political Settlement in Cambodia. See Ratner (1993) 87 A.J.I.L. 1.

20 The UN Transitional Authority in East Timor (UNTAET) was established by S.C. Res. 1272 (2000); (2000) 39 I.L.M. 240. See Traub (2000) 79. Foreign Affairs 74. See also note (2000) 94 A.J.I.L. 105.

21 See Milano (2003) 14 E.J.I.L. 999; Tomuschat, ed., *Kosovo and the International Community* (2002); Weller (1999) 75 Int. Affairs 211. For background, see Malcolm, *Kosovo: A Short History* (2002).

22 There is also the case of Bosnia and Hercegovina. Under the Dayton Agreement, national, federal and regional govern-ments were established, but the Office of the High Representative (OHR) has interpreted its powers extensively, so that it has taken many important decisions and removed officeholders.

23 On the legality of this action, see below, p.784. On the SFRY and the FRY, see below, p.135.

24 S.C. Res. 1244 (1999), para.10.

25 See Cerone (2001) 12 E.J.I.L. 469.

and the US.[26] China, Russia and India and a majority of UN member states had not. Given the likelihood of a Russian veto in the Security Council, the Republic of Kosovo has not applied for admission to the UN. In 2008, the General Assembly requested an advisory opinion from the ICJ on the question: "Is the unilateral declaration of independence by the Provisional Self-Government of Kosovo in accordance with international law?"[27]

8.   An entity is not a state if it declines to be one, which for many years was the position of Taiwan (the Republic of China). Following the 1949 communist revolution in China, the defeated National Government withdrew from mainland China to the island of Taiwan. From that time until recently, both the Beijing and Taiwan Governments claimed to be the government of the one state of China, with Taiwan as a part of it. The Taiwan Government continued to represent China in the United Nations until 1971, when the Beijing Government replaced it.[28] The Beijing Government continues to maintain a "one China policy", regarding Taiwan as a province of the People's Republic of China. In contrast, in 2000 the Taiwan President spoke of Taiwan as an independent state[29] and the Taiwan Government has sought to be represented in the UN not on the basis that it should replace the Beijing Government, but, in effect, as the Government of a new member state.[30]

9.   It is accepted that a new state is automatically bound by international law upon attaining statehood.[31] Is this because it is deemed to consent to its being so bound? Or is it because there is a rule that says that it shall be so bound? If the latter is the case, why is that rule binding upon it? Is a new state's position different from that of an individual born into a state and automatically subject to its laws?[32]

B. Independence

AUSTRO-GERMAN CUSTOMS UNION CASE

Advisory Opinion. P.C.I.J. Reports, Series A/B, No.41 (1931)

By a Protocol of 1931 Austria and Germany reached preliminary agreement on a customs union establishing free trade between the two states. The proposed union "caused such disturbance in international relations that it is no exaggeration to speak of a European crisis."[33]

Article 88 of the Treaty of Saint-Germain 1919 provided:

---

[26]   22 out of 27 EU Member States, acting unilaterally, had recognised it, including the UK.

[27]   General Assembly Resolution A/RES/63/3.

[28]   See the note to App.II, below.

[29]   See Charney and Prescott (2000) 94 A.J.I.L. 453, 464. Election campaign statement. See also note (1999) 93 A.J.I.L. 896. In 2009 Taiwan government policy was to maintain the status quo.

[30]   See the letter accompanying Taiwan's 2003 application for UN membership UN Doc. A/58/197. Like a majority of states, the UK "does not recognise Taiwan as a state or country, nor its authorities as a government," FCO Minister, *Hansard*, HC Vol.463, col.1060 WA (July 24, 2007). The US maintains a "one China" policy, with the Beijing Government as the government; prior to 1979 it recognised the Taiwan Government as such. On Taiwan, see Henckaerts, ed., *The International Legal Status of Taiwan in the New World Order* (1996).

[31]   This is subject to any effect that recognition has; see below, p.130. Although new post-colonial states have objected to particular areas of international law and argue for different rules in those areas, they do not reject the system as a whole.

[32]   See Brierly, p.52; Fitzmaurice, above, p.15, n. 1, pp.165–167; Kelsen, *Principles of International Law* (2nd edn 1967), p.247.

[33]   Fachiri (1932) 13 B.Y.I.L. 68.

"The independence of Austria is inalienable otherwise than with the consent of the Council of the League of Nations. Consequently, Austria undertakes in the absence of the consent of the said Council to abstain from any act which might directly or indirectly or by any means whatever compromise her independence. ..."

A Protocol of 1922 concerning the economic independence of Austria in particular was to the same effect. The Council of the League of Nations asked the PCIJ whether Austria would be acting contrary to these provisions if it went ahead with the proposed union. The Court advised, by eight votes to seven, that the union would be incompatible with the Protocol of 1922. Seven judges who concurred in the Court's opinion (but not a majority of the Court) also thought that it would be contrary to art.88 of the Treaty of Saint-Germain. The following extracts are limited to the Court's discussion of the nature of independence as applied to states. It has been argued that in its assessment of the situation the Court placed as much emphasis upon the likelihood of a political union occurring as a further, separate step after the establishment of the proposed customs union as it did upon the customs union itself.[34]

Opinion of the Court

... irrespective of the definition of the independence of States which may be given by legal doctrine or may be adopted in particular instances in the practice of States, the independence of Austria, according to Article 88 of the Treaty of Saint-Germain, must be understood to mean the continued existence of Austria within her present frontiers as a separate State with sole right of decision in all matters economic, political, financial or other with the result that that independence is violated, as soon as there is any violation thereof, either in the economic, political, or any other field, these different aspects of independence being in practice one and indivisible ...

By "alienation", as mentioned in Article 88, must be understood any voluntary act by the Austrian State which would cause it to lose its independence or which would modify its independence in that its sovereign will would be subordinated to the will of another Power or particular group of Powers, or would even be replaced by such will.

SEPARATE OPINION OF JUDGE ANZILOTTI[35]

Independence ... is really no more than the normal condition of States according to international law; it may also be described as *sovereignty (suprema potestas)*, or *external sovereignty*, by which is meant that the State has over it no other authority than that of international law.

The conception of independence, regarded as the normal characteristic of States as subjects of international law, cannot be better defined than by comparing it with the exceptional and, to some extent, abnormal class of States known as "dependent States". These are States subject to the authority of one or more States. The idea of dependence therefore necessarily implies a relation between a superior State (suzerain, protector, *etc.*) and an inferior or subject State (vassal, *protégé, etc.*); the relation between the State which can legally impose its will and the State which is legally compelled to submit to that will. Where there is no such relation of superiority and subordination, it is impossible to speak of dependence within the meaning of international law.

It follows that the legal conception of independence has nothing to do with a State's subordination to international law or with the numerous and constantly increasing states of *de facto* dependence which characterise the relation of one country to other countries.

It also follows that the restrictions upon a State's liberty, whether arising out of ordinary international law or contractual engagements, do not as such in the least affect its independence. As long as these restrictions do not place the State under the legal authority of another State, the former remains an independent State however extensive and burdensome those obligations may be.

This is obviously the standpoint of the Treaty of Saint-Germain when it proclaims the independence of Austria despite the many serious restrictions it imposes upon her freedom in the economic, military and other spheres.

---

[34] See Borchard (1931) 25 A.J.I.L. 711 at 715.
[35] Judge Anzilotti was one of the seven judges in the majority who found the proposed union incompatible with art.88 of the Treaty of Saint-Germain as well as with the Protocol of 1922.

These restrictions do not put Austria under the authority of the other contracting States, which means that Austria is an independent State within the meaning of international law....

Notes

1. When the Montevideo Convention[36] refers to "capacity to enter into relations with other states" as a requirement of statehood it is referring to independence as that term is understood in Judge Anzilotti's opinion, i.e. independence in law from the authority of any other state (and hence the capacity under its national law to conduct relations with other states).

2. In the *North Atlantic Coast Fisheries* case,[37] the Permanent Court of Arbitration rejected a United States submission in the following terms:

    "... to hold that the United States, the grantee of the fishing right, has a voice under the treaty granting the right in the preparation of fishing legislation, involves recognition of a right in that country to participate in the internal legislation of Great Britain and her Colonies and to that extent would reduce these countries to a state of dependence."

    Elsewhere, dealing with the same submission, the Court stated:

    "... the exercise of such a right of consent by the United States would predicate an abandonment of independence in this respect by Great Britain ..."[38]

3. In the *Wimbledon* case[39] the Permanent Court of International Justice stated:

    "No doubt any convention creating an obligation of this kind [allowing international passage through the Kiel Canal] places a restriction upon the exercise of the sovereign rights of the State, in the sense that it requires them to be exercised in a certain way. But the right of entering into international engagements is an attribute of State sovereignty."

4. Units within a *federal state* may or may not be allowed by the federal constitution some freedom to conduct their own foreign affairs. If, and to the extent that, they are allowed to do so, such units are regarded by international law as having international personality. For example, the Republics of the former USSR were all entitled in law to conduct their own foreign affairs and two of them—Byelorussia (now Belarus) and the Ukraine—to a small extent did so.[40] Such units are not thereby states but international persons sui generis.

5. *Protected or dependent states*. These are a dying species which few seem anxious to preserve. In the nineteenth century, European powers sometimes masked a colonial situation by entering into a treaty of protection with an Asian or African state or chieftain, with the degree of sovereignty left with the protected state or tribe being limited, if not totally surrendered. Generally, the protecting state was responsible for the conduct of foreign relations, although precise terms of

---

[36] Above, p.91.
[37] *G.B. v U.S.*, Scott (1910) *Hague Court Reports* 141 at 170.
[38] Id. above, at 167.
[39] P.C.I.J. Rep, Series A, No.1, at p.25 (1923). See below p.222.
[40] See Dolan (1955) 4 I.C.L.Q. 629. Both of the Republics mentioned were original members of the UN, see below, App.II. On the apparently comparable position under the Russian Federation Constitution, see Gazzini (1996) 17 H.R.L.J. 93 at 94. See also art.32 of the German Basic Law on the treaty-making power of the German *Länder*.

the arrangement varied from case to case.[41] One example of a protected state until recently was the Indian protected state of Bhutan in the Himalayas.[42] Protected states are to be contrasted with independent states that, for reasons of convenience, freely choose to depute certain sovereign powers to other states. For example, certain of Liechtenstein's foreign relations are conducted for it by Switzerland.[43]

FRENCH INDEMNITY OF 1831

US Claims Commission. Moore, 5 Int. Arb. 4447 at 4472

France paid the US compensation to be distributed among US nationals in respect of certain damage caused during the Napoleonic Wars. Some claims were made that related to injuries apparently caused by Holland and Denmark and the question arose whether France was responsible for them. The report of the US Commission that distributed the compensation was supplemented by notes by Commissioner Kane indicating the general principles upon which the Commission had relied. The following extract from these notes concerns the above question.

1. Holland, after some ten years of political changes, during which though nominally independent she was tributary to all the projects of France, had received in the month of June 1806, a king of the Napoleon family. . . . The form of distinct sovereignties was presented to the public eye; but the energies of the Dutch people were directed more than ever to the advancement of the imperial policy. At last, in the concluding month of 1809, a new crisis approached. At a moment when the finances of Holland were in a state of extreme embarrassment, she was required to destroy her commerce with foreign nations, which formed the principal source of her revenues. Louis ventured to remonstrate. . . . He was reminded in reply, that the country of which he was sovereign was a French conquest, and that "his highest and imprescriptible duties were to the imperial crown;" . . .

The tenth article of the [Franco-Dutch] treaty of 16th March 1810 was as follows: "All merchandize, which has arrived in American vessels in the ports of Holland since the 1st of January 1809, shall be placed under sequestration, and shall belong to France, to be disposed of according to circumstances and to the political relations with the United States." . . .

It was for the value of these cargoes, that reclamations were made before the commissioners. The brief account which has been given of the political condition of Holland from the year 1809 till it was formally merged in the French empire [in July 1810], sufficiently explains the reason for allowing them. Holland was already a dependent kingdom, and Louis a merely nominal sovereign. The treaty was a form; in substance it was an imperial decree.

2. The spoliations to which Denmark ministered were of a different character. . . .

It may be, that the conduct of King Frederic was dictated by his anxiety to conciliate the favour of the French emperor; or perhaps he was moved by the portion of the spoil which might fall into his hands: we had nothing to do with his motives or his fears. The act was his own: the kingdom of Denmark was then, as now, independent. . . .

This then is the broad distinction between the cases of Holland and Denmark. The former was a nominal, the latter an actual sovereignty. The intervention of one was merely formal, and was exacted by force; the other was the voluntary pander to French avidity.

---

[41] See the *Nationality Decrees in Tunis and Morocco* case, P.C.I.J. Rep Series B, No.4, p.27 (1923); and the *Rights of Nationals of the U.S. in Morocco* case, I.C.J. Rep. 1952, p. 176. And see Baty (1921–2) 2 B.Y.I.L. 109.

[42] art.2, 1949 Treaty of Friendship between India and Bhutan, 157 B.F.S.P. 214, read: "The Government of India undertakes to exercise no interference in the internal administration of Bhutan. On its part the Government of Bhutan agrees to be guided by the advice of the Government of India in regard to its external relations." The replacement 2007 India-Bhutan Treaty of Friendship does not have such wording, referring instead to "respect of each other's independence" and "sovereignty" (preamble). Bhutan was admitted to the UN in 1971.

[43] See Kohn (1967) 61 A.J.I.L. 547 cf. the position of Western Samoa, whose foreign relations are conducted by New Zealand: see the 1962 Treaty of Friendship (1962) N.Z.T.S. 5.

Notes

1. Independence as a requirement of statehood means, to some extent, factual, as well as legal, independence from other states. Although it is accepted that states may influence the policies and conduct of another state, there may come a point, as this case suggests, where *factual* dependence by one state upon another is so great that it is really no more than a "puppet" state and will not be treated as meeting the requirement of independence. Lauterpacht proposed the following:

    "The first condition of statehood is that there must exist a government actually independent of that of any other State. . . . If a community, after having detached itself from the parent State, were to become, legally or actually, a satellite of another State, it would not be fulfilling the primary condition of independence and would not accordingly be entitled to recognition as a State."[44]

    He gave "Manchukuo" as an example of an entity that was not a state according to this test. "Manchukuo" came into being after Japan invaded Manchuria, a province of China, in 1931.[45] The following year Japan recognised "Manchukuo" as an independent state. Its territory was that of Manchuria. The League of Nations sent the Lytton Commission to "Manchukuo" to discover the facts. The Commission reported:

    "In the 'Government of Manchukuo,' Japanese officials are prominent and Japanese advisers are attached to all important Departments. Although the Premier and his Ministers are all Chinese, the heads of the various Boards of General Affairs, which, in the organisation of the new State, exercise the greatest measure of actual power, are Japanese. At first they were designated as advisers, but recently those holding the most important posts have been made full Government officials on the same basis as the Chinese. . . . They are doubtless not under the orders of the Tokyo Government, and their policy has not always coincided with the official policy either of the Japanese Government or of the Headquarters of the Kwantung Army. But in the case of all-important problems, these officials and advisers, some of whom were able to act more or less independently in the first days of the new organisation, have been constrained more and more to follow the direction of Japanese official authority. This authority, in fact, by reason of the occupation of the country by its troops, by the dependence of the 'Manchukuo Government' on those troops for the maintenance of its authority both internally and externally, in consequence, too, of the more and more important role entrusted to the South Manchuria Railway Company in the management of the railways under the jurisdiction of the 'Manchukuo Government,' and finally by the presence of its consuls, as liaison agents, in the most important urban centres, possesses in every contingency the means of exercising an irresistible pressure."[46]

    The Commission did not pronounce upon the specific question whether "Manchukuo" was an independent state. In the light of the Commission's Report, on February 24, 1933, the League of Nations Assembly resolved that "the sovereignty over Manchuria belongs to China."[47] By 1939,

---

[44] Lauterpacht, *Recognition in International Law* (1948), pp.26–29.
[45] See 1 Hackworth 333–338.
[46] L.N. Doc. C. 663. M 320. 1932, VII.
[47] L.N.O.J. Special Supp. No.112, p.75 (1933). On the Stimson Doctrine of Non-Recognition, which was prompted by the "Manchukuo" situation, see below, p.188.

only El Salvador, Germany, Hungary, Italy and Japan had recognised "Manchukuo." Manchuria was returned to China after the Second World War. Was it at any time an independent state according to the *Customs Union* case? Suppose that at the present time an existing state were to come under the influence of another state to such an extent (in a military, economic, or other sense) that the other state could dictate the composition of its Government and its policies? Would that state continue to be independent for the purposes of statehood?[48] Was Czecho-slovakia in 1969?[49]

2. In 1976, South Africa, in pursuance of its homelands or bantustan policy, granted independence to the Transkei, the homeland of the Xhosa people. Legal sovereignty over the Transkei was transferred to its new African Government which was in control in law of the internal and external affairs of the Transkei. On October 26, 1976, the United Nations General Assembly, by a vote of 134 to 0, with 1 abstention:

    (i)   *Strongly condemns* the establishment of bantustans as designed to consolidate the inhuman policies of *apartheid*, to destroy the territorial integrity of the country, to per-petuate white minority domination and to dispossess the African people of South Africa of their inalienable rights;

    (ii) *Rejects* the declaration of "independence" of the Transkei and declares it invalid;

    (iii) *Calls upon* all Governments to deny any form of recognition to the so-called independent Transkei and to refrain from having any dealings with the so-called independent Transkei or other bantustans;

    (iv) *Requests* all States to take effective measures to prohibit all individuals, corporations and other institutions under their jurisdiction from having any dealings with the so-called independent Transkei or other bantustans.[50]

    No state recognised the Transkei as a state, apart from South Africa.[51] The Transkei and the other homelands no longer exist following the transfer of power in South Africa in the mid-1990s. One interpretation of state practice in the matter is that "the Transkei was not a state because it was the embodiment of a fundamentally unlawful policy of *apartheid*".[52]

3. In 1965, Southern Rhodesia, a British self-governing colony, declared its independence. The rebel Smith Government sought in this way to continue white rule in Rhodesia. This would inevitably have given way to black majority rule if the normal constitutional progress towards independence had been allowed to take its course. The United Kingdom continued to claim sovereignty and applied economic and political sanctions short of the use of armed force to re-assert its authority. The United Nations Security Council imposed a comprehensive régime of economic sanctions upon the rebel Government and "[called] upon all states not to recognise this illegal racist

---

[48] See the discussion in Marek, above, p.91, n.1, pp. 162–180. On the relative nature of the independence of states, see Hart, *The Concept of Law* (2nd edn 1994), pp.221–226.

[49] See below, p.744.

[50] G.A. Res. 31/6, G.A.O.R., 31st Session, Supp. 39, p.10. The US abstained; although agreeing with the recommendation that the Transkei not be recognised, it considered the resolution too strongly worded in other respects. As to the non-recognition of Ciskei, see the *Gur* case, below, p.158.

[51] See Witkin (1977) 18 H.I.L.J. 605.

[52] Crawford, above, p.91, n.1, p.344. See also Richardson, (1978) 17 C.J.T.L. 185. When justifying its non-recognition of another homeland, Bophuthatswana, the UK referred to the question of *apartheid*: see below, p.138.

minority régime."[53] No state recognised Southern Rhodesia as a state. After guerrilla warfare, a political settlement was reached that led to independence in 1980 for Zimbabwe in accordance with the principle of self-determination. Thereupon, Security Council sanctions were terminated. From 1965 onwards, Southern Rhodesia could claim to have met the requirements of statehood in the Montevideo Convention.[54] In terms of the requirement of legal independence, the governing constitution (i.e. the one to look to when deciding who has the capacity to enter into relations with other states) is the one that is effective in the state's territory. In the case of Southern Rhodesia, this was the Smith Government's constitution.[55] The Southern Rhodesian case may, however, indicate that an additional requirement of statehood has evolved, namely that independence be achieved in accordance with the principle of self-determination.[56] A difficulty with requirements of statehood such as this, that look beyond legal independence and effective control of territory to moral or political considerations, is that legal rights and duties may become divorced from reality. In the case of Southern Rhodesia, for example, when Smith Government soldiers destroyed guerrilla bases on the Zambian side of the border, who was responsible in international law? The United Kingdom?

4.   A case in which the response by the United Nations to a colonial rebellion was strikingly different was that of Portuguese Guinea.[57] PAIGC, a national liberation movement, rebelled against the Portuguese administration and had attained control by armed force over two-thirds of the colony by September 1973 when it declared Guinea-Bissau's independence. In November 1973, while Portuguese troops were still in the field, the General Assembly welcomed "the recent accession to independence of the people of Guinea-Bissau, thereby creating the sovereign State of the Republic of Guinea-Bissau."[58] The Portuguese administration was overthrown by PAIGC in March 1974 and Guinea-Bissau was recognised as a state by 84 states by the end of May. Guinea-Bissau was recommended for UN membership by the Security Council in August 1974,[59] shortly before Portugal formally recognised its independence. Referring to the Guinea-Bissau and other cases, Crawford[60] suggests that in cases in which "the metropolitan state forcibly denies self-determination ... the principle of self-determination operates in favour of the statehood of the seceding territory, provided that the seceding government can properly be regarded as representative of the people of that territory ... where the insurgent's control is substantial and their legitimacy or representativeness is acknowledged, self-determination may legitimize recognition that would otherwise be premature."

5.   What if independence is seized by force by rebels with the assistance of another state contrary to art.2(4), United Nations Charter or to the principle of non-intervention? As to which, see below, Ch.11. Crawford[61] suggests:

---

[53]   See below, pp.802, 824. The General Assembly similarly called upon "all states not to recognise any form of independence in Southern Rhodesia without the prior establishment of a government based on majority rule in accordance with General Assembly Resolution 1514 (XX)": G.A. Res. 2379, G.A.O.R., 26th Sess., Supp. 18, p.57 (1968); (1968) 7 I.L.M. 1401. The resolution was adopted by 92 votes to 2, with 17 abstentions.

[54]   Above, p.91.

[55]   In *R. v Ndhlovu* (1968) (4) S.A. 515, the High Court of Rhodesia, Appellate Division, held that the Smith Government's constitution had replaced the British colonial constitution as the valid one, since the Smith Government was in effective control of Southern Rhodesia.

[56]   cf. Crawford, above, p.91, n.1, p.131. On the principle of self-determination, see below, p.104.

[57]   See Rousseau (1974) 78 R.G.D.I.P. 1166.

[58]   G.A. Res. 3061 (XXVIII), G.A.O.R., 28th Session, Supp. 30, p.2.

[59]   S.C. Res. 356 (1974), S.C.O.R., 29th Year, *Resolutions and Decisions*, p.15.

[60]   above, p.91, n.1, p.387.

[61]   above, p.91, n.1 p.148. Footnote omitted. This is one of a list of conclusions that "are to some extent *de lege ferenda*." On the rule as to title to illegally obtained territory, see below, p.188.

"Illegality of intervention in aid of independence of a self-determination unit does not then, as a matter of law, impair the status of the local unit. On the other hand, where a State illegally intervenes in and foments the secession of part of a metropolitan State, other States are under the same duty of non-recognition as in the case of illegal annexation of territory. An entity created in violation of the rules relating to the use of force in such circumstances will not be regarded as a State."

Thus, Indian assistance to Bangladesh, although arguably illegal, did not impair the latter's statehood given that Bangladesh was a unit to which the principle of self-determination applied.[62]

Following the invasion of northern Cyprus by Turkey in 1974[63] 36 per cent of Cyprus, north of a line running through Nicosia and Famagusta, was administered by the Turkish Federated State of Cyprus pending the establishment of an acceptable federal constitution for the one state of Cyprus. In 1983, however, an independent state, called the Turkish Republic of Northern Cyprus (TRNC), with its own constitution, was declared to have been established in the same area. The United Nations Security Council at once deplored "the purported secession of part of the Republic of Cyprus," resolved that the declaration was "legally invalid," and called upon "all states not to recognise any Cypriot State other than the Republic of Cyprus."[64] The Security Council response supports Crawford's view, supposing that Turkey's intervention in 1974 was illegal and the Turkish Cypriot entity was not a self-determination unit. So does the League of Nations' response to "Manchukuo."[65] Such cases do not often arise in practice; most commonly the occupied territory is annexed.

6. *Transdniestria* was formerly an autonomous part of the Moldovian SRR. When, after the dissolution of the USSR, the Republic of Moldova became an independent state, Transdniestria proclaimed its independence of that state as the Moldovian Republic of Transdniestria ("MRT") and, following the Transdniestria War of 1992, in which it was assisted by Russian troops, the MRT established itself as a de facto entity in full control of its territory. This consists mostly of a narrow valley on the eastern bank of the Dniester River and has a population of some 500,000, a large number of whom are of Russian origin. Russian troops remain in MRT territory. In *Ilascu v Moldova and Russia*,[66] the European Court of Human Rights found that:

"the MRT, set up in 1991–92 with the support of the Russian Federation, vested with organs of power and its own administration, remains under the effective authority, or at the very least under the decisive influence, of the Russian Federation, and in any event that it survives by virtue of the military, economic, financial and political support given to it by the Russian Federation."

On this basis, the Court held that Russia could be held responsible for the detention and ill

---

62 above, p.99, n.1, pp.140 et seq. For the facts, see below, p.745.
63 On the Turkish invasion of Cyprus, see below, p.746. See also *Opinion No. 10*, Arbitration Commission, EC Conference on Yugoslavia, below, p.137.
64 S.C. Res. 541 (1983), S.C.O.R., 38th Year, *Resolutions and Decisions*, p.15. cf. S.C. Res. 550 (1984), S.C.O.R., 39th Year, p.12. No state has recognised the TRNC, except Turkey. See Palmer (1986) 4 Boston U.I.L.J. 423. In 2003, the UN brokered Annan Plan for a new constitutional settlement for a single federal state of Cyprus stalled when the Turkish Cypriot Government was unable to agree to it. Negotiations were reactivated in 2004, but the Greek Cypriot population rejected the outcome in a referendum (the Turkish Cypriots approved it).
65 On "Manchukuo," see above, p.100.
66 2004–VIII; 40 E.H.R.R. 1030 para.392.

treatment of the applicants by the MRT authorities under the European Convention on Human Rights. Russia is the only state that has recognised the MRT as a state.

C. Self-determination[67]

The principle of self-determination is a controversial one. It has a long history in international relations as a reason for the cession of territory from one state to another and for the use of plebiscites to establish the wishes of the inhabitants in this connection. Under the United Nations Charter, it became the cornerstone of the General Assembly's decolonisation policy of the 1960s and 1970s. The controversy has concerned both the principle's status in international law and its meaning. It was not a part of international law before the United Nations Charter.[68] The evidence of the following materials suggests that the point has been reached where the principle has generated a rule of international law by which the political future of a colonial or similar non-independent territory should be determined in accordance with the wishes of its inhabitants, within the limits of the principle of *uti posseditis*.[69] It does not extend to claims for independence by minority groups or units in a non-colonial context. The principle may, however, have an internal, as well as an external aspect: it may require that governments generally have a democratic base, and that minorities be allowed political autonomy.[70] The 1966 International Covenants on Human Rights, common art.1, below, p.552, each restate the right to self-determination as a matter of treaty law, although the meaning of the Covenant provisions may differ from that in customary international law.[71] The materials in this section are limited to political self-determination. Economic self-determination is considered in Ch.8.

DECLARATION ON THE GRANTING OF INDEPENDENCE TO COLONIAL TERRITORIES AND PEOPLES[72]

G.A. Res. 1514 (XV). December 14, 1960. G.A.O.R. 15th Sess., Supp. 16, p.66

The General Assembly ... Declares that:

1. The subjection of peoples to alien subjugation, domination and exploitation constitutes a denial of

---

[67] See Cassese, *Self-Determination of Peoples* (1995); Espiell, *The Right to Self-Determination: Implementation of UN Resolutions*, UN Doc. E/CN.4/Sub.2/390 (1980); Klabbers (2006) 28 H.R.Q. 186; Knopp, *Diversity and Self-Determination in International Law* (2002); Koskenniemi (1994) 43 I.C.L.Q. 241; McCorquodale (1994) 43 I.C.L.Q. 857; Müllerson, *International Law, Rights and Politics* (1994), Ch.2; Pomerance, *Self-Determination in Law and Practice* (1982); Quane (1998) 47 I.C.L.Q. 537; Raic, *Statehood and the Law of Self-Determination* (2002); Rigo Sureda, *The Evolution of the Right to Self-Determination* (1973); Shaw, *Title to Territory in Africa* (1986), Ch.3; Tomuschat, ed., *Modern Law of Self-Determination* (1993); Umozurike, *Self-Determination in International Law* (1972).

[68] See the report of the International Committee of Jurists in the *Aaland Islands* case, L.N.O.J., Special Supp. No.3, p.5 (1920), and Oppenheim, Vol.I, p.282.

[69] As to compliance with the rule as a requirement of statehood, see above, p.102. On the legality of the use of force to repress a war of national liberation, i.e. one aimed at furthering the principle of self-determination, see below, p.739.

[70] On internal self-determination, see Cassese, above, p.111, n.70, Ch.5; and Franck (1992) 86 A.J.I.L. 46.

[71] See Cassese above; and McGoldrick, *The Human Rights Committee* (1991), Ch.5.

[72] The resolution was adopted by 89 votes to 0, with nine abstentions. The abstaining states were Australia, Belgium, Dominican Republic, France, Portugal, South Africa, Spain, the UK and the US.

fundamental human rights, is contrary to the Charter of the United Nations and is an impediment to the promotion of world peace and co-operation;

2. All peoples have the right to self-determination; by virtue of that right they freely determine their political status and freely pursue their economic, social and cultural development;

3. Inadequacy of political, economic, social or education preparedness should never serve as a pretext for delaying independence;

4. All armed action or repressive measures of all kinds directed against dependent peoples shall cease in order to enable them to exercise peacefully and freely their right to complete independence, and the integrity of their national territory shall be respected;

5. Immediate steps shall be taken, in Trust and Non-Self-Governing Territories or all other territories which have not yet attained independence, to transfer all powers to the peoples of those territories, without any conditions or reservations, in accordance with their freely expressed will and desire, without any distinction as to race, creed or colour, in order to enable them to enjoy complete independence and freedom;

6. Any attempt aimed at the partial or total disruption of the national unity and the territorial integrity of a country is incompatible with the Purposes and Principles of the Charter of the United Nations;

7. All States shall observe faithfully and strictly the provisions of the Charter of the United Nations, the Universal Declaration of Human Rights and the present Declaration on the basis of equality, non-interference in the internal affairs of all States, and respect for the sovereign rights of all peoples and their territorial integrity.

Notes

1. The 1960 Declaration, which has been the continual point of reference in the General Assembly's decolonisation practice,[73] builds upon arts 1, 55 and 56 of the Charter[74] and has been supplemented by the 1970 Programme of Action for the Full Implementation of the Declaration[75] and the 1970 Declaration on Principles of International Law.[76]

2. Resolution 1514 does not state that title to colonial and similar non-independent territory that is not in accord with the wishes of its people is invalid. The position is instead that "immediate steps" should be taken to achieve independence in accordance with the principle of self-determination. Resolution 1514 proposes self-determination within existing colonial boundaries (para.6). The post-colonial states in particular have taken the view that it would be too disruptive of international stability to allow self-determination within those boundaries for minorities (e.g. the Biafrans in Nigeria).[77] Limited as it is to colonial or similar territories, Resolution 1514 may well have served—very successfully—most of its purpose.

3. On the relationship between the principles of self-determination and *uti possidetis*, with the latter prevailing, as in Resolution 1514, para.6, see the *Frontier Dispute* case, below, p.203, and *Opinion No. 2*, EC Arbitration Commission, below, p.110.

4. In 1961, the General Assembly established the Special Committee on the Situation with Regard to the Implementation of the Declaration on the Granting of Independence to Colonial Countries and Peoples, known as the Special Committee of 24 on Decoloniation, to assist in imple-

---

[73] See the *Western Sahara* case, below, p.106.
[74] Below, App.I.
[75] G.A. Res. 2621, G.A.O.R., 25th Session, Supp. 16, p.10 (1970). See also G.A. Res. 1541 (XV), G.A.O.R., 15th Session, Supp. 16, p.29 (1960).
[76] Below, App.III.
[77] See below, p.131.

mentation of Resolution 1514. It is currently composed of 28 UN member states, none being former colonial powers.

WESTERN SAHARA CASE[78]

Advisory Opinion. I.C.J. Reports 1975, p.12

Western Sahara was colonised by Spain in 1884 and remained until 1976 a Spanish colony known as the Spanish Sahara. Its 1974 census population of 74,900 consisted mostly of nomadic Saharan tribesmen. It is rich in phosphates, in the production of which it is an important competitor of Morocco in the international phosphates industry, and has abundant fishing resources. In 1966, the General Assembly indicated that the decolonisation of the territory should occur on the basis of the right to self-determination as expressed in General Assembly Resolution 1514 (XV) and invited Spain, in consultation with the neighbouring states of Mauritania and Morocco, to "determine at the earliest possible date ... the procedures for the holding of a referendum under United Nations auspices with a view to enabling the indigenous population of the territory to exercise freely its right to self-determination."[79] After much delay, Spain agreed to hold a referendum of the people in the Spanish Sahara under United Nations supervision in 1975. At this point, King Hassan, who had previously supported the application of the principle of self-determination to the Spanish Sahara, claimed the territory for Morocco on the basis of "historic title" predating Spain's colonisation of the territory. Mauritania made a similar, overlapping claim. On the initiative of these two states, the General Assembly requested in 1974 an opinion from the Court on the following questions:

I   Was Western Sahara (Rio de Oro and Sakiet El Hamra) at the time of colonisation by Spain a territory belonging to no one (*terra nullius*)? If the answer to the first question is in the negative,

II   What were the legal ties between this territory and the Kingdom of Morocco and the Mauritanian entity?

In the course of considering whether it should give the requested opinion, the Court found it necessary "to recall briefly the basic principles governing the decolonisation policy of the General Assembly," which it did in the following extract. Further extracts from the Court's opinion are printed below, p.176.

Opinion of the Court

54. The Charter of the United Nations, in Article 1, paragraph 2, indicates, as one of the purposes of the United Nations: "To develop friendly relations among nations based on respect for the principle of equal rights and self-determination of peoples ..." This purpose is further developed in Articles 55 and 56 of the Charter. Those provisions have direct and particular relevance for non-self-governing territories, which are dealt with in Chapter XI of the Charter. As the Court stated in its Advisory Opinion of 21 June 1971 on *The Legal Consequences for States of the Continued Presence of South Africa in Namibia (South West Africa) notwithstanding Security Council Resolutions 276* (1970):

---

[78] See Shaw (1978) 49 B.Y.I.L. 119 and Smith (1977) 9 C. W. R. J.I.L. 135.
[79] G.A. Res. 2229, G.A.O.R., 21st Session, Supp. 16, p.72 (1966).

... the subsequent development of international law in regard to non-self-governing territories, as enshrined in the Charter of the United Nations, made the principle of self-determination applicable to all of them (*I.C.J. Reports* 1971, p.31).

55. The principle of self-determination as a right of peoples, and its application for the purpose of bringing all colonial situations to a speedy end, were enunciated in the Declaration on the Granting of Independence to Colonial Countries and Peoples, General Assembly resolution 1514 (XV). ... The above provisions, in particular paragraph 2, thus confirm and emphasize that the application of the right of self-determination requires a free and genuine expression of the will of the peoples concerned.

56. The Court had occasion to refer to this resolution in the above-mentioned Advisory Opinion of 21 June 1971. Speaking of the development of international law in regard to non-self-governing territories, the Court there stated:

A further important stage in this development was the Declaration on the Granting of Independence to Colonial Countries and Peoples (General Assembly resolution 1514 (XV) of 14 December 1960), which embraces all peoples and territories which "have not yet attained independence." (*I.C.J. Reports* 1971, p. 31).

It went on to state:

... the Court must take into consideration the changes which have occurred in the supervening half-century, and its interpretation cannot remain unaffected by the subsequent development of law, through the Charter of the United Nations and by way of customary law (ibid.).

The Court then concluded:

In the domain to which the present proceedings relate, the last fifty years, as indicated above, have brought important developments. These developments leave little doubt that the ultimate objective of the sacred trust was the self-determination and independence of the peoples concerned. In this domain, as elsewhere, the *corpus iuris gentium* has been considerably enriched, and this the Court, if it is faithfully to discharge its functions, may not ignore. (ibid. pp. 31 et seq.)

57. General Assembly resolution 1514 (XV) provided the basis for the process of decolonization which has resulted since 1960 in the creation of many States which are today Members of the United Nations. It is complemented in certain of its aspects by General Assembly resolution 1541 (XV), which has been invoked in the present proceedings. The latter resolution contemplates for non-self-governing territories more than one possibility, namely:

(a) emergence as a sovereign independent State;

(b) free association with an independent State; or

(c) integration with an independent State.

At the same time, certain of its provisions give effect to the essential feature of the right of self-determination as established in resolution 1514 (XV). Thus principle VII of resolution 1541 (XV) declares that: "Free association should be the result of a free and voluntary choice by the Peoples of the territory concerned expressed through informed and democratic processes." Again, principle IX of resolution 1541 declares that:

Integration should have come about in the following circumstances:

(b) The integration should be the result of the freely expressed wishes of the territory's peoples acting with the full knowledge of the change in their status, their wishes having been expressed through informed and democratic processes, impartially conducted and based on universal adult suffrage. The United Nations could, when it deems it necessary, supervise these processes.

58. General Assembly resolution 2625 (XXV), "Declaration on Principles of International Law concerning

Friendly Relations and Co-operation among States in accordance with the Charter of the United Nations"[80] ... mentions other possibilities besides independence, association or integration. But in doing so it reiterates the basic need to take account of the wishes of the people concerned ...

59. The validity of the principle of self-determination, defined as the need to pay regard to the freely expressed will of peoples, is not affected by the fact that in certain cases the General Assembly has dispensed with the requirement of consulting the inhabitants of a given territory. Those instances were based either on the consideration that a certain population did not constitute a "people" entitled to self-determination or on the conviction that a consultation was totally unnecessary, in view of special circumstances.

Notes

1.   The General Assembly took note "with appreciation"[81] of the Court's opinion. In the *Western Sahara* case, the Court accepted (see para.56) that the principle of self-determination is a part of customary international law. In the *East Timor* case, the Court recognised its *erga omnes* character.[82] Other sources suggest that the principle of self-determination is also *ius cogens*.[83]

2.   The history of the *Western Sahara* case after the Court's opinion shows that the principle of self-determination may not always be easy to implement despite the wishes of the General Assembly.[84] On November 4, 1975, Morocco, which had interpreted the Court's opinion (quite wrongly) as recognising its claim to the territory, began its "Green (i.e. peaceful) March" into Western Sahara. The March was made by about 200,000 unarmed civilians. On November 6, the Security Council, which had earlier vainly called for "restraint and moderation"[85] on the part of the states concerned (including Algeria, which was backing the claims of Polisario—the independence movement of the Saharans—against Morocco and Mauritania) adopted a resolution deploring the March and calling for its termination.[86] This did not occur until a week or so later, after tripartite talks between Spain, Morocco and Mauritania had led to an agreement between the three states whereby Western Sahara would be divided between Morocco (two-thirds) and Mauritania (one-third) and Spain would retain a 35 per cent interest in the phosphates industry.

In December 1975, following the tripartite agreement, the General Assembly adopted two resolutions which are difficult to reconcile. In the first[87] (the "Algerian" resolution), it requested Spain to take immediate steps to enable the Saharans to exercise their right of self-determination and made no reference to the tripartite agreement. In the second[88] (the "Moroccan" resolution), it took note of the tripartite agreement (thereby appearing to recognise the arrangement for the future of Western Sahara which it proposed) and requested the interim administration established in the territory by Spain to take the necessary steps to realise the self-determination of the inhabitants. In 1976, Spain withdrew from the territory and Morocco and Mauritania took over in accordance with the tripartite agreement. In the same year, Polisario proclaimed the Saharwi Arab Democratic Republic (SADR). The SADR has been admitted as a member of the African Union, formerly the OAU,[89] and is recognised by over 70 states, although

---

80   Ed. Below, App.III.
81   G.A. Res. 3458A, G.A.O.R., 30th Session, Supp. 34, p.116, (1975).
82   I.C.J. Rep. 1995, p.90 at 102. See also the *Wall* case, I.C.J. Rep. 2004, p.136 at 172.
83   See, e.g. Brownlie, p.512; and Cassese, above, p.104, n.70, p.203. cf. the Commentary to art,.40, ILC Draft Articles on Responsibility of States for Internationally Wrongful Acts, below, p.451.
84   See Franck (1976) 70 A.J.I.L. 694.
85   S.C. Res. 377 (1975), S.C.O.R., 20th year, *Resolutions and Decisions*, p.8.
86   S.C. Res. 380 (1975), p.9.
87   G.A. Res. 3458A, above, n.84.
88   G.A. Res. 3458B, G.A.O.R., 30th Session, Supp. 34, p.117 (1975).
89   See Naldi (1982) 26 J. African L. 152.

these do not include the US or the UK.[90] In 1979, Mauritania renounced its claims to the Western Sahara. Since then Morocco has taken control of nearly all of the territory of the Western Sahara, although Polisario continued to wage a guerrilla war until a 1991 ceasefire. A 2003 settlement plan (the Baker plan) proposed by the UN Secretary General's Personal Envoy was accepted by Polisario, but not by Morocco.[91] The plan provided for self-determination after a transitional period, following a referendum in which voters would have the choices of independence, integration into Morocco, or self-government or autonomy within Morocco.

3.   Another case of lack of respect for a time for the principle of self- determination by a neighbouring state is that of *East Timor*.[92] East Timor, which was a Portuguese colony, shares an island with Indonesia. In 1974, Indonesia and Australia agreed that the best solution for the security of the region when Portugal relinquished the territory would be for it to join Indonesia. An independence movement within East Timor—Fretilin—opposed this solution. In August 1975, it used force to seize control over the territory from Portugal and declared its independence. In December 1975, Indonesia invaded East Timor and defeated the Fretilin forces, although a guerrilla war continued. Later in the same month the General Assembly[93] and the Security Council[94] called upon Indonesia to withdraw and upon all states to allow the people of East Timor to decide their own future in accordance with the principle of self-determination. For many years, Indonesia refused to withdraw, but in 1999 it allowed a UN supervised referendum in which the people voted for independence. After protracted resistance by anti-independence militia forces supported by the Indonesian army, in 2002 the new state of Timor Leste was internationally recognised.

4.   The Special Committee of 24 on Decolonisation and the General Assembly have not applied Resolution 1514 in the usual way in the case of *Gibraltar*. In 1964, after Spain had raised the question of its status, the Committee reached a consensus inviting Spain and the United Kingdom to conduct "conversations in order to find . . . a negotiated solution, in keeping with the provisions of Resolution 1514 (XV) taking duly into account the opinions expressed by members of the Committee and bearing in mind the interests of the population of the territory."[95] The request for a "negotiated solution" was unusual, as were the references to "the opinions expressed by members of the Committee" (which were not unanimous) and the "interests" (not the wishes) of the inhabitants. The Committee also rejected the 1967 referendum held by the United Kingdom of residents of Gibraltar on their political future.[96] More recently, Spain and the UK agreed on joint sovereignty over Gibraltar, but this was thwarted by a 2003 referendum by the Gibraltar Government of its 29,000 inhabitants who again overwhelmingly favoured remaining British.[97] The Committee and the General Assembly have taken the view that the wishes of the current population should not be paramount in the case of Gibraltar because it is

---

90   The UK recognises neither the Moroccan nor the SADR claim and regards the issue of sovereignty as "undetermined": *Hansard*, HC Vol.442, col.1496 (2004). On the "statehood" of the SADR, see Naldi (1985) 25 Ind. J.I.L. 448.

91   On the Plan, see the Secretary General's Report, UN Doc. S/2003/1016. The Plan is supported by the General Assembly, G.A. 58/109 (2003), and the Security Council, S.C. Res. 1495 (2003). On UN-promoted negotiations between the parties in 2008, see the Secretary General's Report, S/2009/200. The UN operates in the Western Sahara through its Mission for the Referendum in Western Sahara (MINURSO).

92   See Elliott (1978) 27 I.C.L.Q. 238. On the *East Timor* case before the ICJ, see below, p.867.

93   G.A. Res. 3485, G.A.O.R., 30th Session, Supp. 34, p.118 (1975). The resolution was adopted by 72 votes to 10 with 43 abstentions.

94   S.C. Res. 384 (1975), S.C.O.R., 20th year, *Resolutions and Decisions*, p.10. The resolution was adopted unanimously.

95   Cmnd. 2632, p.14. See also G.A. Res. 2070, G.A.O.R. 20th Session, Supp. 14, p.58 (1965).

96   See Cmnd. 3735, p.15. The result of the referendum was that 12,138 wanted Gibraltar to remain in association with the UK; 44 wanted it to become a part of Spain.

97   See the 2003 Special Committee of 24 Report, UN Doc. A/58/23, Pt II, pp.8–9.

an imported, colonial population, replacing the earlier, largely Spanish population which left the territory at the time of its capture in the early eighteenth century.[98] The Committee and the General Assembly have adopted the same approach to the *Falkland Islands*, with Argentina and the UK being invited to seek a negotiation "taking due account of the *interests*" of the population.[99]

5. *Tibet*. Does Tibet have a right to self-determination?[100] The United Kingdom position is as follows:

> "We have made it clear to the Chinese Government, and publicly, that we do not support Tibetan independence. Like every other EU member state, and the United States, we regard Tibet as part of the People's Republic of China."[101]

As to *internal* self-determination, it has stated:

> "We consider the position the Dalai Lama has stated publicly ... that he opposes violence and is seeking meaningful autonomy within the framework of the Chinese constitution, provides a basis for a negotiated settlement."[102]

OPINION NO. 2

Arbitration Commission, EC Conference on Yugoslavia[103]: Badinter, Chairman; Corosaniti, Herzog, Petry, Tomas y Valiente, members. January 11, 1992. 92 I.L.R. 167

Opinion of the Commission

On 20 November 1991 the Chairman of the Arbitration Commission received a letter from Lord Carrington, Chairman of the Conference on Yugoslavia, requesting the Commission's opinion on the following question put by the Republic of Serbia:

> Does the Serbian population in Croatia and Bosnia-Hercegovina, as one of the constituent peoples of Yugoslavia, have the right to self-determination? ...

1. The Commission considers that international law as it currently stands does not spell out all the implications of the right to self-determination.

However, it is well established that, whatever the circumstances, the right to self-determination must not involve changes to existing frontiers at the time of independence (*uti possidetis juris*) except where the States concerned agree otherwise.

2. Where there are one or more groups within a State constituting one or more ethnic, religious or language communities, they have the right to recognition of their identity under international law.

---

[98] Following the occupation of the territory by the British, Gibraltar was populated during the 18th century by Genoese, Maltese, Moroccans, British and others.

[99] Special Committee Resn. A/AC.109/2003/24 (2003). And see G.A. Res. 2065, G.A.O.R. 20th Session, Supp.14, p.57 (1965). Almost all of the 3,000 civilian inhabitants of the island are British nationals who strongly favour retaining their association with the UK: see further below, p.183.

[100] Vanit Van Prag, *The Status of Tibet: History, Rights and Prospects in International Law* (1987), argues that Tibet has a claim to be a state.

[101] Mr Milliband, Foreign Secretary, *Hansard*, HC, Vol.481, col.30 WS (October 29, 2008).

[102] FCO Minister of State, *Hansard*, HC, Vol.485, col.703 WA (December 16, 2008).

[103] On the Commission, see below, p.115.

As the Commission emphasised in its *Opinion No. 1* [below, p.113] ... the—now peremptory—norms of inter-national law require States to ensure respect for the rights of minorities. This requirement applies to all the Republics *vis-à-vis* the minorities on their territory.

The Serbian population in Bosnia-Hercegovina and Croatia must therefore be afforded every right accorded to minorities under international conventions as well as national and international guarantees consistent with the principles of international law and the provisions of Chapter II of the Draft Convention of 4 November 1991,[104] which has been accepted by these Republics.

3. Article 1 of the two 1966 international covenants on human rights establishes that the principle of the right to self-determination serves to safeguard human rights. By virtue of that right every individual may choose to belong to whatever ethnic, religious or language community he or she wishes.

In the Commission's view one possible consequence of this principle might be for the members of the Serbian population in Bosnia-Hercegovina and Croatia to be recognised under agreements between the Republics as having the nationality of their choice, with all the rights and obligations which that entails with respect to the States concerned.

4. The Arbitration Commission is therefore of the opinion:

(i) that the Serbian population in Bosnia-Hercegovina and Croatia is entitled to all the rights accorded to minorities and ethnic groups under international law and under the provisions of the draft Convention of the Conference on Yugoslavia of 4 November 1991, to which the Republics of Bosnia-Hercegovina and Croatia have undertaken to give effect; and

(ii) that the Republics must afford the members of those minorities and ethnic groups all the human rights and fundamental freedoms recognised in international law, including, where appropriate, the right to choose their nationality.

Notes

1. Before 1991, Croatia and Bosnia-Herzegovina were two of the six republics within the one state of the Socialist Federal Republic of Yugoslavia (SFRY). For an account of the dissolution of the SFRY and its replacement by separate states, see below, p.135 et seq.

2. The population of Croatia in the SFRY was ethnically 78 per cent Croat and 12 per cent Serbian, plus other minorities, with the Serbians being in the majority in the areas in which they mostly lived. In the republic of Bosnia-Herzegovina the population was 44 per cent Muslim, 31 per cent Serbian and 17 per cent Croat, again with majorities of each group in areas of concentration. On December 19, 1991, a Serbian Republic of Krajina was declared in Serbian enclaves in Croatia. On January 9, 1992, a Republic of the Serbian People of Bosnia-Hercegovina (*Republika Srpskă*) was declared by Serbs in Bosnia-Hercegovina.

    In *Opinion No.2*, the Arbitration Commission concluded that the principle of self-determination did not extend to the Serbian populations in Croatia and Bosnia-Hercegovina so that they would be entitled to have their political future determined in accordance with their wishes. Instead, the principle of *uti possidetis*, which had been developed in the UN in the colonial context, was applied to the non-colonial context of the SFRY.[105] The approach of the Commission was to emphasise the international law obligations of Croatia and Bosnia-Hercegovina towards mino-rities,[106] rather than to interpret the principle of external self-determination in the Serbs' favour. What if Krajina or *Republika Srpskă* had obtained their independence by armed force (which they did not do)? Would they have been states?

3. Slovenia and Croatia justified their declarations of independence in 1991 by reference to the

---

[104] Ed. See below, p.134.

[105] See further, *Opinion No.3*, below, p.118. For criticism of the Commission approach to self-determination, see Pomerance (1998) 20 Mich..J.I.L. 98.

[106] On the rights of minorities, see the literature below, p.546, n.79. The Commission's characterisation of the rights of minorities as "peremptory" norms (ius cogens) is new. On peremptory norms, see below, p.694.

principle of self-determination. For example, the Croatian declaration refers to the "inalienable ... right of the Croatian nation to self-determination, including the right of disassociation".[107] The Arbitration Commission was not called upon to consider this justification in *Opinion No.2*, or in its other opinions concerning the recognition of the SFRY republics as states.[108] There is little evidence in United Nations or other state practice to suggest that the right to political self-determination would apply outside the colonial or similar context[109] to groups or units within an existing state, such as the SFRY. In other contexts, the principle does not mean that the political status of a minority group (e.g. the Scots, the Kurds, the French Canadians) in an existing state must be determined in accordance with their wishes, which might result in their secession. Everything terms upon the elusive concept of a "people", which Resolution 1514 and subsequent practice identify as the right holder. Higgins considers the question in the non-colonial context as follows[110]:

"... who exactly is entitled to the right to self-determination? We have seen from the Covenant and other instruments that it is 'all peoples' who are entitled to the right. But what are we to understand by that? There are really two possibilities—that 'peoples' means the entire people of a state, or that 'peoples' means all persons comprising distinctive groupings on the basis of race, ethnicity, and perhaps religion.

The emphasis in all the relevant instruments, and in the state practice (by which I mean statements, declarations, positions taken) on the importance of territorial integrity, means that 'peoples' is to be understood in the sense of *all* the peoples of a given territory. Of course, all members of distinct minority groups are part of the peoples of the territory. In that sense they too, as individuals, are the holders of the right of self-determination. But minorities *as such* do not have a right of self-determination. That means, in effect, that they have no right to secession, to independence, or to join with comparable groups in other states."

4.   *Quebec*. In the *Reference re Secession of Quebec* case,[111] the Supreme Court of Canada was asked: "Does international law give the National Assembly, legislature or government of Quebec the right to effect the secession of Quebec from Canada unilaterally?" Answering the question in the negative, the Court stated:

"In summary, the international law right to self-determination only generates, at best, a right to external self-determination in situations of former colonies; where a people is oppressed, as for example under foreign military occupation; or where a definable group is denied meaningful access to government to pursue their political, economic, social and cultural development. In all three situations, the people in question are entitled to a right to external self-determination because they have been denied the ability to exert internally their right to self-determination. Such exceptional circumstances are manifestly inapplicable to Quebec under existing conditions. Accordingly, neither the population of the province of Quebec, even if

---

[107] Blaustein and Flanz, eds, *Constitutions of the Countries of the World*, Release 92–3, pp.119, 123. cf. the Slovenian declaration, Release 92–6, p.55. The Slovenian population is 90 per cent Slovene, with small ethnic minorities of Serbs, Croats and Hungarians.

[108] See *Opinions No.1* and *No.8*, below, pp.113, 114.

[109] The General Assembly has accepted that the Palestinians are a self-determination unit: see, e.g. G.A. Res. ES-7/2, G.A.O.R., 7th Emergency Session, Supp. 1, p.3 (1980). The inhabitants of South Africa were formerly classified in the same way: see, e.g. G.A. Res. 33/24, 33rd Session, Supp. 45 p.137 (1978).

[110] *Problems and Process* (1994), p.124.

[111] (1998) 2 S.C.R. 217 para.138.

characterized in terms of 'people' or 'peoples', nor its representative institutions, the National Assembly, the legislature or government of Quebec, possess a right, under international law, to secede unilaterally from Canada."

D. Extinction and Succession of States

OPINION NO. 1

Arbitration Commission, EC Conference on Yugoslavia: Badinter, Chairman; Corosaniti, Herzog, Petry, Tomas y Valiente, members. November 29, 1991. 92 I.L.R. 162

Opinion of the Commission

The Chairman of the Arbitration Commission received the following letter from Lord Carrington, Chairman of the Conference on Yugoslavia, on 20 November 1991: . . .

Serbia considers that those Republics which have declared or would declare themselves independent or sovereign have seceded or would secede from the SFRY which would otherwise continue to exist.

Other Republics on the contrary consider that there is no question of secession, but the question is one of a disintegration or breaking-up of the SFRY as the result of the concurring will of a number of Republics. They consider that the six Republics are to be considered equal successors to the SFRY, without any of them or group of them being able to claim to be the continuation thereof.

I should like the Arbitration Committee to consider the matter in order to formulate any opinion or recommendation which it might deem useful. . . .

1. The Commission considers:

(a) that the answer to the question should be based on the principles of public international law which serve to define the conditions on which an entity constitutes a State; that in this respect, the existence or disappearance of the State is a question of fact; that the effects of recognition by other States are purely declaratory;

(b) that the State is commonly defined as a community which consists of a territory and a population subject to an organized political authority; that such a State is characterized by sovereignty;

(c) that, for the purpose of applying these criteria, the form of internal political organization and the constitutional provisions are mere facts, although it is necessary to take them into consideration in order to determine the Government's sway over the population and the territory;

(d) that in the case of a federal-type State, which embraces communities that possess a degree of autonomy and, moreover, participate in the exercise of political power within the framework of institutions common to the Federation, the existence of the State implies that the federal organs represent the components of the Federation and wield effective power;

(e) that, in compliance with the accepted definition in international law, the expression "State succession", means the replacement of one State by another in the responsibility for the international relations of territory. This occurs whenever there is a change in the territory of the State. The phenomenon of State succession is governed by the principles of international law, from which the Vienna Conventions of 23 August 1978 and 8 April 1983 have drawn inspiration. In compliance with these principles, the outcome of succession should be equitable, the States concerned being free to settle terms and conditions by agreement. Moreover, the peremptory norms of general international law and, in particular, respect for the fundamental rights of the individual and the rights of peoples and minorities, are binding on all the parties to the succession.

2. The Arbitration Commission notes that:

(a)—although the SFRY has until now retained its international personality, notably inside international organizations, the Republics have expressed their desire for independence;

— in Slovenia, by a referendum in December 1990, followed by a declaration of independence on 25 June 1991, which was suspended for three months and confirmed on 8 October 1991;

— in Croatia, by a referendum held in May 1991, followed by a declaration of independence on 25 June 1991, which was suspended for three months and confirmed on 8 October 1991;

— in Macedonia, by a referendum held in September 1991 in favour of a sovereign and independent Macedonia within an association of Yugoslav States;

— In Bosnia and Hercegovina, by a sovereignty resolution adopted by Parliament on 14 October 1991, whose validity has been contested by the Serbian community of the Republic of Bosnia and Hercegovina.

(b) The composition and workings of the essential organs of the Federation, be they the Federal Presidency, the Federal Council, the Council of the Republics and the Provinces, the Federal Executive Council, the Constitutional Court or the Federal Army, no longer meet the criteria of participation and representativeness inherent in a federal State;

(c) The recourse to force has led to armed conflict between the different elements of the Federation which has caused the death of thousands of people and wrought considerable destruction within a few months. The authorities of the Federation and the Republics have shown themselves to be powerless to enforce respect for the succeeding ceasefire agreements concluded under the auspices of the European Communities or the United Nations Organization.

3. Consequently, the Arbitration Commission is of the opinion:

— that the Socialist Federal Republic of Yugoslavia is in the process of dissolution;

— that it is incumbent upon the Republics to settle such problems of State succession as may arise from this process in keeping with the principles and rules of international law, with particular regard for human rights and the rights of peoples and minorities;

— that it is up to those Republics that so wish, to work together to form a new association endowed with the democratic institutions of their choice.

OPINION NO. 8

Arbitration Commission, EC Conference on Yugoslavia: Badinter, Chairman; Corosaniti, Herzog, Petry, Tomas y Valiente, members. July 4, 1992. 92 I.L.R. 199

Opinion of the Commission

On 18 May the Chairman of the Arbitration Commission received a letter from Lord Carrington, Chairman of the Conference for Peace in Yugoslavia, putting three questions to the Commission. ...

Question No. 2
In its *Opinion No. 1* of 29 November 1991[112] the Arbitration Commission was of the opinion "that the SFRY (was) in the process of dissolution". Can this dissolution now be regarded as complete? ...

2. The dissolution of a State means that it no longer has legal personality, something which has major repercussions in international law. It therefore calls for the greatest caution.

The Commission finds that the existence of a federal State, which is made up of a number of separate entities, is seriously compromised when a majority of these entities, embracing a greater part of the territory and population, constitute themselves as sovereign States with the result that federal authority may no longer be effectively exercised.

By the same token, while recognition of a State by other States has only declarative value, such recognition, along with membership of international organizations, bears witness to these States' conviction that the political entity so recognized is a reality and confers on it certain rights and obligations under international law.

3. The Arbitration Commission notes that since adopting *Opinion No. 1:*

---

[112] Ed. Above, p.113.

— the referendum proposed in *Opinion No. 4*[113] was held in Bosnia-Hercegovina on 29 February and 1 March: a large majority of the population voted in favour of the Republic's independence;

— Serbia and Montenegro, as Republics with equal standing in law, have constituted a new State, the "Federal Republic of Yugoslavia", and on 27 April adopted a new constitution;

— most of the new States formed from the former Yugoslav Republics have recognized each other's independence, thus demonstrating that the authority of the federal State no longer held sway on the territory of the newly constituted States;

— the common federal bodies on which all the Yugoslav Republics were represented no longer exist: no body of that type has functioned since;

— the former national territory and population of the SFRY are now entirely under the sovereign authority of the new States;

— Bosnia-Hercegovina, Croatia and Slovenia have been recognized by all the Member States of the European Community and by numerous other States, and were admitted to membership of the United Nations on 22 May 1992;

— UN Security Council Resolutions Nos. 752 and 757 (1992) contain a number of references to "the former SFRY";

— what is more, Resolution No. 757 (1992) notes that "the claim by the Federal Republic of Yugoslavia (Serbia and Montenegro) to continue automatically (the membership) of the former Socialist Federal Republic of Yugoslavia (in the United Nations) has not been generally accepted";

— the declaration adopted by the Lisbon European Council on 27 June makes express reference to "the former Yugoslavia".

4. The Arbitration Commission is therefore of the opinion:

— that the process of dissolution of the SFRY referred to in *Opinion No. 1* of 29 November 1991 is now complete and that the SFRY no longer exists.

Notes

1. The EC Peace Conference on Yugoslavia was convened following the eruption of civil war in the Socialist Federal Republic of Yugoslavia (SFRY) in 1991.[114] The Arbitration Commission was set up by the Conference as a body to which the "relevant authorities will submit their differences".[115] The Commission, which is known as the Badinter Commission, consisted of five members. At the time that *Opinion Nos. 1–10* were handed down, three members were appointed by the EC and its Member States, and two by the SFRY Presidency. All five were the presidents of European national constitutional courts, or similar bodies.[116] The Opinions of the Commission are not legally binding.

2. The questions considered by the Arbitration Commission of the EC Conference on Yugoslavia in *Opinions No.1* and *No. 8* concerned the extinction of the SFRY and succession to its rights and obligations in international law.

3. On the matter of the extinction of states generally, Oppenheim[117] states:

---

[113] Ed. 92 I.L.R. 173.
[114] For the facts, see below, p.134. See also Weller (1992) 86 A.J.I.L. 569.
[115] Joint Statement, August 28, 1991, 24 EC Bulletin, No.7/8, p.115 (1991).
[116] For the membership rules, and on the Commission generally, see Craven (1995) 66 B.Y.I.L. 333.
[117] Vol.1, pp.204 et seq. Some footnotes omitted.

"§ *59 Extinction of states.* A state ceases to be an international person when it ceases to exist. In practice this may happen:

(a) when one state merges into another and becomes merely a part of it (as occurred when . . . Montenegro [merged] into the Serb-Croat-Slovene State after the First World War), or when two or more states merge to form a single new state.[118]

(b) when a state breaks up so that its whole territory henceforth comprises two or more new states.[119] However, the question whether all the new territorial units are properly to be regarded as new states, or whether one of them constitutes a continuation, much diminished, of the original state is not always easy to answer, and raises complex issues as to the circumstances in which a state ceases to be the same state. Such problems have arisen, for example, over the dissolution of Austria-Hungary after the First World War.[120]

(c) when a state breaks up into parts all of which become part of other—usually sur-rounding—states (as with the absorption of the old State of Poland by Russia, Austria and Prussia in 1795);

(d) formerly,[121] when a state has been subjugated, ie annexed by the victorious state after conquest in war (as when the Orange Free State and the South African Republic were absorbed by Great Britain in 1901)."

4. As to the continued existence of the SFRY, in *Opinion No.1,* the Arbitration Commission considered that on November 29, 1991 it was "in the process of dissolution". By the time of *Opinion No.8,* on July 4, 1992, the Commission considered that the "process" was complete and that "the SFRY no longer exists". One of the events listed in *Opinion No.8* as having occurred between the two *Opinions* was the proclamation on April 27, 1992 of the Federal Republic of Yugoslavia (FRY). This had the territory of Serbia and Montenegro,[122] i.e. the territory of the former SFRY less that of the four republics that had declared their independence. Whereas the FRY recognised that these former SFRY republics had become independent states, the April proclamation maintained that the FRY was the continuation of the "state, international legal and political personality" of the SFRY.[123] This claim was rejected by the Arbitration Commission in *Opinion No.8.*

5. On the question of succession to the rights and duties of the SFRY,[124] the Arbitration Commission referred in *Opinion No.1* to the "principles of international law" and to the Vienna Convention on the Succession of States in respect of Treaties 1978[125] and the Vienna Convention on the Succession of States in respect of State Property, Archives and Debts 1983.[126] These

---

[118] Ed. For examples, see the footnotes to App.II, below.
[119] See, e.g. the break-up of the United Arab Republic in 1961. Ed. For details, see, below, App.II, n.2.
[120] See [on the question whether] . . . the new Austrian Republic was a new state, . . . Marek, *The Identity and Continuity of States in Public International Law* (1954), pp.199–236.
[121] Acquisition of title by conquest is nowadays not permissible. Ed. See below, p.187.
[122] Montenegro seceded from the FRY to become a separate state in 2006.
[123] *Genocide Case (Provisional Measures),* Order of April 8, 1993, I.C.J. Rep. 1993, 3 at 15.
[124] The Arbitration Commission gave its opinion on particular questions of succession in respect of the SFRY in *Opinions Nos. 12–15,* (1993) 32 I.L.M. 1589 et seq.
[125] (1978) 17 I.L.M. 1488. In force 1996. 22 parties. UK not a party.
[126] (1983) 12 I.L.M. 306. Not in force. 15 parties required; 7 ratifications so far, not the UK.

Conventions, which are based upon the work of the International Law Commission, have not met with widespread acceptance.[127] On state succession generally, Oppenheim[128] states:

"It is sometimes helpful to distinguish between universal and partial succession. The former takes place when one international person is completely absorbed by another, either through voluntary merger, or upon the dismemberment of a state which is broken up into parts which either have become separate international persons of their own or have been annexed by surrounding international persons, or (in former times) through subjugation.

Partial succession takes place when a part of the territory of an international person has separated from it in a revolt and by winning its independence has become itself an international person; when one international person has acquired a part of the territory of another through cession; when a hitherto full sovereign state has lost part of its independence through entering into a federal state, or coming under suzerainty or under a protectorate; or when a hitherto partially sovereign state has become fully sovereign. . . .

The practice of states suggests that no *general* succession takes place according to international law. With the extinction of an international person its rights and duties as a person disappear. But certain rights and duties do devolve upon an international person from its predecessor. Since this devolution takes place through the very fact of one international person following another in the possession of state territory, a succession of one international person to those devolved rights and duties clearly takes place. But no general rule can be laid down concerning all the cases in which a succession occurs, and each needs to be examined separately. That examination naturally reflects the historical circumstances of the time, and the major preoccupations of the leading members of the international community in the situations which at the time most frequently give rise to cases of succession. Furthermore, state practice in much of this area has been variable, often dependent on the very special circumstances of particular cases, and based on ad hoc agreements which may not necessarily reflect a view as to the position in customary international law."

As to the particular rules of state succession of customary international law in the subject areas of the 1978 and 1983 Conventions (treaties, property, etc.), which have not been generally accepted as stating custom, and other areas (e.g. succession in respect of nationality and private law rights), Oppenheim states that recent state practice is "insufficiently uniform to provide evidence of clear rules of international law".[129]

6. In the case of the SFRY, in *Opinion No.8* the Arbitration Commission treated the position as one of universal succession, following the dismemberment of the SFRY, not one of partial succession resulting from the separation of some republics from a still continuing SFRY.[130] The same approach of universal succession was adopted within the United Nations in respect of continued SFRY membership. The General Assembly considered that[131]:

---

[127] Even so, they were relied upon in the 2001 Agreement on Succession Issues of the SFRY, (2002) 41 I.L.M. 3. See Stahn (2002) 96 A.J.I.L. 379.

[128] Vol.1, pp.209–210. For a detailed treatment of state succession, see Oppenheim, Vol.1, pp.208–244; and O'Connell, *State Succession in Municipal International Law* (2 Vols., 1967).

[129] Oppenheim, Vol.1, p.236.

[130] On the FRY's status as a new state, see the Commission's *Opinion No.10*, below, p.137.

[131] G.A. Res. 47/1 G.A.O.R., 47th Sess., Supp. 49, p.12 (1992). The Security Council had earlier considered that the SFRY "has ceased to exist" and recommended the position taken by the General Assembly: S.C. Res. 777 (1992), S.C.O.R., 47th Year, *Resolutions and Decisions*, p.34. See Blum (1992) 86 A.J.I.L. 830.

"... the Federal Republic of Yugoslavia (Serbia and Montenegro) cannot continue auto-matically the membership of the former Socialist Federal Republic of Yugoslavia in the United Nations; and therefore decides that the Federal Republic of Yugoslavia (Serbia and Montenegro) should apply for membership of the United Nations and that it shall not participate in the work of the General Assembly ..."

Bosnia-Hercegovina, Croatia, Slovenia and the Former Yugoslav Republic of Macedonia were admitted to the UN in 1992-3. For a time, the FRY declined to apply for membership, continuing to claim succession to the membership of the SFRY. During this period, the SFRY flag and nameplate remained in position at UN Headquarters and there was an unoccupied seat for the SFRY in the General Assembly.[132] The FRY eventually applied for membership and was admitted to the UN in 2000. Since then it has changed its name to Serbia.[133]

7.   In contrast with the position of the SFRY, the position in the former USSR has been treated by the international community as one of partial succession, with the Russian Federation being recognised by states as the successor to the rights and obligations of the USSR, including its membership in the United Nations.[134] Craven distinguishes the two cases as follows:

"The Russian Republic's territory constituted 76% of the total territory of the USSR (22.4 million km^2) and 51% of the total population (148 million). The territory of the FRY, by contrast, comprises 40% of the territory of the SFRY, and its population, 45% (10.5 million). Although it would be wrong to place too much emphasis upon such considerations, they are significant when combined with other factors such as the reactions of other members of the international community (the concurrence of the other former Soviet States being highly determinative in the case of Russia)."[135]

OPINION NO. 3

Arbitration Commission, EC Conference on Yugoslavia: Badinter,
Chairman; Corosaniti, Herzog, Petry, Tomas y Valiente, members. January 11, 1992. 92 I.L.R. 170

Opinion of the Commission

On 20 November 1991 the Chairman of the Arbitration Commission received a letter from Lord Carrington, Chairman of the Conference on Yugoslavia, requesting the Commission's opinion on the following question put by the Republic of Serbia:

Can the internal boundaries between Croatia and Serbia and between Bosnia-Hercegovina and Serbia be regarded as frontiers in terms of public international law?

1.   In its *Opinion No. 1* ... the Commission found that "the Socialist Federal Republic of Yugoslavia is in the process of breaking up". Bearing in mind that the Republics of Croatia and Bosnia-Hercegovina, inter alia, have

---

[132] This was because of a UN Secretariat opinion to the effect that whereas G.A. Res. 47/1 had stated that the FRY could not "continue the membership" of the SFRY, "the resolution neither terminates nor suspends Yugoslavia's membership if the organisation": see the Under-Secretary-General and Legal Counsel letter quoted in the *Genocide* case, see above, n.126. The ICJ described this solution as "not free from legal difficulties": p.15. See further, Gray (1994) 43 I.C.L.Q. 704.

[133] It first changed from the FRY to Serbia and Montenegro, until Montenegro seceded in 2006.

[134] For, e.g. the UK's recognition, see below, p.133.

[135] See above, p.115, n.13, pp.370-371.

sought international recognition as independent States, the Commission is mindful of the fact that its answer to the question before it will necessarily be given in the context of a fluid and changing situation and must therefore be founded on the principles and rules of public international law.

2.   The Commission therefore takes the view that once the process in the SFRY leads to the creation of one or more independent States, the issue of frontiers, in particular those of the Republics referred to in the question before it, must be resolved in accordance with the following principles:

First—All external frontiers must be respected in line with the principle stated in the United Nations Charter, in the Declaration on Principles of International Law concerning Friendly Relations and Co-operation among States in accordance with the Charter of the United Nations (General Assembly Resolution 2625 (XXV)) and in the Helsinki Final Act, a principle which also underlies Article 11 of the Vienna Convention of 23 August 1978 on the Succession of States in Respect of Treaties.

Second—The boundaries between Croatia and Serbia, between Bosnia-Hercegovina and Serbia, and possibly between other adjacent independent States may not be altered except by agreement freely arrived at.

Third—Except where otherwise agreed, the former boundaries become frontiers protected by international law. This conclusion follows from the principle of respect for the territorial status quo and, in particular, from the principle of *uti possidetis*. *Uti possidetis*, though initially applied in settling decolonization issues in America and Africa, is today recognized as a general principle, as stated by the International Court of Justice in its Judgment of 22 December 1986 in the case between *Burkina Faso and Mali* (*Frontier Dispute*, (1986) *I.C.J. Reports* 554 at 565):

> Nevertheless the principle is not a special rule which pertains solely to one specific system of international law. It is a general principle, which is logically connected with the phenomenon of the obtaining of independence, wherever it occurs. Its obvious purpose is to prevent the independence and stability of new States being endangered by fratricidal struggles ...

The principle applies all the more readily to the Republics since the second and fourth paragraphs of Article 5 of the Constitution of the SFRY stipulated that the Republics' territories and boundaries could not be altered without their consent.

Fourth—According to a well-established principle of international law the alteration of existing frontiers or boundaries by force is not capable of producing any legal effect. This principle is to be found, for instance, in the Declaration on Principles of International Law concerning Friendly Relations and Co-operation among States in accordance with the Charter of the United Nations (General Assembly Resolution 2625 (XXV)) and in the Helsinki Final Act; it was cited by the Hague Conference on 7 September, 1991 and is enshrined in the Draft Convention of November 4, 1991 drawn up by the Conference on Yugoslavia.

Notes

In *Opinion No.3*, the Commission stated its conclusion that the boundaries of the successor states to the SFRY are those that existed between the former SFRY republics. For this conclusion, the Commission relied upon the principle of *uti posseditis* and other principles that emphasise the need to respect established boundaries and not to recognise boundary changes obtained by force. See also *Opinion No.2*, above, p.110, where the Commission emphasises that the principle of *uti posseditis* prevails over that of self-determination in this context.

The Dayton Agreement supposes that the old boundaries between the former SFRY republics apply as between the new states. In the case of Croatia, a UN transitional administration arranged for the reintegration of East Slavonia, which had been held by Serbian forces, into Croatia in 1998.

3. MANDATED AND TRUST TERRITORIES

Notes

1. After the First World War, the League of Nations solution to the problem of the future of the overseas possessions of the defeated states of Germany and Turkey in Africa, the Pacific and the Middle East was to place them under mandate (art.22, Covenant). The mandatories were given powers of administration and responsibilities that varied according to the category of mandate, and were to promote their development and ultimate independence. In no case was sovereignty transferred to the mandatory.

2. When the United Nations replaced the League of Nations after the Second World War the system of mandates was replaced by a trusteeship system,[136] which was inspired by the same problem and the same objective. All of the former mandated territories were placed under the trusteeship system by their mandatories (who were then appointed the administering authorities in the same territories) with the exception of (1) those territories—Iraq, Syria, Lebanon and Palestine (now Israel and Jordan)—which had become or were soon to become independent; (2) the islands in the Pacific north of the Equator (which were taken from the former mandatory—Japan—and made into a "strategic trust area" (because of their significance for purposes of defence[137]) administered by the United States; and (3) South West Africa. After many years of conflict between South Africa, the former mandatory, on the one hand, and the United Nations[138] and the national independence movement, on the other hand, in 1990 South West Africa became the independent state of Namibia. All of the trust territories have now become independent states.

---

4. OTHER LEGAL PERSONS

A. *Public International Organisations*[139]

REPARATION FOR INJURIES SUFFERED IN THE SERVICE OF THE UNITED NATIONS CASE

Advisory Opinion. I.C.J. Reports 1949, p.174

On September 17, 1948, Count Bernadotte, a Swedish national, was killed, allegedly by a private gang of terrorists, in the new city of Jerusalem. The new city was then in Israeli possession.[140] Count

---

[136] See Chs XII and XIII, UN Charter, below, App.I.

[137] This was calculated by reference to the experience of the Second World War.

[138] See Dugard, ed., *The South West Africa/Namibia Dispute* (1973); and Slonim, *South West Africa and the United Nations* (1973). The I.C.J. gave four advisory opinions concerning the legal status of South West Africa and UN jurisdiction over it: *International Status of South West Africa* case, I.C.J. Rep. 1950, p.128; *Voting Procedures Case*, I.C.J. Rep. 1955, p.67; *Admissibility of Hearings* case, I.C.J. Rep. 1956, p.23; and *Legal Consequences* case, I.C.J. Rep. 1971, p.16. In the *South West Africa* cases, I.C.J. Rep. 1966, p.6, the I.C.J. found that the applicant states (Ethiopia, Liberia: both LN members) lacked the right or interest required to bring a claim against South Africa alleging that it had infringed its obligations under the mandate.

[139] See Sands and Klein, eds, *Bowett's Law of International Institutions* (5th edn 2001), Ch.15; Hardy (1961) 37 B.Y.I.L. 516; Parry (1949) 26 B.Y.I.L. 108; Schermers and Blokker, *International Institutional Law* (4th edn 2004), Ch.11; White, *The Law of International Organisations* (2nd edn 2005), Ch.2. There are also many *private* international organisations (e.g. the Inter-Parliamentary Union), the members of which are normally private individuals or bodies, although states do participate in some cases.

[140] For a summary of events in the Middle East in 1947–1949, see below, p.191.

Bernadotte was the Chief United Nations Truce Negotiator in the area. In the course of deciding what action to take in respect of his death, the United Nations General Assembly sought the advice of the ICJ. Israel was admitted to the United Nations on May 11, 1949, shortly after the Court gave its opinion.

Opinion of the Court

The first question asked of the Court is as follows:

> In the event of an agent of the United Nations in the performance of his duties suffering injury in circumstances involving the responsibility of a State, has the United Nations, as an Organisation, the capacity to bring an international claim against the responsible *de jure* or *de facto* government with a view to obtaining the reparation due in respect of the damage caused (*a*) to the United Nations, (*b*) to the victim or to persons entitled through him? . . .

The subjects of law in any legal system are not necessarily identical in their nature or in the extent of their rights, and their nature depends upon the needs of the Community. Throughout its history, the development of international law has been influenced by the requirements of international life, and the progressive increase in the collective action of States has already given rise to instances of action upon the international plane by certain entities which are not States. This development culminated in the establishment in June 1945 of an international organisation whose purposes and principles are specified in the Charter of the United Nations. But to achieve these ends the attribution of international personality is indispensable.

The Charter has not been content to make the Organisation created by it merely a centre "for harmonising the actions of nations in the attainment of these common ends" (Article 1, para. 4). It has equipped that centre with organs, and has given it special tasks. It has defined the position of the Members in relation to the Organisation by requiring them to give it every assistance in any action undertaken by it (Article 2, para. 5), and to accept and carry out the decisions of the Security Council; by authorising the General Assembly to make recommendations to the Members; by giving the Organisation legal capacity and privileges and immunities in the territory of each of its Members; and by providing for the conclusion of agreements between the Organisation and its Members. Practice—in particular the conclusions of conventions to which the Organisation is a party—has confirmed the character of the Organisation, which occupies a position in certain respects in detachment from its Members, and which is under a duty to remind them, if need be, of certain obligations. It must be added that the Organisation is a political body, charged with political tasks of an important character, and covering a wide field namely the maintenance of international peace and security, the development of friendly relations among nations, and the achievement of international co-operation in the solution of problems of an economic, social, cultural or humanitarian character (Article 1); and in dealing with its Members it employs political means. The "Convention on the Privileges and Immunities of the United Nations" of 1946 creates rights and duties between each of the signatories and the Organisation (see in particular, section 35). It is difficult to see how such a convention could operate except upon the international plane and as between parties possessing international personality.

In the opinion of the Court, the Organisation was intended to exercise and enjoy, and is in fact exercising and enjoying, functions and rights which can only be explained on the basis of the possession of a large measure of international personality and the capacity to operate upon an international plane. It is at present the supreme type of international organisation, and it could not carry out the intentions of its founders if it was devoid of international personality. It must be acknowledged that its Members, by entrusting certain functions to it, with the attendant duties and responsibilities, have clothed it with the competence required to enable those functions to be effectively discharged.

Accordingly, the Court has come to the conclusion that the Organisation is an international person. That is not the same thing as saying that it is a State, which it certainly is not, or that its legal personality and rights and duties are the same as those of a State. Still less is it the same thing as saying that it is "a super-State", whatever that expression may mean. It does not even imply that all its rights and duties must be upon the international plane, any more than all the rights and duties of a State must be upon that plane. What it does mean is that it is a subject of international law and capable of possessing international rights and duties, and that it has capacity to maintain its rights by bringing international claims.

The next question is whether the sum of the international rights of the Organisation comprises the right to bring the kind of international claim described in the Request for this Opinion. That is a claim against a State to obtain reparation in respect of the damage caused by the injury of an agent of the Organisation in the course of the performance of his duties. Whereas a State possesses the totality of international rights and duties recognised by international law, the rights and duties of an entity such as the Organisation must depend upon its purposes and functions as specified or implied in its constituent documents and developed in practice. The functions of the Organisation are of such a character that they could not be effectively discharged if they involved the concurrent action, on the international plane, of fifty-eight or more[141] Foreign Offices, and the Court concludes that the Members have endowed the Organisation with capacity to bring international claims when necessitated by the discharge of its functions. ...

... It cannot be doubted that the Organisation has the capacity to bring an international claim against one of its Members which has caused injury to it by a breach of its international obligations towards it. The damage specified in Question I (*a*) means exclusively damage caused to the interests of the Organisation itself, to its administrative machine, to its property and assets, and to the interests of which it is the guardian. It is clear that the Organisation has the capacity to bring a claim for this damage. As the claim is based on the breach of an international obligation on the part of the Member held responsible by the Organisation, the Member cannot contend that this obligation is governed by municipal law, and the Organisation is justified in giving its claim the character of an international claim.

When the Organisation has sustained damage resulting from a breach by a Member of its international obligations, it is impossible to see how it can obtain reparation unless it possesses capacity to bring an international claim. It cannot be supposed that in such an event all the Members of the Organisation, save the defendant State, must combine to bring a claim against the defendant for the damage suffered by the Organisation.

In dealing with the question of law which arises out of Question I (*b*) ... The only legal question which remains to be considered is whether, in the course of bringing an international claim of this kind, the Organisation can recover "the reparation due in respect of the damage caused ... to the victim ..."

The traditional rule that diplomatic protection is exercised by the national State does not involve the giving of a negative answer to Question I (*b*).

In the first place, this rule applies to claims brought by a State. But here we have the different and new case of a claim that would be brought by the Organisation.

In the second place, even in inter-State relations, there are important exceptions to the rule, for there are cases in which protection may be exercised by a State on behalf of persons not having its nationality.[142]

In the third place, the rule rests on two bases. The first is that the defendant State has broken an obligation towards the national State in respect of its nationals. The second is that only the party to whom an international obligation is due can bring a claim in respect of its breach. This is precisely what happens when the Organisation, in bringing a claim for damage suffered by its agent, does so by invoking the breach of an obligation towards itself. Thus, the rule of the nationality of claims affords no reason against recognizing that the Organisation has the right to bring a claim for the damage referred to in Question I (*b*). On the contrary, the principle underlying this rule leads to the recognition of this capacity as belonging to the Organisation, when the Organisation invokes, as the ground of its claim, a breach of an obligation towards itself.

Nor does the analogy of the traditional rule of diplomatic protection of nationals abroad justify in itself an affirmative reply. It is not possible, by a strained use of the concept of allegiance, to assimilate the legal bond which exists, under Article 100 of the Charter, between the Organisation on the one hand, and the Secretary-General and the staff on the other, to the bond of nationality existing between a State and its nationals.

The Court is here faced with a new situation. The questions to which it gives rise can only be solved by realizing that the situation is dominated by the provisions of the Charter considered in the light of the principles of international law. ...

The Charter does not expressly confer upon the Organisation the capacity to include, in its claim for reparation, damage caused to the victim or to persons entitled through him. The Court must therefore begin by enquiring whether the provisions of the Charter concerning the functions of the Organisation, and the part played by its agents in the performance of those functions, imply for the Organisation power to afford its agents the limited protection that would consist in the bringing of a claim on their behalf for reparation for damage suffered in such circumstances. Under international law, the Organisation must be deemed to have those powers which, though

---

[141] Ed. Now over 190.

[142] Ed. The Court is probably referring to cases of protected persons, alien members of a state's armed forces and alien crew members of a state's merchant ships. It is also possible to avoid the application of the nationality rule by treaty. See Schwarzenberger, pp.592–596. See further below, p.505.

not expressly provided in the Charter, are conferred upon it by necessary implication as being essential to the performance of its duties.[143] This principle of law was applied by the Permanent Court of International Justice to the International Labour Organisation in its Advisory Opinion No. 13 of July 23rd, 1926 (Series B., No. 13, p. 18) and must be applied to the United Nations.

Having regard to its purposes and functions already referred to, the Organisation may find it necessary, and has in fact found it necessary, to entrust its agents with important missions to be performed in disturbed parts of the world. Many missions, from their very nature, involve the agents in unusual dangers to which ordinary persons are not exposed. For the same reason, the injuries suffered by its agents in these circumstances will sometimes have occurred in such a manner that their national State would not be justified in bringing a claim for reparation on the ground of diplomatic protection, or, at any rate, would not feel disposed to do so. Both to ensure the efficient and independent performance of these missions and to afford effective support to its agents, the Organisation must provide them with adequate protection. ...

In order that the agent may perform his duties satisfactorily, he must feel that this protection is assured to him by the Organisation, and that he may count on it. To ensure the independence of the agent, and, consequently, the independent action of the Organisation itself, it is essential that in performing his duties he need not have to rely on any other protection than that of the Organisation (save of course for the direct and immediate protection due from the State in whose territory he may be). In particular, he should not have to rely on the protection of his own State. If he had to rely on that State, his independence might well be comprised, contrary to the principle applied by Article 100 of the Charter. And lastly, it is essential that—whether the agent belongs to a powerful or to a weak State; to one more affected or less affected by the complications of international life; to one in sympathy or not in sympathy with the mission of the agent—he should know that in the performance of his duties he is under the protection of the Organisation. This assurance is even more necessary when the agent is stateless. ...

The obligations entered into by States to enable the agents of the Organisation to perform their duties are undertaken not in the interest of the agents, but in that of the Organisation. When it claims redress for a breach of these obligations, the Organisation is invoking its own right, the right that the obligations due to it should be respected. On this ground, it asks for reparation of the injury suffered, for "it is a principle of international law that the breach of an engagement involves an obligation to make reparation in an adequate form;" as was stated by the Permanent Court in its Judgment No. 8 of July 26th, 1927 (Series A., No. 9, p. 21). In claiming reparation based on the injury suffered by its agent, the Organisation does not represent the agent, but is asserting its own right, the right to secure respect for undertakings entered into towards the Organisation.

Having regard to the foregoing considerations, and to the undeniable right of the Organisation to demand that its Members shall fulfil the obligations entered into by them in the interest of the good working of the Organisation, the Court is of the opinion that in the case of a breach of these obligations, the Organisation has the capacity to claim adequate reparation, and that in assessing this reparation it is authorised to include the damage suffered by the victim or by persons entitled through him.

The question remains whether the Organisation has "the capacity to bring an international claim against the responsible de jure or de facto government with a view to obtaining the reparation due in respect of the damage caused (a) to the United Nations, (b) to the victim or to persons entitled through him" when the defendant State is not a member of the Organisation.

In considering this aspect of Question I (a) and (b), it is necessary to keep in mind the reasons which have led the Court to give an affirmative answer to it when the defendant State is a Member of the Organisation. It has now been established that the Organisation has capacity to bring claims on the international plane, and that it possessed a right of functional protection in respect of its agents. Here again the Court is authorised to assume that the damage suffered involves the responsibility of a State, and it is not called upon to express an opinion upon the various ways in which that responsibility might be engaged. Accordingly the question is whether the Organisation has capacity to bring a claim against the defendant State to recover reparation in respect of that damage or whether, on the contrary, the defendant State, not being a member, is justified in raising the objection that the Organisation lacks the capacity to bring an international claim. On this point, the Court's opinion is that fifty States,[144] representing the vast majority of the members of the international community, had the power, in conformity with international law, to bring into being an entity possessing objective international personality and not merely personality recognised by them alone, together with capacity to bring international claims. ...

---

[143] Ed. On the doctrine of implied powers, see Campbell (1983) 32 I.C.L.Q. 523. See also the WHO Nuclear Weapons case, I.C.J. Rep. 1996, p.66 at 79.

[144] Ed., i.e. the 50 states that participated in the San Francisco Conference in 1945 at which the UN Charter was drafted.

The Court answered Question I (*a*), unanimously, and I (*b*), by 11 votes to 4,[145] in the affirmative.

Question II is as follows:

"In the event of an affirmative reply on point I (*b*), how is action by the United Nations to be reconciled with such rights as may be possessed by the State of which the victim is a national?"

The affirmative reply given by the Court on point I (*b*) obliges it now to examine Question II. When the victim has a nationality, cases can clearly occur in which the injury suffered by him may engage the interest both of his national State and of the Organisation. In such an event, competition between the State's right of diplomatic protection and the Organisation's right of functional protection might arise, and this is the only case with which the Court is invited to deal.

In such a case, there is no rule of law which assigns priority to the one or to the other, or which compels either the State or the Organisation to refrain from bringing an international claim.

... The Court sees no reason why the parties concerned should not find solutions inspired by goodwill and common sense, and as between the Organisation and its Members it draws attention to their duty to render "every assistance" provided by Article 2, paragraph 5, of the Charter.

Although the bases of the two claims are different, that does not mean that the defendant State can be compelled to pay the reparation due in respect of the damage twice over. International tribunals are already familiar with the problem of a claim in which two or more national States are interested, and they know how to protect the defendant State in such a case.[146]

The risk of competition between the Organisation and the national State can be reduced or eliminated either by a general convention or by agreements entered into in each particular case. There is no doubt that in due course a practice will be developed, and it is worthy of note that already certain States whose nationals have been injured in the performance of missions undertaken for the Organisation have shown a reasonable and co-operative disposition to find a practical solution.

The question of reconciling action by the Organisation with the rights of a national State may arise in another way; that is to say, when the agent bears the nationality of the defendant State.

The ordinary practice whereby a State does not exercise protection on behalf of one of its nationals against a State which regards him as its own national, does not constitute a precedent which is relevant here. The action of the Organisation is in fact based not upon the nationality of the victim but upon his status as agent of the Organisation. Therefore it does not matter whether or not the State to which the claim is addressed regards him as its own national, because the question of nationality is not pertinent to the admissibility of the claim.

In law, therefore, it does not seem that the fact of the possession of the nationality of the defendant State by the agent constitutes any obstacle to a claim brought by the Organisation for a breach of obligations towards it occurring in relation to the performance of his mission by that agent.

The Court answered Question II by 10 votes to 5.[147]

Notes

1.   In the light of the opinion in the *Reparation* case, the United Nations General Assembly authorised the Secretary-General to seek reparation from Israel in connection with the death of Count Bernadotte.[148] In 1950, Israel paid the sum requested by the Secretary-General "as reparation for the damages borne by the United Nations."[149]

2.   What advice do you think the Court would have given on: (i) a claim by the United Nations to exercise sovereignty over territory; (ii) a claim against the United Nations by a state in respect of the breach of a treaty by the United Nations?

---

[145] The judges in the majority were President Basdevant; Vice-President Guerrero; Judges Alvarez, Fabela, Zoričić, de Visscher, Sir Arnold McNair, Klaestad, Read, Hsu Mo and Azevedo. Judges Hackworth, Winiarski, Badawi Pasha and Krylov dissented.
[146] Ed. See below, p.512.
[147] The five dissenting judges were the four who dissented on Question I (*b*) and one other (unknown).
[148] G.A. Res. 365; G.A.O.R., 4th Session, *Resolutions*, p.64.
[149] U.N. Doc. A/1347.

3. Might the Court's opinion on the United Nations right to bring a claim against a non-member have been different if the United Nations had had only six members? How do you reconcile the United Nations "objective international personality" with the rule that treaties (e.g. the United Nations Charter) cannot create obligations for third states without their consent?[150]

4. On the possession and nature of international legal personality by public international organisations, one leading text[151] states:

> "The explicit conferment of international legal personality on intergovernmental organisations has for a long time remained the exception rather than the rule. ... The vast majority of treaties establishing international organisations concluded after the Second World War ... limit the recognition of legal personality to the domestic sphere of member states.[152] The explicit attribution of international legal personality to intergovernmental organisations has, however, become much more frequent since then, including in constituent instruments.[153] Provisions to the same effect may be found in recent treaties establishing autonomous international judicial institutions.[154] This evolution reflects changes in the international society itself, which is increasingly open to the co-existence of various categories of subjects of international law. ... The attribution of international legal personality simply means that the entity upon which it is conferred is a subject of international law and that it is capable of possessing international rights and duties. The precise scope of those rights and duties will vary according to what may reasonably be seen as necessary, in view of the purposes and functions of the organisation in question, to enable the latter to fulfil its tasks. Therefore the test is a functional one; reference to the functions and powers of the organisation exercised on the international plane, and not to the abstract notion of personality, will alone give guidance on what powers may properly be implied."

Powers that are commonly implied on this functional basis include the power to make treaties, including treaties providing for international privileges and immunities for personnel; to bring legal proceedings; and generally to act within the remit of the organisation. Public international organisations have implied duties or liabilities as well as rights or powers. For example, an organisation that sent its personnel into the territory of a state without that state's consent would be in breach of an international duty to respect the territorial sovereignty of states. The United Nations may be responsible in customary international law for human rights violations by UN personnel.[155]

5. There are over 200 intergovernmental organisations (IGOs)[156], the majority of which have come into existence since the Second World War. They range from organisations of universal membership and general competence, such as the United Nations, to regional ones with specialised functions, such as NATO.

---

[150] See Schwarzenberger, pp.128–130.
[151] Sands and Klein, eds, *Bowett's Law of International Institutions* (5th edn 2001), pp.470–473.
[152] See, e.g. IAEA Statute, art. XV WIPO Convention, art.12(1) UNIDO Constitution, art.21.
[153] A classical, and for a long period almost unique, example was the 1951 Treaty establishing the ECSC (art.6), proclaiming the organisation's legal capacity in international relations. More recent examples include the 1976 Agreement establishing IFAD (art.10, section 1), the 1982 United Nations Convention on the Law of the Sea (for the International Seabed Authority; art.176), the 1993 Treaty establishing ECOWAS (art.88, 1), the 1994 COMESA Treaty (art.186, 1) and the 1994 Protocol on the MERCOSUR institutions (art.34).
[154] See in that respect the 1998 Statute of the International Criminal Court (art.4(1)).
[155] See Verdirame (2002) 2 H.R.L.R. 265.
[156] See *Yearbook of International Organizations* 2006–2007 (43rd edn), Appendix 3.

6. *International personality of the European Community.*[157] The Treaty establishing the European Community (EC), Article 281, provides for the EC to have "legal personality", which has been interpreted to mean international personality,[158] and to enter into agreements with non-member states and organisations which can be classified as treaties in international law in a number of particular subject areas.[159] The EC exercises the right of passive legation, with over 150 states having missions accredited to it (or to the EU) in Brussels. The EC does not have a power of active legation, but the European Commission has over 100 non-diplomatic delegations in states and international organisations. It has observer status in the UN General Assembly and participates in international conferences. The European Union (EU), which consists of the 27 EC Member States acting inter-governmentally and not under the Treaty establishing the European Community, is considered by most commentators[160] to have implied international personality, which will have a treaty basis when the 2007 Treaty of Lisbon enters into force.[161] The Member States do, however, take "common positions"[162] and "joint action"[163] under the EU Common Foreign and Security Policy (the Second Pillar).

B. *Individuals*[164]

LAUTERPACHT, SURVEY OF INTERNATIONAL LAW IN RELATION TO THE WORK OF CODIFICATION OF THE INTERNATIONAL LAW COMMISSION

Memorandum prepared for the UN Secretariat, UN Doc. A/CN.4/1/Rev. 1, February 10, 1949, pp.19–20. Reprinted in E. Lauterpacht, *International Law being the Collected Papers of Hersch Lauterpacht*, (1970), Vol.I, pp.469–471

27. The question of the subjects of international law has, in particular in the last twenty-five years, ceased to be one of purely theoretical importance and it is now probable that in some respects it requires authoritative international regulation. Practice has abandoned the doctrine that States are the exclusive subjects of international rights and duties. Although the Statute of the International Court of Justice adheres to the traditional view that only States can be parties' to international proceedings,[165] a number of other international instruments have recognised the procedural capacity of the individual. This was the case not only in the provisions of the Treaty of Versailles relating to the jurisdiction of the Mixed Arbitral Tribunals, but also in other treaties such as the Polish-German Convention of 1922 relating to Upper Silesia in which—as was subsequently held by the Upper Silesian Mixed Tribunal—the independent procedural status of individuals as claimants before an international agency was recognised even as against the State of which they were nationals.[166]

---

[157] See McGoldrick, *International Relations Law of the European Union* (1997), Chs 2 and 8; and Macleod, Hendry and Hyett, *The External Relations of the European Communities* (1996).

[158] Case 22/70 *Commission v Council* [1971] E.C.R. 263.

[159] These include association agreements (art.310) and agreements on commercial policy (art.133) and the environment (art.174(4)).

[160] See Craig and De Burca, *EU Law: Text, Cases and Materials* (4th edn 2008), p.167. See also Neuwahl in Kronenberger, ed., *The European Union and the International Legal Order* (2001), p.3.

[161] See art.47, TEU, as amended by the Treaty of Lisbon.

[162] art.12, Treaty of European Union, e.g. sanctions against the SFRY: Council Decision 94/336/CFSP [1993] OJ L165/1.

[163] art.13, e.g. on the recognition of new states. Note that the power to recognise states remains with the individual Member States, which may act jointly through the EU. See, e.g. the recognition of the republics of the former SFRY, below, p.134.

[164] See Brownlie (1962) 11 I.C.L.Q. 701; Gormley, *The Procedural Status of the Individual before International and Supranational Tribunals* (1966); Higgins (1978) 4 B.J.I.S. 1; Korowicz (1956) 50 A.J.I.L. 533; Lauterpacht (1947) 63 L.Q.R. 438; and (1948) 64 L.Q.R. 97; McCorquodale, in Evans, ed., *International Law* (2nd edn 2006) p.307; Nørgaard, *The Position of the Individual in International Law* (1962); Ochoa (2007) 48 Virg.J.I.L. 119; Orakhelashvili (2001) 31 C.W.I.L.J. 241.

[165] Ed. See below, p.841.

[166] Ed. See *Steiner and Gross v Polish State* (1927–28) 4 A.D. 291.

28. In the sphere of substantive law, the Permanent Court of International Justice recognised, in the advisory opinion relating to the postal service in Danzig,[167] that there is nothing in international law to prevent individuals from acquiring directly rights under a treaty provided that this is the intention of the contracting parties. A considerable number of decisions of municipal courts tendered subsequently to the advisory opinion of the Permanent Court expressly affirmed that possibility.

29. In the field of customary international law the enjoyment of benefits of international law by individuals as a matter of right followed from the doctrine, accepted by a growing number of countries, that generally recognised rules of the law of nations form part of the law of the land.[168] In the sphere of duties imposed by international law the principle that the obligations of international law bind individuals directly regardless of the law of their State and of any contrary order received from their superiors was proclaimed in the Charter annexed to the Agreement of 8 August 1945, providing for the setting up of the International Military Tribunal at Nürnberg as well as in the Charter of the International Military Tribunal at Tokyo of 19th January 1946.[169] That principle was fully affirmed in the judgment of the Nürnberg Tribunal as flowing from the imperative necessity of making international law effective. The Tribunal said: "Crimes against international law are committed by men, not by abstract entities, and only by punishing individuals who commit such crimes can the provisions of international law be enforced."[170] It was reaffirmed in the resolution of the General Assembly of 11 December, 1946,[171] expressing adherence to the principles of the Nürnberg Charter and Judgment. ...

30. On a different plane the Charter of the Nürnberg Tribunal—and the judgment which followed it—proclaimed the criminality of offences against humanity, i.e. of such offences against the fundamental rights of man to life and liberty, even if committed in obedience to the law of the State.[172] To that extent, in a different sphere, positive law has recognised the individual as endowed, under international law, with rights the violation of which is a criminal act.

Notes

1. Although more than 50 years old, this survey of the status of the individual in international law remains accurate today. Most noticeably, although the customary and the treaty law of human rights has developed tremendously since Lauterpacht wrote, the *substantive* legal rights under that law remain vested in states not in individuals, even though individuals may benefit greatly from the state obligations arising under human rights treaties. Exceptionally, art.36(1)(a), Vienna Convention on Consular Relations creates "individual rights" of consular access enforceable by the national state.[173] For an example of a treaty imposing *duties* upon private persons, see the International Convention on Civil Liability for Oil Pollution Damage 1969.[174] Article 1 imposes strict liability for oil pollution on the ship's owner, usually a company. At the same time, the *procedural* rights of individuals (and, in some cases, legal persons and other entities, e.g. churches) have grown greatly, with many more rights to bring claims being available by treaty than when Lauterpacht wrote, again most notably in the field of human rights.[175] To take an important example in a non-human rights context, foreign investors may bring investment claims directly under ICSID or BITs.[176]

2. For the most part, however, the individual remains an object, not a subject, of international law whose most important characteristic for international law purposes is his nationality. It is this, for

---

[167] Ed. P.C.I.J. Rep, Series B, No.11 (1925).
[168] Ed. See above, Ch.3.
[169] Ed. See Woetzel, *The Nuremberg Trials in International Law* (1960); and Horowicz, *The Tokyo Trial*, Int. Conc. No. 465 (1950). On the International Criminal Court, see below, p.537.
[170] Ed. (1947) 41 A.J.I.L. 221.
[171] Ed. G.A. Res. 95(1), G.A.O.R., *Resolutions*, 1st Sess. Pt II, p.188.
[172] Ed. (1947) 41 A.J.I.L. 224.
[173] *LaGrand* case I.C.J. Rep. 2001, p.446 at 494.
[174] 973 U.N.T.S. 3; (1970) 9 I.L.M. 45. In force 1975.
[175] See below, p.547.
[176] See below, p.503.

example that determines which state (his national state) may protect him against the extra-vagances of another (if he is stateless normally no state may do so) and, more ominously, places him within the domestic jurisdiction, and hence the discretionary treatment, of his national state. It is nationality also that decides whether an individual can benefit from treaty guarantees that a state secures for its "nationals".

3.   Other categories of *non state actors* that have some degree of international legal personality are insurgents and national liberation movements.[177] Another important category of actor on the international stage is the transnational company, whose activities affect individuals and the environment across international boundaries and whose wealth and economic power may be greater than that of many states.[178] As yet, these would not seem to have been accorded *substantive* international legal personality, which in this case would consist of duties, as well as rights.[179] Standards regulating the conduct of transnational companies have been spelt out in a series of instruments, but so far these have taken the form of "soft law" rather than legally binding treaty texts.[180]

C. Other Entities

NANNI v PACE AND THE SOVEREIGN ORDER OF MALTA

(1935–37) 8 A.D. 2. Italian Court of Cassation

The Order, the official title of which is the Sovereign Military Order of St. John of Jerusalem, of Rhodes, and of Malta, was established during the Crusades as a nursing brotherhood and military organisation directed against the Muslims. In 1309, the Order conquered the Island of Rhodes, which it then ruled until 1522 when it was ejected by the Ottoman Empire. In 1530, the Order moved to Malta which had been given to it by Emperor Charles V. This it ruled until 1798 when the island was taken by Napoleon. The Order established its headquarters in Rome in 1834. Since that time it has performed work of a humanitarian character for the poor and the sick. In the present case, which raised the question of the personality of the Order in Italian law, the Court examined its history and status in international law.

Judgment of the Court

With the recognition of the Church and of the Byzantine Empire, the Order established, after the conquest of territory of its own, its independence and sovereignty. ... The Grand Master was recognised as Sovereign Head of Rhodes with all the attributes of such a position, which included ... the right of active and passive legation together with the right of negotiating directly with other States and of making conventions and treaties. ... Such attributes of sovereignty and independence have not ceased, in the case of the Order, at the present day—at least

----

[177] See Cassese, *International Law* (2001), pp.87 et seq.

[178] See Muchlinski, *Multinational Enterprises and the Law* (2nd edn 2007).

[179] On the judicial nature of some kinds of agreement between states and transnational companies, see below, p.502.

[180] See the 2003 UN Norms on the Responsibilities of Transnational Corporations and Other Business Enterprises with Regard to Human Rights, UN Doc E/CN.4/Sub.2/2003/12/Rev 2 and the OECD Guidelines for Multinational Enterprises (2000 revision), *www.oecd.org*. See also Addo, ed., *Human Rights Standards and the Responsibilities of Transnational Corporations* (1999); Joseph, *Corporations and Transnational Human Rights Litigation* (2004); Kinley and Chambers (2006) 6 H.R.L.R. 447; Ratner (2001) 111 Yale L.J. 443; Weissbrodt and Kruger (2003) 97 A.J.I.L. 901.

not from the formal point of view in its relations with the Italian State. Nor has its personality in international law come to an end notwithstanding the fact that as a result of the British occupation of Malta such personality cannot be identified with the possession of territory. ... With regard to this second aspect of the matter it is enough to point out that the modern theory of the subjects of international law recognises a number of collective units whose composition is independent of the nationality of their constituent members and whose scope transcends by virtue of their universal character the territorial confines of any single State. It must be admitted that only States can contribute to the formation of international law as an objective body of rules—States as international entities which are territorially identifiable. This is so because the fulfilment of this latter requirement makes them the principal objects and creators of such rules. But it is impossible to deny to other international collective units a limited capacity of acting internationally within the ambit and the actual exercise of their own functions with the resulting international juridical personality and capacity which is its necessary and natural corollary. In accordance with these doctrines, such personality was never denied to the Holy See even before the Lateran Treaty of February 11, 1929,[181] and it is unanimously conceded to the League of Nations, although it is neither a State, nor a super-State, nor a Confederation of States. It is equally conceded to certain international administrative unions.

Notes

1. The Order maintains diplomatic relations with 93 states.[182] Is its practice as to, for example, the extent of diplomatic immunity relevant to the formation of customary international law in the way that state practice is? What about the practice of the United Nations with regard, for example, to treaties it has made with states or other public international organisations? Does that contribute to the customary international law of treaties?

2. *The Holy See and the Vatican City.* Graham[183] states:

   "The view seems to be dominant today ... that the Holy See does, in fact, enjoy international personality. Furthermore, this personality of the Holy See is distinct from the personality of the State of Vatican City. One is a non-territorial institution, and the other a state. The papacy as a religious organ is a subject of international law and capable of international rights and duties. ... The fact that the Holy See is a non-territorial institution is no longer regarded as a reason for denying it international personality. The papacy can act in its own name in the international community. It can enter into legally binding conventions known as concordats. In the world of diplomacy the Pope enjoys the rights of active and passive legation. He can send and receive representatives who are public ministers in the sense of international law."

---

[181] Ed. See now the 1984 Lateran Treaty (1985) 78 *Acta Apostolicae Sedis* 522.

[182] On the Order generally, see Farran (1954) 3 I.C.L.Q. 217; and (1955) 4 I.C.L.Q. 308; O'Connell (1976–77) 48 B.Y.I.L. 433; Theutenberg, *The Holy See, the Order of Malta and International Law* (2003). The UK does not maintain diplomatic relations with the Order.

[183] *Vatican Diplomacy: a Study of Church and State on the International Plane* (1959), pp.186, 201. See also Kunz (1952) 46 A.J.I.L. 308.

5. RECOGNITION OF STATES AND GOVERNMENTS[184]

BRIERLY, THE LAW OF NATIONS

Waldock (6th edn 1963), p.138

The legal significance of recognition is controversial. According to one view it has a "constitutive" effect; through recognition only and exclusively a state becomes an international person and a subject of international law.[185] But there are serious difficulties in this view. The status of a state recognized by state A but not recognized by state B, and therefore apparently both an "international person" and not an "international person" at the same time, would be a legal curiosity. Perhaps a more substantial difficulty is that the doctrine would oblige us to say that an unrecognized state has neither rights nor duties at international law, and some of the consequences of accepting that conclusion might be startling. We should have to say, for example, that an intervention, otherwise illegal, would not have been illegal in Manchukuo,[186] or that if Manchukuo had been involved in war, she would have been under no legal obligation to respect the rights of neutrals. Non-recognition may certainly make the enforcement of rights and duties more difficult than it would otherwise be, but the practice of states does not support the view that they have no legal existence before recognition.[187]

The better view is that the granting of recognition to a new state is not a "constitutive" but a "declaratory" act; it does not bring into legal existence a state which did not exist before. A state may exist without being recognized, and if it does exist in fact, then, whether or not it has been formally recognized by other states, it has a right to be treated by them *as* a state. The primary function of recognition is to acknowledge as a fact something which has hitherto been uncertain, namely the independence of the body claiming to be a state, and to declare the recognizing state's readiness to accept the normal consequences of that fact, namely the usual courtesies of international intercourse. It is true that the present state of the law makes it possible that different states should act on different views of the application of the law to the same state of facts. This does not mean that their differing interpretations are all equally correct, but only that there exists at present no procedure for determining which are correct and which are not. The constitutive theory of recognition gains most of its plausibility from the lack of centralized institutions in the system, and it treats this lack not as an accident due to the stage of development which the law has so far reached, but as an essential feature of the system. It is in fact one more relic of absolutist theories of state sovereignty.

In practice non-recognition does not always imply that the existence of the unrecognized state is a matter of doubt. States have discovered that the granting or withholding of recognition can be used to further a national policy; they have refused it as a mark of disapproval, as nearly all of them did to Manchukuo; and they have granted it in order to establish the very independence of which recognition is supposed to be a mere acknowledgement, as when in 1903 the United States recognized Panama only three days after it had revolted from Colombia or when in 1948 the United States recognized Israel within a few hours of its proclamation of independence.[188]

---

[184] See Blix (1970-II) 130 Hague Recueil 587; Briggs (1949) 43 A.J.I.L. 113; Brownlie (1982) 53 B.Y.I.L. 197; Chen, *The International Law of Recognition* (1951); Dugard, *Recognition and the United Nations* (1987) (states only); Grant, *The Recognition of States* (1999); Jennings (1967-II) 121 Hague Recueil 323 at 346–368; Lauterpacht, *Recognition in International Law* (1947); Peterson, *Recognition of Governments: Legal Doctrine and State Practice 1815–1995* (1995); Roth, *Government Illegitimacy in International Law* (1999); Talmon, *Recognition of Governments in International Law* (1998); Talmon (2004) 75 B.Y.I.L. 101.

[185] Oppenheim, *International Law* (8th edn 1955), Vol.1, para.71.

[186] Ed. See above, p.100.

[187] See on this point Jaffé, *Judicial Aspects of Foreign Relations*, p.98. When Jewish airmen shot down British aeroplanes over Egypt in January 1949 the British Government at once informed the government of the Jewish state, which at that time Britain had not recognized, that they would demand compensation.

[188] In regard to the recognition of Israel, Mr W. R. Austin, the representative of the United States on the Security Council, asserted the political character of the act of recognition in the most unequivocal terms: "I should regard it as highly improper for me to admit that any country on earth can question the sovereignty of the United States of America in the exercise of that high political act of recognition of the *de facto* status of a state. Moreover, I would not admit here, by implication or by direct answer, that there exists a tribunal of justice or of any other kind, anywhere, that can pass upon the legality or the validity of that act of my country" (*New York Times*, May 19, 1948).

Notes

1. The declaratory theory is adopted by most modern writers. It is also supported by arbitral practice. In particular, the *Tinoco Arbitration*, below, p.143, suggests that recognition is simply evidence (to be discounted if politically biased) that the international law requirements are met. State practice confirms this in the sense that states do not refrain from bringing claims under international law against unrecognised states or governments.[189] The Arbitral Commission of the EC Conference on Yugoslavia was of the opinion that recognition of states by other states was "purely declaratory"[190] in effect, although it did "confer certain rights and obligations under international law".[191] An entity that is not recognised by other states will, for example, not have the rights and obligations in the law of diplomatic immunity and will have difficulty functioning in the international community if it is not admitted to international organisations. Although the extract from Brierly is expressed in terms only of the recognition of states, it is clear that the declaratory theory applies to the recognition of governments too. The United Kingdom used formerly to take the view that there was a legal duty to grant recognition to a state or government when the necessary requirements were met.[192] This approach, which is not repeated in the 1980 British statement on the recognition of governments, below, p.139, never found favour with other states.[193] The position would seem to be that recognition is a discretionary act[194] with evidential value in law.

2. On May 30, 1967, Biafra declared its independence of Nigeria, of which it had constituted the Eastern Region. Its war of independence was unsuccessful and Biafra surrendered to the Nigerian Federal Government on January 12, 1970. It is now once again fully a part of Nigeria. Five States— Tanzania, Gabon, Ivory Coast, Zambia and Haiti—recognised it as an independent state during the rebellion, although no state entered into formal diplomatic relations. What effect did these recognitions have in law according to the declaratory and constitutive theories?[195]

---

[189] See the example given by Brierly, n.190 above, and the US response to the seizure of the *Pueblo* by North Korea, which the US did not recognise, below, p.387. In 1957 the UK claimed compensation from the unrecognised Taiwan Government for damage done to British vessels by its forces: see C.P.U.K.I.L. 1957 (1957) 6 I.C.L.Q. 507. In 1954, the US claimed under international law against the unrecognised Government of the Chinese People's Republic for the killing of US nationals when a commercial aircraft was shot down by a Chinese military aircraft: see 2 Whiteman 651. Arab states regard Israel as governed by international law even though they did not recognise Israel as a state (the first to do so was Egypt in 1979).

[190] *Opinion No.1*, above, p.113.

[191] *Opinion No.8*, above, p.114.

[192] See the 1951 Morrison statement of British practice on the recognition of governments, below, p.140. This statement was influenced by Lauterpacht, above, n.187, who argued that there was a duty on the part of states to grant recognition in the absence of an international body competent to do so. Lauterpacht also thought that recognition so granted was constitutive. This view was not clearly adopted in the 1951 statement. In 1948, the UK adopted a declaratory approach in the UN with respect to the recognition of states: ". . . the existence of a state should not be regarded as depending upon recognition but on whether in fact it fulfils the conditions which create a duty for recognition"; UN Doc. A/CN.4/2, p.53, quoted in Crawford, below, p.91, n.1, p.16.

[193] See, e.g. Mr Austin's statement above, n.191. cf. the following statement by the UN Secretariat when considering the question of the representation of members in the UN (UN Doc. S/1466; S.C.O.R., 5th Year, Supp. for Jan/May 1950, p.19): "The recognition of a new state, or a new government of an existing state, is a unilateral act which the recognizing government can grant or withhold. It is true that some legal writers have argued forcibly that when a new government, which comes into power through revolutionary means, enjoys, with a reasonable prospect of permanency, the habitual obedience of the bulk of the population, other states are under a legal duty to recognize it. However, while states may regard it as desirable to follow certain legal principles in according or withholding recognition, the practice of States shows that the act of recognition is still regarded as essentially a political decision, which each state decides in accordance with its own free appreciation of the situation."

[194] cf. *Opinion No.10*, Arbitration Commission, EC Conference on Yugoslavia, below, p.137.

[195] See Ijalaye (1971) 65 A.J.I.L. 551.

3. *Modes of recognition*. Recognition of states or of governments may occur expressly or by implication. There is no precise catalogue of acts that imply recognition.[196] Entry into diplomatic relations clearly implies it, as, normally, does the making of a bilateral treaty arranging for commercial or other relations or support for a state's admission to the United Nations.[197] The crucial question is that of intention. Participation in an international conference with a state or government will not indicate recognition if it is made clear that it is not intended to have this effect. Thus, in 1954, when the Foreign Ministers of France, the United Kingdom, the United States and the USSR proposed the Geneva Conference to discuss Korea and Indochina and invited the Government of the People's Republic of China, the two Koreas and "other interested states", they added: "It is understood that neither the invitation to, nor the holding of, the above mentioned conference shall be deemed to imply diplomatic recognition in any case where it has not already been accorded."[198]

4. *Retroactivity of recognition*. At the time of the recognition of the FRY as a state, the UK Foreign and Commonwealth Office sent the following telegram to its missions: "For legal purposes, in accordance with usual practice, recognition, once granted, dates back to the actual commencement of the activities of the recognised authority".[199]

EC GUIDELINES ON THE RECOGNITION OF NEW STATES IN EASTERN EUROPE AND IN THE SOVIET UNION

December 16, 1991. U.K.M.I.L. 1991, (1991) 62 B.Y.I.L. 559.

In compliance with the European Council's request, Ministers have assessed developments in Eastern Europe and in the Soviet Union with a view to elaborating an approach regarding relations with new States.

In this connection they adopted the following guidelines on the formal recognition of new States in Eastern Europe and in the Soviet Union:

The Community and its Member States confirm their attachment to the principles of the Helsinki Final Act and the Charter of Paris, in particular the principle of self-determination. They affirm their readiness to recognise, subject to the normal standards of international practice and the political realities in each case, those new States which, following the historic changes in the region, have constituted themselves on a democratic basis, have accepted the appropriate international obligations and have committed themselves in good faith to a peaceful process and to negotiations.

Therefore, they adopt a common position on the process of recognition of these new States, which requires:

— respect for the provisions of the Charter of the United Nations and the commitments subscribed to in the Final Act of Helsinki and in the Charter of Paris, especially with regard to the rule of law, democracy and human rights;

---

[196] Apparently, even the sale of blankets may suffice. In 1962, the question arose of the sale to the Republican Government to the Yemen, which had recently come into being by revolution and which had not been recognised by the British Government, of 50,000 surplus blankets. The Lord Privy Seal stated in Parliament: "We could not sell them to the Yemeni republican authorities without recognizing the republican government": *Hansard*, HC Vol.669, cols 1253–1254 (December 19, 1962); C.P.U.K.I.L. 1962, p.152.

[197] e.g. the UK's support for the UN admission of the Democratic People's Republic of Korea "meant that we also now recognise . . . (it) as a state, but we have no plans to establish diplomatic relations": Parliamentary Under-Secretary of State, FCO, *Hansard*, HC, col.156 (October 16, 1991).

[198] Communiqué on the 1954 Berlin Conference dated February 18, 1954, *Documents on American Foreign Relations* (1954), p.219.

[199] U.K.M.I.L. 1996; (1996) 67 B.Y.I.L. 712.

— guarantees for the rights of ethnic and national groups and minorities in accordance with the commitments subscribed to in the framework of the CSCE:

— respect for the inviolability of all frontiers which can only be changed by peaceful means and by common agreement:

— acceptance of all relevant commitments with regard to disarmament and nuclear non-proliferation as well as to security and regional stability:

— commitment to settle by agreement, including where appropriate by recourse to arbitration, all questions concerning state succession and regional disputes.

The Community and its Member States will not recognise entities which are the result of aggression. They would take account of the effects of recognition on neighbouring States.

The commitment to these principles opens the way to recognition by the Community and its Member States and to the establishment of diplomatic relations. It could be laid down in agreements.

Notes

1. Applying these Guidelines,[200] the EC and its Member States recognised as states 11 of the 15 republics of the former USSR[201] The three Baltic states of Estonia, Latvia and Lithuania that had also been USSR republics were recognised by the EC and its Member States before the Guidelines were adopted.[202] The Russian Federation is accepted by the United Kingdom "as the continuing state of the Soviet Union", and hence succeeds to the rights and duties of the former USSR.[203]

   See also the 1991 Declaration that was applied to the states that emerged from the Socialist Federal Republic of Yugoslavia: below, p.134.

2. The Guidelines have in mind the Montevideo Convention requirements of statehood when they refer to "the normal standards of international practice and the political realities in each case".[204] The conditions of respect for the rights of minorities, the inviolability of borders, etc., go beyond the legal requirements of statehood in the Montevideo Convention. Although the Guidelines note that the new states had a "democratic basis", this is not a requirement of statehood.[205] The Guidelines were not intended to be additional legal requirements of statehood. Instead they are political conditions,[206] with recognition being used as a force to achieve

---

[200] On the Guidelines, see Müllerson, *International Law, Rights and Politics* (1994), Ch.4; Rich (1993) 4 E.J.I.L. 36; Warbrick (1992) 41 I.C.L.Q. 473; in Evans, ed., *Aspects of Statehood and Institutionalism in Contemporary Europe* (1997), p.9. For the similar US approach, see the statement by the US Deputy Assistant Secretary of State for European and Canadian Affairs, October 17, 1991, *Foreign Policy Bulletin* 2 (Nov–Dec 1991), p.42.

[201] See the EC Ministerial Statement of December 31, 1991, U.K.M.I.L 1993, (1991) 62 B.Y.I.L. 561. Another recognition condition was that those republics that had nuclear weapons on their territory would adhere to the Nuclear Non-Proliferation Treaty. Armenia, Azerbaijan, Belarus, Kazakhstan, Moldova, Turkmenistan, Ukraine and Uzbekistan were recognised in 1991. Georgia, the Kyrgyz Republic and Tajikstan were recognised in 1992 after they had given assurances to this effect.

[202] See the EC Ministerial Declaration of August 27, 1991, (1991) 62 B.Y.I.L. 558. The EC acted immediately after the Russian Federation had recognised the Baltic states.

[203] Secretary of State FCO (Mr Hurd), *Hansard*, HC Vol.203, col.384 (January 24, 1994); Minister of State, FCO, *id.*, Vol.202, W.A. col. 9 (January 20, 1992).

[204] The "political realities" are those that answer the question whether the claimant state has a government with effective control over its territory.

[205] See Murphy (1999) 48 I.C.L.Q. 545.

[206] But compliance with the principle of self-determination may be a legal requirement of statehood: see the *Southern Rhodesia* case, above, p.101.

political objectives.[207] This is a departure from previous statements of United Kingdom practice on the recognition of states, which generally focus on the Montevideo Convention requirements.[208] The title to the Guidelines limits them geographically. No mention was made of them when Eritrea was recognised by the United Kingdom as a state in 1993.[209]

EC DECLARATION ON YUGOSLAVIA

December 16, 1991. U.K.M.I.L. 1991, (1991) 62 B.Y.I.L. 559.

The European Community and its Member States discussed the situation in Yugoslavia in the light of their guidelines on the recognition of new States in Eastern Europe and in the Soviet Union. They adopted a common position with regard to the recognition of Yugoslav Republics. In this connection they concluded the following:

The Community and its Member States agree to recognise the independence of all the Yugoslav Republics fulfilling all the conditions set out below. The implementation of this decision will take place on January 15, 1992.

They are therefore inviting all Yugoslav Republics to state by 23 December whether:

— they wish to be recognised as independent.
— they accept the commitments contained in the above-mentioned guidelines.
— they accept the provisions laid down in the draft convention[210]—especially those in Chapter II on human rights and rights of national or ethnic groups—under consideration by the Conference on Yugoslavia.
— they continue to support the efforts of the Secretary General and the Security Council of the United Nations, and the continuation of the Conference on Yugoslavia.

The application of those Republics which reply positively will be submitted through the chair of the Conference to the Arbitration Commission for advice before the implementation date ...

The Community and its Member States also require a Yugoslav Republic to commit itself, prior to recognition, to adopt constitutional and political guarantees ensuring that it has no territorial claims towards a neighbouring Community State and that it will conduct no hostile propaganda activities versus a neighbouring Community State, including the use of a denomination which implies territorial claims.

Notes

1.   The question of the recognition of new states in the Balkans arose out of the disintegration of the Socialist Federal Republic of Yugoslavia (SFRY) which had been established after the Second World War.[211] The SFRY was composed of six republics: Bosnia-Hercegovina, Croatia, Macedonia, Montenegro, Serbia and Slovenia. After the death of President Tito in 1980, tension developed between Serbia and other republics, with Croatia and Slovenia, in particular, complaining of increasing Serbian dominance of the SFRY and seeking greater devolved powers. In June 1991, Croatia and Slovenia declared their independence. Civil war then broke out between the federal

---

[207] But see *Opinion No.10*, EC Commission, below, p.137.
[208] The conditions in the Guidelines were a French initiative. Note that some instances of UK non-recognition (e.g. the non-recognition of East Germany until 1973) have had political overtones.
[209] See the letters sent by the Prime Minister and Foreign and Commonwealth Secretary to the Eritrean Provisional Government on May 14 and 17, 1993, U.K.M.I.L 1993, (1993) 64 B.Y.I.L. 602.
[210] Ed. This was an EC Conference Draft Convention of November 4, 1991 that proposed terms for the settlement of the Yugoslav crisis. It was never adopted.
[211] The SFRY succeeded the Kingdom of the Serbs, Croats and Slovenes, which had been established in 1918 by the merger of provinces of the former Austro-Hungarian Empire (mainly Slovenia, Croatia, Bosnia-Hercegovina) with the Kingdom of the Serbs.

army ("JNA") and Slovenian and Croatian forces in the territory of the two republics. Fighting ended in Slovenia in July 1991 when the SFRY presidency ordered the withdrawal of JNA troops from its territory. Fighting continued in Croatia, with the JNA troops being joined by the irregular forces of the Serbian ethnic minority in Croatia. On January 3, 1992, a UN ceasefire was endorsed by Croatia and by Serbian leaders in Belgrade. As part of a UN Security Council peacekeeping plan, a small UN advance force ("UNMLO") arrived in Croatia on January 14, to prepare the way for a UN Protection Force ("UNPROFOR"), which arrived in Croatia in March 1992 with a mandate to secure peace.[212] Sporadic violations of the cease-fire between JNA/ethnic Serbian and Croatian forces continued to occur in parts of Croatia from January until some time after the arrival of UNPROFOR forces.[213]

As regards Bosnia-Hercegovina, fighting broke out on ethnic lines after the February/March 1992 referendum in which Muslims and Croats voted overwhelmingly for independence.[214] Fighting became worse during April 1992 and continued thereafter until the ceasefire prior to the Dayton Agreement in 1995.

2. The EC Declaration on Yugoslavia was adopted on the same day as the general EC Guidelines on the Recognition of New States in Eastern Europe and in the Soviet Union, above, p.132, to which the Declaration refers.[215] The Declaration was preceded by *Opinion No.1* of the Arbitration Commission of the EC Conference on Yugoslavia[216] in which the Arbitration Commission expressed the opinion that the SFRY was "in the process of dissolution". It was in the light of this *Opinion* that the EC and its Member States took the unusual step in the Declaration of inviting republics within the SFRY to apply for recognition as states. Applications for recognition were made by Croatia and Slovenia, which had already declared their independence, and by Bosnia-Hercegovena and Macedonia.[217] These applications were referred to the Arbitration Commission, which, on January 11, 1992, expressed the opinion that Slovenia and Macedonia complied with the Guidelines and the Declaration on Yugoslavia, but that Croatia and Bosnia-Hercegovina did not.[218] The Arbitration Commission did not apply the Montevideo Convention requirements on statehood.[219] On January 15, 1992, the EC and Member States recognised Slovenia and Croatia.[220] They recognised Bosnia-Hercegovina on April 7, 1992[221] and the Former Yugoslav Republic of Macedonia April 8, 1993.[222] All that then remained of the SFRY were Serbia and Montenegro, which reconstituted themselves as the Federal Republic of Yugoslavia (FRY).

---

[212] See S.C. Res. 743 (1992), S.C.O.R., 47th Year. *Resolutions and Decisions*, p.8.

[213] On later developments, see below, p.829.

[214] On the referendum, see below, n.224.

[215] On the Declaration, see Turk (1993) 4 E.J.I.L. 66.

[216] Above, p.113. On the Arbitration Commission and the EC Conference on Yugoslavia, see above, p.115.

[217] Applications were also made, unsuccessfully, by Krajina (a Serbian enclave in Croatia) and Kosovo (a mostly ethnically Albanian autonomous region of Serbia). On Kosovo, see above, p.95.

[218] *Opinions Nos. 4–7*, (1992) 92 I.L.R 173 et seq.. Croatia had not incorporated all of the specified human and minorities' rights into its constitution (to protect mostly Croatian Serbs) and Bosnia-Hercegovina had not determined the "will of the people" on independence.

[219] On the Commission's application of the principle of self-determination, see *Opinion No.2*, above, p.110.

[220] Germany had already unilaterally recognised Croatia and Slovenia on December 23, 1991. On January 15, 1992, Croatia undertook to comply with all of the obligations in the Draft EC Convention on Yugoslavia, and later amended its Constitution, although these amendments did not fully comply with the EC Draft Convention: *Observations on Croatian Constitutional Law*, Arbitration Commission, Conference on Yugoslavia, (1992) 92 I.L.R. 209.

[221] This was after Bosnia-Hercegovina had held a referendum in which over 99 per cent of those voting opted for independence. The 31 per cent ethnic Serbian population boycotted the referendum.

[222] Recognition was implied by support by the UK and other EC states for the Former Yugoslav Republic of Macedonia's UN membership in the General Assembly on that date.

Was the recognition of Croatia and Bosnia-Hercegovina in accordance with the Montevideo Convention requirements of statehood? The Minister of State, FCO, justified United Kingdom recognition of Croatia as follows[223]:

"The criteria are that a country should have a clearly defined territory with a population; a Government with a prospect of retaining control; and independence in its foreign relations. These criteria are always subject to interpretation in the light of circumstances on the ground. In this case we and our E.C. partners recognised Croatia on the basis of advice from the arbitration commission that Croatia largely fulfilled the guidelines on recognition adopted last December. . . . We also took account of additional undertakings from the Croatian Government on minorities legislation."

The recognition of Bosnia-Hercegovina was justified similarly[224]:

"I do not think that the recognition of Bosnia is premature, in the sense that a referendum was held within Bosnia which was a sufficient basis for recognition, and Bosnia complied with all the requirements that were established by Mr Badinter and within the E.C. I think that it was a state that we had to recognise, applying ordinary criteria, in the same way that we recognised both Slovenia and Croatia."

As to Macedonia, SFRY forces withdrew from its territory on March 26, 1992. The delay in recognising it until April 1993 was the result of Greek concerns that the intended use of the historic Greek name of "Macedonia"[225] implied designs on Greek territory across the border. After persistent Greek objection, Macedonia was recognised following amendments to its constitution to indicate its absence of territorial ambition and the change of its name to the "Former Yugoslav Republic of Macedonia".[226]

Generally, it would seem that in the search for a settlement of the Yugoslav crisis, the political consequences of recognition or non-recognition, rather than the legal requirements of statehood, played the crucial role in Balkan recognition decisions.[227] Note, however, that *Opinion No.10* of the EC Commission, below, supposes certain legal limits to the recognition of states.

----

[223] *Hansard*, HC, Vol.203, W.A., col.191 (February 5, 1995). The Secretary of State, FCO, (Mr Hurd) later said: "No one could seriously suggest that we could have gone on pretending that the old Yugoslavia still existed . . . the reality was that Croatia existed. Whether it should have been recognised in the autumn, which is what the Germans wanted, or at the end of the year, which is what happened, or a little later, is a matter of dispute . . ." : Vol.259, col.332 (May 3, 1995).

[224] Mr Hogg, FCO Minister of State, H.C. Foreign Affairs Committee, Parliamentary Papers, 1992–3, H.C. Paper 235–iii, p. 88, December 2, 1992. Earlier, he had explained the situation as follows: " . . . if we recognise Bosnia, there will be the substantial risk that the Serbs will fight . . . if we do not recognise Bosnia we will, in a sense, neglect the fact that we encouraged them to hold a referendum to determine their view, and what would be the view of the Croats and the Muslims who clearly want independence . . . It will be extraordinarily difficult to withhold recognition for any extended period": *Hansard*, HC Vol.205, col.489 (March 5, 1992).

[225] The final paragraph of the EC Declaration on Yugoslavia, above, p.134, reflected Greece's concerns in this regard.

[226] See Craven (1995) 15 A.Y.I.L. 199.

[227] e.g. Mr Hogg, FCO Minister of State stated: ". . . Croatia does not . . . satisfy the [legal] criteria for recognition, but that . . . is a procedural point . . . The essential question . . . to be addressed is the question of minority rights . . . one of the major levers that we have in order to get people to address fully and properly [this question] . . . is recognition": F.C.A., 1st Report, *Central and Eastern Europe: Problems of the Post-Communist Era*, Vol.II, Minutes of Evidence, HC Session 1991–92, p.59.

OPINION NO. 10

Arbitration Commission, EC Conference on Yugoslavia: Badinter,
Chairman; Corosaniti, Herzog, Petry, Tomas y Valiente, members. July 4, 1992. 92 I.L.R. 206.

Opinion of the Commission

On 18 May 1992 the Chairman of the Arbitration Commission received a letter from Lord Carrington, Chairman of the Conference for Peace in Yugoslavia, asking for the Commission's opinion on the following question:

In terms of international law, is the Federal Republic of Yugoslavia a new State calling for recognition by the Member States of the European Community in accordance with the joint statement on Yugoslavia and the Guidelines on the Recognition of new States in Eastern Europe and in the Soviet Union adopted by the Council of the European Communities on 16 December 1991? . . .

1. As the Arbitration Commission found in *Opinion No. 8*,[228] the answer to this question very much depends on that to Question No. 2 from the Chairman of the Conference.

In *Opinion No. 8*, the Arbitration Commission concluded that the dissolution of the Socialist Federal Republic of Yugoslavia ("SFRY") was complete and that none of the resulting entities could claim to be the sole successor to the SFRY.

2. On 27 April this year Montenegro and Serbia decided to establish a new entity bearing the name "Federal Republic of Yugoslavia" and adopted its constitution.

The Arbitration Commission feels that, within the frontiers constituted by the administrative boundaries of Montenegro and Serbia in the SFRY, the new entity meets the criteria of international public law for a State, which were listed in *Opinion No. 1* of 29 November 1991.[229] However, as Resolution 757 (1992) of the UN Security Council points out, "the claim by the Federal Republic of Yugoslavia (Serbia and Montenegro) to continue automatically (the membership) of the former Socialist Federal Republic of Yugoslavia (in the United Nations) has not been generally accepted". As the Arbitration Commission points out in its *Ninth Opinion*,[230] the FRY is actually a new State and could not be the sole successor to the SFRY.

3. This means that the FRY (Serbia and Montenegro) does not *ipso facto* enjoy the recognition enjoyed by the SFRY under completely different circumstances. It is therefore for other States, where appropriate, to recognize the new State.

4. As, however, the Arbitration Commission pointed out in *Opinion No. 1*, while recognition is not a prerequisite for the foundation of a State and is purely declaratory in its impact, it is nonetheless a discretionary act that other States may perform when they choose and in a manner of their own choosing, subject only to compliance with the imperatives of general international law, and particularly those prohibiting the use of force in dealings with other States or guaranteeing the rights of ethnic, religious or linguistic minorities.

Furthermore, the Community and its Member States, in their joint statement of 16 December 1991 on Yugoslavia and the Guidelines, adopted the same day, on the recognition of new States in Eastern Europe and in the Soviet Union, has set out the conditions for the recognition of the Yugoslav republics.

5. Consequently, the opinion of the Arbitration Commission is that:

— the FRY (Serbia and Montenegro) is a new State which cannot be considered the sole successor to the SFRY;

— its recognition by the Member States of the European Community would be subject to its compliance with the conditions laid down by general · international law for such an act and the joint statement and Guidelines of 16 December 1991.

---

228 Ed. Above, p.114.
229 Ed. Above, p.113.
230 Ed. 92 I.L.R. 203.

Notes

1. The EU and its Member States now recognise Serbia (formerly the FRY) and the now separate state of Montenegro as states. Serbia and Montenegro are both UN members: see above, p.118. Although *Opinion No.10* regards recognition as a discretionary act, it supposes certain international law limits to the freedom to recognise states (use of force, rights of minorities).[231]

2. On the recognition of the Republic of Kosovo, see above, p.95.

BRITISH AND US PRACTICE ON THE RECOGNITION OF STATES

Notes

1. *British practice.* In 1986, in response to a question concerning the non-recognition of Bophuthatswana, the Minister of State, Foreign and Commonwealth Office, replied:

    "The normal criteria which the Government apply for recognition as a State are that it should have, and seem likely to continue to have, a clearly defined territory with a population, a Government who are able of themselves to exercise effective control of that territory, and independence in their external relations. Other factors, including some United Nations resolutions, may also be relevant."[232]

    In a later debate, the Minister of State explained why Bophuthatswana did not qualify:

    "Bophuthatswana is a collection of several separate pieces of territory—now six—said to form an independent state. ... the fragmentation of the territory of Bophuthatswana within South Africa, the pattern of the population and the economic dependence on South Africa more than justify our refusal to recognise Bophuthatswana. One of our criteria is that the territory should be clearly defined, which has not been the case."[233]

    In 1988, the Foreign Secretary modified this approach, emphasising *apartheid*[234]:

    "Bophuthatswana's fragmentary nature is only one reason why no country thought it right to recognise its independence. That country is financially dependent on South Africa. The very existence of Bophuthatswana is a consequence of apartheid, and I think that that is the principal reason why recognition has not been forthcoming."

    Other entities which are not recognised as states by the United Kingdom are Palestine,[235] the

---

[231] As to the precipitate recognition of states on Montevideo Convention grounds, see Oppenheim, Vol.I, p.143. As to the duty not to recognise the acquisition of statehood by the use of force, see also the *Northern Cyprus* case, above, p.103.

[232] *Hansard*, HC Vol.102, W.A., col.977 (October 23, 1986); U.K.M.I.L. 1986; (1986) 57 B.Y.I.L. 507. For a relevant UN resolution, see above, p.101.

[233] *Hansard*, HC Vol.105, col.100 (November 12, 1986); U.K.M.I.L. 1986; (1986) 57 B.Y.I.L. 507.

[234] *Hansard*, HC Vol.126, col.760–61 (February 3, 1988); U.K.M.I.L. 1988; (1988) 59 B.Y.I.L. 436–37.

[235] See below, p.193.

Saharwi Arab Democratic Republic,[236] the Turkish Republic of Northern Cyprus,[237] Somaliland[238] Taiwan,[239] Tibet[240] and Transnistria.[241]

2.   *US Practice.* In 1976 the United States Department of State stated[242]:

> "In the view of the United States, international law does not require a state to recognise another entity as a state; it is a matter for the judgment of each state whether an entity merits recognition as a state. In reaching this judgment, the United States has traditionally looked to the establishment of certain facts. These facts include effective control over a clearly-defined territory and population; and organised governmental administration of that territory; and a capacity to act effectively to conduct foreign relations and to fulfill international obligations. The United States has also taken into account whether the entity in question has attracted the recognition of the international community of states."

BRITISH PRACTICE ON THE RECOGNITION OF GOVERNMENTS[243]

Statement by the Foreign Secretary (Lord Carrington), Hansard, HL Vol.
408, cols 1121–1122. April 28, 1980; U.K.M.I.L. 1980, (1980) 51 B.Y.I.L. 367. cf. the statement by the
Lord Privy Seal (Sir Ian Gilmour), ibid. HC Vol.983, cols 277–279.

... we have conducted a re-examination of British policy and practice concerning the recognition of Governments. This has included a comparison with the practice of our partners and allies. On the basis of this review we have decided that we shall no longer accord recognition to Governments. The British Government recognise States in accordance with common international doctrine.

Where an unconstitutional change of régime takes place in a recognised State, Governments of other States must necessarily consider what dealings, if any, they should have with the new régime, and whether and to what extent it qualifies to be treated as the Government of the State concerned. Many of our partners and allies take the position that they do not recognise Governments and that therefore no question of recognition arises in such cases. By contrast, the policy of successive British Governments has been that we should make and announce a decision formally "recognising" the new Government.

This practice has sometimes been misunderstood, and, despite explanations to the contrary, our "recognition" interpreted as implying approval. For example, in circumstances where there might be legitimate public concern about the violation of human rights by the new régime, or the manner in which it achieved power, it has not sufficed to say that an announcement of "recognition" is simply a neutral formality.

We have therefore concluded that there are practical advantages in following the policy of many other countries in not according recognition to Governments. Like them, we shall continue to decide the nature of our dealings with régimes which come to power unconstitutionally in the light of our assessment of whether they are able of themselves to exercise effective control of the territory of the State concerned, and seem likely to continue to do so.

---

[236] See above, p.108.
[237] See above, p.103.
[238] See above, p.93.
[239] See above, p.96.
[240] See above, p.110.
[241] See above, p.103.
[242] (1978) 72 A.J.I.L. 337.
[243] See Davidson, (1981) 32 N.I.L.Q. 22; Dixon (1988) 22 Int. Lawyer 555; Symmons [1981] P.L. 249; Talmon (1992) 63 B.Y.I.L. 231; Warbrick (1981) 30 I.C.L.Q. 568.

Notes

1. This statement is concerned solely with the recognition of new revolutionary governments in existing states. Governments that come into office constitutionally (e.g. by election) in existing states require no recognition in international law. New states (and hence their governments) will, as the statement indicates, continue to be recognised expressly, or formally, "in accordance with common international doctrine." The effect of the statement is that the United Kingdom has abandoned the practice of expressly recognising revolutionary governments. The Foreign Secretary's statement and other parliamentary pronouncements say, in keeping the universal trend towards minimising the role of recognition, that governments will not be recognised at all. It seems more accurate to regard the move as one from express to implied recognition.[244] The new approach is reminiscent of the Estrada doctrine[245] adopted by Mexico in the 1930s and is in line with the practice of an increasing number of other states, including the United States and EU states.[246] Galloway[247] summarises state practice as follows:

   "In each region [of the world] the movement is towards de-emphasizing or completely eliminating the recognition issue. However, it is doubtful that the recognition question will be eliminated in the foreseeable future because, in a significant minority of cases, nations consider the political factors strong enough to make an issue of recognition. This desire to de-emphasize recognition in the majority of cases has resulted in the adherence of over thirty states to the Estrada Doctrine, but with the proviso that in certain situations they grant recognition based on political considerations.[248] The desire to de-emphasize recognition also affects the adherence of well over thirty other states to an ad hoc policy based on political considerations in which recognition is usually downplayed and finessed by the euphemism that relations are continuing, or that relations are being resumed. Taken together, the two approaches account for over 75 of the states included in this study."

2. The 1980 statement does not basically change the criteria upon which the United Kingdom had previously relied in deciding whether to recognise a government and which will continue to be relied upon when deciding whether to have "dealings" with it. These were stated by the Foreign Secretary (Mr Morrison) in 1951:

   "... The conditions under international law for the recognition of a new régime as the *de facto* Government of a State are that the new régime has in fact effective control over most of the State's territory and that this control seems likely to continue. The conditions for the recognition of a new régime as the *de jure* Government of a State are that the new régime should not merely have effective control over most of the State's territory, but that it should, in fact, be firmly established. His Majesty's Government consider that recognition should be accorded when the conditions specified by international law are, in fact, fulfilled and that recognition should not be given when these conditions are not fulfilled. The recognition of a Government

---

[244] See, however, the *Woodhouse* case, below, p.145.
[245] See 2 Whiteman 85.
[246] On US practice, see below, p.142.
[247] *Recognizing Foreign Governments* (1978), p.138. See also Peterson (1983) 77 A.J.I.L. 31, who argues that revolutionary governments should continue to be recognised. See also Nomura (1982) 25 Jap. Ann. I.L. 67; and Ando (1985) 28, Jap. Ann. I.L. 29.
[248] Ed. See the express US recognition of the Chinese Government in 1979, below, p.143.

de jure or *de facto* should not depend on whether the character of the régime is such as to command His Majesty's Government's approval."[249]

The effectiveness of a government is, of course, a sine qua non of recognition of an entity as the government of a state; recognition of an entity before it has become effective is "precipitate" and intervention in a state's affairs contrary to international law.

3.   The 1980 statement differs from that of 1951 in that: (i) there is no suggestion of any duty to recognise; (ii) there is no mention of de jure and de facto governments; and (iii) the words "of themselves" (i.e. without outside assistance) are added. The question of the recognition of a government as the de facto government only arises where there are two competing governments in being. In most cases, the situation is quickly resolved and the question is simply one of recognising the revolutionary government as the new government if the revolution has succeeded. Even where the struggle continues for some time, the United Kingdom has tended in recent years to wait until matters have sorted themselves out rather than grant interim recognition to a revolutionary movement as the de facto government of the territory it controls.[250] Thus in the case of Cambodia in the 1970s, the only step taken was to withdraw recognition from the established government as the de jure government and grant it to the revolutionary Pol Pot Government in 1976 once the latter had reached the capital and was in full control. The latter was not recognised as a de facto government as it gradually gained control of the countryside. It seems likely that, where two governments remain in being, the United Kingdom will henceforth have "dealings" with only one government, even though another government is in control of a part of the state's territory. The words "of themselves" in the 1980 statement reflect a later stage in the Cambodian case, as does the passage in the statement about the "violation of human rights" and the possibility of misunderstandings. The Pol Pot Government, which had grossly ill-treated the Cambodian population, was replaced by force in 1979 by the Heng Samrin Government with the military assistance of Vietnam. In October 1979, the British Government declined to withdraw recognition from the former and to recognise the latter instead. It declined to do so (even though it acknowledged that the latter had "control of the greater part of the territory of Cambodia") for the reason that there was "no other Government which satisfies the criteria for recognition which have been applied by successive British Governments." This would seem to have been a reference to the dependence of the Heng Samrin Government upon Vietnamese support. The British Government stressed that its continued recognition of Pol Pot was not to be taken as "approval of ... the enormity of Pol Pot's human rights violations."[251] By December, the position had changed:

"When we came to power last May, Pol Pot's Government held a dwindling proportion of the territory in Cambodia. Since September that proportion has further dwindled though of course Pol Pot's forces continue to resist. As the House is aware, our normal criteria require us to accord recognition to a Government who enjoy, with a reasonable prospect of permanence, the obedience of the mass of the population and the effective control of much the greater part of the country. ...

---

[249] *Hansard*, HC Vol.485, cols 2410–2411 (March 21, 1951). For further evidence of the adoption of an "effectiveness" test in state practice, see Bundu (1978) 27 I.C.L.Q. 18.
[250] For earlier cases in which the UK recognised de jure and de facto governments, see the facts of *Luther v Sagor* (Russian revolution) below, p.150; *Haile Selassie v Cable and Wireless Ltd (No.2)* (1939) 1 Ch. 182 CA (Italian annexation of Ethiopia) and *The Arantzazu Mendi* [1939] A.C. 256, HL (Spanish civil war).
[251] *Hansard*, HC Vol.972, cols 31–34; col.268 (October 25, 1979). U.K.M.I.L. 1979; (1979) 50 B.Y.I.L. 296.

It will therefore come as no surprise to the House if I say that we can no longer regard Pol Pot as leading an effective Government in Cambodia. By the same token, however, the dependence of the so-called Heng Samrin régime on the Vietnamese occupation army is complete; there is no reason to doubt that without the presence of the occupation troops it would be swept away by resurgent Cambodian nationalism. I therefore make it very clear that we emphatically do not recognise any claim by Heng Samrin. Our position is that there is no Government in Cambodia whom we can recognise. This position is shared by the United States and by some of our leading friends in Europe."[252]

4.   Despite the United Kingdom's adoption of a "face the facts" approach, it may sometimes have been swayed by politics in its judgment.[253] It was noticeable that the United Kingdom recognised the new Obote Government in Uganda in 1979 while the Tanzanian troops that had brought it to power were still in the country, when at the same time the Heng Samrin Government in Cambodia was refused recognition because of Vietnamese support.[254]

5.   In practice, the question of the recognition of governments that have come into being by unconstitutional means in existing states is more common than that of the recognition of new states. As far as the first question is concerned, it is important to distinguish between recognition of a government as the government that can act for a state for international law purposes and entry into diplomatic relations with that government. The latter implies the former, but the former does not require the latter. A not uncommon situation is that in which one government terminates its diplomatic relations with another as an act of retorsion.[255] This by itself does not affect recognition.

US PRACTICE ON THE RECOGNITION OF GOVERNMENTS

1977 US Department of State statement, (1977) 77 U.S. Dept. of State Bull. 462; [1977] U.S.D.I.L. 19

Throughout most of the 19th century, the United States recognized stable governments without thereby attempting to confer approval. U.S. recognition policy grew more complex as various Administrations applied differing criteria for recognition and expressed differently the reasons for their decisions. For example, Secretary of State William Seward (1861–69) added as a criterion the government's ability to honour its international obligations; President Rutherford Hayes (1877–81) required a demonstration of popular support for the new government; and President Woodrow Wilson (1913–21) favored using recognition to spread democracy around the world by demanding free elections.

Other criteria have been applied since then. These include the degree of foreign involvement in the government as well as the government's political orientation, attitude toward foreign investment, and treatment of U.S. citizens, corporations, and government representatives.

One result of such complex recognition criteria was to create the impression among other nations that the United States approved of those governments it recognized and disapproved of those from which it withheld recognition. This appearance of approval, in turn, affected our decisions in ways that have not always advanced U.S. interests. In recent years, U.S. practice has been to deemphasize and avoid the use of recognition in cases of

---

[252] *Hansard*, HC Vol.975, col.723 (December 6, 1979). See Warbrick (1981) 30 I.C.L.Q. 234.

[253] This is true of some of the instances of non-recognition of states cited above, p.138.

[254] See Symmons, above, p.139, n.246, p.250, referring to a letter by Mr Evan Luard, in *The Guardian*, October 5, 1979.

[255] e.g. the UK broke off diplomatic relations with Albania as an act of retorsion in 1946 (now restored) and with Libya in 1984 over the Libyan People's Bureau Incident, below, p.307 (now restored). Diplomatic relations with Argentina were broken off between 1982–90 because of the Falklands War. Diplomatic relations were restored in 1990 with Syria (broken off in 1986 because of Syrian involvement in an attempt in London to blow up an El Al airliner) and Iran (broken off in 1989 over the Salman Rushdie Affair).

changes of governments and to concern ourselves with the question of whether we wish to have diplomatic relations with the new governments.

The Administration's policy is that establishment of relations does not involve approval or disapproval but merely demonstrates a willingness on our part to conduct our affairs with other governments directly.

Notes

1. As the statement indicates, "the United States Government has quietly moved to the Estrada Doctrine" so that "the significance of recognition has faded away."[256] Thus, on the question of the recognition of the Taraki Government in Afghanistan in 1978, the US Government stated that "the question of recognition under the formulation of the last few years doesn't arise *per se*. . . . The important question is not recognition. The question is whether diplomatic relations continue. . . ."[257] On the latter point, it was stated:

    "The Government of the United States of America assumes that the Government of the Democratic Republic of Afghanistan will continue to honour and support the existing treaties and international agreements in force between our two states. On that assumption, it is the intention of the U.S. Government . . . to maintain diplomatic relations. . . ."[258]

    Note, however, that the Governments of the United States and China did expressly agree "to recognise each other and to establish diplomatic relations" as of 1979.[259]

2. On the criterion qualifying a government to be treated as the government of a state, the US would appear to have moved to a simple test of effective control. In 1977, Deputy Secretary of State Christopher[260] stated:

    "We maintain diplomatic relations with many governments of which we do not necessarily approve. The reality is that, in this day and age, coups and other unscheduled changes of government are not exceptional developments. Withholding diplomatic relations from these régimes, after they have obtained effective control, penalizes us. It means that we forsake much of the chance to influence the attitudes and conduct of a new régime. . . . Isolation may well bring out the worst in the new government."

TINOCO ARBITRATION

Great Britain v Costa Rica (1923)

Sole Arbitrator: William H. Taft, Chief Justice of the United States Supreme Court, 1 R.I.A.A. 369

In 1917, Tinoco ousted the Government of Costa Rica by force. Elections were held and "[f]or a full two years Tinoco and the legislative assembly under him peaceably administered the affairs of the

[256] Baxter (1978) 72 A.J.I.L. 875 at 876.
[257] Department of State spokesman, May 1, 1978, (1978) 72 A.J.I.L. 879.
[258] US Embassy in Kabul statement, May 6, 1978, (1978) 72 A.J.I.L. 879.
[259] Joint Communiqué, US Government and the Government of the People's Republic of China: (1979) 73 A.J.I.L. 277. At the same time, the US withdrew its recognition of the Government of Taiwan as the Government of the one state of China. It also expressly recognised the Angolan Government: (1993) 87 A.J.I.L. 595.
[260] Speech at Occidental College, June 11, 1977, [1977] U.S.D.I.L. p.18.

Government of Costa Rica." (at p.379). In 1919, Tinoco was ousted in his turn and the new Government repudiated certain obligations undertaken by the Tinoco Government towards British nationals. In the course of ruling upon the claims brought by Great Britain on the basis of these obligations, the arbitrator discussed the question of recognition.

TAFT C.J.

I must hold that from the evidence ... the Tinoco government was an actual sovereign government.

But it is urged that many leading Powers refused to recognize the Tinoco government, and that recognition by other nations is the chief and best evidence of the birth, existence and continuity of succession of a government. Undoubtedly recognition by other Powers is an important evidential factor in establishing proof of the existence of a government in the society of nations. What are the facts as to this? The Tinoco government was recognized by ... [20 states]. ...

The non-recognition by other nations of a government claiming to be a national personality, is usually appropriate evidence that it has not attained the independence and control entitling it by international law to be classed as such. But when recognition *vel non* of a government is by such nations determined by inquiry, not into its *de facto* sovereignty and complete governmental control, but into its illegitimacy or irregularity of origin,[261] their non-recognition loses something of evidential weight on the issue with which those applying the rules of international law are alone concerned. What is true of the non-recognition of the United States in its bearing upon the existence of a *de facto* government under Tinoco for thirty months is probably in a measure true of the non-recognition by her Allies in the European War. Such non-recognition for any reason, however, cannot outweigh the evidence disclosed by this record before me as to the *de facto* character of Tinoco's government, according to the standard set by international law. ...

It is further objected by Costa Rica that Great Britain by her failure to recognize the Tinoco government is estopped now to urge claims of her subjects dependent upon the acts and contracts of the Tinoco government. ... The contention here ... precludes a government which did not recognize a *de facto* government from appearing in an international tribunal on behalf of its nationals to claim any rights based on the acts of such government.

To sustain this view a great number of decisions in English and American courts are cited to the point that a municipal court cannot, in litigation before it, recognize or assume the *de facto* character of a foreign government which the executive department of foreign affairs of the government of which the court is a branch has not recognized. ... But such cases have no bearing on the point before us. Here the executive of Great Britain takes the position that the Tinoco government which it did not recognize, was nevertheless a *de facto* government that could create rights in British subjects which it now seeks to protect. Of course, as already emphasized, its failure to recognize the *de facto* government can be used against it as evidence to disprove the character it now attributes to that government, but this does not bar it from changing its position. Should a case arise in one of its own courts after it has changed its position doubtless that court would feel it incumbent upon it to note the change in its further rulings.

... It may be urged that it would be in the interest of the stability of governments and the orderly adjustment of international relations, and so a proper rule of international law, that a government in recognizing or refusing to recognize a government claiming admission to the society of nations should thereafter be held to an attitude consistent with its deliberate conclusion in this issue. Arguments for and against such a rule occur to me; but it suffices to say that I have not been cited to text writers of authority or to decisions of significance indicating a general acquiescence of nations in such a rule. Without this, it cannot be applied here as a principle of international law.

---

[261] Ed. The Arbitrator is here referring to the "constitutionality" test of recognition introduced as US policy by President Wilson in 1913 which made "the coming into power of a new government by constitutional means a prerequisite of recognition, particularly with respect to the Central American Republics": 2 Whiteman 69. The test was abandoned by 1931.

Note

This case concerned the recognition of governments. The Tribunal applied the declaratory, not the constitutive, theory of recognition. On the recognition of states, in *Deutsche Continental Gas-Gesell-schaft v Polish State*[262] the German-Polish Mixed Arbitral Tribunal stated:

> "... according to the opinion rightly admitted by the great majority of writers on international law, the recognition of a State is not constitutive but merely declaratory. The State exists by itself (*par lui-même*) and the recognition is nothing else than a declaration of this existence, recognised by the States from which it emanates."

----

6. THE EFFECT OF RECOGNITION IN BRITISH COURTS

REPUBLIC OF SOMALIA v WOODHOUSE DRAKE CAREY SUISSE S.A.

[1993] Q.B. 54; Queen's Bench Division

In January 1991, the Republic of Somalia bought a cargo of rice for delivery by ship to its capital, Mogadishu. By the time the ship arrived offshore, the Somali Government of President Siad Barre had been overthrown and a civil war was in progress. The captain of the ship decided it was too dangerous to deliver the cargo. By order of the Commercial Court in London, it was sold and the proceeds paid into court. In July 1991, the Djibouti Agreement, following an international conference of interested states and parties, nominated Mr Mahdi as the interim President of Somalia. He appointed Mr Qalib as his Prime Minister. In these proceedings, the question was whether the £2 million in court that belonged to the Republic of Somalia could be paid out to Crossman Block, who were the solicitors acting for the interim government of Mr Qalib.

HOBHOUSE J.

The question therefore is whether the interim government is the Government of the Republic of Somalia ... The policy of the United Kingdom is now not to confer recognition on governments as opposed to on states ...

Hobhouse J. then quoted the 1980 Parliamentary Answers, above, p.139

... [Prior to 1980] recognition by Her Majesty's Government was the decisive matter and the courts had no role save to inquire of the executive whether or not it had recognised the government in question.
    Some writers appear still to feel that the criterion remains one of recognition by the government of this country, the difference being that, whereas before 1980 the government would say expressly whether it recognised the foreign government, now it is to be left to be ascertained as a matter of inference: see Professor J. Crawford ... (1986) 57 B.Y. 405, and the continuing references in *Brownlie, Principles of Public International Law*, 4th ed. (1990) and in (1982) 53 B.Y. 197, 209, to the recognition of governments. Mr Richards [for the Treasury Solicitor] did not seek to support that view and it is clearly contrary to or not adopted in other writings: see, for example, Francis Mann, *Foreign Affairs in English Courts* (1986); C. Warbrick, "The New British Policy on Recognition of Governments" (1981) 30 I.C.L.Q. 568; and indeed the general tenor of Professor Brownlie's work itself. The impracticality of the "inferred recognition" theory as a legal concept for forensic use is obvious and it cannot be thought that that was the intention of Her Majesty's Government in giving the Parliamentary answers.

---
[262] (1929) 5 A.D. 11 at 13.

The use of the phrase "left to be inferred" is designed to fulfil a need for information in an international or political, not a judicial, context.

If recognition by Her Majesty's Government is no longer the criterion of the locus standi of a foreign "government" in the English courts and the possession of a legal persona in English law, what criteria is the court to apply? The [1980 Parliamentary] answers do confirm one applicable criterion, namely, whether the relevant régime is able of itself to "exercise effective control of the territory of the state concerned" and is "likely to continue to do so;" and the statement as to what is to be the evidence of the attitude of Her Majesty's Government provides another—to be inferred from the nature of the dealings, if any, that Her Majesty's Government has with it and whether they are on a normal government to government basis. The non-existence of such dealings cannot however be conclusive because their absence may be explained by some extraneous consideration, for example, lack of occasion, the attitude of the régime to human rights, its relationship to another state. As the answers themselves acknowledge, the conduct of governments in their relations with each other may be affected by considerations of policy as well as by considerations of legal characterisation. The courts of this country are now only concerned with the latter consideration. . . .

In relation to Somalia and the present litigation, the Foreign and Commonwealth Office has on three occasions responded to inquiries by solicitors . . .

On 20 February 1992 [in its third letter] the Foreign and Commonwealth Office wrote again to More Fisher Brown. It reconfirmed that Her Majesty's Government was not concerned with the recognition of governments and had not recognised the purported secession. It continued:

> The comment in [the letter of 5 August 1991] has been somewhat overtaken by subsequent events, in particular fighting between rival elements of the United Somalia Congress which broke out in November 1991 and in which thousands of people have been killed and injured. . . . fighting in Mogadishu has continued . . . The United Kingdom maintains formal contact with all the factions involved, but there have been no dealings on a government to government basis.

It is clear from this letter that Her Majesty's Government does not consider that there is at present any effective government in Somalia. It refers to "factions" and treats the interim government as merely one among a number of factions. . . .

Accordingly, if the question before the court is to be decided on the basis of the attitude adopted by Her Majesty's Government, an order cannot be made in favour of the interim government or Crossman Block. The basis for its attitude is clearly not any disapproval of an established régime but rather that there is no régime which has control, let alone any administrative control which has the requisite element of stable continuity.

Mr Richards submitted that particular weight should be given to these communications. I have difficulty in accepting that submission without some qualification. Once the question for the court becomes one of making its own assessment of the evidence, making findings of fact on all the relevant evidence placed before it and drawing the appropriate legal conclusion, and is no longer a question of simply reflecting government policy, letters from the Foreign and Commonwealth Office become merely part of the evidence in the case. In the present case no problem of admissibility of evidence arises. In so far as the letters make statements about what is happening in the territory of some foreign state, such letters may not be the best evidence; but as regards the question whether Her Majesty's Government has dealings with the foreign government it will almost certainly be the best and only conclusive evidence of that fact. Where Her Majesty's Government is dealing with the foreign government on a normal government to government basis as the government of the relevant foreign state, it is unlikely in the extreme that the inference that the foreign government is the government of that state will be capable of being rebutted and questions of public policy and considerations of the interrelationship of the judicial and executive arms of government may be paramount: see *The Arantzazu Mendi* [1939] A.C. 256, 264 and *Gur Corporation v. Trust Bank of Africa Ltd* [1987] Q.B. 599, 625. But now that the question has ceased to be one of recognition, the theoretical possibility of rebuttal must exist.

There is no decided English authority on the effect of the 1980 answers. *Gur Corporation v. Trust Bank of Africa Ltd* was concerned with a question of the recognition of a state and the competence of a subordinate body within the recognised territory of that state under the laws of that state. The 1980 answers were referred to, p. 619, but were not the basis of the decision. Here no question of the recognition of a state is involved. Nor does this case involve any accredited representative of a foreign state in this country. Different considerations would arise if it did, since it would be contrary to public policy for the court not to recognise as a qualified representative of the head of state of the foreign state the diplomatic representative recognised by Her Majesty's Government. There is no recognised diplomatic representative of the Republic of Somalia to the United Kingdom.

The statements of fact in the letters from the Foreign and Commonwealth Office are confirmed by the other evidence that is before the court concerning the actual situation in Somalia. The interim government is not governing that country and does not exercise administrative or any control over its territory and population[263] ...

The criteria of effective control referred to in the Parliamentary answers are clearly not satisfied. In *The Arantzazu Mendi* [1939] A.C. 256, 264–265, Lord Atkin said:

> By "exercising *de facto* administrative control" or "exercising effective administrative control." I understand exercising all the functions of a sovereign government, in maintaining law and order, instituting and main-taining courts of justice, adopting or imposing laws regulating the relations of the inhabitants of the territory to one another and to the government.

The interim government clearly does not satisfy these criteria; the Republic of Somalia currently has no government. However, there are two other aspects on which counsel for the interim government has relied. These are the recognition of the interim government by some other states and international bodies, and the fact that the interim government was set up by the Djibouti Agreement which resulted from an international conference attended by many international states and bodies.[264]

In evaluating these arguments it is relevant to distinguish between regimes that have been the constitutional and established government of a state and a régime which is seeking to achieve that position either displacing a former government or to fill a vacuum. Since the question is now whether a government *exists*, there is no room for more than one government at a time nor for separate *de jure* and *de facto* governments in respect of the same state. But a loss of control by a constitutional government may not immediately deprive it of its status, whereas an insurgent régime will require to establish control before it can exist as a government.

The argument based on the Djibouti Agreement does not assist the interim government. The Djibouti Agreement was not constitutional. It did not create a *de jure* status for the interim government in Somalia. The interim government was not and did not become the constitutional successor of the Government of President Siad Barre. Accordingly, if the interim government is to be treated as the Government of Somalia, it must be able to show that it is exercising administrative control over the territory of the Republic. That it is not able to do. Accordingly, that argument must fail.

As regards the argument of international recognition and recognition by the United Nations, though this does not as such involve control of territory or a population, it does correspond to one aspect of statehood. A classic definition of a state is that contained in article 1 of the Montevideo Convention of 1933 as having: "(a) a permanent population; (b) a defined territory; (c) government; and (d) capacity to enter into relations with other states." Whilst illustrating that it is difficult to separate the recognition of a state from the recognition of a government of that state, this definition also shows that part of the function of a government of a state is to have relations with other states. This is also implicit in the reference in the 1980 Parliamentary answers to dealings on a government to government basis.

Accordingly I consider that the degree of international recognition of an alleged government is a relevant factor in assessing whether it exists as the government of a state. But where, as here, the régime exercises virtually no administrative control at all in the territory of the state, international recognition of an uncon-stitutional regime should not suffice and would, indeed, have to be accounted for by policy considerations rather than legal characterisation; and it is, of course, possible for states to have relations with bodies which are not states or governments of states.

There is evidence from which it appears that the United Nations Organisation considers that there are persons whom it may treat as the representatives of the Republic of Somalia. Resolution 733 started with the words: "Considering the request by Somalia for the Security Council to consider the situation in Somalia." It appears that this request was contained in a letter from Mr Qalib dated December 15, 1991 addressed to the Secretary General to the United Nations and the President of the Security Council. Mr Qalib signed himself as the "Prime Minister of Somalia." ... The text of Resolution 733 was apparently communicated to Mr Mahdi by the Secretary General of the United Nations describing Mr Mahdi as "His Excellency Mr. Ali Mahdi Interim President of Somalia."

This evidence is not wholly satisfactory. The attitude of the United Nations to the interim government could be

---

[263] Ed. Hobhouse J. quoted a report by the Agency for International Development. He had earlier, p.58, noted that the "interim government has been unable to operate in Mogadishu and Mr Qalib has based himself in a hotel in Riyadh in Saudi Arabia".

[264] Ed. The Conference, which was called at Djibouti under the chairmanship of the President of Djibouti, was attended by 16 states, including the United States, the USSR and various African and Arab states, but not the UK; by international organisations such as the OAU and the EEC; and by representatives of six rival groupings within Somalia.

established in a more direct fashion and more authoritatively. The letter of Mr Hassan suggests something less than a fully recognised status. In any event, membership of an international organisation does not amount to recognition nor does a vote on credentials and representation issues: see Warbrick, 30 I.C.L.Q., 568, 583 citing 1950 UN Doc S/1466. But any apparent acceptance of the interim government by the United Nations and other international organisations and states does not suffice in the present case to demonstrate that the interim government is the Government of the Republic of Somalia. The evidence the other way is too strong.

Accordingly, the factors to be taken into account in deciding whether a government exists as the government of a state are: (a) whether it is the constitutional government of the state; (b) the degree, nature and stability of administrative control, if any, that it of itself exercises over the territory of the state; (c) whether Her Majesty's Government has any dealings with it and if so what is the nature of those dealings; and (d) in marginal cases, the extent of international recognition that it has as the government of the state.

On the evidence before the court the interim government certainly does not qualify having regard to any of the three important factors. Accordingly the court must conclude that Crossman Block does not at present have the authority of the Republic of Somalia to receive and deal with the property of the Republic . . . I direct that no part of the sum in court should be paid out to Crossman Block without a further order of the court. . . .

Notes

1.   Before the 1980 statement, the practice of the British courts when called upon to recognise the law or capacity to act of a foreign government was to seek and regard as conclusive a Foreign Office certificate.[265] In this context, recognition was constitutive. When asked in Parliament about the effect of the 1980 statement on legal proceedings concerning new governments, the Foreign Secretary (Lord Carrington) replied:

> "In future cases where a new régime comes to power unconstitutionally our attitude on the question whether it qualifies to be treated as a Government, will be left to be inferred from the nature of the dealings, if any, which we may have with it, and in particular on whether we are dealing with it on a normal Government to Government basis."[266]

It is clear from the *Woodhouse* case that the Foreign Office will, if requested, respond to enquiries as to the dealings, if any, the United Kingdom has with a claimant government and comment on the factual situation in the state concerned. However, the *Woodhouse* case decided that indications given by the Foreign Office as to whether "government to government" dealings have taken place with a claimant government are not conclusive. Instead they are just one consideration for the Court to take into account when deciding whether "a government exists as the government of a state". Was Hobhouse J. correct to reject the "inferred recognition" approach, whereby the 1980 statement would be read simply as intending to signal a move from express to implied recognition? Does the *Woodhouse* approach leave open the possibility that the courts will decide that the government of a state is not that with which the executive is dealing, contrary to the "one voice" approach (which supposes that it is good policy for the courts and the executive to march in step)?[267] If that approach had been followed in the *Woodhouse* case, the Interim Government would have been found not to have been the government of Somalia simply on the basis that the Foreign Office had reported that the United Kingdom did not have dealings with it. Might the *Woodhouse* approach lead to considerable uncertainty in borderline cases, as courts try to apply Hobhouse J.'s list of four factors? Note that the understanding of the Secretary

---

[265] See Lord Reid's speech in the *Carl Zeiss* case below, p.153.
[266] *Hansard*, HL Vol.409, cols 1097–1098, (May 23, 1980); U.K.M.I.L. 1980 (1980) 51 B.Y.I.L. 368.
[267] For criticism of the *Woodhouse* approach, see Talmon, above, p.155, n.37, pp.281 et seq.

of State (Lord Carrington), above, was clearly that the courts would discover the government's "attitude" and follow it.

2. The *Woodhouse* case was followed in *Sierra Leone Telecommunications Co Ltd v Barclays Bank Plc*.[268] In that case, the elected Kabbah Government had been overthrown by coup by a military junta. The plaintiff was a company incorporated in Sierra Leone and wholly owned by the Sierra Leone Government. The company had established a London account with the defendant bank, with signatories mandated to operate it. Following the coup, the defendant refused to make payments requested by those signatories after the junta Government had nominated different signatories and had appointed a new board of directors whose chairman had written to the defendant stating that the requested payments had not been authorised. The plaintiff company, which continued to conduct its business activities from outside Sierra Leone, sought a declaration that the signatories' pre-coup mandate remained valid. Applying the *Woodhouse* criteria, Cresswell J. stated:

> "(a) *Whether it is the constitutional government of the state ...*

On 28 November 1997 the Foreign and Commonwealth Office wrote to Messrs Stephenson Harwood as follows:

> ... The British Government welcomed the election in Sierra Leone of President Ahmad Tejan Kabbah in February 1996. We have consistently condemned the military coup of 25 May 1997 which overthrew the democratically elected government of Sierra Leone. We look forward to the restoration of constitutional order in that country. We continue to deal with the democratically elected government of Sierra Leone under President Kabbah. We have no dealings with the military junta in Freetown. ...

> (b) *The degree, nature and stability of administrative control, if any, that it of itself exercises over the territory of the state*

According to the Sierra Leone High Commissioner the military junta presently has no control whatsoever over the country outside of Freetown and there are civil unrest problems in Freetown. ... The junta has very little real control over the administrative affairs of the country. There were some civil servants left after the coup who had not managed to flee the country. They only number approximately a quarter of the full complement under the legitimate government and therefore none of the departments of government are functioning properly, if at all.

> ... The junta ... do not control the country's only international airport situated at Lungi, near Freetown, nor the main internal airfield at Hastings. Both these airfields are controlled by the forces of ECOMOG [an ECOWAS peacekeeping force]. ... Similarly ECOMOG controls the main routes to and from the capital city, Freetown, and even members of the junta are not allowed to move freely from Freetown to the provinces and back. ... The most recent reports show that forces loyal to President Kabbah are in control of the most important areas up-country. ...

---

[268] [1998] All E.R. 821, QB.

(c) *Whether Her Majesty's government has any dealings with it and if so what is the nature of those dealings.*

See under (a) above.

(d) *In marginal cases, the extent of international recognition that it has as the government of the state*

The United Nations has imposed sanctions relating to the supply of arms and petroleum products to Sierra Leone: see United Nations Resolution SCR 1132 of 8 October 1997. The resolution has been enacted in England by various statutory instruments. In addition the coup has also been condemned by the Commonwealth, the Organisation of African Unity and the European Community. ...

In the light of my analysis of the factors in [the *Woodhouse* case] ... I conclude that the military junta are not the Government of Sierra Leone."

3.   There are cases in which United Kingdom courts have, exceptionally, recognised as legally valid the acts of unrecognised governments or *unrecognised* entities claiming to be states that affect the "private rights" of individuals, provided that the unrecognised government is in effective control of its territory: see below, p.156. Is there any reason why such acts of unrecognised governments of *recognised* states (e.g. Sierra Leone) should not be recognised as legally valid in such circumstances?

4.   It is not clear how the *Woodhouse* approach would apply were the United Kingdom to have dealings with two rival governments.[269] In practice, the United Kingdom had not recognised governments de jure and de facto in the years immediately preceding the 1980 statement and has not had dealings with two governments since then.

LUTHER v SAGOR

[1921] 1 K.B. 456; [1921] 3 K.B. 532. King's Bench Division; Court of Appeal

In 1920, the defendant company bought a quantity of wood from the new Soviet Government of the USSR. The plaintiff Russian company claimed title to the wood on the ground that it had come from a factory in the USSR that had been owned by it before being nationalised by a 1919 decree of the Soviet Government. The plaintiff argued,[270] that the decree should not be recognised by an English court, inter alia, because the Soviet Government had not been recognised by the United Kingdom.

ROCHE J.

The attitude proper to be adopted by a Court of this country with regard to foreign governments or powers I understand to be as follows. ... If a foreign government, or its sovereignty, is not recognized by the Government of this country the Courts of this country either cannot, or at least need not, or ought not, to take notice of, or recognize such foreign government or its sovereignty. This negative proposition is ... established and recognised

---

[269] For the approach of the courts on de jure and de facto governments, see *Luther v Sagor*, below and the cases referred to above, p.141, n.253.

[270] It also argued that the decree was confiscatory.

by the judgment of Kay J. in *Republic of Peru v Dreyfus*.[271] ... In the *City of Berne v Bank of England*[272] the question at issue was the right of an unrecognized foreign government to maintain a suit, but Lord Eldon's judgment is, I think, an authority for the general proposition I have stated. ...

This being the law which must guide and direct my decision, I have to consider whether and in what sense the Government represented by M. Krassin in this matter is recognized by His Majesty's Government. ...

Roche J. then read a letter from the Foreign Office dated November 20, 1920.

Gentlemen,

I am directed by Earl Curzon of Kedleston ... to inform you that for a certain limited purpose His Majesty's Government has regarded Monsieur Krassin as exempt from the process of the Courts, and also for the like limited purpose His Majesty's Government has assented to the claim that that which Monsieur Krassin represents in this Country is a State Government of Russia, but that beyond these propositions the Foreign Office has not gone, nor moreover do these expressions of opinion purport to decide difficult, and it may be very special questions of law upon which it may become necessary for the Courts to pronounce. I am to add that His Majesty's Government has never officially recognised the Soviet Government in any way.

It was said on behalf of the defendants that these communications were vague and ambiguous. I should rather say that they were guarded, but as clear as the indeterminate position of affairs in connection with the subject-matter of the communications enabled them to be ... I am not satisfied that His Majesty's Government has recognized the Soviet Government as the Government of a Russian Federative Republic or of any sovereign state or power. I therefore am unable to recognize it, or to hold it has sovereignty, or is able by decree to deprive the plaintiff company of its property.

Roche J. gave judgment for the plaintiffs. The defendants appealed to the Court of Appeal.

Court of Appeal

BANKES L.J.

Upon the evidence which was before the learned judge I think that his decision was quite right. ...

In this Court the appellants asked leave to adduce further evidence ... It consisted of two letters from the Foreign Office dated respectively April 20 and 22, 1921. The first is ... in these terms: "I am ... to inform you that His Majesty's Government recognize the Soviet Government as the *de facto* Government of Russia." The letter of April 22 ... contains (inter alia) the statement that the Provisional Government came into power on March 14, 1917, that it was recognized by His Majesty's Government as the then existing Government of Russia, and that the Constituent Assembly remained in session until December 13, 1917, when it was dispersed by the Soviet authorities.[273] ...

Under these circumstances the whole aspect of the case is changed, and it becomes necessary to consider matters which were not material in the Court below. The first is a question of law of very considerable importance—namely, what is the effect of the recognition by His Majesty's Government in April, 1921, of the Soviet Government as the *de facto* Government of Russia upon the past acts of that Government, and how far back, if at all, does that recognition extend.

... counsel have been unable to refer the Court to any English authority. Attention has been called to three cases decided in the Supreme Court of the United States: *Williams v. Bruffy*[274] *Underhill v. Hernandez*[275]; and *Oetjen v. Central Leather Co.*[276] In none of these cases is any distinction attempted to be drawn in argument between the effect of a recognition of a government as a *de facto* government and a recognition of a government

---

[271] 38 Ch.D. at 357, 358 and 359.

[272] 9 Ves. 347.

[273] The Provisional Government came into being after the "February Revolution" of 1917, as a result of which the Tsar abdicated. It was led first by Prince Lvov and then by Kerensky. After the "October Revolution" of the same year, the Provisional Government was replaced by the Soviet Government, i.e. the Bolshevik Government led by Lenin.

[274] 96 U.S. 176.

[275] 168 U.S. 250.

[276] 246 U.S. 297.

as a government *de jure*, nor is any decision given upon that point; nor, except incidentally, is any mention made as to the effect of the recognition of a government upon its past acts. The mention occurs in two passages, one in the judgement of … Fuller C.J. in *Underhill v. Hernandez*.[277] He says, in speaking of civil wars: "If the party seeking to dislodge the existing government succeeds, and the independence of the government it has set up is recognized, then the acts of such government from the commencement of its existence are regarded as those of an independent nation." … On principle the views put forward by these learned judges appear to me to be sound, though there may be cases in which the Courts of a country whose government has recognized the government of some other country as the *de facto* government of that country may have to consider at what stage in its development the government so recognized can, to use the language to which I have already referred of those learned judges, be said to have "commenced its existence." No difficulty of that kind arises in the present case, because, upon the construction which I place upon the communication of the Foreign Office to which I have referred, this Court must treat the Soviet Government, which the Government of this country has now recognized as the *de facto* Government of Russia, as having commenced its existence at a date anterior to any date material to the dispute between the parties to this appeal.

… The Government of this country having … recognized the Soviet Government as the Government really in possession of the powers of sovereignty in Russia, the acts of that Government must be treated by the Courts of this country with all the respect due to the acts of a duly recognized foreign sovereign state.

… From the letter from the Foreign Office addressed to Messrs. Linklater of April 22, 1921, it appears that the Soviet authorities dispersed the then Constituent Assembly on December 13, 1917, from which date I think it must be accepted that the Soviet Government assumed the position of the sovereign Government and purported to act as such.

WARRINGTON L.J.

I should have thought that in principle recognition would be retroactive at any rate to such date as our Government accept as that by which the government in question in fact established its authority. It appears from the letter of the Foreign Office dated April 22, 1921, that that date is anterior to any of the events material to the present case.

Scrutton L.J. delivered a concurring judgment. Appeal allowed.

Note

Luther v Sagor established that recognition, once given, was retroactive in effect from the time that the recognised government established itself. It also confirmed that the British courts would not recognise or enforce the laws or other public acts of an unrecognised government. Similarly, an unrecognised government lacked *locus standi* to bring a suit in a British court: *City of Berne v Bank of England* (cited by Roche J., above). Nor was it entitled to sovereign immunity. Thus in *The Annette and the Dora*[278] the plaintiffs brought a writ *in rem* for the attachment of ships belonging to them which had been requisitioned by the Provisional Government of Northern Russia in September 1917 and which were allegedly in that Government's possession. In the light of a Foreign Office certificate to the effect that the Provisional Government had not been formally recognised by the British Government, Hill J. held that it could not plead sovereign immunity so as to have the writ set aside.

The above notes are expressed in terms of the pre-1980 rules concerning recognition. Presumably, under the *Woodhouse* case, these rules continue to apply, with the adaptation that the claimant government of an existing state that is not a government when tested against the *Woodhouse* factors would be in the same position that an unrecognised government was under the pre-1980 case law.

---

[277] 168 U.S. 253. Ed. The other was in the judgment of Field J. in *Williams v Bruffy*.
[278] [1919] P. 105 PD.

As to retroactivity, would the courts regard the claimant government as the lawful government from the moment that it "commenced its existence" (Banks L.J.)?[279]

CARL ZEISS STIFTUNG v RAYNER AND KEELER LTD (NO.2)[280]

[1967] 1 A.C. 853. House of Lords

C.Z.S. is a German charitable foundation that makes optical instruments. Under its constitution, it is run by a Special Board. After the First World War, the Board was the Minister of Education of Thuringia, a state within Germany. In 1945, Thuringia became part of the Russian Zone of Occupied Germany. In 1949, the USSR handed over government of its Zone to the German Democratic Republic. In 1952, the GDR reorganised its local government and Thuringia ceased to exist. The Special Board of C.Z.S., under the new arrangements, became the Council of Gera.

In this case, C.Z.S., acting through its new Board, brought a claim in the English courts. In these interlocutory proceedings, the defendants, now the respondents, asked that the claim be dismissed because it had been brought without the proper authority of the appellants. The requested order was denied by Cross J. but granted by the Court of Appeal after an argument based upon recognition had been put to that court for the first time in the case. The argument was that as the United Kingdom had not recognised the GDR the new Special Board, having been created by the GDR, could not be recognised by an English court. The House of Lords unanimously reversed the Court of Appeal's ruling on appeal.

LORD REID

If the respondents' argument based on non-recognition is well founded, then it must follow that British courts cannot recognise either the existence of the Council of Gera or the validity of anything done by it, and in particular cannot recognise any authority given by it for the raising of the present action. ...

In the normal case a law is made either by the sovereign directly or by some body entitled under the constitution of the country to make it or by some person or body to which the sovereign has delegated authority to make it. On the other hand, there are many cases where laws have been made against the will of the sovereign by persons engaged in a rebellion or revolution: then until such persons or the government which they set up have been granted *de facto* recognition by the Government of this country, their laws cannot be recognised by the courts of this country, but after *de facto* recognition such laws will be recognised. So far there is no difficulty. But the present case does not fit neatly into any of these categories. We are considering whether the law of 1952 under which the Council of Gera was set up can be recognised by our courts and therefore we must ascertain what was the situation in East Germany in 1952.

It is a firmly established principle that the question whether a foreign state ruler or government is or is not sovereign is one on which our courts accept as conclusive information provided by Her Majesty's government: no evidence is admissible to contradict that information.[281]

... In the present case the Court of Appeal twice received ... information from the Foreign Secretary. First on September 16, 1964, it was stated: "Her Majesty's Government has not granted any recognition *de jure* or *de facto* to (a) the 'German Democratic Republic' or (b) its 'Government,' "and secondly on November 6, 1964, a further answer was given ...

In my opinion, this latter answer is decisive on the question which I am now considering and I must therefore

---

[279] For other cases concerning the retroactive effect of recognition that require reconsideration in the light of the *Woodhouse* case, see *Civil Air Transport Inc v Central Air Transport Corporation* [1953] A.C. 70 PC; and *Gdynia Ameriyka Linie Zeglugowe Spolka Akcyjna v Boguslawski* [1953] A.C. 11 HL.

[280] See Greig (1967) 83 L.Q.R. 96; Mann, *Foreign Affairs in English Courts* (1986), pp.56–57; Richter (1968) 6 M.U.L.R. 448.

[281] Ed. Lord Reid cited *Duff Development Co. Ltd v Kelantan Government* [1924] A.C. 797 HL, as authority. See further on this point, above, p.88.

quote the relevant question and the relevant parts of the answer or certificate given by the Foreign Secretary. The question was:

What (a) states or (b) governments or (c) authorities (if any) have since July 1, 1945, up to the present date been recognised by Her Majesty's Government as (a) entitled to exercise or (b) exercising governing authority in the area of Germany outside the zones allocated to the Governments of the United Kingdom, the United States of America and the French Republic by the protocol of September 12, 1944, and the agreement of July 26, 1945, concluded between the Governments of the said states and the Union of Soviet Socialist Republics. Has such recognition been *de jure* or *de facto*.

The relevant parts of the certificate are as follows: ...

(a) From the zone allocated to the Union of Soviet Socialist Republics Allied forces under the Supreme Allied Commander, General Eisenhower, withdrew at or about the end of June, 1945. Since that time and up to the present date Her Majesty's Government have recognised the state and Government of the Union of Soviet Socialist Republics as *de jure* entitled to exercise governing authority in respect of that zone. In matters affecting Germany as a whole, the states and Governments of the French Republic, the United Kingdom of Great Britain and Northern Ireland, the United States of America and the Union of Soviet Socialist Republics were jointly entitled to exercise governing authority. In the period from August 30, 1945, to March 20, 1948, they did exercise such joint authority through the Control Council for Germany. Apart from the states, Governments and Control Council aforementioned, Her Majesty's Government have not recognised either *de jure* or *de facto* any other authority purporting to exercise governing authority in or in respect of the zone. Her Majesty's Government, however, regard the aforementioned Governments as retaining rights and responsibilities in respect of Germany as a whole....

The purpose of a certificate is to provide information about the status of foreign governments and states and therefore the statement that since June, 1945, "Her Majesty's Government have recognised the state and Government of the Union of Soviet Socialist Republics as *de jure* entitled to exercise governing authority in respect of that zone" cannot merely mean that Her Majesty's Government have granted this recognition so as to leave the courts of this country free to receive evidence as to whether in fact the U.S.S.R. are still entitled to exercise governing authority there. The courts of this country are no more entitled to hold that a sovereign, still recognised by our Government, has ceased in fact to be sovereign *de jure*, than they are entitled to hold that a government not yet recognised has acquired sovereign status. So this certificate requires that we must take it as a fact that the U.S.S.R. have been since 1954 and still are *de jure* entitled to exercise that governing authority. The certificate makes no distinction between the period before and the period after the German Democratic Republic was set up. So we are bound to hold that the setting up of that Republic made no difference in the right of the U.S.S.R. to exercise governing authority in the zone. And it must follow from that that the U.S.S.R. could at any time lawfully bring to an end the German Democratic Republic and its Government and could then resume direct rule of the zone. But that is quite inconsistent with there having in fact been any abdication by the U.S.S.R. of its rights when the German Democratic Republic was set up. ...

If we are bound to hold that the German Democratic Republic was not in fact set up as a sovereign independent state, the only other possibility is that it was set up as a dependent or subordinate organisation through which the U.S.S.R. is entitled to exercise indirect rule. I do not think that we are concerned to inquire or to know to what extent the U.S.S.R. in fact exercise their right of control. ...

It was argued that the present case is analogous to cases where subjects of an existing sovereign have rebelled and have succeeded in gaining control of a part of the old sovereign's dominions. When they set up a new government in opposition to the *de jure* sovereign that new government does not and cannot derive any authority or right from the *de jure* sovereign, and our courts must regard its acts and the acts of its organs or officers as nullities until it has established and consolidated its position to such an extent as to warrant our government according *de facto* recognition of it. ...

Lord Reid referred to *Luther v Sagor*, above, p. 150, as an example of this situation and approved of the first instance and the Court of Appeal judgments in that case.

But the present case is essentially different. The German Democratic Republic was set up by the U.S.S.R. and it derived its authority and status from the Government of the U.S.S.R. So the only question could be whether or not it was set up as a sovereign state. But the certificate of our Government requires us to hold that it was not set up as a sovereign state because it requires us to hold that the U.S.S.R. remained *de jure* sovereign and therefore did not voluntarily transfer its sovereignty to the Democratic Republic. And, if the Democratic Republic did not become a sovereign state at its inception, there is no suggestion that it has at any subsequent time attempted to deprive the U.S.S.R. of rights which were not granted to it at its inception. The courts of this country must disregard any declarations of the Government of the U.S.S.R. in so far as they conflict with the certificate of Her Majesty's Secretary of State, and we must therefore hold that the U.S.S.R. set up the German Democratic Republic, not as a sovereign state, but as an organisation subordinate to the U.S.S.R. If that is so, then mere declarations by the Government of the Democratic Republic that it is acting as the government of an independent state cannot be regarded as proof that its initial status has been altered, and we must regard the acts of the German Democratic Republic, its government organs and officers as acts done with the consent of the Government of the U.S.S.R. as the government entitled to exercise governing authority.

It appears to me to be impossible for any *de jure* sovereign governing authority to disclaim responsibility for acts done by subordinate bodies which it has set up and which have not attempted to usurp its sovereignty. So, in my opinion, the courts of this country cannot treat as nullities acts done by or on behalf of the German Democratic Republic. *De facto* recognition is appropriate—and, in my view, is only appropriate—where the new government have usurped power against the will of the *de jure* sovereign. I would think that where a sovereign has granted independence to a dependency any recognition of the new state would be a recognition *de jure*. . . .

I am reinforced in my opinion by a consideration of the consequences which would follow if the view taken by the Court of Appeal were correct. Counsel for the respondents did not dispute that in that case we must not only disregard all new laws and decrees made by the Democratic Republic or its Government, but we must also disregard all executive and judicial acts done by persons appointed by that Government because we must regard their appointments as invalid. The result of that would be far-reaching. Trade with the Eastern Zone of Germany is not discouraged. But the incorporation of every company in East Germany under any new law made by the Democratic Republic or by the official act of any official appointed by its Government would have to be regarded as a nullity, so that any such company could neither sue nor be sued in this country. And any civil marriage under any such new law, or owing its validity to the act of any such official, would also have to be treated as a nullity, so that we should have to regard the children as illegitimate. And the same would apply to divorces and all manner of judicial decisions, whether in family or commercial questions. And that would affect not only status of persons formerly domiciled in East Germany but property in this country the devolution of which depended on East German law.

It was suggested that these consequences might be mitigated if the courts of this country could adopt doctrines which have found some support in the United States of America.[282] . . . In the view which I take of the present case, it is unnecessary to express any opinion whether it would be possible to adopt any similar solutions in this country, if the need should ever arise.

LORD WILBERFORCE

My Lords, if the consequences of non-recognition of the East German "government" were to bring in question the validity of its legislative acts, I should wish seriously to consider whether the invalidity so brought about is total, or whether some mitigation of the severity of this result can be found. As Locke said: "A government without laws is, I suppose, a mystery in politics, inconceivable to human capacity and inconsistent with human society," and this must be true of a society—at least a civilised and organised society—such as we know to exist in East Germany. In the United States some glimmerings can be found of the idea that non-recognition cannot be pressed to its ultimate logical limit, and that where private rights, or acts of everyday occurrence, or perfunctory acts of administration are concerned (the scope of these exceptions has never been precisely defined) the courts may, in the interests of justice and common sense, where no consideration of public policy to the contrary has to prevail, give recognition to the actual facts or realities found to exist in the territory in question. These ideas began to take shape on the termination of the Civil War (see *U.S.* v. *Insurance Companies*), and have been developed and reformulated, admittedly as no more than dicta, but dicta by judges of high authority, in later cases. I mention two of these, *Sokoloff* v. *National City Bank* and *Upright* v. *Mercury Business Machines Co. Inc.*, a case which was concerned with a corporate body under East German law. Other references can be found conveniently assembled in Professor D. P. O'Connell's *International Law* (1965), vol. I, pp. 189 *et seq*. No trace of

---

[282] See Lord Wilberforce, below.

any such doctrine is yet to be found in English law, but equally, in my opinion, there is nothing in those English decisions, in which recognition has been refused to particular acts of non-recognised governments, which would prevent its acceptance or which prescribes the absolute and total invalidity of all laws and acts flowing from unrecognised governments. In view of the conclusion I have reached on the effect to be attributed to non-recognition in this case,[283] it is not necessary here to resort to this doctrine but, for my part, I should wish to regard it as an open question, in English law, in any future case whether and to what extent it can be invoked. ...

Lords Hodson, Guest and Upjohn delivered concurring speeches.

Notes

1. Whereas the *Woodhouse* case and *Luther v Sagor* concerned states recognised by the UK, the *Carl Zeiss* case and the *Gur* case (below) concern unrecognised governments of *unrecognised* states. The decision in the *Carl Zeiss* case is based upon the ingenious but unhappy fiction that the Government of the GDR was acting as the agent of the USSR when legislating to reorganise its local government.[284] Disturbed by the prospects for commercial and private affairs of disregarding all of the legislative and executive acts of a government with which British companies and nationals had substantial dealings (see Lord Reid's speech), the House of Lords seized upon an artificial device that, while doing violence to the concept of agency, at least did not openly undermine the public policy considerations that had led to Foreign Office non-recognition of the GDR. The *Carl Zeiss* case has since been followed in the *Gur* case, below, p.158.

2. The *Carl Zeiss* case is also important for the obiter dicta by Lord Wilberforce to the effect that the courts may, in the interests of justice and common sense, be prepared to recognise and enforce an unrecognised government's acts "where private rights, or acts of everyday occurrence, or perfunctory acts are concerned"—provided that public policy allows. What is not clear, however, is where or how the line will be drawn between recognisable and unrecognisable acts. As Lord Wilberforce states, "the scope of these exceptions has never been precisely defined." One way of avoiding such difficulties of definition would be to see the issue in terms not of recognition but of the "choice of law" rules in the conflict of laws.[285]

3. Lord Wilberforce's view is supported by Sir John Donaldson, M.R. obiter dicta, in the *Gur* case, below p.158. Lord Denning, M.R. expressed a similar view to that of Lord Wilberforce in *Hesperides Hotels v Aegean Holidays Ltd*.[286] This case concerned two hotels owned by the Greek Cypriot plaintiffs which were being run by Turkish Cypriots with the approval of the Turkish Cypriot administration which had governed the part of Cyprus in which the hotels were located since the armed invasion of Cyprus by Turkey in 1974. The plaintiffs' action in trespass was rejected by the Court of Appeal for lack of jurisdiction on the basis of English conflict of law rules. Addressing the fact that the United Kingdom continued to recognise the pre-invasion constitutional government of Cyprus as the de jure government of the whole of Cyprus and did not recognise the Turkish administration de jure or de facto (and had produced to the Court a certificate to this effect), Lord Denning stated obiter dicta:

    "If it were necessary to [do so] ... I would unhesitatingly hold that the courts of this country

---

[283] Ed. That the GDR was acting as the agent of the USSR, the de jure sovereign.

[284] For criticisms of the decision along these and other lines, see the writings cited above, on p.153, n.284, and Jennings, above, p.130, n.187, p.361.

[285] See Greig, above, p.153, n.284, p.138.

[286] [1978] Q.B. 205 CA. The matter was not discussed in the House of Lords: [1979] A.C. 508. See Lloyd Jones (1978) 37 C.L.J. 48; Merrills (1979) 28 I.C.L.Q. 523; and Shaw (1978) 94 L.Q.R. 500.

can recognise the laws or acts of a body which is in effective control of a territory even though it has not been recognised by Her Majesty's Government *de jure* or *de facto*: at any rate, in regard to the laws which regulate the day to day affairs of the people, such as their marriages, their divorces, their leases, their occupations, and so forth; and furthermore that the courts can receive evidence of the state of affairs so as to see whether the body is in effective control or not."[287]

4.   The Foreign Corporations Act 1991 s.1(1), also follows Lord Wilberforce's view in providing for the recognition under United Kingdom law of the corporate status of companies established under "the laws of a territory which is not at the time a recognised state", provided that "it appears that the laws of that territory are at that time applied by a settled court system in the territory". This is intended to cover the position of companies incorporated under, for example, the laws of the Turkish Republic of Northern Cyprus and Taiwan.[288]

5.   In *Caglar v Billingham*,[289] after referring, inter alia, to the *Hesperides* and *Gur* cases, the Special Commissioners of Inland Revenue stated:

> "121. The principle we extract from these authorities is that the courts may acknowledge the existence of an unrecognised foreign government in the context of the enforcement of laws relating to commercial obligations or matters of private law between individuals or matters of routine administration such as the registration of births, marriages or deaths. This principle is in line with that adopted in the Foreign Corporations Act 1991. However, the courts will not acknowledge the existence of an unrecognised state if to do so would involve them in acting inconsistently with the foreign policy or diplomatic stance of this country.
>
>   122. We are not concerned with commercial obligations or matters of private law or matters of administration but with the construction of an Act of the United Kingdom Parliament. In our view it is a matter of basic public policy that we should not take cognisance of the Turkish Republic of Northern Cyprus as that would involve us in acting inconsistently with the foreign policy and diplomatic stance of this country."

6.   The "private rights" exception was applied in *Emin v Yeldag*.[290] In that case, the plaintiff sought ancillary relief under English law on the basis of a divorce granted by a court in the Turkish Republic of Northern Cyprus. A Foreign Office affidavit in the case indicated that the UK Government had no "dealings" with its government. Recognising the divorce, Sumner J. noted that the Attorney-General had intervened in the case and supported the decision. Commenting on the "private rights" exception, Sumner J. stated that "the validity given to such decisions of a court in an unrecognised state must, however, be limited in scope. It must never be inconsistent with the foreign policy or diplomatic stance of the UK Government".[291] Sumner J. distinguished

---

[287] [1978] Q.B. at 218.

[288] Solicitor-General (Sir Nicholas Lyall), *Hansard*, HC Vol.195, col.438 (July 17, 1991).

[289] [1996] S.T.C. 150 at 171. The question in the case was whether the Turkish Republic of Northern Cyprus was a "foreign state" so that staff at its London office were exempt from UK income tax. See Turns (1998) 92 A.J.I.L. 305. See also *North Cyprus Tourism Centre Ltd v Transport for London* [2005] EWHC 1698 (advert by the "Ministry of Tourism TRNC" on London buses did not imply UK recognition). And see *Polly Peck International Plc v Nadir (No.2)* [1992] 4 All E.R. 769 CA.

[290] (2002) 1 F.L.R. 956, Fam D.

[291] (2002) 1 F.L.R. 970. Sumner J. declined to follow *B v B* (2000) 2 F.L.R. 707 Fam D, in which Compton J., deputy High Court judge, refused to recognise a TRNC divorce as being contrary to UK public policy. The Attorney-General did not intervene in *B v B*.

Adams v Adams[292] in which a divorce decree made by a Rhodesian judge—appointed by the unrecognised Smith Government following its breakaway from the UK—was not recognised by an English court on public policy grounds. In that case, Sumner J. agreed, the recognition of a decree issued by a judge in a UK colony who was appointed by a government not recognised by the UK would be "a constitutional anomaly".[293]

GUR CORPORATION v TRUST BANK OF AFRICA LTD[294]

[1987] Q.B. 599. Court of Appeal.

The plaintiff Panamanian company contracted with the Republic of Ciskei to build a hospital and two schools. As the contract required, the plaintiffs obtained a guarantee from the defendant bank in favour of the Ciskei Department of Public Works to cover the cost of remedying any building defects. In these proceedings, the plaintiff sought to recover a sum paid by them to the defendant as security for the guarantee. The defendant joined the Republic of Ciskei as a third party and the Republic of Ciskei brought a counterclaim for the money paid as security. Thereupon, Steyn J. raised the preliminary question whether the Republic of Ciskei had locus standi to sue or be sued in the English courts. In the light of two Foreign Office certificates, Steyn J. held that it did not. The Court of Appeal reversed his decision on the ground that the *Carl Zeiss* case applied: the Ciskei Government was acting as the delegate of the de jure sovereign, South Africa.

SIR JOHN DONALDSON M.R.

The matter came before Steyn J. who ... raised the question of whether it was permissible for the building owners to sue or be sued in the English courts. Let me say at once that the judge was quite right to do so. Although the courts in general, and the Commercial Court in particular, will always do their best to meet the needs and wishes of the litigants, there are certain public policy constraints. So far as is relevant, they are based upon the undesirability, to put it no higher, of the national courts appearing to speak in terms which are not consistent with the nation's foreign policy and diplomatic stance ...

This decision was greeted with some dismay by all three parties. Probably the most dismayed was the bank and for two somewhat different reasons. The first was that the decision opened up the possibility of judgment being given against the bank in favour of the plaintiffs in this country, without the bank being able to obtain a judgment in their own favour against the Republic of Ciskei, which it could use as a defence if sued by Ciskei in the local courts or those of the Republic of South Africa. The second was of more general import. It was that the financial institutions of the City of London which lend money or provide financial services to bodies in a similar position to that of the building owners, and the "Republic of Ciskei" is by no means unique, would have no means of having their rights and obligations determined by the courts of this country.

... the solicitors for the bank wrote to the Foreign and Commonwealth Office on April 10, 1986 on behalf of all parties, asking:

1.   What recognition, if any, does Her Majesty's Government accord to (1) the "Government of the Republic of Ciskei" and/or (2) the Department of Public Works, Republic of Ciskei"?

2.   Would it be contrary to the policy or attitudes of Her Majesty's Government for the English courts to recognise either or both of such bodies as (i) contracting parties and (ii) capable of suing or being sued in an English court under such names ...

---

[292] [1971] P. 188.
[293] (2002) 1 F.L.R. 956 at 969.
[294] See Beck (1987) 36 I.C.L.Q. 350; Crawford (1986) 57 B.Y.I.L. 405; Dixon (1988) 22 Int. Lawyer 555; Mann (1987) 36 I.C.L.Q. 348.

The answer dated May 1, 1986 was:

In answer to the first of your questions, ... consistently with the statements made in Parliament in April 1980[295] ... so far as governments are concerned, the attitude of Her Majesty's Government is to be inferred from the nature of its dealings with the regime concerned and in particular whether Her Majesty's Government deals with it on a normal government to government basis. Her Majesty's Government does not recognise the "Republic of Ciskei" as an independent sovereign state, either *de jure* or *de facto*, and does not have any dealings with the "Government of the Republic of Ciskei" or "the Department of Public Works, Republic of Ciskei."

With regard to the second question, it would appear to the Foreign and Commonwealth Office that the capacity to contract and to sue and be sued is a matter for the court to determine having regard to the answer given to the first question and, therefore, that it would not be appropriate for the Foreign and Commonwealth Office to answer the second question.

In a further letter dated May 9, 1986 Messrs. Durrant Piesse asked a further question:

Which state, if any, does Her Majesty's Government recognise as (a) entitled to exercise or (b) exercising governing authority in respect of the territory in Southern Africa known as Ciskei. Has such recognition been *de jure* or *de facto*?

On May 16, 1986 the Foreign and Commonwealth Office answered:

... I am therefore instructed to reply that beyond making clear that it has not recognised as independent sovereign States Ciskei or any of the other Homelands established in South Africa Her Majesty's Government has not taken and does not have a formal position as regards the exercise of governing authority over the territory of Ciskei. Her Majesty's Government does not have any dealings with the "Government of the Republic of Ciskei", or with "the Department of Public Works. Republic of Ciskei". Her Majesty's Government has made representations to the South African Government in relation to certain matters occurring in Ciskei and others of the Homelands to which South Africa has purported to grant independence, notably on matters relating to individuals, but has not in general received any positive response from the South African Government.

Sir John Donaldson, M.R. next quoted the statement made to Parliament on the recognition of governments in 1980 from which an extract is printed above, p.139. He then considered the *Carl Zeiss* case, above, p.153, and said, inter alia:

The House of Lords [in the *Carl Zeiss* case] held that the English courts could take cognizance of the legislative authority of the G.D.R. because, whilst they could not treat it as a sovereign state with legislative powers as such, they could and should treat it as having effective legislative powers on the footing that its legislative acts were those of a subordinate body which the U.S.S.R. had set up to act on its behalf. ...

Lord Wilberforce ... reserved for further consideration whether the non-recognition of a government or, I think, a state, would necessarily lead to the English courts treating all its legislative activities as being a nullity or whether, in the interests of justice and common sense, where no consideration of public policy to the contrary has to prevail, it might not be possible to take cognizance of the actual facts or realities found to exist in the territory in question and he instanced private rights, or acts of everyday occurrence or perfunctory acts of administration. I see great force in this reservation, since it is one thing to treat a state or government as being "without the law", but quite another to treat the inhabitants of its territory as "outlaws" who cannot effectively marry, beget legitimate children, purchase goods on credit or undertake countless day-to-day activities having legal consequences. However that is not this case. ...

Turning to the question whether the present case came within the *Carl Zeiss* decision, Sir John Donaldson, M.R. continued:

---

[295] See above, p.139.

There is ... an apparent contrast between the two certificates when it comes to *entitlement* to exercise governing authority. In each case the certificates are conclusive that the G.D.R. or, as the case may be, the Republic of Ciskei are not recognised as independent sovereign states. It follows from this that the courts must hold that neither the G.D.R. or its government nor the Republic of Ciskei or its government was in law capable of an executive, administrative or legislative act at the relevant times, unless enabled by some superior authority. In the case of the G.D.R., the certificate pointed expressly to where that superior authority was to be found, namely the sovereign state of the U.S.S.R. The question for our consideration is whether the Ciskei certificates ... point to any superior authority, of which the courts can take cognizance, as supplying the requisite authority to enable the Government of the Republic of Ciskei to undertake executive, administrative or legislative acts. In reviewing and evaluating that other evidence, we must disregard any declarations or Acts of the Republic of South Africa or of the Republic of Ciskei which conflict with the certificates of the Secretary of State, just as the House of Lords disregarded such declarations by the Government of the U.S.S.R.

... We must disregard section 1(1) of the Status of Ciskei Act 1981 which declares the Republic of Ciskei to be a sovereign and independent state ceasing to be part of the Republic of South Africa and section 1(2) which declares that the Republic of South Africa will cease to exercise any authority over the territory since this subsection is clearly consequential upon subsection (1). We must also disregard section 1(1) of the Republic of Ciskei Constitution Act 1981. However, we can, and I think must, take cognizance of the remainder of those Acts, notwithstanding that, absent those sections, they may take on a somewhat different character. Thus section 3(1) of the Status of Ciskei Act 1981, which provides:

> The Legislative Assembly of Ciskei ... may ... make laws (including a constitution) for the Ciskei in the manner prescribed by the said Act. ...

becomes a straightforward delegation of legislative power which could be revoked in the same way as it had been conferred, namely by a subsequent legislative Act of the Republic of South Africa.

We also know the constitutional history of the territory of the Ciskei, to which I have already referred, and we can take judicial notice of the fact that the Republic of South Africa is a sovereign state, recognised by Her Majesty's Government, and that it was entitled to exercise sovereignty over the territory of the Ciskei until the passing of the Status of Ciskei Act 1981. If then we disregard section 1 of that Act, as we must, there are no materials from which we could infer that this situation has changed. Indeed, the certified fact that "Her Majesty's Government has made representation to the South African Government in relation to certain matters occurring in Ciskei and others of the Homelands to which South Africa has purported to grant independence" gives rise to a clear inference that Her Majesty's Government regards the Republic of South Africa as continuing to be *entitled* to exercise sovereign authority over the territory. The further certified fact that the Government of the Republic has not in general made any positive response, gives rise only to an inference that the Government of the Republic is not, in general, willing to exercise the authority which it has *de jure*, preferring to leave this to the Government of Ciskei. This is immaterial for, as Lord Reid said [in the *Carl Zeiss* case] no *de jure* governing authority can disclaim responsibility for acts done by subordinate bodies which it has set up and which have not attempted to usurp its authority. There is no evidence whatever that the Republic of Ciskei or its government has attempted to do that.

It follows that in my judgment the legal status of the Republic of Ciskei and its government is indistinguishable from that which obtained in the case of the G.D.R. and its government at the time with which the *Carl Zeiss* case was concerned.

I would therefore allow the appeal and declare that the Government of the Republic of the Ciskei has *locus standi* in the courts of this country as being a subordinate body set up by the Republic of South Africa to act on its behalf.

Nourse and Glidewell L.JJ. delivered concurring judgments.

Note

In this case, the agency approach which was adopted by the House of Lords in the *Carl Zeiss* case to permit the recognition of the acts of an unrecognised government was used by the Court of Appeal to allow such a government locus standi in an English court. This facilitated commerce without, on the face of it, contradicting public policy. Might it be, however, that to allow the Ciskei Government locus standi was in reality subversive of the public policy (that South Africa's homelands policy should not succeed) that the Foreign Office's refusal to recognise Ciskei was intended to further?[296]

RE AL-FIN CORPORATION'S PATENT[297]

[1970] Ch. 160. Chancery Division

Section 24(1) of the Patents Act 1949 allows a patentee an extension of his patent if he has suffered loss "by reason of hostilities between His Majesty and any foreign state." In this case, the applicants sought an extension under s.24(1) in respect of loss suffered during the Korean War between 1950 and 1953. The Comptroller-General rejected the application partly on the ground that the Korean War did not come within s.24(1) because North Korea, not having been recognised by the United Kingdom, was not a "foreign state". The applicants sought a ruling on this question. The Court had before it a letter from the Foreign Office indicating that North Korea was not then recognised as a state.

GRAHAM J.

The question depends primarily on the proper construction of section 24, and the difference between the parties may be succinctly stated as follows: Must the section be read as if the words "recognised as such by Her Majesty" were included after the words "any foreign state" in subsection (1), or is it correct to read the section in a broader sense without the necessity for the qualification of recognition? . . .

Mr Dillon . . . for the applicants . . . cited the authority of *Luigi Monta of Genoa* v. *Cechofracht Co. Ltd* [1956] 2 Q.B. 552. In that case the question was whether the ship had complied with:

> any orders or directions . . . given by the government of the nation under whose flag the vessel sails . . . or by any other government . . . and compliance with any such orders or directions shall not be deemed to be a variation, and delivery in accordance with such orders or directions shall be a fulfilment of the contract voyage and the freight shall be paid accordingly.

The ship was intercepted and ordered by a general who said he came from "the government of Formosa" to discharge her cargo in that country, and did so. On a case stated by the umpire it was held by Sellers J., see pp. 564, 565 and 566, that the question to be decided was very different from a decision on a question of immunity or other question dependent on recognition, and that there was no such rule of law restricting the evidence to be considered to that provided by the Foreign Office, or which precluded the umpire from finding that there was a government in Formosa on all the evidence which was adduced. He held, on p. 564, that:

> the qualities or character required by the body giving the order or on whose behalf it was given or purported to be given must, therefore, include essentially the exercise of full executive and legislative power over an established territory. . . .

Although it is true that the *Luigi Monta* case is one dealing with the construction of a clause in a charterparty and Mr MacCrindle [for the respondent comptroller] is entitled to draw some distinction between the construction of such a document and of a statute, nevertheless the general principle must be that the true intention of the document, whether it be a commercial document or a statute, is to be ascertained. . . .

. . . in my judgment, the correct principle is that the word must be construed in its context and given the meaning which it is considered was intended by the legislature.

Applying these principles to section 24, I have no hesitation in holding that the phrase "any foreign state",

---

[296] See Beck, above, p.158, n.297, p.358.
[297] See Merrills (1971) 20 I.C.L.Q. 476.

although of course it includes a foreign state which has been given Foreign Office recognition, is not limited thereto. It must at any rate include a sufficiently defined area of territory over which a foreign government has effective control. Whether or not the state in question satisfies these conditions is a matter primarily of fact in each case. . . .

In the present case, apart from paragraph 4 of the Foreign Office Certificate, there is the evidence of Mr Frank in his affidavit of April 24, 1968, which satisfies me, see paragraphs 22 to 25 in particular, that at the relevant time North Korea had a defined territory over which a government had effective control and that His late Majesty was engaged in hostilities with this state albeit his troops were under the command and formed part of the United Nations' forces fighting in the area.

I hold therefore that North Korea was a foreign state within the meaning of section 24. . . .

Notes

1. As this case shows, the English courts exceptionally are prepared to look beyond the terms of a Foreign Office certificate when interpreting or construing the terms "state" in a statute or document on the basis that their function is to discover the intention of Parliament or the draftsman. In contrast, the courts, as the earlier cases in this section show, accept a Foreign Office certificate as conclusive, when recognising the law or the capacity to act of a foreign state.

2. In *Reel v Holder*[298] the Court of Appeal held that it was simply concerned with the interpretation of the rules of the IAAF [the International Amateur Athletic Federation] and not "with the international sphere of statehood and sovereignty" when asked to decide whether Taiwan was a "country" within the meaning of the IAAF rules (held that it was). Accordingly, a Foreign Office statement to the effect that Taiwan was not recognised as a state was not in point. cf. Spinney's Royal Ins. Co.[299] (certificate not sought on question whether hostilities in Lebanon constituted "civil war" for insurance contract purposes).

3. In *Caglar v Billingham*,[300] the Special Commissioners of Inland Revenue held that the term "foreign state" in s.321 of the Income and Corporation Taxes Act 1988 referred only to states recognised by the UK Government, and hence did not include the Turkish Republic of Northern Cyprus. The Commissioners applied the *Al-Fin* "intention" and "context" principle, but reached a different conclusion on the facts.

---

[298] [1981] 1 W.L.R. 1226 CA, per Lord Denning, M.R. at 1228.
[299] [1980] 1 Lloyd's Rep. 406 QB.
[300] [1996] S.T.C 150. See Warbrick (1996) 45 I.C.L.Q. 954.

5 TERRITORY

1. TITLE TO TERRITORY[1]

A. Occupation and Prescription

ISLAND OF PALMAS CASE[2]

Netherlands v U.S. (1928)

Permanent Court of Arbitration. Sole Arbitrator: Huber. 2 R.I.A.A. 829

As a result of the Spanish-American War of 1898, Spain ceded the Philippines to the United States by the Treaty of Paris of that year. In 1906, a United States official visited the island of Palmas (or Miangas), which the United States believed to be a part of the territory ceded to it, and found, to his surprise, a Dutch flag flying there. Palmas lies about 50 miles southeast of Cape San Augustin on the island of Mindanao. It is two miles long and less than a mile wide. In 1928, it had a population of less than 1,000 and was of negligible economic, military or other importance. Nonetheless, the Netherlands and the United States referred the question of sovereignty over the island to arbitration.

Award of the Arbitrator

Sovereignty in the relations between States signifies independence. Independence in regard to a portion of the globe is the right to exercise therein, to the exclusion of any other State, the functions of a State. The development of the national organisation of States during the last few centuries and, as a corollary, the development of international law, have established this principle of the exclusive competence of the State in regard to its own territory in such a way as to make it the point of departure in settling most questions that concern international relations. ... The fact that the functions of a State can be performed by any State within a given zone is, on the other hand, precisely the characteristic feature of the legal situation pertaining in those parts of the globe which, like the high seas or lands without a master, cannot or do not yet form the territory of a State.

... If a dispute arises as to the sovereignty over a portion of territory, it is customary to examine which of the States claiming sovereignty possesses a title—cession, conquest, occupation, *etc.*—superior to that which the other State might possibly bring forward against it. However, if the contestation is based on the fact that the other Party has actually displayed sovereignty, it cannot be sufficient to establish the title by which territorial sovereignty was validly acquired at a certain moment; it must also be shown that the territorial sovereignty has continued to exist and did exist at the moment which for the decision of the dispute must be considered as critical. This demonstration consists in the actual display of State activities, such as belongs only to the territorial sovereign.

... Titles of acquisition of territorial sovereignty in present-day international law are either based on an act of

---

[1] See Castellino and Allen, eds., *Title to Territory in International Law: A Temporal Analysis* (2002); Jennings, *The Acquisition of Territory in International Law* (1963); and Sharma, *Territorial Acquisition, Disputes and International Law* (1997).

[2] See Jessup (1928) 22 A.J.I.L. 735.

effective apprehension, such as occupation or conquest, or, like cession, presuppose that the ceding and the cessionary Powers or at least one of them, have the faculty of effectively disposing of the ceded territory. In the same way natural accretion can only be conceived of as an accretion to a portion of territory where there exists an actual sovereignty capable of extending to a spot which falls within its sphere of activity. It seems therefore natural that an element which is essential for the constitution of sovereignty should not be lacking in its continuation. So true is this, that practice, as well as doctrine, recognizes—though under different legal formulae and with certain differences as to the conditions required—that the continuous and peaceful display of territorial sovereignty (peaceful in relation to other States) is as good as a title. The growing insistence with which international law, ever since the middle of the 18th century, has demanded that the occupation shall be effective would be inconceivable, if effectiveness were required only for the act of acquisition and not equally for the maintenance of the right. If the effectiveness has above all been insisted on in regard to occupation, this is because the question rarely arises in connection with territories in which there is already an established order of things. Just as before the rise of international law, boundaries of lands were necessarily determined by the fact that the power of a State was exercised within them, so too, under the reign of international law, the fact of peaceful and continuous display is still one of the most important considerations in establishing boundaries between States.

Territorial sovereignty, as has already been said, involves the exclusive right to display the activities of a State. This right has as corollary a duty: the obligation to protect within the territory the rights of other States, in particular their right to integrity and inviolability in peace and in war, together with the rights which each State may claim for its nationals in foreign territory. Without manifesting its territorial sovereignty in a manner corresponding to circumstances, the State cannot fulfil this duty....

Although municipal law, thanks to its complete judicial system, is able to recognize abstract rights of property as existing apart from any material display of them, it has none the less limited their effect by the principles of prescription and the protection of possession. International law, the structure of which is not based on any super-State organisation, cannot be presumed to reduce a right such as territorial sovereignty, with which almost all international relations are bound up, to the category of an abstract right, without concrete manifestations. ...

Manifestations of territorial sovereignty assume, it is true, different forms, according to conditions of time and place. Although continuous in principle, sovereignty cannot be exercised in fact at every moment on every point of a territory. The intermittence and discontinuity compatible with the maintenance of the right necessarily differ according as inhabited or uninhabited regions are involved, or regions enclosed within territories in which sovereignty is incontestably displayed or again regions accessible from, for instance, the high seas. It is true that neighbouring States may by convention fix limits to their own sovereignty, even in regions such as the interior of scarcely explored continents where such sovereignty is scarcely manifested, and in this way each may prevent the other from any penetration of its territory. The delimitation of Hinterland may also be mentioned in this connection.[3]

If, however, no conventional line of sufficient topographical precision exists or if there are gaps in the frontiers otherwise established, or if a conventional line leaves room for doubt, or if, as, e.g. in the case of an island situated in the high seas, the question arises whether a title is valid *erga omnes*, the actual continuous and peaceful display of State functions is in case of dispute the sound and natural criterion of territorial sovereignty. ...

The *title alleged by the United States of America* as constituting the immediate foundation of its claim is that of *cession*, brought about by the Treaty of Paris, which cession transferred all rights of sovereignty which Spain may have possessed ... concerning the island of Palmas (or Miangas).

It is evident that Spain could not transfer more rights than she herself possessed ... the United States bases its claim, as successor of Spain, in the first place on *discovery*. ...

It is admitted by both sides that international law underwent profound modifications between the end of the Middle Ages and the end of the 19th century, as regards the rights of discovery and acquisition of uninhabited region or regions inhabited by savages or semi-civilized peoples. Both Parties are also agreed that a juridical fact must be appreciated in the light of the law contemporary with it, and not of the law in force at the time when a dispute in regard to it arises or falls to be settled. The effect of discovery by Spain is therefore to be determined by the rules of international law in force in the first half of the 16th century....

If the view most favourable to the American arguments is adopted—with every reservation as to the soundness

---

3   The reference is to the Hinterland principle of the period of colonial expansion: "... the general principle is that if a national has made a settlement it has a right to assume sovereignty over all the adjacent vacant territory which is necessary to the integrity and security of the Settlement", 1885 British Officers' Opinion, 1 McNair 292.

of such view—that is to say, if we consider as positive law at the period in question the rule that discovery as such, i.e. the mere fact of seeing land, without any act, even symbolical, of taking possession, involved *ipso jure* territorial sovereignty and not merely an "inchoate title", a *jus ad rem*, to be completed eventually by an actual and durable taking of possession within a reasonable time, the question arises whether sovereignty yet existed at the critical date, i.e. the moment of conclusion and coming into force of the Treaty of Paris.

As regards the question which of different legal systems prevailing at successive periods is to be applied in a particular case (the so-called intertemporal law), a distinction must be made between the creation of rights and the existence of rights. The same principle which subjects the act creative of a right to the law in force at the time the right arises, demands that the existence of right, in other words its continued manifestation, shall follow the conditions required by the evolution of law. International law in the 19th century, having regard to the fact that most parts of the globe were under the sovereignty of States members of the community of nations, and that territories without a master had become relatively few, took account of a tendency already existing and especially developed since the middle of the 18th century, and laid down the principle that occupation, to constitute a claim to territorial sovereignty, must be effective, that is, offer certain guarantees to other States and their nationals. It seems therefore incompatible with this rule of positive law that there should be regions which are neither under the effective sovereignty of a State, nor without a master, but which are reserved for the exclusive influence of one State, in virtue solely of a title of acquisition which is no longer recognized by existing law, even if such a title ever conferred territorial sovereignty. For these reasons, discovery alone, without any subsequent act, cannot, at the present time suffice to prove sovereignty over the Island of Palmas (or Miangas); and in so far as there is no sovereignty, the question of an abandonment properly speaking of sovereignty by one State in order that the sovereignty of another may take its place does not arise.

If on the other hand the view is adopted that discovery does not create a definitive title of sovereignty, but only an "inchoate" title, such a title exists, it is true, without external manifestation. However, according to the view that has prevailed at any rate since the 19th century, an inchoate title of discovery must be completed within a reasonable period by the effective occupation of the region claimed to be discovered. This principle must be applied in the present case, for the reasons given above in regard to the rules determining which of successive legal systems is to be applied (the so-called intertemporal law). Now, no act of occupation nor, except as to a recent period, any exercise of sovereignty at Palmas by Spain has been alleged. But even admitting that the Spanish title still existed as inchoate in 1898 and must be considered as included in the cession under Article III of the Treaty of Paris, an inchoate title could not prevail over the continuous and peaceful display of authority by another State; for such display may prevail even over a prior, definitive title put forward by another State ...

In the last place [in examining the United States arguments] there remains to be considered *title arising out of contiguity* ... it is impossible to show the existence of a rule of positive international law to the effect that islands situated outside territorial waters should belong to a State from the mere fact that its territory forms the *terra firma* (nearest continent or island of considerable size). Not only would it seem that there are no precedents sufficiently frequent and sufficiently precise in their bearing to establish such a rule of international law, but the alleged principle itself is by its very nature so uncertain and contested that even Governments of the same State have on different occasions maintained contradictory opinions as to its soundness. The principle of contiguity, in regard to islands, may not be out of place when it is a question of allotting them to one state rather than another, either by agreement between the Parties, or by a decision not necessarily based on law; but as a rule establishing *ipso jure* the presumption of sovereignty in favour of a particular State, this principle would be in conflict with what has been said as to territorial sovereignty and as to the necessary relation between the right to exclude other States from a region and the duty to display therein the activities of a State. Nor is this principle of contiguity admissible as a legal method of deciding questions of territorial sovereignty; for it is wholly lacking in precision and would in its application lead to arbitrary results. This would be especially true in a case such as that of the island in question, which is not relatively close to one single continent, but forms part of a large archipelago in which strict delimitations between the different parts are not naturally obvious.

There lies, however, at the root of the idea of contiguity one point which must be considered also in regard to the Island of Palmas (or Miangas). It has been explained above that in the exercise of territorial sovereignty there are necessarily gaps, intermittence in time and discontinuity in space. This phenomenon will be particularly noticeable in the case of colonial territories, partly uninhabited or as yet partly unsubdued. The fact that a State cannot prove display of sovereignty as regards such a position of territory cannot forthwith be interpreted as showing that sovereignty is inexistent. Each case must be appreciated in accordance with the particular circumstances. ...

As regards groups of islands, it is possible that a group may under certain circumstances be regarded as in law, a unit, and that the fate of the principal part may involve the rest. Here, however, we must distinguish between, on the one hand, the act of first taking possession, which can hardly extend to every portion of territory, and, on the other hand, the display of sovereignty as a continuous and prolonged manifestation which must make itself felt through the whole territory.

As regards the territory forming the subject of the present dispute, it must be remembered that it is a somewhat isolated island, and therefore a territory clearly delimited and individualised. It is moreover an island permanently inhabited, occupied by a population sufficiently numerous for it to be impossible that acts of administration could be lacking for very long periods. The memoranda of both Parties assert that there is communication by boat and even with native craft between the Island of Palmas (or Miangas) and neighbouring regions. The inability in such a case to indicate any acts of public administration makes it difficult to imagine the actual display of sovereignty, even if the sovereignty be regarded as confined within such narrow limits as would be supposed for a small island inhabited exclusively by natives. . . .

The Court then examined the argument put by the Netherlands:

The Netherlands found their claim to sovereignty essentially on the title of peaceful and continuous display of State authority over the island. Since this title would in international law prevail over a title of acquisition of sovereignty not followed by actual display of State authority, it is necessary to ascertain in the first place, whether the contention of the Netherlands is sufficiently established by evidence, and, if so, for what period of time.

In the opinion of the Arbitrator the Netherlands have succeeded in establishing the following facts:

a.   The Island of Palmas (or Miangas) is identical with an island designated by this or a similar name, which has formed, at least since 1700, successively a part of two of the native States of the Island of Sangi (Talautse Isles).

b.   These native States were from 1677 onwards connected with the East Indian Company, and thereby with the Netherlands,[4] by contracts of suzerainty, which conferred upon the suzerain such powers as would justify his considering the vassal State as a part of his territory.

c.   Acts characteristic of State authority exercised either by the vassal State or by the suzerain Power in regard precisely to the Island of Palmas (or Miangas) have been established as occurring at different epochs between 1700 and 1898, as well as in the period between 1898 and 1906.

The acts of indirect or direct display of Netherlands sovereignty at Palmas (or Miangas), especially in the 18th and early 19th centuries are not numerous, and there are considerable gaps in the evidence of continuous display. But apart from the consideration that the manifestations of sovereignty over a small and distant island, inhabited only by natives, cannot be expected to be frequent, it is not necessary that the display of sovereignty should go back to a very far distant period. It may suffice that such display existed in 1898, and had already existed as continuous and peaceful before that date long enough to enable any Power who might have considered herself as possessing sovereignty over the island, or having a claim to sovereignty, to have, according to local conditions, a reasonable possibility for ascertaining the existence of a state of things contrary to her real or alleged rights.

It is not necessary that the display of sovereignty should be established as having begun at a precise epoch; it suffices that it had existed at the critical period preceding the year 1898. It is quite natural that the establishment of sovereignty may be the outcome of a slow evolution, of a progressive intensification of State control. This is particularly the case, if sovereignty is acquired by the establishment of the suzerainty of a colonial Power over a native State, and in regard to outlying possessions of such a vassal state.

Now the evidence relating to the period after the middle of the 19th century makes it clear that the Netherlands Indian Government considered the island distinctly as a part of its possessions and that, in the years immediately preceding 1898, an intensification of display of sovereignty took place.

Since the moment when the Spaniards, in withdrawing from the Moluccas in 1666, made express reservations as to the maintenance of their sovereign rights, up to the contestation made by the United States in 1906, no

---

4   Ed. Elsewhere in his Award the Arbitrator commented on the nature of the acts of the Dutch East India Company as follows: "[They] must, in international law, be entirely assimilated to acts of the Netherlands State itself. From the end of the 16th till the 19th century, companies formed by individuals and engaged in economic pursuits (Chartered Companies), were invested by the State to whom they were subject with public powers for the acquisition and administration of colonies."

contestation or other action whatever or protest against the exercise of territorial rights by the Netherlands over the Talautse (Sangi) Isles and their dependencies (Miangas included) has been recorded. The peaceful character of the display of Netherlands sovereignty for the entire period to which the evidence concerning acts of display relates (1700–1906) must be admitted.

There is moreover no evidence which would establish any act of display of sovereignty over the island by Spain or another Power, such as might counterbalance or annihilate the manifestations of Netherlands sovereignty. As to third Powers, the evidence submitted to the Tribunal does not disclose any trace of such action, at least from the middle of the 17th century onwards. These circumstances, together with the absence of any evidence of a conflict between Spanish and Netherlands authorities during more than two centuries as regards Palmas (or Miangas), are an indirect proof of the exclusive display of Netherlands sovereignty.

This being so, it remains to be considered first whether the display of State authority might not legally be defective and therefore unable to create a valid title of sovereignty, and secondly whether the United States may not put forward a better title to that of the Netherlands.

As to the conditions of acquisition of sovereignty by way of continuous and peaceful display of State authority (so-called prescription), some of which have been discussed in the United States Counter-Memorandum, the following must be said:

The display has been open and public, that is to say that it was in conformity with usages as to exercise of sovereignty over colonial States. A clandestine exercise of State authority over an inhabited territory during a considerable length of time would seem to be impossible. . . .

The conditions of acquisition of sovereignty by the Netherlands are therefore to be considered as fulfilled. It remains now to be seen whether the United States as successors of Spain are in a position to bring forward an equivalent or stronger title. This is to be answered in the negative.

The title of discovery, if it had not been already disposed of by the Treaties of Munster and Utrecht would, under the most favourable and most extensive interpretation, exist only as an inchoate title, as a claim to establish sovereignty by effective occupation. An inchoate title however cannot prevail over a definite title founded on continuous and peaceful display of sovereignty.

The title of contiguity, understood as a basis of territorial sovereignty, has no foundation in international law.

The title of recognition by treaty does not apply, because even if the Sangi States, with the dependency of Miangas, are to be considered as "held and possessed" by Spain in 1648, the rights of Spain to be derived from the Treaty of Munster [1648] would have been superseded by those which were acquired by the Treaty of Utrecht. Now if there is evidence of a state of possession in 1714 concerning the island of Palmas (or Miangas), such evidence is exclusively in favour of the Netherlands. But even if the Treaty of Utrecht could not be taken into consideration, the acquiescence of Spain in the situation created after 1677 would deprive her and her successors of the possibility of still invoking conventional rights at the present time.

The Netherlands title of sovereignty, acquired by continuous and peaceful display of State authority during a long period of time probably going back beyond the year 1700, therefore holds good. . . .

For these reasons the Arbitrator, in conformity with Article I of the Special Agreement of January 23, 1925, decides that: the Island of Palmas (or Miangas) forms in its entirety a part of Netherlands territory.

Notes

1. The Award in the *Palmas* case is of outstanding importance in the law on the acquisition of title to territory because of its full and scholarly treatment of such basic matters as the nature of territorial sovereignty and because of the emphasis placed upon the effect of a "continuous and peaceful display of State authority."[5] As to the latter, the case indicates very clearly that the state that can show such "a display of State authority" in the period leading up to the "critical date" (i.e. the date on which the location of territorial sovereignty is decisive) can defeat any other claim

---

[5] cf. *Eritrea v Yemen* (1998) 114 I.L.R. 1 at 69: "The modern international law of the acquisition (or attribution) of territory generally requires that there be: an intentional display of power and authority over the territory, by the exercise of jurisdiction and State functions, on a continuous and peaceful basis. The latter two criteria are tempered to suit the nature of the territory and the size of its population, if any."

whatever its basis.[6] It has, however, to be a "peaceful" display of such authority, i.e. one without protest by interested states of the sort that prevents prescription and of sufficient duration to establish a prescriptive title.[7] Thus, a state which exercises continuous and peaceful governmental possession has a title by way of occupation if the territory was previously a *res nullius* and by way of prescription if it was not.[8]

As the ICJ noted in the *Pulau Ligitan and Pulau Sipidan* case,[9] the critical date is crucial in that it:

> "cannot take into consideration acts having taken place after the date on which the dispute between the Parties crystallized unless such acts are a normal continuation of prior acts and are not undertaken for the purpose of improving the legal position of the Party which relies on them."

2. *Territorial Sovereignty*.[10] The meaning of territorial sovereignty was discussed by France in its pleadings in the *Nationality Decrees in Tunis and Morocco* case.[11] There M. A. de La Pradelle stated:

> "... territory is neither an object nor a substance; it is a framework. What sort of framework? The framework within which the public power is exercised ... territory as such must not be considered, it must be regarded as the external, ostensible sign of the sphere within which the public power of the state is exercised."[12]

3. *Title by Discovery*. On the possibility of obtaining title by discovery, Keller, Lissitzyn and Mann,[13] referring to the years 1400–1800, state:

> "Throughout this lengthy period, no state appeared to regard mere discovery, in the sense of 'physical' discovery or simple 'visual apprehension,' as being in any way sufficient *per se* to establish a right of sovereignty over, or a valid title to, *terra nullius*. Furthermore, mere disembarkation upon any portion of such regions—or even extended penetration and exploration therein—was not regarded as sufficient itself to establish such a right or title ... the formal ceremony of taking of possession, the symbolic act, was generally regarded as being wholly sufficient *per se* to establish immediately a right of sovereignty over, or a valid title to, areas so claimed and did not require to be supplemented by the performance of other acts, such as, for example, 'effective occupation.' A right or title so acquired and established was deemed good against all subsequent claims set up in opposition thereto unless, perhaps, transferred by conquest or treaty, relinquished, abandoned, or successfully opposed by continued occupation on the part of some other state."

---

[6]   On the concept of the critical date, see Jennings, above, p.163, n.1, p.35; and, more generally, Goldie (1963) 12 I.C.L.Q. 1251. The critical date may change: see the *Land, Island and Maritime Frontier Dispute* case, below, p.204. For recent cases in which the concept has not been decisive, see below, p.168, nn.38, 39.

[7]   See below, p.180.

[8]   Prescription will overcome titles based upon occupation, conquest, cession, etc.

[9]   I.C.J. Rep. 2002, p.625 at p.682.

[10] See Shaw (1982) 13 N.Y.I.L. 61.

[11] P.C.I.J. Rep., Series B, No.4, (1923).

[12] *ibid*. Series C, No.2, pp.106, 108.

[13] *Creation of Rights of Sovereignty through Symbolic Acts 1400–1800* (1938), pp.148–149.

4. *Contiguity*. As stated in the *Palmas* case, above, p.165, contiguity, while not constituting a basis for title in itself, may give rise to a rebuttable presumption of title in some circumstances. Contiguity was relied upon in this way in *Eritrea v Yemen*[14] when the evidence of governmental activity in respect of the disputed islands was sparse and inconclusive. The Tribunal stated:

> "457. ... There is no virtue in relying upon 'very little' when looking at other possible factors might strengthen the basis of decision.
>
> 458. An obvious such factor in the present case is the geographical situation that the majority of the islands and islets and rocks in issue form an archipelago extending across a relatively narrow sea between the two opposite coasts of the sea. So there is some presumption that any islands off one of the coasts may be thought to belong by appurtenance to that coast unless the State on the opposite coast has been able to demonstrate a clearly better title."

In this connection, the Tribunal also considered a Yemeni argument based upon the principle of "natural unity"[15]:

> "461. This 'principle' is described in ... the Yemen Memorial, where impressive authority is cited in support of it, including Fitzmaurice, Waldock and Charles de Visscher. That there is indeed some such concept cannot be doubted. But it is not an absolute principle. ...
>
> 462. Thus, the authorities speak of 'entity' or 'natural entity' in terms of a presumption or of probability and moreover couple it with proximity, contiguity, continuity, and such notions, well known in international law as not in themselves creative of title, but rather of a possibility or presumption for extending to the area in question an existing title already established in another, but proximate or contiguous, part of the same 'unity'.
>
> 463. These ideas, however, have a twofold possible application in the present case. They may indeed, as Yemen would have it, be applied to cause governmental display on one island of a group to extend in its juridical effect to another island or islands in the same group. But by the same rationale a complementary question also arises of how far the sway established on one of the mainland coasts should be considered to continue to some islands or islets off that coast which are naturally 'proximate' to the coast or 'appurtenant' to it. This idea was so well established during the last century that it was given the name of the 'portico doctrine' and recognized 'as a means of attributing sovereignty over off-shore features which fell within the attraction of the mainland'.[16] The relevance of these notions of international law to the legal history of the present case is not far to seek.
>
> 464. Thus the principle of natural and physical unity is a two-edged sword, for if it is indeed to be applied then the question arises whether the unity is to be seen as originating from the one coast or the other. Moreover, as the cases and authorities cited by Yemen clearly show, these notions of unity and the like are never in themselves roots of title, but rather may in certain circumstances raise a presumption about the extent and scope of a title otherwise established."

See also on contiguity, the *Western Sahara* case, below, p.176.

---

[14]   (1998) 114 I.L.R. 1 at 119.
[15]   (1998) 114 I.L.R. 1 at 120–121.
[16]   D. O'Connell, *The International Law of the Sea* 185 (1982).

5. *Intertemporal Law.* Commenting upon Huber's conception of intertemporal law, Jessup[17] wrote:

> "Assume that State A in a certain year acquires Island X from State B by a treaty of peace after a war in which A is the victor.[18] Assume Island X is a barren rocky place, uninhabited and desired by A only for strategic reasons to prevent its fortification by another Power. Assume that A holds Island X, but without making direct use of it, for two hundred years. At the end of that time suppose that the development of international morality has so far progressed as to change the previous rule of international law and that the new rule is that no territory may be acquired by a victor from a vanquished at the close of a war. Under the theory of 'inter-temporal law' as expounded, it would appear that A would no longer have good title to Island X but must secure a new title upon some other basis or in accordance with the new rule. Such a retroactive effect of law would be highly disturbing. Every state would constantly be under the necessity of examining its title to each portion of its territory in order to determine whether a change in the law had necessitated, as it were, a reacquisition."

An extension of the doctrine of intertemporal law from a requirement that title must be valid in accordance with the law in force at the time at which it is claimed to have been established to one by which the validity of title must also be constantly updated as the international law bases for title change would, as Jessup suggests, be extremely disruptive.

6. In the special agreement by which the *Palmas* case was submitted to arbitration, the arbitrator was instructed to determine whether the island formed "a part of Netherlands territory or of territory belonging to the United States of America." Could he, with these instructions, have decided that the island was *res nullius* or that a third state had title to it?[19] Was his ruling in favour of the Netherlands binding upon third states? In the *Frontier Dispute* case,[20] the International Court of Justice noted that its determination of the land border between the parties, Burkina Faso and Mali, would not be opposable to Niger, a neighbouring state whose boundaries might be thought to be affected by the determination, because of art.59, I.C.J. Statute.[21] Is an international judgment or an arbitral award, a further means of acquiring title?[22]

7. The Arbitrator's reliance upon the acts of the Dutch East India Company as evidence of the exercise of authority by the Netherlands makes it relevant to point out the different situation in respect of the acts of individuals unauthorised to act for the state of which they are nationals. In the *Anglo-Norwegian Fisheries* case Judge Sir Arnold McNair stated that:

> "the independent activity of private individuals is of little value unless it can be shown that they

---

17 Above, p.163, n.2, p.735. See also Higgins (1997) 46 I.C.L.Q. 501 at 515–519.

18 Ed. See now art.52 of the Vienna Convention on the Law of Treaties 1969, below, p.691, on treaties the conclusion of which is obtained by armed force.

19 For an arbitration in which such possibilities were left open to the tribunal, see *Eritrea v Yemen* (1998) 114 I.L.R. 1 at 118.

20 I.C.J. Rep. 1986, p.554.

21 Below, App.I.

22 See Brownlie, p.132; and the *Land, Island and Maritime Frontier Dispute* case, I.C.J. Rep. 1992, p.351. In the *Maritime Delimitation and Territorial Questions between Qatar and Bahrain (Merits)* case, I.C.J. Rep. 2001, p.40, although not an arbitration award, a 1939 decision by the British Political Agent on sovereignty over disputed islands taken with the consent of the two parties was held to be legally binding on them. On the competence of the Security Council to determine boundaries in the exercise of its jurisdiction, see Mendelson and Hutton (1993) 64 B.Y.I.L. 135 at 147.

have acted in pursuance of a licence or some other authority received from their Governments or that in some other way their Governments have asserted jurisdiction through them."[23]

CLIPPERTON ISLAND CASE[24]

France v Mexico (1931)

Arbitrator: King Victor Emmanuel III of Italy. (1932) 26 A.J.I.L. 390

Award of the Arbitrator

In fact, we find, in the first place, that on November 17, 1858, Lieutenant Victor Le Coat de Kerwéguen, of the French Navy, commissioner of the French Government, while cruising about one-half mile off Clipperton[25] drew up, on board the commercial vessel *L'Amiral*, an act by which, conformably to the orders which had been given to him by the Minister of Marine, he proclaimed and declared that the sovereignty of the said island beginning from that date belonged in perpetuity to His Majesty the Emperor Napoleon III and to his heirs and successors. During the cruise, careful and minute geographical notes were made; a boat succeeded, after numerous difficulties, in landing some members of the crew; and on the evening of November 20, after a second unsuccessful attempt to reach the shore, the vessel put off without leaving in the island any sign of sovereignty. Lieutenant de Kerwéguen officially notified the accomplishment of his mission to the Consulate of France at Honolulu, which made a like communication to the Government of Hawaii. Moreover, the same consulate had published in English in the journal *The Polynesian*, of Honolulu, on December 8, the declaration by which French sovereignty over Clipperton had already been proclaimed.

Thereafter, until the end of 1887 no positive and apparent act of sovereignty can be recalled either on the part of France or on the part of any other Powers. The island remained without population, at least stable, and no administration was organized there. A concession for the exploitation of guano[26] beds existing there, which had been approved by the Emperor on April 8, 1858, in favor of a certain Mr. Lockart, and which had given rise to the expedition of Lieutenant de Kerwéguen, had not been followed up, nor had its exploitation been undertaken on the part of any other French subjects.

Towards the end of 1897 ... France stated ... that three persons were found in the island collecting guano ... and that they had, on the appearance of the French vessel, raised the American flag. Explanations were demanded on this subject from the United States, which responded that it had not granted any concession to the said company and did not intend to claim any right of sovereignty over Clipperton ...

About a month after this act of surveillance had been accomplished by the French Navy ... Mexico, ignoring the occupation claimed by France and considering that Clipperton was territory belonging to her for a long time, sent to the place a gun-boat, *La Democrata*, which action was caused by the report, afterwards acknowledged to be inaccurate, that England had designs upon the island. A detachment of officers and marines landed from the said ship December 13, 1897, and again found the three persons who resided on the island at the time of the preceding arrival of the French ship. It made them lower the American flag and hoist the Mexican flag in its place. Of the three individuals above mentioned, two consented to leave the island, and the third declared his wish to remain there, and in fact remained there until an unknown date. After that the *Democrata* left on December 15.

On January 8, France, having learned of the Mexican expedition, reminded that Power of its rights over Clipperton. ...

---

[23] I.C.J.Rep. 1951, p.184. cf. the *Pulau Ligitan and Pulau Sipadan* case I.C.J. Rep. 2002, p.625 at p.683, in which Indonesian reliance on fishing in the islands' waters was disregarded because "activities by private persons cannot be seen as *effectivités* if they do not take place on the basis of official regulation under governmental authority." See also the *Kasikili/Sedudu Island* case, below, p.180.

[24] See Dickinson (1933) 27 A.J.I.L. 130.

[25] Ed. Clipperton is "a low coral lagoon reef, less than three miles in diameter, situated in the Pacific Ocean ... some 670 miles south-west of Mexico": Dickinson, p.131.

[26] Ed. Guano is a fertiliser made from the excrement of sea birds, particularly some that nest on islands off the coast of South America. Its discovery in the nineteenth century led to a sort of "Guano-rush".

According to Mexico, Clipperton Island, which had been given the name of the famous English adventurer who, at the beginning of the 18th century, used it as a place of refuge, was none other than Passion Island ... that this island had been discovered by the Spanish Navy and, by virtue of the law then in force, fixed by the Bull of Alexander VII,[27] had belonged to Spain, and afterwards, from 1836, to Mexico as the successor state of the Spanish state.

But according to the actual state of our knowledge, it has not been proven that this island ... had been actually discovered by the Spanish navigators. ... However, even admitting that the discovery had been made by Spanish subjects, it would be necessary, to establish the contention of Mexico to prove that Spain not only had the right, as a state, to incorporate the island in her possessions, but also had effectively exercised the right. But that has not been demonstrated at all. ...

Consequently, there is ground to admit that, when in November, 1858, France proclaimed her sovereignty over Clipperton, that island was in the legal situation of *territorium nullius*, and, therefore, susceptible of occupation.

The question remains whether France proceeded to an effective occupation, satisfying the conditions required by international law for the validity of this kind of territorial acquisition. In effect, Mexico maintains ... that the French occupation was not valid, and consequently [maintains] her own right to occupy the island which must still be considered as *nullius* in 1897.

In whatever concerns this question, there is, first of all, ground to hold as incontestable, the regularity of the act by which France in 1858 made known in a clear and precise manner, her intention to consider the island as her territory.

On the other hand, it is disputed that France took effective possession of the island, and it is maintained that without such a taking of possession of an effective character, the occupation must be considered as null and void.

It is beyond doubt that by immemorial usage having the force of law, besides the *animus occupandi*, the actual, and not the nominal, taking of possession is a necessary condition of occupation. This taking of possession consists in the act, or series of acts, by which the occupying state reduces to its possession the territory in question and takes steps to exercise exclusive authority there. Strictly speaking, and in ordinary cases, that only takes place when the state establishes in the territory itself an organization capable of making its laws respected. But this step is, properly speaking, but a means of procedure to the taking of possession, and, therefore, is not identical with the latter. There may also be cases where it is unnecessary to have recourse to this method. Thus, if a territory, by virtue of the fact that it was completely uninhabited, is, from the first moment when the occupying state makes its appearance there, at the absolute and undisputed disposition of that state, from that moment the taking of possession must be considered as accomplished, and the occupation is thereby complete. ...

The regularity of the French occupation has also been questioned because the other Powers were not notified of it. But it must be observed that the precise obligation to make such notification is contained in art. 34 of the Act of Berlin[28] ... which ... is not applicable to the present case. There is good reason to think that the notoriety given to the act, by whatever means, sufficed at the time, and that France provoked that notoriety by publishing the said act in the manner above indicated.

It follows from these premises that Clipperton Island was legitimately acquired by France on November 17, 1858. There is no reason to suppose that France has subsequently lost her right by *derelictio*, since she never had the *animus* of abandoning the island, and the fact that she has not exercised her authority there in a positive manner does not imply the forfeiture of an acquisition already definitively perfected.

For these reasons, we decide, as arbiter, that the sovereignty over Clipperton Island belongs to France, dating from November 17, 1858.

Notes

1.   This is a classic case of obtaining title to *res nullius* by occupation. What amount of authority does it suggest has to be exercised over an uninhabited island to establish possession?

---

[27]   Ed. This was the Papal Bull *Inter Caetera* of 1493 by which a remarkably generous Pope gave to Spain all land discovered or to be discovered west of a line 100 miles west of the Azores and Cape Verde not in the possession of any Christian king.

[28]   Ed. This required a party to the Act that took possession of land on the coast of Africa to notify the other parties that it had done so.

2. In the *Eastern Greenland* case,[29] Norway "officially confirmed" its "taking possession" of Eastern Greenland, an uncolonised part of the island, by a declaration of July 10, 1931. Denmark, which had colonies elsewhere in Greenland and which claimed sovereignty over the whole of the island, asked the Permanent Court of International Justice to declare that the Norwegian declaration was invalid.

Explaining its approach, the Court stated:

> "a claim to sovereignty based not upon some particular act or title such as a treaty of cession but merely upon continued display of authority, involves two elements each of which must be shown to exist: the intention and will to act as sovereign, and some actual exercise or display of such authority. Another circumstance which must be taken into account ... is the extent to which the sovereignty is also claimed by some other Power. In most of the cases involving claims to territorial sovereignty which have come before an international tribunal, there have been two competing claims to the sovereignty, and the tribunal has had to decide which of the two is the stronger. One of the peculiar features of the present case is that up to 1931 there was no claim by any Power other than Denmark to the sovereignty over Greenland. Indeed, up till 1921, no Power disputed the Danish claim to sovereignty."[30]

Although Denmark had not colonised Eastern Greenland, the Court found sufficient evidence of its claim and of exercise of state authority over the area during many centuries to show that it had established title to it at the "critical date," namely July 10, 1931, when Norway made its claim. In recent history, this evidence consisted from 1814 to 1915 of treaties applying to Greenland as a whole (which showed Denmark's "will and intention to exercise sovereignty"), of the granting of concessions for trading, etc. in Eastern Greenland and of legislation establishing the width of the territorial sea. From 1915 to 1931, it consisted of steps by Denmark to have its title to Greenland recognised by other states as well as various acts of administration and legislation. During both periods, Norwegian expeditions had sometimes wintered in Eastern Greenland and a wireless station and other buildings had been erected. Denmark had protested against the erection of the wireless station. The Court found this evidence sufficient to establish Denmark's sovereignty over the years indicated. Finally, the Court stressed the relative nature of the test to be applied in establishing occupation:

> "It is impossible to read the records of the decisions in cases as to territorial sovereignty without observing that in many cases the tribunal has been satisfied with very little in the way of the actual exercise of sovereign rights, provided that the other State could not make out a superior claim. This is particularly true in the case of claims to sovereignty over areas in thinly populated or unsettled countries."[31]

3. The Court itself added to this jurisprudence in the *Pulau Ligitan and Pulau Sipadan* case[32] in which title was disputed to two very small islands off the coast of Borneo, neither of which had permanent inhabitants when title was claimed. Having found no Indonesian *effectivités* (i.e. exercises of government authority), the Court held that the islands were Malaysian on the basis

---

[29] P.C.I.J. Rep., Series A/B, No.53 (1933). See the discussion of this case in the *Western Sahara* case, below p.177.
[30] P.C.I.J. Rep., Series A/B, No.53 (1933) at pp.45–46. cf. the *Frontier Dispute (Benin/Niger)* case, I.C.J. Rep. 2005, p.90.
[31] P.C.I..J. Rep. Series A/B, No.53 (1933), at p.46. cf. the *Pedra Branca* case, I.C.J. Rep. 2008, paras 63–69, in which the absence of a rival state claim was stressed.
[32] I.C.J. Rep. 2002, p.625.

of "administrative assertions of authority" by way of Malaysian regulation of the collection of turtle eggs on both the islands and of the establishment of a bird sanctuary on one of the islands. Malaysia's provision of lighthouses on the islands was also relevant[33]:

> "147. The Court observes that the construction and operation of lighthouses and navigational aids are not normally considered manifestations of State authority (*Minquiers and Ecrehos, Judgment, I.C.J. Reports 1953*, p.71). The Court, however, recalls that in its Judgment in the case concerning *Maritime Delimitation and Territorial Questions between Qatar and Bahrain (Qatar v. Bahrain)* it stated as follows:
>
>> 'Certain types of activities invoked by Bahrain such as the drilling of artesian wells would, taken by themselves, be considered controversial as acts performed *à titre de souverain*. The construction of navigational aids, on the other hand, can be legally relevant in the case of very small islands. In the present case, taking into account the size of Qit'at Jaradah, the activities carried out by Bahrain on that island must be considered sufficient to support Bahrain's claim that it has sovereignty over it.' (*Judgment, Merits, I.C.J. Reports 2001*, para. 197.)
>
> The Court is of the view that the same considerations apply in the present case."

Commenting generally on Malaysia's activities, the Court stated:

> "the activities ... are modest in number ... but they are diverse in character and include legislative, administrative and quasi-judicial acts. They cover a considerable period of time and show a pattern revealing an intention to exercise State functions in respect of the two islands in the context of the administration of a wider range of islands."

4.   Unlike islands, low tide elevations are not territory that may be appropriated by a state: *Maritime Delimitation and Territorial Questions between Qatar and Bahrain (Merits)* case, below, p.338.

MINQUIERS AND ECREHOS CASE[34]

France v U.K.

I.C.J. Reports 1953, p.47

Judgment of the Court

By Article I of the Special Agreement, signed on December 29th, 1950, the Court is requested:

to determine whether the sovereignty over the islets and rocks (in so far as they are capable of appropriation) of the Minquiers and Ecrehos groups[35] respectively belongs to the United Kingdom or the French Republic.

Having thus been requested to decide whether these groups belong either to France or to the United Kingdom, the Court has to determine which of the Parties has produced the more convincing proof of title to one

---

[33] I.C.J. Rep. 2002, p.685.
[34] See Fitzmaurice (1955–56) 32 B.Y.I.L. 20–76; Johnson (1954) 3 I.C.L.Q. 189; Wade (1954) 40 Trans.Grot. Soc. 97.
[35] Ed. These are in the English Channel, near Guernsey.

or the other of these groups, or to both of them. By the formulation of Article I the Parties have excluded the status of *res nullius* as well as that of *condominium*.

In Article II the Parties have stated their agreement as to the presentation of the Pleadings "without prejudice to any question as to the burden of proof", a question which it is for the Court to decide. Having regard to the position of the Parties, both claiming sovereignty over the same territory, and in view of the formulation of the task of the Court in Article I, and the terms of Article II, the Court is of the opinion that each Party has to prove its alleged title and the facts upon which it relies. . . .

Both Parties contend that they have respectively an ancient or original title to the Ecrehos and the Minquiers, and that their title has always been maintained and was never lost. The present case does not therefore present the characteristics of a dispute concerning the acquisition of sovereignty over *terra nullius*.

The United Kingdom Government derives the ancient title invoked by it from the conquest of England in 1066 by William, Duke of Normandy. By this conquest England became united with the Duchy of Normandy, including the Channel Islands, and this union lasted until 1204 when King Philip Augustus of France drove the Anglo-Norman forces out of Continental Normandy. But his attempts to occupy also the Islands were not successful, except for brief periods when some of them were taken by French forces. On this ground the United Kingdom Government submits the view that all of the Channel Islands, including the Ecrehos and the Minquiers, remained, as before, united with England and that this situation of fact was placed on a legal basis by subsequent Treaties concluded between the English and French Kings . . .

The French Government derives the original title invoked by it from the fact that the Dukes of Normandy were the vassals of the Kings of France, and that the Kings of England after 1066, in their capacity as Dukes of Normandy, held the Duchy in fee of the French Kings. . . .

The Court considers it sufficient to state as its view that even if the Kings of France did have an original feudal title also in respect of the Channel Islands, such a title must have lapsed as a consequence of the events of the year 1204 and following years.[36] Such an alleged original feudal title of the Kings of France in respect of the Channel Islands could today produce no legal effect, unless it had been replaced by another title valid according to the law of the time of replacement. What is of decisive importance, in the opinion of the Court, is not indirect presumptions deduced from events in the Middle Ages, but the evidence which relates directly to the possession of the Ecrehos and Minquiers groups. . . .

The Parties have further discussed the question of the selection of a "critical date" for allowing evidence in the present case. The United Kingdom Government submits that, though the Parties have for a long time disagreed as to the sovereignty over the two groups, the dispute did not become "crystallized" before the conclusion of the Special Agreement of December 29th, 1950, and that therefore this date should be considered as the critical date, with the result that all acts before that date must be taken into consideration by the Court. The French Government, on the other hand, contends that the date of the Convention of 1839 should be selected as the critical date, and that all subsequent acts must be excluded from consideration.

At the date of the [fishery] Convention of 1839, no dispute as to the sovereignty over the Ecrehos and Minquiers groups had yet arisen. The Parties had for a considerable time been in disagreement with regard to the exclusive right to fish oysters, but they did not link that question to the question of sovereignty over the Ecrehos and the Minquiers. In such circumstances there is no reason why the conclusion of that Convention should have any effect on the question of allowing or ruling out evidence relating to sovereignty. A dispute as to sovereignty over the groups did not arise before the years 1886 and 1888, when France for the first time claimed sovereignty over the Ecrehos and the Minquiers respectively. But in view of the special circumstances of the present case, subsequent acts should also be considered by the Court, unless the measure in question was taken with a view to improving the legal position of the Party concerned. In many respects activity in regard to these groups had developed gradually long before the dispute as to sovereignty arose, and it has since continued without interruption and in a similar manner. In such circumstances there would be no justification for ruling out all events which during this continued development occurred after the years 1886 and 1888 respectively. . . .

The Court examined evidence of sovereignty in respect of the Ecrehos presented by each party. In the course of considering the evidence produced by the United Kingdom relating to the nineteenth century, the Court stated that it "attaches, in particular, probative value to the acts which relate to the

---

[36] Ed. The Duchy of Normandy was dismembered after Anglo-Norman forces had been driven out of Normandy in 1204.

exercise of jurisdiction and local administration and to legislation."[37] The Court concluded unanimously as follows:

The Court, being now called upon to appraise the relative strength of the opposing claims to sovereignty over the Ecrehos in the light of the facts considered above, finds that the Ecrehos group in the beginning of the thirteenth century was considered and treated as an integral part of the fief of the Channel Islands which were held by the English King, and that the group continued to be under the dominion of that King, who in the beginning of the fourteenth century exercised jurisdiction in respect thereof. The Court further finds that British authorities during the greater part of the nineteenth century and in the twentieth century have exercised State functions in respect of the group. The French Government, on the other hand, has not produced evidence showing that it has any valid title to the group. In such circumstances it must be concluded that the sovereignty over the Ecrehos belongs to the United Kingdom.

The Court then examined the evidence relating to the Minquiers group and reached the same conclusion.

For these reasons, the Court, unanimously, finds that the sovereignty over the islets and rocks of the Ecrehos and Minquiers groups, in so far as these islets and rocks are capable of appropriation, belongs to the United Kingdom.

Notes

1.   What was the basis for title in this case?

2.   Who was the critical date in this case? Was it decisive? In the *Dubai/Sharjah Border Arbitration*,[38] the role of the critical data was considered limited to "cases where it was necessary to establish exactly and precisely when in the past sovereignty was exercised by a state over a given territory"; in the tribunal's opinion, it did not apply where the question was to whom it belongs today. Is this consistent with the *Miniquiers* case?

3.   Although the pleadings in the case contain lengthy attempts by both parties to trace their title to the islands over many centuries (which must have taken a lot of time and trouble!), the Court decided the case on the basis of recent evidence of the exercise of state authority.[39] Does this confirm the approach taken by the Arbitrator in the *Palmas* case?

WESTERN SAHARA CASE[40]

Advisory Opinion. I.C.J.Reports 1975, p.12

The background to the request for an opinion in this case and the questions put to the Court are indicated above, p.106. In the course of argument, Morocco claimed that it had had "legal ties" (see

---

[37]   It referred to the exercise of criminal jurisdiction, the holding of inquests, the collection of taxes and to a British Treasury Warrant of 1875 including the "Ecrehos Rocks" within the Port of Jersey.

[38]   (1981) 91 I.L.R. 543 at 594. See Bowett (1994) 65 B.Y.I.L. 103 at 111. See also *Eritrea v Yemen* (1998) 114 I.L.R. 1 at 32 (critical date not used when not relied on by parties).

[39]   cf. *Eritrea v Yemen* (1998) 114 I.L.R. 1 at 117. Note, however, that in the *Land, Island and Maritime Frontier Dispute* case, I.C.J. Rep. 1992, p.351 at pp.564–565, the Court Chamber stated that in the *Minquiers and Ecrehos* case, the Court did not "simply disregard the ancient titles, and decide on a basis of more recent display of sovereignty". Instead, it was "examining evidence of possession as confirmatory of title".

[40]   See Shaw (1978) 49 B.Y.I.L. 119; and Note (1977) 9 C.W.R.J.I.L. 135.

Question II put to the Court) with Western Sahara amounting to sovereignty at the time of its colonisation by Spain in 1884. The following extract concerns the Court's treatment of that claim, prefaced by an extract from the Court's answer to Question I. It ends with the general conclusion to the Court's Opinion.

Opinion of the Court

79. Turning to Question 1 ... a determination that Western Sahara was a *"terra nullius"* at the time of colonization by Spain would be possible only if it were established that at that time the territory belonged to no one in the sense that it was then open to acquisition through the legal process of "occupation."

80. Whatever differences of opinion there have been among jurists, the State practice of the relevant period [1884] indicates that territories inhabited by tribes or peoples having a social and political organization were not regarded as *terra nullius*. It shows that in the case of such territories the acquisition of sovereignty was not generally considered as effected unilaterally through "occupation" of *terra nullius* by original title but through agreements concluded with local rulers. Such agreements with local rulers, whether or not considered as an actual "cession" of the territory, were regarded as derivative roots of title, and not original titles obtained by occupation of *terra nullius*.

81. In the present instance, the information furnished to the Court shows that at the time of colonization Western Sahara was inhabited by peoples which, if nomadic, were socially and politically organized in tribes and under chiefs competent to represent them. In its Royal Order of 26 December 1884, far from treating the case as one of occupation of *terra nullius*, Spain claimed that the King was taking the Río de Oro under his protection on the basis of agreements which had been entered into with the chiefs of the local tribes: ...

90. [In respect of Question II], Morocco's claim to "legal ties" with Western Sahara at the time of colonization by Spain has been put to the Court as a claim to ties of sovereignty on the ground of an alleged immemorial possession of the territory. ...

91. In support of this claim Morocco refers to a series of events stretching back to the Arab conquest of North Africa in the seventh century A.D., the evidence of which is, understandably, for the most part taken from historical works ... Stressing that during a long period Morocco was the only independent State which existed in the north-west of Africa, it points to the geographical contiguity of Western Sahara to Morocco and the desert character of the territory. In the light of these considerations, it maintains that the historical material suffices to establish Morocco's claim to a title based "upon continued display of authority" [*Eastern Greenland Case*, P.C.I.J. Rep, Series A/B, No.53, p.43] on the same principles as those applied by the Permanent Court in upholding Denmark's claim to possession of the whole of Greenland [see above p.173].

92. This method of formulating Morocco's claims to ties of sovereignty with Western Sahara encounters certain difficulties. As the Permanent Court stated in the case concerning the *Legal Status of Eastern Greenland*, a claim to sovereignty based upon continued display of authority involves "two elements each of which must be shown to exist: the intention and will to act as sovereign, and some actual exercise or display of such authority". ... True, the Permanent Court recognized that in the case of claims to sovereignty over areas of thinly populated or unsettled countries, "very little in the way of actual exercise of sovereign rights" (ibid. p. 46) might be sufficient in the absence of a competing claim. But in the present instance, Western Sahara, if somewhat sparsely populated, was a territory across which socially and politically organized tribes were in constant movement and where armed incidents between these tribes were frequent. In the particular circumstances ... the paucity of evidence of actual display of authority unambiguously relating to Western Sahara renders it difficult to consider the Moroccan claim as on all fours with that of Denmark in the *Eastern Greenland Case*. Nor is the difficulty cured by introducing the argument of geographical unity or contiguity. In fact, the information before the Court shows that the geographical unity of Western Sahara with Morocco is somewhat debatable, which also militates against giving effect to the concept of contiguity. Even if the geographical contiguity of Western Sahara with Morocco could be taken into account in the present connection, it would only make the paucity of evidence of unambiguous display of authority with respect to Western Sahara more difficult to reconcile with Morocco's claim to immemorial possession.

93. In the view of the Court, however, what must be of decisive importance in determining its answer to Question II is not direct inference drawn from events in past history but evidence directly relating to effective display of authority in Western Sahara at the time of its colonization by Spain and in the period immediately preceding that time (*cf. Minquiers and Ecrehos, Judgment, I.C.J. Reports* 1953, p. 57). As Morocco has also

adduced specific evidence relating to the time of colonization and the period preceding it, the Court will now consider that evidence. ...

The Court then examined this evidence and found that, although there was evidence of *personal* allegiance owed by Saharan tribes to Morocco, there was no *political* authority of the sort associated with sovereignty. The Court also rejected the Moroccan claim that its sovereignty over Western Sahara had been recognised by the international community.

162. The materials and information presented to the Court show the existence at the time of Spanish colonization, of legal ties of allegiance between the Sultan of Morocco and some of the tribes living in the territory of Western Sahara. They equally show the existence of rights, including some rights relating to the land, which constituted legal ties between the Mauritanian entity,[41] as understood by the Court, and the territory of Western Sahara. On the other hand, the Court's conclusion is that the materials and information presented to it do not establish any tie of territorial sovereignty between the territory of Western Sahara and the Kingdom of Morocco or the Mauritanian entity. Thus the Court has not found legal ties of such a nature as might affect the application of resolution 1514 (XV) in the decolonization of Western Sahara and, in particular, of the principle of self-determination through the free and genuine expression of the will of the peoples of the Territory (cf. paragraphs 54–59 above[42])

163. For these reasons ...
The Court Is of Opinion,
with regard to Question I,
unanimously,
that Western Sahara (Río de Oro and Sakiet El Hamra) at the time of colonization by Spain was not a territory belonging to no one (*terra nullius*),
with regard to Question II,
by 14 votes to 2,[43]
that there were legal ties between the territory and the Kingdom of Morocco of the kinds indicated in paragraph 162 of this Opinion,
by 15 votes to 1,[44]
that there were legal ties between this territory and the Mauritanian entity of the kinds indicated in paragraph 162 of this Opinion.

CHAMIZAL ARBITRATION

U.S. v Mexico (1911)

International Boundary Commission: La Fleur, Presiding Commissioner; Mills, U.S. Commissioner; Puga, Mexican Commissioner. (1911) 5 A.J.I.L. 782

By a treaty of 1848, the Rio Grande was made, for part of its length, the boundary between the United States and Mexico. By 1911, the river had changed its course leaving a tract of land of about 600 acres—the Chamizal Tract—between the old and the new beds of the river on the United States side of the new bed over which both states claimed sovereignty. The Commission decided that the part of the Tract that had resulted from a gradual process of accretion belonged to the United States but that the part of it that had resulted from a flood in 1864 belonged to Mexico. The case was decided

---

[41]   Ed. No question of ties amounting to sovereignty in 1884 arose in the case of the "Mauritanian Entity" because it was not then a state.

[42]   For these paragraphs of the Court's judgment, see above, pp.106–108.

[43]   The judges in the majority were President Lachs; Vice-President Ammoun; Judges Forster, Gros, Bengzon, Petrén, Onyeama, Dillard, Ignacio-Pinto, de Castro, Morozov, Jiménez de Aréchaga, Sir Humphrey Waldock and Nagendra Singh. Judge Ruda and Judge ad hoc Boni dissented.

[44]   Only Judge ad hoc Boni dissented.

on the basis of the relevant treaty provisions; an argument based upon prescription was, however, put by the United States and examined by the Commission in the following passage. The United States Commissioner, who dissented from the Commission's decision, concurred in its treatment of this argument.

Opinion of the Commission

... it is contended that the Republic of Mexico is estopped from asserting the national title over the territory known as "El Chamizal" by reason of the undisturbed, uninterrupted, and unchallenged possession of said territory by the United States of America since the Treaty of Guadaloupe Hidalgo.

Without thinking it necessary to discuss the very controversial question as to whether the right of prescription invoked by the United States is an accepted principle of the law of nations, in the absence of any convention establishing a term of prescription, the commissioners are unanimous in coming to the conclusion that the possession of the United States in the present case was not of such a character as to found a prescriptive title. Upon the evidence adduced it is impossible to hold that the possession of El Chamizal by the United States was undisturbed, uninterrupted and unchallenged from the date of the Treaty of Guadaloupe Hidalgo in 1848 until the year 1895, when, in consequence of the creation of a competent tribunal to decide the question, the Chamizal case was first presented. On the contrary it may be said that the physical possession taken by citizens of the United States and the political control exercised by the local and federal governments, have been constantly challenged and questioned by the Republic of Mexico, through its accredited diplomatic agents. ... From ... [1867] until the negotiation of the Convention of 1884, a considerable amount of diplomatic correspondence is devoted to the very question and the Convention of 1884 was an endeavour to fix the rights of the two nations with respect to the changes brought about by the action of the waters of the Rio Grande.

The very existence of that convention precludes the United States from acquiring by prescription against the terms of their title and, as has been pointed out above, the two republics have ever since the signing of that convention treated it as a source of all their rights in respect of accretion to the territory on one side or the other of the river.

Another characteristic of possession serving as a foundation for prescription is that it should be peaceable ...

It is quite clear from the circumstances ... that however much the Mexicans may have desired to take physical possession of the district, the result of any attempt to do so would have provoked scenes of violence and the Republic of Mexico can not be blamed for resorting to the milder forms of protest contained in its diplomatic correspondence.

In private law, the interruption of prescription is effected by a suit, but in dealings between nations this is of course impossible unless and until an international tribunal is established for such a purpose. In the present case, the Mexican claim was asserted before the International Boundary Commission within a reasonable time after it commenced to exercise its functions, and prior to that date the Mexican Government had done all that could be reasonably required of it by way of protest against the alleged encroachment.

Under these circumstances the Commissioners have no difficulty in coming to the conclusion that the plea of prescription should be dismissed.

Notes[45]

1. See also the extract from the *Anglo-Norwegian Fisheries* case, below p.327.

2. In the *Frontier Land* case,[46] Belgium and the Netherlands disputed sovereignty over certain plots of land in the area of the border between them. The Court stated:

    "The final contention of the Netherlands is that if sovereignty over the disputed plots was vested in Belgium by virtue of the Boundary Convention [of 1843], acts of sovereignty exercised by the Netherlands since 1843 have established sovereignty in the Netherlands. This is a claim

---

[45] On acquisitive prescription as a basis for title, see Johnson (1950) 27 B.Y.I.L. 332.

[46] I.C.J. Rep. 1959, p.209. See also the reference to "acquiescence" in the *Land, Island and Maritime Frontier Dispute* case, below, p.204.

to sovereignty in derogation of title established by treaty. ... The question for the Court is whether Belgium has lost its sovereignty by non-assertion of its rights and by acquiescence in acts of sovereignty alleged to have been exercised by the Netherlands at different times since 1843."[47]

The Court examined the evidence and concluded that Belgian sovereignty had not been extinguished. The Court here would seem to be accepting that title may be established by prescription. The same conclusion is implicit in the *Palmas* case, above, p.167.

3.   In the *Kasikili/Sedudu Island* case[48] the ICJ was asked to determine sovereignty over an island in the Chobe River, the "main channel" of which was accepted by the parties, on the basis of an 1890 Anglo-German treaty, as constituting the boundary between them. Having held the "main channel" was such that Botswana had title to the island, the ICJ considered and rejected an alternative Namibian claim to the island based upon prescription:

"94. According to Namibia, four conditions must be fulfilled to enable possession by a State to mature into a prescriptive title:

'1. The possession of the ... state must be exercised *à titre de souverain*.
2. The possession must be peaceful and uninterrupted.
3. The possession must be public.
4. The possession must endure for a certain length of time.' ...

In support of its allegations, Namibia emphasizes the importance of the presence on the Island of Masubia people from the Eastern Caprivi [in Namibia] 'from the beginning of the colonial period at least, and probably a good deal further back than that'. ... Although Namibia admits that, in order to establish sovereignty by operation of prescription, acquiescence and recognition, it must show more than the use of the disputed territory by private individuals for their private ends, it maintains that ... the authority exercised over Kasikili Island by its predecessors was implemented '[f]or the most part ... through the modality of 'indirect rule,' using the chiefs and political institutions of the Masubia to carry out the directives of the ruling power, under the control and supervision of officials of that power' and that '[a]lthough indirect rule was manifested in a variety of ways, its essence was that the acts of administration of the colonial authorities and those of the traditional authorities were acts of a single entity: the colonial government'.

According to Namibia, this situation 'prevailed without any objection, reservation or protest from Botswana or its predecessors in interest [Great Britain] for almost a century until 1984, when Botswana first made formal claim to the Island in private meetings with the South African government'....

96.   The Parties agree between themselves that acquisitive prescription is recognized in international law and they further agree on the conditions under which title to territory may be acquired by prescription, but their views differ on whether those conditions are satisfied in this case. Their disagreement relates primarily to the legal inferences which may be drawn from the presence on Kasikili/Sedudu Island of the Masubia of Eastern Caprivi: while Namibia bases its argument primarily on that presence, considered in the light of the concept of 'indirect rule', to claim that its predecessors exercised title-generating State authority over the Island,

---

[47] I.C.J. Rep. 1959, p.227.
[48] I.C.J. Rep. 1999, p.1045.

Botswana sees this as simply a 'private' activity, without any relevance in the eyes of international law.

97. ... the Court need not concern itself with the status of acquisitive prescription in international law or with the conditions for acquiring title to territory by prescription. It considers, for the reasons set out below, that the conditions cited by Namibia itself are not satisfied in this case ...

98. ... even if links of allegiance may have existed between the Masubia and the Caprivi authorities, it has not been established that the members of this tribe occupied the Island à titre de souverain, i.e., that they were exercising functions of State authority there on behalf of those authorities. Indeed, the evidence shows that Masubia used the Island intermittently, according to the seasons and their needs, for exclusively agricultural purposes; this use, which began prior to the establishment of any colonial administration in the Caprivi Strip, seems to have subsequently continued without being linked to territorial claims on the part of the Authority [South Africa] administering the Caprivi. ... as soon as South Africa officially claimed title, Bechuanaland did not accept that claim, which precluded acquiescence on its part."

4. In the *Pedra Branca* case,[49] the ICJ summarised the position concerning prescription as follows:

"121. Under certain circumstances, sovereignty over territory might pass as a result of the failure of the State which has sovereignty to respond to conduct à titre de souverain of the other State or, as Judge Huber put it in the *Island of Palmas* case, to concrete manifestations of the display of territorial sovereignty by the other State....Such manifestations of the display of sovereignty may call for a response if they are not to be opposable to the State in question. The absence of reaction may well amount to acquiescence. The concept of acquiescence 'is equivalent to tacit recognition manifested by unilateral conduct which the other party may interpret as consent...' (*Delimitation of the Maritime Boundary in the Gulf of Maine Area (Canada/United States of America), Judgment, I.C.J. Reports 1984*, p.305, para.130). That is to say, silence may also speak, but only if the conduct of the other State calls for a response."

In that case, having held that the Sultan of Johore had established original title by occupation of the tiny island of Pedra Blanca situated between Malaysia and Singapore, the ICJ held that sovereignty had passed to Singapore because of the relevant subsequent state conduct, much of which concerned a lighthouse built by the British authorities in Singapore in 1851:

"274. The conduct of the United Kingdom and Singapore was, in many respects, conduct as operator of Horsburgh lighthouse, but that was not the case in all respects. Without being exhaustive, the Court recalls their investigation of marine accidents, their control over visits, Singapore's installation of naval communication equipment and it reclamation plans, all of which include acts à titre de souverain, the bulk of them after 1953. Malaysia and its predecessors did not respond in any way to that conduct, or the other conduct with that character identified earlier in this Judgment, of all of which (but for the installation of the naval communication equipment) it had notice.

275. Further, the Johor authorities and their successors took no action at all on Pedra Branca/Pulau Batu Peteh from June 1850 for the whole of the following century or more. And, when official visits (in the 1970s for instance) were made, they were subject to express

[49] I.C.J. Rep. 2008.

Singapore permission. Malaysia's official maps of the 1960s and 1970s also indicate an appreciation by it that Singapore had sovereignty. Those maps, like the conduct of both Parties which the Court has briefly recalled, are fully consistent with the final matter the Court recalls. It is the clearly stated position of the Acting Secretary of the State of Johor in 1953 that Johor did not claim ownership of Pedra Branca/Pulau Batu Puteh. That statement has major significance.

276. The Court is of the opinion that. . .by 1980[50] sovereignty over Pedra Banca/Pulau Batu Puteh had passed to Singapore."

5. For other cases is which claims based upon acquisitive prescription have arisen, see the *Frontier Dispute* case, the *Land, Island and Maritime Frontier Dispute* case and the *Land and Maritime Boundary between Cameroon and Nigeria* case considered under the heading of "land boundaries", below, pp.202–205.

6. *Historical consolidation.* In the *Land and Maritime Boundary between Cameroon and Nigeria* case, below, p.205, Nigeria relied upon historical consolidation, as an alternative to acquisitive prescription, as a basis for title to land on the Cameroonian side of the land boundary over which it had exercised governmental authority. The concept of historical consolidation is associated especially with De Visscher,[51] who wrote:

"*Consolidation by Historic Titles.* The fundamental interest of the stability of territorial situations from the point of view of order and peace explains the place that consolidation by historic titles holds in international law. ... It is for these situations, especially, that arbitral decisions have sanctioned the principles *quieta non movere*, as much out of consideration for the importance of these situations in themselves in the relations of States as for the political gravity of disputes concerning them. This consolidation, which may have practical importance for territories not yet finally organized under a State regime as well as for certain stretches of sea, such as bays, is not subject to the conditions specifically required in other modes of acquiring territory. Proven long use, which is its foundation, merely represents a complex of interests and relations which in themselves have the effect of attaching a territory or an expanse of sea to a given State."

The Court rejected Nigeria's claim:

"65. The Court ... observes ... that in the *Fisheries* case (*United Kingdom* v. *Norway*) (*I.C.J. Reports 1951*, p. 130) it had referred to certain maritime delimitation decrees promulgated by Norway almost a century earlier which had been adopted and applied for decades without any opposition. These decrees were said by the Court to represent 'a well-defined and uniform system ... which would reap the benefit of general toleration, the basis of an historical consolidation which would make it enforceable as against all States' (ibid., p.137). The Court notes, however, that the notion of historical consolidation has never been used as a basis of title in other territorial disputes, whether in its own or in other case law.

Nigeria contends that the notion of historical consolidation has been developed by academic writers, and relies on that theory, associating it with the maxim *quieta non movere*.

---

[50] Ed. The critical date, when Singapore and Malaysia formally opposed each other's claim to the island.
[51] *Theory and Reality in Public International Law* (rev. edn 1968, trans by Corbett), p. 209. For criticism, see Jennings, above, at p.163, n.1, pp.25–27. See also Johnson 1955 Cam. L.J. 217.

The Court notes that the theory of historical consolidation is highly controversial and cannot replace the established modes of acquisition of title under international law, which take into account many other important variables of fact and law. It further observes that nothing in the *Fisheries* Judgment suggests that the 'historical consolidation' referred to, in connection with the external boundaries of the territorial sea, allows land occupation to prevail over an established treaty title. Moreover, the facts and circumstances put forward by Nigeria with respect to the Lake Chad villages concern a period of some 20 years, which is in any event far too short, even according to the theory relied on by it. Nigeria's arguments on this point cannot therefore be upheld."

Does the Court reject historical consolidation as a basis for title to territory in all cases, or just in cases where there is a treaty title to the contrary? De Visscher's concept of historical consolidation differs from acquisitive prescription as a basis for title in that it does not require acquiescence by the other claimant state or states. Nor does it suppose general recognition by the international community,[52] just "proven long use", which would be treated as sufficient to establish title by a court or tribunal.

REPORT ON THE FALKLANDS ISLANDS[53]

Fifth Report of the Foreign Affairs Committee of the House of Commons, Session 1983–84, HC Papers 268-I, Vol.I, pp.xiv–xvii; Misc. 1 (1985), Cmnd. 9447

15. According to Spanish and Argentine accounts, the Falkland Islands were first discovered by the navigator Esteban Gomez, who sailed with Magellan in 1520. British accounts ascribe the first sighting of the Islands to the mariner John Davis ... in 1592. It is generally agreed, however, that the first recorded landing was made in 1690 by Captain John Strong RN, who named the Islands after Viscount Falkland, then Treasurer of the Navy, but did not take formal possession in the name of the English Crown.

16. ... the Islands remained unoccupied until 1764, when the first effective settlement was established by the French at Port Louis on East Falkland. This settlement was subsequently sold to Spain (and renamed Port Soledad) in 1767, and maintained by that country until 1811. Meanwhile, a British landing in 1765 on Saunders Island, a mile off West Falkland, was followed the next year by the establishment of a settlement at Port Egmont [on West Falkland]. The British settlers were expelled by Spanish forces in 1770, returned in 1771 (following an exchange of declarations between the Spanish and British governments), and subsequently withdrawn in 1774, ostensibly on grounds of cost. Although Spanish and Argentine sources claim that the withdrawal of the British settlement was in accordance with face-saving understandings reached by the Spanish and British governments in 1771[54] and implied British recognition of Spanish title, the settlers left behind them the Union flag and a plaque affirming British ownership and possession in the name of King George III.[55] There is no evidence of the Spanish settlement being extended to West Falkland, nor of the British settlement being extended to East Falkland. ...

17. The Spanish garrison and settlement on East Falkland were withdrawn in 1811, as Spanish rule in southern

---

[52] As to general recognition as a basis for title, see Jennings, above, p.164, n.1.

[53] On sovereignty over the Falklands, see Anon (1982) Rev. I.C.J., No.26, p.26; Beck (1983) 12 Millenium: Jo. Int. Studies 6; Bologna, *id.*, p.39; Franck (1983) 77 A.J.I.L. 109; Myhre (1983) 12 Millenium: Jo. Int. Studies 29; Goebel, *The Struggle for the Falklands* (1927, rev. ed. 1982); Gustafson, *The Sovereignty Dispute over the Falkland (Malvinas) Islands* (1988); Hassan (1982) 23 Virg. J.I.L. 53; Hoffmann and Hoffmann, *Sovereignty in Dispute: the Falklands/Malvinas* (1984); Perl, *The Falkland Islands Dispute in International Law and Politics* (1983); Lindsey (1983) 18 Texas I.L.J. 11; Pinto (1983) 18 Texas I.L.J. 1; Reisman (1983) 93 Yale L.J. 287; Sanchez (1983) 21 Col. J. T. L. 557. On sovereignty over the Falkland Islands Dependencies, see Symmons (1984) 33 I.C.L.Q. 726.

[54] e.g. UN Doc. No. A/37/533.

[55] Ed. The Spanish removed the plaque and razed the remaining buildings to the ground.

America collapsed as an indirect consequence of the Napoleonic Wars. . . . [Argentina's] independence was only formally declared . . . in July 1816. Meanwhile the Falkland Islands remained unoccupied, save by itinerant sealing and whaling ships, until 1820, when Colonel Daniel Jewett took possession of the Islands in the name of the new Government in Buenos Aires, a fact advertised in the London *Times* in August 1821. Thereafter, the Buenos Aires Government made several attempts to establish occupancy, including the appointment of a Governor, who never actually visited the Islands; in 1823, the granting of land, grazing and fishing rights to Louis Vernet; and in 1829 the appointment of Vernet as Political and Military Commander of the Malvinas, an act which prompted Britain's first formal protest to Argentina, Britain having recognised that country only in 1825.

18. In 1831 Vernet seized three American sailing ships for unlawful sealing in Argentine waters and, in retaliation, the United States corvette *Lexington* sailed to the Islands on the instructions of the U.S. Consul in Buenos Aires and physically destroyed the settlement at Port Soledad, declaring the Islands "free of all government." The following year Argentina (prompting further British protests) appointed yet another Governor, Captain Juan Mestivier, who was murdered by mutinous soldiers soon after his arrival in the Islands. Towards the end of 1832 the British Admiralty issued instructions to Captain Onslow of the sloop *Clio* to "exercise Britain's rights of sovereignty." Captain Onslow arrived at Port Soledad early in January 1833 and, according to British accounts, peacefully persuaded the remainder of the Argentine garrison to leave. According to Argentine accounts, however, the Argentine authorities were "forcibly ousted" by the British troops.[56] The Islands thereafter remained in continuous British possession until April 2, 1982. . . .

19. The Argentine Government formally protested against Britain's occupation of the Islands in 1833, 1834, 1841, 1842 and 1849, in the latter year sending a note to the British Government indicating that, although not intending to protest further in view of Britain's inattention to her protests, Argentine silence should not be interpreted as acquiescence. Argentina again issued formal protests in 1884, 1888 and 1908, thereafter protesting regularly both directly to HM Government and, more recently, indirectly at the United Nations and in other international fora.

20. In 1925 Argentina began to formulate claims to the South Orkney Islands, extending the claim to South Georgia in 1927, the remaining areas of what is now the British Antarctic Territory in 1942, and to the South Sandwich Islands in 1948. Britain sought in 1955 to institute proceedings at the International Court of Justice against both Argentina and Chile concerning their respective claims to sovereignty over the Falkland Island Dependencies and British Antarctic Territory, but neither the Argentine nor the Chilean governments agreed to accept the jurisdiction of the Court. The Islands forming the Dependencies were at no time claimed by Spain, and have at no time, prior to 1982, been occupied by Argentina, with the exception of Southern Thule (in the South Sandwich Group) where Argentina maintained a scientific research station, despite British protests, between 1976 and 1982. Notwithstanding, Argentina has since 1937 made a general reservation of rights in respect of the then existing Dependencies, and has subsequently presented her claim to the Falkland Islands in those terms. . . .

22. We sympathise with our predecessors in the difficulties they faced in seeking to reach conclusions on the respective strengths and weaknesses of the Argentine and United Kingdom claims. *The historical and legal evidence demonstrates such areas of uncertainty that we are unable to reach a categorical conclusion on the legal validity of the historical claims of either country.* It is significant in this context that neither country in modern times has sought to refer the question of sovereignty over the Falkland Island themselves to the International Court of Justice or some other form of legal arbitration. This may be due in part to other considerations, such as doubts about whether any judgment would be honoured by the other side, but almost certainly is evidence also of doubts about the solidarity of their respective legal claims. . . .

23. Like our predecessors, we have no difficulty in concluding that *the claims advanced by Argentina in respect of the Dependencies of South Georgia and the South Sandwich Islands are without legal foundation.* None of these islands was at any time claimed by Spain, and none, apart from Southern Thule, has been at any time occupied by Argentina.

Notes

1.   The Falkland Islands, which lie approximately 300 miles off the coast of Argentina, are a Crown Colony in British constitutional law. Sovereignty over them is also claimed by Argentina, which calls them the Malvinas. The small permanent population of about 3,000 persons are mostly

---

[56]   UN Doc. No. A/37/553.

descended from British families settled there from the early 19th Century onwards. The Islands' waters contain valuable fishing grounds[57] and may have commercially viable deposits of oil and gas.[58] As to the 1982 Argentinian invasion of the Falklands, see below, p.749. Diplomatic relations between Argentina and the UK were resumed in 1990 without prejudice to the sovereignty claims of either.[59] In 1994, Argentina's Constituent Assembly approved a provision in its new constitution ratifying its claim to sovereignty over the Malvinas.[60]

2. In its response to the Foreign Affairs Committee Report, the British Government expressed its regret at "the Committee's reluctance to reach a categorical conclusion on the legal validity of Britain's title to the Islands" and justified the British Government claim as follows[61]:

> "Britain's title is derived from early settlement, reinforced by formal claims in the name of the Crown and completed by open, continuous, effective and peaceful possession, occupation and administration of the Islands since 1833 (save for the 10 weeks of forcible Argentine occupation in 1982). The exercise of sovereignty by the United Kingdom over the Falkland Islands has, furthermore, consistently been shown to accord with the wishes of the Islanders, expressed through their democratically elected representatives."

Earlier, the Foreign Secretary had stated in a reply to a letter in 1982:

> "Even leaving aside arguments in our favour based on events before 1833, we have been consistently advised that our title can be soundly based on our possession of the islands from 1833.
> Our case rests on the facts, on prescription and on the principle of self-determination."[62]

With regard to the reference to "events before 1833," would Argentina or the United Kingdom appear to have had the stronger claim to the Falklands before the British action in 1833? Note in this connection the relative nature of the test to be applied when establishing title based upon possession (see the *Eastern Greenland* case, above, p.173) and the rule that *derelicto* requires an intention to abandon (*Clipperton Island* case, above, p.171). On the principle of *uti possidetis*, upon which the Argentinian claim to succeed Spain turns, see below, p.203.

On the United Kingdom's claim to title based upon prescription, Akehurst[63] states:

> "A State, in order to acquire title to territory from another State by prescription, must exercise effective control over that territory for a long period. The UK has clearly satisfied this requirement as regards the Falkland Islands. But international lawyers, with very few exceptions, consider that effective control is not enough on its own; it has to be accompanied by acquiescence on the part of the 'losing' State. There is some disagreement among inter-

---

57 As to the Islands' exclusive fishing zone, see Churchill (1988) 12 Mar. Pol. 343.
58 Exploratory drilling for oil is planned in 2010 by commercial companies under licence from the Falkland Islands Government.
59 See Evans (1991) 40 I.C.L.Q. 473.
60 U.K.M.I.L. 1994, (1994) 65 B.Y.I.L. 636. The UK expressed its "concern" at this development and was "quite clear about British sovereignty over the Falkland Islands": Secretary of State, FCO (Mr Hurd), UN General Assembly, September 27, 1994. Both states maintain their sovereignty claims.
61 *Report on the Falkland Islands*, above, p.213, p.3.
62 U.K.M.I.L. 1982, (1983) 54 B.Y.I.L. 461.
63 HC 31–xv, Session 1982–3. House of Commons Foreign Affairs Committee, *Falkland Islands*, Appendices to the Minutes of Evidence, App. 12.

national lawyers about the meaning of acquiescence; some say that protests are enough to negative acquiescence, while others say that protests need to be supported by further steps such as breaking off diplomatic relations or offering to refer the dispute to arbitration. This controversy is of little importance as far as the present dispute is concerned, because Argentina's protests against Britain's presence on the Falkland Islands have been accompanied by further steps. In the nineteenth century Argentina offered to refer the dispute to arbitration (but the UK did not accept the offer); later Argentina refused to recognise the British nationality of the islanders and tried to conscript them into the Argentinian army when they visited Argentina; in recent years Argentina has taken the dispute to the UN General Assembly.

    The real uncertainty arises from the fact that for long periods (1849–1884, 1888–1908) Argentina remained silent, without protesting or taking other steps to manifest its disapproval of Britain's presence on the Falkland Islands. Normally, in cases of prescription, a State which remains silent for a long time is regarded as acquiescing and therefore as losing its title to the territory in dispute. However, immediately before Argentina fell silent in 1849, she sent a note to the British government in which she said that she did not intend to protest any more because she felt humiliated when Britain paid no attention to her protests; but she added that her silence should not be interpreted as acquiescence. The legal effect of this note is most uncertain. On the one hand Argentina could argue that she was making clear that she did not acquiesce, and that Britain could therefore not acquire title by prescription: on the other hand Britain could argue that protests are the normal way of preserving rights to territory, and that a State which chooses not to protest chooses to deprive itself of the means of preserving its rights, and must therefore be regarded as losing its rights. It is impossible to predict how an international court would decide a case of this sort."

As to the role of the principle of self-determination in deciding the political future of colonial territories generally and as to the approach taken by the UN Decolonisation Committee in applying the principle to the Falklands in particular, see above, pp.109 and 110, respectively. In 1986, 94 per cent of Falklanders voted in a poll to retain their association with the United Kingdom; they did not want independence, nor did they want to merge with Argentina. By virtue of a 1983 amendment to the 1981 British Nationality Act, Falklanders generally are British citizens, with a right of entry to the United Kingdom.

3.   Another possible basis for British sovereignty is conquest. This was a recognised basis for title in 1833 and could therefore be relied upon now in accordance with the doctrine of intertemporal law.[64] A claim based upon conquest could not be defeated by the protests made by Argentina. Moreover, conquest can be established "even where there has been no war or even hostilities in the technical sense, where the territory has nevertheless been seized by a display of armed force, as for example the entry of German troops into Austria in 1938."[65] One reason why the United Kingdom does not rely upon conquest might be that Captain Onslow's instructions were "to exercise rights of sovereignty" impliedly already in existence, thus suggesting the absence of the necessary intention to conquer.[66] Another might be the political delicacy of relying upon such an outdated notion as conquest.

---

[64] As to which, see above, p.170.

[65] Jennings, above, p.163, n.1, p.53.

[66] Note that the UK has made efforts to dispel the "myth" that armed force was used by Captain Onslow's men in 1833. Even so, there would seem to have been a threat of force sufficient for conquest if the necessary *animus* was present.

4. A further ground for title might, whatever the quality of Argentinian protest, be general recognition by the international community of the British claim in the period following 1833. For example, the United Kingdom has extended to the Falklands many multilateral treaties to which large numbers of states, including Latin American states, are parties without attracting comment.[67] Similarly, maritime nations have long accepted British authority over Falklands territorial and internal waters.[68]

B. Conquest

Note

Conquest was a recognised and important basis for title until the early years of this century.[69] It is now well established that the "territory of a state shall not be the object of acquisition by another state resulting from the threat or use of force" contrary to art.2(4) United Nations Charter: see 1970 Declaration on Principles of International Law, section on the principle on the use of force, para.10, below, App.II. As the 1928 Briand-Kellogg Pact and the United Nations Charter have outlawed the use of armed force, see below, pp.721, 723, so the law of conquest has declined in significance to the point where it provides, under the doctrine of intertemporal law, justification only for the titles acquired before the force used to obtain them was declared illegal by customary international law. A different question is whether a state that acts in self-defence to repel armed force used against it contrary to art.2(4) can acquire any territory of the aggressor which it occupies during hostilities. (See, e.g. the Middle East situation below, p.191). Akehurst[70] refers to the wording of the 1970 Declaration (paragraph referred to above) in support of the view that it cannot:

> "In these words, the Declaration makes a significant distinction between military occupation and acquisition of territory. Military occupation (this is the same as in belligerent occupation) is unlawful only if it results from the use of force in contravention of the Charter; *any* threat or use of force, whether it is in contravention of the Charter or not, invalidates acquisition of territory."

Jennings[71] argues differently for the same conclusion:

> "... the suggestion that the state that does not resort to force unlawfully, e.g. resorts to war in self defence, may still acquire a title by conquest ... though not infrequently heard, is to be regarded with some suspicion. It seems to be based upon a curious assumption that, provided a war is lawful in origin, it goes on being lawful to whatever lengths it may afterwards be pursued. The grave dangers of abuse inherent in any such notion are obvious ... Force used in self-defence ... must be proportionate to the threat of immediate danger, and when the threat has been averted the plea of self-defence can no longer be available ... it would be a curious law of self-defence that permitted

---

[67] See, e.g. at different times, the 1904 White Slave Traffic Agreement, U.K.T.S. 24, Cd. 2689; 1 L.N.T.S. 83; the 1973 CITES Convention, U.K.T.S. 101, Cmnd. 6647; 993 U.N.T.S. 243; and 25 I.L.O. Conventions. As to general recognition, see below, p.191.

[68] Only Argentina has protested at the 1986 UK declaration of a Falkland Islands exclusive fishing zone. Vessels from more than 12 states have been granted fishing licences within the zone.

[69] See Korman, *The Right of Conquest: the Acquisition of Territory by Force in International Law and Practice* (1996).

[70] *A Modern Introduction to International Law* (7th edn 1997), p.153. Footnote omitted.

[71] See above, p.163, n.1, p.55. Footnote omitted.

the defender in the course of his defence to seize and keep the resources and territory of the attacker."

THE STIMSON DOCTRINE OF NON-RECOGNITION

1 Hackworth 334

On January 7, 1932, the United States Secretary of State for Foreign Affairs (Stimson) sent a note to the Japanese and Chinese Governments, from which the following extract is taken. It was occasioned by the invasion of Manchuria by Japan and the establishment by the latter of the "puppet state" of "Manchukuo."[72]

The American Government deems it to be its duty to notify both the Imperial Japanese Government and the Government of the Chinese Republic that it can not admit the legality of any situation *de facto* nor does it intend to recognize any treaty or agreement entered into between those Governments, or agents thereof, which may impair the treaty rights of the United States or its citizens in China, including those which relate to the sovereignty, the independence, or the territorial and administrative integrity of the Republic of China, or to the international policy relative to China, commonly known as the open-door policy, and that it does not intend to recognize any situation, treaty, or agreement which may be brought about by means contrary to the covenants and obligations of the Pact of Paris of August 27th, 1928, to which treaty both China and Japan, as well as the United States, are parties.

Notes

1. On March 11, 1932, the Assembly of the League of Nations resolved that "it was incumbent upon the Members of the League of Nations not to recognise any situation, treaty or agreement which may be brought about by means contrary to the Covenant of the League of Nations, or the Pact of Paris."[73] This, however, proved the high-water mark of the Stimson Doctrine. It was applied by some states upon the invasion of Ethiopia in 1935 and in response to German and Russian invasions shortly afterwards but is no longer invoked under this name. It has reappeared in the 1970 Declaration on Principles of International Law, Section on the Principle on the Use of Force, para.10, below, App.III. Article 11 of the Draft Declaration on Rights and Duties of States[74] similarly reads:

    "Every State has the duty to refrain from recognising any territorial acquisition by another State acting in violation of Article 9 [prohibiting resort to war as an instrument of national policy and the threat or use of force contrary to Article 2(4) of the United Nations Charter]."[75]

2. On the UN's non-recognition of the territorial consequences of Turkey's invasion of Northern Cyprus in 1974, see above, p.103.

3. In the *East Timor* case,[76] Australia had agreed with Indonesia by treaty on the allocation of the continental shelf between East Timor and Australia. It acknowledged that by conducting

---

[72] See above, p.100.
[73] L.N.O.J., Special Supp. No.101, pp.87, 88 (1932).
[74] Y.B.I.L.C. 1949, II, pp.286, 288. On the Draft Declaration, see above, p.63.
[75] Below, App.I.
[76] I.C.J. Rep. 1995, p.90.

negotiations on the matter, Australia had recognised the incorporation of East Timor into Indonesia.[77] Although it opposed the manner in which this incorporation had been brought about, i.e. by the use of force, in the Australian Government's view, "there is no binding international legal obligation not to recognise the acquisition of territory that was acquired by force."[78] In his dissenting opinion in the case, Judge Skubiszewski referred to the Stimson doctrine and to Security Council Resolution 384 calling upon "all states to respect the territorial integrity of East Timor" and to allow its inhabitants to exercise their right to self-determination.[79] In his view, recognition of East Timor as a part of Indonesia was contrary to these resolutions and international law: "While recognition of states or government is still a 'free act', it is not so with regard to the irregular acquisition of territory: here the discretionary nature of the act has been changed by the rule on the prohibition of the use of force".[80]

4. On the UN reaction to the 1990 invasion of Kuwait by Iraq, see below, p.809.

THE INVASION OF GOA[81]

S.C.O.R., 16th Yr, 987th and 988th Meetings, December 18, 1961

On December 17–18, 1961, India invaded the Portuguese territories of Goa, Dañao and Diu on the Indian subcontinent. On December 18, Portugal asked the Security Council of the United Nations "to put a stop to the contemnable act of aggression of the Indian Union, ordering an immediate cease-fire and the withdrawal forthwith from Portuguese territories of Goa, Dañao and Diu of all the invading forces of the Indian Union."[82] A draft resolution rejecting the Portugese complaint was rejected by the Security Council by seven votes to five. A second draft resolution recalling the terms of arts 2(3), (4) of the Charter and calling both for the immediate ceasefire and for the withdrawal by India of its forces was vetoed by the USSR. The following are extracts from the Security Council debate.

987th Meeting

46. Mr. Jha (India). I have already said that this is a colonial question, in the sense that part of our country is illegally occupied by right of conquest by the Portuguese. The fact that they have occupied it for 450 years is of no consequence because, during nearly 425 or 430 years of that period we really had no chance to do anything because we were under colonial domination ourselves. But during the last fourteen years, from the very day when we became independent, we have not ceased to demand the return of the peoples under illegal domination to their own countrymen, to share their independence, their march forward to their destiny. I would like to put this matter very clearly before the Council: that Portugal has no sovereign right over this territory. There is no legal frontier—there can be no legal frontier—between India and Goa. And since the whole occupation is illegal as an issue—it started in an illegal manner, it continues to be illegal today and it is even more illegal in the light of

---

[77] I.C.J. Rep. 1995, p.98.

[78] Statement by the Australian Minister for Resources and Energy (Senator Evans), March 20, 1986, quoted by Judge Skubiszewski in his dissenting opinion, p.263. Senator Evans considered the 1970 Declaration on Principles of International Law, below, App.III, on this point as "very hotly contested".

[79] For this and the similar General Assembly position, see above, p.109.

[80] I.C.J. Rep. 1995, p.264. cf. the dissenting Opinion of Judge Weeramantry, p.206. In its majority judgment, the ICJ declined jurisdiction in the case because a third party, Indonesia, would be impleaded, so that the non-recognition point was not decided.

[81] See Wright (1962) 56 A.J.I.L. 617.

[82] UN Doc. S/5030.

resolution 1514 (XV)[83]—there can be no question of aggression against your own frontier, or against your own people, whom you want to keep liberate.

47. That is the situation that we have come to face. If any narrow-minded, legalistic considerations—considerations arising from international law as written by European law writers—should arise, those writers were, after all, brought up on the atmosphere of colonialism. I pay all respect due to Grotius, who is supposed to be the father of international law, and we accept many tenets of international law. They are certainly regulating international life today. But the tenet which ... is quoted in support of colonial Powers having sovereign rights over territories which they won by conquest in Asia and Africa is no longer acceptable. It is the European concept and it must die. It is time, in the twentieth century that it died. ...

72. Mr. Stevenson (United States of America). Let it be perfectly clear what is at stake here; it is the question of the use of armed force by one State against another and against its will, an act clearly forbidden by the Charter. We have opposed such action in the past by our closest friends as well as by others. We opposed it in Korea in 1950, in Suez and in Hungary in 1956 and in the Congo in 1960. And we do so again in Goa in 1961. ...

75. But what is at stake today is not colonialism; it is a bold violation of one of the most basic principles in the United Nations Charter, stated in these words from Article 2, paragraph 4. ...

76. We realize fully the depths of the differences between India and Portugal concerning the future of Goa. We realize that India maintains that Goa by right should belong to India. Doubtless India would hold, therefore, that its action is aimed at a just end. But, if our Charter means anything, it means that States are obliged to renounce the use of force, are obligated to seek a solution of their differences by peaceful means, are obligated to utilize the procedures of the United Nations when other peaceful means have failed.

988th Meeting

77. Mr. Jha (India) ... We are criticized here by various delegations which say, "Why have you used force? The Charter absolutely prohibits force"; but the Charter itself does not completely eschew force, in the sense that force can be used in self-defence, for the protection of the people of a country—and the people of Goa are as much Indians as the people of any other part of India.[84] We cannot accept any other position.

78. If the use of force is a mockery—and many representatives have said that it is not internationally moral—if that is so, I would say that all freedom movements, all independent countries which have attained freedom through violent movements, should also come in that category. If fighting a colonial Power is immoral I am afraid the existence of many States around this table becomes immoral. The use of force, in all circumstances, is regrettable but so far as the achievement of freedom is concerned, when nothing else is available, I am afraid that it is a very debatable proposition to say that force cannot be used at all. ...

79. ... I have said that we accept international law ... International law is not a static institution. It is developing constantly. If international law would be static, it would be dead driftwood, if it did not respond to the public opinion of the world. And it is responding every day, whether we like it or not. General Assembly resolution 1514 (XV),[85] which has been referred to here and elsewhere very frequently, is the embodiment of that great leap forward in the public opinion of the world on these matters. There can be no getting away from that. Just as the process of decolonization is irreversible and irresistible, the embodiment of the principles in resolution 1514 (XV), which has been accepted by virtually every member around this table, is irresistible. One cannot go behind that now. That is the new dictum of international law.

Note

India remains in control of the territories taken in 1961. Portugal recognised Indian title to them in 1974. Who had title to them between 1961 and 1974 in international law? Is the attitude of Portugal or of other states relevant? On the dispute over the legality of external *material* support for a "people" in *its* war of national liberation, see below p.739. Jennings,[86] starting with the assumption that a state cannot now obtain title to territory by action contrary to art.2(4) of the United Nations Charter,

---

[83] Ed. Above, n.104.
[84] Ed. According to a 1950 census, of the 650,000 people living in Goa, 800 were European, 316 were of mixed descent and the rest were Indian: *Hansard*, HC Vol.651, col.1129 (December 19, 1961).
[85] Above, p.104.
[86] See above, p.164, n.1, p.62.

suggests the following "general recognition" approach to the sort of problem exemplified by the Goan situation:

"The traditional procedure by which the law is adjusted to fact—by which indeed, the law when occasion requires may seem to embrace illegality—is the procedure of recognition. In the present context recognition is apt not only because title is *ex hypothesi* a matter that concerns States in general, but also because the principal effect of the change in the law concerning force, is to make the use of force itself a matter of concern to States generally and not only to the States immediately involved. This is a reversal of the previous position in regard to the use of force when it could be said that 'the validity of the title of the subjugating State does not depend upon recognition on the part of other States. Nor is a mere protest of a third State of any legal weight.[87]'"

SECURITY COUNCIL RESOLUTION ON THE MIDDLE EAST, NOVEMBER 22, 1967[88]

S.C. Res. 242 (XXII), S.C.O.R., 22nd Yr, Resolutions and Decisions 1967, p.8

The Security Council

Expressing its continuing concern with the grave situation in the Middle East,

Emphasizing the inadmissibility of the acquisition of territory by war and the need to work for a just and lasting peace in which every State in the area can live in security,

Emphasizing further that all Member States in their acceptance of the Charter of the United Nations have undertaken a commitment to act in accordance with Article 2 of the Charter,

1. Affirms that the fulfilment of Charter principles requires the establishment of a just and lasting peace in the Middle East which should include the application of both the following principles:

(i) Withdrawal of Israeli armed forces from territories occupied in the recent conflict;

(ii) Termination of all claims or states of belligerency and respect for and acknowledgment of the sovereignty, territorial integrity and political independence of every State in the area and their right to live in peace within secure and recognized boundaries free from threats or acts of force;

2. Affirms further the necessity:

(*a*) For guaranteeing freedom of navigation through international waterways in the area;

(*b*) For achieving a just settlement of the refugee problem;

(*c*) For guaranteeing the territorial inviolability and political independence of every State in the area, through measures including the establishment of demilitarized zones;

3. Requests the Secretary-General to designate a Special Representative to proceed to the Middle East to establish and maintain contacts with the States concerned in order to promote agreement and assist efforts to achieve a peaceful and accepted settlement in accordance with the provisions of this resolution;

4. Requests the Secretary-General to report to the Security Council on the progress of the efforts of the Special Representative as soon as possible.

---

[87] Oppenheim, *International Law*, (8th edn) Vol.1, p.573.

[88] See Lapidoth (1992) 26 Israel L.R. 295; Rosenne (1968) 33 L. C.P. 44; and Shapira (1969) 4 Israel L.R. 229.

Notes

1. Resolution 242 (XXII) was made under Chapter VI of the United Nations Charter.[89] It is therefore not binding upon Member States. The term "territories" in para.1(i) was left purposely vague (*some* territories (if so, which)? All?)

2. The history behind Resolution 242 (XXII) may be summarised as follows.[90] In 1947, the United Kingdom gave notice to the United Nations that it was withdrawing forthwith from Palestine, a territory it had administered as mandatory.[91] The General Assembly recommended[92] that Palestine should be partitioned into separate Arab and Jewish states subject to provision for economic union. This was acceptable to the Zionists but not to the Palestinian Arabs. On May 14, 1948, Israel unilaterally declared itself an independent state in respect of that part of Palestine that it occupied. It was immediately attacked by neighbouring Arab states, whom it defeated. During 1949, armistice agreements were made between Israel and each of its neighbours. Under these Israel retained considerably more territory than it would have had under the 1947 plan for partition. Following the war, Egypt occupied and administered Gaza and Jordan occupied and annexed the West Bank of Jordan ("the West Bank") and East Jerusalem.[93] In 1956, after frequent violations of the armistice agreements on all sides, Israel invaded the Egyptian Sinai Peninsula, including the Gaza Strip, during the Suez crisis but later withdrew to the 1949 armistice line on the recommendation of the General Assembly.[94] In the "Six Day War" of June 1967, claiming anticipatory self defence, Israel again invaded the Sinai Peninsula (including the Gaza Strip). It also occupied the West Bank and East Jerusalem,[95] taking them from Jordan, and the strategically important Golan Heights in Syria.

    Hostilities broke out again in the Yom Kippur War[96] of October 1973. Seeking to recover their territories, on October 6, Egypt and Syria launched simultaneous attacks upon Israeli forces in the Sinai Peninsula and the Golan Heights respectively. When a ceasefire was achieved on October 24, Egypt had retaken about 400 square miles of its territory in the Sinai peninsula to the east of the Suez Canal, but had lost about the same amount of territory to Israel on the west bank of the Canal. In the Golan Heights area, Syria had been forced back to within 20 miles of Damascus after initial successes. Security Council Resolution 338 (1973)[97] called for a ceasefire and the implementation of Security Council Resolution 242 (1967).

    In 1979, Egypt and Israel made a Treaty of Peace[98] by which Egypt recognised Israel as a state and Israel returned the Sinai Peninsula (but not the Gaza Strip) to Egypt. Israel has since made a

---

89 See the UK representative (Lord Caradon), UN Doc. No. S/PV. 1379, para.6. The resolution was adopted unanimously.
90 See on the international law issues arising out of the Arab-Israeli conflict, Akehurst (1972–3) 5 N.Z.U.L.R. 231; Blum, *Secure Boundaries and Middle East Peace in the Light of International Law and Practice* (1971); Cattan, *Palestine and International Law* (2nd edn 1976); Feinberg, *The Arab-Israeli Conflict in International Law* (1970); ibid., *Studies in International Law with Special Reference to the Arab Israeli Conflict* (1979); ibid., (1980) 15 Israel L.R. 160; Gainsborough, *The Arab-Israeli Conflict* (1986); Gerson, *Israel, the West Bank and International Law* (1978); Moore, ed., *The Arab-Israeli Conflict* (1974–91) 4 vols.; Pogany, *The Security Council and the Arab-Israeli Conflict* (1984); Quigley, *Palestine and Israel: A Challenge to Justice* (1990); Stone, *Israel and Palestine: Assault on the Law of Nations* (1981); Smith, *Palestine and the Arab-Israeli Conflict* (5th edn 2004); Wright (1968) 33 L. C.P. 5.
91 See above, p.120.
92 G.A. Res. 181 (II), 2 G.A.O.R., *Resolutions 16 Sept–29 Nov 1947*, pp.131–132.
93 Only the UK recognised these annexations (just de facto in the case of East Jerusalem).
94 See Marston (1988) 37 I.C.L.Q. 773; and (1957) Wright 51 A.J.I.L. 257.
95 On the status of Jerusalem, see Cassese (1986) 3 Palestine Y.I.L. 13; Cattan, *Jerusalem* (1981); Jones (1968) 33 L. & C.P. 169; and E. Lauterpacht, *Jerusalem and the Holy Places* (1968).
96 The attacks were launched on *Yom Kippur*, the most sacred Jewish holy day. See Rostow (1975) 69 A.J.I.L. 272.
97 S.C.O.R., 28th Year, *Resolutions and Decisions*, p.10.
98 (1979) 18 I.L.M. 362.

peace treaty with Jordan (1994), but not with Syria. By a 1974 Israeli-Syrian disengagement agreement, Israel withdrew from all of the areas taken in the 1973 War; it remained in the strategically important Golan Heights which it had taken in 1967. Israel retained control of East Jerusalem, the West Bank and the Gaza Strip.

An historic new stage in the Middle East conflict was reached with the adoption of the 1993 Declaration of Principles on Interim Self-Government Arrangements ("the Oslo Accords").[99] The Declaration provided for interim self-government of the West Bank and Gaza Strip by a newly established Palestinian National Authority ("PNA") for a "transitional period not exceeding five years, leading to a permanent settlement based on Security Resolutions 242 and 338" (art.1). Israel undertook to transfer to the PNA responsibility for civil and security administration in urban areas and civil administration in rural areas, except that Israel remained in control of Israeli settlements and "security zones". In return, Mr Arafat, the Palestine Liberation Organisation ("PLO") leader: (i) recognised the right of the state of Israel to exist in peace and security; (ii) undertook that the PLO constitution provision to the contrary would be deleted; and (iii) renounced terrorism.[100]

The PNA has a President elected by popular vote (Mr Abbas, formerly Mr Arafat), a Cabinet and an elected Legislative Council. It has general legislative, administrative and judicial jurisdiction in the West Bank and the Gaza Strip, but does not have all of the powers of government associated with statehood. Thus external security, most foreign relations, and jurisdiction over Israelis in the transferred territories remain matters for Israel, and legislation by the PNA is subject to approval by a joint Israeli/Authority committee.[101]

Whereas the 1993 Declaration's interim self-government arrangements clearly fall short of statehood for the Palestinian people,[102] in 1988, Palestine had already declared itself a state.[103] In 1998, it was given special observer status in the UN General Assembly, with the right to participate in the general debate and the right to sponsor resolutions.[104] Palestine is recognised as a state by over 100 states.[105] The General Assembly recognises the "Palestinian people" as having the right to self determination.[106]

Frustrated by the failure to negotiate the "permanent settlement" envisaged by the 1993 Declaration, the second Palestinian *intifada*, or uprising, began in 2000, leading to increased Israeli security action in the West Bank and the Gaza Strip. In consequence, the 1993 Declaration arrangements lost such momentum and credibility as they had previously had, and later negotiations, resulting in a Road Map (2003) and the Annapolis Israeli-Palestinian Accord (2007) proposing a "two state" solution, have not led to a settlement of the dispute over the territory that lies at the heart of the Middle East problem. Israel continues to occupy most of the territories taken by it in the Six Day War (the West Bank, the Golan Heights and East Jerusalem);

---

[99]   (1993) 32 I.L.M. 1525. On the Declaration, see Blum (1994) 28 Israel L.R. 210 and Benvenisti (1993) 4 E.J.I.L. 541.

[100] See Cotran and Mallat, eds, *The Arab-Israeli Accords: Legal Perspectives* (1996); Giladi (1995) 29 Israel L.R. 506; and Reece Thomas (2000) 29 Anglo-American L.R. 228 at 239.

[101] See Fassberg (1994) 28 Israel L.R. 318; and Singer, 269.

[102] The UK Secretary of State, FCO (Mr Hurd) stated that the new Palestinian entity "is not a state and no-one is claiming it is a state": U.K.M.I.L. 1994, (1994) 65 B.Y.I.L. 594.

[103] Declaration of the Palestine National Council (1988) 27 I.L.M. 1670. See Crawford, (1990) 1 E.J.I.L. 307; and Prince (1989) 25 Stanford I.L.J. 681.

[104] G.A. Res. A/RES/52/250. Adopted by 124 votes to 4 (including Israel and the US), with 10 abstentions. Palestine, originally as the PLO, had earlier had normal observer status as of 1974.

[105] See Cotran in Cotran and Mallat, above, n.100, p.69. Over 50 Palestinian embassies abroad are listed on the Palestine UN Mission website.

[106] See, e.g. G.A. Res. A/RES/52/114 (1997).

it did withdraw, or disengage, from the Gaza Strip in 2005.[107] A major problem has been Israel's housing settlements in the occupied territories. Although these were found to be illegal under international law in the *Wall* case, below, p.600, they continue to be built.

Although no Israeli law mentions annexation, Israeli civil law has been extended by legislation to East Jerusalem (1967) and the Golan Heights (1981),[108] but not to the West Bank or the Gaza Strip. A 1980 Basic Law[109] states that "Jerusalem, complete and united, is the capital of Israel." The General Assembly and the Security Council have declared the above laws invalid.[110] The position in international law would seem to be that Israel is in belligerent occupation of all of the territories taken by it in 1967 and that it has the rights and duties that go with such occupation.[111] As to whether a state that occupies territory in a legitimate exercise of self-defence can continue to occupy or claim sovereignty to it after the attack is repulsed, see above, p.187.

C. Cession

OPPENHEIM'S INTERNATIONAL LAW

(9th edn 1992), Vol.I. Edited by Jennings and Watts

§244 ... Cession of state territory is the transfer of sovereignty over state territory by the owner-state to another state. ...

Every state as a rule can cede a part of its territory to another state, or by ceding the whole of its territory can even totally merge in another state. To constitute a cession it must be intended that *sovereignty* will pass. Acquisition of governmental powers, even exclusive, without an intention to cede territorial sovereignty, will not suffice.[112] But since certain parts of state territory, as for instance rivers and the maritime belt, are inalienable appurtenances of the land, they cannot be ceded without a piece of land.[113]

---

[107] But, although Israel ended its housing settlements in Gaza and has no other presence there, it completely controls access to Gaza by land, sea and air and operates a blockade. Gaza is now controlled internally by Hamas, a Palestinian Islamic organisation which opposes the existence of Israel, that became the majority party in the PNA Legislative Council in its 2006 elections and then took over Gaza by force, ejecting its more moderate PLO Fatah rivals. This left the PNA in some disarray, with Fatah remaining in control of the West Bank.

[108] Jurisdiction and Administration Order No.1, 1967–5727; Golan Heights Law, 5742–1981. The Israeli Supreme Court has stated that from the date of the 1967 Order, "united Jerusalem became an inseparable part of Israel": *Hanzalis v Greek Orthodox Patriarchate Court* (1969) 48 I.L.R. 93, 98.

[109] Basic Law: Jerusalem, Capital of Israel, 5740–1980.

[110] See, e.g. G.A. Res. A/Res/ES-10/13 (2003); S.C. Res. 478 (1980), S.C.O.R., 35th Year, *Resolutions and Decisions*, p.14; and S.C. Res. 497 (1981), S.C.O.R., 36th Year, *Resolutions and Decisions*, p.6. In Resolution 478, the Council decided "not to recognise the 'basic law' and such other actions by Israel that ... seek to alter the character and status of Jerusalem."

[111] See the 1907 Hague Regulations, U.K.T.S. 9 (1910), Cd. 5030; 1 Bevans 631, and the 1949 Fourth Geneva Red Cross Convention, U.K.T.S. 39 (1958), Cmnd. 550; 75 U.N.T.S. 3. Israel's claim no longer to be the occupying power in the Gaza Strip is not accepted by other states: see the *Wall* case, below, p.600. As to the legality of the Israeli settlements, art.49, Fourth Red Cross Convention, reads: "The occupying power shall not ... transfer parts of its own civilian population into the territory it occupies." The UK considers that "all settlements in the occupied territories, including East Jerusalem, are illegal" (Minister of State, FCO, *Hansard*, HC Vol.222, col.579 (April 14, 1993)) and regards "Israel's annexation of East Jerusalem as illegal" (*Hansard*, HC Vol.548, col.27 (July 15, 1993)).

[112] See *U.S. v Ushi Shiroma* (1954) I.L.R. 21 at 82, on the administration of the Ryukyu Islands by the US, also Germany after the Second World War. See also *Puccini v Commissioner-General of the Government of the Territory of Trieste* (1961) I.L.R. 40 at 43.

[113] This proposition appeared in previous editions of this work, but see McNair, I.C.J. Rep (1951), at p.160 for a more cautious statement of the position. [Ed. See below, p.325] Doubtless both rivers and the territorial sea are "appurtenant" to land, but both stretches of river and of territorial sea are not infrequently alienated for the purpose of boundary settlements. But see *U.S. v Angeog* (1961) I.L.R. 32 at 83, for a decision that a cession of the island of Guam necessarily included its territorial sea. ...

Note

Gibraltar[114] Gibraltar is a British Crown Colony. In 1704, it was captured from Spain by a British/Dutch expedition during the War of Spanish Succession. It was later ceded by Spain to Great Britain after the latter had lost the War. Article X of the Treaty of Utrecht 1713 reads:

> "The Catholic King does hereby, for himself, his heirs and successors, yield to the Crown of Great Britain the full and entire property of the town and castle of Gibraltar, together with the port, fortifications, and forts thereunto belonging; and he gives up the said property to be held and enjoyed absolutely with all manner of right for ever, without any exception or impediment whatsoever. ..."[115]

In 1963, Spain raised the question of the status of Gibraltar before the United Nations Decolonisation Committee. The following year the Committee reached a consensus by which it invited Spain and the United Kingdom to conduct "conversations in order to find ... a negotiated solution."[116] During the resulting discussions, the following positions were established.[117] Spain argued that art.X granted to Great Britain "a British military base installed in Spain," not sovereignty over the territory of Gibraltar.[118] The United Kingdom disputed this limited reading of art.X.[119] Spain contended that the United Kingdom had no claim to Gibraltar based on conquest because its seizure in 1704 was not in the name of Great Britain but on behalf of a possible King of Spain—the Pretender to the Spanish Crown, Archduke Charles of Austria—and by an allied force, not an exclusively British one.[120] The United Kingdom reserved its opinion on this question.[121] Spain claimed that certain "neutral ground" to the North of the Rock proper was not included in art.X. The United Kingdom denied this and, in the alternative, claimed a prescriptive title:

> "Her Majesty's Government do not accept that the ground between the Gibraltar frontier fence and the foot of the Rock is Spanish sovereign territory. ... The whole of the territory has in any case been under exclusive British jurisdiction since at least 1838, by which time British sentries were established along the line of the present frontier fence. ...
>
> Notwithstanding occasional protests concerned with specific issues such as the construction by Britain of permanent works on the ground, successive Spanish Governments have, in the view of Her Majesty's Government, demonstrated their acquiescence in these developments and forfeited any title which they may at one time have possessed to the area concerned. Nor has the Spanish Government ever sought to have the matter referred to an international tribunal."[122]

Spain denied that a prescriptive title had been established[123]:

---

[114] See Fawcett (1967) 43 Int. Affairs 236.
[115] 28 C.T.S. 325.
[116] See above, p.109.
[117] For a UK record of the discussion, see Cmnd. 3131.
[118] ibid. p.8.
[119] ibid. p.53.
[120] ibid. p.8.
[121] ibid. p.53.
[122] ibid. p.62. Does the refusal by Spain to refer the question of title to Gibraltar to the I.C.J., as suggested by the UK in 1966, indicate acquiescence? See Fawcett, above, n.114, pp.240–241.
[123] ibid. pp.27–28.

"In addition to prescription being a debatable and vague institution, both in judicial decisions and in doctrine ... in order that prescription may produce legal effects it is necessary to take into account the behaviour of both the interested parties; in other words, the indifference or tacit abandonment on the part of one side, and the occupation as owner on the part of the other. And that is something that has certainly not occurred here. The Spanish Government has continually declared that its acts of tolerance did not imply any extension of the concessions made in the Treaty of Utrecht, and the Government of Great Britain has repeatedly assured it that in their actions there was no intention of altering the 'status quo ante.' Consequently it is not possible to speak to any legitimization of the British presence in part of the neutral ground, by reason of the long series of Spanish protests and refusals which have been made uninterruptedly from 1713 down to the present day."

Spain also claimed sovereignty over Gibraltar's territorial sea. The 1966 (and subsequent) negotiations proved unsuccessful, but in 2002 Spain and the United Kingdom agreed on the principle of their co-sovereignty over Gibraltar.[124] However, the Gibraltar population then overwhelmingly rejected the idea of shared sovereignty in a referendum organised by the Gibraltar Government. Following the referendum, the UK Government confirmed that there would be no change in sovereignty over Gibraltar without the consent of the people given in a UK Government referendum. So, the future of Gibraltar remains unresolved.

Is a title based upon a cession made by a defeated state to a victorious state in 1713 still valid? How does the doctrine of intertemporal law[125] affect the position? Would such a cession be valid if it were to occur now? On the validity of treaties by which one state cedes territory to another after a war or other use of force contrary to art.2(4), United Nations Charter, see below, p.723. What is the relevance of the principle of self-determination?[126]

D. Accretion and Avulsion

Note

A state may also attain sovereignty over new land as a result of natural forces. This may happen slowly (accretion), for example, by the gradual movement of a river bed or suddenly (avulsion), for example, by the creation of an island in territorial waters by volcanic action.[127]

E. New States

Note

Which, if any, of the means of acquiring territorial sovereignty considered in the above materials applies or apply when a new state emerges, either by revolution or, as in the case of many former

---

[124] UK Government statement in UN Doc. A/C.4/57/SR.7, 4, October 2002.
[125] See above, p.170.
[126] See above, p.104.
[127] As in the case of Surtsey: see below, p.338. See further, Oppenheim, Vol.I, pp.697–698. And see the *Chamizal Arbitration*, above, p.178.

colonial territories since the Second World War, by peaceful means? Do these means apply only to the acquisition of additional territory by an existing state, so that the emergence of a new state is to be considered solely by reference to the criteria of statehood considered in Ch.4?[128]

----

2. POLAR REGIONS[129]

A. Antarctica[130]

NEW ZEALAND'S CLAIM TO THE ROSS DEPENDENCY[131]

1 Hackworth 457

The following correspondence concerned Admiral Byrd's second expedition to the Antarctic in 1934. The United Kingdom learnt that a post office was to be established at the expedition's base in the Ross Dependency; that special stamps had been issued for use there; and that certain expedition members had been sworn in to act as United States postmasters. The United Kingdom protested that "such acts could not be regarded otherwise than as infringing the British sovereignty and New Zealand administrative rights in the dependency. ..." The following exchange then occurred.

Note from the United States Secretary of State to the British Ambassador, November 14, 1934

It is understood that His Majesty's Government in New Zealand bases its claim of sovereignty on the discovery of a portion of the region in question ... in the light of long established principles of international law, ... I cannot admit that sovereignty accrues from mere discovery unaccompanied by occupancy and use.

Note from the British Ambassador to the United States Secretary of State, December 27, 1934

1. ... The supposition that the British claim to sovereignty over the Ross Dependency is based on discovery alone, and, moreover on the discovery of only a portion of the region, is based on a misapprehension of the facts of the situation.

2. The Dependency was established and placed under New Zealand Administration by an Order in Council of 1923 in which the Dependency's geographical limits were precisely defined. Regulations have been made by the Governor General of New Zealand in respect of the Dependency and the British title has been kept up by the exercise in respect of the Dependency of administrative and governmental powers, e.g. as regards the issue of whaling licences and the appointment of a special officer to act as magistrate for the Dependency.

3. As I had the honour to state in my note No. 33 of January 29th last, His Majesty's Government in New Zealand recognize the absence of ordinary postal facilities in the Dependency and desire therefore to facilitate as far as possible the carriage of mail by United States authorities to and from the Byrd Expedition. As regards Mr. Anderson's present mission, they understand that he is carrying letters to which are, or will be, affixed special stamps printed in the United States and that these stamps are to be cancelled and date-stamped on board the Expedition's vessel. They also understand that these stamps are intended to be commemorative of the Byrd Expedition and have been issued as a matter of philatelic interest.

4. In the above circumstances His Majesty's Government in New Zealand have no objection to the proposed

---

[128] See Jennings, above, p.163, n.1, pp.7–9.
[129] See Mouton (1962–III) 107 Hague Recueil 169; and Rothwell, *The Polar Regions and the Development of International Law* (1996).
[130] See Auburn, *Antarctic Law and Politics* (1982); Francioni and Scovazzi, eds., *International Law for Antarctica* (2nd edn 1996); Hayton (1960) 54 A.J.I.L. 349; Joyner and Chopra, *The Antarctic Legal Regime* (1988); Myhre, *The Antarctic Treaty System: Politics, Law and Diplomacy* (1986); Sahurie, *The International Law of Antarctica* (1992); Triggs, ed., *The Antarctic Treaty Regime* (1987); Various, Symposium: *The International Legal Regime for Antarctica* (1986) 19 Cornell I.L.J. 155.
[131] See Auburn, *The Ross Dependency* (1972).

visit of Mr. Anderson. They must, however, place it on record that, had his mission appeared to them to be designed as an assertion of United States sovereignty over any part of the Ross Dependency or as a challenge to British sovereignty therein, they would have been compelled to make a protest.

Notes

1. Antarctica is a land mass covered with ice. At certain points (e.g. the Ross Ice Shelf), permanently frozen sea adjoins it. Beyond the land mass and the shelf ice there is a large area of sea that is frozen in some seasons and navigable in others. Official claims to sectors of Antarctica have been made by Argentina, Australia, Chile, France, New Zealand, Norway and the United Kingdom.[132] The only major sector not officially claimed is Marie Byrd Land. Admiral Byrd discovered it and claimed it for the United States, but his claim was not officially adopted. The United States does not recognise the claim of any other state. The claimant states would appear to recognise each others' claims,[133] except that the Argentinian and Chilean sectors overlap with each other, as does each with that of the United Kingdom. In 1955, the United Kingdom instituted proceedings before the International Court of Justice by unilateral application asking the Court to rule on the disputes resulting from this situation between the United Kingdom, on the one hand, and Argentina and Chile, on the other.[134] The applications met with no response from Argentina and Chile and the Court struck them off its list in 1956. Did they nonetheless serve a useful purpose from the standpoint of the United Kingdom?[135] In its applications, the United Kingdom claimed sovereignty over its sector on the basis of "historic British discoveries" followed by "the long-continued and peaceful display of British sovereignty from the date of those discoveries onwards in, and in regard to, the territories concerned."[136]

2. A sector is established by enclosing an area within a line of latitude and two lines of longitude to the point at which the latter lines converge at the South Pole. Thus, applying this method in two stages, the United Kingdom sector, the British Antarctic Territory, consists of "all islands and territories whatsoever which ... are situated south of the 60th parallel of the south latitude between the 20th degree of west longitude and the 80th degree of west longitude."[137]

ANTARCTIC TREATY 1959[138]

U.K.T.S. 97 (1961), Cmnd. 1535, 402 U.N.T.S. 71; (1960) 54 A.J.I.L. 477

Article 1

1. Antarctica shall be used for peaceful purposes only. There shall be prohibited, inter alia, any measures of a military nature, such as the establishment of military bases and fortifications, the carrying out of military manoeuvres, as well as the testing of any type of weapons.

---

[132] For maps of Antarctica with the sectors marked, see the articles by Mouton and Hayton referred to above, nn.129, 130.

[133] See, e.g. the implied mutual recognition of claims by France and by Commonwealth states in the exchange of notes of October 25, 1938, Cmd. 5900.

[134] I.C.J. Pleadings, *Antarctica Cases* (*U.K. v Argentina; U.K. v Chile*).

[135] On the role of protest, see above, pp.178 et seq.

[136] See above, n.134, p.74.

[137] SI 1972/400. Waldock (1948) 25 B.Y.I.L. 311, 328 states that the area "does not seem to have been framed in pursuance of any special sector doctrine. The sector was merely the most convenient geographical definition of the numerous islands and continental territory claimed. ..."

[138] In force 1961. 47 parties, including the UK.

2. The present treaty shall not prevent the use of military personnel or equipment for scientific research or for any other peaceful purpose. . . .

Article 4

1. Nothing contained in the present treaty shall be interpreted as:

(*a*) a renunciation by any Contracting Party of previously asserted rights of or claims to territorial sovereignty in Antarctica;

(*b*) a renunciation or diminution by any Contracting Party of any basis of claim to territorial sovereignty in Antarctica which it may have whether as a result of its activities or those of its nationals in Antarctica, or otherwise;

(*c*) prejudicing the position of any Contracting Party as regards its recognition or non-recognition of any other State's right of or claim or basis of claim to territorial sovereignty in Antarctica.

2. No acts or activities taking place while the present treaty is in force shall constitute a basis for asserting, supporting or denying a claim to territorial sovereignty in Antarctica or create any rights of sovereignty in Antarctica. No new claim, or enlargement of an existing claim, to territorial sovereignty in Antarctica shall be asserted while the present treaty is in force.

Article 5

1. Any nuclear explosions in Antarctica and the disposal there of radioactive waste material shall be prohibited. . . .

Article 6

The provisions of the present treaty shall apply to the area south of 60° South Latitude, including all ice shelves, but nothing in the present treaty shall prejudice or in any way affect the rights, or the exercise of the rights, of any state under international law with regard to the high seas within that area.

Article 7

1. In order to promote the objectives and ensure the observance of the provisions of the present treaty, each Contracting Party whose representatives are entitled to participate in the meetings referred to in Article 9 of the treaty shall have the right to designate observers to carry out any inspection provided for by the present article. . . .

Article 8

1. In order to facilitate the exercise of their functions under the present treaty, and without prejudice to the respective positions of the Contracting Parties relating to jurisdiction over all other persons in Antarctica, observers designated under paragraph 1 of Article 7 and scientific personnel exchanged under subparagraph 1(b) of Article 3 of the treaty, and members of the staffs accompanying any such persons, shall be subject only to the jurisdiction of the Contracting Party of which they are nationals in respect of all acts or omissions occurring while they are in Antarctica for the purpose of exercising their functions.

2. Without prejudice to the provisions of paragraph 1 of this article, and pending the adoption of measures in pursuance of subparagraph 1(e) of Article 9, the Contracting Parties concerned in any case of dispute with regard to the exercise of jurisdiction in Antarctica shall immediately consult together with a view to reaching a mutually acceptable solution.

Notes

1. The Antarctic Treaty's undoubted success stems largely from the "freezing" of territorial claims by art.4.[139] With the issue of sovereignty defused, Antarctica has experienced scientific co-operation rather than political conflict. Other notable features of the Treaty régime are the demilitarised (art.1) and "nuclear free" (art.5) character of Antarctica and the provision for periodic meetings (now annual) of the consultative parties. (art.9).[140] The Consultative Meetings have adopted over 150 (non-binding) recommendations concerning activities in Antarctica and have led to other important conservation measures, particularly the 1972 Convention for the Conservation of Antarctic Seals[141] and the 1980 Convention for the Conservation of Antarctic Marine Living Resources.[142] The latter establishes a Commission charged with promoting the conservation of marine living resources, primarily krill (a small crustacean).

2. The 1959 Treaty contains no provision on the exploitation of mineral resources. It was intended to fill this gap by the 1988 Convention on the Regulation of Antarctic Mineral Resources Activities.[143] This provided for a permit system by which national operators might exploit minerals subject to stringent environmental safeguards. But the Convention did not enter into force because international opinion favoured a complete ban on mineral exploitation. It was quickly replaced by the 1991 Protocol on Environmental Protection to the Antarctic Treaty.[144] This designates Antarctica as "a natural reserve, devoted to peace and science" (art.2), spells out principles and mandatory rules for environmental protection (art.3, Annexes I–IV)) and establishes a Committee on Environmental Protection (art.11). The Protocol imposes a ban on mineral resource activity, except for scientific research (Annex V).

3. The 1959 Treaty has no time limit, but a review conference with a view to modification or amendment may be called by a consultative party (art.12) (none yet). One suggestion is that the present legal régime be replaced by one that regards Antarctica as a part of the "common heritage of mankind."[145] This has been proposed by Malaysia and some other non-aligned countries within the United Nations.[146] Such a régime would make territorial claims to sovereignty inappropriate.

---

[139] What is the effect of art.4(2) for states not parties to it? On treaties establishing objective legal regimes, see below, p.687.

[140] The consultative parties are the 12 named in the Convention preamble (the states with territorial claims, listed above, p.198, and Belgium, Japan, South Africa, US and the Russian Federation) and the 16 other acceding parties that at present conduct "substantial scientific research activity" in Antarctica (art.9(3)).

[141] U.K.T.S. 45 (1978), Cmnd. 7209; 1080 U.N.T.S. 176; 11 I.L.M. 251. In force 1978, 16 parties, including the UK. Whales are protected by the 1946 International Convention for the Regulation of Whaling, U.K.T.S. 5 (1949), Cmnd. 7604; 161 U.N.T.S. 72, which is not restricted to Antarctica. In force 1948, 42 parties, including the UK.

[142] U.K.T.S. 48 (1982), Cmnd. 8714; (1980) 19 I.L.M. 841. In force 1982, 31 parties, including the UK. See Bankes (1981) 19 C.Y.I.L. 303; Frank (1983) 13 O.D.I.L. 291; Gardam (1985) 15 M.U.L.R. 279; Howard (1989) 38 I.C.L.Q. 104.

[143] Misc. 6 (1989), Cm. 634; (1988) 27 I.L.M. 868. Not in force. Ratification by 16 of the 20 drafting conference participants required, including, inter alia, all states with territorial claims. No ratifications. See Redgwell (1990) 39 I.C.L.Q. 474; Watts (1990) 39 I.C.L.Q. 169; and Wolfrum, *The Convention on the Regulation of Antarctic Mineral Resource Activities* (1991). On the exploitation of mineral resources generally, see Francioni (1986) 19 Cornell I.L.J. 163; Lagoni (1979) 39 Z.A.O.R.V. 1; Rich (1982) 31 I.C.L.Q. 709; Tetzeli (1987) 10 Hastings I.C.L.R. 525; Visser (1988) 1 Leiden J.I.L. 171.

[144] (1991) 30 I.L.M. 1455. In force 1998, 27 parties, including the UK. See Blay (1992) 86 A.J.I.L. 377; Francioni (1993) 28 Texas I.L.J. 47; Redgwell (1994) 43 I.C.L.Q. 599; and Rothwell (2000) 11 E.J.I.L. 591. See also the Antarctica Act 1994.

[145] As to which, see below, p.412.

[146] On the Malaysian initiative, see Hayashi (1986) 19 Cornell I.L.J. 275. The consultative parties, who include members of the main political groupings within the UN, are opposed to this attempt to transfer jurisdiction over Antarctica from states actively involved in the continent's development to UN members generally.

B. The Arctic[147]

Notes

1. Two of the states bordering the Arctic Ocean—Canada and the Russian Federation—have made sector claims to land to their north. In 1926, the (then) USSR claimed "sovereignty over all territory, discovered or undiscovered, lying in the Arctic Ocean north of the coast of the Soviet Union to the North Pole, between meridian 32° 4′ 35″ east of Greenwich and meridian 168° 49′ 30″ west of Greenwich."[148] Canada also made sector claims to land in the Arctic for many years,[149] but these have now been replaced by claims to the same islands (the Arctic Archipelago) on the basis of cession (from the UK), occupation and self-determination (indigenous inhabitants).[150] Other states bordering the Ocean with less to gain, namely Denmark, Norway and the US, opposed the use of the sector approach.[151] Neither Canada nor the Russian Federation have officially claimed sovereignty over the ice as well. Thus, in 1956, the Canadian Minister of Northern Affairs and National Resources stated[152]:

    "We have never subscribed to the sector theory in application to the ice. We are content that our sovereignty exists over all the Arctic Island."

    On the question whether a state may acquire sovereignty over ice by other means, (e.g. by occupation), Pharand distinguishes between ice shelves (e.g. those of Ellesmere Island in the Arctic or the Ross Ice Shelf in the Antarctic) and ice islands. As to the former, he states[153]:

    "The legal status of ice shelves in international law has never been determined but there appears to be a consensus among interested states that they ought to be considered as land. ... These huge ice-tongues are partly afloat, but their thickness and quasi-permanency render them much more like land than water ..."

    As to ice islands, since they do not satisfy the definition of an island in art.121, 1982 Law of the Sea Convention, Pharand suggests that the better analogy is with a ship: "The suggestion is that ice islands ought to be considered as ships when occupied [as they may be by research stations] and appropriated."[154]

2. In 1985, Canada drew straight baselines around the outer limits of the islands constituting the Canadian archipelago, claiming the waters on the landward side of the islands, which include

---

[147] See Boczek (1986) 29 G.Y.I.L. 154; Butler, *Northeast Arctic Passage* (1978); Franckx, *Maritime Claims in the Arctic: Canadian and Russian Perspectives* (1993); Pharand, *The Law of the Sea of the Arctic* (1973); *Canada's Arctic Waters in International Law* (1988); (2007) 38 O.D.I.L. 3.

[148] 1 Hackworth 461.

[149] See, e.g. the 1956 statement below at n.152.

[150] *The Arctic: Canada's Legal Claims*, Canadian Government document, 2002, p.1, www.parl.gc.ca.

[151] See 1 Hackworth 463–465.

[152] 1956 Debates, HC, Canada Vol.7, p.6955. See Head (1963) 9 McGill L.J. 200. More recently Canadian Government spokesmen have claimed that waters in the Canadian sector of the Arctic Ocean, although not Canadian, "have a special undefined status because of the presence of ice and do not qualify as high seas": Pharand, *The Law of the Sea of the Arctic* (1973), n.147, p.175. Whereas USSR writers sometimes claimed sovereignty over the ice, see, e.g. Lakhtine (1930) 24 A.J.I.L. 703 at 712, no official claim was made: see Pharand, above, p.170.

[153] Above, n.152, p.170.

[154] Above, n.152, p.196. See also Molde (1982) 51 N.T.I.R. 164.

Hudson Bay and the various routes of the North West Passage, as internal waters.[155] The baselines were said to indicate the outer limit of Canadian "historic internal waters."[156] By a 1988 US-Canadian Agreement on Arctic Co-operation, the US, while objecting to the baselines, agreed to seek Canadian consent before its icebreakers and other vessels navigated the North West Passage.[157]

3.   On continental shelf claims in the Arctic, see below, p.403.

----

3. LAND BOUNDARIES[158]

OPPENHEIM'S INTERNATIONAL LAW

(9th edn 1992), Vol.I. Edited by Jennings and Watts

§ 232 Boundary disputes   Boundaries are, for many reasons, of such importance, that disputes relating thereto are relatively frequent. The location of a land boundary line is usually a matter of the correct interpretation of some instrument, by which the boundary has been established. The commonest way of doing this is by a boundary treaty. In other cases an arbitral award or judicial decision can be the final determination, especially where the meaning of a boundary treaty had been disputed.[159] In that event, the tribunal will have it in mind that "one of the primary objects" of boundary settlement is "to achieve stability and finality".[160] Sometimes international commissions are specially appointed to settle the boundary lines.[161]

§ 233 Boundary and territorial disputes distinguished   Boundary questions are distinguishable from questions of title to territorial sovereignty[162] ... As the International Court of Justice said in the *North Sea Continental Shelf* cases, "The appurtenance of a given area, considered as an entirety, in no way governs the precise delimitations of its boundaries, any more than uncertainty as to boundaries can affect territorial rights".[163] A dispute often involves both kinds of argument, however; and the question which is the correct approach may be one of the

---

[155] See Pharand (1987) 25 C.Y.I.L. 324.

[156] Statement by the Canadian Secretary of State for External Affairs, quoted by Pharand, above, n.155, p.326. cf. the earlier Canadian Government statement in (1970) 9 I.L.M. 607 at 613.

[157] See Pharand, above, n.155, p.327.

[158] See Berstein, *Delimitation of International Boundaries* (1974); Brownlie, *African Boundaries: A Legal and Diplomatic Encyclopaedia* (1979); Prescott, *Boundaries and Frontiers* (1978); Kaikobad, *Interpretation and Revision of International Boundary Decisions* (2007); Sharma, *International Boundary Disputes and International Law* (1976).

[159] See the *Temple of Preah Vihear Case*, p.6, I.C.J. Rep. 1962, 34; see also *Aegean Sea Continental Shelf* case (*Greece v Turkey*), I.C.J. Rep. 1978, p.36. The delimitation of land boundaries was the subject-matter of two Advisory Opinions of the P.C.I.J., P.C.I.J., Series B, No. 8 (Poland and Czechoslovakia), and No. 9 (Albania and the Serb-Croat-Slovene State). ... For later cases, see the *Frontier Land Case*, I.C.J. Rep. 1959, p.209; the *King of Spain Award Case*, I.C.J. Rep. 1960, p.192; the *Rann of Kutch Case*, I.L.M., 7 (1968), p. 633; and see Salmon in A.F.D.I., 14 (1968), p. 217; the *Encuentro/Palena Case, Argentine-Chile Frontier Case* (1966) I.L.R., 38, p. 19 and I.C.L.Q., 12 (1967), p.550, and A.J., 12 (1967), 1071 (a dispute between Argentina and Chile) and Cot, A.F.D.I., 14 (1968), p.237; the *Beagle Channel Case* (1977) I.L.R. 93 (between Argentina and Chile) ...; see also the *Taba Award* (1988) I.L.R. 226, between Egypt and Israel ... I.L.M., 27 (1988), p.1421, I.L.R., 80, p.226. ... [; the] Award in the *Dubai-Sharjah* case (1981) [91 I.L.R. 543] ...; the *Burkina Faso and Mali Frontier Dispute*, I.C.J. Rep. 1986, p.554.

[160] See the *Temple of Preah Vihear Case*, I.C.J. Rep. 1962, p.34. But for the "relativity" of the principle of finality, see Bardonnet, above, pp.67–71.

[161] The work of a boundary commission was crucial to the *Temple of Preah Vihear Case*, I.C.J. Rep. 1962, p.6; see also the Award in the *Argentine/Chile Frontier Case* (1967), Cmnd. 7438 and I.L.R., 38, p.10. See the *Taba Award* (1988) I.L.R., 80, p.226, where it was held that, "If a boundary line is once demarcated jointly by the parties concerned, the demarcation is considered as an authentic interpretation of the boundary agreement even if deviations may have occurred or if there are some inconsistencies with the maps" (para. 210).

[162] "... Nevertheless, some law is common to both kinds of dispute, e.g. the question of the 'critical date'..." (see §273).

[163] I.C.J. Rep. 1969, at p.32; but see also *Burkina Faso and Mali Frontier Dispute*, I.C.J. Rep. 1986, p.554, para.17 for a different view.

points at issue.[164] Even in the strictly territorial dispute the boundaries of the disputed territory must be part of the relevant facts, though not disputed. There is also a sense in which a question of title to territory must always be implicitly involved in a pure boundary dispute; except that in this case it is not the fact and mode of acquisition of territorial title that is disputed but the proper interpretation of some instrument, award or adjudication, or course of historical development, that is claimed to have established the boundary of the territory in question.

§ 234 Third states   Boundary questions, as well as questions of territorial title, often concern more than one state for an international boundary dispute is concerned essentially with rights opposable *erga omnes*; as, for example, where the boundaries of three states converge on a tri-point. When a dispute between two of the states is submitted to a tribunal for settlement, there may therefore also arise questions about the extent of the tribunal's jurisdiction, or, in the International Court of Justice, of intervention under Articles 62 or 63 of the Court's Statute.[165]

Notes

1. Key to the determination of post-colonial boundary disputes is the concept of *uti possidetis juris*, the meaning of which was considered in the *Frontier Dispute* case[166]:

   "23 . . . The essence of the principle lies in its primary aim of securing respect for the territorial boundaries at the moment when independence is achieved. Such territorial boundaries might be no more than delimitations between different administrative divisions or colonies all subject to the same sovereign. In that case, the application of the principle of *uti possidetis* resulted in administrative boundaries being transformed into international frontiers in the full sense of the term. This is true both of the States which took shape in the regions of South America which were dependent on the Spanish Crown, and of the States Parties to the present case, which took shape within the vast territories of French West Africa. *Uti possidetis*, as a principle which upgraded former administrative delimitations, established during the colonial period, to international frontiers, is therefore a principle of a general kind which is logically connected with this form of decolonization wherever it occurs.
   24. The territorial boundaries which have to be respected may also derive from international frontiers which previously divided a colony of one State from a colony of another, or indeed a colonial territory from the territory of an independent State, or one which was under protectorate, but had retained its international personality. There is no doubt that the obligation to respect pre-existing international frontiers in the event of a State succession derives from a general rule of international law whether or not the rule is expressed in the formula *uti possidetis*. . . .
   25. However, it may be wondered how the time-hallowed principle has been able to withstand the new approaches to international law as expressed in Africa, where the successive attainment of independence and the emergence of new States have been accom-

---

[164] See, e.g. the *Rann of Kutch Case*, I.L.M., 7 (1968), pp.633 et seq. (between India and Pakistan). Also the *Aegean Sea Case*, I.C.J. Rep. 1978, p.3, para.84, where the court said: "it would be difficult to accept the broad proposition that delimitation is entirely extraneous to the notion of territorial status. Any disputed delimitation of a boundary entails some determination of entitlement to the areas to be delimited." . . .
[165] See I.C.J. Rep. 1984, p.3, and 1985, p.13 (Libya/Malta continental shelf and Italy); and specifically on land frontiers and a tri-point, see (*Burkina Faso and Mali*) I.C.J. Rep. 1986, p.554, para.49.
[166] I.C.J. Rep. 1986, p.554. Court Chamber decision. See Naldi (1987) 36 I.C.L.Q. 893. The principle of *uti possidetis* has not been applied as state practice in post-colonial Africa in every case, as was pointed out by Judge Luchaire (p.653). He mentioned, inter alia, that British Togoland, a trust territory, was merged with the Gold Coast, a British colony, to become the new state of Ghana.

panied by a certain questioning of traditional international law. At first sight this principle conflicts outright with another one, the right of peoples to self-determination. In fact, however, the maintenance of the territorial status quo in Africa is often seen as the wisest course, to preserve what has been achieved by peoples who have struggled for their independence, and to avoid a disruption which would deprive the continent of the gains achieved by much sacrifice. The essential requirement of stability in order to survive, to develop and gradually to consolidate their independence in all fields, has induced African States judiciously to consent to the respecting of colonial frontiers, and to take account of it in the interpretation of the principle of self-determination of peoples.

26. Thus the principle of *uti possidetis* has kept its place among the most important legal principles, despite the apparent contradiction which explained its coexistence alongside the new norms ...

63. ... the Parties have invoked in support of their respective contentions the 'colonial *effectivités*', in other words, the conduct of the administrative authorities as proof of the effective exercise of territorial jurisdiction in the region during the colonial period. ... The role played in this case by such *effectivités* is complex. Where the act corresponds exactly to law, where effective administration is additional to the *uti possidetis juris*, the only role of *effectivité* is to confirm the exercise of the right derived from a legal title. Where the act does not correspond to the law, where the territory which is the subject of the dispute is effectively administered by a State other than the one possessing the legal title, preference should be given to the holder of the title. In the event that the *effectivité* does not co-exist with any legal title, it must invariably be taken into consideration. Finally, there are cases where the legal title is not capable of showing exactly the territorial expanse to which it relates. The *effectivités* can then play an essential role in showing how the title is interpreted in practice."

On the principle of self-determination, which, as the ICJ notes, gives way to that of *uti possidetis*, see above, p.111. On *uti possidetis* in a non-post colonial context, see *Opinions No.2 and No.3*, EC Arbitration Commission, above, pp.110, 118.

2.   The approach in the *Frontier Dispute* case to the *uti possidetis* principle was followed by another ICJ Chamber in the *Land, Island and Maritime Frontier Dispute* case.[167] In that case, the Chamber also noted that the boundary at the date of independence of states may change as a result of adjudication or the conduct of the parties (treaties, administration, acquiescence):

"67. There has also been some argument between the Parties about the "critical date"[168] in relation to this dispute. The principle of *uti possidetis juris* is sometimes stated in almost absolute terms, suggesting that the position at the date of independence is always deter-minative; in short, that no other critical date can arise. As appears from the discussion above, this cannot be so. A later critical date clearly may arise, for example, either from adjudication or from a boundary treaty. Thus, in the previous Latin American boundary arbitrations it is the award that is now determinative, even though it be based upon a view of the *uti possidetis juris* position. The award's view of the *uti possidetis juris* position prevails and cannot now be questioned juridically, even if it could be questioned historically. So for such a boundary the date of the award has become a new and later critical date. Likewise there can be no question

---

[167] I.C.J. Rep. 1992, p.351 at p.401. See also the *Frontier Dispute (Benin/Niger)* case, I.C.J. Rep. 2005, p.90, and the *Territorial and Maritime Dispute between Nicaragua and Honduras in the Caribbean* case, I.C.J. Rep. 2007, paras 155 et seq.
[168] On the concept of the "critical date", see above, p.167.

that the parts of the El Salvador/Honduras boundary fixed by the General Treaty of Peace of 1980 now constitute the boundary and 1980 is now the critical date. If the *uti possidetis juris* position can be qualified by adjudication and by treaty, the question then arises whether it can be qualified in other ways, for example, by acquiescence[169] or recognition. There seems to be no reason in principle why these factors should not operate, where there is sufficient evidence to show that the parties have in effect clearly accepted a variation, or at least an interpretation, of the *uti possidetis juris* position."

3. In the *Land and Maritime Boundary between Cameroon and Nigeria* case,[170] the plenary Court followed its approach in the above two chamber cases on the significance of *effectivités* that are inconsistent with the legal title (*contra legem*) in the determination of title generally (whether in a land boundary situation or not). In that case, there were examples of Nigerian administration of certain Nigerian inhabited villages that had been settled in an area of dried out land on the shore of Lake Chad on the Cameroonian side of the boundary between the two states that had been established by an Anglo-French treaty. Given the existence of some counter acts of village administration by Cameroon and protest by it as soon as Nigeria formally claimed sovereignty, the Court ruled that the land belonged to Cameroon:

"70. The Court finds that the above events, taken together, show that there was no acquiescence by Cameroon in the abandonment of its title in the area in favour of Nigeria. Accordingly, the Court concludes that the situation was essentially one where the *effectivités* adduced by Nigeria did not correspond to the law, and that accordingly 'preference should be given to the holder of the title' (*Frontier Dispute (Burkina Faso/Republic of Mali), Judgment, I.C.J. Reports 1986*, p.587, para 63)."

4. The boundary between the United Kingdom and France in the Channel Tunnel is at the mid-way point: see s.10 of the Channel Tunnel Act 1987.

----

4. Airspace[171]

CHICAGO CONVENTION ON INTERNATIONAL CIVIL AVIATION 1944[172]

U.K.T.S. 8 (1953), Cmd. 8742; 15 U.N.T.S. 295

Article 1

The contracting States recognize that every State has complete and exclusive sovereignty over the air space above its territory.

---

[169] As to acquiescence, the Court Chamber noted the relevance of "post independence *effectivités*". If a state administers an area and the other state does not object, this goes to prescription.

[170] I.C.J. Rep 2002, p.303. On the historical consolidation claim in this case, see above, p.182.

[171] See Cheng, *The Law of International Air Transport* (1962); Dempsey, *Public International Air Law* (2008); Diederiks-Verschoor, *An Introduction to Air Law* (7th rev. edn. 2001); Johnson, *Rights in Air Space* (1965); Naveau, *International Air Transport in a Changing World* (1989).

[172] In force 1947. 190 parties, including the UK.

Article 2

For the purposes of this Convention the territory of a State shall be deemed to be the land areas and territorial waters adjacent thereto under the sovereignty, suzerainty, protection or mandate of such State.

Article 3

(a) This Convention shall be applicable only to civil aircraft, and shall not be applicable to state aircraft.

(b) Aircraft used in military, customs and police services shall be deemed to be state aircraft.

(c) No state aircraft of a contracting State shall fly over the territory of another State or land thereon without authorization by special agreement or otherwise, and in accordance with the terms thereof.

(d) The contracting States undertake, when issuing regulations for their state aircraft, that they will have due regard for the safety of navigation of civil aircraft.

Article 3 *bis*

(a) The contracting States recognize that every State must refrain from resorting to the use of weapons against civil aircraft in flight and that, in case of interception, the lives of persons on board and the safety of aircraft must not be endangered. This provision shall not be interpreted as modifying in any way the rights and obligations of States set forth in the Charter of the United Nations.

(b) The contracting States recognize that every State, in the exercise of its sovereignty, is entitled to require the landing at some designated airport of a civil aircraft flying above its territory without authority or if there are reasonable grounds to conclude that it is being used for any purpose inconsistent with the aims of this Convention; it may also give such aircraft any other instructions to put an end to such violations. For this purpose, the contracting States may resort to any appropriate means consistent with relevant rules of international law, including the relevant provisions of this Convention, specifically paragraph (a) of this Article. Each contracting State agrees to publish its regulations in force regarding the interception of civil aircraft.

(c) Every civil aircraft shall comply with an order given in conformity with paragraph (b) of this Article. To this end each contracting State shall establish all necessary provisions in its national laws or regulations to make such compliance mandatory for any civil aircraft registered in that State or operated by a person having his principal place of business or permanent residence in that State. Each contracting State shall make any violation of such applicable laws or regulations punishable by severe penalties and shall submit the case to its competent authorities in accordance with its laws or regulations.

(d) Each contracting State shall take appropriate measures to prohibit the deliberate use of any civil aircraft registered in that State or operated by an operator who has his principal place of business or permanent residence in that State for any purpose inconsistent with the aims of this Convention. This provision shall not affect paragraph (a) or derogate from paragraphs (b) and (c) of this article.

Article 5

Each contracting State agrees that all aircraft of the other contracting States, being aircraft not engaged in scheduled international air service, shall have the right, subject to the observance of the terms of this Convention, to make flights into or in transit non-stop across its territory and to make stops for non-traffic purposes without the necessity of obtaining prior permission, and subject to the right of the State flown over to require landing. Each contracting State nevertheless reserves the right, for reasons of safety of flight, to require aircraft desiring to proceed over regions which are inaccessible or without adequate air navigation facilities to follow prescribed routes, or to obtain special permission for such flights.

Such aircraft, if engaged in the carriage of passengers, cargo, or mail for remuneration or hire on other than scheduled international air services, shall also, subject to the provisions of Article 7, have the privilege of taking on or discharging passengers, cargo, or mail, subject to the right of any State where such embarkation or discharge takes place to impose such regulations, conditions or limitations as it may consider desirable.

Article 6

No scheduled international air service may be operated over or into the territory of a contracting State, except with the special permission or other authorization of that State, and in accordance with the terms of such permission or authorization.

Article 17

Aircraft have the nationality of the State in which they are registered.

Article 18

An aircraft cannot be validly registered in more than one State, but its registration may be changed from one State to another.

Article 19

The registration or transfer of registration of aircraft in any contracting State shall be made in accordance with its laws and regulations.

Notes

1. Article 1 of the Chicago Convention reflects a rule of customary international law[173] that developed rapidly in the first part of this century. An example of the violation of airspace of great political importance occurred in the *U-2 Incident*.[174] On May 1, 1960, a U-2, a US high altitude reconnaissance aircraft, was shot down at a height of 20,000 metres over Soviet territory. The aeroplane had taken off from Pakistan and was scheduled to land in Finland after taking aerial photographs while over Soviet territory. The USSR protested at the flight. The US did not try to justify its action in terms of international law or protest at the shooting down or of the subsequent trial of the pilot. The lack of protest by the US in this case is consistent with the view that, other than in the case of entry in distress, intentional trespass by military aircraft (with the exception of military *transport* aircraft) may be met by the use of force without warning.[175]

2. Cases of trespassing *civil* aircraft being shot down are not uncommon.[176] A tragic case was the *Korean Airlines Flight 007 Incident*.[177] In 1983, a Korean Airlines Boeing 747 on a scheduled flight from Alaska to South Korea strayed some 500 kilometres off course over militarily sensitive USSR territory and was intercepted and then shot down by Soviet military aircraft in darkness in the vicinity of Sakalin Island in USSR airspace north of Japan. All 169 passengers and crew, of 14 different nationalities, were killed. Claims for reparation were lodged with the USSR by states in respect of loss of life and damage to property.[178] An International Civil Aviation Organisation (ICAO) fact-finding investigation report[179] concluded that the aircraft's deviation resulted not

---

[173] *Nicaragua Case (Merits)*, I.C.J. Rep. 1986, p.14 at p.111.
[174] See Lissitzyn (1962) 56 A.J.I.L. 135; and Wright (1960) 54 A.J.I.L. 836.
[175] cf. Phelps (1985) 107 Military L.R. 255 at 291.
[176] See Richard (1984) 9 A.A.S.L. 147 at 148.
[177] See Hassan (1984) 33 I.C.L.Q. 712; Martin (1984) 9 Air Law 138; Morgan (1985) 11 Yale J.I.L. 231; Phelps, n.75 above; Richard, n.76 above; Note (1984) 97 H.L.R. 1198; See also the 1973 shooting down of a Libyan Airlines aircraft over sensitive Israeli airspace. Israel was condemned by the ICAO Council: see ICAO Bulletin July 1973, 13. See Hughes (1980) 45 J.A.L.C. 595 at 611.
[178] The UK, for example, claimed £2 million compensation in respect of the deaths of 14 persons entitled to British protection: see U.K.M.I.L. 1985, (1985) 56 B.Y.I.L. 511. For the US claim, see (1984) 78 A.J.I.L. 213. No compensation has been paid.
[179] (1984) 23 I.L.M. 864.

from equipment failure or an intention to trespass but from the negligence of the crew who, through "a considerable degree of lack of awareness and attentiveness," never appreciated that the flight was off course. As to the Soviet response, the ICAO investigation, through lack of co-operation by the USSR, lacked the information necessary to assess the adequacy of the measures (of which, the report concluded, the 747 crew were unaware) taken by the Soviet aircraft to intercept the 747 before shooting it down. The report concluded that the USSR authorities, who were conscious of the admitted presence of a US military intelligence aircraft over the high seas in the area, had assumed, without checking by exhaustive visual inspection, that the 747 was an intelligence aircraft and had interpreted a climb by the 747 as evasive action confirming this assumption. Following the report, the ICAO Council condemned the USSR's "use of armed force".[180]

In a non-trespass case, the *USS Vincennes*, a US naval vessel protecting neutral shipping in the Persian Gulf during the Iran-Iraq War, acting in self defence, shot down over the Gulf an Iranian Airlines civil airliner on a scheduled flight with 290 persons on board in the mistaken belief that it was an Iranian military aircraft that was about to attack the *USS Vincennes*. A claim brought against the US before the I.C.J. was discontinued following a settlement.[181]

3.   *Article 3 bis.* A further consequence of the *Korean Airlines Flight 007 Incident* was the adoption by the ICAO Assembly by unanimous vote of art.3 *bis* of the 1944 ICAO Convention.[182] Article 3 *bis* states an almost absolute rule by which weapons must not be used against civil aircraft in flight except where the UN Charter allows this. This would appear to be a reference to the Charter right of self defence (art.51). Commenting upon this right, the UK representative in the ICAO Assembly stated[183]:

> ". . . can the use of force in self-defence ever be legitimate? Clearly it could be legitimate if the aircraft is making, or is about to make, an attack or is, for example, dropping paratroops. The aircraft would then in effect be operating as a military aircraft. Lives of persons not on board would be endangered. The State would be entitled to use force against it."

On one view, art.3 *bis* is stricter than pre-existing custom. This, it is claimed, permitted the use of deadly force as a last resort (i.e. when attempts by interception to cause an intruding aircraft to land or to leave had failed) in response to a proportionate national security interest.[184] Supposing this view to be correct, it may be that considerations of humanity and the need for public confidence in the safety of civil airflight have precipitated a new consensus favouring the stricter formulation in art.3 *bis* as a customary, as well as a treaty, rule. The Russian Federation has accepted art.3 *bis*.

4.   In 1952, the ICAO Council defined a "scheduled international air service" (see arts 5 and 6, Chicago Convention) as:

---

[180] ICAO Council Resolution of March 6, 1984, (1984) 23 I.L.M. 937.

[181] *Aerial Incident of July 3, 1988 Case*, I.C.J. Rep. 1996, p.9. On the incident, see Linnan (1991) 16 Yale J.I.L. 245. See also the 1996 shooting down by Cuba of two US private aircraft that were dropping anti-Cuban government leaflets over Cuba from outside Cuban airspace. Cuba was condemned by the ICAO Council. (ICAO News Release PIO 3/96, available on: *www.icao.int/icao/en/nr/1996*).

[182] 1984 Protocol Relating to an Amendment to the Convention on International Civil Aviation (1984) 23 I.L.M. 705. In force 1998, 139 parties including the UK.

[183] U.K.M.I.L. 1984, (1984) 55 B.Y.I.L. 591. But see the need for an "armed attack": *Nicaragua (Merits) Case*, below, p.727.

[184] See Hughes (1980) 45 J.A.I.C. 595 at 619.

"a series of flights that possesses all the following characteristics: (a) it passes through the airspace over the territory of more than one State; (b) it is performed by aircraft for the transport of passengers, mail or cargo for remuneration, in such a manner that each flight is open to use by members of the public; (c) it is operated, so as to serve traffic between the same two or more points, either (i) according to a published timetable, or (ii) with flights so regular and frequent that they constitute a recognisably systematic series."[185]

5. Contrast art.17 of the Chicago Convention with the rules on the nationality of ships.[186] The latter contains a "genuine link" requirement, as in the *Nottebohm* case.[187]

CHICAGO INTERNATIONAL AIR SERVICES TRANSIT AGREEMENT 1944[188]

U.K.T.S. 8 (1953) Cmd. 8742, 171 U.N.T.S. 387

Article 1

1. Each contracting State grants to the other contracting States the following freedoms of the air in respect of scheduled international air services.

(1) The privilege to fly across its territory without landing;

(2) The privilege to land for non-traffic purposes. ...

Notes

1. The Chicago International Air Services Transit Agreement is known as the "Two Freedoms" Agreement. More ambitious was the Chicago International Air Transport Agreement 1944[189] which guarantees "Five Freedoms" for its parties. These are the two in the "Two Freedoms" Agreement plus the following:

    "(3) the privilege to put down passengers, mail or cargo taken on in the territory of the State whose nationality the aircraft possesses; (4) The privilege to take on passengers, mail and cargo destined for the territory of the State whose nationality the aircraft possesses; (5) The privilege to take on passengers, mail and cargo destined for the territory of any other contracting State and the privilege to put down passengers, mail and cargo coming from any such territory."[190]

    The "Five Freedoms" Agreement has not been widely ratified and, since the withdrawal of the United States in 1947, has not been of great significance.[191]

2. The exclusion of scheduled flights from the multilateral arrangements of the 1944 Chicago Convention (see art.6) and the failure of the "Five Freedoms" Agreement has led to a network of

---

[185] *Definition of a Scheduled International Air Service*, ICAO Doc. 7278-C/841 (May 10, 1952), p.3.
[186] See below, p.367.
[187] See below, p.505.
[188] In force 1945, 129 parties including the UK.
[189] 149 B.F.S.P. 1; 171 U.N.T.S. 387. In force 1945, 11 parties, UK not a party.
[190] art.5.
[191] See Johnson, above, n.171, p.65.

bilateral and multilateral agreements. It is largely upon the basis of such agreements that international scheduled flights occur.

----

5. OUTER SPACE[192]

TREATY ON THE PRINCIPLES GOVERNING THE ACTIVITIES OF STATES IN THE EXPLORATION AND USE OF OUTER SPACE, INCLUDING THE MOON AND OTHER CELESTIAL BODIES 1967[193]

U.K.T.S. 10 (1968) Cmnd. 3519; 610 U.N.T.S. 205

Article 1

The exploration and use of outer space, including the moon and other celestial bodies, shall be carried out for the benefit and in the interests of all countries, irrespective of their degree of economic or scientific development, and shall be the province of all mankind.

Outer space, including the moon and other celestial bodies, shall be free for exploration and use by all States without discrimination of any kind, on a basis of equality and in accordance with international law, and there shall be free access to all areas of celestial bodies.

There shall be freedom of scientific investigation in outer space, including the moon and other celestial bodies, and States shall facilitate and encourage international co-operation in such investigation.

Article 2

Outer space, including the moon and other celestial bodies, is not subject to national appropriation by claim of sovereignty, by means of use or occupation, or by any other means.

Article 3

States Parties to the Treaty shall carry on activities in the exploration and use of outer space, including the moon and other celestial bodies, in accordance with international law, including the Charter of the United Nations, in the interest of maintaining international peace and security and promoting international co-operation and understanding.

Article 4

States Parties to the Treaty undertake not to place in orbit around the Earth any objects carrying nuclear weapons or any other kinds of weapons of mass destruction, install such weapons on celestial bodies, or station such weapons in outer space in any other manner.

The moon and other celestial bodies shall be used by all States Parties to the Treaty exclusively for peaceful purposes. The establishment of military bases, installations and fortifications, the testing of any type of weapons and the conduct of military manoeuvres on celestial bodies shall be forbidden. The use of military personnel for scientific research or for any other peaceful purposes shall not be prohibited. The use of any equipment or facility necessary for peaceful exploration of the moon and other celestial bodies shall also not be prohibited.

---

[192] See Andem, *International Legal Problems in the Peaceful Exploration and Use of Outer Space* (1992); Cheng, *Studies in International Space Law* (1997); Christol, *Space Law* (1991); Dempsey, ed., *Space Law* (5 vols, 2004); Diederiks-Verschoor, *An Introduction to Space Law* (2nd rev. edn 1999); Fawcett, *Outer Space: New Challenges to Law and Policy* (1984); Gorove, *Developments in Space Law: Issues and Policies* (1991); Jasentuliyana, *International Space Law and the United Nations* (1999); Lafferanderie and Crowther, eds., *Outlook on Space Law over the Next Thirty Years* (1977); McDougal, Lasswell and Vlasic, *Law and Public Order in Space* (1963); Reijnen, *The United Nations Space Treaties Analysed* (1992).

[193] In force 1967, 98 parties, including the five Security Council permanent members. See Darwin (1967) 42 B.Y.I.L. 278; Goedhuis (1968) 15 N.I.L.R. 17; and Cheng (1968) 95 J.D.I. 532.

Article 5

States Parties to the Treaty shall regard astronauts as envoys of mankind in outer space and shall render to them all possible assistance in the event of accident, distress, or emergency landing on the territory of another State Party or on the high seas. When astronauts make such a landing, they shall be safely and promptly returned to the State of registry of their space vehicle.

In carrying on activities in outer space and on celestial bodies, the astronauts of one State Party shall render all possible assistance to the astronauts of other State Parties.

State Parties to the Treaty shall immediately inform the other States Parties to the Treaty or the Secretary-General of the United Nations of any phenomena they discover in outer space, including the moon and other celestial bodies, which could constitute a danger to the life or health of astronauts.

Article 6

States Parties to the Treaty shall bear international responsibility for national activities in outer space, including the moon and other celestial bodies, whether such activities are carried on by governmental agencies or by non-governmental entities, and for assuring that national activities are carried out in conformity with the provisions set forth in the present Treaty. The activities of non-governmental entities in outer space, including the moon and other celestial bodies, shall require authorization and continuing supervision by the appropriate State Party to the Treaty. When activities are carried on in outer space, including the moon and other celestial bodies, by an international organization, responsibility for compliance with this Treaty shall be borne both by the international organization and by the States Parties to the Treaty participating in such organization.

Article 7

Each State Party to the Treaty that launches or procures the launching of an object into outer space, including the moon and other celestial bodies, and each State Party from whose territory or facility an object is launched, is internationally liable for damage to another State Party to the Treaty or to its natural or judicial persons by such object or its component parts on the Earth, in air space or in outer space, including the moon and other celestial bodies.

Article 8

A State Party to the Treaty on whose registry an object launched into outer space is carried shall retain jurisdiction and control over such object, and over any personnel thereof, while in outer space or on a celestial body. Ownership of objects launched into outer space, including objects landed or constructed on a celestial body, and of their component parts, is not affected by their presence in outer space or on a celestial body or by their return to the Earth. Such objects or component parts found beyond the limits of the State Party to the Treaty on whose registry they are carried shall be returned to that State Party, which shall, upon request, furnish identifying data prior to their return.

Article 9

In the exploration and use of outer space, including the moon and other celestial bodies, State Parties to the Treaty shall be guided by the principle of co-operation and mutual assistance and shall conduct all their activities in outer space, including the moon and other celestial bodies, with due regard to the corresponding interests of all other States Parties to the Treaty. States Parties to the Treaty shall pursue studies of outer space, including the moon and other celestial bodies, and conduct exploration of them so as to avoid their harmful contamination and also adverse changes in the environment of the Earth resulting from the introduction of extra terrestrial matter and, where necessary, shall adopt appropriate measures for this purpose. If a State Party to the Treaty has reason to believe that an activity or experiment planned by it or its nationals in outer space, including the moon and other celestial bodies, would cause potentially harmful interference with activities of other States Parties in the peaceful exploration and use of outer space, including the moon and other celestial bodies, it shall undertake appropriate international consultations before proceeding with any such activity or experiment. A State Party to the Treaty which has reason to believe that an activity or experiment planned by another State Party in outer space, including the moon and other celestial bodies, would cause potentially harmful interference with activities in the peaceful exploration and use of outer space, including the moon and other celestial bodies, may request consultation concerning the activity or experiment.

Article 10

In order to promote international co-operation in the exploration and use of outer space, including the moon and other celestial bodies, in conformity with the purposes of this Treaty, the States Parties to the Treaty shall consider on a basis of equality any requests by other States Parties to the Treaty to be afforded an opportunity to observe the flight of space objects launched by those States.

   The nature of such an opportunity for observation and the conditions under which it could be afforded shall be determined by agreement between the States concerned.

Article 11

In order to promote international co-operation in the peaceful exploration and use of outer space, States Parties to the Treaty conducting activities in outer space, including the moon and other celestial bodies, agree to inform the Secretary-General of the United Nations as well as the public and the international scientific community, to the greatest extent feasible and practicable, of the nature, conduct, locations and results of such activities. On receiving the said information, the Secretary-General of the United Nations should be prepared to disseminate it immediately and effectively.

Article 12

All stations, installations, equipment and space vehicles on the moon and other celestial bodies shall be open to representatives of other States Parties to the Treaty on a basis of reciprocity. Such representatives shall give reasonable advance notice of a projected visit, in order that appropriate consultations may be held and that maximum precautions may be taken to assure safety and to avoid interference with normal operations in the facility to be visited.

Notes

1. Acting through the United Nations and greatly helped by the common interest of the US and the USSR, the international community was remarkably quick in agreeing upon the basic legal principles governing activities in outer space.[194] The 1967 Treaty builds upon a number of General Assembly resolutions on space law, particularly Resolutions 1721 (XVI),[195] 1884 (XVIII)[196] and 1962 (XVIII).[197] Resolution 1884 (XVIII) is reproduced in substance in the first paragraph of art.4 of the Treaty; the various principles stated in the other two resolutions form the basis of arts 1–3 and 5–9. All three resolutions were adopted unanimously.

2. Note the following criticism of the 1967 Treaty by Fawcett[198]:

     "In the Outer Space Treaty we have then a rigidly contractual instrument, in essence a bilateral arrangement between the principal space-users. Apart from its provisions for partial demili-tarisation of outer space, tracking and inspection, it does little or nothing to elaborate or secure the principles already set out in General Assembly Resolutions. It may even be that this ill-constructed and precarious instrument is a retrograde step. For in the wise words of Dr.

---

[194] One measure of the importance of a legal régime for outer space is that there are over 10,000 man-made objects in outer space, including 1000 satellites, orbiting the earth.

[195] G.A.O.R., 16th Session, Supp. 17, p.6 (1961).

[196] G.A.O.R., 18th Session, Supp. 15, p.13 (1963).

[197] 1963 Declaration of Legal Principles Governing Activities of States in the Exploration and Use of Outer Space, G.A.O.R., 18th Session, Supp. 15, p.15 (1963).

[198] *International Law and the Uses of Outer Space* (1968), pp.15–16.

Jenks, written before the conclusion of the Outer Space Treaty[199] 'The authority of the Declaration of Legal Principles may be expected to grow with the passage of years. While it is somewhat less than a treaty it must already be regarded as rather more than a statement of custom.'

Though Resolution 1962 (XVIII) is for the most part a declaration, not of rules of international law, but of directive principles, it may like other similar General Assembly Resolutions, be regarded as forming part of an international *ordre public*, to which States should strive to make their policies conform. . . ."

3. *Article* 2 of the Treaty establishes that territory in outer space, like the high seas, is not subject to sovereignty.[200] It is well known that states have reconnaissance satellites used for military spying purposes; these are not prohibited by art.4.[201] Does art.4 prohibit the passage of ballistic missiles through outer space?[202] Article 5 (and to some extent art.8) is supplemented by the 1968 Agreement on the Rescue of Astronauts, the Return of Astronauts and the Return of Objects launched into Outer Space.[203] Article 6 tackles the problem of imputability[204] in respect of any liability that may arise from space activities. Who is responsible under it for the acts or omissions of any private space activities (e.g. by a telecommunications company)?[205] Does the Treaty imagine the possibility of activities by an international organisation, e.g. the European Space Agency? On damage resulting from space activities, art.7 indicates when liability may arise on the part of a state or international organisation responsible under art.6. It has been supplemented by the 1972 Convention on International Liability for Damage caused by Space Objects, see below, n.5. Article 8 gives the state of registry jurisdiction over space objects and persons on board, but does not indicate the extent to which this is exclusive.[206] The best analogy is with the rules concerning ships.[207]

4. By Resolution 1721 (XVI),[208] the General Assembly called upon "states launching objects into orbit to furnish information promptly to the Committee on the Peaceful Uses of Outer Space . . . for the registration of launching" and requested the Secretary General "to maintain a public registry of the information furnished." This voluntary system has not been wholly satisfactory and has been supplemented, for the parties to it, by the 1975 Convention on Registration of Objects launched into Outer Space.[209] Launching states must register every launch, indicating its purpose on a public register kept by the Secretary General.

5. The 1972 Liability Convention[210] establishes *strict* liability (subject to art.VI) for damage caused by

---

[199] Ed., *Space Law* (1965), p.185.
[200] See Christol (1984) 9 A.A.S.L. 217.
[201] See Goedhuis (1978) 27 I.C.L.Q. 576. The American *Samos* satellites provided Israel with important information about Egyptian military installations in hostilities in the Middle East.
[202] See Darwin, above, n.193, p.284.
[203] U.K.T.S. 56 (1969), Cmnd. 3997; (1969) 63 A.J.I.L. 382. In force 1968, 90 parties, including the five Security Council permanent members. See Cheng (1969) 23 Y.B.W.A. 185; and Hall (1969) 63 A.J.I.L. 197.
[204] As to imputability generally in international law, see below, pp.425 et seq.
[205] See Fawcett, above, n.198, pp.23 et seq.
[206] See Czabafi, *The Concept of State Jurisdiction in International Space* (1971).
[207] See below, p.377.
[208] See above, n.195.
[209] U.K.T.S. 70 (1978), Cmnd. 7271; 961 U.N.T.S. 187; (1975) 14 I.L.M. 43. In force 1976, 53 parties, including the five Security Council permanent members. But see Young (1986) 11 A.A.S.L. 287 who describes the Convention as "moribund."
[210] U.K.T.S. 16 (1974), Cmnd. 5551; 961 U.N.T.S. 187; (1971) 10 I.L.M. 965. In force 1973, 86 parties, including the five Security Council permanent members. See Forkosch, *Outer Space and Legal Liability* (1982); and Hurwitz, *State Liability for Outer Space Activities in Accordance with the 1972 Convention on International Liability for Damage caused by Space Objects* (1992). On the measure of damages, see Alexander (1978) 6 J. Space L. 151; and Foster (1972) 10 C.Y.I.L. 137.

a space object to persons or property on the surface of the earth or to an aircraft in flight (art.II) and *fault* liability for damage to other space objects in flight and to persons in them (art.III). It establishes joint and several liability in the case of a joint launch (art.VI). Local remedies need not be exhausted before a claim is brought (art.XI). A claim in respect of damage to individuals is brought by a national state in the first instance, although the place where the damage occurs or where the individual is a resident may act if the national state fails to do so (art.VIII). If a claim cannot be settled diplomatically, it will be determined by a mixed claims commission established at the request of either party (art.XIV). The compensation due:

"shall be determined in accordance with international law, and the principles of justice and equity, in order to provide such reparation in respect of the damage as will restore the person … on whose behalf the claim is brought to the condition which would have existed if the damage had not occurred." (art.XII).

No upper limit to the amount of compensation is set. There have been a number of instances recorded of débris or parts of space objects falling to earth. A part of Sputnik IV weighing 20lb that fell on Manitowoc, Wisconsin, in 1962 was handed back to the USSR at a meeting of the United Nations Committee on the Peaceful Uses of Outer Space.[211] In 1969, some Russian débris broke a kitchen window in Southend. In 1978, a malfunctioning Russian satellite, Cosmos 954, powered by a small nuclear reactor weighing about 100lb, broke up over Canada and came down in a remote part of the North-West Territories. Moderate radiation was reported from the débris, although no other damage is known to have occurred. The USSR agreed to pay C\$ 3 million compensation.[212] Damage of a more far-reaching kind, of the sort that may result from experiments conducted in space (for example, affecting the climate or the atmosphere), is the subject of a very limited undertaking in art.XXI.

6.   *The Moon Agreement*[213] The 1979 Agreement Governing the Activities of States on the Moon and other Celestial Bodies[214] repeats, clarifies and supplements the 1967 Outer Space Treaty. Most significantly, it deals with the question of natural resources. Article 11 reads:

"1. The moon[215] and its natural resources are the common heritage of mankind, which finds its expression in the provisions of this Agreement and in particular in paragraph 5 of this article …

   2. The moon is not subject to national appropriation by any claim of sovereignty, by means of use or occupation, or by any other means.

   3. Neither the surface nor the subsurface of the moon, nor any part thereof or natural resources in place, shall become property of any State, international intergovernmental or non-governmental organization, national organization or non-governmental entity or of any natural person. The placement of personnel, space vehicles, equipment, facilities, stations and installations on or below the surface of the moon, including structures connected with its

---

211   U.N. Doc A/AC. 105/P.V. 15, pp.33–34 (1962), noted in Lay and Taubenfeld, *The Law Relating to the Activities of Man in Space* (1970), p.137, where a number of similar incidents are listed.
212   See (1979) 18 I.L.M. 899 and (1981) 20 I.L.M. 689. See also Cohen (1984) 10 Yale J.I.L. 78; and Gorove (1978) 6 J. Space L.137.
213   See Cheng (1980) 33 C.L.P. 213.
214   (1979) 18 I.L.M. 1434. In force 1984, 13 parties. None of the Security Council permanent members are parties.
215   The Convention provisions "relating to the moon shall also apply to other celestial bodies within the solar system, other than the earth": art.11(1) Agreement.

surface or subsurface, shall not create a right of ownership over the surface or the subsurface of the moon or any areas thereof. The foregoing provisions are without prejudice to the international régime referred to in paragraph 5 of this article.

4. States Parties have the right to exploration and use of the moon without discrimination of any kind, on a basis of equality and in accordance with international law and the terms of this Agreement.

5. States Parties to this Agreement hereby undertake to establish an international régime, including appropriate procedures, to govern the exploitation of the natural resources of the moon as such exploitation is about to become feasible ...

7. The main purposes of the international régime to be established shall include: ...

(d) An equitable sharing by all States Parties in the benefits derived from those resources, whereby the interests and needs of the developing countries, as well as the efforts of those countries which have contributed either directly or indirectly to the exploration of the moon, shall be given special consideration."

This adds to the 1967 Treaty by establishing that the natural resources of celestial bodies are, like those of the deep sea-bed, the "common heritage of mankind" and, as such, to be exploited when technical and commercial considerations permit, in accordance with an international régime. Cheng[216] suggests that, although art.11(5) imposes an obligation to negotiate in good faith to establish the proposed international régime, if no such régime can be agreed upon, the Agreement imposes no moratorium upon unilateral exploitation by the contracting parties.

The Agreement clarifies art.2 of the 1967 Treaty by providing that when carrying out scientific investigations a party has "the right to collect and remove from the moon[217] samples of its minerals and other substances" (art.6(2)). It also confirms (art.11(3)) what is implicit in the characterisation of celestial bodies as *res extra commercium* in art.2 of the 1967 Treaty, namely that private property rights (as well as State sovereignty) may not be acquired over territory or natural resources in outer space, subject, in the case of the latter, to the international régime to be established.

7. The treaties on outer space which have been adopted so far are the work of the United Nations Committee on the Peaceful Uses of Outer Space, a body established in 1958 (then as an ad hoc committee) and composed of 69 states.[218] After its considerable early achievements, the Committee has lost some of its impetus, with few agreed texts emerging from its deliberations in recent years.

8. In order to ensure compliance with United Kingdom international obligations with regard to the launching and operation of space objects, the Outer Space Act 1986 establishes a system of licensing and registration of space activities by United Kingdom nationals.

----

[216] See above, n.213, pp.231–2. On the disagreement concerning a *deep sea-bed* moratorium, see below, p.411.
[217] See above, n.215 on the meaning of "moon".
[218] See Benko, de Graaff, and Reijnen, *Space Law in the United Nations* (1985).

MCMAHON, LEGAL ASPECTS OF OUTER SPACE

(1962) 38 B.Y.I.L. 339. Some footnotes omitted

One school of thought interprets airspace in terms of aerodynamic lift and maintains that a State may only claim sovereignty over the height up to which aircraft can ascend. Such height would be no more than about 20 miles.[219]

The merits of such a common-sense approach are quite evident. However, it fails to offer a sufficiently precise criterion for drawing the line in airspace and is rendered less useful by such hybrid craft as the X-15 which possess characteristics of both aircraft and spacecraft and can attain a height of up to 47 miles. It is also unlikely that States will be content to restrict their claim to sovereignty to 20 miles when they might claim substantially more without unduly interfering with the exploration of outer space by other States.

A number of other writers, invoking what they call the natural principle of interpretation, maintain that airspace is synonymous with atmospheric space and includes any space where air is to be found. As there are traces of air in the atmosphere up to 10,000 miles it would be quite consistent, on the basis of this approach, for States to claim sovereignty up to 10,000 miles. . . .

A third approach, representing an even more exaggerated view than the one above, maintains that State sovereignty extends *usque ad infinitum*. Such a view may be more accurately characterized as *usque ad absurdum* . . .

One or two writers, proceeding by analogy to the law of the sea, suggest the drawing of several lines rather than one. It has been proposed that a State should exercise full sovereignty up to the height to which aircraft can ascend; that then there should be a second area, of up to 300 miles, designated as a contiguous zone and allowing for a right of transit through this zone for all non-military flight instrumentalities; and that finally there should be outer space, free to all. More recently it has been suggested that there be established a neutral zone between the upper limits of airspace and the lower limits of outer space to be known as "Neutralia" in which the right of innocent passage would be recognized. Such an attempt to divide space up into sectors and zones would seem to be too impractical and artificial to commend itself.

A more sensible approach would seem to be the suggestion that a State should only exercise sovereignty over that area whose boundary is the lowest altitude at which an artificial satellite may be put in orbit at least once around the earth. It would seem that the maximum altitude required to do this would be between 70 and 100 miles. The advantage of such an approach is that it takes cognizance of State practice since the launching of the first sputnik, recognizes the legality of those satellites already in orbit and may easily be reconciled with claims to sovereignty up to the height of aerodynamic lift or even up to 70 miles.

A number of other proposals, suggesting more or less arbitrary criteria, have also been advanced. One may note the suggestion that sovereignty should extend as far out as the subjacent State could exercise effective control; that the boundary should be fixed at an altitude approximating to lift or drag; that the sovereignty ceiling should be the line where an object travelling at 25,000 feet per second loses its aerodynamic lift and centrifugal force takes over (the so-called Karman jurisdiction line which would extend up to about 53 miles); and finally that instead of drawing a demarcation line between airspace and outer space there should only be one doctrine, namely freedom of all-inclusive space subject to agreed restrictions.

Most of the above theories presuppose that a demarcation line must be drawn somewhere in space and the problem is to determine where. However, as an alternative, it has been suggested that States should concentrate on the regulation of activities in space, regardless of the location of those activities. The possibility of such an approach was referred to as early as June 1959 by the United Nations *Ad Hoc* Committee on the Peaceful Uses of Outer Space: "There was also discussion as to whether or not further experience might suggest a different approach, namely, the desirability of basing the legal régime governing outer space activities primarily on the nature and type of particular space activities."[220] Of course, the difficulty here is to reach an agreement concerning those activities which are to be permitted and those which are forbidden; such an agreement will be difficult to reach on account of the almost insuperable technical obstacles in disengaging the civil from the

---

[219] The height up to which an aircraft ascends would usually be about 12 miles. However, see "Draft Code of Rules on the Exploration and Uses of Outer Space," in *David Davies Memorial Institute of International Studies* (1962), p.6: "As far as the performance of existing conventional aircraft is a guide to the definition of airspace, the ram jet which makes more efficient use of such air as is available can 'breathe' at greater heights than jet—or piston-engined—aircraft, but 25 miles is probably the outside limit of effective aerodynamic lift."

[220] *Report of the* Ad Hoc *Committee on the Peaceful Uses of Outer Space*, UN Doc. A/4141, July 14, 1959, p.68.

military uses of space vehicles. Secondly, even if such an agreement were reached, it could only be enforced by establishing some form of inspection system. In other words, the whole question merely becomes another facet of the disarmament problem.

Notes

1. The boundary between airspace and outer space has yet to be defined.[221] The question was purposely not dealt with in the seminal General Assembly resolutions and in the 1967 treaty. The Committee on the Peaceful Uses of Outer Space has the question under consideration but has not been able to reach agreement on any particular rule or indeed as to whether a rule is required.[222] The principle of free and equal use of outer space must mean that there is a limit to national sovereignty at some point. It is also significant that states have not protested at the passage of satellites over their territory.[223] This might mean only the acceptance of a right of innocent passage, but this is unlikely.

2. The "perigee" approach, by which the limit of airspace would be the lowest perigee of an orbiting satellite, would appear to be the most likely one to be accepted. It would, in the light of recent studies, probably set the limit at a lower height—between 50 and 60 miles—than that indicated by McMahon.[224]

----

6. RIGHTS IN FOREIGN TERRITORY[225]

NORTH ATLANTIC FISHERIES ARBITRATION

U.S. v Great Britain (1910)

Permanent Court of Arbitration: Lammasch; de Savornin Lohman; Gray; Drago; Fitzpatrick.
11 R.I.A.A. 167

By a treaty of 1818, Great Britain and the United States agreed that "the inhabitants of the said United States shall have forever, in common with the subjects of His Britannic Majesty, the liberty to take fish of every kind on that part of the Southern coast of Newfoundland ... [then described]" (art.1). A dispute arose over Great Britain's competence under the treaty to regulate fishing by United States nationals exercising the liberty granted by it. In the following passage, the Tribunal considered a United States argument that the liberty amounted to a servitude.

---

[221] See the Minister of State, FCO, *Hansard*, HC Vol.546 W.A. 66, (July 23, 1993): "There is no universally agreed precise legal, technical or political definition of either the boundaries separating airspace from outer space or of the term outer space itself".

[222] See the 2008 Report of the Committee on the Peaceful Uses of Outer Space, G.A.O.R., 63rd Session, Supp. 20 (A/63/20), p.28. See also Goedhuis (1982–I) 174 Hague Recueil 377.

[223] cf. the dissenting opinion of Judge Lachs in the *North Sea Continental Shelf* cases, above, p.26, n.44. And see Fawcett, above, n.198, p.22. For the 1976 Bogota Declaration by which 8 equatorial states claimed exclusive jurisdiction and sovereignty over the geostationary orbit over their territories (about 36,000 km high)—a claim rejected by other states, see Gorove, above, n.192, p.362.

[224] See the UN Secretariat background papers on the subject: UN Docs A/AC.105/C.2/7 and A/AC.105/C.2/7/Add.1.

[225] See Reid, *International Servitudes in Law and Practice* (1932); and Vali, *Servitudes in International Law* (2nd edn 1958). See also Brierly, p.191; and McNair (1925) 6 B.Y.I.L. III.

Award of the Tribunal

It is contended by the United States: ...

That the liberties of fishery granted to the United States constitute an International servitude in their favour over the territory of Great Britain, thereby involving a derogation from the sovereignty of Great Britain, the servient State, and therefore Great Britain is deprived, by reason of the grant, of its independent right to regulate the fishery.

The Tribunal is unable to agree with this contention:

(a)   Because there is no evidence that the doctrine of International servitudes was one with which either American or British Statesmen were conversant in 1818, no English publicists employing the term before 1818, and the mention of it in Mr Gallatin's report being insufficient;

(b)   Because a servitude in the French law, referred to by Mr. Gallatin, can, since the Code, be only real and cannot be personal (Code Civil, art.686);

(c)   Because a servitude in International law predicates an express grant of a sovereign right and involves an analogy to the relation of a *praedium dominans* and a *praedium serviens*; whereas by the Treaty of 1818 one State grants a liberty to fish, which is not a sovereign right, but a purely economic right, to the inhabitants of another State;

(d)   Because the doctrine of international servitude in the sense which is now sought to be attributed to it originated in the peculiar and now obsolete conditions prevailing in the Holy Roman Empire of which the *domini terrae* were not fully sovereigns ...

(e)   Because this doctrine being but little suited to the principle of sovereignty which prevails in States under a system of constitutional government such as Great Britain and the United States, and to the present International relations of Sovereign States, has found little, if any, support from modern publicists. It could therefore in the general interest of the Community of Nations, and of the Parties to this Treaty, be affirmed by this Tribunal only on the express evidence of an International contract;

(f)   Because even if these liberties of fishery constituted an International servitude, the servitude would derogate from the sovereignty of the servient State only in so far as the exercise of the rights of sovereignty by the servitude State would be contrary to the exercise of the right by the dominant State. Whereas it is evident that, though every regulation of the fishery is to some extent a limitation, as it puts limits to the exercise of the fishery at will, yet such regulations as are reasonable and made for the purpose of securing and preserving the fishery and its exercise for the common benefit, are clearly to be distinguished from those restrictions and "molestations", the annulment of which was the purpose of the American demands formulated by Mr Adams in 1782, and such regulations consequently cannot be held to be inconsistent with a servitude;

(g)   Because the fishery to which the inhabitants of the United States were admitted in 1783, and again in 1818, was a regulated fishery ...

(h)   Because the fact that Great Britain rarely exercised the right of regulation in the period immediately succeeding 1818 is to be explained by various circumstances and is not evidence of the non-existence of the right;

(i)   Because the words "in common with British subjects" tend to confirm the opinion that the inhabitants of the United States were admitted to a regulated fishery;

(j)   Because the statute of Great Britain, 1819, which gives legislative sanction to the Treaty of 1818, provides for the making of "regulations with relation to the taking, drying and curing of fish by inhabitants of the United States in 'common'."

Notes

1. Does the Tribunal's award give any support to the view that international law recognises servitudes or, in English law terms, easement and profits? Does the extract from *The Wimbledon* case, below p.222.

2. In another case on fishing rights, *Eritrea v Yemen*,[226] the two states disputed sovereignty over islands in the Red Sea. The Tribunal stated:

    "In finding that the Parties each have sovereignty over various of the Islands the Tribunal stresses to them that such sovereignty is not inimical to, but rather entails, the perpetuation of the traditional fishing regime in the region ... requiring free access and enjoyment for the fishermen of both Eritrea and Yemen."

3. In the *Aaland Islands* case,[227] Sweden argued that the provisions in the General Treaty of Peace of 1856 between France, Great Britain and Russia demilitarising the Islands created a servitude binding upon Finland, which had succeeded Russia as the territorial sovereign.

    The International Commission of Jurists which reported on the case stated that "the existence of international servitudes, in the true technical sense of the term, is not generally admitted."[228] Nevertheless, it managed to hold that the demilitarisation provisions were binding upon Finland:

    "The provisions were laid down in European interests. They constituted a special international status relating to military considerations for the Aaland Islands. It follows that, until these provisions are duly replaced by others, every State interested has the right to insist upon compliance with them."[229]

    Earlier the Commission had noted:

    "... the Powers have, on many occasions since 1815, and especially at the conclusion of peace treaties, tried to create true objective law, a real political status the effects of which are felt outside the immediate circle of contracting parties."[230]

4. A recent example of one state being granted rights in the territory of another is found in the 1960 Treaty Concerning the Establishment of the Republic of Cyprus[231] between Greece, Turkey and Great Britain, on the one hand, and Cyprus, on the other hand, which permits the present British military bases in Cyprus. Annex B[232] reads:

    "The Government of the United Kingdom shall have the right to continue to use, without restriction or interference, the Sites in the territories of the Republic of Cyprus listed in Schedule A ..."

---

[226] (1998) 114 I.L.R. 1 at 137.
[227] L.N.O.J., Special Supp. No.3, p.3 (1920).
[228] See above, n.227, p.16.
[229] See above, n.227, p.19.
[230] See above, n.227, p.17.
[231] U.K.T.S. 4 (1961), Cmnd. 1252; 382 U.N.T.S. 8.
[232] s.1(1).

In 1985, the British Minister of State for the Armed Forces stated: "The base is sovereign British territory as laid down in the 1960 treaty. It has the full rights of sovereignty that we associate with the use of that word."[233]

5. In the nineteenth century, China agreed to lease, while retaining sovereignty, several parts of its territory to Western Powers. For example, in 1898 it agreed by treaty[234] to lease to Great Britain the New Territories on the Chinese mainland adjacent to the island of Hong Kong for a period of 99 years. The island of Hong Kong was a British Crown Colony that was ceded by China to Great Britain by the 1842 Treaty of Nanking[235] after the Opium War. See also the 1860 Treaty of Peking[236] by which China ceded Kowloon on the mainland opposite the island of Hong Kong, to Great Britain. By the 1984 Agreement between China and the United Kingdom,[237] all of the above territories passed or reverted to China in 1997.

RIGHT OF PASSAGE CASE[238]

Portugal v India

I.C.J. Reports 1960, p.6

Judgment of the Court

In [its] Application the Government of the Portuguese Republic states that the territory of Portugal in the Indian Peninsula is made up of the three districts of Goa, Daman and Diu.[239] It adds that the district of Daman comprises, in addition to its littoral territory, two parcels of territory completely surrounded by the territory of India which constitutes enclaves: Dadra and Nagar-Aveli. It is in respect of the communications between these enclaves and Daman and between each other that the question arises of a right of passage in favour of Portugal through Indian territory, and of a correlative obligation binding upon India. The Application states that in July 1954, contrary to the practice hitherto followed, the Government of India, in pursuance of what the Application calls "the open campaign which it has been carrying on since 1950 for the annexation of Portuguese territories", prevented Portugal from exercising this right of passage. This denial by India having been maintained, it has followed, according to the Application, that the enclaves of Dadra and Nagar-Aveli have been completely cut off from the rest of the Portuguese territory, the Portuguese authorities thus being placed in a position in which it became impossible for them to exercise Portuguese rights of sovereignty there ...

Portugal claims a right of passage ... to the extent necessary for the exercise of its sovereignty over the enclaves, subject to India's right of regulation and control of the passage claimed, and without any immunity in Portugal's favour. It claims further that India is under obligation so to exercise its power of regulation and control as not to prevent the passage necessary for the exercise of Portugal's sovereignty over the enclaves ...

With regard to Portugal's claim of a right of passage as formulated by it on the basis of local custom, it is objected on behalf of India that no local custom could be established between only two States. It is difficult to see why the number of States between which a local custom may be established on the basis of long practice must necessarily be larger than two. The Court sees no reason why long continued practice between two States

---

[233] *Hansard*, HC Vol.74, col.161 (February 26, 1985) U.K.M.I.L. 1985, (1985) 56 B.Y.I.L. 473.

[234] 90 B.F.S.P. 17.

[235] 30 B.F.S.P. 389.

[236] 50 B.F.S.P. 10

[237] Misc. 20 (1984), Cmnd. 9352; (1984) 23 I.L.M. 1366. See also the Hong Kong Act 1985. See Mushkat (1987) 10 Houston J.I.L. 1.

[238] See Krenz, *International Enclaves and Rights of Passage* (1961); E. Lauterpacht (1958–59) 44 Trans.Grot.Soc. 313, 352–356; 2 Verzijl 368.

[239] Ed. On the subsequent annexation of these territories by India, see above, p.189.

accepted by them as regulating their relations should not form the basis of mutual rights and obligations between the two States ...

The Court ... concludes that, with regard to private persons, civil officials and goods in general there existed during the British and post-British periods a constant and uniform practice allowing free passage between Daman and the enclaves. This practice having continued over a period extending beyond a century and a quarter unaffected by the change in regime in respect of the intervening territory which occurred when India became independent, the Court is, in view of all the circumstances of the case, satisfied that that practice was accepted as law by the Parties and has given rise to a right and a correlative obligation ...

As regards armed forces, armed police and arms and ammunition, the position is different ...

The Court is, therefore, of the view that no right of passage in favour of Portugal involving a correlative obligation on India has been established in respect of armed forces, armed police, and arms and ammunition. The course of dealings established between the Portuguese and the British authorities with respect to the passage of these categories excludes the existence of any such right. The practice that was established shows that, with regard to these categories, it was well understood that passage could take place only by permission of the British authorities. This situation continued during the post-British period.

Portugal also invokes general international custom, as well as the general principles of law recognized by civilized nations, in support of its claim of a right of passage as formulated by it. Having arrived at the conclusion that the course of dealings between the British and Indian authorities on the one hand and the Portuguese on the other established a practice, well understood between the Parties, by virtue of which Portugal had acquired a right of passage in respect of private persons, civil officials and goods in general, the Court does not consider it necessary to examine whether general international custom or the general principles of law recognized by civilized nations may lead to the same result.

As regards armed forces, armed police and arms and ammunition, the finding of the Court that the practice established between the Parties required for passage in respect of these categories the permission of the British or Indian authorities, renders it unnecessary for the Court to determine whether or not, in the absence of the practice that actually prevailed, general international custom or the general principles of law recognized by civilized nations could be relied upon by Portugal in support of its claim to a right of passage in respect of these categories.

The Court is here dealing with a concrete case having special features. Historically the case goes back to a period when, and relates to a region in which, the relations between neighbouring States were not regulated by precisely formulated rules but were governed largely by practice. Where therefore the Court finds a practice clearly established between two States which was accepted by the Parties as governing the relations between them, the Court must attribute decisive effect to that practice for the purpose of determining their specific rights and obligations. Such a particular practice must prevail over any general rules. ...

Having found that Portugal had in 1954 a right of passage over intervening Indian territory between Daman and the enclaves in respect of private persons, civil officials and goods in general, the Court will proceed to consider whether India has acted contrary to its obligation resulting from Portugal's right of passage in respect of any of these categories ...

The events that took place in Dadra on 21–22 July 1954 resulted in the overthrow of Portuguese authority in that enclave. This created tension in the surrounding Indian territory. Thereafter all passage was suspended by India. India contends that this became necessary in view of the abnormal situation which had arisen in Dadra and the tension created in surrounding Indian territory ...

In view of the tension then prevailing in intervening Indian territory, the Court is unable to hold that India's refusal of passage to the proposed delegation and its refusal of visas to Portuguese nationals of European origin and to native Indian Portuguese in the employ of the Portuguese Government was action contrary to its obligation resulting from Portugal's right of passage. Portugal's claim of a right of passage is subject to full recognition and exercise of Indian sovereignty over the intervening territory and without any immunity in favour of Portugal. The Court is of the view that India's refusal of passage in those cases was, in the circumstances, covered by its power of regulation and control of the right of passage of Portugal.

For these reasons,

The Court, ... by eleven votes to four,

finds that Portugal had in 1954 a right of passage over intervening Indian territory between the enclaves of Dadra and Nagar-Aveli and the coastal district of Daman and between these enclaves, to the extent necessary for the exercise of Portuguese sovereignty over the enclaves and subject to the regulation and control of India, in respect of private persons, civil officials and goods in general;

by eight votes to seven,

finds that Portugal did not have in 1954 such a right of passage in respect of armed forces, armed police, and arms and ammunition;

by nine votes to six,

finds that India has not acted contrary to its obligations resulting from Portugal's right of passage in respect of private persons, civil officials and goods in general.[240]

Note

Was the right of passage acknowledged by the Court one that would survive a transfer of title to the territory to which it applied? The Court's judgment was based upon local custom.[241] Does it have any relevance for similar situations, such as that of land-locked states—e.g. Lesotho (surrounded entirely by the one state of South Africa) and Austria (surrounded by several states)—that seek access by land to the sea.[242] Writing about freedom of transit across another state's territory generally, Lauterpacht[243] states:

> "The operative principle, it is believed, is that States, far from being free to treat the establishment or regulation of routes of transit as a substantial derogation from their sovereignty which they are entirely free to refuse, are bound to act in this matter in the fulfilment of an obligation to the community of which they form a part. It is a principle formulated by Grotius over three hundred years ago in the following words: 'Similarly also lands, rivers, and any part of the sea that has become subject to the ownership of a people, ought to be open to those who, for legitimate reasons, have need to cross them; as, for instance, if a people ... desires to carry on commerce with a distant people.'[244] ...
>
> On that view [Grotius's], there exists in customary international law a right to free or innocent passage for purposes of trade, travel and commerce over the territory of all States—a right which derives from the fact of the existence of the international community and which is a direct consequence of the interdependence of States."

THE WIMBLEDON CASE[245]

France, Italy, Japan and the U.K. v Germany (1923)

P.C.I.J. Reports, Series A, No.1

The Kiel Canal is cut through Germany and links the Baltic and North Seas. Article 380 of the Treaty of Versailles of 1919 reads: "The Kiel Canal and its approaches shall be maintained free and open to the vessels of commerce and of war of all nations at peace with Germany on terms of entire equality." The Court discussed the effect of art.380 on the legal status of the Canal in the following passage.

---

[240] It is not clear how every judge voted.

[241] On local custom, see above, p.19.

[242] See the 1982 Convention on the Law of the Sea art.90, below, p.336. See also the 1965 Convention on Transit Trade of Land-Locked States, 597 U.N.T.S. 3; (1965) 4 I.L.M. 957. In force 1967, 39 parties, UK not a party. See Fried (1966) 6 I.J.I.L 9.

[243] E. Lauterpacht, above, p.258, n.238, p.313.

[244] *De Jure Belli ac Pacis*, II, 2, 13, as translated in *Classics of International Law* (1925), pp.196–197.

[245] On international canals generally, see Baxter, *The Law of International Waterways* (1964); and Lee (1968) 33 L. & C.P. 158.

Judgment of the Court

The Court considers that the terms of Article 380 are categorical and give rise to no doubt. It follows that the canal has ceased to be an internal and national navigable waterway, the use of which by the vessels of states other than the riparian state is left entirely to the discretion of that state, and that it has become an international waterway intended to provide under treaty guarantee easier access to the Baltic for the benefit of all nations of the world ...

In order to dispute, in this case, the right of the S.S. "Wimbledon" to free passage through the Kiel Canal under the terms of Article 380, the argument has been urged upon the Court that this right really amounts to a servitude by international law resting upon Germany and that, like all restrictions or limitations upon the exercise of sovereignty, this servitude must be construed as restrictively as possible and confined within its narrowest limits, more especially in the sense that it should not be allowed to affect the rights consequent upon neutrality in an armed conflict. The Court is not called upon to take a definite attitude with regard to the question, which is moreover of a very controversial nature, whether in the domain of international law, there really exist servitudes analogous to the servitudes of private law. Whether the German Government is bound by virtue of a servitude or by virtue of a contractual obligation undertaken towards the Powers entitled to benefit by the terms of the Treaty of Versailles, to allow free access to the Kiel Canal in time of war as in time of peace to the vessels of all nations, the fact remains that Germany had to submit to an important limitation of the exercise of the sovereign rights which no one disputes that she possesses over the Kiel Canal. This fact constitutes a sufficient reason for the restrictive interpretation, in case of doubt, of the clause which produces such a limitation. But the Court feels obliged to stop at the point where the so-called restrictive interpretation would be contrary to the plain terms of the article and would destroy what has been clearly granted.

CONVENTION RESPECTING FREE NAVIGATION OF THE SUEZ CANAL 1888[246]

C. 5623; 79 B.F.S.P. 18; (1909) 3 A.J.I.L. Supp. 123

Article 1

The Suez Maritime Canal shall always be free and open, in time of war as in time of peace, to every vessel of commerce or of war, without distinction of flag.

Consequently, the High Contracting Parties agree not in any way to interfere with the free use of the Canal, in time of war as in time of peace.

The Canal shall never be subjected to the exercise of the right of blockade.

Article 4

The Maritime Canal remaining open in time of war as a free passage, even to the ships of war of belligerents, according to the terms of Article 1 of the present Treaty, the High Contracting Parties agree that no right of war, no act of hostility, nor any act having for its object to obstruct the free navigation of the Canal, shall be committed in the Canal and its ports of access, as well as within a radius of 3 marine miles from those ports, even though the Ottoman Empire should be one of the belligerent Powers ...

Article 10

Similarly, the provisions of Articles 4, 5, 7 and 8 shall not interfere with the measures which His Majesty the Sultan and His Highness the Khedive, in the name of His Imperial Majesty, and within the limits of the Firmans granted, might find it necessary to take for securing by their own forces the defence of Egypt and the maintenance of public order.

In case His Imperial Majesty the Sultan, or His Highness the Khedive, should find it necessary to avail themselves of the exceptions for which this Article provides, the Signatory Powers of the Declaration of London shall be notified thereof by the Imperial Ottoman Government.

It is likewise understood that the provisions of the four Articles aforesaid shall in no case occasion any obstacle

---

[246] The parties are Austria-Hungary, France, Germany, Great Britain, Italy, the Netherlands, Russia, Spain and the Ottoman Empire.

to the measures which the Imperial Ottoman Government may think necessary to take in order to insure by its own forces the defence of its other possessions situated on the eastern coast of the Red Sea.

Article 11

The measures which shall be taken in the cases provided for by Articles 9 and 10 of the present Treaty shall not interfere with the free use of the Canal. In the same cases, the erection of permanent fortifications contrary to the provisions of Article 8 is prohibited.

Article 14

The High Contracting Parties agree that the engagements resulting from the present Treaty shall not be limited by the duration of the Acts of Concession of the Universal Suez Canal Company.

Notes

1. The Suez Canal was built by the Suez Canal Company in accordance with concession agreements made between the Company and the Sultan of Turkey in the 1850s, at a time when Egypt was a part of the Ottoman Empire. Under the terms of these agreements, the Company was to operate the Canal for 99 years from the time that it opened (1869). At the termination of this period, the Egyptian Government was to "take the place of the company and to enter into full possession of the canal." In July 1956, Egypt nationalised the Suez Canal Company and assumed control of the Canal. In August 1956, a conference of 22 interested states was held in London. A proposal supported by 18 of them called for the "efficient and dependable operation, maintenance and development of the Canal as a free, open and secure international waterway in accordance with the principles of the Convention of 1888."[247] On September 26, 1956, the United States Secretary of State for Foreign Affairs (Mr Dulles) said:

    "We believe that the treaty of 1888 internationalises, you might say, the right of use of the canal. It creates a sort of an easement across Egyptian territory, of which we believe the beneficiaries of the treaty as well as the parties to the treaty have the right to make use. And we believe they are also entitled to organise to exercise the right of use and, generally, their rights under the treaty."[248]

    In a Declaration made on April 24, 1957, Egypt stated:

    "It remains the unaltered policy and firm purpose of the Government of Egypt to respect the terms and the spirit of the Constantinople Convention of 1888 and the rights and obligations arising therefrom. The Government of Egypt will continue to respect, observe and implement them."[249]

2. By the 1977 Panama Canal Treaty[250] between Panama and the United States, sovereignty over the Panama Canal Zone was transferred from the United States to Panama, but the United States continued to operate and have the right to defend the Canal, with increasing Panamanian

---

[247] 3 Whiteman 1103.
[248] 3 Whiteman 1102.
[249] (1957) 51 A.J.I.L. 673. On Egypt's acceptance of the ICJ's compulsory jurisdiction concerning Suez Canal disputes, see (1957) 51 A.J.I.L. 675.
[250] (1978) 72 A.J.I.L. 225.

involvement, until the termination of the treaty in 1999. Thereupon, Panama assumed full responsibility for the Canal itself. The Canal "shall remain open to peaceful transit by the vessels of all nations on terms of entire equality."[251]

---

[251] art.2 of the 1977 Treaty concerning the Permanent Neutrality and Operation of the Panama Canal, (1978) 72 A.J.I.L. p.238, which accompanies the main treaty. The canal is declared to be "permanently neutral": art.1.

6 STATE JURISDICTION

1. INTRODUCTORY NOTE[1]

State jurisdiction is the power of a state under international law to govern persons and property by its municipal law. It includes both the power to prescribe rules (prescriptive jurisdiction) and the power to enforce them (enforcement jurisdiction). The latter includes both executive and judicial powers of enforcement. Jurisdiction may be concurrent with the jurisdiction of other states or it may be exclusive. It may be civil or criminal. The rules of state jurisdiction identify the persons and the property within the permissible range of a state's law and its procedures for enforcing that law. They are not concerned with the content of a state's law except in so far as it purports to subject a person to it or to prescribe procedures to enforce it. International organisations have jurisdiction in the above sense to a limited extent (e.g. over employees).

2. CIVIL JURISDICTION

Opinions differ on the limits, if any, that international law sets on the exercise of civil jurisdiction by states. Akehurst[2] states:

> "In practice, the assumption of jurisdiction by a state does not seem to be subject to any requirement that the defendant or the facts of the case need to have any connection with that state; and this practice seems to have met with acquiescence by other states"

Brownlie[3] states:

> "Excessive and abusive assertion of civil jurisdiction could lead to international responsibility or protests at ultra vires acts; indeed, as civil jurisdiction is ultimately reinforced by procedures of enforcement involving criminal sanctions, there is in principle no great difference between problems created by assertion of civil or criminal jurisdiction over aliens."

Whereas, as Akehurst indicates, other states have generally tolerated extra-territorial claims of civil jurisdiction, they have objected to the exercise of extra-territorial jurisdiction by US courts under US anti-trust law (which is partly civil) based just upon the "effects" that acts by foreign companies

---

[1] See Akehurst (1972–73) 46 B.Y.I.L. 145; Bowett (1982) 53 B.Y.I.L. 1; Jennings (1962) 32 N.T.I.R. 209; ibid. (1957) 33 B.Y.I.L. 146; Johnson, in David Davies Memorial Institute of International Studies, *Report of International Law Conference* (1962), p.32; Mann (1964-I) 111 Hague Recueil 1.
[2] See above, n.1, p.176.
[3] Brownlie, p.300.

committed abroad may have in the US, and to the US Helms-Burton Act 1996 which imposes civil and criminal sanctions against foreigners who buy property confiscated by the Cuban government from US nationals.[4] Mann goes further and suggests a general rule by which international law requires a "substantial connection" before civil jurisdiction can be exercised.[5]

Boumediene v Bush[6] concerned an issue of civil jurisdiction of a different kind. In that case, the US Supreme Court held that the federal Military Commissions Act 2006, which provided that US federal courts had no jurisdiction to hear habeas corpus petitions from aliens detained at Guantanamo Bay as "enemy combatants" was unconstitutional. First, although Guantanamo Bay was not de jure US territory, the US constitution applied to the detention of aliens there because the United States had effective de facto control over it. Secondly, habeas corpus could only be suspended in accordance with art.1, para.9 of the US constitution, and the 2006 Act had not met this requirement. Clearly the exercise of jurisdiction in such cases involves a connection with the United States and would be most unlikely to meet with protest from other states.

3. CRIMINAL JURISDICTION

DICKINSON, INTRODUCTORY COMMENT TO THE HARVARD RESEARCH DRAFT CONVENTION ON JURISDICTION WITH RESPECT TO CRIME 1935

(1935) 29 A.J.I.L. Supp. 443

An analysis of modern national codes of penal law and penal procedure, checked against the conclusions of reliable writers and the resolutions of international conferences or learned societies, and supplemented by some exploration of the jurisprudence of national courts, discloses five general principles on which a more or less extensive penal jurisdiction is claimed by states at the present time. These five general principles are: first, the territorial principle, determining jurisdiction by reference to the place where the offence is committed; second, the nationality principle, determining jurisdiction by reference to the nationality or national character of the person committing the offence; third, the protective principle, determining jurisdiction by reference to the national interest injured by the offence; fourth, the universality principle, determining jurisdiction by reference to the custody of the person committing the offence; and fifth, the passive personality principle, determining jurisdiction by reference to the nationality or national character of the person injured by the offence. Of these five principles, the first is everywhere regarded as of primary importance and of fundamental character. The second is universally accepted, though there are striking differences in the extent to which it is used in the different national systems. The third is claimed by most states, regarded with misgivings in a few, and generally ranked as the basis of an auxiliary competence. The fourth is widely, though by no means universally, accepted as the basis of an auxiliary competence, except for the offence of piracy, with respect to which it is the generally recognized principle of jurisdiction. The fifth, asserted in some form by a considerable number of states and contested by others, is admittedly auxiliary in character and is probably not essential for any state if the ends served are adequately provided for on other principles.

Notes

1.   The Harvard Research Draft Convention of 1935 was the product of the unofficial work of a number of American international lawyers. It is not binding upon any state as a treaty and it is not state practice. Nonetheless, both insofar as it is intended to reflect customary international law and in its suggestions *de lege ferenda*, it is of considerable value because of the thorough study of state practice that preceded it. The Draft Convention adopts the first four of the

---

[4]   See Lowe, in Evans, ed., *International Law* (2nd edn 2006), pp.344, 355.
[5]   See the extract below, p.247.
[6]   (2008) 171 L. Ed. 2d. 41. See Jenkins (2009) 9 H.R.L.R. 306.

principles listed in the above extract from the Introductory Comment, all of which were thought to be permitted by international law.[7] The passive personality principle, the permissibility of which was thought to be doubtful,[8] was omitted.

Where more than one state has jurisdiction on a basis permitted by international law, it seems that each state is free to exercise prescriptive jurisdiction when it wishes and that priority to exercise enforcement jurisdiction depends solely upon custody. Even a state with territorial jurisdiction, which is the form of jurisdiction the most firmly rooted in state practice, has no prior claim over another state having custody of a person and relying on some extra-territorial basis for jurisdiction. Two possible limitations upon a state's freedom to exercise enforcement jurisdiction are suggested by the Harvard Research Draft Convention. The first follows from the idea of double jeopardy. Article 13 of the Harvard Research Draft Convention reads:

"In exercising jurisdiction under this Convention, no state shall prosecute or punish an alien after it is proved that the alien has been prosecuted in another State for a crime requiring proof of substantially the same acts or omissions and has been acquitted on the merits, or has been convicted and undergone the penalty imposed, or having been convicted, has been pardoned."

The Commentary refers to considerable support for such a limitation in municipal law.[9] Article 13 does not protect nationals. On this point, the Commentary reads:

"In the present state of international law ... it would seem inappropriate for a convention on jurisdiction with respect to crime to incorporate limitations upon a State's authority over its nationals."[10]

Secondly, a somewhat similar problem arises when a person is placed in a position where under the law of State A he is required to do something which he is prohibited from doing under the law of State B. On this, art.14 of the Harvard Research Draft Convention reads:

"... no state shall prosecute or punish an alien for an act which was required of that alien by the law of the place where the alien was at the time of the act or omission."

The Commentary acknowledges that there were "few precedents" in municipal law for art.14; it was included as "eminently desirable and just."[11] Like art.13, art.14 does not apply to nationals.

2. *The Nationality Principle.* The Commentary to the Draft Convention reads:

"The competence of the State to prosecute and punish its nationals on the sole basis of their nationality is based upon the allegiance which the person charged with crime owes to the State of which he is a national. ... The States which derive their jurisprudence from the civil law assert a competence which is substantially more comprehensive than that exercised by States influenced by the English common law, but all make some use of the principle. ... The

---

[7]   (1935) 29 A.J.I.L. Supp. at 480, 519, 556, 563–564.
[8]   (1935) 29 A.J.I.L. Supp. at p.579.
[9]   (1935) 29 A.J.I.L. Supp. at pp.602 et seq.
[10] (1935) 29 A.J.I.L. Supp. at p.613.
[11] (1935) 29 A.J.I.L. Supp. at p.616.

principle that jurisdiction may be founded either upon nationality at the time of the offence or upon nationality at the time of the prosecution appears to be supported by such legislation as has dealt specifically with the question. If international law permits a state to regard the accused as its national, its competence is not impaired or limited by the fact that he is also a national of another State. ... It is indisputable also that nothing in international law precludes a State from prosecuting and punishing one of its juristic persons for a crime committed outside of its territory.[12]"

In United Kingdom law, some of the small number of offences for which a national can be prosecuted for committing abroad can equally be seen as being based upon the idea of protection (e.g. treason[13] and offences under the Official Secrets Act 1989,[14]) but others (e.g. murder and manslaughter,[15] bigamy,[16] certain sexual offences[17] and bribery and corruption offences[18]) cannot.[19] The nationality principle is also relied upon in English law to give an English court jurisdiction "where any person is charged with having committed any offence ... if he is a British citizen ... on board ... any foreign ship to which he does not belong. ..."[20]

THE LOTUS CASE

France v Turkey (1927)

P.C.I.J. Reports, Series A, No.10

Judgment of the Court

According to the special agreement, the Court has to decide the following questions:

(1) Has Turkey, contrary to Article 15 of the Convention of Lausanne of July 24th, 1923, respecting conditions of residence and business and jurisdiction, acted in conflict with the principles of international law—and if so, what principles—by instituting, following the collision which occurred on August 2nd, 1926, on the high seas between the French steamer *Lotus* and the Turkish steamer *Boz-Kourt* and upon the arrival of the French steamer at Constantinople as well as against the captain of the Turkish steamship, joint criminal proceedings in pursuance of Turkish law against M. Demons, officer of the watch on board the *Lotus* at the time of the collision, in consequence of the loss of the *Boz-Kourt* having involved the death of eight Turkish sailors and passengers?[21]

(2) Should the reply be in the affirmative, what pecuniary reparation is due to M. Demons, provided, according to the principles of international law, reparation should be made in similar cases? ...

---

[12] (1935) 29 A.J.I.L. Supp. at pp.519 et seq.
[13] *R. v Casement* [1917] 1 K.B. 98.
[14] See s.15(1).
[15] Offences against the Person Act 1861 s.9.
[16] Offences against the Person Act 1861 s.57.
[17] Sexual Offences Act 2003 s.72.
[18] Anti-terrorism, Crime and Security Act 2001 s.109.
[19] See Arnell (2001) 50 I.C.L.Q. 955.
[20] Merchant Shipping Act 1995 s.281, which was interpreted (when in the Merchant Shipping Act 1894 s.686(1)) in *R. v Kelly* [1982] A.C. 665 HL as giving jurisdiction to hear charges under the Criminal Damage Act 1971, which otherwise has no extra-territorial effect, against three UK citizens for damage caused by them as passengers on board a Danish North Sea Ferry. See Hirst [1982] Crim.L.R. 496.
[21] Ed. M. Demons was a French national. Both accused were convicted.

3. The prosecution was instituted because the loss of the *Boz-Kourt* involved the death of eight Turkish sailors and passengers. It is clear, in the first place, that this result of the collision constitutes a factor essential for the institution of the criminal proceedings in question; secondly, it follows from the statements of the two Parties that no criminal intention has been imputed to either of the officers responsible for navigating the two vessels; it is therefore a case of prosecution for involuntary manslaughter. ...

... Article 15 of the Convention of Lausanne of July 24th, 1923,[22] ... is as follows:

Subject to the provisions of Article 16, all questions of jurisdiction shall, as between Turkey and the other contracting Powers, be decided in accordance with the principles of international law.

... The French Government contends that the Turkish Courts, in order to have jurisdiction, should be able to point to some title to jurisdiction recognized by international law in favour of Turkey. On the other hand, the Turkish Government takes the view that Article 15 allows Turkey jurisdiction whenever such jurisdiction does not come into conflict with a principle of international law.

The latter view seems to be in conformity with the special agreement itself, No.1 of which asks the Court to say whether Turkey has acted contrary to the principles of international law and, if so, what principles. ...

This way of stating the question is also dictated by the very nature and existing conditions of international law.

International law governs relations between independent States. The rules of law binding upon States therefore emanate from their own free will as expressed in conventions or by usages generally accepted as expressing principles of law and established in order to regulate the relations between these co-existing independent communities or with a view to the achievement of common aims. Restrictions upon the independence of States cannot therefore be presumed.

Now the first and foremost restriction imposed by international law upon a State is that—failing the existence of a permissive rule to the contrary—it may not exercise its power in any form in the territory of another State. In this sense jurisdiction is certainly territorial; it cannot be exercised by a State outside its territory except by virtue of a permissive rule derived from international custom or from a convention.[23]

It does not, however, follow that international law prohibits a State from exercising jurisdiction in its own territory, in respect of any case which relates to acts which have taken place abroad, and in which it cannot rely on some permissive rule of international law. Such a view would only be tenable if international law contained a general prohibition to States to extend the application of their laws and the jurisdiction of their courts to persons, property and acts outside their territory, and if, as an exception to this general prohibition, it allowed States to do so in certain specific cases. But this is certainly not the case under international law as it stands at present. Far from laying down a general prohibition to the effect that States may not extend the application of their laws and the jurisdiction of their courts to persons, property and acts outside their territory, it leaves them in this respect a wide measure of discretion which is only limited in certain cases by prohibitive rules. ...

This discretion left to States by international law explains the great variety of rules which they have been able to adopt without objections or complaints on the part of other States. ...

... Having regard to the terms of Article 15 and to the construction which the Court has just placed upon it, this [the French] contention would apply in regard to civil as well as to criminal cases, and would be applicable on conditions of absolute reciprocity as between Turkey and the other contracting Parties; in practice, it would therefore in many cases result in paralyzing the action of the courts, owing to the impossibility of citing a universally accepted rule on which to support the exercise of their jurisdiction. Nevertheless, it has to be seen whether the foregoing considerations really apply as regards criminal jurisdiction, or whether this jurisdiction is governed by a different principle: this might be the outcome of the close connection which for a long time existed between the conception of supreme criminal jurisdiction and that of a State, and also by the especial importance of criminal jurisdiction from the point of view of the individual.

Though it is true that in all systems of law the principle of the territorial character of criminal law is fundamental, it is equally true that all or nearly all of these systems of law extend their action to offences committed outside the territory of the State which adopts them, and they do so in ways which vary from State to State. The territoriality of criminal law, therefore, is not an absolute principle of international law and by no means coincides with territorial sovereignty.

This situation may be considered from two different standpoints corresponding to the points of view

---

[22]   Ed. Before the First World War, Turkey had been subject to a régime of capitulations (see above, p.10, n.46). The purpose of art.15 was to recognise that Turkey had become a full and equal member of the international community.

[23]   Ed. For examples of exceptions to this principle, see below, p.238.

respectively taken up by the Parties. According to one of these standpoints, the principle of freedom, in virtue of which each State may regulate its legislation at its discretion, provided that in so doing it does not come in conflict with a restriction imposed by international law, would also apply as regards law governing the scope of jurisdiction in criminal cases. According to the other standpoint, the exclusively territorial character of law relating to this domain constitutes a principle which, except as otherwise expressly provided, would *ipso facto*, prevent States from extending the criminal jurisdiction of their courts beyond their frontiers; the exceptions in question, which include for instance extra-territorial jurisdiction over nationals and over crimes directed against public safety, would therefore rest on special permissive rules forming part of international law.

Adopting, for the purposes of the argument, the standpoint of the latter of these two systems, it must be recognized that, in the absence of a treaty provision, its correctness depends upon whether there is a custom having the force of law establishing it. The same is true as regards the applicability of this system—assuming it to have been recognized as sound—in the particular case. It follows that, even from this point of view, before ascertaining whether there may be a rule of international law expressly allowing Turkey to prosecute a foreigner for an offence committed by him outside Turkey, it is necessary to begin by establishing both that the system is well-founded and that it is applicable in this particular case. Now, in order to establish the first of these points, one must, as has just been seen, prove the existence of a principle of international law restricting the discretion of States as regards criminal legislation.

Consequently, whichever of the two systems described above be adopted, the same result will be arrived at in this particular case: the necessity of ascertaining whether or not under international law there is a principle which would have prohibited Turkey, in the circumstances of the case before the Court, from prosecuting Lieutenant Demons. . . .

The arguments advanced by the French Government, other than those considered above, are, in substance, the three following:

(1) International law does not allow a State to take proceedings with regard to offences committed by foreigners abroad, simply by reason of the nationality of the victim; and such is the situation in the present case because the offence must be regarded as having been committed on board the French vessel.

(2) International law recognizes the exclusive jurisdiction of the State whose flag is flown as regards everything which occurs on board a ship on the high seas.

(3) Lastly, this principle is especially applicable in a collision case.

As regards the first argument . . . the Court does not think it necessary to consider the contention that a State cannot punish offences committed abroad by a foreigner simply by reason of the nationality of the victim. For this contention only relates to the case where the nationality of the victim is the only criterion on which the criminal jurisdiction of the State is based. Even if that argument were correct generally speaking—and in regard to this the Court reserves its opinion—it could only be used in the present case if international law forbade Turkey to take into consideration the fact that the offence produced its effects on the Turkish vessel and consequently in a place assimilated to Turkish territory in which the application of Turkish criminal law cannot be challenged, even in regard to offences committed there by foreigners. But no such rule of international law exists. No argument has come to the knowledge of the Court from which it could be deduced that States recognize themselves to be under an obligation towards each other only to have regard to the place where the author of the offence happens to be at the time of the offence. On the contrary, it is certain that the courts of many countries, even of countries which have given their criminal legislation a strictly territorial character, interpret criminal law in the sense that offences, the authors of which at the moment of commission are in the territory of another State, are nevertheless to be regarded as having been committed in the national territory, if one of the constituent elements of the offence, and more especially its effects, have taken place there. French courts have, in regard to a variety of situations, given decisions sanctioning this way of interpreting the territorial principle. Again, the Court does not know of any cases in which governments have protested against the fact that the criminal law of some country contained a rule to this effect or that the courts of a country construed their criminal law in this sense. Consequently, once it is admitted that the effects of the offence were produced on the Turkish vessel, it becomes impossible to hold that there is a rule of international law which prohibits Turkey from prosecuting Lieutenant Demons because of the fact that the author of the offence was on board the French ship. Since, as has already been observed, the special agreement does not deal with the provision of Turkish law under which the prosecution was instituted, but only with the question whether the prosecution should be regarded as contrary to the principles of international law, there is no reason preventing the Court from confining itself to observing that, in this case, a prosecution may also be justified from the point of view of the so-called territorial principle.

Nevertheless, even if the Court had to consider whether Article 6 of the Turkish Penal Code[24] was compatible with international law, and if it held that the nationality of the victim did not in all circumstances constitute a sufficient basis for the exercise of criminal jurisdiction by the State of which the victim was a national, the Court would arrive at the same conclusion for the reasons just set out. For even were Article 6 to be held incompatible with the principles of international law, since the prosecution might have been based on another provision of Turkish law which would not have been contrary to any principle of international law, it follows that it would be impossible to deduce from the mere fact that Article 6 was not in conformity with those principles, that the prosecution itself was contrary to them. The fact that the judicial authorities may have committed an error in their choice of the legal provision applicable to the particular case and compatible with international law only concerns municipal law and can only affect international law in so far as a treaty provision enters into account, or the possibility of a denial of justice arises.

It has been sought to argue that the offence of manslaughter cannot be localized at the spot where the mortal effect is felt; for the effect is not intentional and it cannot be said that there is, in the mind of the delinquent, any culpable intent directed towards the territory where the mortal effect is produced. In reply to this argument it might be observed that the effect is a factor of outstanding importance in offences such as manslaughter, which are punished precisely in consideration of their effects rather than of the subjective intention of the delinquent. But the Court does not feel called upon to consider this question, which is one of the interpretation of Turkish criminal law. It will suffice to observe that no argument has been put forward and nothing has been found from which it would follow that international law has established a rule imposing on States this reading of the conception of the offence of manslaughter.

The second argument put forward by the French Government is the principle that the State whose flag is flown has exclusive jurisdiction over everything which occurs on board a merchant ship on the high seas.

It is certainly true that—apart from certain special cases which are defined by international law—vessels on the high seas are subject to no authority except that of the State whose flag they fly. In virtue of the principle of the freedom of the seas, that is to say, the absence of any territorial sovereignty upon the high seas, no State may exercise any kind of jurisdiction over foreign vessels upon them. Thus, if a war vessel, happening to be at the spot where a collision occurs between a vessel flying its flag and a foreign vessel, were to send on board the latter an officer to make investigations or to take evidence, such an act would undoubtedly be contrary to international law.

But it by no means follows that a State can never in its own territory exercise jurisdiction over acts which have occurred on board a foreign ship on the high seas. A corollary of the principle of the freedom of the seas is that a ship on the high seas is assimilated to the territory of the State of the flag of which it flies, for, just as in its own territory, that State exercises its authority upon it, and no other State may do so. All that can be said is that by virtue of the principle of the freedom of the seas, a ship is placed in the same position as national territory; but there is nothing to support the claim according to which the rights of the State under whose flag the vessel sails may go farther than the rights which it exercises within its territory properly so called. It follows that what occurs on board a vessel on the high seas must be regarded as if it occurred on the territory of the State whose flag the ship flies. If, therefore, a guilty act committed on the high seas produces its effects on a vessel flying another flag or in foreign territory, the same principles must be applied as if the territories of two different States were concerned, and the conclusion must therefore be drawn that there is no rule of international law prohibiting the State to which the ship on which the effects of the offence have taken place belongs, from regarding the offence as having been committed in its territory and prosecuting, accordingly, the delinquent.

This conclusion could only be overcome if it were shown that there was a rule of customary international law which, going further than the principle stated above, established the exclusive jurisdiction of the State whose flag

---

[24] Ed. art.6 reads:

"Any foreigner who, apart from the cases contemplated by Article 4, commits an offence abroad to the prejudice of Turkey or of a Turkish subject, for which offence Turkish law prescribes a penalty involving loss of freedom for a minimum period of not less than one year, shall be punished in accordance with the Turkish Penal Code provided that he is arrested in Turkey. The penalty shall, however, be reduced by one third and instead of the death penalty, twenty years of penal servitude shall be awarded ...

If the offence committed injures another foreigner, the guilty person shall be punished at the request of the Minister of Justice, in accordance with the provisions set out in the first paragraph of this article, provided, however, that: (1) the article in question is one for which Turkish law prescribes a penalty involving loss of freedom for a minimum period of three years; (2) there is no extradition treaty or that extradition has not been accepted either by the government of the locality where the guilty person has committed the offence or by the government of his own country."

was flown. The French Government has endeavoured to prove the existence of such a rule, having recourse for this purpose to the teachings of publicists, to decisions of municipal and international tribunals, and especially to conventions which, whilst creating exceptions to the principle of the freedom of the seas by permitting the war and police vessels of a State to exercise a more or less extensive control over the merchant vessels of another State, reserve jurisdiction to the courts of the country whose flag is flown by the vessel proceeded against.

In the Court's opinion, the existence of such a rule has not been conclusively proved.

In the first place, as regards teachings of publicists, and apart from the question as to what their value may be from the point of view of establishing the existence of a rule of customary law, it is no doubt true that all or nearly all writers teach that ships on the high seas are subject exclusively to the jurisdiction of the State whose flag they fly. But the important point is the significance attached by them to this principle; now it does not appear that in general, writers bestow upon this principle a scope differing from or wider than that explained above and which is equivalent to saying that the jurisdiction of a State over vessels on the high seas is the same in extent as its jurisdiction in its own territory. On the other hand, there is no lack of writers who, upon a close study of the special question whether a State can prosecute for offences committed on board a foreign ship on the high seas, definitely come to the conclusion that such offences must be regarded as if they had been committed in the territory of the State whose flag the ship flies, and that consequently the general rules of each legal system in regard to offences committed abroad are applicable.

In regard to precedents, it should first be observed that, leaving aside the collision cases which will be alluded to later, none of them relates to offences affecting two ships flying the flags of two different countries, and that consequently they are not of much importance in the case before the Court. The case of the *Costa Rica Packet*[25] is no exception, for the prauw on which the alleged depredations took place was adrift without flag or crew, and this circumstance certainly influenced, perhaps decisively, the conclusion arrived at by the arbitrator.

On the other hand, there is no lack of cases in which a State has claimed a right to prosecute for an offence, committed on board a foreign ship, which it regarded as punishable under its legislation. Thus Great Britain refused the request of the United States for the extradition of John Anderson, a British seaman who had committed homicide on board an American vessel, stating that she did not dispute the jurisdiction of the United States but that she was entitled to exercise hers concurrently.[26] This case, to which others might be added, is relevant in spite of Anderson's British nationality, in order to show that the principle of exclusive jurisdiction of the country whose flag the vessel flies is not universally accepted.

The cases in which the exclusive jurisdiction of the State whose flag was flown has been recognized would seem rather to have been cases in which the foreign State was interested only by reason of the nationality of the victim, and in which, according to the legislation of that State itself or the practice of its courts, that ground was not regarded as sufficient to authorize prosecution for an offence committed abroad by a foreigner.

Finally, as regards conventions expressly reserving jurisdiction exclusively to the State whose flag is flown, it is not absolutely certain that this stipulation is to be regarded as expressing a general principle of law rather than as corresponding to the extraordinary jurisdiction which these conventions confer on the state-owned ships of a particular country in respect of ships of another country on the high seas. Apart from that, it should be observed that these conventions relate to matters of a particular kind, closely connected with the policing of the seas, such as the slave trade, damage to submarine cables, fisheries, etc., and not to common-law offences. Above all it should be pointed out that the offences contemplated by the conventions in question only concern a single ship; it is impossible therefore to make any deduction from them in regard to matters which concern two ships and consequently the jurisdiction of two different States. ...

It only remains to examine the third argument advanced by the French Government. ...

In this connection, the Agent for the French Government has drawn the Court's attention to the fact that questions of jurisdiction in collision cases, which frequently arise before civil courts, are but rarely encountered in the practice of criminal courts. He deduces from this that, in practice, prosecutions only occur before the courts of the State whose flag is flown and that that circumstance is proof of a tacit consent on the part of States and, consequently, shows what positive international law is in collision cases.

---

[25] Ed. *G.B. v The Netherlands* (1897) Moore 5 Int.Arb. 4948. Crew from the *Costa Rica Packet*, a British merchant ship, boarded a derelict prauw (a Malayan vessel) on the high seas and took goods (mostly gin and brandy, from which the crew became drunk) from it. When the *Costa Rica Packet* entered a Dutch port in the East Indies, the captain was arrested on charges relating to the seizure of the goods. He was later released without being brought to trial. The Arbitrator (Martens) held that the Netherlands had no jurisdiction to act as it had done—only the flag state of the *Costa Rica Packet* had—and awarded damages against it.

[26] Ed. See the official correspondence of 1879 in 1 Moore 932.

In the Court's opinion, this conclusion is not warranted. Even if the rarity of the judicial decisions to be found among the reported cases were sufficient to prove in point of fact the circumstance alleged by the Agent for the French Government, it would merely show that States had often, in practice, abstained from instituting criminal proceedings, and not that they recognized themselves as being obliged to do so; for only if such abstention were based on their being conscious of having a duty to abstain would it be possible to speak of an international custom. The alleged fact does not allow one to infer that States have been conscious of having such a duty; on the other hand, as will presently be seen, there are other circumstances calculated to show that the contrary is true.

So far as the Court is aware there are no decisions of international tribunals in this matter; but some decisions of municipal courts have been cited. Without pausing to consider the value to be attributed to the judgments of municipal courts in connection with the establishment of the existence of a rule of international law, it will suffice to observe that the decisions quoted sometimes support one view and sometimes the other. . . .

On the other hand, the Court feels called upon to lay stress upon the fact that it does not appear that the States concerned have objected to criminal proceedings in respect of collision cases before the courts of a country other than that the flag of which was flown, or that they have made protests: their conduct does not appear to have differed appreciably from that observed by them in all cases of concurrent jurisdiction. This fact is directly opposed to the existence of a tacit consent on the part of States to the exclusive jurisdiction of the State whose flag is flown, such as the Agent for the French Government has thought it possible to deduce from the infrequency of questions of jurisdiction before criminal courts. It seems hardly probable, and it would not be in accordance with international practice, that the French Government in the *Ortigia-Oncle-Joseph* Case[27] and the German Government in the *Ekbatana-West-Hinder* Case[28] would have omitted to protest against the exercise of criminal jurisdiction by the Italian and Belgian Courts, if they had really thought that this was a violation of international law. . . .

The conclusion at which the Court has therefore arrived is that there is no rule of international law in regard to collision cases to the effect that criminal proceedings are exclusively within the jurisdiction of the State whose flag is flown. . . .

For These Reasons. The Court . . . gives by the President's casting vote—the votes being equally divided[29]— judgment to the effect [that the answer to the first question was in the negative].

DISSENTING OPINION OF JUDGE MOORE.[30]

. . . the countries by which the claim [to jurisdiction based upon the passive personality principle] has been espoused are said to have adopted the "system of protection."

What, we may ask, is this system? In substance, it means that the citizen of one country, when he visits another country, takes with him for his "protection" the law of his own country and subjects those with whom he comes into contact to the operation of that law. In this way an inhabitant of a great commercial city, in which foreigners congregate, may in the course of an hour unconsciously fall under the operation of a number of foreign criminal codes. This is by no means a fanciful supposition; it is merely an illustration of what is daily occurring, if the "protective" principle is admissible. It is evident that this claim is at variance not only with the principle of the exclusive jurisdiction of a State over its own territory, but also with the equally well-settled principle that a person visiting a foreign country, far from radiating for his protection the jurisdiction of his own country, falls under the dominion of the local law and, except so far as his government may diplomatically intervene in case of a denial of justice, must look to that law for his protection.

No one disputes the right of a State to subject its citizens abroad to the operations of its own penal laws, if it sees fit to do so. This concerns simply the citizen and his own government, and no other government can properly interfere. But the case is fundamentally different where a country claims either that its penal laws apply

---

[27] Ed. (1885) 12 J.D.I. 286.
[28] Ed. (1914) 41 J.D.I 1327.
[29] Ed. President Huber; Judges de Bustamante, Oda, Anzilotti, Pessôa; and National Judge Feizi-Daim voted for the Court's judgment. Former President Loder; Vice-President Weiss; and Judges Lord Finlay, Nyholm, Moore and Altimira dissented.
[30] On his reading of the special agreement by which the case was referred to the Court, Judge Moore found it necessary to consider whether art.6 of the Turkish Criminal Code, with its reliance on the passive personality (or "protective") principle, was consistent with international law. It was his conclusion on this question that led to his dissent. Note that by "protective principle" the judge means the "passive personality principle" not the protective principle discussed below, p.246.

to other countries and to what takes place wholly within such countries or, if it does not claim this, that it may punish foreigners for alleged violations, even in their own country, of laws to which they were not subject.

In the discussions of the present case, prominence has been given to the case of the editor Cutting, a citizen of the United States, whose release was demanded when he was prosecuted in Mexico, under a statute precisely similar in terms to Article 6 of the Turkish Penal Code, for a libel published in the United States to the detriment of a Mexican. It has been intimated that this case was "political," but an examination of the public record (*Foreign Relations of the United States*, 1887, p. 751; *idem*, 1888, II, pp. 1114, 1180) shows that it was discussed by both Governments on purely legal grounds, although in the decision on appeal, by which the prisoner was discharged from custody, his release was justified on grounds of public interest.[31] In its representations to the Mexican Government, the Government of the United States, while maintaining that foreigners could not be "protected in the United States by their national laws," and that the Mexican courts might not, without violating international law, "try a citizen of the United States for an offence committed and consummated in his own country, merely because the person offended happened to be a Mexican," pointed out that it nowhere appeared that the alleged libel "was ever circulated in Mexico so as to constitute the crime of defamation under the Mexican law," or "that any copies were actually found ... in Mexico." The United States thus carefully limited its protest to offences "committed and consummated" within its territory; and, in conformity with this view, it was agreed in the extradition treaty between the two countries of February 22nd, 1889, that except in the case of "embezzlement or criminal malversation of public funds committed within the jurisdiction of either Party by public officers or depositaries," neither Party would "assume jurisdiction in the punishment of crimes committed exclusively within the territory of the other." (Moore, *Digest of International Law*, II pp.233, 242.)[32]

Notes

1. On the approach of the Court to the question whether France had to prove a limitation upon Turkey's jurisdiction or whether Turkey had to prove a rule giving it jurisdiction, Brierly[33] states:

   "... their reasoning was based on the highly contentious metaphysical proposition of the extreme positivist school that the law emanates from the free will of sovereign independent States, and from this premiss they argued that restrictions on the independence of States cannot be presumed. Neither, it may be said, can the absence of restrictions; for we are not entitled to deduce the law applicable to a specific state of facts from the mere fact of sovereignty or independence. Further, the reasoning of the majority seems to imply that the process by which the international principles of penal jurisdiction have been formed is by the imposition of certain limitations on an originally unlimited competence, and this is surely historically unsound. The original conception of law was personal, and it was only the rise of the modern territorial State that subjected aliens—even when they happened to be resident in a State not their own—to the law of that State. International law did not start as the law of a society of States each of omnicompetent jurisdiction, but of States possessing a personal jurisdiction over their own nationals and later acquiring a territorial jurisdiction over resident non-nationals. If it is alleged that they have now acquired a measure of jurisdiction over non-resident non-nationals, a valid international custom to that effect should surely be established by those who allege it."

2. What does the Court mean when it says that the "territoriality of criminal law ... is not an absolute principle of international law and by no means coincides with territorial sovereignty?"[34]

---

[31] Ed. Cutting had been convicted by the trial court. An appeal court ordered his release because "the offended party ... has withdrawn from the action": see U.S.For.Rel., 1887, pp.766–767.

[32] Ed. Mexico regarded itself as justified in using the passive personality principle: see the inclosure to the letter from Mr Romero to Mr Bayard, August 30, 1886, U.S.For.Rel., 1887, pp.957 et seq.

[33] (1928) 44 L.Q.R. 154 at 155–156.

[34] Above, p.231.

3. *The territorial principle*. On the question whether the offence could be said to have been committed on Turkish territory to establish Turkish jurisdiction on a territorial basis, Judge Moore agreed with the Court:

> "... it appears to be now universally admitted that, where a crime is committed in the territorial jurisdiction of one State as the direct result of the act of a person at the time corporeally present in another State, international law, by reason of the principle of constructive presence of the offender at the place where his act took effect, does not forbid the prosecution of the offender by the former State, should he come within its territorial jurisdiction."[35]

Consistent with this approach, the Harvard Research Draft Convention proposed that a State be allowed territorial jurisdiction when a crime is committed "in whole or in part" within its territory.[36] A crime is committed "in part" within the territory "when any essential constituent element is consummated there."[37] The Commentary to the Draft Convention reads: "The text of the present article conforms to the modern trend by combining the subjective and objective applications of the territorial principle."[38] According to the "subjective application," a crime occurs in a State when it is "commenced within the State but completed or consummated [in the sense of a constituent element occurring] abroad."[39] The "objective" application is to the effect that it does so in the reverse situation.[40] Thus if X, in state A, shoots and kills Y, in state B, an offence is probably committed (depending upon the constituent elements of murder and related offences in the criminal law of the two states) in each state.

As allowed by the rules as to territorial jurisdiction in international law, the UK Criminal Justice Act 1993 ss.1–2, provides for criminal jurisdiction in respect of listed offences where any act, proof of the commission of which is necessary for a conviction, is committed within the jurisdiction. Section 3(2)(3) of the 1993 Act provides for jurisdiction in respect of extra-territorial conspiracies and attempts in respect of listed offences where the intention is to commit an offence in England, even though no act is committed within the jurisdiction and whether the defendants are British nationals or not.[41] In international law, jurisdiction in these inchoate offence cases may be based on the protective or, possibly, universality principles, depending on the facts. In *D.P.P. v Doot*,[42] the respondents were aliens convicted of conspiracy to import cannabis resin into the United Kingdom. The agreement amounting to the conspiracy had been made abroad before the respondents were arrested in England while in the course of carrying it out. The House of Lords held that the English courts had jurisdiction in the case under English law because the offence continued to occur in England while steps were being taken in concert there to carry out the purpose of the conspiracy.[43] This was so even though the agreement had already been made—

---

[35] P.C.I.J. Rep., Series A, No.10 at p.73.
[36] art.3. See the facts in *R. v Keyn*, above, p.66.
[37] (1935) 29 A.J.I.L. Supp. 495.
[38] (1935) 29 A.J.I.L. Supp. p.494. cf. Lord Diplock in *Treacy v D.P.P.* [1971] A.C. 537, HL.
[39] (1935) 29 A.J.I.L. Supp. p.484.
[40] (1935) 29 A.J.I.L. Supp. p.488.
[41] See *Liangsiriprasert v Govt. of USA* [1991] 1 A.C. 225 PC; and *R. v Sansom* [1991] 2 Q.B. 130 CA (drug importing conspiracy cases to the same effect). On the 1993 Act and international law jurisdiction rules, see Warbrick (1994) 43 I.C.L.Q. 460. It is also an offence under the Offences Against the Person Act 1861 s.4, for any person in *England*, whether a British citizen or not, to solicit a foreigner *abroad* to commit a murder *abroad*: *R. v Abu Hamza* [2006] EWCA Crim 918.
[42] [1973] A.C. 807 HL.
[43] This requirement no longer applies under the 1993 Act: see above.

and hence the constituent elements of the crime completed—abroad. Referring to the question of jurisdiction in the case according to international law, Lord Wilberforce stated:

> "the present case involves 'international elements'—the accused are aliens and the conspiracy was initiated abroad—but there can be no question here of any breach of any rules of international law if they are prosecuted in this country. Under the objective territorial principle (I use the terminology of the Harvard Research in International Law) or the principle of universality (for the prevention of the trade in narcotics falls within this description[44]) or both, the courts of this country have a clear right, if not a duty, to prosecute in accordance with our municipal law."

The Court's application of the territorial principle in the *Lotus* case was based upon the view that a ship, like an aircraft, is to be treated as part of a state's territory for jurisdictional purposes.[45] Lord Finlay took a different view in his dissenting opinion. For him, a ship was not "territory"; it was instead a "moving chattel" of a "very special nature" for which the relevant jurisdictional rule was that "[c]riminal jurisdiction for negligence causing a collision is in the courts of the country of the flag, provided that if the offender is of a nationality different from that of his ship, the prosecution may alternatively be in the courts of his own country."[46]

In *R. v Bates*,[47] the defendant was charged with an offence under the Firearms Act 1937 committed on Rough's Tower, a wartime gun platform on which he was living and located seven miles off the coast of Harwich, then outside United Kingdom territorial waters. The charge was dismissed because "the jurisdiction of the Admiral did not apply to an artificial structure not being a ship and . . . the Firearms Act was intended to operate only within 'the ordinary territorial limits' and on British ships."[48]

As noted by the Court, p.231, above, jurisdiction normally cannot be exercised by one state in the territory of another. Exceptionally, in the *Lockerbie* case judicial jurisdiction was exercised abroad when the two Libyans accused were prosecuted for murder and other offences under Scottish law before the Scottish High Court of Justiciary sitting at The Hague, with the necessary consent of the Netherlands.[49] The trial was conducted in accordance with Scottish law except that the court was composed of three judges and no jury. This was the first time that a Scottish non-military court had sat in the territory of another state.[50] In another exceptional case, the NATO Status of Force Agreement 1951,[51] provides that each party may exercise jurisdiction over its forces stationed in the territory of the other parties.

---

[44] On universality jurisdiction, see the *Arrest Warrant* case, below, p.250.

[45] cf. *R. v Brixton Prison Governor Ex p. Minervini* [1959] 1 Q.B. 155, QBD (Norwegian ship "territory" on which a crime could be committed in the sense of the British-Norwegian extradition treaty; "territory" in the treaty meant "jurisdiction").

[46] P.C.I.J. Rep., Series A, No.10 at p.53.

[47] Unreported case before Essex Assizes; summarised in U.K.M.I.L. 1978, (1978) 49 B.Y.I.L. 393.

[48] See above, n.47. There is a presumption that an Act of Parliament applies only to United Kingdom territory: *Al-Skeini v Secretary of State for Defence* [2007] UKHL 26 per Lord Bingham.

[49] See SI 1998/2251 and the 1998 UK–Netherlands Agreement, reprinted in (1999) 38 I.L.M. 926 et seq. The venue, which was sought by Libya, was endorsed by the Security Council Resolution 1192 (1998). See Aust (2000) 49 I.C.L.Q. 278. On the *Lockerbie* case before the ICJ, see further below, p.878.

[50] The Scottish basis for criminal jurisdiction in the case was territorial since Pan Am flight 103 was blown up while over Scotland: see the Scottish Solicitor General, oral pleadings, *Lockerbie* case (*Interim Measures*), I.C.J. Rep 1992, p.3; U.K.M.I.L. 1992, (1992) 63 B.Y.I.L. 722.

[51] (1955) U.K.T.S. 3, Cmd. 9363, 1999 U.N.T.S. 67. See also the 1991 Sangatte Protocol, see U.K.M.I.L. 1993, (1993) B.Y.I.L. 647; and the 2002 Additional Protocol, Cm 5015, U.K.M.I.L. 2000, (2000) 71 B.Y.I.L. 589, by which the UK and France give their officials jurisdiction in Channel Tunnel "control zones" in each other's territory for immigration purposes.

In *Bankovic v Belgium et al*,[52] the European Court of Human Rights characterised state jurisdiction in international law as "primarily territorial":

> "59. As to the 'ordinary meaning' of the relevant term ['jurisdiction'] in Article 1 of the Convention, the Court is satisfied that, from the standpoint of public international law, the jurisdictional competence of a State is primarily territorial. While international law does not exclude a State's exercise of jurisdiction extra-territorially, the suggested bases of such jurisdiction (including nationality, flag, diplomatic and consular relations, effect, protection, passive personality and universality) are, as a general rule, defined and limited by the sovereign territorial rights of the other relevant States ...
>
> 60. Accordingly, for example, a State's competence to exercise jurisdiction over its own nationals abroad is subordinate to that State's and other States' territorial competence. ... In addition, a State may not actually exercise jurisdiction on the territory of another without the latter's consent, invitation or acquiescence, unless the former is an occupying State in which case it can be found to exercise jurisdiction in that territory, at least in certain repects."

In the *Bankovic* case, NATO had authorised air strikes against targets in the territory of the Former Republic of Yugoslavia ("FRY") in the course of the Kosovo conflict. A missile launched from outside the FRY hit a television/radio building in Belgrade, killing and injuring persons in it. An application alleging a breach of the European Convention on Human Rights (rights to life and expression) was rejected as inadmissible because the Convention only protected persons "within the jurisdiction" of the states parties, and the applicants were not within the jurisdiction of the NATO states concerned, the term "jurisdiction" being interpreted in line with its "primarily territorial" meaning in customary international law.

4. *The passive personality principle*.[53] This was rejected by all of the six dissenting judges. The Commentary to the Harvard Draft Convention in 1935 lists over 20 States that, in one form or another, made, or proposed to make, use of the "passive personality" principle.[54] It had, however, "been vigorously opposed in Anglo-American countries"[55] and, of the five principles "having substantial support in comtemporary national legislation," it was "the most difficult to justify in theory."[56] The principle was not included in the Draft Convention.

However, attitudes have changed; treaties now provide for passive personality jurisdiction in respect of terrorist acts and other matters of general international concern[57] and some states, such as the United States, that were opposed to it now rely upon the principle in such contexts in their national legislation, as noted by a Federal District Court in *US v Yunis (No.2)*.[58] In that case, the defendant, a Lebanese national, and others hijacked a Jordanian airliner at Beirut Airport, with two US nationals and other passengers on board, ultimately blowing it up there. The defendant was arrested by FBI agents on board a yacht in international waters in the Mediterranean. He was convicted in a US court of, inter alia, hostage-taking and air piracy and

---

[52] E.Ct.H.R.R. 2001–XII; 44 E.H.R.R. SE5. See Gondek (2005) 52 N.I.L.R. 349; Happold (2001) 3 H.R.L.R. 77; Markovic (2008) 8 H.R.L.R. 411; O'Boyle in Coomans and Kamminga, eds., *Extraterritorial Application of Human Rights Treaties* (2004), p.125; Trilsch (2003) 97 A.J.I.L. 168; Williams and Shah (2002) E.H.R.L.R 775;

[53] See Watson (1993) 28 Texas I.L.J. 2.

[54] (1935) 29 A.J.I.L. Supp. 578.

[55] (1985) 29 A.J.I.L. Supp. 578 at p.579.

[56] (1985) 29 A.J.I.L. Supp. 578.

[57] e.g. see the 1963 Tokyo Convention on Offences Aboard Aircraft, art.4, (1969) U.K.T.S. 126, Cmnd. 4230; 704 U.N.T.S. 219. In force 1969 (147 parties, including the UK) and the 1984 Torture Convention, below, p.545.

[58] (1988) 82 I.L.R. 344.

sentenced to 30 years imprisonment. On the question of jurisdiction, it was held that the US courts had jurisdiction under the unambiguous wording of the Hostage Taking Act and Anti-Hijacking Act and that the terms of these statutes prevailed over any customary international law jurisdictional rules to the contrary. Nonetheless, the Court went on to suggest that there was jurisdiction in any event in customary international law on the basis of the passive personality and universality principles. As to the former, it stated:

"Although many international legal scholars agree that the principle is the most controversial of the five sources of jurisdiction, they also agree that the international community recognizes its legitimacy. Most accept that 'the extraterritorial reach of a law premised upon the ... principle would not be in doubt as a matter of international law.' Paust, *Jurisdiction and Nonimmunity*, 23 Va.J. of Int'l Law, 191, 203 (1983). More importantly, the international community explicitly approved of the principle as a basis for asserting jurisdiction over hostage takers. As noted above, ... the Hostage Taking Convention set forth certain mandatory sources of jurisdiction. But it also gave each signatory country discretion to exercise extraterritorial jurisdiction when the offense was committed 'with respect to a hostage who is a national of that state if that state considers it appropriate.' Art. 5(a)(d). Therefore, even if there are doubts regarding the international community's acceptance, there can be no doubt concerning the application of this principle to the offense of hostage taking, an offense for which Yunis is charged. *See* M. Bassiouni, II International Criminal Law ch. 4 at 120.

Defendant's counsel correctly notes that the passive personality principle traditionally has been an anathema to United States lawmakers. ... In the past, the United States has protested any assertion of such jurisdiction for fear that it could lead to indefinite criminal liability for its own citizens. This objection was based on the belief that foreigners visiting the United States should comply with our laws and should not be permitted to carry their laws with them. Otherwise Americans would face criminal prosecutions for actions unknown to them as illegal.[59] However, in the most recent draft of the Restatement, the authors noted that the theory 'has been increasingly accepted when applied to terrorist and other organized attacks on a state's nationals by reason of their nationality, or to assassinations of a state's ambassadors, or government officials.' Restatement (Revised) § 402, comment g (Tent.Draft No.6). *See also* McGinley, *The Achillo Lauro Affair—Implications for International Law*, 52 Tenn.L.Rev. 691, 713 (1985). The authors retreated from their wholesale rejection of the principle, recognizing that perpetrators of crimes unanimously condemned by members of the international community, should be aware of the illegality of their actions.[60] Therefore, qualified application of the doctrine to serious and universally condemned crimes will not raise the specter of unlimited and unexpected criminal liabilty.

Finally, this case does not present the first time that the United States has invoked the principle to assert jurisdiction over a hijacker who seized an American hostage on foreign soil.[61] The government relied on this very principle when it sought extradition of Muhammed Abbas

---

[59] The case most widely cited for the United States' rejection of the passive personality principle is known as the *Cutting* case, [above, p.236]. ...

[60] While it might be too much to expect the average citizen to be familiar with all of the criminal laws of every country, it is not unrealistic to assume that he would realize that committing a terrorist act might subject him to foreign prosecution. See Note, Bringing the Terrorist to Justice, 11 Cornell Int'l L.J. 71 (1978).

[61] At least one court has explicitly relied on the passive personality principle to assert jurisdiction over foreigners committing crimes against U.S. nationals overseas. *United States v Benitez* 741 F.2d 1312, 1316 (11th Cir.1984) (Columbian charged with conspiracy to murder DEA agent). ("The nationality of the victims, who are United States government agents, clearly supports jurisdiction.")

Zaiden, the leader of the terrorists who hijacked the Achillo Lauro vessel in Egyptian waters and subsequently killed Leon Klinghoffer, an American citizen. As here, the only connection to the United States was Klinghoffer's American citizenship. Based on that link, an arrest warrant was issued charging Abbas with hostage taking, conspiracy and piracy. *Id.* at 719; ..."

See also the recognition of the passive personality principle in the joint separate opinion, para.47, of Judges Higgins, Kooijmans and Buergenthal, and the separate opinion of President Guillaume, para.16, in the *Arrest Warrant* case, below, p.254.

5.   The ruling of the Court on the question of jurisdiction in cases of collisions on the high seas is contradicted by the 1982 Law of the Sea Convention.[62] The latter probably now reflects customary international law.

ATTORNEY-GENERAL OF THE GOVERNMENT OF ISRAEL v EICHMANN[63]

(1961) 36 I.L.R. 5. District Court of Jerusalem

The accused, who had German nationality,[64] was the Head of the Jewish Office of the German Gestapo. He was the administrator in charge of "the final solution"—the policy that led to the extermination of between 4,200,000 and 4,600,000 Jews in Europe.[65] Eichmann was found in Argentina in 1960 by persons who were probably agents of the Israeli Government[66] and abducted to Israel without the knowledge of the Argentinian Government.[67] There he was prosecuted under the Israeli Nazi and Nazi Collaborators (Punishment) Law of 1951 for war crimes, crimes against the Jewish people, the definition of which was modelled upon the definition of genocide in the Genocide Convention 1949,[68] and crimes against humanity.[69] War crimes were punishable under the 1951 Act if "done, during the period of the Second World War, in an enemy country"; other crimes within the Act were punishable if "done, during the period of the Nazi regime, in an enemy country." He was convicted and sentenced to death. His appeal to the Supreme Court of Israel was dismissed.[70] His ashes "were scattered over the Mediterranean waters—lest they defile Jewish soil."[71]

Judgment of the Court

8. Learned defence counsel ... submits:
(a) that the Israel Law, by imposing punishment for acts done outside the boundaries of the State and before its establishment, against persons who were not Israel citizens, and by a person who acted in the course of duty

---

[62]   art.97, below, p.377.
[63]   See Fawcett (1962) 38 B.Y.I.L. 181; Green (1960) 23 M.L.R. 507; Papadatos, *The Eichmann Trial* (1964); Schwarzenberger (1962) 15 C.L.P. 248; Silving (1961) 55 A.J.I.L. 307.
[64]   This at least was claimed by his counsel in Jerusalem: Rosen, ed., *Six Million Accusers* (1962), p.301. He was born in Germany of German parents and taken to live in Austria as a boy. He entered Argentina with a refugee passport issued by the Red Cross under the false name of Ricardo Klement.
[65]   This estimate is that of Reitlinger in *The Final Solution* (1953), App.I.
[66]   Even supposing they were not, Israel would appear to have adopted their acts.
[67]   Note that there was no extradition treaty between Argentina and Israel.
[68]   U.K.T.S. 58 (1970), Cmnd. 4421; 78 U.N.T.S. 277; (1951) 45 A.J.I.L. Supp. 7.
[69]   These were defined as "... any of the following acts: murder, extermination, enslavement, starvation or deportation and other inhumane acts committed against any civilian population, and persecution on national, racial, religious or political grounds."
[70]   The Supreme Court Judgment is at (1962) 36 I.L.R. 277. The Supreme Court affirmed the reasoning of the District Court.
[71]   Sachar, *A History of the Jews* (1967), p.467.

on behalf of a foreign country ("Act of State") conflicts with international law and exceeds the powers of the Israel Legislature. . . .

10. . . . The law in force in Israel resembles that in force in England in [its application of International Law]. . . .

Our jurisdiction to try this case is based on the Nazi and Nazi Collaborators (Punishment) Law, an enacted Law the provisions of which are unequivocal. The Court has to give effect to a law of the Knesset,[72] and we cannot entertain the contention that this Law conflicts with the principles of international law. . . .

11. We have, however, also considered the sources of international law . . . and have failed to find any foundation for the contention that Israel law is in conflict with the principles of international law. . . .

12. The abhorrent crimes defined in this Law are not crimes under Israel law alone. These crimes, which struck at the whole of mankind and shocked the conscience of nations, are grave offences against the law of nations itself (delicta juris gentium).[73] Therefore, so far from international law negating or limiting the jurisdiction of countries with respect to such crimes, international law is, in the absence of an International Court, in need of the judicial and legislative organs of every country to give effect to its criminal interdictions and to bring the criminals to trial. The jurisdiction to try crimes under international law is universal.

13. This universal authority, namely the authority of the forum deprehensionis (the court of the country in which the accused is actually held in custody), was already mentioned in the Corpus Juris Civilis (see C.3, 15, ubi de criminibus agi oportet) and the towns of northern Italy had already in the Middle Ages followed the practice of trying specific types of dangerous criminals (banniti, vagabundi, assassini) who happened to be within their area of jurisdiction, without regard to the place in which the crimes in question were committed. . . . Maritime nations have also since time immemorial acted on the principle of universal jurisdiction in dealing with pirates, whose crime is known in English law, piracy jure gentium. . . .

The Court quoted from a number of authors[74] who take the view that "crimes against international law" generally or war crimes in particular give rise to universal jurisdiction. It then considered an objection to its jurisdiction based upon Article 6 of the Genocide Convention 1949[75]:

22. . . . It is clear that Article 6, like all other articles which determine the conventional obligations of the contracting parties, is intended for cases of genocide which will occur in the future after the ratification of the treaty or the adherence thereto by the State or States concerned. It cannot be assumed, in the absence of an express provision in the Convention itself, that any of the conventional obligations, including Article 6, will apply to crimes which had been perpetrated in the past. It is of the nature of conventional obligations, as distinct from confirmation of existing principles, that unless another intention is implicit, their application is ex nunc and not ex tunc. . . . We must . . . draw a clear distinction between the first part of Article I, which lays down that "the Contracting Parties confirm that genocide, whether committed in time of peace or in time of war, is a crime under international law"—a general provision which confirms a principle of customary international law "binding on States, even without any conventional obligation"—and Article 6, which comprises a special provision undertaken by the contracting parties with regard to the trial of crimes that may be committed in the future. Whatever may be the purport of this latter obligation within the meaning of the Convention (and in the event of differences of opinion as to the interpretation thereof, each contracting party may, under Article 9, appeal to the International Court of Justice), it is certain that it constitutes no part of the principles of customary international law, which are also binding outside the conventional application of the Convention.

23. Moreover, even with regard to the conventional application of the Convention, it is not to be assumed that Article 6 is designed to limit the jurisdiction of countries to try crimes of genocide by the principle of territoriality. Without entering into the general question of the limits of municipal criminal jurisdiction, it may be pointed out that no one disputes that customary international law does not prohibit a State from trying its own citizens for offences they have committed abroad. . . . Had Article 6 meant to provide that those accused of genocide shall be tried only by "a competent tribunal of the State in the territory of which the act was committed" (or by an "international court" which has not been constituted), then that article would have foiled the very object of the Convention to prevent genocide and inflict punishment therefor. . . .

---

72   Ed. The Israeli Parliament.

73   Ed. On crimes against international law, see the readings below, p.537, n.25.

74   These included Hyde, International Law (2nd edn 1947), Vol.I, p.804; and Cowles (1945) 33 Calif. L. R. 177.

75   art.6 reads: "Persons charged with genocide . . . shall be tried by a competent tribunal of the state in the territory of which the act was committed. . . ."

The Court rejected the defenses of *nullem crimen sine lege, nulla poena sine lege* and "act of state," relying on the reasoning of the International Military Tribunal at Nuremberg.[76]

30. ... The State of Israel's "right to punish" the accused derives, in our view, from two cumulative sources: a universal source (pertaining to the whole of mankind), which vests the right to prosecute and punish crimes of this order in every State within the family of nations; and a specific or national source, which gives the victim nation the right to try any who assault its existence.

This second foundation of criminal jurisdiction conforms, according to accepted terminology, to the protective principle (*compétence réelle*). In England, which until very recently was considered a country that does not rely on such jurisdiction (see also *Harvard Research in International Law*, "Jurisdiction with respect to Crime," 1935, A.J.I.L., vol. 35 (Suppl.), 544) it was said in *Joyce v. Director of Public Prosecutions* [1946] A.C. 347, 372:

> The second point of appeal ... was that in any case no English court has jurisdiction to try an alien for a crime committed abroad. ... There is, I think, a short answer to this point. The statute in question deals with the crime of treason committed within or ... without the realm: ... No principle of comity demands that a state should ignore the crime of treason committed against it outside its territory. On the contrary a proper regard for its own security requires that all those who commit that crime, whether they commit it within or without the realm, should be amenable to its laws.[77]

Oppenheim-Lauterpacht, *op. cit.*, vol. 1, S. 147, p. 333, says that the penal jurisdiction of the State includes "crimes injuring its subjects or serious crimes against its own safety." Most European countries go much further than this (see Harvard Research, loc. cit., pp. 546 et seq.).

31. Dahm says in his *Zur Problematik des Voelkerstrafrechts* (1956), p. 28, that the protective principle is not confined to those foreign offences that threaten the "vital interests" of the State, and goes on to explain (pp. 38–39) in his reference to the "immanent limitations" of the jurisdiction of the State, a departure from which would constitute an "abuse" of its sovereignty, [that]

> Penal jurisdiction is not a matter for everyone to exercise. It requires a "linking point" (*Anknuepfungspunkte*), a legal connection that links the punisher with the punished. The State may, in so far as international law does not contain rules to the contrary, punish only persons and acts *which concern it more than they concern other States*. ...

The Court cited other writers in support of the "linking point" doctrine.[78]

33. ... The "linking point" between Israel and the accused (and for that matter any person accused of a crime against the Jewish people under this Law) is striking in the case of "crime against the Jewish people," a crime that postulates an intention to exterminate the Jewish people in whole or in part. ...

34. The connection between the State of Israel and the Jewish people needs no explanation.

35. ... This crime very deeply concerns the "vital interests" of the State of Israel, and under the "protective principle" this State has the right to punish the criminals. In terms of Dahm's thesis, the acts referred to in this Law of the State of Israel "concern it more than they concern other States," and therefore according also to this author there exists a "linking point." The punishment of Nazi criminals does not derive from the arbitrariness of a country "abusing" its sovereignty but is a legitimate and reasonable exercise of a right of penal jurisdiction.

---

[76] See the Nuremberg Tribunal Judgment, (1947) 41 A.J.I.L. 172.

[77] Ed. Lord Jowitt L.C. The accused, William Joyce, was charged with treason under the Treason Act 1351 for having made propaganda broadcasts to the UK from Germany for the German Government. Although Joyce had spent his adult life in England, the accused was a US citizen born in the US of Irish parents who had emigrated there and become naturalised US nationals. Apart from the "point of appeal" referred to above, it was also contended that the accused did not owe allegiance to the Crown and hence could not be guilty of treason. The House of Lords accepted that allegiance was necessary to the offence but found that the accused, as holder of a British passport in his name still in force at the time of his broadcasts, was entitled to protection by the Crown and, therefore, owed the Crown allegiance. This was so even though the passport had been obtained by fraud. See Lauterpacht (1947) 9 C.L.J. 330.

[78] See also Mann, above, p.228, n.1, pp.49–51.

A people which can be murdered with impunity lives in danger, to say nothing of its "honour and authority" (Grotius). ...

36. Defence counsel contended that the protective principle cannot apply to this Law because that principle is designed to protect only an existing State, its security and its interests, whereas the State of Israel did not exist at the time of the commission of the said crimes. In his submission the same applies to the principle of "passive personality" which stems from the protective principle, and of which some States have made use through their penal legislation for the protection of their citizens abroad. Counsel pointed out that in the absence of a sovereign Jewish State at the time of the catastrophe the victims of the Nazis were not citizens of the State of Israel when they were murdered.

In our view learned Counsel errs when he examines the protective principle in this retroactive Law according to the time of the commission of the crimes, as is usual in the case of an ordinary law. This Law was enacted in 1950, to be applied to a specified period which had terminated five years before its enactment. The protected interests of the State recognized by the protective principle is in this case the interest existing at the time of the enactment of the Law, and we have already dwelt on the importance of the moral and defensive task which this Law is designed to fulfil in the State of Israel. ...

39. We should add that the well-known judgment ... in the *Lotus Case*[79] ruled that the principle of territoriality does not limit the power of a State to try crimes and, moreover, that any argument against such power must point to a specific rule in international law which negates that power. We have followed this principle which, so to speak, shifts the "onus of proof" upon him who pleads against jurisdiction, but have preferred to base ourselves on positive reasons for upholding the jurisdiction of the State of Israel.

40. The second contention of learned defence counsel was that the trial of the accused in Israel following upon his kidnapping in a foreign land, is in conflict with international law and takes away the jurisdiction of this Court.

... with reference to the circumstances of the arrest of the accused and his transfer to Israel, the Republic of Argentina ... lodged a complaint with the Security Council of the United Nations, which resolved on June 23, 1960, as follows (Doc. S/4349) ... :

The Security Council,
   Having examined the complaint that the transfer of Adolf Eichmann to the territory of Israel constitutes a violation of the sovereignty of the Argentine Republic,
   Considering that the violation of the sovereignty of a Member State is incompatible with the Charter of the United Nations,
   Mindful of the universal condemnation of the persecution of the Jews under the Nazis and of the concern of people in all countries that Eichmann should be brought to appropriate justice for the crimes of which he is accused, ...
   1. Declares that acts such as that under consideration, which affect the sovereignty of a Member State and therefore cause international friction, may, if repeated, endanger international peace and security;
   2. Requests the Government of Israel to make appropriate reparation in accordance with the Charter of the United Nations and the rules of international law;
   3. Expresses the hope that the traditionally friendly relations between Argentina and Israel will be advanced.

Pursuant to this Resolution the two Governments reached agreement on the settlement of the dispute between them, and on August 3, 1960, issued the following joint communiqué:

The Governments of Argentina and Israel, animated by a desire to give effect to the resolution of the Security Council of June 23, 1960, in so far as the hope was expressed that the traditionally friendly relations between the two countries will be advanced, resolve to regard as closed the incident which arose out of the action taken by citizens of Israel, which infringed the fundamental rights of the State of Argentina.[80] ...

41. It is an established rule of law that a person being tried for an offence against the laws of a State may not oppose his trial by reason of the illegality of his arrest or of the means whereby he was brought within the

---

[79] Ed. Above, p.230.
[80] Ed. Earlier, Argentina had "requested appropriate reparation for the act, namely the return of Eichmann, for which it set a time limit of one week, and the punishment of those guilty of violating Argentine territory": UN Doc. S/4336.

jurisdiction of that State. The courts in England, the United States and Israel have constantly held that the circumstances of the arrest and the mode of bringing of the accused into the territory of the State have no relevance to his trial, and they have consistently refused in all instances to enter upon an examination of these circumstances. ...

In *Ex p. Elliott* [1949] 1 All E.R. 373, the Court heard an application for habeas corpus by a British soldier who had deserted his unit in 1946, was arrested in Belgium in 1948 by two British military officers accompanied by two Belgian police officers, was transferred by the British military authorities to England and was there held in custody pending his trial for desertion. Counsel for the applicant pleaded inter alia, that the British authorities in Belgium had no power to arrest the applicant and that he was arrested contrary to Belgian law. Lord Goddard dismissed the application, saying in his judgment (at p. 376):

... If a person is arrested abroad and he is brought before a court in this country charged with an offence which that court has jurisdiction to hear, it is no answer for him to say, he being then in lawful custody in this country: "I was arrested contrary to the laws of the State of A or the State of B where I was actually arrested." He is in custody before the court which has jurisdiction to try him. What is it suggested that the court can do? The court cannot dismiss the charge at once without its being heard. He is charged with an offence against English law, the law applicable to the case.

42. That principle is also acknowledged in Palestine case law. ...

In *Afouneh v. Attorney-General*, Cr.A. 14/42, (1942) 9 P.L.R. 63,[81] the Supreme Court [stated]:

In our opinion, the law is correctly stated in volume 4 of Moore's *Digest of International Law*, at p. 311 ... :
"Where a fugitive is brought back by kidnapping, or by other irregular means, and not under an extradition treaty, he cannot, although an extradition treaty exists between the two countries, set up in answer to the indictment the unlawful manner in which he was brought within the jurisdiction of the court. It belongs exclusively to the government from whose territory he was wrongfully taken to complain of the violation of its rights."[82] ...

48. The Anglo-Saxon rule has been accepted by Continental jurists as well. ...[83]

49. Criticism of English and American case law from the point of view of international law has been levelled by Dickinson, "Jurisdiction Following Seizure or Arrest in Violation of International Law," in (1934) 28 *American Journal of International Law*, 231, and Morgenstern, "Jurisdiction in Seizures Effected in Violation of International Law," in (1952) 29 *British Year Book of International Law*, 265. See also Lauterpacht in (1948) 64 *Law Quarterly Review*, 100, note (14). It is not for us to enter into this controversy between international jurists, but we would draw attention to two important points for this case: (1) the critics admit that the established rule is as summarized above; (2) in the case, before us the controversy is immaterial.

... [Dickinson] suggests the following provision, in Harvard Research (p. 653) for which he is responsible, as part of the "Draft Convention on Jurisdiction with Respect to Crime":

---

[81]   Ed. (1941–42) 10 A.D. 327 at 328.

[82]   Ed. Moore relied on *Kerr v Illinois*, 119 U.S. 436 (1886), as his authority for this proposition. In that case, an agent acting for the state of Illinois went to Peru with a warrant for the extradition of Kerr under the extradition treaty between the US and Peru. At the time, Peru was at war with Chile and most of Peru, including Lima, was in Chilean hands. In this confused situation, the agent approached the Chilean military authorities in Lima and, with their assistance, obtained custody of Kerr and took him back to Illinois. No approach was made to the Peruvian Government, which was still in existence in retreat, and no recourse was had to the extradition treaty. Peru did not protest against the agent's action or against Kerr's trial. The US Supreme Court ruled that Kerr's trial was not contrary to the US constitution. For the view that the case involved no violation of Peruvian territorial sovereignty because the Chilean military authorities were competent, in the situation prevailing at the time, to surrender Kerr, see Fairman (1953) 47 A.J.I.L. 678.

[83]   Ed. See, e.g. (after the *Eichmann* case) the decision of the French Court of Cassation (Criminal Chamber) in *Re Argoud* (1964) 45 I.L.R. 90. The accused, a French national, who had been sentenced to death *in absentia* by a French military court for his part in insurrectionist activities and against whom a warrant for arrest was outstanding in respect of subsequent similar conduct, was arrested in Paris after being found there, bound and gagged, following a "tip off". He had been abducted in Munich and brought to Paris by persons who, for the purposes of argument, were taken to be French agents. After noting that the Federal Republic of Germany would have a claim to reparation and that no such claim had been presented, the court ruled that the illegality of the accused's abduction did not rob it of jurisdiction.

Article 16. Apprehension in Violation of International Law. In exercising jurisdiction under this Convention, no State shall prosecute or punish any person who has been brought within its territory or a place subject to its authority by recourse to measures in violation of international law or international convention *without first obtaining the consent of the State or States whose rights have been violated by such measures.* (Emphasis is ours.)

... He proposes this article *de lege ferenda* to ensure "an additional and highly desirable sanction for international law" (p. 624). ...

50. ... the question of the violation of international law by the manner in which the accused was brought into the territory of a country arises at the international level, namely, the relations between the two countries concerned alone, and must find its solution at such level. ...

By the joint decision of the Governments of Argentina and Israel of August 3, 1960 ... the country whose sovereignty was violated has waived its claims, including the claim for the return of the accused, and any violation of international law which might have been involved in the "incident" in question has been "cured." According to the principles of international law no doubt can therefore be cast on the jurisdiction of Israel to bring the accused to trial after August 3, 1960. After that date, no cause remained, in respect of a violation of international law, which could have served to support a plea against his trial in Israel.

Notes

1. *Protective principle*. The Harvard Research found that most, if not all, states used this principle to a greater or lesser extent. Great Britain and the United States used it less than most other states.[84] The Commentary to the Harvard Research Draft Convention suggested that use of the protective principle was justifiable as a basis for jurisdiction because of "the inadequacy of most national legislation punishing offences committed within the territory against the security, integrity and independence of foreign states."[85] It also stated:

    "In view of the fact that an overwhelming majority of States have enacted such legislation, [i.e. legislation relying on the protective principle], it is hardly possible to conclude that such legislation is necessarily in excess of competence as recognised by contemporary international law."[86]

    An example of the general acceptance of the protective principle is found in the doctrine of the contiguous zone.[87] Would the principle allow State A to exercise criminal jurisdiction over the officials of State B in respect of their actions in the execution of an unfriendly policy (e.g. a trade embargo) of State B towards State A?[88] Who has the final word as to the danger to a state's security, etc.? The state concerned?

2. Was Israel justified in relying on the protective principle to prosecute the accused in the *Eichmann* case for acts committed *before* Israel came into being?[89]

3. On the *universality principle*, which was also relied upon as a basis for jurisdiction in the *Eichmann* case, see the *Arrest Warrant* case, below, p.250.

---

[84] For its use in UK law, see, e.g. the *Joyce* case, above, p.243; *Molvan v Att.-Gen. for Palestine* [1948] A.C. 351, PC; the Merchant Shipping Act 1995, s.137 (shipping casualties: oil pollution prevention powers); and the Criminal Jurisdiction Act 1975 s.1, (giving Northern Irish courts jurisdiction over listed offences committed in Ireland across the border).

[85] (1935) 29 A.J.I.L. Supp. 552.

[86] [1935] 29 A.J.I.L. Supp. at p.556.

[87] See below, p.384.

[88] cf. Greig, *International Law* (2nd edn 1976), p.389.

[89] See (1935) 29 A.J.I.L. Supp. 558.

4. On the "linking point" doctrine of jurisdiction (see para.31, *Eichmann* judgment), note the fol-
    lowing suggestion by Mann,[90] who was considering both civil and criminal jurisdiction:

    > "The conclusion, then, is that a State has (legislative) jurisdiction, if its contact with a given set
    > of facts is so close, so substantial, so direct, so weighty, that legislation in respect of them is in
    > harmony with international law and its various aspects (including the practice of States, the
    > principles of non-interference and reciprocity and the demands of inter-dependence). A merely
    > political, economic, commercial or social interest does not in itself constitute a sufficient
    > connection. Whether another State has an equally close or a closer, or perhaps the closest,
    > contact, is not necessarily an irrelevant question, but cannot be decisive where the probability
    > of concurrent jurisdiction is conceded. . . .
    >
    >   It may be said that the test advocated in these pages would substitute vagueness for
    > certainty. This would be formidable criticism if the principles of jurisdiction in fact were at
    > present defined with certainty. . . .
    >
    >   Finally, from the point of view of the progressive evolution of international law it would no
    > doubt be desirable if the principle of exclusivity would come to be accepted for the purpose of
    > jurisdiction, if, in other words, by common consent jurisdiction in respect of a given set of acts
    > were exercised by one State only. Such a development cannot even begin while the doctrine of
    > jurisdiction is embedded in the procrustean law of territoriality. It is, however, likely to be
    > promoted by a doctrine which bases jurisdiction upon closeness of connection."

5. *A fair trial.* It is clear that Eichmann was given a scrupulously fair hearing. Might it nonetheless be
    argued that, in terms of justice not only being done but being seen to be done, a court other than
    an Israeli court should have tried Eichmann?[91]

6. *Illegally obtained custody*[92] In the *Savarkar Case*,[93] an Indian who was being returned to India
    from Great Britain under the Fugitive Offenders Act 1881 escaped and swam ashore in Marseilles
    harbour. A French policeman arrested him and handed him over to the British policeman who
    had come ashore in pursuit. Although the French police in Marseilles had been informed of the
    presence of Savarkar on board, the French policeman who made the arrest thought that he was
    handing back a member of the crew who had committed an offence on board. France alleged a
    violation of its territorial sovereignty and asked for the return of Savarkar to it as restitution. The
    Permanent Court of Arbitration decided in favour of Great Britain for the following reasons:

    > ". . . it is manifest that the case is not one of recourse to fraud or force in order to obtain
    > possession of a person who had taken refuge in foreign territory, and that there was not, in the
    > circumstances of the arrest and delivery of Savarkar to the British authorities and of his
    > removal to India, anything in the nature of a violation of the sovereignty of France, and that all
    > those who took part in the matter certainly acted in good faith and had no thought of doing
    > anything unlawful . . . while admitting that an irregularity was committed by the arrest of
    > Savarkar and by his being handed over to the British police, there is no rule of international
    > law imposing, in circumstances such as those which have been set out above, any obligation

---

90 Above, p.227, n.1, pp.49–51.
91 It would seem that one state with territorial jurisdiction, Poland, offered to try Eichmann: Fawcett, above, n.63, p.206.
92 See Cardozo (1961) 55 A.J.I.L. 127; Evans (1964) 40 B.Y.I.L. 77; O'Higgins (1960) 36 B.Y.I.L. 279.
93 *France v G.B.* Scott, (1911) Hague Court Reports 275.

on the Power which has in its custody a prisoner, to restore him because of a mistake committed by the foreign agent who delivered him up to that Power."[94]

In the *Lawler Incident*,[95] in 1860, a convict escaped from prison in Gibraltar. He was arrested by a British warder across the border in Spain and taken back to Gibraltar without Spanish consent. The British Law Officers advised:

"A plain breach of international law having occurred, we deem it to be the duty of the State, into whose territory the individual, thus wrongfully deported, was conveyed, to restore the aggrieved State, upon its request to that effect, as far as possible, to its original position."[96]

Fawcett[97] suggests the following limitation upon the duty to return:

". . . it might perhaps be said, in the case of irregular capture and removal for trial of a criminal *jure gentium*, that the State, from which he is taken, may only demand his reconduction if two conditions are satisfied: that that State is the *forum conveniens* for his trial, and that it declares an intention to put him on trial. If these conditions are not satisfied, then the State must accept reparation in another form, since otherwise the interest of justice would be defeated."

The same author[98] also points out that in the *Corfu Channel* Case,[99] the International Court of Justice allowed evidence to be introduced, and subsequently relied upon that evidence in its judgment, that had been obtained by a British minesweeping exercise which the Court had ruled to be a violation of Albanian territorial sovereignty.

The Jerusalem court cited *Ex p. Elliott* as an authority for the proposition that it could exercise jurisdiction over Eichmann although he had been illegally abducted from Argentina. There were a number of inconsistent decisions on this point after the *Elliott* case, but the law has now to an extent been clarified by *R. v Horseferry Road Magistrates Court, Ex p. Bennett*,[100] which reaches the opposite conclusion to that in the *Elliott* case. In the *Bennett* case, a New Zealand national who was wanted for fraud offences committed in England was located in South Africa. After consulting with the Crown Prosecution Service, the English police decided not to seek his extradition under the Extradition Act 1989. However, the defendant was arrested by the South African police and deported to New Zealand, via Taipei. On arrival at Taipei, he was arrested by South African police and flown back to Johannesburg. There he was put, handcuffed, on a plane to Heathrow, where he was arrested and committed for trial. His appeal against committal for trial was allowed.[101] On the question of illegal abduction, Lord Griffiths stated:

---

94 Above n.93.
95 1 McNair 78.
96 1 McNair 78. For an incident in which Canada protested at the kidnapping in Toronto and return to Florida of a fugitive suspect, extradition not having been requested, see (1984) 78 A.J.I.L. 207.
97 Fawcett, above, n.63, pp.199–200.
98 Fawcett, above, n.63, p.201.
99 Below, p.341.
100 [1994] 1 A.C. 42 HL. See Choo (1994) 57 M.L.R. 626; and Wedgwood (1995) 89 A.J.I.L. 142. On post-*Bennett* English cases, see Warbrick (2000) 49 I.C.L.Q. 489.
101 However, he was then transferred to Scotland and successfully prosecuted there, the Scottish court deciding that there had *not* been an abuse of process on the facts: *Bennett v HM Advocate*, 1995 S.L.T. 510.

"In the present case there is no suggestion that the appellant cannot have a fair trial, nor could it be suggested that it would have been unfair to try him if he had been returned to this country through extradition procedures. If the court is to have the power to interfere with the prosecution in the present circumstances it must be because the judiciary accept a responsibility for the maintenance of the rule of law that embraces a willingness to oversee executive action and to refuse to countenance behaviour that threatens either basic human rights or the rule of law.

My Lords, I have no doubt that the judiciary should accept this responsibility in the field of criminal law. ... if it comes to the attention of the court that there has been a serious abuse of power it should, in my view, express its disapproval by refusing to act upon it.

... Extradition procedures are designed not only to ensure that criminals are returned from one country to another but also to protect the rights of those who are accused of crimes by the requesting country. Thus sufficient evidence has to be produced to show a prima facie case against the accused and the rule of speciality protects the accused from being tried for any crime other than that for which he was extradited. If a practice developed in which the police or prosecuting authorities of this country ignored extradition procedures and secured the return of an accused by a mere request to police colleagues in another country they would be flouting the extradition procedures and depriving the accused of the safeguards built into the extradition process for his benefit. It is to my mind unthinkable that in such circumstances the court should declare itself to be powerless and stand idly by ...

The courts, of course, have no power to apply direct discipline to the police or the prosecuting authorities, but they can refuse to allow them to take advantage of abuse of power by regarding their behaviour as an abuse of process and thus preventing a prosecution.

In my view your Lordships should now declare that where process of law is available to return an accused to this country through extradition procedures our courts will refuse to try him if he has been forcibly brought within our jurisdiction in disregard of those procedures by a process to which our own police, prosecuting or other executive authorities have been a knowing party.

If extradition is not available very different considerations will arise on which I express no opinion."

As was pointed out by Lord Oliver, dissenting, the defendant had a civil remedy in respect of his abduction. Note also that, in contrast with the *Eichmann* case, the territorial sovereignty of South Africa, which allegedly colluded rather than protested, was not violated. Should it matter that the offence is one that concerns the security of the state, as in the *Eichmann* case, rather than the enforcement of the ordinary criminal law? Might the *Bennett* approach be the only way of preventing abductions or collusion by state agents?[102]

Approaches in other states vary.[103] In the *Bennett* case, the House of Lords had before it decisions from New Zealand[104] and South African[105] courts ruling against the exercise of jur-

---

[102] For other examples of successful abductions, see those by Israel of Mordechai Vanunu (1986) (abducted and convicted for revealing Israeli nuclear secrets) and by France of the terrorist "Carlos the Jackal" (1994) (kidnapped on the street in Sudan for terrorist offences in France).

[103] See Gilbert, *Transnational Fugitive Offenders in International Law* (1998).

[104] *R. v Hartley* [1978] 2 N.Z.L.R. 199 (Australian police put him on a plane to face a murder charge after a telephone call from the New Zealand police).

[105] *S. v Ebrahim*, 1991 (2) S.A. 553, S. African Ct. App. (abduction from Swaziland by South African agents to face a treason trial). See Dugard (1991) 7 S.A.J.L. 199.

isdiction in cases of abduction. In contrast, in *U.S. v Alvarez-Machain*,[106] a Mexican national had been abducted to the US from Mexico by US Drug Enforcement Administration agents to face a charge of murdering another agent of the Administration. Mexico requested his return for criminal prosecution in connection with the murder. Although recognising the abduction as "shocking", the US Supreme Court held that the exercise of criminal jurisdiction in the US was not unconstitutional since there had been no breach of the US-Mexican extradition treaty (which did not prohibit abductions).[107]

THE ARREST WARRANT CASE[108]

Democratic Republic of the Congo v Belgium

I.C.J. Rep 2002, p.3

In April 2000, a Belgian investigating judge, acting under a 1993 Law, issued an international arrest warrant *in absentia* for Abdulaye Yerodia Ndombasi, a national of the Democratic Republic of the Congo (DRC), charging him with offences constituting war crimes amounting to grave breaches of the 1949 Geneva Conventions and crimes against humanity. These were allegedly committed by speeches made by the accused in August 1998 that incited racial hatred and led to murder and lynchings by others.

The accused was not in Belgium when the warrant was issued. In June 2000, it was both sent to the DRC Government and transmitted to Interpol, which circulated it to other states. Under the 1993 Law, Belgium had criminal jurisdiction in respect of the offences concerned "wheresoever they may have been committed." No Belgian national was a victim of the alleged offences. Nor was there any other link between Belgium and the accused.

When the warrant was issued and circulated, the accused was the DRC Minister for Foreign Affairs. In November 2000, he was moved to become Minister of Education, and ceased to hold government office altogether from mid-April 2001.

In this case, the DRC filed an "optional clause" application against Belgium claiming in effect that Belgium lacked jurisdiction in international law to issue and circulate the warrant and that, in any event, Mr Yerodia had diplomatic immunity as a Minister for Foreign Affairs.

The Court upheld the DRC's immunity claim, by 13 votes to 3. Having done so, it did not consider the question of Belgian jurisdiction. However, several of the judges examined the jurisdiction question in their individual opinions, extracts from which are printed below. Extracts from the Court's judgment on the immunity claim are printed below, p.292.

JOINT SEPARATE OPINION OF JUDGES HIGGINS, KOOIJMANS AND BUERGENTHAL

The opinion reviews the Australian and UK war crimes legislation and other national legislation providing for extraterritorial criminal jurisdiction in respect of international crimes and continues:

---

[106] (1992) 119 L.Ed. 2d 441. Illegal abduction was also held irrelevant in the *Yunis* case, above, p.239. In the *Bennett* case, Lord Griffiths distinguished the *Alvarez* case on the ground that it ruled on the question whether criminal jurisdiction actually existed, whereas *Bennett* was about the exercise of judicial discretion not to take a case where jurisdiction existed. On the US case law, see Nadelmann (1993) 25 N.Y.U.J.I.P. 813; and Teson (1994) 31 C.J.T.L. 551.

[107] The *Kerr Case*, above, p.245, n.82, was followed.

[108] See Boister (2000) 7 J.C.S.L. 293; Wickremasinghe (2001) 50 I.C.L.Q. 670.

21. All of these [provisions] illustrate the trend to provide for the trial and punishment under international law of certain crimes that have been committed extraterritorially. But none of them ... represent a classical assertion of a universal jurisdiction over particular offences committed elsewhere by persons having no relationship or connection with the forum State.

22. The case law under these provisions has largely been cautious so far as reliance on universal jurisdiction is concerned. ...

The opinion refers to the *Pinochet* case and cases in other jurisdictions under the above national legislative provisions and concludes:

26. In some of the literature on the subject it is asserted that the great international treaties on crimes and offences evidence universality as a ground for the exercise of jurisdiction recognized in international law. ... This is doubtful. ...

The opinion reviews the common provisions in the 1949 Geneva Conventions and various other treaties on international crimes, including the 1970 Hague Convention on the Seizure of Aircraft and the 1984 Convention against Torture:

28. Article 49 of the First Geneva Convention, Article 50 of the Second Geneva Convention, Article 129 of the Third Geneva Convention and Article 146 of the Fourth Geneva Convention, all of 12 August 1949, provide:

"Each High Contracting Party shall be under obligation to search for persons alleged to have committed, or to have ordered to be committed, ... grave breaches, and shall bring such persons, regardless of their nationality, before its own courts. It may also, if it prefers, and in accordance with the provisions of its own legislation, hand such persons over for trial to another High Contracting Party concerned, provided such High Contracting Party has made out a *prima facie* case." ...

31. No territorial or nationality linkage is envisaged [in the text of the Geneva Conventions], suggesting a true universality principle ... But a different interpretation [of the texts] is given in the authoritative Pictet Commentary: *Geneva Convention for the Amelioration of the Condition of the Wounded and Sick in Armed Forces in the Field* (1952), which contends that this obligation was understood as being an obligation upon States parties to search for offenders who may be on their territory. Is it a true example of universality, if the obligation to search is restricted to the [state's] own territory? Does the obligation to search imply a permission to persecute in absentia, if the search had no result? ...

41. The parties to these treaties agreed both to grounds of jurisdiction and as to the obligation to take the measures necessary to establish such jurisdiction. The specified grounds relied on links of nationality of the offender, or the ship or aircraft concerned, or of the victim. See, for example, Article 4(1) Hague Convention; Article 3(1) Tokyo Convention; Article 5, Hostages Convention; Article 5, Torture Convention. These may properly be described as treaty-based broad extraterritorial jurisdiction. But in addition to these were the parallel provisions whereby a State party in whose jurisdiction the alleged perpetrator of such offences is found, shall prosecute him or extradite him. By the loose use of language the latter has come to be referred to as "universal jurisdiction", though this is really an obligatory territorial jurisdiction over persons, albeit in relation to acts committed elsewhere.

42. Whether this obligation ... is an obligation only of treaty law, *inter partes* or, whether it is now, *at least as regards the offences articulated in the treaties*, an obligation of customary international law was pleaded by the Parties in this case but not addressed in any great detail.

43. Nor was the question of whether any such general obligation applies to crimes against humanity, given that those too are regarded everywhere as comparably heinous crimes. Accordingly, we offer no view on these aspects.

44. However, we note that the inaccurately termed "universal jurisdiction principle" in these treaties is a principle of *obligation*, while the question in this case is whether Belgium had the right to issue and circulate the arrest warrant if it so chose. ...

45. That there is no established practice in which States exercise universal jurisdiction, properly so called,[109] is undeniable. As we have seen, virtually all national legislation envisages links of some sort to the forum State; and no case law exists in which pure universal jurisdiction has formed the basis of jurisdiction. This does not necessarily indicate, however, that such an exercise would be unlawful. In the first place, national legislation reflects the circumstances in which a State provides in its own law the ability to exercise jurisdiction. But a State is not required to legislate up to the full scope of the jurisdiction allowed by international law. The war crimes legislation of Australia and the United Kingdom afford examples of countries making more confined choices for the exercise of jurisdiction. Further, many countries have no national legislation for the exercise of well recognized forms of extraterritorial jurisdiction, sometimes notwithstanding treaty obligations to enable themselves so to act. National legislation may be illuminating as to the issue of universal jurisdiction, but not conclusive as to its legality. Moreover, while none of the national case law to which we have referred happens to be based on the exercise of a universal jurisdiction properly so called, there is equally nothing in this case law which evidences an *opinio juris* on the illegality of such a jurisdiction. In short, national legislation and case law,—that is, State practice—is neutral as to exercise of universal jurisdiction.

46. There are, moreover, certain indications that a universal criminal jurisdiction for certain international crimes is clearly not regarded as unlawful. The duty to prosecute under those treaties which contain the *aut dedere aut prosequi* [extradite or prosecute] provisions opens the door to a jurisdiction based on the heinous nature of the crime rather than on links of territoriality or nationality (whether as perpetrator or victim). The 1949 Geneva Conventions lend support to this possibility, and are widely regarded as today reflecting customary international law. ...

47. The contemporary trends, reflecting international relations as they stand at the beginning of the new century, are striking. The movement is towards bases of jurisdiction other than territoriality. "Effects" or "impact" jurisdiction is embraced both by the United States and, with certain qualifications, by the European Union. Passive personality jurisdiction, for so long regarded as controversial, is now reflected not only in the legislation of various countries (the Unites States, Ch. 113A, 1986 Omnibus Diplomatic and Antiterrorism Act; France, art. 689, Code of Criminal Procedure, 1975), and today meets with relatively little opposition, at least so far as a particular category of offences is concerned. ...

49. Belgium—and also many writers on this subject—find support for the exercise of a universal criminal jurisdiction *in absentia* in the *"Lotus"* case. Although the case was clearly decided on the basis of jurisdiction over damage to a vessel of the Turkish navy and to Turkish nationals, it is the famous dictum of the Permanent Court which has attracted particular attention [see above, p.231]. ...

The Court [in the Lotus case] noted the importance of the territorial character of criminal law but also the fact that all or nearly all systems of law extend their action to offences committed outside the territory of the State which adopts them, and they do so in ways which vary from State to State. After examining the issue the Court finally concluded that for an exercise of extraterritorial criminal jurisdiction (other than within the territory of another State) it was equally necessary to "prove the existences of a principle of international law restricting the discretion of States as regards criminal legislation".

50. ... this celebrated dictum ... represents a continuing potential in the context of jurisdiction over international crimes.

51. That being said, the dictum represents the high water mark of *laissez-faire* in international relations, and an era that has been significantly overtaken by other tendencies. The underlying idea of universal jurisdiction properly so-called (as in the case of piracy, and possibly in the Geneva Conventions of 1949), as well as the *aut dedere aut prosequi* variation, is a common endeavour in the face of atrocities. The series of multilateral treaties with their special jurisdictional provisions reflect a determination by the international community that those engaged in war crimes, hijacking, hostage taking, torture should not go unpunished. Although crimes against humanity are not yet the object of a distinct convention, a comparable international indignation at such acts is not to be doubted. ...

52. We may thus agree with the authors of the Oppenheim, 9th Edition, at page 998, that:

"While no general rule of positive international law can as yet be asserted which gives states the right to punish foreign nationals for crimes against humanity in the same way as they are, for instance, entitled to punish acts of piracy, there are clear indications pointing to the gradual evolution of a significant principle of international law to that effect."

---

[109] Ed., i.e. where the individual is not even on the territory of the state when jurisdiction in exercised.

53. This brings us once more to the particular point that divides the Parties in this case: is it a precondition of the assertion of universal jurisdiction that the accused be within the territory?

54. Considerable confusion surrounds this topic, not helped by the fact that legislators, courts and writers alike frequently fail to specify the precise temporal moment at which any such requirement is said to be in play. Is the presence of the accused within the jurisdiction said to be required at the time the offence was committed? At the time the arrest warrant is issued? Or at the time of the trial itself? An examination of national legislation, cases and writings reveals a wide variety of temporal linkages to the assertion of jurisdiction. This incoherent practice cannot be said to evidence a precondition to any exercise of universal criminal jurisdiction. The fact that in the past the only clear example of an agreed exercise of universal jurisdiction was in respect of piracy, *outside of any territorial jurisdiction*, is not determinative. The only prohibitive rule (repeated by the Permanent Court in the *"Lotus"* case) is that criminal jurisdiction should not be exercised, without permission, within the territory of another State. The Belgian arrest warrant envisaged the arrest of Mr. Yerodia in Belgium, or the possibility of his arrest in third States at the discretion of the States concerned. This would in principle seem to violate no existing prohibiting rule of international law. . . .

57. On what basis is it claimed, alternatively, that an arrest warrant may not be issued for non-nationals in respect of offences occurring outside the jurisdiction? The textual provisions themselves of the 1949 Geneva Convention and the First Additional Protocol give no support to this view. The great treaties on aerial offences, hijacking, narcotics and torture are built around the concept of *aut dedere aut prosequi. Definitionally, this envisages presence on the territory.* There cannot be an obligation to extradite someone you choose not to try unless that person is within your reach. National legislation, enacted to give effect to these treaties, quite naturally also may make mention of the necessity of the presence of the accused. Those sensible realities are critical for the obligatory exercise of *aut dedere aut prosequi* jurisdiction, but cannot be interpreted *a contrario so as to exclude a* voluntary exercise of a universal jurisdiction.

58. If the underlying purpose of designating certain acts as international crimes is to authorize a wide jurisdiction to be asserted over persons committing them, there is no rule of international law (and certainly not the *aut dedere* principle) which makes illegal co-operative overt acts designed to secure their presence within a State wishing to exercise jurisdiction.

59. If, as we believe to be the case, a State may choose to exercise a universal criminal jurisdiction *in absentia*, it must also ensure that certain safeguards are in place. They are absolutely essential to prevent abuse and to ensure that the rejection of impunity does not jeopardize stable relations between States.

No exercise of criminal jurisdiction may occur which fails to respect the inviolability or infringes the immunities of the person concerned. . . . Commencing an investigation on the basis of which an arrest warrant may later be issued does not of itself violate those principles [of inviolability and impunity]. . . .

A State contemplating bringing criminal charges based on universal jurisdiction must first offer to the national State of the prospective accused person the opportunity itself to act upon the charges con-cerned. . . .

Further, such charges may only be laid by a prosecutor or *juge d'instruction* who acts in full independence, without links to or control by the Government of that State. . . .

60. It is equally necessary that universal criminal jurisdiction be exercised only over those crimes regarded as the most heinous by the international community.

61. Piracy is the classical example. This jurisdiction was, of course, exercised on the high seas and not as an enforcement jurisdiction within the territory of a non-agreeing State. But this historical fact does not mean that universal jurisdiction only exists with regard to crimes committed on the high seas or in other places outside national territorial jurisdiction. Of decisive importance is that this jurisdiction was regarded as lawful because the international community regarded piracy as damaging to the interests of all. War crimes and crimes against humanity are no less harmful to the interests of all because they do not usually occur on the high seas. War crimes (already since 1949 perhaps a treaty-based provision for universal jurisdiction) may be added to the list. The specification of their content is largely based upon the 1949 Conventions and those parts of the 1977 Additional Protocols that reflect general international law. Recent years have also seen the phenomenon of an alignment of national jurisdictional legislation on war crimes, specifying those crimes under the statutes of the ICTY, ICTR and the intended ICC. . . .

64. The arrest warrant issued against Mr. Yerodia accuses him both of war crimes and of crimes against humanity. As regards the latter, charges of incitement to racial hatred, which are said to have led to murders and lynchings, were specified. Fitting [. . .] this charge within the generally understood substantive context of crimes against humanity is not without its problems. "Racial hatred" would need to be assimilated to "persecution on racial grounds", or, on the particular facts, to mass murder and extermination. Incitement to perform any of the acts is not in terms listed in the usual definitions of crimes against humanity, nor is it explicitly mentioned in the

Statutes of the ICTY or the ICTR, nor in the Rome Statute for the ICC. However, Article 7(1) of the ICTY and Article 6(1) of the ICTR do stipulate that "any person who planned, instigated, ordered, committed or otherwise aided and abetted in the planning, preparation or execution of a crime referred to [in the relevant articles: crimes against humanity being among them] shall be individually responsible for the crime". In the *Akayesu* Judgment (96-4-T) a Chamber of the ICTR has held that liability for a crime against humanity includes liability through incitement to commit the crime concerned (paras.481–482). The matter is dealt with in a comparable way in Article 25(3) of the Rome Statute.

65. It would seem (without in any way pronouncing upon whether Mr. Yerodia did or did not perform the acts with which he is charged in the warrant) that the acts alleged do fall within the concept of "crimes against humanity" and would be within that small category in respect of which an exercise of universal jurisdiction is not precluded under international law. ...

69. We do not feel it can be said that ... there was no exercise of jurisdiction as such that could attract immunity or infringe the Congo's sovereignty. If a State issues an arrest warrant against the national of another State, that other State is entitled to treat it as such—certainly unless the issuing State draws to the attention of the national State the clauses and provisions said to vacate the warrant of all efficacy. Belgium had conceded that the purpose of the international circulation of the warrant was "to establish a legal basis for the arrest of Mr. Yerodia ... abroad and his subsequent extradition to Belgium". An international arrest warrant, even though a Red Notice[110] has not yet been linked, is analogous to the locking-on of radar to an aircraft: it is already a statement of willingness and ability to act and as such may be perceived as a threat so to do at a moment of Belgium's choosing. Even if the action of a third State is required, the ground has been prepared.

SEPARATE OPINION OF PRESIDENT GUILLAUME

... [customary] international law knows only one true case of universal jurisdiction: piracy. Further, a number of international conventions[111] provide for the establishment of subsidiary universal jurisdiction for purposes of the trial of certain offenders arrested on national territory and not extradited to a foreign country. Universal jurisdiction *in absentia* as applied in the present case is unknown to international law.

13. Having found that neither treaty law not international customary law provide a State with the possibility of conferring universal jurisdiction on its courts where the author of the offence is not present on its territory, Belgium contends lastly that, even in the absence of any treaty or custom to this effect, it enjoyed total freedom of action. To this end it cites from the Judgment of the Permanent Court of International Justice in the *"Lotus"* case:

> "Far from laying down a general prohibition to the effect that States may not extend the application of their laws and the jurisdiction of their courts to persons, property and acts outside their territory, [international law] leaves them in this respect a wide measure of discretion which is only limited in certain cases by prohibitive rules ..."

Hence, so Belgium claimed, in the absence of any prohibitive rule it was entitled to confer upon itself a universal jurisdiction *in absentia*.

14. This argument is hardly persuasive. ...

---

[110]   Ed. The Belgian warrant was circulated by Interpol to states for information purposes only; an Interpol Red Notice is a request for provisional arrest except in those legal systems that do not provide for such arrest.

[111]   Ed. The opinion refers to the 1970 Hague Convention on the Seizure of Aircraft and the following other conventions (para.8):

> "the Montreal Convention for the Suppression of Unlawful Acts against the Safety of Civil Aviation of 23 September 1971; the New York Conevention on the Prevention and Punishment of Crimes against Internationally Protected Persons, including Diplomatic Agents, of 14 December 1973; the New York Convention Against the Taking of Hostages of 17 December 1979; the Vienna Convention on the Physical Protection of Nuclear Materials of 3 March 1980; the New York Convention Against Torture and Other Cruel, Inhuman or Degrading Treatment or Punishment of 10 December 1984; the Montreal Protocol of 24 February 1988 concerning acts of violence at airports; the Rome Convention for the Suppression of Unlawful Acts Against the Safety of Maritime Navigation of 10 March 1988; the Protocol of the same date concerning the safety of platforms located on the continental shelf; the Vienna Convention Against Illicit Traffic in Narcotic Drugs and Pyschotropic Substances of 20 December 1988; the New York Convention for the Suppression of Terrorist Bombings of 15 December 1997; and finally the New York Convention for the Suppression of the Financing of Terrorism of 9 December 1999."

Having noted that this was not the basis for the Court's decision in the *Lotus* case, which was instead that Turkey had territorial jurisdiction because the collision had its effect on a Turkish ship, the opinion states:

15. The absence of a decision by the Permanent Court on the point was understandable in 1927, given the sparse treaty law at that time. The situation is different today, it seems to me—totally different. The adoption of the United Nations Charter proclaiming the sovereign equality of States, and the appearance on the international scene of new States, born of decolonization, have strengthened the territorial principle. International criminal law has itself undergone considerable development and constitutes today an impressive legal *corpus*. It recognizes in many situations the possibility, or indeed the obligation, for a State other than that on whose territory the offence was committed to confer jurisdiction on its courts to prosecute the authors of certain crimes where they are present on its territory. International criminal courts have been created. But at no time has it been envisaged that jurisdiction should be conferred upon the courts of every State in the world to prosecute such crimes, whoever their authors and victims and irrespective of the place where the offender is to be found. To do this would, moreover, risk creating total judicial chaos. It would also be to encourage the arbitrary for the benefit of the powerful, purportedly acting as agent for an ill-defined "international community". Contrary to what is advocated by certain publicists, such a development would represent not an advance in the law but a step backward.

16. States primarily exercise their criminal jurisdiction on their own territory. In classic international law, they normally have jurisdiction in respect of an offence committed abroad only if the offender, or at least the victim, is of their nationality, or if the crime threatens their internal or external security. Additionally, they may exercise jurisdiction in cases of piracy and in the situations of subsidiary universal jurisdiction provided for by various conventions if the offender is present on their territory. But apart from these cases, international law does not accept universal jurisdiction; still less does it accept universal jurisdiction *in absentia*.

Notes

1. These two opinions recognise that "subsidiary universal jurisdiction"[112] has been provided as an *obligation* in a number of treaties on international crimes such as various kinds of terrorist activities, drug trafficking, torture,[113] etc. In all of these cases, a state in whose territory an alleged offender is present must either extradite him or her to a state that has a link with the offence, or prosecute the alleged offender itself (*aut dedere aut prosequi*). National criminal jurisdiction is not provided by treaty for crimes against humanity.[114] Does either of the two opinions take the view that subsidiary universal jurisdiction exists as a matter of *customary* international law? For any treaty-based crime? Or for crimes against humanity?

2. The two opinions differ on the question whether a state has *voluntary* universality jurisdiction of the sort claimed by Belgium in the case of war crimes or crimes against humanity[115] by which it may exercise jurisdiction (by issuing a warrant, etc.) over an alleged offender who is not on its territory and who has no other link with it. Judges Higgins, Kooijmans and Buergenthal rely upon the dictum in the *Lotus* case to conclude that a state can claim such jurisdiction because it is not prohibited by international law. Do you prefer this view or that of Judge Guillaume? Note also that universal jurisdiction, whether of the *aut dedere aut prosequi* or voluntary kind, is likely to be exercised only rarely by a state that has no link with the case, because of its lack of interest in prosecuting the offender and also because of problems of obtaining witness or other evidence.

---

[112] Judge Guillaume's term. Note that Judges Higgins, Kooijmans and Buergenthal characterise this as territorial jurisdiction (on the part of the state in whose territory the alleged offender is), not universal jurisdiction.

[113] As to torture, see art.5, Torture Convention: see below, p.545, n.71.

[114] There is international criminal jurisdiction before the International Criminal Court and the ad hoc tribunals: see the literature below, p.537, n.75.

[115] Note that both opinions agreed that there is "true" criminal universality jurisdiction in the case of piracy, allowing a state to arrest a pirate ship on the high seas.

3. In 2003, Belgium amended its law in the light of the *Arrest Warrant* case. Ratner[116] explains the
    Belgian "saga" as follows:

    "The Belgian statute dates to 1993 when the government . . . amended the penal code to
    include certain violations of the 1949 Geneva Conventions and 1977 Additional Protocols,
    regardless of where such crimes were committed. . . . In 1999 . . . the law was amended to add
    genocide . . . and crimes against humanity. . . . The 1999 amendment also clarified that the
    official immunity of a person would not prevent the application of the law. Belgium's was
    hardly the world's first domestic statute on universal jurisdiction for human rights abuses, but
    it was the broadest in the crimes it covered and its lack of any required link between the
    suspect, victims, or events, on the one hand, and Belgium, on the other.

    In 2001, the government tried two Rwandan nuns and two Rwandan men for participation
    in the genocide; all four were convicted and sentenced to prison terms ranging from twelve to
    twenty years. In June 2001, twenty-three survivors of the 1982 massacre of Palestinian refu-
    gees by Lebanese militiamen at the Sabra and Shatila camps filed a criminal complaint
    against Ariel Sharon, who was the Israeli defense minister in 1982 and since 2001 has been the
    prime minister of Israel, and Amos Yaron, who had been the Israeli general in charge of the
    Beirut sector in 1982. Like that of many states, Belgium's criminal procedure incorporates the
    system of plaintiff-prosecutors or *constitution de partie civil*, whereby victims may initiate cases
    before an investigating judge. . . . thirty-three Israelis and Belgians initiated proceedings
    against Yasir Arafat under the law. The Court also faced criminal complaints against Cuban
    President Fidel Castro, Iraqi President Saddam Hussein, former DRC foreign minister Abul-
    daye Yerodia, former Iranian President Hashemi Rafsanjani, and others.

    . . . As for Sharon's case, a Belgian appeals court ruled in June 2002 that he and Yaron
    could not be tried because such cases were inadmissible when the defendant was not in
    Belgium. Belgian Prime Minister Guy Verhofstadt expressed support for amending the law to
    permit investigations to proceed in the defendant's absence. On February 12, 2003, the
    Belgian Cour de Cassation overruled the court of appeal, finding that the presence of the
    accused was not necessary under Belgian law for the case to proceed. Nonetheless, it found
    the immunity of sitting heads of state and government to be a principle of customary inter-
    national law. It thus dismissed the case against Sharon but allowed the investigation against
    Yaron to proceed. The tribunal left open the possibility that Sharon could be tried after he left
    office. Israel vehemently protested the action and withdrew its ambassador to Belgium.

    Then, in March 2003, seven Iraqi families requested an investigation of former U.S. Pre-
    sident George H. W. Bush, Vice President (and former Secretary of Defense) Dick Cheney,
    Secretary of State (and former chairman of the joint chiefs of staff) Colin Powell, and retired
    general Norman Schwarzkopf for allegedly committing war crimes during the 1991 Gulf war. In
    response, Secretary Powell warned the Belgian government that Belgium was risking its status
    as a diplomatic capital and the host state for the North Atlantic Treaty Organization (NATO)
    by allowing investigations of those who might visit Belgium. Almost immediately, Verhofstadt
    proposed amendments to the statute to limit its scope.

    In April 2003, parliament amended the law . . . such that only the federal prosecutor could
    initiate cases if the violation was overseas, the offender was not Belgian or located in Belgium,
    and the victim was not Belgian or had not lived in Belgium for three years. Furthermore, the
    prosecutor could refuse to proceed if the complaint was 'manifestly unfounded,' or

---

[116] (2003) 97 A.J.I.L. 888.

in the interest of administration of justice and in respect of Belgium's international obligations, this matter should be brought either before international tribunals, or before a tribunal in the place where the acts were committed, or before the tribunals of a State in which the offender is a national or where he may be found, and as long as this tribunal is competent, independent, impartial and fair.

After passage of the amendments, Israel sent its ambassador back to Belgium.

But the amendment did not prove enough for U.S. officials. On June 12, 2003, Secretary of Defense Donald Rumsfeld announced that the United States would refuse to fund a new headquarters building for NATO in Belgium and consider barring its officials from travelling to meetings there unless Belgium rescinded its law. Rumsfeld stated, 'Belgium appears not to respect the sovereignty of other countries.' Verhofstadt agreed within days to submit further amendments to limit the law's reach to cases with a direct link to Belgium. ...

Under the law that entered into force in early August 2003, Belgian courts can hear cases regarding the three sets of crimes when committed outside Belgium only if the defendant or victim is a citizen or resident of Belgium. For defendants, nationality or residence is determined on the date proceedings commence; for victims, it is the date of the crime. If only the victim has the requisite ties to Belgium, the role of the public prosecutor is extensive: only he can move a case forward (without further recourse for plaintiff-prosecutors) ... Moreover, the new law precludes cases against chiefs of state, heads of government, and foreign ministers while they are in office; others whose 'immunity is recognized by international law'; and persons whose immunity is recognized by a treaty to which Belgium is a party. In addition, no act of arrest may be taken during their stay against targets officially invited to Belgium by its government or by an international organization based in Belgium. Pending cases are to be dismissed unless the plaintiff was a Belgian national or the accused had his principal residence in Belgium at the date of the law's entry into force and the case meets the special criteria noted above."

4. *Universal jurisdiction* issues are again before the ICJ in the *Certain Criminal Proceedings in France* case (2003).[117] There a criminal complaint was filed in France on behalf of several human rights organisations against the President of the Democratic Republic of the Congo ("DRC") and three high officials of the DRC, including General Dabira, the Inspector-General of the Armed Forces, alleging crimes against humanity committed by them in the DRC. A French investigating judge initiated an investigation and General Dabira was arrested and questioned while at his residence in France. He was later released and left the country. An unsuccessful attempt was also made to obtain evidence from the DRC President when he visited France. Under French Law, "any person who has committed outside the territory of the Republic, any of the offences enumerated in these Articles [(including torture)], may be prosecuted and tried by the French courts if that person is present in France." The DRC initiated proceedings before the ICJ claiming, in effect, that France lacked criminal jurisdiction in these cases.

---

[117] See the Order refusing Interim Measures, I.C.J. Rep 2003, p.102.

----

4. STATE IMMUNITY[118]

Notes

The following materials are concerned with the question whether a state can be impleaded before the courts of another state without its consent. There used formerly to be a rule of absolute immunity.[119] Since the 1920s, socialist states and others have come to engage in trading activities (acts *iure gestionis*) as well as exercising the public functions traditionally associated with states (acts *iure imperii*). In response, many states have moved in their practice to a doctrine of restrictive immunity by which a foreign state is allowed immunity for acts *iure imperii* only. The bulk of this practice consists of municipal court decisions. A 1982 study[120] shows that the courts of the great majority of states in which the matter has been considered in recent years (mostly Western states) now favour the doctrine of restrictive immunity. The same study also considers state practice in the form of national legislation and treaties. New legislation, such as the United States Foreign Sovereign Immunities Act 1976[121] and the United Kingdom State Immunity Act 1978[122] applies the restrictive immunity doctrine, as do the two main multilateral treaties on the subject, namely the 1972 European Convention on State Immunity. The The 1972 European Convention on State Immunity[123] and the 2004 UN Convention on Jurisdictional Immunities of States and Their Property.[124] These Conventions allow immunity except in certain listed categories of cases. The extensive bilateral treaty practice strongly supports a restrictive immunity approach as well.

Originally, most of the states that followed the restrictive immunity doctrine were from the West; the Soviet bloc and most developing states (which tended to be socialist) did not. With the demise of the USSR and related developments, only China, India and a small number of developing states now follow the absolute immunity approach. The balance has thus shifted in favour of the restrictive immunity approach. O'Connell's 1970 statement remains correct:

---

[118] See Aust (2004) 53 I.C.L.Q. 255; Badr, *State Immunity: An Analytical and Prognostic View* (1984); Bankas, *The State Immunity Controversy in International Law* (2005); Crawford (1983) 54 B.Y.I.L. 75; Dickinson, Lindsay and Loonam, *State Immunity: Selected Materials and Commentary* (2004); Fox, *The Law of State Immunity* (2nd end. 2008); Schreuer, *State Immunity: Some Recent Developments* (1988); Sinclair 113 (1980–II) 167 Hague Recueil; Sucharitkul, *State Immunities and Trading Activities in International Law* (1959); (1976–I) 149 Hague Recueil 87; (1982) 29 N.Y.I.L. 252; Trooboff (1986–V) 200 Hague Recueil 325.'

[119] The absolute immunity rule was at its peak in such 1920s common law cases as *The Porto Alexandre* [1920] P. 30, CA and *The Pesaro*, 271 U.S. 562 (1926). Civil law jurisprudence has always been more diverse: see Schreuer, *op. cit.*, p.306, n.14, above, n.118, p.1.

[120] 4th Report on Jurisdictional Immunities of States and their Property, 1982, prepared for the ILC by its Special Rapporteur (Sucharitkul), Y.B.I.L.C. 1982, II–1, p. 199. See also the surveys in Sinclair, above, n.118, Ch.II; and Badr, above, n.118, Ch.III; *Materials on Jurisdictional Immunities of States and their Property*, UN Legislative Series, UN Doc. ST/LEG/SER.B/20.

[121] (1976) 15 I.L.M. 1388. See Brower, Bistline and Loomis (1979) 73 A.J.I.L. 200; Delaume (1977) 71 A.J.I.L. 399; Feldman (1985) 35 I.C.L.Q. 302.

[122] Below, p.266.

[123] U.K.T.S. 74 (1979), Cmnd. 7742; (1972) 11 I.L.M. 470. In force 1976. Eight parties including the UK. The 1972 Protocol, has six parties. In force 1985. The UK is not a party to the Protocol. The UK Foreign Office has stated that the 1972 Convention reflects "with sufficient accuracy general State practice in the field of sovereign immunity": see Sinclair, above, n.118, p.258, n.443. On the Convention, see Sinclair (1973) 22 I.C.L.Q. 254, and the Explanatory Report in Cmnd. 5081.

[124] (2005) 44 I.L.M. 801. Not yet in force: see below, p.276. See also the 1926 Brussels Convention for the Unification of Certain Rules Relating to the Immunity of State Owned Vessels, Cmnd.7800; 176 L.N.T.S. 199; Hudson, 3 Int. Leg. 1837. In force 1936, 29 parties to the Convention and to its 1934 Protocol, 176 L.N.T.S. 215; Hudson 6 Int. Leg. 868. The UK is a party, 13 states have become parties since 1949. See Thommen, *Legal Status of Government Merchant Ships in International Law* (1962).

"The most that can be said of customary international law is that it enjoins immunity from the judicial process only in respect of governmental activities that pertain to administration, and does not compel it in respect of other activities which are more truly commercial than administrative."[125]

Adoption of the restrictive immunity approach introduces the problem of classifying acts as *iure gestionis* or *iure imperii*. Other problems (which exist whether absolute or restrictive immunity is preferred) lie in deciding (i) which of the many governmental entities (e.g. public corporations) that might claim to act for a state qualify for immunity and (ii) whether a state may be indirectly impleaded.

The following materials in this section examine the doctrine of state (or sovereign)[126] immunity largely as it applies in United Kingdom law. Note that, quite apart from the doctrine of state immunity, United Kingdom courts also refrain from exercising jurisdiction over the acts of other states on the basis of (1) the act of state and (2) the "non-justiciability" doctrines. By the "act of state" doctrine, the United Kingdom courts will not question a legislative or other act of a foreign state with effect in that state's own territory, unless it is contrary to United Kingdom public policy.[127] By the "non-justiciability" doctrine, they will not adjudicate upon the transactions of foreign states, wherever they occur. In *Buttes Gas Oil Co. v Hammer,*[128] applying the "non-justiciability" doctrine, the House of Lords declined to take jurisdiction in a dispute between two oil companies which would have required it to have ruled on transactions in which four Persian Gulf states participated, concerning, inter alia, continental shelf boundaries.

THE SCHOONER EXCHANGE v MCFADDON

7 Cranch 116 (1812). U.S. Supreme Court

A French naval vessel put into Philadelphia for repairs after a storm. The libellants, who sought possession of the vessel, claimed that it was in reality the schooner *Exchange*, an American ship which they owned and which had been seized by France on the high seas in 1810 in accordance with a Napoleonic decree. The United States Attorney-General filed a suggestion to the effect that the court should refuse jurisdiction on the ground of sovereign immunity.

MARSHALL C.J., FOR THE COURT

The jurisdiction of the nation within its own territory is necessarily exclusive and absolute. It is susceptible of no limitation not imposed by itself. . . .

This full and absolute territorial jurisdiction being alike the attribute of every sovereign, and being incapable of conferring extra-territorial power, would not seem to contemplate foreign sovereigns nor their sovereign rights as its objects. One sovereign being in no respect amenable to another, and being bound by obligations of the highest character not to degrade the dignity of his nation, by placing himself or its sovereign rights within the jurisdiction of another, can be supposed to enter a foreign territory only under an express license, or in the confidence that the immunities belonging to his independent sovereign station, though not expressly stipulated, are reserved by implication, and will be extended to him.

This perfect equality and absolute independence of sovereigns, and this common interest impelling them to mutual intercourse, and an interchange of good offices with each other, have given rise to a class of cases in

---

[125] *International Law,* Vol.II (2nd edn. 1970), p.841.
[126] These terms tend to be used interchangeably, although, as Sinclair points out, above, n.118, p.197, "[s]overeign immunity in the strict sense of the term should be taken to refer to the immunity which a personal sovereign or Head of State enjoys when present in the territory of another State."
[127] *Kuwait Airways Corpn v Iraqi Airways Co* [2000] EWCA Civ 281.
[128] [1982] A.C. 888 HL.

which every sovereign is understood to waive the exercise of a part of that complete exclusive territorial jurisdiction, which has been stated to be the attribute of every nation.

1st. One of these is admitted to be the exemption of the person of the sovereign from arrest or detention within a foreign territory. . . .

2nd. A second case, standing on the same principles with the first, is the immunity which all civilised nations allow to foreign ministers. . . .

When private individuals of one nation spread themselves through another as business or caprice may direct, mingling indiscriminately with the inhabitants of that other, or when merchant vessels enter for the purposes of trade, it would be obviously inconvenient and dangerous to society, and would subject the laws to continual infraction, and the government to degradation, if such individuals or merchants did not owe temporary and local allegiance, and were not amenable to the jurisdiction of the country. . . .

But in all respects different is the situation of a public armed ship. She constitutes a part of the military force of her nation; acts under the immediate and direct command of the sovereign; is employed by him in national objects. He has many and powerful motives for preventing those objects from being defeated by the interference of a foreign state. Such interference cannot take place without affecting his power and his dignity. The implied license, therefore, under which such vessel enters a friendly port, may reasonably be construed, and it seems to the court ought to be construed, as containing an exemption from the jurisdiction of the sovereign within whose territory she claims the right of hospitality. . . .

The Court found that the vessel in question was exempt from United States jurisdiction.

Notes

1. The doctrine of state immunity is justified by Marshall C.J. on the basis of the equality, independence, and dignity of states. The maxim *par in parem non habet imperium* (an equal has no authority over an equal) is also commonly invoked. Marshall C.J. marries the doctrine with that of the absolute jurisdiction of the territorial sovereign by assuming the latter's implied consent to immunity from its courts' jurisdiction.

2. Although the move away from absolute to restricted immunity is now well established in the practice of many states, state practice does not suggest that sovereign immunity should be abolished altogether. Note, however, that Lord Denning expressed an opinion in *Rahimtoola v Nizam of Hyderabad*[129] which could be used to support such a development (although Lord Denning did not go so far himself):

   "It is more in keeping with the dignity of a foreign sovereign to submit himself to the rule of law than to claim to be above it, and his independence is better ensured by accepting the decisions of courts of acknowledged impartiality than by arbitrarily rejecting their jurisdiction. In all civilised countries there has been a progressive tendency towards making the sovereign liable to be sued in his own courts; notably in England by the Crown Proceedings Act, 1947. Foreign sovereigns should not be in any different position. There is no reason why we should grant to the departments or agencies of foreign Governments an immunity which we do not grant our own, provided always that the matter in dispute arises within the jurisdiction of our courts and is properly cognizable by them."

   Contrast these arguments against state immunity, which turn upon fairness to individuals affected by state acts and the idea that no one is above the law, with the arguments in its favour in *The Schooner Exchange*. The latter were developed at a time when (1) immunity meant the personal immunity of a sovereign, not the public immunity of a state, and (2) state trading, before socialism, was minimal.

---

[129] [1958] A.C. 379 at 418 PC. See also H. Lauterpacht (1951) 28 B.Y.I.L. 220.

I CONGRESO DEL PARTIDO[130]

[1983] 1 A.C. 244. House of Lords

In 1973, Cubazucar, a Cuban state trading enterprise, contracted to sell sugar to a Chilean company. One shipment made under the contract was carried on the *Playa Larga*—a ship flying the Cuban flag, owned by the Cuban Government and operated by Mambisa, a second Cuban state trading enterprise. Such enterprises are legally independent of the Government and not departments of Government under Cuban law; it was not claimed in argument that they attracted sovereign immunity. The cargo was being discharged in Valparaiso when the socialist Allende Government in Chile was overthrown by the right-wing Pinochet Government, of which Cuba disapproved. Thereupon, the *Playa Larga* left Valparaiso on orders from Mambisa (acting on instructions from the Cuban Government) without discharging the remainder of its cargo, which was later sold to someone else in Cuba. A second shipment under the contract was carried on the *Marble Islands*—a ship then flying the Somali flag and owned by a Liechtenstein company which had been chartered by Mambisa for use by Cubazucar. The *Marble Islands*, which was on the high seas on its way to Valparaiso when the *coup d'état* occurred in Chile, was ordered by Mambisa, on Cuban Government instructions, to sail to North Vietnam. During the journey, it became a Cuban ship owned by the Cuban Government. On arrival in Haiphong, the cargo was (1) sold by the master, on behalf of Mambisa, to Alimport, a third Cuban state trading enterprise, and (2) donated by the latter to the North Vietnamese people. Both of these actions were taken in accordance with Cuban Government instructions.

In this case, the *I Congreso*, another ship owned by the Cuban Government, was arrested in British waters on the application of the plaintiffs, the Chilean owners of the cargoes of the *Playa Larga* and the *Marble Islands*, who had instituted proceedings in rem in the English High Court for breach of contract (non-delivery) and in tort (for detinue or conversion). The Cuban Government entered a defence of state immunity. The defence was upheld by Goff J. and by a divided two man Court of Appeal (in which Waller L.J. and Lord Denning M.R. voted for and against immunity respectively). The plaintiffs appealed to the House of Lords. The case was governed by the common law preceding the 1978 Act.

LORD WILBERFORCE

On the basis of these cases [*The Philippine Admiral* [1977] A.C. 373 and *Trendtex Trading Corp. v. Central Bank of Nigeria*, below, p.273] ... I have no doubt that the "restrictive" doctrine should be applied to the present case. ... The issue is as to the limits of the doctrine. ...

The ... limitation ... under the so called "restrictive theory," arises from the willingness of states to enter into commercial, or other private law, transactions with individuals. It appears to have two main foundations: (a) It is necessary in the interest of justice to individuals having such transactions with states to allow them to bring such transactions before the courts. (b) To require a state to answer a claim based upon such transactions does not involve a challenge to or inquiry into any act of sovereignty or governmental act of that state. It is, in accepted phrases, neither a threat to the dignity of that state, nor any interference with its sovereign functions. ...

The appellants contend that we have here (I take the case of *Playa Larga* for the present ...) a commercial transaction, *viz.*, a trading vessel, owned by the Republic of Cuba, carrying goods, under normal commercial arrangements. Any claim arising out of this situation is, they assert, a claim of private law, and it is irrelevant that the purpose, for which the act giving rise to the claim was committed, may have been of a political character (sc. briefly, to break off trading relations with a state, Chile, with which Cuba was not friendly). ...

In my opinion this argument, though in itself generally acceptable, burkes, or begs, the essential question,

---

[130] See Fox (1982) 98 L.Q.R. 94.

which is "what is the relevant act?" It assumes that this is the initial entry into a commercial transaction and that this entry irrevocably confers upon later acts a commercial, or private law, character. ...

In many cases the process of deciding upon the character of the relevant act presents no difficulty ... In *Trendtex* [1977] Q.B. 529, similarly, and the same is true of the acts in issue in other countries relating to the Nigerian cement purchases, the relevant act was simply a breach of a commercial contract and was treated as such, none the less though committed by a state or department of state for reasons of government. The purpose for which the breach was committed could not alter its clear character.[131] Of cases in other jurisdictions one of great clarity is the leading case of the *Claim against the Empire of Iran Case*, 45 I.L.R. 57 decided by the Federal Constitutional Court of the German Federal Republic in 1963. This was a claim for the cost of repairs to the heating system of the Iranian Embassy. The judgment contains the following passage, at 80:

> As a means for determining the distinction between acts jure imperii and jure gestionis one should rather refer to the nature of the state transaction or the resulting legal relationships, and not to the motive or purpose of the state activity. It thus depends upon whether the foreign state has acted in exercise of its sovereign authority, that is in public law, or like a private person, that is in private law.

And later, at 81:

> This court has therefore examined the argument that the conclusion of the contract for repair is to be regarded as a non-sovereign function of the foreign state, and has accepted this proposition as correct. It is obvious that the conclusion of a contract of this kind does not fall within the essential sphere of state authority. It does not depend ... on whether the conclusion of the contract was necessary for the regular transaction of the embassy's affairs and therefore stood in a recognisable relationship with the sovereign functions of the sending state. Whether a state is entitled to immunity does not depend on the purpose of the function which the foreign state is thereby pursuing.

Clearly a breach of a contract of that character was within the area of private law. ... These are cases which present no difficulty. The problems with which they were concerned were simply (i) whether it could be said that the relevant contract was concluded for governmental purposes, and (ii) whether it was relevant that governmental motives were advanced for breaching the contract.

In other situations it may not be easy to decide whether the act complained of is within the area of non-immune activity or is an act of sovereignty wholly outside it. The activities of states cannot always be compartmentalised into trading or governmental activities; and what is one to make of a case where a state has, and in the relevant circumstances, clearly displayed, both a commercial interest and a sovereign or governmental interest? To which is the critical action to be attributed?

... Under the "restrictive" theory the court has first to characterise the activity into which the defendant state has entered. Having done this, and (assumedly) found it to be of a commercial, or private law, character, it may take the view that contractual breaches, or torts, prima facie fall within the same sphere of activity. It should then be for the defendant state to make a case (*cf. Juan Ysmael*)[132] that the act complained of is outside that sphere, and within that of sovereign action. ...

The conclusion which emerges is that in considering, under the "restrictive" theory whether state immunity should be granted or not, the court must consider the whole context in which the claim against the state is made, with a view to deciding whether the relevant act(s) upon which the claim is based, should, in that context, be considered as fairly within an area of activity, trading or commercial, or otherwise of a private law character, in which the state has chosen to engage, or whether the relevant act(s) should be considered as having been done outside that area, and within the sphere of governmental or sovereign activity. ...

(a) *Playa Larga* ... The appellants are certainly able to show, as a starting point, that this vessel was engaged in trade with the consent, if not with the active participation, of the Republic of Cuba. ... The question is whether

---

[131] Ed. In the *Trendtex Case*, Lord Denning M.R. stated: "It was suggested that the original contracts for cement were ... for the building of barracks for the army. On this account it was said that the contracts of purchase were acts of a governmental nature—*iure imperii*. They were like a contract of purchase of boots for the army. But I do not think this should affect the question of immunity. If a government department goes into the market places of the world and buys boots or cement—as a commercial transaction—that government department should be subject to all the rules of the market place. The seller is not concerned with the purpose to which the purchaser intends to put the goods."

[132] Ed. See below, p.272.

the acts which gave rise to an alleged cause of action were done in the context of the trading relationship, or were done by the government of the Republic of Cuba acting wholly outside the trading relationship and in exercise of the power of the state. ... In my opinion it must be answered on a broad view of the facts as a whole and not upon narrow issues as to Cuba's possible contractual liability. I do not think that there is any doubt that the decision not to complete unloading at Valparaiso, or to discharge at Callao, was a political decision taken by the government of the Republic of Cuba for political and non-commercial reasons. ... The change of government in Chile, and the events at Santiago in which the Cuban Embassy was involved, provoked a determination on the part of the government of Cuba to break off and discontinue trading relations with Chile. There may also have been concern for the safety of *Playa Larga* at Valparaiso. ...

Does this call for characterisation of the act of the Republic of Cuba in withdrawing *Playa Larga* and denying the cargo to its purchasers as done *"jure imperii?"* In my opinion it does not. Everything done by the Republic of Cuba in relation to *Playa Larga* could have been done, and, so far as evidence goes, was done, as owners of the ship: it exercised, and had no need to exercise, sovereign powers. It acted, as any owner of the ship would act, through Mambisa, the managing operators. It invoked no governmental authority. ...

It may well be that those instructions [to Mambisa] would not have been issued, as they were, if the owner of *Playa Larga* had been anyone but a state: it is almost certainly the case that there was no commercial reason for the decision. But these consequences follow inevitably from the entry of states into the trading field. If immunity were to be granted the moment that any decision taken by the trading state were shown to be not commercially, but politically, inspired, the "restrictive" theory would almost cease to have any content and trading relations as to state-owned ships would become impossible. It is precisely to protect private traders against politically inspired breaches, or wrongs, that the restrictive theory allows states to be brought before a municipal court. It may be too stark to say of a state "once a trader always a trader": but, in order to withdraw its action from the sphere of acts done *jure gestionis*, a state must be able to point to some act clearly done *jure imperii*. Though, with much hesitation, I feel obligated to differ on this issue from the conclusion of the learned judge, I respectfully think that he well put this ultimate test [1978] Q.B. 500, 528:

> ... it is not just that the purpose or motive of the act is to serve the purposes of the state, but that the act is of its own character a governmental act, as opposed to an act which any private citizen can perform.

As to the *Playa Larga*, therefore, I find myself in agreement with Lord Denning M.R. and would allow the appeal.

Lord Wilberforce dismissed the appeal in relation to the *Marble Islands*.

Lord Edmund Davies delivered a speech agreeing wholly with Lord Wilberforce. Lords Keith and Bridge agreed with the reasoning of Lord Wilberforce. On the facts, they agreed with Lord Diplock that the appeal should also be allowed in respect of the *Marble Islands* as well as the *Playa Larga*. The claim of immunity was therefore disallowed in respect of both ships.

Appeal allowed.

Notes

1. Lord Wilberforce adopted the approach in the *Empire of Iran* case that the test for the distinction between acts *iure imperii* and *iure gestionis* is the "nature" of the act, not its "purpose", although his quotation from the trial court judge's judgment suggests that the "purpose" is not totally irrelevant. Lord Wilberforce's "nature" of the act in its context approach has been followed in later British cases: see, e.g. the *Holland* case, below, and *Littrell v U.S.A. (No.2)* [1995] 1 W.L.R. 82, HL.

2. In the *I Congreso* case the House of Lords held, in a contractual context, that the courts must look not only to the nature of the contract, but also to the nature of the breach. If a contract is an act *iure imperii*, there is immunity; if it is an act *iure gestionis*, a defence of immunity may still succeed if the act in breach of contract is an act *iure imperii*. The Court, that is, has to consider

whether at any stage in the case the state has acted as a sovereign and hence should not be impleaded. The House of Lords unanimously adopted this approach; they disagreed on the facts concerning the *Marble Islands*, the majority considering that the act in breach of contract was an act *iure gestionis* and the minority classifying it as an act *iure imperii*. This would appear to be the first national court case to look beyond the nature of the contract in this way.[133]

3.   In 1983, in a case[134] that fell very clearly on the *iure imperii* side of the line, a British Royal Navy Sea Harrier made a forced landing on a Spanish container ship on the high seas when it ran out of fuel. When the harrier was taken into a Spanish port, the British government argued before a Spanish court that under the international law of state immunity the harrier could not "be the object of any kind of insurance or preventive measure for guaranteeing payment of any compensation."[135] The Spanish court ordered the release of the Harrier. The container ship owner was later awarded compensation by way of maritime salvage by a London arbitrator.

HOLLAND v LAMPEN-WOLFE

[2000] 1 W.L.R. 1573. House of Lords

The plaintiff, a US citizen, taught, under an agreement between the US Government and the American university at which she was a professor, an international relations course to US military personnel and their families at a US military base in England. She brought defamation proceedings against the defendant, a US citizen, who was a civilian employed by the US Department of Defence as an education services officer at the base who had written a memorandum containing criticisms of the plaintiff's teaching. The US claimed immunity on the defendant's behalf.

LORD MILLETT

It is an established rule of customary international law that one state cannot be sued in the courts of another for acts performed *jure imperii*. ... The existence of the doctrine is confirmed by the European Convention on State Immunity (1972) (Cmnd. 5081), the relevant provisions of which are generally regarded as reflecting customary international law. In according immunity from suit before the English courts to foreign states the State Immunity Act 1978 and the common law give effect to the international obligations of the United Kingdom.

   Where the immunity applies, it covers an official of the state in respect of acts performed by him in an official capacity. In the present case, it is common ground that at all material times the defendant acted in his capacity as an official of the United States Department of Defence, being the department responsible for the armed forces of the United States present in the United Kingdom. ...

   Until 1975 England, almost alone of the major trading nations, continued to adhere to a pure, absolute doctrine of state immunity. In the 1970s, mainly under the influence of Lord Denning M.R., we abandoned that position and adopted the so-called restrictive theory of state immunity under which acts of a commercial nature do not attract state immunity even if done for governmental or political reasons. This development of the common law was confirmed by your Lordships' House in *I Congreso del Partido* in relation to acts committed before the passing of the Act of 1978.

   In the meantime Parliament enacted the Act of 1978, which gave statutory force to a restrictive theory of state immunity. It did this by means of a number of statutory exceptions to a general rule of state immunity. ... Part I of the Act contains detailed exceptions to the rule; there are cases where a state enjoys no immunity. There is no exception in respect of actions for defamation. The exceptions relied upon in the present case are contained in

---

[133] See Mann (1982) 31 I.C.L.Q. 573.
[134] U.K.M.I.L. 1985, (1985) 56 B.Y.I.L. 462.
[135] Ibid., p.463.

section 3,[136] which is concerned with commercial transactions and contracts to be performed in the United Kingdom. . . .

Section 16 excludes certain matters from the operation of Part I of the Act.[137] . . . the subsection disapplies the whole of section 1, so that it disapplies the statutory immunity and leaves the position of visiting forces in the United Kingdom to be governed by the common law. . . .

. . . the defendant must [therefore] either (i) bring the present proceedings within section 16(2) and show that they would attract immunity at common law or (ii) show that they fall outside both section 16(2) and the exceptions contained in section 3.

. . . I am satisfied that the writing and publication of the memorandum were [in the terms of s.16(2)] acts done "in relation to" the armed forces of the United States. The memorandum was concerned with the quality of educational services supplied to members of the armed forces and was written and published by the defendant in the course of his duties to supervise and monitor the supply of those services. . . .

It follows that the defendant's claim to immunity falls to be dealt with under the common law. Accordingly the question is whether, in accordance with the law laid down in *I Congreso del Partido* [1983] 1 A.C. 244, 262, the act complained of was *jure imperii* or *jure gestionis*. This must be judged against the background of the whole context in which the claim is made. . . .

In *Littrell v. United States of America (No.2)* [1995] 1 W.L.R. 82 the plaintiff claimed damages for personal injuries arising from medical treatment which he had received at a United States military hospital in the United Kingdom while a serving member of the United States Air Force. It was conceded that section 16(2) applied, so that the case fell to be decided at common law. The Court of Appeal held that the proceedings were barred by state immunity. . . .

In a careful review of the facts, Hoffman L.J. observed that the acts complained of took place at a military hospital within the control of the United States Air Force. They involved only United States personnel. The operation of a military hospital, although no doubt requiring much the same skills as the operation of a civilian hospital, is a recognised military operation. He concluded that the standard of medical care which the United States should afford its own servicemen was a matter within its own sovereign authority.

The Court of Appeal could find no material distinction between the medical treatment provided in that case and the educational services provided in the present one. I agree with them that the provision of education for members of the armed forces and their families is, in modern conditions, as much a normal and necessary part of the overall activity of maintaining those forces as is the provision of medical treatment. . . .

It is, of course, true that the action is an action for defamation, not for the negligent provision of professional services. The *Littrell* case is clearly distinguishable on this ground. But I do not regard the distinction as material. The defendant was responsible for supervising the provision of educational services to members of the United States armed forces in the United Kingdom and their families. He published the material alleged to be defamatory in the course of his duties. If the provision of the services in question was an official or governmental act of the United States, then so was its supervision by the defendant. I would hold that he was acting as an official of the United States in the course of the performance of its sovereign function of maintaining its armed forces in this country. . . .

This makes it strictly unnecessary to decide whether, if the Act of 1978 were not disapplied by section 16(2), the present proceedings would fall within the exceptions to state immunity contained in section 3. As the matter has been fully argued, however, I will state shortly my reasons for thinking that they would not.

In my opinion, section 3(1)*(a)* is not satisfied because, although the contract between the university and the United States Government is a contract for the supply of services and therefore a commercial contract within the meaning of the section by virtue of section 3(3)*(a)*, the present proceedings do not relate to that contract. They are not about the contract, but about the memorandum. . . . In my opinion the words "proceedings relating to" a transaction refer to claims arising out of the transaction, usually contractual claims, and not tortious claims arising independently of the transaction but in the course of its performance.

For the same reason I doubt that the writing and publication of the memorandum constituted an "activity" of an official character in which the United States engaged through the medium of the defendant, so as to bring the proceedings within section 3(3)*(c)*. The context strongly suggests a commercial relationship akin to but falling short of contract (perhaps because gratuitous) rather than a unilateral tortious act. But even if the defendant's acts of writing and publishing the memorandum can be brought within the opening words of section 3(3)*(c)*, they

---

[136] Ed. For the text, see below, p.266.
[137] Ed. For the text, see below, p.269.

are excluded by the concluding words of the subsection since, for the reasons I have given, they were performed in the exercise of sovereign authority.

Lords Hope, Cooke and Clyde delivered concurring opinions. Lord Hobhouse concurred.

Appeal dismissed.

Notes

1. This case was decided on the basis of the common law distinction between acts *iure imperii* and *iure gestionis* adopted in the *I Congreso* case, above, p.261. This emphasises the nature or context of the act, not its purpose. This common law distinction is also relevant to the interpretation of the 1978 Act, see below, p.270.

2. See also *Hick v US* (1995) 120 I.L.R. 606, EAT (air base recreation facilities on the *iure imperii* side of the line).

STATE IMMUNITY ACT 1978[138]

1.—(1) A State is immune from the jurisdiction of the courts of the United Kingdom except as provided in the following provisions of this Part of this Act.

(2) A court shall give effect to the immunity conferred by this section even though the State does not appear in the proceedings in question.

2.—(1) A State is not immune as respects proceedings in respect of which it has submitted to the jurisdiction of the courts of the United Kingdom. . . .

(2) A State may submit after the dispute giving rise to the proceedings has arisen or by a prior written agreement; but a provision in any agreement that it is to be governed by the law of the United Kingdom is not to be regarded as a submission. . . .

3.—(1) A State is not immune as respects proceedings relating to[139]—

(a) a commercial transaction entered into by the State; or

(b) an obligation of the State which by virtue of a contract (whether a commercial transaction or not) falls to be performed wholly or partly in the United Kingdom.

(2) This section does not apply if the parties to the dispute are States or have otherwise agreed in writing; and subsection (1)(b) above does not apply if the contract (not being a commercial transaction) was made in the territory of the State concerned and the obligation in question is governed by its administrative law.

(3) In this section "commercial transaction" means

(a) any contract for the supply of goods or services;

(b) any loan or other transaction for the provision of finance and any guarantee or indemnity in respect of any such transaction or of any other financial obligation; and

---

[138] See Bird (1979) 13 *Int. Lawyer* 619; Bowett (1978) 37 C.L.J. 193; Delaume (1979) 73 A.J.I.L. 185; Higgins (1979) 10 N.Y.I.L. 35; Hockl, 48 O.Z.O.R.V. 121; Lewis, *State and Diplomatic Immunity* (3rd edn 1990); Mann (1979) 50 B.Y.I.L. 43; Sinclair, above, n.118, pp.257–265; White (1979) 42 M.L.R. 72.

[139] An application to register a foreign judgment for purposes of enforcement involves "proceedings relating to" a commercial transaction: *AIC Ltd v Federal Government of Nigeria* [2003] EWHC 1357, approved in *Svenska Petroleum Exploration AB v Lithuania* [2006] EWCA 1529.

(c) any other transaction or activity (whether of a commercial, industrial, financial, professional or other similar character) into which a State enters or in which it engages otherwise than in the exercise of sovereign authority;

but neither paragraph of subsection (1) above applies to a contract of employment between a State and an individual.

4.—(1) A State is not immune as respects proceedings relating to a contract of employment between the State and an individual where the contract was made in the United Kingdom or the work is to be wholly or partly performed there. . . .
(2) Subject to subsections (3) and (4) below, this section does not apply if—

(a) at the time when the proceedings are brought the individual is a national of the State concerned[140]; or

(b) at the time when the contract was made the individual was neither a national of the United Kingdom nor habitually resident there; or

(c) the parties to the contract have otherwise agreed in writing.

(3) Where the work is for an office, agency or establishment maintained by the State in the United Kingdom for commercial purposes,[141] subsection (2)(a) and (b) above do not exclude the application of this section unless the individual was, at the time when the contract was made, habitually resident in that State.
(4) Subsection (2)(c) above does not exclude the application of this section where the law of the United Kingdom requires the proceedings to be brought before a court of the United Kingdom. . . .

5. A State is not immune as respects proceedings in respect of—

(a) death or personal injury; or

(b) damage to or loss of tangible property,

caused by an act or omission in the United Kingdom.

6.—(1) A State is not immune as respects proceedings relating to—

(a) any interest of the State in, or its possession or use of, immovable property in the United Kingdom; or

(b) any obligation of the State arising out of its interest in, or its possession or use of, any such property.[142]

A state is not immune as respects proceedings relating to patents, trade marks, designs, plant

---

[140] Ed. See *Sengupta v Republic of India* [1983] I.C.R. 221 EAT (Indian national employed at Indian embassy; s.4(2)(a) applied in principle.

[141] Ed. The medical office of the Egyptian embassy, whose function was to procure medical services for Egyptian nationals referred to it by the Egyptian government, was not maintained for "commercial purposes" within s.4(3): *Arab Republic of Egypt v Gamal-Eldin* [1996] 2 All E.R. 237 EAT. So, state immunity prevented an employment law claim by persons employed by the office as drivers. As to contracts of employment generally as an exception to state immunity in international law, see Fox (1995) 66 B.Y.I.L. 97; and Garnett (1997) 46 I.C.L.Q. 81.

[142] Ed. s.16(1)(b) of the 1978 Act, below, p.269, provides that s.6(1) "does not apply to proceedings concerning a state's title to or its possession of property used for the purposes of a diplomatic mission . . ." In *Intpro Properties Ltd v Sauvel* [1983] Q.B. 1019 CA, it was held that the private residence of a French diplomatic agent was not "used for the purposes of a diplomatic mission"; even though the agent used it for official social obligations, that was not sufficient for the residence to be regarded as being used for the professional purposes of the mission, which was what s.16(1)(b) required. Moreover, s.16(1)(b) would not have applied in any event because the claim against the state was for breach of covenant in a lease (preventing access to workmen) and did not concern a question of title or possession. Accordingly, the claim against the defendant state for damages suffered as a result of its breach of covenant could proceed, as s.6 allowed. On a diplomatic immunity point considered in the same case, see below, p.298.

breeders' rights or copyright (art.7), its participation in a company, etc. (art.8), or an arbitration agreement (art.9)

10.—(1) This section applies to—

(a) Admiralty proceedings; and

(b) proceedings on any claim which could be made the subject of Admiralty proceedings.

(2) A State is not immune as respects—

(a) an action in rem against a ship belonging to that State; or

(b) an action in personam for enforcing a claim in connection with such a ship,

if, at the time when the cause of action arose, the ship was in use or intended for use for commercial purposes.[143]

A state is not immune as respects proceedings relating to customs duty, etc. (s.11).

14.—(1) The immunities and privileges conferred by this Part of this Act apply to any foreign or commonwealth State other than the United Kingdom; and references to a State include references to—

(a) the sovereign or other heads of that State in his public capacity;

(b) the government of that State; and

(c) any department of that government,

but not to any entity (hereafter referred to as a "separate entity") which is distinct from the executive organs of the government of the State and capable of suing or being sued.
(2) A separate entity is immune from the jurisdiction of the courts of the United Kingdom if, and only if—

(a) the proceedings relate to anything done by it in the exercise of sovereign authority; and

(b) the circumstances are such that a State (or, in the case of proceedings to which section 10 above applies, a State which is not party to the Brussels Convention) would have been so immune.

(3) If a separate entity (not being a State's central bank or other monetary authority) submits to the jurisdiction in respect of proceedings in the case of which it is entitled to immunity by virtue of subsection (2) above, subsections (1) to (4) of section 13 above shall apply to it in respect of those proceedings as if references to a State were references to that entity.
(4) Property of a State's central bank or other monetary authority shall not be regarded for the purposes of subsection (4) of section 13 above as in use or intended for use for commercial purposes[144]; and where any such bank or authority is a separate entity subsections (1) to (3) of that section shall apply to it as if references to a State were references to the bank or authority.
(5) Section 12 above [service of process and judgments in default of appearance] applies to proceedings against the constituent territories of a federal State; and Her Majesty may by Order in Council provide for the other provisions of this Part of this Act to apply to any such constituent territory specified in the Order as they apply to a State.
(6) Where the provisions of this Part of this Act do not apply to the constituent territory by virtue of any such Order subsections (2) and (3) above shall apply to it as if it were a separate entity.

---

[143] Ed. s.17(1) states that "commercial purposes" means "purposes of such transactions or activities as are mentioned in s.3(3)."
[144] ibid.

16.—(1) This Part of this Act does not affect any immunity or privilege conferred by the Diplomatic Privileges Act 1964 or the Consular Relations Act 1968; and—

(a) section 4 above does not apply to proceedings concerning the employment of the members of a mission within the meaning of the Convention scheduled to the said Act of 1964[145] or of the members of consular post within the meaning of the Convention scheduled to the said Act of 1968;

(b) section 6(1) above does not apply to proceedings concerning a State's title to or its possession of property used for the purposes of a diplomatic mission.[146]

(2) This Part of this Act does not apply to proceedings relating to anything done by or in relation to the armed forces of a State while present in the United Kingdom and, in particular, has effect subject to the Visiting Forces Act 1952.

(3) This Part of this Act does not apply to proceedings to which section 17(6) of the Nuclear Installations Act 1965 applies.

(4) This Part of this Act does not apply to criminal proceedings.

(5) This Part of this Act does not apply to any proceedings relating to taxation other than those mentioned in section 11 above.

20.—(1) Subject to the provisions of this section and to any necessary modifications,[147] the Diplomatic Privileges Act 1964[148] shall apply to—

(a) a sovereign or other head of State;

(b) members of his family forming part of his household; and

(c) his private servants,

as it applies to the head of a diplomatic mission, to members of his family forming part of his household and to his private servants.

(2) The immunities and privileges conferred by virtue of subsection (1)(a) and (b) above shall not be subject to the restrictions by reference to nationality or residence mentioned in Article 37(1) or 38 in Schedule 1 to the said Act of 1964. ...

(5) This section applies to the sovereign or other head of any State on which immunities and privileges are conferred by Part I of this Act and is without prejudice to the application of that Part to any such sovereign or head of State in his public capacity.

21. A certificate by or on behalf of the Secretary of State shall be conclusive evidence on any question—

(a) whether any country is a State for the purposes of Part I of this Act, whether any territory is a constituent territory of a federal State for those purposes or as to the person or persons to be regarded for those purposes as the head or government of a State; ...[149]

---

[145] Ed. A British national working as a secretary in a London embassy was a "member of the mission" as a member of its technical or administrative staff within s.16, so that the exception to state immunity in s.4 of the State Immunity Act 1978 in respect of employment did not apply: *Ahmed v Govt. of the Kingdom of Saudi Arabia* [1996] 2 All E.R. 249 CA. cf. *Arab Republic of Egypt v Gamal-Eldin* [1996] 2 All E.R. 237 EAT.

[146] Ed. See the *Intpro Properties* case, above, n.142.

[147] See the *Pinochet* case, below, p.279.

[148] Ed. Below, p.316.

[149] On judicial review of certificates issued under s.21, see the *Trawnik* case, above, p.88.

Notes

1. At common law, the British courts had abandoned the doctrine of absolute immunity in *The Philippine Admiral* [1977] A.C. 373 JC (actions in rem) and *Trendtex Trading Corpn v Central Bank of Nigeria* [1977] Q.B. 529 CA (actions in personam), just before the 1978 Act was enacted.

2. The Act was introduced partly to permit ratification of the 1926 Brussels Convention and the 1972 European Convention, see above, p.258, and certain of the complications in its text result from this objective. The Act was also a response to the fear in the City that the United Kingdom would increasingly lose business to other jurisdictions if it did not offer better legal security for persons trading with states.[150] The Act applies to all foreign states, except for the provisions about the recognition of judgments (ss.18–19) which apply only to parties to the 1972 European Convention.

3. The pattern of the Act (like that of the 1972 European Convention and the 2004 Convention on Jurisdictional Immunities), is to provide for general immunity (s.1(1)), subject to a list of exceptions (ss.2–11) which accord with the doctrine of restrictive immunity. As a result, the burden is upon the plaintiff to prove that the case falls within one of the listed exceptions. Although the exceptions in the Act are specific to particular contexts (commercial transactions, employment contracts, tort claims, etc.) and are defined in some detail, the Act does not eliminate entirely the general distinction between acts *iure imperii* and acts *iure gestionis* with which the courts have had to grapple at common law since moving to the doctrine of restricted immunity. Thus it is still necessary in some cases, no doubt with the assistance of common law authorities, to interpret the phrase "in the exercise of sovereign authority" when applying s.3(3) in connection with s.3(1)(2) and s.14 or when interpreting (via s.17) the phrase "commercial purposes" in ss.4(3), 10(3), 11, 13(4)(5) and 14(4). Would the wording of s.3(3) permit Lord Wilberforce's approach in the *I Congreso del Partido* case, above, p.261? Can one, that is, look to the nature of the act complained of (the act of breach of contract, of conversion, etc.)? Or must one look only to the nature of the transaction or activity in respect of which it occurs? As to the latter, was there a "commercial transaction" entered into by Cuba in respect of the *Marble Islands* in the *I Congreso del Partido* case? In *Koo Golden East Mongolia v Bank of Nova Scotia*[151] it was held that a contract by which a gold mining company deposited gold with the Mongolian central bank was entered into "in the exercise of sovereign authority" as its purpose was to increase Mongolia's currency resources. A joint venture agreement between a foreign company and a state enterprise to exploit the state's oil reserves was not a "contract for the supply of goods or services" (s.3(3)(a)), and arguably was an "exercise of sovereign authority" (s.3(3)(c)) because of its subject matter, which related to a state's natural resources: *Svenska Petroleum Exploration AB v Lithuania*.[152] A pre-1978 Act case that would be decided the same way on its facts under the Act was *Planmount Ltd v Republic of Zaire*.[153] In that case, a builder sued the defendant for the balance of monies due under a contract for repair work done to the official residence of the ambassador of Zaire in London. A defence of state immunity was rejected at common law, Lloyd J. relying upon the *Trendtex* case, below, p.273. cf. the facts of the *Claim against the Empire of Iran*, see above,

---

[150] See Lord Hailsham L.C., *Hansard*, H.L., Vol.389, col. 1502 March 16, 1978.

[151] [2007] EWCA Civ 1443. O'Keefe (2007) 78 B.Y.I.L. 582, points out that the Court of Appeal erred in considering that the question of "sovereign authority" arose under s.3(3)(c), as the contract was for the "supply of gods or services" and, under s.3(3)(a), any such contract is a "commercial transaction" regardless of its purpose.

[152] [2006] EWCA 1529. Point left undecided.

[153] [1981] 1 All E.R. 1110 QB. In a case under the 1978 Act, a contract for the supply by a British company of the component parts of a super-gun to Iraq was a "commercial transaction" (see s.3(3)(a)) so that the High Court had jurisdiction to make a confiscation order: *Commissioners of Customs and Excise v Ministry of Industries and Military Manufacturing, Republic of Iraq*, unreported, 1992: see Fox (1994) 43 I.C.L.Q. 193 at 194.

p.262. Most of the exceptions in ss.2–11 of the Act are limited by requirements linking the case with the United Kingdom, (e.g. the contract to be performed in the United Kingdom: s.3(1)(b)), but this is *not* true of the "commercial transaction" exception in section 3(1)(a), as to which see below. These requirements are aimed at compliance with the rules limiting the jurisdiction of states in customary international law and hence assisting in the execution of judgments against states that are impleaded. The Act concerns civil proceedings; it does not provide for immunity from criminal liability (e.g. for oil pollution).[154]

4. Section 2(2) reverses the rule in *Kahan v Pakistan Federation* [1951] 2 K.B. 1003, CA by which submission to jurisdiction could only be made before the court and not by prior written agreement. It is quite common for a waiver of immunity to be included in the loan or other financial agreement. A state is deemed to have waived its immunity if it institutes proceedings, or intervenes, or takes any step in the proceedings (s.2(3)).[155]

5. The definition of "commercial transaction" in s.3(3) covers *all* contracts and financial transactions of the kinds listed in s.3(3)(a)(b); there is no need for the court to consider the difficult question whether they result from the "exercise of sovereign authority." They are, by definition, "commercial transactions." Hence neither the purpose for which the goods or services are wanted nor the fact that the contract or loan is one that could only be made by a governmental entity is relevant. A contract for the supply of cement for an army barracks (*Trendtex* case, below, p.273) or of military equipment (or of technicians to train soldiers to use it) would come within s.3(3)(a). A loan to or by a government would similarly fall within s.3(3)(b), as would the letter of credit in the *Trendtex* case. In the case of "any other transaction or activity" in the sense of s.3(3)(c), a court will have to decide whether it results from "an exercise of sovereign authority." Mann[156] argues that the word "activity" allows claims in tort to be brought against a state where they do not result from an "exercise of sovereign authority." Thus a claim in libel, such as that in *Krajina v Tass Agency*, below, p.274, n.170, could not be met by a defence of state immunity unless the tort were committed "in the exercise of sovereign authority." For another example of an "activity" that would probably come within s.3(3)(c), see the facts of *U.S. v Dolfus Mieg*, next note. Section 3(1)(b) adds to s.3(1)(a) by denying immunity in certain non-"commercial transaction" cases in contract. The concurrent or secondary liability of a state under a contract to which it was not a party or the liability of a state as the undisclosed principal of an agent who was a party to a contract would be an "obligation" within s.3(1)(b).[157]

6. Section 6(4) deals with one form of indirect impleading, i.e. the situation in which proceedings are brought against someone other than the state but which concern property within a state's ownership, possession, or control. A defence of state immunity is allowed in such a case under s.6(4) only if the defence would be available if the proceedings had been brought against the state itself. Under the Act, therefore, the plaintiff would still not have succeeded in respect of the 51 gold bars in *U.S. v Dolfus Mieg* [1952] A.C. 582 HL. In that case, the plaintiffs claimed, as owners, the return of gold bars deposited by certain Governments with the Bank of England under a contract of bailment, including 51 bars still in the Bank vaults. Although the proceedings were brought against the Bank, a plea of immunity was upheld because the foreign Governments

---

[154] See the Merchant Shipping (Prevention of Oil Pollution) Regulations 1996 (SI 1996/2154) Regs 12, 13, 36, which create a criminal offence which may be committed by foreign oil tankers that discharge oil into UK. waters.

[155] Waiver must be by the head of mission or other person authorised by the state: *Aziz v Republic of Yemen* [2005] EWCA Civ 735.

[156] See above, n.138, p.52. This is in addition to tort claims allowed by ss.5–6.

[157] *Rayner Ltd v Dept of Trade* [1989] Ch. 72 at 195 per Kerr L.J., CA.

concerned had an immediate right to possession under the contract of bailment and would have been indirectly impleaded had the case gone ahead. Since the bars (which had been taken from the plaintiffs by the German authorities in the Second World War, then recovered by American forces, and finally placed in the possession of the Allied Governments of France, the United Kingdom and the United States, pending restitution proceedings) had undoubtedly been deposited with the Bank by those Governments "in the exercise of sovereign authority," s.3(3)(c) would apply so that immunity would now be available to the American and French Governments if sued themselves in a United Kingdom court.

The prima facie evidence requirement in an "interest" case inserted at the end of s.6(4) confirms *Juan Ismael and Co. v Indonesian Govt.* [1955] A.C. 72 HL.

7. *Section 10*. A second form of indirect pleading, which has often been the subject of claims to state immunity at common law, occurs when an action in rem is brought in admiralty proceedings against a ship belonging to a state, i.e. in its ownership, possession or control. Under s.10, state immunity does not exist "if, at the time when the cause of action arose, the ship was in use or intended for use for commercial purposes" (s.10(2)).[158] How would the *I Congreso del Partido* case, above p.261, have been decided under s.10?

8. Section 13 (not reprinted) lists certain procedural privileges which apply even if a state is not entitled to immunity from jurisdiction. Most significantly, in the absence of a state's consent, (i) a *Mareva* injunction[159] is not available to prevent property being taken out of the jurisdiction pending litigation and (ii) a state's property may not be used for the enforcement of a judgment against it unless it is property that is "for the time being in use or intended for use for commercial purposes."[160]

9. As to the latter, consistently with the dignity of states and the need for good international relations, the common law approach had been to apply a rule of absolute immunity from *execution* so that no property of the state could be attached in satisfaction of a judgment against it. The 1978 Act moderates this approach, in line with some (but not all) civil law jurisdictions,[161] so that execution is permitted (in cases of waiver of immunity from jurisdiction or restricted immunity) against property used "for commercial purposes".[162] Such execution is not permitted, however, against the property of a party to the 1972 European Convention unless it makes an art.24 declaration (s.13(4)(a)). The "commercial purposes" exception in s.13(4) was interpreted so as, in effect, to prevent execution against an embassy bank account in *Alcom v Republic of Colombia*.[163] There it was held that money in an embassy current bank account to pay for the day to day expenses of the Colombian embassy in London was immune from judicial process by virtue of s.13(2)(b). Lord Diplock stated[164]:

---

[158] cf. the similar lack of immunity in respect of *in rem* proceedings against a ship's cargo: s.10(4). Note also that s.10(2)(b) and (4) exclude immunity in actions *in personam* (against the state as third party) in connection with a ship or its cargo where the "commercial purposes" test is met.

[159] See *Mareva Compania Naviera v International Bulkcarriers* [1975] 2 Lloyd's Rep. 509, CA.

[160] See s.13(4). A certificate by the state's head of diplomatic mission as to a property's use or intended use for "commercial purposes" shall be accepted unless the contrary is proved: s.13(5). "Property" means "any right or interest, legal, equitable, or contractual in assets": *AIG Capital Partners v Kazakhstan* [2005] EWCA 2239; [2006] 1 All E.R. 1 at 18. For the meaning of "commercial purposes", see above, p.268, n.143.

[161] On immunity from execution in international law, see Crawford (1981) 75 A.J.I.L. 820 and Fox (1985) 34 I.C.L.Q. 115.

[162] See s.13(4). See also *AIC Ltd v Federal Government of Nigeria* [2003] EWHC 1357.

[163] [1984] A.C. 580, HL.

[164] [1984] A.C. 580 at 604. For criticism of the decision, see Crawford (1983) 54 B.Y.I.L. 75. See also Houtte (1986) 19 R.B.D.I. 70.

"Such expenditure will, no doubt, include *some* moneys due under contracts for the supply of goods or services to the mission ...; but the account will also be drawn upon to meet many other items of expenditure which fall outside even the extended definition of 'commercial purposes' for which section 17(1) and section 3(3) provide. The debt owed by the bank to the foreign sovereign state and represented by the credit balance in the current account kept by the diplomatic mission of that state as a possible subject matter of the enforcement jurisdiction of the court is, however, one and indivisible ... Unless it can be shown by the judgment creditor who is seeking to attach the credit balance by garnishee proceedings that the bank account was earmarked by the foreign state solely (save for de minimis exceptions) for being drawn upon to settle liabilities incurred in commercial transactions ... it cannot ... be sensibly brought within ... Section 13(4) ..."

On the attachment of ships, see s.10.

10. Section 14: see the notes to the *Trendtex* case, below.

11. Section 21(a) is consistent with *Duff Development Co. v Kelantan* [1924] A.C. 797, HL. The statements obiter dicta in that case to the effect that if the Foreign Office did not respond to a request for a certificate the courts would have taken their own decision presumably still apply.

12. A claim of immunity under the Act must be decided as a preliminary issue in favour of the plaintiff before the action can proceed on the merits.[165]

TRENDTEX TRADING CORP. v CENTRAL BANK OF NIGERIA[166]

[1977] Q.B. 529. Court of Appeal

In 1975, the Central Bank of Nigeria issued a letter of credit in favour of the plaintiffs, a Swiss company, for the price of cement to be sold by the plaintiffs to an English company which had secured a contract with the Nigerian Government to supply it with cement for the construction of an army barracks in Nigeria. When, under instructions from the Nigerian Government (which was taking steps to extricate itself from the Nigerian Cement Scandal created by its predecessor Government),[167] the bank refused to honour the letter of credit, the plaintiffs brought an action in personam against the bank in the English High Court. The bank successfully claimed sovereign immunity before Donaldson J. The plaintiffs appealed.

LORD DENNING M.R.

The Central Bank of Nigeria claims that it cannot be sued in this country on the letter of credit; because it is entitled to sovereign immunity.
   ... The doctrine grants immunity to a foreign government or its department of state or any body which can be regarded as an "alter ego or organ" of the government. ... In some countries the government departments conduct all their business through their own offices—even ordinary commercial dealings—without setting up separate corporations or legal entities. In other countries they set up separate corporations or legal entities which

---

[165] *Rayner Ltd v Dept of Trade* [1969] Ch. 72 CA.
[166] See Markesinis (1977) 36 C.L.J. 211 and White (1977) 26 I.C.L.Q. 674.
[167] Huge quantities of cement had been ordered from different sources—far more than Nigeria needed or the port of Lagos could handle. The new Nigerian Government took steps similar to those taken in this case against suppliers in other cases, leading to comparable court proceedings in the US and the FRG: see (1977) 16 I.L.M. 469. A doctrine of restrictive immunity was applied against the defendant's claim of state immunity in those cases also.

are under the complete control of the department, but which enter into commercial transactions, buying and selling goods, owning and chartering ships, just like any ordinary trading concern. This difference in internal arrangements ought not to affect the availability of immunity in international law. A foreign department of state ought not to lose its immunity simply because it conducts some of its activities by means of a separate legal entity. It was so held by this court in *Baccus SRL v. Servicio Nacional del Trigo*.[168]

Another problem arises because of the internal laws of many countries which grant immunities and privileges to their own organisations. Some organisations can sue, or be sued, in their courts. Others cannot. In England we have had for centuries special immunities and privileges for "the Crown," a phrase which has been held to cover many governmental departments and many emanations of government departments but not nationalised commercial undertakings: see *Tamlin v. Hannaford*.[169] The phrase "the Crown" is so elastic that under the Crown Proceedings Act 1947, the Treasury has issued a list of government departments covered by the Act. It includes even the Forestry Commission. It cannot be right that international law should grant or refuse absolute immunity, according to the immunities granted internally. I would put on one side, therefore, our cases about the privileges, prerogatives and exceptions of "the Crown."

It is often said that a certificate by the ambassador, saying whether or not an organisation is a department of state, is of much weight, though not decisive: see *Krajina v. Tass Agency*.[170] But even this is not to my mind satisfactory. What is the test which the ambassador is to apply? In the absence of any test, an ambassador may apply the test of control, asking himself: is the organisation under the control of a minister of state? On such a test, he might certify any nationalised undertaking to be a department of state. He might certify that a press agency or an agricultural corporation (which carried out ordinary commercial dealings) was a department of state, simply because it was under the complete control of the government.

I confess that I can think of no satisfactory test except that of looking to the functions and control of the organisation. I do not think that it should depend on the foreign law alone. I would look to all the evidence to see whether the organisation was under government control and exercised governmental functions. That is the way in which we looked at it in *Mellenger v. New Brunswick Development Corpn.* [1971] 1 W.L.R. 604 (C.A.) ...

At the hearing we were taken through the Act of 1958 under which the Central Bank of Nigeria was established, and the amendments to the Act by later decrees. All the relevant provisions were closely examined; and we had the benefit of expert evidence on affidavit which was most helpful.[171] The upshot of it all may be summarised as follows. (1) The Central Bank of Nigeria is a central bank modelled on the Bank of England. (2) It has governmental functions in that it issues legal tender; it safeguards the international value of the currency; and it acts as banker and financial adviser to the government. (3) Its affairs are under a great deal of government control in that the Federal Executive Council may overrule the board of directors on monetary and banking policy and on internal administrative policy. (4) It acts as banker for other banks in Nigeria and abroad, and maintains accounts with other banks. It acts as banker for the states within the Federation, but has few, if any, private customers.

In these circumstances I have found it difficult to decide whether or not the Central Bank of Nigeria should be considered in international law a department of the Federation of Nigeria, even though it is a separate legal entity. But, on the whole, I do not think it should be.

SHAW L.J.

Whether a particular organisation is to be accorded the status of a department of government or not must depend on its constitution, its powers and duties and its activities. ... The bank is, in the first place, a statutory corporation whose personality, powers and legal attributes are determined by the Central Bank of Nigeria Act 1958. ... Nowhere in that legislation is it called anything but a bank; ... The 52 sections of the principal Act ... contain no direct indication that the bank is a department of the government and there are many indications

---

[168] [1957] 1 Q.B. 438; [1956] 3 All E.R. 715 CA.

[169] [1950] 1 K.B. 18; [1949] 2 All E.R. 327 CA.

[170] [1949] 2 All E.R. 274 CA. In this case, the plaintiff sought damages for an alleged libel in a newspaper published by the defendant. The latter was described in the Russian statute establishing it as "the central information organ of the USSR" and as enjoying "all the rights of a legal person." The Ambassador of the USSR to the UK certified that the defendant was "a department of state of the Soviet State ... exercising the rights of a legal entity." The Court of Appeal held, unanimously, that the defendant was a department of state and entitled to immunity as such under the doctrine of absolute immunity. The Ambassador's certificate, although not conclusive, had sufficiently established this.

[171] Ed. This spoke of the bank as the agent of the government and as being under its control; it did not refer to the bank as a department of government.

which deny it that status. The very name has a commercial ring. Its powers do not identify it with the government and in some respects preclude identification with the government. . . .

Apart from these matters there is an important practical consideration. . . . Those who contemplate entering into transactions with bodies which may be in a position to claim sovereign immunity are entitled at least to the opportunity of assessing any special risk which may arise. How can they know that such a risk lurks in dealing with a body which assumes a guise and bears a title appropriate to a commercial or financial institution? . . . There is no rule of law which demands this; but where the issue of status trembles on a fine edge, the absence of any positive indication that the body in question was intended to possess sovereign status and its attendant privileges must perforce militate against the view that it enjoys that status or is entitled to those privileges. This is especially the case where the opportunity to define the status of the institution concerned in clear and express terms has existed from the very inception, or indeed conception, of that institution—as in this case.

. . . It is clear enough that the bank was the subserving agent of the government in a variety of activities but this is not in my judgment adequate to constitute it as an organ or department of government. I cannot find in the constitution of the bank or in the functions it performs or in the activities it pursues or in all those matters looked at together any compelling or indeed satisfactory basis for the conclusion that it is so related to the Government of Nigeria as to form part of it. Accordingly I would hold that the bank is not entitled to the immunity which it claims. . . .

Notes

1.   The appeal was allowed unanimously. Stephenson L.J. agreed with the other two judges on the status of the bank and that international law had changed to a doctrine of restrictive immunity. Unlike the other two, however, Stephenson L.J. (like the majority in the *Tapioca* case) felt himself bound by precedent to follow the doctrine of absolute immunity.

2.   The current rule indicating whose acts are to be treated as state acts attracting immunity is in the 1978 Act, s.14, above, p.268. A department of government under a foreign state's law is entitled to immunity in respect of its acts even though it has a separate legal personality under that law. This is consistent with *Baccus v S.R.L. Servicio Nacional del Trigo* [1957] 1 Q.B. 438 CA, in which the plaintiff Italian company and the defendants made a contract for the sale of rye which contained an arbitration clause giving jurisdiction over disputes arising under the contract to the English High Court. The plaintiffs initiated proceedings under the clause but the defendants pleaded state immunity on the ground that, although formed as a separate legal person under Spanish law, they were nonetheless a Department of State of the Spanish Government. The Court of Appeal (Jenkins and Parker L.JJ., Singleton L.J. dissenting) upheld this plea in reliance upon affidavit evidence from the Spanish ambassador and a Spanish legal expert to the effect that the defendants were in Spanish law a Department of the Spanish Ministry of Agriculture. Although the same conclusion (that the defendants attracted immunity as a department of government) would be reached under s.14, immunity would nonetheless not be allowed on the facts of the case because the contract was a "commercial transaction": s.3(3)(a).

In the *Trendtex* case, the Court of Appeal looked not only to Nigerian law but also to the functions of the bank and its relationship with the government when deciding whether it should be classified as a department of government.[172] Section 14 would seem to limit itself to the first of these considerations. (If so, it is open to the criticism which Lord Denning makes, namely that differences in "internal arrangements ought not to affect the availability of immunity in international law.") State trading agencies of the sort typical of socialist countries would thus qualify

---

[172] cf. *Czarnikow Ltd v Rolimpex* [1979] A.C. 351 HL (Polish state trading organisation with independent legal personality sufficiently free of government control in its commercial activities so as not to be an organ of the Polish Government).

as departments of state if they are classified as such under the local law,[173] but not otherwise. The Cuban agencies in the *I Congreso* case above, p.261, would not qualify. Nor would United Kingdom public corporations such as the Post Office and the Civil Aviation Authority. It seems likely that, when applying s.14, the courts will continue to rely upon expert evidence and the affidavits of ambassadors to establish the legal status of an entity as they had done at common law: see the *Trendtex* case, the *Baccus* case and the *Krajina* case.

On a wide interpretation of "government", the Australian Federal Police were held to fall within s.14(1) in *Propend Finance Property Ltd v Sing*.[174]

3.   A "separate entity" under s.14 (i.e. one that is not a department of state but that is capable of being sued) is not entitled to state immunity unless it is acting "in the exercise of sovereign authority."[175] Here again (as when interpreting s.3(3)(c)) the courts will have to develop their own distinction between acts *iure imperii* and acts *iure gestionis*: see above, p.263. Sinclair[176] suggests that certain of the functions of a body such as the Civil Aviation Authority (e.g. the licensing of carriers) might qualify for immunity. See also *Kuwait Airways Corpn v Iraqi Airways Co* [1995] 1 W.L.R. 1147 HL.

4.   Under s.14(5) the "constituent territories of a federal state" are treated as "separate entities" and have only immunity under the Act insofar as such entities are granted it under s.14(2), unless and to the extent that an Order in Council is made differently in respect of particular territories.[177] To this extent, the decision in *Mellenger v New Brunswick Development Corp.* [1971] 1 W.L.R. 604 CA (Canadian Province of New Brunswick entitled to immunity) is reversed.

5.   In the *Trendtex* case, the plaintiffs were granted a *Mareva* injunction ordering that assets held by the bank in a bank account in London remain within the jurisdiction pending the outcome of the case. As a result of s.14(4), such an injunction could not now be granted.

Note that s.14(4) means that, unlike other state property, the property of a central bank is not subject to execution *even if it is being used, etc. for commercial purposes*.[178] Section 14(4) also grants central banks the other procedural privileges allowed by s.13. These limitations tend to undermine the effectiveness of the restrictive immunity doctrine as applied to central banks.

UNITED NATIONS CONVENTION ON JURISDICTIONAL IMMUNITIES OF STATES AND THEIR PROPERTY 2004

UN Doc A/RES/59/38; (2005) 44 I.L.M. 801

Article 1. Scope of the present Convention

The present Convention applies to immunity of a State and its property from the jurisdiction of the courts of another State.

---

[173]   Note, however, the good faith control on claims of state immunity suggested in the *Claim against the Empire of Iran* (1963) 45 I.L.R. 57.

[174]   (1997) 111 I.L.R. 611, CA. See *Barker* (1998) 47 I.C.L.Q. 951.

[175]   cf. the approach of the ILC in respect of state responsibility below, p.511.

[176]   See above, n.118, p.259.

[177]   Orders have been made for the constituent territories of Austria (SI 1979/457) and Germany (SI 1993/2809).

[178]   See *AIC Ltd v Federal Government of Nigeria* [2003] EWHC 1357.

Article 2. Use of terms

1. For the purposes of the present Convention:

(a) "court" means any organ of a State, however named, entitled to exercise judicial functions;

(b) "State" means:

> (i) the State and its various organs of government;
> (ii) constituent units of a federal State or political subdivisions of the State, which are entitled to perform acts in the exercise of the sovereign authority and are acting in that capacity;
> (iii) agencies or instrumentalities of the State or other entities, to the extent that they are entitled to perform and are actually performing acts in the exercise of sovereign authority of the State;
> (iv) representatives of the State acting in that capacity;

(c) "commercial transaction" means:

> (i) any commercial contract or transaction for the sale of goods or supply of services;
> (ii) any contract for a loan or other transaction of a financial nature, including any obligation of guarantee or of indemnity in respect of any such loan or transaction;
> (iii) any other contract or transaction of a commercial, industrial trading or professional nature, but not including a contract of employment of persons.

2. In determining whether a contract or transaction is a "commercial transaction" under paragraph 1 (c), reference should be made primarily to the nature of the contract or transaction, but its purpose should also be taken into account if the parties to the contract or transaction have so agreed, or if, in the practice of the State of the forum, that purpose is relevant to determining the non-commercial character of the contract or transaction.

3. The provisions of paragraphs 1 and 2 regarding the use of terms in the present Convention are without prejudice to the use of those terms or to the meanings which may be given to them in other international instruments or in the internal law of any State.

Article 5. State Immunity

A State enjoys immunity, in respect of itself and its property, from the jurisdiction of the courts of another State subject to the provisions of the present Convention.

Article 6. Modalities for giving effect to State immunity

. . .

2. A proceeding before a court of a State shall be considered to have been instituted against another State if that other State:

(a) is named as a party to that proceeding; or

(b) is not named as a party to the proceeding but the proceeding in effect seeks to affect the property, rights, interests or activities of that other State.

Article 10. Commercial transactions

1. If a State engages in a commercial transaction with a foreign natural or juridicial person and, by virtue of the applicable rules of private international law, differences relating to the commercial transaction fall within the jurisdiction of a court of another State, the State cannot invoke immunity from that jurisdiction in a proceeding arising out of that commercial transaction.

2. Paragraph 1 does not apply:

(a) in the case of a commercial transaction between States; or

(b) if the parties to the commercial transaction have expressly agreed otherwise.

3. Where a State enterprise or other entity established by a State which has an independent legal personality and is capable of:

(a) suing or being sued; and

(b) acquiring, owning or possessing and disposing of property, including property which that State has authorized it to operate or manage,

is involved in a proceeding which relates to a commercial transaction in which that entity is engaged, the immunity from jurisdiction enjoyed by that State shall not be affected.

Articles 11–15 exclude immunity in cases concerning employment contracts; personal injury or property damage; property claims; intellectual and industrial property; and participation in companies.

Article 16. Ships owned or operated by a State

1. Unless otherwise agreed between the States concerned, a State which owns or operates a ship cannot invoke immunity from jurisdiction before a court of another State which is otherwise competent in a proceeding which relates to the operation of that ship if, at the time the cause of action arose, the ship was used for other than government non- commercial purposes.

2. Paragraph 1 does not apply to warships, or naval auxiliaries, nor does it apply to other vessels owned or operated by a State and used, for the time being, only on government non-commercial service.

3. Unless otherwise agreed between the States concerned, a State cannot invoke immunity from jurisdiction before a court of another State which is otherwise competent in a proceeding which relates to the carriage of cargo on board a ship owned or operated by the State if, at the time the cause of action arose, the ship was used for other than government non-commercial purposes.

4. Paragraph 3 does not apply to any cargo carried on board the ships referred to in paragraph 2, nor does it apply to any cargo owned by a State and used or intended for use exclusively for government non-commercial purposes.

5. States may plead all measures of defence, prescription and limitation of liability which are available to private ships and cargoes and their owners.

6. If in a proceeding there arises a question relating to the government and non-commercial character of a ship owned or operated by a State or cargo owned by a State, a certificate signed by a diplomatic representative or other competent authority of that State and communicated to the court shall serve as evidence of the character of that ship or cargo.

Notes

1.   The Convention derives from the ILC's Draft Articles on Jurisdictional Immunities of States and Their Property 1991.[179] The draft articles were not well received by all states in the General Assembly Sixth Committee, with some states insisting on the absolute immunity approach and Western states being critical of certain elements of the text, e.g. the reference to "purpose" as well as "nature" in the test of a "commercial transaction". Nonetheless, with acceptance of the restricted immunity doctrine broadening worldwide, the draft articles were referred by the Assembly to an ad hoc Committee. This eventually produced an amended text,[180] which in 2004

[179] (1991) II-2 Y.B.I.L.C. 13; (1991) 30 I.L.M. 1554. The draft articles are based upon reports of the ILC's rapporteurs, Mr Sucharitkul and Mr Motoo Ogiso, for which see the references in (1991) II-2 Y.B.I.L.C. 12. On the draft articles, see Grieg (1989) 38 I.C.L.Q. 242 at 560; Hess (1993) 4 E.J.I.L 269; Morris (1989) 17 Denver J.I.L.P. 395; Tomuschat, *Seidl-Hohenveldern Essays* (1993), p.603. See also the International Law Association's *Revised Draft Articles for a Convention on State Immunity*, Report of the 66th ILA. Conference, Buenos Aires (1994), p.488, and the Institut de droit international's proposals: (1992) 64 *Annuaire de l'Institut de droit international* 388.

[180] For the reports of the Ad Hoc Working Group, see the UN website (General Assembly, Legal (Sixth) Committee).

became the Convention as adopted by the General Assembly. The Convention, which is based upon the restricted immunity doctrine, requires 30 contracting parties to enter into force. By mid-2009, there were only six contracting states, not including the UK.[181] The "general understanding" is that the Convention is limited to matters of civil jurisdiction: it "does not cover criminal proceedings"[182] It will not apply retroactively to proceedings instituted before its entry into force for the state concerned.[183]

2.   The Convention differs only in some details from the draft articles, with changes that respond to concerns expressed by states on some key issues. It maintains the general approach of the draft articles and most of their wording. Accordingly, the Convention follows the pattern of the 1972 European Convention on State Immunity and recent national legislation by stating a general rule of immunity (art.5) and then listing in some detail exceptions or limitations to it (arts 10–17). This is a different and preferable approach to that found (inevitably) in national court decisions in which an attempt is made to spell out an abstract test distinguishing acts *iure imperii* and acts *iure gestionis* which is then applied in all contexts (commercial transactions, contracts of employment, etc.). However, the Convention, like national legislation, cannot totally avoid such concepts as "commercial purposes", so that judicial pronouncements in cases such as the *I Congreso del Partido* remain relevant.

R v BOW STREET MAGISTRATES EX P PINOCHET[184]

[2000] 1 A.C. 147. House of Lords

In 1973, a right wing military coup led by the applicant overthrew the left wing Chilean Government of President Allende. The applicant subsequently became Head of State of Chile until 1990, when he resigned. In 1998, while he was visiting the United Kingdom for medical treatment, Spain requested the applicant's extradition to face charges, inter alia, of torture and conspiracy to torture in the Spanish courts. In judicial review proceedings, the Divisional Court quashed a provisional warrant for the applicant's arrest issued in response to the extradition request, on the ground that the applicant had immunity from prosecution as a former head of state. In these proceedings, the House of Lords heard an appeal against this decision. It held, by six votes to one, that the appeal should be allowed in respect of certain of the charges.

LORD BROWNE-WILKINSON

Since the Nazi atrocities and the Nuremberg trials, international law has recognised a number of offences as being international crimes. Individual states have taken jurisdiction to try some international crimes even in cases

---

[181] The UK has yet to decide whether to ratify the Convention. Foakes and Wilmshurst, *State Immunity: the United Nations Convention and its Effect*, Chatham House Briefing Paper (2005), p.10, while commending the Convention's restricted immunity approach, state: "Some of the wording ... gives rise to doubt as to whether UK ratification would improve the legal position of people or companies wanting to start proceedings in the UK against states". See also Denza (2006) 55 I.C.L.Q. 395; Fox (2006) 55 I.C.L.Q. 399; Gardiner (2006) 55 I.C.L.Q. 407.

[182] GA Resn.A/59/38, para.2 and Report of the ad hoc Committee on Jurisdictional Immunities of States and their Property, G.a.O.R., 59th Sess., Supp.22, para.33.

[183] Convention art.6.

[184] See from a large literature Bianchi (1999) 10 E.J.I.L. 237; Bradley and Goldsmith (1999) 97 Mich.L.R. 2129; Byers (2000) 10 Duke J.C.I.L. 415; Chinkin (1999) 93 A.J.I.L 703; Fox (1999) 48 I.C.L.Q. 687; McLachlan (2002) 51 I.C.L.Q. 959; Nicholls (2000) 41 Virg. J.I.L. 140; O'Neill (2002) 38 Stanford J.I.L. 289; O'Shea (2000) 16 S.A.J.H.R. 642; Powell and Pillay (2001) 16 S.A.J.H.R. 477; Rodley (2000) 69 Nordic J.I.L. 11; Ruffert 48 Neth I.L.R. 171; Van Alebeek (2000) 71 B.Y.I.L. 49; Wedgwood (2000) 40 Virg. J.I.L. 829.

where such crimes were not committed within the geographical boundaries of such states. The most important of such international crimes for present purposes is torture which is regulated by the International Convention against Torture and other Cruel, Inhuman or Degrading Treatment or Punishment 1984 (1990) (Cm. 1775). The obligations placed on the United Kingdom by that Convention (and on the other 110 or more signatory states who have adopted the Convention) were incorporated into the law of the United Kingdom by section 134 of the Criminal Justice Act 1988. That Act came into force on 29 September 1988. Section 134 created a new crime under United Kingdom law, the crime of torture. As required by the Torture Convention "all" torture wherever committed worldwide was made criminal under United Kingdom law and triable in the United Kingdom....Since torture outside the United Kingdom was not a crime under U.K. law until 29 September 1988, the principle of double criminality which requires an act to be a crime under both the law of Spain and of the United Kingdom [for extradition to be possible] cannot be satisfied in relation to conduct before that date if the principle of double criminality requires the conduct to be criminal under United Kingdom law *at the date it was committed*. ...

Lord Browne-Wilkinson held that the relevant date was the date of commission, as opposed to the later date of the extradition request. As a result, most of the charges for which Senator Pinochet's extradition was requested were not extraditable, as torture only became an offence under UK law after they were committed. However, certain alleged offences of torture or conspiracy to torture had occurred after that happened, so that it became necessary to decide whether Senator Pinochet had immunity from prosecution for them.

There is no real dispute that during the period of the Senator Pinochet regime appalling acts of barbarism were committed in Chile and elsewhere in the world: torture, murder and the unexplained disappearance of individuals, all on a large scale. Although it is not alleged that Senator Pinochet himself committed any of those acts, it is alleged that they were done in pursuance of a conspiracy to which he was a party, at his instigation and with his knowledge. He denies these allegations. None of the conduct alleged was committed by or against citizens of the United Kingdom or in the United Kingdom.

...Some of those charges had links with Spain. But most of the charges had no connection with Spain. The background to the case is that to those of left-wing political convictions Senator Pinochet is seen as an arch-devil: to those of right-wing persuasions he is seen as the saviour of Chile. It may well be thought that the trial of Senator Pinochet in Spain for offences all of which related to the State of Chile and most of which occurred in Chile is not calculated to achieve the best justice. But I cannot emphasise too strongly that that is no concern of your Lordships. Although others perceive our task as being to choose between two sides on the grounds of personal preference or political inclination, that is an entire misconception. Our job is to decide two questions of law: are there any extradition crimes and, if so, is Senator Pinochet immune from trial for committing those crimes. ...

...the Republic of Chile accepted before your Lordships that the international law prohibiting torture has the character of jus cogens or a peremptory norm, i.e. one of those rules of international law which have a particular status. In the *Furundzija* case[185], at paragraphs 153 and 154, the tribunal said:

"Because of the importance of the values it protects, [the prohibition of torture] has evolved into a peremptory norm or jus cogens, that is, a norm that enjoys a higher rank in the international hierarchy than treaty law and even 'ordinary' customary rules. The most conspicuous consequence of this higher rank is that the principle at issue cannot be derogated from by states through international treaties or local or special customs or even general customary rules not endowed with the same normative force ..."

The jus cogens nature of the international crime of torture justifies states in taking universal jurisdiction over torture wherever committed. International law provides that offences jus cogens may be punished by any state because the offenders are "common enemies of all mankind and all nations have an equal interest in their apprehension and prosecution:" *Demjanjuk v. Petrovsky* (1985) 603 F.Supp. 1468; 776 F.2d 571. ...

... if Senator Pinochet is not entitled to immunity in relation to the acts of torture alleged to have occurred after 29 September 1988, it will be the first time so far as counsel have discovered when a local domestic court

---

[185] Ed. (1998) 121 I.L.R. 213.

has refused to afford immunity to a head of state or former head of state on the grounds that there can be no immunity against prosecution for certain international crimes. ...

... The issue is whether international law grants state immunity in relation to the international crime of torture and, if so, whether the Republic of Chile is entitled to claim such immunity even though Chile, Spain and the United Kingdom are all parties to the Torture Convention and therefore "contractually" bound to give effect to its provisions for 8 December 1988 at the latest.[186]

... This immunity enjoyed by a head of state in power and an ambassador in post is a complete immunity attaching to the person of the head of state or ambassador and rendering him immune from all actions or prosecutions whether or not they relate to matters done for the benefit of the state. Such immunity is said to be granted ratione personae.

What then when the ambassador leaves his post or the head of state is deposed? The position of the ambassador is covered by [art.39(2) of] the Vienna Convention on Diplomatic Relations (1961).[187] ...

The continuing partial immunity of the ambassador after leaving post is of a different kind from that enjoyed ratione personae while he was in post. Since he is no longer the representative of the foreign state he merits no particular privileges or immunities as a person. However in order to preserve the integrity of the activities of the foreign state during the period when he was ambassador, it is necessary to provide that immunity is afforded to his *official* acts during his tenure in post. If this were not done the sovereign immunity of the state could be evaded by calling in question acts done during the previous ambassador's time. Accordingly under article 39(2) the ambassador, like any other official of the state, enjoys immunity in relation to his official acts done while he was an official. This limited immunity, ratione materiae, is to be contrasted with the former immunity ratione personae which gave complete immunity to all activities whether public or private.

In my judgment at common law a former head of state enjoys similar immunities, ratione materiae, once he ceases to be head of state. He too loses immunity ratione personae on ceasing to be head of state: see Sir Arthur Watts Q.C., Hague Lectures, "The Legal Position in International Law of Heads of State, Heads of Government and Foreign Ministers" 1994-III 247 Recueil des cours, p. 88 and the cases there cited. He can be sued on his private obligations: Ex-King Farouk of Egypt v. Christian Dior (1957) 24 I.L.R. 228; Jimenez v. Aristeguieta (1962) 311 F.2d 547. As ex-head of state he cannot be sued in respect of acts performed whilst head of state in his public capacity: Hatch v. Baez (1876) 7 Hun 596. Thus, at common law, the position of the former ambassador and the former head of state appears to be much the same: both enjoy immunity for acts done in performance of their respective functions whilst in office. ...

Lord Brown-Wilkinson indicated that the immunity of a former head of state in UK law was, like that of a former ambassador, now governed by art.39(2), Vienna Convention on Diplomatic Relations, which applied to heads of state with the "necessary modifications" by virtue of s.20, State Immunity Act 1978, above, p.261.

The correct way in which to apply article 39(2) of the Vienna Convention to a former head of state is baffling. ... The parliamentary history ... discloses no clear indication of what was intended [by s.20, State Immunity Act 1978]. However, in my judgment it does not matter unduly since Parliament cannot have intended to give heads of state and former heads of state greater rights than they already enjoyed under international law. Accordingly, "the necessary modifications" which need to be made will produce the result that a former head of state has immunity in relation to acts done as part of his official functions when head of state. Accordingly, in my judgment, Senator Pinochet as former head of state enjoys immunity ratione materiae in relation to acts done by him as head of state as part of his official functions as head of state.

The question then which has to be answered is whether the alleged organisation of state torture by Senator Pinochet (if proved) would constitute an act committed by Senator Pinochet as part of his official functions as head of state. It is not enough to say that it cannot be part of the functions of the head of state to commit a crime. Actions which are criminal under the local law can still have been done officially and therefore give rise to immunity ratione materiae. The case needs to be analysed more closely.

Can it be said that the commission of a crime which is an international crime against humanity and jus cogens is an act done in an official capacity on behalf of the state? I believe there to be strong ground for saying that the implementation of torture as defined by the Torture Convention cannot be a state function. ...

---

[186] Ed. This was the date on which the UK ratified the Torture Convention; Chile and Spain had done so earlier.
[187] Ed. For the text, see below, p.300.

Lord Browne-Wilkinson quoted Sir Arthur Watts' Hague Lecture, above, p.82, in support of this view.

I have doubts whether, before the coming into force of the Torture Convention, the existence of the international crime of torture as jus cogens was enough to justify the conclusion that the organisation of state torture could not rank for immunity purposes as performance of an official function. At that stage there was no international tribunal to punish torture and no general jurisdiction to permit or require its punishment in domestic courts. Not until there was some form of universal jurisdiction for the punishment of the crime of torture could it really be talked about as a fully constituted international crime. But in my judgment the Torture Convention did provide what was missing: a worldwide universal jurisdiction. Further, it required all member states to ban and outlaw torture: article 2. How can it be for international law purposes an official function to do something which international law itself prohibits and criminalises? Thirdly, an essential feature of the international crime of torture is that it must be committed "by or with the acquiescence of a public official or other person acting in an official capacity." As a result all defendants in torture cases will be state officials. Yet, if the former head of state has immunity, the man most responsible will escape liability while his inferiors (the chiefs of police, junior army officers) who carried out his orders will be liable. I find it impossible to accept that this was the intention.

Finally, and to my mind decisively, if the implementation of a torture regime is a public function giving rise to immunity rationae materiae, this produces bizarre results. Immunity rationae materiae applies not only to ex-heads of state and the ex-ambassadors but to all state officials who have been involved in carrying out functions of the state. Such immunity is necessary in order to prevent state immunity being circumvented by prosecuting or suing an official who, for example, actually carried out the torture when a claim against a head of state would be precluded by the doctrine of immunity. If that applied to the present case, and if the implementation of the torture regime is to be treated as official business sufficient to found an immunity for the former head of state, it must also be official business sufficient to justify immunity for his inferiors who actually did the torturing. Under the Convention the international crime of torture can only be committed by an official or someone in an official capacity. They would all be entitled to immunity. It would follow that there can be no case bought outside Chile in which a successful prosecution for torture can be brought unless the State of Chile is prepared to waive its right to its officials' immunity. Therefore the whole elaborate structure of universal jurisdiction over torture committed by officials is rendered abortive and one of the main objectives of the Torture Convention—to provide a system under which there is no safe haven for torturers—will have been frustrated. In my judgment all these factors together demonstrate that the notion of continued immunity for ex-heads of state is inconsistent with the provisions of the Torture Convention.

For these reasons in my judgment if, as alleged, Senator Pinochet organised and authorised torture after 8 December 1988, he was not acting in any capacity which gives rise to immunity rationae materiae because such actions were contrary to international law, Chile had agreed to outlaw such conduct and Chile had agreed with other parties to the Torture Convention that all signatory states should have jurisdiction to try official torture (as defined in the Convention) even if such torture were committed in Chile. ...

For these reasons, I would allow the appeal so as to permit the extradition proceedings to proceed on the allegation that torture in pursuance of a conspiracy to commit torture, including the single act of torture which is alleged in charge 30, was being committed by Senator Pinochet after 8 December 1988[188] when he lost his immunity.

Lords Hope, Hutton, Saville, Millett, and Phillips delivered concurring opinions. Lord Goff delivered a dissenting opinion.

Appeal allowed.

Notes

1. The *Pinochet* case concerned the question whether state immunity gives way so as to allow criminal prosecutions in cases of serious violations of human rights—a question which has

---

[188] Ed. See above, n.186.

become the subject of much debate (in the context of both criminal and civil proceedings) in recent years.[189]

2. In the *Pinochet* case it was held that a *former* head of state has a limited functional immunity (*ratione materiae*) from criminal prosecution, and the question was whether, in Lord Browne-Wilkinson's words, "the implementation of torture as defined by the Torture Convention cannot be a state function".

3. In contrast, as the *Pinochet* case also confirms, a *current* head of state has complete immunity *ratione personae* from criminal prosecution.[190] Thus in *Tatchell v Mugabe*[191] an application for a warrant for the arrest of President Mugabe, the Head of State of Zimbabwe, was refused. Judge Workman stated:

> "...international customary law which is embodied in our common law currently provides absolute immunity to any Head of State. In addition to the common law our State Immunity Act of 1978 (s.20, above, p.269) which extends the Diplomatic Privileges Act of 1964 provides for immunity from criminal jurisdiction for any Head of State."

This is the position in respect of prosecution in *national* courts. Current Heads of State may not have immunity from prosecution before the international tribunals, such as the International Criminal Court: see the *Arrest Warrant* case, below, p.292, para.55.

4. The immediate consequences in the United Kingdom of the House of Lords decision were summarised by Byers[192] as follows:

> "Following the judgment in Pinochet III, Jack Straw was again faced with the question of whether to grant authority for the extradition to proceed. The fact that he did so, on April 14, 1999, is testimony again to the influence of international and domestic public opinion, and to the constraining effect of his previous assertion—that the extradition was a judicial and not a political issue—on his subsequent behaviour.
>
> An extradition hearing took place in the Bow Street Magistrates Court, with Deputy Chief Stipendiary Magistrate Ronald Bartle considering not only the few charges that had survived the March 24, 1999 judgment in Pinochet III, but also a number of new charges subsequently filed by Judge Garzon [of Spain]. All of the new charges concerned acts of torture committed after 1988, and were thus permissible under the Law Lords' restrictive interpretation of double criminality. On October 8, 1999, the magistrate ruled that Pinochet could indeed be extradited to Spain, and committed him on thirty-four charges of torture and one charge of conspiracy to commit torture.
>
> In response to this decision the Chilean Government requested, on October 14, 1999, that the Home Secretary consider releasing Pinochet on medical grounds. Straw responded by arranging for a medical examination by four prominent British doctors. The examination took place on January 5, 2000 and established that Pinochet was unfit to stand trial—though the

---

[189] See Brohmer, *State Immunity and the Violation of Human Rights* (1997); Caplan (2003) 97 A.J.I.L. 741; Parlett (2006) 2 E.H.R.L.R. 49; Reece Thomas and Small (2003) 50 N.I.L.R. 1; Van Alebeek, *The Immunities of States and Their Officials in International Criminal Law and International Human Rights Law* (2008).

[190] As to this rule in customary international law, see further the *Arrest Warrant* case, below, p.292.

[191] (2004) unreported, Bow Street Magistrates' Court. See O'Keefe (2004) 75 B.Y.I.L. 407. Cf. *SOS Attentats et Beatrice Castelnau d'Esnault c. Gadafy* (2001) 125 I.L.R. 490, French Ct of Cass., *Re Sharon and Yaron* (2003) 127 I.L.R. 110, Belgian Ct of Cass. See Zappali (2001) 12 E.J.I.L. 595.

[192] See above, at p.279, pp.434–435.

report presented to Straw was not released to the press or, more importantly, to the foreign judicial authorities requesting Pinochet's extradition. This, it was explained, was because of medical confidentiality. Instead, Straw merely declared that, on the basis of what he had seen, he was "minded" to order the release of Pinochet.

Human rights organizations and the Belgian government (one of the countries that, in addition to Spain, had an arrest warrant outstanding against Pinochet) challenged Straw's decision not to release the report. This challenge was successful; the Divisional Court ruled on February 15, 2000 that the report had to be shared—under strict confidentiality—with the judicial authorities in each of the requesting states. Despite efforts to prevent the report's content from becoming public knowledge, by February 16, 2000, it had been leaked to the media. It was now apparent that Pinochet was indeed very ill, that he was suffering from extensive brain damage, that his memory had been severely affected, and that he would be incapable of sufficiently following the process of a trial so as to instruct his lawyers. At this point, the way was clear for Straw to do what he had wanted to do all along: to call off the extradition and send Pinochet back to Chile. When this happened, on March 2, 2000, it met with hardly any criticism, even from those who had been most strongly opposed to Pinochet's release."

5.   After his return to Chile, attempts to prosecute Pinochet under Chilean law on charges based on the activities of the notorious Caravan of Death failed when in 2002 the Chilean Supreme Court held, following the finding by a panel of court-appointed doctors that he was suffering from "progressive and incurable dementia", that Pinochet was physically and mentally unfit to stand trial, although leaving open the possibility that he might be tried if his condition improved. In 2004, following a video of an articulate and defiant interview given by him on Miami television, Chilean Supreme Court ruled that Pinochet, then aged 88, was medically fit to stand trial on new charges brought against him. Pinochet was later prosecuted for the torture and murder of political opponents but died in 2006 while proceedings were still pending.

AL-ADSANI v UNITED KINGDOM[193]

European Court of Human Rights. (2001) 34 E.H.R.R. 273

The applicant, who held UK and Kuwaiti nationality, was thought by a relative (the Sheikh) of the Emir of Kuwait to have been responsible for the circulation of videos containing sex scenes involving him. The applicant alleged that, in retaliation, on May 1, 1991 he was taken by the Sheikh by Government transport to the Kuwait state security prison where he was badly beaten by state security guards. On May 7, he was taken by the Sheikh to a royal palace where his head was placed underwater in a swimming pool containing dead bodies and where he suffered severe burns when the Sheikh set fire to mattresses in a cell in which he was detained. The applicant was treated in London for his burns. He was also diagnosed there as suffering from post-traumatic stress disorder. The applicant alleged that while in London he received threats from agents of the Sheikh and from the Kuwaiti Ambassador.

The applicant brought civil proceedings in the English High Court against the Sheikh and the Government of Kuwait for damages for the physical injuries and mental suffering caused by the

---

[193] See Bates (2003) 3 H.R.L.R. 193 and Emberland (2002) 96 A.J.I.L. 699.

assaults in Kuwait and the threats made in London. The applicant obtained a default judgment against the Sheikh. As to the claim against the Government of Kuwait, the Court of Appeal held that it had not been established that the Government of Kuwait had been responsible for any alleged threats made in London. At the same time, there was a possible claim against the Government because of the state's involvement in the assaults in Kuwait on 1 May. But, while the English courts had jurisdiction to hear a claim concerning a tort committed abroad, the Government of Kuwait's claim to state immunity succeeded under s.1 of the State Immunity Act 1978, see above, p.266. As a result, permission to issue a writ against the Government was refused.

The applicant alleged violations by the UK of arts 3 (torture) and 6 (fair trial) of the ECHR. The European Court held unanimously that there was no violation of art.3 because of lack of UK involvement in the alleged torture. As to art.6, the Court ruled, by nine votes to eight, that the right of access to the English courts (that is a part of the art.6 right to a fair trial) had not been violated by the upholding of the defence of state immunity. The following extracts concern only the art.6 claim.

Judgment of the Court

46. The Court reiterates its constant case-law to the effect that Article 6 § 1 does not itself guarantee any particular content for "civil rights and obligations" in the substantive law of the Contracting States. It extends only to *contestations* (disputes) over "civil rights and obligations" which can be said, at least on arguable grounds, to be recognised under domestic law ...

48. The proceedings which the applicant intended to pursue were for damages for personal injury, a cause of action well known to English law. The Court does not accept the Government's submission that the applicant's claim had no legal basis in domestic law since any substantive right which might have existed was extinguished by operation of the doctrine of State immunity. It notes that an action against a State is not barred *in limine*: if the defendant State waives immunity, the action will proceed to a hearing and judgment. The grant of immunity is to be seen not as qualifying a substantive right but as a procedural bar on the national courts' power to determine the right. ...

52. ... Article 6 § 1 secures to everyone the right to have any claim relating to his civil rights and obligations brought before a court.

53. The right of access to a court is not, however, absolute, but may be subject to limitations; these are permitted by implication since the right of access by its very nature calls for regulation by the State. In this respect, the Contracting States enjoy a certain margin of appreciation, although the final decision as to the observance of the Convention's requirements rests with the Court. It must be satisfied that the limitations applied do not restrict or reduce the access left to the individual in such a way or to such an extent that the very essence of the right is impaired. Furthermore, a limitation will not be compatible with Article 6 § 1 if it does not pursue a legitimate aim and if there is no reasonable relationship of proportionality between the means employed and the aim sought to be achieved ...

54. The Court must first examine whether the limitation pursued a legitimate aim. It notes in this connection that sovereign immunity is a concept of international law, developed out of the principle *par in parem non habet imperium*, by virtue of which one State shall not be subject to the jurisdiction of another State. The Court considers that the grant of sovereign immunity to a State in civil proceedings pursues the legitimate aim of complying with international law to promote comity and good relations between States through the respect of another State's sovereignty.

55. The Court must next assess whether the restriction was proportionate to the aim pursued. ...

56. ... measures taken by a High Contracting Party which reflect generally recognised rules of public international law on State immunity cannot in principle be regarded as imposing a disproportionate restriction on the right of access to a court as embodied in Article 6 § 1. Just as the right of access to a court is an inherent part of the fair trial guarantee in that Article, so some restrictions on access must likewise be regarded as inherent, an example being those limitations generally accepted by the community of nations as part of the doctrine of State immunity.

57. The Court notes that the 1978 Act, applied by the English courts so as to afford immunity to Kuwait, complies with the relevant provisions of the 1972 Basle Convention, which, while placing a number of limitations on the scope of State immunity as it was traditionally understood, preserves it in respect of civil proceedings for

damages for personal injury unless the injury was caused in the territory of the forum State. ... Except insofar as it affects claims for damages for torture, the applicant does not deny that the above provision reflects a generally accepted rule of international law. He asserts, however, that his claim related to torture, and contends that the prohibition of torture has acquired the status of a *jus cogens* norm in international law, taking precedence over treaty law and other rules of international law.

58. Following the decision to uphold Kuwait's claim to immunity, the domestic courts were never required to examine evidence relating to the applicant's allegations, which have, therefore, never been proved. However, for the purposes of the present judgment, the Court accepts that the ill-treatment alleged by the applicant against Kuwait in his pleadings in the domestic courts, namely, repeated beatings by prison guards over a period of several days with the aim of extracting a confession ..., can properly be categorised as torture within the meaning of Article 3 of the Convention. ...

61. While the Court accepts ... that the prohibition of torture has achieved the status of a peremptory norm in international law, it observes that the present case concerns not, as in *Furundzija* and *Pinochet*, the criminal liability of an individual for alleged acts of torture, but the immunity of a State in a civil suit for damages in respect of acts of torture within the territory of that State. Notwithstanding the special character of the prohibition of torture in international law, the Court is unable to discern in the international instruments, judicial authorities or other materials before it any firm basis for concluding that, as a matter of international law, a State no longer enjoys immunity from civil suit in the courts of another State where acts of torture are alleged. In particular, the Court observes that none of the primary international instruments referred to (Article 5 of the Universal Declaration of Human Rights, Article 7 of the International Covenant on Civil and Political Rights and Articles 2 and 4 of the UN Convention) relates to civil proceedings or to State immunity.

62. It is true that in its [1999] Report on Jurisdictional Immunities of States and their Property[194] ... the working group of the International Law Commission noted, as a recent development in State practice and legislation on the subject of immunities of States, the argument increasingly put forward that immunity should be denied in the case of death or personal injury resulting from acts of a State in violation of human rights norms having the character of *jus cogens*, particularly the prohibition on torture. However, as the working group itself acknowledged, while national courts had in some cases shown some sympathy for the argument that States were not entitled to plead immunity where there had been a violation of human rights norms with the character of *jus cogens*, in most cases (including those cited by the applicant in the domestic proceedings and before the Court) the plea of sovereign immunity had succeeded.

63. The ILC working group went on to note developments, since those decisions, in support of the argument that a State may not plead immunity in respect of human rights violations: first, the exception to immunity adopted by the United States in the amendment to the Foreign Sovereign Immunities Act (FSIA) which had been applied by the United States courts in two cases; secondly, the *ex parte Pinochet (No.3)* judgment in which the House of Lords "emphasised the limits of immunity in respect of gross human rights violations by State officials". The Court does not, however, find that either of these developments provides it with a firm basis on which to conclude that the immunity of States *ratione personae* is no longer enjoyed in respect of civil liability for claims of acts of torture, let alone that it was not enjoyed in 1996 at the time of the Court of Appeal's judgment in the present case.

64. As to the amendment to the FSIA, the very fact that the amendment was needed would seem to confirm that the general rule of international law remained that immunity attached even in respect of claims of acts of official torture. Moreover, the amendment is circumscribed in its scope: the offending State must be designated as a State sponsor of acts of terrorism, and the claimant must be a national of the United States. The effect of the FSIA is further limited in that after judgment has been obtained, the property of a foreign State is immune from attachment or execution unless one of the statutory exceptions applies. ...

65. As to the *ex parte Pinochet (No.3)* judgment ... the Court notes that the majority of the House of Lords held that, after the UN Convention and even before, the international prohibition against official torture had the character of *jus cogens* or a peremptory norm and that no immunity was enjoyed by a torturer from one Torture Convention State from the criminal jurisdiction of another. But, as the working group of the ILC itself acknowledged, that case concerned the immunity *ratione materiae* from criminal jurisdiction of a former head of State, who was at the material time physically within the United Kingdom. As the judgments in the case made clear, the conclusion of the House of Lords did not in any way affect the immunity *ratione personae* of foreign sovereign States from the civil jurisdiction in respect of such acts (see in particular, the judgment of Lord Millett

---

[194] Ed. See (1999) Y.B.I.L.C., Vol.II (Part Two), Annex.

...). In so holding, the House of Lords cited with approval the judgments of the Court of Appeal in *Al-Adsani* itself.

66. The Court, while noting the growing recognition of the overriding importance of the prohibition of torture, does not accordingly find it established that there is yet acceptance in international law of the proposition that States are not entitled to immunity in respect of civil claims for damages for alleged torture committed outside the forum State. The 1978 Act, which grants immunity to States in respect of personal injury claims unless the damage was caused within the United Kingdom, is not inconsistent with those limitations generally accepted by the community of nations as part of the doctrine of State immunity.

67. In these circumstances, the application by the English courts of the provisions of the 1978 Act to uphold Kuwait's claim to immunity cannot be said to have amounted to an unjustified restriction on the applicant's access to a court. ...

FOR THESE REASONS, THE COURT ... *Holds* by nine votes to eight that there has been no violation of Article 6 § 1 of the Convention.

JOINT DISSENTING OPINION OF JUDGES ROZAKIS AND CAFLISCH JOINED BY JUDGES WILD-HABER, COSTA, CABRAL BARRETO AND VAJIĆ

1. The Court's majority unequivocally accept that the rule on the prohibition of torture had achieved at the material time, namely at the time when civil proceedings were instituted by the applicant before the English courts, the status of a peremptory rule of international law (*jus cogens*). They refer to a number of authorities which demonstrate that the prohibition of torture has gradually crystallised as a *jus cogens* rule. To this conclusion we readily subscribe ...

By accepting that the rule on prohibition of torture is a rule of *jus cogens*, the majority recognise that it is hierarchically higher than any other rule of international law, be it general or particular, customary or conventional, with the exception, of course, of other *jus cogens* norms. For the basic characteristic of a *jus cogens* rule is that, as a source of law in the now vertical international legal system, it overrides any other rule which does not have the same status. In the event of a conflict between a *jus cogens* rule and any other rule of international law, the former prevails. The consequence of such prevalence is that the conflicting rule is null and void, or, in any event, does not produce legal effects which are in contradiction with the content of the peremptory rule.

2. The Court's majority do not seem, on the other hand, to deny that the rules on State immunity, customary or conventional, do not belong to the category of *jus cogens*; and rightly so, because it is clear that the rules of State immunity, deriving from both customary and conventional international law, have never been considered by the international community as rules with a hierarchically higher status. It is common knowledge that, in many instances, States have, through their own initiative, waived their rights of immunity; that in many instances they have contracted out of them, or have renounced them. These instances clearly demonstrate that the rules on State immunity do not enjoy a higher status, since *jus cogens* rules, protecting as they do the "*ordre public*", that is the basic values of the international community, cannot be subject to unilateral or contractual forms of derogation from their imperative contents.

3. The acceptance therefore of the *jus cogens* nature of the prohibition of torture entails that a State allegedly violating it cannot invoke hierarchically lower rules (in this case, those on State immunity) to avoid the consequences of the illegality of its actions. In the circumstances of this case, Kuwait cannot validly hide behind the rules on State immunity to avoid proceedings for a serious claim of torture made before a foreign jurisdiction; and the courts of that jurisdiction (the United Kingdom) cannot accept a plea of immunity, or invoke it *ex officio*, to refuse an applicant adjudication of a torture case. Due to the interplay of the *jus cogens* rule on prohibition of torture and the rules on State immunity, the procedural bar of State immunity is automatically lifted, because those rules, as they conflict with a hierarchically higher rule, do not produce any legal effect. In the same vein, national law which is designed to give domestic effect to the international rules on State immunity cannot be invoked as creating a jurisdictional bar, but must be interpreted in accordance with and in the light of the imperative precepts of *jus cogens*.

4. The majority, while accepting that the rule on the prohibition of torture is a *jus cogens* norm, refuse to draw the consequences of such acceptance. They contend that a distinction must be made between criminal proceedings, where apparently they accept that a *jus cogens* rule has the overriding force to deprive the rules of sovereign immunity from their legal effects, and civil proceedings, where, in the absence of authority, they consider that the same conclusion cannot be drawn. Their position is well summarised in paragraph 66 of the judgment, where they assert that they do not find it established that "there is yet acceptance in international law

of the proposition that States are not entitled to immunity in respect of civil claims for damages for alleged torture committed outside the forum State". Hence, "[t]he 1978 Act, which grants immunity to States in respect of personal injury claims [is] not inconsistent with those limitations generally accepted by the community of nations as part of the doctrine of State immunity".

In our opinion, the distinction made by the majority and their conclusions are defective on two grounds.

Firstly, the English courts, when dealing with the applicant's claim, never resorted to the distinction made by the majority. They never invoked any difference between criminal charges or civil claims, between criminal and civil proceedings, in so far as the legal force of the rules on State immunity or the applicability of the 1978 Act was concerned. The basic position of the Court of Appeal – the last court which dealt with the matter in its essence – is expressed by the observations of Lord Justice Stuart-Smith who simply denied that the prohibition of torture was a *jus cogens* rule. In reading the Lord Justice's observations, one even forms the impression that if the Court of Appeal had been convinced that the rule of prohibition of torture was a norm of *jus cogens*, they could grudgingly have admitted that the procedural bar of State immunity did not apply in the circumstances of the case.

Secondly, the distinction made by the majority between civil and criminal proceedings, concerning the effect of the rule of the prohibition of torture, is not consonant with the very essence of the operation of the *jus cogens* rules. It is not the nature of the proceedings which determines the effects that a *jus cogens* rule has upon another rule of international law, but the character of the rule as a peremptory norm and its interaction with a hierarchically lower rule. The prohibition of torture, being a rule of *jus cogens*, acts in the international sphere and deprives the rule of sovereign immunity of all its legal effects in that sphere. The criminal or civil nature of the domestic proceedings is immaterial. The jurisdictional bar is lifted by the very interaction of the international rules involved, and the national judge cannot admit a plea of immunity raised by the defendant State as an element preventing him from entering into the merits of the case and from dealing with the claim of the applicant for the alleged damages inflicted upon him.

Under these circumstances we believe that the English courts have erred in considering that they had no jurisdiction to entertain the applicant's claim because of the procedural bar of State immunity and the consequent application of the 1978 Act. Accordingly, the applicant was deprived of his right to have access to the English court to entertain his claim of damages for the alleged torture suffered by him in Kuwait, and Article 6 § 1, has, in our view, been violated.

DISSENTING OPINION OF JUDGE FERRARI BRAVO *(TRANSLATION)*

What a pity! The Court, whose task in this case was to rule whether there had been a violation of Article 6 § 1, had a golden opportunity to issue a clear and forceful condemnation of all acts of torture. To do so, it need only have upheld the thrust of the House of Lords' judgment in *Regina v. Bow Street Metropolitan Stipendiary and Others, ex parte Pinochet Ugarte (No.3)* (judgment of 24 March 1999 [2000] Appeal Cases 147), to the effect that the prohibition of torture is now *jus cogens*, so that torture is a crime under international law. It follows that every State has a duty to *contribute* to the punishment of torture and cannot hide behind formalist arguments to avoid having to give judgment.

I say to "contribute" to punishment, and not, obviously, to punish, since it was clear that the acts of torture had not taken place in the United Kingdom but elsewhere, in a State over which the Court did not have jurisdiction.

But it is precisely one of those old formalist arguments which the Court endorsed when it said (in paragraph 61 of the judgment) that it was unable to discern any rules of international law requiring it not to apply the rule of immunity from civil suit where acts of torture were alleged. And the Court went further, notwithstanding its analysis of the cases mentioned in paragraphs 62 to 65, concluding sadly in paragraph 66 that the contrary rule was not *yet* accepted. *Quousque tandem* ...!

There will be other such cases, but the Court has unfortunately missed a very good opportunity to deliver a courageous judgment.

Concurring opinions were delivered by Judge Pellonpää, joined by Judge Bratza, and by Judge Zupancic. A dissenting opinion was also delivered by Judge Loucaides.

Notes

1. Whereas the *Pinochet* case concerned criminal liability for torture, the *Al-Adsani* case concerned *civil* liability.[195] How convincing do you find the court's distinction betweem criminal and civil immunity?

    Like the *Pinochet* case, the *Al-Adsani* case raised the question of the balance to be struck between the international law of human rights and of state immunity in the context of torture.[196] Whereas the *Pinochet* case had, on its facts, come down on the side of human rights, the *Al-Adsani* case, decided a year later, was more cautious, thereby robbing the move towards the punishment of torturers to which *Pinochet* had contributed of some of its momentum. Did the Court miss a "golden opportunity" (Judge Ferrari Bravo)?

2. The ruling in the *Al Adsani* case concerned a claim against the *state*. In *Jones v Ministry of the Interior*,[197] the House of Lords was similarly not persuaded that state immunity gave way in civil claims against *individuals* alleging acts of torture committed by them when acting as servants or agents of the state. The claimants brought claims against the state of Saudia Arabia and certain public officials (a colonel, police officers and a prison governor) for damages for acts of torture committed in Saudia Arabia. As in the *Al Adsani* case, the claim against the state failed under s.1 of the State Immunity Act 1978. Rejecting the claims against the public officials, Lord Bingham stated:

    "10. While the 1978 [State Immunity] Act explains what is comprised within the expression 'State', and both it and the 1972 European Convention govern the immunity of separate entities exercising sovereign powers, neither expressly provides for the case where suit is brought against the servants or agents, officials or functionaries of a foreign state ('servants or agents') in respect of acts done by them as such in the foreign state. There is, however, a wealth of authority to show that in such case the foreign state is entitled to claim immunity for its servants as it could if sued itself. The foreign state's right to immunity cannot be circumvented by suing its servants or agents. Domestic authority for this proposition may be found in ... *R v Bow Street Metropolitan Stipendiary Magistrate, Ex p Pinochet Ugarte (No 3)* [2000] 1 AC 147, 269, 285–286 .... Courts in Germany, the United States, Canada and Ireland have taken the same view: ... The International Criminal Tribunal for the Former Yugoslavia has also taken the same view: *Prosecutor v Blaskic* (1997) 110 ILR 607, 707. In the UN Convention of 2004 [above, p.277] ... this matter is expressly addressed in article 2 where 'State' is defined in (1)(b)(iv) to mean 'representatives of the State acting in that capacity'. It is further provided, in article 6(2)(b), that 'A proceeding before a court of a State shall be considered to have been instituted against another State if that other State ... (b) is not named as a party to the proceeding but the proceeding in effect seeks to affect the property, rights, interests or activities of that other State.'" ...

    17. The claimants' key submissions are that the proscription of torture by international law, having the authority it does, precludes the grant of immunity to states or individuals sued for committing acts of torture, since such cannot be governmental acts or exercises of state

---

[195] On civil liability, see Scott, ed., *Torture as Tort* (2001). On universal jurisdiction for civil claims of torture, Donovan and Roberts (2006) 100 A.J.I.L. 142; Kamminga (2005) 99 A.S.I.L. Proc. 123; Parlett (2007) 4 E.H.R.L.R. 385; Ryngaert (2007) 38 N.Y.I.L. 3; Van Schaack (2005) A.S.I.L. Proc 120.

[196] See the literature cited at n.189.

[197] [2006] UKHL 26. See Bates (2007) 7 H.R.L.R. 651; Fox (2005) 12 L.Q.R. 353 (CA judgment); Seymour (2006) 65 C.L.J. 479; Steinerte and Wallace (2006) 100 A.J.I.L. 901.

authority entitled to the protection of state immunity ratione materiae. In support of this submission the claimants rely on a wide range of materials including: the reasoning of the minority of the Grand Chamber in *Al-Adsani v United Kingdom* (2001) 34 EHRR 273; observations by members of the House in *R v Bow Street Metropolitan Stipendiary Magistrate, Ex p Pinochet Ugarte (No 1)* [2000] 1 AC 61 and *(No 3)* [2000] 1 AC 147 ...; a body of United States authority; the decision of the International Criminal Tribunal for the former Yugoslavia in *Prosecutor v Furundzija* (1998) 38 ILM 317; the decision of the Italian Court of Cassation in *Ferrini v Federal Republic of Germany* (2004) Cass sez un 5044/04; 87 Rivista di diritto internazionale 539; and a recommendation made by the Committee against Torture to Canada on 7 July 2005. ...

18. The Grand Chamber's decision in *Al-Adsani* is very much in point, since it concerned the grant of immunity to Kuwait under the 1978 Act, which had the effect of defeating the applicant's claim in England for damages for torture allegedly inflicted upon him in Kuwait. The claimants are entitled to point out that a powerful minority of the court found a violation of the applicant's right of access to a court under article 6 of the European Convention. The majority, however, ... [w]hile noting the growing recognition of the overriding importance of the prohibition of torture, ... did not find it established that there was yet acceptance in international law of the proposition that states were not entitled to immunity in respect of civil claims for damages for alleged torture committed outside the forum state (para 66). It is of course true, as the claimants contend, that under section 2 of the 1998 Act this decision of the Strasbourg court is not binding on the English court. But ...the House would ordinarily follow such a decision unless it found the court's reasoning to be unclear or unsound, or the law had changed significantly since the date of the decision. Non of these conditions, in my opinion, obtains here.

19. It is certainly true that in ... *Pinochet (No 3)* certain members of the House held that acts of torture could not be functions of a head of state or governmental or official acts. ... references may readily be found in *Pinochet (No 3)*: see, for example, p 205 (Lord Browne-Wilkinson), pp 261–262 (Lord Hutton). I would not question the correctness of the decision reached by the majority in *Pinochet (No 3)*. But the case was categorically different from the present, since it concerned criminal proceedings falling squarely within the universal criminal jurisdiction mandated by the Torture Convention and did not fall within Part 1 of the 1978 Act. The essential ratio of the decision, as I understand it, was that international law could not without absurdity require criminal jurisdiction to be assumed and exercised where the Torture Convention conditions were satisfied and, at the same time, require immunity to be granted to those properly charged. The Torture Convention was the mainspring of the decision, and certain members of the House expressly accepted that the grant of immunity in civil proceedings was unaffected: see p 264 (Lord Hutton), p 278 (Lord Millett) and pp 280, 281, 287 (Lord Phillips of Worth Matravers). It is, I think, difficult to accept that torture cannot be a governmental or official act, since under article 1 of the Torture Convention torture must, to qualify as such, be inflicted by or with the connivance of a public official or other person acting in an official capacity. The claimants' argument encounters the difficulty that it is founded on the Torture Convention; but to bring themselves within the Torture Convention they must show that the torture was (to paraphrase the definition) official; yet they argue that the conduct was not official in order to defeat the claim to immunity. ...

22. In *Ferrini v Federal Republic of Germany*, above, the Italian Court of Cassation entertained a civil claim based on war crimes committed in 1944–1945, partly in Italy but mainly in Germany. In para 9 of its judgment the court found 'no doubt that the principle of universal

jurisdiction also applies to civil actions which trace their origins to such crimes'. In reaching this decision the court distinguished *Al-Adsani v United Kingdom*, above, and *Bouzari v Islamic Republic of Iran* (2002) 124 ILR 527[198] ... It may be, despite the court's closing statement to the contrary, that the decision was influenced by the occurrence of some of the unlawful conduct within the forum state. The decision has been praised by some distinguished commentators (among them Andrea Bianchi in a case note in (2005) 99 Am Jo Int Law 242), but another (Andrea Gattini ... (2005) 3 Jo Int Crim J 224, 231) has accused the court of 'deplorable superficiality': see also Hazel Fox QC ... (2006) 2 EHRLR 142. The *Ferrini* decision cannot in my opinion be treated as an accurate statement of international law as generally understood; and one swallow does not make a rule of international law. The more closely-reasoned decisions in *Bouzari v Islamic Republic of Iran* (2002) 124 ILR 427, (2004) 71 OR (3d) 675 are to the contrary effect. ...

24. In countering the claimants' argument the Kingdom, supported by the Secretary of State, is able to advance four arguments which in my opinion are cumulatively irresistible. First, the claimants are obliged to accept, in the light of the *Arrest Warrant* decision of the International Court of Justice [below, p.292] that state immunity ratione personae can be claimed for a serving foreign minister accused of crimes against humanity. Thus, even in such a context, the international law prohibition of such crimes, having the same standing as the prohibition of torture, does no prevail. It follows that such a prohibition does not automatically override all other rules of international law. The International Court of Justice has made plain that breach of a jus cogens norm of international law does not suffice to confer jurisdiction (*Democratic Republic of the Congo v Rwanda* (unreported) 3 February 2006, para 64). As Hazel Fox QC put it (*The Law of State Immunity* (2004) p 525),

> 'State immunity is a procedural rule going to the jurisdiction of a national court. It does not go to substantive law; it does not contradict a prohibition contained in a *jus cogens* norm but merely diverts any breach of it to a different method of settlement. Arguably, then, there is no substantive content in the procedural plea of State immunity upon which a *jus cogens* mandate can bite.'

Where state immunity is applicable, the national court has no jurisdiction to exercise.

25. Secondly, article 14 of the Torture Convention does not provide for universal civil jurisdiction. ... the natural reading of the article as it stands in my view conforms with the US understanding ... that it requires a private right of action for damages only for acts of torture committed in territory under the jurisdiction of the forum state. This is an interpretation shared by Canada, as its exchanges with the Torture Committee make clear. The correctness of this reading is confirmed when comparison is made between the spare terms of article 14 and the much more detailed provisions governing the assumption and exercise of criminal jurisdiction.

26. Thirdly, the UN Immunity Convention of 2004 provides no exception from immunity where civil claims are made based on acts of torture. The Working Group in its 1999 Report makes plain that such an exception was considered, but no such exception was agreed. Despite its embryonic status, this Convention is the most authoritative statement available on the current international understanding of the limits of state immunity in civil cases, and the

---

[198] Ed. In this case an Iranian national brought a claim in the Canadian courts against the state of Iran for damages in tort for acts of torture committed against him in Iran. The Ontario Appeal Court held that there was "no principle of customary international law which provides an exception from state immunity where an act of torture has been committed outside the forum, even for acts contrary to *jus cogens*." (para.88). See Novogrodsky (2008) 18 E.J.I.L. 939.

absence of a torture or jus cogens exception is wholly inimical to the claimants' contention.[199] ...It may very well be that the claimants' contention will come to represent the law of nations, but it cannot be said to do so now.

27. Fourthly, there is no evidence that states have recognised or given effect to an international law obligation to exercise universal jurisdiction over claims arising from alleged breaches of peremptory norms of international law, not is there any consensus of judical and learned opinion that they should. This is significant, since these are sources of international law. But this lack of evidence is not neutral: since the rule on immunity is well-understood and established, and no relevant exception is generally accepted, the rule prevails.

28. It follows, in my opinion, that Part 1 of the 1978 Act is not shown to be disproportionate as inconsistent with a peremptory norm of international law, and its application does not infringe the claimants' Convention right under article 6 (assuming it to apply). ...."

ARREST WARRANT CASE

Democratic Republic of the Congo v Belgium

I.C.J. Rep 2002, p.3

For the facts of this case, see the extract on the question of jurisdiction, above, p.250.

Judgment of the Court

51. ... in international law it is firmly established that, as also diplomatic and consular agents, certain holders of high-ranking office in a State, such as the Head of State, Head of Government and Minister for Foreign Affairs, enjoy immunities from jurisdiction in other States, both civil and criminal. For the purposes of the present case, it is only the immunity from criminal jurisdiction and the inviolability of an incumbent Minister for Foreign Affairs that fall for the Court to consider. ...

The Court then examined the relevant provisions of the Vienna Conventions on Diplomatic Relations 1961 and on Consular Relations 1963, and the New York Convention on Special Missions 1969.

These conventions ... do not, however, contain any provision specifically defining the immunities enjoyed by Ministers for Foreign Affairs. It is consequently on the basis of customary international law that the Court must decide the questions relating to the immunities of such Ministers raised in the present case.

53. In customary international law, the immunities accorded to Ministers for Foreign Affairs are not granted for their personal benefit, but to ensure the effective performance of their functions on behalf of their respective States. In order to determine the extent of these immunities, the Court must therefore consider the nature of the functions exercised by a Minister for Foreign Affairs. He or she is in charge of his or her Government's diplomatic activities and generally acts as its representative in international negotiations and intergovernmental meetings. Ambassadors and other diplomatic agents carry out their duties under his or her authority. His or her acts may bind the State represented, and there is a presumption that a Minister for Foreign Affairs, simply by virtue of that office, has full powers to act on behalf of the State (see, e.g., art. 7, para.2 (a), of the 1969 Vienna Convention on the Law of Treaties). In the performance of these functions, he or she is frequently required to travel internationally, and thus must be in a position freely to do so whenever the need should arise. He or she must also be in constant communication with the Government, and with its diplomatic missions around the world, and be

---

[199] Ed. Lord Bingham refers to the literature cited above at n.181, welcoming the Convention, and also to Hall (2006) 55 I.C.L.Q. 411 and McGregor 55 I.C.L.Q. 437 criticising the absence of a "torture" exception.

capable at any time of communicating with representatives of other States. The Court further observes that a Minister for Foreign Affairs, responsible for the conduct of his or her State's relations with all other States, occupies a position such that, like the Head of State or the Head of Government, he or she is recognized under international law as representative of the State solely by virtue of his or her office. He or she does not have to present letters of credence: to the contrary, it is generally the Minister who determines the authority to be conferred upon diplomatic agents and countersigns their letters of credence. . . .

54. The Court accordingly concludes that the functions of a Minister for Foreign Affairs are such that, throughout the duration of his or her office, he or she when abroad enjoys full immunity from criminal jurisdiction and inviolability. That immunity and that inviolability protect the individual concerned against any act of authority of another State which would hinder him or her in the performance of his or her duties.

55. In this respect, no distinction can be drawn between acts performed by a Minister for Foreign Affairs in an "official" capacity, and those claimed to have been performed in a "private capacity", or, for that matter, between acts performed before the person concerned assumed office as Minister for Foreign Affairs and acts committed during the period of office. Thus, if a Minister for Foreign Affairs is arrested in another State on a criminal charge, he or she is clearly thereby prevented from exercising the functions of his or her office. The consequences of such impediment to the exercise of those official functions are equally serious, regardless of whether the Minister for Foreign Affairs was, at the time of arrest, present in the territory of the arresting State on an "official" visit or a "private" visit, regardless of whether the arrest relates to acts allegedly performed before the person became the Minister for Foreign Affairs or to acts performed while in office, and regardless of whether the arrest relates to alleged acts performed in an "official" capacity or a "private" capacity. Furthermore, even the mere risk that, by travelling to or transiting another State, a Minister for Foreign Affairs might be exposing himself or herself to legal proceedings could deter the Minister from travelling internationally when required to do so for the purposes of the performance of his or her official functions. . . .

58. The Court has carefully examined State practice, including national legislation and those few decisions of national higher courts, such as the House of Lords or the French Court of Cassation. It has been unable to deduce from this practice that there exists under customary international law any form of exception to the rule according immunity from criminal jurisdiction and inviolability to incumbent Ministers for Foreign Affairs, where they are suspected of having committed war crimes or crimes against humanity.

The Court has also examined the rules concerning the immunity or criminal responsibility of persons having an official capacity contained in the legal instruments creating international criminal tribunals, and which are specifically applicable to the latter (see Charter of the International Military Tribunal of Nuremberg, art. 7; Charter of the International Military Tribunal of Tokyo, art. 6; Statute of the International Criminal Tribunal for the former Yugoslavia, art.7, para.2; Statute of the International Criminal Tribunal for Rwanda, art. 6, para.2; Statute of the International Criminal Court, art. 27). It finds that these rules likewise do not enable it to conclude that any such an exception exists in customary international law in regard to national courts.

Finally, none of the decisions of the Nuremberg and Tokyo international military tribunals, or of the International Criminal Tribunal for the former Yugoslavia, cited by Belgium deal with the question of the immunities of incumbent Ministers for Foreign Affairs before national courts where they are accused of having committed war crimes or crimes against humanity. The Court accordingly notes that those decisions are in no way at variance with the findings it has reached above. . . .

59. It should further be noted that the rules governing the jurisdiction of national courts must be carefully distinguished from those governing jurisdictional immunities: jurisdiction does not imply absence of immunity, while absence of immunity does not imply jurisdiction. Thus, although various international conventions on the prevention and punishment of certain serious crimes impose on States obligations of prosecution or extradition, thereby requiring them to extend their criminal jurisdiction, such extension of jurisdiction in no way affects immunities under customary international law, including those of Ministers for Foreign Affairs. These remain opposable before the courts of a foreign State, even where those courts exercise such a jurisdiction under these conventions.

60. The Court emphasizes, however, that the *immunity* from jurisdiction enjoyed by incumbent Ministers for Foreign Affairs does not mean that they enjoy *impunity* in respect of any crimes they might have committed, irrespective of their gravity. Immunity from criminal jurisdiction and individual criminal responsibility are quite separate concepts. While jurisdictional immunity is procedural in nature, criminal responsibility is a question of substantive law. Jurisdictional immunity may well bar prosecution for a certain period or for certain offences; it cannot exonerate the person to whom it applies from all criminal responsibility.

61. Accordingly, the immunities enjoyed under international law by an incumbent or former Minister for Foreign Affairs do not represent a bar to criminal prosecution in certain circumstances.

First, such persons enjoy no criminal immunity under international law in their own countries, and may thus be tried by those countries' courts in accordance with the relevant rules of domestic law.

Secondly, they will cease to enjoy immunity from foreign jurisdiction if the State which they represent or have represented decides to waive that immunity.

Thirdly, after a person ceases to hold the office of Minister for Foreign Affairs, he or she will no longer enjoy all of the immunities accorded by international law in other States. Provided that it has jurisdiction under international law, a court of one State may try a former Minister for Foreign Affairs of another State in respect of acts committed prior or subsequent to his or her period of office, as well as in respect of acts committed during that period of office in a private capacity.

Fourthly, an incumbent or former Minister for Foreign Affairs may be subject to criminal proceedings before certain international criminal courts, where they have jurisdiction. Examples include the International Criminal Tribunal for the former Yugoslavia, and the International Criminal Tribunal for Rwanda ... and the future International Criminal Court created by the 1998 Rome Convention. The latter's Statute expressly provides, in Article 27, paragraph 2, that "[i]mmunities or special procedural rules which may attach to the official capacity of a person, whether under national or international law, shall not bar the Court from exercising its jurisdiction over such a person".

62. Given the conclusions it has reached above concerning the nature and scope of the rules governing the immunity from criminal jurisdictions enjoyed by incumbent Ministers for Foreign Affairs, the Court must now consider whether in the present case the issue of the arrest warrant of 11 April 2000 and its international circulation violated those rules. ...

70. The Court notes that the *issuance*, as such, of the disputed arrest warrant represents an act by the Belgian judicial authorities intended to enable the arrest on Belgian territory of an incumbent Minister for Foreign Affairs on charges of war crimes and crimes against humanity. The fact that the warrant is enforceable is clearly apparent from the order given to "all bailiffs and agents of public authority ... to execute this arrest warrant" ... and from the assertion in the warrant that "the position of Minister for Foreign Affairs currently held by the accused does not entail immunity from jurisdiction and enforcement". The Court notes that the warrant did admittedly make an exception for the case of an official visit by Mr. Yerodia to Belgium, and that Mr. Yerodia never suffered arrest in Belgium. The Court is bound, however, to find that given the nature and purpose of the warrant, its mere issue violated the immunity which Mr. Yerodia enjoyed as the Congo's incumbent Minister for Foreign Affairs. ...

71. The Court also notes that Belgium admits that the purpose of the international *circulation* of the disputed arrest warrant was "to establish a legal basis for the arrest of Mr. Yerodia ... abroad and his subsequent extradition to Belgium". The Respondent maintains, however, that the enforcement of the warrant in third States was "dependent on some further preliminary steps having been taken" and that, given the "inchoate" quality of the warrant as regards third States, there was no "infringe[ment of] the sovereignty of the [Congo]". It further points out that no Interpol Red Notice was requested until 12 September 2001, when Mr. Yerodia no longer held ministerial office.

The Court cannot subscribe to this view. As in the case of the warrant's issue, its international circulation from June 2000 by the Belgian authorities, given its nature and purpose, effectively infringed Mr. Yerodia's immunity as the Congo's incumbent Minister for Foreign Affairs and was furthermore liable to affect the Congo's conduct of its international relations. Since Mr. Yerodia was called upon in that capacity to undertake travel in the performance of his duties, the mere international circulation of the warrant, even in the absence of "further steps" by Belgium, could have resulted, in particular, in his arrest while abroad. The Court observes in this respect that Belgium itself cites information to the effect that Mr. Yerodia, "on applying for a visa to go to two countries, [apparently] learned that he ran the risk of being arrested as a result of the arrest warrant issued against him by Belgium", adding that "[t]his, moreover, is what the [Congo] ... hints when it writes that the arrest warrant 'sometimes forced Minister Yerodia to travel by roundabout routes'". Accordingly, the Court concludes that the circulation of the warrant, whether or not it significantly interfered with Mr. Yerodia's diplomatic activity, constituted a violation of an obligation of Belgium towards the Congo, in that it failed to respect the immunity of the incumbent Minister for Foreign Affairs of the Congo and, more particularly, infringed the immunity from criminal jurisdiction and the inviolability then enjoyed by him under international law.

72. The Court will now address the issue of the remedies sought by the Congo on account of Belgium's violation of the above-mentioned rules of international law. ...

76. ... as the Permanent Court of International Justice stated in its Judgment of 13 September 1928 in the case concerning the *Factory at Chorzów*:

"[t]he essential principle contained in the actual notion of an illegal act... is that reparation must, as far as possible, wipe out all the consequences of the illegal act and reestablish the situation which would, in all probability, have existed if that act had not been committed" *(P.C.I.J., Series A, No.17, p. 47).*

In the present case, "the situation which would, in all probability, have existed if [the illegal act] had not been committed" cannot be re-established merely by a finding by the Court that the arrest warrant was unlawful under international law. The warrant is still extant, and remains unlawful, notwithstanding the fact that Mr. Yerodia has ceased to be Minister for Foreign Affairs. The Court accordingly considers that Belgium must, by means of its own choosing, cancel the warrant in question and so inform the authorities to whom it was circulated. ...

78. For these reasons,

THE COURT ...

(2) By thirteen votes to three,[200]

Finds that the issue against Mr. Abdulaye Yerodia Ndombasi of the arrest warrant of 11 April 2000, and its international circulation, constituted violations of a legal obligation of the Kingdom of Belgium towards the Democratic Republic of the Congo, in that they failed to respect the immunity from criminal jurisdiction and the inviolability which the incumbent Minister for Foreign Affairs of the Democratic Republic of Congo enjoyed under international law; ...

(3) By ten votes to six,[201]

Finds that the Kingdom of Belgium must, by means of its own choosing, cancel the arrest warrant of 11 April 2000 and so inform the authorities to whom the warrant was circulated. ...

Notes

1. See the notes on the jurisdictional aspects of this case, above, p.255. In 2003, Belgium amended its law so as to give immunity to heads of state and governments, foreign ministers and certain others immunity while in office.

2. The *Arrest Warrant* (or *Yerodia*) case.[202] was the third in a trilogy of cases (following *Pinochet* and *Al-Adsani*) in which the impact of the modern law of human rights on the traditional law of state immunity was tested. The *Arrest Warrant* case differs from *Pinochet* in that it concerned a current Minister for Foreign Affairs. For indications of the impact that a rule by which *current* office holders were not immune from prosecution abroad for war crimes and crimes against humanity would have, see Ratner's summary of the cases against Messrs Sharon and Arafat that were commenced in the Belgian courts, above, p.255. Does the difficulty for the conduct of foreign relations justify a bar to prosecutions for such heinous offences while a Minister for Foreign Affairs remains in post? Is it sufficient that, following *Pinochet*, former heads of state, etc. need to be careful where they travel?

3. Whereas current and former Heads of State and other senior government office holders such as Ministers for Foreign Affairs may have personal or functional immunity from prosecution in *national* courts, such persons do not have immunity from prosecution before the International Criminal Court or other international tribunals, as the ICJ points out (para.55). See the prosecution of the former Yugoslav President Milosevic before the International Criminal Tribunal for the Former Yugoslavia[203] for international crimes in Bosnia, Croatia and Kosovo and the arrest

---

[200] The judges in the majority were: President Guillaume; Vice-President Shi; Judges Ranjeva, Herczegh, Fleischhauer, Koroma, Vereshchetin, Higgins, Parra-Aranguren, Kooijmans, Rezek, Buergenthal; Judge ad hoc Bula-Bula. Judges Oda, Al-Khasawneh; Judge ad hoc Van den Wyngaert dissented.

[201] The judges in the majority were: President Guillaume; Vice-President Shi; Judges Ranjeva, Herczegh, Fleischhauer, Koroma, Vereshchetin, Parra-Aranguren, Rezek; Judge ad hoc Bula-Bula. Judges Oda, Higgins, Kooijmans, Al-Khasawneh, Buergenthal; Judge ad hoc Van den Wyngaert dissented.

[202] For literature on the case, see above, n.100.

[203] See Milošević (IT-01-54) Kosovo, Croatia and Bosnia.

warrant issued by the International Criminal Court against the current Sudanese President Al-Bashir for international crimes in Darfur.[204]

----

5. DIPLOMATIC IMMUNITY[205]

VIENNA CONVENTION ON DIPLOMATIC RELATIONS 1961[206]

U.K.T.S. 19 (1965), Cmnd. 2565; 500 U.N.T.S. 95; (1961) 55 A.J.I.L. 1064

The States Parties to the present Convention, ...

Realizing that the purpose of such privileges and immunities is not to benefit individuals but to ensure the efficient performance of the functions of diplomatic missions as representing States,

Affirming that the rules of customary international law should continue to govern questions not expressly regulated by the provisions of the present Convention,

Have agreed as follows:

Article 1

For the purpose of the present Convention, the following expressions shall have the meanings hereunder assigned to them:

(a) the "head of the mission" is the person charged by the sending State with the duty of acting in that capacity;

(b) the "members of the mission" are the head of the mission and the members of the staff of the mission;

(c) the "members of the staff of the mission" are the members of the diplomatic staff, of the administrative and technical staff and of the service staff of the mission;

(d) the "members of the diplomatic staff" are the members of the staff of the mission having diplomatic rank;

(e) a "diplomatic agent" is the head of the mission or a member of the diplomatic staff of the mission;

(f) the "members of the administrative and technical staff" are the members of the staff of the mission employed in the administrative and technical service of the mission[207];

(g) the "members of the service staff" are the members of the staff of the mission in the domestic service of the mission[208];

(h) a "private servant" is a person who is in the domestic service of a member of the mission and who is not an employee of the sending State;

(i) the "premises of the mission" are the buildings or parts of buildings and the land ancillary thereto, irrespective of ownership, used for the purposes of the mission including the residence of the head of the mission.[209]

---

[204] See ICC-02/05-01/09 of March 4, 2009 (*The Prosecutor v Omar Hassan Ahmad Al Bashir*).

[205] See Barker, *The Protection of Diplomatic Personnel* (2006); Dembinski, *The Modern Law of Diplomacy* (1988), Pt IV; Denza, *Diplomatic Law* (3rd edn 2008); Hardy, *Modern Diplomatic Law* (1967); *Satow's Diplomatic Practice* (6th edn 2009, by Roberts); Mahmoudi, in *Festskift till Lars Hjerner* (1990), p.327; 2nd edn Sen, *A Diplomat's Handbook of International Law and Practice* (3rd rev. edn 1988), Ch.V; McClanahan, *Diplomatic Immunity* (1989); Wilson, *Diplomatic Privileges and Immunities* (1967); Young (1964) 40 B.Y.I.L. 141. On consular immunity, see Lee, *Consular Law and Practice* (2nd edn 1991).

[206] In force 1964, 186 parties, including the UK. See Kerley (1962) 56 A.J.I.L. 88.

[207] Ed., e.g. archivists, clerical and secretarial staff, translators.

[208] Ed., e.g. chauffeurs, porters, kitchen staff.

[209] The "premises of the mission" do not include the private residence of a diplomatic agent other than the head of the mission: *Intpro Properties Ltd v Sauvel* [1983] Q.B. 1019, CA.

Article 9

1. The receiving State may at any time and without having to explain its decision, notify the sending State that the head of the mission or any member of the diplomatic staff of the mission is *persona non grata* or that any other member of the staff of the mission is not acceptable. In any such case, the sending State shall, as appropriate, either recall the person concerned or terminate his functions with the mission. A person may be declared *non grata* or not acceptable before arriving in the territory of the receiving State. ...

Article 22

1. The premises of the mission[210] shall be inviolable. The agents of the receiving State may not enter them, except with the consent of the head of the mission.
2. The receiving State is under a special duty to take all appropriate steps to protect the premises of the mission against any intrusion or damage and to prevent any disturbance of the peace of the mission or impairment of its dignity.
3. The premises of the mission, their furnishings and other property thereon and the means of transport of the mission shall be immune from search, requisition, attachment or execution.

Article 23

[Exemption from taxes on the premises of the mission.]

Article 24

The archives and documents of the mission shall be inviolable at any time and wherever they may be.

Article 25

The receiving State shall accord full facilities for the performance of the functions of the mission.

Article 26

Subject to its laws and regulations concerning zones entry into which is prohibited or regulated for reasons of national security, the receiving State shall ensure to all members of the mission freedom of movement and travel in its territory.

Article 27

1. The receiving State shall permit and protect free communication on the part of the mission for all official purposes. In communicating with the Government and the other missions and consulates of the sending State, wherever situated, the mission may employ all appropriate means, including diplomatic couriers and messages in code or cipher. However, the mission may install and use a wireless transmitter only with the consent of the receiving State.
2. The official correspondence of the mission shall be inviolable. Official correspondence means all correspondence relating to the mission and its functions.
3. The diplomatic bag shall not be opened or detained.
4. The packages constituting the diplomatic bag must bear visible external marks of their character and may contain only diplomatic documents or articles intended for official use. ...

---

[210] art.22 only applies to premises that are currently used as the premises of a mission: *Westminster City Council v Govt. of Iran* [1986] 1 W.L.R. 979 Ch D (premises of Iranian Embassy gutted by fire not within art.22).

Article 29

The person of a diplomatic agent shall be inviolable. He shall not be liable to any form of arrest or detention. The receiving State shall treat him with due respect and shall take all appropriate steps to prevent any attack on his person, freedom or dignity.[211]

Article 30

1. The private residence of a diplomatic agent shall enjoy the same inviolability and protection as the premises of the mission.

2. His papers, correspondence and, except as provided in paragraph 3 of Article 31, his property,[212] shall likewise enjoy inviolability.

Article 31

1. A diplomatic agent shall enjoy immunity from the criminal jurisdiction of the receiving State. He shall also enjoy immunity from its civil and administrative jurisdiction, except in the case of:

(a) a real action relating to private immovable property situated in the territory of the receiving State, unless he holds it on behalf of the sending State for the purposes of the mission[213];

(b) an action relating to succession in which the diplomatic agent is involved as executor, administrator, heir or legatee as a private person and not on behalf of the sending State;

(c) an action relating to any professional or commercial activity exercised by the diplomatic agent in the receiving State outside his official functions.

2. A diplomatic agent is not obliged to give evidence as a witness.

3. No measures of execution may be taken in respect of a diplomatic agent except in the cases coming under subparas (a), (b) and (c) of paragraph 1 of this Article, and provided that the measures concerned can be taken without infringing the inviolability of his person or of his residence.

4. The immunity of a diplomatic agent from the jurisdiction of the receiving State does not exempt him from the jurisdiction of the sending State.

Article 32

1. The immunity from jurisdiction of diplomatic agents and of persons enjoying immunity under Article 37 may be waived by the sending State.

2. Waiver must always be express.

3. The initiation of proceedings by a diplomatic agent or by a person enjoying immunity from jurisdiction under

---

[211] Article 29 applies to a diplomatic agent and (by virtue of s.20 of the State Immunity Act 1978, above, p.269) to a head of state, etc. in his personal, as well as his official, capacity: *Aziz v Aziz and the Sultan of Brunei* [2007] EWCA Civ 712. On "inviolability" of the person, see the *Arrest Warrant* case, above p.292. Revealing the identity of a head of state or information about him in the context of a claim by his former wife to have been defrauded by a third party was not an "attack" on his "dignity", and speech that is lawful in English law will never be such an "attack": *Aziz v Aziz and the Sultan of Brunei* [2007] EWCA Civ 712. The duty to "prevent" an attack applies only to state actors; there is no positive obligation upon a state to take "steps" to prevent one by a private person: per Collins L.J., obiter. See also the *US Diplomatic and Consular Staff* case, below, p.312.

[212] Ed. The UK takes the view that this does not prevent the towing away of a diplomatic agent's car that is causing an obstruction; but wheel-clamping has been discontinued on the basis that it is a penal measure contrary to art.31(1), below: *Diplomatic Immunities and Privileges*, Misc. 5 (1985), Cmnd. 9497, p.26. See also U.K.M.I.L. 1985, (1985) 56 B.Y.I.L. 435.

[213] Ed. A "real action," which is a literal translation of the French text of art.31 and which is a term not known to English law since the Middle Ages, is an action in which the ownership or possession (as opposed to use) of real property is in issue; hence an action to enforce a covenant under a lease authorising entry to effect repairs does not qualify: *Intpro Properties Ltd v Sauvel* [1983] Q.B. 1019 CA. In the same case it was held that the private residence of a diplomatic agent other than a head of mission is not held for the "purposes of the mission". For the state immunity aspect of this case (the plaintiff sued both France and its agent), see above, n.142.

Article 37 shall preclude him from invoking immunity from jurisdiction in respect of any counter-claim directly connected with the principal claim.

4. Waiver of immunity from jurisdiction in respect of civil or administrative proceedings shall not be held to imply waiver of immunity in respect of the execution of the judgment, for which a separate waiver shall be necessary.

Article 34

[Exemption from taxation of diplomatic agents.]

Article 36

[Exemption from customs duties for the mission and diplomatic agents and their families.]

Article 37

1. The members of the family of a diplomatic agent forming part of his household shall, if they are not nationals of the receiving State, enjoy the privileges and immunities specified in Articles 29 to 36.

2. Members of the administrative and technical staff of the mission, together with members of their families forming part of their respective households, shall, if they are not nationals of or permanently resident in the receiving State, enjoy the privileges and immunities specified in Articles 29 to 35, except that the immunity from civil administrative jurisdiction of the receiving State specified in paragraph 1 of Article 31 shall not extend to acts performed outside the course of their duties. They shall also enjoy the privileges specified in Article 36, paragraph 1, in respect of articles imported at the time of first installation.

3. Members of the service staff of the mission who are not nationals of or permanently resident in the receiving State shall enjoy immunity in respect of acts performed in the course of their duties, exemption from dues and taxes on the emoluments they receive by reason of their employment and the exemption contained in Article 33 [concerning social security provisions].

4. Private servants of members of the mission shall, if they are not nationals of or permanently resident in the receiving State, be exempt from dues and taxes on the emoluments they receive by reason of their employment. In other respects, they may enjoy privileges and immunities only to the extent admitted by the receiving State. However, the receiving State must exercise its jurisdiction over those persons in such a manner as not to interfere unduly with the performance of the functions of the mission.

Article 38

1. Except insofar as additional privileges and immunities may be granted by the receiving State, a diplomatic agent who is a national of or permanently resident[214] in that State shall enjoy only immunity from jurisdiction, and inviolability, in respect of official acts performed in the exercise of his functions.

2. Other members of the staff of the mission and private servants who are nationals of or permanently resident in the receiving State shall enjoy privileges and immunities only to the extent admitted by the receiving State. However, the receiving State must exercise its jurisdiction over those persons in such a manner as not to interfere unduly with the performance of the functions of the mission.

Article 39

1. Every person entitled to such privileges and immunities shall enjoy them from the moment he enters the territory of the receiving State on proceeding to take up his post or, if already in its territory, from the moment when his appointment is notified to the Ministry of Foreign Affairs or such other ministry as may be agreed.[215]

---

[214] Ed. The UK considers that the test of permanent residence "should normally be whether or not he would be in the United Kingdom but for the requirements of the sending state": 1969 FCO Note to Missions, reprinted in *First Report from the Foreign Affairs Committee*, (1984–85) H.C. 127, p.14. The Note gives guidance in the application of the test. See *Lutgarda Jimenez v Commrs of Inland Revenue* [2004] UKSPC 00419.

[215] See *R. v Secretary of State for the Home Dept Ex p. Bagga* [1991] 1 Q.B. 485 CA and *Lutgarda Jimenez v Commrs of Inland Revenue* [2004] UKSPC 001419.

2. When the functions of a person enjoying privileges and immunities have come to an end, such privileges and immunities shall normally cease at the moment when he leaves the country, or on expiry of a reasonable period in which to do so, but shall subsist until that time, even in case of armed conflict. However, with respect to acts performed by such a person in the exercise of his functions as a member of the mission, immunity shall continue to subsist.[216] ...

Article 40

1. If a diplomatic agent passes through or is in the territory of a third State, which has granted him a passport visa if such visa was necessary, while proceeding to take up or return to his post, or when returning to his own country, the third State shall accord him inviolability and such other immunities as may be required to ensure his transit or return. The same shall apply in the case of any members of his family enjoying privileges or immunities who are accompanying the diplomatic agent, or travelling separately to join him or to return to their country.

2. In circumstances similar to those specified in paragraph 1 of this Article, third States shall not hinder the passage of members of the administrative and technical or service staff of a mission, and of members of their families, through the territories.

3. Third States shall accord to official correspondence and other official communications in transit, including messages in code or cipher, the same freedom and protection as is accorded by the receiving State. They shall accord to diplomatic couriers, who have been granted a passport visa if such visa was necessary, and diplomatic bags in transit the same inviolability and protection as the receiving State is bound to accord.

4. The obligations of third States under paragraphs 1, 2 and 3 of this Article shall also apply to the persons mentioned respectively in those paragraphs, and to official communications and diplomatic bags, whose presence in the territory of the third State is due to *force majeure*.

Article 41

1. Without prejudice to their privileges and immunities, it is the duty of all persons enjoying such privileges and immunities to respect the laws and regulations of the receiving State. They also have a duty not to interfere in the internal affairs of that State. ...

3. The premises of the mission must not be used in any manner incompatible with the functions of the mission as laid down in the present Convention or by other rules of general international law or by any special agreements in force between the sending and the receiving State.

Article 44

The receiving State must, even in case of armed conflict, grant facilities in order to enable persons enjoying privileges and immunities, other than nationals of the receiving State, and members of the families of such persons irrespective of their nationality, to leave at the earliest possible moment. It must, in particular, in case of need, place at their disposal the necessary means of transport for themselves and their property.

Article 45

If diplomatic relations are broken off between two States, or if a mission is permanently or temporarily recalled:

(a) the receiving State must, even in case of armed conflict, respect and protect the premises of the mission, together with its property and archives[217];

(b) the sending State may entrust the custody of the premises of the mission, together with its property and archives, to a third State acceptable to the receiving State;

---

[216] An embassy police liaison officer exercises a "function as a member of the mission" so that his immunity continues after departure: *Propend Finance Pty Ltd v Sing and the Commissioner of the Australian Federal Police* (1997) 111 I.L.R. 611 CA.

[217] Ed. Under the Diplomatic and Consular Premises Act 1987, s.2, former diplomatic premises may be vested in the Secretary of State. This was done to deal with squatters in the premises of the former Cambodian Embassy when the UK did not recognise the Cambodian Government at the time of Pol Pot: see *R. v Secretary of State for Foreign Affairs Ex p Samuel*, *The Times*, September 10, 1988, QB.

(c)   the sending State may entrust the protection of its interests and those of its nationals to a third State acceptable to the receiving State.

Article 47

1. In the application of the provisions of the present Convention, the receiving State shall not discriminate as between States.

2. However, discrimination shall not be regarded as taking place:

(a)   where the receiving State applies any of the provisions of the present Convention restrictively because of restrictive application of that provision to its mission in the sending State;

(b)   where by custom or agreement States extend to each other more favourable treatment than is required by the provisions of the present Convention.

Notes

1.   The Convention was adopted at the United Nations Conference on Diplomatic Intercourse and Immunities in Vienna in 1961.[218] The Conference based its work upon Draft Articles prepared by the International Law Commission.[219] Optional Protocols concerning the Acquisition of Nationality[220] and the Compulsory Settlement of Disputes[221] were also adopted. It is not stated in the Convention whether or not it was intended to be declaratory of the customary international law existing in 1961. As far as the law concerning diplomatic immunity is concerned, it is probably correct to regard it as a combination of codification and progressive development. It would seem both to incorporate clearly established rules (see the *U.S. Diplomatic and Consular Staff in Tehran Case*, below, p.312) and to fill in gaps or to spell out rules where practice was uncertain or inconsistent. Whether the Convention, so far as it engages in progressive development, has yet had sufficient impact upon the attitudes and practice of states to have affected customary international law is impossible to say. What is clear is that its impact upon the legal rights and duties of states has already been great because of the very large number of states that have become parties to it.

The above extracts from the Convention concern the immunity, inviolability and protection afforded to the premises of the mission, to certain property relating to the mission's functioning[222] and to certain persons representing states diplomatically or concerned with such representation. Immunity and inviolability overlap to some extent (see art.22(1)(3), Vienna Convention for example). The former term is applied mainly to jurisdictional immunity, i.e. immunity from the process of the courts, and to immunity from taxes. The latter is concerned mainly with questions of trespass.

The question of abuse of diplomatic immunity has been a frequent theme in recent years.[223] While there has always been concern at the abuse by a small number of individual diplomats of their jurisdictional immunity, the question has become more serious in the light of convincing evidence that a few states use the inviolability of their mission premises and their diplomatic bag

---

[218] For the Conference Records, see *U.N. Conference on Diplomatic Intercourse and Immunities, Vienna*, March 2—April 15, 1961. *Official Records*, Vols I and II, 1962, UN Docs.A/CONF.20/14 and A/CONF.20/14 Add. 1.

[219] Y.B.I.L.C., 1958, II, p.89.

[220] Misc. 6 (1961), Cmnd. 1368; 500 U.N.T.S. 223. In force 1964, 51 parties. UK not a party.

[221] U.K.T.S. 19 (1965), Cmnd. 565; 500 U.N.T.S. 241. In force 1964, 66 parties, including the UK.

[222] The rules on the availability and immunity of such premises and property are rules of *state*, rather than *diplomatic*, immunity. They are included here for convenience.

[223] See Barker, *The Abuse of Diplomatic Privileges and Immunities* (1996).

to facilitate the commission of acts of violence against their political opponents abroad or to assist terrorists. It is noticeable, however, that even those states, such as the United Kingdom, that have expressed concern at these newer forms of abuse would not want, on balance, to limit the immunities and inviolability that exists at present because of the value they place upon them to protect their own missions abroad from other kinds of interference with their functioning.[224] Indeed, codification proposals since 1961 (e.g. the ILC Draft Articles on the Diplomatic Bag, see below, p.370) are the result of initiatives by states that wish to strengthen diplomatic immunity, not reduce it.

2. *Jurisdictional immunity.* In 2006, 24,000 individuals in the United Kingdom were entitled to diplomatic immunity.[225] Article 37(2) of the Convention, on the immunities of administrative and technical staff, was the subject of disagreement at Vienna.[226] Several states have made reservations agreeing to allow the immunity granted by it only on condition of reciprocity and several others have made reservations not accepting it at all; some other states, including the United Kingdom, have deposited objections to reservations of the latter kind.[227] Note that the International Law Commission had appreciated in its Commentary that art.37(2) would be an example of "progressive development":

> "(2) It is the general practice to accord to members of the diplomatic staff of a mission the same privileges and immunities as are enjoyed by heads of mission, and it is not disputed that this is a rule of international law. But beyond this there is no uniformity in the practice of States in deciding which members of the staff of a mission shall enjoy privileges and immunities. Some States include members of the administrative and technical staff among the beneficiaries, and some even include members of the service staff. ...
>
> (4) In view of the differences in State practice, the Commission had to choose between two courses: either to work on the principle of a bare minimum, and stipulate that any additional rights to be accorded should be decided by bilateral agreement; or to try to establish a general and uniform rule based on what would appear to be necessary and reasonable.
>
> (5) A majority of the Commission favoured the latter course, believing that the rule proposed would represent a progressive step.
>
> (6) The Commission differentiated between members of the administrative and technical staff on the one hand, and members of the service staff on the other.
>
> (7) As regards persons belonging to the administrative and technical staff, it took the view that there were good grounds for granting them the same privileges and immunities as members of the diplomatic staff. ...
>
> (8) The reasons relied on may be summarized as follows. It is the function of the mission as an organic whole which should be taken into consideration, not the actual work done by each person. Many of the persons belonging to the services in question perform confidential tasks which, for the purposes of the mission's function, may be even more important than the tasks entrusted to some members of the diplomatic staff. An ambassador's secretary or an archivist may be as much the repository of secret or confidential knowledge as members of the

---

[224] For the UK view, see *Diplomatic Immunities and Privileges*, above, n.212, p.6. For an argument that immunity should be limited to protect human rights, see Vicuna (1991) 40 I.C.L.Q. 34.
[225] U.K.M.I.L. 2006 (2006) 78 B.Y.I.L. 785.
[226] See above, n.218, Vol.I, 32nd and 33rd Meetings, pp.193–201.
[227] For the reservations and objections to them, see *http:/treaties.un.org/*.

diplomatic staff. Such persons equally need protection of the same order against possible pressure by the receiving State."[228]

Would a "diplomatic agent" who negligently injured a pedestrian while driving his car on holiday in the receiving state be entitled to claim immunity under the Convention in respect of any civil or criminal proceedings arising therefrom? Would a code clerk or a cook employed in an embassy be entitled to do so in the same situation? Would the wife or private employee of any of the above be entitled to do so?[229] Might the nationality or the place of permanent residence of the person claiming immunity in any of the above cases be relevant?

Article 40 of the Convention was interpreted in *R. v Guildhall Magistrates Court Ex p. Jarrett-Thorpe.*[230] The applicant was the husband of the counsellor to the Sierra Leone Embassy in Rome. His wife travelled to London to buy furnishings for the Rome Embassy. It was intended that the applicant would join her later for the purpose of travelling back to Rome with her and to help with her luggage. It was not intended that he should enter the United Kingdom for any other purpose. When he arrived in the United Kingdom, the applicant received a message to the effect that his wife had already left for Rome. While he was waiting for a flight to Rome the applicant was arrested by the police at Heathrow in connection with criminal proceedings pending against him in London. Lawton J. held that art.40 applied so that the applicant was entitled to immunity. The Court rejected the argument that art.40 only applied to diplomatic agents and members of their families when they were in transit between the sending state and the receiving state.

3.   *Waiver of immunity.* A resolution adopted at Vienna recommended:

> "that the sending State should waive the immunity of members of its diplomatic mission in respect of civil claims of persons in the receiving State when this can be done without impeding the performance of the functions of the mission, and that, when immunity is not waived, the sending State should use its best endeavours to bring about a just settlement of the claims."[231]

The following is a 1952 statement of British practice, based upon "the principle that diplomatic immunity is accorded not for the benefit of the individual in question, but for the benefit of the State in whose service he is, in order that he may fulfil his diplomatic duties with the necessary independence":

> "... when a dispute arises between a person living in this country and a person possessing diplomatic immunity here and the dispute cannot be settled directly between the parties, it is commonly reported to the Foreign Office and the Foreign Office then approaches the diplomatic mission concerned with the request that the Head of the Mission will either waive the immunity of the member of his staff so that the dispute can be decided in the ordinary way in the courts or that the matter should be decided by a private arbitration conducted under conditions which are fair to both sides. Such requests are commonly acceded to, and the cases where this approach has not brought about a proper settlement of the matter have generally

---

[228] Y.B.I.L.C., 1958, II, pp.101–102.
[229] On the status of the family of a diplomatic agent, see O'Keefe (1976) 25 I.C.L.Q. 329.
[230] *The Times*, October 5, 1977, QBD.
[231] UN Doc. A/CONF. 20/14, Add. 1, v. 90.

been cases where, owing to delay, the foreign diplomat in question has already left the country before the matter can be dealt with, a delay which is generally due to a failure of the party who thinks he is injured to approach the Foreign Office promptly. If a case arose where the foreign mission concerned was neither willing to waive immunity nor to persuade the foreign diplomat to accept a reasonable arbitration and the foreign diplomat remained in this country, the Foreign Office would in the circumstances feel obliged, unless there were exceptional features in the case, to inform the foreign mission concerned that this individual could no longer be accepted as a person holding a diplomatic immunity appointment in this country.

If a person possessing diplomatic immunity is alleged to have committed a criminal offence and there is a prima facie case which, in the ordinary way, would lead to the institution of a prosecution, the Foreign Office approaches the foreign mission concerned and, unless the offence is such that it is considered that an admonition by the Head of the Mission is sufficient, the Foreign Office requests a waiver of immunity in order that the case may be tried, on the footing that, if the immunity is not waived, it may be impossible for the Foreign Secretary to continue to accept the individual concerned as a person possessing diplomatic status in this country."[232]

In 2006, in the United Kingdom there were 15 occasions on which persons claimed diplomatic immunity to avoid arrest or prosecution for serious offences (i.e. offences with a possible sentence of 12 or more months' imprisonment); there were also 5,484 outstanding parking and other minor traffic violation fines, and 74,198 fines for non-payment of the London congestion charge.[233]

4. *Inviolability of the premises of the mission.* An amendment[234] to the Convention to require the head of a mission to: "co-operate with the local authorities in case of fire, epidemic or other extreme emergency" was not adopted at Vienna. In the International Law Commission it had been suggested that "[i]t was hardly conceivable that a head of mission would fail to co-operate ... in an emergency"[235] and that the sanction of declaring him *persona non grata* would be available if he did.[236] In addition, the fear was that "if specific exceptions were made in the Convention this would give ... a certain power of appreciation to the receiving state which it was thought might ... be undesirable."[237] Commenting upon an incident in 1929, when French officials entered the Soviet Embassy in Paris after allegations that persons were being detained and might be executed there, Sibert argues that the intervention was consistent with international law:

"because no civilised state could permit a foreign legation to be made a place of imprisonment, or, *a fortiori*, a place of execution."[238]

---

[232] Interdepartmental Committee on State Immunities, *Report on Diplomatic Immunity*, Cmnd. 8460, pp.3–4. The statement still represents British practice.

[233] U.K.M.I.L. 2006, (2006) 78 B.Y.I.L. 784-5. With regard to drunken driving, a diplomatic agent cannot be required to undergo a blood test or other medical examination, such as a breathalyser test, because of art.29: *Hansard*, HC Vol.101, col.64 WA (July 7, 1986). For more recent figures see U.K.M.I.L. 2001, 73 B.Y.I.L. 68.

[234] U.N. Doc. A/CONF. 20/C.I.L.129.

[235] Y.B.I.L.C., 1958, I, 129 (Mr Amado).

[236] See above, n.14, p.130 (Mr Bartos).

[237] Sir Francis Vallat, Foreign Affairs Committee Report, above, n.214, p.25.

[238] *Traité de droit international public*, Vol.II, 1951, p.25. Translation.

In the *Sun Yat Sen Incident*,[239] in 1896, a Chinese national who was not in any way connected with the Chinese Embassy in London was kept there against his will. A writ of habeas corpus was refused by Wright J. because he doubted "the propriety of making any order or granting any summons against a foreign legation".[240] The British Government referred to the detention as "an abuse of ... diplomatic privilege" and a "flagrant ... violation of municipal and international law." It added that

> "if persisted in or repeated, it would justify the use of whatever measures might be necessary for the liberation of the captive, and a demand for the immediate departure from this country of any persons responsible for his imprisonment."

Denza[241] considers the problem of "abuse" as follows:

> "There have, however, been a very few occasions where a State in the face of a serious threat to national security or a flagrant abuse of diplomatic immunity has deliberately authorized forcible entry of mission premises. In 1973 the Pakistan Ministry of Foreign Affairs informed the Iraqi Ambassador of evidence that arms were being brought into Pakistan under diplomatic immunity and stored at the Embassy of Iraq in Islamabad. When the ambassador refused permission for a search, a raid by armed police took place and huge consignments of arms—apparently destined for rebel tribes in Baluchistan—were found stored in crates. The Pakistan Government sent a strong protest to the Iraq Government, declared the Ambassador *persona non grata*, and recalled their own Ambassador. Ten weeks later relations were restored at ambassadorial level by a joint communiqué in which Iraq declared its respect for the territorial integrity of Pakistan."

In the *Libyan People's Bureau Incident*, below, p.307, in answer to the question whether, following the shooting from the Bureau window, "we had a right to go in immediately in self-defence and seize persons and articles", Sir John Freeland, the Legal Adviser to the British Foreign Office stated[242]:

> "I certainly would not exclude the possibility of its being justifiable in a case where, for example, there is continued firing of weapons from the premises of an embassy, where every other method has been tried and has failed to stop that, for it then to be lawful to go into the embassy to stop it ..."

How is this consistent with the absolute inviolability rule in art.22? Could it be argued that since the right of self defence at customary international law is not expressly excluded by art.22 it is

---

[239] 1 McNair 85. The person detained gave notice of his plight by placing a slip of paper in a bread roll which he then threw on to the street below through the bars of his window: Viscount Alverstone, *Recollections of Bar and Bench* (1914), pp.168–169.
[240] 1 McNair 88.
[241] See above, n.205, p.149. Footnote omitted.
[242] Foreign Affairs Committee Report, above, n.214, p.28. On the issues raised in the Report, see Cameron (1985) 34 I.C.L.Q. 610; and Higgins (1985) 79 A.J.I.L. 641. For the UK Government response to the Report, see *Diplomatic Immunities and Privileges*, above, p.212. On the response, see Higgins (1986) 80 A.J.I.L. 135.

available?[243] Another approach is to regard the shooting as a material breach of the 1961 Convention so that the United Kingdom's obligation under art.22 was, as a state specially affected, suspended (see art.60(2)(b), Vienna Convention on the Law of Treaties, below, n.700). The Foreign Affairs Committee, however, pointed out that "the drafting history of the Vienna Convention [on Diplomatic Relations] probably makes this principle inappropriate, especially as a 'remedy' for violation is provided in the form of a severing of diplomatic relations."[244]

The question of *diplomatic asylum*[245] within the premises of a mission was purposely not dealt with in the Convention.[246] Article 41(3) states that the mission should not be used "in any manner incompatible with the functions of the mission," which begs the question. According to British practice at the turn of the century:

> "[i]t is in no way necessary for the discharge of an Ambassador's duty that his house should be an asylum for persons charged with crime of any description, and no such privilege can be asserted. . . .

But, according to the same practice, asylum is in fact (although without legal authority) allowed in certain exceptional cases:

> ". . . the practice of harbouring political refugees is an objectionable one and should be resorted to only from motives of humanity in cases of instant or imminent personal peril. In such cases the refugee should not be allowed to communicate with his partisans from the shelter of His Majesty's Legation and should be removed the moment he is no longer exposed to summary treatment at the hands of his pursuers.
>
> Protection must, of course, sometimes be afforded to British subjects in time of danger but this is an wholly different matter from harbouring political refugees who are citizens or subjects of the country. In cases where British subjects have committed an offence against the local laws and have sought refuge in His Majesty's Legation they should be given up only to the competent authorities and on satisfactory guarantees being given that they will still receive proper treatment and a fair trial. . . ."[247]

The Harvard Research Draft Convention on Diplomatic Privileges and Immunities 1932[248] reads:

> "*Article 6.* A sending state shall not permit the premises occupied or used by its mission or by a member of its mission to be used as a place of asylum for fugitives from justice."

Diplomatic asylum is also granted by the US. Cardinal Mindszenty, for example, took refuge in

---

[243] See Beaumont (1991) 29 C.Y.I.L. 391; cf. Colonel Draper's memorandum, *Diplomatic Immunities and Privileges*, above, p.212, pp.71–72. Neither Sir John Freeland nor Colonel Draper considered self-defence was available on the facts of the *Libyan People's Bureau Incident* because there was only one round of firing. The persons who left the Bureau on evacuation were searched on the grounds of self-defence in case they were armed: p.xxxii.

[244] See Draper, above, n.243, p.xxix. Cf. *Partial Award: Diplomatic Claim: Eritrea's Claim 20*, below, p.316.

[245] See Morgenstern (1948) 25 B.Y.I.L. 236; Porcino (1975–76) 8 N.Y.U.J.I.P. 435; Ronning, *Diplomatic Asylum* (1965); Symonides (1986) 15 Pol. Y.I.L. 217.

[246] See Y.B.I.L.C. 1958, II, p.104.

[247] Sir E. Grey to H.M. Minister in Haiti, May 30, 1913, 7 B.D.I.L. 922. The exception probably covers all cases, whether political or not. The UK continues to grant diplomatic asylum on the same basis. Between 1979 and 1984 there were seven cases of foreign citizens seeking sanctuary in British embassies, etc.: *Hansard*, HC Vol.65, col.813 (October 19, 1984).

[248] (1932) 26 A.J.I.L. Suppl. 19.

the United States Embassy in Budapest after the failure of the Hungarian Uprising in 1956 and remained there until 1970 when he was allowed to leave the country to take up residence in Rome.[249] Although the granting of diplomatic asylum has been common practice in Latin American states and is regulated by treaties between them[250] it would not seem that any rules of American customary international law have developed: see the *Asylum* case, above, p.21. In 1980, following a revolution, Liberian soldiers entered the French Embassy in Monrovia and arrested the son of the former Liberian President who had been granted asylum. France protested against "a blatant and unacceptable violation of the status of diplomatic missions and of international customs.[251] On diplomatic asylum generally, Ronning[252] states:

"The only generalization which seems at all acceptable is that the practice of states in this regard is not based upon any generally recognized *right of asylum* so far as general international law is concerned. Instead, it is a *de facto* result of the fact that international law accords to the various accredited diplomatic officers certain well-recognized immunities from local jurisdiction, such as immunity of their official residences and offices from invasion by local authorities. Humanitarian, political or other motives may lead to the original grant of asylum but once the refugee is inside the legation the territorial state is faced with an insoluble dilemma. Assuming the state of refuge will not surrender the refugee, the territorial state can apprehend him only by violating the immunity of the diplomatic premises or, possibly, by breaking diplomatic relations. The fact is that such extreme measures are considered too high a price to pay for apprehension of the refugee."

In 1999, the Chinese Embassy in Belgrade was hit by a United States missile during the Kosovo crisis. The United States apologised for this accident and agreed to pay $28 million compensation. China agreed to pay $2.876 million compensation for damage to the United States embassy and consular buildings in China caused by rioting following the Belgrade incident.[253]

5. *Protection of the premises of the mission.* The "special duty" to protect the premises of the mission set out in art.22 of the Convention is well established in customary international law and is very important at the present time when such premises prove convenient settings for political demonstrations. See the *U.S. Diplomatic and Consular Staff in Iran* case, below, p.312. See also an incident in 1965 when the United States Embassy in Moscow was attacked by students; the USSR expressed regret, indicated stricter measures of protection and agreed to pay compensation for property damage.[254]

In 1984, in the *Libyan People's Bureau Incident*, a demonstration by about 70 Libyan opponents of Colonel Kadhafi's Government was held in St. James Square opposite the Libyan People's Bureau, the Libyan diplomatic mission in London. The demonstration, which the Bureau had unsuccessfully asked the Foreign Office to have banned, was countered by a 20 strong pro-Kadhafi group, the two groups being separated by barriers and a large number of police. During the peaceful demonstration, a burst of automatic gunfire from a Bureau window killed WPC Fletcher and injured 11 demonstrators. The United Kingdom severed diplomatic relations with

---

[249] US policy is "to grant temporary refuge for humanitarian reasons in extreme or exceptional circumstances when the life or safety of a person is put in immediate danger, such as pursuit by a mob": (1981) 75 A.J.I.L. 142.
[250] See, e.g. the 1954 Caracas Convention on Diplomatic Asylum, P.A.U.T.S. 18; 161 B.F.S.P. 570. In force 1954, 14 parties.
[251] *Keesings Archives* p.30407.
[252] See above, p.245, p.22.
[253] U.S.D.I.L. 2000, pp.421 et seq.
[254] 7 Whiteman 387.

Libya as a result of the shooting. When the Bureau building was evacuated, it was searched[255] and guns were found. As to whether the United Kingdom had done sufficient to comply with its "special duty" under art.22 to protect the Libyan mission, the House of Commons Foreign Affairs Committee stated[256]:

> "Our view is that although the 'peace of the mission' may not be entirely identical to the Queen's peace, *the receiving state's duty to protect the peace of the mission cannot be given so wide an interpretation as to require the mission to be insulated from expressions of public opinion within the receiving state. Provided always that work at the mission can continue normally, that there is untrammelled access and egress, and that those within the mission are never in fear that the mission might be damaged or its staff injured, the requirements of Article 22 are met.* A breakdown of the public order outside mission premises would put in jeopardy the fulfilling of obligations under Article 22; an orderly expression of opposition to the policies of the sending state cannot of itself do so."

The Committee also referred to the unreported case of *R v Roques*[257] (1984) in which anti-apartheid demonstrators who demonstrated, contrary to police orders, on the east pavement of Trafalgar Square, immediately outside the South African embassy, were charged with obstruction of a police officer, the demonstration being in breach of the Diplomatic Privileges Act 1964 (which incorporates art.22) which it was the police's duty to apply. Dismissing the charges, the magistrates took the view that impairment of the "dignity" of the mission (see art.22) "required abusive or insulting behaviour, and that political demonstrations do not themselves amount to such."

The duty of protection extends, under art.30, to the private residence of a diplomatic agent and was interpreted in this context in *Agbor v Metropolitan Police Commissioner*.[258] There, a dispute arose over the occupation of a flat in a house in London owned by the Nigerian Government and used to house diplomatic agents. Shortly after Biafra purported to secede from Nigeria, a Biafran family managed to gain possession of the flat while its next official tenant was awaited. At the request of the Nigerian Government, the family was evicted by the police. The Court was asked in the application before it to allow the family to return to the flat pending a decision by it on the right of possession. The application was granted because the flat was not at the time the residence of a diplomatic agent. Lord Denning added that even if it had been he was

> "not at all satisfied that the [Diplomatic Privileges] Act of 1964 gives to the executive any right to evict a person in possession who claims as of right to occupation of the premises. It enables

---

[255] On the obligation to protect, but not to treat as inviolable, the premises of a mission after diplomatic relations are terminated, see art.45, 1961 Convention. As to whether the mission might have been entered prior to its evacuation, see above, p.305.

[256] Report, above, p.214, p.xvii. Giving evidence to the Committee the Head of the British Diplomatic Service, Sir Antony Acland, stated: "I think the essential thing is that demonstrations should be adequately controlled and policed so that there is no damage done physically or otherwise to the premises of the mission or to the people within that mission. In the case of the tragic St James Square incident there were certainly enough police present": pp.21–22. See also on the incident, Sutton [1985] P.L. 191. There are 300 demonstrations outside London embassies annually; police practice is to restrict them to the opposite side of the road from the embassy in full compliance with art.22: *Diplomatic Immunities and Privileges*, above, n.212, p.17.

[257] ibid., p.xvii.

[258] [1969] 1 W.L.R. 703 CA.

the police to defend the premises against intruders. But not to turn out people who are in possession and claim as of right to be there."[259]

6. *Freedom of communication.* Before the 1961 Convention, "it was certainly accepted international practice, and probably international law, that in exceptional cases where the receiving state had grounds for suspecting abuse" it had a right of challenge in respect of the diplomatic bag.[260] It could, that is, ask for permission to inspect its contents. The sending state could either allow the bag to be opened and inspected, or have the bag returned to its place of origin. Article 27(3) requires that the bag be allowed through without inspection.[261] Reservations to the Convention insisting upon a power of inspection have been made,[262] but have met with protest by some other parties. In the opinion of the United Kingdom Foreign Office, art.27 does not prohibit electronic scanning of the diplomatic bag or sniffing by dogs.[263] Scanning would seem to be a practice followed by some receiving states, although it "would not necessarily pick up a weapon in a diplomatic bag."[264] In 1985, the United Kingdom Government, which had previously not conducted any scannings, stated that it would "be ready to scan any bag on specific occasions where the grounds for suspicion are sufficiently strong."[265]

In 1984, Mr Dikko, a minister in the overthrown Nigerian Government, was kidnapped in London and found drugged in a crate at Stansted Airport awaiting shipment to Nigeria, where he was wanted on criminal charges.[266] Although labelled "diplomatic baggage," the crate lacked the "visible external marks" required by art.27(4), 1961 Convention to be a diplomatic bag (in particular, it lacked a seal). Accordingly, there was no breach of art.27 when customs officials, alerted by medical odours, opened it. The United Kingdom Foreign Secretary stated that even if the crate were a diplomatic bag, "the overriding duty to preserve and protect human life" might have justified its opening in appropriate circumstances.[267] Following the incident, two members of the Nigerian High Commission were expelled and one of the kidnappers, who had unsuccessfully claimed diplomatic immunity,[268] was sentenced to 12 years imprisonment for attempted kidnapping.

Another remarkable incident occurred in 1964 when an Israeli national was found drugged,

---

[259] [1969] 1 W.L.R. 703 at 707. Salmon L.J. agreed, at 710.

[260] Denza, above, 296, p.227. The diplomatic bag consists of packages, sacks, or possibly trunks and is usually sent in the custody of a diplomatic courier "who shall be provided with an official document indicating his status and the number of packages constituting the diplomatic bag" (art.27(6), Vienna Convention), although it may be entrusted to the safe keeping of the aircraft's captain (art.27(7), 1961 Convention). There is no limit on the size or shape of the bag. A USSR lorry was opened for inspection by the West German authorities in 1984 not because of its size or shape but because, being capable of movement, it could not be a bag: Foreign Affairs Committee Report, above, n.214, p.xii.

[261] In a rare case of disregard for the need for consent, in 2000 Zimbabwe officials insisted on opening the UK diplomatic bag at Harare airport despite UK protest: U.K.M.I.L. 2000, (2000) 71 B.Y.I.L. 587.

[262] By six Arab states, including Libya. For texts of reservations and objections to them, see *http://treaties.un.org/*. The UK objected to certain of the reservations, but not that by Libya. Accordingly, it could, in accordance with the principle of reciprocity, see below, p.319, have relied upon the Libyan reservation to have requested the opening (or return unopened) of the Libyan diplomatic bag in the context of the *Libyan People's Bureau Incident.* The decision not to do so was a "political judgment": Foreign Affairs Committee Report, above, p.358, n.92, p.xxxii.

[263] Foreign Affairs Committee Report, above, p.358, n.92, pp.xii, 5. Although scanning is regarded by some states as a form of constructive opening, the Foreign Office notes that art.27, does not refer to inviolability: ibid. Note that scanning "might put at risk sensitive cipher or coding materials contained in the bag:" p.xiii.

[264] *Hansard,* HC Vol.985, col.1219, (June 2, 1980); U.K.M.I.L. 1980; (1980) 51 B.Y.I.L. 419.

[265] *Diplomatic Immunities and Privileges,* above, n.212, p.21.

[266] For an account of the Dikko Case, see Akinsanya (1985) 34 I.C.L.Q. 602.

[267] Foreign Affairs Committee Report, above, p.358, n.92, p.xxxiv Note that the "material breach" remedy of suspension of treaty obligations would not have been available: see below, p.839.

[268] *R. v Lambeth JJ, Ex p. Yusufu* [1985] Crim.L.R. 510 QBD.

bound and gagged at Rome airport in a trunk marked "diplomatic mail" that was being sent by the Egyptian mission to Cairo. Italy declared a First Secretary at the Egyptian Embassy *persona non grata* and expelled two others. The Egyptian Ambassador deplored the incident and claimed ignorance of it.[269]

The status of the diplomatic bag has been considered by the International Law Commission. Its Draft Articles on the Status of the Diplomatic Courier and the Diplomatic Bag not Accompanied by Diplomatic Courier[270] read:

"Article 28

1. The diplomatic bag shall be inviolable wherever it may be; it shall not be opened or detained and shall be exempt from examination directly or through electronic or other technical devices.

2. Nevertheless, if the competent authorities of the receiving or the transit State have serious reason to believe that the consular bag contains something other than the correspondence, documents or articles referred to in paragraph 1 of article 25, they may request that the bag be opened in their presence by an authorized representative of the sending State. If this request is refused by the authorities of the sending State, the bag shall be returned to its place of origin."

The Commentary to art.28 reads:

"The extent of the principle of inviolability of the diplomatic bag is further clarified by the words 'and shall be exempt from examination directly or through electronic or other technical devices.' The view prevailed in the Commission that the inclusion of this phrase was necessary as the evolution of technology had created very sophisticated means of examination which might result in the violation of the confidentiality of the bag, means which furthermore were at the disposal of only the most developed States. On the other hand, the paragraph does not extend to an external examination of the bag and of its marks or visible indications of its character as such, to the extent that such an external examination would be conducted for identification purposes only and with a view to ascertaining that a given container claimed to be a diplomatic bag actually bears such a character. The paragraph does not rule out non-intrusive means of examination, such as sniffing dogs, in case of suspicion that the bag is used for the transport of narcotic drugs. ...

    Paragraph 2 applies only to the consular bag *stricto sensu*. It introduces, in connection with the consular bag, a balance between the interests of the sending State in ensuring the protection, safety and confidentiality of the contents of its bag and the security interests of the receiving or transit State.

    ... the Commission has been fully aware that the cases of possible abuses of the bag ... may extend also to the diplomatic bag *stricto sensu* or to the bags of missions or delegations. Contemporary international practice has witnessed cases of diplomatic bags being used or

---

[269] *Keesings Archives*, p.20580. In 1980 £500,000 worth of cannabis was found in diplomatic baggage bound for the Moroccan Embassy in London when a crate marked "household effects" split open at Harwich; *The Times*, June 13, 1980. The prohibited import of drugs is the most common abuse of the diplomatic bag in UK experience; Foreign Affairs Committee, above, n.214, p.6.

[270] The draft articles were finally adopted by the ILC in 1989. For text and commentary, see the Report of the ILC on its 41st Session, G.A.O.R., 44th Sess., Supp. 10, pp.26 et seq.

attempted to be used for the illicit import or export of currency, narcotic drugs,[271] arms or other items, and even for the transport of human beings, which have violated the established rules regarding the permissible contents of the bag and adversely affected the legitimate interests of the receiving or transit States. The Commission is of the view that while the protection of the diplomatic bag is a fundamental principle for the normal functioning of official communications between States, the implementation of this principle should not provide an opportunity for abuse which may affect the legitimate interests of the receiving or transit States. ...

In this connection, the Commission considered the possibility of extending to all diplomatic bags the régime of the consular bag as reflected in paragraph 2. Some members, however, were of the view that the establishment of a uniform régime for all bags should be done on the basis of the existing régime for the diplomatic bag *stricto sensu* as reflected in the Convention on Diplomatic Relations, which does not provide the receiving or transit State with the right laid down in paragraph 2. Some intermediate solutions were also considered. In the end and after extensive consideration of the problem, the Commission opted for the present formulation, which maintains the existing régime as contained in the four codification conventions on diplomatic and consular law as a compromise solution capable of ensuring better prospects for a wide adherence by States to the present draft articles."

7. *The basis for diplomatic immunity.* In its Commentary on its draft articles the International Law Commission stated:

> "(1) Among the theories that have exercised an influence on the development of diplomatic privileges and immunities, the Commission will mention the 'exterritoriality' theory, according to which the premises of the mission represent a sort of extension of the territory of the sending State; and the 'representative character' theory, which bases such privileges and immunities on the idea that the diplomatic mission personifies the sending State.
>
> (2) There is now a third theory which appears to be gaining ground in modern times, namely, the 'functional necessity' theory, which justifies privileges and immunities as being necessary to enable the mission to perform its functions.
>
> (3) The Commission was guided by this third theory in solving problems on which practice gave no clear pointers, while also bearing in mind the representative character of the head of the mission and of the mission itself."[272]

In *Radwan v Radwan*[273] it was held that the Egyptian consulate in London was not a part of the territory of the United Arab Republic so that a divorce obtained there was not obtained "in any country outside the British Isles" for the purposes of the Recognition of Divorces and Legal Separations Act 1971. After reviewing the literature on the subject, which he found rejected the extraterritoriality theory, Cumming-Bruce J. referred to the Vienna Convention:

> "If it was the view of the high contracting parties that the premises of missions were part of the territory of the sending state, that would undoubtedly be formulated and it would have been quite unnecessary to set out the immunities in the way in which it has been done."[274]

---

[271] See above, n.270, pp.109–110.
[272] Y.B.I.L.C., 1958, II, pp.94–95.
[273] [1973] Fam. 24.
[274] [1973] Fam. 24 at 34.

U.S. DIPLOMATIC AND CONSULAR STAFF IN TEHRAN CASE[275]

U.S. v Iran

ICJ Reports 1980, p.3

On November 4, 1979, several hundred Iranian students and other demonstrators took possession of the US Embassy in Tehran by force. They did so in protest at the admission of the deposed Shah of Iran into the US for medical treatment. The demonstrators were not opposed by the Iranian security forces who "simply disappeared from the scene". US consulates elsewhere in Iran were similarly occupied. The demonstrators were still in occupation when the present judgment was given. They had seized archives and documents and continued to hold 52 US nationals. (Women and black people had been released.) Fifty were diplomatic or consular staff; two were private citizens. In an earlier judgment,[276] the Court had indicated interim measures at the request of the US In the present judgment, the Court ruled on the US request for a declaration that Iran had infringed a number of treaties, including the 1961 and 1963 Vienna Conventions on Diplomatic and Consular Relations respectively. It also asked for a declaration calling for the release of the hostages, the evacuation of the Embassy and consulates, the punishment of the persons responsible and the payment of reparation. In April 1980, while the case was pending, US military forces entered Iran by air and landed in a remote desert area in the course of an attempt to rescue the hostages. The attempt was abandoned because of equipment failure. US military personnel were killed in an air collision as the units withdrew. No injury was done to Iranian nationals or property.

Judgment of the Court

The events which are the subject of the United States' claims fall into two phases ...

57. The first ... covers the armed attack on the United States Embassy by militants on 4 November 1979.

58. No suggestion has been made that the militants, when they executed their attack on the Embassy, had any form of official status as recognized "agents" or organs of the Iranian State. Their conduct in mounting the attack, overrunning the Embassy and seizing its inmates as hostages cannot, therefore, be regarded as imputable to that State on that basis. ... Their conduct might be considered as itself directly imputable to the Iranian State only if it were established that, in fact, on the occasion in question the militants acted on behalf of the State, having been charged by some competent organ of the Iranian State to carry out a specific operation. The information before the Court does not, however, suffice to establish with the requisite certainty the existence at that time of such a link. ...

59. Previously, it is true, the religious leader of the country, the Ayatollah Khomeini, had made several public declarations inveighing against the United States as responsible for all his country's problems. ... In ... [a November 1, 1979] message the Ayatollah Khomeini had declared that it was "up to the dear pupils, students and theological students to expand with all their might their attacks against the United States and Israel, so they may force the United States to return the deposed and criminal shah. ... In the view of the Court, however, it would be going too far to interpret such general declarations of the Ayatollah Khomeini to the people or students of Iran as amounting to an authorization from the State to undertake the specific operation of invading and seizing the United States Embassy. ...

61. [This] ... does not mean that Iran is, in consequence, free of any responsibility in regard to those attacks; for its own conduct was in conflict with its international obligations. By a number of provisions of the Vienna Conventions of 1961 and 1963, Iran was placed under the most categorical obligations, as a receiving State, to

---

[275] See Gross (1980) 74 A.J.I.L. 395.
[276] I.C.J. Rep 1979, p.7. The Court called for the vacation of the Embassy and other premises; the release of the hostages; and the restoration of full diplomatic protection. In 1979, the Security Council also called upon Iran to release the hostages: S.C. Resn. 457 (1979), S.C.O.R. 24th Year, *Resolutions and Decisions*, p.24.

take appropriate steps to ensure the protection of the United States Embassy and Consulates, their staffs, their archives, their means of communication and the freedom of movement of the members of their staffs. ...

62. ... In the view of the Court, the obligations of the Iranian Government here in question are not merely contractual obligations established by the Vienna Conventions of 1961 and 1963, but also obligations under general international law.

63. The facts ... establish to the satisfaction of the Court that on 4 November 1979 the Iranian Government failed altogether to take any "appropriate steps" to protect the premises, staff and archives of the United States' mission against attack by the militants, and to take any steps either to prevent this attack or to stop it before it reached its completion. They also show that on 5 November 1979 the Iranian Government similarly failed to take appropriate steps for the protection of the United States Consulates at Tabriz and Shiraz. In addition they show, in the opinion of the Court, that the failure of the Iranian Government to take such steps was due to more than mere negligence or lack of appropriate means. ...

67. This inaction of the Iranian Government by itself constituted clear and serious violation of Iran's obligations to the United States under the provisions of Article 22, paragraph 2, and Articles 24, 25, 26, 27 and 29 of the 1961 Vienna Convention on Diplomatic Relations, and Articles 5 and 36 of the 1963 Vienna Convention on Consular Relations. Similarly, with respect to the attacks of the Consulates at Tabriz and Shiraz, the inaction of the Iranian authorities entailed clear and serious breaches of its obligations under the provisions of several further articles of the 1963 Convention on Consular Relations ...

69. The second phase of the events ... comprises the whole series of facts which occurred following the completion of the occupation of the United States Embassy by the militants, and the seizure of the Consulates at Tabriz and Shiraz. The occupation having taken place and the diplomatic and consular personnel of the United States' mission having been taken hostage, the action required of the Iranian Government by the Vienna Conventions and by general international law was manifest. Its plain duty was at once to make every effort, and to take every appropriate step, to bring these flagrant infringements of the inviolability of the premises, archives and diplomatic and consular staff of the United States Embassy to a speedy end, to restore the Consulates at Tabriz and Shiraz to United States control, and in general to re-establish the status quo and to offer reparation for the damage.

70. No such step was, however, taken by the Iranian authorities. ...

73. The seal of official government approval was finally set on this situation by a decree issued on 17 November 1979 by the Ayatollah Khomeini. His decree began with the assertion that the American Embassy was "a centre of espionage and conspiracy" and that "those people who hatched plots against our Islamic movement in that place do not enjoy international diplomatic respect." He went on expressly to declare that the premises of the Embassy and the hostages would remain as they were until the United States had handed over the former Shah for trial and returned his property to Iran. ...

74. ... The approval given to these facts by the Ayatollah Khomeini and other organs of the Iranian State, and the decision to perpetuate them, translated continuing occupation of the Embassy and detention of the hostages into acts of that State. The militants, authors of the invasion and jailers of the hostages, had now become agents of the Iranian State for whose acts the State itself was internationally responsible. ...

77. ... these facts constituted breaches additional to those already [held to have committed of art.22(2) of the 1961 Convention, viz additional breaches of arts 22(1)(3) and 33 of the 1963 Convention] ...

91. ... Wrongfully to deprive human beings of their freedom and to subject them to physical constraint in conditions of hardship is in itself manifestly incompatible with the principles of the Charter of the United Nations, as well as with the fundamental principles enunciated in the Universal Declaration of Human Rights. But what has above all to be emphasized is the extent and seriousness of the conflict between the conduct of the Iranian State and its obligations under the whole corpus of the international rules for which diplomatic and consular law is comprised, rules the fundamental character of which the Court must here again strongly affirm.

92. ... The frequency with which at the present time the principles of international law governing diplomatic and consular relations are set at naught by individuals or groups of individuals is already deplorable. But this case is unique and of very particular gravity because here it is not only private individuals or groups of individuals that have disregarded and set at naught the inviolability of a foreign embassy, but the government of the receiving State itself. ... Such events cannot fail to undermine the edifice of law carefully constructed by mankind over a period of centuries, the maintenance of which is vital for the security and well-being of the complex international community of the present day, to which it is more essential than ever that the rules developed to ensure the ordered progress of relations between its members should be constantly and scrupulously respected.

93. ... the Court ... cannot let pass without comment the incursion into the territory of Iran made by United

States military units on 24–25 April 1980 ... No doubt the United States Government may have had under-standable preoccupations with respect to the well-being of its nationals held hostage in its Embassy for over five months. No doubt also the United States Government may have had understandable feelings of frustration at Iran's long-continued detention of the hostages, notwithstanding two resolutions of the Security Council as well as the Court's own Order of 15 December 1979 calling expressly for their immediate release. Nevertheless ... the Court cannot fail to express its concern in regard to the United States' incursion into Iran. ... the Court was in course of preparing the present judgment adjudicating upon the claims of the United States against Iran when the operation of 24 April 1980 took place. The Court therefore feels bound to observe that an operation undertaken in those circumstances, from whatever motive, is of a kind calculated to undermine respect for the judicial process in international relations and to recall that in paragraph 47, 1 B, of its Order of 15 December 1979 the Court had indicated that no action was to be taken by either party which might aggravate the tension between the two countries.

94. At the same time, however, the Court must point out that neither the question of the legality of the operation of 24 April 1980, under the Charter of the United Nations and under general international law, nor any possible question of responsibility flowing from it, is before the Court.

95. For these reasons, The Court, ... By thirteen votes to two,[277]

Decides that the Islamic Republic of Iran has violated obligations owed by it to the United States of America under international conventions in force between the two countries, as well as under long-established rules of general international law; ...

Notes

1. The Court also decided (i) unanimously, that Iran "must immediately take all steps to redress the situation resulting from the events of November 4, 1979," including the release of the hostages and the return of the premises, documents, etc., to the US and (ii) by 12 votes to 3,[278] that Iran was "under an obligation to make reparation" to the US. Iran, which declined to participate in the proceedings, did not comply with the Court's judgment in any respect. The hostages were ultimately released in January 1981 as a result of a negotiated settlement with the US.

2. In the *Armed Activities* case,[279] the Democratic Republic of the Congo ("DRC") successfully claimed that Uganda had used armed force in breach of international law by its invasion of the DRC in August 1998 and subsequent activities on its territory. In a counterclaim, Uganda claimed that the related storming and long-term occupation of the Ugandan embassy in Kinshasa by DRC troops and other acts were in violation of the Vienna Convention. Ruling for Uganda, the Court stated[280]:

    "307. ... Uganda contends that on or around 11 August 1998 Congolese soldiers stormed the Ugandan Embassy in Kinshasa, threatened the ambassador and other diplomats, demanding the release of certain Rwandan nationals. According to Uganda, the Congolese soldiers also stole money found in the Chancery. Uganda alleges that, despite protests by Ugandan Embassy officials, the Congolese Government took no action.

    308. Uganda further asserts that, prior to their evacuation from the DRC on 20 August 1998, 17 Ugandan nationals and Ugandan diplomats were likewise subjected to inhumane treatment by FAC troops stationed at Ndjili International Airport. Uganda alleges that, before releasing the Ugandans, the FAC troops confiscated their money, valuables and briefcases. ...

---

[277] Ed. The judges in the majority were President Sir Humphrey Waldock; Vice-President Elias; Judges Forster, Gros, Lachs, Nagendra Singh, Ruda, Mosler, Oda, Ago, El-Erian, Sette-Camara and Baxter. Judges Morozov and Tarazi dissented.
[278] Judge Lachs joined the dissenting judges.
[279] I.C.J. Rep. 2005, p.168.
[280] I.C.J. Rep. 2005. Referring to arts 44 and 45, Vienna Convention, the court confirmed that the Convention applies in armed conflict.

309. Uganda claims that in September 1998, following the evacuation of the remaining Ugandan diplomats from the DRC, . . . [DRC] troops forcibly seized the Ugandan Chancery and the official residence of the Ugandan Ambassador in Kinshasa. Uganda maintains that the Congolese troops stole property from the premises, including four embassy vehicles. According to Uganda, on 23 November 1998 FAC troops again forcibly entered the Ugandan Chancery and the official residence of the Ugandan Ambassador in Kinshasa and stole property, including embassy furniture, household and personal effects belonging to the Ambassador and to other diplomatic staff, embassy office equipment, Ugandan flags and four vehicles belonging to Ugandan nationals. Uganda alleges that the Congolese army also occupied the Chancery and the official residence of the Ugandan Ambassador. . . .

311. Uganda alleges, moreover, that '[t]he Congolese government permitted WNBF commander Taban Amin, the son of former Ugandan dictator Idi Amin, to occupy the premises of the Uganda Embassy in Kinshasa and establish his official headquarters and residence at those facilities'. . . .

337. . . . the Court finds that, as regards the attacks on Uganda's diplomatic premises in Kinshasa, the DRC has breached its obligations under Article 22 of the Vienna Convention on Diplomatic Relations.

338. Acts of maltreatment by DRC forces of persons within the Ugandan Embassy were necessarily consequential upon a breach of the inviolability of the Embassy premises prohibited by Article 22 of the Vienna Convention on Diplomatic Relations. This is true regardless of whether the persons were or were not nationals of Uganda or Ugandan diplomats. In so far as the persons attacked were in fact diplomats, the DRC further breached its obligations under Article 29 of the Vienna Convention.

339. . . .The Court . . . finds that, through acts of maltreatment inflicted on Ugandan diplomats at the airport when they attempted to leave the country, the DRC acted in violation of is obligations under international law on diplomatic relations [under art.29 of the Vienna Convention]. . . .

342 . . . [As to the claim concerning Ugandan public property] the Status Report on the Residence and Chancery, jointly prepared by the DRC and Uganda under the Luanda Agreement, provides sufficient evidence for the Court to conclude that Ugandan property was removed from the premises of the official residence and Chancery. It is not necessary for the Court to make a determination as to who might have removed the property reported missing. The Vienna Convention on Diplomatic Relations not only prohibits any infringements of the inviolability of the mission by the receiving State itself but also puts the receiving State under an obligation to prevent others—such as armed militia groups—from doing so (see *United States Diplomatic and Consular Staff in Tehran, Judgment, I.C.J. Reports 1980*, pp30–32, paras.61–67). . . .Similarly, the Court need not establish a precise list of items removed—a point of disagreement between the Parties—in order to conclude at this stage of the proceedings that the DRC breached its obligations under the relevant rules of international law. Although these issues will become important should there be a reparation stage, they are not relevant for the Court's finding on the legality or illegality of the acts of the DRC.

343. In addition to the issue of the taking of Ugandan public property described in paragraph 309, above, Uganda has specifically pleaded that the removal of 'almost all of the documents in their archives and working files' violates Article 24 of the Vienna Convention on Diplomatic Relations. The same evidence discussed in paragraph 342 also supports this contention, and the Court accordingly finds the DRC in violation of its obligations under Article 24 of the Vienna Convention."

3.   A breach of art.22, Vienna Convention, was also found by the Eritrea-Ethiopia Claims Commission in *Partial Award: Diplomatic Claim: Eritrea's Claim 20*[281]:

> "46. The Commission concludes that ... Eritrea has presented clear and convincing evidence that Ethiopian security agents entered, ransacked, searched and seized the Eritrean Embassy Residence, as well as vehicles and other property, without Eritrea's consent. ... Even if the Respondent Government had presented evidence supporting the reasonableness of its suspicion of criminal activity taking place in the Residence, for example, by submitting redacted intelligence reports, there would still be no legal defence for Ethiopia's admitted 'sealing off' of the Residence in the face of such suspected illegal activity without Eritrea's consent. The Residence, as part of the diplomatic premises, is absolutely inviolable under Article 22 of the Vienna Convention on Diplomatic Relations.
>
> 47. This conclusion does not mean that Ethiopia was defenceless in the face of allegedly illegal Eritrean activity in the Residence. Ethiopia was at all times free to terminate diplomatic relations with Eritrea and hence to close its mission, including the Residence, subject to Ethiopia's obligations under Article 43, paragraph (a), of the Vienna Convention on Diplomatic Relations to 'respect and protect the premises of the mission, together with its property and archives'."

DIPLOMATIC PRIVILEGES ACT 1964

(1964, c. 81)

1. The following provisions of this Act shall, with respect to the matters dealt with therein, have effect in substitution for any previous enactment or rule of law.

2.—(1) Subject to section 3 of this Act, the Articles set out in Schedule 1 to this Act[282] ... shall have the force of law in the United Kingdom ...
(3) For the purposes of Article 32 a waiver by the head of the mission of any State or any person for the time being performing his functions shall be deemed to be a waiver by that State. ...

3.—(1) If it appears to Her Majesty that the privileges and immunities accorded to a mission of Her Majesty in the territory of any State, or to persons connected with that mission, are less than those conferred by this Act on the mission of that State or on persons connected with that mission, Her Majesty may by an Order in Council withdraw such of the privileges and immunities so conferred from the mission of that State or from such persons connected with it as appears to Her Majesty to be proper. ...

4. If in any proceedings any question arises whether or not any person is entitled to any privilege or immunity under this Act a certificate issued by or under the authority of the Secretary of State stating any fact relating to that question shall be conclusive evidence of that fact.

7.—(1) Where any special agreement or arrangement between the Government of any State and the Government of the United Kingdom in force at the commencement of this Act provides for extending—

(a) such immunity from jurisdiction and from arrest or detention, and such inviolability of residence, as are conferred by this Act on a diplomatic agent; or

---

[281] PCA 2005, *www.pca-cpa.org*.
[282] Ed. Vienna Convention, arts 1, 22–24, 27–40.

(b) such exemption from customs duties, taxes and related charges as is conferred by this Act in respect of articles for the personal use of a diplomatic agent;

to any class of person, or to articles for the personal use of any class of person, connected with the mission of that State, that immunity and inviolability or exemption shall so extend, so long as that agreement or arrangement continues in force. ...

EMPSON v SMITH

[1966] 1 Q.B. 426. Court of Appeal

In 1963, the plaintiff brought a county court action against the defendant for breach of a tenancy agreement. The action was stayed after the Ministry of Commonwealth Relations had certified that the defendant was an administrative officer employed by the High Commissioner for Canada.[283] In December 1964 an application by the plaintiff, made in August 1964, to have the stay removed was heard by the county court, together with an application by the defendant, made in November 1964, to have the writ dismissed as a nullity. By that time the Diplomatic Privileges Act had come into force, on October 1, 1964. The county court granted the defendant's application. The plaintiff appealed to the Court of Appeal.

DIPLOCK L.J.:

[The 1964] Act makes radical amendments in the previously existing law on diplomatic privileges and immunity and in particular draws a distinction between the immunities enjoyed by "members of the diplomatic staff" and "members of the administrative and technical staff" of a mission. Section 4 of that Act provides that a certificate issued by or under the authority of the Secretary of State shall be conclusive evidence of any fact relevant to any person's entitlement to any privilege or immunity. A further certificate dated October 20, 1964, was issued under that Act certifying that the defendant was on October 1, and had continued to be, a member of the administrative and technical staff of the Diplomatic Mission of Canada in the United Kingdom.

When the action was commenced in March 1963, the defendant was entitled under section 1(1)(a) of the Act of 1952 "to the like immunity from suit and legal process as is accorded to members of the official staff of an envoy of a foreign sovereign power." He was thus entitled so long as he remained en poste to complete immunity from civil suit in the United Kingdom, both as respects acts done in his official capacity on behalf of his government and as respects acts done in his private capacity. ...

If the defendant had applied before the passing of the Diplomatic Privileges Act 1964, to have the plaintiff's action dismissed there would have been no answer to his application. But he delayed until November, 1964. By that date his right to immunity from civil suit had been curtailed by that Act which applies to the United Kingdom the provisions of the Vienna Convention on Diplomatic Relations, 1961, contained in the Schedule to the Act. By the combined effect of Articles 31 and 37 of the Convention as a member of the administrative and technical staff of the mission his immunity from the civil jurisdiction of the courts of the United Kingdom does not extend to acts performed outside the course of his duties. Whether he is entitled to immunity in any particular suit no longer depends solely upon his status but also upon the subject-matter of the suit.

It is elementary law that diplomatic immunity is not immunity from legal liability but immunity from suit. If authority is needed for this it is to be found in *Dickinson v. Del Solar*[284] ... Statutes relating to diplomatic immunity from civil suit are procedural statutes. The Diplomatic Privileges Act, 1964, is in my view clearly applicable to suits brought after the date on which that statute came into force in respect of acts done before that date. If, therefore, the plaintiff had issued her plaint after October 1, 1964, instead of before, the action could not have been dismissed upon the ground of diplomatic privilege unless and until the court had determined the issue: whether or not the defendant's acts alleged by the plaintiff to constitute her cause of action against him

---

[283] The certificate was issued under the Diplomatic Immunities (Commonwealth Countries and Republic of Ireland) Act 1952 s.1(1), as amended by the Diplomatic Privileges Act 1964, Sch.2, which gives the missions of the Commonwealth countries listed the same immunities as those of other states.

[284] [1930] 1 K.B. 376, 380. Ed. cf. *Shaw v Shaw* [1979] Fam. 62 CA: petition for divorce presented by a wife when her husband was a diplomatic agent could not be struck out on the basis of diplomatic immunity after he had ceased to be such.

were acts performed outside the course of his duties. It is, to say the least, arguable that acts done by the defendant in relation to his tenancy of his private residence in London were performed by him outside the course of his duties. But this issue is one which can be decided only upon evidence. It has not yet been considered, for the deputy county court judge found it unnecessary to go into it. He dismissed the plaintiff's action upon other grounds. He took the view that "the proceedings were a nullity at the time they were commenced, they are not affected by the 1964 Act which came into operation subsequently."

The deputy county court judge did not refer to section 3 of the Diplomatic Privileges Act, 1708[285] but counsel for the defendant has in this court relied strongly upon it in support of the proposition that Mrs. Empson's plaint was void *ab initio*. The Act of Anne ... has been repeatedly held to be declaratory of the common law, and must therefore be construed according to the common law of which the law of nations must be deemed a part ... it was decided in *Re Suarez*[286] that notwithstanding that Act a writ issued in the High Court against an ambassador was not void ab initio. If it were it would, indeed, be impossible for the privilege ever to be waived for, as was decided in *Kahan v. Pakistan Federation*[287] there can be no effective waiver until the court is actually seised of the proceedings. The waiver is an undertaking given not to the other party to the proceedings but to the court itself. It can effectively be given only after the proceedings have commenced. *Kahan's* case was one of state immunity, but it is well settled that diplomatic immunity is governed by the same principles for it is claimed by the head of the mission on behalf of his state.

It follows therefore that until steps were taken to set aside or to dismiss the action the plaintiff's plaint was no nullity: it was a valid plaint. If the defendant had, with the permission of his High Commissioner, appeared to it before October 1, 1964, the procedural bar to the hearing would have been removed. So, too, if the defendant had ceased to be en poste while the plaint was still outstanding the action could then have proceeded against him. I can see no reason in logic or the law of nations why the position should be any different when the procedural bar has been removed by Act of Parliament—particularly when that Act of Parliament gives statutory effect to an international convention, by which sovereign states have mutually waived in part immunities for members of the staff of their foreign missions to which they were formerly entitled by the law of nations.

In holding, in my view, incorrectly, that the proceedings were a nullity at the time they were commenced, the deputy county court judge founded himself upon a passage in the judgment of Lord Parker C.J. in *Reg. v. Madan*[288] in which he referred to the proceedings being "null and void unless and until there is a valid waiver which, as it were, would bring the proceedings to life and give jurisdiction to the court." Lord Parker was clearly not using the words "null and void" in a precise sense for what is null and void is not a phoenix, there are no ashes from which it can be brought to life. In that case he was concerned only with waiver as removing the procedural bar of diplomatic immunity. His words should not be read that *only* waiver can, as it were, bring the proceedings to life. The removal of the procedural bar from any other cause will have the same effect.

I am therefore of opinion that the deputy county court judge was wrong in dismissing the action as he did.[289]
...

Appeal allowed.

---

[285] Section 3 reads: "And to prevent the like insolences for the future be it further declared by the authority aforesaid that all writs and processes that shall at any time hereafter be sued forth or prosecuted whereby the person of any ambassador or other publick minister of any foreign prince or state authorized and received as such by her Majesty her heirs or successors or the domestick or domestick servant of any such ambassador or other publick minister may be arrested or imprisoned or his or their goods or chattels may be distrained seized or attached shall be deemed and adjudged to be utterly null and void to all intents constructions and purposes whatsoever."

[286] [1918] 1 Ch.176.

[287] [1951] 2 K.B. 1003; [1951] 2 T.L.R. 697 CA.

[288] [1961] 2 Q.B. 1 at 7.

[289] Sellers and Danckwerts L.JJ. delivered concurring judgments.

Notes[290]

1. Would the question whether the breach of the tenancy agreement by the defendant was an act "performed outside the course of" his duties have been a question of *fact* with which an executive certificate could have dealt and upon which such a certificate would have been conclusive under s.4 of the Diplomatic Privileges Act?

2. *Empson v Smith* indicates one respect in which the 1964 Act changes the previous English law on diplomatic immunity. Have the following pre-1964 rules also been changed:

    (a) That a diplomatic agent can claim immunity in a civil action for the payment of rates on his private residence?[291]

    (b) That a diplomatic agent can claim immunity in a civil action concerning his private commercial activities?[292]

    (c) That a British subject accredited as a diplomatic agent to a foreign mission in the United Kingdom has immunity from distraint of goods for non-payment of rates unless the contrary has been indicated by the British Government when he is received?[293]

    (d) That immunity can be deemed to have been waived by entry of appearance in an action?[294]

3. British Foreign Office practice is to treat a diplomat's "family" as including the spouse or civil partner and minor children [under 18], and certain other persons "in exceptional circumstances". In practice, the "exceptional" cases fall into two categories:

    > "1. the child of a diplomat between the ages of eighteen and twenty-five clearly resident with and financially dependent on him or her, in full time education at a recognised educational establishment and not engaged in paid full time employment;
    > 2. in certain cases, a dependent parent of a diplomat normally resident with him or her"[295]

    In *Re C (An Infant)*[296] Harman J., considering whether the son of a person entitled to immunity was himself entitled to it, ruled that the test was whether "he is ordinarily resident with, or is under his father's control."

4. *Reciprocity.* Sections 3 and 7 of the 1964 Act follow from art.47 of the Convention which recognises that immunity may be based upon reciprocity. No orders in council have been made under s.3.[297] The United Kingdom has reciprocal arrangements under s.7(1)(a) with three states.[298] The arrangement with the Russian Federation reads in part ". . . members of the staff of Her Majesty's Embassy in Moscow below the rank of attaché (apart from those who are Russian nationals), their wives and families, the personal servants of the Ambassador and

---

[290] On the 1964 Act, see Buckley (1965–66) 41 B.Y.I.L. 321.
[291] *Parkinson v Potter* (1885) 16 Q.B.D. 152.
[292] *Taylor v Best* (1854) 14 C.B. 487.
[293] *MacCartney v Garbutt* (1890) 24 Q.B.D. 368.
[294] *Dickinson v Del Solar* [1930] 1 K.B. 376.
[295] Denza, above, n.205, p.394.
[296] [1959] 1 Ch.363, 367.
[297] Foreign Affairs Committee Report, above, n.214, p.6. See, however, the Diplomatic Immunities Restriction Order 1956 (SI 1956/84) which continued in force by virtue of Diplomatic Privileges Act 1964, s.8(5) and which removes from junior staff and servants of missions personal immunity from suit or legal process to the extent necessary to achieve reciprocity with the treatment given to British members of diplomatic missions in the states concerned.
[298] Bulgaria, Czechoslavakia and the Russian Federation.

servants employed in the Embassy Offices (again, apart from those who are Russian nationals) will henceforth enjoy immunity from personal arrest or other legal process and from the civil and criminal jurisdiction of the Russian courts and inviolability of residence, provided that the corresponding categories of the staff of the Russian Embassy in London continue to enjoy these same immunities."[299] The United Kingdom has arrangements under s.7(1)(b) with nine states.[300]

---

[299] Note from the Foreign Office to the Russian Ambassador in London, April 20, 1956, 1964 B.P.I.L., pp.226, 227. The arrangements were justified by the British Under Secretary of State for Foreign Affairs as follows: "... the threat of legal proceedings, in other words, blackmail, is a weapon which can be and is used to subvert members of diplomatic missions in some countries," *Hansard*, HC Vol.697, col.1362 (July 1, 1964).

[300] Belgium, Bulgaria, France, Germany, Indonesia, Luxembourg, the Netherlands, Poland, US Lauterpacht suggests that the arrangements made under s.7(1)(a) and (b) are not regarded as treaties by the parties: 1964 B.P.I.L., p.226.

7 THE LAW OF THE SEA

1. INTRODUCTORY NOTE[1]

A. The 1958 Conventions on the Law of the Sea

The law of the sea was the subject of the first completed attempt of the International Law Commission to place a large segment of international law on a multilateral treaty basis. Four Conventions resulting from its work[2] were produced by the first and second Geneva Conferences on the Law of the Sea of 1958[3] and 1960.[4] They are the Geneva Conventions on the Territorial Sea and the Contiguous Zone,[5] on the High Seas,[6] on the Continental Shelf[7] and on Fishing and Conservation of the Living Resources of the High Seas.[8] All four have entered into force and have been ratified by a large, though not overwhelming, number of states.[9]

The High Seas Convention is said in its Preamble to be "generally declaratory of established principles of international law."[10] No such claim is made for any of the other Conventions and it is clear that they are a mixture of "codification" and "progressive development" in the sense of the terms of reference of the International Law Commission.[11] It is often difficult to be sure within which of these two categories a particular rule falls and whether, if within the latter, practice has so developed since its adoption at Geneva that it now states a rule of customary international law. The *North Sea*

---

[1]   See Anderson, *Modern Law of the Sea: Selected Essays* (2007); Bowett, *The Law of the Sea* (1967); Brown, *The International Law of the Sea* (2 vols, 1994); Churchill and Lowe, *The Law of the Sea* (3rd edn. 1999); McDougal and Burke, *The Public Order of the Oceans* (1967, reprinted 1987, with new introduction); O'Connell, *The International Law of the Sea* (2 vols, ed., Shearer, 1982, 1984). See also the *UN Law of the Sea Bulletin*, which contains law of the sea treaties and national laws, etc.

[2]   In 1956 the Commission submitted to the UN General Assembly 73 *Draft Articles Concerning the Law of the Sea*, together with a Commentary upon them: for the text of the Draft Articles and the Commentary, see Y.B.I.L.C., 1956, II, pp.256 et seq.

[3]   See *UN Conference on the Law of the Sea, Geneva*, February 24–April 27, 1958, *Official Records*, Vols I–VII, UN Doc. A/CONF. 13/37–43. (Referred to in this chapter as *1958 Sea Conference Records*.)

[4]   See *2nd UN Conference on the Law of the Sea, Geneva*, March 17–April 26, 1960, *Official Records*, UN Doc. A/CONF. 19/8 and 9. See Dean (1960) 54 A.J.I.L. 751.

[5]   U.K.T.S. 3 (1965), Cmnd. 2511; 516 U.N.T.S. 205; (1958) 52 A.J.I.L. 834.

[6]   U.K.T.S. 5 (1963), Cmnd. 1929; 450 U.N.T.S. 82; (1958) 52 A.J.I.L. 842.

[7]   U.K.T.S. 39 (1964), Cmnd. 2422; 499 U.N.T.S. 311; (1958) 52 A.J.I.L. 858.

[8]   U.K.T.S. 39 (1966), Cmnd. 3208; 599 U.N.T.S. 285; (1958) 52 A.J.I.L. 851.

[9]   The Territorial Sea Convention entered into force in 1964; there are 52 parties. The High Seas Convention entered into force in 1962; there are 63 parties. The Continental Shelf Convention entered into force in 1964; there are 58 parties. The Fisheries Convention entered into force in 1966; there are 38 parties. The UK is a party to all four Conventions. The Conference also adopted an Optional Protocol on the Compulsory Settlement of Disputes, (1963) U.K.T.S. 60, Cmnd. 2112; 450 U.N.T.S. 169; (1958) 52 A.J.I.L. 862. This entered into force in 1962; 38 parties, including the UK. On the Conventions, see Dean (1958) 52 A.J.I.L. 607; Fitzmaurice (1959) 8 I.C.L.Q. 73; Jessup (1959) 59 Col.L.R. 234; Sørensen, *The Law of the Sea*, Int.Conc., No. 520 (1958).

[10]   Note that there are some provisions of the Convention, e.g. art.15 on piracy (see new art.101, 1982 Convention, below, p.178), that were clearly instances of "progressive development" of the law and not "codification".

[11]   See above, p.63.

Continental Shelf cases[12] have shown that it must not be too readily assumed that a treaty provision even in a "law-making" treaty states a rule of customary international law.

Although the Geneva Conventions were a considerable achievement, they were not perfect. In particular, they did not contain a rule on the basic question of the width of the territorial sea or on the related question of the fishing rights, if any, of coastal states beyond their territorial sea. They also have been overtaken by events, both scientific and political. The development of new techniques for underwater exploitation of oil and other mineral resources has made it necessary to reconsider the régime of the continental shelf and to establish a régime for the deep sea-bed. Concern for the conservation of fishing resources and the prevention of pollution has grown and has led to general approval of an approach based upon control by the coastal state over wide areas of the sea adjacent to its coastline. State practice on the width of the territorial sea has changed, again in favour of the coastal state and with consequential problems for innocent passage and overflight. Archipelagic and landlocked states have pressed their claims for better treatment. These, and other considerations, including the fact that most post-colonial states had had no say in the drafting of the Geneva Conventions of 1958,[13] led to the decision to call a Third United Nations Conference on the Law of the Sea (UNCLOS III).[14]

B. The 1982 Convention on the Law of the Sea

After nine long years of negotiation,[15] the Conference adopted the 1982 Convention on the Law of the Sea.[16] The 1982 Convention is a remarkable instrument. The Convention covers, in its 320 articles and nine annexes, all of the ground of the four 1958 Conventions and quite a lot more. Many of its provisions repeat verbatim or in essence those of the Geneva Conventions. Some contain different or more detailed rules on matters covered by them. Others, most strikingly those on the exclusive economic zone and the deep sea-bed, spell out new legal régimes. The main changes or additions are the acceptance of a 12-mile territorial sea; provision for transit passage through international straits; increased rights for archipelagic and landlocked states; stricter control of marine pollution; further provision for fisheries conservation; acceptance of a 200–mile exclusive economic zone for coastal states; changes in the continental shelf régime; and provision for the development of deep sea-bed mineral resources.[17]

An underlying theme of the Convention is that it should "contribute to the realisation of a just and equitable international economic order which takes into account the interests and needs of mankind

---

12   Above, p.24.
13   86 states participated in the 1958 Conference; over 150 states participated in UNCLOS III.
14   On the Conference, see Ganz (1977) 26 I.C.L.Q. 1; Oxman (1977) 71 A.J.I.L. 247; Stevenson and Oxman (1974) 68 A.J.I.L. 1; (1975) 69 A.J.I.L. 1 and 763; Oxman (1977) 71 A.J.I.L. 247; (1978) 72 A.J.I.L. 57; (1979) 73 A.J.I.L. 1; (1980) 74 A.J.I.L. 1; (1981) 75 A.J.I.L. 211; (1982) 76 A.J.I.L. 1.
15   The records of debates and documents of the Conference are published in *Third UN Conference on the Law of the Sea: Official Records*, Vols I–XVII, 1975–84. Referred to in this Chapter as *UNCLOS III Records*, these official records are less useful than the equivalent publications for UNCLOS I and II because most of the drafting at UNCLOS III was done at informal meetings for which there is no official record of debates. See, however, the series of studies being prepared by the UN Office for Ocean Affairs and the Law of the Sea on the legislative history of some of the articles of the Convention (e.g. the 1987 study on the legislative history of Pt X on rights of access of land-locked states). For a more extensive set of conference documents, see Platzöder, ed., *Third United Nations Conference on the Law of the Sea*, 18 vols, 1982–1988. For another collection of documents relevant to UNCLOS III, see Lay, Churchill and Nordquist, eds, *New Directions in the Law of the Sea* (11 vols, 1973–81 and 2nd edn. looseleaf, 1983-). For accounts of UNCLOS III, see Friedheim, *Negotiating the New Ocean Regime* (1993); and Sanger, *Ordering the Oceans: The Making of the Law of the Sea* (1986).
16   UKTS 81 (1999), Cm. 4524; 1833 U.N.T.S. 3; (1982) 21 I.L.M. 1261. See *Bernaerts' Guide to the Law of the Sea: The 1982 United Nations Convention* (1988); and Nordquist, ed., *United Nations Convention on the Law of the Sea 1982: A Commentary* (Vols I–VI, 1985–2002).
17   On the effect of some of these changes on freedom of the air, see Hailbronner (1983) 77 A.J.I.L. 490.

as a whole and, in particular, the special interests and needs of developing countries, whether coastal or land-locked" (Preamble). The parts of the Convention in which this theme is most evident are those on the exclusive economic zone, the continental shelf and, above all, the deep sea-bed.

The Convention contains machinery for the settlement of disputes arising under it, including an International Tribunal for the Law of the Sea, with its seat at Hamburg (art.287 and Annex VI).

The Convention is a distinctive document in that none of its particular provisions were voted upon. Articles were drafted in the working Committees and presented as stating the common, predominant, or accepted view, with the complete text of the Convention seen as an intricate and delicately balanced bargain between the different interests of the participating states. States opposed to provision A were prepared to accept it either in return for the inclusion of provision B or in the interest of an agreed régime for the law of the sea that taken as a whole was acceptable. The intention was that the complete text would be adopted by the same process of consensus too.[18] The thought was that general acceptance of the complete package would increase its chances of ratification and strengthen its claim to be regarded as "instant" customary international law.[19] In the event, this expectation was not realised. At the eleventh hour, the newly elected United States Government asked for time to review the draft text and, when it was unable to obtain all of the changes (almost entirely in respect of the deep sea-bed) that it wanted, requested a vote. The Convention was then adopted, in accordance with traditional Conference practice, by a majority vote.[20]

Dissatisfaction with the deep sea-bed regime in Pt XI of the Convention led the US to vote against the adoption of the Convention and, together with the FRG and the UK, not to become a signatory to it. During the 1980s and early 1990s, the Convention was ratified by developing states, but, because of the deep sea-bed regime, not by developed states. In order to obtain more general ratification of the Convention and to ensure its success, steps were taken within the UN which ultimately led to the adoption of the 1994 New York Implementing Agreement.[21] This amends Pt XI to the satisfaction of developed states and has secured the future of the 1982 Convention as a generally accepted statement of the law of the sea. The 1982 Convention entered into force in 1994[22] and 160 states are now parties, including many developed states.[23]

It seems likely, even allowing for the *North Sea Continental Shelf* cases, that state practice will confirm or come to accept many of the particular Convention rules (whether those duplicating or building upon the relevant 1958 Convention or those adding to them) as being binding as custom.[24] But caution is in order since the consensus favouring the inclusion of a particular rule *as a part of the overall package* at UNCLOS III may have masked opposition to the rule taken by itself. A number of provisions in the area of the more traditional law of the sea,[25] as well as the acceptance of com-

---

[18] On the merits of the consensus approach, see Plant (1987) 36 I.C.L.Q. 525.

[19] See Caminos and Molitor (1985) 79 A.J.I.L. 871.

[20] The vote was 130 to four, with 17 abstentions. Israel, Turkey, the US, and Venezuela voted against. Seven West European states (Belgium, the FRG, Italy, Luxembourg, the Netherlands, Spain and the UK), eight East European States (Bulgaria, Byelorussia, Czechoslovakia, the GDR, Hungary, Poland, Ukraine, and the USSR), Mongolia, and Thailand abstained.

[21] On the Agreement, see below, p.411.

[22] When the 1982 Convention entered into force, a complicated set of treaty relations resulted, with the 1958 Conventions continuing fully in force for the states, such as the US, parties to them and not parties to the 1982 Convention. The 1958 Conventions also continue to govern states parties to both the 1958 and the 1982 Conventions in their relations with states parties to the 1958 Conventions only. The 1982 Convention replaces completely the 1958 Conventions for the parties to both. See art.311, 1982 Convention.

[23] These include Australia, France, Germany, Japan and the UK. The US is not a party.

[24] See, e.g., the US-USSR statement on innocent passage, below, p.419. On the relationship between the 1982 Convention and custom, see Bernhardt (1987–V); 205 Hague Receuil 247; Butler (1988) 12 Mar. Pol. 182; Gamble and Frankowska (1984) 21 San Diego L.R. 491; Larson (1994) 25 O.D.I.L. 75; Lee (1983) 77 A.J.I.L. 541; Macrae (1983) 13 Cal. West I.L.J. 181; Mendelson (1988) 12 Mar. Pol. 192; Sohn (1985) 34 A.U.L.R. 271.

[25] e.g. those on the right of transit passage through international straits: see below, p.355.

pulsory judicial and arbitral settlement, were, for example, concessions by developing states to which acceptance of the (original) deep sea-bed régime was a necessary counterweight.

A package approach to the relationship between the 1982 Convention and custom is suggested by the following remarks of the UNCLOS III President (Mr T. Koh) at the closing ceremony[26]:

"Although the Convention consists of a series of compromises, they form an integral whole. This is why the Convention does not provide for reservations.[27] It is therefore not possible for States to pick what they like and disregard what they do not like. In international law, as in domestic law, rights and duties go hand in hand. It is therefore legally impermissible to claim rights under the Convention without being willing to assume the correlative duties."

On this view, either the whole of the package in the 1982 Convention is likely to be custom or none.[28] The ICJ, which has found itself almost magnetically drawn to the Convention in a series of cases, mostly on maritime boundaries, has tended not to follow a package approach but, in the more usual way, to assess separately the status of particular rules or régimes as they arise for consideration. In the *Gulf of Maine Case*,[29] a Chamber of the Court stated:

"Turning lastly to the proceedings of the Third United Nations Conference on the Law of the Sea and the final result of that Conference, the Chamber notes in the first place that the Convention adopted at the end of the Conference has not yet come into force and that a number of States do not appear inclined to ratify it. This, however, in no way detracts from the consensus reached on large portions of the instrument and, above all, cannot invalidate the observation that certain provisions of the Convention concerning the continental shelf and the exclusive economic zone ... were adopted, without any objections ... these provisions, even if in some respects they bear the mark of the compromise surrounding their adoption, may nevertheless be regarded as consonant at present with general international law on the question."

In view of the entry into force of the 1982 Convention and the fact that a large majority of states are parties, the materials in the present chapter are based upon it. Its relation with custom and with the rules in the 1958 Conventions is also considered.

---

[26] *The Law of the Sea: Official Text of the UN Convention on the Law of the Sea* (1983), UN Publication, p.xxxiv. On the "package deal" principle, see also Brown (1984) 2 J.E.N.R.L. 258 at 260.

[27] Ed. See art.309.

[28] Note, however, that Pt XI of the 1982 Convention on the deep sea-bed, which was a crucial part of the bargain for developing states, concerns an issue that is not now as important for them as during UNCLOS III and has, in any event, been revised so as to favour developed states. As a result, the package in the 1982 Convention as a whole now clearly favours developed states.

[29] I.C.J. Rep. 1984, 246 at p.294. See also *Continental Shelf* (*Tunisia v Libya*) case, I.C.J. Rep. 1982, p.18 at 74 (reference to the Draft 1982 Convention as confirming the definition of the continental shelf); and the *Continental Shelf* (*Libya v Malta*) case, I.C.J. Rep. 1985, p.13, at 30 ("... the 1982 Convention is of major importance, having been adopted by an overwhelming majority of states; hence it is clearly the duty of the Court ... to consider in what degree any of its relevant provisions are binding upon the Parties as rules of customary international law"). And see the *Nicaragua* case, I.C.J. Rep. 1986, p.14, at p.111 (1982 Convention codifies innocent passage rule).

2. THE TERRITORIAL SEA[30]

A. *Sovereignty in the Territorial Sea*

CONVENTION ON THE LAW OF THE SEA 1982

UN Doc. A/CONF. 62/122; (1982) 21 I.L.M. 1261

Article 2

1. The sovereignty of a coastal State extends, beyond its land territory and internal waters and, in the case of an archipelagic State, its archipelagic waters, to an adjacent belt of sea, described as the territorial sea.

2. This sovereignty extends to the air space over the territorial sea as well as to its bed and subsoil.

3. The sovereignty over the territorial sea is exercised subject to this Convention and to other rules of international law.

Notes

1. There can be little doubt that the above rules[31] represent customary international law.[32] The "other rules of international law" referred to in art.2(3) presumably include both customary rules (e.g. concerning the treatment of aliens) and treaty obligations (e.g. concerning navigation at sea).

2. In the *Grisbadarna Case*,[33] the Permanent Court of Arbitration held that when certain land territory was ceded to Sweden "the radius of maritime territory constituting an inseparable appurtenance of this land territory must have automatically formed a part of this cession." Judge Sir Arnold McNair, in his dissenting opinion in the *Anglo-Norwegian Fisheries* case,[34] stated: "International law does not say to a State: 'You are entitled to claim territorial waters if you want them.' No maritime state can refuse them. International law imposes upon a maritime State certain obligations and confers upon it certain rights arising out of the sovereignty which it exercises over its maritime territory."

B. *Width of the Territorial Sea*

CONVENTION ON THE LAW OF THE SEA 1982

UN Doc. A/CONF. 62/122; (1982) 21 I.L.M. 1261

Article 3

Every State has the right to establish the breadth of its territorial sea up to a limit not exceeding 12 nautical miles,[35] measured from baselines determined in accordance with this Convention.

---

[30] The term "territorial sea" is interchangeable with "territorial waters".

[31] Article 2 is identical to arts 1, 2, of the 1958 Territorial Sea Convention, except for the references to archipelagic states.

[32] On the development of the rule of sovereignty over the seabed of the territorial sea, see Marston (1976–7) 48 B.Y.I.L. 321. On the evolution of British practice, see Marston, *The Marginal Seabed: United Kingdom Legal Practice* (1981).

[33] *Norway v Sweden*, Scott (1909) *Hague Court Reports* 121 at 127.

[34] I.C.J. Rep. 1951, p.116 at 160. See also above, p.194.

[35] Ed. A nautical mile is 1.1508 statute miles.

Notes

1. Lack of agreement prevented the inclusion in the 1958 Territorial Sea Convention of a rule on the width of the territorial sea. This absence of agreement reflected the uncertainty which has existed in customary international law for a number of years. It is arguable that at the turn of the century there was a rule of general application, originating for some states and writers in the distance from the coastline that a cannon could fire (and hence protect[36]), by which the territorial sea was three miles in width (the "cannon shot" rule). State practice now does not support such a rule or any other that specifies a single distance as the width of the territorial sea. Most coastal states claim 12 miles. Information available in 2008 showed that four states claimed from three to six miles[37]; 137 claimed 12 miles[38] and seven claimed 200 miles.[39] Compared with earlier figures,[40] these show a marked swing from three miles to 12 miles as the width most commonly claimed. At UNCLOS III, Ecuador argued for a 200 mile territorial sea but found little support.[41] The 1982 Convention probably states the present customary international law position. Agreement upon a 200 mile exclusive economic zone[42] takes away much of the argument for a territorial sea wider than 12 miles. The validity of claims to territorial seas wider than 12 miles depends upon the response of other states: see the *Anglo-Norwegian Fisheries* case, below, p.329.

2. The extension of the territorial sea to 12 miles has important consequences for the right of innocent passage for ships; it also affects aircraft which have no right of innocent passage over the territorial sea.[43] The following factors, referred to by the United States representative at Geneva in 1958, are worth bearing in mind:

    "One of the merits of the three mile limit was that it was safest for shipping. Many landmarks still used for visual piloting by small craft were not visible at a range of 12 miles; only 20 per cent of the world's lighthouses had a range exceeding that distance; radar navigation was of only marginal utility beyond 12 miles; and many vessels (which frequently did not wish to enter the territorial sea) did not carry sufficient cable or appropriate equipment to anchor at the depths normally found outside the 12-mile limit. In addition, any extension of the breadth of the territorial sea would mean an increase in the cost of patrolling the larger area. ... One further objection to extending the territorial sea was that, in time of war, a neutral State would have greater difficulty in safeguarding the broader belt of territorial waters against the incursions of ships of belligerents."[44]

---

[36] See the Preamble to the Territorial Waters Jurisdiction Act 1878, above, p.68.

[37] *UN Law of the Sea Bulletin*, No.67 (2008). Greece, Jordan, Palau and Turkey (in the Aegean Sea).

[38] These included most Afro-Asian and Latin American states. Most Western states, including Australia, Canada, France, Ireland, Japan, New Zealand, the UK and the US, also claimed 12 miles, as did China. The UK extended its territorial sea from three miles by the Territorial Sea Act 1987. See Churchill (1987) 37 I.C.L.Q. 412. The UK and Denmark claim only three miles for some overseas territories.

[39] 200 miles were claimed by four Latin American states and three African states, including Somalia. It is not clear to what extent these are claims to full territorial sovereignty in all cases. Togo claimed 30 miles.

[40] Figures produced by the UN Secretariat for the 1960 Conference showed that 22 states claimed three miles; 18 claimed 4–10 miles; 11 claimed 12 miles; and two claimed more than 12 miles: 4 Whiteman 21. 1973 FAO figures showed 21 claims to three miles and 56 claims to 12 miles.

[41] See *UNCLOS III Records*, Vol.IV, pp.75–80.

[42] See below, p.391.

[43] The 1982 Convention right of transit passage through international straits, see below, p.355, responds to these problems.

[44] *1958 Sea Conference Records*, Vol.III, p.26.

Note also Judge Sir Gerald Fitzmaurice in his dissenting opinion in the *Fisheries Jurisdiction* case (*Jurisdiction*)[45]:

> "the territorial sea involves responsibilities as well as rights, which many countries were unable to discharge satisfactorily outside a relatively narrow belt, such as for example policing and maintaining order; buoying and marking channels and reefs, sandbanks and other obstacles; keeping navigable channels clear, and giving notice of dangers to navigation; providing rescue services, lighthouses, lightships, bell-buoys, etc."

And see the following comment by the representative of Byelorussia at the 1960 Geneva Conference:

> "The main objective of the champions of the six-mile limit (the 1960 Canadian/United States proposal) was to obtain for their naval forces unconditional, so-called legitimate, access to foreign waters close to coasts in which they were interested for strategic or political reasons."[46]

Clearly, if passage through the territorial sea by warships in order to check on a coastal state's security or of demonstrating a state's "presence" as a form of political pressure is not an exercise of the right of innocent passage,[47] the wider the territorial sea the less the sea can be used effectively for such purposes.

C. Delimitation of the Territorial Sea

ANGLO-NORWEGIAN FISHERIES CASE[48]

U.K. v Norway

I.C.J. Reports 1951, p.116

A Norwegian Decree of 1935 delimited Norway's "Fishery Zone" (by which was meant its territorial sea) along almost 1,000 miles of coastline north of latitude 66° 28.8′ North. The Zone, which the United Kingdom agreed was, as a matter of historic title, four (not three) miles wide, was measured not from the low-water mark at every point along the coast (as is the normal practice) but from straight baselines linking the outermost points of land (sometimes "drying rocks" above water only at low-tide) along it. The preamble to the Decree justified this system on grounds of "well-established national titles of right," "the geographical conditions prevailing on the Norwegian coasts," and "the safeguard of the vital interests of the inhabitants of the northernmost parts of the country." The first of these grounds related to the use of straight baselines in Norwegian decrees of 1869 and 1889 (though for different parts of the coastline totalling only 89 miles) and acquiescence in that use by other states. The "geographic conditions" were that the coastline concerned is deeply indented by *fjords* and *sunds* (sounds) and, for part of its length south of North Cape, is fronted by a fringe of

---

[45] *UK v Iceland* I.C.J. Rep. 1973, p.28, n.8. And see art.24(2), 1982 Convention, below, p.346.
[46] UN Doc. A/CONF. 19/C.1/SR.17, p.13.
[47] See below, p.352. On security zones, see below, p.386.
[48] See Johnson (1952) 1 I.C.L.Q. 145; and Waldock (1951) 28 B.Y.I.L. 114.

islands and rocks (the *skjærgaard*) that is difficult to separate from the mainland. The third ground is explained in the Court's statement that "[i]n these barren regions the inhabitants of the coastal zone derive their livelihood essentially from fishing." By using straight baselines Norway enclosed waters within its territorial sea that would have been high seas, and hence open to foreign fishing, if it had used the low-water mark line. Several baselines were over 30 miles long; the longest was 44 miles long.[49] In this case, the United Kingdom challenged the legality of Norway's straight baseline system and the choice of certain baselines used in applying it. The question was important for British fishing interests. Norwegian enforcement of its system had given rise to disputes involving British fishing vessels.

Judgment of the Court

The Court has no difficulty in finding that, for the purpose of measuring the breadth of the territorial sea, it is the low-water mark as opposed to the high-water mark, or the mean between two tides, which has generally been adopted in the practice of States. This criterion is the most favourable to the coastal State and clearly shows the character of territorial waters as appurtenant to the land territory. The Court notes that the Parties agree as to this criterion, but that they differ as to its application.

The Parties also agree that in the case of a low-tide elevation (drying rock) the outer edge at low water of this low-tide elevation may be taken into account as a base-point for calculating the breadth of the territorial sea. . . .

The Court finds itself obliged to decide whether the relevant low-water mark is that of the mainland or of the "skjærgaard." Since the mainland is bordered in its western sector by the "skjærgaard" which constitutes a whole with the mainland, it is the outer line of the "skjærgaard," which must be taken into account in delimiting the belt of Norwegian territorial waters. This solution is dictated by geographic realities.

Three methods have been contemplated to effect the application of the low-water mark rule. The simplest would appear to be the method of the *tracé parallèle*, which consists of drawing the outer limit of the belt of territorial waters by following the coast in all its sinuosities. This method may be applied without difficulty to an ordinary coast, which is not too broken. Where a coast is deeply indented and cut into, as is that of Eastern Finnmark, or where it is bordered by an archipelago such as the "skjærgaard" along the western sector of the coast here in question, the baseline becomes independent of the low-water mark, and can only be determined by means of geometric construction. In such circumstances the line of the low-water mark can no longer be put forward as a rule requiring the coast line to be followed in all its sinuosities. Nor can one characterise as exceptions to the rule the very many derogations which would be necessitated by such a rugged coast; the rule would disappear under the exceptions. Such a coast, viewed as a whole, calls for the application of a different method; that is, the method of baselines which, within reasonable limits, may depart from the physical line of the coast.[50]

It is true that the experts of the Second Sub-Committee of the Second Committee of the 1930 Conference for the codification of international law formulated the low-water mark rule somewhat strictly ("following all the sinuosities of the coast"). But they were at the same time obliged to admit many exceptions relating to bays, islands near the coast, groups of islands. In the present case this method of the *tracé parallèle*, which was invoked against Norway in the Memorial, was abandoned in the written Reply, and later in the oral argument of the Agent of the United Kingdom Government. Consequently, it is no longer relevant to the case. "On the other hand," it is said in the Reply, "the *courbe tangente*—or, in English, 'envelopes of arcs of circles'—method is the method which the United Kingdom considers to be the correct one."

The arcs of circles method, which is constantly used for determining the position of a point or object at sea, is a new technique in so far as it is a method for delimiting the territorial sea. This technique was proposed by the United States delegation at the 1930 Conference for the codification of international law. Its purpose is to secure the application of the principle that the belt of territorial waters must follow the line of the coast. It is not obligatory by law, as was admitted by Counsel for the United Kingdom Government in his oral reply. . . .

The principle that the belt of territorial waters must follow the general direction of the coast makes it possible to fix certain criteria valid for any delimitation of the territorial sea; these criteria will be elucidated later. The

---

[49] For a map showing the baselines, see Waldock, above, n.48, p.115.

[50] Ed. These last two sentences are a revised translation by the ICJ Registry of the authoritative French text: see Y.B.I.L.C., 1956, II, p.267.

Court will confine itself at this stage to noting that, in order to apply this principle, several States have deemed it necessary to follow the straight baselines method and that they have not encountered objections of principle by other States. This method consists of selecting appropriate points on the low-water mark and drawing straight lines between them. This has been done, not only in the case of well-defined bays, but also in cases of minor curvatures of the coastline where it was solely a question of giving a simpler form to the belt of territorial waters.

It has been contended, on behalf of the United Kingdom, that Norway may draw straight lines only across bays. The Court is unable to share this view. If the belt of territorial waters must follow the outer line of the "skjærgaard," and if the method of straight baselines must be admitted in certain cases, there is no valid reason to draw them only across bays, as in Eastern Finnmark, and not also to draw them between islands, islets and rocks, across the sea areas separating them, even when such areas do not fall within the conception of a bay. It is sufficient that they should be situated between the island formations of the "skjærgaard," *inter fauces terrarum*.

In the opinion of the United Kingdom Government, Norway is entitled, on historic grounds, to claim as internal waters all fjords and sunds which have the character of a bay. . . .

By "historic waters" are usually meant waters which are treated as internal waters but which would not have that character were it not for the existence of an historic title. . . . In its [the United Kingdom's] opinion Norway can justify the claim that these waters are . . . internal on the ground that she has exercised the necessary jurisdiction over them for a long period without opposition from other States, a kind of *possessio longi temporis*, with the result that her jurisdiction over these waters must now be recognised although it constitutes a derogation from the rules in force. . . . But the United Kingdom Government concedes this only on the basis of historic title; it must therefore be taken that that Government has not abandoned its contention that the 10-mile rule is to be regarded as a rule of international law.

In these circumstances the Court deems it necessary to point out that although the 10-mile rule has been adopted by certain States both in their national law and in their treaties and conventions, and although certain arbitral decisions have applied it as between these States, other States have adopted a different limit. Consequently, the 10-mile rule has not acquired the authority of a general rule of international law.

In any event the 10-mile rule would appear to be inapplicable as against Norway inasmuch as she has always opposed any attempt to apply it to the Norwegian coast.

The Court now comes to the question of the length of the baselines drawn across the waters lying between the various formations of the "skjærgaard." Basing itself on the analogy with the alleged general rule of 10 miles relating to bays, the United Kingdom Government still maintains on this point that the length of straight lines must not exceed 10 miles.

In this connection, the practice of States does not justify the formulation of any general rule of law. The attempts that have been made to subject groups of islands or coastal archipelagoes to conditions analogous to the limitations concerning bays (distance between the islands not exceeding twice the breadth of the territorial waters, or 10 or 12 sea miles), have not got beyond the stage of proposals.

Furthermore, apart from any question of limiting the lines to 10 miles, it may be that several lines can be envisaged. In such cases the coastal State would seem to be in the best position to appraise the local conditions dictating the selection.

Consequently, the Court is unable to share the view of the United Kingdom Government, that "Norway, in the matter of baselines, now claims recognition of an exceptional system." As will be shown later, all that the Court can see therein is the application of general international law to a specific case. . . .

It does not at all follow that, in the absence of rules having the technically precise character alleged by the United Kingdom Government, the delimitation undertaken by the Norwegian Government in 1935 is not subject to certain principles which make it possible to judge as to its validity under international law. The delimitation of sea areas has always an international aspect; it cannot be dependent merely upon the will of the coastal State as expressed in its municipal law. Although it is true that the act of delimitation is necessarily a unilateral act, because only the coastal State is competent to undertake it, the validity of the delimitation with regard to other States depends upon international law.

In this connection, certain basic considerations inherent in the nature of the territorial sea, bring to light certain criteria which, though not entirely precise, can provide courts with an adequate basis for their decisions, which can be adapted to the diverse facts in question.

Among these considerations, some reference must be made to the close dependence of the territorial sea upon the land domain. It is the land which confers upon the coastal State a right to the waters off its coasts. It follows that while such a State must be allowed the latitude necessary in order to be able to adapt its delimitation to practical needs and local requirements, the drawing of baselines must not depart to any appreciable extent from the general direction of the coast.

Another fundamental consideration, of particular importance in this case, is the more or less close relationship existing between certain sea areas and the land formations which divide or surround them. The real question raised in the choice of baselines is in effect whether certain sea areas lying within these lines are sufficiently closely linked to the land domain to be subject to the regime of internal waters. This idea, which is at the basis of the determination of the rules relating to bays, should be liberally applied in the case of a coast, the geographical configuration of which is as unusual as that of Norway.

Finally, there is one consideration not to be overlooked, the scope of which extends beyond purely geographical factors: that of certain economic interests peculiar to a region, the reality and importance of which are clearly evidenced by a long usage.

Norway puts forward the 1935 Decree as the application of a traditional system of delimitation, a system which she claims to be in complete conformity with international law. The Norwegian Government has referred in this connection to an historic title, the meaning of which was made clear by Counsel for Norway at the sitting on October 12, 1951: "The Norwegian Government does not rely upon history to justify exceptional rights, to claim areas of sea which the general law would deny; it invokes history, together with other factors, to justify the way in which it applies the general law." This conception of an historic title is in consonance with the Norwegian Government's understanding of the general rules of international law. In its view, these rules of international law take into account the diversity of facts and, therefore, concede that the drawing of baselines must be adapted to the special conditions obtaining in different regions. In its view, the system of delimitation applied in 1935, a system characterised by the use of straight lines, does not therefore infringe the general law: it is an adaptation rendered necessary by local conditions.

The Court examined the Norwegian system.

The Court ... finds that this system was consistently applied by Norwegian authorities. ...

The Court considers that too much importance need not be attached to the few uncertainties or contradictions, real or apparent, which the United Kingdom Government claims to have discovered in Norwegian practice. They may be easily understood in the light of the variety of the facts and conditions prevailing in the long period which has elapsed since 1812, and are not such as to modify the conclusions reached by the Court. ...

From the standpoint of international law, it is now necessary to consider whether the application of the Norwegian system encountered any opposition from foreign States.

Norway has been in a position to argue without any contradiction that neither the promulgation of her delimitation Decrees in 1869[51] and in 1889, nor their application, gave rise to any opposition on the part of foreign States. Since, moreover, these Decrees constitute, as has been shown above, the application of a well-defined and uniform system, it is indeed this system itself which would reap the benefit of general toleration, the basis of an historical consolidation which would make it enforceable as against all States.

The general toleration of foreign States with regard to the Norwegian practice is an unchallenged fact. For a period of more than 60 years the United Kingdom Government itself in no way contested it. ... It would appear that it was only in its Memorandum of July 27, 1933, that the United Kingdom made a formal and definite protest on this point.

The United Kingdom Government has argued that the Norwegian system of delimitation was not known to it and that the system therefore lacked the notoriety essential to provide the basis of an historic title enforceable against it. The Court is unable to accept this view. ...

The notoriety of the facts, the general toleration of the international community, Great Britain's position in the North Sea, her own interest in the question, and her prolonged abstention would in any case warrant Norway's enforcement of her system against the United Kingdom.

The Court is thus led to conclude that the method of straight lines, established in the Norwegian system, was imposed by the peculiar geography of the Norwegian coast; that even before the dispute arose, this method had been consolidated by a constant and sufficiently long practice, in the face of which the attitude of governments bears witness to the fact that they did not consider it to be contrary to international law.

The question now arises whether the Decree of July 12, 1935, which in its preamble is expressed to be an application of this method, conforms to it in its drawing of the baselines, or whether, at certain points, it departs from this method to any considerable extent. ...

---

[51]   Ed. France, which had been in dispute with Norway on a related matter, did ask for an explanation of the 1869 Decree. Norway replied, arguing that the enactment was lawful, and France "did not pursue the matter": I.C.J. Rep. 1951, p.136.

The Norwegian Government admits that the baselines must be drawn in such a way as to respect the general direction of the coast and that they must be drawn in a reasonable manner. . . .

The delimitation of the Lopphavet basin has also been criticised by the United Kingdom. . . . The Lopphavet basin constitutes an ill-defined geographic whole. It cannot be regarded as having the character of a bay. It is made up of an extensive area of water dotted with large islands which are separated by inlets that terminate in the various fjords. The baseline has been challenged on the ground that it does not respect the general direction of the coast.[52] It should be observed that, however justified the rule in question may be, it is devoid of any mathematical precision. In order properly to apply the rule, regard must be had for the relation between the deviation complained of and what, according to the terms of the rule, must be regarded as the *general* direction of the coast. Therefore, one cannot confine oneself to examining one sector of the coast alone, except in a case of manifest abuse. . . . In the case in point, the divergence between the baseline and the land formations is not such that it is a distortion of the general direction of the Norwegian coast.

Even if it were considered that in the sector under review the deviation was too pronounced, it must be pointed out that the Norwegian Government has relied upon an historic title clearly referable to the waters of Lopphavet. . . . The Court considers that, although it is not always clear to what specific areas they apply, the historical data produced. . . . lend some weight to the idea of the survival of traditional rights reserved to the inhabitants of the Kingdom over fishing grounds included in the 1935 delimitation, particularly in the case of Lopphavet. Such rights, founded on the vital needs of the population and attested by very ancient and peaceful usage, may legitimately be taken into account in drawing a line which, moreover, appears to the Court to have been kept within the bounds of what is moderate and reasonable. . . .

For these reasons, the Court . . . finds by 10 votes to two[53] that the method employed for the delimitation of the fisheries zone by the Royal Norwegian Decree of July 12, 1935, is not contrary to international law; and by eight votes to four,[54] that the baselines fixed by the said Decree in application of this method are not contrary to international law.

Notes

1. The judgment in the case was greeted with dismay by British commentators who felt that it did not do justice to the not insignificant body of state practice on the questions in issue.[55] Although, as those commentators suggest, it may have been an example of judicial legislation, the judgment has undoubtedly been accepted by states and now almost certainly reflects customary international law on most points.[56]

2. *Measurement of the outer limit of the territorial sea*. The two methods discussed by the Court for finding the outer limit of the territorial sea are the *tracé parallèle* and *the arcs of circles (courbe tangente)* methods. The former, which is apparently not used in practice,[57] involves drawing a line parallel to the baseline. The line is established by projections the width of the territorial sea from every point along the baseline made outwards in the general direction of the coast. The method is difficult to apply with exactness on any irregular stretch of coastline. With regard to the latter, which Judge Read, disagreeing with the Court, thought was not new but "the way in which the coastline rule has been applied in the international practice of the last century and a half,"[58] Waldock[59] states:

---

52 Ed. The baseline across the Lopphavet basin is 44 miles long. One of the points from which it is drawn is a drying rock 18 miles from the next point, which is also a drying rock.

53 The judges in the majority were President Basdevant; Vice-President Guerrero; Judges Alvarez, Hackworth, Winiarski, Zoričić, de Visscher, Klaestad, Badawi Pasha and Hsu Mo. The dissenting judges were Judges Sir Arnold McNair and Read. Judge Hackworth voted with the majority on both rulings solely on the basis that Norway had established an historic title.

54 Judge Hsu Mo joined the dissenting judges. It is not clear who the fourth dissenting judge was.

55 See the articles by Johnson and Waldock cited above, n.47.

56 Note the different rule in the 1982 Convention, art.7(4), below, p.333, on drying rocks, or low-tide elevations.

57 Waldock, above, n.47, pp.134–135.

58 I.C.J. Rep. 1951, p.192.

59 See above, n.47, pp.134–135.

"To apply the rule you take a pair of dividers (compasses) opened to give a three-mile measurement and then draw a three-mile arc either from the land towards the given position at sea or from the position at sea towards the nearest points of land. If the arcs fall short, the position at sea is not within territorial waters. ... That this was the procedure found in state practice is demonstrated by the fact that very few states indeed ever drew either the outer limit of their territorial waters or their baseline. Without a precise delimitation of territorial waters, the only possible course is to determine the outer limit by taking three-mile arcs from the land. ... It is nothing but the application to territorial waters of the method used by seamen the world over for measuring distances at sea. ..."

Although easier to apply than the *tracé parallèle* method, the "arcs of circles" method may still lead to awkward pockets of high seas on exceptionally irregular coastlines.[60] It remains the standard method used by mariners in applying the low-water mark baseline, which also remains the baseline used by states along regular coastlines.

3. *Straight baselines.* Did the Court find for Norway because its system for the delimitation of its territorial sea was permitted by customary international law or because, although not permitted by it, Norway had established an historic title?[61] Or both? How long and how irregular does a coastline have to be for the Court's straight baseline approach to be applicable? Is it, where applicable, obligatory or can a state still use the low-water mark method instead? What is the precise relevance of economic factors in the Court's approach? Do they permit a state to be bolder than it might otherwise be in choosing its base points? As far as bays are concerned, might economic factors there too justify a longer closing line than would otherwise be permissible? Does the Court set any upper limit in terms of miles to the length of a straight baseline or of a closing line for a bay?

CONVENTION ON THE LAW OF THE SEA 1982

UN Doc. A/CONF. 62/122; (1982) 21 I.L.M. 1261

Article 4

The outer limit of the territorial sea is the line every point of which is at a distance from the nearest point of the baseline equal to the breadth of the territorial sea.

Article 5

Except where otherwise provided in this Convention, the normal baseline for measuring the breadth of the territorial sea is the low-water line along the coast as marked on large-scale charts officially recognized by the coastal State.

Article 6

In the case of islands situated on atolls or of islands having fringing reefs, the baseline for measuring the breadth of the territorial sea is the seaward low-water line of the reef, as shown by the appropriate symbol on charts officially recognized by the coastal State.

---

[60] For a proposal made some years ago by the US to prevent such pockets arising, see Boggs (1930) 24 A.J.I.L. 541 at 547 (Fig.6).

[61] See further on "historic waters," the *Continental Shelf* (*Tunisia v Libya*) case, below, p.337.

Article 7

1. In localities where the coastline is deeply indented and cut into, or if there is a fringe of islands along the coast in its immediate vicinity, the method of straight baselines joining appropriate points may be employed in drawing the baseline from which the breadth of the territorial sea is measured.

2. Where because of the presence of a delta and other natural conditions the coastline is highly unstable, the appropriate points may be selected along the furthest seaward extent of the low-water line and, notwithstanding subsequent regression of the low-water line, the straight baselines shall remain effective until changed by the coastal State in accordance with this Convention.

3. The drawing of straight baselines must not depart to any appreciable extent from the general direction of the coast, and the sea areas lying within the lines must be sufficiently closely linked to the land domain to be subject to the régime of internal waters.

4. Straight baselines shall not be drawn to and from low-tide elevations, unless lighthouses or similar installations which are permanently above sea level have been built on them or except in instances where the drawing of baselines to and from such elevations has received general international recognition.

5. Where the method of straight baselines is applicable under paragraph 1, account may be taken, in determining particular baselines, of economic interests peculiar to the region concerned, the reality and the importance of which are clearly evidenced by long usage.

6. The system of straight baselines may not be applied by a State in such a manner as to cut off the territorial sea of another State from the high seas or an exclusive economic zone.

Article 8

1. Except as provided in Part IV,[62] waters on the landward side of the baseline of the territorial sea form part of the internal waters of the State.

2. Where the establishment of a straight baseline in accordance with the method set forth in article 7 has the effect of enclosing as internal waters areas which had not previously been considered as such, a right of innocent passage as provided in this Convention shall exist in those waters.

Article 9

If a river flows directly into the sea, the baseline shall be a straight line across the mouth of the river between points on the low-water line of its banks.

Article 10

1. This article relates only to bays the coasts of which belong to a single State.

2. For the purposes of this Convention, a bay is a well-marked indentation whose penetration is in such proportion to the width of its mouth as to contain land-locked waters and constitute more than a mere curvature of the coast. An indentation shall not, however, be regarded as a bay unless its area is as large as, or larger than, that of the semi-circle whose diameter is a line drawn across the mouth of that indentation.

3. For the purpose of measurement, the area of an indentation is that lying between the low-water mark around the shore of the indentation and a line joining the low-water mark of its natural entrance points. Where, because of the presence of islands, an indentation has more than one mouth, the semi-circle shall be drawn on a line as long as the sum total of the lengths of the lines across the different mouths. Islands within an indentation shall be included as if they were part of the water area of the indentation.

4. If the distance between the low-water marks of the natural entrance points of a bay does not exceed 24 nautical miles, a closing line may be drawn between these two low-water marks, and the waters enclosed thereby shall be considered as internal waters.

5. Where the distance between the low-water marks of the natural entrance points of a bay exceeds 24 nautical miles, a straight baseline of 24 nautical miles shall be drawn within the bay in such a manner as to enclose the maximum area of water that is possible with a line of that length.

6. The foregoing provisions do not apply to so-called "historic" bays, or in any case where the system of straight baselines provided for in article 7 is applied.

---

[62] Ed. arts 46–54 on archipelagic states.

Article 11

For the purpose of delimiting the territorial sea, the outermost permanent harbour works which form an integral part of the harbour system are regarded as forming part of the coast.[63] Off-shore installations and artificial islands shall not be considered as permanent harbour works.

Article 12

Roadsteads which are normally used for the loading, unloading and anchoring of ships, and which would otherwise be situated wholly or partly outside the outer limit of the territorial sea, are included in the territorial sea.

Article 13

1. A low-tide elevation is a naturally formed area of land which is surrounded by and above water at low tide but submerged at high tide. Where a low-tide elevation is situated wholly or partly at a distance not exceeding the breadth of the territorial sea from the mainland or an island, the low-water line on that elevation may be used as the baseline for measuring the breadth of the territorial sea.

2. Where a low-tide elevation is wholly situated at a distance exceeding the breadth of the territorial sea from the mainland or an island, it has no territorial sea of its own.

Article 14

The coastal State may determine baselines in turn by any of the methods provided for in the foregoing articles to suit different conditions.

Article 15

Where the coasts of two States are opposite or adjacent to each other, neither of the two States is entitled, failing agreement between them to the contrary, to extend its territorial sea beyond the median line every point of which is equidistant from the nearest points on the baselines from which the breadth of the territorial seas of each of the two States is measured.[64] The above provision does not apply, however, where it is necessary by reason of historic title or other special circumstances to delimit the territorial seas of the two States in a way which is at variance therewith.[65]

Article 121

1. An island is a naturally formed area of land, surrounded by water, which is above water at high tide.

2. Except as provided for in paragraph 3, the territorial sea, the contiguous zone, the exclusive economic zone and the continental shelf of an island are determined in accordance with the provisions of this Convention applicable to other land territory.

3. Rocks which cannot sustain human habitation or economic life of their own shall have no exclusive economic zone or continental shelf.

---

[63]   Ed. Permanent harbour works were used as basepoints for drawing an equi-distance boundary line between adjacent states in *Dubai v Sharjah* (1981) 91 I.L.R. 543 at 662. Dykes or jetties may constitute harbour works if not "of excessive length": see *Maritime Delimitation in the Black Sea* case, I.C.J. Rep. 2009, para.134.

[64]   For the median line between the UK and French territorial seas in the area of the Dover Straits, which are less than 24 miles wide, see the Territorial Sea (Limits) Order 1989 (SI 1989/482), which implements a 1988 UK—France Agreement, Cm. 557.

[65]   The "special circumstances" exception was applied in the *Territorial and Maritime Dispute in the Caribbean Sea* case, I.C.J. Rep. 2007, p.441, para.277. This was because the equidistance line would be distorted by the unusual geographical configuration and because sediment accretion along the coastline would render it "arbitrary and unreasonable" over time.

Notes

Baselines.[66]

1. In the *Maritime Delimitation in the Black Sea* case, I.C.J. Rep. 2009, para.137, the ICJ stated that "the coastal state, in conformity with the provisions of Articles 7, 9, 10, 12 and 15, UNCLOS, may determine the relevant base points" although it is "nevertheless an exercise that always has an international aspect".

    The 1982 Convention follows the approach of the International Court of Justice in the *Anglo-Norwegian Fisheries* case.[67] It differs only in requiring (art.7(4)) that low-tide elevations be permanently above sea level to be used as the beginning of a straight baseline[68]; art.7(6) supplements the judgment. As permitted by art.7, the United Kingdom now uses straight baselines from Cape Wrath to the Mull of Kintyre on the west coast of Scotland.[69] The result is to enclose as internal waters areas of water between the Outer Hebrides and the mainland which, when a low-water mark baseline was used, were high seas. Because of this result, the right of innocent passage in art.8(2) applies.

    States generally have not been slow to seize the opportunity allowed by straight baselines of, in effect, extending seawards the limits of their territorial sea and other areas of maritime jurisdiction (exclusive economic zone, etc.). More than 60 coastal states now draw straight baselines, not always consistently with the limitations as to their use in art.7, 1982 Convention.[70] Indeed, Prescott,[71] after analysing state practice, describes art.7, 1982 Convention as a "dead-letter" and states:

    > "Because the rules covering baselines in the 1958 and 1982 Conventions are ambiguous and because there is no international authority charged with their supervision there has been widespread abuse of the system. Indeed it would now be possible to draw a straight baseline along any section of coast in the world and cite an existing straight baseline as a precedent."

    The abuses he refers to include drawing straight baselines along coasts that are not noticeably irregular or fronted by a fringe of (as opposed to a few) islands. However, the exceptional character of straight baselines was stressed by the ICJ in *Qatar v Bahrain*[72]:

    > "212. The Court observes that the method of straight baselines, which is an exception to the normal rules for the determination of baselines, may only be applied if a number of conditions are met. This method must be applied restrictively. Such conditions are primarily that either the coastline is deeply indented and cut into, or that there is a fringe of islands along the coast in its immediate vicinity.
    >   213. The fact that a State considers itself a multiple-island State or a *de facto* archipelagic

---

[66] See Reisman and Westerman, *Straight Baselines in International Maritime Boundary Delimitation* (1992); and Roach and Smith, *United States Response to Excessive Maritime Claims* (2nd edn. 1996)

[67] The 1982 Convention (arts 5, 8, 4, 12, 15 and 19) also repeats almost exactly nearly all of the provisions of the 1958 Convention (arts 3, 5, 6, 9, 12 and 13 respectively) on baselines. It retains the wording of art.4 too (1982 Convention, art.7), but adds to the end of art.4(4) a new "general recognition" exception (1982 Convention, art.7(4)). It also adds an additional paragraph to art.4 (1982 Convention, art.7(2)) on deltas. The 1982 Convention (art.11) similarly retains art.8 of the 1958 Convention, but supplements it by an additional final sentence.

[68] On low-tide elevations and straight baselines, see Marston (1972–73) 46 B.Y.I.L. 405.

[69] Territorial Waters Order in Council 1964, art.3, SI 1965, Pt III, s.2, p.6452A.

[70] UK Hydrographic Office notice, January 1, 2002, U.K.M.I.L. (2001), 72 B.Y.I.L. 634.

[71] In Blake, ed., *Maritime Boundaries and Ocean Resources* (1987), pp.38, 49.

[72] I.C.J. Rep. 2001, p.40.

State does not allow it to deviate from the normal rules for the determination of baselines unless the relevant conditions are met. The coasts of Bahrain's main islands do not form a deeply indented coast, nor does Bahrain claim this. It contends, however, that the maritime features off the coast of the main islands may be assimilated to a fringe of islands which constitute a whole with the mainland.

214. The Court does not deny that the maritime features east of Bahrain's main islands are part of the overall geographical configuration; it would be going too far, however, to qualify them as a fringe of islands along the coast. The islands concerned are relatively small in number. Moreover, in the present case it is only possible to speak of a "cluster of islands" or an "island system" if Bahrain's main islands are included in that concept. In such a situation, the method of straight baselines is applicable only if the State has declared itself to be an archipelagic State under Part IV of the 1982 Convention on the Law of the Sea, which is not true of Bahrain in this case.

215. The Court, therefore, concludes that Bahrain is not entitled to apply the method of straight baselines."

On the use of straight baselines by archipelagic states, see below, p.340.

Exceptionally, the 1986 Falkland Islands Interim Fishery Zone[73] is measured not from the low-water line or from straight baselines but by drawing a circle 150 miles in circumference from a point on the Islands.

2. *Deltas.* Article 7(2), 1982 Convention has a rule concerning deltas that was not in the 1958 Convention. It benefits such states as Bangladesh, which suggested it, and Egypt, whose Nile delta is regressing and would be within the "notwithstanding" clause.[74]

3. *Bays.*[75] If an area of water satisfies the requirements of art.10, 1982 Convention for a bay, it becomes internal waters so that there is no right of innocent passage through it.[76] On the closing line for bays, the Second Sub-Committee of the Second Committee of the 1930 Hague Codification Conference proposed a closing line of 10 miles.[77] In its 1956 Draft Articles, on which the 1958 Territorial Sea Convention was based, the International Law Commission at one stage proposed a closing line of 25 miles, but later reduced it to 15. It explained in its Commentary:

"The proposal to extend the closing line to 25 miles had found little support; a number of Governments stated that, in their view, such an extension was excessive. By a majority, the Commission decided to reduce the 25 miles figure, proposed in 1955, to 15 miles. While appreciating that a line of 10 miles had been recognised by several Governments and established by international conventions, the Commission took account of the fact that the origin of the 10 mile line dates back to a time when the breadth of the territorial sea was much more commonly fixed at three miles than it is now."[78]

The 24 miles rule was inserted in the 1958 Convention at Geneva[79], and is repeated in Article 10,

[73] *Law of the Sea Bulletin*, above, n.1, No.9 (1987), p.19. See Symmons (1987) 37 I.C.L.Q. 283.
[74] See Churchill and Lowe, above, n.1, p.38.
[75] See Bouchez, *The Regime of Bays in International Law* (1964); Strohl, *The International Law of Bays* (1963); Westerman, *The Juridical Bay* (1987).
[76] 1982 Convention art.10, is identical to art.7, 1958 Convention.
[77] L.N.Doc. C. 351 (b). M. 145 (b). 1930. V, p.217.
[78] Y.B.I.L.C., 1956, II. p.269.
[79] *1958 Sea Conference Records*, Vol.III, p.146.

1982 Convention. On the relation between the 24–mile rule and customary international law, the following statement in 1963 by the United States Secretary of State on the status of Bristol Bay off the coast of Alaska is of interest:

"Although the Convention is not yet in force ... it must be regarded in view of its adoption (at Geneva) by a large majority of the States of the world as the best evidence of international law on the subject at the present time. This is particularly so in view of the rejection by the International Court of Justice in the *Anglo-Norwegian Fisheries Case* of the so-called 10-mile rule previously considered as international law by the United States and other countries. ... Since the line drawn ... [across the Bay] is over 162 miles long ... there is no basis in international law ... for Alaska's claim ... unless these waters can be considered an 'historic bay'."[80]

As to *bays bordered by more than one state*, Colombos[81] states:

"There exists a good deal for controversy on the subject, but the correct view is that territorial waters should follow the sinuosities of the coast ... subject to any special agreement. ..."

An example of such a bay is the controversial Gulf of Aqaba in the Red Sea which is bordered by the states of Egypt, Israel, Jordan and Saudi Arabia.[82] Neither the 1958 nor the 1982 Conventions govern such bays or historic bays.

Historic bays undoubtedly may exist at customary international law.[83] Thus in the *Land, Island and Maritime Frontier Dispute* case,[84] an ICJ Chamber held that the Gulf of Foncesa, which is surrounded by Nicaragua, Honduras and El Salvador and which is about 19 miles across at its mouth, was an historic bay with the three coastal states concerned sharing joint sovereignty over the waters landward of the closing line. In 1974, the US protested at a claim made by Libya that the Gulf of Sirte within a closing line of approximately 300 miles was Libyan internal or territorial waters as a "violation of international law."[85] The Gulf did not "meet the international law standards of past open, notorious and effective exercise of authority, and acquiescence of foreign nations necessary to be regarded historically as Libyan internal or territorial waters."[86] In the *Continental Shelf (Tunisia v Libya)* case,[87] Tunisia, in the course of developing its continental shelf claim, argued that it had historic rights to the exploitation of fixed fisheries (to catch swimming species) and sponges in the waters off its coastline beyond its territorial sea. After noting that "historic titles," including titles to historic bays, "must enjoy respect and be preserved as they always have been by long usage"; that the juridical régime of "historic waters" had purposely been left for separate, later consideration when the 1958 Convention was being drafted; and that UNCLOS III had not tackled the question either, the Court stated:

---

[80] (1963) 2 I.L.M. 528.

[81] Colombos, *The International Law of the Sea* (6th edn. 1967), p.188.

[82] On the right of passage through the Gulf, see below, p.424.

[83] For examples of claims to historic bays—some contested (e.g. Canadian claim to Hudson Bay, contested by US), others accepted (e.g. US claim to Delaware Bay), see UN Secretariat Memorandum, *1958 Sea Conference Records*, Vol.I, p.1.

[84] I.C.J. Rep. 1992, p.351. See Gioia (1993) 24 N.Y.I.L. 81; Scobbie (1994) Mar. Pol. 249; and Shaw (1993) 42 I.C.L.Q. 929. cf. *El Salvador v Honduras* (1917) 11 A.J.I.L. 674, Central American Court of Justice.

[85] (1974) 68 A.J.I.L. 510.

[86] (1974) 68 A.J.I.L. 510. cf. the UK reaction: *Hansard*, HC Vol.91, col.506 (February 13, 1986). In 1981, two Libyan military aircraft were shot down when they attacked US military aircraft engaged in exercises in the disputed area of the Gulf.

[87] I.C.J. Rep. 1982, pp.73–74.

"It seems clear that the matter continues to be governed by general international law which does not provide for a *single 'régime'* for 'historic waters' or 'historic bays,' but only for a particular régime for each of the concrete, recognised cases of 'historic waters' or 'historic bays.' It is clearly the case that, basically, the notion of historic rights or waters and that of the continental shelf are governed by distinct legal régimes in customary international law. The first régime is based on acquisition and occupation, while the second is based on the existence of rights *'ipso facto* and *ab initio.'* No doubt both may sometimes coincide in part or in whole, but such coincidence can only be fortuitous ... it may be that Tunisia's historic rights and titles are more nearly related to the concept of the exclusive economic zone, which may be regarded as part of modern international law. ..."

The requirement of "respect" or "acquiescence" points to a distinction between bays that conform to art.10, 1982 Convention and historic bays, namely that whereas the former are valid irrespective of the response of other states, the latter depend upon consent. Consistent with the Court's comment in the *Tunisia v Libya* case that there is no "single régime" for historic bays, there does not appear to be any maximum length for a closing line for such a bay; a line of any length may be accepted by other states.

See also on bays, *Post Office v Estuary Radio Ltd.*[88]

4. *Islands.*[89] A case of an island being created by natural forces was the creation of Surtsey by volcanic activity in 1963 in Icelandic territorial waters. Would land which is permanently above the sea as a result of dredging operations be an island under the 1982 Convention? Artificial islands, installations and structures are stated by the 1982 Convention not to be islands.[90] Small islands have become more important in recent years because of the possibility of exploiting oil and gas resources in the seabed surrounding them.

    The 1982 Convention (art.121), which was stated by the Conciliation Commission in the *Jan Mayen* case[91] to "reflect the present status of international law," repeats the definition of an island and the rule about its territorial sea in art.10, 1958 Territorial Sea Convention, but restricts the circumstances in which it may have an exclusive economic zone of continental shelf, see below, p.397.

5. *Low tide elevations.*[92] The role of low tide elevations in the law of the sea (see art.13) was summarised in *The Maritime Delimitation and Territorial Questions between Qatar and Bahrain* case[93] as follows:

    "201. According to the relevant provisions of the Conventions on the Law of the Sea, which reflect customary international law ..., the low-water line of a low-tide elevation may be used as the baseline for measuring the breadth of the territorial sea if it is situated wholly or partly at a distance not exceeding the breadth of the territorial sea from the mainland or an island. If a low-tide elevation is wholly situated at a distance exceeding the breadth of the territorial

---

[88] [1968] 2 Q.B. 740 CA.

[89] See Bowett, *The Legal Regime of Islands in International Law* (1979); Jayewardene, *The Regime of Islands in International Law* (1990); Symmons, *The Maritime Zones of Islands in International Law* (1979); and Symonides (1987) 65 R.D.I. 161.

[90] Article 60(8), below, p.393. cf. art.5(4), Continental Shelf Convention 1958. See also Papadakis, *The International Regime of Artificial Islands* (1977).

[91] (1981) 20 I.L.M. 797, 803. See also *Eritrea v Yemen (Phase two: Maritime Delimitation)* (1999) 119 I.L.R. 417, 489–61.

[92] See Marston (1972–3) 46 B.Y.I.L. 405 and Weil, in Ando, McWhinney, Wolfrum, eds., *Liber Amicorum Judge Oda* (2002), Vol.1, p.307.

[93] I.C.J. Rep. 2001, p.40. See Mendelson (1991) 72 B.Y.I.L. 183. See also the *Sovereignty over Pedra Branca* case, I.C.J. Rep. 2008, para.291.

sea, it has no territorial sea of its own. The above-mentioned Conventions further provide that straight baselines shall not be drawn to and from low-tide elevations, unless lighthouses or similar installations which are permanently above sea level have been built on them (1958 Convention, paragraph 3 of Article 4; 1982 Convention, paragraph 4 of Article 7) . . .

202. When a low-tide elevation is situated in the overlapping area of the territorial sea of two States, whether with opposite or with adjacent coasts, both States in principle are entitled to use its low-water line for the measuring of the breadth of their territorial sea. The same low-tide elevation then forms part of the coastal configuration of the two States. That is so even if the low-tide elevation is nearer to the coast of one State than that of the other, or nearer to an island belonging to one party than it is to the mainland coast of the other. For delimitation purposes the competing rights derived by both coastal States from the relevant provisions of the law of the sea would by necessity seem to neutralize each other . . .

204. . . . Nor is there any doubt that a coastal State has sovereignty over low-tide elevations which are situated within its territorial sea, since it has sovereignty over the territorial sea itself, including its sea-bed and subsoil. . . .

205. International treaty law is silent on the question whether low-tide elevations can be considered to be 'territory'. Nor is the Court aware of a uniform and widespread State practice which might have given rise to a customary rule which unequivocally permits or excludes appropriation of low-tide elevations. It is only in the context of the law of the sea that a number of permissive rules have been established with regard to low-tide elevations which are situated at a relatively short distance from a coast.

206. The few existing rules do not justify a general assumption that low-tide elevations are territory in the same sense as islands. It has never been disputed that islands constitute terra firma, and are subject to the rules and principles of territorial acquisition; the difference in effects which the law of the sea attributes to islands and low-tide elevations is considerable. It is thus not established that in the absence of other rules and legal principles, low-tide elevations can, from the viewpoint of the acquisition of sovereignty, be fully assimilated with islands of other land territory.

207. . . . A low-tide elevation . . . as such does not generate the same rights as islands or other territory. Moreover, it is generally recognized and implicit in the words of the relevant provisions of the Conventions on the Law of the Sea that, whereas a low-tide elevation which is situated within the limits of the territorial sea may be used for the determination of its breadth, this does not hold for a low-tide elevation which is situated less than 12 nautical miles from that low-tide elevation but is beyond the limits of the territorial sea. The law of the sea does not in these circumstances allow application of the so-called 'leap-frogging' method. In this respect it is irrelevant whether the coastal State has treated such a low-tide elevation as its property and carried out some governmental acts with regard to it; it does not generate a territorial sea.

208. Paragraph 3 of Article 4 of the 1958 Convention on the Territorial Sea and the Contiguous Zone and paragraph 4 of Article 7 of the 1982 Convention on the Law of the Sea provide that straight baselines shall not be drawn to and from low-tide elevations unless lighthouses or similar installations which are permanently above sea level have been built on them. These provisions are another indication that low-tide elevations cannot be equated with islands, which under all circumstances qualify as basepoints for straight baselines."

6. *Archipelagos.*[94] In 1957, Indonesia announced that its territorial sea would henceforth be "measured from straight baselines connecting the outermost points of the islands of the Republic of Indonesia."[95] The waters within the baselines would be "national waters subject to the absolute sovereignty of Indonesia," except that the "peaceful passage of foreign vessels would be guaranteed as long as and in so far as it is not contrary to the sovereignty of the Indonesian state or harmful to her security."[96] A number of states, including the United Kingdom,[97] protested. The International Law Commission felt itself unable, for lack of information, to reach any conclusion on the question of a special rule for archipelagos, and there are no provisions on the matter in the 1958 Convention.

The 1982 Convention contains provisions allowing the use of straight baselines by "mid-ocean" archipelagic states[98] (but not by continental states with "off-lying archipelagos"). These read in part (art.47):

1. An archipelagic state may draw straight archipelagic baselines joining the outermost points of the outermost islands and drying reefs of the archipelago provided that within such baselines are included the main islands and an area in which the ratio of the area of the water to the area of the land, including atolls, is between one to one and nine to one.

2. The length of such baselines shall not exceed 100 nautical miles, except that up to three per cent of the total number of baselines enclosing any archipelago may exceed that length, up to a maximum length of 125 nautical miles.

3. The drawing of such baselines shall not depart to any appreciable extent from the general configuration of the archipelago.

The "archipelagic waters" thus enclosed are stated to be within the sovereignty of the archipelagic state (art.49, 1982 Convention), but are subject to the Convention right of innocent passage (art.52, 1982 Convention), and to the right of archipelagic sea-lanes passage (art.53).[99] The latter is comparable to the right of transit passage through international straits, see below, p.356, and includes a right of overflight for aircraft.[100] The right of innocent passage is suspendable for security reasons only (art.52(2)); there is no provision for the right of archipelagic

[94] See Dubner, *The Law of Territorial Waters of Mid-Ocean Archipelagos and Archipelagic States* (1976); Munavvar, *Ocean States: Archipelagic Regimes in the Law of the Sea* (1995); and Rodgers, *Mid-Ocean Archipelagos and International Law* (1981).

[95] 4 Whiteman 284. The Philippines had made a similar announcement in 1955; p.282. See Sørensen, *Varia Juris Gentium* (1959), p.315.

[96] 4 Whiteman 284.

[97] See *Hansard*, HC, Vol.582, col.1185, (February 19, 1958).

[98] Article 46 reads: "For the purposes of this Convention: (a) 'Archipelagic State' means a State constituted wholly by one or more archipelagos and may include other islands; (b) 'Archipelago' means a group of islands, including parts of islands, interconnecting waters and other natural features which are so closely interrelated with such islands, waters and other natural features form an intrinsic geographical, economic and political entity, or which historically have been regarded as such." As Churchill and Lowe, above, n.1, p.121, state, although this definition might include such island states as Japan and the UK, the 1:1 rule in art.47(1) would prevent them from drawing archipelagic baselines. Excluding such states, there remain 25–35 archipelagic states, of whom 15 (e.g. Antigua, Fiji, Papua, Cape Verde, Indonesia and the Philippines) have drawn archipelagic baselines: pp.106–107. As to "off-lying archipelagos," (e.g. the Canadian Archipelago, around which, Canada has now drawn *Anglo-Norwegian Fisheries* case straight baselines: see above, p.201), see Herman (1985) 23 C.Y.I.L. 172. Note that Denmark has drawn archipelagic baselines around the Faroes and Portugal has done so around the Azores. Is this consistent with the 1982 Convention? See Alexander (1987) 18 O.D.I.L. 333 at 337.

[99] But note that on signing the 1982 Convention, the Philippines made a declaration equating archipelagic waters with internal waters. Australia, the USSR, the Ukranian SSR and the Byelorussian SSR objected: UN Doc. ST/LEG/SER. E/7, pp.764 et seq.

[100] See de Vries Lentsch (1983) 14 N.Y.I.L. 165.

sea-lane passage to be suspended. An archipelagic state must "recognise traditional fishing rights and other legitimate activities of the immediately adjacent neighbouring states" (art.51(1)) and "respect existing submarine cables" (art.51(2)). These limitations are more extensive than those upon a coastal state in respect of its territorial sea. Although maritime states were opposed to archipelagic baselines in the 1950s, the rights of passage written into the 1982 Convention would seem to have overcome their doubts[101]; moreover, it has been suggested that the area of exclusive economic zone that results from the use of archipelagic baselines is only 1 or 2 per cent greater than that which would result by the drawing of such zones around each island.[102]

D. Jurisdiction over Foreign Ships in the Territorial Sea

CORFU CHANNEL CASE (MERITS)

U.K. v Albania

I.C.J. Reports 1949, p.4

The facts of the case, so far as they concern the Albanian counterclaim, are indicated in the following extract from the Court's judgment. The United Kingdom brought the case claiming compensation for damage caused by mines to the *Saumarez* and the *Volage* during their passage through the Corfu Channel on October 22, 1946.[103]

Judgment of the Court

In the second part of the Special Agreement, the following question is submitted to the Court:

(2) Has the United Kingdom under international law violated the sovereignty of the Albanian People's Republic by reason of the acts of the Royal Navy in Albanian waters on the 22nd October and on the 12th and 13th November 1946 and is there any duty to give satisfaction? . . .

On May 15, 1946, the British cruisers *Orion* and *Superb*, while passing southward through the North Corfu Channel, were fired at by an Albanian battery in the vicinity of Saranda. . . .

The United Kingdom Government at once protested to the Albanian Government, stating that innocent passage through straits is a right recognised by international law. There ensued a diplomatic correspondence in which the Albanian Government asserted that foreign warships and merchant vessels had no right to pass through Albanian territorial waters without prior notification to, and the permission of, the Albanian authorities. . . .

It was in such circumstances that these two cruisers together with the destroyers *Saumarez* and *Volage* were sent through the North Corfu Strait on . . . [October 22, 1946].

The Court will now consider the Albanian contention that the United Kingdom Government violated Albanian sovereignty by sending the warships through this Strait without the previous authorisation of the Albanian Government.

It is, in the opinion of the Court, generally recognised and in accordance with international custom that States in time of peace have a right to send their warships through straits used for international navigation between two parts of the high seas without the previous authorisation of a coastal State, provided that the passage is

---

[101] The US considers that the 1982 Convention regime for archipelagic states reflects custom: (1989) 83 A.J.I.L. 559.

[102] See Hodson and Smith (1976) 3 O.D.I.L. 225 at 244.

[103] See Verzjil, *The Jurisprudence of the World Court*, vol. 2 (1966), p.22.

innocent. Unless otherwise prescribed in an international convention, there is no right for a coastal State to prohibit such passage through straits in time of peace.

The Albanian Government does not dispute that the North Corfu Channel is a strait in the geographical sense; but it denies that this Channel belongs to the class of international highways through which a right of passage exists, on the grounds that it is only of secondary importance and not even a necessary route between two parts of the high seas, and that it is used almost exclusively for local traffic to and from the ports of Corfu and Saranda.

It may be asked whether the test is to be found in the volume of traffic passing through the Strait or in its greater or lesser importance for international navigation. But in the opinion of the Court the decisive criterion is rather its geographical situation as connecting two parts of the high seas and the fact of its being used for international navigation. Nor can it be decisive that this Strait is not a necessary route between two parts of the high seas, but only an alternative passage between the Ægean and the Adriatic Seas. It has nevertheless been a useful route for international maritime traffic.[104] ...

One fact of particular importance is that the North Corfu Channel constitutes a frontier between Albania and Greece, that a part of it is wholly within the territorial waters of these States, and that the Strait is of special importance to Greece by reason of the traffic to and from the port of Corfu.

Having regard to these various considerations, the Court has arrived at the conclusion that the North Corfu Channel should be considered as belonging to the class of international highways through which passage cannot be prohibited by a coastal State in time of peace.

On the other hand, it is a fact that the two coastal States did not maintain normal relations, that Greece had made territorial claims precisely with regard to a part of Albanian territory bordering on the Channel, that Greece had declared that she considered herself technically in a state of war with Albania, and that Albania, invoking the danger of Greek incursions, had considered it necessary to take certain measures of vigilance in this region. The Court is of opinion that Albania, in view of these exceptional circumstances, would have been justified in issuing regulations in respect of the passage of warships through the Strait, but not in prohibiting such passage or in subjecting it to the requirement of special authorisation.

For these reasons the Court is unable to accept the Albanian contention that the Government of the United Kingdom has violated Albanian sovereignty by sending the warships through the Strait without having obtained the previous authorisation of the Albanian Government.

In these circumstances, it is unnecessary to consider the more general question, much debated by the Parties, whether States under international law have a right to send warships in time of peace through territorial waters not included in a strait.

The Albanian Government has further contended that the sovereignty of Albania was violated because the passage of the British warships on October 22, 1946, was not an *innocent passage*. ...

It is shown by the Admiralty telegram of September 21 ... that the object of sending the warships through the Strait was not only to carry out a passage for purposes of navigation, but also to test Albania's attitude ... The legality of this measure taken by the Government of the United Kingdom cannot be disputed, provided that it was carried out in a manner consistent with the requirements of international law. ... The Government of the United Kingdom was not bound to abstain from exercising its right of passage, which the Albanian Government had illegally denied.

It remains, therefore, to consider whether the *manner* in which the passage was carried out was consistent with the principle of innocent passage and to examine the various contentions of the Albanian Government in so far as they appear to be relevant.

The Court found, contrary to Albania's contention, that the warships were neither in combat formation nor manoeuvering and that there were no soldiers on board.

... The guns were ... "trained fore and aft, which is their normal position at sea in peace time, and were not loaded." ... In the light of this evidence, the Court cannot accept the Albanian contention that the position of the guns was inconsistent with the rules of innocent passage.

In the ... telegram of October 26, the Commander-in-Chief reported that the passage "was made with ships at action stations in order that they might be able to retaliate quickly if fired upon again." In view of the firing from the Albanian battery on May 15, this measure of precaution cannot, in itself, be regarded as unreasonable.

---

[104] Ed. The Court noted that 2,884 ships passed through the Channel in one 21–month period, flying seven different flags.

But four warships—two cruisers and two destroyers—passed in this manner, with crews at action stations, ready to retaliate quickly if fired upon. They passed one after another through this narrow channel, close to the Albanian coast, at a time of political tension in this region. The intention must have been, not only to test Albania's attitude, but at the same time to demonstrate such force that she would abstain from firing again on passing ships. Having regard, however, to all the circumstances of the case, as described above, the Court is unable to characterise these measures taken by the United Kingdom authorities as a violation of Albania's sovereignty.

... In a report of the commander of *Volage*, dated October 23, 1946—a report relating to the passage on the 22nd—it is stated: "The most was made of the opportunities to study Albanian defences at close range. ..."

With regard to the observations of coastal defences made after the explosions, these were justified by the fact that two ships had just been blown up and that, in this critical situation, their commanders might fear that they would be fired on from the coast, as on May 15.

Having thus examined the various contentions of the Albanian Government in so far as they appear to be relevant, the Court has arrived at the conclusion that the United Kingdom did not violate the sovereignty of Albania by reason of the acts of the British Navy in Albanian waters on October 22, 1946.

In addition to the passage of the United Kingdom warships on October 22, 1946, the second question in the Special Agreement relates to the acts of the Royal Navy in Albanian waters on November 12 and 13, 1946. This is the minesweeping operation called "Operation Retail." ...

The United Kingdom Government does not dispute that "Operation Retail" was carried out against the clearly expressed wish of the Albanian Government. It recognises that the operation had not the consent of the international mine clearance organisations, that it could not be justified as the exercise of a right of innocent passage, and lastly that, in principle, international law does not allow a State to assemble a large number of warships in the territorial waters of another State and to carry out minesweeping in those waters. The United Kingdom Government states that the operation was one of extreme urgency, and that it considered itself entitled to carry it out without anybody's consent.

... the explosions of October 22, 1946, in a channel declared safe for navigation, and one which the United Kingdom Government, more than any other government, had reason to consider safe, raised quite a different problem from that of a routine sweep carried out under the orders of the mine clearance organisations. These explosions were suspicious; they raised a question of responsibility.

Accordingly, this was the ground on which the United Kingdom Government chose to establish its main line of defence. According to that Government, the *corpora delicti* must be secured as quickly as possible, for fear they should be taken away, without leaving traces, by the authors of the minelaying or by the Albanian authorities. This justification took two distinct forms in the United Kingdom Government's arguments. It was presented first as a new and special application of the theory of intervention, by means of which the State intervening would secure possession of evidence in the territory of another State, in order to submit it to an international tribunal and thus facilitate its task.

The Court cannot accept such a line of defence. The Court can only regard the alleged right of intervention as the manifestation of a policy of force, such as has, in the past, given rise to most serious abuses and such as cannot, whatever be the present defects in international organisation, find a place in international law. Intervention is perhaps still less admissible in the particular form it would take here; for, from the nature of things, it would be reserved for the most powerful States, and might easily lead to perverting the administration of international justice itself.

The United Kingdom Agent, in his speech in reply, has further classified "Operation Retail" among methods of self-protection or self-help. The Court cannot accept this defence either. Between independent States, respect for territorial sovereignty is an essential foundation of international relations. The Court recognises that the Albanian Government's complete failure to carry out its duties after the explosions, and the dilatory nature of its diplomatic notes, are extenuating circumstances for the action of the United Kingdom Government. But to ensure respect for international law, of which it is the organ, the Court must declare that the action of the British Navy constituted a violation of Albanian sovereignty.

This declaration is in accordance with the request made by Albania through her Counsel, and is in itself appropriate satisfaction.

The method of carrying out "Operation Retail" has also been criticised by the Albanian Government, the main ground of complaint being that the United Kingdom, on that occasion, made use of an unnecessarily large display of force, out of proportion to the requirements of the sweep. The Court thinks that this criticism is not justified. It does not consider that the action of the British Navy was a demonstration of force for the purpose of exercising political pressure in Albania. The responsible naval commander, who kept his ships at a distance from the coast, cannot be reproached for having employed an important covering force in a region where twice within a few months his ships had been the object of serious outrages.

For these reasons, the Court, ... by 14 votes to two,[105] gives judgment [for the United Kingdom in respect of the passage on October 22, 1946] and, unanimously, gives judgment [for Albania in respect of the minesweeping of November 13, 1946].

CONVENTION ON THE LAW OF THE SEA 1982

UN Doc. A/CONF. 62/122; (1982) 21 I.L.M. 1261

Part II

Territorial Sea and Contiguous Zone

Section 3. Innocent Passage in the Territorial Sea

Subsection A. Rules Applicable to All Ships

Article 17

Subject to this Convention, ships of all States, whether coastal or land-locked enjoy the right of innocent passage through the territorial sea.

Article 18

1. Passage means navigation through the territorial sea for the purpose of:

(a) traversing that sea without entering internal waters or calling at a roadstead or port facility outside internal waters; or

(b) proceeding to or from internal waters or a call at such roadstead or port facility.

2. Passage shall be continuous and expeditious. However, passage includes stopping and anchoring, but only in so far as the same are incidental to ordinary navigation or are rendered necessary by *force majeure* or distress or for the purpose of rendering assistance to persons, ships or aircraft in danger or distress.

Article 19

1. Passage is innocent so long as it is not prejudicial to the peace, good order or security of the coastal State. Such passage shall take place in conformity with this Convention and with other rules of international law.

2. Passage of a foreign ship shall be considered to be prejudicial to the peace, good order or security of the coastal State if in the territorial sea it engages in any of the following activities:

(a) any threat or use of force against the sovereignty, territorial integrity or political independence of the coastal State, or in any other manner in violation of the principles of international law embodied in the Charter of the United Nations;

(b) any exercise or practice with weapons of any kind;

(c) any act aimed at collecting information to the prejudice of the defence or security of the coastal state;

(d) any act of propaganda aimed at affecting the defence or security of the coastal State;

(e) the launching, landing or taking on board of any aircraft;

---

[105] The judges in the majority were Acting President Guerrero; President Basdevant; Judges Alvarez, Fabela, Hackworth, Winiarski, Zoričić, de Visscher, Sir Arnold McNair, Klaestad, Badawi Pasha, Read and Hsu Mo; Judge ad hoc Ečer. Judges Krylov and Azevedo dissented.

(*f*)   the launching, landing or taking on board of any military device;

(*g*)   the loading or unloading of any commodity, currency or person contrary to the customs, fiscal, immigration or sanitary laws and regulations of the coastal State;

(*h*)   any act of wilful and serious pollution contrary to this Convention;

(*i*)   any fishing activities;

(*j*)   the carrying out of research or survey activities;

(*k*)   any act aimed at interfering with any systems of communication or any other facilities or installations of the coastal State;

(*l*)   any other activity not having a direct bearing on passage.

Article 20

In the territorial sea, submarines and other underwater vehicles are required to navigate on the surface and to show their flag.

Article 21

1. The coastal State may adopt laws and regulations, in conformity with the provisions of this Convention and other rules of international law, relating to innocent passage through the territorial sea, in respect of all or any of the following:

(*a*)   the safety of navigation and the regulation of maritime traffic;

(*b*)   the protection of navigational aids and facilities and other facilities or installations;

(*c*)   the protection of cables and pipelines;

(*d*)   the conservation of the living resources of the sea;

(*e*)   the prevention of infringement of the fisheries laws and regulations of the coastal State;

(*f*)   the preservation of the environment of the coastal State and the prevention, reduction and control of pollution thereof;

(*g*)   marine scientific research and hydrographic surveys;

(*h*)   the prevention of infringement of the customs, fiscal, immigration or sanitary laws and regulations of the coastal State.

2. Such laws and regulations shall not apply to the design, construction, manning or equipment of foreign ships unless they are giving effect to generally accepted international rules or standards.

3. The coastal State shall give due publicity to all such laws and regulations.

4. Foreign ships exercising the right of innocent passage through the territorial sea shall comply with all such laws and regulations and all generally accepted international regulations relating to the prevention of collisions at sea.

Article 22

1. The coastal State may, where necessary having regard to the safety of navigation, require foreign ships exercising the right of innocent passage through its territorial sea to use such sea lanes and traffic separation schemes as it may designate or prescribe for the regulation of the passage of ships.

2. In particular, tankers, nuclear-powered ships and ships carrying nuclear or other inherently dangerous or noxious substances or materials may be required to confine their passage to such sea lanes.

3. In the designation of sea lanes and the prescription of traffic separation schemes under this article, the coastal State shall take into account:

(a) the recommendations of the competent international organization;

(b) any channels customarily used for international navigation;

(c) the special characteristics of particular ships and channels; and

(d) the density of traffic.

4. The coastal State shall clearly indicate such sea lanes and traffic separation schemes on charts to which due publicity shall be given.

Article 23

Foreign nuclear-powered ships and ships carrying nuclear or other inherently dangerous or noxious substances shall, when exercising the right of innocent passage through the territorial sea, carry documents and observe special precautionary measures established for such ships by international agreements.

Article 24

1. The coastal State shall not hamper the innocent passage of foreign ships through the territorial sea except in accordance with this Convention. In particular, in the application of this Convention or of any laws or regulations adopted in conformity with this Convention, the coastal State shall not:

(a) impose requirements on foreign ships which have the practical effect of denying or impairing the right of innocent passage; or

(b) discriminate in form or in fact against the ships of any State or against ships carrying cargoes to, from or on behalf of any State.

2. The coastal State shall give appropriate publicity to any danger to navigation, of which it has knowledge, within its territorial sea.

Article 25

1. The coastal State may take the necessary steps in its territorial sea to prevent passage which is not innocent.
2. In the case of ships proceeding to internal waters or a call at a port facility outside internal waters, the coastal State also has the right to take the necessary steps to prevent any breach of the conditions to which admission of those ships to internal waters or such a call is subject.
3. The coastal State may, without discrimination in form or in fact among foreign ships, suspend temporarily in specified areas of its territorial sea the innocent passage of foreign ships if such suspension is essential for the protection of its security, including weapons exercises. Such suspension shall take effect only after having been duly published.

Article 26

1. No charge may be levied upon foreign ships by reason only of their passage through the territorial sea.
2. Charges may be levied upon a foreign ship passing through the territorial sea as payment only for specific services rendered to the ship. These charges shall be levied without discrimination.

Subsection B. Rules Applicable to Merchant Ships and Government Ships Operated for Commercial Purposes

Article 27

1. The criminal jurisdiction of the coastal State should not be exercised on board a foreign ship passing through the territorial sea to arrest any person or to conduct any investigation in connection with any crime committed on board the ship during its passage, save only in the following cases:

(a) if the consequences of the crime extend to the coastal State;

(b) if the crime is of a kind to disturb the peace of the country or the good order of the territorial sea;

(c) if the assistance of the local authorities has been requested by the master of the ship or by a diplomatic agent or consular officer of the flag State; or

(d) if such measures are necessary for the suppression of illicit traffic in narcotic drugs or psychotropic substances.

2. The above provisions do not affect the right of the coastal State to take any steps authorized by its laws for the purpose of an arrest or investigation on board a foreign ship passing through the territorial sea after leaving internal waters.

3. In the cases provided for in paragraphs 1 and 2, the coastal state shall, if the master so requests, notify a diplomatic agent or consular officer of the flag State before taking any steps, and shall facilitate contact between such agent or officer and the ship's crew. In cases of emergency this notification may be communicated while the measures are being taken.

4. In considering whether or in what manner an arrest should be made, the local authorities shall have due regard to the interests of navigation.

5. Except as provided in Part XII or with respect to violations of laws and regulations adopted in accordance with Part V, the coastal State may not take any steps on board a foreign ship passing through the territorial sea to arrest any person or to conduct any investigation in connection with any crime committed before the ship entered the territorial sea, if the ship, proceeding from a foreign port, is only passing through the territorial sea without entering internal waters.

Article 28

1. The coastal State should not stop or divert a foreign ship passing through the territorial sea for the purpose of exercising civil jurisdiction in relation to a person on board the ship.

2. The coastal State may not levy execution against or arrest the ship for the purpose of any civil proceedings, save only in respect of obligations or liabilities assumed or incurred by the ship itself in the course or for the purpose of its voyage through the waters of the coastal State.

3. Paragraph 2 is without prejudice to the right of the coastal State, in accordance with its laws, to levy execution against or to arrest, for the purpose of any civil proceedings, a foreign ship lying in the territorial sea, or passing through the territorial sea after leaving internal waters.

Subsection C. Rules Applicable to Warships and Other Government Ships Operated for Non-Commercial Purposes

Article 29

For the purposes of this Convention, "warship" means a ship belonging to the armed forces of a state bearing the external marks distinguishing such ships of its nationality, under the command of an officer duly commissioned by the government of the State and whose name appears in the appropriate service list or its equivalent, and manned by a crew which is under regular armed forces discipline.

Article 30

If any warship does not comply with the laws and regulations of the coastal State concerning passage through the territorial sea and disregards any request for compliance therewith which is made to it, the coastal State may require it to leave the territorial sea immediately.

Article 31

The flag State shall bear international responsibility for any loss or damage to the coastal State resulting from the non-compliance by a warship or other government ship operated for non-commercial purposes with the laws and regulations of the coastal State concerning passage through the territorial sea or with the provisions of this Convention or other rules of international law.

Article 32

With such exceptions as are contained in subsection A and in articles 30 and 31, nothing in this Convention affects the immunities of warships and other government ships operated for non-commercial purposes.

Part III

Straits used for International Navigation

Section 1. General Provisions

Article 34

1. The régime of passage through straits used for international navigation established in this Part shall not in other respects affect the legal status of the waters forming such straits or the exercise by the States bordering the straits of their sovereignty or jurisdiction over such waters and their air space, bed and subsoil.

2. The sovereignty or jurisdiction of the States bordering the straits is exercised subject to this Part and to other rules of international law.

Article 35

Nothing in this Part affects:

(a) any areas of internal waters within a strait, except where the establishment of a straight baseline in accordance with the method set forth in article 7 has the effect of enclosing as internal waters areas which had not previously been considered as such;

(b) the legal status of the waters beyond the territorial seas of States bordering straits as exclusive economic zones or high seas; or

(c) the legal régime in straits in which passage is regulated in whole or in part by long-standing international conventions in force specifically relating to such straits.

Article 36

This Part does not apply to a strait used for international navigation if there exists through the strait a route through the high seas or through an exclusive economic zone of similar convenience with respect to navigational and hydrographical characteristics; in such routes, the other relevant Parts of this Convention, including the provisions regarding the freedoms of navigation and overflight, apply.

Section 2. Transit Passage

Article 37

This section applies to straits which are used for international navigation between one part of the high seas or an exclusive economic zone and another part of the high seas or an exclusive economic zone.

Article 38

1. In straits referred to in article 37, all ships and aircraft enjoy the right of transit passage, which shall not be impeded; except that, if the strait is formed by an island of a State bordering the strait and its mainland, transit passage shall not apply if there exists seaward of the island a route through the high seas or through an exclusive economic zone of similar convenience with respect to navigational and hydrographical characteristics.

2. Transit passage means the exercise in accordance with this Part of the freedom of navigation and overflight solely for the purpose of continuous and expeditious transit of the strait between one part of the high seas or an exclusive economic zone and another part of the high seas or an exclusive economic zone. However, the

requirement of continuous and expeditious transit does not preclude passage through the strait for the purpose of entering, leaving or returning from a State bordering the strait, subject to the conditions of entry to that State.

3. Any activity which is not an exercise of the right of transit passage through a strait remains subject to the other applicable provisions of this Convention.

Article 39

1. Ships and aircraft, while exercising the right of transit passage, shall:

(a) proceed without delay through or over the strait;

(b) refrain from any threat or use of force against the sovereignty, territorial integrity or political independence of States bordering the strait, or in any other manner in violation of the principles of international law embodied in the Charter of the United Nations;

(c) refrain from any activities other than those incident to their normal modes of continuous and expeditious transit unless rendered necessary by *force majeure* or by distress;

(d) comply with other relevant provisions of this Part.

2. Ships in transit passage shall:

(a) comply with generally accepted international regulations, procedures and practices for safety at sea, including the International Regulations for Preventing Collisions at Sea;

(b) comply with generally accepted international regulations, procedures and practices for the prevention, reduction and control of pollution from ships.

3. Aircraft in transit passage shall:

(a) observe the Rules of the Air established by the International Civil Aviation Organization as they apply to civil aircraft; state aircraft will normally comply with such safety measures and will at all times operate with due regard for the safety of navigation;

(b) at all times monitor the radio frequency assigned by the competent internationally designated air traffic control authority or the appropriate international distress radio frequency.

Article 40

During transit passage, foreign ships, including marine scientific research and hydrographic survey ships, may not carry out any research or survey activities without the prior authorization of the States bordering straits.

Article 41

1. In conformity with this Part, States bordering straits may designate sea lanes and prescribe traffic separation schemes for navigation in straits where necessary to promote the safe passage of ships. . . .

Article 42

1. Subject to the provisions of this section, States bordering straits may adopt laws and regulations relating to transit passage through straits, in respect of all or any of the following:

(a) the safety of navigation and the regulation of maritime traffic, as provided in article 41;

(b) the prevention, reduction and control of pollution, by giving effect to applicable international regulations regarding the discharge of oil, oily wastes and other noxious substances in the strait;

(c) with respect to fishing vessels, the prevention of fishing, including the stowage of fishing gear;

(*d*) the loading or unloading of any commodity, currency or person in contravention of the customs, fiscal, immigration or sanitary laws and regulations of States bordering straits.

2. Such laws and regulations shall not discriminate in form or in fact among foreign ships or in their application have the practical effect of denying, hampering or impairing the right of transit passage as defined in this section.

3. States bordering straits shall give due publicity to all such laws and regulations.

4. Foreign ships exercising the right of transit passage shall comply with such laws and regulations.

5. The flag State of a ship or the State or registry of an aircraft entitled to sovereign immunity which acts in a manner contrary to such laws and regulations or other provisions of this Part shall bear international responsibility for any loss or damage which results to States bordering straits.

Article 44

States bordering straits shall not hamper transit passage and shall give appropriate publicity to any danger to navigation or overflight within or over the strait of which they have knowledge. There shall be no suspension of transit passage.

Section 3. Innocent Passage

Article 45

1. The régime of innocent passage, in accordance with Part II, section 3,[106] shall apply in straits used for international navigation:

(*a*) excluded from the application of the régime of transit passage under article 38, paragraph 1; or

(*b*) between a part of the high seas or an exclusive economic zone and the territorial sea of a foreign State.

2. There shall be no suspension of innocent passage through such straits.

JOINT STATEMENT BY THE U.S. AND THE USSR ON UNIFORM INTERPRETATION OF RULES OF INTERNATIONAL LAW GOVERNING INNOCENT PASSAGE 1989[107]

(1989) 28 I.L.M. 1444. Reprinted in Schachte (1993) 24 O.D.I.L. 179 at 194

1. The relevant rules of international law governing innocent passage of ships in the territorial sea are stated in the 1982 United Nations Convention on the Law of the Sea (Convention of 1982), particularly in Part II, Section 3.

2. All ships, including warships, regardless of cargo, armament or means of propulsion, enjoy the right of innocent passage through the territorial sea in accordance with international law, for which neither prior notification nor authorization is required.

3. Article 19 of the Convention of 1982 sets out in paragraph 2 an exhaustive list of activities that would render passage not innocent. A ship passing through the territorial sea that does not engage in any of those activities is in innocent passage.

4. A coastal State which questions whether the particular passage of a ship through its territorial sea is innocent shall inform the ship of the reason why it questions the innocence of the passage, and provide the ship an opportunity to clarify its intention or correct its conduct in a reasonably short period of time.

5. Ships exercising the right of innocent passage shall comply with all laws and regulations of the coastal State adopted in conformity with relevant rules of international law as reflected in Articles 21, 22, 23 and 25 of the Convention of 1982. These include the laws and regulations requiring ships exercising the right of innocent passage through its territorial sea to use such sea lanes and traffic separation schemes as it may prescribe where

---

[106] Ed. arts 17–32.

[107] The Joint Statement was the result of discussions between the US and the USSR over several years and is based upon and interprets the provisions of the 1982 Convention, which the two states consider, "with respect to traditional uses of the oceans, generally constitute international law and practice".

needed to protect safety of navigation. In areas where no such sea lanes or traffic separation schemes have been prescribed, ships nevertheless enjoy the right of innocent passage.

6. Such laws and regulations of the coastal State may not have the practical effect of denying or impairing the exercise of the right of innocent passage as set forth in Article 24 of the Convention of 1982.

7. If a warship engages in conduct which violates such laws or regulations or renders its passage not innocent and does not take corrective action upon request, the coastal state may require it to leave the territorial sea, as set forth in Article 30 of the Convention of 1982. In such case the warship shall do so immediately.

8. Without prejudice to the exercise of rights of coastal and flag states, all differences which may arise regarding a particular case of passage of ships through the territorial sea shall be settled through diplomatic channels or other agreed means.

Notes

1. *Vessels entitled to innocent passage.*[108] In 1896, the British Law Officers referred to "an accepted principle of international law that the innocent passage of *merchant vessels* for the purposes of navigation should be permitted through territorial waters."[109] With regard to *warships*,[110] in the *Corfu Channel* case the Court held that they had a right of innocent passage through international straits in the territorial sea but did not consider their position beyond that. In 1956, the International Law Commission proposed a draft article which permitted coastal states to make the passage of warships "subject to previous authorisation or notification."[111] In its Commentary, the Commission stated that since "a number of States do require previous notification or authorisation" it could not "dispute the right of States to take such a measure."[112] At Geneva, the draft article, which was intended to precede that which became art.23 of the 1958 Convention (now art.30, 1982 Convention[113]), was rejected without a replacement text being inserted.[114] In this situation, is there a right of innocent passage for warships under the Territorial Sea Convention? Note the wording, "all ships" preceding art.14[115] and the reference to "submarines" in it. When ratifying the 1958 Convention, the USSR made the following declaration in respect of art.23: "The ... [USSR] considers that the coastal state has the right to establish procedures for the authorisation of the passage of foreign warships through its territorial waters."[116] In contrast, in 1967 the British Foreign Secretary, in response to the question "what steps are being taken to prevent the deliberate violation of British territorial waters off Gibraltar by Spanish warships?" stated in Parliament:

    "Under international law Spanish and other warships enjoy the right of innocent passage

---

[108] On innocent passage generally, see Brown, *Passage through the Territorial Sea, Straits used for International Navigation, and Archipelagos* (1974); Lee (1961) 55 A.J.I.L. 77; and Ngantcha, *The Right of Innocent Passage and the Evolution of the International Law of the Sea* (1990).

[109] 1 McNair 343. Italics added.

[110] The definition of "warship" in art.29, 1982 Convention (above, p.347), which is repeated from art.8(2), 1958 High Seas Convention, is based upon arts 3 and 4, Hague Convention on the Conversion of Merchantships into Warships 1907, (1910) U.K.T.S. 11 Cd. 5115; (1908) 2 A.J.I.L. Supp. 1933. On the regime of warships in the 1982 Convention, see Lowe (1986) 10 Mar. Pol. 171; and Oxman (1984) 24 Virg. J.I.L. 809.

[111] art.24, I.L.C. Draft Articles.

[112] Y.B.I.L.C., 1956, II, p. 277.

[113] With the word "immediately" added. For art.30, see above, p.347.

[114] An amendment to the Commission's text to omit "authorisation or" was carried by the Plenary Session by 45 votes to 27, with six abstentions. The text as thus amended was then voted on as a whole and failed to obtain the necessary two-thirds majority (the vote was 43 in favour, 24 against, with 12 abstentions): *1958 Sea Conference Records*, Vol.II, pp.67–68.

[115] This is now art.19, 1982 Convention.

[116] UN Doc. ST/LEG/SER. E/7, p.731. Similar declarations were made by a number of other East European states and by Colombia; Some states objected, including Australia and Thailand who refer to one or more of the declarations as reservations; pp. 730–31.

through Gibraltar's territorial sea. Exercise of this right is subject to compliance with the local regulations and with normal navigational practice."[117]

The 1982 Convention also contains no provision expressly allowing or denying a right of innocent passage for warships. Several attempts were made to add a provision requiring prior notification and authorisation, but it proved impossible to obtain the necessary consensus,[118] most states preferring not to press a delicate question.[119] Like the 1958 Convention, the 1982 Convention has a heading "all ships" before the articles on innocent passage and requires "submarines" to navigate on the surface.[120]

The balance of state practice on the question of a right of innocent passage for warships was greatly changed in 1989, when in the US–USSR Joint Statement, above, p.350, the USSR accepted that there was such a right.[121] But the position remains unresolved; writing in 1990, Kwiatowska[122] notes that the position taken in the Joint Statement

"is not shared by a relatively large number of over 40 coastal states, as evidenced by national legislation and declarations made by these states upon signing and ratifying the 1982 ... Convention. These states consist of 4 Eastern European states, 5 Western European states, 32 developing states (including Brazil, China, and India), as well as Albania, Malta, and Yugoslavia, all of which ... presently claim a right to control entry of warships into their territorial seas by means of prior notification, authorization, or limitations on number of warships present at any one time ... This practice, to which the pre-*glasnost* Soviet position ... importantly contributed, appears irreversible."

2. *Passage through internal waters*.[123] There is no right of innocent passage through *internal* waters.[124] As to entry into a state's ports, in *Saudi Arabia v Aramco*,[125] the arbitrator stated: "According to a great principle of public international law, the ports of every state must be open to foreign vessels and can only be closed when the vital interests of the state so require." O'Connell,[126] however, states:

"... it is questionable whether the rule of international law to which he [the arbitrator] referred is a rule that ports must be open to trade, or the corollary of a different rule of international

---

[117] *Hansard*, HC Vol.754, col.20 (November 13, 1967); (1967) B.P.I.L. 95. The UK interprets the 1958 and the 1982 Conventions as allowing innocent passage for warships: *Hansard*, HL Vol.388, cols.846–847 (February 1, 1978); UKM.I.L. 1978, (1978) 49 B.Y.I.L. 395.

[118] See Oxman (1981) 75 A.J.I.L. 235. The 1982 Convention took the text of the 1958 Convention as its starting point.

[119] Several states (e.g. Cape Verde, Democratic Yemen, Iran, Romania, Sao Tomé, Sudan) made declarations upon signature or ratification of the 1982 Convention to the effect that authorisation of warship passage may be required: UN Doc. ST/LEG/SER.E./15, pp.822 et seq. Others (Albania, China, Pakistan) made similar statements at UNCLOS III: *UNCLOS III Records*, Vol.XVI, pp.155 et seq. Note that certain of these pronouncements (e.g. that by Sao Tomé) can be read, *quaere* unintentionally, as reservations to the Convention rather than mere interpretative declarations.

[120] 1982 Convention, art.20, which adds "other underwater vehicles" to submarines for this purpose.

[121] See Juda (1990) 21 O.D.I.L. 111.

[122] (1990) 21 O.D.I.L. 447. cf. the list of states requiring authorisation in Froman (1984) 21 San Diego L.R. 630 at 652. On China, see Zou Keyuan (1998) 29 O.D.I.L. 195.

[123] See Degan (1986) 17 N.Y.I.L. 3.

[124] cf. Colombos, above, n.81, p.176.

[125] (1963) 27 I.L.R. 117 at 212.

[126] See above, n.1, Vol.II, p.848. cf. Lowe (1977) 14 San Diego L.R. 597. It is generally accepted that warships have no right to enter a foreign port. On New Zealand's exclusion of US warships carrying nuclear weapons contrary, in the US view, to the 1951 ANZUS Pact (1952) 46 A.J.I.L. Supp. 93, see Woodliffe (1986) 35 I.C.L.Q. 730.

law which forbids discrimination among foreign ships using ports. ... If a country chooses to close its ports altogether that would seem to be an act of sovereignty; but if it opens them, it must open them ... arguably ... to all-comers, on a non-discriminatory basis."

In the *Nicaragua (Merits)* case,[127] the ICJ stated that "by virtue of its sovereignty ... a coastal state may regulate access to its ports." Coastal states may make entry to their ports or internal waters subject to compliance with requirements for the control of pollution of the marine environment.[128]

3. *Meaning of passage.* Passage is defined in art.18, 1982 Convention.[129] In the *Nicaragua* case,[130] the ICJ stated that "in order to enjoy access to ports, foreign vessels possess a customary right of innocent passage in territorial waters for the purposes of entering or leaving internal waters ..."

   Is the right of innocent passage in art.18, 1982 Convention, the same in scope as that applied by the Court in the *Corfu Channel* case?[131] Were the British warships that swept the Corfu Channel for mines on November 13, 1946, engaged in "passage" in the sense of art.18? Were those that earlier went through the Channel on October 22, 1946, to test Albanian reaction?[132]

4. *Innocence of passage.* After adopting a general definition of "innocent" in art.19(1), the 1982 Convention adds a long list of prejudicial activities in art.19(2).[133] This list was regarded as "exhaustive" in the US–USSR Joint Statement, above, p.350. Was the passage of British warships through the Corfu Channel on October 22, 1946, "innocent" according to art.19? Would it have been if they had been taking arms to a third state which was then at war with Albania?[134] Suppose a merchant ship of State A wishes to pass through the territorial sea of State B at a time when the nationals of State B are inclined to demonstrate against State A. Could State B exclude the ship if it feared demonstrations against it? Would it matter whether the captain of the ship knew that demonstrations were likely to occur? Article 20 requires submarines (warships or otherwise) to navigate on the surface and to show their flag. It is not stated that non-compliance with this requirement renders passage non-innocent. O'Connell suggests that "[w]hile it is possible ... for a submerged submarine to be in innocent passage ... this is a matter for evaluation ... of ... the submarine's behaviour, and the chances of its not being in innocent passage are high."[135]

   The passage of nuclear powered ships and ships carrying nuclear substances (presumably including nuclear weapons) is regulated by art.23, 1982 Convention but is not non-innocent in itself.[136] In the 1982 Convention, "fishing activities" render passage non-innocent (art.19(2)(i)), but non-compliance with fishing regulations generally does not.

   If compliance by a foreign ship with the requirements of the right of innocent passage is not

---

[127] I.C.J. Rep. 1986, p.14 at 111.
[128] See art.211(3), 1982 Convention. See also Keselj (1999) 30 O.D.I.L. 127; and Kasoulides, *Port State Control and Jurisdiction* (1993).
[129] cf. art.14(2)(3), 1958 Territorial Sea Convention.
[130] I.C.J. Rep. 1986, p.14 at 111. The Court states that art.18(1)(b) "does no more than codify customary international law."
[131] Although that case was only concerned with the innocent passage of warships through international straits, it seems permissible to regard the Court's understanding of the nature of innocent passage as of general application.
[132] Is the distinction between motive and intention for the purpose of mens rea in criminal law helpful here?
[133] Above, p.344. Article 14, 1958 Convention has a general obligation, but no list.
[134] Non-innocent passage is expressly limited in art.19(2) to conduct *in* the territorial sea: contrast art.14, 1958 Convention.
[135] See above, n.1, p.297. The suggestion concerned the same provision as submarines in art.14(6), 1958 Convention. On USSR submarines in Swedish waters, see below, p.354.
[136] See, however, the declarations by Egypt and Yemen upon signature or ratification of the 1982 Convention requiring authorisation of passage: UN Doc. ST/LEG/SER.E/15, pp.822 et seq.

clear, upon whom is the burden of proof? The coastal state? Or the state claiming a right of passage for its ships? O'Connell[137] suggests:

> "The Draft Convention (1980), by linking innocence explicitly with the list of subject-matters within coastal State competence, could have the effect of reversing the presumption of innocence. If passage is innocent until the commission of a prejudicial act, the burden of proving non-innocence could logically rest on the coastal State, which should be required to establish the fact and its prejudicial implications. But if no overt act need be committed for passage to be non-innocent then logically the burden of proving innocence would tend to shift to the ship."

5. *Laws governing passage.* Arts 21–24, 1982 Convention contains much more detailed provisions on the laws and regulations that a coastal State may make governing passage, than the equivalent art.17, 1958 Territorial Sea Convention.

    Article 21, 1982 Convention must be read in the context of a difference of opinion between common law and civil law states on the extent of the prescriptive (legislative) jurisdiction of coastal states over foreign ships passing through their territorial sea.[138]

    The common law view is that, since the territorial sea is sovereign territory, coastal states have an unlimited power to legislate on civil and criminal law matters for all ships that venture therein,[139] although as a matter of comity they will exercise self-restraint.

    The civil law view, which is influenced by the fact that, for jurisdictional purposes, a ship is the territory of the flag state, is that coastal states have only such prescriptive jurisdiction as states generally agree, and that agreement exists only in respect of matters that are of their nature related to passage. Since it lists only such matters, it might be inferred from the text of art.21 that it favours the civil law view so that, for example, a coastal state may legislate to prevent dangerous navigation by a ship in innocent passage, but not the murder of crew members on board.

    As to the duty to give publicity to dangers to navigation (art.24(2), 1982 Convention), there is a customary international law duty to warn of mines: see the *Corfu Channel* case, above, p.341.

6. *Enforcement powers in respect of non-innocent passage.* Article 25(1), 1982 Convention, authorises a coastal state to "take the necessary steps" to prevent non-innocent passage.[140] Such steps may include the use of reasonable force as a last resort,[141] even against warships since "entry of a warship for purposes other than the purpose of innocent passage is an intrusion upon national territory and may be repelled just as a military intrusion on land may be."[142]

    Non-innocent passage may involve a breach of the coastal state's criminal law so as to bring the

---

[137] See above, n.1, p.273. Footnote omitted.
[138] See the Report of the Sub-committee (M. Schücking, *Rapporteur*) of the L.N. Committee of Experts for the Progressive Codification of International Law, L.N. Doc. C. 44.M.21. 1926, V, s.XII. See also O'Connell, n.1, above, Vol.II, Ch.19. cf. the similar difference of opinion as to enforcement jurisdiction in the territorial sea: see below, p.358.
[139] See, e.g. the Territorial Waters Jurisdiction Act 1878, following the decision in *R. v Keyn*, above, p.66.
[140] Article 25 repeats verbatim art.16(1), 1958 Convention.
[141] On the "reasonable force" rule, see the *Saiga* case, below, p.369.
[142] O'Connell, above, n.1, Vol.I, p.297. Accordingly, the legality of the use of depth charges by Sweden to cause submerged USSR submarines suspected of non-innocent passage in Swedish internal and territorial waters to come to the surface could not be "ruled out": ibid. See also on Sweden's action, Sadurska (1984) 10 Yale J.I.L. 34. And see the Swedish declaration on signature of the 1982 Convention: UN Doc. ST/LEG/SER.E/15, p.839.

power of arrest in art.27, 1982 Convention, discussed below, p.357, into play if the ship is a merchant ship or a government ship operated for commercial purposes.

7.   *Passage through international straits.*[143] In the *Corfu Channel* case, the ICJ recognised that at customary international law the right of innocent passage cannot be suspended on grounds of security in a part of the territorial sea that is an international strait used for navigation from one part of the high seas to another, as it can in other parts of the territorial sea. This rule, which underlines the importance placed upon access to the high seas, was extended by art.16(4), 1958 Convention, to straits which lead from the high seas into the territorial sea of a state. This extension is repeated in art.45, 1982 Convention. An important example of such straits are the Straits of Tiran in the Red Sea. These lead into the Gulf of Aqaba, which is about 17 miles wide at its widest point and which is bordered by Egypt, Israel, Jordan and Saudi Arabia. Given the claims to a 12 mile territorial sea of both Egypt and Saudi Arabia, which border the Gulf at its mouth and along most of its length, all of the Gulf is territorial sea.[144] Accordingly, whereas the *Corfu Channel* case does not recognise an unrestricted right of innocent passage for ships bound for Israel or Jordan, at the end of the Gulf, art.16(4), Territorial Sea Convention and art.45, 1982 Convention do. While Israel is a party to the Territorial Sea Convention, the other three states are not; the reverse is true of the 1982 Convention. In 1967, the decision of the United Arab Republic (now Egypt) to prevent Israeli and other ships carrying strategic material to Israel from passing through the Straits of Tiran was the *casus belli* of the "Six Day War." At the time of the closure, the British Prime Minister was reported as saying: "It is the view of Her Majesty's Government . . . that the Straits of Tiran must be regarded as an international waterway through which the vessels of all nations have a right of passage."[145] The Security Council Resolution of November 22, 1967,[146] setting out a basis for the settlement of the Arab-Israeli conflict, refers to the need to guarantee "freedom of navigation through international waterways in the area." By the 1979 Treaty of Peace between Egypt and Israel,[147] it is provided:

"The Parties consider the Straits of Tiran and the Gulf of Aqaba to be international waterways open to all nations for unimpeded and non-suspendable freedom of navigation and overflight. The Parties will respect each other's right to navigation and overflight for access to either country through the Straits of Tiran and the Gulf of Aqaba."

Passage through a number of other straits is also guaranteed in varying degrees by particular

---

[143] See Brown, above, n.108, Caminos (1987-V) 205 Hague Recueil 9; Jia, *The Regime of Straits in International Law* (1998); Koh, *Straits in International Navigation: Contemporary Issues* (1982); Nandan and Anderson (1989) 60 B.Y.I.L. 159; Reisman (1989) 60 B.Y.I.L. 48; Schachte (1993) 24 O.D.I.L. 179; Schachte and Bernhardt (1993) 33 Virg.J.I.L. 527. For particular straits, see the books in the *International Straits of the World Series*, edited by Mangone and published by Nijthoff.

[144] The water-line across the Straits of Tiran is about seven miles long. It is interrupted by the island of Tiran which is about three miles from the Egyptian side of the Straits and four miles from the Saudi Arabian side. The only navigable channel is on the Egyptian side of the island. See Gross (1959) 53 A.J.I.L. 564; (1968) 33 L. C.P. 125; Johnson (1968) 31 M.L.R. 153; Selak (1958) 52 A.J.I.L. 660.

[145] UN Doc. 5/PV 1342, p.20, May 23, 1967.

[146] Above, p.191.

[147] Article 5(2), (1979) 18 I.L.M. 362. See El Baradei (1982) 76 A.J.I.L. 532; and Lapidoth (1983) 77 ibid. 84.

treaty régimes. For example, passage through the Bosphorus and the Dardanelles is fully guaranteed for merchant ships by the 1936 Treaty of Montreux.[148]

8. *The right of transit passage.*[149] The question of passage through international straits has become more important as states have widened their territorial seas. The English Channel and the Straits of Gibraltar, for example, are not more than 24 miles wide at their narrowest points.[150] Responding to Western concern at this encroachment upon freedom of the high seas, the 1982 Convention contains provisions allowing a new right of *transit passage* through an international strait within the territorial sea of one or more coastal states.

The right of *transit passage* in the 1982 Convention has no counterpart in the 1958 Convention. The wording "used for international navigation" in art.37 of the 1982 Convention follows the wording of the judgment in the *Corfu Channel* case (and that of 1958 Convention, art.16(4)). The right of transit passage does not apply (i) to a strait through which there exists "a route through the high seas or through an exclusive economic zone of similar convenience with respect to navigational and hydrographical characteristics" (art.36); (ii) in the "island" situation described in art.38(1)[151]; and (iii) to straits between a part of the high seas or an exclusive economic zone and the territorial sea of a foreign state (like the Straits of Tiran: see art.37). In (ii) and (iii), the ordinary right of innocent passage through the territorial sea applies, except that, as in the case of international straits in the 1958 Convention, that right cannot be suspended (1982 Convention, art.45).[152]

The right of *transit passage* through international straits is more generous than the right of innocent passage through other parts of the territorial sea in both the 1958 and 1982 Conventions.[153] It expressly allows passage by aircraft including, it seems, military aircraft—"all ... aircraft" (art.38(1))[154]; "state aircraft" (art.5 39(3))—and it appears to allow underwater transit by submarines (no provision comparable to 1982 Convention, art.20, above, p.345, on innocent passage). There are also fewer Convention restrictions on conduct during passage (see arts 39–41) and less power is given to the coastal state to regulate passage (see arts 41, 42) than is the case with innocent passage. The right of transit passage probably allows passage by warships,[155] as in the case of the previously established customary international law, right of innocent passage through international straits (*Corfu Channel* case).

The United Kingdom regards the right of transit passage as already stating customary law. In the

---

[148] (1937) U.K.T.S. 30 , Cmd. 5551; (1937) 173 L.N.T.S. 213; 31 A.J.I.L. Supp. 1. In force 1936. 12 parties, including Turkey, the UK and the Russian Federation but not the US. The Treaty's restrictions on the passage of warships (arts 8–22) are not now being strictly observed: see Froman (1977) 14 San Diego L.R. 681. For the British view (not shared by Turkey) that the passage of aircraft carriers is prohibited, see *Hansard*, HL Vol.472, col.498 (March 10, 1986). See generally, Rozakis and Stagos, *The Turkish Straits* (1987).

[149] See George (2002) 33 O.D.I.L. 189; Said (1989) 20 O.D.I.L. 157; Treve in Bos and Siblesz, eds, *Realism in Lawmaking* (1986) p.247.

[150] There are over 100 straits less than 24 miles in width: see Ganz, above, n.14, p.7.

[151] On the "routes of similar convenience" exception in arts 36 and 38(1), see Alexander (1987) 18 O.D.I.L. 479. The exception in art.38(1) was introduced "in response to Italy's concern over the status of the Strait of Messina": p.484.

[152] The 1982 provisions on the right of transit and innocent passage through international straits do not affect "the legal régime in straits in which passage is regulated in whole or in part by long-standing international conventions in force specifically relating to such straits" (art.35(c), 1982 Convention). See, e.g. the Treaty of Montreux, above, n.148.

[153] Although the reason for this is that the right of transit passage was prompted by the extension of the territorial sea into waters in which freedom of the high seas formerly applied, the right applies over the whole of the territorial sea, even within three miles of the coast.

[154] Note that there is no provision equivalent to arts 27–28, 1982 Convention (arts 19–20, 1958 Convention) on innocent passage on the question of enforcement jurisdiction during transit passage. See Shearer (1986) 35 I.C.L.Q. 320 at 332, who concludes that it does not exist.

[155] On the passage of warships through the straits of Hormuz, see Mahmoudi (1991) 15 Mar. Pol. 338.

debate on the bill extending British territorial waters to 12 miles, a Government spokesman stated[156]:

> "International law and practice have now developed to the point where, if the United Kingdom extends to 12 miles, we should afford to others the essential rights in some internationally important straits for which there is no alternative route; namely, the Straits of Dover, the North Channel lying between Scotland and Northern Ireland, and the passage between Shetland and Orkney. These rights, which are widely recognised as necessary, include: a right of unimpeded passage through such straits for merchant vessels and warships; a right of overflight; the right of submarines to pass through the straits submerged; and appropriate safeguards for the security and other interests of the coastal state.
>
> In other straits used for international navigation, such as the Pentland Firth south of Orkney and the passage between the Scilly Isles and the mainland of Cornwall, as in other parts of the territorial sea, a right of innocent passage will continue to exist in accordance with the practice of states."

The "right of unimpeded transit passage" through the Dover Straits is recognised by the 1988 Anglo-French Joint Declaration.[157]

9.   *Civil and criminal jurisdiction over foreign merchant ships in the territorial sea*. This is provided for in arts 27 and 28, 1982 Convention, which follow arts 19 and 20, 1958 Convention respectively very closely. According to some commentators, the use of the word "should", as opposed to "may", in art.19(1), 1958 Convention, and now art.27, 1982 Convention, indicates that the rule it contains is one of comity and not of law.[158] The International Law Commission had proposed "may."[159] The wording was changed at Geneva on the suggestion of the United States, which explained its suggestion as follows:

> "It was the practice of most states not to arrest or conduct criminal investigations on board foreign ships passing through their territorial waters save in the instances mentioned in sub-paragraphs *a, b* and *c,* but the declaration in the Commissions text that 'A State may not take any steps . . .' was a departure from the doctrine of international law that the coastal State had unlimited criminal jurisdiction within its territorial seas."[160]

The United States also successfully proposed the use of "should" in place of "may" in art.20, 1958 Convention, now art.28, 1982 Convention, for the same reason.[161] Note, however, that in both cases the United States full proposal was "should, generally." The word "generally" was deleted in the First Committee in respect of art.20[162] and in the Plenary Meetings in respect of art.19.[163] At least one delegate opposing that word would seem to have thought that its exclusion had the effect of confirming that a coastal state "*could* not stop a ship for the purpose

---

[156] *Hansard*, HL Vol.484, col.382 (February 5, 1987). cf. the US recognition of the "right of transit passage" in a note concerning passage through the Persian Gulf: (1984) 78 A.J.I.L. 884.
[157] Cm. 557 (1989), p.4.
[158] See Fitzmaurice, above, n.9, p.104 and Lee (1961) 55 A.J.I.L. 77 at 83–86; but see McDougal and Burke, above, n.1, p.300. The French text, which, like the English, is one of five authentic texts, uses "devrait."
[159] Y.B.I.L.C., 1956, II, p.274.
[160] *1958 Sea Conference Records*, Vol.III, p.81.
[161] *1958 Sea Conference Records*, Vol.III, p.82
[162] *1958 Sea Conference Records*, Vol.III, p.125.
[163] *1958 Sea Conference Records*, Vol.I, p.66.

of exercising its *civil* jurisdiction in respect of an individual on board."[164] This uncertainty is parallelled by a difference in state practice between common law and civil law states. Generally, common law states follow the rules in the 1958 and 1982 Conventions in practice as rules of comity whereas civil law states regard them as binding in law.[165] Articles 27 and 28, 1982 Convention, following arts 19 and 20, 1958 Convention, give enforcement jurisdiction only in respect of merchant ships and government ships used for commercial purposes; warships and government ships used for non-commercial purposes are immune from enforcement jurisdiction for non-compliance with the local law, except[166] that measures may be taken to remove them from the territorial sea.[167]

In *Pianka v The Queen*,[168] the appellants, United States citizens, had been given clearance to head from a Jamaican port to Montego Bay in Jamaica in their United States registered motor boat. The next night they were discovered in Jamaican territorial waters with a large quantity of the drug ganja on board. Their appeal in these proceedings against conviction by a Jamaican court, inter alia, for illegal possession of the drug in Jamaican territorial waters was unsuccessful. A part of their defence was that their arrest conflicted with art.19 of the 1958 Convention (which had been incorporated by statute into Jamaican law). The Jamaican Court of Appeal rejected this defence[169]:

"... even if the 'Star Baby' was not bound for Montego Bay ... but rather was making for the high seas this was not in right of innocent passage through the territorial sea for the appellants had received into their possession while on the territorial sea a dangerous drug, the possession and conveyance of which were prohibited under the criminal law ... of Jamaica, and its receipt and conveyance by the appellants in that event was prejudicial to the good order of Jamaica. The consequences of the crime, therefore, extended to Jamaica and additionally was such as to disturb the good order of the territorial sea. That being so, and these being within the exceptions contained in art. 19, there was no contravention of art. 19 in seeking to invoke the criminal jurisdiction of the Court."

The Privy Council upheld the Court of Appeal judgment on the application of art.19, adding only that "these provisions [of that Article] should receive a liberal construction" and that the case could have been dealt with under art.19(1)(*d*)[170] because Jamaica was a party to the 1961 Single Convention on Narcotic Drugs[171] which covers ganja.

In *The David*,[172] the facts were that *The David*, a Panamanian merchant ship, was arrested in 1925 in the territorial sea of the Panama Canal Zone, within the territorial jurisdiction of the United States, in connection with civil proceedings against it concerning a collision that had occurred in

---

[164] M. Petrén (Sweden), 1958 Sea Conference Records, Vol.I, p.125. Italics added. He was discussing art.20, in particular.

[165] cf. the difference of opinion as to prescriptive jurisdiction, see above, p.354, and as to jurisdiction in ports, see below, p.361.

[166] See the heading to Pt I, S.III, Subs.B and arts 21 and 22, 1958 Convention and the heading to Pt I, S.3, Subs.B and art.32, 1982 Convention.

[167] Article 23, 1958 Convention and art.30, 1982 Convention. These provisions apply only to warships. There is a lacuna in respect of government ships operated for non-commercial purposes, which constitute an a fortiori case. The flag state of a warship or a government ship operated for non-commercial purposes is responsible for damage resulting from a breach of the local law: art.31, 1982 Convention. As to permissible enforcement action against a warship engaged in non-innocent passage, see above, p.354.

[168] [1979] A.C. 107 PC.

[169] (1975) 24 W.I.R. 285 at 292–293.

[170] cf. art.27(1)(d), 1982 Convention.

[171] 520 U.N.T.S. 204; U.K.T.S. 23 (1979), Cmnd. 7466.

[172] (1933) 6 R.I.A.A. 382.

1923. The United States-Panama General Claims Commission rejected Panama's claim that the arrest had been contrary to international law. It said:

"There is no clear pre-ponderance of authority to the effect that such vessels [foreign merchant vessels] when passing through territorial waters are exempt from civil arrest. In the absence of such authority, the Commission cannot say that a country may not under the rules of international law, assert the right to arrest on civil process merchant ships passing through its territorial waters."[173]

The Panamanian Commissioner (Alfaro), dissenting, stated:

"It is proper to point out also that the claimant does not maintain that absolute immunity exists from the jurisdiction of the littoral authorities; that it does not allege, for example, lack of jurisdiction in the case of an offence committed within territorial waters in the course of innocent passage, although some writers deny jurisdiction even in such cases. The claimant also accepts that the ship is obliged to comply with orders and maritime regulations which contribute to the safety of navigation, or that are of a sanitary or police character. The claimant maintains only that in case of a civil action growing out of a collision occurring previously beyond the jurisdiction of the littoral authorities, the latter were without jurisdiction later to interfere with the passage of the same ship by means of a civil suit not affecting in any way territorial sovereign interests."[174]

Presumably "the consequences of the crime extend to the coastal state" (art.28(1)(a), 1982 Convention) in such cases as smuggling, illegal immigration, pollution and violations of security laws. Would it do so just because the perpetrator or the victim "of the crime" (which presumably refers to a crime under the law of the coastal state) on board a foreign ship is a national of the coastal state? The International Law Commission's draft of art.19(1)(a), 1958 Convention[175] read "beyond the ship." It was changed to "to the coastal state" at Geneva. Does the wording finally adopted exclude the coastal state's jurisdiction in cases of collisions between two ships neither of which is flying its flag?[176] What if the effect, as in some cases of pollution, is felt only in the territorial sea and not on land or in inland waters? On the meaning of the terms "peace" and "good order", see the cases on jurisdiction over foreign ships in internal waters immediately below. Are the limitations upon the coastal state's jurisdiction in arts 28 and 29, 1982 Convention limitations upon executive enforcement jurisdiction only? Would, for example, a prosecution under the Territorial Waters Jurisdiction Act 1878 in the circumstances of *R. v Keyn* be prohibited by art.28 of the 1982 Convention?[177]

---

173 (1933) 6 R.I.A.A. 382 at 384.
174 (1933) 6 R.I.A.A. 382 at p.386.
175 Now art.28(1)(a), 1982 Convention.
176 See McDougal and Burke, above, n.1, p.300.
177 See above, p.66.

E. Jurisdiction Over Foreign Ships in Internal Waters[178]

R. v ANDERSON

(1868) 11 Cox's Criminal Cases 198. Court of Criminal Appeal

The defendant, a United States national, was found guilty by the Central Criminal Court of manslaughter on board a British merchant ship of which he was a crew member. The offence was committed on the River Garonne in France some 300 yards from shore when the ship was on its way to Bordeaux. The defendant appealed on the ground that the Court had lacked jurisdiction to try him.

BOVILL C.J.:

There is no doubt that the place where the offence was committed was within the territory of France, and that the prisoner was therefore subject to the laws of France, which the local authorities of that realm might have enforced if so minded; but at the same time, in point of law, the offence was also committed within British territory, for the prisoner was a seaman on board a merchant vessel, which, as to her crew and master, must be taken to have been at the time under the protection of the British flag, and, therefore, also amenable to the provisions of the British law. It is true that the prisoner was an American citizen, but he had with his own consent embarked on board a British vessel as one of the crew. Although the prisoner was subject to the American jurisprudence as an American citizen, and to the law of France as having committed an offence within the territory of France, yet he must also be considered as subject to the jurisdiction of British law, which extends to the protection of British vessels, though in ports belonging to another country. From the passage in the treatise of Ortolan[179] ... it appears that, with regard to offences committed on board of foreign vessels within the French territory, the French nation will not assert their police law unless invoked by the master of the vessel, or unless the offence leads to a disturbance of the peace of the port. ... The place where the offence was committed was in a navigable part of the river below bridge, and where the tide ebbs and flows, and great ships do lie and hover. An offence committed at such a place, according to the authorities, is within the Admiralty jurisdiction, and it is the same as if the offence had been committed on the high seas. On the whole I come to the conclusion that the prisoner was amenable to the British law, and that the conviction was right.

BYLES J.:

I am of the same opinion. ... A British ship is, for the purposes of this question, like a floating island; and, when a crime is committed on board a British ship, it is within the jurisdiction of the Admiralty Court, and therefore of the Central Criminal Court, and the offender is as amenable to British law as if he had stood on the Isle of Wight and committed the crime. ...

Channel B. and Lush J. delivered concurring judgments.

WILDENHUS'S CASE

120 U.S. 1 (1887). US Supreme Court

W., a Belgian crew member of a Belgian merchant ship, was found guilty by an American state court of the murder of another Belgian crew member on board the ship when it was docked in the port of Jersey City, New Jersey. It was argued in this application for habeas corpus that, under a consular convention of 1880 between Belgium and the United States, the United States court had lacked jurisdiction. The application was rejected by the United States Supreme Court.

---

[178] See Charteris (1920–21) 1 B.Y.I.L. 45; Degan (1986) 17 N.Y.I.L. 3; Francioni (1975) 1 It. Y.I.L. 27; Jessup, *The Law of Territorial Waters and Maritime Jurisdiction* (1927), pp.144–194. On entry into foreign ports, see above, p.352.

[179] *Règles internationales et diplomatie de la mer* (4th edn 1864), Vol.I, pp.269–271.

WAITE C.J.:

It is part of the law of civilised nations that when a merchant vessel of one country enters the ports of another for the purposes of trade, it subjects itself to the law of the place to which it goes, unless by treaty or otherwise the two countries have come to some different understanding or agreement. ... As the owner has voluntarily taken his vessel for his own private purposes to a place within the dominion of a government other than his own, and from which he seeks protection during his stay, he owes that government such allegiance for the time being as is due for the protection to which he becomes entitled.

From experience, however, it was found long ago that it would be beneficial to commerce if the local government would abstain from interfering with the internal discipline of the ship and the general regulation of the rights and duties of the officers and crew towards the vessel or among themselves. And so by comity it came to be generally understood among civilised nations that all matters of discipline and all things done on board which affected only the vessel or those belonging to her, and did not involve the peace or dignity of the country, or the tranquillity of the port, should be left by the local government to be dealt with by the authorities of the nation to which the vessel belonged as the laws of that nation or the interests of its commerce should require. But if crimes are committed on board of a character to disturb the peace and tranquillity of the country to which the vessel has been brought, the offenders have never by comity or usage been entitled to any exemption from the operation of the local laws for their punishment, if the local tribunals see fit to assert their authority. Such being the general public law on this subject, treaties and conventions have been entered into by nations having commercial intercourse, the purpose of which was to settle and define the rights and duties of the contracting parties with respect to each other in these particulars, and thus prevent the inconvenience that might arise from attempts to exercise conflicting jurisdictions. ...

The Treaty [now before the court] is part of the supreme law of the United States, and has the same force and effect in New Jersey that it is entitled to elsewhere. If it gives the Consul of Belgium exclusive jurisdiction over the offence which it is alleged has been committed within the territory of New Jersey, we see no reason why he may not enforce his rights under the Treaty by writ of *habeas corpus* in any proper court of the United States. This being the case, the only important question left for our determination is whether the thing which has been done—the disorder that has arisen—on board this vessel is of a nature to disturb the public peace, or, as some writers term it, the "public repose" of the people who look to the State of New Jersey for their protection. If the thing done—"the disorder," as it is called in the Treaty—is of a character to affect those on shore or in the port when it becomes known, the fact that only those on the ship saw it when it was done, is a matter of no moment. Those who are not on the vessel pay no special attention to the mere disputes or quarrels of the seamen while on board, whether they occur under deck or above. Neither do they as a rule care for anything done on board which relates only to the discipline of the ship, or to the preservation of order and authority. Not so, however, with crimes which from their gravity awaken a public interest as soon as they become known, and especially those of a character which every civilised nation considers itself bound to provide a severe punishment for when committed within its own jurisdiction. In such cases inquiry is certain to be instituted at once to ascertain how or why the thing was done, and the popular excitement rises or falls as the news spreads and the facts become known. It is not alone the publicity of the act, or the noise and clamour which attends it, that fixes the nature of the crime, but the act itself. If that is of a character to awaken public interest when it becomes known, it is a "disorder" the nature of which is to affect the community at large, and consequently to invoke the power of the local government whose peoples have been disturbed by what was done. The very nature of such an act is to disturb the quiet of a peaceful community, and to create, in the language of the Treaty, a "disorder" which will "disturb tranquillity and public order on shore or in the port." The principle which governs the whole matter is this: Disorders which disturb only the peace of the ship or those on board are to be dealt with exclusively by the sovereignty of the home of the ship, but those which disturb the public peace may be suppressed, and, if need be, the offenders punished by the proper authorities of the local jurisdiction. It may not be easy at all times to determine to which of the two jurisdictions a particular act of disorder belongs. Much will undoubtedly depend on the attending circumstances of the particular case, but all must concede that felonious homicide is a subject for the local jurisdiction, and that if the proper authorities are proceeding with the case in a regular way the consul has no right to interfere to prevent it. That, according to the petition for the *habeas corpus*, is this case.

Notes

1.   *Wildenhus's* case adopts the common law view as to a coastal state's enforcement jurisdiction over crimes committed by foreign ships in international water, namely that the coastal state may

in law exercise jurisdiction in all criminal matters but that as a matter of comity it should not do so unless the crime disturbs its "peace or tranquillity".[180] The civil law view is that this is a limitation of international law, not comity.[181] It would appear generally agreed that the coastal state's enforcement jurisdiction in civil matters is unrestricted.[182]

2. In the *Eisler* case,[183] in 1949, Eisler was arrested and taken off a Polish ship at Southampton for extradition to the United States. Poland protested "on the ground that Eisler was a political refugee entitled under international law to asylum and protection under the Polish flag, and that a state's jurisdiction over territorial and national waters did not entitle the state to arrest persons on board a foreign vessel for the purpose of extradition to a third state."[184] The British Government is reported as rejecting Poland's argument for the following reason:

    "it would mean ... that States could grant to persons on board their merchant or passenger ships in foreign ports or waters the same asylum that a State can grant to persons on its territory. It was, however, quite contrary to the practice of States to recognise any principle of asylum in connexion with merchant ships, and the Polish Government had refused it in the case of offences committed by persons who subsequently went on board a foreign ship in a Polish port. The absence of any right to grant asylum on board merchant ships sprang from a universally recognised principle of international law that a merchant ship in the ports or roadsteads of another country falls under the jurisdiction of the coastal State."[185]

    What if the Polish ship in question had been stopped for the purpose of arresting Eisler while it was passing through British territorial waters?

3. On criminal jurisdiction over foreign warships in port, see *The Schooner Exchange v McFaddon*.[186]

    In 1977, while H.M.S. *Danae* was in Rio de Janeiro on a goodwill visit, some junior ratings invited Ronald Biggs, the Great Train Robber and a United Kingdom citizen, on board. When it was discovered who he was, Mr Biggs was asked to leave the ship. Later the question was asked in Parliament why he had not been arrested. The following Government explanation was given:

    "Since Mr Biggs did not commit an offence while on board HMS 'Danae' the only powers under which he could have been arrested would have been the powers of 'citizen's arrest' under the provisions of the Criminal Law Act 1967. The relevant provisions of this Act, however, apply only to England and Wales.
        Whilst one of Her Majesty's ships in a foreign port has extra-territoriality—that is, it is immune from local jurisdiction and enforcement of local laws—it is not correct to regard it as floating United Kingdom territory, and all laws of the United Kingdom do not necessarily apply to all persons on board that ship. The relevant provisions of the Criminal Law Act are such an example."[187]

---

[180] See the 1929 *Harvard Draft Convention on Territorial Waters*, art.18 and Commentary thereto, (1929) 23 A.J.I.L. Sp. Supp. 243 at 307; and the 1929 Report of the Sub-committee (M. Schücking, *rapporteur*) of the L.N. Committee of Experts for the Progressive Codification of International law, L.N. Doc. C.44. M.21. 1926. V, Section XI.
[181] ibid.
[182] ibid.
[183] Jennings (1949) 26 B.Y.I.L. 468.
[184] Jennings (1949) 26 B.Y.I.L. 468
[185] *The Times*, June 9, 1949, p.3. See also the *Medvid* case (1986) 80 A.J.I.L. 622.
[186] Above, p.259.
[187] *Hansard*, HC Vol.930, col.450, (April 29, 1977).

----

3. THE HIGH SEAS

A. *Freedom of the High Seas*

CONVENTION ON THE LAW OF THE SEA 1982

UN Doc. A/CONF. 62/122; (1982) 21 I.L.M. 1261

Article 86

The provisions of this Part [Pt VII: arts 86–120] apply to all parts of the sea that are not included in the exclusive economic zone, in the territorial sea or in the internal waters of a State, or in the archipelagic waters of an archipelagic State. This article does not entail any abridgement of the freedoms enjoyed by all States in the exclusive economic zone in accordance with article 58.

Article 87

1. The high seas are open to all States, whether coastal or land-locked. Freedom of the high seas is exercised under the conditions laid down by this Convention and by other rules of international law. It comprises, inter alia, both for coastal and land-locked States:

(a) freedom of navigation;

(b) freedom of overflight;

(c) freedom to lay submarine cables and pipelines, subject to Part VI;

(d) freedom to construct artificial islands and other installations permitted under international law, subject to Part VI[188];

(e) freedom of fishing, subject to the conditions laid down in section 2;

(f) freedom of scientific research, subject to Parts VI[189] and XIII.[190]

2. These freedoms shall be exercised by all States with due regard for the interests of other States in their exercise of the freedom of the high seas, and also with due regard for the rights under this Convention with respect to activities in the Area.

Article 88

The high seas shall be reserved for peaceful purposes.

Article 89

No State may validly purport to subject any part of the high seas to its sovereignty.

Notes

1. *Freedom of the high seas.* Article 86, 1982 Convention takes into account the emergence of the concept of the exclusive economic zone and the new provisions as to archipelagic states. Whereas under the equivalent art.1, 1958 High Seas Convention, the high seas begin where the

---

[188] Ed. arts 76–85 (on the continental shelf).
[189] Ed. arts 116–120 (on conservation and management of the living resources).
[190] Ed. arts 238–265 (on marine scientific research).

territorial sea ends, the 1982 Convention concept of the high seas is a more limited one, applying only beyond the limit of the exclusive economic zone.

2.   Other freedoms additional to those in art.87, 1982 Convention, include the freedom to use the high seas for weapon testing and naval exercises. To this should be added the freedom to observe the naval exercises of other states. Whiteman records:

"When a Soviet 'electronics ship,' supposedly operating as a Soviet trawler, cruised through a Polaris submarine test area off Long Island in April 1960 ... Rear Admiral Charles C. Kirkpatrick ... emphasised at a Pentagon news conference that, since the ship was in international waters at all times, the Soviet ship remained unmolested ... 'We are a legal people and abide by international law,' he said ... As reported, it was explained by an officer present that the Soviet ship with its electronic gear could monitor radio information for 'hundreds of miles.'"[191]

States sometimes use the high seas to make a show of strength off the coast of other states. The 1982 Convention limits the use of the high seas to "peaceful purposes" (art.88). The United Kingdom Government takes the view that rocket and other weapons testing on the high seas does not contravene this provision.[192]

In 1954, radiation from hydrogen bomb tests conducted by the United States on the high seas in the area of the Eniwetok Atoll in the Trust Territory then administered by the United States[193] caused the death of a Japanese fisherman and caused injury to other Japanese fishermen, to some inhabitants of the Rongelap Atoll within the Territory and to some United States nationals.[194] The tests took place in a danger zone, within which shipping was advised not to go, of 50,000 square miles. Both the Japanese fishing vessel concerned and the Rongelap Atoll were outside this zone. They were affected because the force of the explosion had been miscalculated and because of a sudden change of wind. The United States gave medical and other assistance and paid monetary compensation. In the case of the Japanese nationals, the compensation, which was for personal injuries and for economic loss resulting from the contamination of Japanese fishing catches, was expressly stated to be ex gratia. At the time of a later test series in 1958, the United States took the following legal position:

"The high seas have long been used by the nations of the world for naval manoeuvres, weapons tests, and other matters of this kind. Such measures no doubt result in some inconvenience to other users of the high seas but they are not proscribed by international law."[195]

When plans for the 1958 United States tests were announced, Japan stated that it was "greatly concerned" and expressed the view that "the United States Government has the responsibility of compensating for economic losses that may be caused by the establishment of a danger zone and for all losses and damages that may be inflicted on Japan and the Japanese people as a result of the nuclear tests."[196] Japan did not refer expressly to international law. On July 2, 1958,

---

[191] 4 Whiteman, 516–517.
[192] *Hansard*, HL Vol.388, col.842 (February 1, 1978); UKM.I.L. 1978, (1978) 49 B.Y.I.L. 397.
[193] See above, p.120.
[194] See generally 4 Whiteman 553 et seq. See also McDougal and Schlei (1955) 64 Yale L.J. 648 ("for" the legality of the tests); and Margolis (1955) 64 Yale L.J. 629 ("against" their legality).
[195] 4 Whiteman 595.
[196] 4 Whiteman pp.585–586.

a United States national entered the danger zone in a yacht as a protest. He was prosecuted under United States law applying to United States nationals only. Could the United States have legislated to have excluded an alien? Could the national state of an alien injured by radiation in a danger zone successfully claim compensation under international law if the alien (a) deliberately ignores the warning or (b) is unaware of it?

An amendment to what became art.2 of the High Seas Convention[197] proposed by the USSR, which was conducting most of its nuclear tests in Siberia,[198] to make nuclear testing on the high seas a violation of the Convention was not voted upon at Geneva; instead the Conference adopted the proposal of India that the matter should be referred to the General Assembly "for appropriate action."[199] In 1963, the Nuclear Test Ban Treaty[200] was signed and came into force. This prohibits the testing of nuclear weapons, inter alia, on the high seas. France, which is not a party to the Treaty, continued to conduct tests in the South Pacific until 1973 when it completed its final series of tests in the atmosphere.[201] The 1972 and 1973 tests were the subject of protests by several states and led to the *Nuclear Tests* cases.[202] These were brought by Australia and New Zealand against France. The cases were taken off the Court's list without a decision being given on the merits when France announced that it would not conduct further tests after 1973; despite argument to the contrary by the applicant states, the Court found that their claims no longer had any object.[203] The applicants had asked the Court for a declaration that the carrying out of further nuclear tests in the South Pacific was not consistent with international law.[204]

In order to develop its long range missiles, the United States found it necessary to arrange for test sites in the territory of other states[205] in the Atlantic area and to fire the missiles over the high seas. One writer records:

"None of the missiles ... carry warheads, atomic or otherwise; they are loaded with concrete blocks instead. A missile weighing many tons can, however, do considerable damage ... accidents can occur, as in the case of the errant flight of a Snark into the wilds of Brazil in December 1956. ... Thus far no official complaints from other governments, comparable to those voiced in and out of the United Nations with respect to the nuclear weapons testing, have apparently been made to the government of the United States. ..."[206]

3. *Land-locked states.* Article 90, 1982 Convention[207] contains the right of land-locked states (of which there are over 30) to have ships flying their flag. In addition, the 1982 Convention has other

---

[197] See now art.87, 1982 Convention.
[198] But some were conducted in the Barents Sea: 4 Whiteman p.574.
[199] Resolution on Nuclear Tests on the High Seas, *1958 Sea Conference Records*, Vol.II, p.24, p.101 (text).
[200] U.K.T.S. 3 (1964), Cmnd. 2245; 480 U.N.T.S. 43. In force 1963. 123 parties, including the UK.
[201] For a discussion of the legality of these tests, see Mercer (1968) N.Z.L.J. 405–408, 418–421; and Swan (1973–74) 9 M.U.L.R. 296.
[202] I.C.J. Rep. 1974, p.253 (*Australia v France*); I.C.J. Rep. 1974, p.457 (*New Zealand v France*).
[203] France began testing again in 1981. The I.C.J. dismissed a request by New Zealand to examine the situation in connection with the French 1995 tests: I.C.J. Rep. 1995, p.288.
[204] This was specifically the Australian request; for the similar New Zealand request, see I.C.J. Rep. 1974, p.460.
[205] The UK, for example, agreed to a US base in the Bahamas. See generally 4 Whiteman 619–623.
[206] Reiff, *The United States and the Treaty Law of the Sea* (1959), p.371.
[207] Below, p.366. cf. art.4, 1958 High Seas Convention.

detailed provisions on the transit trade of land-locked states and their access to the high seas which are stronger than their equivalent in the 1958 High Seas Convention (art.3).[208]

B. Nationality of Ships

CONVENTION ON THE LAW OF THE SEA 1982

UN Doc. A/CONF. 62/122; (1982) 21 I.L.M. 1261

Article 90

Every State, whether coastal or land-locked, has the right to sail ships flying its flag on the high seas.

Article 91

1. Every State shall fix the conditions for the grant of its nationality to ships, for the registration of ships in its territory, and for the right to fly its flag. Ships have the nationality of the State whose flag they are entitled to fly. There must exist a genuine link between the State and the ship.
2. Every State shall issue to ships to which it has granted the right to fly its flag documents to that effect.

Article 92

1. Ships shall sail under the flag of one State only and, save in exceptional cases expressly provided for in international treaties or in this Convention, shall be subject to its exclusive jurisdiction on the high seas. A ship may not change its flag during a voyage or while in a port of call, save in the case of a real transfer of ownership or change of registry.
2. A ship which sails under the flags of two or more States, using them according to convenience, may be assimilated to a ship without nationality.

Article 94

1. Every State shall effectively exercise its jurisdiction and control in administrative, technical and social matters over ships flying its flag.
2. In particular every State shall:

(a) maintain a register of ships containing the names and particulars of ships flying its flag, except those which are excluded from generally accepted international regulations on account of their small size; and

(b) assume jurisdiction under its internal law over each ship flying its flag and its master, officers and crew in respect of administrative, technical and social matters concerning the ship.

3. Every State shall take such measures for ships flying its flag as are necessary to ensure safety at sea with regard, inter alia, to:

(a) the construction, equipment and seaworthiness of ships;

(b) the manning of ships, labour conditions and the training of crews, taking into account the applicable international instruments;

---

[208] 1982 Convention, arts 124–132. See Caflisch (1978) 49 B.Y.I.L. 71; Menefee (1992) 23 Cal.West.I.L.J. 1; Sinjela, *Land-Locked States and the UNCLOS Regime* (1983); Sulaiman (1984) 10 S.A.Y.I.L. 144; Vasciannie, *Land-Locked and Geographically Disadvantaged States in the International Law of the Sea* (1990); Wani (1982) 22 Virg.J.I.L. 627. As to the rights of land-locked states in the exclusive economic zone, see art.69, 1982 Convention. See also the 1965 Convention on Transit Trade of Land-Locked States, and art.3, 1958 High Seas Convention.

(c) the use of signals, the maintenance of communications and the prevention of collisions.

4. Such measures shall include those necessary to ensure:

(a) that each ship, before registration and thereafter at appropriate intervals, is surveyed by a qualified surveyor of ships, and has on board such charts, nautical publications and navigational equipment and instruments as are appropriate for the safe navigation of the ship;

(b) that each ship is in the charge of a master and officers who possess appropriate qualifications, in particular in seamanship, navigation, communications and marine engineering, and that the crew is appropriate in qualification and numbers for the type, size, machinery and equipment of the ship;

(c) that the master, officers and, to the extent appropriate, the crew are fully conversant with and required to observe the applicable international regulations concerning the safety of life at sea, the prevention of collisions, the prevention, reduction and control of marine pollution, and the maintenance of communications by radio.

5. In taking the measures called for in paragraphs 3 and 4 each State is required to conform to generally accepted international regulations, procedures and practices and to take any steps which may be necessary to secure their observance.

6. A State which has clear grounds to believe that proper jurisdiction and control with respect to a ship have not been exercised may report the facts to the flag State. Upon receiving such a report, the flag State shall investigate the matter and, if appropriate, take any action necessary to remedy the situation.

7. Each State shall cause an inquiry to be held by or before a suitably qualified person or persons into every marine casualty or incident of navigation on the high seas involving a ship flying its flag and causing loss of life or serious injury to nationals of another State or serious damage to ships or installations of another State or to the marine environment. The flag State and the other State shall co-operate in the conduct of any inquiry held by that other State into any such marine casualty or incident of navigation.

Notes

1. *Nationality of ships*. Ships are deemed to have a nationality for international law purposes.[209] Normally, a ship is registered under the law of a particular state and is then, under that state's law, both entitled to fly its flag and deemed to have its nationality. On the application of the rules in art.91 concerning the nationality of ships, see the *Saiga* case, below, p.369. Articles 90–92 retain almost entirely the wording of arts 4–6 of the 1958 High Seas Convention; the only significant change is the omission of the final part of the third sentence of art.5 concerning the "genuine link" requirement, as explained below.

2. *Genuine link requirement*. This requirement in art.91(1) was first introduced in art.5(1), 1985 High Seas Convention. It was prompted by the advent of "flags of convenience" or "open registry" states. Of these, Sørenson[210] writes:

    "Owners register their ships in such countries for various reasons. Taxation is very low, or practically non-existent. Operating costs are lower because the legislation and collective agreements on wages, labour conditions, and social security of the traditionally maritime countries do not apply. Lack of adequate administrative machinery, especially inspection services, means that the countries concerned are unable to enforce effectively such laws and regulations as they may have enacted with respect to safety standards, accommodation and protection of crews, and so forth."

---

[209] See Myers, *The Nationality of Ships* (1967).
[210] Above, n.9, pp.202–203. See generally Bozcek, *Flags of Convenience* (1962); and Osieke (1979) 73 A.J.I.L. 604.

The leading "flags of convenience" states are Liberia, Panama and the Bahamas, each of which has more registered tonnage (much of it Greek or US beneficially owned) than the leading maritime powers.

3. The reasons for concern about "flags of convenience" are (i) the abuse of the concept of nationality involved in a ship having a state's nationality for international law purposes regardless of the nationality of its owner, operator or crew; (ii) the reputation of the "flags of convenience" states for failing to enforce health and safety standards; and (iii) the fact that "the expansion of open-registry fleets has adversely affected the development and competitiveness of fleets of countries which do not offer open-registry facilities, including those of developing countries."[211] This last, economic reason led UNCTAD to sponsor the 1986 UN Convention on Conditions for Registration of Ships.[212] This requires a party to have a "competent and adequate national maritime administration" which must, inter alia, ensure that ships flying its flag comply with international rules concerning the safety of ships and marine pollution. A party must also (i) include in its register of shipping information identifying those owning and managing its ships and hence accountable for them; (ii) ensure that its nationals participate to a required degree in *either* the ownership *or* the manning of its ships; and (iii) ensure that those responsible for the management of its ships are able to meet operational financial obligations. These requirements to some extent supplement those in art.5, 1958 High Seas Convention and art.94, 1982 Convention and add an extra dimension to the concept of a genuine link. They nonetheless represent a compromise between the interests of developed and developing states, the Group of 77 states having argued, inter alia, for *both* ownership *and* manning obligations in the 1986 Convention.

4. The genuine link requirement was retained in art.91(1) of the 1982 Convention, but the "jurisdiction and control" obligation in the final part of the third sentence of art.5(1), 1958 High Seas Convention[213] was moved to art.94(1), 1982 Convention and spelt out in detail in art.94(2). The purpose and meaning of the genuine link requirement and the effect of its absence on the recognition of a ship's nationality are explored in the *Saiga* case, below, p.369.

5. Whether the "genuine link" requirement is a part of customary international law is unclear. The *travaux préparatoires* of the 1986 Registration Convention shows widespread support for it. However, Liberia—a leading "flag of convenience" state, which is a party to the 1982 Convention—has asserted that "[a]ny limitation on the rights of states to determine the conditions under which vessels should be accepted on national shipping registers would be contrary to customary international law."[214]

6. In its advisory opinion in the *IMCO* case,[215] the International Court of Justice advised that the term "largest ship-owning nations" in the IMCO Constitution (art.28(*a*)) referred to registered tonnage and not beneficially owned tonnage. On this basis, it advised that Liberia and Panama should have been elected to membership of the Maritime Safety Committee of IMCO. The Court limited itself to the particular issue of treaty interpretation before it and did not consider the question of the nationality of ships and flags of convenience generally.

---

[211] 1978 Resolution of an ad hoc intergovernmental working group of the UNCTAD Committee on Shipping, quoted in Marston (1986) 20 J.W.T.L. 576.

[212] (1987) 26 I.L.M. 1236. Not in force. The Convention requires 40 parties with 25 per cent of the world's tonnage to enter into force: 14 parties, the UK is not a party. On the Convention generally, see Bettink (1987) 18 N.Y.I.L. 69; Egiyan (1988) 12 Mar. Pol. 314; Marston, above, n.211.

[213] The third sentence of art.5(1) reads: "There must exist a genuine link between the state and the ship; in particular, the state must effectively exercise its jurisdiction and control in administrative, technical and social matters over ships flying its flag."

[214] UN Doc. TD/RS/CONF/15, pp.7–8, quoted in Marston, above, n.211, p.578.

[215] I.C.J. Rep. 1960, p.150.

7.   A different kind of "flag of convenience" emerged in the context of the Iran-Iraq War, in response to the danger to shipping in the Persian Gulf,[216] when Kuwaiti tankers were re-registered under the UK and US flags to benefit from the protection of the UK and US naval presence in the Gulf.[217]

8.   A ship is not prohibited from sailing without a flag. If it does so, however, it is, for the purpose of protection at least, treated as the equivalent of a stateless person. Thus, in *Naim Molvan v Att.- Gen. for Palestine*,[218] the Judicial Committee of the Privy Council stated:

> "No question of comity nor of any breach of international law can arise if there is no State under whose flag the vessel sails ... having no [flag] ... the *Asya* could not claim the protection of any State nor could any State claim that any principle of international law was broken by her seizure."

Nonetheless the State of which the owner of a ship without a flag was a national could intervene on the ground of injury to a national's property.[219]

THE M/V SAIGA (NO 2) CASE[220]

St Vincent and the Grenadines v Guinea

International Tribunal for the Law of the Sea (1999) 120 I.L.R. 143.

The *Saiga* was an oil tanker owned by a Cypriot company, managed by a Scottish company, and chartered to a Swiss company. Having formerly been registered as a Maltese ship, its six month certificate of provisional registration as a St Vincent and Grenadines ship expired on September 12, 1997; a permanent Vincentian certificate was issued on November 28, 1997. The *Saiga*'s work was to sell gas oil as bunker to fishing vessels off the West African coast. On October 27, 1997, the *Saiga* supplied gas oil to Senegalese and Greek flag fishing vessels in the Guinean EEZ, about 22 miles from the nearest point of land, a Guinean island. On October 28, while it was stationed outside the Guinean EEZ awaiting other fishing vessels, the *Saiga* was boarded and arrested by Guinean patrol boats and taken to Conraky, Guinea, where the tanker and its crew were detained. On December 4, 1997, at the request of St Vincent and the Grenadines, the Tribunal gave judgment under art.292 of the 1982 Convention, ordering the prompt release of the *Saiga* and its crew on the posting of a reasonable bond. The *Saiga* and most of its crew had not been released by December 17, 1997 when its Master, a Ukrainian national, was convicted by a Guinean court of the offence of the "illegal import, buying and selling of fuel in the Republic of Guinea", resulting from the *Saiga*'s activities in Guinea's EEZ. The Master was given a suspended prison sentence and a large fine. The *Saiga* was confiscated as security for the fine, but released on March 4, 1998.

In this case, St Vincent and the Grenadines claimed that, by its arrest of the *Saiga* and its subsequent actions, Guinea had violated various provisions of the 1982 Convention, to which both

---

[216] See below, p.750.
[217] See Gray (1988) 37 I.C.L.Q. 420 at 424.
[218] [1948] A.C. 351 at 369–370.
[219] See below, Ch.8.
[220] See Kwiatkowska (1999) 30 O.D.I.L. 43; and Oxman and Bantz (2000) 94 A.J.I.L. 40. On the "prompt release" judgment, see Lowe (1999) 48 I.C.L.Q. 187; and Wegelein (1999) 30 O.D.I.L. 255.

states were parties. Although neither state had made declarations under art.286(1), they referred the case to the Tribunal by agreement. The following extract from the Tribunal's judgment begins with its rulings against certain objections to admissibility by Guinea. The first of these was based on the fact that when the arrest occurred the *Saiga* had no Vincentian certificate of registration.

Judgment of the Tribunal

62. The question for consideration is whether the *Saiga* had the nationality of Saint Vincent and the Grenadines at the time of its arrest. ...

63. Article 91 [1982 Convention] leaves to each State exclusive jurisdiction over the granting of its nationality to ships. In this respect, article 91 codifies a well-established rule of general international law.

Under this article, it is for Saint Vincent and the Grenadines to fix the conditions for the grant of its nationality to ships, for the registration of ships in its territory and for the right to fly its flag. ...

66. The Tribunal considers that the nationality of a ship is a question of fact to be determined, like other facts in dispute before it, on the basis of evidence adduced by the parties.

67. Saint Vincent and the Grenadines has produced evidence before the Tribunal to support its assertion that the *Saiga* was a ship entitled to fly its flag at the time of the incident giving rise to the dispute. In addition to making references to the relevant provisions of the Merchant Shipping Act, Saint Vincent and the Grenadines has drawn attention to several indications of Vincentian nationality on the ship or carried on board. These include the inscription "Kingstown" as the port of registry on the stern of the vessel, the documents on board and the ship's seal which contained the words "SAIGA Kingstown" and the then current charter-party which recorded the flag of the vessel as "Saint Vincent and the Grenadines".

68. The evidence adduced by Saint Vincent and the Grenadines has been reinforced by its conduct. Saint Vincent and the Grenadines has at all times material to the dispute operated on the basis that the *Saiga* was a ship of its nationality. It has acted as the flag State of the ship during all phases of the proceedings. It was in that capacity that it invoked the jurisdiction of the Tribunal in its Application for the prompt release of the *Saiga* and its crew under article 292 of the Convention and in its Request for the prescription of provisional measures under article 290 of the Convention.

69. As far as Guinea is concerned, the Tribunal cannot fail to note that it did not challenge or raise any doubts about the registration or nationality of the ship at any time until the submission of its Counter-Memorial in October 1998. ...

72. On the basis of the evidence before it, the Tribunal finds that Saint Vincent and the Grenadines has discharged the initial burden of establishing that the *Saiga* had Vincentian nationality at the time it was arrested by Guinea. Guinea had therefore to prove its contention that the ship was not registered in or did not have the nationality of Saint Vincent and the Grenadines at that time. The Tribunal considers that the burden has not been discharged and that it has not been established that the *Saiga* was not registered in or did not have the nationality of Saint Vincent and the Grenadines at the time of the arrest.

73. The Tribunal concludes:

(a) it has not been established that the Vincentian registration or nationality of the *Saiga* was extinguished in the period between the date on which the Provisional Certificate of Registration was stated to expire and the date of issue of the Permanent Certificate of Registration;

(b) in the particular circumstances of this case, the consistent conduct of Saint Vincent and the Grenadines provides sufficient support for the conclusion that the *Saiga* retained the registration and nationality of Saint Vincent and the Grenadines at all times material to the dispute;

(c) in view of Guinea's failure to question the assertion of Saint Vincent and the Grenadines that it is the flag State of the *Saiga* when it had every reasonable opportunity to do so and its other conduct in the case, Guinea cannot successfully challenge the registration and nationality of the *Saiga* at this stage;

(d) in the particular circumstances of this case, it would not be consistent with justice if the Tribunal were to decline to deal with the merits of the dispute.

74. For the above reasons, the Tribunal rejects Guinea's objection to the admissibility of the claims of Saint Vincent and the Grenadines based on the ground that the *Saiga* was not registered in Saint Vincent and the

Grenadines at the time of its arrest and that, consequently, the *Saiga* did not have Vincentian nationality at that time. . . .

75. The next objection to admissibility raised by Guinea is that there was no genuine link between the *Saiga* and Saint Vincent and the Grenadines. . . .

79. Article 91, paragraph 1, of the Convention provides: "There must exist a genuine link between the State and the ship." Two questions need to be addressed in this connection. The first is whether the absence of a genuine link between a flag State and a ship entitles another State to refuse to recognize the nationality of the ship. The second question is whether or not a genuine link existed between the *Saiga* and Saint Vincent and the Grenadines at the time of the incident.

80. With regard to the first question, the Tribunal notes that the provision in article 91, paragraph 1, of the Convention, requiring a genuine link between the State and the ship, does not provide the answer. Nor do articles 92 and 94 of the Convention, which together with article 91 constitute the context of the provision, provide the answer. The Tribunal, however, recalls that the International Law Commission, in article 29 of the Draft Articles on the Law of the Sea adopted by it in 1956, proposed the concept of a "genuine link" as a criterion not only for the attribution of nationality to a ship but also for the recognition by other States of such nationality. After providing that "[s]hips have the nationality of the State whose flag they are entitled to fly", the draft article continued: "Nevertheless, for purposes of recognition of the national character of the ship by other States, there must exist a genuine link between the State and the ship". This sentence was not included in article 5, paragraph 1, of the Convention on the High Seas of 29 April 1958 (hereinafter "the 1958 Convention"), which reads, in part, as follows:

There must exist a genuine link between the State and the ship; in particular, the State must effectively exercise its jurisdiction and control in administrative, technical and social matters over ships flying its flag.

Thus, while the obligation regarding a genuine link was maintained in the 1958 Convention, the proposal that the existence of a genuine link should be a basis for the recognition of nationality was not adopted.

81. The Convention follows the approach of the 1958 Convention. Article 91 retains the part of the third sentence of article 5, paragraph 1, of the 1958 Convention which provides that there must be a genuine link between the State and the ship. The other part of that sentence, stating that the flag State shall effectively exercise its jurisdiction and control in administrative, technical and social matters over ships flying its flag, is reflected in article 94 of the Convention, dealing with the duties of the flag State.

82. Paragraphs 2 to 5 of article 94 of the Convention outline the measures that a flag State is required to take to exercise effective jurisdiction as envisaged in paragraph 1. Paragraph 6 sets out the procedure to be followed where another State has "clear grounds to believe that proper jurisdiction and control with respect to a ship have not been exercised". That State is entitled to report the facts to the flag State which is then obliged to "investigate the matter and, if appropriate, take any action necessary to remedy the situation". There is nothing in article 94 to permit a State which discovers evidence indicating the absence of proper jurisdiction and control by a flag State over a ship to refuse to recognize the right of the ship to fly the flag of the flag State.

83. The conclusion of the Tribunal is that the purpose of the provisions of the Convention on the need for a genuine link between a ship and its flag State is to secure more effective implementation of the duties of the flag State, and not to establish criteria by reference to which the validity of the registration of ships in a flag State may be challenged by other States.

84. This conclusion is not put into question by the United Nations Convention on Conditions for Registration of Ships of 7 February 1986 invoked by Guinea. This Convention (which is not in force) sets out as one of its principal objectives the strengthening of "the genuine link between a State and ships flying its flag". In any case, the Tribunal observes that Guinea has not cited any provision in that Convention which lends support to its contention that "a basic condition for the registration of a ship is that also the owner or operator of the ship is under the jurisdiction of the flag State."

85. The conclusion is further strengthened by the Agreement for the Implementation of the Provisions of the United Nations Convention on the Law of the Sea of 10 December 1982 Relating to the Conservation and Management of Straddling Fish Stocks and Highly Migratory Fish Stocks open for signature on 4 December 1995 and the Agreement to Promote Compliance with International Conservation and Management Measures by Fishing Vessels on the High Seas of 24 November 1993. These Agreements, neither of which is in force, set out, inter alia, detailed obligations to be discharged by the flag States of fishing vessels but do not deal with the conditions to be satisfied for the registration of fishing vessels.

86. In the light of the above considerations, the Tribunal concludes that there is no legal basis for the claim of

Guinea that it can refuse to recognize the right of the *Saiga* to fly the flag of Saint Vincent and the Grenadines on the ground that there was no genuine link between the ship and Saint Vincent and the Grenadines.

87. With regard to the second question, the Tribunal finds that, in any case, the evidence adduced by Guinea is not sufficient to justify its contention that there was no genuine link between the *Saiga* and Saint Vincent and the Grenadines at the material time.

88. For the above reasons, the Tribunal rejects the objection to admissibility based on the absence of a genuine link between the Saiga and Saint Vincent and the Grenadines. ...

The Tribunal rejected, by 18 votes to 2, Guinea's admissibility objection that local remedies had to be exhausted before it could hear a claim alleging the unlawful detention of a ship, and continued:

103. In its last objection to admissibility, Guinea argues that ... the claims of Saint Vincent and the Grenadines in respect of loss or damage sustained by the ship ... the Master and other members of the crew and other persons, including the owners of the cargo, are clearly claims of diplomatic protection. In its view, Saint Vincent and the Grenadines is not competent to institute these claims on behalf of the persons concerned since none of them is a national of Saint Vincent and the Grenadines. ...

105. In dealing with this question, the Tribunal finds sufficient guidance in the Convention. The Convention contains detailed provisions concerning the duties of flag States regarding ships flying their flag. Articles 94 and 217, in particular, set out the obligations of the flag State which can be discharged only through the exercise of appropriate jurisdiction and control over natural and juridical persons such as the Master and other members of the crew, the owners or operators and other persons involved in the activities of the ship. No distinction is made in these provisions between nationals and non-nationals of a flag State. Additionally, articles 106, 110, paragraph 3, and 111, paragraph 8, of the Convention contain provisions applicable to cases in which measures have been taken by a State against a foreign ship. These measures are, respectively, seizure of a ship on suspicion of piracy, exercise of the right of visit on board the ship, and arrest of a ship in exercise of the right of hot pursuit. In these cases, the Convention provides that, if the measures are found not to be justified, the State taking the measures shall be obliged to pay compensation "for any loss or damage" sustained. In these cases, the Convention does not relate the right to compensation to the nationality of persons suffering loss or damage. Furthermore, in relation to proceedings for prompt release under article 292 of the Convention, no significance is attached to the nationalities of persons involved in the operations of an arrested ship.

106. The provisions referred to in the preceding paragraph indicate that the Convention considers a ship as a unit, as regards the obligations of the flag State with respect to the ship and the right of a flag State to seek reparation for loss or damage caused to the ship by acts of other States and to institute proceedings under article 292 of the Convention. Thus the ship, every thing on it, and every person involved or interested in its operations are treated as an entity linked to the flag State. The nationalities of these persons are not relevant.

107. The Tribunal must also call attention to an aspect of the matter which is not without significance in this case. This relates to two basic characteristics of modern maritime transport: the transient and multinational composition of ships' crews and the multiplicity of interests that may be involved in the cargo on board a single ship. A container vessel carries a large number of containers, and the persons with interests in them may be of many different nationalities. This may also be true in relation to cargo on board a break-bulk carrier. Any of these ships could have a crew comprising persons of several nationalities. If each person sustaining damage were obliged to look for protection from the State of which such person is a national, undue hardship would ensue.

108. The Tribunal is, therefore, unable to accept Guinea's contention that Saint Vincent and the Grenadines is not entitled to present claims for damages in respect of natural and juridical persons who are not nationals of Saint Vincent and the Grenadines. ...

116. The main charge against the *Saiga* was that it violated article 1 of Law L/94/007 by importing gas oil into the customs radius (*rayon des douanes*) of Guinea. Guinea justifies this action by maintaining that the prohibition in article 1 of Law L/94/007 "can be applied for the purpose of controlling and suppressing the sale of gas oil to fishing vessels in the customs radius according to article 34 of the Customs Code of Guinea". ...

120. In the view of the Tribunal, there is nothing to prevent it from considering the question whether or not, in applying its laws to the *Saiga* in the present case, Guinea was acting in conformity with its obligations towards Saint Vincent and the Grenadines under the Convention and general international law. In its Judgment in the *Case Concerning Certain German Interests in Polish Upper Silesia*, the Permanent Court of International Justice stated:

From the standpoint of International Law and of the Court which is its organ, municipal laws are merely facts which express the will and constitute the activities of the States, in the same manner as do legal decisions or administrative measures. The Court is certainly not called upon to interpret the Polish law as such; but there is nothing to prevent the Court's giving judgment on the question whether or not, in applying that law, Poland is acting in conformity with its obligations towards Germany under the Geneva Convention. (*Certain German Interests in Polish Upper Silesia, Merits, Judgment No. 7, 1926, P.C.I.J., Series A, No. 7*, p.19)

121. A denial of the competence of the Tribunal to examine the applicability and scope of national law is even less acceptable in the framework of certain provisions of the Convention. One such provision, which is also relied upon by Guinea, is article 58, paragraph 3 ...

Under this provision, the rights and obligations of coastal and other States under the Convention arise not just from the provisions of the Convention but also from national laws and regulations "adopted by the coastal State in accordance with the provisions of this Convention". Thus, the Tribunal is competent to determine the compatibility of such laws and regulations with the Convention.

122. The Tribunal notes that Guinea produces no evidence in support of its contention that the laws cited by it provide a basis for the action taken against the *Saiga* beyond the assertion that it reflects the consistent practice of its authorities, supported by its courts. Even if it is conceded that the laws of Guinea which the *Saiga* is alleged to have violated are applicable in the manner that is claimed by Guinea, the question remains whether these laws, as interpreted and applied by Guinea, are compatible with the Convention. ...

127. The Tribunal notes that, under the Convention, a coastal State is entitled to apply customs laws and regulations in its territorial sea (articles 2 and 21) ... [and its] contiguous zone ... (article 33, paragraph 1).

In the exclusive economic zone, the coastal State has jurisdiction to apply customs laws and regulations in respect of artificial islands, installations and structures (article 60, paragraph 2). In the view of the Tribunal, the Convention does not empower a coastal State to apply its customs laws in respect of any other parts of the exclusive economic zone not mentioned above.

128. Guinea further argues that the legal basis of its law prohibiting the supply of gas oil to fishing vessels in the customs radius is to be found in article 58 of the Convention. It relies on the reference, contained in paragraph 3 of that article, to the "other rules of international law" to justify the application and enforcement of its customs and contraband laws to the customs radius. These "other rules of international law" are variously described by Guinea as "the inherent right to protect itself against unwarranted economic activities in its exclusive economic zone that considerably affect its public interest", or as the "doctrine of necessity", or as "the customary principle of self-protection in case of grave and imminent perils which endanger essential aspects of its public interest".

129. The Tribunal finds it necessary to distinguish between the two main concepts referred to in the submissions of Guinea. The first is a broad notion of "public interest" or "self-protection" which Guinea invokes to expand the scope of its jurisdiction in the exclusive economic zone, and the second is "state of necessity" which it relies on to justify measures that would otherwise be wrongful under the Convention.

130. The main public interest which Guinea claims to be protecting by applying its customs laws to the exclusive economic zone is said to be the "considerable fiscal losses a developing country like Guinea is suffering from illegal off-shore bunkering in its exclusive economic zone". Guinea makes references also to fisheries and environmental interests. In effect, Guinea's contention is that the customary international law principle of "public interest" gives it the power to impede "economic activities that are undertaken [in its exclusive zone] under the guise of navigation but are different from communication".

131. According to article 58, paragraph 3, of the Convention, the "other rules of international law" which a coastal State is entitled to apply in the exclusive economic zone are those which are not incompatible with Part V of the Convention. In the view of the Tribunal, recourse to the principle of "public interest", as invoked by Guinea, would entitle a coastal State to prohibit any activities in the exclusive economic zone which it decides to characterize as activities which affect its economic "public interest" or entail "fiscal losses" for it. This would curtail the rights of other States in the exclusive economic zone. The Tribunal is satisfied that this would be incompatible with the provision of articles 56 and 58 of the Convention regarding the rights of the coastal State in the exclusive economic zone.

132. It remains for the Tribunal to consider whether the otherwise wrongful application by Guinea of its customs laws to the exclusive economic zone can be justified under general international law by Guinea's appeal to "state of necessity".

133. In the *Case Concerning the Gabčíkovo-Nagymaros Project (Gabčíkovo-Nagymaros Project (Hungary/Slovenia), Judgment, I.C.J. Reports 1997*, pp.40 and 41, paragraphs 51 and 52), the International Court of Justice

noted with approval two conditions for the defence based on "state of necessity" which in general international law justifies an otherwise wrongful act. These conditions, as set out in article 33, paragraph 1, of the International Law Commission's Draft Articles on State Responsibility, are:

(a) the act was the only means of safeguarding an essential interest of the State against a grave and imminent peril; and

(b) the act did not seriously impair an essential interest of the State towards which the obligation existed.

134. In endorsing these conditions, the Court stated that they "must be cumulatively satisfied" and that they "reflect customary international law".

135. No evidence has been produced by Guinea to show that its essential interests were in grave and imminent peril. But, however essential Guinea's interest in maximizing its tax revenue from the sale of gas oil to fishing vessels, it cannot be suggested that the only means of safeguarding that interest was to extend its customs laws to parts of the exclusive economic zone.

136. The Tribunal, therefore, finds that, by applying its customs laws to a customs radius which includes parts of the exclusive economic zone, Guinea acted in a manner contrary to the Convention. Accordingly, the arrest and detention of the *Saiga*, the prosecution and conviction of its Master, the confiscation of the cargo and the seizure of the ship were contrary to the Convention. ...

139. Saint Vincent and the Grenadines contends that, in arresting the *Saiga*, Guinea did not lawfully exercise the right of hot pursuit under article 111 of the Convention. ...

146. The Tribunal notes that the conditions for the exercise of the right of hot pursuit under article 111 of the Convention are cumulative; each of them has to be satisfied for the pursuit to be legitimate under the Convention. In this case, the Tribunal finds that several of these conditions were not fulfilled.

147. With regard to the pursuit alleged to have commenced on 27 October 1997, the evidence before the Tribunal indicates that, at the time the Order for the Joint Mission of the Customs and Navy of Guinea was issued, the authorities of Guinea, on the basis of information available to them, could have had no more than a suspicion that a tanker had violated the laws of Guinea in the exclusive economic zone. The Tribunal also notes that, in the circumstances, no visual or auditory signals to stop could have been given to the *Saiga*. Furthermore, the alleged pursuit was interrupted. According to the evidence given by Guinea, the small patrol boat P35 that was sent out on 26 October 1997 on a northward course to search for the *Saiga* was recalled when information was received that the *Saiga* had changed course. This recall constituted a clear interruption of any pursuit, whatever legal basis might have existed for its commencement in the first place.

148. As far as the pursuit alleged to have commenced on 28 October 1998 is concerned, the evidence adduced by Guinea does not support its claim that the necessary auditory or visual signals to stop were given to the *Saiga* prior to the commencement of the alleged pursuit, as required by article 111, paragraph 4, of the Convention; Although Guinea claims that the small patrol boat (P35) sounded its siren and turned on its blue revolving light signals when it came within visual and hearing range of the *Saiga*, both the Master who was on the bridge at the time and Mr. Niasse who was on the deck, categorically denied that any such signals were given. In any case, any signals given at the time claimed by Guinea cannot be said to have been given at the commencement of the alleged pursuit.

149. The Tribunal has already concluded that no laws or regulations of Guinea applicable in accordance with the Convention were violated by the *Saiga*. It follows that there was no legal basis for the exercise of the right of hot pursuit by Guinea in this case.

150. For these reasons, the Tribunal finds that Guinea stopped and arrested the *Saiga* on 28 October 1997 in circumstances which did not justify the exercise of the right of hot pursuit in accordance with the Convention.

151. The Tribunal notes that Guinea, in its pleadings and submissions, suggests that the actions against the *Saiga* could, at least in part, be justified on the ground that the *Saiga* supplied gas oil to the fishing vessels in the contiguous zone of the Guinean island of Alcatraz. ...

152. The Tribunal has not based its consideration of the question of the legality of the pursuit of the *Saiga* on the suggestion of Guinea that a violation of its customs law occurred in the contiguous zone. The Tribunal would, however, note that its conclusion on this question would have been the same if Guinea had based its action against the *Saiga* solely on the ground of an infringement of its customs laws in the contiguous zone. For, even in that case, the conditions for the exercise of the right of hot pursuit, as required under article 111 of the Convention, would not have been satisfied for the reasons given in paragraphs 147 and 148. ...

155. In considering the force used by Guinea in the arrest of the *Saiga*, the Tribunal must take into account the

circumstances of the arrest in the context of the applicable rules of international law. Although the Convention does not contain express provisions on the use of force in the arrest of ships, international law, which is applicable by virtue of article 293 of the Convention, requires that the use of force must be avoided as far as possible and, where force is unavoidable, it must not go beyond what is reasonable and necessary in the circumstances. Considerations of humanity must apply in the law of the sea, as they do in other areas of international law.

156. These principles have been followed over the years in law enforcement operations at sea. The normal practice used to stop a ship at sea is first to give an auditory or visual signal to stop, using internationally recognized signals. Where this does not succeed, a variety of actions may be taken, including the firing of shots across the bows of the ship. It is only after the appropriate actions fail that the pursuing vessel may, as a last resort, use force. Even them appropriate warning must be issued to the ship and all efforts should be made to ensure that life is not endangered (*S.S. "I'm Alone"* case (*Canada/United States, 1935*), *U.N.R.I.A.A., Vol.III*, p.1609; *The Red Crusader* case (*Commission of Enquiry, Denmark – United Kingdom, 1962*), *I.L.R., Vol.35*, p.485). The basic principle concerning the use of force in the arrest of a ship at sea has been reaffirmed by the Agreement for the Implementation of the Provisions of the United Nations Convention on the Law of the Sea of 10 December 1982 Relating to the Conservation and Management of Straddling Fish Stocks and Highly Migratory Fish Stocks. Article 22, paragraph 1(f), of the Agreement states:

1.   The inspecting State shall ensure that its duly authorized inspectors:

   . . .

   (f)   avoid the use of force except when and to the degree necessary to ensure the safety of the inspectors and where the inspectors are obstructed in the execution of their duties. The degree of force used shall not exceed that reasonably required in the circumstances.

157. In the present case, the Tribunal notes that the *Saiga* was almost fully laden and was low in the water at the time it was approached by the patrol vessel. Its maximum speed was 10 knots. Therefore it could be boarded without much difficulty by the Guinean officers. At one stage in the proceedings Guinea sought to justify the use of gunfire with the claim that the *Saiga* had attempted to sink the patrol boat. During the hearing, the allegation was modified to the effect that the danger of sinking to the patrol boat was from the wake of the *Saiga* and not the result of a deliberate attempt by the ship. But whatever the circumstances, there is no excuse for the fact that the officers fired at the ship itself with live ammunition from a fast-moving patrol boat without issuing any of the signals and warnings required by international law and practice.

158. The Guinean officers also used excessive force on board the *Saiga*. Having boarded the ship without resistance, and although there is no evidence of the use or threat of force from the crew, they fired indiscriminately while on the deck and used gunfire to stop the engine of the ship. In using firearms in this way, the Guinean officers appeared to have attached little or no importance to the safety of the ship and the persons on board. In the process, considerable damage was done to the ship and to vital equipment in the engine and radio rooms. And, more seriously, the indiscriminate use of gunfire caused severe injuries to two of the persons on board.

159. For these reasons, the Tribunal finds that Guinea used excessive force and endangered human life before and after boarding the *Saiga*. . . .

163. Saint Vincent and the Grenadines requests the Tribunal to find that Guinea violated Articles 292, paragraph 4, and 296 of the Convention by failing to release the *Saiga* promptly after the posting of the security, in the term of a bank guarantee, in compliance with the Judgment of the Tribunal of 4 December 1997.

165. The Tribunal notes that the ship was released on 28 February 1998. The release was expressly stated in the Deed of Release to be in execution of the Judgment of 4 December 1997. A release of the ship [and its remaining crew] 80 days after the posting of the bond cannot be considered as a prompt release. However, a number of factors contributed to the delay in releasing the ship and not all of them can be said to be due to the fault of Guinea. Therefore, the Tribunal does not find that, in the circumstances of this case, Guinea failed to comply with the Judgment of 4 December 1997.

166. Accordingly, the Tribunal does not find that Guinea failed to comply with articles 292, paragraph 4, and 296 of the Convention. . . .

183. For the above reasons, the Tribunal . . .

(3) By 18 votes to 2,

Rejects the objection to the admissibility of the claims of Saint Vincent and the Grenadines based on Guinea's contention that the *Saiga* was not registered in Saint Vincent and the Grenadines at the time of its arrest; ...

(4) By 18 votes to 2,

Rejects the objections to the admissibility of the claims of Saint Vincent and the Grenadines based on Guinea's contention that there was no genuine link between Saint Vincent and the Grenadines and the *Saiga* at the time of its arrest; ...

(6) By 18 votes to 2,

Rejects the objection to the admissibility of certain of the claims of Saint Vincent and Grenadines based on Guinea's contention that the persons in respect of whom Saint Vincent and the Grenadines brought the claims were not its nationals;

(7) By 18 votes to 2,

Decides that Guinea violated the rights of Saint Vincent and the Grenadines under the Convention in arresting the *Saiga*, and in detaining the *Saiga* and members of its crew, in prosecuting and convicting its Master and in seizing the *Saiga* and confiscating its cargo; ...

(8) By 18 votes to 2,

Decides that in arresting the *Saiga* Guinea acted in contravention of the provisions of the Convention on the exercise of the right of hot pursuit and thereby violated the rights of Saint Vincent and the Grenadines; ...

(9) By 18 votes to 2,

Decides that while stopping and arresting the *Saiga* Guinea used excessive force contrary to international law and thereby violated the rights of Saint Vincent and the Grenadines; ...

(11) By 17 votes to 3,

Rejects the claim by Saint Vincent and the Grenadines that Guinea violated its rights under the Convention by failing to release promptly the *Saiga* and members of its crew in compliance with the Judgment of the Tribunal of 4 December 1997; ...

(12) By 18 votes to 2,

Decides that Guinea shall pay compensation to Saint Vincent and the Grenadines in the sum of US$2,123,357 (United States Dollars Two Million One Hundred and Twenty-Three Thousand Three Hundred and Fifty-Seven) with interest, as indicated in paragraph 175; ...

Notes

1.   The *Saiga* case touches upon a number of law of the sea issues, including the nationality of ships, the genuine link requirement, the right of hot pursuit and the EEZ regime. As to the nationality of ships, it confirms that under art.91 1982 Convention the criteria for nationality is left to the flag state, which may grant its nationality to a ship even though it lacks much or any connection with it, and that this nationality will be recognised in international law for the purposes of protecting the ship under the 1982 Convention. Although the genuine link requirement in art.91(1) may have had its inspiration in the *Nottebohm* case,[221] which held that a state may only offer diplomatic protection for a national who is an individual where there is a genuine connection between the two, the genuine link requirement for ships does not have the same limiting effect.[222] A state may not refuse to recognise a ship's nationality because of the absence of a genuine link; instead the purpose of the requirement is to "secure more effective implementation of the duties of the flag State" (para.83). Did the Tribunal in the *Saiga* case suppose that the content or meaning of the genuine connection requirement is to be found in art.94?

2.   In the *Saiga* case, the absence of current Vincentian registration was not decisive on the facts of the case and considerations of "justice" led the Tribunal to consider the claim on the merits. For a Tribunal case in which, in the absence of current registration of the detained ship, the applicant

---

[221] See below, p.505.

[222] The link between St Vincent and the Grenadines was minimal.

state failed to establish that it was competent to bring a "prompt release" claim under the 1982 Convention as the flag state, see the *Grand Prince* case (*Belize v France*).[223]

3. On hot pursuit and the EEZ, see below, pp.388 and 391.

4. *Prompt release proceedings*. Requests for orders for the release of arrested vessels that have not been released promptly on the posting of a reasonable bond where this is required by the 1982 Convention,[224] such as that made by St Vincent and the Grenadines at an early stage of this case, have been made to the Tribunal in five cases, constituting the bulk of the Tribunal's work so far.[225]

C. Jurisdiction on the High Seas[226]

CONVENTION ON THE LAW OF THE SEA 1982

UN Doc. A/CONF. 62/122; (1982) 21 I.L.M. 1261

Article 95

Warships[227] on the high seas have complete immunity from the jurisdiction of any State other than the flag State.

Article 96

Ships owned or operated by a State and used only on government non-commercial service shall, on the high seas, have complete immunity from the jurisdiction of any State other than the flag State.

Article 97

1. In the event of a collision or any other incident of navigation concerning a ship on the high seas, involving the penal or disciplinary responsibility of the master or of any other person in the service of the ship, no penal or disciplinary proceedings may be instituted against such person except before the judicial or administrative authorities either of the flag State or of the State of which such person is a national.

2. In disciplinary matters, the State which has issued a master's certificate or a certificate of competence or licence shall alone be competent, after due legal process, to pronounce the withdrawal of such certificates, even if the holder is not a national of the State which issued them.

3. No arrest or detention of the ship, even as a measure of investigation, shall be ordered by any authorities other than those of the flag State.

Article 98

1. Every State shall require the master of a ship flying its flag, in so far as he can do so without serious danger to the ship, the crew or the passengers:

(a) to render assistance to any person found at sea in danger of being lost;

---

[223] (2001). See Oxman and Banz (2002) 96 A.J.I.L. 219.
[224] "Prompt release" requirements of this kind are found in art.73(2), below, p.394; and in art.226(1)(b) (concerning arrest for pollution infringements). See also art.220(7) (pollution).
[225] See Oxman and Bantz (2002) 96 A.J.I.L. 219.
[226] See Van Zwanenberg (1961) 10 I.C.L.Q. 785.
[227] Ed. For the definition of a "warship", see art.29, 1982 Convention, above, p.347.

(b) to proceed with all possible speed to the rescue of persons in distress, if informed of their need of assistance, in so far as such action may reasonably be expected of him;

(c) after a collision, to render assistance to the other ship, its crew and its passengers and, where possible, to inform the other ship of the name of his own ship, its port of registry and the nearest port at which it will call.

2. Every coastal State shall promote the establishment, operation and maintenance of an adequate and effective search and rescue service regarding safety on and over the sea and, where circumstances so require, by way of mutual regional arrangements co-operate with neighbouring States for this purpose.

Article 99

Every State shall take effective measures to prevent and punish the transport of slaves in ships authorized to fly its flag and to prevent the unlawful use of its flag for that purpose. Any slave taking refuge on board any ship, whatever its flag, shall *ipso facto* be free.

Article 100

All States shall co-operate to the fullest possible extent in the repression of piracy on the high seas or in any other place outside the jurisdiction of any State.

Article 101

Piracy consists of any of the following acts:

(a) any illegal acts of violence or detention, or any act of depredation, committed for private ends by the crew or the passengers of a private ship or a private aircraft, and directed:
   (i) on the high seas against another ship or aircraft, or against persons or property on board such ship or aircraft;
   (ii) against a ship, aircraft, persons or property in a place outside the jurisdiction of any State;

(b) any act of voluntary participation in the operation of a ship or of an aircraft with knowledge of facts making it a pirate ship or aircraft;

(c) any act of inciting or of intentionally facilitating an act described in sub-paragraph (a) or (b).

Article 102

The acts of piracy, as defined in Article 101, committed by a warship, government ship or government aircraft whose crew has mutinied and taken control of the ship or aircraft are assimilated to acts committed by a private ship or aircraft.

Article 103

A ship or aircraft is considered a pirate ship or aircraft if it is intended by the persons in dominant control to be used for the purpose of committing one of the acts referred to in Article 101. The same applies if the ship or aircraft has been used to commit any such act, so long as it remains under the control of the persons guilty of that act.

Article 104

A ship or aircraft may retain its nationality although it has become a pirate ship or aircraft. The retention or loss of nationality is determined by the law of the State from which such nationality was derived.

Article 105

On the high seas, or in any other place outside the jurisdiction of any State, every State may seize a pirate ship or aircraft, or a ship or aircraft taken by piracy and under the control of pirates, and arrest the persons and seize the property on board. The courts of the State which carried out the seizure may decide upon the penalties to be imposed, and may also determine the action to be taken with regard to the ships, aircraft or property, subject to the rights of third parties acting in good faith.

Article 106

Where the seizure of a ship or aircraft on suspicion of piracy has been effected without adequate grounds, the State making the seizure shall be liable to the State the nationality of which is possessed by the ship or aircraft for any loss or damage caused by the seizure.

Article 107

A seizure on account of piracy may be carried out only by warships or military aircraft, or other ships or aircraft clearly marked and identifiable as being on government service and authorized to that effect.

Article 108

1. All States shall co-operate in the suppression of illicit traffic in narcotic drugs and psychotropic substances engaged in by ships on the high seas contrary to international conventions.
2. Any State which has reasonable grounds for believing that a ship flying its flag is engaged in illicit traffic in narcotic drugs or psychotropic substances may request the co-operation of other States to suppress such traffic.

Article 109

1. All States shall co-operate in the suppression of unauthorized broadcasting from the high seas.
2. For the purposes of this Convention, "unauthorized broadcasting" means the transmission of sound radio or television broadcasts from a ship or installation on the high seas intended for reception by the general public contrary to international regulations, but excluding the transmission of distress calls.
3. Any person engaged in unauthorized broadcasting may be prosecuted before the court of:

(a) the flag State of the ship;

(b) the State of registry of the installation;

(c) the State of which the person is a national;

(d) any State where the transmissions can be received; or

(e) any State where authorized radio communication is suffering interference.

4. On the high seas, a State having jurisdiction in accordance with paragraph 3 may, in conformity with Article 110, arrest any person or ship engaged in unauthorized broadcasting and seize the broadcasting apparatus.

Article 110

1. Except where acts of interference derive from powers conferred by treaty, a warship which encounters on the high seas a foreign ship, other than a ship entitled to complete immunity in accordance with Articles 95 and 96, is not justified in boarding it unless there is reasonable ground for suspecting that;

(a) the ship is engaged in piracy;

(b) the ship is engaged in the slave trade;

(c) the ship is engaged in unauthorized broadcasting and the flag State of the warship has jurisdiction under Article 109;

(*d*) the ship is without nationality; or

(*e*) though flying a foreign flag or refusing to show its flag, the ship is, in reality, of the same nationality as the warship.

2. In the cases provided for in paragraph 1, the warship may proceed to verify the ship's right to fly its flag. To this end, it may send a boat under the command of an officer to the suspected ship. If suspicion remains after the documents have been checked, it may proceed to a further examination on board the ship, which must be carried out with all possible consideration.

3. If the suspicions prove to be unfounded, and provided that the ship boarded has not committed any act justifying them, it shall be compensated for any loss or damage that may have been sustained.

4. These provisions apply *mutatis mutandis* to military aircraft.

5. These provisions also apply to any other duly authorized ships or aircraft clearly marked and identifiable as being on government service.

Notes

1.   The basic rule of customary international law that "vessels on the high seas are subject to no authority except that of the State whose flag they fly" is stated and elaborated upon by the Permanent Court of International Justice in the *Lotus* case.[228] Accordingly arts 95 and 96, 1982 Convention[229] provide for the absolute immunity of warships and other state ships not used for commercial purposes. For other vessels, art.110, 1982 Convention lists five exceptions to the exclusive administrative jurisdiction of the flag state on the high seas. As to customary international law, Smith,[230] writing in 1959, states that, provided that a merchant vessel, when "approached" at sea by a warship, "responds by showing her flag the captain of the warship is not justified in boarding her or taking any further action, unless there is reasonable ground for suspecting that she is engaged in piracy or some other improper activity."

On the coastal state's right to visit ships in the exclusive economic zone under art.73, 1982 Convention, see below, p.394. Other customary international law powers exist under the doctrines of hot pursuit[231] and the contiguous zone[232] and, possibly, for the purpose of self-defence[233] or to deal with marine casualties threatening pollution.[234] As far as treaty exceptions are concerned, treaty powers of jurisdiction[235] exist for the parties inter se in respect, inter alia, of fishing practices and conservation[236], and of interference with submarine cables[237] and drug trafficking.[238] The severe penalty in art.110(3), 1982 Convention, which probably reflects customary international law,[239] was thought by the International Law Commission to be "justified in order to prevent the right of visit being abused."[240]

---

[228] See above, p.230.

[229] These are identical to arts 8(1) and 9, 1958 High Seas Convention.

[230] *The Law and Custom of the Sea* (3rd edn 1959) p.64. On the position under the treaties on slavery, see Gutteridge (1957) 6 I.C.L.Q. 449.

[231] See below, p.388.

[232] See below, p.384.

[233] See below, p.754.

[234] See Smith, above, n.230, pp.221–222.

[235] These powers are generally very limited and depend upon the consent of the flag state or state of registration.

[236] See, e.g. Canada-US Convention for the Preservation of the Halibut Fishery of the North Pacific Ocean and the Bering Sea 1953, art.II, U.S.T.I.A.S. 2900.

[237] See, e.g. Convention for the Protection of Submarine Cables 1884, art.X, 75 B.F.S.P.356; 2 Malloy 1949.

[238] See the 1988 UN Convention Against Illicit Traffic in Narcotic Drugs and Psychotropic Substances, art.17, 1582 UNTS 165.

[239] See Smith, above, n.230, p.65.

[240] Y.B.I.L.C., 1956, II, p.284.

2. *Weapons of Mass Destruction ("WMD").*[241] There is no exception to the exclusive administrative jurisdiction of the flag state so as to permit the exercise of jurisdiction by other states on the high seas to prevent the transport of WMDs. In the *So San* incident (2002),[242] Spanish naval vessels approached the *So San*, a freighter registered in Cambodia but not flying a flag, on the high seas in the Gulf of Aden. They did so at the request of the US, which suspected that the *So San* was carrying a missile shipment from North Korea to a rogue state. When the *So San* did not stop, despite warning shots, it was boarded by helicopter by Spanish marines who, joined on board by US arms experts, found hidden SCUD missiles parts that were not on the cargo manifest. When a US naval vessel began escorting the *So San* to a base in the UK Chagos Islands, Yemen protested to the US and Spain. Once the US was satisfied by the Yemeni government that the parts had been lawfully bought by it from North Korea for its own legitimate defence purposes, the *So San* was released with its missile cargo and allowed to continue to its Yemeni destination, the US acknowledging that it had no administrative jurisdiction to do otherwise. Was even the boarding and search of the vessel lawful under art.110, 1982 Convention?

    Following this incident, in 2003 the US introduced the Proliferation Security Initiative ("PSI") by which participating states agreed to co-operative to prevent the transport of WMDs to states or non-state actors "engaged in proliferation".[243] Participation in the PSI involves a political, not a legal, obligation and the exercise of administrative jurisdiction by non-flag states on the high seas is dependent upon flag state consent. Security Council Resolution 1540[244] takes matters further by imposing legal obligations on states to prevent WMD proliferation, including transportation by sea, but contains no power to exercise administrative jurisdiction on the high seas for non-flag states. The 2005 Protocol to the IMO Convention for the Suppression of Unlawful Acts against the Safety of Navigation[245] provides inter alia for an offence of transporting on board a ship any biological, chemical or nuclear ("BCN") weapon (art.3 *bis* (1)(b)(ii)), but the exercise of administrative jurisdiction by non-flag states on the high seas again requires flag state consent (art.8 bis).

3. *Penal Jurisdiction in Collisions.* Article 97, 1982 Convention, which conflicts with the decision in the *Lotus Case*,[246] probably states the customary international law rule.

4. *Piracy.*[247] Articles 100–107, 1982 Convention repeat the rules on piracy in arts 14–21, 1958 High Seas Convention. They are binding on most states, as parties thereto. They can probably be taken generally[248] to indicate the elements of the offence of piracy *iure gentium* in present day customary international law and the legal regime applicable to it. The definition of piracy in art.101, 1982 Convention, requires the piratical act to be committee for all "private ends". This extends piracy beyond its original meaning of acts committed "with intent to plunder" (*animus*

---

[241] See Byers (2004) 98 A.J.I.L. 526; Guilfoyle (2007) J.C.S.L. 1; and Joyner (2005) 30 Y.J.I.L. 507.

[242] Joyner (2005) 30 Y.J.I.L. 508.

[243] Participants include the UK and most other western states. For details and PSI activities, see Guilfoyle (2007) J.C.S.L. 11.

[244] UN doc S/RES/1540 (2004).

[245] For the text, see *www.imo.org*, 6 parties. Not yet in force. See also below, n.256.

[246] See above, p.230. Essentially the same rule as that in art.97 is included in the Brussels Convention on Penal Jurisdiction in Matters of Collision 1952, art.1, (1960) U.K.T.S. 47; Cmnd. 1128; 429 U.N.T.S. 233; (1959) 53 A.J.I.L. 536. In force 1955. 66 parties, including the UK. Article 97 reproduces verbatim art.11, 1958 High Seas Convention.

[247] See Azubuike (2009) 15 Ann. Survey I.C.L. 43; Bahar (2007) 40 Vand. J.T.L. 1; Dubner, *The Law of International Sea Piracy* (1980); Keyuan (2005) 59 J.I.A. 118; (2009) C.J.I.L. 323; Stiles, 27 Suffolk Transnational L.R. 299; Symposium articles in (199091) 21 Cal. W.L.J. 104.

[248] The extension of the offence in the 1958 and 1982 Conventions to cover aircraft was an instance of "progressive development".

furandi).[249] There are different views as to whether the "private means" limitation excludes acts by terrorists or other political acts of violence. Guilfoyle[250] states:

> "It is commonly and mistakenly presumed that these words must exclude all politically motivated violence. In fact, the words 'for private ends' simply denote that the violence involved is not *public* and were originally included to acknowledge the historic exception for civil war [insurgents] who attacked only the vessels of the government they sought to overthrow. All acts of violence lacking State sanction are acts undertaken for 'private ends'."

Piracy may only be committed on the "high seas" or "any other place outside the jurisdiction of any state" (art.101(a))[251]; it may not be committed in the territorial sea. The "high seas" means waters beyond the outer limit of the territorial sea, including the EEZ.[252]

Piracy requires two ships or aircraft; the taking over of a ship or aircraft by its crew or others on board is not piracy.[253] Consequently the *Santa Maria* and *Achille Lauro Incidents* did not involve piracy. In the *Santa Maria Incident*,[254] in 1961, a Portuguese passenger vessel called the *Santa Maria* was seized in the Atlantic on the high seas by armed men who had boarded it as passengers. One member of the crew was killed and others injured. The men were supporters of General Delgado, a political opponent of President Salazar of Portugal. The ship was eventually handed over to Brazil and returned to Portugal. The men were given political asylum by Brazil.

In a similar incident in 1985, the *Achille Lauro*,[255] an Italian liner, was seized in Port Said beyond the limit of Egyptian territorial waters by PLO hijackers on board as passengers. The crew and passengers were held hostage and a Jewish US national among the passengers was killed when demands for the release of Palestinian prisoners held by Israel were not met. Later, an Egyptian civil aircraft carrying the hijackers to Tunis was intercepted by a US military aircraft over the high seas in the Mediterranean and forced to land in Italy. The hijackers were handed over to the Italian authorities and convicted of terrorist offences in the Italian courts. In response to the *Achille Lauro Incident*, the 1988 IMO Convention on the Suppression of Unlawful Acts against the Safety of Maritime Navigation[256] was adopted. This, inter alia, makes it an offence to seize control of a ship by the use or threat of force where the ship "is navigating or is scheduled to navigate into, through or from waters beyond the outer limit of the territorial sea of a single state, or the lateral limits of its territorial sea with adjacent states." (arts 3–4). This covers the taking over of a ship by its crew or passengers, whether on the high seas or in the territorial sea

---

[249] Oppenheim, Vol.1, p.74.

[250] (2008) 57 I.C.L.Q. 690 at 693. Contrast Passman (2008–9) 33 Tul. M.L.J. 1, 12 ("attacks for public or political motives, including terrorism", excluded).

[251] By a "place outside the jurisdiction of any state", the ILC "had chiefly in mind acts committed ... on an island constituting *terra nullius* or on the shores of an unoccupied territory: Y.B.I.L.C., 1956, II, p.282.

[252] Article 86, as read with art.58(2), 1882 Convention.

[253] Article 101, 1982 Convention. For the warship exception, see art.102.

[254] 4 Whiteman 665. See Franck (1961) 36 N.Y.U.L.R. 839 and Green (1961) 37 B.Y.I.L. 496.

[255] See Green, in Dinstein, ed., *International Law in a Time of Perplexity: Essays in Honour of Shabtai Rosenne* (1989), p.249; Halberstam (1988) 82 A.J.I.L. 269; Paust (1987) 20 Vand. J.T.L. 235; note (1986) 26 Virg. J.I.L. 723.

[256] 1678 U.N.T.S. 221 (1988) 27 I.L.M. 668. In force 1992, 152 parties, including the UK. The Convention was accompanied by a 1988 Protocol for the Suppression of Unlawful Acts against the Safety of Fixed Platforms Located on the Continental Shelf: p.685. In force 1992, 140 parties, including the UK. See Freestone (1988) 3 I.J.E.C.L. 305. The Convention applies to acts committed by persons on ship A against ship B (in which case the law of piracy may also apply if the acts occur on the high seas), as well to the taking of control of ship A by persons on it. Accordingly, it applies to the many armed robberies at sea (but not on the high seas) in the Straits of Malacca between Indonesia and Malaysia (see Beckmann (2002) 33 O.D.I.L. 317) and to Somalian hijackings (see below).

(except where the ship is navigating just from one port to another within the same state's territorial sea), and terrorist and other political, as well as private, acts. State parties must establish jurisdiction over Convention offences and consider prosecution or extradition of offenders found on their territory.

The powers of arrest, etc. that all states have on the high seas in respect of pirate ships and the powers then of their courts to impose penalties on the offenders and to dispose of the pirate ship and the ship seized are indicated in arts.105–107, 1982 Convention.[257]

The precise role of piracy *jure gentium* is also uncertain. According to one view, piracy is a crime under international law in respect of which all states are allowed jurisdiction.[258] According to another view, there is no international crime of piracy; instead international law authorises states to exercise criminal jurisdiction under their municipal law on a universality basis in respect of acts which come within the definition of *piracy jure gentium*.[259]

Piracy still occurs, with piracy *off the coast of Somalia* presenting the international community with a considerable problem,[260] particularly in the absence of an effective government in that state. In 2008, a total of 42 vessels were seized for ransom by Somali pirates on the high seas or in Somali territorial waters and 815 crew taken hostage.[261] Although the seizing of ships for ransom is clearly "for private means", many of the Somalia cases have not involved piracy because they have been committed in Somalia's territorial sea.[262] To assist in tackling the problem, the UN Security Council, acting under Ch.VII, UN Charter has adopted resolutions deciding that states and regional organisations may enter and take action in Somalia's territorial sea in respect of "piracy and armed robbery at sea" and on Somali land territory, with the consent of the Transitional Federal Government ("TFG") of Somalia.[263] In response to the concerns of some states (e.g. Indonesia) that such resolutions should not be regarded as "legislation" changing the 1982 Convention rules on piracy, these resolutions, which are limited in time, are stated to be specific to Somalia and not to establish custom. Resolution 1846 reads:

"The Security Council ...
  Determining that the incidents of piracy and armed robbery against vessels in the territorial waters of Somalia and the high seas off the coast of Somalia exacerbate the situation in Somalia which continues to constitute a threat to international peace and security in the region,
  Acting under Chapter VII of the Charter of the United Nations ...
  10 *Decides* that for a period of 12 months from the date of this resolution States and

---

[257] On the "reasonable force" rule, see below, p.390. An arresting state may agree with another state for that state to prosecute (e.g. Kenya has tried Somali pirates arrested by the US navy).

[258] See, e.g. 2 Moore 951. On universality jurisdiction for piracy, see the two separate opinions in the *Arrest Warrant* case, above, p.250.

[259] See, e.g. Schwarzenberger (1950) 3 C.L.P. 263.

[260] See Guilfoyle (2008) 57 I.C.L.Q. 691; Treves (2009) 20 E.J.I.L. 399; Keyuan (2009) 24 I.J.M.C.L. 583. Piracy also occur off the coast of some West African and Latin American states. See the reports of the ICC International Maritime Bureau Piracy Reporting Centre.

[261] Somalia claims a 200-mile territorial sea. Somalia is a party to the 1982 Convention, which, probably reflecting custom, allows only a 12-mile territorial sea (art.3): see above, p.326. Hijackings more than 12 miles off the Somali coast may constitute piracy. In such cases, the 1988 IMO Convention (see above, n.382) applies; Somalia is not a party.

[262] ICC International Maritime Bureau: Piracy and Armed Robbery against Ships Annual Report 2008, p.26.

[263] See S.C. resns 1816 (2008); 1828 (2008); (1846) (2008); and 1851 (2008). Resolution 1851 was the first to extend the authorisation to Somalia land territory ("all necessary measures that are appropriate in Somalia", at the request of the TFG (para.6)). As to the TFG, see above, p.94. These powers are to be exercised consistently with the right of innocent passage: SC resn 1846 para.6.

regional organizations cooperating with the TFG in the fight against piracy and armed robbery at sea off the coast of Somalia, for which advance notification has been provided by the TFG to the Secretary-General, may:

(a) Enter into the territorial waters of Somalia for the purpose of repressing acts of piracy and armed robbery at sea, in a manner consistent with such action permitted on the high seas with respect to piracy under relevant international law; and

(b) Use, within the territorial waters of Somalia, in a manner consistent with such action permitted on the high seas with respect to piracy under relevant international law, all necessary means to repress acts of piracy and armed robbery at sea;

11. *Affirms* that the authorizations provided in this resolution apply only with respect to the situation in Somalia and shall not affect the rights or obligations or responsibilities of Member States under international law, including any rights or obligations under the Convention with respect to any other situation, and underscores in particular that this resolution shall not be considered as establishing customary international law; and *affirms further* that such authorizations have been provided only following the receipt of the 20 November letter conveying the consent of the TFG; ...

14 *Calls upon* all States, and in particular flag, port and coastal States, States of the nationality of victims and perpetrators of piracy and armed robbery, and other States with relevant jurisdiction under international law and national legislation, to cooperate in determining jurisdiction, and in the investigation and prosecution of persons responsible for acts of piracy and armed robbery off the coast of Somalia, consistent with applicable international law including international human rights law, and to render assistance by, among other actions, providing disposition and logistics assistance with respect to persons under their jurisdiction and control, such victims and witnesses and persons detained as a result of operations conducted under this resolution; ..."

5. *Pirate Radio Stations.*[264] Article 109, 1982 Convention gives wide powers of enforcement jurisdiction over pirate radio stations on the high seas. See also the European Agreement for the Prevention of Broadcasting from Stations outside National Waters 1965[265] which permits the exercise of criminal jurisdiction but does not give a right to visit.

D. The Contiguous Zone[266]

CONVENTION ON THE LAW OF THE SEA 1982

UN Doc. A/CONF. 62/122; (1982) 21 I.L.M. 1261

Article 33

1. In a zone contiguous to its territorial sea, described as the contiguous zone, the coastal State may exercise the control necessary to:

---

[264] See Hunnings (1965) 14 I.C.L.Q. 410; Van Panhuys and Van Emde Boas (1966) 60 A.J.I.L. 303; Woodliffe (1986) 1 I.J.E.C.L. 402.

[265] E.T.S. No. 53; 634 U.N.T.S. 239; (1968) U.K.T.S. 1, Cmnd. 1497. In force 1967, 18 parties, including the UK.

[266] See Fitzmaurice, above, n.9, above, p.108; Lowe (1981) 52 B.Y.I.L. 109; Oda (1962) 11 I.C.L.Q. 131.

(a) prevent infringement of its customs, fiscal, immigration or sanitary laws and regulations within its territory or territorial sea;

(b) punish infringement of the above laws and regulations committed within its territory or territorial sea.

2. The contiguous zone may not extend beyond 24 nautical miles from the baselines from which the breadth of the territorial sea is measured.

Notes

1. The 1982 Convention (art.33) retains the contiguous zone and gives coastal states the same powers as they have under art.24, 1958 Territorial Sea Convention, except that the contiguous zone can be used to control traffic in archeological and historical objects found at sea by virtue of art.303(2), 1982 Convention:

> "In order to control traffic in such objects, the coastal state may, in applying article 33, presume that their removal from the sea-bed in the zone referred to in that article without its approval would result in an infringement within its territory or territorial sea of the laws and regulations referred to in that article."

The zone may, however, extend to 24 miles from the territorial sea baseline, instead of 12 miles which is the 1958 Convention limit. In the 12 miles beyond the limit of a 12 miles territorial sea, therefore, a coastal state may exercise powers that are additional to those (applying to different kinds of activities) that exist under the exclusive economic zone régime in the 1982 Convention.[267]

2. The International Law Commission's Commentary on its Draft Articles reads:

> "(1) International law accords States the right to exercise preventative or protective control for certain purposes over a belt of the high seas contiguous to their territorial sea. It is of course, understood that this power of control does not change the legal status of the waters over which it is exercised. These waters are and remain a part of the high seas and are not subject to the sovereignty of the coastal State, which can exercise over them only such rights as are conferred on it by the present draft or are derived from international treaties.
>
> (2) Many States have adopted the principle that in the contiguous zone the coastal State may exercise customs control in order to prevent attempted infringements of its customs and fiscal regulations within its territory or territorial sea, and to punish infringements of those regulations committed within its territory or territorial sea. The Commission considered that it would be impossible to deny to States the exercise of such rights.
>
> (3) Although the number of States which claim rights over the contiguous zone for the purpose of applying sanitary regulations is fairly small, the Commission considers that, in view of the connexion between customs and sanitary regulations, such rights should also be recognised for sanitary regulations.
>
> (4) The Commission did not recognise special security rights in the contiguous zone. It considered that the extreme vagueness of the term "security" would open the way for abuses and that the granting of such rights was not necessary. The enforcement of customs and sanitary regulations will be sufficient in most cases to safeguard the security of the State. In so

---

[267] See below, p.391. The contiguous zone and the exclusive economic zone physically overlap.

far as measures of self-defence against an imminent and direct threat to the security of the State are concerned, the Commission refers to the general principles of international law and the Charter of the United Nations.

(5) Nor was the Commission willing to recognise any exclusive rights of the coastal State to engage in fishing in the contiguous zone. The Preparatory Committee of the Hague Codification Conference found, in 1930, that the replies from Governments offered no prospect of an agreement to extend the exclusive fishing rights of the coastal State beyond the territorial sea. The Commission considered that in that respect the position has not changed."[268]

A proposal at Geneva to add "and violations of security" to art.24(1)(a), 1958 Convention was defeated.[269] A number of states have nonetheless established security zones; these have met with protest by the US.[270] On the right of self-defence, see below. Note in this connection the practice of some states of having an aircraft carrier or other warship stationed offshore on the high seas as a "reminder" to a coastal state of its interest in events taking place within it. On the use of spy ships, see n.4, below. The reference to immigration regulations was added at Geneva. The International Law Commission had thought it unsupported by state practice and otherwise undesirable.[271] It also thought that the reference to sanitary regulations would cover immigration so far as the latter related to questions of public health.[272]

In *U.S. v Fishing Vessel Taiyo Maru No.28*,[273] in which a Japanese ship was found fishing illegally in the United States exclusive fishing zone nine miles offshore and beyond the United States territorial sea limit, it was held that the list of purposes in art.24 for which a contiguous zone may be established is not exhaustive[274]:

"Article 24 ... is permissive, rather than restrictive. It provides that a coastal state 'may' establish a contiguous zone for the purposes of enforcing its customs, fiscal, immigration or sanitary regulations. Although Article 24 only affirmatively recognises the right of a coastal state to create a contiguous zone for one of the four enumerated purposes, nothing in the Article precludes the establishment of such a zone for other purposes, including the enforcement of domestic fisheries law."

3.   Article 33(1)(b), which gives enforcement jurisdiction to the coastal state after an offence has been committed in its territory or territorial sea, clearly must be read as giving a power of arrest. Does art.33(1)(a), which applies before an offence is committed, do so too? Shearer states[275]:

"Since laws on the substantive subjects of customs, fiscal, immigration and sanitary matters cannot be applied to the contiguous zone, it follows that an offence cannot be committed until the boundary of territorial waters is crossed by inward-bound ships. 'Control' therefore must be limited to such measures as inspections and warnings, and cannot include arrest or forcible taking into port. It is arguable, however, and probably sustainable on the history of the British

---

[268] Y.B.I.L.C., 1956, II, pp.294–295.
[269] *1958 Sea Conference Records*, Vol.II, p.40. See also p.117.
[270] See Churchill and Lowe, above, p.381, n.1, p.138
[271] Y.B.I.L.C. 1956, II, pp.76–78.
[272] Y.B.I.L.C. 1956, II, pp.76–78.
[273] 395 F.Supp.413 (D.Me. 1975). See Fidell (1976) 70 A.J.I.L. 95.
[274] 395 F.Supp.419.
[275] (1986) 35 I.C.L.Q. 320 at 330. For other views, see Fitzmaurice, above, n.9, pp.113–115; and McDougal and Burke, above, n.1, pp.621–630.

Hovering Acts and similar legislation elsewhere, that a coastal State might lawfully legislate to make it an offence to hover or to trans-ship dutiable cargoes in the contiguous zone and to carry out an arrest there because these activities are within the connotations of 'prevention.' "[276]

Although the wording of art.33 is framed in terms of enforcement jurisdiction, some states have claimed legislative jurisdiction also, apparently without protest by other states.[277]

4. On January 23, 1968, the *Pueblo*, a U.S. "Navy intelligence collection auxiliary ship," was ordered to heave to by North Korean patrol ships off the coast of North Korea.[278] It was boarded and escorted into Wonsan. In December 1968, the crew of the *Pueblo* were returned to the US after detention without trial and after the US had signed a document indicating that the *Pueblo* had been spying in North Korean territorial waters.[279] The body of the crew member who had died after being injured in the struggle during the capture of the *Pueblo* was also returned. Earlier, in February 1968, Secretary of State Rusk had sent this telegram to all U.S. diplomatic posts:

"The ship was seized slightly more than 15 miles from the nearest land, Ung Do Island, which lies slightly seaward of a straight line across the mouth of Wonsan Bay. The geographic situation of Wonsan Bay is such as to warrant treating the bay as internal waters. The outer limits of the territorial waters would, therefore, be measured from a straight line across the mouth of Wonsan Bay or from Ung Do Island, to the extent measurement from the island increases the area within the territorial sea. ...

The United States Government has no official information concerning breadth of territorial sea claimed by North Korea, but we assume it claims 12 miles in line with claims of most other communist countries and in view of the position it took in the 1953 armistice talks. ...

The *Pueblo* was a commissioned vessel of the United States Navy and therefore entitled to the immunities recognised by article eight of the 1958 convention on the high seas.[280] Absolute immunity from any jurisdiction other than that of the flag state is, of course, the traditional rule of international law, and the fact that North Korea is not a party to the 1958 convention is irrelevant.

The United States Government recognises only the three-mile limit, North Korea has never alleged that the *Pueblo* was within three miles of the North Korean coast. Thus from the United States view of international law even if the Pueblo had been at the position alleged by North Korea (7.1 miles offshore), it would still have been on the high seas. Nonetheless, the Pueblo was under orders to stay at least 13 miles from North Korea, i.e. at least one mile beyond waters presumably claimed by North Korea.

Even if the *Pueblo* had been in the territorial waters of North Korea, its seizure would have been improper. On numerous occasions similar Soviet ships have intruded into United States territorial waters; we have warned them to leave and, when appropriate, have submitted protest through diplomatic channels. In the absence of immediate threat of armed attack (the *Pueblo* was armed with only two machine guns), escorting foreign naval vessels out of territorial waters is the strongest action a coastal state should take. The seizure of foreign war ships or other attacks upon them are much too dangerous and provocative acts to be per-

---

[276] O'Connell, above, n.1, Vol.II, at p.1060.
[277] See Churchill and Lowe, above, p.381, n.1, p.138.
[278] For the facts, see *Keesings Archives*, p.23120A. See also Butler (1969) 63 Proc.A.S.I.L. 7; and Rubin (1969) 18 I.C.L.Q. 961.
[279] See (1969) 8 I.L.M. 199. This admission was later retracted.
[280] Ed. On art.8, see above, p.333.

mitted by international law. This restriction on the use of force by a coastal state is set forth in article 23 of the 1958 convention on the territorial sea, which authorises, as the sole remedy, requiring a war ship to leave the territorial sea."[281]

Had North Korea violated international law? Has the US?

5. In 2008, 77 states claimed 24-miles contiguous zones; another six states claimed zones less than 24 miles in width.[282] The UK does not claim a contiguous zone. Would the exercise of any powers justified by art.33 be regarded as lawful by a British court with UK legislation?[283]

E. Hot Pursuit[284]

CONVENTION ON THE LAW OF THE SEA 1982

UN Doc. A/CONF. 62/122; (1982) 21 I.L.M. 1261

Article 111

1. The hot pursuit of a foreign ship may be undertaken when the competent authorities of the coastal State have good reason to believe that the ship has violated the laws and regulations of that State. Such pursuit must be commenced when the foreign ship or one of its boats is within the internal waters, the archipelagic waters, the territorial sea or the contiguous zone of the pursuing State, and may only be continued outside the territorial sea or the contiguous zone if the pursuit has not been interrupted. It is not necessary that, at the time when the foreign ship within the territorial sea or the contiguous zone receives the order to stop, the ship giving the order should likewise be within the territorial sea or the contiguous zone. If the foreign ship is within a contiguous zone, as defined in Article 33, the pursuit may only be undertaken if there has been a violation of the rights for the protection of which the zone was established.

2. The right of hot pursuit shall apply *mutatis mutandis* to violations in the exclusive economic zone or on the continental shelf, including safety zones around continental shelf installations, of the laws and regulations of the coastal State applicable in accordance with this Convention to the exclusive economic zone or the continental shelf, including such safety zones.

3. The right of hot pursuit ceases as soon as the ship pursued enters the territorial sea of its own State or of a third State.

4. Hot pursuit is not deemed to have begun unless the pursuing ship has satisfied itself by such practicable means as may be available that the ship pursued or one of its boats or other craft working as a team and using the ship pursued as a mother ship is within the limits of the territorial sea, or, as the case may be, within the contiguous zone or the exclusive economic zone or above the continental shelf. The pursuit may only be commenced after a visual or auditory signal to stop has been given at a distance which enables it to be seen or heard by the foreign ship.

5. The right of hot pursuit may be exercised only by warships or military aircraft, or other ships or aircraft clearly marked and identifiable as being on government service and authorized to that effect.

6. Where hot pursuit is effected by an aircraft:

(a) the provisions of paragraphs 1 to 4 shall apply *mutatis mutandis*;

(b) the aircraft giving the order to stop must itself actively pursue the ship until a ship or another aircraft of the coastal State, summoned by the aircraft, arrives to take over the pursuit, unless the aircraft is itself

---

[281] (1968) 62 A.J.I.L. 756.
[282] *UN Law of the Sea Bulletin*, No.67 (2008).
[283] See *R. v Keyn*, above, p.66.
[284] See Allen (1989) 20 O.D.I.L. 309; Poulantzas, *The Right of Hot Pursuit in International Law* (2nd edn 2002); and Williams (1939) 20 B.Y.I.L. 83.

able to arrest the ship. It does not suffice to justify an arrest outside the territorial sea that the ship was merely sighted by the aircraft as an offender or suspected offender, if it was not both ordered to stop and pursued by the aircraft itself or other aircraft or ships which continue the pursuit without interruption.

7. The release of a ship arrested within the jurisdiction of a State and escorted to a port of that State for the purposes of an inquiry before the competent authorities may not be claimed solely on the ground that the ship, in the course of its voyage, was escorted across a portion of the exclusive economic zone or the high seas, if the circumstances rendered this necessary.

8. Where a ship has been stopped or arrested outside the territorial sea in circumstances which do not justify the exercise of the right of hot pursuit, it shall be compensated for any loss or damage that may have been thereby sustained.

Notes

1. The 1982 Convention repeats art.23, High Seas Convention with alterations to allow for the right of hot pursuit in cases of violations of the coastal state's law and regulations applicable to the exclusive economic zone or continental shelf where the violations occur in or on those places (art.111(2)).[285] It also permits hot pursuit where the ship is in archipelagic waters (art.111(1)). In the 1982 Convention, "other ships or aircraft" in government service must be "clearly marked and identifiable" as such, as well as "authorised", to exercise the right of hot pursuit.

2. Does "ship" in art.111(1) include warships?[286] Can the hot pursuit of a ship be undertaken under the Convention when the violation of the local law has occurred not in the current passage but on some previous one? Can it be undertaken under the Convention where a violation is not by the ship but by a crew member or passenger on board?

3. In US v Fishing Vessel Taiyo Maru No.28,[287] a Japanese ship found fishing illegally nine miles offshore in the US exclusive fishing zone was pursued by United States coastguard vessels and seized some 68 miles off land on the high seas. The Court held that "neither the language nor the history of the [1958] Conventions shows that the signatory parties intended to limit the right of a coastal state to … conduct hot pursuit from … [an exclusive fishing] zone." This decision must apply equally to hot pursuit from an EEZ. For those states, like the United Kingdom, that have an EFZ but not an EEZ, the above case remains directly relevant.

4. The art.23(3) 1958 High Seas Convention requirement, now in art.111(4), 1982 Convention, that hot pursuit only commences once "a visual or auditory signal" was interpreted so as to allow a radio communication to be sufficient in R v Mills,[288] and this may now be sufficient in customary international law. Devonshire J. stated:

"It is clear from Poulantzas at 204 that both the Hague Codification Conference of 1930 and the Geneva Conference of 1958 accepted that signals by radio should not be regarded as lawful for the commencement of the pursuit. It was thought that this exclusions was justified to prevent abuse from radio signals sent from a considerable distance. …
      Craig Allen said[289]:

'… Most modern publicists agree that enforcing craft should be permitted to give the initial signal by radio, even before the pursuing vessel comes within sight. Where it is clear by the

---

[285] See the Saiga case, above, p.369.
[286] See art.95, 1982 Convention, above, p.377.
[287] See above, p.386. See Sisco (1977) 14 San Diego L.R. 656.
[288] (1995), QBD, unreported. See Gilmore (1995) 44 I.C.L.Q. 949.
[289] Ed. (1989) 20 O.D.I.L. 309.

offending vessel's acknowledgement or otherwise that the vessel received and understood a signal to stop given by radio, such a signal meets the underlying policy goal of providing adequate notice to the vessel.'

Modern technology has moved on since 1958 and the law must take account of those changes. Mr Montalto told me that VHF radio is now the standard method of communication between vessels at sea which are required by International Radio Regulations to keep a watch on Channel 16. I hold that messages sent by this medium comply with the pre-conditions of the Convention to the exercise of the right of hot pursuit."

5. The pursuit does not have to commence immediately the ship enters the territorial sea or other jurisdictional zone (see art.111(4)); it may be delayed to ensure that an offence has been committed or because of sea conditions: *R v Mills*, above.

6. Neither the 1958 High Seas Convention nor the 1982 Convention contains any rule about the use of force to effect arrest, either in the particular context of hot pursuit or generally. The "reasonable and necessary in the circumstances" rule stated in the *Saiga* case, above, p.369, can be taken to state the position in customary international law, both in respect of arrests following hot pursuit and other lawful arrests at sea as well.

In *The Red Crusader Case*,[290] a Danish fisheries inspection vessel arrested a Scottish trawler, *The Red Crusader*, off the Faroes and ordered it to proceed to the Faroes for trial for fishing in an area in which this was prohibited by a Danish–UK treaty. After obeying for a while, *The Red Crusader*, with Danish crew from the fisheries inspection vessel stationed on board, sought to escape. Thereupon, the Danish vessel fired warning shots close to *The Red Crusader* and ordered it to stop. When these warnings were not heeded, *The Red Crusader* was fired upon directly with solid shot and damaged (but not sunk). All of the firing occurred in Faroese territorial waters. In its Report, an Anglo-Danish Commission of Enquiry found:

"In opening fire at 03.22 hours up to 03.53 hours, the Commanding Officer of the *Niels Ebbesen* exceeded legitimate use of armed force on two counts: (a) firing without warning of solid gun-shot; (b) creating danger to human life on board the Red Crusader without proved necessity, by the effective firing at the *Red Crusader* after 03.40 hours.

The escape of the *Red Crusader* in flagrant violation of the order received and obeyed, the seclusion on board the trawler of an officer and rating of the crew of *Niels Ebbesen*, and Skipper Wood's refusal to stop may explain some resentment on the part of Captain Sølling. Those circumstances, however, cannot justify such violent action.

The Commission is of the opinion that other means should have been attempted, which, if duly persisted in, might have finally persuaded Skipper Wood to stop and revert to the normal procedure which he himself had previously followed."

---

[290] (1962) 35 I.L.R. 485. Following the Commission of Enquiry Report, the purpose of which was to establish the facts, a mutual waiver of claims for compensation for trawler damage and of criminal charges was agreed: p.500. See also the *I'm Alone* (1935) 3 R.I.A.A. 1609; (1935) 29 A.J.I.L. 326.

----

4. THE EXCLUSIVE ECONOMIC ZONE[291]

The exclusive economic zone has its roots in the concept of the exclusive fishing zone and the doctrine of the continental shelf. It combines and develops the two. The emergence of the concept of the exclusive fishing zone and its translation into the exclusive economic zone is considered in the following materials. The doctrine of the continental shelf is considered separately below, p.399.

The exclusive fishing zone is a zone of the sea adjacent to a coastal state's territorial sea within which the coastal state has exclusive jurisdiction over fishing. The concept can be traced to the (then) extravagant 200-mile claims of certain Latin American states in the late 1940s to protect whaling and other fishing interests.[292] These were the subject of protest and were not thought to be lawful.[293] Then, as now, such claims were motivated by a genuine concern for conservation (international action not proving effective) as well as other national considerations. A turning point came with the failure of the 1958 Conference on the Law of the Sea and the supplementary 1960 Conference to agree upon a wider territorial sea than the traditional three-mile sea or upon fishing jurisdiction for coastal states beyond their territorial sea.[294] The majority view in 1958 was that, in the absence of agreement to the contrary, fishing beyond the limit of a lawful territorial sea was open to all states in accordance with "freedom of fishing" on the high seas. Unilateral action by Iceland and other states in the years that followed led gradually to an acceptance of a 12-mile[295] exclusive fishing zone,[296] the legality of which was recognised in the *Fisheries Jurisdiction (Merits)* cases.[297] Thereafter, claims became more ambitious so that by 1978, 23 states claimed 200-mile exclusive fishing zones and another 38 claimed exclusive economic zones.[298] Indicative of the speed of events is the fact that the United Kingdom, which had fought a "war" over Iceland's claim to a 200-mile exclusive fishing zone just 12 months previously, claimed its own 200-mile exclusive fishing zone as of 1977.[299] By 2008, the point had been reached where 105 states, from all political groupings, claimed 200-mile exclusive economic zones, without protest from other states.[300]

---

[291] See Attard, *The Exclusive Economic Zone in International Law* (1987); Extavour, *The Exclusive Economic Zone* (2nd edn 1981); Franckx and Gautier, eds, *The Exclusive Economic Zone and the United Nations Law of the Sea Convention 1982–2000* (2003); Kwiatkowska, *The 200 Mile EEZ in the New Law of the Sea* (1989); Orrego Vicuna, *The Exclusive Economic Zone* (1989); Pharand and Leanza, eds., *The Continental Shelf and the Exclusive Economic Zone* (1993); and Smith, *Exclusive Economic Claims: An Analysis and Primary Documents* (1986).

[292] See Hollick (1977) 71 A.J.I.L. 494.

[293] See Kunz (1956) 50 A.J.I.L. 828.

[294] See 4 Whiteman 91–137.

[295] i.e. 12 miles as measured from the same baselines as those used for the territorial sea.

[296] A 1967 survey showed that exclusive fishing zones (mostly for 12 miles) were claimed by 33 states, including the UK (Fishery Limits Act 1964): *Limits and Status of the Territorial Sea, Exclusive Zone, Fisheries Conservation Zones and the Continental Shelf*, FAO Legislative Series No.8, 1969, as revised. Other states had achieved the same result by claiming a 12-mile territorial sea. Most coastal states making such claims allowed other states to fish, permanently or for a phasing-out period, in the areas claimed where they could show that their fishermen had long done so.

[297] I.C.J. Rep.1974, p.3 (*U.K. v Iceland*); p.175 (*F.R.G. v Iceland*). But the ICJ ruled that Iceland's 1971 claim to a 50-mile exclusive fishing zone was illegal.

[298] FAO figures published in *Lay et al*, above, n.15, Vol.X, p.472.

[299] Fishery Limits Act 1976. The Act allows certain states to fish within the 200-mile limit and in accordance with the Fishery Limits Act 1964. These include EC states and the Russian Federation.

[300] *UN Law of the Sea Bulletin*, No.67 (2008).

CONVENTION ON THE LAW OF THE SEA 1982

UN Doc. A/CONF. 62/122; (1982) 21 I.L.M. 1261

Article 55

The exclusive economic zone is an area beyond and adjacent to the territorial sea, subject to the specific legal régime established in this Part [Part V], under which the rights and jurisdiction of the coastal State and the rights and freedoms of other States are governed by the relevant provisions of this Convention.

Article 56

1. In the exclusive economic zone, the coastal State has:

(a) sovereign rights for the purpose of exploring and exploiting, conserving and managing the natural resources, whether living or non-living, of the waters superjacent to the sea-bed and of the sea-bed and subsoil, and with regard to other activities for the economic exploitation and exploration of the zone, such as the production of energy from the water, currents and winds;

(b) jurisdiction as provided for in the relevant provisions of this Convention with regard to:

   (i) the establishment and use of artificial islands, installations and structures;
   (ii) marine scientific research;
   (iii) the protection and preservation of the marine environment;

(c) other rights and duties provided for in this Convention.

2. In exercising its rights and performing its duties under this Convention in the exclusive economic zone, the coastal State shall have due regard to the rights and duties of other States and shall act in a manner compatible with the provisions of this Convention.

3. The rights set out in this article with respect to the sea-bed and subsoil shall be exercised in accordance with Part VI [on the continental shelf].

Article 57

The exclusive economic zone shall not extend beyond 200 nautical miles from the baselines from which the breadth of the territorial sea is measured.

Article 58

1. In the exclusive economic zone, all States, whether coastal or landlocked, enjoy, subject to the relevant provisions of this Convention, the freedoms referred to in article 87[301] of navigation and overflight and of the laying of submarine cables and pipelines, and other internationally lawful uses of the sea related to these freedoms, such as those associated with the operation of ships, aircraft and submarine cables and pipelines, and compatible with the other provisions of this Convention.[302]

2. Article 88 to 115 and other pertinent rules of international law apply to the exclusive economic zone in so far as they are not incompatible with this Part [Pt V].

3. In exercising their rights and performing their duties under this Convention in the exclusive economic zone, States shall have due regard to the rights and duties of the coastal State and shall comply with the laws and

---

[301] See above, p.363.

[302] Ed. In the *Saiga* case, above, p.369, the International Tribunal for the Law of the Sea declined to rule on the question whether, in the absence of any specific provision in the 1982 Convention, bunkering (i.e. the sale of gas oil to vessels at sea) in the EEZ was an exercise of freedom of navigation, or a related lawful use of the sea.

regulations adopted by the coastal State in accordance with the provisions of this Convention and other rules of international law in so far as they are not incompatible with this Part.[303]

Article 59

In cases where this Convention does not attribute rights or jurisdiction to the coastal State or to other States within the exclusive economic zone, and a conflict arises between the interests of the coastal State and any other State or States, the conflict should be resolved on the basis of equity and in the light of all the relevant circumstances, taking into account the respective importance of the interests involved to the parties as well as to the international community as a whole.

Article 60

1. In the exclusive economic zone, the coastal State shall have the exclusive right to construct and to authorise and regulate the construction, operation and use of:

(*a*) artificial islands;

(*b*) installations and structures for the purposes provided for in article 56 and other economic purposes;

(*c*) installations and structures which may interfere with the exercise of the rights of the coastal State in the zone.

2. The coastal State shall have exclusive jurisdiction over such artificial islands, installations and structures, including jurisdiction with regard to customs, fiscal, health, safety and immigration laws and regulations. . . .
7. Artificial islands, installations and structures and the safety zones around them may not be established where interference may be caused to the use of recognised sea lanes essential to international navigation.
8. Artificial islands, installations and structures do not possess the status of islands. They have no territorial sea of their own, and their presence does not affect the delimitation of the territorial sea, the exclusive economic zone or the continental shelf.

Article 61

1. The coastal State shall determine the allowable catch of the living resources in its exclusive economic zone.
2. The coastal State, taking into account the best scientific evidence available to it, shall ensure through proper conservation and management measures that the maintenance of the living resources in the exclusive economic zone is not endangered by over-exploitation. As appropriate, the coastal State and competent international organisations, whether subregional, regional, or global, shall co-operate to this end.
3. Such measures shall also be designed to maintain or restore populations of harvested species at levels which can produce the maximum sustainable yield, as qualified by relevant environmental and economic factors, including the economic needs of coastal fishing communities and the special requirements of developing states, and taking into account fishing patterns, the interdependence of stocks and any generally recommended international minimum standards, whether subregional, regional or global. . . .

Article 62

1. The coastal State shall promote the objective of optimum utilisation of the living resources in the exclusive economic zone without prejudice to Article 61.
2. The coastal State shall determine its capacity to harvest the living resources of the exclusive economic zone. Where the coastal State does not have the capacity to harvest the entire allowable catch, it shall, through agreements or other arrangements and pursuant to the terms, conditions, laws and regulations referred to in

---

[303] The 1982 Convention does not require notification of presence in the EEZ by a foreign fishing vessel. For a French legal requirement to this effect, see the *Camouco* case (*Panama v France*) (2000) *www.itlos.org* (judgments), discussed in Oxman and Bantz (2000) 94 A.J.I.L. 713.

paragraph 4, give other States access to the surplus of the allowable catch, having particular regard to the provisions of Articles 69 and 70,[304] especially in relation to the developing states mentioned therein.

3. In giving access to other States to its exclusive economic zone under this article, the coastal State shall take into account all relevant factors, including, inter alia, the significance of the living resources of the area to the economy of the coastal State concerned and its other national interests, the provisions of Articles 69 and 70, the requirements of developing countries in the subregion or region in harvesting part of the surplus and the need to minimise economic dislocation in States whose nationals have habitually fished in the zone or which have made substantial efforts in research and identification of stocks.

4. Nationals of other States fishing in the exclusive economic zone shall comply with the conservation measures and with the other terms and conditions established in the regulations of the coastal State. ...

Articles 64–67 make special provision for highly migratory species (e.g. tuna, swordfish), marine mammals (e.g. whales, seals), anadromous stocks (e.g. salmon), and catadromous species (e.g. eels)

Article 68

This Part [arts 55–75] does not apply to sedentary species as defined in Article 77, paragraph 4.

Article 73

1. The coastal State may, in the exercise of its sovereign rights to explore, exploit, conserve and manage the living resources in the exclusive economic zone, take such measures, including boarding, inspection, arrest and judicial proceedings, as may be necessary to ensure compliance with the laws and regulations adopted by it in conformity with this Convention.

2. Arrested vessels and their crews shall be promptly released upon the posting of reasonable bond or other security.

3. Coastal State penalties for violations of fisheries laws and regulations in the exclusive economic zone may not include imprisonment, in the absence of agreements to the contrary by the States concerned, or any other form of corporal punishment.

4. In cases of arrest or detention of foreign vessels the coastal State shall promptly notify the flag State, through appropriate channels, of the action taken and of any penalties subsequently imposed.

Article 74

1. The delimitation of the exclusive economic zone between States with opposite or adjacent coasts shall be effected by agreement on the basis of international law, as referred to in Article 38 of the Statute of the International Court of Justice, in order to achieve an equitable solution.

2. If no agreement can be reached within a reasonable period of time, the States concerned shall resort to the procedures provided for in Part XV [on the settlement of disputes].[305]

3. Pending agreement as provided for in paragraph 1, the States concerned, in a spirit of understanding and co-operation, shall make every effort to enter into provisional arrangements of a practical nature and, during this transitional period, not to jeopardise or hamper the reaching of the final agreement. Such arrangements shall be without prejudice to the final delimitation. ...

Notes

1.   It is clear that the international community allows coastal states a 200–mile exclusive economic zone. A consensus to this effect quickly emerged at UNCLOS III and provision is accordingly

---

[304] Ed. On the rights of land-locked states and states "with special geographical characteristics" (who together constituted about one-third of the states at UNCLOS III). The latter are defined in 1982 Convention, art.70(2).

[305] See below, p.414. For the approach adopted by international courts and tribunals in resolving maritime boundary disputes in the absence of agreement, see below, p.405.

made for such a zone in the 1982 Convention. In the *Continental Shelf (Libya v Malta)* case,[306] the International Court of Justice observed that "the institution of the exclusive economic zone ... is shown by the practice of states to have become part of customary law." What is not clear is whether the whole of the 1982 Convention régime on the exclusive economic zone may be considered as custom or only parts of it.[307] Churchill and Lowe,[308] after concluding that a state may claim a 200–mile exclusive economic zone, state:

> "What is much less certain is whether the coastal State's fishery management duties set out in articles 61 and 62 have become part of customary law. Relatively few States' national legislation refers to these duties. This may be, not because the duties are not accepted, but because these duties are not considered as an appropriate matter for legislation, since they relate to administrative practices. On the other hand, the duties may be too vague and insufficiently of a 'norm-creating character' to pass into customary law."

2. The 1982 Convention intentionally refrains from describing the exclusive economic zone as a part of the high seas. The zone is treated instead as an intermediate area of sea between the high seas and the territorial sea with a distinct régime of its own. This régime accords the coastal state (i) sovereign rights of exploitation of zone resources and (ii) ancillary and other powers of exclusive jurisdiction, notably in respect of marine research and the control of pollution (1982 Convention, art.56). Although the position of the coastal state in an area previously regarded as being fully subject to the "freedom of the high seas" is thus greatly strengthened, it falls far short of sovereignty. In particular, states generally may continue to exercise within the zone freedom of navigation and overflight and other freedoms[309] not covered by art.56, 1982 Convention that form part of the established concept of "freedom of the high seas" (art.58). To this large extent, the 1982 Convention does not revert to Selden's idea of the closed sea in respect of the zone.[310] Foreign ships in passage are, however, subject to the coastal state's enforcement jurisdiction in respect of illegal fishing (art.73) and the control of pollution (art.220). An unresolved question is whether foreign warships, which enjoy freedom of navigation through the exclusive economic zone, may conduct naval exercises therein, as they can on the high seas.[311] Several states[312] made declarations when signing the 1982 Convention to the effect that such exercises were not permitted by it. A number of other uses of the economic zone are not regulated by the 1982

---

[306] I.C.J. Rep. 1985, p.13 at 33. Earlier in the *Continental Shelf (Tunisia v Libya)* case, I.C.J. Rep. 1982, p.18 at p.74, the Court had stated that the zone "may be regarded as part of modern international law." cf. the *Gulf of Maine* case, extract above, p.324.

[307] cf. the distinction drawn in the *North Sea Continental Shelf* cases, above, p.21, between arts 1 and 2 and art.6, Continental Shelf Convention.

[308] See above, n.1, p.291.

[309] See those listed in art.87, 1982 Convention, above, p.363. On freedom of navigation in the EEZ, see Burke (1983) 20 San Diego L.R. 595; and Robertson (1984) 24 Virg. J.I.L. 865.

[310] See Ganz, above, n.14, p.53. Selden was a 17th-century English lawyer who argued unsuccessfully that the seas might be subjected to territorial sovereignty. The opposing view of Grotius, propounded when the Netherlands was the dominant maritime power, prevailed.

[311] The UNCLOS III President (Mr Koh) has stated that there was a general understanding at UNCLOS III that military activities in the EEZ would not require coastal state permission: in Van Dyke, ed., *Consensus and Confrontation: the U.S. and the Law of the Sea Convention* (1985), pp.303–304.

[312] Brazil, Cape Verde, Uruguay: UN Doc. ST/LEG/SER. E/15, pp.822, et seq. Italy made a contrary declaration. Cape Verde and Uruguay stated that naval exercises are "non-peaceful" uses of the EEZ which are prohibited without the coastal state's consent. Note (i) that although there is no express prohibition of "non-peaceful" uses of the EEZ, there is such a prohibition in respect of the high seas (art.87), and presumably therefore an implied one in respect of the EEZ, but (ii) that naval exercises on the high seas are thought to be lawful: see above, p.364.

Convention. Examples given by Churchill and Lowe[313] are "the emplacement of underwater listening devices for submarines ... the recovery of historic wrecks beyond the contiguous zone ... and jurisdiction over buoys used for pure scientific research." In the case of such unregulated uses, any conflict between a coastal and other state "should be resolved on the basis of equity," etc. (art.59).

3. Well over 90 per cent of the world's annual catch of fish is harvested within 200 miles of land.[314] Accordingly, the exclusive fishing rights given to the coastal state in the EEZ by art.56 are economically very valuable.[315] The obligations placed upon the coastal state to conserve fisheries (art.61) are matched by rights of exploitation that make little concession to the interests of other states. The coastal state is entitled under art.62 to reserve all of the allowable catch for its fishermen if they are capable of exploiting it. The access of fishermen of other states, including landlocked and geographically disadvantaged states (art.69), to the surplus (art.62(3)) depends on "agreements or other arrangements" (art.62(2)). Disputes concerning a coastal state's rights over fisheries within its exclusive economic zone are not subject to compulsory arbitration or adjudication; *extreme* cases are subject to compulsory but non-binding conciliation (art.297(3)). The consequent absence of binding, third-party procedures makes it difficult to enforce conservation and other limitations on a coastal state's fishing rights.[316] Note also its wide powers of enforcement jurisdiction (boarding, arrest, etc.) over foreign ships suspected of illegal fishing (art.73).

4. The coastal state's rights to exploit continental shelf (i.e. sea-bed and subsoil) resources in its exclusive economic zone are exercised in accordance with the separate régime for the continental shelf in Pt VI (arts 76–85) of the 1982 Convention, below, p.400.[317] Some of the rules in Pt VI are identical to those in the exclusive economic zone régime in Pt V.[318] But the exploitation of shelf resources, including sedentary species (see art.68), within the 200–mile limit is not subject to the conservation and sharing restrictions that apply under the exclusive economic zone régime (arts 61–62) applicable to fish.

5. *Prompt release of arrested vessels.* Ships and their crews that are arrested under art.73(1) must be "promptly released upon the posting of reasonable bond or security" (art.73(2)). In the *Monte Confurco* case (*Seychelles v France*),[319] the International Tribunal for the Law of the Sea summarised the meaning of "reasonable" developed in its jurisprudence as follows:

> "76. In the *"Camouco"* Case,[320] the Tribunal specified the factors relevant in an assessment of the reasonableness of bonds or other financial security as follows:

---

[313] See above, n.1, pp.175–6.

[314] Gulland (1979) 22 *Oceanus* 36.

[315] On the EEZ fishing regime generally, see Burke (1984) 63 Oregon L.R. 73; Dahmani, *The Fisheries Régime of the Exclusive Economic Zone* (1987); Ulfstein (1983) 52 N.T.I.R. 3.

[316] Before the EEZ evolved, the standard medium for fisheries conservation was the international fisheries commission (e.g. the North Atlantic Salmon Conservation Organisation). The limitations of such commissions are that states are generally unwilling to give them sufficient legislative or enforcement powers. The problem with reliance upon coastal states for conservation is that fish move inconveniently from one maritime zone to another and that not all states take their obligations to control fishermen seriously. See Juda (1987) 18 O.D.I.L. 305.

[317] See art.56(3), 1982 Convention. Although inelegantly drafted, a separate continental shelf régime was necessary to provide for (i) states that have a continental shelf but not an exclusive economic zone and (ii) states with a continental shelf beyond the 200–mile limit of the exclusive economic zone. The UK is an example of both kinds of states.

[318] The same rules apply in respect of artificial structures, etc. (arts 60 and 80), the delimitation of boundaries (arts 74 and 83) and the publishing of charts (arts 75 and 84).

[319] (2002) www.itlos.org (judgments).

[320] Ed. (2000) ibid.

'The Tribunal considers that a number of factors are relevant in an assessment of the reasonableness of bonds or other financial security. They include the gravity of the alleged offences, the penalties imposed or imposable under the laws of the detaining State, the value of the detained vessel and of the cargo seized, the amount of the bond imposed by the detaining State and its form. (Judgment of 7 February 2000, paragraph 67).'

This is by no means a complete list of factors. Nor does the Tribunal intend to lay down rigid rules as to the exact weight to be attached to each of them. These factors complement the criterion of reasonableness specified by the Tribunal in the *M/V "SAIGA" Case*[321] as follows:

'In the view of the Tribunal, the criterion of reasonableness encompasses the amount, the nature and the form of the bond or financial security. The overall balance of the amount, form and nature of the bond or financial security must be reasonable. (Judgment of 4 December 1997, paragraph 82).'"

6. *Exclusive Fishing Zones*. In 2002, four states, including the United Kingdom, claimed 200–mile exclusive fishing zones, but not exclusive economic zones.[322] Such EFZ claims, although much wider than the 12 miles EFZ's recognised as valid in the *Fisheries Jurisdiction* Cases *(Merits)*[323] in 1974, have not met with protest and are clearly permissible in customary international law. If a 200-mile exclusive economic zone is lawful, then *a fortiori* an equivalent fishing zone is lawful too. However, it is not clear precisely what this entails. Whereas there is in the 1982 Convention a detailed régime in respect of conservation, access to fisheries, enforcement jurisdiction, etc. in respect of fishing within the exclusive economic zone, the 1982 Convention has no separate régime in respect of exclusive fishing zones that could apply to parties to the Convention as treaty rules or to states generally as custom. It would be surprising, however, if the same regime did not apply as a matter of custom to fishing in the same waters, whether the waters were classified as an exclusive economic or fishing zone.

The United Kingdom, now a party to the 1982 Convention, explained its decision not to replace its EFZ and continental shelf (within its first 200 miles) by an EEZ as follows[324]:

"We see no point at present in creating one in order to secure resources. The United Kingdom already has a fishery zone extending to a maximum of 200 nautical miles and, since rights over our continental shelf (which extends well beyond 200 miles) are inherent and do not have to be proclaimed, there would be no advantage to the United Kingdom in declaring such a zone."

An exclusive economic zone does, nonetheless, bring with it certain other benefits, particularly (i) art.56 jurisdiction in respect of marine research and pollution control and (ii) clearly defined enforcement jurisdiction in respect of illegal fishing (art.73). Such a zone might, however, also bring additional conservation and "access to foreign fishermen" obligations, unless the rules in arts 61 and 62 come to be accepted as applicable equally to EEZs and EFZs.

7. *Islands*. The 1982 Convention (art.121(3)) provides that an island may have an exclusive economic zone or a continental shelf with the following exceptions: "Rocks which cannot sustain human

---

[321] Ed. See above, p.369.
[322] *UN Law of the Sea Bulletin*, No.67 (2008).
[323] See above, p.391.
[324] *Hansard*, HL Vol.473, col.46 (April 7, 1986).

habitation or economic life of their own shall have no exclusive economic zone or continental shelf."[325] In the *Jan Mayen* case,[326] the Conciliation Commission stated that art.121 "reflects the present status of international law." The meaning of "economic life" is obscure. An island such as Rockall[327] would not qualify for an exclusive economic zone under art.121(3).[328] Such an island close to the mainland may, however, be taken into account when drawing baselines for an exclusive economic zone or continental shelf.[329] France has declared a 200-mile EEZ around Clipperton Island.[330]

8. The EEZ régime was seen as one of the vehicles in the 1982 Convention for achieving a new international economic order that would redress the economic balance in the interest of developing states.[331] According to Wijkman,[332] however, it is unlikely to have this result. Writing in 1982, he states:

"The draft Convention would redistribute income from long distance fishing fleets and other foreign fishermen to those states with long coasts bordering on rich fishing grounds. The richest fishing grounds, like the richest countries, are located in the temperate zones, and three-quarters of the world catch is taken from waters off the developed countries. ... About one-third of the catch in developing countries' waters is taken by non-local fishermen, and these are largely from developed countries.

... a total of at least 1.2 billion dollars annually is to be redistributed to coastal states, and of this the developed countries would enjoy the major part. Developing coastal countries do gain somewhat at the expense of the developed. The major losers are long-distance fishing fleets and those fishermen who historically have fished in waters that now are declared 'foreign.'

Whether this redistribution of income is fair is a matter of opinion. Coastal countries claim ownership of the fishing stocks by right of proximity. Less fortunately located nations stress that this resource, too, should be part of the common heritage in which they have a share. Undeniably, the proposed treaty fails to compensate those fishing nations that lose historical rights, and favours currently rich coastal countries over poor ones, and coastal states over others."

---

[325] Such rocks do have a territorial sea under the 1982 Convention, as under the Territorial Sea Convention, if they come within the definition of an island common to both texts: see above, p.338. See Charney (1999) 93 A.J.I.L. 863.
[326] (1981) 20 I.L.M. 797 at 803.
[327] Rockall is a bare, uninhabitable rock that rises 70 feet out of the North East Atlantic 170 miles from the nearest Scottish island of St Kilda and over 200 miles from Ireland. It was annexed by the UK in 1955 and made a part of Scotland for legal purposes by the Island of Rockall Act 1972. British sovereignty over Rockall is not disputed.
[328] The UK claims a 12-mile territorial sea around Rockall. Upon acceding to the 1982 Convention, the UK withdrew an earlier questionable 200 mile exclusive fishing zone around the island, since "Rockall was not a valid base point for (fishing) ... limits under article 121(3)": U.K.M.I.L. 1997, (1997) 68 B.Y.I.L. 600. This change had "no effect" on the UK continental shelf claim to the west of Scotland, which was formerly justified both because of Rockall and as a natural prolongation of Scotland; it is now based solely on the latter ground: U.K.M.I.L. 1994, (1994) 65 B.Y.I.L. 655. The UK continental shelf claim is disputed by Denmark. Ireland and the UK have agreed on their shelf boundaries: UK-Ireland 1998 Agreement, Cm.535. On the Spratly islands in the South China Sea, which may also be subject to art.121(3), see Gjetnes (2000) 32 O.D.I.L. 190.
[329] See the *Anglo-French Continental Shelf* case (1978) Misc. 15, Cmnd. 7438; (1979) 18 I.L.M. 397, 434: 54 I.L.R. 6 (use of the Eddystone Rocks).
[330] See Van Dyke and Brooks (1983) 12 O.D.I.L. 265. On Clipperton Island, see above, p.171.
[331] See above, p.391.
[332] (1982) 16 J.W.T.L. 27.

5. THE CONTINENTAL SHELF[333]

THE TRUMAN PROCLAMATION ON THE CONTINENTAL SHELF 1945

4 Whiteman 756

Whereas the Government of the United States of America, aware of the long range world-wide need for new sources of petroleum and other minerals, holds the view that efforts to discover and make available new supplies of these resources should be encouraged; and. . . .

Whereas recognised jurisdiction over these resources is required in the interest of their conservation and prudent utilisation when and as development is undertaken; and

Whereas it is the view of the Government of the United States that the exercise of jurisdiction over the natural resources of the subsoil and sea bed of the continental shelf by the contiguous nation is reasonable and just, since the effectiveness of measures to utilise or conserve these resources would be contingent upon cooperation and protection from the shore, since the continental shelf may be regarded as an extension of the land mass of the coastal nation and thus naturally appurtenant to it, since these resources frequently form a seaward extension of a pool or deposit lying within the territory, and since self-protection compels the coastal nation to keep close watch over activities off its shores which are of the nature necessary for utilisation of these resources:

Now therefore, I, Harry S. Truman, President of the United States of America, do hereby proclaim the following policy of the United States of America with respect to the natural resources of the subsoil and sea bed of the continental shelf.

Having concern for the urgency of conserving and prudently utilising its natural resources, the Government of the United States regards the natural resources of the subsoil and sea bed of the continental shelf beneath the high seas but contiguous to the coasts of the United States as appertaining to the United States, subject to its jurisdiction and control. In cases where the continental shelf extends to the shores of another state, or is shared with an adjacent state, the boundary shall be determined by the United States and the state concerned in accordance with equitable principles. The character as high seas of the waters above the continental shelf and the right to their free and unimpeded navigation are in no way thus affected.

Notes

1. The Truman Proclamation, which was the first of its kind, was quickly followed by similar declarations made by other states. By 1945, it had become technically possible to drill for oil and other mineral resources in the seabed from the sea and the Truman Proclamation was aimed at filling a gap in international law on the legal rights and duties of states arising from that possibility.

2. Geomorphologically, the continental shelf is the gently sloping platform of submerged land surrounding the continents and islands. Normally it extends to a depth of approximately 200 metres or 100 fathoms[334] at which point the seabed falls away sharply. In some places it continues beyond a depth of 200 metres. It varies in width from less than five miles (off the coast of California, for example), to 750 miles (below the Barents Sea). The continental shelf west of the United Kingdom has an outer limit at a depth of about 200 metres and extends to about 300 miles off Land's End. Shelves occupy about 7.5 per cent of the total ocean area.

3. The status of the continental shelf doctrine in customary international law was considered by the Arbitrator, Lord Asquith, in the *Abu Dhabi Arbitration* in 1951.[335] In the light of the declarations then in existence, he concluded:

---

[333] Cook and Carleton, eds., *Continental Shelf Limits* (2000).

[334] This was the depth that the US had in mind in the Truman Proclamation.

[335] (1952) 1 I.C.L.Q. 247; (1951) 18 I.L.R. 144. See now, however, the *North Sea Continental Shelf* cases, above, p.21.

"... there are in this field so many ragged ends and unfilled blanks, so much that is merely tentative and exploratory, that in no form can the doctrine claim as yet to have assumed hitherto the hard lineaments or the definitive status of an established rule of international law."

CONVENTION ON THE LAW OF THE SEA 1982

UN Doc. A/CONF. 62/122; (1982) 21 I.L.M. 1261

Article 76

1. The continental shelf of a coastal State comprises the sea-bed and subsoil of the submarine areas that extend beyond its territorial sea throughout the natural prolongation of its land territory to the outer edge of the continental margin, or to a distance of 200 nautical miles from the baselines from which the breadth of the territorial sea is measured where the outer edge of the continental margin does not extend up to that distance.

2. The continental shelf of a coastal State shall not extend beyond the limits provided for in paragraphs 4 to 6.

3. The continental margin comprises the submerged prolongation of the land mass of the coastal State, and consists of the sea-bed and subsoil of the shelf, the slope and the rise. It does not include the deep ocean floor with its oceanic ridges or the subsoil thereof.

4. (a) For the purposes of this Convention, the coastal State shall establish the outer edge of the continental margin wherever the margin extends beyond 200 nautical miles from the baselines from which the breadth of the territorial sea is measured, by either:

(i) a line delineated in accordance with paragraph 7 by reference to the outermost fixed points at each of which the thickness of sedimentary rocks is at least 1 per cent of the shortest distance from such point to the foot of the continental slope; or

(ii) a line delineated in accordance with paragraph 7 by reference to fixed points not more than 60 nautical miles from the foot of the continental slope.

(b) In the absence of evidence to the contrary, the foot of the continental slope shall be determined as the point of maximum change in the gradient at its base.

5. The fixed points comprising the line of the outer limits of the continental shelf on the sea-bed, drawn in accordance with paragraph 4(a)(i) and (ii), either shall not exceed 350 nautical miles from the baselines from which the breadth of the territorial sea is measured or shall not exceed 100 nautical miles from the 2,500 metre isobath, which is a line connecting the depth of 2,500 metres.

6. Notwithstanding the provisions of paragraph 5, on submarine ridges, the outer limit of the continental shelf shall not exceed 350 nautical miles from the baselines from which the breadth of the territorial sea is measured. This paragraph does not apply to submarine elevations that are natural components of the continental margin, such as its plateaux, rises, caps, banks and spurs.

7. The coastal State shall delineate the outer limits of its continental shelf, where that shelf extends beyond 200 nautical miles from the baselines from which the breadth of the territorial sea is measured, by straight lines not exceeding 60 nautical miles in length, connecting fixed points, defined by co-ordinates of latitude and longitude.

8. Information on the limits of the continental shelf beyond 200 nautical miles from the baselines from which the breadth of the territorial sea is measured shall be submitted by the coastal State to the Commission on the Limits of the Continental Shelf set up under Annex II on the basis of equitable geographical representation. The Commission shall make recommendations to coastal States on matters related to the establishment of the outer limits of their continental shelf. The limits of the shelf established by a coastal State on the basis of these recommendations shall be final and binding.

9. The coastal State shall deposit with the Secretary-General of the United Nations charts and relevant information, including geodetic data, permanently describing the outer limits of its continental shelf. The Secretary-General shall give due publicity thereto.

10. The provisions of this article are without prejudice to the question of delimitation of the continental shelf between States with opposite or adjacent coasts.

Article 77

1. The coastal State exercises over the continental shelf sovereign rights for the purpose of exploring it and exploiting its natural resources.

2. The rights referred to in paragraph 1 are exclusive in the sense that if the coastal State does not explore the continental shelf or exploit its natural resources, no one may undertake these activities without the express consent of the coastal State.

3. The rights of the coastal State over the continental shelf do not depend on occupation, effective or notional, or on any express proclamation.

4. The natural resources referred to in this Part consist of the mineral and other non-living resources of the sea-bed and subsoil together with living organisms belonging to sedentary species, that is to say, organisms which, at the harvestable stage, either are immobile on or under the sea-bed or are unable to move except in constant physical contact with the sea-bed or the subsoil.

Article 78

1. The rights of the coastal State over the continental shelf do not affect the legal status of the superjacent waters or of the air space above those waters.

2. The exercise of the rights of the coastal State over the continental shelf must not infringe or result in any unjustifiable interference with navigation and other rights and freedoms of other States as provided for in this Convention.

Article 79

1. All States are entitled to lay submarine cables and pipelines on the continental shelf, in accordance with the provisions of this article.

2. Subject to its right to take reasonable measures for the exploration of the continental shelf, the exploitation of its natural resources and the prevention, reduction and control of pollution from pipelines, the coastal State may not impede the laying or maintenance of such cables or pipelines.

3. The delineation of the course for the laying of such pipelines on the continental shelf is subject to the consent of the coastal State.

4. Nothing in this Part affects the right of the coastal State to establish conditions for cables or pipelines entering its territory or territorial sea, or its jurisdiction over cables and pipelines constructed or used in connection with the exploration of its continental shelf or exploitation of its resources or the operations of artificial islands, installations and structures under its jurisdiction.

5. When laying submarine cables or pipelines, States shall have due regard to cables or pipelines already in position. In particular, possibilities of repairing existing cables or pipelines shall not be prejudiced.

Article 80

Article 60 applies *mutatis mutandis* to artificial islands, installations and structures on the continental shelf.

Article 81

The coastal State shall have the exclusive right to authorize and regulate drilling on the continental shelf for all purposes.

Article 82

1. The coastal State shall make payments or contributions in kind in respect of the exploitation of the non-living resources of the continental shelf beyond 200 nautical miles from the baselines from which the breadth of the territorial sea is measured.

2. The payments and contributions shall be made annually with respect to all production at a site after the first five years of production at that site. For the sixth year, the rate of payment or contribution shall be 1 per cent of the value or volume of production at the site. The rate shall increase by 1 per cent for each subsequent year

until the twelfth year and shall remain at 7 per cent thereafter. Production does not include resources used in connection with exploitation.

3. A developing State which is a net importer of a mineral resource produced from its continental shelf is exempt from making such payments or contributions in respect of that mineral resource.

4. The payments or contributions shall be made through the Authority, which shall distribute them to States Parties to this Convention, on the basis of equitable sharing criteria, taking into account the interests and needs of developing States, particularly the least developed and the land-locked among them.

Article 83

1. The delimitation of the continental shelf between States with opposite or adjacent coasts shall be effected by agreement on the basis of international law, as referred to in Article 38 of the Statute of the International Court of Justice, in order to achieve an equitable solution.

2. If no agreement can be reached within a reasonable period of time, the States concerned shall resort to the procedures provided for in Part XV [on the settlement of disputes: see below, p.496].

3. Pending agreement as provided for in paragraph 1, the States concerned, in a spirit of understanding and co-operation, shall make every effort to enter into provisional arrangements of a practical nature and, during this transitional period, not to jeopardize or hamper the reaching of the final agreement. Such arrangements shall be without prejudice to the final delimitation. ...

Article 84

1. Subject to this Part, the outer limit lines of the continental shelf and the lines of delimitation drawn in accordance with article 83 shall be shown on charts of a scale or scales adequate for ascertaining their position. Where appropriate, lists of geographical co-ordinates of points, specifying the geodetic datum, may be substituted for such outer limit lines or lines of delimitation.

2. The coastal State shall give due publicity to such charts or lists of geographical co-ordinates and shall deposit a copy of each such chart or list with the Secretary-General of the United Nations and, in the case of those showing the outer limit lines of the continental shelf, with the Secretary-General of the Authority.

Article 85

This Part does not prejudice the right of the coastal State to exploit the subsoil by means of tunnelling, irrespective of the depth of water above the subsoil.

Notes

1.   The legal definition of the continental shelf in art.96, 1982 Convention, differs from that in art.1, 1958 Continental Shelf Convention, which reads:

"For the purpose of these articles, the term 'continental shelf' is used as referring (a) to the seabed and subsoil of the submarine areas adjacent to the coast but outside the area of the territorial sea, to a depth of 200 metres or, beyond that limit, to where the depth of the superjacent waters admits of the exploitation of the natural resources of the said areas; (b) to the seabed and subsoil of similar submarine areas adjacent to the coasts of islands."

Under art.76(3), 1982 Convention, the continental shelf extends to the outer edge of the "continental margin", which includes the shelf itself and "the slope and the rise" beyond it.[336] The "continental slope" is the steep slope with which the shelf proper terminates; the "continental

---

[336] See Kwiatkowska (1991) 22 O.D.I.L. 153. On the customary international law status of the 1982 Convention régime, see the *Gulf of Maine* case, above, p.324. Article 76 was assumed to state custom in the *St Pierre and Miquelon* case (1992) 31 I.L.M. 1149. See contra the dissenting opinion of Mr Weil as to art.76(4)–(9).

rise" is the less sharply sloping area between the "slope" and the deep seabed. Unlike the 1958 Convention, the 1982 Convention does not define the shelf in terms of "exploitability." It also differs in providing that the shelf extends a distance of 200 miles from the coast whether it reaches that distance in nature or not. The 1982 Convention retains an advantage, however, for the 60 or so naturally favoured states in that the shelf extends beyond that distance in law to the "outer edge" of the continental shelf *if* geomorphologically that point is more than 200 miles out. This was an advantage which such states have under the 1958 Convention and which they were not prepared to surrender; its inclusion was for them an essential part of the package in the 1982 Convention. Even so, the advantage is limited in two respects. First, no shelf may in law extend more than 350 miles from the territorial sea baseline or, beyond that (subject to art.76(6), the "2500 metres depth plus 100 miles" limit set in art.76(5). Article 76(6) concerns the role of submarine ridges that geomorphologically are not "natural components of the continental margin" but rise from the deep seabed. The shallower depths that these cause cannot be used to extend the "margin" into an area that is really a part of the deep seabed.[337] Secondly, art.82(1) of the 1982 Convention provides that a state shall make "payments or contributions in kind" in respect of the exploitation of shelf resources more than 200 miles from its coast. These payments or contributions go to the International Sea-bed Authority for distribution "on the basis of equitable sharing criteria, taking into account the interests and needs of developing states, particularly the least developed and the land-locked among them." (art.82(4)). Payments commence after five years of production and increase from 1 per cent to 7 per cent in the following years (art.82(2)).

2.   In other respects, the 1982 Convention mostly follows the 1958 Convention. Arts 2, 3, 4 and 7 of the latter are repeated in arts 77, 78(1), 79(2) and 87 respectively of the former.[338]

3.   As noted above, p.396, the continental shelf régime in Pt VI of the 1982 Convention (arts 76–85) applies to shelf resources of states that have made an exclusive economic zone claim (art.56(3)) as well as states that have not done so. It also applies to the continental shelf resources that any state has beyond the 200 mile limit.

In 2007, the Russian Federation made widely publicised natural resources claims to the Arctic seabed on the basis that it was a continuation of its continental shelf; Russian submarines placed a Russian flag in a container on the seabed at the North Pole.

4.   *Islands.* Islands have a continental shelf in the 1982 Convention unless they are just "rocks which cannot sustain human habitation or economic life of their own."[339]

5.   *No territorial sovereignty.* Article 77, 1982 Convention gives only limited rights to the coastal state in the continental shelf, not sovereignty.[340] The Truman Proclamation and most others had not

---

[337] For further details on the rules for the drawing of outer limits beyond 200 miles, see art.76(7), 1982 Convention. A state must submit details of a "beyond 200 mile" claim to the Commission on the Limits of the Continental Shelf for its "recommendations": see art.76(8). The Commission has 21 members who are independent scientific and technical (but not legal) experts elected by the states parties: 1982 Convention, Annex II. The Commission makes "recommendations". These are not legally binding, but a shelf limit established by a coastal state on the basis of them is "final and binding": art.78(8). Submissions to the Commission have included one by Russia and one by Australia and a joint submission by France, Ireland, Spain and the UK. See Llewellyn (2007) 56 I.C.L.Q. 677. On the ambiguities in art.76, see Macnab (2004) 35 O.D.I.L. 1.

[338] The rules concerning artificial structures, etc. in art.5 of the 1958 Convention re-appear (by virtue of art.80, 1982 Convention) with modification in art.60, 1982 Convention, above, p.393, although there is no full equivalent of art.5(1), 1958 Convention. art.6, 1958 Convention, is replaced by a different rule in art.83, 1982 Convention.

[339] 1982 Convention, art.121(3). See also p.398.

[340] cf. art.2, 1958 Continental Shelf Convention.

claimed sovereignty. In contrast, the claims of some Latin American states are to "national sovereignty."[341]

6. *Living resources.* The phrase "living organisms belonging to the sedentary species" in art.77(4), 1982 Convention, was said at Geneva[342] to include, inter alia, "coral, sponges, oysters, including pearl oysters, pearl shell, the sacred chank of India and Ceylon, the trocus and plants."[343] It probably also includes clams[344] and scallops. It excludes bottom fish, shrimps, prawns and, probably, octopuses. Crabs and lobsters have caused problems. The United Kingdom position has been expressed as follows:

> "... lobsters swim and crabs do not. Therefore, crabs are within the Convention, and lobsters are not."[345]

The intention of at least one of the states sponsoring the text adopted was, however, to exclude all crustacea, including crabs.[346] In 1963, a dispute occurred between France and Brazil over the fishing of crawfish (*langoustes*) by Breton fishermen on the Brazilian continental shelf. It would seem that adult crawfish normally stay in rock holes or clamber about, but will swim if pursued. It is interesting that, although neither France nor Brazil were then parties to the Convention, both relied on their (differing) interpretations of art.2(4), 1958 Convention to support their claims in respect of freedom to fish for the crawfish.[347]

The inclusion in the 1958 and 1982 Conventions of living resources as well as mineral resources was probably an instance of "progressive development" rather than "codification." The Truman Proclamation is clearly concerned with mineral resources only and the customary international law position before the Convention was probably that claims to exploit living resources, such as pearls, sponges and oysters had to be based upon occupation.[348]

7. Provision is made by the Continental Shelf Act 1964 for the granting of licences for the exploration and exploitation of oil and natural gas in the United Kingdom continental shelf.

8. *Tunnelling.* The 1982 Convention does not affect tunnelling through the subsoil of the continental shelf from the territory of the coastal state (see art.85).[349] Colombos suggests that "the subsoil under the bed of the sea may be considered capable of occupation" and that it would "be unreasonable to withhold recognition of the right of a State to drive mines or build tunnels in the subsoil, even when they extend considerably beyond the three-mile limit of territorial waters,

---

[341] See the claims made by Chile and Peru in 1947; such claims have been the subject of protests: 4 Whiteman 794–799.

[342] i.e. during the adoption of the same wording in art.2(4), 1958 Continental Shelf Convention.

[343] Mr Bailey (Australia), *1958 Sea Conference Records*, Vol.VI, p.57. See Scott (1992) 41 I.C.L.Q. 788.

[344] This is the US view: 4 Whiteman 863.

[345] *Hansard*, HC Vol.688, col.277 (January 28, 1964); 1964 B.P.I.L. 58–59 (but see the attitude taken by the UK on lobster fishing off the Bahamas: 4 Whiteman 863). The US distinguishes between lobsters and crabs in the same way; 4 Whiteman 863. Zoologically, this clear cut distinction between lobsters and crabs is an oversimplification. France stated that it understood art.2(4) to exclude all crustacea except for one kind of crab (*le crabe anatife*) when it ratified the Convention: see Hartingh (1965) 11 *Annuaire Français* 725.

[346] See Mr Bailey, Australia, above, n.343.

[347] A compromise was reached in 1964 allowing a limited number of French boats to fish for crawfish for the following five years. See Goldie, in Alexander, ed., *The Law of the Sea* (1967), pp.286–287. See also Azzam (1964) 13 I.C.L.Q. 1453. Zoologically, the crawfish, although sometimes known as the rock lobster, is not a lobster at all. On the US–Japanese dispute over the king crab, see 4 Whiteman 864.

[348] Young (1961) 55 A.J.I.L. 359 at 360–362. See the Tunisian claim to historic rights in the *Continental Shelf* (*Tunisia v Libya*) case, extract above, p.338.

[349] cf. art.7, 1958 Continental Shelf Convention.

provided that they do not affect or endanger the surface of the sea."[350] He also suggests that "in the case of a tunnel between two different States, the territorial property and jurisdiction of that part of the tunnel which runs under the bed of the high seas would have to be regulated by agreement between the two States chiefly concerned."[351] Tunnelling for mining purposes beyond the three-mile limit has occurred in Cornwall, for example, under the Cornwall Submarine Mines Act 1858. Section 2 states that "all mines and minerals lying below low-water mark under the open sea adjacent to, but not being part of the county of Cornwall, are vested in Her Majesty the Queen in right of her Crown as part of the soil and territorial possession of the Crown." The Channel Tunnel Act 1987, s.10, which was enacted when the United Kingdom claimed only a three-mile territorial sea (so that a part of the Straits of Dover was high seas) provides that the Channel "tunnel system as far as the frontier ... shall, as it becomes occupied by ... the concessionaires working from England ... be incorporated into England."[352]

9. In 2008, 91 states had continental shelf claims in place; they were mostly for 200 miles, to the edge of the continental margin or to a line of delimitation with another state.[353]

----

6. MARITIME BOUNDARIES[354]

CASE CONCERNING MARITIME DELIMITATION IN THE BLACK SEA

Romania v Ukraine

I.C.J. Rep. 2009

Romania and Ukraine requested the Court to draw "in accordance with international law" a single maritime boundary line between their continental shelf and exclusive economic zones in the Black Sea. The case was referred to the Court by Romania under a treaty between the two states, their negotiations to draw a line having failed. The Court applied the 1982 Convention, as both states were parties to it.

Judgment

115. When called upon to delimit the continental shelf or exclusive economic zones, or to draw a single delimitation line, the Court proceeds in defined stages.

116. ... First the Court will establish a provisional delimitation line, using methods that are geometrically objective and also appropriate for the geography of the area in which the delimitation is to take place. So far as delimitation between adjacent coasts is concerned, an equidistance line will be drawn unless there are compelling reasons that make this unfeasible in the particular case (see *Territorial and Maritime Dispute between Nicaragua and Honduras in the Caribbean Sea (Nicaragua v. Honduras,* Judgment of 8 October 2007, para.281).[355] So far as opposite coasts are concerned, the provisional delimitation line will consist of a median line between the two coasts. ...

---

[350] *The International Law of the Sea* (6th edn, 1967), p.69.
[351] Ibid.
[352] On the Channel Tunnel, see further above, p.205.
[353] *UN Law of the Sea Bulletin,* No.67 (2008).
[354] See Charney and Alexander, eds, *International Maritime Boundaries* (5 vols, 1993–2005, Vols 4 and 5, edited by Charney and Smith and Colson and Smith respectively); Charney (1994) 88 A.J.I.L. 227; Evans, *Relevant Circumstances and Maritime Delimitations* (1989); *id.* (1993) 64 B.Y.I.L. 283; Tanja, *The Legal Delimitation of International Maritime Boundaries* (1990); Thirlway (1994) 65 B.Y.I.L. 2; Weil, *The Law of Maritime Delimitation: Reflections* (1989).
[355] Ed. On its non-application in this case, see above, n.65.

120. The course of the final line should result in an equitable solution (Articles 74 and 83 of UNCLOS). Therefore, the Court will at the next second stage consider whether there are factors calling for the adjustment or shifting of the provisional equidistance line in order to achieve an equitable result (*Land and Maritime Boundary between Cameroon and Nigeria (Cameroon v. Nigeria: Equatorial Guinea intervening), judgment, I.C.J. Reports 2002*, p.411, para.288). ...

122. Finally, and at a third stage, the Court will verify that the line (a provisional equidistance line which may or may not have been adjusted by taking into account the relevant circumstances) does not, as it stands, lead to an inequitable result by reason of any marked disproportion between the ratio of the respective coastal lengths and the ratio between the relevant maritime area of each State by reference to the delimitation line ...

This is not to suggest that these respective areas should be proportionate to coastal lengths—as the Court has said "the sharing out of the area is therefore the consequence of the delimitation, not vice versa" (*Maritime Delimitation in the Area between Greenland and Jan Mayen) Denmark v. Norway), Judgment, I.C.J. Reports 1993*, p.67, para.64). ...

155. As the Court indicated above [paragraph 120] ... once the provisional equidistance line has been drawn, it shall "then [consider] whether there are factors calling for the adjustment or shifting of that line in order to achieve an 'equitable result'" ... Such factors have usually been referred to in the jurisprudence of the Court ... as the relevant circumstances ...

164. Where disparities in the lengths of coasts are particularly marked, the Court may choose to treat that fact of geography as a relevant circumstance that would require some adjustments to the provisional equidistance line to be made.

165. In the case concerning *Land and Maritime Boundary between Cameroon and Nigeria*, the Court acknowledged "that a *substantial* difference in the lengths of the parties' respective coastlines *may* be a factor to be taken into consideration in order or adjust of shift the provisional delimitation line" (*Judgment, I.C.J. Report 2002*, p.446, para.301; emphasis added), although it found that in the circumstances there was no reason to shift the equidistance line.

166. In the case concerning *Maritime Delimitation in the Area between Greenland and Jan Mayen (Denmark v. Norway)*, the Court found that the disparity between the lengths of the coasts of Jan Mayen and Greenland (approximately 1:9) constituted a "special circumstance" requiring modification of the provisional median line, by moving it closer to the coast of Jan Mayen, to avoid inequitable results for both the continental shelf and the fisheries zone. The Court stated that:

> "It should, however, be made clear that taking account of the disparity of coastal lengths does not mean a direct and mathematical application of the relationship between the length of the coastal front of eastern Greenland and that of Jan Mayen." (*Judgment, I.C.J. Reports 1993*, p.69, para.69). ...

168. In the present case ... the Court sees no such particularly marked disparities between the relevant coasts of Ukraine and Romania that would require it to adjust the provisional equidistance line at this juncture. ...

185 ... In this [relevant circumstances] phase the Court may be called upon to decide whether this line should be adjusted because of the presence of small islands in its vicinity. As the jurisprudence has indicated, the Court may on occasion decide not to take account of very small islands or decide not to give them their full potential entitlement to maritime zones, should such an approach have a disproportionate effect on the delimitation line under consideration (see ... *Territorial and Maritime Dispute between Nicaragua and Honduras in the Caribbean Sea (Nicaragua v. Honduras)*, Judgment of 8 October 2007, paras.302 *et seq.*) ...

[On the facts, the Court decided that the presence of Serpent's Island was not a relevant circumstance requiring an adjustment. It then rejected Ukraine's claim that its oil exploration licensing and fishing activities were relevant circumstances as follows:]

198. ... As the Arbitral Tribunal in the case between Barbados and Trinidad and Tobago observed, "[r]esource-related criteria have been treated more cautiously by the decisions of international courts and tribunals, which have not generally applied this factor as a relevant circumstance" (*Award of 11 April 2006, RIAA*, Vol.XXVII, p.214, para.241). With respect to fisheries, the Court adds that no evidence has been submitted to it by Ukraine that any delimitation line other than that claimed by it would be "likely to entail catastrophic repercussions for the livelihood and economic well-being of the population" (*Delimitation of the Maritime Boundary in the Gulf of Maine Area (Canada/United States of America), Judgment, I.C.J. Reports 1984*, p.342, para.237). ...

204. ... the legitimate security considerations of the parties may play a role in determining the final delimitation line (see *Continental Shelf (Libyan Arab Jamahiriya/Malta), Judgment, I.C.J. Reports 1985*, p.42, par.51). ... in the present case however, the provisional equidistance line ... determined by the Court fully respects the legitimate security interest of either Party. Therefore, there is no need to adjust the line on the basis of this consideration. ...

210. The Court now turns to check that the result thus far arrived at, so far as the envisaged delimitation line is concerned, does not lead to any significant disproportionality by reference to the respective coastal lengths and the apportionment of areas that ensue. This Court agrees with the observation that

> "it is disproportion rather than any general principle of proportionality which is the relevant criterion or factor ... there can never be a question of completely refashioning nature ... it is rather a question of remedying the disproportionality and inequitable effects produced by particular geographical configurations or features" (*Anglo-French Continent Shelf Case, RIAA*, Vol.XVIII, p.58, para.101) ...

212. This checking can only be approximate. Diverse techniques have in the past been used for assessing coastal lengths, with no clear requirements of international law having been shown as to whether the real coastline should be followed, or baselines used, or whether or not coasts relating to internal waters should be excluded.

213. The Court cannot but observe that various tribunals, and the Court itself, have drawn different conclusions over the years as to what disparity in coastal lengths would constitute a significant disproportionality which suggested the delimitation line was inequitable, and still required adjustment. This remains in each case a matter for the Court's appreciation, which it will exercise by reference to the overall geography of the area. ...

215. It suffices for this third stage for the Court to note that the ratio of the respective coastal lengths for Romania and Ukraine, measured as described above, is approximately 1:2.8 and the ratio of the relevant area between Romania and Ukraine is approximately 1:2.1.

216. The Court is not of the view that this suggests that the line as constructed, and checked carefully for any relevant circumstances that might have warranted adjustment, requires any alteration.

Notes

1. The delimitation of maritime boundaries between states has generated much litigation before the ICJ and arbitral tribunals because of the importance of the fishing, oil and other economic resources at stake. The jurisprudence is complicated in that cases have concerned opposite or adjacent states; different maritime boundaries—territorial sea, EEZ, continental shelf—or a combination of them; and the application of customary international law or of the 1958 or 1982 Conventions.

2. As is now common, the parties to the *Black Sea* case requested the drawing of a single maritime boundary for the adjoining EEZ and continental shelves.[356] As the Court noted in *Qatar v Bahrain*,[357] the concept of a single maritime boundary applying to two or more jurisdictional zones is not provided for in the 1982 Convention (or the 1958 Convention). The Court equates the delimitation rules governing such a boundary with those that apply to EEZ or continental shelf boundaries separately (paras 115 et seq.).[358] The Court would appear to have read this approach into the 1982 Convention, which it stated was the applicable law, given that Romania and Ukraine were parties to it.

---

[356] Other single boundary cases include the *Gulf of Maine* case, I.C.J. Rep. 1984, p.246; *Qatar v Bahrain*, I.C.J. Rep. 2001, p.40; and *Land and Maritime Boundary between Cameroon and Nigeria*, I.C.J. Rep. 2002, p.303. In *Barbados v Trinidad and Tobago*, PCA 2006, www.pca-cpa.org, para.235, the Tribunal notes that "State practice ... has overwhelmingly resorted to the establishment of single maritime boundaries". On single maritime boundaries, see Legault and Hankey (1985) 79 A.J.I.L. 961 and Sharma (1987) 2 I.J.E.C.L. 203.

[357] See above, n.356.

[358] See the provisions for EEZ and continental shelf boundaries in arts 74 and 83 respectively.

3.   As to customary international law, it is noticeable that the ICJ refers in its maritime boundary judgments[359] to earlier cases decided on the basis of custom or of treaty law without making any distinction. What appears to be emerging is a single "equidistance/special circumstances" rule for the drawing of all maritime boundaries, formulated in the *Black Sea* case, that is applicable under the 1982 Convention and is customary law too.[360] As far as territorial sea boundaries are concerned, the "equidistance/special circumstances" rule in art.15, 1982 Convention (above, p.334) that applies to them has been declared by the Court to be custom[361] and to be "very similar" to the "equitable principles/relevant circumstances" rule that applies to EEZ and continental shelf boundaries in arts 74 and 83, 1982 Convention.[362]

4.   As to "relevant circumstances" that might call for a deviation from the equidistance line in order to obtain an "equitable result", in the *Black Sea* case the Court identified a "substantial difference" in coastline length,[363] the impact of small islands (see below) and security interest as circumstances that might qualify, although they did not result in an adjustment on the facts of that case. The Court confirmed that "resource-related criteria" are relevant only where the equidistance line will have "catastrophic repercussions" (para.198).[364] In *Tunisia v Libya*,[365] the ICJ rejected a continental shelf claim based in part on one state party's relative poverty vis-à-vis the other on the basis that it is not engaged in redistributive justice when determining maritime boundaries.

5.   As to *islands*, in the *Anglo-French Continental Shelf* case,[366] allowance was made for the Scilly Isles and the Channel Islands in the drawing of a continental shelf boundary. The Court of Arbitration stated that in the case of the former, "[w]hat equity calls for is an appropriate abatement of the disproportionate effects" of a full application (favouring the United Kingdom) of the equidistance method. Taking a lead from examples of state practice "in which only partial effect has been given to offshore islands situated outside the territorial sea of the mainland," the Court accorded a "half effect" to the Scilly Islands.[367] The Channel Islands presented the problem of islands on the wrong side of the median line and "wholly detached geographically from the United Kingdom".[368] The solution adopted by the Court, in its search for a "more equitable balance" than would have resulted from the arguments put by either party, was to give the Channel Islands a continental shelf of 12 miles from its territorial sea baselines as an enclave

---

[359] See, e.g. the *Land and Maritime Boundary between Cameroon and Nigeria*, I.C.J. Rep. 2002, p.303.

[360] In *Qatar v Bahrain*, above n.356, para.167, the parties agreed that "most of the provisions of the 1982 Convention which are relevant for the present case reflect custom", which was the applicable law in that case. Contrast the approach in the *North Sea Continental Shelf*, cases, above, p.21 (the equidistance/special circumstances rule in art.6, Continental Shelf Convention, not custom), which might be decided differently now.

[361] *Qatar v Bahrain*, above p.356, para.176.

[362] *Land and Maritime Boundary between Cameroon and Nigeria*, I.C.J. Rep. 2002, p.303 at p.441. Cf. *Qatar v Bahrain*, above n.356, para.231 (rules "closely interrelated"). Although "very similar", and despite a general move to a single rule, under art.15 "special circumstances" may, as in the *Territorial and Maritime* dispute in the *Caribbean Sea Dispute* case, see above, n.65, lead to the non-use, rather than, as under the *Black Sea* case approach, the modification of an equidistance line.

[363] The concavity of the coastline within the area to be delimited is another geographical feature that may be relevant if it has a sufficiently distorting effect: *Land and Maritime Boundary between Cameroon and Nigeria*, I.C.J. Rep. 2002, p.303, para.297. Geological features within the 200-mile zone (e.g. "natural prolongation") are not relevant to continental shelf claims: *Libya v Malta*, I.C.J. Rep 1985, p.35. Contrast the earlier *North Sea Continental Shelf* cases, above, p.21.

[364] This *Gulf of Maine* case exception was applied, exceptionally and controversially, to protect fishing interests in the *Jan Mayen* case, I.C.J. Rep. 1993, p.38 at p.72. Oil concession practice is relevant if common to both parties: *Land and Maritime Boundary between Cameroon and Nigeria*, I.C.J. Rep. 2002, p.303.

[365] I.C.J. Rep.1982, p.77. Likewise, a Maltese argument based on its absence of land-based resources was not relevant: *Libya v Malta*, I.C.J. Rep. 1985, p.41.

[366] (1979) 18 I.L.M. 397.

[367] (1979) 18 I.L.M. 397 at 455. See also *Qatar v Bahrain*, above, p.356, para.219.

[368] (1979) 18 I.L.M.397 at 444.

within the French continental shelf. In the *Jan Mayen* case,[369] the Conciliation Commission noted that in state practice where both coastal states have islands along their coasts, examples are found where a "trade off" takes place by ignoring the islands on each side of the line when drawing the boundary "line".

----

7. THE DEEP SEA-BED[370]

CONVENTION ON THE LAW OF THE SEA 1982

UN Doc. A/CONF. 62/122; (1982) 21 I.L.M. 1261

Article 135

Neither this Part [XI] nor any rights granted or exercised pursuant thereto shall affect the legal status of the waters superjacent to the Area[371] or that of the air space above those waters.

Article 136

The Area and its resources[372] are the common heritage of mankind.

Article 137

1. No state shall claim or exercise sovereignty or sovereign rights over any part of the Area or its resources, nor shall any State or natural or juridical person appropriate any part thereof. No such claim or exercise of sovereignty or sovereign rights nor such appropriation shall be recognised.

2. All rights in the resources of the Area are vested in mankind as a whole, on whose behalf the Authority shall act. These resources are not subject to alienation. The minerals recovered from the Area, however, may only be alienated in accordance with this Part and the rules, regulations and procedures of the Authority.

3. No State or natural or juridical person shall claim, acquire or exercise rights with respect to the minerals recovered from the Area except in accordance with this Part. Otherwise, no such claim, acquisition or exercise of such rights shall be recognised. ...

Article 140

1. Activities in the Area shall ... be carried out for the benefit of mankind as a whole, irrespective of the geographical location of States, whether coastal or land-locked, and taking into particular consideration the interests and needs of developing States and of peoples who have not attained full independence or other self-governing status recognised by the United Nations in accordance with General Assembly 1514 (XV)[373] and other relevant General Assembly resolutions.

2. The Authority shall provide for the equitable sharing of financial and other economic benefits derived from

---

[369] (1981) 20 I.L.M. 797 at 824.

[370] See Andrassy, *International Law and the Resources of the Sea* (1970); Brown above, n.1, Vol.1, Ch.17; Mahmoudi, *The Law of Deep Sea-Bed Mining* (1987); Meese (1986) 17 O.D.I.L. 131; Paolillo (1984–IV) 188 Hague Recueil 135; Post, *Deepsea Mining and the Law of the Sea* (1983); Young (1968) 62 A.J.I.L. 641.

[371] Ed. The "area" is the "sea-bed and ocean floor and subsoil thereof beyond the limits of national jurisdiction" (1982 Convention, art.1(1)), i.e. the area beyond the edge of the "continental margin": see above, p.402.

[372] Ed. 1982 Convention, art.133, reads: "For the purposes of this Part: (a) 'resources' means all solid, liquid or gaseous mineral resources *in situ* in the Area at or beneath the sea-bed, including polymetallic nodules; (b) resources, when recovered from the Area, are referred to as 'minerals.'" The definition of "resources" is very generally phrased to allow for the future discovery in commercial quantities of resources other than "polymetallic" (or manganese) nodules.

[373] Ed. Above, p.104.

activities in the Area through any appropriate mechanism, on a non-discriminatory basis, in accordance with article 160, paragraph 2(f)(i).[374]

Article 141

The Area shall be open to use exclusively for peaceful purposes by all States, whether coastal or land-locked, without discrimination and without prejudice to the other provisions of this Part. ...

Article 150

Activities in the Area shall ... be carried out in such a manner as to foster healthy development of the world economy and balanced growth of international trade, and to promote international co-operation for the over-all development of all countries, especially developing States, and with a view to ensuring:

(a) the development of the resources of the Area;

(b) orderly, safe and rational management of the resources of the Area ...

(d) participation in revenues by the Authority and the transfer of technology to the Enterprise and developing States as provided for in this Convention; ...

(f) the promotion of just and stable prices remunerative to producers and fair to consumers for minerals derived both from the Area and from other sources, and the promotion of long-term equilibrium between supply and demand;

(g) the enhancement of opportunities for all States Parties, irrespective of their social and economic systems or geographical location, to participate in the development of the resources of the Area and the pre-vention of monopolization of activities in the Area;

(h) the protection of developing countries from adverse effects on their economies or on their export earnings resulting from a reduction in the price of an affected mineral, or in the volume of exports of that mineral, to the extent that such reduction is caused by activities in the Area ...

(i) the development of the common heritage for the benefit of mankind as a whole ...

Article 153

1. Activities in the Area shall be organised, carried out and controlled by the Authority on behalf of mankind as a whole in accordance with this article as well as other relevant provisions of this Part and the relevant Annexes, and the rules, regulations and procedures of the Authority.

2. Activities in the Area shall be carried out: ...

(a) by the Enterprise, and

(b) in association with the Authority by States Parties, or state enterprises or natural or juridical persons which possess the nationality of States Parties or are effectively controlled by them or their nationals, when sponsored by such States, or any group of the foregoing which meets the requirements provided in this Part and in Annex III. ...

Notes

1.   Part XI (arts 133–191) of the 1982 Convention was prompted by the wish to establish rules governing the exploitation of the mineral resources of the deep sea-bed, which was viewed in the period before the adoption of the Convention as having become a practical, if expensive, pro-position. Manganese nodules and other resources are to be found in the Pacific and Indian

---

[374] Ed. This gives the Authority power to make regulations for "equitable sharing", "taking into particular consideration the interests and needs of developing states and peoples who have not attained full independence or other self-governing status."

Oceans and elsewhere in the seas of the world. Most attention would seem to be concentrated on an area of the sea-bed of the North Pacific, between the United States mainland and Hawaii. During the drafting of the 1982 Convention, a number of international consortia composed of companies from developed states made substantial investments in research and development with a view to beginning production when this proved economically worthwhile, and a stable legal régime prevailed. But investment has since been severely cut back as the market price of deep sea-bed minerals has declined and the high cost of underwater mining has been confirmed. There seems little prospect of such mining in the foreseeable future.

2. The United Nations had had the question of the legal régime of the deep sea-bed under discussion from 1967. It was not long before the analogy with "freedom of fishing" on the high seas, with each state controlling its own nationals, was abandoned (but see the UK Deep Sea Mining (Temporary Provisions) Act 1981 and similar legislation, below) in favour of the idea of an international régime. Even developed states preferred the security that a limited international régime would offer their national undertakings[375] to the hazards of a "free for all." In 1969, the General Assembly, by a majority,[376] declared a moratorium on sea-bed exploitation "beyond the limits of national jurisdiction" pending the establishment of an international régime. Similarly, the 1970 General Assembly Declaration of Principles Governing the Sea-Bed[377] rules out the possibility of a "free for all" and indicates some principles upon which an international régime should be based.[378] Above all, it establishes, in a text that attracted no dissent, the principle that the resources of the deep sea-bed are "the common heritage of mankind." They are, that is, to be used to benefit all states, not just those with the technology and capital to recover them. The understanding in 1970 was that a share of the profits from deep sea-bed mining should, in accordance with this principle, be distributed among developing states. The emergence of a new area in which there were no vested interests was seen to offer a good opportunity of progress towards a more equitable international economic order. What the 1970 Declaration did not do was to indicate whether the mining should be done by national undertakings under the aegis of an international body or by the international body itself. This, and other details, could only be formulated in a Convention.

3. Part XI 1982 Convention, established the "international regime" on the deep sea-bed referred to in the 1970 Declaration. Unfortunately, it proved not to be acceptable to the US and other developed states, who declined to sign and/or ratify the 1982 Convention because of it.[379] Although enough developing states had ratified the Convention to bring it into force in 1994, these states lacked the financial capacity to fund both the deep sea-bed regime in Pt XI of the Convention and other institutions created by the 1982 Convention.[380] Anticipating this and other threats to the success of the 1982 Convention regime as a whole caused by the non-involvement in it of developed states, the UN took steps[381] in the early 1990s to facilitate their acceptance of the 1982 Convention, resulting in the 1994 New York Agreement Relating to the Implementation

---

[375] This term is used to include public and private undertakings at the national level, including consortia of companies of different nationalities.

[376] G.A. Resn. 2574D (XXIV), G.A.O.R., 24th Session, Supp. 30 (1969). The resolution was adopted by 62 votes to 28, with 28 abstentions.

[377] G.A. Resn. 2749 (XXV) (1970); (1971) 10 I.L.M. 220.

[378] On the impact of the Declaration upon custom, see Brown (1983) 20 San Diego L.R. 521.

[379] See above, p.323.

[380] These are the International Tribunal for the Law of the Sea and the Commission on the Limits of the Continental Shelf.

[381] See Anderson (1993) 42 I.C.L.Q. 654; (1994) 43 I.C.L.Q. 886; (1995) 44 I.C.L.Q. 313.

of Pt XI.[382] In effect, the Agreement modifies Pt XI in such a way as to meet the objections of developed states to the Convention's original deep sea-bed regime. Developing states were willing to accept this mainly because changed economic circumstances have meant that the exploitation of deep sea-bed mineral resources, with resulting payments for them (see arts 140(2) and 160(2)(f)(i), 1982 Convention), is unlikely in the foreseeable future[383] and because of the financial need to involve developed states in the 1982 Convention generally.[384]

The 1994 Agreement entered into force in 1996[385] and Pt XI of the 1982 Convention is in its early stages of implementation in accordance with its terms. The following notes on Pt XI take account of the changes made by the 1994 Agreement.

4.   The 1982 Convention adopts the idea of the 1970 Declaration that the deep sea-bed and its resources are "the common heritage of mankind"[386] not open to claims of sovereignty or sovereign rights. This was not controversial. The problem was to take the matter further and to devise a system for the exploitation of resources that was both consistent with this idea and met the demands of developed and developing states alike. Developing states pressed for a system by which exploitation would be conducted by an international body—the Authority (see below)— and not by states or national undertakings. Developed states preferred the idea by which exploitation would be by states or national undertakings subject to a system of registration or, at most, licensing. The system of "parallel access" adopted in the Convention is a compromise between the two approaches, although one that, in the original text of Pt XI, leans mostly towards the approach of the developing states. Under art.153, 1982 Convention, control of all sea-bed activities is placed in the hands of the Authority, which may exploit resources itself or contract with a national undertaking[387] to do so. Under the 1994 Agreement, the Enterprise,[388] acting for the Authority, "shall conduct its initial deep sea-bed operations through joint ventures" with national undertakings, not by itself, and must act in accordance with "sound commercial principles" when doing so.[389] The original Pt XI contains provisions for the setting of production levels (to protect land-based producers) and for the transfer to technology by national under-takings to the Enterprise and to developing countries. The 1994 Agreement states that these

---

[382] (1994) 33 I.L.M. 1309. See Brown (1995) 19 Mar. Pol. 5; Oxman (1994) 88 A.J.I.L. 687; Platzöder, ed., *The 1994 United Nations Convention on the Law of the Sea* (1995); (1993) 4 E.J.I.L. 390; and Sohn (1994) 88 A.J.I.L. 696. The Agreement and Pt XI "shall be interpreted and applied together as a single instrument" and in the event "of any inconsistency . . . the provisions of the agreement shall prevail": art.2, 1994 Agreement.

[383] These minerals now command lower prices with the development of artificial substitutes and for other reasons.

[384] Other factors which strengthened the hand of developed states were the disintegration of the USSR; the reduction in the political power of developing states in the UN; and the worldwide move from state to private enterprise: see de Marffy-Mantuano (1995) 89 A.J.I.L. 814.

[385] There are 136 parties, including the UK. States that become parties to the 1982 Convention after the Agreement entered into force on July 28, 1994 thereby become parties to the Agreement also; parties to the 1982 Convention prior to that date became parties to the Agreement by signing it by July 28, 1995: G. A. Resn. 48/263 (1994) 33 I.L.M. 1309. On this ingenious application of the law concerning the acceptance of treaties, see de Marffy-Mantuano, above, at n.384. However, there are some pre-July 28, 1994 Convention parties, including some who abstained in the voting on Resn. 48/263, that did not sign the 1994 Agreement within the 12 month period and have not otherwise become parties to it.

[386] On the concept of the "common heritage of mankind", see Larshan and Brennan (1983) 21 Col. J.T.L. 305; Goldie (1983) 10 Syracuse J.I.L.C. 69; Joyner (1986) 35 I.C.L.Q. 190; Kiss (1985) 40 Int. Jo. 423; Schmidt, *Common Heritage or Common Burden?* (1989); Van Hoof (1986) 7 Grotiana 49; White (1982) 14 C.W.R.J.I.L. 509; Wolfrum (1983) 43 Z.A.O.R.V. 312.

[387] Only national undertakings that meet the (i) nationality or control and (ii) sponsorship requirements of art.153(2)(b) and Annex III of the 1982 Convention (linking the undertaking enterprise with a Convention party) are eligible for a contract. art.4(2) of Annex III makes particular provision for partnerships or consortia from more than one state.

[388] This is the body provided for in the 1982 Convention, art.151(2)(a), to conduct mining for the Authority. It has not yet been established.

[389] Annex, s.2, para.2.

provisions shall not apply.[390] These changes made by the 1994 Agreement clearly reflect the wishes and interests of developed states.

Other changes made by the 1994 Agreement respond to the financial concerns of developed states. The "cost effectiveness" principle and other new rules governing the operation of the Authority[391] and the establishment of a finance committee to oversee the budget[392] reduce the financial contributions due from Convention parties.

5. The Convention (arts 156–168) provides for an independent International Sea-Bed Authority, with its seat in Jamaica, which has overall responsibility for the deep sea-bed regime. The Authority was established in 1994 following the entry into force of the 1982 Convention.[393] The Authority has two political organs, the Assembly and the Council. The Assembly, of which all Convention parties are members, was originally conceived as the policy-making body. It takes decisions by a two thirds majority. Under the 1994 Agreement, "the general policies of the Authority shall be established by the Assembly in collaboration with the Council" and most decisions by the Assembly shall be "based on the recommendation of the Council", thereby shifting the balance of political power between the Assembly and the Council significantly towards the latter.[394]

The Council, which is composed of 36 members elected by the Assembly to represent various interest groups, is the executive body. Members are elected on the basis of a system that ensures a reasonable representation of interested groups, including states that are the leading consumers or importers of sea-bed minerals, the main investors in sea-bed activities or the main land-based exporters of sea-bed minerals. Under the 1994 Agreement, the US will be assured membership once it becomes a 1982 Convention party (at present it is an Authority observer). Under the 1994 Agreement, decisions by the Council on questions of substance are taken by a two-thirds majority, provided that they are not opposed by a majority in any one of the Council chambers.[395] These chambers, composed of groupings of states with specified interests, are provided for by the 1994 Agreement; some of them will be controlled by the developed states.

The amendments made by the 1994 Agreement to the original Pt XI provisions on decision making that are indicated above, which increase the power of the Council at the expense of the Assembly and the influence in the Council of developed states, again follow the wishes and interests of that group of states.

6. Another criticism of the original Pt XI regime was the absence of any protection for pre-Convention investment in exploration. This problem was tackled by Resolution II of the Final Act of UNCLOS III.[396] This permits the registration of states and national undertakings that have spent $30 million on seabed activities as pioneer investors. As such, they have priority over other applicants in the allocation of contracts.

---

[390] Annex, s.6, para.7, and s.5, para.2. Production is to occur instead on the basis of "sound commercial principles" and the provisions of the GATT (s.6, para.1); developing states that suffer serious adverse effects on their export earnings or economies are to be compensated from the proceeds of mining (s.7). The Enterprise and developing states are to obtain technology on commercial terms on the open market; if they are unable to do so, the Authority may "request" the assistance of contractors or their sponsoring state, subject to "the effective protection of intellectual property rights": Annex, s.5, para.1.

[391] Annex, s.1.

[392] Annex, s.9.

[393] For documents on the Preparatory Committee for the Sea-bed Authority, see Platzöder, ed., *The Law of the Sea: Documents 1983–9* (13 Vols, 1983).

[394] Annex, s.3, paras 1, 4.

[395] Annex, s.3, para. 5.

[396] Reprinted in Brown, above, n.1, Vol.2, p.343. See Kimball (1986) 17 O.D.I.L. 367, and Larson (1986) 17 O.D.I.L. 271.

7. As yet, the Authority, which meets for just two sessions a year, has made little progress. In 2000 it adopted regulations on the exploitation of polymetallic nodules and in 2001 entered into exploration contracts with seven pioneer investors.[397] It is currently engaged in drafting regulations on polymetallic sulphides and cobalt rich crusts. The Enterprise has yet to be established and the seven contract holders have no immediate plans for exploitation.

8. *The reciprocating states régime.* Following its rejection of the 1982 Convention régime for the deep sea-bed, the United States enacted the Deep Sea-bed Hard Mineral Resources Act 1980,[398] by which the United States may issue licences to exploit deep sea-bed resources. Similar legislation has since been enacted by the United Kingdom[399] and a number of other developed states.[400] The United Kingdom legislation remains in force for the present.

----

8. SETTLEMENT OF DISPUTES

CONVENTION ON THE LAW OF THE SEA 1982

UN Doc. A/CONF. 62/122; (1982) 21 I.L.M. 1261

Article 286

Subject to section 3 [arts 297–299], any dispute concerning the interpretation or application of this Convention shall, where no settlement has been reached by recourse to section 1,[401] be submitted at the request of any party to the dispute to the court or tribunal having jurisdiction under this section.

Article 287

1. When signing, ratifying or acceding to this Convention or at any time thereafter, a State shall be free to choose, by means of a written declaration, one or more of the following means for the settlement of disputes concerning the interpretation or application of this Convention:

(a) the International Tribunal for the Law of the Sea established in accordance with Annex VI:

(b) the International Court of Justice;

(c) an arbitral tribunal constituted in accordance with Annex VII;

(d) a special arbitral tribunal constituted in accordance with Annex VIII for one or more of the categories of disputes specified therein [i.e. fisheries, marine environment, marine scientific research and navigation, including pollution from vessels and dumping].

2. A declaration made under paragraph 1 shall not affect or be affected by the obligation of a State Party to accept the jurisdiction of the Sea-Bed Disputes Chamber of the International Tribunal for the Law of the Sea to the extent and in the manner provided for in Part XI, section 5 [concerning the deep sea-bed].

3. A State Party, which is a party to a dispute not covered by a declaration in force, shall be deemed to have accepted arbitration in accordance with Annex VII.

---

[397] See *www.isa.org.*
[398] (1980) 19 I.L.M. 1003.
[399] Deep Sea Mining (Temporary Provisions) Act 1981.
[400] The FRG (1981) 20 I.L.M. 393; France (1982) 21 I.L.M. 808; the USSR (1982) 21 I.L.M. 551; Japan (1983) 22 I.L.M. 102; and Italy (1985) 24 I.L.M. 983.
[401] Ed. s.1 (arts 279–285) provides for the settlement of disputes by the peaceful means listed in art.33, UN Charter, other than judicial settlement or arbitration.

4. If the parties to a dispute have accepted the same procedure for the settlement of the dispute, it may be submitted only to that procedure, unless the parties otherwise agree.

5. If the parties to a dispute have not accepted the same procedure for the settlement of the dispute, it may be submitted only to arbitration in accordance with Annex VII, unless the parties otherwise agree.

6. A declaration made under paragraph 1 shall remain in force until three months after notice of revocation has been deposited with the Secretary-General of the United Nations.

7. A new declaration, a notice of revocation or the expiry of a declaration does not in any way affect proceedings pending before a court or tribunal having jurisdiction under this article, unless the parties otherwise agree.

8. Declarations and notices referred to in this article shall be deposited with the Secretary-General of the United Nations, who shall transmit copies thereof to the States Parties.

Article 288

1. A court or tribunal referred to in article 287 shall have jurisdiction over any dispute concerning the interpretation or application of this Convention which is submitted to it in accordance with this Part.

2. A court or tribunal referred to in article 287 shall also have jurisdiction over any dispute concerning the interpretation or application of an international agreement related to the purposes of this Convention, which is submitted to it in accordance with the agreement.

3. The Sea-Bed Disputes Chamber of the International Tribunal for the Law of the Sea established in accordance with Annex VI, and any other chamber or arbitral tribunal referred to in Part XI, section 5, shall have jurisdiction in any matter which is submitted to it in accordance therewith.

4. In the event of a dispute as to whether a court or tribunal has jurisdiction, the matter shall be settled by decision of that court or tribunal.

Article 290

1. If a dispute has been duly submitted to a court or tribunal which considers that *prima facie* it has jurisdiction under this Part or Part XI, section 5, the court or tribunal may prescribe any provisional measures which it considers appropriate under the circumstances to preserve the respective rights of the parties to the dispute or to prevent serious harm to the marine environment, pending the final decision. . . .

5. Pending the constitution of an arbitral tribunal to which a dispute is being submitted under this section, any court or tribunal agreed upon by the parties or, failing such agreement within two weeks from the date of the request for provisional measures, the International Tribunal for the Law of the Sea or, with respect to activities in the Area, the Sea-Bed Disputes Chamber, may prescribe, modify or revoke provisional measures in accordance with this article if it considers that *prima facie* the tribunal which is to be constituted would have jurisdiction and that the urgency of the situation so requires. Once constituted, the tribunal to which the dispute has been submitted may modify, revoke or affirm those provisional measures, acting in conformity with paragraphs 1 to 4.

6. The parties to the dispute shall comply promptly with any provisional measures prescribed under this article.

Article 291

1. All the dispute settlement procedures specified in this Part shall be open to States Parties.

2. The dispute settlement procedures specified in this Part shall be open to entities other than States Parties only as specifically provided for in this Convention.

Article 292

Where the authorities of a State Party have detained a vessel flying the flag of another State Party and it is alleged that the detaining State has not complied with the provisions of this Convention[402] for the prompt release of the vessel or its crew upon the posting of a reasonable bond or other financial security, the question of release from detention may be submitted to any court or tribunal agreed upon by the parties or failing such

---

[402] Ed. See art.73(2), above, p.471, and arts 220(6)(7) (pollution arrests) and 226(1)(c) (seaworthiness arrests).

agreement within 10 days from the time of detention, to a court or tribunal accepted by the detaining State under article 287 or to the International Tribunal for the Law of the Sea, unless the parties otherwise agree.

Article 293

1. A court or tribunal having jurisdiction under this section shall apply this Convention and other rules of international law not incompatible with this Convention.

2. Paragraph 1 does not prejudice the power of the court or tribunal having jurisdiction under this section to decide a case *ex aequo et bono*, if the parties so agree.

Article 295

Any dispute between States Parties concerning the interpretation or application of this Convention may be submitted to the procedures provided for in this section only after local remedies have been exhausted where this is required by international law.

Article 296

1. Any decision rendered by a court or tribunal having jurisdiction under this section shall be final and shall be complied with by all the parties to the dispute.

2. Any such decision shall have no binding force except between the parties and in respect of that particular dispute.

Article 297

1. Disputes concerning the interpretation or application of this Convention with regard to the exercise by a coastal State of its sovereign rights or jurisdiction provided for in this Convention shall be subject to the procedures provided for in section 2 [arts 286–296] in the following cases:

1. (a) when it is alleged that a coastal State has acted in contravention of the provisions of this Convention in regard to the freedoms and rights of navigation, overflight or the laying of submarine cables and pipelines, or in regard to other internationally lawful uses of the sea specified in article 58 [above, p.448];

   (b) when it is alleged that a State in exercising the aforementioned freedoms, rights or uses has acted in contravention of this Convention or of laws or regulations adopted by the coastal State in conformity with this Convention and other rules of international law not incompatible with this Convention; or

   (c) when it is alleged that a coastal State has acted in contravention of specified international rules and standards for the protection and preservation of the marine environment which are applicable to the coastal State and which have been established by this Convention or through a competent inter-national organization or diplomatic conference in accordance with this Convention.

2. (a) Disputes concerning the interpretation or application of the provisions of this Convention with regard to marine scientific research shall be settled in accordance with section 2, except that the coastal State shall not be obliged to accept the submission to such settlement of any dispute arising out of:

   (i) the exercise by the coastal State of a right or discretion in accordance with article 246 [marine scientific research in the EEZ and on the continental shelf]; or

   (ii) a decision by the coastal State to order suspension or cessation of a research project in accordance with article 253 [marine scientific research in the deep sea-bed area].

   (b) A dispute arising from an allegation by the researching State that with respect to a specific project the coastal state is not exercising its rights under articles 246 and 253 in a manner compatible with this Convention shall be submitted, at the request of either party, to conciliation under Annex V, section 2, provided that the conciliation commission shall not call in question the exercise by the coastal State of its discretion to designate specific areas as referred to in article 246, paragraph 6, or of its discretion to withhold consent in accordance with article 246, paragraph 5.

3.   (*a*) Disputes concerning the interpretation or application of the provisions of this Convention with regard to fisheries shall be settled in accordance with section 2, except that the coastal State shall not be obliged to accept the submission to such settlement of any dispute relating to its sovereign rights with respect to the living resources in the exclusive economic zone or their exercise, including its discretionary powers for determining the allowable catch, its harvesting capacity, the allocation of surpluses to other States and the terms and conditions established in its conservation and management laws and regulations.

  (*b*) Where no settlement has been reached by recourse to section 1 of this Part, a dispute shall be submitted to conciliation under Annex V, section 2, at the request of any party to the dispute, when it is alleged that:

    (i) a coastal State has manifestly failed to comply with its obligations to ensure through proper conservation and management measures that the maintenance of the living resources in the exclusive economic zone is not seriously endangered;

    (ii) a coastal state has arbitrarily refused to determine, at the request of another State, the allowable catch and its capacity to harvest living resources with respect to stocks which that other State is interested in fishing; or

    (iii) a coastal State has arbitrarily refused to allocate to any State, under articles 62 [above, p.470], 69 and 70 [on the rights of land-locked and geographically disadvantaged states respectively] and under the terms and conditions established by the coastal State consistent with this Convention, the whole or part of the surplus it has declared to exist.

  (*c*) In no case shall the conciliation commission substitute its discretion for that of the coastal State.

  (*d*) The report of the conciliation commission shall be communicated to the appropriate international organizations.

  (*e*) In negotiating agreements pursuant to articles 69 and 70, States Parties, unless they otherwise agree, shall include a clause on measures which they shall take in order to minimize the possibility of a disagreement concerning the interpretation or application of the agreement, and on how they should proceed if a disagreement nevertheless arises.

Article 298

1. When signing, ratifying or acceding to this Convention or at any time thereafter, a State may, without prejudice to the obligations arising under section 1, declare in writing that it does not accept any one or more of the procedures provided for in section 2 with respect to one or more of the following categories of disputes:

  (*a*) (i) disputes concerning the interpretation or application of articles 15, 74 and 83 relating to sea boundary delimitations, or those involving historic bays or titles, provided that a State having made such a declaration shall, when such a dispute arises subsequent to the entry into force of this Convention and where no agreement within a reasonable period of time is reached in negotiations between the parties, at the request of any party to the dispute, accept submission of the matter to conciliation under Annex V, section 2; and provided further that any dispute that necessarily involves the concurrent consideration of any unsettled dispute concerning sovereign or other rights over continental or insular land territory shall be excluded from such submission;

    (ii) after the conciliation commission has presented its report, which shall state the reasons on which it is based, the parties shall negotiate an agreement on the basis of that report; if these negotiations do not result in an agreement, the parties shall, by mutual consent, submit the question to one of the procedures provided for in section 2, unless the parties otherwise agree;

    (iii) this subparagraph does not apply to any sea boundary dispute finally settled by an arrangement between the parties, or to any such dispute which is to be settled in accordance with a bilateral or multilateral agreement binding upon those parties;

  (*b*) disputes concerning military activities, including military activities by government vessels and aircraft engaged in non-commercial service, and disputes concerning law enforcement activities in regard to the exercise of sovereign rights or jurisdiction excluded from the jurisdiction of a court or tribunal under article 297, paragraph 2 or 3;

(c) disputes in respect of which the Security Council of the United Nations is exercising the functions assigned to it by the Charter of the United Nations, unless the Security Council decides to remove the matter from its agenda or calls upon the parties to settle it by the means provided for in this Convention.

2. A State Party which has made a declaration under paragraph 1 may at any time withdraw it, or agree to submit a dispute excluded by such declaration to any procedure specified in this Convention.

3. A State Party which has made a declaration under paragraph 1 shall not be entitled to submit any dispute falling within the excepted category of disputes to any procedure in this Convention as against another State Party, without the consent of that party.

4. If one of the State Parties has made a declaration under paragraph 1(a), any other State Party may submit any dispute falling within an excepted category against the declarant party to the procedure specified in such declaration.

5. A new declaration, or the withdrawal of a declaration, does not in any way affect proceedings pending before a court or tribunal in accordance with this article, unless the parties otherwise agree.

6. Declarations and notices of withdrawal of declarations under this article shall be deposited with the Secretary-General of the United Nations, who shall transmit copies thereof to the States Parties.

Notes

1.   The 1982 Convention is notable for the provision it makes for the settlement of disputes by judicial settlement or arbitration if negotiation, conciliation or other means of peacefully settling disputes listed in art.33, UN Charter are unsuccessful.[403] A considerable achievement is the provision as the general rule for the *compulsory* judicial settlement or arbitration of disputes that may arise under the Convention, at the request of just one of the parties to the dispute (art.286). Exceptionally, some kinds of disputes concerning the exercise by a coastal state of its sovereign rights, powers, and jurisdiction are not subject to compulsory jurisdiction (art.297). In addition a contracting state or party may make a declaration excluding certain other kinds of disputes (territorial sea, continental shelf, exclusive economic zone boundary disputes; disputes concerning military activities; and disputes before the Security Council) from compulsory jurisdiction (art.298). The 1958 Conventions make no such provision for compulsory jurisdiction; the *Optional* Protocol that accompanies these Conventions is all that drafting Conferences normally achieve. Since many of the 1982 Convention rules contain lacunae[404] or, inevitably, are generally phrased,[405] and since some state practice is of doubtful consistency with them,[406] the availability of judicial or arbitral proceedings offers an exceptional opportunity to clarify the law and resolve disputes between the parties.

2.   As to the forum competent to hear cases subject to compulsory jurisdiction, a state party may make a declaration by which it accepts the jurisdiction of the International Tribunal for the Law of the Sea (ITLOS), the ICJ or an arbitral tribunal constituted under Annexes VII or VIII, or more than one of these (art.287(1)). Where one or both of the two states parties to a dispute has or have not made a declaration, or if their declarations do not accept a common forum,[407] an arbitral

---

[403] See Adede, *The System for Settlement of Disputes under the United Nations Convention on the Law of the Sea* (1987); Birnie, in Butler, ed., *The Law of the Sea and International Shipping* (1985), p.39; Carnegie (1979) 28 I.C.L.Q. 669; Charney (1990) 90 A.J.I.L. 69; Gamble (1991) 9 B.U.I.L.J. 39; Jaenicke (1983) 43 Z.A.O.R.V. 813; Janis (1992) 16 Mar. Pol. 102; Treves in Schneiber, ed., *Law of the Sea* (2000), p.61.

[404] e.g. on innocent passage for warships: see above, p.351.

[405] e.g. the "routes" of similar convenience" exception to the right of transit passage: see above, p.356.

[406] e.g. on the use of straight baselines: see above, p.335.

[407] As in the *Mox Plant* case (*Ireland v UK*) (2001).

tribunal default option applies (art.187(3)(5)). Only 32 contracting parties have made declarations, with choices varying widely among the possible options.

3. ITLOS was established by the 1982 Convention (see Annex VI). It has its seat in Hamburg and came into being in 1996.[408] ITLOS has 21 judges who are elected for nine year terms of office. Judges must be of "recognised competence in the field of the law of the sea."[409] The Tribunal as a whole must be representative in its membership of "the principal legal systems of the world" and have "an equitable geographical distribution."[410] As agreed by the contracting parties, the judges are distributed as follows: Africa and Asia, five each; Latin America and the Caribbean, four each; Western European states and others, four each; Eastern Europe, three.

4. As well as jurisdiction to decide cases on their merits, ITLOS may order provisional measures in cases brought before it or in cases to be decided by an arbitral tribunal, pending the establishment of the tribunal (art.290).[411] It also has jurisdiction in prompt release cases (art.292); and in some deep sea-bed cases (arts 187–188).

5. Sixteen cases have been submitted to ITLOS. It has given one judgment on the merits, in the *Saiga* case, above, p.369. Most of its decisions have concerned provisional measures and prompt release claims. In early 2010, ITLOS had just one case on its docket.[412] As this low case load indicates, as yet ITLOS "has not yet been put to full use."[413] This is not unusual in the early years of a new international court or tribunal.

6. The parallel jurisdiction of ITLOS and the ICJ on law of the sea issues has raised the question whether the result will be a lack of consistency of jurisprudence on the law of the sea.[414] So far, ITLOS has been careful to take into account World Court case law in its decisions.[415]

---

[408] On ITLOS, see Eiriksson, *The International Tribunal for the Law of the Sea* (2000).

[409] ITLOS Statute, art.2(1).

[410] ITLOS Statute, art.2(2).

[411] Provisional measures are legally binding: art.290(6) of the 1982 Convention.

[412] The *Delimitation of the Maritime Boundary between Bangladesh and Madagascar in the Bay of Bengal* case.

[413] Statement by the ITLOS President to the 13th Meeting of the State Parties, June 13, 2003.

[414] See Boyle (1997) 46 I.C.L.Q. 37. See also Charney (1998) 271 Hague Receuil 101; Oxman (2001) 95 A.J.I.l. 277 at 280; Higgins (2001) 50 I.C.L.Q. 121 at 122. On the question of the multiplicity of international courts and tribunals generally, see below, p.837.

[415] See the *Saiga* case, above, p.369.

8 STATE RESPONSIBILITY

1. INTRODUCTORY NOTE

In any legal system there must be liability for failure to observe obligations imposed by its rules. Such liability is known in international law as *responsibility*. The materials in this chapter directly concern the responsibility of states. Other international persons are, of course, responsible for violating their obligations also.[1]

In municipal law, a division is made between civil and criminal liability and, within the former, between liability in contract and in tort. From a different standpoint, liability is based upon intentional or negligent conduct or arises without fault at all. There are also rules about such matters as imputability (e.g. rules about the liability of employers for the ultra vires actions of their employees), remedies and locus standi. Some of these divisions and rules exist in international law, but, until recently, the theory of the law of state responsibility was not well developed.[2] The position has now changed with the adoption by the ILC in 2001, after many years of endeavour,[3] of its Draft Articles on Responsibility of States for Internationally Wrongful Acts.[4] The final text omits a controversial text (art.19) in an earlier draft providing for the criminal responsibility of states, taking the view instead that international law knows no such concept.[5] It also does not distinguish between liability in contract and tort (see art.12). The Draft Articles are presented as a combination of codification and progressive development. They are concerned with the *secondary*, not the *primary*, rules of state responsibility, a distinction which is explained as follows[6]:

---

[1] On the responsibility of international organisations for acts attributable to them, see the ILC Draft Articles on the Responsibility of International Organisations, art.3, G.A.O.R. A/58/19 (2003). See also above, p.125 and below, p.423. On the question whether a state is responsible for the acts of its armed forces, etc. as UN force members, see Amerasinghe, *Principles of the International Law of International Organisations* (2nd edn 2005), Ch.13. See also *Behrami and Behrami v France*, Hudoc (2007); (2007) 45 E.H.R.R. SE 10.

[2] See Brownlie, *State Responsibility* (Pt I, 1983); Borchard (1929) 1 Z.A.O.R.V. 223; Cheng, *General Principles of Law as Applied by International Courts and Tribunals* (1953), Chs 6–10; Eagleton, *The Responsibility of States in International Law* (1928); Fitzmaurice and Sarooshi, eds, *Issues of State Responsibility before International Judicial Institutions* (2004); Garcia Amador (1958–II) 94 Hague Recueil 365; Ragazzi, ed., *International Responsibility Today: Essays in Memory of Oscar Schachter* (2005); Thirlway (1995) 66 B.Y.I.L. 1 at 38. Among textbooks, see, in particular, Brownlie, Ch.21; and Schwarzenberger, Chs 31–36. See also the reports of the ILC Special Rapporteurs on state responsibility, Ago, Riphagen, Arangio Ruiz and Crawford printed in the Yearbooks of the Y.B.I.L.C. from 1969 onwards.

[3] For an account of the ILC's work since 1956, see Crawford, *The International Law Commission's Articles on State Responsibility* (2002), pp.1–60.

[4] See Crawford, above, at n.2; symposium, (2002) 96 A.J.I.L. 773; and symposium, (2002) 13 E.J.I.L. 1053. See also Rosenne, ed., *The International Law Commission's Draft Articles on State Responsibility* (1991) (on an earlier version of arts 1–35) and id. (2004) 75 B.Y.I.L. 363.

[5] See the ILC commentary, below, p.450.

[6] Commentary, ILC Draft Articles, below, p.505, para.1.

"The emphasis is on the secondary rules of State responsibility: that is to say, the general conditions under international law for the State to be considered responsible for wrongful actions or omissions, and the legal consequences which flow therefrom. The articles do not attempt to define the content of the international obligations breach of which gives rise to responsibility. This is the function of the primary rules, whose codification would involve restating most of substantive international law, customary and conventional."

The materials in the following section of this Chapter consist of the text of most of the Draft Articles together with the ILC commentaries on them. The General Assembly has "commended" the Draft Articles to the attention of governments, but left unresolved the question of a possible Convention based upon them, most recently deferring it to its 65th session in 2010.[7] While some states favour a Convention, others do not. The United Kingdom, for example, has stated:

"...reaching agreement on the text of the Articles was not easy, and required intense negotiation and compromise. Consequently, the text...in its entirety is not wholly satisfactory to any state. Nevertheless, states generally have accepted the Articles in their current form. At present, many of the Articles reflect an authoritative statement of international law and have been referred to by international courts and tribunals, writers and...domestic courts[8]...there is a real risk that in moving towards the adoption of a convention...old issue may be re-opened...If few states were to ratify a Convention, that instrument would have less legal force than the Articles...and stifle the process of development and consolidation of the law that the Articles...have set in train."[9]

As to *primary* rules of state responsibility, responsibility arises for the breach of any obligation owed under international law. A state is responsible, for example, if it fails to honour a treaty, if it violates the territorial sovereignty of another state, if it damages the territory or property of another state, if it employs armed force against another state, if it injures the diplomatic representatives of another state, or if it mistreats the nationals of another state. For some writers the term state responsibility has been used only in connection with the last of these examples. Although it is not used in this limited sense here, the only particular category of state responsibility dealt with in this Chapter, in section 3, is, in fact, the treatment of aliens. Materials on other categories of responsibility are included in other Chapters of this book. Section 3 of this Chapter concerns only the admission and expulsion of aliens and the expropriation of their property. The customary international law of state responsibility concerning such other matters such as the detention and physical ill-treatment of aliens and their right to a fair trial has been rendered less important than formerly by the development of international human rights law, which applies to all individuals, whether aliens or nationals.[10]

---

[7]   A/RES/62/61 (2007). See also A/RES/56/83 (2001).

[8]   Ed. The UK statement refers to the UN Secretary General's *Compilation of Decisions of International Courts, Tribunals and Other Bodies*, A/62/62 (2007) and the British Institute of International and Comparative Law's report (by Olleson), *The Impact of the ILC's Articles on Responsibility of States for Internationally Wrongful Acts* (2007). See also the *Gabčikovo-Nagymaros Project* case, below, n.216.

[9]   UK statement at the General Assembly's 6th Committee, 62nd session, October 23, 2007, U.K.M.I.L. 2007; (2007) 78 B.Y.I.L. 649. See also Crawford and Olleson (2005) 54 I.C.L.Q. 959.

[10] See below, Ch.9. On the customary international law on the treatment of aliens in these areas, see the literature cited below, p.564, n.2.

2. THE THEORY OF RESPONSIBILITY

ILC DRAFT ARTICLES ON RESPONSIBILITY OF STATES FOR INTERNATIONALLY WRONGFUL ACTS

Report of the 53rd Sess., ILC (2001), G.A.O.R. 56th Sess., Supp. 10.

Part One: The Internationally Wrongful Act of a State

Chapter I: General Principles

Article 1

Every internationally wrongful act of a State entails the international responsibility of that State.

Commentary

(1) Article 1 states the basic principle underlying the articles as a whole, which is that a breach of international law by a State entails its international responsibility.[11] ...

(2) The International Court of Justice has applied the principle on several occasions, for example in the *Corfu Channel* case[12] ...

(7) The articles deal only with the responsibility of States. Of course, as the International Court of Justice affirmed in the *Reparation for Injuries* case, the United Nations "is a subject of international law and capable of possessing international rights and duties ... it has the capacity to maintain its rights by bringing international claims."[13] The Court has also drawn attention to the responsibility of the United Nations for the conduct of its organs or agents.[14] It may be that the notion of responsibility for wrongful conduct is a basic element in the possession of international legal personality. Nonetheless special considerations apply to the responsibility of other international legal persons, and these are not covered in the articles ...

Article 2

There is an internationally wrongful act of a State when conduct consisting of an action or omission:

(a) is attributable to the State under international law; and

(b) constitutes a breach of an international obligation of the State.

Commentary

... (3) The element of attribution has sometimes been described as "subjective" and the element of breach as "objective", but the articles avoid such terminology. Whether there has been a breach of a rule may depend on the intention or knowledge of relevant State organs or agents and in that sense may be "subjective". For example article II of the Genocide Convention states that: "In the present Convention, genocide means any of the following acts committed with intent to destroy, in whole or in part, a national, ethnical, racial or religious group, as such ..." In other cases, the standard for breach of an obligation may be "objective", in the sense that the advertence or otherwise of relevant State organs or agents may be irrelevant. Whether responsibility is "objective" or "subjective" in this sense depends on the circumstances, including the content of the primary obligation in question. The articles lay down no general rule in that regard. The same is true of other standards, whether they involve some degree of fault, culpability, negligence or want of due diligence. Such standards vary

---

[11] Ed. On the succession of new states to the responsibility of their predecessors, see Dumberry, *State Succession to International Responsibility* (2007).

[12] *Corfu Channel, Merits, ICJ Reports 1949, p. 4, at p.23.*

[13] I.C.J. Rep. 1949, p.174 at 179.

[14] *Difference Relating to Immunity from Legal Process of a Special Rapporteur of the Commission on Human Rights*, I.C.J. Rep. 1999. p.62 at pp.88–89, para.66.

from one context to another for reasons which essentially relate to the object and purpose of the treaty provision or other rule giving rise to the primary obligation. Nor do the articles lay down any presumption in this regard as between the different possible standards. Establishing these is a matter for the interpretation and application of the primary rules engaged in the given case.

(4) Conduct attributable to the State can consist of actions or omissions. Cases in which the international responsibility of a State has been invoked on the basis of the omission are at least as numerous as those based on positive acts, and no difference in principle exists between the two. Moreover it may be difficult to isolate an "omission" from the surrounding circumstances which are relevant to the determination of responsibility. For example in the *Corfu Channel* case, the International Court of Justice held that it was a sufficient basis for Albanian responsibility that it knew, or must have known, of the presence of the mines in its territorial waters and did nothing to warn third States of their presence.[15] In the *Diplomatic and Consular Staff* case, the Court concluded that the responsibility of Iran was entailed by the "inaction" of its authorities which "failed to take appropriate steps", in circumstances where such steps were evidently called for.[16] In other cases it may be the combination of an action and an omission which is the basis for responsibility.[17] ...

(9) ... It is sometimes said that international responsibility is not engaged by conduct of a State in disregard of its obligations unless some further element exists, in particular, "damage" to another State. But whether such elements are required depends on the content of the primary obligation, and there is no general rule in this respect. For example, the obligation under a treaty to enact a uniform law is breached by the failure to enact the law, and it is not necessary for another State party to point to any specific damage it has suffered by reason of that failure. Whether a particular obligation is breached forthwith upon a failure to act on the part of the responsible State, or whether some further event must occur, depends on the content and interpretation of the primary obligation and cannot be determined in the abstract.[18]

(10) A related question is whether fault constitutes a necessary element of the internationally wrongful act of a State. This is certainly not the case if by "fault" one understands the existence, for example, of an intention to harm. In the absence of any specific requirement of a mental element in terms of the primary obligation, it is only the act of the State that matters, independently of any intention.

Article 3

The characterization of an act of a State as internationally wrongful is governed by international law. Such characterization is not affected by the characterization of the same act as lawful by internal law.

Commentary[19]

(1) Article 3 makes explicit a principle already implicit in article 2, namely that the characterization of a given act as internationally wrongful is independent of its characterization as lawful under the internal law of the State concerned. There are two elements to this. First, an act of a State cannot be characterized as internationally wrongful unless it constitutes a breach of an international obligation, even if it violates a provision of the State's own law. Secondly and most importantly, a state cannot, by pleading that its conduct conforms to the provisions of its internal law, escape the characterization of that conduct as wrongful by international law. ...

---

[15] *Corfu Channel, Merits,* ICJ Reports 1949, p. 4 at pp. 22–23.

[16] *Diplomatic and Consular Staff,* ICJ Reports 1980, p. 3, at pp. 31–32, paras 63, 67. See also *Velásquez Rodríguez, Inter-Am.Ct.H.R., Series C, No. 4* (1989), para. 170: "under international law a State is responsible for the acts of its agents undertaken in their official capacity and for their omissions ..."

[17] For example, under Article 4 of the Hague Convention (VIII) of 18 October 1907 Relative to the Laying of Automatic Submarine Contact Mines, a neutral Power which lays mines off its coasts but omits to give the required notice to other States Parties would be responsible accordingly. ...

[18] For examples of analysis of different obligations, see e.g. *Diplomatic and Consular Staff,* ICJ Reports 1980, p. 3, at pp. 30–33, paras. 62–68; *Rainbow Warrior, R.I.A.A.,* vol. XX, p. 217 (1990), at pp. 266–267, paras 107–110; ...

[19] Ed. On the principle in art.3, see above, p.63.

Chapter II: Attribution of Conduct to a State

Article 4

1. The conduct of any State organ shall be considered an act of that State under international law, whether the organ exercises legislative, executive, judicial or any other functions, whatever position it holds in the organization of the State, and whatever its character as an organ of the central government or of a territorial unit of the State.

2. An organ includes any person or entity which has that status in accordance with the internal law of the State.

Commentary

(6) ... the reference to a State organ in article 4 is ... not limited to the organs of the central government, to officials at a high level or to persons with responsibility for the external relations of the State. It extends to organs of government of whatever kind or classification, exercising whatever functions, and at whatever level in the hierarchy, including those at provincial or even local level. ...

The International Court has ... confirmed the rule in categorical terms. In *Difference Relating to Immunity from Legal Process of a Special Rapporteur of the Commission on Human Rights*, it said:

> "According to a well-established rule of international law, the conduct of any organ of a State must be regarded as an act of that State. This rule ... is of a customary character ..."[20]

In that case the Court was principally concerned with decisions of State courts, but the same principle applies to legislative and executive acts.

(7) Nor is any distinction made at the level of principle between the acts of "superior" and "subordinate" officials, provided they are acting in their official capacity. ... No doubt lower level officials may have a more restricted scope of activity and they may not be able to make final decisions. But conduct carried out by them in their official capacity is nonetheless attributable to the State for the purposes of article 4. Mixed commissions after the Second World War often had to consider the conduct of minor organs of the State, such as administrators of enemy property, mayors and police officers, and consistently treated the acts of such persons as attributable to the State.

(8) Likewise, the principle in article 4 applies equally to organs of the central government and to those of regional or local units ... the Franco-Italian Conciliation Commission in the *Heirs of the Duc de Guise* case said:

> "For the purposes of reaching a decision in the present case it matters little that the decree of 29 August 1947 was not enacted by the Italian State but by the region of Sicily. For the Italian State is responsible for implementing the Peace Treaty, even for Sicily, notwithstanding the autonomy granted to Sicily in internal relations under the public law of the Italian Republic."[21] ...

(9) It does not matter for this purpose whether the territorial unit in question is a component unit of a federal State or a specific autonomous area, and it is equally irrelevant whether the internal law of the State in question gives the federal parliament power to compel the component unit to abide by the State's international obligations. ... The France/Mexico Claims Commission in the *Pellat* case reaffirmed "the principle of the international responsibility ... of a federal State for all the acts of its separate States which give rise to claims by foreign States" and noted specially that such responsibility "... cannot be denied, not even in cases where the federal Constitution denies the central Government the right of control over the separate States or the right to require them to comply, in their conduct, with the rules of international law".[22] That rule has since been consistently applied. Thus for example in the *LaGrand* case, the International Court said:

---

[20] ... *ICJ Reports 1999*, p. 62, at p. 87, para. 62, referring to the Draft Articles on State Responsibility, art. 6, now embodied in art. 4. Ed. cf. the *Genocide Convention* case, I.C.J. Rep. 2007 and the *OSPAR Arbitration* P.C.A. 2003, p.45 *www.pca-cpa.org*.

[21] *R.I.A.A.*, vol XIII, p. 150 (1951), at p. 161 ...

[22] *R.I.A.A.*, vol. V, p. 534 (1929), at p. 536.

"Whereas the international responsibility of a State is engaged by the action of the competent organs and authorities acting in that State, whatever they may be; whereas the United States should take all measures at its disposal to ensure that Walter LaGrand is not executed pending the final decision in these proceedings; whereas, according to the information available to the Court, implementation of the measures indicated in the present Order falls within the jurisdiction of the Governor of Arizona; whereas the Government of the United States is consequently under the obligation to transmit the present Order to the said Governor; whereas the Governor of Arizona is under the obligation to act in conformity with the international undertakings of the United States ..."[23]

(10) The reasons for this position are reinforced by the fact that federal States vary widely in their structure and distribution of powers, and that in most cases the constituent units have no separate international legal personality of their own (however limited), nor any treaty-making power. In those cases where the constituent unit of a federation is able to enter into international agreements on its own account,[24] the other party may well have agreed to limit itself to recourse against the constituent unit in the event of a breach. In that case the matter will not involve the responsibility of the federal State and will fall outside the scope of the present articles. Another possibility is that the responsibility of the federal State under a treaty may be limited by the terms of a federal clause in the treaty.[25] ...

(11) ... while the powers of an entity and its relation to other bodies under internal law will be relevant to its classification as an "organ", internal law will not itself perform the task of classification. ... For example, under some legal systems the term "government" refers only to bodies at the highest level such as the head of State and the cabinet of ministers. In others, the police have a special status, independent of the executive; this cannot mean that for international law purposes they are not organs of the State.[26] Accordingly, a State cannot avoid responsibility for the conduct of a body which does not in truth act as one of its organs merely by denying it that status under its own law. ...

(13) Although the principle stated in article 4 is clear and undoubted, difficulties can arise in its application. A particular problem is to determine whether a person who is a State organ acts in that capacity. It is irrelevant for this purpose that the person concerned may have had ulterior or improper motives or may be abusing public power. Where such a person acts in an apparently official capacity, or under colour of authority, the actions in a question will be attributable to the State. The distinction between unauthorized conduct of a State organ and purely private conduct has been clearly drawn in international arbitral decisions. For example, the award of the United States/Mexico General Claims Commission in the *Mallén* case (1927) involved, first, the act of an official acting in a private capacity, and secondly, another act committed by the same official in his official capacity, although in an abusive way.[27] The latter action was, and the former was not, held attributable to the State. The French-Mexican Claims Commission in the *Caire* case excluded responsibility only in cases where "the act had no connexion with the official function and was, in fact, merely the act of a private individual".[28] The case of purely private conduct should not be confused with that of an organ functioning as such but acting ultra vires or in breach of the rules governing its operation. In this latter case, the organ is nevertheless acting in the name of the State: this principle is affirmed in article 7. ...

Article 5

The conduct of a person or entity which is not an organ of the State under article 4 but which is empowered by the law of that State to exercise elements of the governmental authority shall be considered an act of the State under international law, provided the person or entity is acting in that capacity in the particular instance.

---

[23]   ... *Provisional Measures, ICJ Reports 1999*, p. 9, at p. 16, para 28.

[24]   See e.g. arts. 56(3), 172(3) of the Constitution of the Swiss Confederation, 18 April 1999.

[25]   See e.g. Convention for the Protection of the World Cultural and Natural Heritage, Paris, 16 November 1972, *U.N.T.S.*, vol. 1037, p. 152. art. 34.

[26]   See e.g. the *Church of Scientology* case in the German Bundesgerichtshof, Judgment of 26 September 1978, *VI ZR 267/76*, *N.J.W.* 1979, p. 1101; *I.L.R.*, vol 65, p. 193. ...

[27]   *R.I.A.A.*, vol. IV, p. 173 (1927), at p. 175.

[28]   *R.I.A.A.*, vol. V, p. 516 (1929), at p. 531. ...

Commentary

(1) Article 5 ... is intended to take account of the increasingly common phenomenon of para-statal entities, which exercise elements of governmental authority in place of State organs, as well as situations where former State corporations have been privatized but retain certain public or regulatory functions.

(2) ... They may include public corporations, semi-public entities, public agencies of various kinds and even, in special cases, private companies, provided that in each case the entity is empowered by the law of the State to exercise functions of a public character normally exercised by State organs, and the conduct of the entity relates to the exercise of the governmental authority concerned. For example in some countries private security firms may be contracted to act as prison guards and in that capacity may exercise public powers such as powers of detention and discipline pursuant to a judicial sentence or to prison regulations. Private or State-owned airlines may have delegated to them certain powers in relation to immigration control or quarantine. In one case before the Iran-United States Claims Tribunal, an autonomous foundation established by the State held property for charitable purposes under close governmental control; its powers included the identification of property for seizure. It was held that it was a public and not a private entity, and therefore within the Tribunal's jurisdiction; with respect to its administration of allegedly expropriated property, it would in any event have been covered by article 5.[29] ...

(5) The justification for attributing to the State under international law the conduct of "para-statal" entities lies in the fact that the internal law of the State has conferred on the entity in question the exercise of certain elements of the governmental authority. If it is to be regarded as an act of the State for purposes of international responsibility, the conduct of an entity must accordingly concern governmental activity and not other private or commercial activity in which the entity may engage. Thus, for example, the conduct of a railway company to which certain police powers have been granted will be regarded as an act of the State under international law if it concerns the exercise of those powers, but not if it concerns other activities (e.g. the sale of tickets or the purchase of rolling-stock).

(6) Article 5 does not attempt to identify precisely the scope of "governmental authority" for the purpose of attribution of the conduct of an entity to the State. Beyond a certain limit, what is regarded as "governmental" depends on the particular society, its history and traditions. Of particular importance will be not just the content of the powers, but the way they are conferred on an entity, the purposes for which they are to be exercised and the extent to which the entity is accountable to government for their exercise. These are essentially questions of the application of a general standard to varied circumstances. ...

Article 6

The conduct of an organ placed at the disposal of a State by another State shall be considered an act of the former State under international law if the organ is acting in the exercise of elements of the governmental authority of the State at whose disposal it is placed.

Commentary

... (3) Examples of situations that could come within this limited notion of a State organ "placed at the disposal" of another State might include a section of the health service or some other unit placed under the orders of another country to assist in overcoming an epidemic or natural disaster, or judges appointed in particular cases to act as judicial organs of another State. On the other hand, mere aid or assistance offered by organs of one State to another on the territory of the latter is not covered by article 6. For example armed forces may be sent to assist another State in the exercise of the right of collective self-defence or for other purposes. Where the forces in question remain under the authority of the sending State, they exercise elements of the governmental authority of that State and not of the receiving State. Situations can also arise where the organ of one State acts on the joint instructions of its own and another State, or there may be a single entity which is a joint organ of several States. In these cases, the conduct in question is attributable to both States ...

(8) A further, long-standing example, of a situation to which article 6 applies is the Judicial Committee of the Privy Council, which has acted as the final court of appeal for a number of independent States within the Commonwealth. Decisions of the Privy Council on appeal from an independent Commonwealth State will be attributable to that State and not to the United Kingdom. The Privy Council's role is paralleled by certain final

---

[29] *Hyatt International Corporation v Government of the Islamic Republic of Iran* (1985) 9 *Iran-U.S.C.T.R. 72*, at pp. 88–94.

courts of appeal acting pursuant to treaty arrangements.[30] There are many examples of judges seconded by one State to another for a time: in their capacity as judges of the receiving State, their decisions are not attributable to the sending State, even if it continues to pay their salaries. ...

Article 7

The conduct of an organ of a State or of a person or entity empowered to exercise elements of the governmental authority shall be considered as an act of the State under international law if the organ, person or entity acts in that capacity, even if it exceeds its authority or contravenes instructions.

Commentary

(1) Article 7 deals with the important question of unauthorized or ultra vires acts of State organs or entities. ...

(2) The State cannot take refuge behind the notion that, according to the provisions of its internal law or to instructions which may have been given to its organs or agents, their actions or omissions ought not to have occurred or ought to have taken a different form. This is so even where the organ or entity in question has overtly committed unlawful acts under the cover of its official status or has manifestly exceeded its competence. It is so even if other organs of the State have disowned the conduct in question.[31] Any other rule would contradict the basic principle stated in article 3, since otherwise a State could rely on its internal law in order to argue that conduct, in fact carried out by its organs, was not attributable to it. ...

(4) The modern rule is now firmly established in this sense by international jurisprudence, State practice and the writings of jurists.[32] It is confirmed, for example, in article 91 of the 1977 Geneva Protocol I Additional to the Geneva Conventions of 12 August 1949,[33] which provides that: "A Party to the conflict ... shall be responsible for all acts by persons forming part of its armed forces": this clearly covers acts committed contrary to orders or instructions. The commentary notes that article 91 was adopted by consensus and "correspond[s] to the general principles of law on international responsibility".[34]

(5) A definitive formulation of the modern rule is found in the *Caire* case. The case concerned the murder of a French national by two Mexican officers who, after failing to extort money, took Caire to the local barracks and shot him. The Commission held ...

"that the two officers even if they are deemed to have acted outside their competence ... and even if their superiors countermanded an order, have involved the responsibility of the State, since they acted under cover of their status as officers and used means placed at their disposal on account of that status."[35] ...

(7)...Cases where officials acted in their capacity as such, albeit unlawfully or contrary to instructions, must be distinguished from cases where the conduct is so removed from the scope of their official functions that it should be assimilated to that of private individuals, not attributable to the State. In the words of the Iran-United States Claims Tribunal, the question is whether the conduct has been "carried out by persons cloaked with governmental authority."[36]

(8) The problem of drawing the line between unauthorized but still "official" conduct, on the one hand, and "private" conduct on the other, may be avoided if the conduct complained of is systematic or recurrent, such that the State knew or ought to have known of it and should have taken steps to prevent it. However, the distinction between the two situations still needs to be made in some cases, for example when considering isolated instances of outrageous conduct on the part of persons who are officials. That distinction is reflected in the

---

[30] E.g. the Agreement between Nauru and Australia relating to Appeals to the High Court of Australia from the Supreme Court of Nauru, 21 September 1976, *U.N.T.S.*, vol. 1216, p. 151.

[31] See e.g. the "Star and Herald" controversy. Moore, *Digest*, vol VI, p. 775.

[32] For example, the 1961 revised draft by Special Rapporteur F.V. García Amador provided that "an act or omission shall likewise be imputable to the State if the organs or officials concerned exceeded their competence but purported to be acting in their official capacity". *Yearbook ... 1961*, vol. II, p. 53. Ed. Cf. Meron (1957) 33 B.Y.I.L. 851.

[33] Protocol Additional to the Geneva Conventions of 12 August 1949, and relating to the protection of victims of international armed conflicts (Protocol I), 8 June 1977, *U.N.T.S.*, vol 1124, p. 3.

[34] International Committee of the Red Cross, *Commentary on the Additional Protocols* (Geneva 1987), pp. 1053–1054.

[35] *R.I.A.A.*, vol. V, p. 516 (1929), at p. 531. ... Ed. Cf. *Ilascu v Moldova and Russia*, E.Ct.H.R. 2004–VII; 40 E.H.R.R. 1030, para.391.

[36] *Petrolane, Inc. v. Islamic Republic of Iran* (1991) 27 *Iran-U.S.C.T.R.* 64, at p.92. See also commentary to article 4, para.(13).

expression "if the organ, person or entity acts in that capacity" in article 7. This indicates that the conduct referred to comprises only the actions and omissions of organs purportedly or apparently carrying out their official functions, and not the private actions or omissions of individuals who happen to be organs or agents of the State.[37] In short, the question is whether they were acting with apparent authority....

Article 8

The conduct of a person or group of persons shall be considered an act of a State under international law if the person or group of persons is in fact acting on the instructions of, or under the direction or control of, that State in carrying out the conduct.

Commentary

... (2) The attribution to the State of conduct in fact authorized by it is widely accepted in international jurisprudence.[38] In such cases it does not matter that the person or persons involved are private individuals nor whether their conduct involves "governmental activity". Most commonly cases of this kind will arise where State organs supplement their own action by recruiting or instigating private persons or groups who act as "auxiliaries" while remaining outside the official structure of the State. These include, for example, individuals or groups of private individuals who, though not specifically commissioned by the State and not forming part of its police or armed forces, are employed as auxiliaries or are sent as "volunteers" to neighbouring countries, or who are instructed to carry out particular missions abroad.

(3) More complex issues arise in determining whether conduct was carried out "under the direction or control" of a State. Such conduct will be attributable to the State only if it directed or controlled the specific operation and the conduct complained of was an integral part of that operation. The principle does not extend to conduct which was only incidentally or peripherally associated with an operation and which escaped from the State's direction or control.

(4) The degree of control which must be exercised by the State in order for the conduct to be attributable to it was a key issue in the *Military and Paramilitary Activities* case.[39] The question was whether the conduct of the *contras* was attributable to the United States so as to hold the latter generally responsible for breaches of international humanitarian law committed by the *contras*. This was analysed by the Court in terms of the notion of "control". On the one hand, it held that the United States was responsible for the "planning, direction and support" given by United States to Nicaraguan operatives.[40] But it rejected the broader claim of Nicaragua that all the conduct of the *contras* was attributable to the United States by reason of its control over them. ...

Thus while the United States was held responsible for its own support for the *contras*, only in certain individual instances were the acts of the *contras* themselves held attributable to it, based upon actual participation of and directions given by that State. The Court confirmed that a general situation of dependence and support would be insufficient to justify attribution of the conduct to the State.

(5) The Appeals Chamber of the International Criminal Tribunal for the Former Yugoslavia has also addressed these issues.[41] In *Prosecutor v. Tadić*, the Chamber stressed that:

"The requirement of international law for the attribution to States of acts performed by private individuals is that the State exercises control over the individuals. The *degree of control* may, however, vary according to the factual circumstances of each case. The Appeals Chamber fails to see why in each and every circumstance international law should require a high threshold for the test of control."[42]

The Appeals Chamber held that the requisite degree of control by the Yugoslavian authorities over these armed forces required by international law for considering the armed conflict to be international was "*overall control* going beyond the mere financing and equipping of such forces and involving also participation in the planning

---

[37] One form of ultra vires conduct covered by article 7 would be for a State official to accept a bribe to perform some act or conclude some transaction....
[38] See, e.g. The "Zafiro", *R.I.A.A.*, vol. VI p. 160 (1925). ...
[39] ... *ICJ Reports 1986*, p. 14.
[40] Ibid., p. 51, para 86.
[41] Case IT-94-1, *Prosecutor v. Tadić*, (1999) *I.L.M.*, vol. 38, p. 1518. ...
[42] Case IT-94-1, *Prosecutor v. Tadić*, (1999) *I.L.M.*, vol. 38, p. 1518, at p. 1541, para. 11 (emphasis in original).

and supervision of military operations".[43] In the course of their reasoning, the majority considered it necessary to disapprove the International Court's approach in *Military and Paramilitary Activities*. But the legal issues and the factual situation in that case were different from those facing the International Court in *Military and Paramilitary Activities*. The Tribunal's mandate is directed to issues of individual criminal responsibility, not State responsibility, and the question in that case concerned not responsibility but the applicable rules of international humanitarian law.[44] ...

Article 9

The conduct of a person or group of persons shall be considered an act of a State under international law if the person or group of persons is in fact exercising elements of the governmental authority in the absence or default of the official authorities and in circumstances such as to call for the exercise of those elements of authority.

Commentary

... (2) The principle underlying article 9 owes something to the old idea of the *levée en masse*, the self-defence of the citizenry in the absence of regular forces:[45] in effect it is a form of agency of necessity. Instances continue to occur from time to time in the field of State responsibility. Thus the position of the Revolutionary Guards or "Komitehs" immediately after the revolution in the Islamic Republic of Iran was treated by the Iran-United States Claims Tribunal as covered by the principle expressed in article 9. *Yeager v. Islamic Republic of Iran* concerned, inter alia, the action of performing immigration, customs and similar functions at Tehran airport in the immediate aftermath of the revolution. The Tribunal held the conduct attributable to the Islamic Republic of Iran, on the basis that, if it was not actually authorized by the Government, then the Guards ...

"at least exercised elements of the governmental authority in the absence of official authorities, in operations of which the new Government must have had knowledge and to which it did not specifically object ..."[46]

Article 10

1. The conduct of an insurrectional movement which becomes the new government of a State shall be considered an act of that State under international law.
2. The conduct of a movement, insurrectional or other, which succeeds in establishing a new State in part of the territory of a pre-existing State or in a territory under its administration shall be considered an act of the new State under international law.
3. This article is without prejudice to the attribution to a State of any conduct, however related to that of the movement concerned, which is to be considered an act of that State by virtue of articles 4 to 9.

Commentary

... (3) ... International arbitral bodies, including mixed claims commissions and arbitral tribunals[47] have uniformly affirmed what Commissioner Nielsen in the *Solis* case described as a "well-established principle of international law", that no government can be held responsible for the conduct of rebellious groups committed in violation of its authority, where it is itself guilty of no breach of good faith, or of no negligence in suppressing insurrection.[48] Diplomatic practice is remarkably consistent in recognizing that the conduct of an insurrectional movement cannot be attributed to the State. ...

---

[43]   Ibid., at p. 1546, para. 145 (emphasis in original). Ed. In the *Genocide Convention* case, I.C.J. Rep. 2007, paras 403 et seq. the ICJ confirmed its approach in the *Nicaragua* case, disagreeing with the *Tadic* case, though, like the ILC, distinguishing it on the facts.

[44]   See the explanation given by Judge Shahabuddeen, ibid., at pp. 1614–1615.

[45]   This principle is recognized as legitimate by article 2 of the 1907 Hague Regulations Respecting the Laws and Customs of War on Land; ... and by article 4, paragraph A (6), of the Geneva Convention of 12 August 1949 on the Treatment of Prisoners of War, *U.N.T.S.*, vol 75, p. 135.

[46]   (1987) 17 *Iran-U.S.C.T.R.* 92, at p. 104, para 43.

[47]   See e.g. *British Claims in the Spanish Zone of Morocco*, *R.I.A.A.*, vol. II, p. 615 (1925), at p. 642 ... Ed. See on art.10, Dumberry (2006) 17 E.J.I.L. 605.

[48]   *R.I.A.A.*, vol. IV, p. 358 (1928), at p. 361 (referring to *Home Missionary Society*, *R.I.A.A.*, vol. VI, p. 42 (1920) ...

(4) The general principle ... is premised on the assumption that the structures and organization of the movement are and remain independent of those of the State. This will be the case where the State successfully puts down the revolt. In contrast, where the movement achieves its aims and either installs itself as the new government of the State or forms a new State in part of the territory of the pre-existing State or in a territory under its administration, it would be anomalous if the new regime or new State could avoid responsibility for conduct earlier committed by it. In these exceptional circumstances, article 10 provides for the attribution of the conduct of the successful insurrectional or other movement to the State. The basis for the attribution of conduct of a successful insurrectional or other movement to the State under international law lies in the continuity between the movement and the eventual government. Thus the term "conduct" only concerns the conduct of the movement as such and not the individual acts of members of the movement, acting in their own capacity. ...

(12) Arbitral decisions, together with State practice and the literature, indicate a general acceptance of the two positive attribution rules in article 10. ... In the *Pinson* case, the French-Mexican Claims Commission ruled that ...

> "if the injuries originated, for example, in requisitions or forced contributions demanded ... by revolutionaries before their final success, or if they were caused ... by offences committed by successful revolutionary forces, the responsibility of the State ... cannot be denied."[49] ...

(16) A further possibility is that the insurrectional movement may itself be held responsible for its own conduct under international law, for example for a breach of international humanitarian law committed by its forces. The topic of the international responsibility of unsuccessful insurrectional or other movements, however, falls outside the scope of the present Articles, which are concerned only with the responsibility of States.

Article 11

Conduct which is not attributable to a State under the preceding articles shall nevertheless be considered an act of that State under international law if and to the extent that the State acknowledges and adopts the conduct in question as its own.

Commentary

... (3) ... [L]ike article 10, article 11 is based on the principle that purely private conduct cannot as such be attributed to a State. But it recognizes "nevertheless" that conduct is to be considered as an act of a State "if and to the extent that the State acknowledges and adopts the conduct in question as its own". Instances of the application of the principle can be found in judicial decisions and State practice. For example, in the *Lighthouses* arbitration, a tribunal held Greece liable for the breach of a concession agreement initiated by Crete at a period when the latter was an autonomous territory of the Ottoman Empire, partly on the basis that the breach had been "endorsed by [Greece] as if it had been a regular transaction ... and eventually continued by her, even after the acquisition of territorial sovereignty over the island ..."[50] In the context of State succession, it is unclear whether a new State succeeds to any State responsibility of the predecessor State with respect to its territory.[51] However, if the successor State, faced with a continuing wrongful act on its territory, endorses and continues that situation, the inference may readily be drawn that it has assume responsibility for it.

(4) Outside the context of State succession, the *Diplomatic and Consular Staff* case[52] provides a further example of subsequent adoption by a State of particular conduct. There the Court drew a clear distinction between the legal situation immediately following the seizure of the United States embassy and its personnel by the militants, and that created by a decree of the Iranian State which expressly approved and maintained the situation.[53] ...

(5) As regards State practice, the capture and subsequent trial in Israel of Adolf Eichmann may provide an example of the subsequent adoption of private conduct by a State. On 10 May 1960, Eichmann was captured by a

---

[49] *R.I.A.A.*, vol. V, p. 327 (1928), at p. 353.
[50] *R.I.A.A.*, vol. XII, p. 155 (1956), at p. 198.
[51] The matter is reserved by art. 39, Vienna Convention on Succession of States in Respect of Treaties, 23 August 1978, *U.N.T.S.*, vol. 1946, p. 3.
[52] *United States Diplomatic and Consular Staff in Tehran*, ICJ Reports 1980, p. 3.
[53] Ed. See above, p.312.

group of Israelis in Buenos Aires. He was held in captivity in Buenos Aires in a private home for some weeks before being taken by air to Israel. Argentina later charged the Israeli Government with complicity in Eichmann's capture, a charge neither admitted nor denied by the Israeli Foreign Minister, Ms. Meir, during the Security Council's discussion of the complaint. She referred to Eichmann's captors as a "volunteer group".[54] Security Council resolution 138 of 23 June 1960 implied a finding that the Israeli Government was at least aware of, and consented to, the successful plan to capture Eichmann in Argentina. It may be that Eichmann's captors were "in fact acting on the instructions of or under the direction or control of" Israel, in which case their conduct was more properly attributed to the State under article 8. But where there are doubts about whether certain conduct falls within article 8, these may be resolved by the subsequent adoption of the conduct in question by the State.

(6) The phrase "acknowledges and adopts the conduct in question as its own" is intended to distinguish cases of acknowledgement and adoption from cases of mere support or endorsement.[55] ...

Chapter III: Breach of an International Obligation

Article 12

There is a breach of an international obligation by a State when an act of that State is not in conformity with what is required of it by that obligation, regardless of its origin or character.

Commentary

(5) ... [T]here is no room in international law for a distinction, such as is drawn by some legal systems, between the regime of responsibility for breach of a treaty and for breach of some other rule, i.e. for responsibility arising *ex contractu* or *ex delicto*. In the *Rainbow Warrior* arbitration, the Tribunal affirmed that "in the international law field there is no distinction between contractual and tortuous responsibility".[56] As far as the origin of the obligation breached is concerned, there is a single general régime of State responsibility. Nor does any distinction exist between "civil" and "criminal" responsibility as is the case in internal legal systems.[57]

(6) State responsibility can arise from breaches of bilateral obligations or of obligations owed to some States or to the international community as a whole. It can involve relatively minor infringements as well as the most serious breaches of obligations under peremptory norms of general international law. ...

(11) Article 12 also states that there is a breach of an international obligation when the act in question is not in conformity with what is required by that obligation, "regardless of its ... character". In practice, various classifications of international obligations have been adopted. For example a distinction is commonly drawn between obligations of conduct and obligations of result. That distinction may assist in ascertaining when a breach has occurred. But it is not exclusive,[58] and it does not seem to bear specific or direct consequences as far as the present articles are concerned. ...

(12) The question often arises whether an obligation is breached by the enactment of legislation by a State, in cases where the content of the legislation *prima facie* conflicts with what is required by the international obligation, or whether the legislation has to be implemented in the given case before the breach can be said to have occurred. Again, no general rule can be laid down applicable to all cases.[59] Certain obligations may be breached by the mere passage of incompatible legislation.[60] Where this is so, the passage of the legislation without more entails the international responsibility of the enacting State, the legislature itself being an organ of the State for the purposes of the attribution of responsibility.[61] In other circumstances, the enactment of

---

[54] *S.C.O.R., Fifteenth Year*, 865th Mtg., 22 June 1960, p. 4.

[55] The separate question of aid or assistance by a State to internationally wrongful conduct of another State is dealt with in article 16.

[56] *R.I.A.A.*, vol. XX, p. 217 (1990), at p. 251, para 75.

[57] Ed. On the absence of criminal responsibility, see below, p.451.

[58] Cf., *Gabčíkovo-Nagymaros Project, ICJ Reports 1997*, p. 7, at p. 77, para. 135, where the Court referred to the parties having accepted "obligations of conduct, obligations of performance, and obligations of result".

[59] Cf. *Applicability of the Obligation to Arbitrate under Section 21 of the United Nations Headquarters Agreement of 26 June 1947, ICJ Reports 1988*, p. 12, at p. 30, para. 42.

[60] A uniform law treaty will generally be construed as requiring immediate implementation, i.e. as embodying an obligation to make the provisions of the uniform law a part of the law each State party. ...

[61] See article 4 and commentary. For illustrations see, e.g. the findings of the European Court of Human Rights in *Norris v. Ireland, E.C.H.R., Series A, No. 142* (1988), para. 31. ...

legislation may not in and of itself amount to a breach,[62] especially if it is open to the State concerned to give effect to the legislation in a way which would not violate the international obligation in question. In such cases, whether there is a breach will depend on whether and how the legislation is given effect.

Article 13

An act of a State does not constitute a breach of an international obligation unless the State is bound by the obligation in question at the time the act occurs.

Commentary

(1) Article 13 ... is but the application in the field of State responsibility of the general principle of inter-temporal law, as stated by Judge Huber in another context in the *Island of Palmas* case:

> "A juridical fact must be appreciated in the light of the law contemporary with it, and not of the law in force at the time when a dispute in regard to it arises or falls to be settled."[63] ...

Article 14

1. The breach of an international obligation by an act of a State not having a continuing character occurs at the moment when the act is performed, even if its effects continue.

2. The breach of an international obligation by an act of a State having a continuing character extends over the entire period during which the act continues and remains not in conformity with the international obligation.

3. The breach of an international obligation requiring a State to prevent a given event occurs when the event occurs and extends over the entire period during which the event continues and remains not in conformity with that obligation.

Commentary

... (4) Whether a wrongful act is completed or has a continuing character will depend both on the primary obligation and the circumstances of the given case. For example, the Inter-American Court of Human Rights has interpreted forced or involuntary disappearance as a continuing wrongful act, one which continues for as long as the person concerned is unaccounted for.[64] The question whether a wrongful taking of property is a completed or continuing act likewise depends to some extent on the content of the primary rule said to have been violated. Where an expropriation is carried out by legal process, with the consequence that title to the property concerned is transferred, the expropriation itself will then be a completed act. ...

(8) The consequences of a continuing wrongful act will depend on the context, as well as on the duration of the obligation breached. For example, the *Rainbow Warrior* arbitration involved the failure of France to detain two agents on the French Pacific island of Hao for a period of three years, as required by an agreement between France and New Zealand. The Arbitral Tribunal referred with approval to the Commission's draft articles (now amalgamated in article 14) and to the distinction between instantaneous and continuing wrongful acts, and said:

> "Applying this classification to the present case, it is clear that the breach consisting in the failure of returning to Hao the two agents has been not only a material but also a continuous breach. And this classification is not purely theoretical, but, on the contrary, it has practical consequences since the seriousness of the breach and its prolongation in time cannot fail to have considerable bearing on the establishment of the reparation which is adequate for a violation presenting these two features."[65]

---

[62] As the International Court held in *LaGrand (Germany v. United States of America), Merits*, judgment of 27 June 2001, paras. 90–91.

[63] *R.I.A.A.*, vol II, p. 829 (1949), at p. 845. Ed. see further above, p.170.

[64] *Blake v. Guatemala, Inter-Am Cr.H.R., Series C, No. 36* (1998), para. 67.

[65] *Rainbow Warrior (New Zealand/France), R.I.A.A.*, vol. XX, p. 217 (1990), at p. 264, para. 101. Ed. art.14(3) states "a general rule of the law of state responsibility": *Genocide Convention* case, I.C.J. Rep. 2007, para.431. The obligation to act to prevent genocide commences when the state learns, or should normally have learnt, of the existence of a serious risk of its commission and will continue while this risk remains, though no breach will occur if genocide does not actually take place.

The Tribunal went on to draw further legal consequences from the distinction in terms of the duration of French obligations under the agreement.[66]

(9) The notion of continuing wrongful acts has also been applied by the European Court of Human Rights to establish its jurisdiction *ratione temporis* in a series of cases. The issue arises because the Court's jurisdiction may be limited to events occurring after the respondent State became a party to the Convention or the relevant Protocol and accepted the right of individual petition. ...

Article 15

1. The breach of an international obligation by a State through a series of actions or omissions defined in aggregate as wrongful, occurs when the action or omission occurs which, taken with the other actions or omissions, is sufficient to constitute the wrongful act.

2. In such a case, the breach extends over the entire period starting with the first of the actions or omissions of the series and lasts for as long as these actions or omissions are repeated and remain not in conformity with the international obligation.

Commentary

... (2) Composite acts covered by article 15 are limited to breaches of obligations which concern some aggregate of conduct and not individual acts as such. In other words their focus is "a series of acts or omissions defined in aggregate as wrongful". Examples include the obligations concerning genocide, *apartheid* or crimes against humanity, systematic acts of racial discrimination, systematic acts of discrimination prohibited by a trade agreement, etc. Some of the most serious wrongful acts in international law are defined in terms of their composite character. The importance of these obligations in international law justifies special treatment in article 15.[67]

Chapter IV: Responsibility of a State in Connection with the Act of Another State

Article 16[68]

A State which aids or assists another State in the commission of an internationally wrongful act by the latter is internationally responsible for doing so if:

(a) that State does so with knowledge of the circumstances of the internationally wrongful act; and

(b) the act would be internationally wrongful if committed by that State.

Commentary

...(7) State practice supports assigning international responsibility to a State which deliberately participates in the internationally wrongful conduct of another through the provision of aid or assistance, in circumstances where the obligation breached is equally opposable to the assisting State. For example, in 1984 Iran protested against the supply of financial and military aid to Iraq by the United Kingdom, which allegedly included chemical weapons used in attacks against Iranian troops, on the ground that the assistance was facilitating acts of aggression by Iraq.[69] The British government denied both the allegation that it had chemical weapons and that it had supplied them to Iraq.[70] ...

(8) The obligation not to use force may also be breached by an assisting State through permitting the use of its territory by another State to carry out an armed attack against a third State. An example ... arises from the Tripoli bombing incident in April 1986. Libya charged the United Kingdom with responsibility for the event, based on the fact that the United Kingdom had allowed several of its air bases to be used for the launching of American

---

[66] Ibid., at pp. 265–266, paras 105–106. ...

[67] Ed. On "composite acts" partly before and after a treaty enters into force, see Gallus (2007) 56 I.C.L.Q. 491.

[68] Ed. art.16 reflects customary international law: *Genocide Convention* case, I.C.J. Rep. 2007 para.420. On art.16, see Nolte and Aust (2009) 58 I.C.L.Q. 1.

[69] See *New York Times*, 6 March 1984, p. A1, col. 1.

[70] See *New York Times*, 5 March 1984, p. A3, col. 1

fighter planes to attack Libyan targets.[71] Libya asserted that the United Kingdom "would be held partly responsible" for having "supported and contributed in a direct way" to the raid.[72] The United Kingdom denied responsibility on the basis that the raid by the United States was lawful as an act of self-defence against Libyan terrorist attacks on American targets.[73] A proposed Security Council resolution concerning the attack was vetoed, but the United Nations General Assembly issued a resolution condemning the "military attack" as "a violation of the Charter of the United Nations and of international law", and calling upon all States "to refrain from extending any assistance or facilities for perpetrating acts of aggression against the Libyan Arab Jamahiriya."[74]

(9) The obligation not to provide aid or assistance to facilitate the commission of an internationally wrongful act by another State is not limited to the prohibition on the use of force. For instance, a State may incur responsibility if it assists another State to circumvent sanctions imposed by the United Nations Security Council[75] or provides material aid to a State that uses the aid to commit human rights violations. In this respect, the United Nations General Assembly has called on member States in a number of cases to refrain from supplying arms and other military assistance to countries found to be committing serious human rights violations.[76] ...

Article 17

A State which directs and controls another State in the commission of an internationally wrongful act by the latter is internationally responsible for that act if:

(a) that State does so with knowledge of the circumstances of the internationally wrongful act; and

(b) the act would be internationally wrongful if committed by that State.

Commentary

... (2) Some examples of international responsibility flowing from the exercise of direction and control over the commission of a wrongful act by another State are now largely of historical significance. International dependency relationships such as "suzerainty" or "protectorate" warranted treating the dominant Sate as internationally responsible for conduct formally attributable to the dependent State. ...

(5) Nonetheless, instances exist or can be envisaged where one State exercises the power to direct and control the activities of another State, whether by treaty or as a result of a military occupation or for some other reason. For example, during the belligerent occupation of Italy by Germany in the Second World War, it was generally acknowledged than the Italian police in Rome operated under the control of the occupying Power. Thus the protest by the Holy See in respect of wrongful acts committed by Italian police who forcibly entered the Basilica of St Paul in Rome in February 1944 asserted the responsibility of the German authorities.[77] In such cases the occupying State is responsible for acts of the occupied State which it directs and controls. ...

Article 18

A State which coerces another State to commit an act is internationally responsible for that act if:

(a) the act would, but for the coercion, be an internationally wrongful act of the coerced State; and

(b) the coercing State does so with knowledge of the circumstances of the act.

---

[71] See United States of America *Department of State Bulletin*, No. 2111. June 1986, p. 8.

[72] See the statement of Ambassador Hamed Houdeiry, Libyan People's Bureau, Paris, *The Times*, 16 April 1986, p. 6, col. 7.

[73] Statement of Mrs. Margaret Thatcher, Prime Minister, *House of Commons Debates*, 6th series, vol. 95, col. 737 (15 April 1986), reprinted in *B.Y.I.L.*, vol. 57 (1986), p. 638.

[74] See G.A. Res. 41/38 of 20 November 1986, paras. 1, 3.

[75] See, e.g., Report by President Clinton, *A.J.I.L.*, vol. 91 (1997), p. 709.

[76] *Report of the Economic and Social Council, Report of the Third Committee of the General Assembly*, Draft Resolution XVII, 14 December 1982, A.37.745, p. 50.

[77] See R. Ago, *"L'occupazione bellica di Roma e il Trattato lateranense"*, *Comunicazioni e Studi* (Milan, Giuffré, 1946) vol. II, pp. 167–168.

Commentary

... (7) State practice lends support to the principle that a State bears responsibility for the internationally wrongful conduct of another State which it coerces. In the *Romano-Americana* case, the claim of the United States Government in respect of the destruction of certain oil storage and other facilities owned by an American company on the orders of certain oil storage and other facilities owned by an American company on the orders of the Romanian Government during the First World War was originally addressed to the British Government. At the time the facilities were destroyed, Romania was at war with Germany, which was preparing to invade the country, and the United States claimed that the Romanian authorities had been "compelled" by Great Britain to take the measures in question. In support of its claim, the United States Government argued that the circumstances of the case revealed "a situation where a strong belligerent for a purpose primarily its own arising from its defensive requirements at sea, compelled a weaker Ally to acquiesce in an operation which it carried out in the territory of that Ally."[78] The British Government denied responsibility, asserting that its influence over the conduct of the Romanian authorities "did not in any way go beyond the limits of persuasion and good counsel as between governments associated in a common cause"[79]. The point of disagreement between the governments of the United States and of Great Britain was not as to the responsibility of a State for the conduct of another State which it has coerced, but rather the existence of "compulsion" in the particular circumstances of the case. ...

Chapter V: Circumstances Precluding Wrongfulness[80]

Article 20

Valid consent by a State to the commission of a given act by another State precludes the wrongfulness of that act in relation to the former State to the extent that the act remains within the limits of that consent.

Article 21[81]

The wrongfulness of an act of a State is precluded if the act constitutes a lawful measure of self-defence taken in conformity with the Charter of the United Nations.

Commentary

...(3) This not to say that self-defence precludes the wrongfulness of conduct in all cases or with respect to all obligations. Examples relate to international humanitarian law and human rights obligations. The Geneva Conventions of 1949 and Protocol I of 1977 apply equally to all the parties in an international armed conflict, and the same is true of customary international humanitarian law.[82] Human rights treaties contain derogation provisions for times of public emergency, including actions taken in self-defence. As to obligations under international humanitarian law and in relation to non-derogable human rights provisions, self-defence does not preclude the wrongfulness of conduct.

(4) The International Court in its advisory opinion on the *Legality of the Threat or Use of Nuclear Weapons* provided some guidance on this question. One issue before the Court was whether a use of nuclear weapons would necessarily be a breach of environmental [treaty] obligations because of the massive and long-term damage such weapons can cause. The Court said:

"...The Court does not consider that the treaties in question could have intended to deprive a State of the exercise of its right of self-defence under international law because of its obligations to protect the environment. Nonetheless, States must take environmental considerations into account when assessing what is necessary and proportionate in the pursuit of legitimate military objectives. Respect for the environment is one

---

[78]   Note from the United States Embassy in London, 16 February 1925 in Hackworth, *Digest*, vol. V, p. 702.
[79]   Note from the British Foreign Office dated 5 July 1928, ibid., p. 704
[80]   Ed. See Lowe (1999) 10 E.J.I.L. 405.
[81]   Ed. On the right to self defence under art.51, UN Charter, see below, p.746.
[82]   As the Court said of the rules of international humanitarian law in the advisory opinion of the *Legality of the Threat of Use of Nuclear Weapons*, *I.C.J. Reports 1996*, p.226, at p.257, para.79, they constitute "intransgressible principles of international customary law"....

of the elements that go to assessing whether an action is in conformity with the principles of necessity and proportionality."[83]

A State acting in self defence is "totally restrained" by an international obligation if that obligation is expressed or intended to apply as a definitive constraint even to States in armed conflict.[84]

Article 22

The wrongfulness of an act of a State not in conformity with an international obligation towards another State is precluded if and to the extent that the act constitutes a countermeasure taken against the latter State in accordance with Chapter II of Part Three [arts 49–54, below pp.456 et seq.].

Article 23

1. The wrongfulness of an act of a State not in conformity with an international obligation of that State is precluded if the act is due to *force majeure,* that is the occurrence of an irresistible force or of an unforeseen event, beyond the control of the State, making it materially impossible in the circumstances to perform the obligation.
    2. Paragraph 1 does not apply if:

(a) the situation of *force majeure* is due, either alone or in combination with other factors, to the conduct of the State invoking it; or

(b) the State has assumed the risk of that situation occurring.

Commentary

(1) *Force majeure* ... differs from a situation of distress (article 24) or necessity (article 25) because the conduct of the State which would otherwise be internationally wrongful is involuntary or at least involves no element of free choice ...
    (3) Material impossibility of performance giving rise to *force majeure* may be due to a natural or physical event (e.g., stress of weather which may divert State aircraft into the territory of another State, earthquakes, floods or drought) or to human intervention (e.g., loss of control over a portion of the State's territory as a result of an insurrection or devastation of an area by military operations carried out by a third State), or some combination of the two. ... *Force majeure* does not include circumstances in which performance of an obligation has become more difficult, for example due to some political or economic crisis. Nor does it cover situations brought about by the neglect or default of the State concerned, even if the resulting injury itself was accidental and unintended. ...
    (7) The principle has ... been accepted by international tribunals. Mixed claims commissions have frequently cited the unforeseeability of attacks by rebels in denying the responsibility of the territorial State for resulting damage suffered by foreigners.[85] In the *Lighthouses* arbitration, a lighthouse owned by a French company had been requisitioned by the Greek Government in 1915 and was subsequently destroyed by enemy action. The arbitral tribunal denied the French claim for restoration of the lighthouse on grounds of *force majeure.*[86] ...

Article 24

1. The wrongfulness of an act of a State not in conformity with an international obligation of that State is precluded if the author of the act in question has no other reasonable way, in a situation of distress, of saving the author's life or the lives of other persons entrusted to the author's care.
    2. Paragraph 1 does not apply if:

---

[83] *I.C.J. Reports 1996,* p.226, at p.242, para.30.
[84] See, e.g., Multilateral Convention on the Prohibition of Military or any other Hostile Use of Environmental Modification Techniques, 10 December 1976, *U.N.T.S.,* vol.1108, p.151.
[85] See e.g., ... the *Gill* case: *R.I.A.A.,* vol V, p. 157 (1931). ...
[86] *Ottoman Empire Lighthouses Concession, R.I.A.A.,* vol. XII, p. 155 (1956), at pp. 219–220.

(a) the situation of distress is due, either alone or in combination with other factors, to the conduct of the State invoking it, or

(b) the act in question is likely to create a comparable or greater peril.

Commentary

(1) ... Unlike situations of *force majeure* dealt with in article 23, a person acting under distress is not acting involuntarily, even though the choice is effectively nullified by the situation of peril.[87] Nor is it a case of choosing between compliance with international law and other legitimate interests of the state, such as characterize situations of necessity under article 25. The interest concerned is the immediate one of saving people's lives, irrespective of their nationality.

(2) In practice, cases of distress have mostly involved aircraft or ships entering State territory under stress of weather or following mechanical or navigational failure. ...

(4) ... The *Rainbow Warrior* arbitration involved a plea of distress as a circumstance precluding wrongfulness outside the context of ships or aircraft. France sought to justify its conduct in removing the two officers from the island of Hao on the ground of "circumstances of distress in a case of extreme urgency involving elementary humanitarian considerations affecting the acting organs of the State".[88] The Tribunal unanimously accepted that this plea was admissible in principle, and by majority that it was applicable to the acts of one of the two cases. ...

(6) Article 24 is limited to cases where human life is at stake. The Tribunal in the *Rainbow Warrior* arbitration appeared to take a broader view of the circumstances justifying a plea of distress, apparently accepting that a serious health risk would suffice. The problem with extending article 24 to less than life-threatening situations is where to place any lower limit. ...

Article 25

1. Necessity may not be invoked by a State as a ground for precluding the wrongfulness of an act not in conformity with an international obligation of that State unless the act:

(a) is the only means of the State to safeguard an essential interest against a grave and imminent peril; and

(b) does not seriously impair an essential interest of the State or States towards which the obligation exists, or of the international community as a whole.

2. In any case, necessity may not be invoked by a State as a ground for precluding wrongfulness if:

(a) the international obligation in question excludes the possibility of invoking necessity; or

(b) the State has contributed to the situation of necessity.

Commentary

... (2) The plea of necessity is exceptional in a number of respects. Unlike consent (article 20), self-defence (article 21) or countermeasures (article 22), it is not dependent on the prior conduct of the injured State. Unlike force majeure (article 23), it does not involve conduct which is involuntary or coerced. Unlike distress (article 24), necessity consists not in danger to the lives of individuals in the charge of a State official but in a grave danger either to the essential interests of the state or of the international community as a whole. It arises where there is an irreconcilable conflict, between an essential interest on the one hand and an obligation of the State invoking

---

[87] For this reason, writers who have considered this situation have often defined it as one of "relative impossibility" of complying with the international obligation. See, e.g., O.J. Lissitzyn, "The Treatment of Aerial Intruders in Recent Practice and International Law", *A.J.I.L.*, vol. 47 (1953), p. 559.

[88] *Rainbow Warrior (New Zealand/France)*, *R.I.A.A.*, vol. XX, p. 217 (1990), at pp. 254–255, para. 78.

necessity on the other. These special features mean that necessity will only rarely be available to excuse non-performance of an obligation and that it is subject to strict limitations to safeguard against possible abuse.[89]

(5) The *"Caroline"* incident of 1837, though frequently referred to as an instance of self-defence, really involved the plea of necessity at a time when the law concerning the use of force had a quite different basis than it now has.[90] ...

(9) In March 1967 the Liberian oil tanker *Torrey Canyon* went aground on submerged rocks off the coast of Cornwall outside British territorial waters, spilling large amounts of oil which threatened the English coastline. After various remedial attempts had failed, the British Government decided to bomb the ship to burn the remaining oil. This operation was carried out successfully. The British Government did not advance any legal justification for its conduct, but stressed the existence of a situation of extreme danger and claimed that the decision to bomb the ship had been taken only after all other means had failed.[91] No international protest resulted. A convention was subsequently concluded to cover future cases where intervention might prove necessary to avert serious oil pollution.[92] ...

(10) In the *Rainbow Warrior* arbitration, the Arbitral Tribunal expressed doubt as to the existence of the excuse of necessity. It noted that the Commission's draft article "allegedly authorizes a State to take unlawful action invoking a state of necessity" and described the Commission's proposal as "controversial".[93]

(11) ... in the *Gabčíkovo-Nagymaros Project* case,[94] the International Court carefully considered an argument based on the Commission's draft article (now article 25), expressly accepting the principle while at the same time rejecting its invocation in the circumstances of that case:

"The Court considers ... that the state of necessity is a ground recognized by customary international law for precluding the wrongfulness of an act not in conformity with an international obligation. It observes moreover that such ground for precluding wrongfulness can only be accepted on an exceptional basis. The International Law Commission ... conditions [now in Article 25] reflect customary international law."[95] ...

(13) The existence and limits of a plea of necessity have given rise to a long-standing controversy among writers. It was for the most part explicitly accepted by the early writers, subject to strict conditions. In the nineteenth century, abuses of necessity associated with the idea of "fundamental rights of States" led to a reaction against the doctrine. During the twentieth century, the number of writers opposed to the concept of state of necessity in international law increased, but the balance of doctrine has continued to favour the existence of the plea.[96]

(14) On balance, State practice and judicial decisions support the view that necessity may constitute a circumstance precluding wrongfulness under certain very limited conditions, and this view is embodied in article 25. The cases show that necessity has been invoked to preclude the wrongfulness of acts contrary to a broad range of obligations, whether customary or conventional in origin. It has been invoked to protect a wide variety of interests, including safeguarding the environment, preserving the very existence of the State and its people in

---

[89] Perhaps the classic case of such an abuse was the occupation of Luxembourg and Belgium by Germany in 1914, which Germany sought to justify on the ground of necessity. See ... the speech in the Reichstag by the German Chancellor, von Bethmann-Hollweg, on 4 August 1914, containing the well-known words ... "we are in a state of self-defence and necessity knows no law" ... *Jahrbuch des Völkerrechts*, vol. III (1916), p. 728.

[90] Ed. On the *Caroline* case, see below, p.746.

[91] The *"Torrey Canyon"*, Cmnd. 3246 (London, Her Majesty's Stationery Office, 1967).

[92] International Convention Relating to Intervention on the High Seas in Cases of Oil Pollution Casualties, 29 November 1969, *U.N.T.S.*, vol. 970, p. 211.

[93] *Rainbow Warrior (New Zealand/France)*, R.I.A.A., vol.XX, p.217 (1990) at p.254....

[94] *Gabčíkovo-Nagymaros Project (Hungary/Slovakia)*, ICJ Reports 1997, p. 7.

[95] Ibid., at pp. 40–41, paras. 51–52.

[96] For a review of the earlier doctrine, see *Yearbook ... 1980*, vol.II, Part One, pp.47–49; and see also...J. Barboza, "Necessity (Revisted) in International Law", in J. Makarczyk (ed), *Essays in Honour of Judge Mafred Lachs* (The Hague, Martinus Nijhoff, 1984), p.27; R. Boed, "State of Necessity as a Justification for Internationally Wrongful Conduct", *Yale Human Rights & Development Law Journal*, vol.3 (2000), p.1.

time of public emergency, or ensuring the safety of a civilian population.[97] But stringent conditions are imposed before any such plea is allowed. This is reflected in article 25. In particular, to emphasise the exceptional nature of necessity and concerns about its possible abuse, article 25 is cast in negative language ("Necessity may not be invoked ... unless").

(15) ... The extent to which a given interest is "essential" depends on all the circumstances, and cannot be prejudged. It extends to particular interests of the state and its people, as well as of the international community as a whole. Whatever the interest may be, however, it is only when it is threatened by a grave and imminent peril that this condition is satisfied. The peril has to be objectively established and not merely apprehended as possible. In addition to being grave, the peril has to be imminent in the sense of proximate. However, as the Court said in the *Gabčíkovo-Nagymaros Project* case:

"This does not exclude ... that a 'peril' appearing in the long term might be held to be 'imminent' as soon as it is established, at the relevant point in time, that the realization of that peril, however far off it might be, is not thereby any less certain and inevitable."[98]

Moreover the course of action taken must be the "only way" available to safeguard that interest. The plea is excluded if there are other (otherwise lawful) means available, even if they may be more costly or less convenient. Thus in the *Gabčíkovo-Nagymaros Project* case, the Court was not convinced that the unilateral suspension and abandonment of the Project was the only course open in the circumstances, having regard in particular to the amount of work already done and the money expended on it, and the possibility of remedying any problems by other means.[99] The word "way" in *paragraph (1)(a)* is not limited to unilateral action but may also comprise other forms of conduct available through cooperative action with other States or through international organizations (for example, conservation measures for a fishery taken through the competent regional fisheries agency). Moreover the requirement of necessity is inherent in the plea: any conduct going beyond what is strictly necessary for the purpose will not be covered.

(16) ... By definition, in cases of necessity the peril will not yet have occurred. In the *Gabčíkovo-Nagymaros Project* case the Court noted that the invoking State could not be the sole judge of the necessity,[100] but a measure of uncertainty about the future does not necessarily disqualify a State from invoking necessity, if the peril is clearly established on the basis of the evidence reasonably available at the time. ...

(19) ... *Paragraph (2)(a)* concerns cases where the international obligation in question explicitly or implicitly excludes reliance on necessity. Thus certain humanitarian conventions applicable to armed conflict expressly exclude reliance on military necessity.

(20) According to *paragraph (2)(b)*, necessity may not be relied on if the responsible State has contributed to the situation of necessity. Thus in the *Gabčíkovo-Nagymaros Project* case, the court considered that because Hungary had "helped, by act or omission to bring" about the situation of alleged necessity, it could not now rely on that situation as a circumstance precluding wrongfulness.[101] ...

(21) As embodied in article 25, the plea of necessity is not intended to cover conduct which is in principle

---

[97] Ed. Necessity was pleaded by Argentina unsuccessfully in a series of ICSID arbitrations to justify measures taken by it in 2001–3 in breach of legal obligations owed to foreign investors in response to its severe economic crisis. In *CMS Gas v Argentina* (2005) 44 I.L.M. 1205 at 1240–1241, referring to art.25, which it regarded as customary international law, the tribunal, while accepting that there was a "grave and imminent peril" to an "essential interest", i.e. to prevent "total economic collapse", considered that the measures taken were not "the only means" available and that the state had "contributed to the situation of necessity" by its "government policies and their shortcomings". Cf. *Enron Corp v Argentina*, ICSID Case No.ARB/01/3 (2007). Exceptionally, the defence was accepted in *LG and E Energy v Argentina* (2007) 46 I.L.M. 36. See Reinisch (2007) 8 J. World Investment and Trade 191. See also Rudolf and Hufken (2007) 101 A.J.I.L. 857. In the *Wall* case, para.140, below, p.600, referring to art.25, the ICJ was "not convinced that the construction of the wall along the route chosen was the only means to safeguard the interests of Israel against the peril which it has invoked as justification for that construction".
[98] *ICJ Reports 1997*, p. 7, at p. 42, para 54. 426 Ibid., at pp. 42–43, para 55.
[99] Ibid., at p. 40, para 51.
[100] Ibid., at p. 40, para 51.
[101] *Gabčíkovo-Nagymaros Project, ICJ Reports 1997*, p. 7, at p. 46, para. 57.

regulated by the primary obligations. This has a particular importance in relation to the rules relating to the use of force in international relations and to the question of "military necessity". It is true that in a few cases, the plea of necessity has been invoked to excuse military action abroad, in particular in the context of claims to humanitarian intervention.[102] The question whether measures of forcible humanitarian intervention, not sanctioned pursuant to Chapters VII or VIII of the Charter of the United Nations, may be lawful under modern international law is not covered by article 25.[103] ...

Article 26

Nothing in this Chapter precludes the wrongfulness of any act of a State which is not in conformity with an obligation arising under a peremptory norm of general international law.

Commentary

... (4) It is ... desirable to make it clear that the circumstances precluding wrongfulness in Chapter V of Part One do not authorize or excuse any derogation from a peremptory norm of general international law. For example, a State taking countermeasures may not derogate from such a norm: for example, a genocide cannot justify a counter-genocide.[104] The plea of necessity likewise cannot excuse the breach of a peremptory norm. ...

(5) The criteria for identifying peremptory norms of general international law are stringent. Article 53 of the Vienna Convention [on the Law of Treaties] requires not merely that the norm in question should meet all the criteria for recognition as a norm of general international law, binding as such, but further that it should be recognised as having a peremptory character by the international community of States as a whole. So far, relatively few peremptory norms have been recognised as such. But various tribunals, national and international, have affirmed the idea of peremptory norms in contexts not limited to the validity of treaties. Those peremptory norms that are clearly accepted and recognised include the prohibitions of aggression, genocide, slavery, racial discrimination, crimes against humanity and torture, and the right to self-determination.[105] ...

Article 27

The invocation of a circumstance precluding wrongfulness in accordance with the Chapter is without prejudice to:

(a) compliance with the obligation in question, if and to the extent that the circumstance precluding wrongfulness no longer exists;

(b) the question of compensation for any material loss caused by the act in question ...

Part Two: Content of the International Responsibility of a State

Chapter I: General Principles

Article 28

The international responsibility of a State which is entailed by an internationally wrongful act in accordance with the provisions of Part One involves legal consequences as set out in this Part.

---

[102] E.g. in 1960 Belgium invoked necessity to justify its military intervention in the Congo. The matter was discussed in the Security Council but not in terms of the plea of necessity as such. See *S.C.O.R., Fifteenth Year*, 873rd mtg., 13/14 July 1960, paras. 144, 182, 192; 877th mtg., 20/21 July 1960, paras. 31ff, 142; 878th mtg., 21 July 1960, paras. 23, 65; 879th mtg., 21/22 July 1960, paras 80ff, 118, 151. ...

[103] See also article 26 and commentary for the general exclusion of from the scope of circumstances precluding wrongfulness of conduct in breach of a peremptory norm.

[104] As the International Court noted in its decision on counterclaims in the case concerning the *Application of the Convention on the Prevention and Punishment of the Crime of Genocide*, "in no case could one breach of the Convention serve as an excuse for another": *Application of the Convention on the Prevention and Punishment of the Crime of Genocide, Counter-Claims, ICJ Reports 1997*, p. 243, at p. 258, para 35.

[105] Ed. For details, see below, pp.451–452.

Article 29

The legal consequences of an internationally wrongful act under this Part do not affect the continued duty of the responsible State to perform the obligation breached.

Article 30

The State responsible for the internationally wrongful act is under an obligation:

(a) to cease that act, if it is continuing:

(b) to offer appropriate assurances and guarantees of non-repetition, if circumstances so require.

Commentary

... (3) The Tribunal in the *Rainbow Warrior* arbitration stressed "two essential conditions intimately linked" for the requirement of cessation of wrongful conduct to arise, "namely that the wrongful act has a continuing character and that the violated rule is still in force at the time in which the order is issued."[106] While the obligation to cease wrongful conduct will arise most commonly in the case of a continuing wrongful act,[107] article 30 also encompasses situations where a State has violated an obligation on a series of occasions, implying the possibility of further repetitions. The phrase "if it is continuing" at the end of paragraph (a) of the article is intended to cover both situations.

(4) Cessation of conduct in breach of an international obligation is the first requirement in eliminating the consequences of wrongful conduct. With reparation, it is one of the two general consequences of an internationally wrongful act. Cessation is often the main focus of the controversy produced by conduct in breach of an international obligation.[108] It is frequently demanded not only by States but also by the organs of international organizations such as the General Assembly and Security Council in the face of serious breaches of international law. By contrast reparation, important though it is in many cases, may not be the central issue in a dispute between States as to questions of responsibility.[109] ...

(7) The question of cessation often arises in close connection with that of reparation, and particularly restitution. The result of cessation may be indistinguishable from restitution, for example in cases involving the freeing of hostages or the return of objects or premises seized. Nonetheless the two must be distinguished. Unlike restitution, cessation is not subject to limitations relating to proportionality.[110] It may give rise to a continuing obligation, even when literal return to the *status quo ante* is excluded or can only be achieved in an approximate way. ...

(10) The question whether the obligation [in article 30(b)] to offer assurances or guarantees of non-repetition may be a legal consequence of an internationally wrongful act was debated in the *LaGrand* case.[111] This concerned an admitted failure of consular notification contrary to article 36 of the Vienna Convention on Consular Relations of 1963. In its fourth submission Germany sought both general and specific assurances and guarantees as to the means of future compliance with the Convention. The United States argued that ... no assurances or guarantees were appropriate in light of the extensive action it had taken to ensure that federal and state officials would in future comply with the Conven-tion ...

On the question of appropriateness, the Court noted that an apology would not be sufficient in any case in which a foreign national had been "subjected to prolonged detention or sentenced to severe penalties" following a failure of consular notification.[112] But in the light of information provided by the United States as to the steps taken to comply in future, the Court held ...

---

[106] Ibid., at p. 270, para. 114.

[107] For the concept of a continuing wrongful act, see commentary to article 14 ...

[108] The focus of the W.T.O. Dispute Settlement Mechanism is on cessation rather than reparation: Agreement establishing the World Trade Organisation, 15 April 1994, Annex 2 ...

[109] For cases where the International Court has recognised that this may be so see, e.g., ... *Gabčikovo-Nagymaros Project, ICJ Reports 1997*, p. 7, at p. 81, para 153. See further C. Gray, *Judicial Remedies in International law* (Oxford, Clarendon Press, 1987), pp. 77–92.

[110] See article 35(b) and commentary.

[111] *LaGrand (Germany v. United States of America), Merits*, judgment of 27 June 2001.

[112] *LaGrand, Merits*, judgment of 27 June 2001, para. 123.

"that the commitment expressed by the United States to ensure implementation of the specific measures adopted in performance of its obligations under Article 36, paragraph 1(b), must be regarded as meeting Germany's request for a general assurance of non-repetition."[113]

As to the specific assurances sought by Germany, the Court limited itself to stating that . . .

". . . if the United States, notwithstanding its commitment referred to . . . should fail in its obligation of consular notification to the detriment of German nationals, an apology would not suffice in cases where the individuals concerned have been subjected to prolonged detention or convicted and sentenced to severe penalties. In the case of such a conviction and sentence, it would be incumbent upon the United States to allow the review and reconsideration of the conviction and sentence by taking account of the violation of the rights set forth in the Convention."[114] . . .

The Court thus upheld its jurisdiction on Germany's fourth submission and responded to it in the dispositif. It did not, however, discuss the legal basis for assurances of non-repetition . . .

Article 31

1. The responsible State is under an obligation to make full reparation for the injury caused by the internationally wrongful act.
2. Injury includes any damage, whether material or moral, caused by the internationally wrongful act of a State.

Commentary

(1) . . . The general principle of the consequences of the commission of an internationally wrongful act was stated by the Permanent Court in the *Factory at Chorzów* case:

"It is a principle of international law that the breach of an engagement involves an obligation to make reparation in an adequate form. Reparation therefore is the indispensable complement of a failure to apply a convention and there is no necessity for this to be stated in the convention itself. Differences relating to reparations, which may be due by reason of failure to apply a convention, are consequently differences relating to its application."[115] . . .

(2) In a subsequent phase of the same case, the Court went on to specify in more detail the content of the obligation of reparation. It said:

"The essential principle contained in the actual notion of an illegal act—a principle which seems to be established by international practice and in particular by the decisions of arbitral tribunals—is that reparation must, so far as possible, wipe out all the consequences of the illegal act and re-establish the situation which would, in all probability, have existed if that act had not been committed. Restitution in kind, or, if this is not possible, payment of a sum corresponding to the value which a restitution in kind would bear; the award, if need be, of damages for loss sustained which would not be covered by restitution in kind or payment in place of it—such are the principles which should serve to determine the amount of compensation due for an act contrary to international law."[116]

In the first sentence, the Court gave a general definition of reparation, emphasizing that its function was the re-establishment of the situation affected by the breach. In the second sentence it dealt with that aspect of reparation encompassed by "compensation" for an unlawful act—that is, restitution or its value, and in addition damages for loss sustained as a result of the wrongful act.

---

[113] Ibid., para. 124; see also the dispositif, para. 128(6).
[114] Ibid., para. 125. See also ibid., para. 127, and the dispositif, para 28(7).
[115] *Factory at Chorzów, Jurisdiction*, 1927, P.C.I.J., Series A, No. 9, p. 21.
[116] *Factory at Chorzów, Jurisdiction*, 1927, P.C.I.J., Series A, No. 9, p. 21.

(3) The obligation placed on the responsible State by article 31 is to make "full reparation" in the *Factory at Chorzów* sense. In other words, the responsible State must endeavour to "wipe out all the consequences of the illegal act and reestablish the situation which would, in all probability, have existed if that act had not been committed"[117] through the provision of one or more of the forms of reparation set out in Chapter II of this Part. . . .

(4) . . . The general obligation of reparation arises automatically upon commission of an internationally wrongful act and is not, as such, contingent upon a demand or protest by any State, even if the form which reparation should take in the circumstances may depend on the response of the injured State or States.

(5) The responsible State's obligation to make full reparation relates to the "injury caused by the internationally wrongful act" . . . in accordance with paragraph 2, "injury" includes any material or moral damages caused thereby. This formulation is intended both as inclusive, covering both material and moral damage broadly understood, and as limitative, excluding merely abstract concerns or general interests of a State which is individually unaffected by the breach.[118] "Material" damage here refers to damage to property or other interests of the State and its nationals which is assessable in financial terms. "Moral" damage includes such things as individual pain and suffering, loss of loved ones or personal affront associated with an intrusion on one's home or private life. . . .

(7) . . . there is no general requirement of material harm or damage for a State to be entitled to seek some form of reparation. In the *Rainbow Warrior* arbitration it was initially argued that "in the theory of international responsibility, damage is necessary to provide a basis for liability to make reparation", but the parties subsequently agreed that . . .

"[u]nlawful action against non-material interests, such as acts affecting the honour, dignity or prestige of a State, entitle the victim State to receive adequate reparation, even if those acts have not resulted in a pecuniary or material loss for the claimant State."[119]

The Tribunal held that the breach by France had "provoked indignation and public outrage in New Zealand and caused a new, additional non-material damage . . . of a moral, political and legal nature, resulting from the affront to the dignity and prestige not only of New Zealand as such, but of its highest judicial and executive authorities as well".[120] . . .

(10) . . . Various terms are used to describe the link which must exist between the wrongful act and the injury in order for the obligation of reparation to arise. For example, reference may be made to losses "attributable [to the wrongful act] as a proximate cause",[121] or to damage which is "too indirect, remote, and uncertain to be appraised"[122] or to "any direct loss, damage, including environmental damage and the depletion of natural resources, or injury to foreign Governments, nationals and corporations as a result of the wrongful act.[123] Thus causality in fact is a necessary but not a sufficient condition for reparation. There is a further element, associated with the exclusion of injury that is too "remote" or "consequential" to be the subject of reparation. In some cases, the criterion of "directness" may be used,[124] in others "foreseeability"[125] or "proximity".[126] But other factors may

---

[117] *Factory at Chorzów, Merits, 1928 P.C.I.J., Series A, No. 17*, p. 47.

[118] Although not individually injured, such States may be entitled to invoke responsibility in respect of breaches of certain classes of obligation in the general interest, pursuant to article 48. Generally on notions of injury and damage see A. Tanzi, "Is Damage a Distinct Condition for the Existence of an Internationally Wrongful Act?", in M. Spinedi & B. Simma (eds.) *United Nations Codification of State Responsibility* (New York, Oceana, 1987), p. 1; I. Brownlie, *System of the Law of Nations: State Responsibility (Part 1)* (Oxford, Clarendon Press, 1983), pp. 53–88.

[119] *Rainbow Warrior (New Zealand/France), R.I.A.A.*, vol XX, p. 217 (190), at p. 267, para. 109.

[120] Ibid., at p. 267, para. 110.

[121] See United States-Germany Mixed Claims Commission, *Administrative Decision No. II R.I.A.A.*, vol. VII, p. 23 (1923), at p. 30. See also . . . the Canadian statement of claim following the disintegration of the *Cosmos 954* Soviet nuclear-powered satellite over its territory in 1978. *I.L.M.*, vol. 18(1979), p. 907, para. 23.

[122] See the *Trail Smelter* arbitration, *R.I.A.A.*, vol III, p. 1905 (1938, 1941), at p. 1931 . . .

[123] Security Council resolution 687 (1991), para. 16. This was a Chapter VII resolution, but it is expressed to reflect Iraq's liability "under international law . . . as a result of its unlawful invasion and occupation of Kuwait". The United Nations Compensation Commission and the Governing Council have provided some guidance on the interpretation of the requirements of directness and causation under para. 16 . . .

[124] As in Security Council resolution 687 (1991), para. 16.

[125] See, e.g., the *"Naulilaa" case (Responsibility of Germany for damage caused in the Portuguese colonies in the south of Africa) (Portugal v. Germany), R.I.A.A.*, vol II, p. 1011 (1928), at p. 1031.

[126] For comparative reviews of issues of causation and remoteness see, e.g. H.L.A. Hart & A.M. Honoré *Causation in the Law* (2nd end.) (Oxford, Clarendon Press, 1985) . . .

also be relevant: for example, whether State organs deliberately caused the harm in question, or whether the harm caused was within the ambit of the rule which was breached, having regard to the purpose of that rule.[127] In other words, the requirement of a causal link is not necessarily the same in relation to every breach of an international obligation. In international as in national law, the question of remoteness of damage "is not a part of the law which can be satisfactorily solved by search for a single verbal formula".[128] The notion of a sufficient causal link which is not too remote is embodied in the general requirement in article 31 that the injury should be in consequence of the wrongful act, but without the addition of any particular qualifying phrase.

(11) . . . [A] failure to mitigate by the injured party may preclude recovery to that extent. The point was clearly made in this sense by the International Court in the *Gabčikovo-Nagymaros Project* case:

"Slovakia also maintained that it was acting under a duty to mitigate damages when it carried out Variant C. It stated that 'It is a general principle of international law that a party injured by the non-performance of another contract party must seek to mitigate the damage he has sustained.' It would follow from such a principle that an injured State which has failed to take the necessary measures to limit the damage sustained would not be entitled to claim compensation for that damage which could have been avoided. While this principle might thus provide a basis for the calculation of damages, it could not, on the other hand, justify an otherwise wrongful act."[129] . . .

Article 32

The responsible State may not rely on the provisions of its internal law as justification for failure to comply with its obligations under this Part.

Commentary

. . . (2) Article 32 is modelled on article 27 of the 1969 Vienna Convention on the Law of Treaties, which provides that a party may not invoke the provisions of its internal law as justification for its failure to perform a treaty. This general principle is equally applicable to the international obligations deriving from the rules of State responsibility set out in Part Two. . . .

Chapter II: Reparation for Injury

Article 34

Full reparation for the injury caused by the internationally wrongful act shall take the form of restitution, compensation and satisfaction, either singly or in combination, in accordance with the provisions of this Chapter.

Article 35

A State responsible for an internationally wrongful act is under an obligation to make restitution, that is, to re-establish the situation which existed before the wrongful act was committed, provided and to the extent that restitution:

(a) is not materially impossible;

(b) does not involve a burden out of all proportion to the benefit deriving from restitution instead of compensation.

---

[127] See e.g. the decision of the Iran-United States Claims Tribunal in *Islamic Republic of Iran v. United States of America (Cases A15(IV) and A24)*, (1996) 32 *Iran-U.S.C.T.R.*, 115.

[128] P.S. Atiyah, *An Introduction to the Law of Contract* (5th edn) (Oxford, Clarendon Press, 1995), p. 466.

[129] *Gabčikovo-Nagmaros Project (Hungary.Slovakia)*, ICJ Reports 1997, p. 7, at p. 55, para. 80.

Commentary

... (3) ... The primacy of restitution was confirmed by the Permanent Court in the *Factory at Chorzów* case when it said that the responsible State was under "the obligation to restore the undertaking and, if this be not possible, to pay its value at the time of the indemnification, which value is designed to take the place of restitution which has become impossible".[130] The Court went on to add that "[t]he impossibility, on which the Parties are agreed, of restoring the Chorzów factory could therefore have no other effect but that of substituting payment of the value of the undertaking for restitution".[131] It can be seen in operation in the cases where tribunals have considered compensation only after concluding that, for one reason or another, restitution could not be effected.[132] Despite the difficulties restitution may encounter in practice, States have often insisted upon claiming it in preference to compensation. Indeed in certain cases, especially those involving the application of peremptory norms, restitution may be required as an aspect of compliance with the primary obligation.

(4) On the other hand there are often situations where restitution is not available or where its value to the injured State is so reduced that other forms of reparation take priority .... quite apart from valid election by the injured State or other entity, the possibility of restitution may be practically excluded, e.g. because the property in question has been destroyed or fundamentally changed in character or the situation cannot be restored to the *status quo ante* for some reason. ... In the *Aminoil* arbitration, the parties agreed that restoration of the *status quo ante* following the annulment of the concession by the Kuwait decree would be impracticable.[133]

(5) Restitution may take the form of material restoration or return of territory, persons or property, or the reversal of some juridical act, or some combination of them. Examples of material restitution include the release of detailed individuals, the handing over to a State of an individual arrested in its territory,[134] the restitution of ships,[135] or other types of property[136] including documents, works of art, share certificates, etc.[137] The term "juridical restitution" is sometimes used where restitution requires or involves the modification of a legal situation either within the legal system of the responsible State or in its legal relations with the injured State. Such cases include the revocation, annulment or amendment of a constitutional or legislative provision enacted in violation of a rule of international law,[138] the rescinding or reconsideration of an administrative or judicial measure unlawfully adopted in respect of the person or property of a foreigner[139] or a requirement that steps be taken (to the extent allowed by international law) for the termination of a treaty.[140] ...

(8) Under *article 35(a)*, restitution is not required if it is "materially impossible". ...

(9) Material impossibility is not limited to cases where the object in question has been destroyed, but can cover more complex situations. In the *Forests of Central Rhodope* case, the claimant was entitled to only a share in the forestry operations and no claims had been brought by the other participants. The forests were not in the same condition as at the time of their wrongful taking, and detailed inquiries would be necessary to determine their

---

[130] *Factory at, Chorzów Merits, 1928, P.C.I.J. Series A, No. 17*, p. 48.

[131] Ibid.

[132] See, e.g., *British Claims in the Spanish Zone of Morocco, R.I.A.A.*, vol. II, p. 615 (1925), at pp. 621–625, 651–742 ...

[133] *Government of Kuwait v. American Independent Oil Company*, (1982) I.L.R., vol. 66, p. 529, at p. 533.

[134] Examples of material restitution involving persons include ... the *Diplomatic and Consular Staff* case in which the International Court ordered Iran to immediately release every detained United States national: *United States Diplomatic and Consular Staff in Tehran, ICJ Reports 1980*, p. 3, at pp. 44–45.

[135] See e.g. the "*Giaffarieh*" incident (1886) which originated in the capture in the Red Sea by an Egyptian warship of four merchant ships from Masawa under Italian registry: Società Italiana per l'Organizzazione Internazionale Consiglio Nazionale delle Ricerche, *La prassi italiana di diritto internazionale* (1st series) (Dobbs Ferry, Oceana, 1970), vol. II, pp. 901–902.

[136] E.g., *Temple of Preah Vihear, Merits, ICJ Reports 1962*, p. 6, at pp. 36–37, where the International Court decided in favour of a Cambodian claim which included restitution of certain objects removed from the area and the temple by Thai authorities ...

[137] In the *Buzau-Hehoiasi Railway* case, an arbitral tribunal provided for the restitution to a German company of shares in a Romanian railway company: *R.I.A.A.*, vol III, p. 1839 (1939).

[138] For cases where the existence of a law itself amounts to a breach of an international obligation see commentary to article 12, para. (12)

[139] E.g. the *Martini* case, *R.I.A.A.*, vol. II, p. 973 (1930).

[140] In the *Bryan-Chamorro Treaty* case (*Costa Rica v. Nicaragua*), the Central American Court of Justice decided that "the Government of Nicaragua, by availing itself of measures possible under the authority of international law, is under the obligation to re-establish and maintain the legal status that existed prior to the Bryan-Chamorro Treaty between the litigant republics in so far as relates to matters considered in this action ..." *A.J.I.L.*, vol. 11 (1917), p. 674, at p. 696; see also at p. 683.

condition. Since the taking, third parties had acquired rights to them. For a combination of these reasons, restitution was denied.[141] ...

(11) ... restitution may not be required if it would "involve a burden out of all proportion to the benefit deriving from restitution instead of compensation". This applies only where there is a grave disproportionality between the burden which restitution would impose on the responsible State and the benefit which would be gained, either by the injured State or by any victim of the breach. It is thus based on considerations of equity and reasonableness,[142] although with a preference for the position of the injured State in any case where the balancing process does not indicate a clear preference for compensation as compared with restitution. The balance will invariably favour the injured State in any case where the failure to provide restitution would jeopardize its political independence or economic stability.

Article 36

1. The State responsible for an internationally wrongful act is under an obligation to compensate for the damage caused thereby, insofar as such damage is not made good by restitution.

2. The compensation shall cover any financially assessable damage including loss of profits insofar as it is established.

Commentary

(1) Article 36 deals with compensation for damage caused by an internationally wrongful act, to the extent that such damage is not made good by restitution. The notion of "damage" is defined inclusively in article 31(2) as any damage whether material or moral. ... The qualification "financially assessable" [in Article 36(2)] is intended to exclude compensation for what is sometimes referred to as "moral damage" to a State, i.e., the affront or injury caused by a violation of rights not associated with actual damage to property or persons: this is the subject matter of satisfaction, dealt with in article 37.

(2) Of the various forms of reparation, compensation is perhaps the most commonly sought in international practice. ...

(3) ... Restitution, despite its primacy as a matter of legal principle, is frequently unavailable or inadequate. it may be partially or entirely ruled out either on the basis of the exceptions expressed in article 35, or because the injured State prefers compensation or for other reasons. Even where restitution is made, it may be insufficient to ensure full reparation. The role of compensation ... was articulated by the Permanent Court in the following terms:

> "Restitution in kind or, if this is not possible, payment of a sum corresponding to the value which a restitution in kind would bear; the award, if need be, of damages for loss sustained which would not be covered by restitution in kind or payment in place of it—such are the principles which should serve to determine the amount of compensation due for an act contrary to international law."[143] ...

(4) As compared with satisfaction, the function of compensation is to address the actual losses incurred ... It is not concerned to punish the responsible State, nor does compensation have an expressive or exemplary character.[144] ... It is true that monetary payments may be called for by way of satisfaction under article 37, but they perform a function distinct from that of compensation. Monetary compensation is intended to offset, as far as may be, the damage suffered by the injured State as a result of the breach. Satisfaction is concerned with non-material injury, specifically non-material injury to the State on which a monetary value can be put only in a highly approximate and notional way ...

(7) As to the appropriate heads of compensable damage and the principles of assessment to be applied in

---

[141] R.I.A.A., vol. III, p. 1405 (1933), at p. 1432.

[142] See, e.g. J.H.W. Verzijl, *International Law in Historical Perspective* (Leyden, Sijthoff, 1973), part VI, p. 744 ...

[143] *Factory at Chorzów, Merits, 1928*, P.C.I.J., Series A, No. 17, p. 47. ... Ed. Cf. the *Genocide Convention* case, I.C.J. Rep. 2007, para.460, citing Draft Articles, arts 31 and 36.

[144] In *Velásquez Rodríguez v. Honduras (Compensation)*, the Inter-American Court of Human Rights held that international law did not recognize the concept of punitive or exemplary damages: *Inter-Am. Ct.H.R., Series C, No. 7* (1989), p. 52 ...

quantification, these will vary, depending upon the content of particular primary obligations, an evaluation of the respective behaviour of the parties and, more generally, a concern to reach an equitable and acceptable outcome.[145] ...

(8) Damage to the State as such might arise out of the shooting down of its aircraft or the sinking of its ships, attacks on its diplomatic premises and personnel, damage caused to other public property, the costs incurred in responding to pollution damage, or incidental damage arising, for example, out of the need to pay pensions and medical expenses for officials injured as the result of a wrongful act. Such a list cannot be comprehensive and the categories of compensable injures suffered by states are not closed. ...

(16) Within the field of diplomatic protection, a good deal of guidance is available as to appropriate compensation standards and methods of valuation, especially as concerns personal injury and takings of, or damage to, tangible property. It is well-established that a State may seek compensation in respect of personal injuries suffered by its officials or nationals, over and above any direct injury it may itself have suffered in relation to the same event. Compensable personal injury encompasses not only associated material losses, such as loss of earnings and earning capacity, medical expenses and the like, but also non-material damage suffered by the individual (sometimes, though not universally, referred to as "moral damage" in national legal systems). Non-material damage is generally understood to encompass loss of loved ones, pain and suffering as well as the affront to sensibilities associated with an intrusion on the person, home or private life. No less than material injury sustained by the injured State, non-material damage is financially assessable and may be the subject of a claim of compensation, as stressed in the *"Lusitania"* case.[146]

Article 37

1. The State responsible for an internationally wrongful act is under an obligation to give satisfaction for the injury caused by that act insofar as it cannot be made good by restitution or compensation.

2. Satisfaction may consist in an acknowledgement of the breach, an expression of regret, a formal apology or another appropriate modality.

3. Satisfaction shall not be out of proportion to the injury and may not take a form humiliating to the responsible State.

Commentary

(1) ... The rather exceptional character of the remedy of satisfaction, and its relationship to the principle of full reparation, are emphasized by the phrase "insofar as [the injury] cannot be made good by restitution or compensation". It is only in these cases where those two forms have not provided full reparation that satisfaction may be required. ...

(3) ... Material and moral damage resulting from an internationally wrongful act will normally be financially assessable and hence covered by the remedy of compensation. Satisfaction, on the other hand, is the remedy for those injuries, not financially assessable, which amount to an affront to the State. These injuries are frequently of a symbolic character, arising from the very fact of the breach of the obligation, irrespective of its material consequences for the State concerned.

(4) The availability of the remedy of satisfaction for injury of this kind, sometimes described as "non-material injury", is well-established in international law. The point was made, for example, by the Tribunal in the *Rainbow Warrior* arbitration:

"There is a long established practice of States and international Courts and Tribunals of using satisfaction as a remedy or form of reparation (in the wide sense) for the breach of an international obligation. This practice relates particularly to the case of moral or legal damage done directly to the State, especially as opposed to the case of damage to persons involving international responsibilities".[147]

State practice also provides many instances of claims for satisfaction in circumstances where the internationally

---

[145] Cf. G.H. Aldrich, *The Jurisprudence of the Iran-United States Claims Tribunal* (Oxford, Clarendon Press, 1996), p. 242 ... C.D. Gray, *Judicial Remedies in International Law* (Oxford, Clarendon Press, 1987), pp. 33–34 ...

[146] *R.I.A.*, vol. VII, p. 32 (1923). International tribunals have frequently granted pecuniary compensation for moral injury to private parties. E.g. *Chevreau (France v. United Kingdom)*, *R.I.A.A.*, vol. II p. 1113 (1923); *A.J.I.L.* vol, 27 (1933), p. 153 ...

[147] *Rainbow Warrior (New Zealand/France) R.I.A.A.* vol. XX, p. 217 (1990), at pp. 272–273, para. 122.

wrongful act of a State causes non-material injury to another State. Examples include situations of insults to the symbols of the State, such as the national flag,[148] violations of sovereignty or territorial integrity,[149] attacks on ships or aircraft,[150] ill treatment of or deliberate attacks on heads of State or Government or diplomatic or consular representatives or other protected persons[151] and violations of the premises of embassies or consulates or of the residences of members of the mission.[152]

(5) *Paragraph 2* of article 37 provides that satisfaction may consist in acknowledgement of the breach, an expression of regret, a formal apology or another appropriate modality. The forms of satisfaction listed in the article are no more than examples. The appropriate form of satisfaction will depend on the circumstances and cannot be prescribed in advance.[153] Many possibilities exist, including the due inquiry into the causes of an accident resulting in harm or injury,[154] a trust fund to manage compensation payments in the interests of the beneficiaries, disciplinary or penal action against the individuals whose conduct caused the internationally wrongful act[155] or the award of symbolic damages for non-pecuniary injury.[156] Assurances or guarantees of non-repetition, which are dealt with in the articles in the context of cessation [in Article 30], may also amount to a form of satisfaction. ...

Chapter III: Serious Breaches of Obligations under Peremptory Norms of General International Law

[INTRODUCTORY NOTE]

... (2) Whether a qualitative distinction should be recognized between different breaches of international law has been the subject of a major debate.[157] The issue was underscored by the International Court of Justice in the *Barcelona Traction* case, when it said that:

"an essential distinction should be drawn between the obligations of a State towards the international community as a whole, and those arising vis-à-vis another State in the field of diplomatic protection. By their very nature the former are the concern of all States. In view of the importance of the rights involved, all States can be held to have a legal interest in their protection: they are obligations *erga omnes*."[158]

The Court was there concerned to contrast the position of an injured State in the context of diplomatic protection with the position of all States in respect of the breach of an obligation towards the international community as a whole.[159] Although no such obligation was at stake in that case, the Court's statement clearly indicates that for

---

[148] Examples are ... the case that arose from the insult to the French flag in Berlin in 1920 (C. Eagleton, *The Responsibility of States in International Law* (New York, New York University Press, 1928). pp. 186–187).

[149] As occurred in the *Rainbow Warrior* arbitration, *R.I.A.A.*, vol. XX, p. 217 (1990).

[150] Examples include the attack carried out in 1961 against a Soviet aircraft transporting President Brezhnev by French fighter planes over the international waters of the Mediterranean (*R.G.D.I.P.*, vol. 65 (1961), p. 603). ...

[151] See F. Przetacznic, "La responsabilité internationale de l'Etat à raison des préjudices de caractère moral et politique causés à un autre Etat", *R.G.D.I.P.*, vol. 78 (1974), p. 917, at p. 951.

[152] Examples include the attack by demonstrators in 1851 on the Spanish Consulate in New Orleans (Moore, *Digest*, vol. VI, p. 811, at p. 812) ...

[153] In the *Rainbow Warrior* arbitration the Tribunal, while rejecting New Zealand's claims for restitution and/or cessation and declining to award compensation, made various declarations by way of satisfaction, and in addition a recommendation "to assist [the parties] in putting an end to the present unhappy affair". Specifically it recommended that France contribute US$2 million to a fund to be established "to promote close and friendly relations between the citizens of the two countries". See *R.I.A.A.* vol. XX, p. 217 (1990), at p. 274, paras 126–127 ...

[154] E.g. the United States naval inquiry into the causes of the collision between an American submarine and the Japanese fishing vessel, the *Ehime Maru*, in waters off Honolulo: *New York Times*, 8 Feb. 2001, section 1, p. 1, col. 6.

[155] Action against the guilty individuals was requested in the case of the killing in 1948, in Palestine, of Count Bernadotte while he was acting in the service of the United Nations (Whiteman, *Digest*, vol. 8, pp. 724–743). ...

[156] See, e.g., *The "I'm Alone", R.I.A.A.*, vol. III, p. 1609 (1935); *Rainbow Warrior, R.I.A.A.*, vol. XX, p. 217 (1990).

[157] For full bibliographies see M. Spinedi, "Crimes of States: A Bibliography", in J.J.H. Weiler, A. Cassese & M. Spinedi (eds.), *International Crimes of States* (Berlin/New York, De Gruyter, 1989), pp. 339–353 and N. Jøgensen, *The Responsibility of States for International Crimes* (Oxford, Oxford University Press, 2000) pp.299–314.

[158] *Barcelona Traction, Light and Power Company, Limited, Second Phase, ICJ Reports 1970*, p. 3, at p. 32, para. 33. See M. Ragazzi *The Concept of International Obligations Erga Omnes* (Oxford, Clarendon Press, 1997). Ed. On the *Barcelona* case, see below, p.632.

[159] Ed. On this distinction, see Vermeer-Kunzli (2007) 56 I.C.L.Q. 182.

the purposes of State responsibility certain obligations are owed to the international community as a whole, and that by reason of "the importance of the rights involved" all States have a legal interest in their protection.

(3) On a number of subsequent occasions the Court has taken the opportunity to affirm the notion of obligations to the international community as a whole, although it has been cautious in applying it. In the *East Timor* case, the Court said that "Portugal's assertion that the right of peoples to self-determination, as it evolved from the Charter and from United Nations practice, has an *erga omnes* character, is irreproachable." [160] At the preliminary objections stage of the *Application of the Convention on the Prevention and Punishment of the Crime of Genocide* case, it stated that "the rights and obligations enshrined by the [Genocide] Convention are rights and obligations *erga omnes*":[161] this finding contributed to its conclusion that its temporal jurisdiction over the claim was not limited to the time after which the parties became bound by the Convention.

(4) A closely related development is the recognition of the concept of peremptory norms of international law in articles 53 and 64 of the Vienna Convention on the Law of Treaties. These provisions recognise the existence of substantive norms of a fundamental character, such that no derogation from them is permitted even by treaty.

(5) From the first it was recognised that these developments had implications for the secondary rules of State responsibility which would need to be reflected in some way in the articles. Initially it was thought this could be done by reference to a category of "international crimes of State", which would be contrasted with all other cases of internationally wrongful acts ("international delicts").[162] There has been, however, no development of penal consequences for States of breaches of these fundamental norms. For example, the award of punitive damages is not recognised in international law even in relation to serious breaches of obligations arising under peremptory norms. In accordance with article 34 the function of damages is essentially compensatory. Overall it remains the case, as the International Military Tribunal said in 1946, that:

"Crimes against international law are committed by men, not by abstract entities, and only by punishing individuals who commit such crimes can the provisions of international law be enforced."[163]

(6) In line with this approach, despite the trial and conviction by the Nuremberg and Tokyo Military Tribunals of individual government officials for criminal acts committed in their official capacity, neither Germany nor Japan were treated as "criminal" by the instruments creating these tribunals.[164] As to more recent international practice, a similar approach underlies the establishment of the ad hoc tribunals for Yugoslavia and Rwanda by the United Nations Security Council. Both tribunals are concerned only with the prosecution of individuals. In its decision relating to a *subpoena duces tecum* in *Prosecutor v Blaskić*, the Appeals Chamber of the International Criminal Tribunal for the Former Yugoslavia stated that "[u]nder present international law it is clear that States, by definition, cannot be the subject of criminal sanctions akin to those provided for in national criminal systems,"[165] The Rome Statute of the International Criminal Court of 17 July 1998 likewise establishes jurisdiction over the "most serious crimes of concern to the international community as a whole", but limits this jurisdiction

---

[160] *East Timor (Portugal v. Australia), ICJ Reports 1995*, p. 90, at p. 102, para. 29.

[161] *Application of the Convention on the Prevention and Punishment of the Crime of Genocide, Preliminary Objections, ICJ Reports 1996*, p. 595, at p. 616, para. 31.

[162] See *Yearbook ... 1976*, vol II Part 2. pp. 95–122, especially paras 6–34 ... Ed. At one stage the Draft Articles provided for international crimes by states. Article 19(3) stated: "An internationally wrongful act that results from the breach by a state of an international obligation so essential for the protection of fundamental interests of the international community that its breach is recognised as a crime by that community as a whole, constitutes an international crime". Article 19(3) then listed as international crimes serious breaches of obligations prohibiting aggression, the maintenance of colonialism by force, slavery, genocide, apartheid and massive pollution of the environment. Article 19 was omitted from the final text in the face of considerable opposition by states and in academic literature. See Allott (1988) 29 H.J.I.L. 1; Crawford, above, n.3, pp.16–20, 35–38; Gilbert (1990) 39 I.C.L.Q. 345; Gray (1983) 56 B.Y.I.L. 25; Jorgensen, *The Responsibility of States for International Crimes* (2003); Weller, Cassese, Spinedi, *International Crimes of States* (1989).

[163] International Military Tribunal for the Trial of the Major War Criminals, judgment of 1 October 1946, reprinted in *A.J.I.L.*, vol. 41 (1947), p. 172, at p. 221.

[164] This despite the fact that the London Charter of 1945 specifically provided for the condemnation of a "group or organization" as "criminal", cf. Charge of the International Military Tribunal, London, 8 August 1945, *U.N.T.S.*, vol. 82 p. 279, arts. 9, 10.

[165] Case IT-95-14-AR 108*bis, Prosecutor v. Blaskić, I.L.R.* vol., 110, p. 688 (1997), at p. 698, para. 25. Cf. *Application of the Convention on the Prevention and Punishment of the Crime of Genocide, Preliminary Objections, ICJ Reports 1996*, p. 595, in which neither of the parties treated the proceedings as being criminal in character. See also the commentary to article 12, para. (6).

to "natural persons" (art. 25 (1)). The same article specifies that no provision of the Statute "relating to individual criminal responsibility shall affect the responsibility of States under international law".[166]

(7) Accordingly the present articles do not recognise the existence of any distinction between State "crimes" and "delicts" for the purposes of Part One. On the other hand, it is necessary for the articles to reflect that there are certain *consequences* flowing from the basic concepts of peremptory norms of general international law and obligations to the international community as a whole within the field of State responsibility. Whether or not peremptory norms of general international law and obligations to the international community as a whole are aspects of a single basic idea, there is at the very least substantial overlap between them. The examples which the International Court has given of obligations towards the international community as a whole[167] all concern obligations which, it is generally accepted, arise under peremptory norms of general international law. Likewise the examples of peremptory norms given by the Commission in its commentary to what became article 53 of the Vienna Convention[168] involve obligations to the international community as a whole. But there is at least a difference in emphasis. While peremptory norms of general international law focus on the scope and priority to be given to a certain number of fundamental obligations, the focus of obligations to the international community as a whole is essentially on the legal interest of all States in compliance—i.e., in terms of the present articles, in being entitled to invoke the responsibility of any State in breach. Consistently with the difference in their focus, it is appropriate to reflect the consequences of the two concepts in two distinct ways. First, serious breaches of obligations arising under peremptory norms of general international law can attract additional consequences, not only for the responsible State but for all other States. Secondly, all States are entitled to invoke responsibility for breaches of obligations to the international community as a whole. The first of these propositions is the concern of the present Chapter. ...

Article 40

1. This Chapter applies to the international responsibility which is entailed by a serious breach by a state of an obligation arising under a peremptory norm of general international law.

2. A breach of such an obligation is serious if it involves a gross or systematic failure by the responsible State to fulfil the obligation.

Commentary

... (3) It is not appropriate to set out examples of the peremptory norms referred to in the text of article 40 itself ... The obligations referred to in article 40 arise from those substantive rules of conduct that prohibit what has come to be seen as intolerable because of the threat it presents to the survival of States and their peoples and the most basic human values.

(4) Among these prohibitions, it is generally agreed that the prohibition of aggression is to be regarded as peremptory. This is supported, for example, by the Commission's commentary to what was to become article 53,[169] uncontradicted statements by governments in the course of the Vienna Conference,[170] the submissions of both parties in *Military and Paramilitary Activities* and the Court's own position in that case.[171] There also seems to be widespread agreement with other examples listed in the (Commission's commentary to article 53: viz, the prohibitions against slavery and the slave trade, genocide, and racial discrimination and *apartheid*. These

---

[166] Rome Statute of the International Criminal Court, 17 July 1998, A/CONF. 183/9, art 25(4) ...

[167] According to the International Court of Justice, obligations *erga omnes* "derive, for example, in contemporary international law, from the outlawing of acts of aggression, and of genocide, as also from the principles and rules concerning the basic rights of the human person, including protection from slavery and racial discrimination": *Barcelona Traction, Light and Power Company, Limited, Second Phase, ICJ Reports 1970*, p. 3, at p. 32, para. 34. See also *East Timor (Portugal v. Australia), ICJ Reports 1995*, p. 90, at p. 102, para 29; *Legality of the Threat or Use of Nuclear Weapons, ICJ Reports 1996*, p. 226, at 258, para. 83; *Application of the Convention on the Prevention and Punishment of the Crime of Genocide, Preliminary Objections, ICJ Reports 1996*, p. 595, at pp. 615–616, paras, 31–32.

[168] Ed. See the *Barcelona* case below, p.515.

[169] *Yearbook ... 1966*, vol. II, p. 247.

[170] In the course of the Vienna conference, a number of governments characterized as peremptory the prohibitions against aggression and the illegal use of force: see *United Nations Conference on the Law of Treaties, First Session*, A/CONF.39/11, pp. 294, 296–7, 300, 301, 302, 303, 304, 306, 307, 311, 312, 318, 320, 322, 323–4, 326.

[171] *Military and Pramilitary Activities in and against Nicaragua (Nicaragua v. United States of America), Merits, ICJ Reports 1986*, p. 14, at pp. 100–1, para 190. See also President Nagendra Singh, ibid., at p. 153.

practices have been prohibited in widely ratified international treaties and conventions admitting of no exception. There was general agreement among governments as to the peremptory character of these prohibitions at the Vienna conference. As to the peremptory character of the prohibition against genocide, this is supported by a number of decisions by national and international courts.[172]

(5) Although not specifically listed in the Commission's commentary to article 53 of the Vienna Convention, the peremptory character of certain other norms seems also to be generally accepted. This applies to the prohibition against torture as defined in article 1 of the Convention against Torture and Other Cruel, Inhuman or Degrading Treatment or Punishment of 10 December 1984.[173] The peremptory character of this prohibition has been confirmed by decisions of international and national bodies.[174] In the light of the International Court's description of the basic rules of international humanitarian law applicable in armed conflict as "intransgressible" in character, it would also seem justified to treat these as peremptory.[175] Finally, the obligation to respect the right of self-determination deserves to be mentioned. As the International Court noted in the *East Timor* case, "[t]he principle of self-determination ... is one of the essential principles of contemporary international law", which gives rise to an obligation to the international community as a whole to permit and respect its exercise.[176]
...

(7) Apart from its limited scope in terms of the comparatively small number of norms which qualify as peremptory, article 40 applies a further limitation for the purposes of the Chapter, viz. that the breach should itself have been "serious". A "serious" breach is defined in paragraph 2 as one which involves "a gross or systematic failure by the responsible State to fulfil the obligation" in question. The word "serious" signifies that a certain order of magnitude of violation is necessary in order not to trivialize the breach and it is not intended to suggest that any violation of these obligations is not serious or is somehow excusable. But relatively less serious cases of breach of peremptory norms can be envisaged, and it is necessary to limit the scope of this Chapter to the more serious or systematic breaches. Some such limitation is supported by State practice. For example, when reacting against breaches of international law, States have often stressed their systematic, gross or egregious nature. Similarly, international complaint procedures, for example in the field of human rights, attach different consequences to systematic breaches, e.g. in terms of the non-applicability of the rule of exhaustion of local remedies.[177] ...

Article 41

1. States shall cooperate to bring to an end through lawful means any serious breach within the meaning of article 40.

2. No State shall recognize as lawful a situation created by a serious breach within the meaning of article 40, nor render aid or assistance in maintaining that situation.

3. This article is without prejudice to the other consequences referred to in this Part and to such further consequences that a breach to which this Chapter applies may entail under international law.

Commentary

... (2) Pursuant to *paragraph 1* of article 41, States are under a positive duty to cooperate in order to bring to an end serious breaches in the sense of article 40. ...

---

[172] See, for example, the International Court of Justice in *Application of the Convention or the Prevention and Punishment of the Crime of Genocide Provisional Measures*, I.C.J. Rep. 1993, p. 325, at pp. 439–440; *Counter-claims*, I.C.J. Rep. 43, The District Court of Jerusalem 1997 p. 2 in *Attorney-General of the Government of Israel v Eichmann*, (1961) I.L.R., vol. 36 p5.

[173] *U.N.T.S.* vol. 1460, p. 112.

[174] Cf. the U.S. Court of Appeals, 2nd Circuit, in *Siderman de Blake v. Argentina*, 965 F 2d 699; (1992) *I.L.R.*, vol. 103, p. 455, at p. 471; the United Kingdom Court of Appeal in *Al Adsani v. Government of Kuwait*, (1996) *I.L.R.*, vol. 107, p. 536 at pp. 540–541; the United Kingdom House of Lords in *R. v. Bow Street Metropolitan Magistrate, ex parte Pinochet Ugarte (No. 3)*, [1999] 2 W.L.R. 827, at pp. 841, 881, Cf. the U.S. Court of Appeals, 2nd Circuit in *Filartiga v. Pena-Irala*, 630 F.2d 876; (1980) *I.L.R.* vol. 77, p. 169, at pp. 177–179.

[175] *Legality of the Threat or Use of Nuclear Weapons, ICJ Reports 1996*, p. 226, at p. 257, para. 79.

[176] *East Timor (Portugal v Australia), ICJ Reports 1995*, p. 90, at p. 102, para. 29. See Declaration on Principles of International Law concerning Friendly Relations and Cooperation among States in accordance with the Charter of the United Nations, G.A. Res. 2625 (XXV) of 24 October 1970, fifth principle.

[177] See *Ireland v United Kingdom, E.C.H.R. Series A, No 25* (1978), para 159; cf. e.g. the procedure established under ECOSOC resolution 1503 (XXVIII), which requires a "consistent pattern of gross violations of human rights".

(3) . . . Such cooperation must be through lawful means, the choice of which will depend on the circumstances of the given situation. It is, however, made clear that the obligation to cooperate applies to States whether or not they are individually affected by the serious breach. What is called for in the face of serious breaches is a joint and coordinated effort by all States to counteract the effects of these breaches. It may be open to question whether general international law at present prescribes a positive duty of cooperation, and paragraph 1 in that respect may reflect the progressive development of international law. But in fact such cooperation, especially in the framework of international organizations, is carried out already in response to the gravest breaches of international law and it is often the only way of providing an effective remedy. Paragraph 1 seeks to strengthen existing mechanisms of cooperation, on the basis that all States are called upon to make an appropriate response to the serious breaches referred to in article 40. . . .

(6) The existence of an obligation of non-recognition in response to serious breaches of obligations arising under peremptory norms already finds support in international practice and in decisions of the International Court of Justice. The principle that territorial acquisitions brought about by the use of force are not valid and must not be recognized found a clear expression during the Manchurian crisis of 1931–1932,[178] . . .

The Declaration of Principles of International Law Concerning Friendly Relations and Co-operation Among States in Accordance with the Charter of the United Nations affirms this principle by stating unequivocally that States shall not recognize as legal any acquisition of territory brought about by the use of force.[179] As the International Court of Justice held in *Military and Paramilitary Activities*, the unanimous consent of States to this declaration "may be understood as an acceptance of the validity of the rule or set of rules declared by the resolution by themselves."[180]

(7) An example of the practice of non-recognition of acts in breach of peremptory norms is provided by the reaction of the Security Council to the Iraqi invasion of Kuwait in 1990. Following the Iraqi declaration of a "comprehensive and eternal merger" with Kuwait, the Security Council in Resolution 662 (1990), decided that the annexation had "no legal validity and is considered null and void", and called upon all States, international organizations and specialized agencies not to recognize that annexation and to refrain from any action or dealing that might be interpreted as a recognition of it, whether direct or indirect. In fact no State recognized the legality of the purported annexation, the effects of which were subsequently reversed.

(8) As regards the denial by a State of the right of self-determination of peoples, the International Court's advisory opinion in *Namibia (South West Africa)* is similarly clear in calling for a non-recognition of the situation.[181] The same obligations are reflected in Security Council and General Assembly resolutions concerning the situation in Rhodesia[182] and the Bantustans in South Africa.[183] These examples reflect the principle that where a serious breach in the sense of article 40 has resulted in a situation that might otherwise call for recognition, this has nonetheless to be withheld. Collective non-recognition would seem to be a prerequisite for any concerned community response against such breaches and marks the minimum necessary response by States to the serious breaches referred to in article 40. . . .

(10) The consequences of the obligation of non-recognition are, however, not unqualified. In the *Namibia (South West Africa)* advisory opinion the Court, despite holding that the illegality of the situation was opposable *erga omnes* and could not be recognised as lawful even by States not members of the United Nations, said that:

"the non-recognition of South Africa's administration of the Territory should not result in depriving the people of Namibia of any advantages derived from international co-operation. In particular, while official acts performed by the Government of South Africa on behalf of or concerning Namibia after the termination of the Mandate are illegal and invalid, this invalidity cannot be extended to those acts, such as, for instance, the

---

[178] Ed. See above, p.188.

[179] G.A. Res. 2625 (XXV), first principle, para. 10.

[180] *Military and Paramilitary Activities in and Against Nicaragua (Nicaragua v. United States of America), Merits, ICJ Reports 1986*, p. 14, at p. 100, para. 188.

[181] *Legal Consequences for States of the Continued Presence of South Africa in Namibia (South West Africa) notwithstanding Security Council Resolution 276 (1970), ICJ Reports 1971*, p. 16, at p. 56, para. 126, where the Court held that "the termination of the Mandate and the declaration of the illegality of South Africa's presence in Namibia are opposable to all States in the sense of barring *erga omnes* the legality of a situation which is maintained in violation of international law.

[182] Cf. SC Res. 216 (1965).

[183] See e.g. GA Res. 31/6A (1976), endorsed by SC Res. 402 (1976); GA Res. 32/105N (1977); GA Res. 34/93G (1979); see also the statements issued by the respective presidents of the U.N. Security Council in reaction to the "creation" of Venda and Ciskei; S/13549, 21 September 1979; S/14794, 15 December 1981.

registration of births, deaths and marriages, the effects of which can be ignored only to the detriment of the inhabitants of the Territory."[184] ...

(11) The second obligation contained in paragraph 2 prohibits States from rendering aid or assistance in maintaining the situation created by a serious breach in the sense of article 40. This goes beyond the provisions dealing with aid or assistance in the commission of an internationally wrongful act, which are covered by article 16. It deals with conduct "after the fact" which assists the responsible State in maintaining a situation "opposable to all States in the sense of barring *erga omnes* the legality of a situation which is maintained in violation of international law".[185] It extends beyond the commission of the serious breach itself to the maintenance of the situation created by that breach, and it applies whether or not the breach itself is a continuing one. As to the elements of "aid or assistance", article 41 is to be read in connection with article 16. In particular, the concept of aid or assistance in article 16 presupposes that the State has "knowledge of the circumstances of the internationally wrongful act". There is no need to mention such a requirement in article 41(2) as it is hardly conceivable that a State would not have notice of the commission of a serious breach by another State.

(12) In some respects the prohibition contained in paragraph 2 may be seen as a logical extension of the duty of non-recognition. However, it has a separate scope of application insofar as actions are concerned which would not imply recognition of the situation created by serious breaches in the sense of article 40. This separate existence is confirmed, for example, in the Security Council's resolutions prohibiting any aid or assistance in maintaining the illegal *apartheid* regime in South Africa or Portuguese colonial rule.[186] ...

Part Three: The Implementation of the Responsibility of a State

Chapter I: Invocation of the Responsibility of a State

Article 42

A State is entitled as an injured State to invoke the responsibility of another State if the obligation breached is owed to:

(a) that State individually; or

(b) a group of States including the State, or the international community as a whole, and the breach of the obligation:

    (i) specially affects that State; or
    (ii) is of such a character as radically to change the position of all the other States to which the obligation is owed with respect to the further performance of the obligation.

Article 48

1. Any State other than an injured State is entitled to invoke the responsibility of another State in accordance with paragraph 2 if:

(a) the obligation breached is owed to a group of States including that State, and is established for the protection of a collective interest of the group; or

(b) the obligation breached is owed to the international community as a whole.

2. Any State entitled to invoke responsibility under paragraph 1 may claim from the responsible State:

---

[184] *Legal Consequences for States of the Continued Presence of South Africa in Namibia (South West Africa) notwithstanding Security Council Resolution 276 (1970), ICJ Reports 1971*, p. 16, at p. 56. para. 125.

[185] *Legal Consequences for States of the Continued Presence of South Africa in Namibia (South West Africa) notwithstanding Security Council Resolution 276 (1970), ICJ Reports 1971*, p. 16, at p. 56, para. 125.

[186] *Cf.* e.g. SC Res. 218 (1965) on the Portuguese colonies and SC Res. 418 (1977) and 569 (1985) on South Africa.

(a) cessation of the internationally wrongful act, and assurances and guarantees of non-repetition in accordance with article 30; and

(b) performance of the obligation of reparation in accordance with the preceding articles, in the interest of the injured State or of the beneficiaries of the obligation breached.

3. The requirements for the invocation of responsibility by an injured State under articles 43, 44 and 45 apply to an invocation of responsibility by a State entitled to do so under paragraph 1.

Chapter II: Countermeasures

[INTRODUCTORY NOTE]

... (2) It is recognised both by governments and by the decisions of international tribunals that counter-measures are justified under certain circumstances.[187] ...

(3) As to terminology, traditionally the term "reprisals" was used to cover otherwise unlawful action, including forcible action, taken by way of self-help in response to a breach. More recently the term "reprisals" has been limited to action taken in time of international armed conflict; i.e., it has been taken as equivalent to belligerent reprisals. The term "countermeasures" covers that part of the subject of reprisals not associated with armed conflict, and in accordance with modern practice and judicial decisions the term is used in that sense in this Chapter.[188] Countermeasures are to be contrasted with retorsion, i.e., "unfriendly" conduct which is not inconsistent with any international obligation of the State engaging in it even though it may be a response to an internationally wrongful act. Acts of retorsion may include the prohibition of or limitations upon normal dip-lomatic relations or other contacts, embargos of various kinds or withdrawal of voluntary aid programs. Whatever their motivation, so long as such acts are not incompatible with the international obligations of the States taking them towards the target State, they do not involve countermeasures and they fall outside the scope of the present articles. The term "sanction" is also often used as equivalent to action taken against a State by a group of States or mandated by a international organization. But the term is imprecise: Chapter VII of the United Nations Charter refers only to "measures", even though these can encompass a very wide range of acts, including the use of armed force.[189] Questions concerning the use of force in international relations and of the legality of belligerent reprisals are governed by the relevant primary rules. ...

(4) Countermeasures are to be clearly distinguished from the termination or suspension of treaty relations on account of the material breach of a treaty by another State, as provided for in article 60 of the Vienna Convention on the Law of Treaties. Where a treaty is terminated or suspended in accordance with article 60, the substantive legal obligations of the States parties will be affected, but this is quite different from the question of respon-sibility that may already have arisen from the breach. Countermeasures involve conduct taken in derogation from a subsisting treaty obligation but justified as a necessary and proportionate response to an internationally wrongful act of the State against which they are taken. They are essentially temporary measures, taken to achieve a specified end, whose justification terminates once the end is achieved.

(5) This Chapter does not draw any distinction between what are sometimes called "reciprocal counter-measures" and other measures. That term refers to countermeasures which involve suspension of performance of obligations towards the responsible State "if such obligations correspond to, or are directly connected with, the obligation breached".[190] There is no requirement that States taking countermeasures are limited to suspension

---

[187] For the substantial literature see the bibliographies in E. Zoller, *Peaceitme Unilateral Remedies: An Analysis of Counter-measures* (Dobbs Ferry, N.Y. Transnational Publishers, 1984), pp. 179–189; O.Y. Elagab, *The Legality of Non-Forcible Counter-Measures in International Law* (Oxford, Clarendon Press, 1988), pp.37–41; L-A Sicilianos, *Les Réactions décen-tralisées à l'illicite* (Paris, L.D.G.J., 1990), pp. 501–525; D. Alland, *Justice privée et ordre juridique international; Etude théorique des contre-mesures en droit international public,* (Paris Pedone, 1994). Ed. White and Abass, in Evans, ed., *International Law* (2003), Ch.16.

[188] See *Air Services Agreement of 27 March 1946 (United States v. France), R.I.A.A.*, vol. XVIII, p. 416 (1979), at p. 416, para. 80; *United States Diplomatic and Consular Staff in Tehran, ICJ Reports 1980*, p. 3, at p. 27, para. 53; *Military and Paramilitary Activities in and against Nicaragua (Nicaragua v. United States of America), Merits, ICJ Reports 1986*, p. 14, at p. 102, para 201; *Gabčikovo-Nagymaros Project (Hungary/Slovakia), ICJ Reports 1997*, p. 7, at p. 55, para 82.

[189] Charter of the United Nations, Arts, 39, 41, 42.

[190] See *Yearbook ... 1985* vol. II, Part 1, p. 10.

of performance of the same or a closely related obligation.[191] A number of considerations support this conclusion. First, for some obligations, for example those concerning the protection of human rights, reciprocal countermeasures are inconceivable. The obligations in question have a non-reciprocal character and are not only due to other States but to the individuals themselves.[192] Secondly, a limitation to reciprocal countermeasures assumes that the injured State will be in a position to impose the same or related measures as the responsible State, which may not be so. The obligation may be a unilateral one or the injured State may already have performed its side of the bargain. Above all, considerations of good order and humanity preclude many measures of a reciprocal nature. This conclusion does not, however, end the matter. Countermeasures are more likely to satisfy the requirements of necessity and proportionality if they are taken in relation to the same or a closely related obligation, as in the *Air Services* arbitration. ...

Article 49

1. An injured State may only take countermeasures against a State which is responsible for an internationally wrongful act in order to induce that State to comply with its obligations under Part Two.
2. Countermeasures are limited to the non-performance for the time being of international obligations of the State taking the measures towards the responsible State.
3. Countermeasures shall, as far as possible, be taken in such a way as to permit the resumption of performance of the obligations in question.

Commentary

(1) ... Countermeasures may only be taken by an injured State in order to induce the responsible State to comply with its obligations under Part Two, namely, to cease the internationally wrongful conduct, if it is continuing, and to provide reparation to the injured State. Countermeasures are not intended as a form of punishment for wrongful conduct but as an instrument for achieving compliance with the obligations of the responsible State under Part Two. ...

(3) *Paragraph 1* of article 49 presupposes an objective standard for the taking of countermeasures. ... A State which resorts to countermeasures based on its unilateral assessment of the situation does so at its own risk and may incur responsibility for its own wrongful conduct in the event of an incorrect assessment. ...

(4) ... Countermeasures may not be directed against States other than the responsible State. In a situation where a third State is owed an international obligation by the State taking countermeasures and that obligation is breached by the countermeasure, the wrongfulness of the measure is not precluded as against the third State. ...

(5) This does not mean that countermeasures may not incidentally affect the position of third States or indeed other third parties. For example, if the injured State suspends transit rights with the responsible state in accordance with this Chapter, other parties, including third States, may be affected thereby. If they have no individual rights in the matter they cannot complain. ... Such indirect or collateral effects cannot be entirely avoided. ...

(7) The phrase "for the time being" in paragraph 2 indicates the temporary or provisional character of countermeasures. ... Countermeasures are taken as a form of inducement, not punishment: if they are effective in inducing the responsible State to comply with its obligations of cessation and reparation, they should be discontinued and performance of the obligation resumed. ...

(9) ... States should as far as possible choose countermeasures that are reversible. In the *Gabčíkovo-Nagymaros Project* case, the existence of this condition was recognised by the Court, although it found it was not necessary to pronounce on the matter. After concluding that "the diversion of the Danube carried out by Czechoslovakia was not a lawful countermeasure because it was not proportionate", the Court said:

"It is therefore not required to pass upon one other condition for the lawfulness of a countermeasure, namely that its purpose must be to induce the wrongdoing State to comply with its obligations under international law, and that the measure must therefore be reversible."[193]

---

[191] Contrast the exception of non-performance in the law of treaties, which is so limited ...
[192] Cf. *Ireland v United Kingdom*, E.C.H.R., Series A, No 25 (1978).
[193] *Gabčíkovo-Nagymaros Project*, ICJ Reports 1997, p. 7, at pp. 56–57, para. 87.

However, the duty to choose measures that are reversible is not absolute. It may not be possible in all cases to reverse all of the effects of countermeasures after the occasion for taking them has ceased. For example, a requirement of notification of some activity is of no value after the activity has been undertaken. ...

Article 50

1. Countermeasures shall not affect:

(a) the obligation to refrain from the threat or use of force as embodied in the Charter of the United Nations[194];

(b) obligations for the protection of fundamental human rights;

(c) obligations of a humanitarian character prohibiting reprisals;

(d) other obligations under peremptory norms of general international law.

2. A State taking countermeasures is not relieved from fulfilling its obligations:

(a) under any dispute settlement procedure applicable between it and the responsible State;

(b) to respect the inviolability of diplomatic or consular agents, premises, archives and documents.

Commentary

(1) Article 50 specifies certain obligations the performance of which may not be impaired by countermeasures. ... So far as the law of countermeasures is concerned, they are sacrosanct. ...

(5) The prohibition of forcible countermeasures is spelled out in the Declaration on Principles of International Law concerning Friendly Relations and Cooperation (among States) in accordance with the Charter of the United Nations, by which the General Assembly of the United Nations proclaimed that "States have a duty to refrain from acts of reprisal involving the use of force."[195] The prohibition is also consistent with prevailing doctrine as well as a number of authoritative pronouncements of international judicial[196] and other bodies.[197]

(6) *Paragraph (1)(b)* provides that countermeasures may not affect obligations for the protection of fundamental human rights. ...

(7) In its General Comment 8 (1997) the Committee on Economic, Social and Cultural Rights discussed the effect of economic sanctions on civilian populations and especially on children. It dealt both with the effect of measures taken by international organizations, a topic which falls outside the scope of the present articles, as well as with measures imposed by individual States or groups of States. It stressed that "whatever the circumstances, such sanctions should always take full account of the provisions of the International Covenant on Economic, Social and Cultural Rights",[198] and went on to state that:

"it is essential to distinguish between the basic objective of applying political and economic pressure upon the governing élite of a country to persuade them to conform to international law, and the collateral infliction of suffering upon the most vulnerable groups within the targeted country."[199]

Analogies can be drawn from other elements of general international law. For example, Additional Protocol 1 of 1977, article 54(1) stipulates unconditionally that "[s]tarvation of civilians as a method of warfare is pro-

---

[194] See *Guyana v Suriname*, P.C.A. 2007, p.147, *www.pca/cpa.org.*

[195] G.A. Res. 2625 (XXV) of 24 October 1970, first principle, para. 6 ...

[196] See esp. *Corfu Channel, Merits, ICJ Reports 1949*, p. 4, at p. 35; *Military and Paramilitary Activities in and against Nicaragua (Nicaragua v. United States of America), Merits ICJ Reports 1986*, p. 16, at p. 127, para. 249.

[197] See, e.g. Security Council resolution 111 (1956), resolution 171 (1962), resolution 188 (1964), resolution 316 (1972), resolution 332 (1973), resolution 573 (1985) and resolution 1322 (2000) ...

[198] E/C.12/1997/8, 5 December 1997, para. 1.

[199] Ibid., para. 4.

hibited."[200] Likewise, the final sentence of article 1(2) of the two United Nations Covenants on Human Rights states that "In no case may a people be deprived of its own means of subsistence".[201] ...

(8) *Paragraph (1)(c)* ... reflects the basic prohibition of reprisals against individuals, which exists in international humanitarian law. In particular, under the 1929 Hague and 1949 Geneva Conventions and Additional Protocol I of 1977, reprisals are prohibited against defined classes of protected persons, and these prohibitions are very widely accepted.[202]

(9) *Paragraph (1)(d)* prohibits countermeasures affecting obligations under peremptory norms of general international law. Evidently a peremptory norm, not subject to derogation as between two States even by treaty, cannot be derogated from by unilateral action in the form of countermeasures. ...

Article 51

Countermeasures must be commensurate with the injury suffered, taking into account the gravity of the internationally wrongful act and the rights in question.

Commentary

... (2) Proportionality is a well-established requirement for taking countermeasures, being widely recognized in State practice, doctrine and jurisprudence. ...

(3) In the *Air Services* arbitration,[203] the issue of proportionality was examined in some detail. In that case there was no exact equivalence between France's refusal to allow a change of gauge in London on flights from the west coast of the United States and the Untied States' countermeasure which suspended Air France flights to Los Angeles altogether. The Tribunal nonetheless held the United States measures to be in conformity with the principle of proportionality because they "do not appear to be clearly disproportionate when compared to those taken by France".[204] In particular the majority said:

"It is generally agreed that all counter-measures must, in the first instance, have some degree of equivalence with the alleged breach: this is a well-known rule ... It has been observed, generally, that judging the 'proportionality' of counter-measures is not an easy task and can at best be accomplished by approximation. In the Tribunal's view, it is essential, in a dispute between States, to take into account not only the injuries suffered by the companies concerned but also the importance of the questions of principle arising from the alleged breach. The Tribunal thinks that it will not suffice, in the present case, to compare the losses suffered by Pan Am on account of the suspension of the projected services with the losses which the French companies would have suffered as a result of the counter-measures; it will also be necessary to take into account the importance of the positions of principle which were taken when the French authorities prohibited changes of gauge in third countries. If the importance of the issue is viewed within the framework of the general air transport policy adopted by the United States Government and implemented by the conclusion of a large number of international agreements with countries other than France, the measures taken by the United States do not appear to be clearly disproportionate when compared to those taken by France. Neither Party has provided the Tribunal with evidence that would be sufficient to affirm or reject the existence of pro-portionality in these terms, and the Tribunal must be satisfied with a very approximate appreciation."[205]

In that case the countermeasures taken were in the same field as the initial measures and concerned the same

---

[200] Protocol Additional to the Geneva Conventions of 12 August 1949, and relating to the Protection of Victims of International Armed Conflicts (Protocol), 8 June 1977, *U.N.T.S.*, vol. 1125, p. 3 ...

[201] art. 1(2) of the International Covenant on Economic, Social and Cultural Rights, 16 December 1966, *U.N.T.S.*, vol. 993, p. 3, and art. 1(2) of the International Covenant on Civil and Political Rights, 16 December 1966, *U.N.T.S.*, vol. 999, p. 171.

[202] See K.J. Partsch, "Reprisals" in R. Bernhardt (ed.) *Encyclopedia of Public International Law* (Amsterdam, North Holland, 2000) vol, 4, p, 200, at pp. 203–204; ... Ed. The suspension of prisoner of war exchanges by Ethiopia, as required by 1949 Geneva Red Cross Convention III, art.118, until Eritrea clarified the fate of unlisted missing persons captured by it could not be justified as a countermeasure because of art.50(1)(b) and (c): *Partial Award, Prisoners of War, Eritrea's Claim 17*, 2003, Eritrea-Ethiopia Claims Commission, paras 159–160, *www.pca-cpa.org*.

[203] *Air Services Agreement of 27 March 1946 (United States v. France), R.I.A.A.*, vol. XVIII, p. 417 (1978).

[204] Ibid., at p. 444, para. 83.

[205] Ibid...

routes, even if they were rather more severe in terms of their economic effect on the French carriers than the initial French action.

(4) The question of proportionality was again central to the appreciation of the legality of possible counter-measures taken by Czechoslovakia in the *Gabčíkovo-Nagmaros Project* case.[206] The International Court, having accepted that Hungary's actions in refusing to complete the Project amounted to an unjustified breach of the 1977 Agreement, went on to say:

> "In the view of the Court, an important consideration is that the effects of a countermeasure must be commensurate with the injury suffered, taking account of the rights in question. In 1929, the Permanent Court of International Justice, with regard to navigation on the River Oder, stated as follows:
>
> > '[the] community of interest in a navigable river becomes the basis of a common legal right, the essential features of which are the perfect equality of all riparian States in the user of the whole course of the river and the exclusion of any preferential privilege of any one riparian State in relation to the others' ...
>
> Modern development of international law has strengthened this principle for nonnavigational uses of international watercourses as well ...
>
> The Court considers that Czechoslovakia, by unilaterally assuming control of a shared resource, and thereby depriving Hungary of its right to an equitable and reasonable share of the natural resources of the Danube—with the continuing effects of the diversion of these waters on the ecology of the riparian area of the Szigetköz—failed to respect the proportionality which is required by international law ... The Court thus considers that the diversion of the Danube carried out by Czechoslovakia was not a lawful countermeasure because it was not proportionate."[207]

Thus the Court took into account the quality or character of the rights in question as a matter of principle and (like the Tribunal in the *Air Services* case) did not assess the question of proportionality only in quantitative terms ...

(6) Considering the need to ensure that the adoption of countermeasures does not lead to inequitable results, proportionality must be assessed taking into account not only the purely "quantitive" element of the injury suffered, but also "qualitative" factors such as the importance of the interest protected by the rule infringed and the seriousness of the breach ...

Article 52

1. Before taking countermeasures, an injured State shall:

(a) call on the responsible State, in accordance with article 43, to fulfil its obligations under Part Two;

(b) notify the responsible State of any decision to take countermeasures and offer to negotiate with that State.

2. Notwithstanding paragraph 1(b), the injured State may take such urgent countermeasures as are necessary to preserve its rights.

3. Countermeasures may not be taken, and if already taken must be suspended without undue delay if:

(a) the internationally wrongful act has ceased, and

(b) the dispute is pending before a court or tribunal which has the authority to make decisions binding on the parties.

4. Paragraph 3 does not apply if the responsible State fails to implement the dispute settlement procedures in good faith.

---

[206] *Gabčíkovo-Nagmaros Project (Hungary.Slovakia), ICJ Reports 1997*, p. 7.
[207] Ibid., at p. 56, paras. 85, 87 ...

Commentary

... (3) The system of article 52 builds upon the observations of the Tribunal in the *Air Services* arbitration. The first requirement, set out in *paragraph (1)(a)*, is that the injured State must call on the responsible State to fulfil its obligations of cessation and reparation before any resort to countermeasures. This requirement (sometimes referred to as "*sommation*") was stressed both by the Tribunal in the *Air Services* arbitration[208] and by the International Court in the *Gabčikovo-Nagmaros Project* case.[209] It also appears to reflect a general practice. ...

(6) Under *paragraph 2* ... the injured State may take "such urgent countermeasures as are necessary to preserve its rights" even before any notification of the intention to do so. Under modern conditions of communications, a State which is responsible for an internationally wrongful act and which refuses to cease that act or provide any redress therefore may also seek to immunize itself from countermeasures, for example by withdrawing assets from banks in the injured State. Such steps can be taken within a very short time, so that the notification required by *paragraph (1)(b)* might frustrate its own purpose. Hence *paragraph 2* allows for urgent countermeasures which are necessary to preserve the rights of the injured State: this phrase includes both its rights in the subject-matter of the dispute and its right to take countermeasures. Temporary stay orders, the temporary freezing of assets and similar measures could fall within *paragraph 2*, depending on the circumstances. ...

Article 53

Countermeasures shall be terminated as soon as the responsible State has complied with its obligations under Part Two in relation to the internationally wrongful act.

Article 54

This Chapter does not prejudice the right of any State, entitled under article 48, paragraph 1 to invoke the responsibility of another State, to take lawful measures against that State to ensure cessation of the breach and reparation in the interest of the injured State or of the beneficiaries of the obligation breached.

Commentary

(1) Chapter II deals with the right of an injured State to take countermeasures ... However, "injured" States, as defined in article 42 are not the only States entitled to invoke the responsibility of a State for an internationally wrongful act under Chapter I of this Part. Article 48 allows such invocation by any State, in the case of the breach of an obligation to the international community as a whole, or by any member of a group of States, in the case of other obligations established for the protection of the collective interest of the group. ... Thus with respect to the obligations referred to in article 48, such States are recognised as having a legal interest in compliance. The question is to what extent these States may legitimately assert a right to react against unremedied breaches.[210]

(2) It is vital for this purpose to distinguish between individual measures, whether taken by one State or by a group of States each acting in its individual capacity and through its own organs on the one hand, and institutional reactions in the framework of international organisations on the other. The latter situation, for example where it occurs under the authority of Chapter VII of the United Nations Charter, is not covered by the articles. ...

(3) Practice on this subject is limited and rather embryonic. In a number of instances, States have reacted against what were alleged to be breaches of the obligations referred to in article 48 without claiming to be individually injured. Reactions have taken such forms as economic sanctions or other measures (e.g. breaking off air links or other contacts). Examples include the following: ...

---

[208] Ibid., at p. 444, paras. 85–7.
[209] *Gabčikovo-Nagmaros Project (Hungary/Slovakia), ICJ Reports 1997*, p. 7, at p. 56, para. 84.
[210] See e.g., M. Akehurst, "Reprisals by Third States", *B.Y.I.L.*, vol. 44 (1970), p. 1; J.I. Charney, "Third State Remedies in International Law", *Michigan Journal of International Law*, vol. 10 (1988), p. 57; D.N. Hutchinson, "Solidarity and Breaches of Multilateral Treaties", *B.Y.I.L.*, vol. 59 (1989), p. 151; L.-A. Sicilianos, *Les réactions décentralisées à l'illicite* (Paris, L.D.G.J., 1990) pp. 110–175; J.A. Frowein, "Reactions by Not Directly Affected States to Breaches of Public International Law", *Recueil des cours*, vol. 248 (1994–IV), p. 345; B. Simma, "From Bilateralism to Community Interest in International law", *Recueil des cours*, vol. 250 (1994–VI), p. 217.

Collective measures against Iraq (1990). On 2 August 1990, Iraqi troops invaded and occupied Kuwait. The UN Security Council immediately condemned the invasion. EC Member States and the United States adopted trade embargos and decided to freeze Iraqi assets.[211] This action was taken in direct response to the Iraqi invasion with the consent of the Government of Kuwait.

Collective measures against Yugoslavia (1998). In response to the humanitarian crisis in Kosovo, the member States of the European Community adopted legislation providing for the freezing of Yugoslav funds and an immediate flight ban.[212] For a number of countries, such as Germany, France and the United Kingdom, the latter measure implied the non-performance of bilateral aviation agreements. Because of doubts about the legitimacy of the action, the British government initially was prepared to follow the one-year denunciation procedure provided for in article 17 of its agreement with Yugoslavia. However, it later changed its position and denounced flights with immediate effect. Justifying the measure, it stated that "President Milosevic's ... worsening record on human rights, means that, on moral and political grounds, he has forfeited the right of his Government to insist on the 12 months notice which would normally apply."[213] The Federal Republic of Yugoslavia protested these measures as "unlawful, unilateral and an example of the policy of discrimination".[214] ...

(4) In some other cases certain States similarly suspended treaty rights in order to exercise pressure on States violating collective obligations. However, they did not rely on a right to take countermeasures but asserted a right to suspend the treaty because of a fundamental change of circumstances. ...

EC Member States—Yugoslavia (1991). In the autumn of 1991, in response to resumption of fighting within Yugoslavia, EC members suspended and later denounced the 1983 Co-operation Agreement with Yugoslavia. This led to a general repeal of trade preferences on imports and thus went beyond the weapons embargo ordered by the Security Council in Resolution 713 of 25 September 1991. The reaction was incompatible with the terms of the Co-operation Agreement, which did not provide for the immediate suspension but only for denunciation upon six months' notice. Justifying the suspension, EC members States explicitly mentioned the threat to peace and security in the region. But ... they relied on fundamental change of circumstances, rather than asserting a right to take countermeasures. ...

(6) As this review demonstrates, the current state of international law on countermeasures taken in the general or collective interest is uncertain. State practice is sparse and involves a limited number of States.[215] At present there appears to be no clearly recognised entitlement of States referred to in article 48 to take countermeasures in the collective interest. Consequently it is not appropriate to include in the present articles a provision concerning the question whether other States, identified in article 48, are permitted to take countermeasures in order to induce a responsible State to comply with its obligations. Instead Chapter II includes a saving clause which reserves the position and leaves the resolution of the matter to the further development of international law.

(7) Article 54 accordingly provides that the Chapter on countermeasures does not prejudice the right of any State, entitled under article 48(1) to invoke the responsibility of another State, to take lawful measures against the responsible State to ensure cessation of the breach and reparation in the interest of the injured State or of the beneficiaries of the obligation breached. The article speaks of "lawful measures" rather than "countermeasures" so as not to prejudice any position concerning measures taken by States other than the injured State

---

[211] See e.g. President Bush's Executive Orders of 2 August 1990, reproduced in *A.J.I.L., vol 84 (1990) p. 903.*

[212] Common positions of 7 May & 29 June 1998, *O.J.E.C.* 1998 L 143, p. 1 and *O.J.E.C.* 1998, L 190 p. 3; implemented through EC Regulations 1295/98 (*O.J.E.C.* 1998 L 178, p. 33) & 1901/98 (*O.J.E.C.* 1998 L248, p. 1).

[213] See *B.Y.I.L.*, vol. 69 (1998), pp. 580–1; *B.Y.I.L.*, vol. 70 (1999), pp. 555–6.

[214] Statement of the Government of the Federal Republic of Yugoslavia on the Suspension of Flights of Yugoslav Airlines, 10 October 1999: S/1999/216.

[215] Ed. For a later survey of many examples of third party countermeasures in state practice, see Dawidowicz (2007) 77 B.Y.I.L. 333.

in response to breaches of obligations for the protection of the collective interest or those owed to the international community as a whole. ...

3. THE TREATMENT OF ALIENS[216]

A. Introductory Note

The treatment of aliens (or, more accurately, the treatment of the nationals of other states) is as controversial a subject as any in international law. The controversy stems from a difference of approach between those states that consider that there is an "international minimum standard" of treatment which must be accorded to aliens by all states irrespective of how they treat their own nationals and those that argue that aliens may only insist upon "national treatment", i.e. treatment equal to that given by the state concerned to its own nationals.[217] Generally speaking, developed states follow the "international minimum standard" approach while the developing states favour "national treatment".[218] At the turn of the century, the latter states consisted mainly of Latin American states; more recently they have been joined by most of the post-colonial Afro-Asian states. The former USSR rejected the "international minimum standard" approach also. The support for both points of view makes it difficult to determine many of the rules of international law in this area.

Whether an "international minimum standard" or a "national treatment" rule applies, it is commonly agreed by states that international law does not control their treatment of aliens in every area of activity. Whereas, on either basis, states are limited in their treatment of aliens in the areas indicated in the materials in this section, in certain other areas states may at customary international law treat aliens *qua* aliens[219] in their discretion. For example, aliens may be, and commonly are, restricted in the ownership of property, participation in public life and the taking of public employment. In the United Kingdom, an alien may not own a British ship, vote in a parliamentary election, or hold any office under the Crown.[220]

B. An Injury to the State

MAVROMMATIS PALESTINE CONCESSIONS CASE (JURISDICTION)

Greece v U.K. (1924)

P.C.I.J. Reports, Series A, No. 2, p.12

Judgment of the Court

In the case of the Mavrommatis concessions it is true that the dispute was at first between a private person and a State—i.e. between M. Mavrommatis and Great Britain. Subsequently, the Greek Government took up the

---

[216] See Amerasinghe, *State Responsibility for Injuries to Aliens* (1967); Borchard, *The Diplomatic Protection of Citizens Abroad* (1915); Dunn, *The Protection of Nationals* (1932); Eagleton, *The Responsibility of States in International Law* (1928); Freeman, *The International Responsibility of States for Denial of Justice* (1938); Jessup, *A Modern Law of Nations* (1946), Ch.V; Lillich, ed., *International Law of State Responsibility for Injuries to Aliens* (1983); Parry (1956–II) 90 Hague Recueil 653; Paulson, *Denial of Justice in International Law* (2005); and Tiburcio, *The Human Rights of Aliens under International and Comparative Law* (2001).

[217] On the position of stateless persons, see below, p.514.

[218] On the approach now adopted by developing states in the particular case of expropriation, see below, p.477.

[219] Aliens may, as individuals, have some protection at customary international law and by treaty on a human rights basis: see below, Ch.9.

[220] Bradley and Ewing, *Constitutional and Administrative Law* (14th edn 2007), p.449.

case. The dispute then entered upon a new phase; it entered the domain of international law, and became a dispute between two States.

... It is an elementary principle of international law that a State is entitled to protect its subjects, when injured by acts contrary to international law committed by another State, from whom they have been unable to obtain satisfaction through the ordinary channels. By taking up the case of one of its subjects and by resorting to diplomatic action or international judicial proceedings on his behalf, a State is in reality asserting its own rights—its right to ensure, in the person of its subjects, respect for the rules of international law.

The question, therefore, whether the present dispute originates in an injury to a private interest, which in point of fact is the case in many international disputes, is irrelevant from this standpoint. Once a State has taken up a case on behalf of one of its subjects before an international tribunal, in the eyes of the latter the State is sole claimant.

Note

The Commentary to art.1 of the Draft Articles on Diplomatic Protection, comments on the rule stated in *Mavrommatis* case as follows:

"(3) ... Obviously it is a fiction...to say than an injury to a national is an injury to the State itself. Many of the rules of diplomatic protection contradict the correctness of this fiction, notably the rule of continuous nationality which requires a State to prove that the injured national remained its national after the injury itself and up to the date of presentation of the claim.[221]...

(4) ... The fiction was...no more than a means to an end, the end being the protection of the rights of an injured national....

(5) Draft Article 1 is formulated in such a way[222] as to leave open the question whether the State exercising diplomatic protection does so in its own right or that of its national—or both...."

The Commentary argues that the recognition in international law of substantive and procedural rights for private persons (see below, p.504), have made this fiction less necessary. What consequences would there be for the law of diplomatic protection if the *Mavrommatis* fiction were abandoned?

ADMINISTRATIVE DECISION NO. V

U.S. v Germany (1924)

Mixed Claims Commission: Parker, Umpire; Anderson, American Commissioner; Kiesselbalch, German Commissioner. (1924) 7 R.I.A.A. 119

Opinion of the Umpire

Ordinarily a nation will not espouse a claim on behalf of its national against another national unless requested so to do by such national. When on such request a claim is espoused, the nation's absolute right to control it is necessarily exclusive. In exercising such control it is governed not only by the interest of the particular claimant but by the larger interests of the whole people of the nation and must exercise an untrammelled discretion in determining when and how the claim will be presented and pressed, or withdrawn or compromised, and the

---

[221] Ed. Note also that the cases in Section 3 of this Chapter suggest that compensation is normally assessed by tribunals by reference to the injury suffered by the national, not the state.

[222] Ed. In particular, the final version of art.1, below, p.503, omits wording ("in its own right") found in the *Mavrommatis* case, above, and included in an earlier version of draft art.1.

private owner will be bound by the action taken. Even if payment is made to the espousing nation in pursuance of an award, it has complete control over the fund so paid to and held by it and may, to prevent fraud, correct a mistake, or protect the national honour, at its election return the fund to the nation paying it or otherwise dispose of it. ...

Notes

1.   It is evident from the above extract that diplomatic protection is a matter of discretion for the national state. This was confirmed by the ICJ in the *Barcelona Traction* case, paras.78–79.[223] Any limitation upon a state's control or discretion at all stages of a case is a matter for municipal, not international, law. However, some limitations upon a state's discretion may be emerging. In *R. (Abassi) v Secretary of State for Foreign and Commonwealth Affairs*,[224] the Court of Appeal held that, under United Kingdom law, the Government had no duty to intervene by diplomatic or other means to protect a citizen injured by a foreign state, but that a government "decision or inaction" in this connection was subject to judicial review if it could be shown that it was "irrational or contrary to legitimate expectation; but the Court cannot enter the forbidden areas, including decisions affecting foreign policy".

While recognising that diplomatic protection is discretionary in customary international law, in *Kaunda v President of the Republic of South Africa*[225] the South African Constitutional Court stated:

> "There may...be a duty on government, consistent with its obligations under international law to take action to protect one of its citizens against a gross abuse of international human rights norms. A request to government for assistance in such circumstances where the evidence is clear would be difficult, and in extreme cases possibly impossible to refuse. It is unlikely that such a request would ever be refused by government, but if it were, the decision would be justiciable and a court would order the government to take appropriate action."

See also art.19, Draft Articles on Diplomatic Protection:

> "A state entitled to exercise diplomatic protection according to the present draft articles, should:
>
> (a) Give due consideration to the possibility of exercising diplomatic protection, especially when a significant injury has occurred;
> (b) Take into account, wherever feasible, the views of injured persons with regard to resort to diplomatic protection and the reparation to be sought; and
> (c) Transfer to the injured person any compensation obtained for the injury."

2.   Article 19(c), Draft Articles is an example of progressive development. A state is not obliged by long-established international law to hand over to a claimant compensation received in his case; the question is one of municipal law. As far as English law is concerned, in *Rustomjee v The Queen*,[226] Lush J. stated:

---

[223] See below, p.515.
[224] [2002] EWCA Civ 1598, para.69.
[225] 2005 (4) S.A.L.R. 235 (CC); (2005) 44 I.L.M. 173, para.69, Chaskalson C.J. for the Court. See Coombs (2005) 99 A.J.I.L. 681.
[226] (1876) 1 Q.B.D. 487 at 497. See also *Civilian War Claimants' Association Ltd v The King* [1932] A.C. 14 HL.

No doubt a duty arose as soon as the money was received to distribute that money amongst the persons towards whose losses it was paid by the Emperor of China; but then the distribution when made would be, not the act of an agent accounting to a principal, but the act of the sovereign in dispensing justice to her subjects. For any omission of that duty the sovereign cannot be held responsible.

The case concerned money paid to Great Britain by China by treaty as compensation for damage suffered by British nationals in China. Similarly, as regards art.19(a), in United Kingdom law the Crown owes no legal duty to provide protection so that failure to obtain the release of a British citizen is not actionable in the British courts.[227]

C. International Minimum Standard or National Treatment?

NEER CLAIM

U.S. v Mexico (1926)

U.S.-Mexican General Claims Commission: for the Commissioners
4 R.I.A.A. 60

In this case the United States claimed that Mexico had failed to exercise due diligence in finding and prosecuting the murderer of a United States national. In the course of rejecting the claim, the Commission indicated the standard that it would have to apply. The Commission was unanimous.

Opinion of the Commission

The Commission recognises the difficulty of devising a general formula for determining the boundary between an international delinquency of this type and an unsatisfactory use of power included in national sovereignty ... Without attempting to announce a precise formula, it is in the opinion of the Commission possible ... to hold (first) that the propriety of governmental acts should be put to the test of international standards, and (second) that the treatment of an alien, in order to constitute an international delinquency, should amount to an outrage, to bad faith, to wilful neglect of duty, or to an insufficiency of governmental action so far short of international standards that every reasonable and impartial man would readily recognize its insufficiency. Whether the insufficiency proceeds from deficient execution of an intelligent law or from the fact that the laws of the country do not empower the authorities to measure up to international standards is immaterial.

Notes

1. The great majority of arbitration awards are like that in the *Neer Claim* in supporting the view that international law requires states to treat aliens according to an "international minimum standard".[228] In the *Chevreau* case, for instance, in which France claimed on behalf of a French national in respect of his arrest and treatment in detention by Great Britain, the Arbitrator (Beichmann) said: "The detained man must be treated in a manner fitting his station, and which

---

[227] *Mutasa v Att.-Gen.* [1980] Q.B. 114.
[228] *France v Great Britain* (1931) 2 R.I.A.A. 1113. English translation in (1933) 27 A.J.I.L. 153.

conforms to the standard habitually practised among civilized nations."[229] More recently the tribunal in the *Asian Agricultural Products Ltd* case[230] applied the "'due diligence' obligation under the *minimum standard* of customary international law". The majority of arbitrators in such awards have in the past tended to be from developed states.

2. How persuasive is the argument that an alien who visits, takes up residence in, or does business in a foreign state must take conditions as he finds them?

PREPARATORY STUDY CONCERNING A DRAFT DECLARATION ON RIGHTS AND DUTIES OF STATES

Memorandum submitted by the UN Secretary-General, UNDoc. A/CN. 4/2, p.71, 1949

Early discussion in the International Law Commission on a Draft Declaration on Rights and Duties of States was based upon a Panamanian draft upon which governments were asked to comment. Article 7 of that draft reads in part: "Foreigners may not claim rights different from, or more extensive than, those enjoyed by nationals." The following is the response by the United Kingdom Government to that Article. The sentence was finally omitted from the Commission's Draft Declaration on the separate ground that the question should be dealt with in the course of codifying the law of state responsibility.

The second sentence of this article is not in accord with existing international law, as His Majesty's Government apprehend it. There is much international authority for the existence of a minimum international standard, with which States are obliged to comply in their treatment of foreigners, whether or not they do so in the treatment of their nationals. If, and in so far as international law develops so as to limit the domestic jurisdiction of States in the treatment of their nationals to such an extent that every treatment of a national, which falls below the international standard, is a breach of international law (and therefore a matter on which other States may intervene), then the existing principle of international law with regard to the "international standard" will apply to both nationals and foreigners. Unless and until that position is reached, His Majesty's Government consider that the doctrine of the minimum international standard, with regard to the treatment of foreigners, remains part of international law and that agreement to abolish that doctrine will not be attained.

Notes

1. At the Hague Codification Conference in 1930 the following text on the particular question of injury to aliens at the hands of private persons was rejected by 23 votes to 17:

    "A state is only responsible for damage caused by private persons to the persons or property of foreigners if it has manifestly failed to take such preventive or punitive measures as in the circumstances might reasonably be expected of it had the persons injured been its own nationals."

    A text on the same question favouring an international minimum standard was then adopted by 21 votes to 17.[231] On the other hand, art.9 of the 1933 Montevideo Convention on Rights and Duties of States,[232] which would still represent the view of most developing states, reads in part:

---

[229] (1933) 27 A.J.I.L. at 160.
[230] (1990) 30 I.L.M. 577 at 608. See also the Court Chamber ("minimum international standard") in the *ELSI* case, I.C.J. Rep. 1989, p.14.
[231] See Hackworth (1930) 24 A.J.I.L. 500 at 513–514.
[232] See above, p.92. There are 16 parties to the Convention, including the US. See, however, the US reservation, 4 Malloy 4810.

"Nationals and foreigners are under the same protection of the law and the national authorities and the foreigners may not claim rights other or more extensive than those of the nationals."

2. For a robust, Victorian statement favouring the international minimum standard in the administration of justice, note that of Lord Palmerston (Foreign Secretary) in 1850:

"We shall be told, perhaps, as we have already been told, that if the people of the country are liable to have heavy stones placed upon their breasts, and police officers to dance upon them; if they are liable to have their heads tied to their knees, and to be left for hours in that state; or to be swung like a pendulum and to be bastinadoed as they swing, foreigners have no right to be better treated than the natives, and have no business to complain if the same things are practised upon them. We may be told this, but this is not my opinion, nor do I believe it is the opinion of any reasonable man."[233]

3. In 1957, the International Law Commission debated the Second Report on State Responsibility of its Special Rapporteur (Garcia Amador).[234] The Rapporteur proposed in his Report the following draft article:

"*Article* 5.1. The State is under a duty to ensure to aliens the enjoyment of the same civil rights, and to make available to them the same individual guarantees as are enjoyed by its nationals. These rights and guarantees shall not, however, in any case be less than the 'fundamental human rights' recognized and defined in contemporary international instruments."

This ambitious proposal would, in a sense, have married the international minimum standard and national treatment approaches. Its human right basis, which would have made substantial inroads upon the domestic jurisdiction of states, was too far out of line with state practice to have had any real hope of approval. Despite redrafting, it was felt to be impracticable for purposes of codification and not pursued further.[235] Later the Commission changed its approach and, as indicated earlier,[236] concentrated upon the secondary rules of state responsibility.

With the remarkable development of customary and treaty based international human rights law since 1945, the value for nationals of diplomatic protection under the law of state responsibility for the treatment of aliens has undoubtedly diminished in those areas of ill-treatment to which international human rights law applies. Nonetheless, the law of state responsibility is not made totally redundant by this development. This follows from the difficulties in enforcing customary human rights law[237] and the less than perfect remedies and universal acceptance of human rights treaties. For the time being at least, the possibility of diplomatic protection by one's

---

[233] 6 B.D.I.L. 290. Parl. Deb., ser.4, col.387, CXII.

[234] Y.B.I.L.C., 1957, II, p.104. The debate was a famous one, in which nationals from developing and developed states put different points of view most forcefully: Vol.I, pp.155 et seq.

[235] For another approach, see the General Assembly's 1985 Declaration on the Human Rights of Individuals who are not Nationals of the Country in which They Live, G.A. Resn. 40/144, G.A.O.R., 40th Sess., Supp. 53, p.252 (1985). This is limited and tailored to the human rights of aliens (e.g. provisions concerning the right to transfer assets home), and was a response to the ill-treatment of aliens in Amin's Uganda in the late 1970s. It has not proved significant in practice. On the Declaration, see Lillich and Neff (1978) 21 G.Y.I.L. 97; and Lillich, *The Human Rights of Aliens in Contemporary International Law* (1984), pp.55–56

[236] See above, p.422.

[237] See below, p.626.

national state is a valuable supplement to such procedures as exist under international human rights law.

The following materials are limited to areas of primary rules in which the law of state responsibility clearly remains of value for nationals. Freedom from the arbitrary exclusion and, to a lesser extent, of the expulsion of aliens is not well guaranteed by human rights law, and the right to property—and hence protection from expropriation—is not guaranteed at all in the ICCPR or as fully as it might be for foreign companies in most other human rights treaties.

D. Admission and Expulsion[238]

REPORT ON ADMISSION TO LOUISIANA

Report by J. Dodson, Queen's Advocate, to the Foreign Secretary, August 4, 1843. 2 McNair 105

... The purport of the Act in question [a Louisiana State Statute] is to prohibit free persons of colour from entering the State of Louisiana by sea, and of punishing them with great severity in case of their arrival within the territory contrary to the tenor of this inhospitable law.

The provisions of this extraordinary and illiberal Act are calculated to operate with peculiar harshness as regards the free coloured subjects of Her Majesty; and I therefore think that Her Majesty's Government would be justified in making a representation against it, in the shape of a remonstrance to the Government of the United States. Whether Her Majesty's Government would have a right to go further and insist upon the repeal of this specimen of Louisianian legislation, may be a matter not altogether free from doubt, but upon the best consideration I have been able to give the subject, I incline to think that Great Britain does not possess such right. It cannot be denied that every independent State or nation is entitled to admit or exclude from its territories the subjects and citizens of foreign States, unless it has entered into any engagement by treaty on the subject, in which case the treaty must of course prescribe the rule to be observed.

Note

In *Att.-Gen. for Canada v Cain*,[239] the Judicial Committee of the Privy Council said:

"One of the rights possessed by the supreme power in every State is the right to refuse to permit an alien to enter that State, to annex what conditions it pleases to the permission to enter it, and to expel or deport from the State, at pleasure, even a friendly alien, especially if it considers his presence in the State opposed to its peace, order, and good government, or to its social or material interests."

---

[238] See Dowty, *Closed Borders* (1987); Goodwin-Gill, *International Law and the Movement of Persons between States* (1978); Henckaerts, *Mass Expulsion in Modern International Law and Practice* (1995); Plender, *International Migration Law* (2nd edn 1988); Pellonpää, *Expulsion in International Law* (1984); Tiburcio, above, n.216, pp.210 et seq.

[239] [1906] A.C. 542 at 546.

RANKIN v IRAN

U.S. v Iran (1987)

Iran-US Claims Tribunal. Chamber Two: Briner, Chairman; Aldrich, Bahrami, Members. 17 Iran-U.S.C.T.R. 135

The claimant was an American national employed by BHI, an American company, in Iran at the time of the fall of the Shah's Government and its replacement by the Islamic Revolutionary Government in February 1979. On February 12, the day after the new Government took office, the claimant, who was still under contract to work for BHI in Iran, requested and was granted by BHI permission to be evacuated from the country with other BHI employees whom BHI had arranged to be repatriated. In this case, he claimed compensation for loss of salary and abandoned personal property resulting from his alleged expulsion from Iran contrary to international law.

Award of the Tribunal

22. According to the practice of States, the writings of scholars, the decisions of international tribunals, and bilateral treaty provisions such as those contained in the [1955] Treaty of Amity ... between Iran and the United States ..., international law imposes certain restraints on the circumstances and the manner in which a State may expel aliens from its territory. A claimant alleging expulsion has the burden of proving the wrongfulness of the expelling State's action, in other words that it was arbitrary, discriminatory, or in breach of the expelling State's obligations. These restraints have usually been considered in the context of specific measures directed against an individual emanating directly from the State or legally attributable to it. However, these general principles apply equally to a situation in which, while there is no law, regulation, or directive which forces the individual alien to leave, his or her continued presence in the host country is made impossible because of conditions generated by wrongful acts of the State or attributable to it ...

30. ... a. A distinction must be made between the period prior to February 1979 and thereafter, when the Ayatollah Khomeini returned to Iran from exile and the new Islamic Government replaced that of the Shah.

b. During the earlier period, the leaders of the Revolution fostered anti-American attitudes ... However, the evidence before us is inadequate to show that in the period prior to February 1979 there existed a general expulsion policy towards foreigners. The thrust of the Revolutionary Movement was then aimed at the overthrow of the regime of the Shah. ...

d. However, when the Ayatollah Khomeini returned to Iran on February 1, 1979, he was reported to have called for the departure of all foreigners. Shortly thereafter, the newly-formed Government began to take action to cancel contracts with non-Iranian persons and companies and to implement a policy to lessen the influence of foreigners in Iran and cause the departure of, among others, most Americans.

e. The implementation of this policy could, in general terms, be violative of both procedural and substantive limitations on a State's right to expel aliens from its territory, as found in the provisions of the Treaty of Amity and in customary international law.[240] However, it ... is necessary to examine the circumstances of each departure and to identify the general and specific acts relied on and evidenced to determine how they affected or motivated at that time the individual who now is alleging expulsion and whether such acts are attributable to Iran (*See* Articles 5–10, Draft Articles on State Responsibility ...). In this regard the Tribunal notes the significance of the general turmoil and disorder which ensued after the return of Ayatollah Khomeini as competing groups vied for power in the revolutionary environment which existed in Iran at that time. The Tribunal considers this a factor which could have caused an individual's decision to leave and which could not be attributed to the State or its agents or organs. ...

39. [Having reviewed the evidence] ... the Tribunal finds that the Claimant has not satisfied the burden of proving that the implementation of the new policy of the Respondent ... was a substantial causal factor in his departure from Iran. Neither has the Claimant satisfied the burden of proving that his decision to leave was caused by specific acts or omissions of or attributable to the Respondent. Rather, the turmoil and generally

---

[240] e.g. by expelling an alien who had a continued right to residence in Iran or by depriving an alien of a reasonable opportunity to protect his property interests prior to his expulsion.

chaotic conditions associated with this crucial stage of the Revolution would appear to have been the motivating factor in the Claimant's decision to leave.

Claim dismissed

Note

The requirements for "constructive expulsion" were expressed as follows by Chamber Three of the Tribunal in *International Technical Products Corp. v Iran*[241]:

"Such cases would seem to presuppose at least (1) that the circumstances in the country of residence are such that the alien cannot reasonably be regarded as having any real choice, and (2) that behind the events or acts leading to the departure there is an intention of having the alien ejected and these acts, moreover, are attributable to the State in accordance with principles of state responsibility."

DR BREGER'S CASE

Letter of December 15, 1961, from the U.S. Department of State to a Congressman. 8 Whiteman 861

As to Dr Breger's expulsion from the Island of Rhodes in 1938, it may be pointed out that under generally accepted principles of international law, a state may expel an alien whenever it wishes, provided it does not carry out the expulsion in an arbitrary manner, such as by using unnecessary force to effect the expulsion or by otherwise mistreating the alien or by refusing to allow the alien a reasonable opportunity to safeguard property. In view of Dr Breger's statement to the effect that he was ordered by the Italian authorities to leave the Island of Rhodes within six months, it appears doubtful that international liability of the Italian Government could be based on the ground that he was not given enough time to safeguard his property.

Notes

1. In *Yeager v Iran*,[242] the Tribunal awarded compensation to an American expelled from Iran who "was given only 30 minutes to pack a few personal belongings without advance notice" on the basis that customary international law recognised "that a state must give the foreigner to be expelled sufficient time to wind up his affairs."

    Goodwin-Gill[243] suggests that there are substantive as well as procedural limitations upon the power to expel aliens:

    "State practice accepts that expulsion is justified:

    (a) for entry in breach of law;
    (b) for breach of the conditions of admission;
    (c) for involvement in criminal activities;
    (d) in the light of political and security considerations.

---

[241] (1985) 9 Iran-U.S.C.T.R. 18. See also *Yeager v Iran* (1987) 17 Iran-U.S.T.R. 92 and *Short v Iran* (1987) 16 id. 76. On the Iranian "constructive expulsion" cases, see Cove (1987–8) 11 Fordham I.L.J. 802.

[242] (1987) 17 Iran-U.S.C.T.R. 92 at 106.

[243] See above, n.238, p.262. As to procedure, he suggests that the expulsion must be in accordance with the local law and not arbitrary: p.263.

In determining whether its interests are adversely affected by the continuing presence of the alien, or whether there is a threat to 'ordre public,' the expelling State enjoys under international law a fairly wide margin of appreciation.

'Ordre public' remains a 'general legal conception,' the content of which is determined by law. Whether or not reasons of 'ordre public' exist is open to impartial adjudication in the light of the prescribed function of expulsion and of the international obligations which each State owes.

The principle of good faith and the requirement of justification, or 'reasonable cause,' demand that due consideration be given to the interests of the individual, including his basic human rights, his family, property, and other connections with the State of residence, and his legitimate expectations. These must be weighed against the competing claims of 'ordre public.'"

2. On the expulsion of refugees, see the 1951 Convention relating to the Status of Refugees.[244] Although there is no duty to admit a refugee, contracting parties "shall not expel a refugee lawfully in their territory save on grounds of national security or public order" (art.32(1)). Further, a refugee, whether lawfully or unlawfully present, must not be returned "to the frontiers of territories where his life or freedom would be threatened on account of his race, religion, nationality, membership of a particular social group or political opinion." (art.33(1)).[245] It is arguable that the Convention now states rules of customary international law.[246]

3. With regard to the deportation of stateless persons, British practice has been expressed as follows:

"H.M. Government observe the principle that an alien should not be deported except to the country of which he is a national. Accordingly, it is not the practice to deport stateless aliens resident in the United Kingdom."[247]

4. The admission and expulsion of aliens is regulated by a number of bilateral and multilateral treaties. The 1962 Anglo-Japanese Treaty of Commerce, Establishment and Navigation,[248] for example, reads:

"Nationals of one High Contracting Party shall be accorded, with respect to entry into, residence in and departure from any territory of the other, treatment not less favourable than that accorded to the nationals of any other foreign country."

---

[244] (1954) U.K.T.S. 39, Cmd. 9171; 189 U.N.T.S. 150. In force 1954. 144 parties, including the UK. See also the 1967 Protocol, (1969) U.K.T.S. 15, Cmnd. 3906, 606 U.N.T.S. 267, to which there are 144 parties, including the UK. A refugee is defined, art.1A(2), as amended by the 1967 Protocol, as a person who "owing to well-founded fear of being persecuted for reasons of race, religion, nationality, membership of a particular social group or political opinion, is outside the country of his nationality and is unable or, owing to such fear, is unwilling to avail himself of the protection of that country, or who, not having a nationality and being outside the country of his former habitual residence is unable or, owing to such fear, is unwilling to return to it." See further Goodwin-Gill and McAdams, *The Refugee in International Law* (3rd edn 2007), Ch.2.

[245] This is unless he is reasonably suspected of being a security risk or, having been finally convicted of a particularly serious crime, constitutes a danger to the community: art.33(2).

[246] See Goodwin-Gill, above, n.238, p.141.

[247] L.N.O.J. 1934, p.373. This remains British practice.

[248] (1963) U.K.T.S. 17, Cmnd. 1979, art.3(1).

See also the European Convention on Establishment 1955.[249] EU law allows freedom of movement within the EU for EU citizens for employment and residential purposes for citizens of Member States.[250] Human rights treaties contain some guarantees concerning the expulsion (but not the entry) of aliens.[251]

5. In a press release dated May 21, 1951,[252] the United States Department of State expressed its concern "over the continued denial by Chinese Communist authorities of exit permits to certain Americans, including a number of Shanghai businessmen, some of whom have been endeavouring for over a year to leave China." It continued: "Arbitrary refusal to permit aliens to depart from a country is of course a violation of the elementary principles of international law and practice."

6. Whereas a state may exclude aliens in its discretion, it is obliged to admit its own nationals who have been expelled from another state, at least where they have nowhere else to go.[253] When Kenya and Uganda became independent, some East African Asians chose (as, exceptionally, the constitutional arrangements for independence allowed them to do) to remain citizens of the United Kingdom and Colonies or British protected persons[254] and not to take the nationality of the newly independent state. This possibility was provided because of the fears of such persons for the treatment that they would receive within the new states; it was understood that as United Kingdom citizens or protected persons they would have a right of entry into the United Kingdom if need be. By the Commonwealth Immigrants Act 1968 (now the Immigration Act 1971), United Kingdom citizens and British protected persons who did not, mainly by birth or ancestry, have certain defined ties with the United Kingdom lost their right of entry into the United Kingdom in United Kingdom law and were made the subject of a system of controlled entry. In consequence, a large number of East African Asians who *voluntarily* left Kenya and Uganda after the 1968 Act came into force were refused entry. When, in 1972, Uganda *expelled* all East African Asians who were not Ugandan nationals, the United Kingdom acknowledged and acted upon an international law obligation to admit them. The Lord Chancellor (Lord Hailsham) stated:

"If I may now turn to the position in international law more generally, the Attorney General, acting in his capacity as the professional legal advisor to the Government, and not, as quite improperly suggested, instigated by his political colleagues, advised us that in international law a State is under a duty as between other States to accept in its territories those of its nationals who have nowhere else to go. If a citizen of the United Kingdom is expelled, as I think illegally from Uganda, and is not accepted for settlement elsewhere, we could be required by any State where he then was to accept him."[255]

[249] (1971) U.K.T.S. 1, Cmnd. 453; 529 U.N.T.S. 141. In force 1965. 12 parties, including the UK.
[250] See Craig and De Burca, *EU Law: Text and Materials* (4th edn 2008), p.852.
[251] See, e.g. art.13, I.C.C.P.R., below, p.555.
[252] 18 Whiteman 874.
[253] Although the admission, etc. of nationals does not properly come within this section, it is considered here for convenience.
[254] On UK nationality see Bradley and Ewing, *Constitutional and Administrative Law* (14th edn 2007), p.445.
[255] *Hansard*, HL Vol.335, col.497. But see Lord Denning M.R., in *R. v Immigration Officer Ex p. Thakrar* [1974] Q.B. 684 CA (no duty to admit British subjects expelled *en masse* from a British overseas territory). See Akehurst (1975) 38 M.L.R. 72; and Sharma and Wooldridge (1974) 23 I.C.L.Q. 397. See also the *East African Asians Cases* (1973) 3 E.H.R.R. 76.

Was the refusal to admit East African Asians who had *voluntarily* left Kenya and Uganda a breach of customary international law? In *Van Duyn v Home Office*,[256] the European Court of Justice stated that "it is a principle of international law. .. that a State is precluded from refusing to its own nationals the right of entry or residence."[257] To whom is the resulting duty owed? All states?[258]

7. On the *expulsion* of nationals, Weiss states:

> "As between national and State of nationality the question of the right of sojourn is not a question of international law. It may, however, become a question bearing on the relations between States. The expulsion of nationals forces other States to admit aliens, but, according to the accepted principles of international law, the admission of aliens is in the discretion of each State. ... It follows that the expulsion of a national may only be carried out with the consent of the State to whose territory he is to be expelled, and that the State of nationality is under a duty towards other States to receive its nationals back on its territory."[259]

See also art.13 of the Universal Declaration of Human Rights 1948,[260] and art.12 of the International Covenant on Civil and Political Rights 1966.[261]

8. The right of "[e]veryone to be free to leave any country, including his own," subject to public order, etc., limitations is recognised on a human rights basis (for nationals and aliens) in international human rights treaties[262] and, although difficult to enforce, may be protected by customary international law too.[263] Departure from a state's territory will in most cases be dependent upon the possession of a passport.[264] In 1976, the British Government withdrew the passports of United Kingdom citizens who had fought as mercenaries in the Angolan war of independence. "The Foreign Office said that these will not be returned, and that future applications will be refused unless the men sign a declaration they will not work as mercenaries."[265]

---

[256] [1974] E.C.R. 1337. The statement was made in the context of freedom of movement for employment, not expulsion from another state.

[257] cf. art.13, U.D.H.R., below, p.849; art.12(4), I.C.C.P.R., below, p.555.

[258] See Goodwin-Gill, above, n.238 p.137.

[259] *Nationality and Statelessness in International Law* (2nd edn. 1979), pp.45–46. Footnote omitted.

[260] Below, p.549.

[261] Below, p.555.

[262] See, e.g. art.12(2), I.C.C.P.R., below, p.555. See also art.13, U.D.H.R., below, p.549.

[263] On the right to leave and return, see Dinstein (1974) 4 Is. Y.H.R. 266; Hannum, *The Right to Leave and Return in International Law and Practice* (1987); Higgins (1974) 4 Is. Y.H.R. 275; Ingles, *Study of Discrimination in Respect of the Right of Everyone to Leave any Country, etc.*, UN Doc. E/CN.4/Sub.2/229/Rev. 1 (1963); Jagerskold, in Henkin, ed., *The International Bill of Rights* (1981), Ch.7; and Torovsky (1962–63) 4 J.I.C.J. 63.

[264] On the law concerning passports, see Turack, *The Passport in International Law* (1972). On the UK position, see Williams (1974) 23 I.C.L.Q. 642.

[265] *The Times*, February 20, 1976.

E. Expropriation[266]

Note

Expropriation, or the compulsory taking of private property by the state, is a phenomenon that became especially important in international law with the spread of socialism and the emergence of the post-colonial state. If the typical nineteenth century case was the occasional taking of the property of a single foreigner in the context of a particular project or dispute, more recently it has been the general expropriation by law of enterprises with a view to their public management in the national interest. It is normally in this last context that the twentieth century term "nationalisation" is used. Whereas expropriation and nationalisation are sometimes treated as separate concepts, the view taken in the following pages is that the latter is a species of the former. Unfortunately, the political differences between capitalist and socialist states coupled with the economic differences between developed and developing states have led to a situation in which there has been little agreement on the rules on expropriation, as the following extracts show. Whereas it is generally agreed that expropriation may occur, developed states suggest that it must take place in accordance with an "international minimum standard" set by international law while developing states deny that this is so. In their opinion, the circumstances and conditions of expropriation are matters to be left largely to the expropriating state to regulate in its discretion under its law. However, as the comment by Walde, below, p.477, suggests, these divisions are becoming less sharp as developing states have both moved from state ownership and sought to encourage foreign investment.

RESOLUTION ON PERMANENT SOVEREIGNTY OVER NATURAL RESOURCES 1962[267]

G.A. Res. 1803 (XVII), G.A.O.R., 17th Sess., Supp. 17, p. 15

The General Assembly

Declares that:

1. The rights of peoples and nations to permanent sovereignty over their natural wealth and resources must be exercised in the interest of their national development and of the well-being of the people of the State concerned; ...

3. In cases where authorization is granted, the capital imported and the earnings on that capital shall be governed by the terms thereof, by the national legislation in force, and by international law. The profits derived must be shared in the proportions freely agreed upon, in each case, between the investors and the recipient State, due care being taken to ensure that there is no impairment, for any reason, of that State's sovereignty over its natural wealth and resources;

4. Nationalization, expropriation or requisitioning shall be based on grounds or reasons of public utility,

---

[266] Among the extensive literature, see Akinsanya, *The Expropriation of Multinational Property in the Third World* (1980); Asante (1988) 37 I.C.L.Q. 588; Beveridge, *The Treatment and Taxation of Foreign Investment under International Law* (2000); Fatouros, *Government Guarantees to Foreign Investors* (1962); Higgins (1982–II) 176 Hague Recueil 259; Jain, *Nationalisation of Foreign Property* (1983); Jimenez de Aréchega (1978) 11 N.Y.U.J.I.L.P. 179; Katzarov, *The Theory of Nationalisation* (1964); Lillich, ed., *The Valuation of Nationalised Property in International Law*, 4 vols (1972–1987); Norton (1991) 85 A.J.I.L. 474; Pellonpää and Fitzmaurice (1988) 19 N.Y.I.L. 53; Ratner (2008) 102 A.J.I.L. 475; Schrijver, *Sovereignty over Natural Resources* (1997); Sornarajah, *The Pursuit of Nationalised Property* (1986); *The International Law on Foreign Investment* (2nd edn. 2004); Verwey, and Schrijver (1984) 15 N.Y.I.L. 3; Weston, in Lillich, ed., *International Law of State Responsibility for Injuries to Aliens* (1983), p.89; White, *Nationalisation of Foreign Property* (1961); Wortley, *Expropriation in Public International Law* (1959). The *U.S. Restatement, 3d, Foreign Relations Law of the U.S.* (1987), Vol.2, para.712, contains an excellent treatment of the subject.

[267] See Gess (1964) 13 I.C.L.Q. 398; and O'Keefe (1974) 8 J.W.T.L. 239.

security or the national interest which are recognized as overriding purely individual or private interests, both domestic and foreign. In such cases the owner shall be paid appropriate compensation in accordance with the rules in force in the State taking such measures in the exercise of its sovereignty and in accordance with international law. In any case where the question of compensation gives rise to a controversy, the national jurisdiction of the State taking such measures shall be exhausted. However, upon agreement by sovereign States and other parties concerned, settlement of the dispute should be made through arbitration or international adjudication; ...

8. Foreign investment agreements freely entered into by, or between, sovereign States shall be observed in good faith; States and international organizations shall strictly and conscientiously respect the sovereignty of peoples and nations over their natural wealth and resources in accordance with the Charter and the principles set forth in the present resolution.

Notes

1. The resolution was adopted by 87 votes to 2, with 12 abstentions. France and South Africa voted against it; the Soviet bloc, Burma, Cuba and Ghana abstained.

2. Resolution 1803 has been accepted in a number of arbitration awards as reflecting customary international law.[268] It recognises the right to expropriate foreign property. That there is such a right is common ground among states generally, with developed, as well as developing, states availing themselves of it.[269] The Resolution's public purpose ("public utility", etc.) and compensation requirements are considered later, as is its lack of a "non-discrimination" guarantee.

CHARTER OF ECONOMIC RIGHTS AND DUTIES OF STATES 1974[270]

G.A. Res. 3281 (XXIX). (1975) 14 I.L.M. 251

Article 2

1. Every State has and shall freely exercise full permanent sovereignty, ... including possession, use and disposal, over all its wealth, natural resources and economic activities.

2. Each State has the right:

(a) To regulate and exercise authority over foreign investment within its national jurisdiction in accordance with its laws and regulations and in conformity with its national objectives and priorities. No State shall be compelled to grant preferential treatment to foreign investment;

(b) To regulate and supervise the activities of transnational corporations within its national jurisdiction and

---

[268] See, e.g. the *Texaco* case, below, p.494; the *Aminoil* case, below p.498; the *Amoco* case, below, p.481; and the *Sedco* case (*Second Interlocutory Award*) (1986) 10 Iran-U.S. C.T.R. 180 at 198.

[269] On the 1982 French nationalisations, see Borde and Eggleston (1982) 68 A.B.A.J. 422.

[270] The Charter was adopted by 120 votes to six, with 10 abstentions. The states voting against were Belgium, Denmark, the FRG, Luxembourg, the UK and the US. The abstaining states were Austria, Canada, France, Ireland, Israel, Italy, Japan, the Netherlands, Norway, and Spain. A separate vote was taken on art.2(2)(c). The majority in favour of it was 104 to 16, with six abstentions. The votes against were by the six states that later voted against the Charter as a whole and by nine of the 10 states that later abstained on the Charter as whole plus Sweden (instead of Israel). The six states that abstained on art.2(2)(c) were Australia, Barbados, Finland, Israel, New Zealand and Portugal. An amendment to art.2(2)(c) which would have replaced the present wording by "to nationalise, expropriate, or requisition foreign property for a public purpose, provided that just compensation in the light of all the relevant circumstances shall be paid" was proposed by a group of western states in the Second Committee: UN Doc. A/C.2/L.1404 (1974). It was defeated by 87 votes to 19, with 11 abstentions. On the Charter, see Brower and Tepe (1975) 9 Int. Lawyer 295; De Waart (1977) 24 N.I.L.R. 304; Fatouros and Meagher (1980) 12 N.Y.U.J.I.L.P. 653; Jain (1979) 19 Ind. J.I.L. 544; McWhinney (1976) 14 C.Y.I.L. 57; Weston (1981) 75 A.J.I.L. 437; White (1975) 24 I.C.L.Q. 542.

take measures to ensure that such activities comply with its laws, rules and regulations and conform with its economic and social policies. . . .

(c) To nationalize, expropriate or transfer ownership of foreign property in which case appropriate compensation should be paid by the State adopting such measures, taking into account its relevant laws and regulations and all circumstances that the State considers pertinent. In any case where the question of compensation gives rise to a controversy, it shall be settled under the domestic law of the nationalizing State and by its tribunals, unless it is freely and mutually agreed by all States concerned that other peaceful means be sought on the basis of the sovereign equality of States and in accordance with the principle of free choice of means.

Notes

1. The Charter was prepared by the United Nations Conference on Trade and Development (UNCTAD), an organ of the General Assembly whose function is primarily "to promote international trade . . . particularly trade between countries at different stages of development, between developing countries and between countries with different systems of economic and social organisation."[271] The Charter sets out economic rights and duties of states over the whole spectrum of international trade, including the right to engage without discrimination in international trade; the right to participate fully in the international decision-making process in the solution of world economic, financial and monetary problems; and the duty to co-operate in the expansion of world trade. Only the Article on expropriation is printed above.

2. The Charter was preceded by General Assembly Resolution 3171 (XXVIII)[272] of 1973 and by the Declaration on the Establishment of a New International Economic Order 1974[273] which follow the same pattern on expropriation.

3. Clearly, the 1974 Charter favours the view of developing states—much more so than the earlier Resolution 1803. It does not mention any public purpose limitation upon the power to expropriate and the compensation provision contradicts developed states' views. These points are taken up later. What should be emphasised for the moment is that the Charter's value as a statement of custom is doubtful. In the *Texaco* case, below, p.494, the arbitrator considered that art.2 was put forward *de lege ferenda* and not as a statement of current law. In any event, he considered that the opposition to it was of sufficient size and significance to deny it the status of custom. Other arbitration awards have drawn the same distinction between Resolution 1803 and the 1974 Charter, taking the view that the latter is not reflective of custom.[274]

   Writing in 1979, Brownlie states[275]:

   "It is fairly clear that the Charter does not purport to be a declaration of pre-existing principles and overall it has a strong programmatic, political and didactic flavour. Nonetheless, there can

---

[271] G.A. Resn. 1995, G.A.O.R., 19th Sess., Supp. 15, p.1. (1964).

[272] G.A.O.R., 28th Sess., Supp. 30, p.52 (1973); (1974) 68 A.J.I.L. 381. The Resolution was adopted by 108 votes to 1, with 16 abstentions. The vote on para.3 was 86 to 11, with 28 abstentions. The states voting against were, predictably, 11 of the developed states that later voted against or abstained in respect of art.2(2)(c), Charter of Economic Rights and Duties of States, above, including the UK and the US. The 28 abstaining states consisted of such states also and some developing states as well.

[273] G.A. Resn. 3201 (S-VI); (1974) 13 I.L.M. 715. The Declaration was adopted without a vote. The FRG, France, Japan, the UK and the US made reservations to it: pp.744 et seq. (1974).

[274] See the arbitration awards referred to in n.268 above. But in the *Liamco* case, the arbitrator concluded that Resolution 1803 and the 1974 Charter "if not a unanimous source of law", were both "evidence of the recent dominant trend of international opinion concerning the sovereign right of states over their natural resources": (1981) 20 I.L.M. 53.

[275] (1979–I) 162 Hague Recueil 255 at 268.

be little doubt that Article 2, paragraph 2(c), is regarded by many States as an emergent principle, a statement of presently applicable rules."

The New International Economic Order (NIEO) had very little success in causing developed states to alter their ways generally and in establishing a new consensus on the international law of expropriation in particular. Moreover, since its adoption, the attitudes of developing countries have changed so that the NIEO is no longer central to their approach. Commenting on the present situation, Walde states[276]:

"This paper has followed the comprehensive onslaught of the Third World [through the NIEO] on a world economic system dominated in law, in institutions and in key concepts by Western countries. This onslaught can be explained by decolonisation and by the alliance among developing countries keen to have economic emancipation follow political association with the socialist countries competing with Western capitalism. An often historically rooted view of the State as the proper guardian and director of economic development propelled a very statist view of how economic development should be brought about, and in its wake an exaggerated concept of national sovereignty, seen as a defense against the overwhelming economic power of multinational companies and the Western school of international law protecting them.

Within the space of twenty years, this dominant paradigm of international economic relations has changed dramatically. On many issues one can see in fact a complete reversal—from statism to market liberalism, from nationalisation to privatisation,[277] from foreign investment restriction to deregulated open-door policies. The failure of high expectations for the State-driven model of economic development, the collapse of communism and the emergence of new commercially-oriented middle-classes challenging the NIEO-focussed State classes in developing countries have contributed to this complete change of paradigm."

STARRETT HOUSING CORP. v IRAN (INTERLOCUTORY AWARD)

U.S. v Iran (1983)

Iran-US Claims Tribunal.[278] Chamber One: Lagergren, Chairman; Kashani, Holtzmann, Members. 4 Iran-U.S.C.T.R. 122; (1984) 23 I.L.M. 1090

In 1974, the claimant American company, operating through Shah Goli, an Iranian subsidiary company, entered into an agreement with an Iranian development bank to buy land in Iran and build houses upon it. The project was proceeding on schedule when harassment during the 1979 revolution caused the withdrawal of most of the American and other foreign personnel working on it. This, coupled with general revolutionary disruption and government intervention (e.g. by making Shah Goli forgo contractual payments under duress and freezing its bank account), caused the project to fall behind schedule and Shah Goli to be in financial difficulties. In this situation, on January 30, 1980, the

[276] Al-Nauimi and Meese, eds, *International Legal Issues Arising under the United Nations Decade of International Law* (1995), p.1301, p.1335.
[277] Ed. Note, however, in 2004 plans were announced by Zimbabwe to nationalise all farmland. This followed land reforms in Zimbabwe initiated in 2002, in which white-owned farms, some foreign-owned, were expropriated and handed over to private black Zimbabweans.
[278] On the Iran-US Claims Tribunal, see below, p.834, n.14. On expropriation, see Mouri, *The International Law of Expropriation as Reflected in the Work of the Iran-U.S. Claims Tribunal* (1994).

Iranian Government, acting under a July 1979 decree, placed Shah Goli under the control of a temporary manager. The claimants sought compensation for the expropriation of their property rights in the project and in Shah Goli. In this interlocutory award, the Tribunal determined that there had been a "taking" of the claimant's property as of the end of January 1980 and appointed experts to evaluate the loss.

Award of the Tribunal

It is undisputed in this case that the Government of Iran did not issue any law or decree according to which the Zomorod Project or Shah Goli expressly was nationalized or expropriated. However, it is recognized in international law that measures taken by a State can interfere with property rights to such an extent that these rights are rendered so useless that they must be deemed to have been expropriated, even though the State does not purport to have expropriated them and the legal title to the property formally remains with the original owner.

... There can be little doubt that at least at the end of January 1980 the claimants had been deprived of the effective use, control and benefits of their property rights in Shah Goli. By that time the Ministry of Housing had appointed Mr Erfan as Temporary Manager of Shah Goli to direct all further activities in connection with the Project on behalf of the Government. ... As a result of these measures the Claimants could no longer exercise their rights to manage Shah Goli and were deprived of their possibilities of effective use and control of it.

It has, however, to be borne in mind that assumption of control over property by a government does not automatically and immediately justify a conclusion that the property has been taken by the government, thus requiring compensation under international law. In this case it cannot be disregarded that Starrett has been requested to resume the Project. The Government of Iran argues that it would have been possible for Starrett to appoint managers from any country other than the United States, but the evidence does not in other respects indicate on what conditions Starrett has been afforded any possibility to resume the Project. The completion of the Project was dependent upon a large number of American construction supervisors and subcontractors whom it would have been necessary to replace and the right freely to select management, supervisors and subcontractors is an essential element of the right to manage a project. Further, given the contents of the [January 1980] Construction Completion Bill it must be taken for granted that Starrett can only resume the Project subject to the provisions of that Bill, which entail far-reaching restrictions in the right of former owners to manage housing projects. Indeed, the language of that bill seems to indicate that the right to manage such projects ultimately rests with the Ministry of Housing and Bank Maskan. ...

There is an allegation that Starrett abandoned the Project for economic reasons. The Tribunal does not go into this issue because it is notorious that at least after November 4, 1979, the date when the hostage crisis began, all American companies with projects in Iran were forced to leave their projects and had to evacuate their personnel. Therefore, at least as regards the situation subsequent to that date the Government of Iran cannot possibly rely on any withdrawal of personnel as a justification for the appointment of a new manager. In fact, the evidence shows that Starrett maintained staff in Iran longer than most other American companies, obviously in an attempt to secure future possibilities to complete the Project.

However, in this case the Claimants assert that [before January 1980] the effects of what is referred to as "virulent anti-American and other policies and actions of the Revolutionary Group and the Islamic Republic"— both before and after the establishment of the new Government —rendered it impossible for Starrett to continue operations at the Project and that this amounted to an unlawful expropriation under general principles of international law ...

There is no reason to doubt that the events in Iran prior to January 1980 to which the Claimants refer, seriously hampered their possibilities to proceed with the construction work and eventually paralysed the Project. But investors in Iran, like investors in all other countries, have to assume a risk that the country might experience strikes, lock-outs, disturbances, changes of the economic and political system and even revolution. That any of these risks materialized does not necessarily mean that property rights affected by such events can be deemed to have been taken. A revolution as such does not entitle investors to compensation under international law ... the Tribunal does not find that any of these events individually or taken together can be said to amount to a taking of the Claimants' contractual rights and shares. ...

The next question for the Tribunal is to determine the exact nature of the property rights that were taken. The Claimants contend that it was neither the land and the buildings only nor their shares in Shah Goli that were taken. The Claimants assert that the expropriated rights comprised the assets and contractual rights and the other property of, in the first instance, Shah Goli as a controlled subsidiary of Starrett Housing. The Claimants define the principal assets of Shah Goli as the buildings and the principal contractual rights as including the rights to complete the Project and to earn reasonable profits which Starrett anticipated, and to recover the funds which it loaned and which were used to build the Project.

There is nothing unique in the Claimants' position in this regard. They rely on precedents in international law in which cases measures of expropriation or taking, primarily aimed at physical property, have been deemed to comprise also rights of a contractual nature closely related to the physical property. In this case it appears from the very nature of the measures taken by the Government of Iran in January 1980 that these measures were aimed at the taking of Shah Goli. The Tribunal holds that the property interest taken by the Government of Iran must be deemed to comprise the physical property as well as the right to manage the Project and to complete the construction in accordance with the Basic Project Agreement and related agreements, and to deliver the apartments and collect the proceeds of the sale as provided in the Apartment Purchase Agreements.

Mr Holtzmann, US arbitrator, filed a concurring opinion. Mr Kashani, Iranian arbitrator, dissented but would not appear to have filed an opinion.

Notes

1.   The *Starrett* case considers the meaning of a *taking* of property,[279] a question not addressed in General Assembly Resolution 1803 or the 1974 Charter. A taking may be effected by the transfer of title by law, as in the typical case of nationalisation or of the expropriation for example, of land, to build a road. The physical seizure of property may suffice,[280] as may its transfer under duress[281] or by confiscatory taxation.[282] However, "[i]t is an accepted principle of international law that a state is not liable for economic injury which is a consequence of bona fide 'regulation' within the accepted police power of states."[283] Accordingly, economic measures such as non-confiscatory taxation, exchange control regulation and currency revaluation do not normally result in expropriation. In addition, the forfeiture of property as a criminal sanction is in principle lawful.

The kind of taking illustrated by the *Starrett* case is the taking of the "effective use" of property, variously also known as indirect, "creeping" or "constructive" expropriation.[284] In *Tippetts v TAMS–ATTA*,[285] the Iran-US Claims Tribunal suggested that "constructive expropriation" occurs when "events demonstrate that the owner was deprived of fundamental rights of ownership and it appears that this deprivation is not merely ephemeral." In the same case, the Tribunal took the view that an objective theory of state responsibility applies[286]:

"The intent of the government is less important than the effects of the measures on the owner, and the form of the measures of control or interference is less important than the reality of their impact."

[279] See Christie (1962) 38 B.Y.I.L. 307; and, on the US-Iran Claims Tribunal case law, Aldrich (1994) 88 A.J.I.L. 585.

[280] See *Daley v Iran* (1988) 18 Iran-U.S.C.T.R. 232 (car seized by Revolutionary Guards); and *Dames and Moore v Iran* (1983) 4 *id.* 212 at 223 ("The unilateral taking of possession of property [in that case field laboratory equipment] and the denial of its use to the rightful owners may amount to an expropriation even without a formal decree regarding title to the property").

[281] *American Bell International Inc. v Iran* (1984) 6 Iran-U.S.C.T.R. 74 (threats of "serious personal consequences" for company representative).

[282] e.g. in 1964, the UK Government characterised a Burmese profits tax of 99 per cent as "de facto expropriation without compensation": 1964 B.P.I.L. 202.

[283] *Sedco Inc. v N.I.O.C.* (*First Interlocutory Award*) (1985) 9 Iran-U.S.C.T.R. 248 at 275.

[284] cf. *United Painting Co. Inc. v Iran* (1989) 23 Iran-U.S.C.T.R. 351; and *Biloune and Marine Drive Complex Ltd v Ghana Investments Centre* (1989) 95 I.L.R. 183. See Dolzer (1986) 1 I.C.S.I.D. Rev.-F.I.L.J. 4; Reisman and Sloane (2003) 74 B.Y.I.L. 115; Vagts (1978) 72 A.J.I.L. 17; Weston (1975–6) 16 Virg. J.I.L. 103.

[285] (1985) 6 Iran-U.S.C.T.R. 219 at 225.

[286] ibid., p.226. cf. the *Starrett* case, above.

"Constructive expropriation" is also considered in the Explanatory Note to the 1961 Harvard Draft Convention, art.10[287]:

"There are a variety of methods by which an alien natural or juridical person may have the use or enjoyment of his property limited by State action, even to the extent of the State's forcing the alien to dispose of his property at a price representing only a fraction of what its value would be had not the alien's use of it been subjected to interference by the State.[288]

... A State may make it impossible for an alien to operate a factory which he owns by blocking the entrances on the professed ground of maintaining order. It may, through its labor legislation and labor courts, designedly set the wages of local employees of the enterprise at a prohibitively high level. If technical personnel are needed from outside the country, entry visas may be denied them. Essential replacement parts or machinery may be refused entrance, or allocations of foreign exchange may deliberately be denied with the purpose of making it impossible to import the requisite machinery. Any one of these measures ... could make it impossible for the alien owner to use or enjoy his property. More direct interferences may also be imagined. The alien may simply be forbidden to employ a certain portion of a building which he occupies, either on a wholly arbitrary basis or on the authority of some asserted requirement of the local law. A government, while leaving ownership of an enterprise in the alien owner, might appoint conservators, managers, or inspectors who might interfere with the free use by the alien of its premises and its facilities. Or, simply by forbidding an alien to sell his property, a government could effectively deprive that property of its value.

Whether an interference with the use, enjoyment, or disposal of property constitutes a 'taking' or a 'taking of use' will be dependent upon the duration of the interference.[289] Although a restriction on the use of property may purport to be temporary, there obviously comes a stage at which an objective observer would conclude that there is no immediate prospect that the owner will be able to resume the enjoyment of his property. Considerable latitude has been left to the adjudicator of the claim to determine what period of interference is unreasonable and when the taking therefore ceases to be temporary.

The unreasonableness of an interference with the use, enjoyment, or disposal of property must be determined in conformity with the general principles of law recognized by the principal legal systems of the world."

2.   Expropriation was distinguished from *regulation* in *Myers Inc v Canada*[290]:

"In general, the term 'expropriation' carries with it the connotation of 'taking' by a govern-mental-type authority of a person's 'property' with a view to transferring ownership of that property to another person, usually the authority that exercised its *de jure* or *de facto* power to

---

[287] (1961) 55 A.J.I.L. 558–59.

[288] Ed. On the forced sale of foreign owned commercial enterprises to nationals under West African indigenisation pro-grammes, see Akinsanya, *Economic Independence and Indigenisation of Private Foreign Investments: the Experience of Nigeria and Ghana* (1982); and Beveridge (1991) 40 I.C.L.Q. 302.

[289] In the *ELSI Case*, I.C.J. Rep. 1989, p.14 at 71, a court chamber held that the requisition of a firm's plant and machinery that was for a limited period of six months and was subject to administrative appeal was not by itself a "significant deprivation" of the firm's property so as to amount to a "taking". On the case, see Hamrock (1992) 27 Tex.I.L.J. 837; and Murphy (1991) 18 Yale J.I.L. 291.

[290] (2000) 121 I.L.R. 73. NAFTA Tribunal (ban on cross border traffic in PCB waste affecting claimant's business not expro-priation).

do the 'taking'. ... The general body of precedent usually does not treat regulatory action as amounting to expropriation. ...

Expropriations tend to involve the deprivation of ownership rights; regulations a lesser interference. The distinction between expropriation and regulation screens out most potential cases of complaints concerning economic intervention by a State and reduces the risk that governments will be subject to claims as they go about their business of managing public affairs."

3.   The *Starrett* case also examines what is property for the purpose of expropriation. The 1961 Harvard Draft Convention defines it as comprising "all movable and immovable property, whether tangible or intangible, including industrial, literary, and artistic property, as well as rights and interests in any property" (art.10(7)). The definition excludes contractual rights; these are regarded as being subject to a different rule. But in the *Anglo-Iranian Oil Co.* case, the claimant United Kingdom Government argued[291]:

"The Government of the United Kingdom does not consider it necessary to elaborate the proposition that rights acquired by foreign nationals by virtue of concessionary contracts are property rights and that as such they are entitled to the same protection as international law grants to the property rights of foreigners."

Note also that in the *Shufeldt* claim, the arbitrator, in awarding compensation for the premature termination by Guatemala by legislative decree of a concession contract for the exploitation of chicle, stated:

"There cannot be any doubt that property rights are created under and by virtue of a contract."[292]

This view is confirmed by the jurisprudence of the Iran-US Claims Tribunal. Although the *Starrett* case extends only to contract rights which are "closely related" to physical property which has also been expropriated, the *Amoco International Finance Corp.* case[293] is not so limited.

AMOCO INTERNATIONAL FINANCE CORP. v IRAN

U.S. v Iran (1987)

Iran–US Claims Tribunal. Chamber Three: Virally, Chairman; Brower, Ansari, members. 15 Iran–U.S.C.T.R. 189. Footnote omitted.

The claimant Swiss company, a wholly-owned subsidiary of Standard Oil, a US company, entered into a 1966 joint venture agreement (the Khemco Agreement) with NPC, an Iranian company controlled by the Iranian Government, to form Khemco, an Iranian company jointly owned and managed by the

---

[291] *Anglo-Iranian Oil Co.* case (1951) ICJ Pleadings, p.83. The UK took the generally accepted view that a state can only expropriate an alien's property that is within its territory: p.81.

[292] *U.S. v Guatemala* (1930) 2 R.I.A.A. 1083 at 1097.

[293] Award, para.108, below. cf. *Mobil Oil Iran Inc. v Iran* (1987) 16 Iran-U.S.C.T.R. 3 at 25 ("the expropriation ... of contractual rights").

contracting companies, to process and sell Iranian natural gas, each contracting company having a 50 per cent stake in Khemco's profits. In 1980, the Khemco Agreement, which by its terms was valid for 35 years, was declared null and void by the Iranian Government following the 1979 Iranian revolution and in implementation of Iranian legislation (the 1980 Single Article Act) that was intended to complete the nationalisation of the Iranian Oil Industry. The claimant sought compensation for the loss of its interests in Khemco arising under the Khemco Agreement as a result of the 1980 nationalisation.

Award of the Tribunal

108 ... Expropriation, which can be defined as a compulsory transfer of property rights, may extend to any right which can be the object of a commercial transaction, i.e. freely sold and bought, and thus has a monetary value. It is because Amoco's interests under the Khemco Agreement have such an economic value that the nullification of those interests by the Single Article Act can be considered as a nationalisation ...

113 ... A leading expression of these rules [of customary international law on expropriation] is the judgment ... in the *Case Concerning Certain German Interests in Polish Upper Silesia* ..., 1926 P.C.I.J., Ser. A, No. 7 ... As reflected in this case, the principles of international law generally accepted some sixty years ago in regard to the treatment of foreigners recognized very few exceptions to the principle of respect for vested rights. The Court listed among such exceptions only "expropriation for reasons of public utility, judicial liquidation and similar measures." *Id*: at 22. A very important evolution in the law has taken place since then, with the progressive recognition of the right of States to nationalize foreign property for a public purpose. This right is today unanimously accepted, even by States which reject the principle of permanent sovereignty over natural resources, considered by a majority of States as the legal foundation of such a right.

114. The importance of this evolution derives from the fact that nationalization is generally defined as the transfer of an economic activity from private ownership to the public sector. It is realized through expropriation of the assets of an enterprise or of its capital stock, with a view to maintaining such enterprise as a going concern under State control. Modern nationalization often brings into State ownership a number of enterprises of the same kind and may even be applied to all enterprises in a particular industry. It may result, therefore, in a taking of private property of much greater magnitude than the traditional expropriation for reasons of public utility, and is also of a very different nature, since it is always linked to determined political choices. For these reasons, and because it applies to going concerns, taken as such, modern nationalization raises specific legal problems, notably in relation to the issue of compensation.

The Tribunal then considered the particular grounds upon which the claimant argued that the nationalisation was unlawful in international law, including grounds of discrimination and absence of a public purpose considered below. A claim that the expropriation was in breach of "stabilisation clauses" in the contract was rejected, inter alia, because these did not bind Iran because it was not a party to the contract.

139. In support of its contention that the expropriation was discriminatory, the Claimant relies on the fact that, in another of NPC's joint ventures, the Japanese share of a consortium [IJPC] ... was not expropriated. In contrast, all American interests in petrochemical joint ventures with NPC were expropriated. ...

140. Discrimination is widely held as prohibited by customary international law in the field of expropriation. ... the Respondents recognize that a discriminatory expropriation is wrongful, but deny that the expropriation was discriminatory in the instant case.

141. The Respondents assert that the Single Article Act applied to the entire oil industry, irrespective of the nationality of the foreign companies involved in this industry. In the event, it was applied to non-United States corporations as well as United States corporations. Therefore, it can not be held to be discriminatory. That the Special Commission did not include the contract with IJPC among those which were nullified, the Respondents submit, was an exception due to specific circumstances. They mention specifically the fact that the operation of the IJPC joint venture was not closely linked with other contracts relating to the exploitation of oil fields, whereas the operation of the Khemco plant was linked to the supply of gas from the oil fields operated jointly by Amoco

and NIOC pursuant to the JSA [joint structure agreement]. Furthermore, the Respondents emphasize that IJPC was not yet an operational concern at the relevant time, a point that was confirmed by the Claimant.

142. The Tribunal finds it difficult, in the absence of any other evidence, to draw the conclusion that the expropriation of a concern was discriminatory only from the fact that another concern in the same economic branch was not expropriated. Reasons specific to the non- expropriated enterprise, or to the expropriated one, or to both, may justify such a difference of treatment. Furthermore, as observed by the arbitral tribunal in *Kuwait v. American Independent Oil Company (AMINOIL)*[294] ... a coherent policy of nationalization can reasonably be operated gradually in successive stages. In the present Case, the peculiarities discussed by the Parties can explain why IJPC was not treated in the same manner as Khemco. The Tribunal declines to find that Khemco's expropriation was discriminatory. ...

145. A precise definition of the "public purpose" for which an expropriation may be lawfully decided has neither been agreed upon in international law nor even suggested. It is clear that, as a result of the modern acceptance of the right to nationalize, this term is broadly interpreted, and that States, in practice, are granted extensive discretion. An expropriation, the only purpose of which would have been to avoid contractual obligations of the State or of an entity controlled by it, could not, nevertheless be considered as lawful under international law. See *Aminoil*, para.109.[295] ... Such an expropriation, indeed, would be contrary to the principle of good faith and to accept it as lawful would run counter to the well-settled rule that a State has the right to commit itself by contract to foreign corporations. *Id.* para. 90. ... It is also generally accepted that a State has no right to expropriate a foreign concern only for financial purposes. It must, however, be observed that, in recent practice and mostly in the oil industry, States have admitted expressly ... that they were nationalizing foreign properties primarily in order to obtain a greater share, or even the totality, of the revenues drawn from the exploitation of a national natural resource, which, according to them, should accrue to the development of the country. Such a purpose has not generally been denounced as unlawful and illegitimate.

146. ... It cannot be doubted that the Single Article Act was adopted for a clear public purpose, namely to complete the nationalization of the oil industry in Iran initiated by the 1951 Nationalization of the Iranian Oil Industry Act, with a view to implementing one of the main economic and political objectives of the new Islamic Government. The decision of the Special Commission relative to Khemco was taken in apparent conformity with the Single Article Act. Even if financial considerations were considered in the adoption of such a decision—which would have been only natural, but which has not been evidenced—this fact would not be sufficient, in the opinion of the Tribunal, to prove that this decision was not taken for a public purpose. ...

192. For the reasons set forth above, the Tribunal finds that Amoco's rights and interests under the Khemco Agreement, including its shares in Khemco, were lawfully expropriated by Iran. ... The next issue, therefore, relates to the rules to be applied in determining the compensation to be paid in such a circumstance.

191. ... [T]he leading case in this context is [the *Chorzów Factory Case*, above, p.446]. In spite of the fact that it is nearly sixty years old, this judgment is widely regarded as the most authoritative exposition of the principles applicable in this field, and is still valid today. ...

192. ... [T]he first principle established by the Court is that a clear distinction must be made between lawful and unlawful expropriations, since the rules applicable to the compensation to be paid by the expropriating State differ according to the legal characterization of the taking. *Id.* at 46–47. Such a principle has been recently and expressly confirmed by the celebrated *Aminoil* case. ...

193. According to the Court in the *Chorzów Factory Case* an obligation of reparation of all the damages sustained by the owner of expropriated property arises from an unlawful expropriation [as on the facts in the *Chorzów Factory Case*]. The rules of international law relating to international responsibility of States apply in such a case. They provide for *restitutio in integrum*: restitution in kind or, if impossible, its monetary equivalent. If need be, "damages for loss sustained which would not be covered by restitution" should also be awarded. See *Chorzów Factory*, [see above, p.446]. ... On the other hand, a lawful expropriation must give rise to "the payment of fair compensation," *id.* at 46, or of "the just price of what was expropriated." *Id.* at 47. ...

---

[294] Ed. Below, p.498. Rejecting the claimant's argument that the nationalisation measure in issue was invalid because it related only to the claimant's concession, the *Aminoil* Tribunal did "not see why a Government that is pursuing a coherent policy of nationalisation should not have been entitled to do so progressively, ... in step with the development of the necessary administrative and technical availabilities": below, para.86. In the *Aminoil* case, the Tribunal found good reasons why, 90 per cent of the oil industry having already been nationalised, only the claimant, of the two remaining concessionaires, was nationalised in 1977. These were that the other concession was for offshore operations, requiring special expertise that Kuwait lacked, and was a concession granted jointly with Saudi Arabia: para.87.

[295] Ed. para.109 reads: "... it can be conceded in its [Aminoil's] favour that a nationalisation whose alleged justification lies *solely* in the advantages to be derived from putting a term to a contractual dispute would not be regular."

197. Obviously the value of an expropriated enterprise does not vary according to the lawfulness or the unlawfulness of the taking. ... In the traditional language of international law it equates the *damnum emergens*, which must be compensated in any case. ... The difference is that if the taking is lawful the value of the undertaking at the time of the dispossession is the measure and the limit of the compensation, while if it is unlawful, this value is, or may be, only a part of the reparation to be paid. In any event, even in case of unlawful expropriation the damage actually sustained is the measure of the reparation, and there is no indication that "punitive damages" could be considered.

198. What can be added to the value of the enterprise in order to meet the requirements of *restitutio?* An answer to this question can be found in the formulation of the questions on which an expert inquiry was arranged by the Court. *See Chorzów Factory, supra*, at 51. ...

200. ... The clear implication is that ... the compensation would include the two elements: the value of the undertaking at the date of the expropriation, plus the profits which would have been earned after this date, had the taking not occurred, until the date of the judgment. Equally clear is the consequence to be drawn from this finding: that this lost profit was not included in the valuation of the enterprise as of the date of the taking. Otherwise, there would be double recovery.

201. Of paramount interest is the list of the components enumerated by the Court as included in the value of the undertaking. They appertain to three categories: corporeal properties (lands, buildings, equipment, stocks), contractual rights (supply and delivery contracts) and other intangible valuables (processes, goodwill and "future prospects"). Using today's vocabulary, this would mean "going concern value," which is not a new concept after all. Only one component relates to the future: "future prospects" ...

203. ... "future prospects" does not equal lost profit (*lucrum cessans*). Those are two different concepts. The first one clearly refers to the fact that the undertaking was a "going concern" which had demonstrated a certain ability to earn revenues and was, therefore, to be considered as keeping such ability for the future: this is an element of its value at the time of the taking. The second relates to the amount of the earnings hypothetically accrued from the date of the taking to the date of the expert opinion, had the enterprise remained in the hands of its former owner. ...

205. It is relevant to note that, even for the purpose of *restitutio*, the Court takes into consideration *lucrum cessans* (in the meaning previously defined) only for a limited and rather short period of time. Furthermore, the quantification of *lucrum cessans* implies no projection into the future, since it finds its *dies ad quem* at the date of the judgment.

206. The case law developed since the judgment of the Court has generally followed the principles set forth in this judgment, at least on the distinction between lawful and unlawful expropriation. It is particularly remarkable that all the awards which adopted the standard of *restitutio* relate to expropriation found unlawful. ...[296]

217. For the purpose of valuing the compensation due in case of the lawful expropriation of an asset, market value, apparently, is the most commendable standard, since it is also the most objective and the most easily ascertained when a market exists for identical or similar assets. ...

219. Market value, on the other hand, is an ambiguous concept, to say the least ..., when an open market does not exist for the expropriated asset or for goods identical or comparable to it. ...

220. ... The Tribunal is therefore of the view that the ... choice between all the available methods must rather be made in view of the purpose to be attained, in order to avoid arbitrary results and to arrive at an equitable compensation in conformity with the applicable legal standards. ...

226. This conclusion is fully in conformity with the practice of international arbitral tribunals, which, in considering lawful expropriation, have consistently tried to determine according to the law, by all the available means, often using several methods, the appropriate compensation to be paid in the circumstances of each case. ... *See, e.g.* liamco, *supra*, at 146–51, 62 I.L.R. at 208–10; aminoil, *supra*, paras. 146–49, 153, 21 *Int'l Legal Mat'ls* at 1033–35.

The tribunal then considered and rejected the discounted cash flow (DCF) and net book value methods of valuation proposed by the US and Iran respectively and continued:

262. In the instant Case ... the Claimant was deprived of its contractual rights under the Khemco Agreement, and the compensation due relates to these rights. It is not disputed, however, that the value of such rights equals

---

[296] Ed. The tribunal refers, inter alia, to the *Lighthouses Arbitration* (1956) 23 I.L.R. 299; *Sapphire Int. Petroleums v NIOC* (1967) 35 I.L.R. 136; the *BP* case, below, p.486; the *Texaco* case, below, p.494; and the *AGIP* case (1982) 21 I.L.M. 726.

the value of the shares owned by Amoco in the joint stock company incorporated pursuant to the Khemco Agreement. ...

263. Khemco was a going concern at the time of the expropriation. ... Going concern value, accordingly, is the measure of compensation in this case.

264. Going concern value encompasses not only the physical and financial assets of the undertaking, but also the intangible valuables which contribute to its earning power, such as contractual rights (supply and delivery contracts, patent licences and so on), as well as goodwill and commercial prospects. Although those assets are closely linked to the profitability of the concern, they cannot and must not be confused with the financial capitalization of the revenues which might be generated by such a concern after the transfer of property resulting from the expropriation (*lucrum cessans*). ...

341. For the foregoing reasons, the Tribunal awards as follows:

(a) The shareholding interest of Amoco International S.A. in Kharg Chemical Company Limited was lawfully expropriated by the Government of the Islamic Republic of Iran as of 24 December 1980,

(b) The Government of the Islamic Republic of Iran shall pay to the Claimant ... a compensation measured at fifty per cent ... of the going concern value of Khemco ... as of 31 July 1979,[297] without the addition of future lost profits beyond such value. ...

Judge Brower, the US arbitrator, filed a concurring opinion.[298] The signature of Mr Ansari, the Iranian Arbitrator, was accompanied by the words: "Concurring opinion in part, Dissenting opinion in part."

Notes

1. *Public purpose*. The *Amoco* case supports the view adopted in most international judicial and arbitral decisions[299] that, to be lawful, an expropriation must have a public purpose. Exceptionally, in the *Liamco* case,[300] the arbitrator held that, although there was a requirement of non-discrimination, as to which, see below, p.487, there was no separate public purpose requirement in international law, at least in the case of *nationalisation*:

    "As to the contention that the said measures were politically motivated and not in pursuance of a legitimate public purpose, it is the general opinion in international theory that the public utility principle is not a necessary requisite for the legality of a nationalisation. This principle was mentioned by Grotius and other later publicists, but now there is no international authority, from a judicial or any other source, to support its application to nationalisation. ...

    However, political motivation may take the shape of discrimination as a result of political retaliation. ...

    It is clear and undisputed that non-discrimination is a requisite for the validity of a lawful nationalisation. This is a rule well established in international legal theory and practice (V.

---

[297] Ed. The date chosen for the valuation of the expropriated property was that on which measures depriving the claimant of its rights in the management of Khemco were effective, not the later date when the process of expropriation was completed [December 24, 1980].

[298] Although concurring, Judge Brower disagreed with the Tribunal's reasoning in several respects. He considered, inter alia, that the expropriation was unlawful under customary international law because insufficient guarantees of compensation had been given at the time of the taking and that the Tribunal had misinterpreted the *Chorzów Factory* case when concluding that it excluded lost profits from the compensation due for a lawful expropriation.

[299] Other Iran–US Claims Tribunal cases are to the same effect. See, e.g. the *INA* case (1985) 8 Iran–U.S.C.T.R. 373 at 378. cf. the *Certain German Interests* case, extract in the *Amoco* case, above, p.481; the *Aminoil* case, below, p.498; and the *BP* case, below, p.486.

[300] (1981) 20 I.L.M. 1 at 58–59. The sole arbitrator was Dr Mahamssani, a Lebanese lawyer.

White . . . [above, at n.266] pp. 119 *et. seq.*). Therefore, a purely discriminatory nationalisation is illegal and wrongful."

The *Liamco* case was very similar on its facts to the *Texaco* case, below, p.494, with a United States oil company complaining of Libya's nationalisation of property contrary to the terms of an oil concession contract. The company claimed in part that the nationalisation: (i) had been effected as "part of an overall program of political retaliation against those nations including the United States whose politics were contrary to those of the new Libyan regime"; and (ii) was discriminatory against "selected foreign companies." After examining evidence of Libyan policy and practice, the arbitrator concluded that the nationalisation was not discriminatory because "Libya's motive for nationalisation was its desire to preserve the ownership of its oil. . . . The political motive [complained of] was not the predominant motive for nationalisation, and . . . such motive per se does not constitute a sufficient proof of a purely discriminatory measure."[301]

The *Liamco* case is not in accord with General Assembly Resolution 1803, which affirms the need for a public purpose. Although the 1974 Declaration on Economic Rights and Duties of States, adopting the view of developing states, makes no mention of such a requirement, it probably does not reflect present customary law in this respect.[302] However, although a public purpose may be necessary, the *Amoco* case suggests that this is a requirement that is easily satisfied, by virtue, in effect, of a wide "margin of appreciation" doctrine.[303] The *Amoco* case does, none-theless, give examples (Award, para.145) of situations in which the requirement might not be complied with, and the *BP* case[304] may indicate another. In that case, in 1971, Libya had nationalised the property, rights and assets under an oil concession contract of British Petro-leum, a British company in which the British Government then held 49 per cent of the shares. The British Government protested to Libya that its action infringed international law for the following reasons[305]:

"An act of nationalisation is not legitimate in international law unless it satisfies the following requirements:

(i) it must be for a public purpose related to the internal needs of the taking State[306]; and

(ii) it must be followed by the payment of prompt, adequate and effective compensation.

Nationalisation measures which are arbitrary or discriminatory or which are motivated by considerations of a political nature unrelated to the internal well being of the taking state are, by a reference to those principles, illegal and invalid."

In the *BP* case, the nationalisation was not accompanied by that of property held by other foreign

---

[301] (1981) 20 I.L.M. 1 at p.60. Note that in the *Texaco* case, allegations of political motivation for the nationalisations were not examined; it was neither thought necessary nor, in Libya's absence, appropriate to do so.

[302] On the *de lege ferenda* character of the 1974 Declaration, see above, p.476.

[303] See also the *American International Group* case, (1983) 4 Iran–U.S.C.T.R. 96 at 105, which supposes that the burden of proof is upon the owner to show that there is no valid public purpose.

[304] (1974) 53 I.L.R. 297.

[305] (1974) 53 I.L.R. 297 at p. 317. cf. the terms of the official US protest at one of several 1973 Libyan nationalisations, which it thought to be motivated by political opposition to US policies in the Middle East and US protest at the Arab oil boycott: "Under established principles of international law, measures taken against the rights and property of foreign nationals which are arbitrary, discriminatory, or based on considerations of political reprisal and economic coercion are invalid and not entitled to recognition by other states": quoted in Von Mehren and Kourides (1981) 75 A.J.I.L. 476 at 486.

[306] Ed. The limitation "related to the internal needs" of the taking state is used in UK bilateral investment protection treaties: see, e.g. art.5(1), 1989 U.K.–Guyana, below, n.341.

oil companies under concession contracts (or even property held by British Petroleum itself under other concessions). The reason for the nationalisation was the refusal of the United Kingdom shortly before the nationalisation to intervene to prevent Iran from forcibly occupying the Tunb Islands in the Persian Gulf.[307] The islands were the territory of the trucial state of Ras Al-Khaymah (now within the United Arab Emirates) which at the time of the occupation was still a state entitled by treaty to protection from the United Kingdom. The treaty of protection expired the day following the occupation. The dispute was referred to arbitration by British Petroleum under the contract.[308] The sole arbitrator held[309]:

> "The BP Nationalisation Law, and the actions taken thereunder by the Respondent, do con-
> stitute a fundamental breach of the BP Concession as they amount to a total repudiation of
> the agreement and the obligations of the Respondent thereunder, and, on the basis of rules of
> applicable systems of law too elementary and voluminous to require or permit citation, the
> Tribunal so holds. Further, the taking by the Respondent of the property, rights and interests
> of the Claimant clearly violates public international law as it was made for purely extraneous
> political reasons and was arbitrary and discriminatory in character. Nearly two years have now
> passed since the nationalisation, and the fact that no offer of compensation has been made
> indicates that the taking was also confiscatory."

In 1979, Nigeria expropriated BP assets because it was continuing to supply oil to South Africa contrary to Nigerian policy on trade with South Africa.[310] Would this motive render the expropriation illegal according to the *BP* case?

2. *Non-discrimination.* The *Aramco* case also suggests that non-discrimination is a condition of a lawful expropriation.[311] However, the tribunal recognises (para.142) that it is not an absolute requirement; discrimination that is reasonably related to the public purpose that underlies the expropriation is not illegal.

Neither General Assembly Resolution 1803 nor the 1974 Declaration on Economic Rights and Duties of States mention non-discrimination. Developed states continue to insist that discrimination against or between foreigners vitiates an expropriation. See, e.g. the United Kingdom and United States protests against the Libyan nationalisations, above, p.486. Earlier, in the *Anglo-Iranian Oil Co.* case,[312] the United Kingdom submitted that a "measure of expropriation or nationalisation ... becomes unlawful in international law, if in effect it is exclusively or primarily directed against foreigners as such, and it cannot be shown that, but for the measure of expropriation or nationalisation, public interests of vital importance would suffer." On the basis of the above submission, the United Kingdom challenged the legality of the Iranian Oil Nationalisation Act 1951. That Act "resolved that the oil industry throughout all parts of the country, without exception, be nationalised. ..." In fact, the "oil industry" consisted only of the Anglo-Iranian Oil Co.[313] When can a state nationalise an industry that is wholly owned by foreign

---

[307] Libya justified the nationalisation thus in the Security Council: S.C.O.R. 1610th Meeting, p.20, December 9, 1971.
[308] Libya declined to appoint an arbitrator or otherwise participate in the proceedings so that a sole arbitrator (Largergren, a Swedish national) was appointed. Although the *BP* case does not refer expressly to a "public purpose" requirement, the references to expropriations that are "arbitrary" and "for purely extraneous political reasons" imply one.
[309] 53 I.L.R. 329.
[310] *Keesings Archives*, p.29902.
[311] Other Iran–US Claims Tribunal cases are to the same effect: see, e.g. the *American International Group Case*, above, n.303, n.26, cf. the *BP* case, above, p.486; the *Liamco* case, above, p.486; and the *Aminoil* case, below, p.498.
[312] *Anglo-Iranian Oil Co.* case, ICJ Pleadings, p.81.
[313] A small concession owned partly by a Russian company was understood to have stopped working.

interests consistently with the British submission in the *Anglo-Iranian Oil Co.* case? Baade[314] argues against a non-discrimination requirement:

"Since states are free to decide with whom to trade, they must also be free to decide with whom to stop dealing—subject, of course, to as yet unexpired treaty obligations. ... Discrimination can be dictated by a number of reasons: preferences based on consideration of foreign policy, military alliances, and the like; ethnic or cultural preferences or aversions; retaliation; or, more importantly for present purposes, decolonization in fact as well as in law. Independence would seem an empty gesture or even a cruel hoax to many a new country if it were prevented from singling out the key investments of the former colonial power for nationalization. There is no support in law or reason for the proposition that a taking that meets other relevant tests of legality is illegal under international law merely because it is discriminatory."

Does the non-discrimination requirement spelt out in the *Amoco* case meet Baade's objections? Pellonpää and Fitzmaurice[315] suggest that, as formulated in that case, the requirement is not a difficult one to meet:

"Justification is probably quite easily available in so far as distinctions, made between foreigners as a class on the one hand, and the State and its nationals on the other, are concerned, and specific reasons may also justify differential treatment of various classes of foreigners. In similarity to the condition of public purpose, the State's assertion that such reasons exist creates a strong presumption of the correctness of such an assertion. Thus, while both the public purpose and non-discrimination requirements are well established, a certain shift in favour of the State's economic sovereignty appears to be discernible in the way they are interpreted today."

3. *Expropriation contrary to a treaty obligation.* This clearly engages responsibility, as illustrated in the *Chorzów Factory* case (*Indemnity*) (*Merits*).[316]

4. *Compensation for a lawful expropriation.*[317] As stated in the *Amoco* case, the rules on the compensation to be paid for a lawful expropriation are "the object of heated controversies" (Award para.117), with fundamental disagreement between developed and developing states. The long-standing view of developed states was expressed in a note from the United States Secretary of State Hull to the Mexican Government in 1940 on the expropriation by Mexico of foreign oil interests:

---

[314] In Miller & Stanger, eds. *Essays on Expropriations* (1967), p.24. Footnotes omitted.
[315] See above, n.266, p.67.
[316] P.C.I.J. Reports, Series A, No. 17, pp.46–8. On expropriation in breach of an "internationalised contract", see below, p.606.
[317] See Claggett, in Lillich, above, n.266, Vol.4, p. 31; Francioni (1975) 24 I.C.L.Q. 255; Gann (1985) 23 C.J.T.L. 615; Mavroidis (1992) 45 R.H.D.I. 69; Mendelson (1985) 79 A.J.I.L. 414; Muller (1981) 19 C.J.T.L. 35; Murphy (1993) 110 S.A.L.J. 79; Schachter (1984) 78 A.J.I.L. 121 and (1985) 79 A.J.I.L. 420; Westberg (1993) 8 For.Invest.L.J. 1 and (1990) 5 I.C.S.I.D. Rev-F.I.L.J. 256.

"... the right to expropriate property is coupled with and conditioned on the obligation to make adequate, effective and prompt compensation. The legality of an expropriation is in fact dependent upon the observance of this requirement."[318]

Developed states still keep to the Hull compensation formula (which appears in various permutations) and condition the legality of an expropriation upon the payment of compensation complying with it.[319] See, e.g. the United Kingdom protest in the *BP* case, above, p.486. When Resolution 1803 was being debated, the United States repeatedly said that it understood "appropriate compensation" (para.4) as incorporating the "international minimum standard" of the Hull formula.[320] In truth, the use of such a general and undefined phrase probably was an exercise in evasion. It is significant that the following amendment[321] to para.4 proposed by the USSR, although defeated, received 28 votes.[322]

"The question of compensation to the owners shall in such cases be decided in accordance with the national law of the country taking these measures in the exercise of its sovereignty."

If the 1974 Charter, which is generally taken to present the views of developing states, takes a very different stance on compensation from that in the Hull formula, it does not, in the opinion of Jimenez de Aréchaga,[323] a former ICJ President and Argentinian international lawyer, assert that the question of compensation ceases to be regulated by international law at all:

"The *travaux préparatoires* of the Charter ... show that ... paragraph 2(c) is not based on a position which denies the existence of any obligation to pay compensation. This position, originally adopted by the working group which drafted the Charter, was abandoned during discussion. ... The text as finally adopted not only imposes the duty to pay 'appropriate compensation' ... it also provides that such compensation shall be determined by 'taking into account ... all circumstances that the State considers pertinent.' ...

Thus, it is clear that the basic features of Article 2, paragraph 2(c)—the recognition of an international duty to pay compensation and the determination of the amount due in light of the particular circumstances of each case—are rooted in equitable considerations. ...

However, this interpretation of the Charter provision has been widely criticized, especially by writers from industrialized countries. The main criticism ... is 'the absence of any references in Article 2 to the applicability of international law to the treatment of foreign investment.' ...[324] Other critics have concluded that the only obligation 'is to grant such compensation, if any, as it is subjectively thought to be "appropriate," considering only local law and "circumstances," to which international law is not necessarily "pertinent."'[325] ... It is true that Article 2,

---

[318] 3 Hackworth 662. More recently, the US Restatement stated that the "Executive Branch and the Congress of the United States have held resolutely to the view that international law requires compensation that is 'prompt, adequate and effective'": *Third Restatement of U.S. Foreign Relations Law*, Vol.2, (1987), para.712, reporters' notes, p.207. By "adequate," the US means "fair market value," which in the case of an enterprise is its "going concern" value: US Department of State Legal Adviser's Memorandum (1983) 22 I.L.M. 1406 at 1407, n.42. There is no express mention of "lost profits".

[319] This last point is important for the question whether restitution can be claimed.

[320] See, e.g. UN Doc. A/C.2/SR. 835, para.10.

[321] UN Doc. A/C.2/L670.

[322] The full vote was 28 to 39, with 21 abstentions: UN Doc. A/C.2/SR.858, para.41.

[323] (1978) 11 N.Y.U.J.I.L.P. 179 at 183–187. Some footnotes omitted. cf. Brownlie (1979–I) 162 Hague Recueil 255 at 268–269.

[324] Statement by the delegate of Canada, 29 U.N.G.A.O.R., C.2 (1649th Mtg.) 446, UN Doc.A/C.2/SR. 1649 (1974).

[325] Browner and Tepe (1975) 9 Int. Lawyer 295 at 305.

paragraph 2(c) does not include the provision of . . . Resolution 1803 requiring . . . the payment of appropriate compensation '. . . *in accordance with international law*.' . . .

Article 2 of the Charter also refers to the application by the expropriating State of its laws and regulations and to its appreciation of all pertinent circumstances. It is perfectly legitimate to accept this determination as the one to be made in the first instance since under the local remedies rule national law and local remedies must be applied and exhausted. But the requirement of Article 2, paragraph 2(c) for the payment of an 'appropriate compensation' remains.

Thus, if a nationalizing State, in application of its laws and in its appreciation of the circumstances, were to offer compensation which was not considered 'appropriate' by the other interested State (and not just by the individual party), the subjective determination by the host State would not be final. The State of nationality of the expropriated owner would become authorized under the existing rules of international law to take up the case of its national and to make a claim on its behalf, based on the host State's noncompliance with the international duty to pay 'appropriate' compensation."

Supposing that the Hull formula did at one time state a customary rule of compensation of general application, it no longer does so in the absence of support by states as a whole. The problem is that the view of developing states, as indicated in art.2(2)(c), 1974 Charter, above, p.476, has, by the same token, by no means replaced it. This creates difficulties for international arbitral tribunals, which have struggled to find a middle way.

The 1974 Charter has found little favour in international arbitral awards.[326] Nor has the Western "prompt, adequate and effective" compensation standard been adopted. Instead tribunals have recently been attracted by the "appropriate compensation" rule upon which states generally were able to agree in Resolution 1803. It was used, for example, in the *Aminoil* case,[327] and in the *Amoco* case and other Iran–United States Claims Tribunal cases. The problem is to know what "appropriate compensation" means. Adopted in Resolution 1803 to achieve the appearance of agreement, "appropriate compensation" was used in the *Aminoil* case as a standard that permitted by its generality a flexible and equitable response to the legitimate expectations of the parties, taking into account, on the facts of that case, such considerations as the presence of a stabilisation clause[328] and the history of the particular investment.[329] Its interpretation by the Iran–United States Claims Tribunal has varied according to the views of the particular chairman of the Chamber of the Tribunal concerned. For the most part, "appropriate compensation" has been understood by the Tribunal in a way that approximates more closely to the views of Western states than to those of developing states. In the *Sola Tiles* case,[330] Bocksteigel, Chairman of Chamber One, having settled on the "appropriate compensation" formula as having achieved "widespread use in recent years", interpreted it as the equivalent of "adequate" compensation and regarded Resolution 1803, which incorporated the "appropriate compensation" formula, as intending "no break with prevailing customary law". "Appropriate compensation"

---

[326] They have generally questioned its standing as evidence of custom: see above, p.476.
[327] Below, p.498.
[328] As to stabilisation clauses, see below, p.497.
[329] Note that most of the cases concern the expropriation of enterprises. Where what is taken is the private property of an individual, (e.g. his car), fewer complications arise.
[330] (1987) 14 Iran–U.S.C.T.R. 223. cf. the *American International Group* case, (1983) 4 ibid. 96 ("the former owner of the nationalised property is normally entitled to compensation for the value of the property taken", in that case regarded as the "going concern" value).

was, however, to be determined in the light of the particular circumstances of the case so that if, as on the facts of the *Sola Tiles* case, a company's prospects were poor, no compensation should be awarded for its going concern value. In the *Amoco* case, Virally, Chairman of Chamber Three, understood that the payment, in the normal case, of the market value of an enterprise in the application of the *damnum emergens* approach in the *Chorzow Factory* case to be in accord with the "appropriate compensation" standard.

However, in the *INA* case,[331] in a separate opinion, Lagergren, an earlier Chairman of Chamber One, adopted a more flexible approach, drawing a distinction between "large-scale nationalisations" and other lawful expropriations:

> "I conclude from the foregoing that an application of current principles of international law, as encapsulated in the 'appropriate compensation' formula, would in a case of lawful large-scale nationalisations in a state undergoing a process of radical economic restructuring normally require the 'fair market value' standard to be discounted in taking account of 'all circumstances.' However, such discounting may, of course, never be such as to bring the compensation below a point which would lead to 'unjust enrichment' of the expropriating state. It might also be added that the discounting often will be greater in a situation where the investor has enjoyed the profits of his capital outlay over a long period of time, but less, or none, in the case of a recent investor, such as INA."

But Lagergren also raised the question whether the standard of "appropriate compensation" with the above meaning may have replaced the Hull formula for other lawful expropriations too[332]:

> "Whether this standard is more correctly characterised as an exception to a still subsisting—though admittedly shrinking—Hull doctrine, or as evidence of a more general tendency towards the wholesale displacement of that doctrine as the repository of the *opinio juris*, is still the subject of debate. But the latter view appears by now to have achieved a rather solid basis in arbitral decisions and in writings."

The *World Bank 1992 Guidelines on the Treatment of Foreign Directive Investment*[333] take a Western position, regarding "appropriate" compensation as having the Hull formila meaning and "adequate" compensation as the "market value":

> "1. A State may not expropriate or otherwise take in whole or in part a foreign private investment in its territory, or take measures, which have similar effects, except where this is done in accordance with applicable legal procedures, in pursuance in good faith of a public purpose, without discrimination on the basis of nationality and against the payment of appropriate compensation.
>
> 2. Compensation for a specific investment taken by the State will, according to the details provided below, be deemed 'appropriate' if it is adequate, effective and prompt.

---

[331] (1985) 8 Iran–U.S.C.T.R. 373 at 390. cf. *Lithgow v U.K.*, Eur. Ct. H.R. Rep, Ser. A, No.102, para.121 (1986).

[332] (1985) 8 Ivan-U.S.C.T.R. 373 at p.387. But see the *Sedco* case (*Second Interlocutory Award*) (1986) 10 Iran–U.S.C.T.R. 180 at 187 in which it was noted that the view of writers, upon which no opinion was expressed, that custom no longer required full compensation was limited mostly to "large-scale nationalisation, e.g. of an entire industry or natural resource;" in the case of a "discrete expropriation of alien property," it was not disputed that full compensation was required.

[333] Section II (1992) 31 I.L.M. 1376. Cf. UNCTAD, *International Investment Agreements: Key Issues*, (2004), Vol.1, p.239. On "market value", see Marboet (2006) 7 J. World Investment and Trade 723.

3. Compensation will be deemed 'adequate' if it is based on the fair market value of the taken asset as such value is determined immediately before the time at which the taking occurred or the decision to take the asset became publicly known....

5. In the absence of a determination agreed on by, or based on the agreement of, the parties, the fair market value will be acceptable if determined by the State according to reasonable criteria related to the market value of the investment, i.e., in an amount that a willing buyer would normally pay to a willing seller after taking into account the nature of the investment, the circumstances in which it would operate in the future and its specific characteristics, including the period in which it has been in existence, the proportion of tangible assets in the total investment and other relevant factors pertinent to the specific circumstances of each case."

As important as the *standard* of compensation (full, partial) is the *method of valuation* of the expropriated property.[334] How does the "going concern" value applied in the *Amoco* case differ from the "net book" claimed by the respondent? Might recovery for "future prospects" as allowed in the *Amoco* case to some extent mitigate the lack of compensation for lost profits?

On the question whether, as claimed by developed states,[335] the payment of the required compensation is a condition of the legality of an expropriation, the jurisprudence of the Iran–US Claims Tribunal suggests that it is not. For example, in the *INA* case,[336] the Tribunal distinguished between the public purpose requirement, non-compliance with which renders an expropriation "*per se* unlawful," and the requirement to pay compensation in the case of a "lawful expropriation." The inference is that if compensation is not paid as required, the position is simply that the obligation to pay it continues, with interest to the time of payment; the rules as to reparation for an illegal act[337] do not apply. There may, however, be a duty to make sufficient provision for the payment of compensation at the time of the expropriation.[338] Judge Brower, an American arbitrator, while doubting that the payment of compensation was a condition of legality, stated in his separate opinion in the *Sedco* (*Second Interlocutory Award*) case[339]:

"If ... no provision for compensation is made contemporaneously with the taking, or one is made which clearly cannot produce the required compensation, or unreasonably insufficient compensation is paid at the time of taking, it would seem appropriate to deem the taking itself wrongful."

5. *Lump sum settlement agreements and bilateral investment treaties.* In lump sum settlement agreements, as to which, see below, p.504, the sum paid consistently falls short of "adequate compensation" in the sense of the Hull formula. Many such bilateral agreements have been made since World War II and it has been argued that they constitute state practice indicative of the customary international law on compensation for a lawful expropriation.[340] A similar

---

[334] See Lillich, above, n.266.
[335] See above, 489.
[336] See above, n.331, at p.378. See also the *American International Group* case, above, n.303.
[337] See below, p.494.
[338] See Pellonpää and Fitzmaurice, above, n.266 at p.69.
[339] (1986) 10 Iran-U.S. C.T.R. 180 at 204, n.39.
[340] See, e.g. Lillich and Weston (1988) 82 A.J.I.L. 69.

argument can be made in respect of bilateral investment treaties (BITs), although to the contrary effect, since they generally require compensation according to the Hull formula.[341] The value of both kinds of evidence of state practice was considered in the *Sedco* (*Second Interlocutory Award*) case[342]:

> "Assessment of the present state of customary law on this subject on the basis of the conduct of States in actual practice is difficult, inter alia, because of the questionable evidentiary value for customary international law of much of the practice available. This is particularly true in regard to 'lump sum' agreements between States (a practice often claimed to support the position of less than full compensation), as well as to compensation settlements negotiated between States and foreign companies. Both types of agreements can be so greatly inspired by non-judicial considerations—e.g. resumption of diplomatic or trading relations—that it is extremely difficult to draw from them conclusions as to *opinio juris, i.e.* the determination that the content of such settlements was thought by the States involved to be required by international law. The International Court of Justice[343] and international arbitral tribunals[344] have cast serious doubts on the value of such settlements as evidence of custom. . . . The bilateral investment treaty practice of States, which much more often than not reflects the traditional international law standard of compensation for expropriation, more nearly constitutes an accurate measure of the High Contracting Parties' views as to customary international law, but also carries with it some of the same evidentiary limitations as lump sum agreements. Both kinds of agreements involve in some degree bargaining in a context to which '*opinio juris* seems a stranger.'[345]"

Calamita[346] points out that in "second generation BITs between capital importing states [on both sides]...[which] now account for over 45 per cent of all BITs in force...the parties are routinely, consistently and overwhelmingly adopting the Hull formula or some similar market value variant and argues that as a result, when considering whether BIT standards reflect custom, it is not longer possible to discount this practice "on the ground of unequal bargaining power between capital-exporting and capital-importing states." Might capital-importing states nonetheless accept the Hull formula *in a treaty* for other reasons?[347]

6. *Effective compensation*. In terms of the Hull formula, there has been little consideration by tribunals of the "promptness" or "effectiveness" of compensation. As to "effective compensation, in the *Anglo-Iranian Oil* case[348] the United Kindom argues:

> "The third requirement is summed up in the word 'effective' and means that the recipient of the compensation must be able to make use of it. He must, for instance, be able, if he wishes,

---

[341] See, e.g. art.5(1), 1989 U.K.–Guyana Agreement, Cm 909. On UK bilateral investment treaties, of which there are now over 90 in force, see Denza and Brooks (1987) 36 I.C.L.Q. 908; and Warbrick, (1987) 36 I.C.L.Q. 929. More generally, see Dolzer and Stevens, *Bilateral Investment Treaties* (1995). See also below, p.503.

[342] (1986) 10 Iran–U.S. C.T.R. 180 at 184–185.

[343] See, e.g. *Barcelona Traction* (*Belg. v. Spain*), I.C.J. Rep. 1970, p.3 at p.40. . .Ed. The ICJ there states: "Far from evidencing any norm as to the classes of beneficiaries of compensation, such arrangements are *sui generis* and provide no guidance in the present case."

[344] See, [the *Aminoil* case below, p.498]...paras. 156–157....

[345] *Aminoil* [case] . . . at para.157.

[346] (2009) 58 I.C.L.Q. 119 at 134–135.

[347] See Guxman (1998) 38 Virg.J.I.L. 639.

[348] I.C.J. Pleadings, pp.105–106.

to use it to set up a new enterprise to replace the one that has been expropriated or to use it for such other purposes as he wishes. Monetary compensation which is in blocked currency is not effective because, where the person to be compensated is a foreigner, he is not in a position to use it or to obtain the benefit of it. The compensation therefore must be freely transferable from the country paying it and, so far as that country's restrictions are concerned, convertible into other currencies."

7. *Reparation for an illegal expropriation*. The *Amoco* case follows the *Chorzów Factory* and *Aminoil* cases in recognising that in a case of illegal expropriation the ordinary rules of state responsibility apply.[349] Restitution was awarded in the *Texaco* case, although the claimant eventually accepted compensation. Restitution will seldom be possible where an enterprise is expropriated. As to compensation, the *Amoco* case follows the *Chorzów Factory* case in supposing that damages by way of reparation for any illegal expropriation may include lost profits, although apparently only to the time of judgment. If the intention is to place the claimant in the position that existed before expropriation, why, in the case of an enterprise with the prospect of doing business into the foreseeable future, should directly attributable lost profits be limited to those accruing at the date of the judgment? Should punitive damages be available in an appropriate case of illegal expropriation?[350]

TEXACO v LIBYA[351]

Texaco Overseas Petroleum Co. and California Asiatic Oil Co. v. Libya (1977) 53 I.L.R. 389; (1978) 17 I.L.M. 1

In 1973 and 1974, Libya nationalised all of the properties, rights, assets and interests of the two claimant United States companies under certain concession contracts made between Libya and the claimants for the exploitation of oil in Libya. Each contract (cl.16) provided that "the contractual rights expressly created by this concession shall not be altered except by mutual consent of the parties." Each indicated the law of the contract (cl.28):

"This concession shall be governed by and interpreted in accordance with the principles of the law of Libya common to the principles of international law and in the absence of such common principles then by and in accordance with the general principles of law, including such of those principles as may have been applied by international tribunals."

The contracts provided for the reference of any dispute arising under them to "two arbitrators, one of whom shall be appointed by each such party, and an Umpire who shall be appointed by the Arbitrators" (ibid.). In the event of either party failing to appoint an arbitrator, a sole arbitrator was to be appointed by the President of the ICJ (ibid.). In this case, Professor Dupuy, a French international

---

[349] For these rules, see arts 31–37, ILC Draft Articles, above, pp.443 et seq.

[350] See the *Amoco* case, para.197, above; and Arbitrator Brower in *Sedco v Iran* (*Second Interlocutory Award*) (1986) 10 Iran–U.S. C.T.R. 180 at 205. On punitive damages, see the ILC Draft Articles Commentary, above, p.447.

[351] See Bowett (1978) 37 C.L.J. 5; Fatouros (1980) 74 A.J.I.L. 134; Greenwood (1982) 53 B.Y.I.L. 27; Von Mehren and Kourides, above, n.305; Varma (1979) 18 Col. J.T.L. 259; White (1981) 30 I.C.L.Q. 1. See also Benton (1974) 11 Houston L.R. 924. On international contracts generally, see Asante (1979) 28 I.C.L.Q. 401; Friedmann, *Expropriation in International Law* (1953) pp.200–210; Hyde (1962–I) 105 Hague Recueil 267; Lalive (1964) 13 I.C.L.Q. 987; McNair (1957) 33 B.Y.I.L. 1; Mann (1959) 35 B.Y.I.L. 34; Schwebel (1959) 53 Proc. A.S.I.L. 266.

lawyer, was appointed as a sole arbitrator after Libya had failed to act. Libya did not participate in the proceedings at any stage, except by way of memorandum to the President of the ICJ objecting to the proceedings.

The arbitrator held that the concessions were "internationalised" contracts and that the law applying to them was that chosen by the parties in cl.28. In the following extract, the arbitrator indicates more fully when a contract between a state and an alien may be characterised as an "internationalised" one, and what the consequences of such a characterisation are. He then considers whether the contracts are binding under the applicable law and whether the Libyan nationalisation measures in breach of the contracts can be justified on other grounds.

Award of the Arbitrator

40. The internationalisation of contracts entered into between States and foreign private persons can result in various ways ...

42. International arbitration case law confirms that the reference to the general principles of law [in its proper law clause] is always regarded to be a sufficient criterion for the internationalisation of a contract.[352]

44. ... Another process for the internationalisation of a contract consists in inserting a clause providing that possible differences which may arise in respect of the interpretation and the performance of the contract shall be submitted to arbitration.

... It is ... unquestionable that the reference to international arbitration is sufficient to internationalise a contract, in other words, to situate it within a specific legal order—the order of the international law of contracts.

45. ... A third element of the internationalisation of the contracts in dispute results from the fact that it takes on a dimension of a new category of agreements between States and private persons: economic development agreements. ...

Several elements characterise these agreements: in the first place, their subject matter is particularly broad: they are not concerned only with an isolated purchase or performance, but tend to bring to developing countries investments and technical assistance. ... Thus, they assume a real importance in the development of the country where they are performed. ...

In the second place, the long duration of these contracts implies close co-operation between the State and the contracting party and requires permanent installations as well as the acceptance of extensive responsibilities by the investor.

Finally, because of the purpose of the co-operation in which the contracting party must participate with the State and the magnitude of the investments to which it agreed, the contractual nature of this type of agreement is reinforced. ... This investor must in particular be protected against legislative uncertainties, that is to say the risks of the municipal law of the host country being modified, or against any government measures which would lead to an abrogation or rescission of the contract. Hence, the insertion, as in the present case, of so-called stabilisation clauses: these clauses tend to remove all or part of the agreement from the internal law and to provide for its correlative submission to *sui generis* rules ... or to a system which is properly an international law system. ...

47. ... [S]tating that a contract between a State and a private person falls within the international legal order means that for the purposes of interpretation and performance of the contract, it should be recognized that a private contracting party has specific international capacities. But, unlike a State, the private person has only a limited capacity and his quality as a subject of international law does enable him only to invoke, in the field of international law, the rights which he derives from the contract.

The arbitrator next applied the law of the contracts in cl.28 and held that the concessions were binding. This was because both Libyan and international law accepted that contracts were binding (*pacta sunt servanda*).

---

[352] Ed. The arbitrator cited the following cases: the *Lena Goldfields Arbitration* (1930) 5 A.D. 3, 426; the *Abu Dhabi Arbitration*, above, n.339; the *Qatar* case (1953) 20 I.L.R. 534; and the *Sapphire* case (1963) 35 I.L.R. 136. See also the *Aramco* case (1963) 27 I.L.R. 117.

53. The Tribunal must now rule on the point whether ... the defendant Government has, or has not, breached its obligations arising from the contracts it executed. For this purpose, this Tribunal should examine the various reasons which could be envisaged in order to justify the defendant Government's behaviour. ...

After rejecting the possibility that Libya could be excused from its obligations in accordance with the law applicable to administrative contracts (so that the obligations could be altered or terminated unilaterally by the state),[353] the arbitrator considered an argument based upon "the concept of sovereignty and the nature of measures of nationalisation."

61. ... It is clear from an international point of view that it is not possible to criticize a nationalisation measure concerning nationals of the State concerned, or any measure affecting aliens in respect of whom the State concerned has made no particular commitment to guarantee and maintain their position. On the assumption that the nationalising State has concluded with a foreign company a contract which stems from the municipal law of that State and is completely governed by that law the resolution of the new situation created by nationalisation will be subject to the legal and administrative provisions then in force.

62. But the case is totally different where the State has concluded with a foreign contracting party an internationalised agreement. ...

71. ... the recognition by international law of the right to nationalise is not sufficient ground to empower a State to disregard its commitments, because the same law also recognises the power of a State to commit itself internationally, especially by accepting the inclusion of stabilisation clauses in a contract entered into with a foreign private party. ...

73. Thus, in respect of the international law of contracts, a nationalisation cannot prevail over an inter-nationalised contract, containing stabilisation clauses, entered into between a State and a foreign private company. ...

The arbitrator then considered, thirdly and finally, whether "resolution concerning natural resources and wealth adopted by the General Assembly" justified Libya's conduct.

87. ... On the basis of the circumstances of adoption ... and by expressing an *opinio juris communis*, Resolution 1803 (XVII)[354] seems to this Tribunal to reflect the state of customary law existing in this field. ... The consensus by a majority of States belonging to the various representative groups indicates without the slightest doubt universal recognition of the rules therein incorporated, i.e. with respect to nationalisation and compensation the use of the rules in force in the nationalising State, but all this in conformity with international law.

88. While Resolution 1803 (XVII) appears to a large extent as the expression of a real general will, this is not at all the case with respect to the other Resolutions mentioned above.[355] ... In particular, as regards the Charter of Economic Rights and Duties of States, several factors contribute to denying legal value to those provisions of the document which are of interest in the instant case.

—In the first place, Article 2 of this Charter must be analysed as a political rather than as a legal declaration concerned with the ideological strategy of development and, as such, supported only by non-   industrialised States.

—In the second place, this Tribunal notes that in the draft submitted by the Group of 77 to the Second Commission ... the General Assembly was invited to adopt the Charter "as a first measure of codification and progressive development" within the field of the international law of development. However, because of the opposition of several States, this description was deleted from the text submitted to the vote of the Assembly. ...

The absence of any connection between the procedure of compensation and international law and the subjection of this procedure solely to municipal law cannot be regarded by this Tribunal except as a *de lege*

---

[353] The arbitrator held that (i) the concessions were not administrative contracts under Libyan law and (ii) the theory of administrative contracts was not a part of international law. French in origin, it was not a general principle of law found in all of the main kinds of legal systems.

[354] Ed. Above, p.474.

[355] Ed. Resolutions 3171, 3201, and 3281, above, pp.475–476.

ferenda formulation, which even appears *contra legem* in the eyes of many developed countries.[356] Similarly, several developing countries, although having voted favorably on the Charter of Economic Rights and Duties of States as a whole, in explaining their votes regretted the absence of any reference to international law. ...

90. The argument of the Libyan Government ... is also negated by a complete analysis of the whole text of the Charter of Economic Rights and Duties of States.

Analysing the scope of these various provisions, Ambassador Castañeda, who chaired the Working Group charged with drawing up the Charter of Economic Rights and Duties of States, formally stated that the principle of performance in good faith of international obligations laid down in Chapter I(j) of the Charter applies to all matters governed by it, including, in particular, matters referred to in Article 2. Following his analysis, this particularly competent and eminent scholar concluded as follows[357]:

> The Charter accepts that international law may operate as a factor limiting the freedom of the State should foreign interests be affected, even though Article 2 does not state this explicitly. This stems legally from the provisions included in other Articles of the Charter which should be interpreted and applied jointly with those of Article 2.

The arbitrator, having found no justification for Libya's acts, held that the appropriate remedy was restitutio in integrum, as claimed by the concessionaires, so that Libya was "legally bound to perform" the contracts. In fact, the claimants subsequently accepted an offer of compensation in full settlement of their claim.[358]

Note

Most contracts between states and aliens are governed by municipal law—normally, but not always,[359] the municipal law of the contracting states.[360] Nonetheless, some—particularly concession contracts for the exploitation of natural resources—are governed by other legal rules indicated usually in a choice of law clause in the contract. The contract in the *Texaco* case—(which is also known as the *Topco* case) was typical of the latter kind of contract.

According to a theory developed by some Western writers[361] and adopted in the *Texaco* case, such a contract may qualify as an "internationalised contract" or "economic development agreement" with the result that the contracting state is deemed to have surrendered the power to expropriate contrary to its terms, by virtue of the contract's "stabilisation clauses." This theory is questioned by other Western writers[362] and is strongly contested in the developing world.[363] For a different approach, see the *Aminoil* case, below.

----

[356] Ed. Earlier, the arbitrator had examined the voting record of the 1974 Charter and similar resolutions and concluded that they "were supported by a majority of states but not by any of the developed countries with market economies which carry on the largest part of international trade" (para.86).

[357] Ed. 20 *Annuaire Français* 31 at 54 (1974). Translation in Award. Chapter I(j) reads "Economic as well as political and other relations among States shall be governed, inter alia, by the following principles ... (j) Fulfillment in good faith of international obligations." 1974 Charter, art. 32(2), states that "[i]n their interpretation and application, the provisions of the present Charter are interrelated and each provision should be construed in the context of other provisions."

[358] See (1978) 17 I.L.M. 2.

[359] See, e.g. *R. v International Trustee for the Protection of Bondholders Aktiengesellschaft* [1937] A.C. 500 HL.

[360] On the question whether the breach by a state of a contract between it and an alien that is governed by municipal law is contrary to international law, see Jennings (1961) 37 B.Y.I.L. 156; and Mann (1960) 54 A.J.I.L. 572. On the position where such a breach is by way of nationalisation, see the *Texaco* case, above, para.61.

[361] See, e.g. Schwebel, in *International Law at the Time of its Codification: Essays in Honour of Robert Ago* (1989), Vol.3, p.401; and Curtis (1988) 29 H.I.L.J. 317.

[362] See, e.g. Bowett (1988) 69 B.Y.I.L. 49, 51.

[363] See, e.g. Jimenez de Aréchaga, above, n.266.

AMINOIL CASE[364]

Kuwait v American Independent Oil Co. (1982)

Arbitration Tribunal: Reuter, President; Sultan, Fitzmaurice, members. 21 I.L.M. 976

In 1948, Aminoil, an American company, was granted by Kuwait an oil concession of 60 years duration. In 1977, Kuwait terminated the concession by Decree Law No.124 and transferred to itself the company's concession assets against compensation to be assessed by a Kuwaiti "Compensation Committee." Aminoil declined to co-operate with the Committee, contesting instead the legality of the Decree Law. The parties referred the case to arbitration under a special Arbitration Agreement which provided in art.III(2):

"The law governing the substantive issues between the Parties shall be determined by the Tribunal, having regard to the quality of the Parties, the transnational character of their relations and the principles of law and practice prevailing in the modern world."

Interpreting art.III(2), the Tribunal decided that it was required to apply Kuwaiti law, of which international law—with its rules governing the legality of an expropriation—formed a part. The Tribunal rejected Aminoil's claim that the nationalisation did not satisfy the international law requirements, the existence of which the tribunal did not question, that it be for a public purpose and non-discriminatory. The Tribunal then, in the following extracts, considered whether the nationalisation was contrary to international law because it was inconsistent with the stabilisation clauses in the contract and discussed the compensation that was payable in respect of what it held to be a lawful taking.

Award of the Tribunal

88. .... Nevertheless, Aminoil's concessionary contract contained specific provisions in the light of which it may be queried whether the nationalisation was in truth lawful. .... The relevant part of *Article 1 of 1948* provided that:

"The period of this Agreement shall be sixty (60) years from the date of signature."

Article 17 of 1948 provided as follows:

"The Shaikh shall not by general or special legislation or by administrative measures or by any other act whatever annul this Agreement except as provided in Article 11. No alteration shall be made in the terms of this Agreement by either the Shaikh or the Company except in the event of the Shaikh and the Company jointly agreeing that it is desirable in the interest of both parties to make certain alterations, deletions or additions to this Agreement."

Finally, ... [as amended in 1961] *Article 11*, after indicating in a first paragraph (A) certain events (not here relevant) in which the Ruler of Kuwait would be entitled to terminate the Concession, went on in a second paragraph (B) to state

"(B) Save as aforesaid this Agreement shall not be terminated before the expiration of the period specified in Article 1 thereof except by surrender as provided in Article 12 or if the Company shall be in default under the arbitration provisions of Article 18."

---

[364] See Mann (1983) 54 B.Y.I.L. 213; Marston (1983) 17 J.W.T.L. 177; Redfern (1984) 55 B.Y.I.L. 65; Teson (1984) 24 Virg. J.I.L. 323; Tschanz (1984) 18 Int. Lawyer 245; Young and Owen, in Lillich, ed., *Valuation of Nationalised Property in International Law* (1987), Vol.4, p.3.

These clauses combined, but especially Article 17, constituted what are sometimes called the "stabilisation" clauses of the contract. A straightforward and direct reading of them can lead to the conclusion that they prohibit any nationalisation. ...

90. [In contrast, Kuwait] ... claimed that permanent sovereignty over natural resources has become an imperative rule of *jus cogens* prohibiting States from affording, by contract or by treaty, guarantees of any kind against the exercise of the public authority in regard to all matters relating to natural riches. This contention lacks all foundation. Even if Assembly Resolution 1803 [above, p.474] ... is to be regarded, by reason of the circumstance of its adoption, as reflecting the then state of international law, such is not the case with subsequent resolutions which have not had the same degree of authority. Even if some of their provisions can be regarded as codifying rules that reflect international practice, it would not be possible from this to deduce the existence of a rule of international law prohibiting a State from undertaking not to proceed to a nationalisation during a limited period of time. It may indeed well be eminently useful that "host" States should, if they so desire, be able to pledge themselves not to nationalise given foreign undertakings within a limited period; and no rule of public international law prevents them from doing so. ...

95. ... contractual limitations on the State's right to nationalise are juridically possible, but what that would involve would be a particularly serious undertaking which would have to be expressly stipulated for, and be within the regulations governing the conclusion of State contracts; and it is to be expected that it should cover only a relatively limited period. In the present case however, the existence of such a stipulation would have to be presumed as being covered by the general language of the stabilisation clauses, and over the whole period of an especially long concession since it extended to 60 years. A limitation on the sovereign rights of the State is all the less to be presumed where the concessionaire is in any event in possession of important guarantees regarding its essential interests in the shape of a legal right to eventual compensation.

96. Such is the case here,—for if the Tribunal thus holds that it cannot interpret Articles 17 and ... revised 11 as absolutely forbidding nationalisation, it is nevertheless the fact that these provisions are far from having lost all their value and efficacy on that account since, by impliedly requiring that nationalisation shall not have any confiscatory character, they re-inforce the necessity for a proper indemnification as a condition of it.

97. There is another aspect of the matter which has weighed with the Tribunal. While attributing its full value to the fundamental principle of *pacta sunt servanda*, the Tribunal has felt obliged to recognize that the contract of Concession has undergone great changes since 1948: changes conceded—often unwillingly, but conceded nevertheless—by the Company. These changes have ... been the consequence of ... a profound and general transformation in the terms of oil concessions that occurred in the Middle-East, and later throughout the world. ... They were introduced into the contractual relations between the Government and Aminoil through the play of Article 9 [i.e. by textual amendment], or else as the result of at least tacit acceptances by the Company. ...

98. This Concession—in its origin a mining concession granted by a State whose institutions were still incomplete and directed to narrow patrimonial ends—became one of the essential instruments in the economic and social progress of a national community in full process of development. This transformation, progressively achieved, took place at first by means of successive increases in the financial levies going to the State, and then through the growing influence of the State in the economic and technical management of the undertaking ... and the regulation of works and investment programmes. The contract of Concession thus changed its character and became one of those contracts in regard to which, in most legal systems, the State, while remaining bound to respect the contractual equilibrium, enjoys special advantages. ...

100. The faculty of nationalising the Concession could not thenceforward be excluded in relation to the régime of the undertaking as it resulted from the sum total of the considerations relevant to its functioning. ...

102. The Tribunal thus arrives at the conclusion that the "take-over" of Aminoil's enterprise was not, in 1977, inconsistent with the contract of concession, provided always that the nationalisation did not possess any confiscatory character. ...

The Tribunal then considered the compensation due for what was a lawful taking:

143. The most general formulation of the rules applicable for a lawful nationalisation was contained in the United Nations General Assembly Resolution No 1803 (XVII) of December 14, 1962, on Permanent Sovereignty over Natural Resources, Article 4 ...

This text which obtained a unanimous vote in the General Assembly, codifies positive principles, recognised by the Constitution and Law of Kuwait, that have not been contested in the present proceedings. It calls for a concrete interpretation of the term "appropriate compensation." Other disputes have long since turned upon different terms such as "fair," "just," "equitable," not to speak of "adequate," "effective," "prompt," etc. There are indeed, several tendencies, all appealing to the same principle, one of which however reduces compensation almost to the status of a symbol, and the other of which assimilates the compensation due for a legitimate take-over to that due in respect of an illegitimate one. These tendencies were in mutual opposition in the United Nations when the Resolutions following No 1803 were voted, none of which obtained unanimous acceptance, and some of which, such as the Charter of the Economic Rights and Duties of States, have been the subject of divergent interpretations.

144. The Tribunal considers that the determination of the amount of an award of "appropriate" compensation is better carried out by means of an enquiry into all the circumstances relevant to the particular concrete case, than through abstract theoretical discussion. Moreover the Charter of the Economic Rights and Duties of States, even in its most disputed clause (Article 2, paragraph 2c) [above, p.475]—and the one that occasioned reservations on the part of the industrialized States—recommended taking account of "all circumstances" in order to determine the amount of compensation—which does not in any way exclude a substantial indemnity.[365]

145. Careful consideration of the circumstances proper to each case sometimes enables certain difficulties to be set aside. Thus the opposition manifested by some States to any but the most incomplete compensation may be explicable on the basis that their object is to do away with foreign investments entirely, because they do not welcome foreign capital and are even less favourable to investing abroad themselves. ...

146. ... In this respect it is not disputed that Kuwait is a country favouring foreign investment, and itself an important investor abroad . ... The Tribunal will therefore confine itself to registering that in the case of the present dispute there is no room for rules of compensation that would make nonsense of foreign investment. ...

148. Both Parties to the present litigation have invoked the notion of "legitimate expectations" for deciding on compensation. That formula is well-advised, and justifiably brings to mind the fact that, with reference to every long-term contract, especially such as involve an important investment, there must necessarily be economic calculations, and the weighing-up of rights and obligations, of chances and risks, constituting the contractual equilibrium. ...

149. For assessment of that equilibrium itself, and of the legitimate expectations to which it gives rise ... it is not only a question of the original text; there are also the amendments, the interpretations, and the behaviour manifested along the course of its existence, that indicate (often fortuitously) how the legitimate expectations of the Parties are to be seen, and sometimes seen as becoming modified according to the circumstances. ...

158. The Tribunal now comes to the basis on which the evaluation of the legitimate expectations of Aminoil must proceed. ...

159. To start with ... whereas the contract of concession did not forbid nationalisation, the stabilisation clauses inserted in it ... were nevertheless not devoid of all consequence, for they prohibited any measures that would have had a confiscatory character. These clauses created for the concessionaire a legitimate expectation that must be taken into account. ...

160. But above all, account must be taken of the position of Aminoil in its relations with the Government of Kuwait. From the time when its rate of production reached a satisfactory level, Aminoil was in the position of an undertaking whose aim was to obtain a "reasonable rate of return" and not speculative profits which, in practice, it never did realise. ...

161. ... [O]ver the years, Aminoil had come to accept the principle of a moderate estimate of profits, and ... it was this that constituted its legitimate expectations ...

164. Having thus described the place occupied by the notion of a reasonable rate of return in the indemnification of Aminoil, the Tribunal must now indicate what principles are, in its view, valid for determining the compensation due in respect of the Company's assets. As the Tribunal has stated earlier, it considers it to be just and reasonable to take some measure of account of all the elements of an undertaking. This leads to a separate appraisal of the value, on the one hand of the undertaking itself, as a source of profit, and on the other of the totality of the assets, and adding together the results obtained. ...

178. *Amounts due to Aminoil—*

(1) These are made up of the values of the various components of the undertaking separately considered, and

---

[365] As stated by the United States Court of Appeals for the Second Circuit in *Banco Nacional de Cuba v Chase Manhattan Bank*, (August 4, 1981). "It may well be the consensus of nations that full compensation need not be paid 'in all circumstances' ... and that requiring an expropriating state to pay 'appropriate compensation'—even considering the lack of precise definition of that term,—would come closest to reflecting what international law requires. But the adoption of an 'appropriate compensation' requirement would not exclude the possibility that in some cases full compensation would be appropriate."

of the undertaking itself considered as an organic totality—or going concern—therefore as a unified whole, the value of which is greater than that of its component parts, and which must also take account of the legitimate expectations of the owners. These principles remain good even if the undertaking was due to revert, free of cost, to the concessionary Authority in another 30 years, the profits having been restricted to a reasonable level.

(2) As regards the evaluation of the different concrete components that constitute the undertaking, the Joint Report furnishes acceptable indications concerning the assets other than fixed assets. But as regards the fixed assets, the "net book value" used as a basis merely gives a formal accounting figure which, in the present case, cannot be considered adequate.

(3) For the purposes of the present *case*, and *for the fixed assets*, it is a depreciated replacement value that seems appropriate. In consequence, taking that basis for the fixed assets, taking the order of value indicated in the Joint Report for the non-fixed assets, and taking into account the legitimate expectations of the concessionaire, the Tribunal comes to the conclusion that, at the date of 19 September, 1977, a sum estimated at $206,041,000 represented the reasonably appraised value of what constituted the object of the takeover. . . .

179. For these reasons,

THE TRIBUNAL, unanimously, having regard to all of the above mentioned considerations,

AWARDS to Aminoil,

THE SUM OF ONE HUNDRED AND SEVENTY NINE MILLION, SEVEN HUNDRED AND FIFTY THOUSAND, SEVEN HUNDRED AND SIXTY FOUR UNITED STATES DOLLARS[366]

Separate Opinion of Sir Gerald Fitzmaurice[367]

21. The Award however holds that, despite their unambiguous language, these provisions did not operate to prevent an eventual nationalisation by unilateral legislative act—or at least, that whatever the original position, they had ceased to do so by the date of the take-over in 1977—(this is probably the vital point in the reasoning). . . .

23. I know of no general legal principle . . . which would require something to be expressly stated rather than left to be implied from representative language clearly covering it according to normal canons of interpretation; or rather, and more correctly, which would prohibit something from being inferred from such language *merely because* it was not expressly stated.

24. There is absolutely nothing in the stabilization clauses to warrant the view that they were intended to be confined in the manner suggested—i.e. to the case of confiscatory measures only. . . .

25. In my opinion, so far was it from being the case that the Parties in 1948 had not got the eventuality of an ultimate nationalisation in mind, that I feel confident that, at least on Aminoil's side, it was precisely one of the principal contingencies foreseen as possible. The language of Article 17, though general, smacks strongly of it. . . .

26. It is an illusion to suppose that monetary compensation alone, even on a generous scale, necessarily removes the confiscatory element from a take-over, whether called nationalisation or something else. It is like paying compensation to a man who has lost his leg. Unfortunately it does not restore the leg. When a company such as Aminoil procures the insertion in its Concession of a clause like Article 17, its aim is not to obtain money if the Article is breached, but to guarantee if possible that it is not breached. . . .

28. . . . [with regard to the "evolution" argument in paras. 97–100 Award], the argument seems to me to break down in one crucial respect: whatever changes were consented to by the Company, and whatever the quality of that consent, they were changes that were to take place within the framework of a *continuing* Concession—not of one that was to come, and did come, to an end without any such consent, but by the sole will of the other Party. It was change, not termination that Aminoil agreed to. . . .

30. In consequence, . . . although the nationalisation of Aminoil's undertaking may otherwise have been perfectly lawful, considered simply in its aspect of being an act of the State, it was nevertheless irreconcilable with the stabilization clauses of a Concession that was still in force at the moment of the take-over.

---

[366] Ed. This final figure allows for certain Aminoil debts.

[367] Sir Gerald Fitzmaurice agreed with the operative section (*dispositif*) of the tribunal's award (which is limited to the amount of compensation due to Aminoil) and so did not dissent.

Notes

1. *Stabilisation clauses.*[368] The *Aminoil* case makes no mention of the theory of internationalised contracts that was at the heart of the award in the *Texaco* case, above, p.494. It does accept that a state may surrender its power to expropriate property by agreeing to a stabilisation clause in a contract—but only if (as is unlikely) the clause is expressly and specifically to this effect.[369] Note, however, Sir Gerald Fitzmaurice's more *Texaco*-like view. Although other arbitrations have followed or are consistent with the *Texaco* case in supposing that a generally worded stabilisation clause may prevent expropriation,[370] the more balanced view in the *Aminoil* case seems likely to prevail. The fact that expropriation runs counter to a stabilisation clause may, however, be relevant to the determination of "appropriate compensation."

    A study of practice in the late 1960s and 1970s shows that, because of the increased bargaining power of producer states, the majority of oil contracts then made were governed by the law of the contracting state and subject to the jurisdiction of its courts.[371] To the extent that this practice continues, the role of stabilisation clauses is likely to decline.

2. *Compensation.* The *Aminoil* case is a notable example of the increasing use by tribunals of the "appropriate compensation" formula in Resolution 1803 as the standard of compensation required by international law. See further on compensation, above, pp.488, 494.

F. Diplomatic Protection[372]

i. Introductory Note

When an alien is ill treated contrary to the law of state responsibility, the injury is to his national state, which may raise the question of the delinquent state's liability by the exercise of its right to diplomatic protection. This will require compliance with the law on the admissibility of claims. In particular, the state exercising its right of protection must satisfy the rules concerning the nationality of claims, and the injured alien must have exhausted local remedies available in the law of the delinquent state.

In 2006, the International Law Commission adopted a set of Draft Articles on Diplomatic Protection.[373] In 2007 the General Assembly drew states' attention to them and decided to consider in 2010 whether a convention on diplomatic protection should be drafted on the basis of them.[374] Whereas some states favour the drafting of such a convention, others would prefer state practice to evolve in the light of the Draft Articles. The Draft Articles are accompanied by a Commentary, which records that some of the Articles are instances of progressive development,[375] rather than a state-

---

[368] See Garcia-Amador (1993) 2 Fla.St.U.J. Trans.L.P. 23; and Paasivirta (1989) 60 B.Y.I.L. 315. See also Mariruzzaman (1992) 9 J.Int.Arb. 141.

[369] cf. the *Amoco* case, above, p.481, para.179.

[370] See *Revere Copper Inc. v OPIC* (1978) 17 I.L.M. 1321; and *AGIP v Congo* (1982) 21 I.L.M.726. See also the concurring opinion of Arbitrator Brower in *Mobil v Iran* (1987) 16 Iran-U.S. C.T.R. 3 at 64–68.

[371] See Kuusi, *The Host State and the Transnational Corporation* (1979), pp.140–145.

[372] See Amerasinghe, *Diplomatic Protection* (2008).

[373] For the text and Commentary, see Report of the 58th Sess. I.L.C. (2006), G.A.O.R. A/61/10, pp. 22 et seq. See also the seven reports of the ILC Special Rapporteur on Diplomatic Protection, Professor Dugard, as to which see Report of the 58th Sess. I.L.C. (2006), G.A.O.R. A/61/10, pp.14–15. See also art.44, I.L.C. Draft Articles on Responsibility of States for InternationallyWrongful Acts, above, n.4. On the Diplomatic Protection Draft Articles, see Dugard (2005) 24 A.Y.I.L. 75; Kateka (2007) 20 I.L.J.I.L. 921; Zieck (2001) 14 L.I.J.L. 209.

[374] G.A.Res. A/62/67.

[375] A controversial example is art.8, below, p.514, on the protection of refugees and stateless persons.

ment of current customary international law. The Draft Articles are based on the following definition of "diplomatic protection" in art.1, which reflects customary international law[376]:

"For the purposes of the present draft articles, diplomatic protection consists of the invocation by a State, through diplomatic action or other means of peaceful settlement, of the responsibility of another State for an injury caused by an internationally wrongful act of that State to a natural or legal person that is a national of the former State with a view to the implementation of such responsibility".

The Commentary to art.1 reads[377]:

"'Diplomatic action' covers all the lawful procedures employed by a State to inform another State of its views and concerns, including protest, request for an inquiry or for negotiations aimed at the settlement of disputes. 'Other means of peaceful settlement' embraces all forms of lawful dispute settlement, from negotiation, mediation and conciliation to arbitral and judicial dispute settlement. The use of force, prohibited by Article 2, paragraph 4, of the Charter of the United Nations, is not a permissible method for the enforcement of the right of diplomatic protection. Diplomatic protection does not include démarches or other diplomatic action that do not involve the invocation of the legal responsibility of another State, such as informal requests for corrective action."

Diplomatic protection may lead to arbitration awards or judicial decisions, although resort to arbitration on this basis is now much less common that formerly,[378] and very few cases of diplomatic protection have ever been taken to the World Court.[379] In the last few decades, other mechanisms than diplomatic protection have evolved for the settlement of disputes concerning the treatment of aliens. In the case of investment disputes, available methods of settlement have been supplemented by the Convention on the Settlement of Investment Disputes between States and Nationals of Other States 1965.[380] This establishes an International Centre for the Settlement of Investment Disputes (in Washington DC). Conciliation and arbitration facilities are available through the centre to settle cases between contracting parties and companies of the nationality of a contracting party where both sides consent, with the company being able to bring a claim directly without the need for diplomatic protection. In addition, bilateral investment treaties ("BITs"), of which there are now more than 2,500,[381] similarly may allow the investor to bring a claim directly to an ICSID or other tribunal. As noted by the ILC:

"the dispute settlement procedures provided for in BITs and ICSID offer greater advantages to the foreign investor than the customary international law system of diplomatic protection, as they give the investor direct access to international arbitration, avoid the political uncertainty inherent in the

---

[376] *Diallo* case, I.C.J. Rep. 2007, para.39.
[377] See above, n.373.
[378] Many of the arbitration cases in this Chapter are arbitration awards resuling from diplomatic protection. As to the current US–Iranian Claims Tribunal, see below, p.834, n.14.
[379] Examples are the *Nottebohm, Barcelona Traction* and *Diallo* cases in this Chapter.
[380] (1967) U.K.T.S. 25, Cmnd. 3255; 575 U.N.T.S. 159; (1965) 4 I.L.M. 532. In force 1966, 143 parties. These include France, the UK and the US among developed states and most African and some Asian and Latin American developing states. See Schreuer, *The ICSID Convention: A Commentary* (2001). Private persons may also bring investment claims directly under the North American Free Trade Agreement 1992 ("NAFTA"): see Kinnear, Bjorklund and Hannaford, *Investment Disputes under NAFTA* (2006).
[381] UNCTAD, *World Investment Report 2007*, p.16.

discretionary nature of diplomatic protection and dispense with the conditions for the exercise of diplomatic protection."[382]

The result is that, in the context of the protection of companies and shareholders, "the role of diplomatic protection" has "somewhat faded".[383] Another mechanism that has replaced diplomatic protection leading to arbitration has been the "lump sum settlement agreement".[384] By such agreements, one state agrees by treaty to pay another a "lump sum" in full satisfaction of out-standing claims by the nationals of the latter against the former. The latter then arranges itself for the distribution of the settlement sum, typically by a national claims commission. Settlements between the United Kingdom and East European states arising out of the nationalisations of British nationals' property of the late 1940s, for example, were reached in this way, the "lump sum" being distributed by the Foreign Compensation Commission.[385] Such settlements are invariably of a compromise character so that claims are not fully met.

A further development has been the emergence of remedies directly available to private persons before international courts or other bodies under international human rights law—the subject matter of which overlaps in some areas (e.g. rights to life, freedom of the person, fair trial, property) with that to which the right to diplomatic protection applies under the law of state responsibility.[386]

ii. Nationality of Claims[387]

(1) The General Rule

PANEVEZYS-SALDUTISKIS CASE[388]

Estonia v Lithuania (1939)

P.C.I.J. Reports, Series A/B, No. 76

Judgment of the Court

... In taking up the case of one of its nationals, by resorting to diplomatic action or international judicial proceedings on his behalf, a State is in reality asserting its own right, the right to ensure in the person of its nationals respect for the rules of international law. This rule is necessarily limited to intervention on behalf of its own nationals because, in the absence of a special agreement, it is the bond of nationality between the State and the individual which alone confers upon the State the right of diplomatic protection, and it is as a part of the function of diplomatic protection that the right to take up a claim and to ensure respect for the rules of international law must be envisaged. Where the injury was done to the national of some other State, no claim to which such injury may give rise falls within the scope of the diplomatic protection which a State is entitled to afford nor can it give rise to a claim which that State is entitled to espouse.

---

[382] Commentary to art.17, I.L.C. Draft Articles on Diplomatic Protection, above, at n.373.

[383] *Diallo* case, para.88, below, p.525.

[384] See Lillich and Weston, *International Claims: Their Settlement by Lump Sum Agreements*, 2 vols, 1975; and *International Claims, Contemporary European Practice* (1982). See also the UN Compensation Commission, below, p.835, n.15.

[385] On British practice generally, see Lillich, *International Claims: Post-war British Practice* (1967). On the Foreign Compensation Commission, see Magnus (1988) 37 I.C.L.Q. 975.

[386] See the *Diallo* case, para.39, below, p.525. And see McGoldrick, in Fitzmaurice and Sarooshi, eds, *Issues of State Repon-sibility before International Judicial Institutions* (2004), p.161. See further, below, Ch.9.

[387] See Donner, *The Regulation of Nationality in International Law* (2nd edn 1994), Ch.2; Hurst (1926) 7 B.Y.I.L. 163; Joseph, *Nationality and Diplomatic Protection: The Commonwealth of Nations* (1969); Leigh (1971) 20 I.C.L.Q. 453; Sinclair (1950) 27 B.Y.I.L. 124.

[388] See also the *Barcelona Traction* case, below, p.515.

Note

Article 3 Draft Articles on Diplomatic Protection provides:

"1. The State entitled to exercise diplomatic protection is the State of nationality.

2. Notwithstanding paragraph 1, diplomatic protection may be exercised by a State in respect of a person that is not its national in accordance with draft article 8."

Article 8, below, p.515, concerns the diplomatic protection of refugees and stateless persons. See also the special rule for the protection of ship's crews in art.18, Draft Articles:

"The right of the State of nationality of the members of the crew of a ship to exercise diplomatic protection is not affected by the right of the State of nationality of a ship to seek redress on behalf of such crew members, irrespective of their nationality, when they have been injured in connection with an injury to the vessel resulting from an internationally wrongful act."

This right of the national state of the ship to protect crew members regardless of their nationality is supported by state practice and recognised in *The M/V Saiga (No.2)* case, above, p.369. Although not "diplomatic protection in the absence of the bond of nationality",[389] it is a valuable supplement to the right of diplomatic protection of particular crew members by their national states.

---

(2) Protection of Natural Persons
NOTTEBOHM CASE[390]

Liechtenstein v Guatemala

ICJ Reports 1955, p.4

Judgment of the Court

By the application filed on December 17, 1951, the Government of Liechtenstein instituted proceedings before the Court in which it claimed restitution and compensation on the ground that the Government of Guatemala had "acted towards the person and property of Mr. Friedrich Nottebohm, a citizen of Liechtenstein, in a manner contrary to international law."[391] In its Counter-Memorial, the Government of Guatemala contended that this claim was inadmissible on a number of grounds, and one of its objections to the admissibility of the claim related to the nationality of the person for whose protection Liechtenstein had seised the Court. ...

Guatemala has referred to a well-established principle of international law, which it expressed in Counter-Memorial, where it is stated that "it is the bond of nationality between the State and the individual which alone confers upon the State the right of diplomatic protection." ...

Nottebohm was born at Hamburg on September 16, 1881. He was German by birth, and still possessed German nationality when, in October 1939, he applied for naturalization in Liechtenstein.

In 1905 he went to Guatemala. He took up residence there and made that country the headquarters of his business activities. ... After 1905 he sometimes went to Germany on business and to other countries for holidays.

---

[389] Commentary to art.18, Draft Articles on Diplomatic Protection, above, p.373. For other exceptional cases in which a state other than the national state may protect a person, see above, p.122, n.145.

[390] See Jones (1956) 5 I.C.L.Q. 230; Kunz (1960) 54 A.J.I.L. 536; Verzijl, *The Jurisprudence of the World Court*, Vol.2 (1965), p.210.

[391] Ed. The Court was asked to "adjudge and declare that the Government of Guatemala in arresting, detaining, expelling and refusing to re-admit Mr Nottebohm and in seizing and retaining his property without compensation acted in breach of their obligations under international law": I.C.J. Rep. 1955, pp.6–7.

He continued to have business connections in Germany. He paid a few visits to a brother who had lived in Liechtenstein since 1931. Some of his other brothers, relatives and friends were in Germany, others in Guatemala. He himself continued to have his fixed abode in Guatemala until 1943, that is to say, until the occurrence of the events which constitute the basis of the present dispute. . . .

The Liechtenstein Law of January 4, 1934, lays down the conditions for the naturalization of foreigners. . . . The Law specifies certain mandatory requirements, namely, that the applicant for naturalization should prove: (1) "that the acceptance into the Home Corporation (*Heimatverband*) of a Liechtenstein commune has been promised to him in case of acquisition of the nationality of the State (2) that he will lose his former nationality as a result of naturalization, although this requirement may be waived under stated conditions. It further makes naturalization conditional upon compliance with the requirement of residence for at least three years in the territory of the Principality, although it is provided that "this requirement can be dispensed with in circumstances deserving special consideration and by way of exception." In addition, the applicant for naturalization is required to submit a number of documents, such as . . ., if he is not a resident in the Principality, proof that he has concluded an agreement with the Revenue authorities. . . . The Law further provides for the payment by the applicant of a naturalization fee. . . .

On October 9, 1939, Nottebohm, "resident in Guatemala since 1905 (at present residing as a visitor with his brother, Hermann Nottebohm, in Vaduz)," applied for admission as a national of Liechtenstein. . . . He sought dispensation from the condition of three years' residence as prescribed by law, without indicating the special circumstances warranting such waiver. . . .

Lastly, he requested "that naturalization proceedings be initiated and concluded before the Government of the Principality and before the Commune of Mauren without delay. . . .

A certificate of nationality has . . . been produced . . . to the effect that Nottebohm was naturalized by Supreme Resolution of the Reigning Prince dated October 13, 1939.

Having obtained a Liechtenstein passport, Nottebohm had it visaed by the Consul General of Guatemala in Zurich on December 1, 1939, and returned to Guatemala at the beginning of 1940, where he resumed his former business activities. . . .

In order to decide upon the admissibility of the Application, the Court must ascertain whether the nationality conferred on Nottebohm by Liechtenstein by means of a naturalization which took place in the circumstances which have been described, can be validly invoked as against Guatemala, whether it bestows upon Liechtenstein a sufficient title to the exercise of protection in respect of Nottebohm as against Guatemala and therefore entitles it to seise the Court of a claim relating to him. In this connection, Counsel for Liechtenstein said: "the essential question is whether Mr. Nottebohm, having acquired the nationality of Liechtenstein, that acquisition of nationality is one which must be recognised by other States." This formulation is accurate, subject to the twofold reservation that, in the first place, what is involved is not recognition for all purposes but merely for the purposes of the admissibility of the Application, and, secondly, that what is involved is not recognition by all States but only by Guatemala.

The Court does not propose to go beyond the limited scope of the question which it has to decide, namely whether the nationality conferred on Nottebohm can be relied upon as against Guatemala in justification of the proceedings instituted before the Court. . . .

In order to establish that the Application must be held to be admissible, Liechtenstein has argued that Guatemala formerly recognized the naturalization which it now challenges and cannot therefore be heard to put forward a contention which is inconsistent with its former attitude. . . .

The Court considered and rejected this contention on the evidence. It dismissed part of the evidence as irrelevant because it referred to "the control of aliens in Guatemala and not to the exercise of diplomatic protection."

It is for Liechtenstein, as it is for every sovereign State, to settle by its own legislation the rules relating to the acquisition of its nationality, and to confer that nationality by naturalization granted by its own organs in accordance with that legislation. It is not necessary to determine whether international law imposes any limitations on its freedom of decision in this domain. Furthermore, nationality has its most immediate, its most far-reaching and, for most people, its only effects within the legal system of the State conferring it. Nationality serves above all to determine that the person upon whom it is conferred enjoys the rights and is bound by the obligations which the law of the State in question grants to or imposes on its nationals. This is implied in the wider concept that nationality is within the domestic jurisdiction of the State.

But the issue which the Court must decide is not one which pertains to the legal system of Liechtenstein. It does not depend on the law or on the decision of Liechtenstein whether that State is entitled to exercise its protection in the case under consideration. To exercise protection, to apply to the Court, is to place oneself on the plane of international law. It is international law which determines whether a State is entitled to exercise protection and to seise the Court. . . .

International practice provides many examples of acts performed by States in the exercise of their domestic jurisdiction which do not necessarily or automatically have international effect, which are not necessarily and automatically binding on other States or which are binding on them only subject to certain conditions: this is the case, for instance, of a judgment given by the competent court of a State which it is sought to invoke in another State. . . .

International arbitrators have decided . . . numerous cases of dual nationality, where the question arose with regard to the exercise of protection. They have given their preference to the real and effective nationality, that which accorded with the facts, that based on stronger factual ties between the person concerned and one of the States whose nationality is involved. Different factors are taken into consideration, and their importance will vary from one case to the next: the habitual residence of the individual concerned is an important factor, but there are other factors such as the centre of his interests, his family ties, his participation in public life, attachment shown by him for a given country and inculcated in his children, etc.

Similarly, the courts of third States, when they have before them an individual whom two other States hold to be their national, seek to resolve the conflict by having recourse to international criteria and their prevailing tendency is to prefer the real and effective nationality.

The same tendency prevails in the writings of publicists and in practice. This notion is inherent in the provisions of Article 3, paragraph 2, of the Statute of the Court.[392] National laws reflect this tendency when, inter alia, they make naturalization dependent on conditions indicating the existence of a link, which may vary in their purpose or in their nature but which are essentially concerned with this idea. The Liechtenstein Law of January 4, 1934, is a good example.

The practice of certain States which refrain from exercising protection in favour of a naturalized person when the latter has in fact, by his prolonged absence, severed his links with what is no longer for him anything but his nominal country, manifests the view of these States that, in order to be capable of being invoked against another State, nationality must correspond with the factual situation. A similar view is manifested in the relevant provisions of the bilateral nationality treaties concluded between the United States of America and other States since 1868, such as those sometimes referred to as the Bancroft Treaties, and in the Pan-American Convention, signed at Rio de Janeiro on August 13, 1906, on the status of naturalized citizens who resume residence in their country of origin.

The character thus recognized on the international level as pertaining to nationality is in no way inconsistent with the fact that international law leaves it to each State to lay down the rules governing the grant of its own nationality. The reason for this is that the diversity of demographic conditions has thus far made it impossible for any general agreement to be reached on the rules relating to nationality, although the latter by its very nature affects international relations. It has been considered that the best way of making such rules accord with the varying demographic conditions in different countries is to leave the fixing of such rules to the competence of each State. On the other hand, a State cannot claim that the rules it has thus laid down are entitled to recognition by another State unless it has acted in conformity with this general aim of making the legal bond of nationality accord with the individual's genuine connection with the State which assumes the defence of its citizens by means of protection as against other States.

The requirement that such a concordance must exist is to be found in the studies carried on in the course of the last thirty years upon the initiative and under the auspices of the League of Nations and the United Nations. It explains the provisions which the Conference for the Codification of International Law, held at The Hague in 1930, inserted in Article I of the Convention relating to the Conflict of Nationality Laws. . . .[393] In the same spirit, Article 5 of the Convention refers to criteria of the individual's genuine connections for the purpose of resolving questions of dual nationality which arise in third States.

According to the practice of States, to arbitral and judicial decisions and to the opinions of writers, nationality is a legal bond having as its basis a social fact of attachment, a genuine connection of existence, interests and sentiments, together with the existence of reciprocal rights and duties. It may be said to constitute the juridical expression of the fact that the individual upon whom it is conferred, either directly by the law or as the result of

---

[392] Ed. Below, App.I.
[393] Ed. Below, p.510.

an act of the authorities, is in fact more closely connected with the population of the State conferring nationality than with that of any other State. Conferred by a State, it only entitles that State to exercise protection *vis-à-vis* another State, if it constitutes a translation into juridical terms of the individual's connection with the State which has made him its national.

Diplomatic protection and protection by means of international juridical proceedings constitute measures for the defence of the rights of the State. ...

Since this is the character which nationality must present when it is invoked to furnish the State which has granted it with a title to the exercise of protection and to the institution of international judicial proceedings, the Court must ascertain whether the nationality granted to Nottebohm by means of naturalization is of this character or, in other words, whether the factual connection between Nottebohm and Liechtenstein in the period preceding, contemporaneous with and following his naturalization appears to be sufficiently close, so preponderant in relation to any connection which may have existed between him and any other State, that it is possible to regard the nationality conferred upon him as real and effective, as the exact juridical expression of a social fact of a connection which existed previously or came into existence thereafter.

Naturalization is not a matter to be taken lightly. To seek and to obtain it is not something that happens frequently, in the life of a human being. It involves his breaking of a bond of allegiance and his establishment of a new bond of allegiance. It may have far-reaching consequences and involve profound changes in the destiny of the individual who obtains it. It concerns him personally, and to consider it only from the point of view of its repercussions with regard to his property would be to misunderstand its profound significance. In order to appraise its international effect, it is impossible to disregard the circumstances in which it was conferred, the serious character which attaches to it, the real and effective, and not merely the verbal preference of the individual seeking it for the country which grants it to him.

At the time of his naturalization does Nottebohm appear to have been more closely attached by his tradition, his establishment, his interests, his activities, his family ties, his intentions for the near future to Liechtenstein than to any other State? ...

The essential facts are as follows:

At the date when he applied for naturalization Nottebohm had been a German national from the time of his birth. He had always retained his connections with members of his family who had remained in Germany and he had always had business connections with that country. His country had been at war for more than a month, and there is nothing to indicate that the application for naturalization then made by Nottebohm was motivated by any desire to dissociate himself from the Government of his country.

He had been settled in Guatemala for 34 years. He had carried on his activities there. It was the main seat of his interests. He returned there shortly after his naturalization, and it remained the centre of his interests and of his business activities. He stayed there until his removal as a result of war measures in 1943. He subsequently attempted to return there, and he now complains of Guatemala's refusal to admit him. There, too, were several members of his family who sought to safeguard his interests.

In contrast, his actual connections with Liechtenstein were extremely tenuous. No settled abode, no prolonged residence in that country at the time of his application for naturalization: the application indicates that he was paying a visit there and confirms the transient character of this visit by its request that the naturalization proceedings should be initiated and concluded without delay. No intention of settling there was shown at that time or realized in the ensuing weeks, months or years—on the contrary, he returned to Guatemala very shortly after his naturalization and showed every intention of remaining there. If Nottebohm went to Liechtenstein in 1946, this was because of the refusal of Guatemala to admit him. No indication is given of the grounds warranting the waiver of the condition of residence, required by the 1934 Nationality Law, which waiver was implicitly granted to him. There is no allegation of any economic interest or of any activities exercised or to be exercised in Liechtenstein and no manifestation of any intention whatsoever to transfer all or some of his interests and business activities to Liechtenstein. It is unnecessary in this connection to attribute much importance to the promise to pay the taxes levied at the time of his naturalization. The only links to be discovered between the Principality and Nottebohm are the short sojourns already referred to and the presence in Vaduz of one of his brothers: but his brother's presence is referred to in his application for naturalization only as a reference to his good conduct. Furthermore, other members of his family have asserted Nottebohm's desire to spend his old age in Guatemala.

These facts clearly establish, on the one hand, the absence of any bond of attachment between Nottebohm and Liechtenstein and, on the other hand, the existence of a long-standing and close connection between him and Guatemala, a link which his naturalization in no way weakened. That naturalization was not based on any real prior connection with Liechtenstein, nor did it in any way alter the manner of life of the person upon whom it was conferred in exceptional circumstances of speed and accommodation. In both respects, it was lacking in the genuineness requisite to an act of such importance, if it is to be entitled to be respected by a State in the position of Guatemala. It was granted without regard to the concept of nationality adopted in international relations.

Naturalization was asked for not so much for the purpose of obtaining a legal recognition of Nottebohm's membership in fact in the population of Liechtenstein, as it was to enable him to substitute for his status as a national of a belligerent State that of a national of a neutral State, with the sole aim of thus coming within the protection of Liechtenstein but not of becoming wedded to its traditions, its interests, its way of life or of assuming the obligations—other than fiscal obligations—and exercising the rights pertaining to the status thus acquired.

Guatemala is under no obligation to recognise a nationality granted in such circumstances. Liechtenstein consequently is not entitled to extend its protection to Nottebohm *vis-à-vis* Guatemala and its claim must, for this reason, be held to be inadmissible. . . .

For these reasons, THE COURT, by eleven votes to three,[394] holds that the claim submitted by the Government of the Principality of Liechtenstein is inadmissible.

Notes

1. Nottebohm had lost his German nationality upon taking that of Liechtenstein. What state could have protected him against Guatemala in accordance with the "genuine connection" requirement insisted upon by the Court? Could Liechtenstein have protected Nottebohm against any state? Could Guatemala ever have protected him?

2. How important do you think it was in the *Nottebohm* case that Nottebohm's nationality was a "nationality of convenience?" Suppose he had been a Liechtenstein national by birth who had emigrated to Guatemala?[395]

3. Should there be a "genuine connection" requirement, or should international law allow a state to protect any of its nationals without question? The Court supported its "genuine connection" requirement largely by reference to practice concerning dual nationality. Might that be a special case? Note that the requirement had an immediate impact upon the rule concerning the nationality of ships in the 1958 High Seas Convention.[396]

4. Article 4, I.L.C. Draft Articles on Diplomatic Protection (below), rejects the genuine connection requirement for natural persons.

I.L.C. DRAFT ARTICLES ON DIPLOMATIC PROTECTION

Report of the 58th Sess. I.L.C. (2006) G.A.O.R. A/61/10, pp. 22 et seq.

Article 4

For the purposes of the diplomatic protection of a natural person, a State of nationality means a State whose nationality that person has acquired, in accordance with the law of that State, by birth, descent, naturalization, succession of States, or in any other manner not inconsistent with international law.

---

[394] The judges in the majority were President Hackworth; Vice-President Badawi; Judges Basdevant, Zoričić, Hsu Mo, Armand-Ugon, Kojevnikov, Sir Muhammad Zafrulla Khan, Moreno Quintana and Cordova; Judge ad hoc Garcia Bauer. Judges Klaestad and Read and Judge ad hoc Guggenheim dissented.

[395] See the *Diallo* case, below, p.525.

[396] See above, p.367.

Commentary

(2)...In 1923 the Permanent Court of International Justice stated in the *Nationality Decrees in Tunis and Morocco* case that:

> "in the present state of international law, questions of nationality are...in principle within the reserved domain".[397]

This principle was confirmed by article 1 of the 1930 Hague Convention on Certain Questions Relating to the Conflict of Nationality Laws:

> "It is for each State to determine under its own law who are its nationals."[398]...

(3) The connecting factors for the conferment of nationality listed in draft article 4...include the connecting factors most commonly employed by States for the grant of nationality: birth (*jus soli*), descent (*just sanguinis*) and naturalization. Marriage to a national is not included in this list as in most circumstances marriage per se is insufficient for the grant of nationality: it requires in addition a period of residence, following which nationality is conferred by naturalization....

(5) Draft article 4 does not require a State to prove an effective or genuine link between itself and its national, along the lines suggested in the *Nottebohm* case, as an additional factor for the exercise of diplomatic protection, even where the national possesses only one nationality....[T]he Commission took the view that there were certain factors that served to limit *Nottebohm* to the facts of the case in question, particularly the fact that the ties between Mr. Nottebohm and Liechtenstein (the Applicant State) were "extremely tenuous" compared with the close ties between Mr. Nottebohm and Guatemala (the Respondent State) for a period of over 34 years, which led the International Court of Justice to repeatedly assert that Liechtenstein was "not entitled to extend its protection to Nottebohm vis-à-vis Guatemala". This suggests that the Court did not intend to expound a general rule[399] applicable to all States but only a relative rule according to which a State in Liechtenstein's position was required to show a genuine link between itself and Mr. Nottebohm in order to permit it to claim on his behalf against Guatemala with whom he had extremely close ties. Moreover,...if the genuine link requirement proposed by *Nottebohm* was strictly applied it would exclude millions of persons from the benefit of diplomatic protection as in today's world of economic globalization and migration there are millions of persons who have moved away from their State of nationality and made their lives in States whose nationality they never acquire or have acquired nationality by birth or descent from States with which they have a tenuous connection.

(6) The final phrase in draft article 4 stresses that the acquisition of nationality must not be inconsistent with international law....Article 1 of the 1930 Hague Convention on Certain Questions Relating to the Conflict of Nationality Law confirmed this...with the proviso "[t]his [state] law shall be recognized by other States insofar as it is consistent with international conventions, international custom and the principles of law generally recognized with regard to nationality". Today, conventions, particularly in the field of human rights, require States to comply with international standards in the granting of nationality. For example, article 9, paragraph 1, of the Convention on the Elimination of All Forms of Discrimination against Women provides that:

> "States parties shall grant women equal rights to men to acquire, change or retain their nationality. They shall ensure in particular that neither marriage to an alien nor change of nationality by the husband during marriage shall automatically change the nationality of the wife, render her stateless or force upon her the nationality of the husband."[400]...

---

[397] *Nationality Decrees issued in Tunis and Morocco (French Zone)*, advisory opinion, P.C.I.J. Reports, Series B, No.4, 1923, at p.24. Ed. See generally Donner, *The Regulation of Nationality in International Law* (2nd edn 1994).

[398] League of Nations, *Treaty Series*, vol.179, p.89. Ed. In force 1937. 20 parties, including the UK.

[399] This interpretation [not a general rule] was placed on the *Nottebohm* case by the Italian–United State Conciliation Commission in the *Flegenheimer* case: I.L.R. vol.25 (1958), p.148.

[400] See also art.20 of the American Convention on Human Rights, United Nations, *Treaty Series*, vol.1144, p.123; art.5(d)(iii) of the International Convention on the Elimination of All Forms of Racial Discrimination, United Nations, *Treaty Series*, vol.660, p.195; and art.1 of the Convention on the Nationality of Married Women.

Article 5

1. A State is entitled to exercise diplomatic protection in respect of a person who was a national of that State continuously from the date of injury to the date of the official presentation of the claim. Continuity is presumed if that nationality existed at both these dates.

2. Notwithstanding paragraph 1, a State may exercise diplomatic protection in respect of a person who is its national at the date of the official presentation of the claim but was not a national at the date of injury, provided that the person had the nationality of a predecessor State or lost his or her previous nationality and acquired, for a reason unrelated to the bringing of the claim, the nationality of the former State in a manner not inconsistent with international law.

3. Diplomatic protection shall not be exercised by the present State of nationality in respect of a person against a former State of nationality of that person for an injury caused when that person was a national of the former State of nationality and not of the present State of nationality.

4. A State is no longer entitled to exercise diplomatic protection in respect of a person who acquires the nationality of the State against which the claim is brought after the date of the official presentation of the claim.

Commentary

(1) Although the continuous nationality rule is well established, it has been subjected to considerable criticism[401] on the ground that it may produce great hardship in cases in which an individual changes his or her nationality for reasons unrelated to the bringing of a diplomatic claim. Suggestions that it be abandoned have been resisted [in these articles] out of fear that this might be abused and lead to "nationality shopping" for the purpose of diplomatic protection....

(2) Paragraph 1 asserts the traditional principle that a State is entitled to exercise diplomatic protection in respect of a person who was its national both at the time of the injury and at the date of the official presentation of the claim. State practice and doctrine are unclear on whether the national must retain the nationality of the claimant State between these two dates, largely because in practice this issue seldom arises....It is, however, incongruous to require that the same nationality be shown both at the date of injury and at the date of the official presentation of the claim without requiring it to continue between these two dates....[I]n an exercise in progressive development of the law, the rule has been drafted to require that the injured person be a national continuously from the date of the injury to the date of the official presentation of the claim....

(3) The first requirement is that the injured national be a national of the claimant State at the date of the injury. The date of injury need not be a precise date but could extend over a period of time if the injury consists of several acts or a continuing act committed over a period of time....

(5) The *dies ad quem* for the exercise of diplomatic protection is the date of the official presentation of the claim. There is, however, support for the view that if the individual should change his nationality between this date and the making of an award or a judgment he ceases to be a national for the purposes of diplomatic protection.[402] In 2003 in *Loewen Group Inc. v. USA*[403] an ICSID arbitral tribunal held that "there must be continuous material identity from the date of the events giving rise to the claim, which date is known as the *dies a quo*, through to the date of the resolution of the claim, which date is known as the *dies ad quem*". On the facts, the Loewen case dealt with the situation in which the person sought to be protected changed nationality after the presentation of the claim to that of the respondent State, in which circumstances a claim for diplomatic protection can clearly not be upheld, as is made clear in draft article 5, paragraph (4). However, the Commission was not prepared to follow the Loewen tribunal in adopting a blanket rule that nationality must be maintained to the date of resolution of the claim.[404] Such a rule could be contrary to the interests of the individual, as many years may pass between the presentation of the claim and its final resolution and it could be unfair to penalize the individual for changing nationality, through marriage or naturalization, during this period. Instead, preference is given to the date of the official presentation of the claim as the *dies ad quem*. This date is significant as it is the

---

[401] See the comment of Judge Sir Gerald Fitzmaurice in the *Barcelona Traction* case, at pp.101–102...

[402] R.Y. Jennings and A.Watts, *Oppenheim's International Law*, ... at p.512. *Eschauzier* claim (*Great Britain v Mexico*) UNRIAA vol.V, p.207.

[403] ICSID Reports, vol.7 (2005), p.442 at para.225.

[404] For criticism of the *Loewen* case, see J.Paulsson, *Denial of Justice in International Law* (New York: Cambridge University Press, 2005), pp.183–184.

date on which the State of nationality shows its clear intention to exercise diplomatic protection—a fact that was hitherto uncertain. Moreover, it is the date on which the admissibility of the claim must be judged....

(13) Paragraph 4 provides that if a person in respect of whom a claim is brought becomes a national of the respondent State after the presentation of the claim, the applicant State loses its right to proceed with the claim as in such a case the respondent State would in effect be required to pay compensation to its own national. There was the situation in *Loewen Group Inc v. USA*...

Article 6

1. Any State of which a dual or multiple national is a national may exercise diplomatic protection in respect of that national against a State of which that person is not a national.

2. Two or more States of nationality may jointly exercise diplomatic protection in respect of a dual or multiple national.

Commentary

(1)...Although the laws of some States do not permit their nationals to be nationals of other States, international law does not prohibit dual or multiple nationality[405]: indeed such nationality was given approval by article 3 of the 1930 Hague Convention on Certain Questions Relating to the Conflict of Nationality Laws, which provides:

> "...a person having two or more nationalities may be regarded as its national by each of the States whose nationality he possesses."...

(2) Paragraph 1 allows a State of nationality to exercise diplomatic protection in respect of its national [against a State of which that person is not a national] even where that person is a national of one or more other States.[406]...

(3) Although there is support for the requirement of a genuine or effective link between the State of nationality and a dual or multiple national in the case of the exercise of diplomatic protection against a State of which the injured person is not a national, in both arbitral decisions[407] and codification endeavours,[408] the weight of authority does not require such a condition. In the *Salem* case an arbitral tribunal held that Egypt could not raise the fact that the injured individual had effective Persian nationality against a claim from the United States, another State of nationality. It stated that:

> "the rule of International Law [is] that in a case of dual nationality a third Power is not entitled to contest the claim of one of the two powers whose national is interested in the case by referring to the nationality of the other power"[409]

This rule has been followed in other cases[410] and has more recently been upheld by the Iran-United States ClaimTribunal.[411] The decision not to require a genuine or effective link in such circumstances accords with reason. Unlike the situation in which one State of nationality claims from another State of nationality in respect of a dual national, there is no conflict over nationality where one State of nationality seeks to protect a dual national against a third State....

---

[405] Ed. See Boll, *Multiple Nationality and International Law* (2007).

[406] Ed. On the protection of dual nationals in extraordinary rendition cases, see Forcese (2006) 17 B.J.I.L. 369.

[407] See the decision of the Yugoslav–Hungarian Mixed Arbitral Tribunal in the *de Born* case, *Annual Digest of Public International Law Cases*, vol.3, 1925–1926, case No.205 of 12 July 1926.

[408] See article 5 of the 1930 Hague Convention on Certain Questions Relating to the Conflict of Nationality Laws;...1960 Harvard Draft Convention on the International Responsibility of States for Injuries to Aliens, article 23(3), in L.B. Sohn and R.R. Baxter, "Responsibility of States for Injuries to the Economic Interests of Aliens", AJIL, vol.55 (1961), p.548;...

[409] Award of 8 June 1932, UNRIAA vol.II, p.1165 at p.1188.

[410] See the decisions of the Italian–United States Conciliation Commission in the *Mergé* claim of 10 June 1955, ILR vol.22 (1955), p.443 and p.456; the *Vereano* claim, decision No.172 of 17 May 1957, ILR vol.24)(1957), pp.464–465; and the *Stankovic* claim of 26 July 1963, ILR vol.40 (1963) p.153 at p.155.

[411] See *Dallal v Iran*, Iran, U.S. C.T.R., vol.3 (1983), p.23

Article 7

A State of nationality may not exercise diplomatic protection in respect of a person against a State of which that person is also a national unless the nationality of the former State is predominant, both at the date of injury and at the date of the official presentation of the claim.

Commentary

. . .

(2) In the past there was strong support for the rule of non-responsibility according to which one State of nationality might not bring a claim in respect of a dual national against other State of nationality. The 1930 Hague Convention on Certain Questions Relating to the Conflict of Nationality Laws declares in article 4 that:

"A State may not afford diplomatic protection to one of its nationals against a State whose nationality such person also possesses."

Later codification proposals adopted a similar approach[412] and there was also support for this position in arbitral awards.[413] In 1949 in its advisory opinion in the case concerning *Reparation for Injuries*, the International Court of Justice described the practice of States not to protect their nationals against another State of nationality as "the ordinary practice".[414]

(3) Even before 1930 there was, however, support in arbitral decisions for another position, namely that the State of dominant or effective nationality might bring proceedings in respect of a national against another State of nationality.[415] This jurisprudence was relied on by the International Court of Justice in another context in the *Nottebohm* case[416] and was given explicit approval by the Italian–United States Conciliation Commission in the *Mergé* claim in 1955. Here the Conciliation Commission stated that:

"The principle, based on the sovereign equality of States, which excludes diplomatic protection in the case of dual nationality, must yield before the principle of effective nationality whenever such nationality is that of the claiming State. But it must not yield when such predominance is not proved, because the first of these two principles is generally recognized and may constitute a criterion of practical application for the elimination of any possible uncertainty."[417]

In its opinion, the Conciliation Commission held that the principle of effective nationality and the concept of dominant nationality were simply two sides of the same coin. The rule thus adopted was applied by the Conciliation Commission in over 50 subsequent cases concerning dual nationals. Relying on these cases, the Iran–United States Claims Tribunal has applied the principle of dominant and effective nationality in a number of cases.[418] . . .

(4) Even though the two concepts are different the authorities use the term "effective" or "dominant" without distinction to describe the required link between the claimant State and its national. . .Draft article 7 does not use either of these words to describe the required link but instead uses the term "predominant" as it conveys the element of relativity and indicates that the individual has stronger ties with one State rather than another. . . .It is moreover the term used by the Italian–United States Conciliation Commission in the *Mergé* claim which may be seen as the starting point for the development of the present customary rule.

---

[412] See art.23(5) of the 1960 Harvard Draft Convention reproduced in AJIL, vol.55 on the International Responsibility of State for Injuries to Aliens, reproduced in *AJIL*, vol.55 (1961), p.548. . .

[413] See *Alexander* case (1898) 3 Moore, *International Arbitrations*, p.2529 (United States–British Claims Commission). . .*Adams and Blackmore* case, decision No.64 of 3 July 1931, UNRIAA vol.V, pp.216–217 (British–Mexican Claims Commission).

[414] *I.C.J. Reports 1949*, p.186.

[415] . . . *Carnevaro* case (Permanent Court of Arbitration, 1912) reported in Scott, *The Hague Court Reports*, vol.1, at p.284. . .*Tellech* case of 25 May 1928 (United States–Austria and Hungary Tripartite Claim Commission) 6 UNRIAA, vol.VI, p.248.

[416] *I.C.J. Reports 1955*, pp.22–23. *Nottebohm* was not concerned with dual nationality but the Court found support for its finding that Nottebohm had no effective link with Liechtenstein in cases dealing with dual nationality. . . .

[417] IRL, vol.22 (1955), p.443 at p.455 (para.V.5). . . .

[418] See, in particular, *Esphahanian v. Bank Tejarat*, Iran-U.S.C.T.R., vol.2 (1983), p.166; case No.A/18, Iran-U.S.C.T.R., vol.5 (1984), p.251. . .

(5) No attempt is made to describe the factors to be taken into account in deciding which nationality is predominant. The authorities indicate that such factors include habitual residence, the amount of time spent in each country of nationality, date of naturalization (i.e., the length of the period spent as a national of the protecting State before the claim arose); place, curricula and language of education; employment and financial interests; place of family life; family ties in each country; participation in social and public life; use of language; taxation, bank account, social security insurance; visits to the other State of nationality; possession and use of passport of the other State; and military service. None of these factors is decisive and the weight attributed to each factor will vary according to the circumstances of each case.

Article 8

1. A State may exercise diplomatic protection in respect of a stateless person who, at the date of injury and at the date of the official presentation of the claim, is lawfully and habitually resident in that State.

2. A State may exercise diplomatic protection in respect of a person who is recognized as a refugee by that State, in accordance with internationally accepted standards, when that person, at the date of injury and at the date of the official presentation of the claim, is lawfully and habitually resident in that State.

3. Paragraph 2 does not apply in respect of an injury caused by an internationally wrongful act of the State of nationality of the refugee.

Commentary

(1)...In 1931 the United States–Mexican Claims Commission in *Dickson Car Wheel Company v. United Mexican States* held that a stateless person could not be the beneficiary of diplomatic protection when it stated:

"A State...does not commit an international delinquency in inflicting an injury upon an individual lacking nationality, and consequently, no State is empowered to intervene or complain on his behalf either before or after the injury."[419]

This dictum no longer reflects the accurate position of international law for both stateless persons and refugees. Contemporary international law reflects a concern for the status of both categories of persons. This is evidenced by such conventions as the Convention on the Reduction of Statelessness of 1961 and the Convention Relating to the Status of Refugees of 1951

(2) Draft article 8 [is] an exercise in progressive development of the law[420]...

(10) Paragraph 3 provides that the State of refuge may not exercise diplomatic protection in respect of a refugee against the State of nationality of the refugee. To have permitted this would have contradicted the basic approach of the present draft articles, according to which nationality is the predominant basis for the exercise of diplomatic protection. The paragraph is also justified on policy grounds. Most refugees have serious complaints about their treatment at the hand of their State of nationality, from which they have fled to avoid persecution. To allow diplomatic protection in such cases would be to open the floodgates for international litigation. Moreover, the fear of demands for such action by refugees might deter States from accepting refugees.

---

[419] UNRIAA, vol.IV, p.669 at p.678.
[420] In *Al Rawi & Others, R (on the Application of) v. Secretary of State for Foreign Affairs* and *Another* [2006] EWHC (Admin) an English court held that draft article 8 was to be considered *lex ferenda* and "not yet part of international law" (para.63).

(3) Protection of Companies and Shareholders

BARCELONA TRACTION, LIGHT AND POWER CO. CASE[421]

Belgium v Spain

ICJ Reports 1970, p.3

The company concerned was established under Canadian law in 1911 in connection with the development of electricity supplies in Spain. In 1948, it was declared bankrupt by a Spanish court and, at about the same time, other steps were taken by Spanish authorities injuring it. Canada intervened on its behalf to begin with but later withdrew. At all relevant times, 88 per cent of the shares in the company were, Belgium claimed, owned by Belgian nationals. Belgium brought this claim in respect of the injury to its nationals who were shareholders resulting from the injury to the company. Spain objected that since the injury was to the company, not the shareholders, Belgium lacked locus standi to bring the claim. In a judgment in 1964,[422] the Court joined this preliminary objection to the merits.

Judgment of the Court

33. When a State admits into its territory foreign investments or foreign nationals, whether natural or juristic persons, it is bound to extend to them the protection of the law and assumes obligations concerning the treatment to be afforded them. These obligations, however, are neither absolute nor unqualified. In particular, an essential distinction should be drawn between the obligations of a State towards the international community as a whole, and those arising *vis-à-vis* another State in the field of diplomatic protection. By their very nature the former are the concern of all States. In view of the importance of the rights involved, all States can be held to have a legal interest in their protection; they are obligations *erga omnes*.

34. Such obligations derive, for example, in contemporary international law, from the outlawing of acts of aggression, and of genocide, as also from the principles and rules concerning basic rights of the human person including protection from slavery and racial discrimination. Some of the corresponding rights of protection have entered into the body of general international law (*Reservations to the Convention on the Prevention and Punishment of the Crime of Genocide, Advisory Opinion, ICJ Reports* 1951, p. 23); others are conferred by international instruments of a universal or quasi-universal character.

35. Obligations the performance of which is the subject of diplomatic protection are not of the same category. It cannot be held, when one such obligation in particular is in question, in a specific case, that all States have a legal interest in its observance. In order to bring a claim in respect of the breach of such an obligation, a State must first establish its right to do so, for the rules on the subject rest on two suppositions:

"The first is that the defendant State had broken an obligation towards the national State in respect of its nationals. The second is that only the party to whom an international obligation is due can bring a claim in respect of its breach." (*Reparation for Injuries Suffered in the Service of the United Nations, Advisory Opinion, ICJ Reports* 1949, pp. 181–182).

In the present case it is therefore essential to establish whether the losses allegedly suffered by Belgian shareholders in Barcelona Traction were the consequence of the violation of obligations of which they were the beneficiaries. In other words: has a right of Belgium been violated on account of its nationals' having suffered infringement of their rights as shareholders in a company not of Belgian nationality?

36. Thus it is the existence or absence of a right, belonging to Belgium and recognized as such by international law, which is decisive for the problem of Belgium's capacity. ...

38. In this field international law is called upon to recognize institutions of municipal law that have an important and extensive role in the international field. This...means...that international law has had to

---

[421] See Briggs (1971) 65 A.J.I.L. 327; Higgins (1971) 11 Virg. J.I.L. 327; Lee (2006) 42 Stanford J.I.L. 237; Lillich (1971) 65 A.J.I.L. 522; Staker (1990) 61 B.Y.I.L. 155.
[422] I.C.J. Rep. 1964, p.6.

recognize the corporate entity as an institution created by States in a domain essentially within their domestic jurisdiction. This in turn requires that, whenever legal issues arise concerning the rights of States with regard to the treatment of companies and shareholders, as to which rights international law has not established its own rules, it has to refer to the relevant rules of municipal law. ...

41. ... The concept and structure of the [limited liability] company are founded on and determined by a firm distinction between the separate entity of the company and that of the shareholder, each with a distinct set of rights. The separation of property rights as between company and shareholder is an important manifestation of this distinction. So long as the company is in existence the shareholder has no right to the corporate assets.

44. Notwithstanding the separate corporate personality, a wrong done to the company frequently causes prejudice to its shareholders. But the mere fact that damage is sustained by both company and shareholder does not imply that both are entitled to claim compensation. ... Thus whenever a shareholder's interests are harmed by an act done to the company, it is to the latter that he must look to institute appropriate action; for although two separate entities may have suffered from the same wrong, it is only one entity whose rights have been infringed. ...

47. The situation is different if the act complained of is aimed at the direct rights of the shareholder as such. It is well known that there are rights which municipal law confers upon the latter distinct from those of the company, including the right to any declared dividend, the right to attend and vote at general meetings, the right to share in the residual assets of the company on liquidation. Whenever one of his direct rights is infringed, the shareholder has an independent right of action. ...

48. The Belgian Government claims that shareholders of Belgian nationality suffered damage in consequence of unlawful acts of the Spanish authorities and, in particular, that the Barcelona Traction shares, though they did not cease to exist, were emptied of all real economic content. It accordingly contends that the shareholders had an independent right to redress, notwithstanding the fact that the acts complained of were directed against the company as such. Thus the legal issue is reducible to the question of whether it is legitimate to identify an attack on company rights, resulting in damage to shareholders, with the violation of their direct rights. ...

50. In turning now to the international legal aspects of the case, the Court must, as already indicated, start from the fact that the present case essentially involves factors derived from municipal law—the distinction and the community between the company and the shareholder—which the Parties, however widely their inter-pretations may differ, each take as the point of departure of their reasoning. If the Court were to decide the case in disregard of the relevant institutions of municipal law it would, without justification, invite serious legal difficulties. It would lose touch with reality, for there are no corresponding institutions of international law to which the Court could resort. Thus the Court has, as indicated, not only to take cognizance of municipal law but also to refer to it. It is to rules generally accepted by municipal legal systems which recognize the limited company whose capital is represented by shares, and not to the municipal law of a particular State, that international law refers. In referring to such rules, the Court cannot modify, still less deform them.

51. On the international plane, the Belgian Government has advanced the proposition that it is inadmissible to deny the shareholder's national State a right of diplomatic protection merely on the ground that another State possesses a corresponding right in respect of the company itself. In strict logic and law this formulation of the Belgian claim to *jus standi* assumes the existence of the very right that requires demonstration. In fact the Belgian Government has repeatedly stressed that there exists no rule of international law which would deny the national State of the shareholders the right of diplomatic protection for the purpose of seeking redress pursuant to unlawful acts committed by another State against the company in which they hold shares. This, by emphasizing the absence of any express denial of the right, conversely implies the admission that there is no rule of international law which expressly confers such a right on the shareholders' national State.

52. International law may not, in some fields, provide specific rules in particular cases. In the concrete situation, the company against which allegedly unlawful acts were directed is expressly vested with a right, whereas no such right is specifically provided for the shareholder in respect of those acts. Thus the position of the company rests on a positive rule of both municipal and international law. As to the shareholder, while he has certain rights expressly provided for him by municipal law ..., appeal can, in the circumstances of the present case, only be made to the silence of international law. Such silence scarcely admits of interpretation in favour of the shareholder.

53. It is quite true, as was recalled in the course of oral argument in the present case, that concurrent claims are not excluded in the case of a person who, having entered the service of an international organization and retained his nationality, enjoys simultaneously the right to be protected by his national State and the right to be protected by the organization to which he belongs. This however is a case of one person in possession of two separate bases of protection, each of which is valid (*Reparation for Injuries Suffered in the Service of the United*

Nations, Advisory Opinion, ICJ Reports 1949, p. 185). There is no analogy between such a situation and that of foreign shareholders in a company which has been the victim of a violation of international law which has caused them damage. ...

55. The Court will now examine other grounds on which it is conceivable that the submission by the Belgian Government of a claim on behalf of shareholders in Barcelona Traction may be justified. ...

The Court then refers to municipal law again and the practice of "lifting the veil" for some purposes to take account of the identity of persons behind the company.

58. In accordance with the principle expounded above, the process of lifting the veil, being an exceptional one admitted by municipal law in respect of an institution of its own making, is equally admissible to play a similar role in international law. It follows that on the international plane also there may in principle be special circumstances which justify the lifting of the veil in the interest of shareholders. ...

64. ... In this connection two particular situations must be studied: the case of the company having ceased to exist and the case of the company's national State lacking capacity to take action on its behalf.

65. As regards the first of these possibilities the Court observes that ... Barcelona Traction has lost all its assets in Spain, and was placed in receivership in Canada, a receiver and manager having been appointed. It is common ground that from the economic viewpoint the company has been entirely paralyzed. ...

66. It cannot however, be contended that the corporate entity of the company has ceased to exist, or that it has lost its capacity to take corporate action. ... It has not become incapable in law of defending its own rights and the interests of the shareholders. In particular, a precarious financial situation cannot be equated with the demise of the corporate entity, which is the hypothesis under consideration: the company's status in law is alone relevant, and not its economic condition, nor even the possibility of its being "practically defunct"—a description on which argument has been based but which lacks all legal precision. Only in the event of the legal demise of the company are the shareholders deprived of the possibility of a remedy available through the company; it is only if they became deprived of all such possibility that an independent right of action for them and their government could arise.

67. In the present case, Barcelona Traction is in receivership in the country of incorporation. Far from implying the demise of the entity or of its rights, this much rather denotes that those rights are preserved for so long as no liquidation has ensued. Though in receivership, the company continues to exist. Moreover, it is a matter of public record that the company's shares were quoted on the stock-market at a recent date.

68. ... The Court is thus not confronted with the first hypothesis contemplated in paragraph 64, and need not pronounce upon it.

69. The Court will now turn to the second possibility, that of the lack of capacity of the company's national State to act on its behalf. The first question which must be asked here is whether Canada—the third apex of the triangular relationship—is, in law, the national State of Barcelona Traction.

70. In allocating corporate entities to States for purposes of diplomatic protection, international law is based, but only to a limited extent, on an analogy with the rules governing the nationality of individuals. The traditional rule attributes the right of diplomatic protection of a corporate entity to the State under the laws of which it is incorporated and in whose territory it has its registered office. These two criteria have been confirmed by long practice and by numerous international instruments. This notwithstanding, further or different links are at times said to be required in order that a right of diplomatic protection should exist. Indeed, it has been the practice of some States to give a company incorporated under their law diplomatic protection solely when it has its seat (*siège social*) or management or centre of control in their territory, or when a majority or a substantial proportion of the shares has been owned by nationals of the State concerned. Only then, it has been held, does there exist between the corporation and the State in question a genuine connection of the kind familiar from other branches of international law. However, in the particular field of the diplomatic protection of corporate entities, no absolute test of the "genuine connection" has found general acceptance. Such tests as have been applied are of a relative nature, and sometimes links with one State have had to be weighed against those with another. In this connection reference has been made to the *Nottebohm* case.[423] ... However, given both the legal and factual aspects of protection in the present case the Court is of the opinion that there can be no analogy with the issues raised or the decision given in that case.

71. In the present case, it is not disputed that the company was incorporated in Canada and has its registered

---

[423] Ed. See above, p.505.

office in that country. The incorporation of the company under the law of Canada was an act of free choice. Not only did the founders of the company seek its corporation under Canadian law but it has remained under that law for a period of over 50 years. It has maintained in Canada its registered office, its accounts and its share registers. Board meetings were held there for many years; it has been listed in the records of the Canadian tax authorities. Thus a close and permanent connection has been established, fortified by the passage of over half a century. This connection is in no way weakened by the fact that the company engaged from the very outset in commercial activities outside Canada, for that was its declared object. Barcelona Traction's links with Canada are thus manifold.

72. Furthermore, the Canadian nationality of the company has received general recognition. Prior to the institution of proceedings before the Court, three other governments apart from that of Canada (those of the United Kingdom, the United States and Belgium) made representations concerning the treatment accorded to Barcelona Traction by the Spanish authorities. The United Kingdom Government intervened on behalf of bondholders and of shareholders. Several representations were also made by the United States Government, but not on behalf of the Barcelona Traction company as such. ...

73. Both Governments acted at certain stages in close co-operation with the Canadian Government. ...

74. As to the Belgian Government, its earlier action was also undertaken in close co-operation with the Canadian Government. The Belgian Government admitted the Canadian character of the company in the course of the present proceedings. It explicity stated that Barcelona Traction was a company of neither Spanish nor Belgian nationality but a Canadian company incorporated in Canada. The Belgian Government has even conceded that it was not concerned with the injury suffered by Barcelona Traction itself, since that was Canada's affair. ...

76. In sum, the record shows that from 1948 onwards the Canadian Government made to the Spanish Government numerous representations which cannot be viewed otherwise than as the exercise of diplomatic protection in respect of the Barcelona Traction company. Therefore this was not a case where diplomatic protection was refused or remained in the sphere of fiction. It is also clear that over the whole period of its diplomatic activity the Canadian Government proceeded in full knowledge of the Belgian attitude and activity.

77. It is true that at a certain point the Canadian Government ceased to act on behalf of Barcelona Traction, for reasons which have not been fully revealed, though a statement made in a letter of July 19, 1955 by the Canadian Secretary of State for External Affairs suggests that it felt the matter should be settled by means of private negotiations.[424] The Canadian Government has nonetheless retained its capacity to exercise diplomatic protection; no legal impediment has prevented it from doing so: no fact has arisen to render this protection impossible. It has discontinued its action of its own free will.

78. The Court would here observe that, within the limits prescribed by international law, a State may exercise diplomatic protection by whatever means and to whatever extent it thinks fit, for it is its own right that the State is asserting. Should the natural or legal persons on whose behalf it is acting consider that their rights are not adequately protected, they have no remedy in international law. All they can do is to resort to municipal law, if means are available, with a view to furthering their cause or obtaining redress. The municipal legislator may lay upon the State an obligation to protect its citizens abroad, and may also confer upon the national a right to demand the performance of that obligation, and clothe the right with corresponding sanctions. However, all these questions remain within the province of municipal law and do not affect the position internationally.

79. The State must be viewed as the sole judge to decide whether its protection will be granted, to what extent it is granted, and when it will cease. It remains in this respect a discretionary power the exercise of which may be determined by considerations of a political or other nature, unrelated to the particular case. Since the claim of the State is not identical with that of the individual or corporate person whose cause is espoused, the State enjoys complete freedom of action. Whatever the reasons for any change of attitude, the fact cannot in itself constitute a justification for the exercise of diplomatic protection by another government, unless there is some independent and otherwise valid ground for that. ...

81. The cessation by the Canadian Government of the diplomatic protection of Barcelona Traction cannot, then, be interpreted to mean that there is no remedy against the Spanish Government for the damage done by the allegedly unlawful acts of the Spanish authorities. ... Therefore there is no substance in the argument that for the Belgian Government to bring a claim before the Court represented the only possibility of obtaining redress for the damage suffered by Barcelona Traction and, through it, by its shareholders. ...

---

[424] Ed. "By late 1951 the Canadian Secretary of State for External Affairs told the Spanish Consul in Canada that 'Canadian interests in this case are so slight that it is of little interest to us'": *Barcelona Traction* case (*Preliminary Objections*), Separate Opinion of Judge Wellington Koo, I.C.J. Rep. 1964, pp.61–62.

83. The Canadian Government's right of protection in respect of the Barcelona Traction company remains unaffected by the present proceedings. The Spanish Government has never challenged the Canadian nationality of the company, either in the diplomatic correspondence with the Canadian Government or before the Court. Moreover it has unreservedly recognized Canada as the national State of Barcelona Traction in both written pleadings and oral statements made in the course of the present proceedings. Consequently, the Court considers that the Spanish Government has not questioned Canada's right to protect the company. . . .

92. Since the general rule on the subject does not entitle the Belgian Government to put forward a claim in the case, the question remains to be considered whether nonetheless, as the Belgian Government has contended during the proceedings, considerations of equity do not require that it be held to possess a right of protection . . . [A] theory has been developed to the effect that the State of the shareholders has a right of diplomatic protection when the State whose responsibility is invoked is the national State of the company. Whatever the validity of this theory may be, it is certainly not applicable to the present case, since Spain is not the national State of Barcelona Traction.

93. On the other hand, the Court considers that, in the field of diplomatic protection as in all other fields of international law, it is necessary that the law be applied reasonably. It has been suggested that if in a given case it is not possible to apply the general rule that the right of diplomatic protection of a company belongs to its national State, considerations of equity might call for the possibility of protection of the shareholders in question by their own national State. This hypothesis does not correspond to the circumstances of the present case.

94. In view, however, of the discretionary nature of diplomatic protection, considerations of equity cannot require more than the possibility for some protector State to intervene, whether it be the national State of the company, by virtue of the general rule mentioned above, or, in a secondary capacity, the national State of the shareholders who claim protection. In this connection, account should also be taken of the practical effects of deducing from considerations of equity any broader right of protection for the national State of the shareholders. It must first of all be observed that it would be difficult on an equitable basis to make distinctions according to any quantitative test: it would seem that the owner of 1 per cent and the owner of 90 per cent of the share-capital should have the same possibility of enjoying the benefit of diplomatic protection. The protector State may, of course, be disinclined to take up the case of a single small shareholder, but it could scarcely be denied the right to do so in the name of equitable considerations. In that field, protection by the national State of the shareholders can hardly be graduated according to the absolute or relative size of the shareholding involved. . . .

96. The Court considers that the adoption of the theory of diplomatic protection of shareholders as such, by opening the door of competing diplomatic claims, could create an atmosphere of confusion and insecurity in international economic relations. The danger would be all the greater inasmuch as the shares of companies whose activity is international are widely scattered and frequently change hands. It might perhaps be claimed that, if the right of protection belonging to the national States of the shareholders were considered as only secondary to that of the national State of the company, there would be less danger of difficulties of the kind contemplated. However, the Court must state that the essence of a secondary right is that it only comes into existence at the time when the original right ceases to exist. As the right of protection vested in the national State of the company cannot be regarded as extinguished because it is not exercised, it is not possible to accept the proposition that in case of its non-exercise the national States of the shareholders have a right of protection secondary to that of the national State of the company. Furthermore, study of factual situations in which this theory might possibly be applied gives rise to the following observations.

97. The situations in which foreign shareholders in a company wish to have recourse to diplomatic protection by their own national State may vary. It may happen that the national State of the company simply refuses to grant it its diplomatic protection, or that it begins to exercise it (as in the present case) but does not pursue its action to the end. It may also happen that the national State of the company and the State which has committed a violation of international law with regard to the company arrive at a settlement of the matter, by agreeing on compensation for the company, but that the foreign shareholders find the compensation insufficient. Now, as a matter of principle, it would be difficult to draw a distinction between these three cases so far as the protection of foreign shareholders by their national State is concerned, since in each case they may have suffered real damage. Furthermore, the national State of the company is perfectly free to decide how far it is appropriate for it to protect the company, and is not bound to make public the reasons for its decision. To reconcile this discretionary power of the company's national State with a right of protection falling to the shareholders' national State would be particularly difficult when the former State has concluded, with the State which has contravened international law with regard to the company, an agreement granting the company compensation which the foreign share-holders find inadequate. If, after such a settlement, the national State of the foreign shareholders could in its turn put forward a claim based on the same facts, this would be likely to introduce into the negotiation of this

kind of agreement a lack of security which would be contrary to the stability which it is the object of international law to establish in international relations.

98. It is quite true, as recalled in paragraph 53, that international law recognizes parallel rights of protection in the case of a person in the service of an international organization. Nor is the possibility excluded of concurrent claims being made on behalf of persons having dual nationality, although in that case lack of a genuine link with one of the two States may be set up against the exercise by that State of the right of protection. It must be observed, however, that in these two types of situation the number of possible protectors is necessarily very small, and their identity normally not difficult to determine. In this respect such cases of dual protection are markedly different from the claims to which recognition of a general right of protection of foreign shareholders by their various national States might give rise.

99. It should also be observed that the promoters of a company whose operations will be international must take into account the fact that States have, with regard to their nationals, a discretionary power to grant diplomatic protection or to refuse it. When establishing a company in a foreign country, its promoters are normally impelled by particular considerations; it is often a question of tax or other advantages offered by the host State. It does not seem to be in any way inequitable that the advantages thus obtained should be balanced by the risks arising from the fact that the protection of the company and hence of its shareholders is thus entrusted to a State other than the national State of the shareholders.

100. In the present case, it is clear from what has been said above that Barcelona Traction was never reduced to a position of impotence such that it could not have approached its national State, Canada, to ask for its diplomatic protection, and that, as far as appeared to the Court, there was nothing to prevent Canada from continuing to grant its diplomatic protection to Barcelona Traction if it had considered that it should do so.

101. For the above reasons, the Court is not of the opinion that, in the particular circumstances of the present case, *jus standi* is conferred on the Belgian Government by considerations of equity. ...

103. Accordingly, the Court rejects the Belgian Government's claim by fifteen votes to one, twelve votes of the majority being based on the reasons set out in the present Judgment.[425]

Notes

1. *The Protection of Companies*.[426] The Barcelona Traction Company continued legally in existence, although it did not trade, until 1980 when it was dissolved under Canadian law. It would seem to have been understood by states before the *Nottebohm* case that they could protect any company having their nationality according to their law. In 1911, for example, when it became known that the Government of Siam, in interpreting a treaty between Siam and the United Kingdom guaranteeing "British subjects" national treatment in respect of land in Siam, was of a mind to treat British companies, to which the treaty undoubtedly extended, differently from other British subjects because non-British interests were incorporating British companies in order to take advantage of its terms, the Foreign Office responded in the following terms: "The Siamese Government could not be permitted to maintain that a company, duly incorporated as British, was really foreign and that His Majesty's Government had no right to protect it."[427] Is this approach supported by the *Barcelona Traction* case? Article 9, ILC Draft Articles, below, p.522, generally follows the approach in the *Barcelona Traction* case.

2. *Protection of Shareholders*.[428] Do you find the reasons given by the Court for rejecting the argument for a secondary power of protection on the part of the national state of shareholders in a foreign company when the national state of the company will not act convincing? Should the case be regarded as indicating one situation in which the general rule of protection in inter-

---

[425] The judges in the majority were President Bustamante y Rivero; Vice-President Koretsky; Judges Sir Gerald Fitzmaurice, Tanaka, Jessup, Morelli, Padilla Nervo, Forster, Gros, Ammoun, Bengzon, Petrén, Lachs and Onyeama; Judge ad hoc Armand-Ugon. The dissenting judge was Judge ad hoc Riphagen. The three judges in the majority who did not concur in the reasoning of the Court were Judges Tanaka, Jessup and Gros.

[426] See Beckett (1931) 17 Trans.Grot.Soc. 175; and Harris (1969) 18 I.C.L.Q. 275.

[427] (1911) 5 B.D.I.L. 510 at 511.

[428] See Jones (1949) 26 B.Y.I.L. 225.

national law, leaving the interests of individuals as a discretionary matter in the hands of their national state, can lead to injustice? The Court suggests in its judgment (para.99) that the promoters of companies should take into account the risk of non-protection as well as considerations such as tax advantage. Is the Court also suggesting that persons thinking of investing in foreign companies should bear in mind the same factor?

In 1925, in the *Romano-Americana* case,[429] the United States sought compensation from the United Kingdom for the destruction in 1916 of the assets in Roumania of a Roumanian subsidiary company of an American parent company. The assets had been destroyed by "the Roumanian authorities with the collaboration of certain British Officers acting under instructions from the British Government"[430] to prevent them coming into the hands of the enemy. In denying responsibility, the United Kingdom argued:

"... it will be found upon examination that the cases in which the right of a Government to intervene on behalf of the shareholders of such a corporation for the purpose of establishing a claim against another Government, has been admitted, are few in number and exhibit certain marked characteristics, none of which are present in the case now under consideration. Cases of this kind fall generally speaking into two cases: (1) where the action of the Government against whom the claim is made has, in law or in fact, put an end to the Company's existence, or by confiscating its property, has compelled it to suspend operations; (2) where by special agreement between the two Governments a right to compensation has been accorded to the shareholders. ... The first class, so far from being an exception to the general rule, is in fact an example of its application; for it is not until a company has ceased to have an active existence or has gone into liquidation that the interest of its shareholders ceases to be merely the right to share in the company's profits and becomes a right to share in its actual surplus assets."[431]

The United States later discontinued its claim against the United Kingdom and took up its case against Roumania, which eventually agreed to pay compensation. Is the British argument consistent with the Court's judgment?[432]

In 1938, in the *Mexican Eagle Co.* case,[433] Mexico expropriated the assets of an oil company registered in Mexico the shares in which were almost entirely foreign owned. When Mexico protested at British intervention on behalf of the substantial British interests in the company, the United Kingdom replied: "If the doctrine were admitted that a government can first make the operation of foreign interests in its territories depend upon their incorporation under local law, and then plead such incorporation as the justification for rejecting foreign diplomatic intervention, it is clear that the means would never be wanting whereby foreign governments could be prevented from exercising their undoubted right under international law to protect the commercial interests of their nationals abroad." Eventually arrangements for the payment of compensation were made. Does the Court's judgment in the *Barcelona Traction* case leave open the possibility that the British argument here would be acceptable to it? See para.92, judgment. Note that several of the judges delivering separate, concurring opinions express the view that a

---

[429] 5 Hackworth 840.
[430] 5 Hackworth p.841.
[431] 5 Hackworth p.843.
[432] Note also that in 1889, in the *Delagoa Bay* case, the UK and the US successfully intervened to protect Anglo-American shareholders in a Portuguese company on the ground that the Portuguese company was "practically defunct": (1888–89) B.F.S.P. 691. Was *this* consistent with the Court's judgment?
[433] Cmd. 5758, p.9.

state could protect its shareholders in a foreign company where the defendant state is the national state of the company.[434]

I.L.C. DRAFT ARTICLES ON DIPLOMATIC PROTECTION

Report of the 28th Sess. I.L.C. (2006), G.A.O.R. A/61/10 pp.22 et seq.

Article 9

For the purposes of the diplomatic protection of a corporation, the State of nationality means the State under whose law the corporation was incorporated. However, when the corporation is controlled by nationals of another State or States and has no substantial business activities in the State of incorporation, and the seat of management and the financial control of the corporation are both located in another State, that State shall be regarded as the State of nationality.

Commentary

. . .

(3) As with natural persons, the granting of nationality to a corporation is "within the reserved domain" of a State. . .[435]. . .But, it is for international law to determine the circumstances in which a State may exercise diplomatic protection on behalf of a corporation or its shareholders. This matter was addressed by the International Court of Justice in *Barcelona Traction* when it stated that international law "attributes the right of diplomatic protection of a corporate entity to the State under the laws of which it is incorporated and in whose territory it has its registered office".[436]. . .As the laws of most States require a company incorporated under its laws to maintain a registered office in its territory, even if this is a mere fiction, incorporation is the most important criterion for the purposes of diplomatic protection. The Court in *Barcelona Traction* was not, however, satisfied with incorporation as the sole criterion for the exercise of diplomatic protection. Although it did not reiterate the requirement of a "genuine connection" as applied in the *Nottebohm* case, and acknowledged that "in the particular field of the diplomatic protection of corporate entities, no absolute test of the 'genuine connection' has found general acceptance,"[437] it suggested that in addition to incorporation and a registered office, there was a need for some "permanent and close connection" between the State exercising diplomatic protection and the corporation.[438]. . .

(4) Draft article 9 accepts the basic premise of *Barcelona Traction* that it is incorporation that confers nationality on a corporation for the purposes of diplomatic protection. However, it provides an exception in a particular situation where there is no other significant link or connection between the State of incorporation and the corporation itself, and where certain significant connections exist with another State, in which case that other State is to be regarded as the State of nationality for the purpose of diplomatic protection. Policy and fairness dictate such a solution. It is wrong to place the sole and exclusive right to exercise diplomatic protection in a State with which the corporation has the most tenuous connection as in practice such a State will seldom be prepared to protect such a corporation. . . .

(6) In *Barcelona Traction* the International Court of Justice warned that the granting of the right of diplomatic protection to the States of nationality of shareholders might result in a multiplicity of actions which "could create an atmosphere of confusion and insecurity in international economic relations".[439] The same confusion might result from the granting of the right to exercise diplomatic protection to several States with which a corporation

---

[434] Judge Sir Gerald Fitzmaurice, I.C.J. Rep. 1970, p.73; Judge Tanaka, ibid., p.134; and Judge Jessup, ibid. at p.192. Judge Sir Gerald Fitzmaurice draws no distinction between enforced and voluntary local incorporations; Judge Jessup notes that the equities are particularly strong in the former case. Judge Tanaka does not refer to the point. Certain other judges were strongly opposed to an exception: see the Commentary to art.9, I.L.C. Draft Articles, below.

[435] *Barcelona Traction* case, at pp.33–34, para.38.

[436] *Ibid.*, p.42, para.70.

[437] *I.C.J. Reports 1970*, p.42, para.70.

[438] *Ibid.*, p.42, para.71.

[439] *Ibid.*, p.49, para.96.

enjoys a link or connection. Draft article 9 does not allow such multiple actions. The State of nationality with the right to exercise diplomatic protection is either the State of incorporation or, if the required conditions are met, the State of the seat of management and financial control of the corporation. If the seat of management and the place of financial control are located in different States, the State of incorporation remains the State entitled to exercise diplomatic protection.

Article 10

1. A State is entitled to exercise diplomatic protection in respect of a corporation that was a national of that State, or its predecessor State, continuously from the date of injury to the date of the official presentation of the claim. Continuity is presumed if that nationality existed at both these dates.

2. A State is no longer entitled to exercise diplomatic protection in respect of a corporation that acquires the nationality of the State against which the claim is brought after the presentation of the claim.

3. Notwithstanding paragraph 1, a State continues to be entitled to exercise diplomatic protection in respect of a corporation which was its national at the date of injury and which, as the result of the injury, has ceased to exist according to the law of the State of incorporation.

Commentary

(1) The general principles relating to the requirement of continuous nationality are discussed in the commentary to draft article 5. In practice problems of continuous nationality arise less in the case of corporations than with natural persons....

(6) Difficulties arise in respect of the exercise of diplomatic protection of a corporation that has ceased to exist according to the law of the State in which it was incorporated and of which it was a national. If one takes the position that the State of nationality of such a corporation may not bring a claim as the corporation no longer exists at the time of presentation of the claim, then no State may exercise diplomatic protection in respect of an injury to the corporation....This matter troubled several judges in the *Barcelona Traction* case[440] and it has troubled certain courts and arbitral tribunals[441] and scholars.[442] Paragraph 3 adopts a pragmatic approach and allows the State of nationality of a corporation to exercise diplomatic protection in respect of an injury suffered by the corporation when it was its national and has ceased to exist—and therefore ceased to be its national—as a result of the injury....

Article 11

The State of nationality of shareholders in a corporation shall not be entitled to exercise diplomatic protection in respect of such shareholders in the case of an injury to the corporation unless:

(a) The corporation has ceased to exist according to the law of the State of incorporation for a reason unrelated to the injury; or

(b) The corporation had, at the date of injury, the nationality of the State alleged to be responsible for causing the injury, and incorporation in that State was required by it as a precondition for doing business there.

Commentary

...

(3) The Court in *Barcelona Traction* accepted that the State(s) of nationality of shareholders might exercise diplomatic protection on their behalf in two situations: first, where the company had ceased to exist in its place of incorporation[443]—which was not the case with the *Barcelona Traction*; secondly, where the State of incorporation was itself responsible for inflicting injury on the company and the foreign shareholders' sole means of protection

---

[440] Judges Jessup, *I.C.J. Reports 1970*, at p.193, Gros, *ibid.*, at p.277, and Fitzmaurice, *ibid.*, at pp.101–102, and Judge *ad hoc* Riphagen, *ibid.*, at p.345.

[441] See the *Kunhardt and co.*, case (Opinions in the American–Venezuelan Commission of 1903), UNRIAA, vol.XII, p.171,...

[442] ...Beckett, "Diplomatic Claims in Respect of Injuries to Companies", *Transactions of the Grotus Society*, vol.17 (1932), p.158 at p.191;...

[443] [I.C.J. Reports 1970] pp.40–41, paras.65–68.

on the international level was through their State(s) of nationlity[444]—which was not the case with *Barcelona Traction*. These two exceptions, which were not thoroughly examined by the Court in *Barcelona Traction* because they were not relevant to the case, are recognized in paragraphs (a) and (b) of draft article 11....

(5) Draft article 11, paragraph (a) requires that the corporation shall have "ceased to exist" before the State of nationality of the shareholders shall be entitled to intervene on their behalf. Before the *Barcelona Traction* case the weight of authority favoured a less stringent test, one that permitted intervention on behalf of shareholders when the company was "practically defunct".[445] The Court in *Barcelona Traction*, however, set a higher threshold for determining the demise of a company....The Court stated: "Only in the event of the legal demise of the company are the shareholders deprived of the possibility of a remedy available through the company..."[446] Subsequent support has been given to this test by the European Court of Human Rights.[447]

(8) Draft article 11, paragraph (b), gives effect to the exception allowing the State of nationality of the shareholders in a corporation to exercise diplomatic protection on their behalf where the State of incorporation is itself responsible for inflicting injury on the corporation. The exception is limited to cases where incorporation was required by the State inflicting the injury on the corporation as a precondition for doing business there.

(9) There is support for such an exception in State practice, arbitral awards[448] and doctrine. Significantly the strongest support for intervention on the part of the State of nationality of the shareholders comes from three claims in which the injured corporation had been *compelled* to incorporate in the wrongdoing State: *Delagoa Bay Railway, Mexican Eagle* and *El Triunfo....*

(10) In *Barcelona Traction*, Spain, the respondent State, was not the State of nationality of the injured company. Consequently, the exception under discussion was not before the Court. Nevertheless, the Court did make passing reference to this exception [*Barcelona Traction*, para.92, above, p.515]....Judges Fitzmaurice,[449] Tanaka[450] and Jessup[451] expressed full support in their separate opinions in *Barcelona Traction* for the right of the State of nationality of the shareholders to intervene when the company was injured by the State of incorporation.[452]...Judges Padilla Nervo,[453] Morelli[454] amd Ammoun,[455] on the other hand, were vigorously opposed to the exception.

(11) Developments relating to the proposed exception in the post-*Barcelona Traction* period have occurred mainly in the context of treaties. Nevertheless they do indicate support for the notion that the shareholders of a company may intervene against the State of incorporation of the company when it has been responsible for causing injury to the company.[456]...

(12)...In these circumstances it would be possible to sustain a general exception on the basis of judicial opinion. However, draft article 11, paragraph (b), does not go this far....It limits the exception to the situation in which the corporation had, <u>at the date of the injury</u> (a further restrictive feature), the nationality of the State alleged to be responsible for causing the injury and incorporation in that State was required by it as a pre-

---

[444] *Ibid.*, p.48, para.92.

[445] *Delagoa Bay Railway Co.* case, B.J. Moore, *Digest of International Law*, vol.VI (1906), p.648; *El Triunfo* claim; B.J. Moore, *Digest of International Law*, vol.VI (1906), p.649; *Baasch & Romer* case, Neherlands–Venezuelan Mixed Coimmission, 28 February 1903, UNRIAA, vol.X,p.713 at p.723.

[446] [I.C.J. Reports 1970, p.41, para.66]..., see also the separate opinions of Judges Nervo, *ibid.*, p.256 and Ammoun, *ibid.*, pp,319–320.

[447] *Agrotexim* case, ECHR., *Series A* (1995), No.330-A, p.25, para.68.

[448] *Delagoa Bay Railway Company; Mexican Eagle (El Aguila)*, M. Whiteman, *Digest of International Law*, vol.VIII, pp.1272–1274; *Romano–Americano*, Hackworth, *Digest of International Law*, vol.V, p.841; *El Triunfo* award of 8 May 1902, UNRIAA, vol.XV, p.467...

[449] [I.C.J. Reports 1970]...pp.72–75.

[450] *Ibid.*, p.134.

[451] *Ibid.*, pp.191–193.

[452] Judge Wellington Koo likewise supported this position in the *Case concerning the Barcelona Traction, Light and Power Company Limited, Preliminary Objections, I.C.J. Reports 1964*, p.58, para.20.

[453] *Ibid;*, pp.257–259.

[454] *Ibid.*, pp.240–241.

[455] *Ibid.*, p.318.

[456] See *SEDCO Inc. v. National Iranian Oil Company and the Islamic Republic of Iran* case No.129, of 24 October 1985, ILR, vol.84, pp.484, 496 (interpreting article VII(2) of the Algiers Claims Settlement Declaration); *Liberian Eastern Timber Corporation (LETCO) v. The Government of the Republic of Liberia* ICSID Reports, vol.2 (1994), p.346 (interpreting art.25 of the Convention on the Settlement of Investment Disputes between States and Nationals of Other States, United Nations, *Treaty Series*, vol.575, p.159). Ed. The Commentary also refers to the *ELSI* case, I.C.J. Rep. 1989, p.14. But see now the *Diallo* case, below, p.525.

condition for doing business there. It is not necessary that the law of that State require incorporation. Other forms of compulsion might also result in a corporation being "required" to incorporate in that State.

Article 12

To the extent that an internationally wrongful act of a State causes direct injury to the rights of shareholders as such, as distinct from those of the corporation itself, the State of nationality of any such shareholders is entitled to exercise diplomatic protection in respect of its nationals.

Commentary

(1) That shareholders qualify for diplomatic protection when their own rights are affected was recognized by the Court in *Barcelona Traction*[457]...

(3) Draft article 12 makes no attempt to provide an exhaustive list of the rights of shareholders as distinct from those of the corporation itself. In *Barcelona Traction* the International Court mentioned the most obvious rights of shareholders—the right to a declared dividend, the right to attend and vote at general meetings and the right to share in the residual assets of the company on liquidation—but made it clear that this list is not exhaustive....That draft article 12 is to be interpreted restrictively is emphasized by the phrases "the rights of the shareholders as such" and rights "as distinct from those of the corporation itself".

DIALLO CASE (PRELIMINARY OBJECTIONS)[458]

Guinea v Democratic Republic of the Congo (2007)

I.C.J. Reports 2007

Mr Diallo was a national of Guinea who had settled in the DRC (then Zaire) in 1964, aged 17, and had remained resident there ever since, engaging in commercial activities through his two companies, Africom-Zaire and Africontainers-Zaire, both of which were incorporated under DRC law and had DRC nationality under that law. He was arrested in 1995 and detained prior to his deportation two months or so later in 1996 (to Guinea) on "public order" grounds. Acting by way of diplomatic protection of a national, Guinea brought this case under the "optional clause" (both states had made declaration under art.36(2), Statute of the Court), claiming that the arrest, detention and deportation of Mr Diallo were the "culmination of a DRC policy to prevent him from recovering debts owing to his companies" and were contrary to the principle that aliens should be treated in accordance with a "minimum standard of civilization". Guinea's claims concerned the DRC's treatment of (i) Mr Diallo as an individual and as an *associé* of the two companies and (ii) his companies. In this judgment, the Court ruled, inter alia, on the preliminary objection as to admissibility raised by the DRC to the effect that Guinea lacked standing to exercise diplomatic protection in the case.

Judgment of the Court

34. The Court will first address the question of the admissibility of Guinea's Application in so far as it concerns protection of Mr. Diallo's rights as an individual....

39....Owing to the substantive development of international law over recent decades in respect of the rights it accords to individuals, the scope *ratione materiae* of diplomatic protection, originally limited to alleged violations of the minimum standard of treatment of aliens, has subsequently widened to include, inter alia, internationally guaranteed human rights.

40. In the present case Guinea seeks to exercise its diplomatic protection on behalf of Mr. Diallo in respect of the DRC's alleged violation of his rights as a result of his arrest, detention and expulsion, that violation allegedly constituting an internationally wrongful act by the DRC giving rise to its responsibility. It therefore falls to the Court to ascertain whether the Applicant has met the requirements for the exercise of diplomatic protection, that is to say whether Mr. Diallo is a national of Guinea...

---

[457] Ed. Paragraph 47, above, p.516. See also the *Diallo* case, below.
[458] See Knight and O'Brien (2008) 9 M.J.I.L. 40; Okowa (2008) 57 I.C.L.Q. 219; and Vermeer-Kunzli (2007) 20 L.J.I.L. 941.

41. ... it is not disputed by the DRC that Mr. Diallo's sole nationality is that of Guinea and that he has continuously held that nationality from the date of the alleged injury to the date the proceedings were initiated.

49. The Court now turns to the question of the admissibility of Guinea's Application in so far as it concerns protection of Mr. Diallo's rights as *associé*[459] of the two companies Africom-Zaire and Africontainers-Zaire....

60....the *Barcelona Traction* [case] ...involved a public limited company whose capital was represented by shares. The present case concerns SPRLs who capital is composed of *parts sociales*....

61. As the Court recalled in the *Barcelona Traction* case, "[t]here is...no need to investigate the many different forms of legal entity provided for by the municipal laws of States" (*I.C.J. Reports 1970*, p.34, para.40). What matters, from the point of view of international law, is to determine whether or not these have a legal personality independent of their members. Conferring independent corporate personality on a company implies granting it rights over its own property, rights which it alone is capable of protecting. As a result, only the State of nationality may exercise diplomatic protection on behalf of the company when its rights are injured by a wrongful act of another State. In determining whether a company possesses independent and distinct legal personality, international law looks to the rules of the relevant domestic law....

63. Congolese law accords and SPRL independent legal personality distinct from that of its *associés*, particularly in that the property of the *associé* is completely separate from that of the company, and in that the *associés* are responsible for the debts of the company only to the extent of the resources they have subscribed. Consequently, the company's debts receivable from and owing to third parties relate to its respective rights and obligations. As the Court pointed out in the *Barcelona Traction* case: "So long as the company is in existence the shareholder has no right to the corporate assets." (*I.C.J. Reports 1970*, p.34, para.41.) This remains the fundamental rule in this respect, whether for a SPRL or for a public limited company.

64. The exercise by a State of diplomatic protection on behalf of a natural or legal person, who is *associé* or shareholder, having its nationality, seeks to engage the responsibility of another State for an injury caused to that person by an internationally wrongful act committed by that State. Ultimately, this is no more than the diplomatic protection of a natural or legal person as defined by Article 1 of the ILC draft Articles; what amounts to the internationally wrongful act, in the case of *associés* or shareholders, is the violation by the respondent State of their direct rights in relation to a legal person, direct rights that are defined by the domestic law of that State, as accepted by both Parties, moreover. On this basis, diplomatic protection of the direct rights of *associés* of a SPRL or shareholders of a public limited company is not to be regarded as an exception to the general legal régime of diplomatic protection for natural or legal persons, as derived from customary international law.

65. ... the Court finds that Guinea does indeed have standing in this case in so far as its action involves a person of its nationality, Mr. Daiallo, and is directed against the allegedly unlawful acts of the DRC which are said to have infringed his rights, particularly his direct rights as *associé* of the two companies ...

76. The Court will now consider the question of the admissibility of Guinea's Application as it relates to the exercise of diplomatic protection with respect of Mr. Diallo "by substitution" for Africom-Zaire and Africontainers-Zaire and in defence of their rights....

82....Guinea contends that, in the *Barcelona Traction* case, the Court referred, in a dictum, to the possibility of an exception, founded on reasons of equity, to the general rule of the protection of a company by its national State, "when the State whose responsibility is invoked is the national State of the company". In this connection, it quotes the following passage from the Judgment,...:

"...if in a given case it is not possible to apply the general rule that the right of diplomatic protection of a company belongs to its national State, consideration of equity might call for the possibility of protection of the shareholders in question by their own national State." (*I.C.J. Reports 1970*, p.48, para.93.)

... Guinea recognizes that the Court did not definitively settle the question of the existence of diplomatic protection by substitution in the *Barcelona Traction* case. It nevertheless considers that the text of the Judgment, read in the light of the opinions of the Members of the Court appended to it, leads one "to believe that a majority of the Judges regarded the exception as established in law"....

87. Since its dictum in the *Barcelona Traction case* (...para.93)..., the Court has not had occasion to rule on whether, in international law, there is indeed an exception to the general rule "that the right of diplomatic protection of a company belongs to its national State" (...para.93), which allows for protection of the shareholders by their own national State "by substitution", and on the reach of any such exception. It is true that in the

---

[459] Ed. Under DRC law, the two companies were not public listed companies, but SPRLs, in which shares (*parts sociales*) were not freely transferrable and were held by shareholders known as *associés*.

case concerning *Elettronica Sicula S.p.A. (ELSI) (United States of America v. Italy)*,[460] the Chamber of the Court allowed a claim by the United States of America on behalf of two United States corporation (who held 100 per cent of the shares in an Italian company), in relation to alleged acts by the Italian authorities injuring the rights of the latter company. However, in doing so, the Chamber based itself not on customary international law but on a Treaty of Friendship, Commerce and Navigation between the two countries directly granting to their nationals, corporations and associations certain rights in relation to their participation in corporations and associations having the nationality of the other State....

88. The Court is bound to note, that in contemporary international law, the protection of the rights of companies and the rights of their shareholders, and the settlement of the associated disputes, are essentially governed by bilateral or multilateral agreements for the protection of foreign investments, such as the treaties for the promotion and protection of foreign investments, and the Washington Convention of 18 March 1965 on the Settlement of Investment Disputes between States and Nationals of Other States,[461] which created an International Centre for Settlement of Investment Disputes (ICSID), and also by contracts between State and foreign investors. In that context, the role of diplomatic protection somewhat faded, as in practice recourse is only made to it in rare cases where treaty régimes do not exist or have proved inoperative. It is in this particular and relatively limited context that the question of protection by substitution might be raised. The theory of protection by substitution seeks indeed to offer protection to the foreign shareholders of a company who could not rely on the benefit of an international treaty and to whom no other remedy is available, the allegedly unlawful acts having been committed against the company by the State of its nationality. Protection by "substitution" would therefore appear to constitute the very last resort for the protection of foreign investments.

89. The Court, having carefully examined State practice and decisions of international courts and tribunals in respect of diplomatic protection of *associé* and shareholders, is of the opinion that these do not reveal—at least at the present time—an exception in customary international law allowing for protection by substitution, such as is relied on by Guinea.

90. The fact invoked by Guinea that various international agreements, such as agreements for the promotion and protection of foreign investments and the Washington Convention, have established special legal régimes governing investment protection, or that provisions in this regard are commonly included in contracts entered into directly between States and foreign investors, is not sufficient to show that there has been a change in the customary rules of diplomatic protection; it could equally show the contrary. The arbitrations relied on by Guinea are also special cases, whether based on specific international agreements between two or more States, including the one responsible for the allegedly unlawful acts regarding the companies concerned (see, for example, the special agreement concluded between the American, British and Portuguese Governments in the *Delagoa* case[462] or the one concluded between El Salvador and the United States of America in the *Salvador Commercial Company* case[463]) or based on agreements concluded directly between a company and the State allegedly responsible for the prejudice to it (see, for example, the *Biloune v. Ghana Investment Centre* case[464]).

91. It is a separate question whether customary international law contains a more limited rule of protection by substitution, such as that set out by the ILC in its draft Articles on Diplomatic Protection, which would apply only where a company's incorporation in the State having committed the alleged violation of international law "was required by it as a precondition for doing business there" (Article 11, paragraph *(b)*).

92. However, this very special case does not seem to correspond to the one the Court is dealing with here....it has not satisfactorily been established before the Court that...incorporation [of the two companies] in that country, as legal entities of Congolese nationality, would have been required of their founders to enable the founders to operate in the economic sectors concerned.

93. The Court concludes on the facts before it that the companies, Africom-Zaire and Africontainers-Zaire, were not incorporated in such a way that they would fall within the scope of protection by substitution in the sense of Article 11, paragraph *(b)*, of the ILC draft Articles on Diplomatic Protection referred to by Guinea. Therefore, the question of whether or not this paragraph of Article 11 reflects customary international law does not arise in this case.

94. In view of the foregoing, the Court cannot accept Guinea's claim to exercise diplomatic protection by substitution....

---

[460] Ed. I.C.J. Rep. 1989, p.15.
[461] Ed. See above, p.503.
[462] Ed. See above, n.432.
[463] Ed. (1902 15 R.I.A.A. 467.
[464] Ed. (1993) 95 I.L.R. 207.

The Court declared that the application was admissible insofar as it concerned the protection of Mr Diallo's (i) rights as an individual (unanimous ruling) and (ii) as an *associé* of the two companies (by 14 votes to one). It declared the application to be inadmissible, by 14 votes to one, insofar as it concerned Mr Diallo's protection in respect of alleged violations of rights of the two companies.

Notes

1. Insofar as Guinea was acting to protection Mr Diallo as an individual, it is noticeable that, despite the fact that he had made the DRC his place of residence and business activities for the whole of his adult life, the Court does not refer to the "genuine connection" requirement in the *Nottebohm* case, when holding (see para.41) that Guinea may protect him as his national state against the DRC, which supports the view that it is a requirement that has limited application, just to exceptional factual situations such as those in *Nottebohm* case.[465] Cf. the approach in art.4, I.L.C. Draft Articles, above, p.509.

2. The case contains a clear ruling on the question left open in the *Barcelona Traction* case (para.93), concerning the protection of shareholders in existing companies. The Court held in the *Diallo* case that there is no general exception to the general rule governing the protection of companies by which the national state of a shareholder may offer that shareholder protection where, as on the facts of the *Diallo* case, the national state of an existing company is the state against which protection is sought (para.89). The question whether the more limited exception suggested in art.11 (b), I.L.C. Draft Articles (below, p.523) is custom was left open (para.93). Judge ad hoc Mahiou suggested in his declaration that, although there may not have been a legal requirement under DRC law, in practice Mr Diallo had to incorporate his companies in the DRC in order to do business there. Does the exception in art.11(c) cover this situation? Should it?

3. Would Mr Diallo or his national state have had an international remedy available in his case under international human rights law (e.g. the ICCPR or the African Charter on Human and Peoples' Rights (see below, Ch.9) as well as under the law of state responsibility?

---

iii. Exhaustion of Local Remedies[466]

I.L.C. DRAFT ARTICLES ON DIPLOMATIC PROTECTION

Report of the 58th Sess.I.L.C. (2006),G.A.O.R., A/61/10, pp.22 et seq.

Article 14

1. A State may not present an international claim in respect of an injury to a national or other person referred to in draft article 8 before the injured person has, subject to draft article 15, exhausted all local remedies.

2. "Local remedies" means legal remedies which are open to the injured person before the judicial or administrative courts or bodies, whether ordinary or special, of the State alleged to be responsible for causing the injury.

3. Local remedies shall be exhausted where an international claim, or request for a declaratory judgment related to the claim, is brought preponderantly on the basis of an injury to a national or other person referred to in draft article 8.

---

[465] The ICJ noted, however, para.41, that the DRC had not disputed Guinea's right to protect its national.
[466] See Amerasinghe, *Local Remedies in International Law* (2nd edn., 2004); Law, *The Local Remedies Rule in International Law* (1961); Trindade, *The Application of the Rule of Exhaustion of Local Remedies in International Law* (1983).

Commentary

(1)...This rule was recognized by the International Court of Justice in the *Interhandel* case as "a well-established rule of customary international law"[467] and by a Chamber of the International Court in the *Elettronica Sicula (ELSI)* case as "an important principle of customary international law".[468] The exhaustion of local remedies rule ensures that "the State where the violation occurred should have an opportunity to redress it by its own means, within the framework of its own domestic system".[469]...

(4)...In the first instance it is clear that the foreign national must exhaust all the available judicial remedies provided for in the municipal law of the respondent State. If the municipal law in question permits an appeal in the circumstances of the case to the highest court, such an appeal must be brought in order to secure a final decision in the matter.[470] Even if there is no appeal as of right to a higher court, but such a court has a discretion to grant leave to appeal, the foreign national must still apply for leave to appeal to that court.[471] Courts in this connection include both ordinary and special courts since "the crucial question is not the ordinary or extraordinary character of a legal remedy but whether it gives the possibility of an effective and sufficient means of redress".[472]

(5) Administrative remedies must also be exhausted. The injured alien is, however, only required to exhaust such remedies which may result in a binding decision. He is not required to approach the executive for relief in the exercise of its discretionary powers. Local remedies do not include remedies whose "purpose is to obtain a favour and not to vindicate a right"[473] nor do they include remedies of grace[474] unless they constitute an essential prerequisite for the admissibility of subsequent contentious proceedings. Requests for clemency and resort to an ombudsman generally fall into this category.

(6)...the foreign litigant must raise the basic arguments he intends to raise in international proceedings in the municipal proceedings. In the *ELSI* case the Chamber of the International Court of Justice stated that:[475]

"for an international claim to be admissible, it is sufficient if the essence of the claim has been brought before the competent tribunals and pursued as far as permitted by local law and procedure, and without success".[476]

This test is preferable to the stricter test enunciated in the *Finnish Ships Arbitration* that:

"all the contentions of fact and propositions of law which are brought forward by the claimant Government...must have been investigated and adjudicated upon by the municipal courts".[477]...

(9) Paragraph 2 provides that the exhaustion of local remedies rule applies only to cases in which the claimant State has been injured "indirectly", that is, through its national. It does not apply where the claimant State is directly injured by the wrongful act of another State, as here the State has a distinct reason of its own for bringing an international claim.

(10) In practice it is difficult to decide whether the claim is "direct" or "indirect" where it is "mixed", in the sense that it contains elements of both injury to the State and injury to the nationals of the State. Many disputes before the International Court of Justice have presented the phenomenon of the mixed claim. In the *Hostages* case,[478]

---

[467] *Interhandel* case (*Switzerland v. United States of America*) Preliminary objections, *I.C.J. Reports 1959*, p.6 at p.27.

[468] *I.C.J. Reports 1989*, p.15 at p.42, para.50.

[469] *Interhandel* case, at p.27.

[470] Ed. See the *Ambatielos* case, 12 R.I.A.A. 83; (1956) 23 I.L.R. 306 (non-exhaustion for failure to appeal to House of Lords).

[471] This would include the *certiorari* process before the United States Supreme Court.

[472] B. Schouw Nielsen v. Denmark, Application No.343/57 (European Commission of Human Rights) (1958–1959), *Yearbook of the European Convention on Human Rights*, vol.2, p.412 at p.438...

[473] *De Becker v. Belgium*, Application No.214/56, 1958–1959, *Yearbook of the European Convention on Human Rights*, vol.2, p.214 at 238.

[474] Claim of Finnish Shipowners against Great Britain in respect of the Use of Certain Finnish Vessels During the War ("*Finnish Ships Arbitration*") 1934, UNRIAA, vol.III, p.1479.

[475] See *Avena and Other Mexican Nationals (Mexico v. United States of America*, at paras.135–143.

[476] *I.C.J. Reports 1989*, p.15 at para.59.

[477] UNRIAA, vol.III, at p.1502. Ed. See Adler (1990) 39 I.C.L.Q. and Mann (1992) 86 A.J.I.L. 92. Local remedies must also be used effectively: *Ambatielos* case 12 R.I.A.A. 83; (1956) 23 I.R.L. 306 (non-exhaustion for failure to call a key witness).

[478] *Case concerning United States Diplomatic and Consular Staff in Tehran (United States of America v. Iran*), Judgment, *I.C.J. Reports 1980*, p.3.

there was a direct violation on the part of the Islamic Republic of Iran of the duty it owed to the United State of America to protect its diplomats and consuls, but at the same time there was injury to the person of the nationals (diplomats and consuls) held hostage; and in the *Interhandel* case, there were claims brought by Switzerland relating to a direct wrong to itself arising out of breach of a treaty and to an indirect wrong resulting from an injury to a national corporation. In the *Hostages* case the Court treated the claim as a direct violation of international law; and in the *Interhandel* case the Court found that the claim was preponderantly indirect and that *Interhandel* had failed to exhaust local remedies. In the *Arrest Warrant of 11 August 2000* case there was a direct injury to the Democratic Republic of the Congo (DRC) and its national (the Foreign Minister) but the Court held that the claim was not brought within the context of the protection of a national so it was not necessary for the DRC to exhaust local remedies.[479] In the *Avena* case Mexico sought to protect its nationals on death row in the United States through the medium of the Vienna Convention on Consular Relations, arguing that it had "itself suffered, directly and through its nationals" as a result of the United States' failure to grant consular access to its nationals under article 36(1) of the Convention. The Court upheld this argument because of the "interdependence of the rights of the State and individual rights".[480]

(11) In the case of a mixed claim it is incumbent upon the tribunal to examine the different elements of the claim and to decide whether the direct or indirect element is preponderant. In the *ELSI* case a Chamber of the International Court of Justice rejected the argument of the United States that part of its claim was premised on the violation of a treaty and that it was therefore unnecessary to exhaust local remedies, holding that:

> "the Chamber has no doubt that the matter which colours and pervades the United States claim as a whole, is the alleged damage to Raytheon and Machlett [United States corporations]".[481]

Closely related to the preponderance test is the *sine qua non* or "but for" test, which asks whether the claim comprising elements of both direct and indirect injury would have been brought were it not for the claim on behalf of the injured national. If this question is answered negatively, the claim is an indirect one and local remedies must be exhausted. There is, however, little to distinguish the preponderance test from the "but for" test. If the claim is preponderantly based on injury to a national this is evidence of the fact that the claim would not have been brought but for the injury to the national. In these circumstances one test only is provided for in paragraph 3, that of preponderance....

Article 15

Local remedies do not need to be exhausted where:

(a) There are no reasonably available local remedies to provide effective redress, or the local remedies provide no reasonable possibility of such redress;

(b) There is undue delay in the remedial process which is attributable to the State alleged to be responsible;

(c) There was no relevant connection between the injured person and the State alleged to be responsible at the date of injury;

(d) The injured person is manifestly precluded from pursuing local remedies; or

(e) The State alleged to be responsible has waived the requirement that local remedies be exhausted.

Commentary

...

(2) Paragraph (a) deals with the exception to the exhaustion of local remedies rule sometimes described, in broad terms, as the "futility" or "ineffectiveness" exception. Three options require consideration for the formulation of a rule describing the circumstances in which local remedies need not be exhausted because of failures in the administration of justice...

---

[479] *Case concerning the Arrest Warrant of 11 April 200* (*Democratic Republic of Congo v. Belgium*), Judgment, *I.C.J. Reports 2002*, p.3 at p.18, para.40.

[480] *I.C.J. Reports 2004*, p.12, para.40.

[481] *I.C.J. Reports 1989*, p.15 at p.43, para.52. See also the *Interhandel* case *I.C.J. Reports 1959*, at p.28.

(3) The "obvious futility" test, expounded by Arbitrator Bagge in the *Finnish Ships Arbitration*, sets too high a threshold. On the other hand, the test of "no reasonable prospect of success", accepted by the European Commission of Human Rights in several decisions,[482] is too generous to the claimant. This leaves the third option which avoids the stringent language of "obvious futility" but nevertheless imposes a heavy burden on the claimant by requiring that he prove that in the circumstances of the case, and having regard to the legal system of the respondent State, there is no reasonable possibility of effective redress offered by the local remedies. This test has its origin in a separate opinion of Sir Hersch Lauterpacht in the *Norwegian Loans* case[483] and is supported by the writings of jurists.[484] The test, however, fails to include the element of availability of local remedies which was endorsed by the Commission in its articles on Responsibility of States for Internationally Wrongful Acts[485] and is sometimes considered as a component of this rule by courts[486] and writers.[487] For this reason the test in paragraph (a) is expanded to require that there are no "reasonably available local remedies" to provide effective redress or that the local remedies provide no reasonable possibility of such redress. In this form the test is supported by judicial decisions which have held that local remedies need not be exhausted where the local court has no jurisdiction over the dispute in question;[488] the national legislation justifying the acts of which the alien complains will not be reviewed by local courts;[489] the local courts are notoriously lacking in independence;[490] there is a consistent and well-established line of precedents adverse to the alien;[491] the local courts do not have the competence to grant an appropriate and adequate remedy to the alien;[492] or the respondent State does not have an adequate system of judicial protection.[493]

(4) In order to meet the requirements of paragraph (a) it is not sufficient for the injured person to show that the possibility of success is low or that further appeals are difficult or costly. The test is not whether a successful outcome is likely or possible but whether the municipal system of the respondent State is reasonably capable of providing effective relief. This must be determined in the context of the local law and the prevailing circumstances....

(5) [Paragraph (b).] That the requirement of exhaustion of local remedies may be dispensed with in cases in which the respondent State is responsible for an unreasonable delay in allowing a local remedy to be

---

[482] *Retimag S.A. v. Federal Republic of Germany*, Application No.712/60, *Yearbook of the European Convention on Human Rights*, vol.4, p.385 at p.400; *X, Y and X v. UK*, Application Nos.8022/77. 8027/77, *European Court on Human Rights, Decisions and Reports*, vol.18, p.66 at p.74...

[483] *Case of certain Norwegian Loans (France v. Norway)*, Judgment, *I.C.J. Reports 1957*, at p.39.

[484] G. Fitzmaurice "Hersch Lauterpacht—The Scholar a Judge", BYBIL, vol.37 (1961), p.1 at pp.60–61...

[485] Article 44 requires local remedies to be "available and effective".

[486] In *Loewen Group Inc v. USA*, the tribunal stated that the exhaustion of local remedies rule obliges the injured person "to exhaust remedies which are effective and adequate and are reasonably available" to him (at para.168).

[487] C.F. Amerasinghe, *Local Remedies in International Law, op.cit.*, pp.181–2, 203–4.

[488] *Panevezys-Saldutiskis Railway* case, at p.18, *Arbitration under Article 181 of the Treaty of Neuilly*, reported in AJIL., vol.28 (1934), p.760 at p.789; *Claims of R. Gelbtrunk and "Salvador Commercial Co." et al.*, UNRIAA, vol.XV, p.467 at pp.476–477;...*Finnish Ships Arbitration*, UNRIAA, vol.III, p.1535.

[489] *Arbitration under Article 181 of the Treaty of Neuilly*, AJIL., vol.28 (1934), p.789. See also *Affaire de Forets du Rhodope Central (Fond)* 1933, UNRIAA, vol.III, p.1405; *Ambatielos* claim, UNRIAA, vol.XII, p.119; *Interhandel* case, *I.C.J. Reports 1959*, at p.28.

[490] *Robert E. Brown Claim* of 23 November 1923, UNRIAA, vol.VI, p.120; *Vélasquez Rodriguez* case, Inter-American Court of Human Rights, Series C, No.4, paras.56–78, p.291 at pp.304–309.

[491] *Panevezys-Saldutiskis Railway* case, at p.18; *S.S. "Lisman"*, UNRIAA, vol.III, p.1769 at p.1773; *S.S. "Seguranca"*, UNRIAA, vol.III, p.1861 at p.1868; *Finnish Ships Arbitration*, at p.1495; *X. v Federal Republic of Germany*, 1956, *Yearbook of the European Convention on Human Rights*, vol.1, p.138...

[492] *Finnish Ships Arbitration*, at pp.1496–1497; *Vélasquez Rodriguez* case; *Yagci and Sargin v. Turkey*, Judgment of 8 June 1995, *European Court on Human Rights, Decisions and Reports*, No.319, p.3 at p.17, para.42...

[493] *Mushikiwabo and others v. Barayagwiza*, 9 April 1996, ILR, vol.107, p.457 at 460. During the military dictatorship in Chile the Inter-American Commission on Human Rights resolved that the irregularities inherent in legal proceedings under military justice obviated the need to exhaust local remedies; resolution 1a/88, case 9755, *Ann.Rep.Int. Am. Com HR* 1987/88.

implemented is confirmed by codification attempts,[494] human rights instruments and practice,[495] judicial decisions[496] and scholarly opinion. It is difficult to give an objective content or meaning to "undue delay", or attempt to prescribe a fixed time limit within which local remedies are to be implemented. Each case must be judged on its own facts. As the British Mexican Claims Commission stated in the *El Oro Mining* case:

> "The Commission will not attempt to lay down with precision just within what period a tribunal may be expected to render judgment. This will depend upon several circumstances, foremost amongst them ... the volume of the work involved by a thorough examination of the case, in other words, upon the magnitude of the latter."[497] ...

(8) [Paragraph (c).] There is support in the literature for the proposition that in all cases in which the exhaustion of local remedies has been required there has been some link between the injured individual and the respondent State, such as voluntary physical presence, residence, ownership of property or a contractual relationship with the respondent State.[498] Proponents of this view maintain that the nature of diplomatic protection and the local remedies rule has undergone major changes in recent times. Whereas the early history of diplomatic protection was characterized by situations in which a foreign national resident and doing business in a foreign State was injured by the action of that State and could therefore be expected to exhaust local remedies in accordance with the philosophy that the national going abroad should normally be obliged to accept the local law as he finds it, including the means afforded for the redress of wrong, an individual may today be injured by the act of a foreign State outside its territory or by some act within its territory in circumstances in which the individual has no connection with the territory. Examples of this are afforded by transboundary environmental harm (for example, the explosion at the Chernobyl nuclear plant near Kiev in the Ukraine in 1986, which caused radioactive fallout as far away as Japan and Scandinavia) and the shooting down of an aircraft that has accidentally strayed into a State's airspace (as illustrated by the *Aerial Incident* in which Bulgaria shot down an El Al flight that had accidentally entered its airspace). The basis for such a voluntary link or territorial connection rule is the assumption of risk by the alien in a foreign State. It is only where the alien has subjected himself voluntarily to the jurisdiction of the respondent State that he would be expected to exhaust local remedies.

(9) Neither judicial authority nor State practice provide clear guidance on the existence of such an exception to the exhaustion of local remedies rule. While there are tentative dicta in support of the existence of such an exception in the *Interhandel*[499] and *Salem*[500] cases, in other cases[501] tribunals have upheld the applicability of the local remedies rule despite the absence of a voluntary link between the injured alien and the respondent State. In both the *Norwegian Loans* case[502] and the *Aerial Incident* case (*Israel v. Bulgaria*)[503] arguments in favour of the voluntary link requirement were forcefully advanced, but in neither case did the International Court make a decision on this matter....

(10) Paragraph (c) does not use the term "voluntary link" to describe this exception as this emphasizes the

---

[494] See the discussion of early codifications attempts by *F.V. Garcia-Amador* in First Report, *Yearbook...1956*, vol.II, p.173 at 223–226; art.19(2) of the 1960 Draft Convention on the International Responsibility of States for Injuries to Aliens prepared by the Harvard Research on International Law, reproduced in AJIL, vol.55 (1961), p.545 at p.577.

[495] International Covenant on Civil and Political Rights, United Nations, *Treaty Series*, vol.999, p.171, article (1)(c); American Convention on Human Rights (article 46(2)(c)); *Weinberger v Uruguay*, Communication 28/1978, Human Rights Committee, *Selected Decisions*, vol.1, p.57 at p.59; *Las Palmeras*, American Court of Human Rights, Series C, *Decisions and Judgments*, No.67, para.38 (4 Feburary 2000); *Erdogan v. Turkey*, Application No.19807/92, No.84A, European Commission of Human Rights (1996), *Decisions and Reports*, p.5 at p.15.

[496] *El Oro Mining and Railway Company (Limited)* (*Great Britain v. United Mexican States*), decision No.55 of 18 June 1931, UNRIAA, vol.V, p.191 at p.198. See also *Case concerning the Administration of the Prince von Pless*, Preliminary objections, *P.C.I.J. Series A/B*, 1933, No.52, p.4.

[497] *Ibid.*, at p.198.

[498] See Amerasinghe, *Local Remedies in International Law*, p.169; T. Meron, "The Incidence of the Rule of Exhaustion of Local Remedies", BYBIL, vol.35, 1959, p.83 at p.94.

[499] Here the International Court stated: "it has been considered necessary that the *State where the violation occurred* should also have an opporunity to redress it by its own means", *I.C.J. Reports 1959*, at p.27. Emphasis added

[500] In the *Salem* case an arbitral tribunal declared that "[a]s a rule, a foreigner must acknowledge as applicable to himself the kind of justice instituted in the country in which he did choose his residece", UNRIAA, vol.II, p.1165 at p.1202.

[501] *Finnish Ships Arbitration*, at p.1504; *Ambatielos Claim*, at p.99.

[502] *Case of certain Norwegian Loans* (*France v. Norway*), Oral Pleadings of France, *I.C.J. Pleadings 1957*, vol.1, p.408.

[503] *Case concerning the Aerial Incident of 27 July 1955* (*Israel v. Bulgaria*) (Pdeliminary objections), Oral Pleadings of Israel, *I.C.J. Pleadings 1959*, pp.531–532.

subjective intention of the injured individual rather than the absence of an objectively determinable connection between the individual and the host State. In practice it would be difficult to prove such a subjective criterion. Hence paragraph (c) requires the existence of a "relevant connection" between the injured alien and the host State and not a voluntary link. This connection must be "relevant" in the sense that it must relate in some way to the injury suffered. A tribunal will be required to examine not only the question whether the injured individual was present, resided or did business in the territory of the host State but whether, in the circumstances, the individual by his conduct, had assumed the risk that if he suffered an injury it would be subject to adjudication in the host State....

(11) Paragraph (d)..., which is an exercise in progressive development, must be narrowly construed, with the burden of proof on the injured person to show not merely that there are serious obstacles and difficulties in the way of exhausting local remedies but that he is "manifestly" precluded from pursuing such remedies....Circumstances that may manifestly preclude the exhaustion of local remedies possibly include the situation in which the injured person is prevented by the respondent State from entering its territory, either by law or by threats to his or her personal safety, and thereby denying him the opportunity to bring proceedings in local courts. Or where criminal syndicates in the respondent State obstruct him from bringing such proceedings. Although the injured person is expected to bear the costs of legal proceedings before the courts of the respondent State there may be circumstances in which such costs are prohibitively high and "manifestly preclude" compliance with the exhaustion of local remedies rule.[504]

(12) [Paragraph (e).] A state may be prepared to waive the requirement that local remedies be exhausted....

(13) Waiver of local remedies may take many different forms. It may appear in a bilateral or multilateral treaty entered into before or after the dispute arises; it may appear in a contract between the alien and the respondent State; it may be express or implied; or it may be inferred from the conduct of the respondent State in circumstances in which it can be described as estoppel or forfeiture....

(16) Waiver of local remedies must not be readily implied. In the *ELSI* case a Chamber of the International Court of Justice stated in this connection that it was:

"unable to accept that an important principle of customary international law should be held to have been tacitly dispensed with, in the absence of any words making clear an intention to do so".[505]

---

[504] On the implications for costs for exhaustion of local remedies, see *Loewen Group Inc. v. United States of America*, at para.166.

[505] *I.C.J. Reports 1989*, at p.42, para.50.

9   HUMAN RIGHTS

1. INTRODUCTION[1]

International law rules framed in terms of the protection of human rights against state interference are very largely a post-1945 phenomenon. Before then individuals were seen mostly as aliens and nationals, not as individuals. Some protection was afforded to them as aliens,[2] but the treatment of nationals was regarded as being within the domestic jurisdiction of sovereign states. By the nineteenth century, some writers recognised an exception in the case of humanitarian intervention, although state practice shows that intervention by a state on that ground was usually justified on other grounds at the same time.[3] After the First World War, efforts were made to protect minority groups by treaty,[4] but no protection of individuals generally was attempted. Events in Europe in the 1930s and in the Second World War focused attention upon this wider question and the guarantee of human rights became one of the purposes for which the Allied Powers fought.[5] It was therefore no surprise when the promotion of human rights became one of the purposes of the United Nations[6] and when the Charter imposed obligations upon the UN and its members to this end.[7] The Charter was followed by the Universal Declaration of Human Rights 1948[8] and a series of multilateral treaties and other declarations concluded through the United Nations (see below). At a regional level, the European Convention on Human Rights 1950,[9] the European Social Charter 1961[10] and the Revised

---

[1]   On the international law of human rights generally, see Donnelly, *International Human Rights* (3rd edn 2006); Hannum, ed., *Guide to International Human Rights Practice* (4th edn 2004); Kälin and Künzli, *The Law of International Human Rights Protection* (2009); Krause and Scheinin, eds, *International Protection of Human Rights: a Textbook* (2009); Lauterpacht, *International Law and Human Rights* (1950); Marks and Clapham, *International Law Lexicon* (2005); Nowak, *Introduction to the International Human Rights Regime* (2003); Rehman, *International Human Rights Law* (2nd edn 2009); Smith, *Textbook on International Human Rights* (3rd edn, 2007); Steiner, Alston and Goodman, *International Human Rights in Context* (3rd edn 2008); Tomuschat, *Human Rights: Between Idealism and Realism* (2nd edn 2008).
[2]   See above, Ch.8.
[3]   On humanitarian intervention, see below, p.777.
[4]   See Oppenheim, Vol.I, p.973.
[5]   See the UN Declaration of January 1, 1942: (1942) 36 A.J.I.L., Supp. 191.
[6]   UN Charter, art.1, below, App.I.
[7]   UN Charter, arts 55–56.
[8]   See below, p.548.
[9]   (1953) U.K.T.S. 71, 213 U.N.T.S. 221. In force 1953, 47 parties, including the U.K. See Harris, O'Boyle and Warbrick, *The Law of the European Convention on Human Rights* (2nd edn by Harris, O'Boyle, Bates and Buckley, 2009); Jacobs and White, *The European Convention on Human Rights* (4th edn by Ovey and White, 2006); Van Dijk, Van Rijn, Van Hoof and Zwaak, eds, *Theory and Practice of the European Convention on Human Rights* (4th edn 2006).
[10]   (1965) U.K.T.S., Cmnd. 2643; 529 U.N.T.S. 89. In force 1965.

European Social Charter 1996,[11] the American Convention on Human Rights 1969[12] and the African Charter on Human Rights and Peoples' Rights 1981[13] and the Revised Arab Charter on Human Rights 2004[14] are the main treaties have been adopted; all are now in force. There are also International Labour Conventions that contain human rights guarantees.[15] The Human Dimension of the Final Act of the Conference on Security and Co-operation in Europe 1975 (the Helsinki Declaration)[16] and later OSCE texts and developments are also relevant.

The following two sections concern, firstly, the action taken at a universal level to protect human rights within the United Nations, mainly by the UN Human Rights Council (formerly the UN Commission on Human Rights) through the adoption and implementation of treaties and by other means and, second, the protection of human rights in customary international law.

Writers commonly refer to human rights as belonging to one of three generations. The "first generation" consists of those civil and political rights that derive from the natural rights philosophy of Locke, Rousseau and others and that have been given priority by Western states. The "second generation" are those economic, social and cultural rights that attained recognition in the twentieth century with the advent of socialism. Although there is jurisprudential debate[17] and scepticism on the part of some Western states[18] as to the human rights character of "second generation" human rights, the Universal Declaration on Human Rights catalogues rights within both generations as human rights, and the International Covenants on Civil and Political Rights and on Economic, Social and Cultural Rights impose legal obligations in respect of each. Moreover, the premise underlying all United Nations human rights texts is that civil and political rights and economic, social and cultural rights are of equal priority, with the realisation of the two groups of rights being interdependent.[19] The idea of a "third generation" of human rights emerged as recently as the 1970s and is supported predominantly by developing states. It is the idea that in addition to the individual rights of the first two "generations," there are collective, group rights, such as the right to development, that may properly qualify as human rights.[20]

The evolution of the international law of human rights has been one of the more remarkable features of the development of international law since 1945. Whereas progress has so far been made

---

[11] E.T.S. 163. In force 1999. There are 42 parties to the 1961 Charter and/or the Revised Charter (the latter will eventually replace the former). The UK is a party to the 1961 Charter. See Harris, *The European Social Charter* (2nd ed. by Harris and Darcy, 2001).

[12] P.A.U.T.S. 36; (1970) 9 I.L.M. 673. In force 1978. 25 parties. See Buergenthal and Shelton, eds, *Protecting Human Rights in the Americas* (4th edn 1995); Caminos, in Symonides, ed., *Human Rights: International Protection, Monitoring, Enforcement* (2003), Ch.5; Davidson, *The Inter-American Human Rights System* (1997); Harris and Livingstone, eds, *The Inter-American System of Human Rights* (1998); Pasqualucci, *The Practice and Procedure of the Inter-American Court of Human Rights* (2003).

[13] (1982) 21 I.L.M. 59. In force 1986, 53 parties. See Evans and Murray, eds, *The African Charter on Human and Peoples' Rights* (2nd edn 2008); Heyns (2004) 108 Penn. State L.R. 679; Okafor, *The African Human Rights System, Activist Forces and International Institutions* (2007); Viljoen, *International Human Rights Law in Africa* (2007).

[14] (2005) 12 I.H.R.R. 893. In force 2008, 10 parties. See Hassan, in Symonides, ed., *Human Rights: International Protection, Monitoring, Enforcement* (2003), Ch.7; Rishmawi, in Krause and Scheinin, eds, above, n.1, p.529; Rishmawi (2005) H.R.L.R. 261; id. (2010) 10 H.R.L.R. 169.

[15] See Samson, in Matscher, ed., *The Implementation of Economic and Social Rights* (1991), p.123 and Swepston, in Symonides, ed., *Human Rights: International Protection, Monitoring, Enforcement* (2003), Ch.2.

[16] (1975) 14 I.L.M. 1292. The declaration is not binding in law: see Russell (1976) 70 A.J.I.L. 242. On the OSCE and human rights, see Brett (1996) 18 H.R.Q. 668.

[17] See, e.g. Beetham (1995) 43 Pol. Studies 41; Cranston, *What are Human Rights* (1973); McFarlane, *The Theory and Practice of Human Rights* (1985); Raphael, ed., *Political Thought and the Rights of Man* (1967); Vincent, *Human Rights and International Relations* (1986).

[18] During the Reagan Presidency, the US took the view that such rights were "societal goals" rather than human rights: see the US statement in UN Doc.A/40/C.3/36, p.5 (1985).

[19] On their interdependency, see Scott (1999) 21 H.R.Q. 633.

[20] On third generation human rights, see below, p.623.

mainly through treaties, the customary international law of human rights is in the process of evolution too. However, it remains uncertain how far customary law extends beyond some fundamental civil and political rights and who in law holds or may enforce the resulting substantive legal rights. As to human rights treaties, most states have accepted some of the increasing number of universal and regional human rights treaties protecting either human rights generally, or one "generation" of human rights or just one particular right. Such treaties typically provide for bodies to monitor compliance, although the powers of enforcement granted to them vary greatly, ranging from the competence of a court to take a legally binding decision following an individual petition,[21] to that of a committee to make only non-binding general comments or recommendations after the examination of national reports.[22] Nonetheless all such supervisory bodies contribute in their functioning to the meaning of the rights their treaties guarantee and to the corpus of practice applying international human rights standards.

Finally mention should be made of the establishment of the International Criminal Court, with jurisdiction to try individuals for international crimes.[23] Although the Court's decisions will clearly have relevance for the international law of human rights,[24] the subject of international criminal justice is a specialist one and is not dealt with here.[25]

HIGGINS, PROBLEMS AND PROCESS: INTERNATIONAL LAW AND HOW WE USE IT

1994, pp.96–97.

It is sometimes suggested that there can be no fully universal concept of human rights, for it is necessary to take into account the diverse cultures and political systems of the world.[26] In my view this is a point advanced mostly by states, and by liberal scholars anxious not to impose the Western view of things on others. It is rarely advanced by the oppressed, who are only too anxious to benefit from perceived universal standards. The non-universal, relativist view of human rights is in fact a very state-centred view and loses sight of the fact that human rights are *human* rights and not dependent on the fact that states, or groupings of states, may behave differently from each other so far as their politics, economic policy, and culture are concerned. I believe, profoundly, in the universality of the human spirit. Individuals everywhere want the same essential things: to have sufficient food and shelter; to be able to speak freely; to practise their own religion or to abstain from religious belief; to feel that their person is not threatened by the state; to know that they will not be tortured, or detained without charge, and that, if charged, they will have a fair trial. I believe there is nothing in these aspirations that is dependent upon culture, or religion or stage of development. They are as keenly felt by the African tribesman as by the European city-dweller, by the inhabitant of a Latin American shanty-town as by the resident of a Manhattan apartment.

Notes

1. Ahead of the Vienna World Conference on Human Rights 1993, Asian states adopted the Bangkok Declaration 1993[27] which challenged what was perceived as the western concept of

---

[21] e.g. the European and Inter-American Courts of Human Rights.

[22] e.g. the Children's Rights Committee.

[23] In contrast, international human rights courts and treaty monitoring bodies determine the *civil* liability of *states*.

[24] The same is true of the International Criminal Tribunals for the Former Yugoslavia and Rwanda, the Special Court for Sierra Leone, etc. See Jones, *International Criminal Practice* (2003).

[25] On the ICC, see Cassese, *International Criminal Law* (2nd edn 2008); Cassese, Gaeta and Jones, *The Rome Statute of the International Criminal Court* (2002); Schabas, *An Introduction to the International Criminal Court* (3rd edn 2007); Triffterer, ed., *Commentary on the Rome Statute of the International Criminal Court* (2nd edn 2008).

[26] On this see, inter alia, I. Nguema, "Human Rights Perspective in Africa" (1990) 11 H.R.L.J. 261; D. Donoho, "Relativism Versus Universalism in Human Rights: The Search for Meaningful Standards" (1991) 27 *Stanford Law Journal* 345; H. Gros Espiel, "The Evolving Concept of Human Rights: Western Socialist and Third World Approaches", in B. Ramcharan (ed.), *Human Rights Thirty Years after the Universal Declaration* (1979), pp.41 et seq.

[27] (1993) 14 H.R.L.J. 370.

human rights. The Declaration stressed the need to consider human rights in their national and regional contexts and emphasised the principles of respect for national sovereignty and non-interference in the internal affairs of states. However, the universality of human rights and their place beyond the limits of domestic jurisdiction were reaffirmed by the Vienna Declaration and Programme of Action on Human Rights 1993[28] that was adopted by the Vienna World Conference:

> "1. The World Conference on Human Rights reaffirms the solemn commitment of all States to fulfil their obligations to promote universal respect for, and observance and protection of, all human rights and fundamental freedoms for all in accordance with the Charter of the United Nations, other instruments relating to human rights, and international law. The universal nature of these rights and freedoms is beyond question. ...
>
>   5. All human rights are universal, indivisible and interdependent and interrelated. The international community must treat human rights globally in a fair and equal manner, on the same footing, and with the same emphasis. While the significance of national and regional particularities and various historical, cultural and religious backgrounds must be borne in mind, it is the duty of States, regardless of their political, economic and cultural systems, to promote and protect all human rights and fundamental freedoms."

2. Whereas no one argues that states may torture or arbitrarily detain or kill individuals, there are some contexts in which religious and other cultural differences do disclose genuine disagreement.[29] In some Islamic states, apostasy and adultery are capital criminal offences.[30] Discrimination against women in respect of property and marital rights has led certain Islamic states to make reservations to key provisions of the 1979 Convention on the Elimination of Discrimination against Women.[31] Discrimination on the basis of sexual orientation is strong in some cultures, but less so in others.[32] Catholic states may take a different view from others about abortion and the right to life of the unborn child. Female genital circumcision is a traditional cultural practice in some African and other states.[33]

Does corporal punishment present a problem of cultural diversity? In 1994, despite President Clinton's intervention and much public outcry in the US, a criminal judicial sentence of four strokes of the cane for vandalising cars by spray paint was carried out against an American youth of 18 years in Singapore,[34] which is one of many states in which corporal punishment remains lawful. In *Tyrer v U.K.*,[35] three strokes of the birch as a penalty for assault were held to be degrading punishment in breach of art.3, European Convention on Human Rights. Interpreting art.7, ICCPR, the Human Rights Committee has stated that "the prohibition extends to corporal punishment, including excessive chastisement": General Comment No.20, below, p.574.

---

[28] (1994) 1–1 I.H.R.R. 240.

[29] See further on cultural relativism, Brems, *Human Rights: Universality and Diversity* (2001); Muskat (2002) 6 Sing. J.I.C.L. 1028; Rehman and Breau, eds, *Religion, Human Rights and International Law* (2007); Renteln, *International Human Rights: Universalism versus Relativism* (1990).

[30] See below, p.572. See generally Baderin, *International Human Rights and Islamic Law* (2003).

[31] e.g. Egypt has made a reservation to art.16 "concerning the equality of men and women in all matters relating to marriage and family relations" in so far as it runs counter to the "Islamic Sharia's provisions whereby women are accorded rights subject to those of their spouses so as to ensure a just balance between them": UN Doc. ST/LEG/Ser.E/15, p.171.

[32] See the *Toonen* case, below, p.596.

[33] See *Harmful and Traditional Practices Affecting the Health of Women and Children*, UN Human Rights Fact Sheet No.23, p.7.

[34] *Keesings Archives*, p.40013.

[35] E. Ct. H.R. R. A 28 (1978).

----

2. ACTION THROUGH THE UNITED NATIONS[36]

A. Introductory Note

Articles 55 and 56, UN Charter, impose upon the United Nations and its members respectively obligations "to promote" respect for and observance of human rights. The UN organs or bodies with jurisdiction in respect of human rights include:

1. The General Assembly, which can adopt resolutions that declare human rights standards (eg the Universal Declaration of Human Rights) or condemn particular breaches of human rights (e.g. in the Former Republic of Yugoslavia[37]);

2. the Security Council, which may take enforcement action (e.g. in Iraq[38]) in respect of human rights violations that amount to a threat or a breach of the peace;

3. the Economic and Social Council (ECOSOC), which may make recommendations for the promotion of respect for human rights[39]; and

4. above all, the Human Rights Council.[40]

B. The Human Rights Council

BOYLE, THE UNITED NATIONS HUMAN RIGHTS COUNCIL: ORIGINS, ANTECEDENTS, AND PROSPECTS

Extract from Boyle, ed., *New Institutions for Human Rights Protection*, 2009, p.12–46. Some footnotes omitted

Like its predecessor, the Human Rights Council is an intergovernmental body and is comprised of representatives of 47 member states. At its abolition the [UN Commission on Human Rights] had 53 members. The differences between the two bodies…which, taken together, may give rise to some optimism for [the Council's] prospect of strengthening international human rights protection [include the following]. First, the new Council is established as a subsidiary organ of the General Assembly, whereas the former Commission was one of a number of subsidiary bodies of ECOSOC. This enhanced status for the Council is intended to, and should have, the effect of making its deliberations more authoritative, visible, and influential within the United Nations as well as outside it….Secondly, the Council is virtually a standing body; it is required to meet for 10 weeks per year over a least three sessions with the option of holding special sessions at the request of a third of its membership. In contrast, the Commission on Human Rights met for a single six-week session each year. Thirdly, the Council has been given a new task of immense potential, that of establishing and conducting for all states a peer review system, the Universal Periodic Review (UPR), in respect of their human rights obligations and commitments….

An important difference between the former Commission and the Council lies in the system of election of its members and the standards to be met by candidate states. Members of the Council are to be elected for the allocated regional distribution of seats 'directly and individually' by secret ballot and by a simple majority of the General Assembly's 192 members. The Commission's membership had been elected by the smaller electorate of ECOSOC with its 54 members and was often agreed upon without election from previously agreed regional

---

[36] See Alston, *The United Nations and Human Rights* (1992); Bayefsky, ed., *The UN Human Rights System in the 21st Century* (2000); *id.*, *The UN Human Rights Treaty System* (2001).

[37] E.g. G.A. Res.50/192 (1995) (rape and abuse of women).

[38] See below, p.797.

[39] UN Charter, art.62.

[40] The ICJ also has jurisdiction: see e.g. the *Wall* case, below, p.600.

'clean slates' of candidates. Where this resulted in the presence on the Commission of states with questionable human rights records, controversy flared.

When electing members of the Council, states are directed to weigh candidate states' human rights records and voluntary pledges that they have made on improving national human rights protection. No such standards existed for election to the Commission. All elected Council members will be considered under the UPR process during their tenure on the Council. Where a state elected to the Council is responsible for gross and systematic violations of human rights, the General Assembly could suspend that state from the Council.[41] To encourage rotation of its members no state can be elected for more tha[n] two terms without leaving the Council.[42] One effect of the latter rule is to put an end to a convention or practice that had operated intermittently under the Commission on Human Rights, whereby the Permanent Five on the Security Council would be assured of a seat. At present [in 2009] all five are elected members of the new Council[43]...

The mandate given to the Commission was that of standard setting beginning with 'the formulation of an international bill of rights'. It was also tasked with the protection of minorities and the prevention of discrimination and with a residual authority that allowed the Commission to address 'any other matter concerning human rights'. The Commission's achievement across the bulk of this range of tasks, particularly in standard setting, is accepted even by its fiercest detractors as impressive. Most of the agreements that constitute modern international law on human rights involved the Commission and its Sub-Commission.[44]

...while the intergovernmental engagement with establishing binding norms in international law...worked effectively, the opposite...proved the case in seeking to involve the same states in exercising judgment over each other in respect of compliance with such norms. From the outset the...Commission resisted taking on the function of examining the numerous individual complaints and petitions which streamed into the United Nations from all over the world appealing for action over human rights violations....Complaints which raised labour rights issues were referred to the International Labour Organisation Committee on Freedom of Association, but otherwise the thousands of petitions which flooded into the UN remained un-opened and unanswered...initial resistance to giving the new Commission any investigative or protective function came from the major Powers, including the United States, USSR, and the United Kingdom....those states which had crafted Article 2(7) of the Charter intended to rule out UN involvement in domestic affairs saw the Commission's role as confined to proposing and promoting international standards and as a forum for debate on such standards. ...

The Commission's denial to itself of jurisdiction to address complaints was to persist for two decades ending only when the process of decolonization from the 1960s brought the newly independent African and Asian countries a majority in the General Assembly. These countries pushed for action on issues of relevance to them, especially South Africa and the Apartheid system, and in pressing for the comprehensive achievement of self-determination of peoples ...

It was thus developing countries that were the progenitors of Commission Resolution [1235] (1967) establishing mechanisms for the Commission and its Sub-Commission to publicly debate situations of large-scale human rights violations, 'including policies of racial discrimination and segregation and apartheid in all countries'[45] It was the same states which sponsored Resolution 1503 (1970) that gave the Commission the competence to receive and adjudicate on communications alleging gross and systematic violation of human rights.[46] It was equally the pressure for action on Apartheid which began what became known as the Commission's system of special procedures....

While the NAM (Non-Aligned Movement) countries—supported primarily by the USSR—had in mind racism and Apartheid, their success created the precedent for the development of the Commission's mandate to address any situation of human rights violation in the world. The new Human Rights Council retains that

---

41   ...A two-thirds majority vote of members present and voting is required.

42   Ibid. para.7. However it seems that absence from the Council need be for no more than one year after serving a second term. A term is for a period of three years.

43   Ed. The US did not stand for membership in the first round of elections because of its opposition to the Council as conceived in General Assembly resolution 60/251. It was elected as a member in 2009.

44   Ed. See the list of treaties and declarations, below, p.545. The Council has the same standard setting mandate. It has adopted the International Convention for the Protection of all Persons from Forced Disappearances 2006, the Declaration on the Rights of Indigenous Peoples 2007 and the Optional Protocol to the International Covenant on Economic Social and Cultural Rights 2008.

45   ECOSOC Res 1235 (XLII) adopted 6 June 1967 ...

46   ECOSOC Res 1503 (XLVIII) of 27 May 1970 revised by ECOSOC Resolution 2003/3 of 9 June 2000.

competence of the former Commission in its permanent agenda.[47] In turn, the Council inherited the confidential complain mechanism of the Commission. It has replaced the '1503 procedure' with a new complaint mechanism which is largely similar in nature. ...

One of the complaints over the Commission on Human Rights was that it was 'politicized' in its treatment of human rights...it became the principal charge that finally brought the Commission down....States large and small resent or reject 'finger pointing' or attention being drawn to their shortcomings. The awareness of serious human rights suffering in member states, with the Commission pressed to act by NGOs, brings the political differences between [regional] blocs openly to the surface. One part of the resentment concerns complaints of 'selectivity' that certain states which are less powerful are targeted for condemnation where no such measures are addressed to the powerful.[48]

[The membership and powers of the Human Rights Council are now discussed.]

First Elections to the Council....The first elections to the 47 member Council were held on 9 May 2006, NGOs were active in pressing the candidate states to make 'voluntary pledges' on upholding human rights. All states ultimately did so and according to observers the pledge may have also dissuaded states with notorious records from standing. The Council's marginally smaller membership than the former Commission (47 rather than 53) resulted in a more pronounced redistribution of seats between the five regional groupings under the equitable geographical distribution formula. The reduction of Latin American and Caribbean seats .,.. and the Western Group seats...meant that these countries 'have lost the power to win a vote...unless their proposals attract the support of at least three African and Asian States.'[49]

Following the elections...the newly elected Council spent a large portion of its first year 2006–7 in agreeing on the architecture of the body. The results, referred to as the Institution Building text, were...adopted by Resolution on 18 June 2007.[50]...

Universal Periodic Review Mechanism...The cycle for review of all [UN member] states will be four years, which will require 48 states to be reviewed each year over three sessions of the Council. All members of the Council are to be reviewed during their period in office and the equitable geographic distribution principle will operate in the selection of countries for review....

Resolution 5/1 provides that there will be three documents generated as the basis of the review of the state. First, a national report is prepared by the state with a maximum length of 20 pages. The second document will be information from treaty bodies and the Special Procedures prepared by the OHCHR with a maximum length of 10 pages. A third 10-page document also prepared by the OHCHR will be based on information provided by 'other stakeholders', including NGOs and National Human Rights Institutions. ...

The review hearing is conducted in a plenary working group of the Council chaired by the President with member and observer states being free to participate in the interactive dialogue. NGOs and other stakeholders may attend but may not participate at this stage. The rules provide for three rapporteurs chosen by drawing lots from different regional groups (the troika) who have the task of facilitating the review and preparing the working group report on the state in question. The review hearing is allocated three hours and a further hour is allocated for the adoption of the working group's report. The outcome report considered by the plenary Council at a later meeting comprises a summary of the review process along with recommendations and/or conclusions and voluntary commitments. The opportunity is also provided for NGOs to comment at this stage. Prior to the adoption of the 'outcome' document of the review, the state is to be fully involved and may make further comments on the draft report. Recommendations accepted by the state in question will be identified and those which it does not accept will also be recorded. ...

---

[47] Item 4, Human rights situations that require the Council's attention. Agenda and Framework from the Program of Work, A/HRC/Res/5/1.

[48] See, for example, the view of Pakistan; 'Politicization and selective targeting...the arbitrary naming of countries and submission of country-specific resolutions, mostly against developing countries, especially Islamic countries, is the most negative feature of the Commission's work'. Statement by Ambassador Munir Akram, Permanent Representative of Pakistan to the United Nations at the Human Rights negotiations on the Establishment of Human Rights Council, New York, 18 October 2005. ...

[49] Y. Terlingen...(2006) 21 Ethics and International Affairs 167,171...Ed. Seats are allocated by regional groups as follows: African states 13; Asian states 13; Latin American and Caribbean states 8; Western and other states 7; East European states 6.

[50] A/HRC/Res/5/1, Human Rights Council Resolution 5/1, United Nations Human Rights Council Institution Building, 18 June 2007, paras 1–38.

The true test of the effectiveness of UPR will emerge only with evidence of fulfilment of commitments made by states. UPR will be a standing item on the Council's agenda and it is the intention that there should be scrutiny on the extent to which recommendations are implemented by the state reviewed. In formal terms, that must await the second cycle of UPR, namely after four years, when it is planned that the focus will be on the implementation of commitments. Proposals in the negotiations that a follow up rapporteur might be appointed or that the state reviewed might report to the Council on implementation of the review were not accepted. Persistent non-cooperation by a state with the mechanism, including failure to fulfil recommendations accepted, will be addressed by the Council.

...While the mechanism is at an early stage it is clear that states under review and Council members in the three hours of interactive dialogue have made serious efforts to give the process meaning and depth. The atmosphere has been constructive and the issues raised for scrutiny have addressed both strengths and weaknesses of the countries in question. What is most interesting and of longer term significance, has been the extent to which countries under review have been both self-critical and have accepted recommendations made by other states for positive action, including the ratification of international instruments. The frankness with which some countries accepted that they have human rights problems and agreed to address them is genuinely new and encouraging. The United Kingdom, considered in the first session, accepted most of the UPR recommendations in whole or in part. Pakistan, considered in the second session of UPR, announced that it was in the process of ratifying the United Nations Civil and Political Covenant and the Convention against Torture. It had ratified the Covenant on Economic and Social and Cultural Rights on its election to the Council. It is also establishing a Human Rights Commission and had incorporated a human rights education curriculum in schools. The interactive dialogue with Pakistan did address many issues including the violation of rights of women, the rights of religious minorities, and capital punishment, subjects which were also documented powerfully in the NGO submissions to the review. ...

Special Procedures. The most important institutional creation of the former Commission on Human Rights was that of the system of Special Procedures and it is an institution that has been preserved in the new Human Rights Council. ...

The Special Procedures (Special Rapporteurs, Representatives, Independent Experts, and Working Groups) are independent and unpaid experts appointed by the Commission and now the Council, who have a variety of protection functions including monitoring, investigating, advising, reporting, and making recommendations on the implementation of human rights by governments. They are categorized as thematic, dealing globally with specific human rights or human rights concerns, or are appointed in respect of the human rights situation in particular countries. In addition to protection functions the special rapporteurs, as they are most commonly known, have played a significant role in developing international human rights law standards through their analysis of particular norms and their conceptualization and reflections on the problems of securing protection of those norms. However, the work of experts has not always been appreciated and some states represented on the Council harbour reservations and hostility to the special procedures system, especially those appointed to monitor and investigate violations in particular countries....Some states did press for the abolition of country rapporteurs based on the argument that the system of UPR rendered them unnecessary.[51] Among the first decisions of the Council was not to re-appoint the country rapporteurs for Cuba and Belarus. However, the remaining 39 rapporteurs had their mandates renewed for one year.[52] UN Resolution 60/251 had directed the Council to 'review and where necessary improve and rationalize' the system of special procedures, a process which is ongoing. The Council has now adopted a Code of Conduct for Special Procedure mandate holders.[53] The Council has also set out rules to ensure transparent selection and appointment of qualified mandate holders.[54] Given that more time is available, the experience of the interactive dialogue with the special procedures during the presentation of their reports in the Council sessions to date has been a considerable improvement in terms of time and content, compared with the former Commission. ...

The Human Rights Council Advisory Committee. This new body replacing the former Sub-Commission on the

---

[51] Algeria (on behalf of the African Group), Bangladesh, Belarus, China, Cuba, the Democratic People's Republic of Korea, India, Iran, Malaysia ...

[52] Ed. The mandates for the independent experts for the DRC and Liberia were discontinued in 2008, leaving 8 *country* mandates: Burundi, Cambodia, North Korea, Haiti, Myanmar, Occupied Palestinian Territories, Somalia and the Sudan. There are 31 *thematic* mandates, covering civil and political rights and, increasingly, economic, social and cultural rights. They include the Special Rapporteurs on Torture, Extrajudicial, Summary or Arbitrary Executions, Education, and Health, and the Working Group on Arbitrary Detention.

[53] A/HRC/Res/5/2, 18 June 2007.

[54] Ibid., paras 39–64.

Promotion and Protection of Human Rights [consists]...of 18 experts and is explicitly termed a think tank for the Council. It will work at the Council's direction and under guidelines set out in the institution-building resolution. The clear subordination of the Advisory Committee to the Council spelled out in these guidelines is the culmination of what has been happening to the autonomy of its predecessor body.

The Advisory Committee is elected by the Council in secret ballot based on a set allocation by geographical region.[55] All member states of the UN may nominate candidates for the Advisory Committee but from their own region only. While civil society organizations may not nominate, the guidelines recommend that states consult with NHRIs and NGOs and that the names of those supporting proposed candidates should be included with the nomination. Due consideration should be given in nominations and elections to gender balance and 'an appropriate representation of different civilizations and legal systems'.[56]

Members of the Advisory Committee are required to have recognized competence in the field of human rights, to be of high moral standing, and to have independence and impartiality. Regrettably, the guidelines do not exclude candidates holding government appointment but rather only where such individuals hold positions that could give rise to a conflict of interests with their responsibilities in the Advisory Committee. Members will serve for three years and may be re-elected once.

The Advisory Committee may not adopt resolutions or decisions and its work, studies, and research-based advice, will be requested by the Council. However, it may suggest further research proposals for approval by the Council. At its abolition, the Sub-Commission met for a single session of three weeks. The Advisory Committee is reduced to two weeks of meetings, which should be different sessions, although it may request approval for additional ad hoc sessions from the Council. In addition to states, NGOs, NIHRIs, intergovernmental organizations and others are encouraged to participate in the Committee's meetings on the same basis as their involvement with the Council. The Advisory Committee will have a function under the new complaints procedure of the Council ...

Complaint Procedure. Resolution 5/1 sets out a complaint procedure, 'to address consistent patterns of gross and reliably tested violations of all human rights and all fundamental freedoms occurring in any part of the world and under any circumstances.'[57] In effect, the complaint procedure reproduces the 1503 complaint procedure of the former Commission on Human Rights. However, it is expressed to be 'improved where necessary so as to ensure that the complaint procedure be impartial, objective, efficient, and victims-oriented and conducted in a timely manner'. The entire procedure will remain a confidential one 'with a view to enhancing cooperation with the State concerned'. The mechanism is directed at situations of violation and is not for a complaint of an individual violation for which there are other avenues at national and international levels.

As under the 1503 procedure, there are two stages in the process of addressing a complaint. The Human Rights Advisory Committee will constitute a five-member Working Group on Communications, with one member from each regional group. Its function is to determine the admissibility and merits of a communication. The other body, the Working Group on Situations, is made up from the Council itself. It receives from the Advisory Committee a file of all admissible communications with its recommendations. The Working Group on Situations may then provide a report to the Council with recommendations on a course of action. The range of actions open to the Council are, as with the former Commission, to keep the matter under review, appoint an expert to monitor and to report back to the Council, or to decide to discontinue the confidential procedure and bring the case before the Council in public session. The Council may recommend that the OHCHR provide capacity-building assistance or advisory services to the state concerned. A positive improvement on the 1503 procedure is that the complainant is to be kept informed at all states of the process, including being informed as to the outcome. ...

Special Sessions. The idea of mandating the new Human Rights Council to convene special sessions outside its agreed schedule of meetings was intended to increase its relevance and that of the United Nations in addressing human rights emergencies.[58]

The Human Rights Council was authorized to hold special sessions at the request of a member of the Council with the support of one-third of the membership. Within a period of less than two years the Council has convened in special session no less than seven times. ...

---

[55] A/HRC/Res/5/1, paras 70–84. The regional allocation on the Advisory Committee is African States 5; Asian States 5; Eastern European States 2; Latin American and Caribbean States 3; Western European and other States 3. ...

[56] A/HRC/Res/5/1, para 72

[57] A/HRC/Res/5/1, paras 85–109.

[58] Ed. The Commission was authorised to hold exceptional sessions only in 1990, but held very few, e.g. on the former Yugoslavia in 1992

[By October 2009, the Council had held 12 special sessions. Five were on Palestine. Other country specific sessions were on Lebanon, Darfur, the DRC, Myanmar and Sri Lanka. Two were on general themes: the right to food and the world food crisis, and the global economic and financial crisis and human rights.]

A perceptive and experienced observer of the transition from Commission on Human Rights to Human Rights Council summed up the first year of the Council as 'neither a mountain nor a mole hill'.[59] That continues to be an apposite verdict after the second year of its existence. The Human Rights Council has neither fulfilled the highest expectations nor has it dashed them completely. ...

The Council's achievements in making a successful transition from the former Commission, by establishing its own institutional architecture, procedures, and agenda for work is rightly praised. ...That is not to say that there are not major differences within the Council over human rights, as has been evident in its sessions to date. But members understand that the credibility of the Council requires that differences are negotiated through dialogue, particularly across regions. The membership of the Council is by a considerable majority representative of the developing world. The Western members cannot dominate its decisions and need to negotiate to achieve their goals. But the commitment to a culture of dialogue and cooperation must not lead to a position where the Council avoids addressing the realities of states flagrantly violating human rights. The efforts to abolish country rapporteurs have been resisted so far, but if the pressure to do so from some states (including China) succeed, not only the credibility, but also the relevance, of the Council could come into question.

The long-term success of the Council rests with the one true innovation achieved through its creation: the system of Universal Periodic Review. UPR is at an early stage but the success to date of the on-adversarial but frank and detailed dialogue between states holds real promise for the advancement of universal human rights protection. The continued engagement of civil society and of other 'stakeholders' such as NHRIs with the Council is vital for the effectiveness of UPR. Their engagement across the entire mandate of the Council is equally vital if its potential as a new beginning in the promotion and protection of universal human rights is to be realized.

Notes

1. UN human rights action is centred on the Human Rights Council, which replaced the UN Commission on Human Rights in 2006.[60] There was a need for change because, as noted by Boyle, the Commission had become discredited: increasing politicisation had undermined its "credibility and professionalism", with states seeking membership "not to strengthen human rights but to protect themselves against criticism or to criticise others".[61] But, despite these flaws, any obituary for the Commission should record its undoubted achievements in standard setting, through the adoption of human rights treaties and declarations, and the development of its Charter-based system of special procedures. More generally, it was mainly through the work of the Commission that the idea that the treatment of a state's own nationals was a matter within its domestic jurisdiction[62] has been abandoned: its practice showed clearly that the protection of human rights is within the domain of international law with states now routinely responding to allegations against them without pleading national sovereignty.

2. Whether the new Council will in the long term prove an improvement on the Council can only be conjecture at this stage. Like its predecessor, the Council is a highly political animal, composed of the same diplomats and subject to the same practice of bloc voting based on the common

[59] R. Brett, 'Neither Mountain Nor Mole Hill: Review of the Human Rights Council One Year On', Quaker United Nations Office, Geneva, August 2007, at 8.
[60] The Council was established by General Assembly Resolution 60/151 (2006).
[61] *In Larger Freedom: Towards Development, Security and Human Rights for All*, report of the Secretary-General, A/59/2005, para.182. The election of Libya as chair of the Commission in 2003 and the re-election of Sudan to the Commission in 2004 underlined a further criticism by western states that states with bad human rights records should not be on the Commission.
[62] On the domestic jurisdiction limitation to UN competence, see art.2(7), UN Charter, below, p.826.

interests of diverse regional groups. More positively, the new Council has retained the Commission's system of special procedures[63] and the new UPR procedure provides for the review of the human rights record of *all* UN member states[64] and does so even in the subject areas of human rights treaties to which they are not parties.[65] As noted by Boyle, the UPR procedure has made a more encouraging start than might have been predicted, although in the "interactive dialogue" politics clearly underlie some comments by states on other states.

C. UN Human Rights Standards and Treaty Monitoring Bodies

i. Treaties and Declarations

UN human rights standards have been spelt out in a series of human rights treaties and declarations. These are the Universal Declaration and the two Covenants, covering civil and political, and economic, social and cultural rights respectively,[66] and other treaties and declarations that are subject or person specific. Altogether, the following nine treaties have been adopted:

1. Convention on the Elimination of all Forms of Racial Discrimination 1966 ("CERD")[67];

2. International Covenant on Civil and Political Rights 1966 ("ICCPR")[68];

3. International Covenant on Economic, Social and Cultural Rights 1966 ("ICESCR")[69];

4. Convention on the Elimination of All Forms of Discrimination Against Women 1979 ("CEDAW")[70];

5. Convention Against Torture 1984 ("CAT")[71];

---

[63]   On this system, see Gutter (2007) 7 H.R.L.R. 93 and Hannum (2007) 7 H.R.L.R. 73.

[64]   A fair criticism of the Commission was that the records of only some states were reviewed by it, other states with questionable records being able to prevent that by mustering sufficient bloc votes or in other ways.

[65]   States may also prove more responsive to criticism by their peers than by independent treaty monitoring bodies.

[66]   The three are known as the international bill of rights.

[67]   60 U.N.T.S. 195; (1966) 60 A.J.I.L. 650; (1966) 5 I.L.M. 352. In force 1969, 173 parties, including the UK. See Banton, *International Action against Racial Discrimination* (1966); Banton, in Alston and Crawford, eds, *The Future of UN Human Rights Treaty Reporting* (2002), Ch.3; Meron (1985) 79 A.J.I.L. 283; Partsch, in Alston, ed., *The UN and Human Rights* (1992) pp. 339 et seq.; Lerner, *The UN Convention on the Elimination of Racial Discrimination* (1980); Thornberry (2005) 5 H.R.L.R. 239.

[68]   See below, p.552.

[69]   See below, p.607.

[70]   1249 U.N.T.S. 13; (1980) 19 I.L.M. 33. In force 2000, 186 parties, including the UK. See Bayefsky (2000) 94 A.S.I.L. Proc. 197; Bustelo, in Alston and Crawford, eds, *The Future of UN Human Rights Treaty Reporting* (2002), Ch.4; Byrnes (1989) Yale J.I.L. 1; Jacobson, in Alston, ed., *The UN and Human Rights* (1992), Ch.11. See also the 1999 Optional Protocol, 2131 U.N.T.S. 83; (2007) 7 I.H.R.R. 294, which provides for a right of individual petition. In force 2000, 99 parties, including the UK. See Bijnsdorp (2000) 18 N.H.R.Q. 328 and Sokhi-Bulley (2006) 6 H.R.L.R. 143.

[71]   1465 U.N.T.S. 85; (1984) 23 I.L.M. 1027 and (1985) 535. In force 1987, 146 parties, including the UK. See Boulesbaa, *The UN Convention on Torture and Prospects for Enforcement* (1999); Burgers and Danelius, *The UN Convention Against Torture* (1988); Ingelse, *The UN Committee Against Torture* (2001); Nowak and McArthur, *The UN Convention Against Torture* (2008). See also the 2003 Optional Protocol ("OPCAT"), A/RES/57/199; (2003) 42 I.L.M. 26; (20003) 10 I.H.R.R. 593, which provides for prison monitoring visits by a CAT sub-committee and by national bodies. In force 2006, 50 parties, including the UK. See Evans and Haenni-Dale (2004) 4 H.R.L.R. 19.

6.   Convention on the Rights of the Child 1989 ("CRC")[72];

7.   Convention on the Protection of the Rights of All Migrant Workers 1999 ("CRMW")[73];

8.   Convention on the Rights of Persons with Disabilities 2006 ("CRPD")[74];

9.   Convention for the Protection of All Persons from Enforced Disappearance 2006.[75]

General Assembly human rights declarations on matters on which there are not subject or person specific treaties include:

(1)   Universal Declaration on Human Rights 1948[76];

(2)   Declaration on the Elimination of Religious Freedom 1981[77];

(3)   Declaration on the Right to Development 1986[78];

(4)   Declaration on the Rights of Minorities 1992[79];

(5)   Declaration on the Rights and Responsibilities of Individuals, Groups and Organs of Society to Promote and Protect Universally Recognised Human Rights 1998[80];

(6)   Declaration on the Rights of Indigenous Peoples 2007.[81]

ii. Treaty Monitoring Bodies[82]

Each of the nine human rights treaties listed above[83] has a committee of independent experts,[84] which monitors compliance with it. These are known as treaty monitoring bodies (TMBs). The most well know in the Human Rights Committee, which monitors compliance with the ICCPR. The

---

[72] 1577 U.N.T.S. 3; (1989) 28 I.L.M. 1448. In force 1990, 193 parties, including the UK. See McGoldrick (1991) 5 I.J.L.F. 132; and Van Bueren, *The International Law on the Rights of the Child* (1998). See also the 2000 Protocols on Children in Armed Conflict and on the Sale of Children, Child Prostitution and Child Pornography, A/RES/54/263; (2000) 8 I.H.R.R. 288. Both in force 2002, with 130 and 135 parties respectively, including the UK.

[73] A/RES/45/158; (1991) 30 I.L.M. 117. In force 2003, 42 parties, not including the UK. See Cholewinski, *Migrant Workers in International Human Rights Law* (1997); and De Guchteneire, Pecoud and Cholewinski, eds, *Migration and Human Rights: the UN Convention on Migrant Workers' Rights* (2009).

[74] A/61/611; (2008) 15 I.H.R.R. 255. In force 2008. 78 parties, including the UK. See Kayess and French (2008) 8 H.R.L.R. 1; Lawson (2007) 34 S.J.I.L.C. 563; Megret (2008) 30 H.R.Q. 494; Stein (2007) 95 C.L.R. 75. See also the 2008 Optional Protocol, A/61/611; (2008) 15 I.H.R.R. 277, which provides for a right of individual petition. In force 2008, 46 parties, including the UK.

[75] A/61/488; (2007) 14 I.H.R.R. 582. 18 contracting states, not including the UK. Not yet in force (20 parties required). See McCrory (2007) 7 H.R.L.R. 545.

[76] See below, p.548.

[77] A/36/51. See Boyle and Sheen, *Freedom of Religion and Belief: A World Report*; Lerner (1981) 11 Is Y.H.R. 82; 12 Is Y.H.R. 185; Liskofsy, in Wood, ed., *Religion and the State* (1985); Taylor, *Freedom of Religion* (2005).

[78] See below, p.621.

[79] A/47/135. See Phillips and Rosas, *The UN Minority Rights Declaration* (1993); *Universal Minority Rights* (1995); Rehman, *The Weaknesses in the International Protection of Minority Rights* (2000); Thornberry, *International Law and the Protection of Minorities* (1991); Weller, *Universal Minority Rights* (2007).

[80] A/53/144; (1999) 6 I.H.R.R. 880.

[81] (2008) 15 I.H.R.R. 280. See Errico (2007) 7 H.R.L.R. 741 at 756.

[82] See O'Flaherty, *Human Rights and the UN* (2nd edn 2002) and Vandenhole, *The Procedures Before the UN Human Rights Treaty Bodies* (2004).

[83] There is a 10th TMB, the Sub-Committee on Prevention of Torture, which operates under OPCAT, above n.71. There is no machinery to monitoring compliance with General Assembly declarations, which are not legally binding: see above, p.52.

[84] They vary in size from 10 (CRC, CRMW) to 23 (CEDAW) members. The OPCAT Sub-Committee has 25 members. TMB membership is allocated by UN regional groups.

composition and powers of the HRC, which are typical of TMBs generally are considered below, p.560.

Monitoring is done in the case of each treaty through a reporting procedure by which contracting parties submit periodic reports on their law and practice in the areas covered by the treaty. The TMB holds a public oral hearing at which a government delegation from the state concerned presents its report and responds to questions. NGOs may present shadow national reports.[85] The TMB then adopts "concluding observations"[86] in which it comments on the positive and negative aspects of the state's record of compliance with its treaty obligations. It makes recommendations to the reporting state, which are not legally binding.[87] All TMBs call on states to report on their implementation of recommendations made to them in their next periodic reports and some TMBs have more focused procedures, using a rapporteur on "follow up".[88]

Outside of the reporting system, all TMBs adopt general comments or recommendations in which they state their interpretation of particular articles or address other matters. Although not legally binding upon states' parties, general comments are of considerable importance in practice.[89]

In the case of all but one of the nine human rights treaties,[90] provision is made for monitoring, or enforcement, by the provision of an optional right of individual petition alleging a violation of the treaty. If the petition is declared admissible, the TMB will make a finding as to whether there has been a violation. These findings are not legally binding.[91] In some treaties,[92] provision is also made for state petitions by one state party against another, but no such petition has ever been brought. Some treaties[93] also provide the TMB with a power to undertake an inquiry upon receipt of "reliable information indicating grave or systematic violations by a state party" of treaty rights.

For some time, the treaty-based reporting mechanism for these human rights treaties has been the subject of concern because of the large workload that it imposes for states parties, and the failure of states to submit full reports on time or at all.[94] A proposal for a single national report for all treaties , possibly examined by a single unified TMB,[95] has now given way to the idea of an expanded core document, supplemented by the treaty specific reports responding to the particular guarantees of each treaty that are already required.[96]

Other UN treaties with a human rights character but that do not provide for monitoring machinery

---

[85] On the other varying possibilities for NGO participation in each TMB, see Gaer (2003) 2 J.H.R. 339.

[86] On "concluding comments", see generally O'Flaherty (2006) 6 H.R.L.R. 27.

[87] The Human Rights Council makes use of concluding observations during UPR.

[88] See the 10th Inter-Committee Meeting of the Human Rights Treaty Bodies, HRI/ICM/2009/6.

[89] On HRC general comments, which are typical, see below, p.561.

[90] The exception is the CRC: a working group has the drafting of an optional protocol providing for a right of petition under consideration. Rights of individual petition are currently in force for six of the eight other treaties. Those provided for the ICESCR and the Convention on the Rights of Disappeared Persons are not operational: the ICESCR Optional Protocol and the Disappeared Persons Convention are not yet in force.

[91] Some TMBs, e.g. the HRC, have rapporteurs on "follow up" who review a state's response to findings of violations.

[92] See, e.g. the ICCPR, below, p.562.

[93] e.g. CAT and CEDAW. States may opt out.

[94] See Alston and Crawford, eds, above, at n.70. As of January 2004, 185 initial reports (114 for over five years) and 660 periodic reports to the (then) six human rights treaty committees were overdue: *Effective Functioning of Human Rights Mechanisms Treaty Bodies*, E/CN.4/2004/98, p.2.

[95] For a more ambitious proposal for an International Court of Human Rights, see Nowak (2007) 7 H.R.L.R. 251.

[96] See *Effective Functioning of Human Rights Mechanisms Treaty Bodies*, E/CN.4/2004/98 and the 2004 Report of the UN Secretariat on Guidelines for an Expanded Core Document, HRI/MC/2004/3. See also Johnstone (2007) 7 H.R.L.R. 173 and O'Flaherty and O'Brien (2007) 7 H.R.L.R. 141. For the most recent reform initiative, see the *Dublin Statement on the Process of Strengthening of the UN Human Treaty Body System* (2009), on which see O'Flaherty (2010) 10 H.R.L.R. (in press).

are the Genocide Convention 1948,[97] the Convention Relating to the Status of Refugees 1951[98] and the Convention on the Crime of Apartheid.[99]

D. The UN High Commissioner for Human Rights

In 1993 the post of UN High Commissioner for Human Rights was established, as a result of the Vienna World Conference on Human Rights. The Commissioner's responsibilities are very generally phrased. They include the following[100]:

(a) To promote and protect the effective enjoyment by all of all civil, cultural, economic, political and social rights;

(b) To carry out the tasks assigned to him/her by the competent bodies of the United Nations system in the field of human rights and to make recommendations to them with a view to improving the promotion and protection of all human rights; . . .

(f) To play an active role in removing the current obstacles and in meeting the challenges to the full realization of all human rights and in preventing the continuation of human rights violations throughout the world, as reflected in the Vienna Declaration and Programme of Action
. . .

UNIVERSAL DECLARATION OF HUMAN RIGHTS 1948[101]

G.A. Resolution 217A (III), G.A.O.R., 3rd Sess., Part I, Resns, p.71

The General Assembly proclaims
This Universal Declaration of Human Rights as a common standard of achievement for all peoples and all nations, to the end that every individual and every organ of society, keeping this Declaration constantly in mind, shall strive by teaching and education to promote respect for these rights and freedoms and by progressive measures, national and international, to secure their universal and effective recognition and observance, both among the peoples of Member States themselves and among the peoples of territories under their jurisdiction.

Article 1

All human beings are born free and equal in dignity and rights. They are endowed with reason and conscience and should act towards one another in a spirit of brotherhood.

---

[97] 78 U.N.T.S. 277; (1951) 45 A.J.I.L. Supp 6. In force 1951, 141 parties, including the UK. See Wright 1949) 43 A.J.I.L. 738; Lemkin (1947) 41 A.J.I.L.145; Robinson, *The Genocide Convention: a Commentary* (1960). On the crime of genocide, see Cassese, *International Criminal Law* (2nd edn 2008), Ch.5.

[98] 189 U.N.T.S. 150. In force 1965, 144 parties, including the UK. See Goodwin-Gill and McAdam, *The Refugee in International Law* (3rd edn 2007).

[99] (1974) 13 I.L.M. 50. In force 1976, 107 parties, not including the UK.

[100] G.A. Resn. 48/141, G.A.O.R., Supp. 49, p.261. See also the annual reports of the Commissioner in G.A.O.R., Supp. 36. The present Commissioner is Navanethem Pillay (2008). She was formerly an International Criminal Court and ICTR judge and human rights lawyer in South Africa. See Alston (1997) 8 E.J.I.L. 321; Boyle (2004) 22 N.Q.H.R. 310; Clapham (1994) 5 E.J.I.L. 556; and Ramcharran, *The United Nations High Commissioner for Human Rights* (2002).

[101] See Alfredsson and Eide, eds, *The Universal Declaration of Human Rights: A Common Standard of Achievement* (1999); Baehr, Flinterman and Senders, eds, *Innovation and Inspiration: Fifty Years of the Universal Declaration of Human Rights* (1999); Johnson and Symonides, *The Universal Declaration of Human Rights: A History of its Creation and Implementation* (1998); Van der Heijden and Tahzib-Lie, eds, *Reflections on the Universal Declaration of Human Rights* (1998); Morsink, *The Universal Declaration of Human Rights: Origins, Drafting Intent* (2000); Von Bernstorff, 19 E.J.I.L. 903 (203).

Article 2

Everyone is entitled to all the rights and freedoms set forth in this Declaration, without distinction of any kind, such as race, colour, sex, language, religion, political or other opinion, national or social origin, property, birth or other status. Furthermore, no distinction shall be made on the basis of the political, jurisdictional or international status of the country or territory to which a person belongs, whether it be independent, trust, non-self-governing or under any other limitation of sovereignty.

Article 3

Everyone has the right of life, liberty and security of person.

Article 4

No one shall be held in slavery or servitude; slavery and the slave trade shall be prohibited in all their forms.

Article 5

No one shall be subjected to torture or to cruel, inhuman or degrading treatment or punishment.

Article 6

Everyone has the right to recognition everywhere as a person before the law.

Article 7

All are equal before the law and are entitled without any discrimination to equal protection of the law. All are entitled to equal protection against any discrimination in violation of this Declaration and against any incitement to such discrimination.

Article 8

Everyone has the right to an effective remedy by the competent national tribunals for acts violating the fundamental rights granted him by the constitution or by law.

Article 9

No one shall be subjected to arbitrary arrest, detention or exile.

Article 10

Everyone is entitled in full equality to a fair and public hearing by an independent and impartial tribunal, in the determination of his rights and obligations and of any criminal charge against him.

Article 11

1. Everyone charged with a penal offence has the right to be presumed innocent until proved guilty according to law in a public trial at which he has had all the guarantees necessary for his defence.
2. No one shall be held guilty of any penal offence on account of any act or omission which did not constitute a penal offence, under national or international law, at the time when it was committed. Nor shall a heavier penalty be imposed than the one that was applicable at the time the penal offence was committed.

Article 12

No one shall be subjected to arbitrary interference with his privacy, family, home or correspondence, nor to attacks upon his honour and reputation. Everyone has the right to the protection of the law against such interference or attacks.

Article 13

1. Everyone has the right to freedom of movement and residence within the borders of each state.
2. Everyone has the right to leave any country, including his own, and to return to his country.

Article 14

1. Everyone has the right to seek and to enjoy in other countries asylum from persecution.
2. This right may not be invoked in the case of prosecutions genuinely arising from non-political crimes or from acts contrary to the purposes and principles of the United Nations.

Article 15

1. Everyone has the right to a nationality.
2. No one shall be arbitrarily deprived of his nationality nor denied the right to change his nationality.

Article 16

1. Men and women of full age, without limitation due to race, nationality or religion, have the right to marry and to found a family. They are entitled to equal rights as to marriage, during marriage and at its dissolution.
2. Marriage shall be entered into only with the free and full consent of the intending spouses.
3. The family is the natural and fundamental group unit of society and is entitled to protection by society and the State.

Article 17

1. Everyone has the right to own property alone as well as in association with others.
2. No one shall be arbitrarily deprived of his property.

Article 18

Everyone has the right to freedom of thought, conscience and religion; this right includes freedom to change his religion or belief, and freedom, either alone or in community with others and in public or private, to manifest his religion or belief in teaching, practice, worship and observance.

Article 19

Everyone has the right to freedom of opinion and expression; this right includes freedom to hold opinions without interference and to seek, receive and impart information and ideas through any media and regardless of frontiers.

Article 20

1. Everyone has the right to freedom of peaceful assembly and association.
2. No one may be compelled to belong to an association.

Article 21

1. Everyone has the right to take part in the government of his country, directly or through freely chosen representatives.

2. Everyone has the right of equal access to public service in his country.

3. The will of the people shall be the basis of the authority of government; this will shall be expressed in periodic and genuine elections which shall be by universal and equal suffrage and shall be held by secret vote or by equivalent free voting procedures.

Article 22

Everyone, as a member of society, has the right to social security and is entitled to realisation through national effort and international co-operation and in accordance with the organisation and resources of each State, of the economic, social and cultural rights indispensable for his dignity and the free development of his personality.

Article 23

1. Everyone has the right to work, to free choice of employment, to just and favourable conditions of work and to protection against unemployment.

2. Everyone, without any discrimination, has the right to equal pay for equal work.

3. Everyone who works has the right to just and favourable remuneration ensuring for himself and his family an existence worthy of human dignity, and supplemented, if necessary, by other means of social protection.

4. Everyone has the right to form and to join trade unions for the protection of his interests.

Article 24

Everyone has the right to rest and leisure including reasonable limitation of working hours and periodic holidays with pay.

Article 25

Everyone has the right to a standard of living adequate for the health and well-being of himself and of his family, including food, clothing, housing and medical care and necessary social services, and the right to security in the event of unemployment, sickness, disability, widowhood, old age or other lack of livelihood in circumstances beyond his control.

2. Motherhood and childhood are entitled to special care and assistance. All children, whether born in or out of wedlock, shall enjoy the same social protection.

Article 26

1. Everyone has the right to education. Education shall be free, at least in the elementary and fundamental stages. Elementary education shall be compulsory. Technical and professional education shall be made generally available and higher education shall be equally accessible to all on the basis of merit.

2. Education shall be directed to the full development of the human personality and to the strengthening of respect for human rights and fundamental freedoms. It shall promote understanding, tolerance and friendship among all nations, racial or religious groups, and shall further the activities of the United Nations for the maintenance of peace.

3. Parents have a prior right to choose the kind of education that shall be given to their children.

Article 27

1. Everyone has the right freely to participate in the cultural life of the community, to enjoy the arts and to share in scientific advancement and its benefits.

2. Everyone has the right to protection of the moral and material interests resulting from any scientific, literary or artistic production of which he is the author.

Article 28

Everyone is entitled to a social and international order in which the rights and freedoms set forth in the Declaration can be fully realised.

Article 29

1. Everyone has duties to the community in which alone the free and full development of his personality is possible.

2. In the exercise of his rights and freedoms, everyone shall be subject only to such limitations as are determined by law solely for the purpose of securing due recognition and respect for the rights and freedoms of others and of meeting the just requirements of morality, public order and the general welfare in a democratic society.

3. These rights and freedoms may in no case be exercised contrary to the purposes and principles of the United Nations.

Article 30

Nothing in this Declaration may be interpreted as implying for any State, group or person any right to engage in any activity or to perform any act aimed at the destruction of any of the rights and freedoms set forth herein.

Notes

One of the first steps taken by the United Nations was the adoption by the General Assembly of the Universal Declaration of Human Rights, by 48 votes to none, with eight abstentions.[102] The Declaration contains a comprehensive list of civil, political, economic, social and cultural rights. According to Mrs Eleanor Roosevelt, United States representative to the General Assembly and Chairman of the United Nations Commission on Human Rights during the drafting of the Declaration, it "is not, and does not purport to be a statement of law or of legal obligation"; it is instead, she continued, "a common standard of achievement for all peoples of all nations."[103] Despite this, the Declaration has undoubtedly had considerable impact in shaping subsequent treaties on human rights, and has been relied upon extensively by persons putting forward claims for fair treatment in terms of human rights; it has also had some impact upon the content of the constitutions of new states and upon decisions of municipal courts.[104] The status of the Declaration as a source of rules of customary international law was considered in the *Filartiga* case.[105]

INTERNATIONAL COVENANT ON CIVIL AND POLITICAL RIGHTS 1966[106]

999 U.N.T.S. 171; (1977) U.K.T.S. 6, Cmnd. 6702; (1967) 61 A.J.I.L. 870

Article 1

1. All people have the right of self-determination. By virtue of that right they freely determine their political status and freely pursue their economic, social and cultural development.

2. All peoples may, for their own ends, freely dispose of their natural wealth and resources without prejudice to

---

[102] The abstaining states were, the Byelorussian SSR, Czechoslovakia, Poland, Saudi Arabia, South Africa, the Ukrainian SSR, the USSR and Yugoslavia.

[103] (1948) 19 *US Dept. of State Bull.* 751.

[104] See *Measures taken within the United Nations in the field of Human Rights* UN Doc. A/CONF. 32/5, pp.28–30.

[105] Below, p.630.

[106] In force 1976. 165 parties, including the UK. See Bair, *The International Covenant on Civil and Political Rights and its (First) Optional Protocol* (2005); Conte, Davidson and Burchill, *Defining Civil and Political Rights: the Jurisprudence of the United Nations Human Rights Committee* (2004); Joseph, Schultz and Castan, eds, *The International Covenant on Civil and Political Rights* (2nd edn 2004); McGoldrick, *The Human Rights Committee* (1991); and Nowak, *UN Covenant on Civil and Political Rights: CCPR Commentary* (2nd edn 2005).

any obligations arising out of international economic co-operation, based upon the principle of mutual benefit, and international law. In no case may a people be deprived of its own means of subsistence.

3. The States Parties to the present Covenant, including those having responsibility for the administration of Non-Self-Governing and Trust Territories, shall promote the realisation of the right of self-determination, and shall respect that right, in conformity with the provisions of the Charter of the United Nations.

Article 2

1. Each State Party to the present Covenant undertakes to respect and to ensure to all individuals within its territory and subject to its jurisdiction the rights recognised in the present Covenant, without distinction of any kind, such as race, colour, sex, language, religion, political or other opinion, national or social origin, property, birth or other status.

2. Where not already provided for by existing legislative or other measures, each State Party to the present Covenant undertakes to take the necessary steps, in accordance with its constitutional processes and with the provisions of the present Covenant, to adopt such legislative or other measures as may be necessary to give effect to the rights recognised in the present Covenant.

3. Each State Party to the present Covenant undertakes:

(a) To ensure that any person whose rights or freedoms as herein recognized are violated shall have an effective remedy, notwithstanding that the violation has been committed by persons acting in an official capacity;

(b) To ensure that any person claiming such a remedy shall have his right thereto determined by competent judicial, administrative or legislative authorities, or by any other competent authority provided for by the legal system of the State, and to develop the possibilities of judicial remedy;

(c) To ensure that the competent authorities shall enforce such remedies when granted.

Article 3

The States Parties to the present Covenant undertake to ensure the equal right of men and women to the enjoyment of all civil and political rights set forth in the present Covenant.

Article 4

1. In time of public emergency which threatens the life of the nation and the existence of which is officially proclaimed, the States Parties to the present Covenant may take measures derogating from their obligations under the present Covenant to the extent strictly required by the exigencies of the situation, provided that such measures are not inconsistent with their other obligations under international law and do not involve discrimination solely on the ground of race, colour, sex, language, religion or social origin.

2. No derogation from articles 6, 7, 8 (paragraphs 1 and 2), 11, 15, 16 and 18 may be made under this provision.

3. Any State Party to the present Covenant availing itself of the right of derogation shall immediately inform the other States Parties to the present Covenant, through the intermediary of the Secretary-General of the United Nations, of the provisions from which it has derogated and of the reasons by which it was actuated. A further communication shall be made, through the same intermediary, on the date on which it terminates such derogation.

Article 5

1. Nothing in the present Covenant may be interpreted as implying for any State, group or person any right to engage in any activity or perform any act aimed at the destruction of any of the rights and freedoms recognised herein or at their limitation to a greater extent than is provided for in the present Covenant.

2. There shall be no restriction upon or derogation from any of the fundamental human rights recognised or existing in any State Party to the present Covenant pursuant to law, conventions, regulations or custom on the pretext that the present Covenant does not recognise such rights or that it recognises them to a lesser extent.

Article 6

1. Every human being has the inherent right to life. This right shall be protected by law. No one shall be arbitrarily deprived of his life.

2. In countries which have not abolished the death penalty, sentence of death may be imposed only for the most serious crimes in accordance with the law in force at the time of the commission of the crime and not contrary to the provisions of the present Covenant and to the Convention on the Prevention and Punishment of the Crime of Genocide. This penalty can only be carried out pursuant to a final judgment rendered by a competent court.

3. When deprivation of life constitutes the crime of genocide, it is understood that nothing in this article shall authorise any State Party to the present Covenant to derogate in any way from any obligation assumed under the provisions of the Convention on the Prevention and Punishment of the Crime of Genocide.

4. Anyone sentenced to death shall have the right to seek pardon or commutation of the sentence. Amnesty, pardon or commutation of the sentence of death may be granted in all cases.

5. Sentence of death shall not be imposed for crimes committed by persons below 18 years of age and shall not be carried out on pregnant women.

6. Nothing in this article shall be invoked to delay or to prevent the abolition of capital punishment by any State Party to the present Covenant.

Article 7

No one shall be subjected to torture or to cruel, inhuman or degrading treatment or punishment. In particular, no one shall be subjected without his free consent to medical or scientific experimentation.

Article 8

1. No one shall be held in slavery; slavery and the slave-trade in all their forms shall be prohibited.

2. No one shall be held in servitude.

3.   (a) No one shall be required to perform forced or compulsory labour;

   (b) Paragraph 3(a) shall not be held to preclude, in countries where imprisonment with hard labour may be imposed as a punishment for a crime, the performance of hard labour in pursuance of a sentence to such punishment by a competent court;

   (c) For the purpose of this paragraph the term "forced or compulsory labour" shall not include:

      (i) Any work or service, not referred to in subparagraph (b), normally required of a person who is under detention in consequence of a lawful order of a court, or of a person during conditional release from such detention;

      (ii) Any service of a military character and, in countries where conscientious objection is recognised, any national service required by law of conscientious objectors;

      (iii) Any service exacted in cases of emergency or calamity threatening the life or well-being of the community;

      (iv) Any work or service which forms part of normal civil obligations.

Article 9

1. Everyone has the right to liberty and security of person. No one shall be subjected to arbitrary arrest or detention. No one shall be deprived of his liberty except on such grounds and in accordance with such procedure as are established by law.

2. Anyone who is arrested shall be informed, at the time of arrest, of the reasons for his arrest and shall be promptly informed of any charges against him.

3. Anyone arrested or detained on a criminal charge shall be brought promptly before a judge or other officer authorised by law to exercise judicial power and shall be entitled to trial within a reasonable time or to release. It shall not be the general rule that persons awaiting trial shall be detained in custody, but release may be subject to guarantees to appear for trial, at any other stage of the judicial proceedings, and, should occasion arise, for execution of the judgment.

4. Anyone who is deprived of his liberty by arrest or detention shall be entitled to take proceedings before a

court, in order that that court may decide without delay on the lawfulness of his detention and order his release if the detention is not lawful.

5. Anyone who has been the victim of unlawful arrest or detention shall have an enforceable right to compensation.

Article 10

1. All persons deprived of their liberty shall be treated with humanity and with respect for the inherent dignity of the human person.

2. (a) Accused persons shall, save in exceptional circumstances, be segregated from convicted persons and shall be subject to separate treatment appropriate to their status as unconvicted persons;

  (b) Accused juvenile persons shall be separated from adults and brought as speedily as possible for adjudication.

3. The penitentiary system shall comprise treatment of prisoners the essential aim of which shall be their reformation and social rehabilitation. Juvenile offenders shall be segregated from adults and be accorded treatment appropriate to their age and legal status.

Article 11

No one shall be imprisoned merely on the ground of inability to fulfil a contractual obligation.

Article 12

1. Everyone lawfully within the territory of a State shall, within that territory, have the right to liberty of movement and freedom to choose his residence.

2. Everyone shall be free to leave any country, including his own.

3. The above-mentioned rights shall not be subject to any restrictions except those which are provided by law, are necessary to protect national security, public order (*ordre public*), public health or morals or the rights and freedoms of others, and are consistent with the other rights recognised in the present Covenant.

4. No one shall be arbitrarily deprived of the right to enter his own country.

Article 13

An alien lawfully in the territory of a State Party to the present Covenant may be expelled therefrom only in pursuance of a decision reached in accordance with law and shall, except where compelling reasons of national security otherwise require, be allowed to submit the reasons against his expulsion and to have his case reviewed by, and be represented for the purpose before, the competent authority or a person or persons especially designated by the competent authority.

Article 14

1. All persons shall be equal before the courts and tribunals. In the determination of any criminal charge against him, or of his rights and obligations in a suit of law, everyone shall be entitled to a fair and public hearing of a competent, independent and impartial tribunal established by law. The Press and the public may be excluded from all or part of a trial for reasons of morals, public order (*ordre public*) or national security in a democratic society, or where the interest of the private lives of the parties so requires, or the extent strictly necessary in the opinion of the court in special circumstances where publicity would prejudice the interests of justice; but any judgment rendered in a criminal case or in a suit at law shall be made public except where the interest of juvenile persons otherwise requires or the proceedings concern matrimonial disputes or the guardianship of children.

2. Everyone charged with a criminal offence shall have the right to be presumed innocent until proved guilty according to law.

3. In the determination of any criminal charge against him, everyone shall be entitled to the following minimum guarantees, in full equality:

(a) To be informed promptly and in detail in a language which he understands of the nature and cause of the charge against him;

(b) To have adequate time and facilities for the preparation of his defence and to communicate with counsel of his own choosing;

(c) To be tried without undue delay;

(d) To be tried in his presence, and to defend himself in person or through legal assistance of his own choosing; to be informed, if he does not have legal assistance, of this right; and to have legal assistance assigned to him, in any case where the interests of justice so require, and without payment by him in any such case if he does not have sufficient means to pay for it;

(e) To examine, or have examined, the witnesses against him and to obtain the attendance and examination of witnesses on his behalf under the same conditions as witnesses against him;

(f) To have the free assistance of an interpreter if he cannot understand or speak the language used in court;

(g) Not to be compelled to testify against himself or to confess guilt.

4. In the case of juvenile persons, the procedure shall be such as will take account of their age and the desirability of promoting their rehabilitation.

5. Everyone convicted of a crime shall have the right to his conviction and sentence being reviewed by a higher tribunal according to law.

6. When a person has by a final decision been convicted of a criminal offence and when subsequently his conviction has been reversed or he has been pardoned on the ground that a new or newly discovered fact shows conclusively that there has been a miscarriage of justice, the person who has suffered punishment as a result of such conviction shall be compensated according to law, unless it is proved that the non-disclosure of the unknown fact in time is wholly or partly attributable to him.

7. No one shall be liable to be tried or punished again for an offence for which he has already been finally convicted or acquitted in accordance with the law and penal procedure of each country.

Article 15

1. No one shall be held guilty of any criminal offence on account of any act or omission which did not constitute a criminal offence, under national or international law, at the time when it was committed. Nor shall a heavier penalty be imposed than the one that was applicable at the time when the criminal offence was committed. If, subsequent to the commission of the offence, provision is made by law for imposition of a lighter penalty, the offender shall benefit thereby.

2. Nothing in this article shall prejudice the trial and punishment of any person for any act or omission which, at the time when it was committed, was criminal according to the general principles of law recognised by the community of nations.

Article 16

Everyone shall have the right to recognition everywhere as a person before the law.

Article 17

1. No one shall be subjected to arbitrary or unlawful interference with his privacy, family, home or correspondence, nor to unlawful attacks on his honour and reputation.

2. Everyone has the right to the protection of the law against such interference or attacks.

Article 18

1. Everyone shall have the right to freedom of thought, conscience and religion. This right shall include freedom to have or adopt a religion or belief of his choice, and freedom, either individually or in community with others and in public or private, to manifest his religion or belief in worship, observance, practice and teaching.

2. No one shall be subject to coercion which would impair his freedom to have or to adopt a religion or belief of his choice.

3. Freedom to manifest one's religion or beliefs may be subject only to such limitations as are prescribed by law and are necessary to protect public safety, order, health, or morals or the fundamental rights and freedoms of others.

4. The States Parties to the present Covenant undertake to have respect for the liberty of parents and, when applicable, legal guardians to ensure the religious and moral education of their children in conformity with their own convictions.

Article 19

1. Everyone shall have the right to hold opinions without interference.

2. Everyone shall have the right to freedom of expression; this right shall include freedom to seek, receive and impart information and ideas of all kinds, regardless of frontiers, either orally, in writing or in print, in the form of art, or through any other media of his choice.

3. The exercise of the rights provided for in paragraph 2 of this article carries with it special duties and responsibilities. It may therefore be subject to certain restrictions, but these shall only be such as are provided by law and are necessary:

(a) For respect of the rights or reputations of others;

(b) For the protection of national security or of public order (*ordre public*), or of public health or morals.

Article 20

1. Any propaganda for war shall be prohibited by law.

2. Any advocacy of national, racial or religious hatred that constitutes incitement to discrimination, hostility or violence shall be prohibited by law.

Article 21

The right of peaceful assembly shall be recognised. No restrictions may be placed on the exercise of this right other than those imposed in conformity with the law and which are necessary in a democratic society in the interests of national security or public safety, public order (*ordre public*), the protection of public health or morals or the protection of the rights and freedoms of others.

Article 22

1. Everyone shall have the right to freedom of association with others, including the right to form and join trade unions for the protection of his interests.

2. No restrictions may be placed on the exercise of this right other than those which are prescribed by law and which are necessary in a democratic society in the interests of national security or public safety, public order (*ordre public*), the protection of public health or morals or the protection of the rights and freedoms of others. This article shall not prevent the imposition of lawful restrictions on members of the armed forces and of the police in their exercise of this right.

3. Nothing in this article shall authorise States Parties to the International Labour Organisation Convention of 1948 concerning Freedom of Association and Protection of the Right to Organize to take legislative measures which would prejudice, or to apply the law in such a manner as to prejudice, the guarantees provided for in that Convention.

Article 23

1. The family is the natural and fundamental group unit of society and is entitled to protection by society and the State.

2. The right of men and women of marriageable age to marry and to found a family shall be recognised.

3. No marriage shall be entered into without the free and full consent of the intending spouses.

4. State Parties to the present Covenant shall take appropriate steps to ensure equality of rights and responsibilities of spouses as to marriage, during marriage and at its dissolution. In the case of dissolution, provision shall be made for the necessary protection of any children.

Article 24

1. Every child shall have, without any discrimination as to race, colour, sex, language, religion, national or social origin, property or birth, the right to such measures of protection as are required by his status as a minor, on the part of his family, society and the State.
2. Every child shall be registered immediately after birth and shall have a name.
3. Every child has the right to acquire a nationality.

Article 25

Every citizen shall have the right and the opportunity, without any of the distinctions mentioned in article 2 and without unreasonable restrictions:

(a) To take part in the conduct of public affairs, directly or through freely chosen representatives;

(b) To vote and to be elected at genuine periodic elections which shall be by universal and equal suffrage and shall be held by secret ballot, guaranteeing the free expression of the will of the electors;

(c) To have access, on general terms of equality, to public service in his country.

Article 26

All persons are equal before the law and are entitled without any discrimination to the equal protection of the law. In this respect, the law shall prohibit any discrimination and guarantee to all persons equal and effective protection against discrimination on any ground such as race, colour, sex, language, religion, political or other opinion, national or social origin, property, birth or other status.

Article 27

In those States in which ethnic, religious or linguistic minorities exist, persons belonging to such minorities shall not be denied the right, in community with the other members of their group, to enjoy their own culture, to profess and practice their own religion, or to use their own language.

Article 50

The provisions of the present Covenant shall extend to all parts of federal States without any limitations or exceptions.

SECOND OPTIONAL PROTOCOL TO THE INTERNATIONAL COVENANT ON CIVIL AND POLITICAL RIGHTS, AIMING AT THE ABOLITION OF THE DEATH PENALTY 1989[107]

(2000) U.K.T.S. 39, Cm.4676; 26 I.L.M. 1464

Article 1

1. No one within the jurisdiction of a State Party to the present Optional Protocol shall be executed.
2. Each State party shall take all necessary measures to abolish the death penalty within its jurisdiction.

---

[107] In force 1991, 72 parties, including the UK.

Article 2

1. No reservation is admissible to the present Protocol, except for a reservation made at the time of ratification or accession that provides for the application of the death penalty in time of war pursuant to a conviction for a most serious crime of a military nature committed during wartime. ...

Notes

1.   The ICCPR has 165 parties. Of the missing states, a significant number are from Asia, including China, Malaysia, Myanmar, Pakistan, Saudi Arabia and Singapore. A number of the states parties are successor states to the former USSR and the Federal Republic of Yugoslavia. In General Comment No.26,[108] the Human Rights Committee ("HRC") took the view that the such states automatically succeed to the obligations of their predecessors:

> "4. ... The Human Rights Committee has consistently taken the view, as evidenced by its long-standing practice, that once the people are accorded the protection of the rights under the Covenant, such protection devolves with territory and continues to belong to them, notwith-standing change in government of the State party, including dismemberment in more than one State or State succession or any subsequent action of the State party designed to divest them of the rights guaranteed by the Covenant."

In 1997, North Korea informed the UN Secretary General, as depositary, of its withdrawal from the ICCPR.[109] The Secretary General responded that "a withdrawal from the Covenant would not appear possible unless all of the States Parties ... agree."[110] The HRC then adopted General Comment No.26 (above), in which it similarly took the view that the ICCPR and its Second Optional Protocol, neither of which has a withdrawal clause, are not open to withdrawal. The HRC continues to regard North Korea as an ICCPR party and North Korea has since reported again under the ICCPR. In contrast, the First Optional Protocol, which provided for a right of individual petition, expressly permits withdrawal (art.12). Jamaica withdrew from the First Protocol in 1997. Trinidad and Tobago and Guyana did so in 1998 and 1999, but then became parties once more, with new reservations excluding death penalty cases. When the Trinidad and Tobago reservation was declared invalid,[111] it withdrew from the Protocol again.

2.   The basic obligation of states parties in art.2(1) ICCPR was commented upon by the HRC in General Comment No.31. This reads:

> "5. The article 2, paragraph 1, obligation to respect and ensure the rights recognized by the Covenant has immediate effect for all States parties. ...
>
>   6. The legal obligation under article 2, paragraph 1, is both negative and positive in nature. States Parties must refrain from violation of the rights recognized by the Covenant, and any restrictions on any of those rights must be permissible under the relevant provisions of the Covenant. Where such restrictions are made, States must demonstrate their necessity and only take such measures as are proportionate to the pursuance of legitimate aims in order to

---

[108] (1998) 5 I.H.R.R. 301. Similarly, the HRC regards China, which is not otherwise an ICCPR party, as obliged to report, which China does, under the ICCPR in respect of Hong Kong, following its transfer from the UK.
[109] See Evatt (1999) 5 A.J.H.R. 215. See also Crawford, in Alston and Crawford, above, n.70, p.10.
[110] C.N.467 1997. Treaties-10, November 12, 1997.
[111] See below, p.667.

ensure continuous and effective protection of Covenant rights. In no case may the restrictions be applied or invoked in a manner that would impair the essence of a Covenant right. . . .

8. The article 2, paragraph 1, obligations are binding on States Parties and do not, as such, have direct horizontal effect as a matter of international law. The Covenant cannot be viewed as a substitute for domestic criminal or civil law. However the positive obligations on States Parties to ensure Covenant rights will only be fully discharged if individuals are protected by the State, not just against violations of Covenant rights by its agents, but also against acts committed by private persons or entities that would impair the enjoyment of Covenant rights in so far as they are amenable to application between private persons or entities. There may be circumstances in which a failure to ensure Covenant rights as required by article 2 would give rise to violations by States Parties of those rights, as a result of States Parties' permitting or failing to take appropriate measures or to exercise due diligence to prevent, punish, investigate or redress the harm caused by such acts by private persons or entities. States are reminded of the interrelationship between the positive obligations imposed under article 2 and the need to provide effective remedies in the event of breach under article 2, paragraph 3. The Covenant itself envisages in some articles certain areas where there are positive obligations on States Parties to address the activities of private persons or entities. For example, the privacy-related guarantees or article 17 must be protected by law. It is also implicit in article 7 that States Parties have to take positive measures to ensure that private persons or entities do not inflict torture or cruel, inhuman or degrading treatment or punishment on others within their power. In fields affecting basic aspects of ordinary life such as work or housing, individuals are to be protected from discrimination within the meaning of article 26. . . .

10. States Parties are required by article 2, paragraph 1, to respect and to ensure the Covenant rights to all persons who may be within their territory and to all persons subject to their jurisdiction. This means that a State party must respect and ensure the rights laid down in the Covenant to anyone within the power or effective control of that State Party, even if not situated within the territory of the State Party. As indicated in General Comment 15 adopted at the twenty-seventh session (1986), the enjoyment of Covenant rights is not limited to citizens of State parties but must also be available to all individuals, regardless of nationality or statelessness, such as asylum seekers, refugees, migrant workers and other persons, who may find themselves in the territory or subject to the jurisdiction of the State Party. [See also the *Wall* case, para.109, below, p.601.] This principle also applies to those within the power or effective control of the forces of a State Party acting outside its territory, regardless of the circumstances in which such power or effective control was obtained, such as forces constituting a national contingent of a State Party assigned to an international peace-keeping or peace-enforcement operation.

11. As implied in General Comment 29 . . . on States of Emergencies . . . paragraph 3 [below, p.597], the Covenant applies also in situations of armed conflict to which the rules of international humanitarian law are applicable. While, in respect of certain Covenant rights, more specific rules of international humanitarian law may be specially relevant for the purposes of the interpretation of Covenant rights, both spheres of law are complementary, not mutually exclusive."

As para.10 makes clear, the term "jurisdiction" in art.2(1) means that the ICCPR applies to Al Quaeda and Taliban suspects detained by the US at its base in Guantanamo Bay, quite apart from the US lease of the territory from Cuba.[112]

3. The system of implementation of the ICCPR centres upon the HRC.[113] This consists of 18 members elected from among the nationals of the contracting parties.[114] In the election, "consideration shall be given to equitable geographic distribution of membership and to the representation of the different forms of civilisation and of the principal legal systems" (art.31(2), ICCPR).[115] The members are independent experts; they do not represent their governments. They nearly all have a legal background. As to the independence of members, Joseph, Schultz and Castan state[116]:

> "A survey of the curricula vitae of the eighteen current members (as at October 2003) reveals that almost all members have expert human rights qualifications, and no direct connections with their governments. Thus, the current Committee seems to fulfil the requisite criteria of independence and expertise. This was not perhaps the case with early Committees, which had too many diplomats as members, who may have been inclined to push the 'official' view of their home States."

4. The parties to the Covenant "undertake to submit periodic reports on the measures they have adopted which give effect to the rights recognised herein and on the progress made in the enjoyment of those rights" (art.40(1)).[117] The Committee has decided that, after a state's initial report, subsequent reports shall be submitted whenever the Committee so requests, in most cases every four or five years. The Committee has experienced the same problems of unsubmitted, late or inadequate reports as other international bodies that operate reporting systems to monitor international human rights treaty obligations.[118] Its practice is to consider reports at public hearings to which the state whose report is being discussed is invited to send representatives to introduce the report and respond to questions.[119] The exchanges have generally been courteous, with the Committee emphasising that its role is to achieve "constructive dialogue" in order to define the obligations in the Covenant and to encourage compliance rather than to criticise.[120]

---

[112] As of 1903, the US has held a permanent lease of the territory at Guantanamo Bay on which it has a military base. The lease was granted by Cuba by two 1903 agreements and a 1934 treaty with the US, on payment of an annual rent of about $4,000.

[113] On the Committee, see Joseph, Schultz and Castan, above, n.105, pp.16 et seq.; Steiner, in Alston and Crawford, eds, *The Future of UN Human Rights Treaty Reporting* (2000), Ch.2; and Opsahl, in Alston, ed., *The United Nations and Human Rights* (1992), Ch.10. See also Schmidt (1992) 41 I.C.L.Q. 645.

[114] Article 28. Members, who serve part-time, are elected for renewable four year terms.

[115] In 2009, the Committee was composed of nationals of the following states: African states: Algeria, Egypt, Mauritius, Morocco, Tunisia, South Africa; Asian states: India, Japan; European and other Western states: France, Ireland, Romania, Sweden, Switzerland, UK, US; Latin American and Caribbean states: Argentina, Colombia, Peru.

[116] See above, n.105, p.17.

[117] On the reporting system, see Boerefijn, *The Reporting Procedure under the Covenant on Civil and Political Rights: Practice and Procedures of the Human Rights Committee* (1999); Joseph (1995) 13 N.Q.H.R. 5.

[118] See above, p.681.

[119] The HRC may, in its discretion, review a state's compliance with the ICCPR in the absence of a report: General Comment No.30 (2003) 10 I.H.R.R. 1, para.4.

[120] For a notable exception, see the hearing of the first Iranian report which the Iranian representative described as "a political inquisition"; S.R. 368, para.58. The 1994 hearing of the Egyptian report, S.R. 1244–7, was brought to life—hearings can seem less than exciting to the outside observer—by persistent questioning that led to some unexpectedly frank answers on issues such as the superiority of shari'a law over the ICCPR and the treatment of the Baha'i.

An important matter is the information that the Committee may have recourse to when considering a state's report. Given that national reports inevitably present the government point of view, the question arises whether the Committee may rely upon information from specialised agencies (particularly the ILO and UNESCO) that operate in areas covered by the ICCPR and from NGOs, such as Amnesty International and Human Rights Watch. Under current arrangements, specialised agencies may provide the HRC with information as the latter prepares for it's consideration of national reports.[121] Whereas before the end of the Cold War NGOs could only submit information to individual members privately, it is now established practice for them to submit to the HRC, documents and "shadow reports", and for the HRC to take them into account. Information provided by NGOs plays a very large part in the work of the Committee.

Having completed its examination of national reports, the HRC "shall transmit ... such general comments as it may consider appropriate ... to the States Parties" to the ICCPR (art.40(4)). It is by reference to this duty that the Committee now completes its consideration of national reports by adopting Concluding Observations on the state's human rights record.[122]

On the basis of the same duty, the Committee also adopts General Comments that are not specific to particular states. So far the General Comments made by the Committee have concerned the reporting process (e.g. on the kind of information required) and the Committee's interpretation of the Covenant guarantee. General Comments of the latter kind have varied a great deal, with General Comment No.6 on the right to life (art.6), see below, p.569, for example, including a controversial statement about nuclear weapons, and others containing either little more than a wordy restatement of the relevant text (e.g. General Comment No.10 on freedom of speech (art.19)),[123] or useful elaboration upon its meaning (e.g. General Comment No.7 on freedom from torture (art.7), below, p.574). General Comments are being increasingly supplemented as interpretations of the ICCPR by Committee "views" expressed in Optional Protocol cases (see below) in which the concept of consensus is not so predominant.

5.   The Covenant also provides in art.41 for an optional system of *state* applications.[124] A contracting party *may*, on condition of reciprocity, accept the right of the other contracting parties to bring a claim to the Committee alleging a violation of the Covenant by it. So far 48 parties (including the United Kingdom) have accepted it. No state applications have been brought so far, states generally preferring to deal with inter-state disputes by diplomacy.

6.   113 of the parties to the ICCPR are parties also to its 1966 First Protocol.[125] By this, a party

"recognises the competence of the Committee to receive and consider communications from

---

[121] See Vandenhole, above, n.82, p.91.

[122] This practice dates from 1992, following the end of the Cold War. Earlier, East European members had opposed such a practice, so that the Committee, which operates by consensus, did not make collective comments on particular states. The Observations review a state's human rights record and may identify a breach of the Covenant by it. The HRC employs a "follow up" procedure, using a Special Rapporteur, to discuss with states their response to its Observations: General Comment No.30, para.5 (2003) 10 I.H.R.R. 1.

[123] HRC Report, G.A.O.R. 38th Sess., Supp. 40, p.109 (1983). Freedom of speech has been an area in which the UN has found it difficult to make progress because of differences of approach on the part of Western and other states. For the 33 General Comments adopted so far, see the UN website: www.un.org (human rights) and *International Human Rights Reports* (cumulative index).

[124] See Leckie (1988) 10 H.R.Q. 249.

[125] Misc. 4 (1976), Cmnd. 3320; (1967) 61 A.J.I.L. 887; 999 U.N.T.S. 302. The UK is not a party. It takes the view that an individual has a sufficient remedy through the European Convention on Human Rights. On the Committee's practice under the Optional Protocol, see Ghandi, *The Human Rights Committee and the Right of Individual Communication* (1998); id. Ghandi (2008) 48 Ind. J.I.L. 208; Young, *The Law and Process of the UN Human Rights Committee* (2002).

individuals subject to its jurisdiction who claim to be victims of a violation by that State Party of any of the rights set forth in the Covenant. (Article 1)."[126]

Aumeeruddy-Cziffra v Mauritius (the Mauritian Women case)[127] is the leading case on the meaning of "victim". There the Committee stated:

"9.2 ... A person can only claim to be a victim in the sense of article 1 of the Optional Protocol if he or she is actually affected. It is a matter of degree how concretely this requirement should be taken. However, no individual can in the abstract, by way of an *actio popularis*, challenge a law or practice claimed to be contrary to the Covenant. If the law or practice has not already been concretely applied to the detriment of that individual, it must in any event be applicable in such a way that the alleged victim's risk of being affected is more than a theoretical possibility."

On the fact of that case, women whose husbands were at risk of deportation because their residence permits might be withdrawn at any time were considered "victims", but unmarried women, who might be affected in the future, were not.[128] Only individuals are "victims" for the purposes of a communication under the First Protocol (art.1); companies and other legal persons are not "victims". Another individual, NGO, etc. may bring a claim on behalf of an individual victim, provided that authorisation can be shown or there is good reason for its absence (e.g. that the victim is in detention).[129]

The overlap between the Protocol and petition systems under other human rights treaties is the subject of a rule by which the Committee may not consider a communication unless the "same matter is not being examined under another procedure of international investigation or settlement."[130] Thus an application pending at Strasbourg[131] or before the Inter-American Commission on Human Rights[132] is excluded. The Committee has, however, held that where the conduct of a state has resulted in more than one alleged victim, it may receive a communication from one of the victims even though the same conduct is the subject of a pending petition submitted elsewhere by another victim.[133] Consideration of communications under Resolution 1503 or its successor, the Resolution 5/1 complaint procedure[134], and country studies by the Inter-American Commission on Human Rights or the ILO Freedom of Association Committee do not relate to the

---

[126] The Committee may also hear claims under the 1966 Protocol that arise under the 1989 Second Optional Protocol: art.5 of the latter.

[127] (1981) 1 Selected Decisions H.R.C. 67. Cf. *Picq v France* (2009) 16 I.H.R.R. 955 at 960: "Any person claiming to be a victim ... must demonstrate either that a state party has by an act or omission already impaired the exercise of his right or that such impairment is imminent, basing his argument for example on legislation in force or on a judicial or administrative decision or practice."

[128] See also the *Toonen* case, below, p.590; and *Hertzberg v Finland* (1982) 1 Selected Decisions H.R.C. 124, where persons whose conduct was inhibited by laws which created the threat of prosecution were "victims" even though they had not been prosecuted.

[129] See *Y v Australia* (2000) 7 I.H.R.R. 906.

[130] Article 5(2)(a), First Optional Protocol. The Human Rights Committee will consider a claim "if it has been withdrawn from or is no longer being examined under ... [another] procedure at the time that the Committee reaches a decision on the admissibility" of it: HRC Report, G.A.O.R., 33rd Sess., Supp. 40, p.100 (1978).

[131] *D.F. v Sweden* (1985) 2 Selected Decisions H.R.C., p.55. The Committee may consider a case the examination of which at Strasbourg has been completed, unless the state concerned has made a reservation to its acceptance of the Optional Protocol excluding such cases: see, e.g. *Valentjin v France* (1997) 4 I.H.R.R. 273.

[132] *Millàn v Uruguay*, (1980) 1 Selected Decisions H.R.C. 52.

[133] *Fanali v Italy*, (1983) 2 Selected Decisions H.R.C. 99.

[134] *A v S.* (1978) 1 Selected Decisions H.R.C. 17.

"same matter"[135] as an individual communication under the Optional Protocol and so do not exclude the Committee's jurisdiction. The Committee's competence is also subject to other admissibility requirements, including the exhaustion of local remedies (art.5(2)(b)). There is no time limit on the bringing of a claim.[136] Legal aid is not available in the preparation or presentation of a communication.[137]

7.   The Committee considers both the admissibility and the merits of communications in private on the basis of written statements or explanations by the complainant and the respondent state.[138] There is no provision for oral hearings. The Committee has discussed the possibility of inviting the complainant and the respondent state to participate in oral hearings, which would undoubtedly assist in the elucidation of the facts and the consideration of legal argument.[139]

8.   The Committee's early jurisprudence was dominated by cases against Uruguay in which the then Government, which was accused of gross ill-treatment of political opponents, did not co-operate fully with the Committee, often failing to respond to requests for information.[140] It was in this context that the Committee established its rules concerning the burden of proof. In *Bleier v Uruguay*,[141] in which Uruguay's denial that a disappeared person was in its custody was contradicted by other evidence, the Committee stated:

"13.3 With regard to the burden of proof, this cannot rest alone on the author of the communication, especially considering that the author and the State Party do not always have equal access to the evidence and that frequently the State Party alone has access to relevant information. It is implicit in Article 4(2) of the Optional Protocol that the State Party has the duty to investigate in good faith all allegations of violation of the Covenant made against it and its authorities, especially when such allegations are corroborated by evidence submitted by the author of the communication, and to furnish to the Committee the information available to it. In cases where the author has submitted to the Committee allegations supported by substantial witness testimony, as in this case, and where further clarification of the case depends on information exclusively in the hands of the State Party, the Committee may consider such allegations as substantiated in the absence of satisfactory evidence and explanations to the contrary submitted by the State Party."

The Committee continues to decide cases on the basis of the author's uncontested, but corroborated allegations, sometimes in situations where the state cannot be said to have exclusive access to any relevant evidence in the sense of the *Bleier* case but where the state simply refuses to respond.[142]

---

[135] *Baboeram v Suriname* (1985) 2 Selected Decisions H.R.C. 172.

[136] A late communication may be rejected as an abuse of the right of submission, see, e.g. *Kudrna v Czech Republic* (2009) 17 I.H.R.R. 1 (seven years, no good reason), but generally the HRC does not reject communications on this ground.

[137] See Butler (2000) 49 I.C.L.Q. 360 at 370.

[138] As of 1997, the admissibility and merits stages have been merged so as (successfully) to speed up proceedings; whereas cases used to take four years to decide on the merits, on average they now take just over two: see Jospeh, Schultz and Castan, above, at n.105, p.47.

[139] See Tomuschat (1980) 1 H.R.L.J. 249 at 354, a former Committee member, who notes the inadequacy of written proceedings, but points to the burden that oral proceedings would add for a hard-pressed, part-time body.

[140] The Uruguayan Government that accepted the Optional Protocol in 1970 was overthrown by a revolutionary Government whose acts resulted in the numerous cases against Uruguay. In 1984 that Government was itself overthrown and replaced the following year by an elected Government which has been commended for its co-operation with the Committee: *Conteris v Uruguay* (1985) 2 Selected Decisions H.R.C. 168 at 171.

[141] (1982) 1 Selected Decisions H.R.C. 109 at 112.

[142] See, *e.g.* *Reid v Jamaica* (1995) 2 I.H.R.R. 57.

9. The Committee may suggest interim measures "to avoid irreparable damage to the victim",[143] as it did when it successfully requested a stay of execution of the death penalty in *Pratt and Morgan v Jamaica*.[144] States do not always comply with requests. In *Piandiong v Philippines*[145] sentences of capital punishment were carried out in pending cases despite the Committee's request to the contrary.

10. The Committee is required to formulate its "views" on the question whether a breach has occurred and to send them to the respondent state and the complainant (art.5(4)). In deciding on its "views" (and when taking decisions as to admissibility), the Committee "strives to reach its decisions by consensus, without resorting to voting. However, ... members can append their individual opinions to the Committee's decisions of a final nature."[146] The Committee's "views" are not legally binding and there is no provision in the ICCPR for a court or any other body to take binding decisions. The Committee has explained its functions as follows[147]:

> "11. While the function of the Human Rights Committee in considering individual communications is not, as such, that of a judicial body, the views issued by the Committee under the Optional Protocol exhibit some important characteristics of a judicial decision. They are arrived at in a judicial spirit, including the impartiality and independence of Committee members, the considered interpretation of the language of the Covenant, and the determinative character of the decisions."

Although its "views" are not legally binding, the Committee has received information from some respondent states indicating that they have taken, or are in the process of taking, action in response to findings against them.[148] But in many cases, states have not implemented the Committee's views.[149] As a result, the Committee has appointed a "special rapporteur for the follow up on views"[150] to monitor the situation and list states that have not responded to requests for information.

11. By July 2009, 1888 communications, naming 83 respondent states, had been registered since 1977.[151] The Committee had adopted views on the merits in 681 of these cases, in 543 of which breaches had been found. 533 cases had been declared inadmissible. The remainder were pending or had been withdrawn. Eighty-eight communications were registered in 2008. These low total and annual numbers are partly because cases may be brought instead before the

---

[143] Rule 86, HRC Rules of Procedure, UN Doc. CCPR/C/3/Rev.6 (2001). See Harrington (2003) 48 McGill L.J. 55.

[144] HRC Report, G.A.O.R., 44th Sess., Supp.40, p.222 (1989). Rule 86 is also used to prevent extradition to face treatment contrary to the ICCPR: see, *e.g. Cox v Canada* (1994) 2 I.H.R.R. 307.

[145] (2001) 8 I.H.R.R. 349. For similar execution cases, see *Ashby v Trinidad* (2002) 9 I.H.R.R. 906; and *Mansaraj v Sierra Leone* (2001) 8 I.H.R.R. 947.

[146] HRC Report, G.A.O.R., 44th Sess., Supp. 40, p. 14 (1989).

[147] General Comment No.33: Obligations of States Parties under the Optional Protocol, CCPR/C/GC/33.

[148] See *Aumeeruddy-Cziffra v Mauritius* (1981) 1 Selected Decisions H.R.C. 67; *Lovelace v Canada* (1981) 2 Selected Decisions H.R.C. 28; and *Vuolanne v Finland*, below, p.589. In 1984, Uruguay sent the Committee a list of detainees who had been released, including two in whose cases the Committee had found breaches of the Covenant: see HRC Report, G.A.O.R., 39th Sess., Supp. 40, p.126 (1984). The Committee had also learnt unofficially of the release of three other such detainees.

[149] The 2002 HRC Report states: "Roughly 30 per cent of the replies received could be considered satisfactory in that they display the State party's willingness to implement the Committee's Views or to offer the applicant an appropriate remedy": A/57/40, Vol.1, para.225.

[150] Rule 95, HRC Rules of Procedure.

[151] H.R.C. Report for 2008–9, A/64/40, Vol.1, p.94. Many obviously inadmissible cases are disposed of without registration.

European and Inter-American Courts of Human Rights, which can give legally binding judg-ments.[152]

GUERRERO v COLOMBIA

Human Rights Committee (1982) 1 Selected Decisions H.R.C. 112

In this case, the Colombian police raided a house in which it was thought that a kidnap victim was being detained. The victim was not found, but the police hid in the house awaiting the arrival of the suspected kidnappers. Seven persons, who were never proved to have been connected with the kidnapping, were shot without warning as they arrived at intervals at the house. The police action was justified by the government on the basis of Legislative Decree No.0070 which, for so long as "the national territory is in a state of siege," provided the police with a defence to any criminal charge arising out of acts committed "in the course of operations planned with the object of preventing and curbing kidnapping."

Views of the Committee

13.1 ... The right enshrined in [Article 6] ... is the supreme right of the human being. It follows that the deprivation of life by the authorities of the State is a matter of the utmost gravity. This follows from the article as a whole and in particular is the reason why paragraph 2 of the article lays down that the death penalty may be imposed only for the most serious crimes. The requirements that the right shall be protected by law and that no one shall be arbitrarily deprived of his life mean that the law must strictly control and limit the circumstances in which a person may be deprived of his life by the authorities of a State.

13.2 In the present case it is evident from the fact that seven persons lost their lives as a result of the deliberate action of the police that the deprivation of life was intentional. Moreover, the police action was apparently taken without warning to the victims and without giving them any opportunity to surrender to the police patrol or to offer any explanation of their presence or intentions. There is no evidence that the action of the police was necessary in their own defence or that of others, or that it was necessary to effect the arrest or prevent the escape of the persons concerned. Moreover, the victims were no more than suspects of the kidnapping which had occurred some days earlier and their killing by the police deprived them of all the protections of due process of law laid down by the Covenant. In the case of Mrs. María Fanny Suárez de Guerrero, the forensic report showed that she had been shot several times after she had already died from a heart attack. There can be no reasonable doubt that her death was caused by the police patrol.

13.3 For these reasons it is the Committee's view that the action of the police resulting in the death of Mrs. María Fanny Suárez de Guerrero was disproportionate to the requirements of law enforcement in the circumstances of the case and that she was arbitrarily deprived of her life contrary to article 6(1). ... Inasmuch as the police action was made justifiable as a matter of Colombian law by Legislative Decree No. 0070 ..., the right to life was not adequately protected by the law of Colombia as required by article 6(1). ...

15. The Committee is accordingly of the view that the State Party should take the necessary measures to compensate the husband of Mrs. María Fanny Suárez de Guerrero for the death of his wife and to ensure that the right to life is duly protected by amending the law.

----

[152] Note, however, that the Optional Protocol does not impose a time limit on the bringing of cases, whereas the American and European Conventions have a six–month time limit.

Notes

1.   The *Guerrero* case stresses the pre-eminent importance of the right to life and imposes strict standards for the taking of life by the state.[153] The Committee gives some indication of the meaning of a taking of life that is "arbitrary" contrary to art.6(1). The fact that it is lawful under national law is not such as to prevent it from being "arbitrary." The self defence, arrest and prevention of escape justifications that the Committee implies are acceptable are ones commonly allowed in national law and expressly permitted (on a basis of absolute necessity) by the European Convention on Human Rights, art.2.

The HRC has expressed its concern at Israel's practice of "targeted" killings of terrorist suspects[154]

"15. ... This practice would appear to be used at least in part as a deterrent or punishment, thus raising issues under article 6. While noting the delegation's observations about respect for the principle of proportionality in any response to terrorist activities against civilians and its affirmation that only persons taking direct part in hostilities have been targeted, the Committee remains concerned about the nature and extent of the responses by the Israeli Defence Force (IDF) to Palestinian terrorist attacks.

The State party should not use 'targeted killings' as a deterrent or punishment. The State party should ensure that the utmost consideration is given to the principle of proportionality in all its responses to terrorist threats and activities. State policy in this respect should be spelled out clearly in guidelines to regional military commanders, and complaints about disproportionate use of force should be investigated promptly by an independent body. Before resorting to the use of deadly force, all measures to arrest a person suspected of being in the process of committing acts or terror must be exhausted."

2.   An important problem concerning the right to life is that of "disappeared persons". In General Comment No. 6,[155] the Committee commented on this problem as follows:

"4. States parties should also take specific and effective measures to prevent the disappearance of individuals, something which unfortunately has become all too frequent and leads too often to arbitrary deprivation of life. Furthermore, States should establish effective facilities and procedures to investigate thoroughly cases of missing and disappeared persons in circumstances which may involve a violation of the right to life."

---

[153] cf. para. 4, HRC. General Comment No. 6 (1981), (1994) 1–2 I.H.R.R. 4. cf. also *Baboeram v Suriname* (1985) 2 Selected Decisions H.R.C. 172, in which 15 prominent Surinamese citizens associated with attempts to introduce democracy into Suriname were taken from their homes at night by the military and killed. The Government claimed that they had been killed trying to escape following an attempted coup. In view of evidence provided by the authors of the communications of injuries to the bodies that were not consistent with this explanation and in the absence of any medical reports from the Government to the contrary, the Committee concluded that "the victims were arbitrarily deprived of their lives" contrary to art.6(1).

[154] Concluding Observations on Israel, August 21, 2003, CCPR/CO/78/ISR. The practice is also followed by the US in the Afghanistan/Pakistan border region and in Yemen to kill Al Qaeda suspects, using drones. On the international human rights and international humanitarian law implications, see Kretzmer (2005) 16 E.J.I.L. 171 and Murphy and Radsan (2009) 31 Cardozo L.R. 405.

[155] (1994) 1–2 I.H.R.R. 4. See also the Convention for the Protection of All Persons from Enforced Disappearance 2006, above, n.95.

In *Bleir v Uruguay*,[156] in which the defendant state's denial that a disappeared person was in its custody was contradicted by other evidence, the Committee, applying its burden of proof rule, see above, p.563, stated:

"13.4 The Committee finds that the disappearance of Eduardo Bleier in October 1975 does not alone establish that he was arrested by Uruguayan authorities. But, the allegation that he was so arrested and detained is confirmed (i) by the information, unexplained and substantially unrefuted by the State party, that Eduardo Bleier's name was on a list of prisoners read out once a week at an army unit in Montevideo where his family delivered clothing for him and received his dirty clothing until the summer of 1976, and (ii) by the testimony of other prisoners that they saw him in Uruguayan detention centres. Also there are the reports of several eyewitnesses that Eduardo Bleier was subjected to severe torture while in detention.

14. It is therefore the Committee's view that the information before it reveals breaches of articles 7, 9 and 10(1) of the International Covenant on Civil and Political Rights and that there are serious reasons to believe that the ultimate violation of article 6 has been perpetrated by the Uruguayan authorities.

15. As regards the latter point the Human Rights Committee urges the Uruguayan Government to reconsider its position in this case and to take effective steps (i) to establish what has happened to Eduardo Bleier since October 1975; to bring to justice any persons found to be responsible for his death, disappearance or ill-treatment; and to pay compensation to him or his family for any injury which he has suffered; and (ii) to ensure that similar violations do not occur in the future."

3. The Committee has considered several cases in which individuals have died after being taken into custody but in which the respondent state has denied that death was attributable to its agents. In *Herrera Rubio v Colombia*,[157] the author's parents were taken from their home by "individuals wearing military uniforms, identifying themselves as members of the counter-guerilla." After the parents had later been found dead, a state investigation "established that no member of the armed forces had taken part in the killings". The Committee stated[158]:

"10.3. Whereas the Committee considers that there is reason to believe, in the light of the author's allegations, that Colombian military persons bear responsibility for the deaths of José Herrera and Emma Rubio de Herrera, no conclusive evidence has been produced to establish the identity of the murderers. In this connection the Committee refers to its general comment No. 6 (16) concerning article 6 of the Covenant, [para. 4, note 2 above]. . . The Committee has duly noted the State Party's submissions concerning the investigations carried out in this case, which, however, appear to have been inadequate in the light of the State Party's obligations under article 2 of the Covenant . . .

11. The Human Rights Committee, . . . is of the view that the facts as found by the Committee disclose violations of the Covenant with respect to:

Article 6, because the State Party failed to take appropriate measures to prevent the

---

[156] (1982) 1 Selected Decisions H.R.C. 109 at 112. For other cases of disappearances resulting in findings of breaches of arts 6, 7 and 9, see *Mojica v Dominican Rep.* (1995) 2 I.H.R.R. 86; *Bautista de Arellana v Colombia* (1996) 3 I.H.R.R. 315; and *Celis Laureano v Peru* (1997) 4 I.H.R.R. 54.

[157] (1985) 2 Selected Decisions H.R.C. 192. cf. *Barbato v Uruguay*, (1985) 2 Selected Decisions H.R.C. p.112 (1982); and *Miango v Zaire*, (1985) 2 Selected Decisions H.R.C. p.219 (1987). See also *Burrell v Jamaica* (1997) 4 I.H.R.R. 350.

[158] (1985) 2 Selected Decisions H.R.C. p.195.

disappearance and subsequent killings of José Herrera and Emma Rubio de Herrera and to investigate effectively the responsibility for their murders; . . ."

4.   Article 6 imposes an obligation to provide medical care to ensure the lives of prisoners, and to do so regardless of cost. In *Lantsov v Russia*,[159] the applicant's son died in pre-trial detention. While healthy on being detained, he fell ill because of the poor conditions of detention. Finding a breach of art.6, the HRC stated:

> "9.2. . . . The Committee notes that the State party has not refuted the causal link between the conditions of the detention or Mr. Lantsov and the fatal deterioration of his state of health. Further, even if the Committee starts from the assertion of the State party that neither Mr. Lantsov himself nor his co-detainees had requested medical help in time, the essential fact remains that the State party by arresting and detaining individuals takes the responsibility to care for their life. It is up to the State party by organizing its detention facilities to know about the state of health of the detainees as far as may be reasonable expected. Lack of financial means cannot reduce this responsibility. The Committee considers that a properly functioning medical service within the detention centre could and should have known about the dangerous change in the state of health of Mr. Lantsov. It considers that the State party failed to take appropriate measures to protect Mr. Lantsov's life during the period he spent in the detention centre."

5.   In General Comment No. 6, para.2, the Committee noted the link between non-compliance with the international law rules prohibiting resort to armed force and the loss of innocent lives.[160] The matter was taken up again in the Second General Comment (No.14)[161] on art.6, in which the Committee focused on the dangers of nuclear weapons:

> "4. . . . It is evident that the designing, testing, manufacture, possession and deployment of nuclear weapons are among the greatest threats to the right to life which confront mankind today. This threat is compounded by the danger that the actual use of such weapons may be brought about, not only in the event of war, but even through human or mechanical error or failure. . . .
> 6. The production, testing, possession, deployment and use of nuclear weapons should be prohibited and recognised as crimes against humanity.
> 7. The Committee accordingly, in the interest of mankind, calls upon all States whether parties to the Covenant or not, to take urgent steps, unilaterally and by agreement, to rid the world of this menace."

Although a number of individual applications alleging a violation of art.6 resulting from the threat of nuclear weapons have failed for various reasons, in *Bordes and Temeharo v France*,[162] the HRC indicated that "it wishes to reiterate" what it had stated in General Comment No.14, para.4. In its Advisory Opinion in the *Legality of Nuclear Weapons* case,[163] the ICJ took a different

---

[159] (2002) 9 I.H.R.R. 935.
[160] See above, n.194.
[161] (1994) 1-2 I.H.R.R. 15. Paragraph 6 of the General Comment was the subject of criticism by some states in the General Assembly Third Committee: see G.A.O.R., 39th Sess., A/C.3/SR 46, 48–51 (1984).
[162] (1997) 4 I.H.R.R. 284.
[163] I.C.J. Rep. 1996, p.226 at 240.

approach, suggesting that the question was not one of interpretation of art.6 by the Committee, but of the application of international humanitarian law:

"25. The Court observes that the protection of the International Covenant of Civil and Political Rights does not cease in times of war, except by operation of Article 4 of the Covenant whereby certain provisions may be derogated from in a time of national emergency. Respect for the right to life is not, however, such a provision. In principle, the right not arbitrarily to be deprived of one's life applies also in hostilities. The test of what is an arbitrary deprivation of life, however, then falls to be determined by the applicable *lex specialis*, namely, the law applicable in armed conflict which is designed to regulate the conduct of hostilities. Thus whether a particular loss of life, through the use of a certain weapon in warfare, is to be considered an arbitrary deprivation of life contrary to Article 6 of the Covenant, can only be decided by reference to the law applicable in armed conflict and not deduced from the terms of the Covenant itself."

6.   In General Comment No.6, the Committee also interpreted art.6 in such a way as to impose a positive obligation upon states of the kind more normally associated with the protection of economic, social and cultural rights[164]:

"5. Moreover, the Committee has noted that the right to life has been too often narrowly interpreted. The expression 'inherent right to life' cannot properly be understood in a restrictive manner, and the protection of this right requires that States adopt positive measures. In this connection, the Committee considers that it would be desirable for States Parties to take all possible measures to reduce infant mortality and to increase life expectancy, especially in adopting measures to eliminate malnutrition and epidemics."

JUDGE v CANADA

Human Rights Committee. (2004) 11 I.H.R.R. 125. Footnotes omitted.

In 1987, the author, a US citizen, was convicted of murder and sentenced to death by the electric chair (later changed to lethal injection) by a Pennsylvania court. He escaped from prison and fled to Canada, where, in 1988, he was convicted of robberies and sentenced to 10 years imprisonment. In 1993, a deportation order was issued against him, not to be executed until his sentence expired in 1998. His request not to be returned to the US until extradition was sought and assurances had been given that he would not be executed was rejected by the Canadian Minister of Citizenship and Immigration. In 1998, the author was deported without assurances, before he was able to appeal a Quebec court decision rejecting a stay of execution of his deportation. The author alleged that his deportation was, inter alia, a breach of art.6.

Views of the Committee

10.2 In considering Canada's obligations, as a State party which has abolished the death penalty, in removing persons to another country where they are under sentence of death, the Committee recalls its previous jur-

---
[164] See above n.154.

isprudence in *Kindler v. Canada*, [(1993) 1–2 I.H.R.R. 98], that it does not consider that the deportation of a person from a country which has abolished the death penalty to a country where he/she is under sentence of death amounts per se to a violation or article 6 of the Covenant. The Committee's rationale in this decision was based on an interpretation of the Covenant which read article 6, paragraph 1, together with article 6, paragraph 2, which does not prohibit the imposition of the death penalty for the most serious of crimes. It considered that as Canada itself had not imposed the death penalty but had extradited the author to the United States to face capital punishment, a state which had not abolished the death penalty, the extradition itself would not amount to violation by Canada unless there was a real risk that the author's rights under the Covenant would be violated in the United States. On the issue of assurance, the Committee found that the terms or article 6 did not necessarily require Canada to refuse to extradite or to seek assurances but that such a request should at least be considered by the removing state.

10.3 While recognizing that the Committee should ensure both consistency and coherence of its jurisprudence, it notes that there may be exceptional situations in which a review of the scope of application of the rights protected in the Covenant is required, such as where an alleged violation involves the most fundamental of rights—the right to life—and in particular if there have been notable factual and legal developments and changes in international opinion in respect of the issue raised. The Committee is mindful of the fact that the above-mentioned jurisprudence was established some 10 years ago, and that since that time there has been a broadening international consensus in favour of abolition of the death penalty, and in states which have retained the death penalty, a broadening consensus not to carry it out. Significantly, the Committee notes that since *Kindler* the State party itself has recognized the need to amend its own domestic law to secure the protection of those extradited from Canada under sentence of death in the receiving state, in the case of *United States v. Burns* [(2001) S.C.J. 8]. There, the Supreme Court of Canada held that the government *must* seek assurances, in all but exceptional cases, that the death penalty will not be applied prior to extraditing an individual to a state where he/she faces capital punishment. It is pertinent to note that under the terms of this judgment, "Other abolitionist countries do not, in general, extradite without assurances." The Committee considers that the Covenant should be interpreted as a living instrument and the rights protected under it should be applied in context and in the light of present-day conditions.

10.4 In reviewing its application of article 6, the Committee notes that, as required by the Vienna Convention on the Law of Treaties, a treaty should be interpreted in good faith and in accordance with the ordinary meaning to be given to the terms of the treaty in their context and in the light of its object and purpose. Paragraph 1 of article 6, which states that "Every human being has the inherent right to life . . .", is a general rule: its purpose is to protect life. States parties that have abolished the death penalty have an obligation under this paragraph to so protect in all circumstances. Paragraphs 2 to 6 of article 6 are evidently included to avoid a reading of the first paragraph of article 6, according to which that paragraph could be understood as abolishing the death penalty as such. This construction of the article is reinforced by the opening words of paragraph 2 ("In countries which have not abolished the death penalty . . .") and by paragraph 6 ("Nothing in this article shall be invoked to delay or to prevent the abolition of capital punishment by and State Party to the present Covenant."). In effect, paragraphs 2 to 6 have the dual function of creating an exception to the right to life in respect of the death penalty and laying down limits on the scope of that exception. Only the death penalty pronounced when certain elements are present can benefit from the exception. Among these limitations are those found in the opening words of paragraph 2, namely, that only States parties that "have not abolished the death penalty" can avail themselves of the exceptions created in paragraphs 2 to 6. For countries that *have* abolished the death penalty, there is an obligation not to expose a person to the real risk of its application. Thus, they may not remove, either by deportation or extradition, individuals from their jurisdiction if it may be reasonably anticipated that they will be sentenced to death, without ensuring that the death sentence would not be carried out.

10.5 The Committee acknowledges that by interpreting paragraphs 1 and 2 of article 6 in this way, abolitionist and retentionist States parties are treated differently. But it considers that this is an inevitable consequence of the wording of the provision itself, which, as becomes clear from the *travaux préparatories*, sought to appease very divergent views on the issue of the death penalty, in an effort at compromise among the drafters of the provision. The Committee notes that it was expressed in the *travaux* that, on the one hand, one of the main principles of the Covenant should be abolition, but on the other, it was pointed out that capital punishment existed in certain countries and that abolition would create difficulties for such countries. The death penalty was seen by many delegates and bodies participating in the drafting process as an "anomaly" or a "necessary evil". It would appear logical, therefore, to interpret the rule in article 6, paragraph 1, in a wide sense, whereas paragraph 2, which addresses the death penalty, should be interpreted narrowly.

10.6 For these reasons, the Committee considers that Canada, as a State party which has abolished the death penalty, irrespective of whether it has not yet ratified the Second Optional Protocol to the Covenant Aiming at the Abolition of the Death Penalty [Canada ratified it in 2005], violated the author's right to life under article 6, paragraph 1, by deporting him to the United States, where he is under sentence of death, without ensuring that the death penalty would not be carried out. The Committee recognizes that Canada did not itself impose the death penalty on the author. But by deporting him to a country where he was under sentence of death, Canada established the crucial link in the causal chain that would make possible the execution of the author. ...

10.8 As to whether the State party violated the author's rights under articles 6, and 2, paragraph 3, by deporting him to the United States where he is under sentence of death, before he could exercise his right to appeal the rejection of his application for a stay of deportation before the Québec Court of Appeal and, accordingly, could not pursue further available remedies, the Committee notes that the State party removed the author from its jurisdiction within hours after the decision of the Superior Court of Québec, in what appears to have been an attempt to prevent him from exercising his right of appeal to the Court of Appeal. It is unclear from the submissions before the Committee to what extent the Court of Appeal could have examined the author's case, but the State party itself concedes that as the author's petition was dismissed by the Superior Court for procedural and substantive reasons ..., the Court of Appeal could have reviewed the judgment on merits.

10.9 The Committee recalls its decision in *A.R.J. v. Australia*, a deportation case where it did not find a violation of article 6 by the returning state as it was not foreseeable that he would be sentenced to death and "because the judicial and immigration instances seized of the case heard extensive arguments" as to a possible violation of article 6. In the instant case, the Committee finds that, by preventing the author from exercising an appeal available to him under domestic law, the State party failed to demonstrate that the author's contention that his deportation to a country where he faces execution would violate his right to life, was sufficiently considered. The State party makes available an appellate system designed to safeguard any petitioner's, including the author's, rights and in particular the most fundamental of rights—the right to life. Bearing in mind that the State party has abolished capital punishment, the decision to deport the author to a state where he is under sentence of death without affording him the opportunity to avail himself of an available appeal, was taken arbitrarily and in violation or article 6, together with article 2, paragraph 3, of the Covenant.

10.10 Having found a violation or article 6, paragraph 1 alone and, read together with article 2, paragraph 3 of the Covenant, the Committee does not consider it necessary to address whether the same facts amount to a violation of article 7 of the Covenant.

Notes

1. In the *Judge* case, the Committee for the first time expressly overruled one of its earlier pre-cedents.[165] The case shows a strong abolitionist tendency on the part of the Committee, which is in line with the restrictive provisions of art.6(2)–(6) and the prohibition of the death penalty in the 2nd ICCPR Optional Protocol, above, p.588. Would a state that does not provide for capital punishment be free under art.6 to introduce or re-introduce it for any offence (supposing it is not a party to the 2nd Optional Protocol)?[166]

2. With regard to the death penalty generally, the Committee's General Comment No.6 reads[167]:

    "6. While it follows from article 6(2) to (6) that States Parties are not obliged to abolish the death penalty totally, they are obliged to limit its use and, in particular, to abolish it for other than the 'most serious crimes.' Accordingly, they ought to consider reviewing their criminal laws in this light and, in any event, are obliged to restrict the application of the death penalty to the 'most serious crimes.' The article also refers generally to abolition in terms which strongly suggest (paras. 2(2) and (6)) that abolition is desirable. The Committee concludes that all measures of abolition should be considered as progress in the enjoyment of the right

---

[165] There were earlier cases of implied overruling. See Joseph (2004) 4 H.R.L.R. 109 at 111.
[166] See *Judge* case, para.10.4. Article 4(3), American Convention on Human Rights expressly prohibits the re-introduction of capital punishment.
[167] See above, n.154.

to life within the meaning of article 40, and should as such be reported to the Committee. The Committee notes that a number of States have already abolished the death penalty or suspended its application. Nevertheless, States' reports show that progress made towards abolishing or limiting the application of the death penalty is quite inadequate.

7. The Committee is of the opinion that the expression 'most serious crimes' must be read restrictively to mean that the death penalty should be a quite exceptional measure. It also follows from the express terms of article 6 that it can only be imposed in accordance with the law in force at the time of the commission of the crime and not contrary to the Covenant. The procedural guarantees therein prescribed must be observed, including the right to a fair hearing by an independent tribunal, the presumption of innocence, the minimum guarantees for the defence, and the right to review by a higher tribunal. These rights are applicable in addition to the particular right to seek pardon or commutation of the sentence."

104 states retain the death penalty, although it is not used in practice in many of them.[168] It exists for political offences (e.g. treason), military offences (e.g. mutiny), terrorist offences (e.g. hijacking), drug trafficking offences, ordinary offences (e.g. murder, kidnapping), economic offences (e.g. public corruption) and rape. Some Islamic states make apostasy, adultery, sodomy, drinking liquor and sex between a Muslim and non-Muslim capital offences.[169] Many of these offences do not qualify as "the most serious offences" as that phrase has been restrictively interpreted by the Committee. Joseph, Schultz and Castan[170] summarise its practice as follows:

"The HRC has ... confirmed that the following are not 'most serious crimes', and cannot therefore attract the death penalty without violating article 6: treason, piracy, robbery, traffic in toxic or dangerous wastes, abetting suicide, drug-related offences, property offences, multiple evasion of military service, apostasy, committing a third homosexual act, embezzlement by officials, theft by force, 'abduction not resulting in death', crimes of an economic nature, adultery, corruption, and 'crimes that do not result in the loss of life'. Messrs Klein and Kretzmer, in the minority in *T.T. v Australia* (706/96), implied that drug offences were not serious enough to attract the death penalty. In Concluding Observations on Iraq, the HRC strongly implied that 'non-violent' infringements are not serious enough to attract the death penalty. The HRC has also stated that 'political and economic' offences are not 'most serious crimes' for the purposes of article 6(2). ... In summary, it appears that only intentional killings or attempted killings, and *perhaps* the intentional infliction of grievous bodily harm, may attract the death penalty under article 6(2)."

Jospeh, Schultz and Castan also state that, "contrary to the practice in a number of Islamic States, the victim's family, considering their inherent partiality, should not have a role in deciding whether or not the death penalty will be imposed and/or executed".[171]

As to "procedural guarantees",[172] in *Mbenge v Zaire*,[173] having found breaches of the fair trial

---

[168] Hood, *The Death Penalty: A World Wide Perspective* (4th edn by Hood and Hoyle, 2008)), p.14. See generally, Schabas, *The Abolition of the Death Penalty in International Law* (3rd edn 2002); and Naldi (1991) 38 N.I.L.R. 373. No European state uses capital punishment. 46 of the 47 Council of Europe member states have abolished it and Russia applies a moratorium. The ICC, the ICTY and ICTR may not impose the death penalty.
[169] See the survey in Hood, above, n.167, Ch.3.
[170] See above, n.105, p.167. Footnotes omitted.
[171] See above, n.105, p.168.
[172] See General Comment No.6, para.7, above, n.154.
[173] (1983) 2 Selected Decisions H.R.C. 76 at 79. cf. *Pratt and Morgan v Jamaica* below, p.578.

guarantees in art.14(3)(a)(b)(d) and (e), the Committee concluded that as a result of these findings "the death sentences pronounced against the author ... were imposed contrary to the provisions of the Covenant, and therefore in violation of Article 6(2)."

A *mandatory* death penalty for a particular offence, regardless of the facts of the case, is an "arbitrary" taking of life in breach of art.6(1). In *Thompson v St Vincent and the Grenadines*,[174] the Committee held that a mandatory death penalty for murder (defined as an intentional killing) was contrary to art.6:

> "8.2 ... The Committee notes that the mandatory imposition of the death penalty under the laws of the State party is based solely upon the category of crime for which the offender is found guilty, without regard to the defendant's personal circumstances or the circumstances of the particular offense. The death penalty is mandatory in all cases of 'murder' (intentional acts of violence resulting in the death of a person). The Committee considers that such a system of mandatory capital punishment would deprive the author of the most fundamental of rights, the right to life, without considering whether this exceptional form of punishment is appropriate in the circumstances of his or her case. The existence of a right to seek pardon or commutation, as required by article 6, paragraph 4, of the Covenant, does not secure adequate protection to the right to life, as these discretionary measures by the executive are subject to a wide range of other considerations compared to appropriate judicial review of all aspects of a criminal case. The Committee finds that the carrying out of the death penalty in the author's case would constitute an arbitrary deprivation of his life in violation of article 6, paragraph 1, of the Covenant."

4. In view of the art.6(5) prohibition of capital punishment for offenders under 18, the US made a reservation[175] when ratifying the ICCPR to safeguard US states that make juveniles of 16 or 17 liable for the death penalty.

GENERAL COMMENT NO.20 ON ARTICLE 7 ICCPR: FREEDOM FROM TORTURE, ETC.

Human Rights Committee. 47 UN G.A.O.R., Supp.40 (A/47/40) Annex VI; (1994) 1–2 I.H.R.R. 26.

2. The aim of the provisions of article 7 of the International Covenant on Civil and Political Rights is to protect both the dignity and the physical and mental integrity of the individual. It is the duty of the State party to afford everyone protection through legislative and other measures as may be necessary against the acts prohibited by article 7, whether inflicted by people acting in their official capacity, outside their official capacity or in a private capacity. The prohibition in article 7 is complemented by the positive requirements of article 10, paragraph 1, of the Covenant, which stipulates that "All persons deprived of their liberty shall be treated with humanity and with respect for the inherent dignity of the human person."

3. ... even in situations of public emergency such as those referred to in article 4 of the Covenant, no derogation from the provision of article 7 is allowed ... The Committee likewise observes that no justification or extenuating circumstances may be invoked to excuse a violation of article 7 for any reasons, including those based on an order from a superior officer or public authority.

4. The Covenant does not contain any definition of the concepts covered by article 7, nor does the Committee

---

[174] (2000) 8 I.H.R.R. 336. Five Committee members dissented. cf. *Kennedy v Trinidad and Tobago* (2002) 9 I.H.R.R. 944 (death penalty for felony involving violence inadvertently resulting in death).

[175] See UN Doc ST/LEG/Ser.E/15, p.130. But see now *Roper v Simmons* (2005) 543 U.S. 551 (death penalty for juveniles under 18 unconstitutional).

consider it necessary to draw up a list of prohibited acts or to establish sharp distinctions between the different kinds of punishment or treatment; the distinctions depend on the nature, purpose and severity of the treatment applied.

5. The prohibition in article 7 relates not only to acts that cause physical pain but also to acts that cause mental suffering to the victim. In the Committee's view, moreover, the prohibition must extend to corporal punishment, including excessive chastisement ordered as punishment for a crime or as an educative or disciplinary measure. It is appropriate to emphasize in this regard that article 7 protects, in particular, children, pupils and patients in teaching and medical institutions.

6. The Committee notes that prolonged solitary confinement of the detained or imprisoned person may amount to acts prohibited by article 7 . . . . When the death penalty is applied by a State party for the most serious crimes, it must not only be strictly limited in accordance with article 6 but it must be carried out in such a way as to cause the least possible physical and mental suffering.

7. Article 7 expressly prohibits medical or scientific experimentation without the free consent of the person concerned. . . . Special protection in regard to such experiments is necessary in the case of persons not capable of giving valid consent, and in particular those under any form of detention and imprisonment. Such persons should not be subjected to any medical or scientific experimentation that may be detrimental to their health.

8. The Committee notes that it is not sufficient for the implementation of article 7 to prohibit such treatment or punishment or to make it a crime. States parties should inform the Committee of the legislative, administrative, judicial and other measures they take to prevent and punish acts of torture and cruel, inhuman and degrading treatment in any territory under their jurisdiction.

9. In the view of the Committee, States parties must not expose individuals to the danger of torture or cruel, inhuman or degrading treatment or punishment upon return to another country by way of their extradition, expulsion or refoulement . . .

11. . . . To guarantee the effective protection of detained persons, provisions should be made for detainees to be held in places officially recognized as places of detention and for their names and places of detention, as well as for the names of persons responsible for their detention, to be kept in registers readily available and accessible to those concerned, including relatives and friends. To the same effect, the time and place of all interrogations should be recorded, together with the names of all those present and this information should also be available for purposes of judicial or administrative proceedings. Provisions should also be made against incommunicado detention. In that connection, States parties should ensure that any places of detention be free from any equipment liable to be used for inflicting torture or ill-treatment. The protection of the detainee also requires that prompt and regular access be given to doctors and lawyers and, under appropriate supervisions when the investigation so requires, to family members.

12. It is important for the discouragement of violations under article 7 that the law must prohibit the use or admissibility in judicial proceedings of statements or confessions obtained through torture or other prohibited treatment. . . .

Notes

1.   Although the Committee has not adopted any abstract definition of "torture" in its jurisprudence, it is probable that the definition in the 1984 UN Torture Convention applies.[176] As General Comment No.20, para.4 indicates, the Committee has not been concerned to distinguish between "torture" and other forms of conduct contrary to art.7. This is surprising in view of the effect of a finding of "torture" on a state's reputation. Nor, in cases in which the victim is in

---

[176] Article 1 reads: ". . . the term 'torture' means any act by which severe pain or suffering, whether physical or mental, is inflicted on a person for such purposes of obtaining from him or a third person information or a confession, punishing him for an act he or a third person has committed or is suspected of having committed, or intimidating or coercing him or a third person, or for any reason based on discrimination of any kind, when such pain or suffering is inflicted by or at the instigation of or with the consent or acquiescence of a public official or other person acting in an official capacity. It does not include pain or suffering arising only from, inherent or to incidental lawful sanctions. However, that the UN Torture Convention definition does not extend to private acts of ill-treatment or "lawful sanctions". Article 7 ICCPR controls the latter and imposes a positive obligation upon states to prevent or investigate the former. A controversial form of torture is "waterboarding", in which a person is made to believe he is suffocating to death under water. The US Bush Government denied that it was "torture". It was banned by the Obama administration.

detention, has the Committee sought to draw an exact line between breaches of arts 7 and 10. Prison conditions are generally dealt with under art.10, but art.7 is sometimes invoked. In the *Estrella* case, below, prison conditions which the Committee described as "inhuman" were found to be contrary to art.10, not art.7, with no consideration being given to the boundary or overlap between the two.

As the Committee stated in *Vuolanne v Finland*[177]:

> "the assessment of what constitutes inhuman or degrading treatment falling within the meaning of article 7 depends on all the circumstances of the case, such as the duration and manner of the treatment, its physical or mental effects as well as the sex, age and state of health of the victim."

2.   Consistent with its concern at the number of Optional Protocol cases in which a violation of art.7 has been found, the Committee indicated in General Comment No.20 that states are required by art.7 to do more than just make torture, etc. illegal; they must also act to prevent, investigate and punish acts of torture, etc. (para.8), and provide a remedy for a victim (para.14).

3.   The prohibition of corporal punishment in General Comment No.20, para.5, refers to "excessive" chastisement. However, the Committee has in some concluding observations seemed to go further than this, regarding all kinds of corporal punishment (judicial, school, parental) to be a breach, regardless of the level of severity.[178] In *Higginson v Jamaica*,[179] the Committee stated:

> "... it is the consistent opinion of the Committee that corporal punishment constitutes cruel, inhuman and degrading treatment or punishment contrary to article 7 of the Covenant. The Committee finds that the imposition or the execution of a sentence [by a court] of whipping with the tamarind switch [six strokes] constitutes a violation of the author's rights under article 7."

4.   In the case of Yemen, the Committee was "extremely concerned to find that amputation" was "still prescribed by law and practised, contrary to Article 7."[180]

ESTRELLA v URUGUAY

Human Rights Committee. (1983) 2 Selected Decisions H.R.C. 93

The author, an Argentinian national, was a professional pianist living in Uruguay. He was officially informed that, as a Peronist, he was regarded as an opponent of the Uruguayan Government and his concerts and teaching were cancelled. While he was preparing to leave Uruguay, the author was arrested and taken to a place of detention with others and later transferred to Libertad prison.

Views of the Committee

1.6. The author claims that in that place, the four of them were subjected to torture:

[177] HRC Report, G.A.O.R., 44th Sess., Supp. 40, p.249 (1989).
[178] Jospeh, Schultz and Castan, above, n.105, p.249.
[179] (2002) 9 I.H.R.R. 959.
[180] Concluding Observations of July 24, 2002, UN Doc. CCPR/CO/75/YEM.

The tortures consisted of electric shocks, beatings with rubber truncheons, punches and kicks, hanging us up with our hands tied behind our backs, pushing us into water until we were nearly asphyxiated, making us stand with legs apart and arms raised for up to 20 hours, and psychological torture. The latter consisted chiefly in threats of torture or violence to relatives or friends, or of dispatch to Argentina to be executed, in threats of making us witness the torture of friends, and in inducing in us a state of hallucination in which we thought we could see and hear things which were not real. In my own case, their point of concentration was my hands. For hours upon end, they put me through a mock amputation with an electric saw, telling me, "we are going to do the same to you as Victor Jara."[181] Amongst the effects from which I suffered as a result were a loss of sensitivity in both arms and hands for 11 months, discomfort that still persists in the right thumb, and severe pain in the knees. I reported the fact to a number of military medical officers in the barracks and in the "Libertad" prison.

The author alleges that he was interrogated for the purpose of forcing him to admit that he had been involved in plans to carry out armed operations in Uruguay and Argentina. . . .

1.10. In the second part of his communication . . . the author gives a detailed description of [prison conditions at Libertad prison, to which he was transferred]. He states, in particular, that five floors of the prison are divided into very small cells; that two detainees share each cell (except on the second floor, which is reserved for detainees held in solitary confinement); that these cells are so small that "when one detainee walks, the other has to sit"; that detainees are usually kept in their cells 23 hours per day, that they are not allowed to lie on their beds from 6.30 a.m. to 9 p.m. or to do any exercise and that they are allowed to go into the open air for only one hour per day, provided that they have not been punished. . . .

1.11. The author states that the reasons for punishment at Libertad prison are endless (for example, for walking without having their hands behind their back; for looking directly at a prison guard; for trying to share food or clothes . . .).

1.12. The author maintains that in fact a policy of arbitrary sanctions is continually applied for the purpose of generating moments of hope followed by frustration. He alleges that the whole system at Libertad is aimed at destroying the detainees' physical and psychological balance, that detainees are continuously kept in a state of anxiety, uncertainty and tension. . . . He claims that many detainees are psychologically ill . . . Up to three times a day during alarms, detainees have to lie down on the floor wherever they are, face downward, hands over their heads and any movement could mean being shot by a prison guard. Shooting exercises are carried out in the prison yard and the dummy targets wear exactly the same uniforms as the prisoners. The author also maintains that even Sunday masses were discontinued in 1975 for being moments shared by most detainees. . . .

8.1. The Human Rights Committee has considered the present communication in the light of all information made available to it by the parties as provided in article 5(1) of the Optional Protocol. The Committee bases its views on the following facts, which, in the absence of any substantive clarifications from the State Party, are unrefuted. . . .

8.3. On December 15, 1977, at a time when the author was about to leave Uruguay, he and his friend, Luis Bracony, were kidnapped at his home in Montevideo by some 15 strongly armed individuals in civilian clothes. They were brought blindfolded to a place where . . . the author was subjected to severe physical and psychological torture, including the threat that the author's hands would be cut off by an electric saw, in an effort to force him to admit subversive activities. This ill-treatment had lasting effects, particularly to his arms and hands.

8.4. On December 23, 1977, the author was transferred to a military barracks, probably of Batallón 13, where he continued to be subjected to ill-treatment. In particular, he was threatened with death and he was denied medical attention. On January 20, 1978 he was taken to Libertad prison. He spent the first 10 days in solitary confinement in a cell which was a kind of cage in a section known as "La Isla." He remained imprisoned at Libertad until February 13, 1980.

8.5. At Libertad prison the author was subjected to continued ill-treatment and to arbitrary punishments including 30 days in solitary confinement in a punishment cell and seven months without mail or recreation and subjected to harassment and searches. . . .

9.1. On the basis of the detailed information submitted by the author . . ., the Committee is in a position to conclude that the conditions of imprisonment to which Miguel Angel Estrella was subjected at Libertad prison were inhuman. In this connection, the Committee recalls its consideration of other communications . . . which confirm the existence of a practice of inhuman treatment at Libertad.

---

[181] A well-known Chilean singer and guitarist who was found dead with his hands badly broken at the end of a September 1973 concert in a stadium in Santiago, Chile.

10. The Human Rights Committee ... is of the view that the facts, as found by the Committee, disclose violations of the ... Covenant in particular of:

Article 7, because Miguel Angel Estrella was subjected to torture during the first days of his detention (December 15–23, 1977);

Article 10(1), because he was detained under inhuman prison conditions; ...

11. The Committee, accordingly, is of the opinion that the State party is under an obligation to provide the victim with effective remedies, including compensation, for the violations he has suffered and to take steps to ensure that similar violations do not occur in the future.

Notes

1.   The *Estrella* case is one of many that have alleged torture or other ill- treatment contrary to art.7. Most cases have involved allegations of physical ill-treatment of the kind found to have been inflicted in the *Estrella* case or of inhuman conditions of detention or lack of medical treatment in prison. The Committee's general approach to the assessment of prison conditions was stated and applied in *Mukong v Cameroon*[182]:

> "9.3 As to the conditions of detention in general, the Committee observes that certain minimum standards regarding the conditions of detention must be observed regardless of a State party's level of development. These include, in accordance with Rules 10, 12, 17, 19 and 20 of the *U.N. Standard Minimum Rules for the Treatment of Prisoners*,[183] minimum floor space and cubic content of air for each prisoner, adequate sanitary facilities, clothing which shall be in no manner degrading or humiliating, provision of a separate bed, and provision of food of nutritional value adequate for health and strength. It should be noted that these are *minimum* requirements which the Committee considers should always be observed, even if economic or budgetary considerations may make compliance with these obligations difficult. It transpires from the file that these requirements were not met during the author's detention in the summer of 1988 and in February/March 1990.
>
> 9.4 The Committee further notes that quite apart from the general conditions of detention, the author has been singled out for exceptionally harsh and degrading treatment. Thus, he was kept detained *incommunicado*, was threatened with torture and death and intimidated, deprived of food, and kept locked in his cell for several days on end without the possibility of recreation. In this context, the Committee recalls its General Comment 20[44] which recommends that States parties should make provision against *incommunicado* detention and notes that total isolation of a detained or imprisoned person may amount to acts prohibited by article 7. In view of the above, the Committee finds that Mr. Mukong has been subjected to cruel, inhuman and degrading treatment, in violation of article 7 of the Covenant."

Note that the Committee makes no allowance for a state's economic circumstances.

---

[182] (1995) 2 I.H.R.R. 131.
[183] Ed. Printed in *Human Rights: A Compilation of International Instruments*, Vol.I, Pt I, UN Publication, 1993, p.243.

The infliction of mental suffering may be sufficient to infringe art.7. In the death penalty case of *Pratt and Morgan v Jamaica*,[184] the Committee stated:

> "13.7 The second issue under article 7 concerns the issue of warrants for execution and the notification of the stay of execution. The issue of a warrant for execution necessarily causes intense anguish to the individual concerned. In the authors' case, death warrants were issued twice by the Governor General, first on February 13, 1987 and again on February 23, 1988. It is uncontested that the decision to grant a first stay of execution, taken at noon on February 23, 1987, was not notified to the authors until 45 minutes before the scheduled time of the execution on February 24, 1987. The Committee considers that a delay of close to 20 hours from the time the stay of execution was granted to the time the authors were removed from their death cell constitutes cruel and inhuman treatment within the meaning of article 7."

NG v CANADA

Human Rights Committee. (1994) 1–2 I.H.R.R. 161

In 1990, the author, a UK citizen, was extradited by Canada to stand trial in California for kidnapping and 12 murders. He claimed that his extradition was, inter alia, in breach of art.7 because, if convicted and sentenced to death, he would be executed by gas asphyxiation. He had not been tried by the time that the Committee's views were adopted.

Views of the Committee

16.1 In determining whether, in a particular case, the imposition of capital punishment constitutes a violation of article 7, the Committee will have regard to the relevant personal factors regarding the author, the specific conditions of detention on death row, and whether the proposed method of execution is particularly abhorrent. In the instant case, it is contented that execution by gas asphyxiation is contrary to internationally accepted standards of humane treatment, and that it amounts to treatment in violation of article 7 of the Covenant. The Committee begins by noting that whereas article 6, paragraph 2, allows for the imposition of the death penalty under certain limited circumstances, any method of execution provided for by law must be designed in such a way as to avoid conflict with article 7.

16.2 The Committee is aware that, by definition, every execution of a sentence of death may be considered to constitute cruel and inhuman treatment within the meaning of article 7 of the Covenant; on the other hand, article 6, paragraph 2, permits the imposition of capital punishment for the most serious crimes. Nonetheless, the Committee reaffirms, as it did in its General Comment 20[44] on article 7 of the Covenant (CCPR/C/21Add.3, paragraph 6) that, when imposing capital punishment, the execution of the sentence "... must be carried out in such a way as to cause the least possible physical and mental suffering".

16.3 In the present case, the author has provided detailed information that execution by gas asphyxiation may cause prolonged suffering and agony and does not result in death as swiftly as possible, as asphyxiation by cyanide gas may take over 10 minutes. The State party had the opportunity to refute these allegations on the facts; it has failed to do so. Rather, the State party has confined itself to arguing that in the absence of a norm of

---

[184] HRC Report, G.A.O.R., 44th Sess., Supp. 40, p.222 at 230 (1989). The Committee also accepted that in a death penalty case "undue delay" in proceedings in breach of art.14(3)(c) might be "cruel, inhuman and degrading treatment" contrary to art.7, although this was not established on the facts of the *Pratt and Morgan* case. cf. *Quinteros v Uruguay*, (1983) 2 Selected Decisions H.R.C. 138 at 142, in which a daughter was arrested and held incommunicado: "The Committee understands the anguish and stress caused to the mother by the disappearance of her daughter and by the continuing uncertainty concerning her fate and whereabouts. The author has the right to know what has happened to her daughter. In these respects, she too is a victim of the violations of the Covenant suffered by her daughter in particular of art. 7." cf. *Schedko v Belarus* (2003) 10 I.H.R.R. 679 (mother not told of son's place of execution or burial: inhuman treatment).

international law which expressly prohibits asphyxiation by cyanide gas, "it would be interfering to an unwarranted degree with the internal laws and practices of the United States to refuse to extradite a fugitive to face the possible imposition of the death penalty by cyanide gas asphyxiation".

16.4 In the instant case and on the basis of the information before it, the Committee concludes that execution by gas asphyxiation, should the death penalty be imposed on the author, would not meet the test of "least possible physical and mental suffering", and constitutes cruel and inhuman treatment, in violation of article 7 of the Covenant. Accordingly, Canada which could reasonably foresee that Mr. Ng, if sentenced to death, would be executed in a way that amounts to a violation of article 7, failed to comply with its obligations under the Covenant, by extraditing Mr. Ng without having sought and received assurances that he would not be executed.

16.5 The Committee need not pronounce itself on the compatibility, with article 7, of methods of execution other than that which is at issue in this case.

17. The Human Rights Committee, acting under article 5, paragraph 4, of the International Covenant on Civil and Political Rights, is of the view that the facts as found by the Committee reveal a violation by Canada of article 7 of the Covenant.

Dissenting Opinion of Messrs Mavrommatis and Sadi

We do not believe that, on the basis of the material before us, execution by gas asphyxiation could constitute cruel and inhuman treatment within the meaning of article 7 of the Covenant. A method of execution such as death by stoning, which is intended to and actually inflicts prolonged pain and suffering, is contrary to article 7.

Every known method of judicial execution in use today, including execution by lethal injection, has come under criticism for causing prolonged pain or the necessity to have the process repeated. We do not believe that the Committee should look into such details in respect of execution such as whether acute pain of limited duration or less pain of longer duration is preferable and could be a criterion for a finding of violation of the Covenant.

Dissenting Opinion of Mr. Ando

In the view of the Committee ... (paragraph 16.3) ... the swiftness of death seems to be the very criterion by which the Committee has concluded that execution by gas asphyxiation violates article 7.

In many of the States parties to the Covenant where death penalty has not been abolished, other methods of execution such as hanging, shooting, electrocution or injection of certain materials are used. Some of them may take a longer time and others shorter than gas asphyxiation, but I wonder if, irrespective of the kind and degree of suffering inflicted on the executed, all those methods that may take over ten minutes are in violation of article 7 and all others that take less are in conformity with it. In other words I consider that the criteria of permissible suffering under article 7 should not solely depend on the swiftness of death.

The phrase "least possible physical and mental suffering" comes from the Committee's General Comment 20 on article 7, which states that the death penalty must be carried out in such a way as to cause the least possible physical and mental suffering. This statement, in fact, implies that there is no method of execution which does not cause any physical or mental suffering and that every method of execution is bound to cause some suffering.

However, I must admit that it is impossible for me to specify which kind of suffering is permitted under article 7 and what degree of suffering is not permitted under the same article. I am totally incapable of indicating any absolute criterion as to the scope of suffering permissible under article 7. What I can say is that article 7 prohibits any method of execution which is *intended for* prolonging suffering of the executed or causing unnecessary pain to him or her. As I do not believe that gas asphyxiation is so intended, I cannot concur with the Committee's view that execution by gas asphyxiation violates article 7 of the Covenant.

Notes

1. In contrast with the *Ng* case, in *Cox v Canada*[185] the Committee held that execution by lethal injection of cyanide was not a breach of art.7. Are such fine distinctions defensible? Or would you agree with either of the different approaches in the dissenting opinions in the *Ng* case?

2. The Human Rights Committee has long taken the view that detention for a long period of time on death row does not per se amount to a breach of art.7 or art.10 (concerning the treatment of

---

[185] (1995) 2 I.H.R.R. 98 (another extradition to the US case).

prisoners); there have to be further "compelling circumstances". In *Barrett and Sutcliffe v Jamaica*,[186] the Committee justified this view as follows:

> "The Committee ... reiterates that prolonged judicial proceedings do not *per se* constitute cruel, inhuman and degrading treatment, even if they may be a source of mental strain and tension for detained persons. This also applies to appeal and review proceedings in cases involving capital punishment, although an assessment of the particular circumstances of each case would be called for. In States whose judicial system provides for a review of criminal convictions and sentences, an element of delay between the lawful imposition of a sentence of death and the exhaustion of available remedies is inherent in the review of the sentence; thus, even prolonged periods of detention under a severe custodial regime on death row cannot generally be considered to constitute cruel, inhuman or degrading treatment if the convicted person is merely availing himself of appellate remedies."

Aware of the Committee's view, in *Pratt v Att.-Gen. of Jamaica*,[187] the UK Privy Council took a different stance. In its opinion, "in any case in which execution is to take place more than five years after sentence there will be strong grounds for believing that the delay is such as to constitute 'inhuman or degrading punishment or other treatment'."

The Committee rejected the Privy Council approach in *Johnson v Jamaica*,[188] in which it gave further reasons for its position, including the argument that if the length of detention on death row may per se amount to a breach of art.7, "the implication is that if a State party executes a condemned prisoner after he has spent a certain period of time on death row, it will not be in violation of its obligations under the Covenant, whereas if it refrains from doing so, it will violate the Covenant." In the *Johnson* case, the author had been on death row for 11 years. The Committee found no breach of arts 7 and 10, there being "no compelling circumstances, over and above the length of the detention on death row".

AGIZA v SWEDEN

Committee against Torture (2005) 12 I.H.R.R. 958

Decision of the Committee

2.1 [The facts as presented by the complainant.] In 1982, the complainant [an Egyptian national] was arrested on account of his family connection to his cousin, who had been arrested for suspected involvement in the assassination of the former Egyptian President, Anwar Sadat. Before his release in March 1983, he was allegedly subjected to torture. ...

2.2 In 1991, the complainant left Egypt for Saudi Arabia on security grounds [fear of arrest etc] ...

2.3 In 1998, the complainant was tried in Egypt for terrorist activity directed against the State before a "Superior Court Martial" *in absentia*, along with over one hundred other accused. He was found guilty of belonging to the terrorist group "Al Gihad", and was sentenced, without possibility of appeal, to 25 years' imprisonment. In 2000...the complainant...claimed asylum...in Sweden ...

---

[186] HRC Report, G.A.O.R., 47th Sess., Supp. 40, p.246 at 250 (1992). Mme Chanet, dissenting, preferred the approach of the European Court of Human Rights in *Soering v U.K.* E.Ct.H.R.R., Ser.A, No.161, para.105 (1989), that no allowance should be made to the benefit of the state for the fact that the delay was caused by the convicted person exercising a right of appeal, because it is "part of human nature that the person will cling to life by exploiting those safeguards to the full".

[187] [1994] 2 A.C. 1 at 35.

[188] (1997) 4 I.H.R.R. 21 at 27.

2.5 On 18 December 2001, the Government rejected the asylum application ...On 18 December 2001, the complainant was deported. ...

12.28 Counsel [for the complainant] provides the conclusions...of the investigations of the [Swedish] Parliamentary Ombudsman into the circumstances of deportation from Sweden to Cairo...According to the Ombudsman's summary,...the [US] Central Intelligence Agency offered the Swedish Security Police the use of an aircraft for direct expulsion to Egypt. The Security Police...accepted. ...

12.29 Immediately after the Government's decision in the afternoon of December 18, the expellees were apprehended by Swedish police and subsequently transported to Bromma airport....A number of American security personnel, wearing masks conducted [a] security check...The expellees[189] had their clothes cut up and removed with a pair of scissors, their bodies were searched, their hands and feet were fettered, they were dressed in overalls and their heads were covered with loosely fitted hoods. Finally, they were taken, with bare feet, to the airplane where they were strapped to mattresses. They were kept in this position during the entire flight to Egypt. It had been alleged that the expellees were also given a sedative per rectum which the Ombudsman was unable to substantiate during the investigation. The Ombudsman found that the Security Police had remained passive throughout the procedure. ...

12.30 In the Ombudsman's view, the investigation disclosed that the...American security personnel took charge and were allowed to perform the security check on their own. Such total surrender of power to exercise public authority on Swedish territory was, according to the Ombudsman, clearly contrary to Swedish law. In addition, at least some of the coercive measures taken during the security check were not in conformity with Swedish law. Moreover, the treatment of the expellees, taken as a whole, must be considered to have been inhuman and thus unacceptable and may amount to degrading treatment within the meaning of Article 3 of the European Convention [on Human Rights]. ...

13.3 ...The Committee recalls that the aim of the determination is to establish whether the individual concerned was personally at risk of being subjected to torture in the country to which he was returned. It follows that the existence of a consistent pattern of gross, flagrant or mass violations of human rights in a country does not as such constitute a sufficient ground for determining that a particular person was in danger of being subjected to torture upon his return to that country; additional grounds must exist to show that the individual concerned was personally at risk. Similarly, the absence of a consistent pattern of gross violations of human rights does not mean that a person could not be considered to be in danger of being subjected to torture in his or her specific circumstances.

13.4 The Committee considers at the outset that it was known, or should have been known, to the State party's authorities at the time of complainant's removal that Egypt resorted to consistent and widspread use of torture against detainees, and that the risk of such treatment was particularly high in the case of detainees held for political and security reasons. The State party was also aware that its own security intelligence services regarded the complainant as implicated in terrorist activities and a threat to its national security, and for these reasons its ordinary tribunals referred the case to the Government for a decision at the highest executive level, from which no appeal was possible. The State party was also aware of the interest in the complainant by the intelligence services of two other States: according to the facts submitted by the State party to the Committee, the first foreign State [the US] offered through its intelligence service an aircraft to transport the complainant to the second State, Egypt, where to the State party's knowledge, he had been sentenced *in absentia* and was wanted for alleged involvement in terrorist activities. In the Committee's view, the natural conclusion from these combined elements, that is, that the complainant was at real risk of torture in Egypt in the event of expulsion, was confirmed when, immediately preceding expulsion, the complainant was subjected on the State party's territory to treatment in breach of, at least, article 16[190] of the Convention by foreign agents but with the acquiescence of the State party's police. It follows that the State party's expulsion of the complainant was in breach of article 3 of the Convention.[191] The procurement of diplomatic assurances, which, moreover, provided no mechanism for their enforcement, did not suffice to protect against this manifest risk.

---

[189] Ed. the other "expellee" brought the case of *Alzery v Sweden*, below, p.582.

[190] Ed. Article 16(1) requires states "to prevent...acts of cruel, inhuman or degrading treatment or punishment which do not amount to torture".

[191] Ed. Article 3 reads: "1. No State Party shall expel, return ('*refouler*') or extradite a person to another State where there are substantial grounds for believing that he would be in danger of being subjected to torture. 2. For the purpose of determining whether there are such grounds, the competent authorities shall take into account all relevant considerations including, where applicable, the existence in the State concerned of a consistent pattern of gross, flagrant or mass violations of human rights."

Notes

1. In this case there was a violation of the obligation in art.3 CAT not to return an individual to another state where there are "substantial grounds for believing that he would be in substantial danger of being subjected to torture".[192] A similar obligation has been read into the prohibition of torture in art.7 ICCPR, and a case was later brought before the Human Rights Committee (HRC) under that provision in *Alzery v Sweden*[193] in which the victim was the other "expellee" (see above para.12.29) referred to in the *Agiza* case.[194] In the *Alzery* case, the author, an Egyptian national, claimed that he had fled Egypt after being arrested and tortured by the Egyptian authorities for his involvement in an Islamic organisation that opposed the government. He was refused asylum in Sweden for "security reasons", and ordered to be deported to Egypt. He was searched and transferred to Egypt under the same conditions and in the same aircraft as the complainant in the *Agiza* case. The HRC found a violation of art.7 as follows:

    > "11.3 The first substantive issue before the Committee is whether the author's expulsion from Sweden to Egypt exposed him to a real risk of torture or other ill-treatment in the receiving State, in breach of the prohibition on refoulement contained in article 7 of the Covenant. In determining the risk of such treatment in the present case, the Committee must consider all relevant elements, including the general situation of human rights in a State. The existence of diplomatic assurances, their content and the existence and implementation of enforcement mechanisms are all factual elements relevant to the overall determination of whether, in fact, a real risk of proscribed ill-treatment exists.[195]
    >
    > 11.4 The Committee notes that, in the present case, the State party itself has conceded that there was a risk of ill-treatment that—without more—would have prevented the expulsion of the author consistent with its international human rights obligations. . .The State party in fact relied on the diplomatic assurances alone for its belief that the risk of proscribed ill-treatment was sufficiently reduced to avoid breaching the prohibition on refoulement.
    >
    > 11.5 The Committee notes that the assurances procured contained no mechanism for monitoring of their enforcement. Nor were any arrangements made outside the text of the assurances themselves which would have provided for effective implementation. The visits by the State party's ambassador and staff commenced five weeks after the return, neglecting altogether a period of maximum exposure to risk of harm. The mechanics of the visits that did take place, moreover, failed to conform to key aspects of international good practice by not insisting on private access to the detainee and inclusion of appropriate medical and forensic expertise, even after substantial allegations of ill-treatment emerged. In light of these factors, the State party has not shown that the diplomatic assurances procured were in fact sufficient in the present case to eliminate the risk of ill-treatment to a level consistent with the

---

[192] The prohibition is an absolute one; a state cannot justify returning an individual to face torture because, for example, he is a danger to the public order of the returning state: *Chahal v UK*, 1996-V 1831; (1997) 23 E.H.R.R. 413; *Ahani v Canada* (2004) 112 I.H.R.R. 941; *Tapia Paez v Sweden* (1998) 5 I.H.R.R. 318.

[193] (2007) 14 I.H.R.R. 341.

[194] On the *Agiza* case, see Joseph (2005) 5 H.R.L.R. 339.

[195] Cf. the *Arar* case in which a Canadian and Syrian dual national, born in Syria but living in Canada, was detained at a US airport in transit while returning home from a holiday in Tunisia because his name was on the US Watch List of suspected terrorists. He was flown by the US to Jordan, then driven to Syria, where he was kept for nearly a year and tortured. Canada paid him $10.5m, after a judicial inquiry found that Arar had been wrongly identified by the RCMP as an Islamic extremist with links with Al-Qaida, this information being passed on to the US and contributing to his being on the list.

requirements of article 7 of the Covenant. The author's expulsion thus amounted to a violation of article 7 of the Covenant.

11.6 On the issue of the treatment by the author at Bromma airport, the Committee must first assess whether the treatment suffered by the author at the hands of foreign agents is properly imputable to the State party under the terms of the Covenant and under applicable rules of State responsibility. The Committee notes that, at a minimum, a State party is responsible for acts of foreign officials exercising acts of sovereign authority on its territory, if such acts are performed with the consent or acquiescence of the State party (see also article 1 of the Convention against Torture). It follows that the acts complained of, which occurred in the course of performance of official functions in the presence of the State party's officials and within the State party's jurisdiction, are properly imputable to the State party itself, in addition to the State on whose behalf the official were engaged. Insofar as the State party accepts the finding of its Parliamentary Ombudsman that the treatment suffered was disproportionate to any legitimate law enforcement purpose, it is evident that the use of force was excessive and amounted to a breach of article 7 of the Covenant. It follows that the State party violated article 7 of the Covenant as a result of the treatment suffered by the author at Bromma airport."

2.   The *Agiza* and *Alzery* cases[196] are cases of "extraordinary rendition", one definition of which is "the deliberate transfer of terrorist suspects to foreign countries for interrogation, knowing that torture may be used".[197] It involves the bypassing of the law of extradition and deportation, which contain substantive and procedural limitations upon the removal of an individual from one state to another.[198] There is evidence[199] that, following 9/11, many suspected terrorists were extra-judicially flown from one state to another[200] to places of secret detention for interrogation in the "war on terror".

LLANTOY HUAMÁN v PERU

Human Rights Committee (2006) 13 I.H.R.R. 355

The author, aged 17, became pregnant. Her gynaecologist recommended a termination when a scan revealed the foetus was anencephalic. The state hospital director refused permission on the ground that a therapeutic abortion was only lawful in Peru if it was the only way to save the life of the mother or to avoid serious and permanent damage to her health. Permission was refused despite evidence from a social worker and a psychiatrist as to the effect of the pregnancy on the author's

---

[196] Ed. Cf. *Saadi v Italy* hudoc (2008) and *AS and DD (Libya) v Secretary of State for the Home Dept* [2008] EWCA Civ 289 (diplomatic assurances by Tunisia and Libya). On diplomatic assurances, see Hawkins (2006) 20 Georgetown Im.L.J. 213; Jones (2006) 8 E.J.M.L. 9; Larsaeus, *The Use of Diplomatic Assurances in the Prevention of Prohibited Treatment*, Refugee Studies Centre, Working Paper 32 (2006); Noll (2006) 7 M.J.I.L. 104; Skolund (2008) 77 Nordic J.I.L. 319. Neither the *Agiza* nor *Alzery* cases could have been brought against the US as it had not accepted the CAT or ICCPR right of petition.

[197] UK House of Commons Select Committee on Foreigtn Affairs, 6th Report of 2004-5, HC 36-I, para.89. On extraordinary rendition, see Button (2007) 19 Flor. J.I.L. 531; Satterthwaite (2007) 75 G.W.L.R. 1333; Sands (2006) E.H.R.L.R. 408; Sadat (2006) 37 C.W.J.I.L. 309; Weissbrodt and Bergquist (2006) 19 Harv. H.R.J. 123; Winkler (2008) 30 L.L.A.I.C.L.R. 33.

[198] Cf. cases such as *Eichmann*, above, p.241, where an individual is illegally abducted for prosecution, not interrogation.

[199] See *Secret Detentions and Illegal Transfers of Detainees involving Council of Europe Member States*, 2nd Report of the Report of Committee on Legal Affairs and Human Rights, Council of Europe, 2007, Rapporteur Dick Marty.

[200] Sometimes this has involved stopovers at the airports of third states (e.g. the UK).

mental health. The author gave birth to an anencephalic baby girl who survived for only four days. The HRC found violations of arts 2, 7, 17 and 24.

Views of the Committee

6.2 The Committee notes that the author attached a doctor's statement confirming that her pregnancy exposed her to a life-threatening risk. She also suffered severe psychological consequences exacerbated by her status as a minor, as the psychiatric report of 20 August 2001 confirmed. The Committee notes that the State party has not provided any evidence to challenge the above. It notes that the authorities were aware of the risks to the author's life, since a gynaecologist and obstetrician in the same hospital had advised her to terminate the pregnancy, with the operation to be carried out in the same hospital. The subsequent refusal of the competent medical authorities to provide the service may have endangered the author's life. The author states that no effective remedy was available to her to oppose that decision. In the absence of any information from the State party, due weight must be given to the author's claims.

6.3 The author also claims that, owing to the refusal of the medical authorities to carry out the therapeutic abortion, she had to endure the distress of seeing her daughter's marked deformities and knowing that she would die very soon. This was an experience which added further pain and distress to that which she had already borne during the period when she was obliged to continue with the pregnancy. The author attaches a psychiatric certificate dated 20 August 2001, which confirms the state of deep depression into which she fell and the severe consequences this caused, taking her age into account. The Committee notes that this situation could have been foreseen, since a hospital doctor had diagnosed anencephaly in the foetus, yet the hospital director refused termination. The omission on the part of the State in not enabling the author to benefit from a therapeutic abortion, was, in the Committee's view, the cause of the suffering she experienced. The Committee has pointed out in its General Comment No.20 that the right set out in article 7 of the Covenant relates not only to physical pain but also to mental suffering, and that the protection is particularly important in the case of minors. In the absence of any information from the State party in this regard, due weight must be given to the author's complaints. Consequently, the Committee considers that the facts before it reveal a violation of article 7 of the Covenant. In the light of this finding the Committee does not consider it necessary in the circumstances to ma[k]e a finding on article 6 of the Covenant.

6.4 The author states that the State party, in denying her the opportunity to secure medical intervention to terminate the pregnancy, interfered arbitrarily in her private life. The Committee notes that a public-sector doctor told the author that she could either continue with the pregnancy or terminate it in accordance with domestic legislation allowing abortions in cases of risk to the life of the mother. In the absence of any information from the State party, due weight must be given to the author's claim that at the time of this information, the conditions for a lawful abortion as set out in the law were present. In the circumstances of the case, the refusal to act in accordance with the author's decision to terminate her pregnancy was not justified and amounted to a violation of article 17 of the Covenant.

6.5 The author claims a violation of article 24 of the Covenant, since she did not receive from the State party the special care she needed as a minor. The Committee notes the special vulnerability of the author as a minor girl. It further note that, in the absence of any information from the State party, due weight must be given to the author's claim that she did not receive, during and after her pregnancy, the medical and psychological support necessary in the specific circumstances of her case. Consequently, the Committee considers that the facts before it reveal a violation of article 24 of the Covenant.

6.6 The author claims to have been a victim of violation of article 2 of the Covenant on the grounds that she lacked an adequate legal remedy. In the absence of information from the State party, the Committee considers that due weight must be given to the author's claims as regards lack of any adequate legal remedy and consequently concludes that the facts before it also reveal a violation of article 2 in conjunction with articles 7, 17 and 24.

Dissenting Opinion by Committee Member Solari-Yrigoyen

...The Committee notes that when the author was a minor, she and her mother were informed by the obstetric gynaecologist at Lima National Hospital...that the foetus suffered from anencephaly which would inevitably cause its death at birth. The doctor told the author that she had two options: (1) continue the pregnancy, which would endanger her own life; or (2) terminate the pregnancy by a therapeutic abortion. He recommended the second option. Given this conclusive advice from the specialist who had told her of the risks to her life if the pregnancy continued, the author decided to follow his professional advice and accepted the second option. . . .

The author substantiated with medical and psychological certificates all her claims about the fatal risk she ran if the pregnancy continued. In spite of the risk, the director of the public hospital would not authorize the therapeutic abortion which the law of the State party allowed, arguing that it would not be a therapeutic abortion but rather a voluntary and unfounded abortion punishable under the Criminal Code. The hospital director did not supply any legal ruling in support of his pronouncements outside his professional field or challenging the medical attestations to the serious risk to the mother's life. . . .Refusing a therapeutic abortion not only endangered the author's life but had grave consequences which the author has also substantiated to the Committee by means of valid supporting documents.

It is not only taking a person's life that violates article 6 of the Covenant but also placing a person's life in grave danger, as in this case. Consequently, I consider that the facts in the present case reveal a violation of article 6 of the Covenant.

Notes

1. In this case, the HRC found multiple violations of the ICCPPR, but considered it unnecessary to apply art.6. Would you agree with Mr Solari-Yrigoyen that art. 6 had been violated?

2. The HRC did find a violation of art.17, on the basis that there was an interference with the author's right to privacy in terms of her personal autonomy. Does the case establish a right to abortion under art.17? If so, is it an absolute right (giving the pregnant woman freedom to have an abortion in her discretion[201]), or just one where her life or health is threatened?

3. As to the HRC's approach to the question whether the unborn foetus may have a right to life under art.6, Joseph, Schutz and Castan[202] summarise the HRC's position as follows:

    "Anti-abortion advocates argue that abortion constitutes a breach of the right to life of an unborn baby. However, the HRC has not adopted this position. Rather, it has focused on the detrimental human rights effects of anti-abortion laws, as recently occurred in General Comment 28 [on art.3: Equality of Rights between Men and Women].[203] The issue has also been raised in Concluding Observations. . . .

    'Regarding Chile:

    15. The criminalisation of all abortions, without exception, raises serious issues, especially in the light of unrefuted reports that many women undergo illegal abortions that pose a threat to their lives. The legal duty imposed upon health personnel to report on cases of women who have undergone abortions may inhibit women from seeking medical treatment, thereby endangering their lives. The State party is under a duty to ensure the life of all persons, including pregnant women whose pregnancies are terminated. In this regard: the Committee recommends that the law be amended so as to introduce exceptions to the general prohibition on all abortions and to protect the confidentiality of medical information.' . . .

---

[201] Cf. *Roe v Wade* (1973) 410 U.S. 174 (unqualified discretion in the first trimester).

[202] See above, at n.105, pp.189–191. Footnotes omitted.

[203] Ed. General Comment No.28 reads: "10. When reporting on the right to life protected by article 6, States parties should provide data on birth rates and on pregnancy- and childbirth-related deaths of women. Gender-disaggregated data should be provided on infant mortality rates. States parties should give information on any measures taken by the State to help women prevent unwanted pregnancies, and to ensure that they do not have to undergo life-threatening clandestine abortions. States parties should also report on measures to protect women from practices that violate their right to life, such as female infanticide, the burning of widows and dowry killings. The Committee also wishes to have information on the particular impact on women of poverty and deprivation that may pose a threat to their lives."

The UN Committee on the Elimination of All Forms of Discrimination Against Women (CEDAW Committee) has cited compulsory abortion as a danger to the mental and physical health of women in its General Recommendation 19, and also condemned the criminalising of abortion in the same General Comment. The CEDAW Committee clearly endorses freedom of choice for women in the abortion debate."

MUKONG v CAMEROON

Human Rights Committee (1995) 2 I.H.R.R. 131

The author was a journalist who had long advocated multi-party democracy in the one party state of Cameroon. He was arrested in 1988 following a BBC broadcast in which he criticised the President of Cameroon and the Government. The reason for the arrest was that his remarks were subversive contrary to an Ordinance under which he was later charged with an offence. He was re-arrested in 1990 following a public meeting in which he advocated multi-party democracy. The Committee found that the conditions of his detention infringed art.7, ICCPR and that the limitation on his freedom of speech was in breach of art.19, ICCPR (see below, p.679). The following extract concerns the meaning of "arbitrary" in art.9(1) and the permissible public interest reasons for detaining an accused on remand.

Views of the Committee

9.8 The Committee notes that the State party has dismissed the author's claim under article 9 by indicating that he was arrested and detained in application of the rules of criminal procedure, and that the police detention and preliminary enquiries by the examining magistrate were compatible with article 9. It remains however to be determined whether other factors may render an otherwise lawful arrest and lawful detention "arbitrary" within the meaning of article 9. The drafting history of article 9, paragraph 1, confirms that "arbitrariness" is not to be equated with "against the law", but must be interpreted more broadly to include elements of inappropriateness, injustice, lack of predictability and due process of law. As the Committee has observed on a previous occasion,[204] this means that remand in custody pursuant to lawful arrest must not only be lawful but reasonable in all the circumstances. Remand in custody must further be necessary in all the circumstances, for example to prevent flight, interference with evidence or the recurrence of crime. In the present case, the State party has not shown that any of these factors was present. It has merely contended that the author's arrest and detention were clearly justified by reference to article 19, paragraph 3, i.e. permissible restrictions on the author's freedom of expression. ... the Committee finds that the author's detention in 1988–1989 and 1990 was neither reasonable nor necessary in the circumstances of the case, and thus in violation of article 9, paragraph 1, of the Covenant.

Notes

1.   There have been many cases brought under art.9 in which the arrested person had been given no reason for arrest, had no judicial remedy available to challenge the legality of his detention and was eventually released without being charged. *Carballal v Uruguay*[205] is one of a number of such cases involving multiple breaches of art.9. The uncontested facts were:

> "Leopoldo Buffo Carballal was arrested on January 4, 1976 and held incommunicado for more than five months, much of the time tied and blindfolded, in several places of detention.

---

[204] See ... *Van Alpen v The Netherlands* ... 27 July 1990. ...
[205] (1981) 1 Selected Decisions H.R.C. 63 at 64–65.

Recourse to habeas corpus was not available to him. He was brought before a military judge on May 5, 1976 and again on June 28, or July 28, 1976, when an order was issued for his release. He was, however, kept in detention until January 26, 1977."

The Committee found breaches of art.9 as follows:

"Article 9(1), because he was not released until approximately six or seven months after an order for his release was issued by the military court;
Article 9(2), because he was not informed of the charges brought against him;
Article 9(3), because he was not brought before a judge until four months after he was detained and 44 days after the Covenant entered into force for Uruguay;
Article 9(4), because recourse to habeas corpus was not available to him."

2.   Article 9 protects all categories of persons detained by the state, including illegal immigrants and the mentally disabled, not just suspected criminals. In *A v Australia*,[206] the author was a Cambodian national who had applied for asylum in Australia after entering the country illegal by boat. The author was detained for over four years, under a government policy of detaining boat people during all of the time that their asylum applications were being considered. The Committee held that the author's detention was "arbitrary", in breach of art.9(1):

"9.2 ... the Committee recalls that the notion of 'arbitrariness' must not be equated with 'against the law' but be interpreted more broadly to include such elements as inappropriateness and injustice. ... The State party however, seeks to justify the author's detention by the fact that he entered Australia unlawfully and by the perceived incentive for the applicant to abscond if left in liberty. ...
9.3 The Committee agrees that there is no basis for the author's claim that it is *per se* arbitrary to detain individuals requesting asylum. Nor can it find any support for the contention that there is a rule of customary international law which would render all such detention arbitrary.
9.4 The Committee observes however, that every decision to keep a person in detention should be open to review periodically so that the grounds justifying the detention can be assessed. In any event, detention should not continue beyond the period for which the State can provide appropriate justification. For example, the fact of illegal entry may indicate a need for investigation and there may be other factors particular to the individual, such as the likelihood of absconding and lack of cooperation, which may justify detention for a period. Without such factors detention may be considered arbitrary, even if entry was illegal. In the instant case, the State party has not advanced any grounds particular to the author's case, which would justify his continued detention for a period of four years ..."

In contrast, the detention of a mentally disabled person was held not to be arbitrary on the facts in *A v New Zealand*[207]:

"7.2 The main issue before the Committee is whether the author's detention under the Mental Health Act from 1984 to 1993 constituted a violation of the Covenant, in particular of article 9.

---

[206] (1998) 5 I.H.R.R. 78. See also *C v Australia* (2003) 10 I.H.R.R. 364.
[207] (2000) 7 I.H.R.R. 44.

The Committee notes that that author's assessment under the Mental Health Act followed threatening and aggressive behaviour on the author's part, and that the committal order was issued according to law, based on the opinion of three psychiatrists. Further, a panel of psychiatrists continued to review the author's situation periodically. The Committee is therefore of the opinion that the deprivation of the author's liberty was neither unlawful nor arbitrary and thus not in violation of article 9, paragraph 1 of the Covenant."

3. Article 9(3) requires that an arrested person in criminal cases be brought "promptly" before a judge, etc. The meaning of "promptly" in the Committee's practice is summarised by Joseph, Schultz and Castan[208] as follows:

> "In *Van der Houwen v The Netherlands* (583/94), seventy-three hours of detention without being brought before a judge was held not to be a violation of article 9(3). However, in the later case of *Borisenko v Hungary* (852/99), the author's unexplained detention for three days prior to presentation before a judicial officer constituted a breach of article 9(3).[209] Furthermore, in *Freemantle v Jamaica* (625/95), the Committee found a violation of article 9(3) when the author was held incommunicado for four days without being brought before a judge and without having access to counsel. ... HRC jurisprudence therefore indicates that the limit of 'promptness' for the purposes of the article 9(3) guarantee of judicial review lies somewhere around three days. ... However, in recent Concluding Observations, the HRC has taken a stricter view. For example, in its 2000 Observations on Gabon, the HRC stated[210]:
>
> > '13. ... The State party should take action to ensure that detention in police custody never lasts longer than 48 hours and that detainees have access to lawyers from the moment of their detention. The State party must ensure full de facto compliance with the provisions of article 9, paragraph 3, of the Covenant.'"

4. Under art.9(3), a person arrested on a criminal charge must be brought promptly before a judge or "other officer authorised by law to exercise judicial power". The latter term does not include a public prosecutor in the sense of the former Soviet procuratura system, who had a role in the prosecution of offenders as well as the power to take remand decisions. In *Kulomin v Hungary*[211] the Committee stated:

> "11.3 The Committee notes that, after his arrest on 20 August 1988, the author's pre-trial detention was ordered and subsequently renewed on several occasions by the public prosecutor, until the author was brought before a judge on 29 May 1989. The Committee considers that it is inherent to the proper exercise of judicial power, that it be exercised by an authority which is independent, objective and impartial in relation to the issues dealt with. In the circumstances of the instant case, the Committee is not satisfied that the public prosecutor could be regarded as having the institutional objectivity and impartiality necessary to be considered an 'officer authorized to exercise judicial power' within the meaning of article 9(3)."

---

[208] See above, n.105, pp.324–325. Some footnotes omitted.
[209] Para 7.4. Messrs Ando and Bhagwati dissented, noting that the State Party had failed to put forward justifications for the 3-day detention as the author had not complained about that period of detention.
[210] UN Doc. CCPR/CO/70/GAB ...
[211] (1997) 4 I.H.R.R. 11.

5. Whether a detained person is tried "within reasonable time" (art.9(3)) depends on the facts of each case; a period of four years and four months was not "reasonable" when there were no special circumstances.[212] In *Teesdale v Jamaica*,[213] 16 months pre-trial detention was unreasonable:

> "9.3 ... the Committee notes that the author was detained on 28 May 1988 and formally charged with murder on 2 June 1988. His trial began on 6 October 1989 and he was sentenced to death on 2 November 1989. ... It appears from the transcript of the trial. ... that all evidence for the case of the prosecution was gathered by 1 June 1988 and no further investigations were carried out. The Committee is of the view that in the context of article 9, paragraph 3, in the specific circumstances of the present case and in the absence of any explanation for the delay by the State party, the length of time that the author was in pre-trial detention is unreasonable and, therefore, constitutes a violation of this provision."

In *Fillastre and Bizouarn v Bolivia*,[214] the Committee stated: "The lack of adequate budgetary appropriations for the administration of criminal justice ... does not justify unreasonable delays".

6. Article 9(4), which applies to detention for any reason (criminal suspect, mentally disabled, deportation, etc.) is the habeas corpus provision of the Covenant. In *Voulanne v Finland*,[215] the Committee found a breach where a soldier was arrested for a military disciplinary charge:

> "The Committee does not accept the contention of the State Party that the request for review before a superior military officer according to the Law on Military Disciplinary Procedure currently in effect in Finland is comparable to judicial scrutiny of an appeal and that the officials ordering detention act in a judicial or quasi-judicial manner. The procedure followed in the case of Mr. Vuolanne did not have a judicial character, and the supervisory military officer who upheld the decision of July 17, 1987 against Mr. Vuolanne cannot be deemed to be a 'court' within the meaning of article 9, paragraph 4; therefore, the obligations laid down therein have not been complied with by the authorities of the State Party. ..."

TOONEN v AUSTRALIA[216]

Human Rights Committee (1994) 1–3 I.H.R.R. 97

The author alleged that sections of the Tasmanian Criminal Code that made private homosexual conduct a criminal offence were in breach of arts 17 and 26, ICCPR. Although the author had not been prosecuted and the police had not brought any prosecutions for several years, the Committee considered that the author was a "victim" competent to bring the communication. This was because the "threat of enforcement [he was a gay rights activist and a practising homosexual] and the

---

[212] *Kone v Senegal* (1995) 2 I.H.R.R. 279. A period of 30 months between arrest and the beginning of the trial was a breach of art.9(3) on the facts: *Douglas v Jamaica* (1997) 4 I.H.R.R. 387. So was four years between an appeal court decision ordering retrial and the retrial starting: *Shalto v Trinidad* (1995) 2 I.H.R.R. 568.

[213] (2002) 9 I.H.R.R. 962. The pre-trial detention conditions were in breach of art.10 ICCPR.

[214] HRC Report, G.A.O.R., 48th Sess., Supp. 40, p.294 (1992) (four years unreasonable).

[215] HRC Report, G.A.O.R., 44th Sess., Supp. 40, p.249 (1989).

[216] Joseph (1994) 13 U.Tas.L.R. 392.

pervasive impact of the continued existence of these provisions on administrative practices and public opinion had affected him and continued to affect him personally." Whereas the state of Tasmania argued that there was no breach of art.17, ICCPR, the Australian Federal Government (the "state party" referred to in para.8.4, HRC Views, below) accepted that there was. The HRC did not consider the claim under art.26.

Views of the Committee

8.2 Inasmuch as article 17 is concerned, it is undisputed that adult consensual sexual activity in private is covered by the concept of "privacy", and that Mr. Toonen is actually and currently affected by the continued existence of the Tasmanian laws. The Committee considers that Sections 122(a), (c) and 123 of the Tasmanian Criminal Code "interfere" with the author's privacy, even if these provisions have not been enforced for a decade. In this context, it notes that the policy of the Department of Public Prosecutions not to initiate criminal proceedings in respect of private homosexual conduct does not amount to a guarantee that no actions will be brought against homosexuals in the future, particularly in the light of undisputed statements of the Director of Public Prosecutions of Tasmania in 1988 and those of members of the Tasmanian Parliament. The continued existence of the challenged provisions therefore continuously and directly "interferes" with the author's privacy.

8.3 The prohibition against private homosexual behaviour is provided for by law, namely, Sections 122 and 123 of the Tasmanian Criminal Code. As to whether it may be deemed arbitrary, the Committee recalls that pursuant to its General Comment 16[32] on article 17, the "introduction of the concept of arbitrariness is intended to guarantee that even interference provided for by the law should be in accordance with the provisions, aims and objectives of the Covenant and should be, in any event, reasonable in the circumstances". The Committee interprets the requirements of reasonableness to imply that any interference with privacy must be proportional to the end sought and be necessary in the circumstances of any given case.

8.4 While the State party acknowledges that the impugned provisions constitute an arbitrary interference with Mr. Toonen's privacy, the Tasmanian authorities submit that the challenged laws are justified on public health and moral grounds, as they are intended in part to prevent the spread of HIV/AIDS in Tasmania, and because, in the absence of specific limitation clauses in article 17, moral issues must be deemed a matter for domestic decision.

8.5 As far as the public health argument of the Tasmanian authorities is concerned, the Committee notes that the criminalization of homosexual practices cannot be considered a reasonable means or proportionate measure to achieve the aim of preventing the spread of HIV/AIDS. The Australian Government observes that statutes criminalizing homosexual activity tend to impede public health programmes "by driving underground many of the people at the risk of infection". Criminalization of homosexual activity thus would appear to run counter to the implementation of effective education programmes in respect of the HIV/AIDS prevention. Secondly, the Committee notes that no link has been shown between the continued criminalization of homosexual activity and the effective control of the spread of the HIV/AIDS virus.

8.6 The Committee cannot accept either that for the purposes of article 17 of the Covenant, moral issues are exclusively a matter of domestic concern, as this would open the door to withdrawing from the Committee's scrutiny a potentially large number of statutes interfering with privacy. It further notes that, with the exception of Tasmania, all laws criminalizing homosexuality have been repealed throughout Australia and that, even in Tasmania, it is apparent that there is no consensus as to whether Sections 122 and 123 should not also be repealed. Considering further that these provisions are not currently enforced, which implies that they are not deemed essential to the protection of morals in Tasmania, the Committee concludes that the provisions do not meet the "reasonableness" test in the circumstances of the case, and that they arbitrarily interfere with Mr. Toonen's right under article 17, paragraph 1. . . .

9. The Human Rights Committee, acting under article 5, paragraph 4, of the Optional Protocol to the International Covenant on Civil and Political Rights, is of the view that the facts before it reveal a violation of articles 17, paragraph 1, *juncto* 2, paragraph 1, of the Covenant.

10. Under article 2(3)(a) of the Covenant, the author, victim of a violation of articles 17, paragraphs 1, *juncto* 2, paragraph 1, of the Covenant, is entitled to a remedy. In the opinion of the Committee, an effective remedy would be the repeal of Sections 122(a), (c) and 123 of the Tasmanian Criminal Code.

Notes

1. Criminal laws prohibiting homosexual acts are actively enforced in some states. Would a conviction in such a state be in breach of art.17, or might it be justified as being for the enforcement of that state's public morals?

2. In the absence of any intention of the Tasmanian Government to change its law to comply with *Toonen*, the Australian Government enacted a federal law, the Human Rights (Sexual Conduct) Act 1994, which provides that sexual conduct involving only consenting adults in private shall not be an offence under any law of the Commonwealth, a State or a Territory.[217]

3. See also on art.17 *Llantoy Huamán v Peru*, above, p.584.

FAURISSON v FRANCE[218]

Human Rights Committee. (1996) 4 I.H.R.R. 444

The Gayssot Act 1990 made it a criminal offence to challenge the correctness of the conviction of war criminals at Nuremberg for crimes against humanity. As a result of an interview published in a French magazine in which he repeated his view that there were no homicidal gas chambers for the extermination of jews in Nazi concentration camps, the author, who was a professor of literature, was convicted of a criminal offence under this Act. The author alleged, inter alia, a breach of art.19, ICCPR.

Views of the Committee

9.2 The Committee takes note of public debates in France, including negative comments made by French parliamentarians on the Gayssot Act, as well as of arguments put forward in other, mainly European, countries which support and oppose the introduction of similar legislations.

9.3 Although it does not contest that the application of the terms of the Gayssot Act, which, in their effect, make it a criminal offence to challenge the conclusions and the verdict of the International Military Tribunal at Nuremberg, may lead, under different conditions than the facts of the instant case, to decisions or measures incompatible with the Covenant, the Committee is not called upon to criticize in the abstract laws enacted by States parties. ...

9.4 Any restriction on the right of freedom of expression must cumulatively meet the following conditions: it must be provided by law, it must address one of the aims set out in paragraph 3(a) and (b) of article 19, and must be necessary to achieve a legitimate purpose.

9.5 The restriction on the author's freedom of expression was indeed provided by law i.e. the Act of 13 July 1990. It is the constant jurisprudence of the Committee that the restrictive law itself must be in compliance with the provisions of the Covenant. In this regard the Committee concludes, on the basis of the reading of the judgment of the 17th *Chambre correctionnelle du Tribunal de grande instance de Paris* that the finding of the author's guilt was based on his following two statements: "... I have excellent reasons not to believe in the policy of extermination of Jews or in the magic gas chambers ... I wish to see that 100 per cent of the French citizens realize that the myth of the gas chambers is a dishonest fabrication". His conviction therefore did not encroach upon his right to hold and express an opinion in general, rather the court convicted Mr. Faurisson for having violated the rights and reputation of others. For these reasons the Committee is satisfied that the Gayssot Act, as read, interpreted and applied to the author's case by the French courts, is in compliance with the provisions of the Covenant.

---

[217] See 1996 HRC Report, A/51/40, para.456.

[218] On the *Faurisson* case and race hate speech generally, see McGoldrick and O'Donnell (1998) 18 Legal Studies 453.

9.6 To assess whether the restrictions placed on the author's freedom of expression by his criminal conviction were applied for the purposes provided for by the Covenant, the Committee begins by noting, as it did in its General Comment 10 [on Article 19] that the rights for the protection of which restrictions on the freedom of expression are permitted by article 19, paragraph 3, may relate to the interests of other persons or to those of the *community as a whole*. Since the statements made by the author, read in their full context, were of such a nature as to raise or strengthen anti-semitic feelings, the restriction served the respect of the Jewish community to live free from fear of an atmosphere of anti-semitism. The Committee therefore concludes that the restriction of the author's freedom of expression was permissible under article 19, paragraph 3(a), of the Covenant.

9.7 Lastly the Committee needs to consider whether the restriction of the author's freedom of expression was necessary. The Committee noted the State party's argument contending that the introduction of the Gayssot Act was intended to serve the struggle against racism and anti-semitism. It also noted the statement of a member of the French Government, the then Minister of Justice, which characterized the denial of the existence of the Holocaust as the principal vehicle for anti-semitism. In the absence in the material before it of any argument undermining the validity of the State party's position as to the necessity of the restriction, the Committee is satisfied that the restriction of Mr. Faurisson's freedom of expression was necessary within the meaning of article 19, paragraph 3, of the Covenant.

10. The Human Rights Committee, acting under article 5, paragraph 4, of the Optional Protocol to the International Covenant on Civil and Political Rights, is of the view that the facts as found by the Committee do not reveal a violation by France of article 19, paragraph 3, of the Covenant.

Notes

1. Would censorship of, or a conviction for publishing, the Danish Cartoons or Salmon Rushdie's *Satanic Verses*, which were very offensive to Muslims, have been a violation of art.19.

2. In *Mukong v Cameroon*,[219] a journalist had been detained because of his advocacy of political views contrary to those of the Government. Rejecting the Government's argument that this restriction upon freedom of expression could be justified under art.19(3) in terms of national security and/or public order, the Committee stated:

> "9.7 ... Any restriction of the freedom of expression pursuant to paragraph 3 of article 19 must cumulatively meet the following conditions: it must be provided for by law, it must address one of the aims enumerated in paragraph 3(a) and (b) of article 19, and must be necessary to achieve the legitimate purpose. The State party has indirectly justified its actions on grounds of national security and/or public order, by arguing that the author's right to freedom of expression was exercised without regard to the country's political context and continued struggle for unity. While the State party has indicated that the restrictions on the author's freedom of expression were provided for by law, it must still be determined whether the measures taken against the author were necessary for the safeguard of national security and/ or public order. The Committee considers that it was not necessary to safeguard an alleged vulnerable state of national unity by subjecting the author to arrest, continued detention and treatment in violation of article 17. It further considers that the legitimate objective of safe-guarding and indeed strengthening national unity under difficult political circumstances cannot be achieved by attempting to muzzle advocacy of multi-party democracy, democratic tenets and human rights; in this regard, the question of deciding which measures might meet the 'necessity' test in such situations does not arise. In the circumstances of the author's case, the Committee concludes that there has been a violation of article 19 of the Covenant."

It is noticeable that in this case the Committee made its own objective assessment of the needs

---

[219] For further facts of the case, see above, p.586.

of national security and public order in Cameroon. In contrast, under the ECHR, the European Court of Human Rights, while making the final determination, allows states a certain measure of discretion, or "margin of appreciation", when assessing whether a particular restriction upon human rights can be justified as being in the interest of, for example, national security or public morals.[220] The Committee has decided not to adopt a "margin of appreciation" approach when interpreting the Covenant generally. In *Lansmann v Finland*,[221] the Committee expressly rejected a state argument that it should apply a "a margin of appreciation" when deciding whether quarrying that allegedly interfered with the rights of the Sami to engage in reindeer husbandry was in breach of their minority rights under art.27, Covenant. Should it apply a "margin of appreciation", perhaps on the basis that states have local knowledge and responsibilities? Or does such a doctrine run the risk of abuse by states?

3.   In *Singer v Canada*,[222] the author, whose business clientele were mostly anglophonic, claimed that Quebec legislation requiring that all outdoor advertising be in French, not in English, was in breach of art.19. Ruling in his favour, the Committee "concluded that a State party to the Covenant may choose one or more official languages, but it may not exclude, outside the spheres of public life, the freedom to express oneself in a language of one's choice".

BROEKS v NETHERLANDS

Human Rights Committee. (1987) 2 Selected Decisions H.R.C. 196

The author was dismissed from her employment as a nurse because of illness. Under Dutch social security law, in order to receive unemployment benefit beyond a certain period, she had, as a married woman, to show that she was the "breadwinner," a condition which did not apply to a married man. The author claimed that this discrimination was in breach of art.26, ICCPR.

Views of the Committee

12.1. The State Party contends that there is considerable overlapping of the provisions of article 26 with the provisions of article 2 of the International Covenant on Economic, Social and Cultural Rights. The Committee is of the view that the International Covenant on Civil and Political Rights would still apply even if a particular subject-matter is referred to or covered in other international instruments. ... Notwithstanding the interrelated drafting history of the two Covenants, it remains necessary for the Committee to apply fully the terms of the International Covenant on Civil and Political Rights. The Committee observes in this connection that the provisions of article 2 of the International Covenant on Economic, Social and Cultural Rights do not detract from the full application of article 26 of the International Covenant on Civil and Political Rights.

12.2. The Committee has also examined the contention of the State Party that article 26 of the International Covenant on Civil and Political Rights cannot be invoked in respect of a right which is specifically provided for under article 9 of the International Covenant on Economic, Social and Cultural Rights (social security, including social insurance). ... The discussions, at the time of drafting, concerning the question whether the scope of article 26 extended to rights not otherwise guaranteed by the Covenant, were inconclusive and cannot alter the conclusion arrived at by the ordinary means of interpretation referred to in paragraph 12.3 below.

12.3. For the purpose of determining the scope of article 26, the Committee has taken into account the

---

[220] No "margin of appreciation" was referred to by the Committee in the *Toonen* case, above, p.590, in a public morals case. Under the European Convention a wide "margin of appreciation is generally allowed in public morality cases because of the differences across Europe on such matters as obscenity legislation: see Harris, O'Boyle and Warbrick, above, at n.9, p.11.

[221] (1995) 2 I.H.R.R. 287. The Committee did apply a "margin of appreciation" in a public morals context in the early case of *Hertzberg v Finland* (1982) 1 Selected Decisions H.R.C. 124, but has not done so since.

[222] (1995) 2 I.H.R.R. 149 at 156. The requirement had been repealed by the time the Committee adopted its views.

"ordinary meaning" of each element of the article in its context and in the light of its object and purpose (art. 31 of the Vienna Convention on the Law of Treaties). The Committee begins by noting that article 26 does not merely duplicate the guarantees already provided for in article 2. It derives from the principle of equal protection of the law without discrimination, as contained in article 7 of the Universal Declaration of Human Rights, which prohibits discrimination in law or in practice in any field regulated and protected by public authorities. Article 26 is thus concerned with the obligations imposed on States in regard to their legislation and the application thereof.

12.4. Although article 26 requires that legislation should prohibit discrimination, it does not of itself contain any obligation with respect to the matters that may be provided for by legislation. Thus it does not, for example, require any State to enact legislation to provide for social security. However, when such legislation is adopted in the exercise of a State's sovereign power, then such legislation must comply with article 26 of the Covenant.

12.5. The Committee observes in this connection that what is at issue is not whether or not social security should be progressively established in the Netherlands, but whether the legislation providing for social security violates the prohibition against discrimination contained in article 26 of the International Covenant on Civil and Political Rights and the guarantee given therein to all persons regarding equal and effective protection against discrimination.

13. The right to equality before the law and to equal protection of the law without any discrimination does not make all differences of treatment discriminatory. A differentiation based on reasonable and objective criteria does not amount to prohibited discrimination within the meaning of article 26.

14. It therefore remains for the Committee to determine whether the differentiation in Netherlands law at the time in question and as applied to Mrs. Broeks constituted discrimination within the meaning of article 26. The Committee notes that in Netherlands law the provisions of articles 84 and 85 of the Netherlands Civil Code impose equal rights and obligations on both spouses with regard to their joint income. Under section 13, subsection 1(1), of the Unemployment Benefits Act (WWV), a married woman, in order to receive WWV benefits, had to prove that she was a "breadwinner"—a condition that did not apply to married men. Thus a differentiation which appears on one level to be one of status is in fact one of sex, placing married women at a disadvantage compared with married men. Such a differentiation is not reasonable; and this seems to have been effectively acknowledged even by the State Party by the enactment of a change in the law on April 29, 1985, with retroactive effect to December 23, 1984. . . .

15. The circumstances in which Mrs. Broeks found herself at the material time and the application of the then valid Netherlands law made her a victim of a violation, based on sex, of article 26 of the International Covenant on Civil and Political Rights, because she was denied a social security benefit on an equal footing with men.

16. The Committee notes that the State Party had not intended to discriminate against women and further notes with appreciation that the discriminatory provisions in the law applied to Mrs. Broeks have, subsequently, been eliminated. Although the State Party has thus taken the necessary measures to put an end to the kind of discrimination suffered by Mrs. Broeks at the time complained of, the Committee is of the view that the State Party should offer Mrs. Broeks an appropriate remedy.

Notes

1. The *Broeks* case confirms that art.26 prohibits discrimination in any area of law, not just in areas relating to rights protected in the ICCPR. One consequence is that, as on the facts of the *Broeks* case, discrimination in areas of law covered by rights within the ICESCR may be the subject of an Optional Protocol communication in so far as the claim is one of sexual, racial, etc. inequality in the guarantee of the right concerned. See also General Comment No.31, para.8, above, p.560.

2. The *Broeks* case establishes that art.26 does not prohibit "differentiation based upon reasonable and objective criteria." In *Danning v Netherlands*,[223] in which a social security benefit for an unemployed disabled person was higher for a married man than, as in the case of the victim, for

---

[223] (1987) 2 Selected Decisions H.R.C. 205. A breach of art.26 was found in *Zwaan-de Vries v Netherlands* (1987) 2 Selected Decisions H.R.C. 209 (another social security "breadwinner" case); *Gueye v France*, HRC Report, G.A.O.R., 44th Sess., Supp. 40, p.189 at p.194 (1989) (army pensions); and *Sprenger v Austria*, HRC Report, G.A.O.R., 47th Sess., Supp. 40, p.319 (1992) (public health insurance).

a person co-habiting without being married, the Committee found that there were "reasonable and objective criteria" for the discrimination and hence no breach of art.26:

> "The Committee observes, in this connection, that the decision to enter into a legal status by marriage, which provides, in Netherlands law, both for certain benefits and for certain duties and responsibilities, lies entirely with the cohabiting persons. By choosing not to enter into marriage, Mr. Danning and his cohabitant have not, in law, assumed the full extent of the duties and responsibilities incumbent on married couples. Consequently, Mr. Danning does not receive the full benefits provided for in Netherlands law for married couples. The Committee concludes that the differentiation complained of by Mr. Danning does not constitute discrimination in the sense of article 26 of the Covenant."

The Committee's jurisprudence in this area has worried states[224] and there are signs that the Committee is not unanimous, with some members taking the view that economic and social rights can be realised only progressively.[225]

3. In *Young v Australia*,[226] the author had been in a same sex relationship with Mr C for 38 years. When Mr C, a war veteran, died, the author claimed a pension under war veterans legislation as Mr C's dependant. His claim was rejected; whereas unmarried partners of different sexes could qualify as dependants, same sex partners could not. The Committee found for the author under art.26:

> "10.4 The Committee recalls its earlier jurisprudence that the prohibition against discrimination under article 26 comprises also discrimination based on sexual orientation.[227] It recalls that in previous communications the Committee found that differences in the receipt of benefits between married couples and heterosexual unmarried couples were reasonable and objective, as the couples in question had the choice to marry with all the entailing consequences.[228] It transpires for the contested sections of the VEA that individuals who are part of a married couple or of a heterosexual cohabiting couple (who can prove that they are in a 'marriage-like' relationship) fulfil the definition of 'member of a couple' and therefore of a 'dependant', for the purpose of receiving pension benefits. In the instant case, it is clear that the author, as a same sex partner, did not have the possibility of entering into marriage. Neither was he recognized as a cohabiting partner of Mr. C, for the purposes of receiving pension benefits, because of his sex or sexual orientation. The Committee recalls its constant jurisprudence that not every distinction amounts to prohibited discrimination under the Covenant, as long as it is based on reasonable and objective criteria. The State party provides no arguments on how this distinction between same-sex partners, who are excluded from pension benefits under law, and unmarried heterosexual partners, who are granted such benefits, is reasonable and objective, and no evidence which would point to the existence of factors justifying such a distinction has been advanced. In this context, the Committee finds

---

[224] Germany made a reservation intended to exclude such art.26 cases when it ratified the First Optional Protocol: for the text, see ST/LEG/SER.E/15, p.160.

[225] See Schmidt, in Harris and Joseph, eds, *The International Covenant on Civil and Political Rights and United Kingdom Law* (1995), p.637 and Joseph, Schultz and Castan, above, n.105, p.686.

[226] (2004) 11 I.H.R.R. 146 at 157. In their individual concurring opinions, Mrs Wedgwood and Mr De Pasquale stressed that the case did not decide that there could not be any "objective and reasonable" justification for the distinction, only that the claim succeeded because Australia had not argued for one.

[227] *Toonen v Australia*, ... [above, p.590].

[228] *Danning v the Netherlands*, ... [above, p.595].

that the State party has violated article 26 of the Covenant by denying the author a pension on the basis of his sex or sexual orientation."

4. As well as marital status and "sex or sexual orientation" (*Danning* and *Young* cases), the HRC has interpreted "other status" as including a number of other kinds of distinction, including age[229] and conscientious objection to military service.[230]

5. Article 26 has been found to be infringed in other various contexts. A breach of art.26, as well as of arts 3 and 14(1), was found in *Avellanal v Peru*,[231] in which a married woman was not allowed to sue in respect of matrimonial property. There was also a breach of art.26 when a law provided for the restitution of property confiscated from persons fleeing from Czechoslovakia under the former communist Government only to Czech citizens resident in the Czech Republic.[232] In *Hoyos y Martinez de Irujo v Spain*,[233] in which the daughter and first born child of a nobleman challenged a rule of male supremacy in succession to titles of nobility, the HRC held that art.26 did not apply as an hereditary title, because of its exclusive nature, did not fall within the principles of equality before the law and non-discrimination in art.26.

STATES OF EMERGENCY (ARTICLE 4)[234]

General Comment No.29, Human Rights Committee. UN Doc. CCPR/C/21/Rev.1/Add.11 2001. (2002) 9 I.H.R.R. 303

4. A fundamental requirement for any measures derogating from the Covenant, as set forth in article 4, paragraph 1, is that such measures are limited to the extent strictly required by the exigencies of the situation. This requirement relates to the duration, geographical coverage and material scope of the state of emergency and any measures of derogation resorted to because of the emergency ... the obligation to limit any derogations to those strictly required by the exigencies of the situation reflects the principle of proportionality which is common to derogation and limitation powers. ... When considering States parties' reports the Committee has expressed its concern over insufficient attention being paid to the principle of proportionality.[235]

5. ... If States purport to invoke the right to derogate from the Covenant during, for instance, a natural catastrophe, a mass demonstration including instances of violence, or a major industrial accident, they must be able to justify not only that such a situation constitutes a threat to the life of the nation, but also that all their measures derogating from the Covenant are strictly required by the exigencies of the situation. In the opinion of the Committee, the possibility of restricting certain Covenant rights under the terms of, for instance, freedom of movement (article 12) or freedom of assembly (article 21) is generally sufficient during such situations and no derogation from the provisions in question would be justified by the exigencies of the situation. ...

7. ... Conceptually, the qualification of a Covenant provision as a non-derogable one does not mean that no limitations or restrictions would ever be justified. The reference in article 4, paragraph 2, to article 18, a provision that includes a specific clause on restrictions in its paragraph 3, demonstrates that the permissibility of restrictions is independent of the issue of derogability. Even in times of most serious public emergencies, States

---

[229] *Hinostroza Solis v Peru* (2006) 13 I.H.R.R. 944.
[230] *Foin v France* (2000) 7 I.H.R.R. 354.
[231] H.R.C. Report, G.A.D.R. 44th Sess., Supp. 40, p.196 (1989).
[232] *Simunek v Czech Republic* (1996) 3 I.H.R.R. 28.
[233] (2004) 11 I.H.R.R. 916.
[234] On General Comment No.29, see Joseph (2002) 2 H.R.L.R. 81. On human rights in emergencies, see De Zayas, in Premont, Stenersen and Oseredczuk, eds, *Non-Derogable Rights and States of Emergency* (1996), p.225; Fitzpatrick, *Human Rights in Crisis* (1994); McGoldrick (2004) 2 I.J.C.L. 380; Oraa, *Human Rights in States of Emergency in International Law* (1992); Svensson-McCarthy, *The International Law of Human Rights and States of Emergency* (1998).
[235] See, for example, concluding observations on Israel (1998), CCPR/C/79/Add.93, para. 11.

that interfere with the freedom to manifest one's religion or belief must justify their actions by referring to the requirements specified in article 18, paragraph 3. ...

8. According to article 4, paragraph 1, one of the conditions for the justifiability of any derogation from the Covenant is that measures taken do not involve discrimination solely on the ground of race, colour, sex, language, religion or social origin. Even though article 26 or the other Covenant provisions related to non-discrimination (articles 2, 3, 14, paragraph 1, 23, paragraph 4, 24, paragraph 1, and 25) have not been listed among the non-derogable provisions in article 4, paragraph 2, there are elements or dimensions of the right to non-discrimination that cannot be derogated from in any circumstances. In particular, this provision of article 4, paragraph 1, must be complied with if any distinctions between persons are made when resorting to measures that derogate from the Covenant.

9. Furthermore, article 4, paragraph 1, requires that no measure derogating from the provisions of the Covenant may be inconsistent with the State party's other obligations under international law, particularly the rules of international humanitarian law. Article 4 of the Covenant cannot be read as justification for derogation from the Covenant if such derogation would entail a breach of the State's other international obligations, whether based on treaty or general international law. This is reflected also in article 5, paragraph 2, of the Covenant according to which there shall be no restriction upon or derogation from any fundamental rights recognized in other instruments on the pretext that the Covenant does not recognize such rights or that it recognizes them to a lesser extent. ...

11. The enumeration of non-derogable provisions in article 4 is related to, but not identical with, the question whether certain human rights obligations bear the nature of peremptory norms of international law. The proclamation of certain provisions of the Covenant as being of a non-derogable nature, in article 4, paragraph 2, is to be seen partly as recognition of the peremptory nature of some fundamental rights ensured in treaty form in the Covenant (e.g., articles 6 and 7). However, it is apparent that some other provisions of the Covenant were included in the list of non-derogable provisions because it can never become necessary to derogate from these rights during a state of emergency (e.g., articles 11 and 18). Furthermore, the category of peremptory norms extends beyond the list of non-derogable provisions as given in article 4, paragraph 2. States parties may in no circumstances invoke article 4 of the Covenant as justification for acting in violation of humanitarian law or peremptory norms of international law, for instance by taking hostages, by imposing collective punishments, through arbitrary deprivations of liberty or by deviating from fundamental principles of fair trial, including the presumption of innocence.

12. In assessing the scope of legitimate derogation from the Covenant, one criterion can be found in the definition of certain human rights violations as crimes against humanity. If action conducted under the authority of a State constitutes a basis for individual criminal responsibility for a crime against humanity by the persons involved in that action, article 4 of the Covenant cannot be used as justification that a state of emergency exempted the State in question from its responsibility in relation to the same conduct. Therefore, the recent codification of crimes against humanity, for jurisdictional purposes, in the Rome Statute of the International Criminal Court is of relevance in the interpretation of article 4 of the Covenant.

13. In those provisions of the Covenant that are not listed in article 4, paragraph 2, there are elements that in the Committee's opinion cannot be made subject to lawful derogation under article 4. Some illustrative examples are presented below.

(a) All persons deprived of their liberty shall be treated with humanity and with respect for the inherent dignity of the human person. Although this right, prescribed in article 10 of the Covenant, is not separately mentioned in the list of non-derogable rights in article 4, paragraph 2, the Committee believes that here the Covenant expresses a norm of general international law not subject to derogation. This is supported by the reference to the inherent dignity of the human person in the preamble to the Covenant and by the close connection between article 7 and 10.

(b) The prohibitions against taking of hostages, abductions or unacknowledged detention are not subject to derogation. The absolute nature of these prohibitions, even in times of emergency, is justified by their status as norms of general international law.

(c) The Committee is of the opinion that the international protection of the rights of persons belonging to minorities includes elements that must be respected in all circumstances. This is reflected in the pro-hibition against genocide in international law, in the inclusion of a non-discrimination clause in article 4 itself (paragraph 1), as well as in the non-derogable nature of article 18.

(d) As confirmed by the Rome Statute of the International Criminal Court, deportation or forcible transfer of population without grounds permitted under international law, in the form of forced displacement by expulsion or other coercive means from the area in which the persons concerned are lawfully present, constitutes a crime against humanity. The legitimate right to derogate from article 12 of the Covenant during a state of emergency can never be accepted as justifying such measures.

(e) No declaration of a state of emergency made pursuant to article 4, paragraph 1, may be invoked as justification for a State party to engage itself, contrary to article 20, in propaganda for war, or in advocacy of national, racial or religious hatred that would constitute incitement to discrimination, hostility or violence.

14. Article 2, paragraph 3, of the Covenant requires a State party to the Covenant to provide remedies for any violation of the provisions of the Covenant. ... Even if a State party, during a state of emergency, and to the extent that such measures are strictly required by the exigencies of the situation, may introduce adjustments to the practical functioning of its procedures governing judicial or other remedies, the State party must comply with the fundamental obligation, under article 2, paragraph 3, of the Covenant to provide a remedy that is effective.

15. It is inherent in the protection of rights explicitly recognized as non-derogable in article 4, paragraph 2, that they must be secured by procedural guarantees, including, often, judicial guarantees. The provisions of the Covenant relating to procedural safeguards may never be made subject to measures that would circumvent the protection of non-derogable rights. Article 4 may not be resorted to in a way that would result in derogation from non-derogable rights. Thus, for example, as article 6 of the Covenant is non-derogable in its entirety, any trial leading to the imposition of the death penalty during a state of emergency must conform to the provisions of the Covenant, including all the requirements of articles 14 and 15.

16. ... As certain elements of the right to a fair trial are explicitly guaranteed under international humanitarian law during armed conflict, the Committee finds no justification for derogation from these guarantees during other emergency situations. The Committee is of the opinion that the principles of legality and the rule of law require that fundamental requirements of fair trial must be respected during a state of emergency. Only a court of law may try and convict a person of a criminal offence. The presumption of innocence must be respected. In order to protect non-derogable rights, the right to take proceedings before a court to enable the court to decide without delay on the lawfulness of the detention, must not be diminished by a State party's decision to derogate from the Covenant.

SILVA v URUGUAY

Human Rights Committee. (1981) 1 Selected Decisions H.R.C. 65

The authors alleged breaches of art.25, ICCPR because they were banned by a 1976 executive decree from engaging in "any activity of a political nature, including the right to vote, for a term of 15 years." The authors, who were professors, an accountant and an engineer, had been candidates for elective office for political groups which had since been banned by decree. The respondent state relied unsuccessfully on a notice of derogation made under art.4.

Views of the Committee

In its note of June 28, 1979 to the Secretary-General of the United Nations[236] ... which was designed to comply with the formal requirements laid down in article 4(3) of the Covenant, the Government of Uruguay has made reference to an emergency situation in the country which was legally acknowledged in a number of "Institutional Acts." However, no factual details were given at that time. The note confined itself to stating that the existence of the emergency situation was "a matter of universal knowledge"; no attempt was made to indicate the nature and the scope of the derogations actually resorted to with regard to the rights guaranteed by the Covenant, or to show that such derogations were strictly necessary.

Although the sovereign right of a State Party to declare a state of emergency is not questioned, yet, in the specific context of the present communication, the Human Rights Committee is of the opinion that a State, by

---

[236] Ed. Text in UN Doc. ST/LEG/SER.E/15, p.155.

merely invoking the existence of exceptional circumstances, cannot evade the obligations which it has under-taken by ratifying the Covenant. Although the substantive right to take derogatory measures may not depend on a formal notification being made pursuant to article 4(3) of the Covenant, the State Party concerned is duty-bound to give a sufficiently detailed account of the relevant facts when it invokes article 4(1) of the Covenant in proceedings under the Optional Protocol. It is the function of the Human Rights Committee, acting under the Optional Protocol, to see to it that States Parties live up to their commitments under the Covenant. In order to discharge this function and to assess whether a situation of the kind described in article 4(1) of the Covenant exists in the country concerned, it needs full and comprehensive information. If the respondent Government does not furnish the required justification itself, as it is required to do under article 4(2) of the Optional Protocol and article 4(3) of the Covenant, the Human Rights Committee cannot conclude that valid reasons exist to legitimise a departure from the normal legal régime prescribed by the Covenant.

The Committee considered the merits of the claims and found breaches of art.25.

Notes

1. Did the Committee take the view that non-compliance with the notification requirement in art.4(3) would invalidate a derogation that was consistent with art.4(1)? What would Uruguay had to have done to satisfy the Committee under art.4?

2. Since the ICCPR entered into force, more than 20 states have submitted to the UN Secretary General notices of derogation, some of which have since been terminated.[237] For some years, the UK had a notice of derogation in place concerning art.9(3) ICCPR for the detention of terrorist suspects in Northern Ireland. This was finally terminated in 2001, only to be replaced by a notice of derogations from art.9(1) ICCPR addressing the terrorist threat following 9/11, which was withdrawn in 2005.[238]

3. Trinidad and Tobago has made a reservation to the Covenant reserving the right "not to apply in full" art.4(2).[239] This reservation which permits derogation from a non-derogable provision, has been objected to as being contrary to the object and purpose of the Covenant.[240]

LEGAL CONSEQUENCES OF THE CONSTRUCTION OF A WALL IN THE OCCUPIED PALESTINIAN TERRITORY[241]

Advisory Opinion I.C.J. Rep. 2004, p.136

By G.A. Resolution ES-10/14 (2003), the General Assembly requested an opinion on the following question:

"What are the legal consequences arising from the construction of the wall being built by Israel, the occupying Power, in the Occupied Palestinian Territory, including in and around East Jerusalem, as described in the report of the Secretary-General, considering the rules and principles of international law, including the Fourth Geneva Convention of 1949, and relevant Security Council and General Assembly resolutions?"

---

[237] UN Doc. ST/LEG/SER.E/21.
[238] See above, n.236, p.204. See the dialogue between the HRC and the UK concerning this notice of derogation in Concluding Observations: UK, CCPTR/CO/73/UK (2001) and the UK Comments, Add.2.
[239] See above, n.236, p.128.
[240] Objections by Germany and the Netherlands: See above, n.236, p.132. Note also the French reservation to art.4(1): p.132.
[241] See Danmrosch and Oxman, et al (2005) A.J.I.L. p.1 et seq.

In 2002, Israel began the construction of a wall to "enable it effectively to combat terrorist attacks launched from the West Bank" (advisory opinion, para.116). In the north, the wall largely follows the Green Line that was established by the 1949 armistice agreement between Israel and Jordan as the border between Israel and the territory on the West Bank then occupied by Jordan, now the Palestinian Occupied Territory.[242] Further south, the wall is mostly to the east of the Green Line, resulting in a "Closed Area" of the West Bank between the Green Line and the wall.

In the following extract from its opinion, the Court first examines whether only international humanitarian law, including the Fourth Geneva Convention, applies in a situation of armed conflict, such as that existing in the Occupied Palestinian Territory, or whether international human rights law applies also. It then considers whether international human rights law has extraterritorial application, so as to apply to the Occupied Palestinian Territory occupied by Israel since the 1967 war, but not a part of the territory of the state of Israel. The Court next gives its opinion as to whether the wall is in violation of international law. Finally, the Court considers the legal consequences of any such violations for Israel and third states.

Opinion of the Court

102. The participants in the proceedings before the Court ... disagree whether the international human rights conventions to which Israel is party apply within the Occupied Palestinian Territory [Israel claimed that they did not.] ...

104. In order to determine whether these texts are applicable in the Occupied Palestinian Territory, the Court will first address the issue of the relationship between international humanitarian law and human rights law and then that of the applicability of human rights instruments outside national territory.

[On the relationship of international humanitarian law and international human rights law, the Court quoted from its opinion in the *Legality of the Threat or use of Force* case, para.25, above, p.569, and continued:]

106. More generally, the Court considers that the protection offered by human rights conventions does not cease in case of armed conflict, save through the effect of provisions for derogation of the kind to be found in Article 4 of the International Covenant on Civil and Political Rights. As regards the relationship between international humanitarian law and human rights law, there are thus three possible situations: some rights may be exclusively matters of international humanitarian law; others may be exclusively matters of human rights law; yet others may be matters of both these branches of international law. In order to answer the question put to it, the Court will have to take into consideration both these branches of international law, namely human rights law, and as *lex specialis*, international humanitarian law.

107. It remains to be determined whether the two international Covenants and the Convention on the Rights of the Child are applicable only on the territories of the States parties thereto or whether they are also applicable outside those territories and, if so, in what circumstances.

108. The scope of application of the International Covenant on Civil and Political Rights is defined by Article 2, paragraph 1, thereof, which provides:

"Each State Party to the present Covenant undertakes to respect and to ensure to all individuals within its territory and subject to its jurisdiction the rights recognized in the present Covenant. ...

This provision can be interpreted as covering only individuals who are both present within a State's territory and subject to that State's jurisdiction. It can also be construed as covering both individuals present within a State's territory and those outside that territory but subject to that State's jurisdiction ...

109 The Court would observe that, while the jurisdiction of States is primarily territorial, it may sometimes be exercised outside the national territory. Considering the object and purpose of the International Covenant on Civil

---

[242] For the background generally, see above, pp.191 et seq.

and Political Rights, it would seem natural that, even when such is the case, States parties to the Covenant should be bound to comply with its provisions.

The constant practice of the Human Rights Committee is consistent with this. Thus, the Committee has found the Covenant applicable where the State exercises its jurisdiction on foreign territory. It has ruled on the legality of acts by Uruguay in cases of arrests carried out by Uruguayan agents in Brazil or Argentina (case No.52/79, *López Burgos* v. *Uruguay*; case No.56/79, *Lilian Celiberti de Casariego* v. *Uruguay*). It decided to the same effect in the case of the confiscation of a passport by a Uruguayan consulate in Germany (case No.106/81, *Montero* v. *Uruguay*).

The *travaux préparatoires* of the Covenant confirm the Committee's interpretation of Article 2 of that instrument. These show that, in adopting the wording chosen, the drafters of the Covenant did not intend to allow States to escape from their obligations when they exercise jurisdiction outside their national territory. They only intended to prevent persons residing abroad from asserting, vis-à-vis their State of origin, rights that do not fall within the competence of that State, but of that of the State of residence ...

110. ...In 2003 in face of Israel's consistent position to the effect that "the Covenant does not apply beyond its own territory, notably in the West Bank and Gaza ...", the Committee reached the following conclusion:

"in the current circumstances, the provisions of the Covenant apply to the benefit of the population of the Occupied Territories, for all conduct by the State party's authorities or agents in those territories that affect the enjoyment of rights enshrined in the Covenant and fall within the ambit of State responsibility of Israel under the principles of public international law" (CCPR/C/78/ISR, para.11).

111. In conclusion, the Court considers that the International Covenant on Civil and Political Rights is applicable in respect of acts done by a State in the exercise of its jurisdiction outside its own territory.

112. The International Covenant on Economic, Social and Cultural Rights contains no provision on its scope of application. This may be explicable by the fact that this Covenant guarantees rights which are essentially territorial. However, it is not to be excluded that it applies both to territories over which a State party has sovereignty and to those over which that State exercises territorial jurisdiction. Thus Article 14 makes provision for transitional measures in the case of any State which "at the time of becoming a Party, has not been able to secure in its metropolitan territory or other territories under its jurisdiction compulsory primary education, free of charge". ...

[In response to Israel's view that the ICCSCR did not apply to the occupied territories] the Committee... reaffirmed its view that the State party's obligations under the Covenant apply to all territories and populations under its effective control" (E/C/12/1/Add.90, paras.15 and 31).

For the reasons explained in paragraph 106 above, the Court cannot accept Israel's view. It would also observe that the territories occupied by Israel have for over 37 years been subject to its territorial jurisdiction as the occupying Power. In the exercise of the powers available to it on this basis, Israel is bound by the provisions of the International Covenant on Economic, Social and Cultural Rights. Furthermore, it is under an obligation not to raise any obstacle to the exercise of such rights in those fields where competence has been transferred to Palestinian authorities.

113. As regards the Convention on the Rights of the Child of 20 November 1989, that instrument contains an Article 2 according to which "States Parties shall respect and ensure the rights set forth in the...Convention to each child within their jurisdiction ...". That Convention is therefore applicable within the Occupied Palestinian Territory.

114. Having determined the rules and principles of international law relevant to reply to the question posed by the General Assembly, and having ruled in particular on the applicability within the Occupied Palestinian Territory of international humanitarian law and human rights law, the Court will now seek to ascertain whether the construction of the wall has violated those rules and principles. ...

118. As regards the principle of the right of peoples to self-determination, the Court observes that the existence of a "Palestinian people" is no longer in issue. Such existence has moreover been recognized by Israel...The Israeli-Palestinian Interim Agreement on the West Bank and Gaza Strip of 28 Septemher 1995...refers a number of times to the Palestinian people and its "legitimate rights"...The Court considers that those rights include the right to self-determination, as the General Assembly has moreover rcognized on a number of occasions (see, for example, resolution 58/163 of 22 December 2003).

119. The Court notes that the route of the wall as fixed by the Israeli Government includes within the "Closed Area"...some 80 per cent of the [Israeli] settlers living in the Occupied Palestinian Territory. Moreover, it is apparent...that the wall's sinuous route has been traced in such a way as to include within that area the great majority of Israeli settlements in the occupied Palestinian Territory (including East Jerusalem).

120. As regards these settlements, the Court notes that Article 49, paragraph 6, of the Fourth Geneva Convention provides: "The Occupying Power shall not deport or transfer parts of its own civilian population into the territory it occupies." ...

...the information provided to the Court shows that, since 1977, Israel has conducted a policy and developed practices involving the establishment of settlements in the Occupied Palestinian Territory, contrary to the terms of Article 49, paragraph 6 just cited.

The Security Council has thus taken the view that such policy and practices "have no legal validity". It has also called upon "Israel, as the occupying Power, to abide scrupulously" by the Fourth Geneva Convention and:

"to rescind its previous measures and to desist from taking any action which would result in changing the legal status and geographical nature and materially affecting the demographic composition of the Arab territories occupied since 1967, including Jerusalem and, in particular, not to transfer parts of its own civilian population into the occupied Arab territories" (resolution 446 (1979) of 22 March 1979).

The Council reaffirmed its position in resolutions 452 (1979) of 20 July 1979 and 465 (1980) of 1 March 1980. Indeed, in the latter case it described "Israel's policy and practices of settling parts of its population and new immigrants in [the occupied] territories" as a "flagrant violation" of the Fourth Geneva Convention.

The Court concludes that the Israeli settlements in the Occupied Palestinian Territory (including East Jerusalem) have been established in breach of international law.

121. Whilst the Court notes the assurance given by Israel that the construction of the wall does not amount to annexation and that the wall is of a temporary nature ..., it nevertheless cannot remain indifferent to certain fears expressed to it that the route of the wall will prejudge the future frontier between Israel and Palestine, and the fear that Israel may integrate the settlements and their means of access. The Court considers that the construction of the wall and its associated regime create a "fait accompli" on the ground that could well become permanent, in which case, and notwithstanding the formal characterization of the wall by Israel, it would be tantamount to *de facto* annexation.

122. The Court recalls moreover that, according to the report of the Secretary-General, the planned route would incorporate in the area between the Green Line and the wall more than 16 per cent of the territory of the West Bank. Around 80 per cent of the settlers living in the Occupied Palestinian Territory, that is 320,000 individuals, would reside in that area, as well as 237,000 Palestinians. Moreover, as a result of the construction of the wall, around 160,000 other Palestinians would reside in almost completely encircled communities ...

In other terms, the route chosen for the wall gives expression *in loco* to the illegal measures taken by Israel with regard to Jerusalem and the settlements, as deplored by the Security Council. ...There is also a risk of further alterations to the demographic composition of the Occupied Palestinian Territory resulting from the construction of the wall inasmuch as it is contributing...to the departure of Palestinian populations from certain areas. That construction, along with measures taken previously, thus severely impedes the exercise by the Palestinian people of its right to self-determination, and is therefore a breach of Israel's obligation to respect that right.

123. The construction of the wall also raised a number of issues in relation to the relevant provisions of international humanitarian law and of human rights instruments. ...

[As to international humanitarian law, the Court referred to the 1907 Hague Regulations and arts 47, 49, 52, 53 and 59, Fourth Geneva Protocol. It then referred to international human rights law as follows:]

127 The International Covenant on Civil and Political Rights...contains several relevant provisions. ...

[The Court referred to arts 9, 12, 17, ICCPR]

130. As regards the International Covenant on Economic, Social and Cultural Rights, that instrument includes a number of relevant provisions, namely: the right to work (Arts.6 and 7); protection and assistance accorded to the family and to children and young persons (art.10); the right to an adequate standard of living, including adequate food, clothing and housing, and the right "to be free from hunger" (art.11); the right to health (art.12); the right to education (Arts.13 and 14).

131. Lastly, the United Nations Convention on the Rights of the Child of 20 November 1989 includes similar provisions in Articles 16, 24, 27 and 28. . . .

134 To sum up, the Court is of the opinion that the construction of the wall and its associated régime impede the liberty of movement of the inhabitants of the Occupied Palestinian Territory (with the exception of Israeli citizens and those assimilated thereto) as guaranteed under Article 12, paragraph 1, of the International Covenant on Civil and Political Rights. They also impede the exercise by the persons concerned of the right to work, to health, to education and to an adequate standard of living as proclaimed in the International Covenant on Economic, Social and Cultural Rights and in the United Nations Convention on the Rights of the Child. Lastly, the construction of the wall and it associated régime, by contributing to the demographic changes referred to in paragraphs 122 and 133 above, contravene Article 49, paragraph 6, of the Fourth Geneva Convention and the Security Council resolutions cited in paragraph 120 above . . .

136. . . .some human rights conventions, and in particular the International Covenant on Civil and Political Rights, contain provisions which States parties may invoke in order to derogate, under various conditions, from certain of their conventional obligations. In this respect, the Court would however recall that the communication notified by Israel to the Secretary-General of the United Nations under Article 4 of the International Covenant on Civil and Political Rights concerns only Article 9 of the Covenant, relating to the right to freedom and security of person . . .; Israel is accordingly bound to respect all the other provisions of that instrument.

The Court would note, moreover, that certain provisions of human rights conventions contain clauses qualifying the rights covered by those provisions. There is no clause of this kind in Article 17 of the International Covenant on Civil and Political Rights. On the other hand, Article 12, paragraph 3 of that instrument provides that restrictions on liberty of movement as guaranteed under that Article . . .

As for the International Covenant on Economic, Social and Cultural Rights, Article 4 thereof contains a general [limitation] provision . . .

The Court would observe that the restrictions provided for under Article 12, paragraph 3, of the International Covenant on Civil and Political Rights are, by the very terms of that provision, exceptions to the right of freedom of movement contained in paragraph 1. In addition, it is not sufficient that such restrictions be directed to the ends authorized; they must also be necessary for the attainment of those ends. As the Human Rights Committee put it, they "must conform to the principle of proportionality" and "must be the least intrusive instrument amongst those which might achieve the desired result" (CCPR/C/21/Rev.1/Add.9, General Comment No.27, para.14). On the basis of the information available to it, the Court finds that these conditions are not met in the present instance.

The Court would further observe that the restrictions on the enjoyment by the Palestinians living in the territory occupied by Israel of their economic, social and cultural rights, resulting from Israel's construction of the wall, fail to meet a condition laid down by Article 4 of the International Covenant on Economic, Social and Cultural Rights, that is to say that their implementation must be "solely for the purpose of promoting the general welfare in a democratic society".

137. To sum up, the Court, from the material available to it, is not convinced that the specific course Israel has chose for the wall was necessary to attain its security objectives. The wall, along the route chosen, and its associated régime gravely infringe a number of rights of Palestinians residing in the territory occupied by Israel, and the infringements resulting from that route cannot be justified by military exigencies or by the requirements of national security or public order. The construction of such a wall accordingly constitutes breaches by Israel of various of its obligations under the applicable international humanitarian law and human rights instruments.

138. . . .However. . .Israel's Permanent Representative to the United Nations asserted in the General Assembly on 20 October 2003 that "the fence is a measure wholly consistent with the right of States to self-defence enshrined in Article 51 of the Charter"; the Security Council resolutions referred to, he continued, "have clearly recognized the right of States to use force in self-defence against terrorist attacks", and therefore surely recognize the right to use non-forcible measures to that end (A/ES-10/PV.21, p.6).

139. . . .Article 51 of the Charter. . .recognizes the existence of an inherent right of self-defence in the case of armed attack by one State against another State. However, Israel does not claim that the attacks against it are imputable to a foreign State.

The Court also notes that Israel exercise control in the Occupied Palestinian Territory and that, as Israel itself states, the threat which it regards as justifying the construction of the wall originates within, and not outside, that territory. The situation is thus different from that contemplated by Security Council resolutions 1368 (2001) and 1373 (2001), and therefore Israel could not in any event invoke those resolutions in support of its claim to be exercising a right of self-defence.

Consequently, the Court concludes that Article 51 of the Charter has no relevance in this case.

140. The Court has, however, considered whether Israel could rely on a state of necessity which would preclude the wrongfulness of the construction of the wall. In this regard the Court is bound to note that some of the conventions at issue in the present instance include qualifying clauses of the rights guaranteed or provisions for derogation (see paragraph...136, above). Since those treaties already address considerations of this kind within their own provisions, it might be asked whether a state of necessity as recognized in customary international law could be invoked with regard to those treaties as a ground for precluding the wrongfulness of the measures or decisions being challenged. However, the Court will not need to consider that question. As the Court observed in the case concerning the *Gabčíkovo-Nagymaros Project (Hungary/Slovakia)*, "the state of necessity is a ground recognised by customary international law that "can only be accepted on an exceptional basis"; it "can only be invoked under certain strictly defined conditions which must be cumulatively satisfied; and the State concerned is not the sole judge of whether those conditions have been met" (*I.C.J. Reports 1997*, p.40, para.51) One of those conditions was stated by the Court in terms used by the International Law Commission, in a text which in its present form requires that the act being challenged be "the only way for the State to safeguard an essential interest against a grave and imminent peril" (Article 25 of the International Law Commission's Articles on Responsibility of States for Internationally Wrongful Acts [above, p.438]...In the light of the material before it, the Court is not convinced that the construction of the wall along the route chosen was the only means to safeguard the interests of Israel against the peril which it has invoked as justification for that construction. ...

142. In conclusion, the Court considers that Israel cannot rely on a right of self-defence or on a state of necessity in order to preclude the wrongfulness of the construction of the wall resulting from the considerations mentioned in paragraphs 122 and 137 above. The Court accordingly finds that the construction of the wall, and its associated régime, are contrary or international law. ...

148. The Court will now examine the legal consequences resulting from the violations of international law by Israel ...

149. The Court notes that Israel is first obliged...to comply with its obligation to respect of the right of the Palestinian people to self-determination and its obligations under international humanitarian law and international human rights law. Furthermore, it must ensure freedom of access to the Holy Places that came under its control following the 1967 War ...

150. The Court observes that Israel also has an obligation to put an end to the violation of its international obligations flowing from the construction of the wall in the Occupied Palestinian Territory. ...

151. Israel accordingly has the obligation to cease forthwith the works of construction of the wall being built by it in the Occupied Palestinian Territory, including in and around East Jerusalem. Moreover, in view of the Court's finding...that Israel's violations of its international obligations stem from the construction of the wall and from its associated régime, cessation of those violations entails the dismantling forthwith of those parts of that structure situated within the Occupied Palestinian Territory, including in and around East Jerusalem. All legislative and regulatory acts adopted with a view to its construction, and to the establishment of its associated regime, must forthwith be repealed or rendered ineffective ...

152. Moreover, given that the construction of the wall in the Occupied Palestinian Territory has, inter alia, entailed the requisition and destruction of homes, businesses and agricultural holdings, the Court finds further that Israel has the obligation to make reparation for the damage caused to all the natural or legal persons concerned. ...

153. Israel is accordingly under an obligation to return the land, orchards, olive groves and other immovable property seized from any natural or legal person for the purposes of construction of the wall in the Occupied Palestinian Territory. In the event that such restitution should prove to be materially impossible, Israel has an obligation to compensate the persons in question for the damage suffered. The Court considers that Israel also has an obligation to compensate, in accordance with the applicable rules of international law, all natural or legal persons having suffered any form of material damage as a result of the wall's construction.

154. The Court will now consider the legal consequences of the internationally wrongful acts flowing from Israel's construction of the wall as regards other States.

155. The Court would observe that the obligations violated by Israel include certain obligations *erga omnes*. As the Court indicated in the *Barcelona Traction* case, such obligations are by their very nature "the concern of all States" and, "In view of the importance of the rights involved, all States can be held to have a legal interest in their protection" (*Barcelona Traction, Light and Power Company, Limited, Second Phase, Judgment, I.C.J. Reports 1970*, p.32, para.33). The obligations *erga omnes* violated by Israel are the obligation to respect the right of the Palestinian people to self-determination, and certain of its obligations under international humanitarian law. ...

159. Given the character and the importance of the rights and obligations involved, the Court is of the view

that all States are under an obligation not to recognize the illegal situation resulting from the construction of the wall in the Occupied Palestinian Territory, including in and around East Jerusalem. They are also under an obligation not to render aid or assistance in maintaining the situation created by such construction. It is also for all States, while respecting the United Nations Charter and international law, to see to it that any impediment, resulting from the construction of the wall, to the exercise by the Palestinian people of its right to self-determination is brought to an end. In addition, all the States parties to the Geneva Convention relative to the Protection of Civilian Persons in Time of War of 12 August 1949 are under an obligation, while respecting the United Nations Charter and international law, to ensure compliance by Israel with international humanitarian law as embodied in that Convention.

160. Finally, the Court is of the view that the United Nations, and especially the General Assembly and the Security Council, should consider what further actions is required to bring to an end the illegal situation result from the construction of the wall and the associated régime taking due account of the present Advisory Opinion.
. . .

163. For these reasons,
THE COURT . . .
(3) *Replies* in the following matter to the question put by the General Assembly:
A. By fourteen voles to one,[243]
The construction of the wall being built by Israel, the occupying Power, in the Occupied Palestinian Territory, including in and around East Jerusalem, and its associated régime, are contrary to international law; . . .
B. By fourteen votes to one,[244]
Israel is under an obligation to terminate its breaches of international law; it is under an obligation to cease forthwith the works of construction of the wall being built in the Occupied Palestinian Territory, including in and around East Jerusalem, to dismantle forthwith the structure therein situated, and to repeal or render ineffective forthwith all legislative and regulatory acts relating thereto, in accordance with paragraph 151 of this Opinion; . . .
C. By fourteen votes to one,[245]
Israel is under an obligation to make reparation for all damage caused by the construction of the wall in the Occupied Palestinian Territory, including in and around East Jerusalem; . . .
D. By thirteen voles to two,[246]
All states are under an obligation not to recognize the illegal situation resulting from the construction of the wall and not render aid or assistance in maintaining the situation created by such construction; all States parties to the Fourth Geneva Convention relative to the Protection of Civilian Persons in Time of War of 12 August 1949 have in addition the obligation, while respecting the United National Charter and international law, to ensure compliance by Israel with international humanitarian law as embodied in that Convention; . . .
E. By fourteen votes to one,[247]
The United Nations, and especially the General Assembly and the Security Council, should consider what further action is required to bring to an end the illegal situation resulting from the construction of the wall and the associated régime, taking due account of the present Advisory Opinion.

Notes

1.   The General Assembly responded to the Court's Opinion as follows[248]:

" The General Assembly . . .

1.   *Acknowledges* the advisory opinion of the International Court of Justice of 9 July 2004 on the *Legal Consequences of the Construction of a Wall in the Occupied Palestinian Territory*, including in and around East Jerusalem;

---

[243] Judge Buergenthal dissented
[244] Judge Buergenthal dissented.
[245] Judge Buergenthal dissented.
[246] Judges Kooijmans and Buergenthal dissented.
[247] Judge Buergenthal dissented.
[248] A/RES/ES-10/15. The resolution was adopted by 150 votes to 6 with 10 abstentions. Australia, Israel, Marshall Islands, Micronesia, Palau and the US voted against. Cameroon, Canada, El Salvador, Nauru, Papua New Guinea, Solomon Islands, Tonga Uganda, Uruguay and Vanuatu abstained.

2. *Demands* that Israel, the occupying Power, comply with its legal obligations as mentioned in the advisory opinion.

3. *Calls upon* all States Members of the United Nations to comply with their legal obligations as mentioned in the advisory opinion; ..."

Israel continued to build the wall and has not otherwise fulfilled the obligations identified by the Court.

2. The opinion is significant for the position taken by the Court on the inter-relationship of international human rights law and international humanitarian law,[249] the extraterritorial application of human rights treaties,[250] the application of the relevant human rights guarantees and the right to self-defence.[251]

INTERNATIONAL COVENANT ON ECONOMIC, SOCIAL AND CULTURAL RIGHTS 1966[252]

993 U.N.T.S. 3; (1977) U.K.T.S. 6, Cmnd. 6702; (1967) 6 I.L.M. 360

Article 1

Identical to Article 1, ICCPR, above, p. 668.

Article 2

1. Each State Party to the present Covenant undertakes to take steps, individually and through international assistance and co-operation, especially economic and technical, to the maximum of its available resources, with a view to achieving progressively the full realisation of the rights recognised in the present Covenant by all appropriate means, including particularly the adoption of legislative measures.

2. The States Parties to the present Covenant undertake to guarantee that the rights enunciated in the present Covenant will be exercised without discrimination of any kind as to race, colour, sex, language, religion, political or other opinion, national or social origin, property, birth or other status.

3. Developing countries, with due regard to human rights and their national economy, may determine to what extent they would guarantee the economic rights recognised in the present Covenant to non-nationals.

---

[249] See Doswald-Beck and Vite (1993) I.R.R.C. 94; Lubell (2005) 87 I.R.R.C. 737; Hampson, in Meyer, ed., *Armed Conflict and the New Law* (Vol.2, 1993); Meron, *Human Rights in International Strife* (1987); Provost, *International Human Rights and Humanitarian Law* (2002); Sayapin (2009) 9 H.R.L.R. 95; Vinuesa, in (1998) 1 Y.I.H.L. 69. And see HRC General Comment 31, para.11, above, p.560.

[250] See HRC General Comment 31, para.10, above, p.560.

[251] On the right to self-defence, see below, p.746.

[252] In force 1976. 160 parties, including the UK. See Alston and Quinn (1987) 9 H.R.Q. 156; Craven, *The International Covenant on Economic, Social and Cultural Rights* (1995); (1993) 40 N.I.L.R. 367; Henkaerts, in Trindade, ed., *The Modern World of Human Rights: Essays in Honour of Thomas Buergenthal* (1996), p.267; Sepulveda, *The Nature of the Obligations under the International Covenant on Economic, Social and Cultural Rights* (2003); Simma, in Matscher, ed., *The Implementation of Economic and Social Rights* (1991), p.75. See generally on economic, social and cultural rights, Chapman and Russell, eds, *Core Obligations: Building a Framework for Economic, Social and Cultural Rights* (2002); Eide, Krause and Rosas, eds, *Economic, Social and Cultural Rights: A Textbook* (2nd edn 2001); Hunt, *Reclaiming Social Rights* (1996); Ssenyonjo, *Economic, Social and Cultural Rights in International Law* (2009); Van der Auweraert, Oelsmaeker, Sarkin, Vande Lanotte, eds, *Social, Economic and Cultural Rights: An Appraisal of Current European and International Developments* (2002). Simma, in Matscher, ed., *The Implementation of Economic and Social Rights* (1991), p.75. See also the 1986 Limburg Principles on the Implementation of the International Covenant on Economic, Social and Cultural Rights and Commentaries thereto: (1987) 9 H.R.Q. 121 and the Maastricht Guidelines on Violations of Economic, Social and Cultural Rights (1998) 20 H.R.Q. 691

Article 3

The States Parties to the present Covenant undertake to ensure the equal right of men and women to the enjoyment of all economic, social and cultural rights set forth in the present Covenant.

Article 4

The States Parties to the present Covenant recognise that, in the enjoyment of those rights provided by the State in conformity with the present Covenant, the State may subject such rights only to such limitations as are determined by law only in so far as this may be compatible with the nature of these rights and solely for the purpose of promoting the general welfare in a democratic society.

Article 5

1. Nothing in the present Covenant may be interpreted as implying for any State, group or person any right to engage in any activity or to perform any act aimed at the destruction of any of the rights or freedoms recognised herein, or at their limitation to a greater extent than is provided for in the present Covenant.

2. No restriction upon or derogation from any of the fundamental human rights recognised or existing in any country in virtue of law, conventions, regulations or custom shall be admitted on the pretext that the present Covenant does not recognise such rights or that it recognises them to a lesser extent.

Article 6

1. The States Parties to the present Covenant recognise the right to work, which includes the right of everyone to the opportunity to gain his living by work which he freely chooses or accepts, and will take appropriate steps to safeguard this right.

2. The steps to be taken by a State Party to the present Covenant to achieve the full realisation of this right shall include technical and vocational guidance and training programmes, policies and techniques to achieve steady economic, social and cultural development and full and productive employment under conditions safeguarding fundamental political and economic freedoms to the individual.

Article 7

The States Parties to the present Covenant recognise the right of everyone to the enjoyment of just and favourable conditions of work, which ensure, in particular:

(a) Remuneration which provides all workers, as a minimum, with:

(i) Fair wages and equal remuneration for work of equal value without distinction of any kind, in particular women being guaranteed conditions of work not inferior to those enjoyed by men, with equal pay for equal work;

(ii) A decent living for themselves and their families in accordance with the provisions of the present Covenant;

(b) Safe and healthy working conditions;

(c) Equal opportunity for everyone to be promoted in his employment to an appropriate higher level, subject to no considerations other than those of seniority and competence;

(d) Rest, leisure and reasonable limitation of working hours and periodic holidays with pay, as well as remuneration for public holidays.

Article 8

1. The States Parties to the present Covenant undertake to ensure:

(a) The right of everyone to form trade unions and join the trade union of his choice, subject only to the rules of the organisation concerned, for the promotion and protection of his economic and social interests. No restrictions may be placed on the exercise of this right other than those prescribed by law and which are necessary in a democratic society in the interests of national security or public order or for the protection of the rights and freedoms of others;

(b) The right of trade unions to establish national federations or confederations and the right of the latter to form or join international trade-union organisations;

(c) The right of trade unions to function freely subject to no limitations other than those prescribed by law and which are necessary in a democratic society in the interests of national security or public order or for the protection of the rights and freedoms of others;

(d) The right to strike, provided that it is exercised in conformity with the laws of the particular country.

2. This article shall not prevent the imposition of lawful restrictions on the exercise of these rights by members of the armed forces or of the police or of the administration of the State.

3. Nothing in this article shall authorise States Parties to the International Labour Organization Convention of 1948 concerning Freedom of Association and Protection of the Right to Organize to take legislative measures which would prejudice, or apply the law in such a manner as would prejudice, the guarantees provided for in that Convention.

Article 9

The States Parties to the present Covenant recognise the right of everyone to social security, including social insurance.

Article 10

The States Parties to the present Covenant recognise that:

1. The widest possible protection and assistance should be accorded to the family, which is the natural and fundamental group unit of society, particularly for its establishment and while it is responsible for the care and education of dependent children. Marriage must be entered into with the free consent of the intending spouses.

2. Special protection should be accorded to mothers during a reasonable period before and after childbirth. During such period working mothers should be accorded paid leave or leave with adequate social security benefits.

3. Special measures of protection and assistance should be taken on behalf of all children and young persons without any discrimination for reasons of parentage or other conditions. Children and young persons should be protected from economic and social exploitation. Their employment in work harmful to their morals or health or dangerous to life or likely to hamper their normal development should be punishable by law. States should also set age limits below which the paid employment of child labour should be prohibited and punishable by law.

Article 11

1. The States Parties to the present Covenant recognise the right of everyone to an adequate standard of living for himself and his family, including adequate food, clothing and housing, and to the continuous improvement of living conditions. The States Parties will take appropriate steps to ensure the realisation of this right, recognising to this effect the essential importance of international co-operation based on free consent.

2. The States Parties to the present Covenant, recognising the fundamental right of everyone to be free from hunger, shall take, individually and through international co-operation, the measures, including specific programmes, which are needed:

(a) To improve methods of production, conservation and distribution of food by making full use of technical and scientific knowledge by disseminating knowledge of the principles of nutrition and by developing or reforming agrarian systems in such a way as to achieve the most efficient development and utilisation of natural resources;

(b) Taking into account the problems of both food-importing and food-exporting countries, to ensure an equitable distribution of world food supplies in relation to need.

Article 12

1. The States Parties to the present Covenant recognise the right of everyone to the enjoyment of the highest attainable standard of physical and mental health.

2. The steps to be taken by the States Parties to the present Covenant to achieve the full realisation of this right shall include those necessary for:

(a) The provision for the reduction of the stillbirth-rate and of infant mortality and for the healthy development of the child;

(b) The improvement of all aspects of environmental and industrial hygiene;

(c) The prevention, treatment and control of epidemic, endemic, occupational and other diseases;

(d) The creation of conditions which would assure to all medical service and medical attention in the event of sickness.

Article 13

1. The States Parties to the present Covenant recognise the right of everyone to education. They agree that education shall be directed to the full development of the human personality and the sense of its dignity, and shall strengthen the respect for human rights and fundamental freedoms. They further agree that education shall enable all persons to participate effectively in a free society, promote understanding, tolerance and friendship among all nations and all racial, ethnic or religious groups, and further the activities of the United Nations for the maintenance of peace.

2. The States Parties to the present Covenant recognise that, with a view to achieving the full realisation of this right:

(a) Primary education shall be compulsory and available free to all;

(b) Secondary education in its different forms, including technical and vocational secondary education, shall be made generally available and accessible to all by every appropriate means, and in particular by the progressive introduction of free education;

(c) Higher education shall be made equally accessible to all, on the basis of capacity, by every appropriate means, and in particular by the progressive introduction of free education;

(d) Fundamental education shall be encouraged or intensified as far as possible for those persons who have not received or completed the whole period of their primary education;

(e) The development of a system of schools at all levels shall be actively pursued, an adequate fellowship system shall be established, and the material conditions of teaching staff shall be continuously improved.

3. The States Parties to the present Covenant undertake to have respect for the liberty of parents and, when applicable, legal guardians, to choose for their children schools, other than those established by the public authorities, which conform to such minimum educational standards as may be laid down or approved by the State and to ensure the religious and moral education of their children in conformity with their own convictions.

4. No part of this article shall be construed so as to interfere with the liberty of individuals and bodies to establish and direct educational institutions, subject always to the observance of the principles set forth in paragraph 1 of this article and to the requirement that the education given in such institutions shall conform to such minimum standards as may be laid down by the State.

Article 14

Each State Party to the present Covenant which, at the time of becoming a Party, has not been able to secure in its metropolitan territory or other territories under its jurisdiction compulsory primary education, free of charge, undertakes, within two years, to work out and adopt a detailed plan of action for the progressive implementation, within a reasonable number of years, to be fixed in the plan, of the principle of compulsory education free of charge for all.

Article 15

1. The States Parties to the present Covenant recognise the right of everyone:

(*a*) To take part in cultural life;

(*b*) To enjoy the benefits of scientific progress and its applications;

(*c*) To benefit from the protection of the moral and material interests resulting from any scientific, literary or artistic production of which he is the author.

2. The steps to be taken by the States Parties to the present Covenant to achieve the full realisation of this right shall include those necessary for the conservation, the development and the diffusion of science and culture.

3. The States Parties to the present Covenant undertake to respect the freedom indispensable for scientific research and creative activity.

4. The States Parties to the present Covenant recognise the benefits to be derived from the encouragement and development of international contacts and co-operation in the scientific and cultural fields.

Article 23

The States Parties to the present Covenant agree that international action for the achievement of the rights recognised in the present Covenant includes such methods as the conclusion of conventions, the adoption of recommendations, the furnishing of technical assistance and the holding of regional meetings and technical meetings for the purpose of consultation and study organised in conjunction with the Governments concerned.

Article 28

The provisions of the present Covenant shall extend to all parts of federal States without any limitations or exceptions.

Notes

1.   The ICESCR protects "second generation" human rights, as to which see above, p.536. After early attempts to include both "first" and "second" generation rights in one document, it was decided to guarantee civil and political rights and economic, social and cultural rights in two separate Covenants. This was because there were seen to be differences in the nature of the legal obligations and the systems of supervision that could be imposed. As to the former, the obligations appropriate to civil and political rights (e.g. not to torture) were typically negative and capable of immediate implementation by all states, whereas those suitable for economic, social and cultural rights (e.g. to provide adequate housing) were mostly positive and susceptible only of progressive and differential compliance as each state's economy permitted.[253] As to remedies, it was thought to follow from the differing nature of the obligations described above that whereas breaches of civil and political rights could properly be challenged through a system of

---

[253] Although this analysis is helpful as a generalisation, there are civil and political rights that require positive action and money (e.g. the right to a fair trial supposes court buildings and legal aid) and some economic, social and cultural rights (e.g. the right to form a trade union) call only for non-intervention by states. Moreover, civil and political rights may, although theoretically capable of immediate implementation, require a change in "societal structures" or attitudes, which takes time (see Alston and Quinn, above, n.25, p.172) and are increasingly understood to impose positive obligations of protection (see, e.g. the obligation to prevent and investigate the arbitrary taking of life: see above, p.568). The concern about economic cost relates to social rights: individual and collective economic rights, which mostly involve positive state obligations to control private employers, or negative obligations concerning state employees or state interference with trade union rights, and cultural rights generally do not raise special issues of cost.

petitions, the essentially programmatic and conditional nature of economic, social and cultural rights obligations made them "non-justiciable," so that only a system of reports was possible.

2. The analysis of the different nature of the legal obligations of states (positive/negative, immediate/progressive) in respect of civil and political rights and of economic, social and cultural rights is, as suggested in note 1 above, not without important exceptions. A more helpful analysis, that applies to all categories of human rights, is explained and applied by the CESCR in its General Comment No.14[254] on the right to health:

> "33. The right to health, like all human rights, imposes three types or levels of obligation on States parties: the obligations to *respect, protect* and *fulfil*. In turn, the obligation to fulfil contains obligations to facilitate, provide and promote.[255] The obligation to *respect* requires States to refrain from interfering directly or indirectly with the enjoyment of the right to health. The obligation to *protect* requires States to take measures that prevent third parties from interfering with article 12 guarantees. Finally, the obligation to *fulfil* requires States to adopt appropriate legislative, administrative, budgetary, judicial, promotional and other measures towards the full realization of the right to health. ...
>
> 37. The obligation to *fulfil (facilitate)* requires the States inter alia to take positive measures that enable and assist individuals and communities to enjoy the right to health. States parties are also obliged to *fulfil (provide)* a specific right contained in the Covenant when individuals or a group are unable, for reasons beyond their control, to realize that right themselves by the means at their disposal. The obligation to *fulfil (promote)* the right to health requires States to undertake actions that create, maintain and restore the health of the population. Such obligations include: (i) fostering recognition of factors favouring positive health results, e.g. research and provision of information ..."

3. The rights guaranteed in the ICESCR begin with individual (arts 6 and 7) and collective (art.8) economic rights, the meaning of which has been elaborated in many ILO conventions and recommendations.[256] The innovation of the ICESCR is the guarantee of the social rights in arts 9 to 14. While some of the guarantees of social rights contain detailed obligations (e.g. art.13(2)(a)), most are very generally phrased (e.g. arts 9 and 11(1)). The meaning of some of these guarantees has been spelt out by the Committee on Economic, Social and Cultural Rights (CESCR) in General Comments[257] and is generally to be distilled from the practice of the CESCR in examining and commenting upon state reports.

4. Primary responsibility for the implementation of the ICESCR is placed on the UN Economic and Social Council (ECOSOC) (arts 16–22). Originally, ECOSOC delegated this responsibility to a Working Group composed of government representatives. Partly because of its representative character, the Working Group was not a success. With effect from 1987, it was replaced by the Committee on Economic, Social and Cultural Rights (CESCR), which is comparable to the ICCPR

---

[254] (2001) 8 I.H.R.R. 1. See on this now well established tripartite classification, Eide, UN Doc. E/CN.4/Sub.2/1983/24; Schue, *Basic Rights* (2nd edn. 1996), Ch.2; Van Hoof, in Alston and Tomasevski, eds, *The Right to Food* (1984), pp.106–107.

[255] According to General Comments Nos. 12 [on adequate food: 6 IHRR 902 (1999)] and 13 [on education: 7 IHRR 303 (2003)], the obligation to fulfil incorporates an obligation to *facilitate* and an obligation to *provide*. In the present General Comment, the obligation to fulfil also incorporates an obligation to *promote* because of the critical importance of health promotion in the work of WHO and elsewhere.

[256] See Valticos and Von Potobsky, *International Labour Law* (2nd rev. edn 1995).

[257] There are general comments on the rights to work, social security, housing, food, water, health, education, equality of men and women and non-discrimination disabilities, older persons and cultural rights. For the texts, see *www.un.org* (human rights).

Human Rights Committee.[258] The CESCR is composed of 18 part-time members elected by the ICESCR parties, with "due consideration" being "given to equitable geographic distribution and to the representation of different forms of social and legal systems."[259] As with the Human Rights Committee, members are independent experts who do not represent their national governments. Most have a legal background.

5. Each party must submit "reports on the measures which they have adopted and the progress made in achieving the observance of the rights recognised" in the ICESCR (art.16(1)). Following an initial report, parties must submit reports for consideration by the CESCR every five years.[260] Many reports have been submitted late or not at all. As with the Human Rights Committee, there is little that the CESCR can do except remind such parties of their reporting obligations or publish the names or express criticism of defaulting states.[261] The CESCR examines reports at public hearings to which reporting states are invited to send representatives to introduce their reports and answer questions. The CESCR has made good progress in ensuring the availability of information from sources other than national reports to assist it in their examination. Specialised agencies, parti-cularly the ILO, UNESCO and WHO, may provide the CESCR with information, both in writing and orally.[262] More significantly in practice, NGOs may do the same. International and national NGO "shadow reports" and other documents play an important role in the CESCR's functioning.[263]

Following its consideration of a state's report, the Committee adopts Concluding Observations in which it reviews a state's performance.[264] These both praise and criticise a state's record, and have, so far only in a few cases, contained findings of non-compliance with the Covenant.

An important CESCR innovation outside the context of the reporting system was the introduction of a day of General Discussion in each session, in which general themes (concerning particular rights or other CESCR matters) are considered, with the oral participation of specialised agen-cies, NGOs, and individual experts.[265]

6. Implementation of the ICESCR is currently based exclusively upon national reports. This was thought to follow from the generally progressive character of the obligations in the ICESCR, which in turn were considered to result from the nature of economic, social and cultural rights. However, the 2008 Optional Protocol to the ICESCR provides for rights of individual and state petition to the CESCR.[266]

----

[258] On the CESCR see Alston (1987) 9 H.R.Q. 332; id., in Alston, ed., *The United Nations and Human Rights* (1992), Ch.12; Arambulo, *Strengthening the Supervision of the International Covenant on Economic, Social and Cultural Rights* (1999); Leckie, in Alston and Crawford, eds, *The Future of UN Treaty Monitoring* (2000), Ch.6.

[259] ECOSOC Resolution 1985/17, para.(b). Not being treaty-based, the CESCR's mandate could be terminated by ECOSOC.

[260] Article 17, ICESCR. The requirement of quinquennial reports on all of the rights in the ICESCR was introduced in 1988: ECOSOC Resolution 88/4, E/C.12/1988/4, p.58. Earlier, parties had reported every three years on one of three groups of rights for second and later reports.

[261] The CESCR may also examine a party's compliance with the Covenant during a reporting period in the absence of a state report, using available evidence from IGO and NGO sources: see UN Doc. E/1994/23, para.44(c). For examples, see Arambulo, above, at n.257, p.44.

[262] See Vadenhole, above, n.82, p.129.

[263] See Vadenhole, above, n.82, pp.127–129.

[264] The Covenant or ECOSOC Resolution basis for this power is unclear: see Craven, above, n.251, p.87. No party has objected to the Committee's practice, which is comparable to that of other human rights treaty bodies: see, e.g. the Human Rights Committee, above, p.561.

[265] See Alston, above, at n.257, p.493.

[266] A/Res/63/117, 30 signatories, not including the UK. No contracting parties; 10 required for entry into force. The Protocol also provides for a power to conduct an inquiry into "grave or systematic violations": art.11. See Mahon (2008) 8 H.R.L.R. 617.

THE NATURE OF STATES PARTIES OBLIGATIONS: ARTICLE 2(1) OF THE COVENANT

General Comment No.3, Committee on Economic, Social and Cultural Rights. UN Doc. E/1991/23; (1994) 1–1 I.H.R.R. 6

1. Article 2 ... describes the nature of the general legal obligations undertaken by States parties to the Covenant. Those obligation include both what may be termed (following the work of the International Law Commission) obligations of conduct and obligations of result.[267] While great emphasis has sometimes been placed on the difference between the formulations used in this provision and that contained in the equivalent article 2 of the International Covenant on Civil and Political Rights, it is not always recognized that there are also significant similarities. In particular, while the Covenant provides for progressive realization and acknowledges the constraints due to the limits of available resources, it also imposes various obligations which are of immediate effect. Of these, two are of particular importance in understanding the precise nature of States parties obligations. One of these ... is the "undertaking to guarantee" that relevant rights "will be exercised without discrimination" [art.2(2)].

2. The other is the undertaking in article 2(1) "to take steps", which in itself, is not qualified or limited by other considerations ... Thus while the full realization of the relevant rights may be achieved progressively, steps towards that goal must be taken within a reasonably short time after the Covenant's entry into force for the States concerned. Such steps should be deliberate, concrete and targeted as clearly as possible towards meeting the obligations recognized in the Covenant.[268]

3. The means which should be used in order to satisfy the obligation to take steps are stated in article 2(1) to be "all appropriate means, including particularly the adoption of legislative measures". The Committee recognizes that in many instances legislation is highly desirable and in some cases may even be indispensable. For example, it may be difficult to combat discrimination effectively in the absence of a sound legislative foundation for the necessary measures. In fields such as health, the protection of children and mothers, and education, as well as in respect of the matters dealt with in articles 6 to 9, legislation may also be an indispensable element for many purposes. ...

5. Among the measures which might be considered appropriate, in addition to legislation, is the provision of judicial remedies with respect to rights which may, in accordance with the national legal system, be considered justiciable. The Committee notes, for example, that the enjoyment of the rights recognized, without discrimination, will often be appropriately promoted, in part, through the provision of judicial or other effective remedies. Indeed, those States parties which are also parties to the International Covenant on Civil and Political Rights are already obliged (by virtue of arts. 2 (paras. 1 and 3), 3 and 26) of the Covenant to ensure that any person whose rights or freedoms (including the right to equality and non-discrimination) recognized in that Covenant are violated, "shall have an effective remedy" (art. 2(3)(a)). In addition, there are a number of other provisions in the International Covenant on Economic, Social and Cultural Rights, including articles 3, 7(a)(i). 8, 10(3), 13(2)(a), (3) and (4) and 15(3) which would seem to be capable of immediate application by judicial and other organs in many national legal systems. Any suggestion that the provisions indicated are inherently non-self-executing would seem to be difficult to sustain.

6. Where specific policies aimed directly at the realization of the rights recognized in the Covenant have been adopted in legislative form, the Committee would wish to be informed, inter alia, as to whether such laws create any right of action on behalf of individuals or groups who feel that their rights are not being fully realized. In cases where constitutional recognition has been accorded to specific economic, social and cultural rights, or where provisions of the Covenant have been incorporated directly into national law, the Committee would wish to receive information as to the extent to which these rights are considered to be justiciable (i.e. able to be invoked before the courts). ...

7. Other measures which may also be considered "appropriate" for the purposes of article 2(1) include, but are not limited to, administrative, financial, educational and social measures.

8. The Committee notes that the undertaking "to take steps ... by all appropriate means including particularly the adoption of legislative measures" neither requires nor precludes and particular form of government or economic system being used as the vehicle for the steps in question, provided only that it is democratic and that

---

[267] Ed. On "obligations of conduct" (to do or not do something specified) and "result" (to take action to achieve a required result), see Goodwin-Gill, in Alston and Tomasevski, eds., above, n.253, p.111. Although the distinction between the two kinds of obligations was not retained in the final draft of the I.L.C. Draft Articles on State Responsibility: see Crawford, above, p.421, n.3, pp.20, 129, it continues to be used in international human rights law.

[268] Ed. cf. the Limburg Principles, principle 21, above, n.251.

all human rights are thereby respected. Thus, in terms of political and economic systems the Covenant is neutral and its principles cannot accurately be described as being predicated exclusively upon the need for, of the desirability of a socialist or a capitalist system, or a mixed, centrally planned, or laisser-faire economy, or upon any other particular approach. In this regard, the Committee reaffirms that the rights recognized in the Covenant are susceptible of realization within the context of a wide variety of economic and political systems, provided only that the interdependence and indivisibility of the two sets of human rights, as affirmed inter alia in the preamble to the Covenant, is recognized and reflected in the system in question. The Committee also notes the relevance in this regard of other human rights and in particular the right to development.

9. ... The concept of progressive realization constitutes a recognition of the fact that full realization of all economic, social and cultural rights will generally not be able to be achieved in a short period of time. In this sense the obligation differs significantly from that contained in article 2 of the International Covenant on Civil and Political Rights which embodies an immediate obligation to respect and ensure all of the relevant rights. Nevertheless, the fact that realization over time, or in other words progressively, is foreseen under the Covenant should not be misinterpreted as depriving the obligation of all meaningful content. It is on the one hand a necessary flexibility device, reflecting the realities of the real world and the difficulties involved for any country in ensuring full realization of economic, social and cultural rights. On the other hand, the phrase must be read in the light of the overall objective, indeed the raison d'être of the Covenant, which is to establish clear obligations for States parties in respect of the full realization of the rights in question. It thus imposes an obligation to move as expeditiously and effectively as possible towards that goal. Moreover, any deliberately retrogressive measures in that regard would require the most careful consideration and would need to be fully justified by reference to the totality of the rights provided for in the Covenant and in the context of the full use of the maximum available resources.

10. ... the Committee is of the view that a minimum core obligation to ensure the satisfaction of, at the very least, minimum essential levels of each of the rights is incumbent upon every State party. Thus, for example, a State party in which any significant number of individuals is deprived of essential foodstuffs, of essential primary health care, of basic shelter and housing, or of the most basic forms of education is, prima facie, failing to discharge its obligations under the Covenant. If the Covenant were to be read in such a way as not to establish such a minimum core obligation, it would largely be deprived of its raison d'être. By the same token, it must be noted that any assessment as to whether a State has discharged its minimum core obligation must also take account of resource constraints applying within the country concerned. Article 2(1) obligates each State party to take the necessary steps "to the maximum of its available resources". In order for a State party to be able to attribute its failure to meet at least its minimum core obligations to a lack of available resources it must demonstrate that every effort has been made to use all resources that are at its disposition in an effort to satisfy, as a matter of priority, those minimum obligations.

11. The Committee wishes to emphasize, however, that even where the available resources are demonstrably inadequate, the obligation remains for a State party to strive to ensure the widest possible enjoyment of the relevant rights under the prevailing circumstances. ...

12. Similarly, the Committee underlines the fact that even in times of severe resources constraints whether caused by a process of adjustment, of economic recession, or by other factors the vulnerable members of society can and indeed must be protected by the adoption of relatively low-cost targeted programmes. In support of this approach the Committee takes note of the analysis prepared by UNICEF entitled "Adjustment with a human face: protecting the vulnerable and promoting growth",[269] the analysis by UNDP in its Human Development Report 1990 and the analysis by the World Bank in the World Development Report 1990.

13. A final element of article 2(1), to which attention must be drawn, is that the undertaking given by all States parties is "to take steps, individually and through international assistance and cooperation, especially economic and technical ...". The Committee notes that the phrase "to the maximum of its available resources" was intended by the drafters of the Covenant to refer to both the resources existing within a State and those available for the international community through international cooperation and assistance. Moreover, the essential role of such cooperation in facilitating the full realization of the relevant rights is further underlined by the specific provisions contained in articles 11, 15, 22 and 23. With respect to article 22 the Committee has already drawn attention, in General Comment 2 (1990), to some of the opportunities and responsibilities that exist in relation to international cooperation. Article 23 also specifically identifies "the furnishing of technical assistance" as well as other activities, as being among the means of "international action for the achievement of rights recognized.

14. The Committee wishes to emphasize that in accordance with Articles 55 and 56 of the Charter of the

---

[269] G.A. Cornia, R. Jolly and F. Stewart, eds., Oxford, Clarendon Press, 1987.

United Nations, with well-established principles of international law, and with the provisions of the Covenant itself, international cooperation for development and thus for the realization of economic, social and cultural rights is an obligation of all States. It is particularly incumbent upon those States which are in a position to assist others in this regard. The Committee notes in particular the importance of the Declaration on the Right to Development adopted by the General Assembly in its resolution 41/128 of 4 December 1986[270] and the need for States parties to take full account of all the principles recognized therein. It emphasizes that, in the absence of an active programme of international assistance and cooperation on the part of all those States that are in a position to undertake one, the full realization of economic, social and cultural rights will remain an unfulfilled aspiration in many countries. ...[271]

Notes

1. The CESCR's General Comment No.3 interprets the basic obligations of parties under art.2 ICESCR. As noted by the CESCR (para.2), the obligation to "take steps" is an immediate one, as well as being a continuing or dynamic one, with an unceasing expectation of incremental progress within the limits of the economy. Moreover, to the extent that an article in the Covenant guaranteeing a particular right details the steps to be taken, the obligation in respect of that right becomes an "obligation of conduct", not one of "result".

2. As to "appropriate means" (see para.3) legislation, although singled out in art.2(1) as particularly important, is neither required nor in every case sufficient. Exceptionally, repealing legislation may be necessary where existing legislation is contrary to an ICESCR obligation (see, e.g. art.2(2)). Realisation of a right in the sense of art.2(1), however, means realisation in fact, so that for example, legislation requiring, "fair wages" (art.7(a)(i)) may not be necessary if these can be achieved by collective agreements between employers and trades unions.

3. The question whether the obligations in the ICESCR are "justiciable" (see paras 5–6) was crucial to the debate when a right of individual petition claiming violations of the ICESCR was under consideration.[272] Whereas it was considered that such a right was not feasible when the ICESCR was drafted (see above), attitudes have changed and the 2008 Protocol to the ICESCR provides for a right of individual petition in respect of all ICESCR rights. On the justiciability of economic, social and cultural rights, see further the *South African* cases, below, p.618.

4. Compliance with the obligations in the ICESCR does not suppose that a state has a particular kind of government or economic system (capitalist, socialist) (see para.8). What is required instead is that, whatever system it has, a state uses its "available resources"[273] to achieve "progressively" the realisation of the rights recognised in the ICESCR.[274]

    When a state is determining the amount of "available resources" that it has to devote to the realisation of the ICESCR rights, does it have a complete discretion as to how it allocates its gross national product between, for example, the right to social security and national defence? The Limburg Principles read[275]:

    "28. In the use of the available resources due priority shall be given to the realisation of rights

---

[270] Ed. See below, p.767.

[271] On arts 2(2)(3), see Klerk (1987) 9 H.R.Q. 250. On the art.2(3) exception concerning developing states, see Dankwa, ibid., 230.

[272] On the justiciability of economic, social and cultural rights, see Craven in Burchill, Harris and Owers, eds, *Economic, Social and Cultural Rights: Their Implementation in UK Law* (1999), Ch.1.

[273] On "maximum available resources" see Robertson (1994) 16 H.R.Q. 693.

[274] For an excellent example of the use of "indicators" to assess achievement in realizing social rights, see Backman, Hunt et al, (2008) 372 *The Lancet* 2047 (right to health).

[275] See above, n.151.

recognised in the Covenant, mindful of the need to assure to everyone satisfaction of sub-sistence requirements as well as the provision of essential services."

Alston and Quinn suggest[276]:

"The discretion to which a state is entitled is, however, not unlimited, and its position is clearly not immune from scrutiny by the international body charged with responsibility for supervising States Parties' compliance with their treaty obligations. While the Covenant itself is, inevitably, devoid of specific allocational benchmarks, there is presumably a process requirement by which states might be requested to show that adequate consideration has been given to the possible resources available to satisfy each of the Covenant's requirements, even if the effort was ultimately unsuccessful. If a state is unable to do so then it fails to meet its obligation of conduct to ensure a principled policy-making process—one reflecting a sense of the impor-tance of the relevant rights."

As to the "minimum core" obligation (para.10), see the *TAC* case, below, p.619. What if a state's economy is in recession? Or if the cost of providing social welfare benefits becomes unsus-tainable because of demographic change (more older people)? In such circumstances, may a party *reduce* its public spending on health, education, social security, etc. without violating the ICESCR? See para.12.

5. With regard to "international assistance and co-operation," does art.2(1) impose an obligation on developed states to assist developing states to realise economic, social and cultural rights, in particular by providing financial aid? See General Comment No.3, para.13. If so, is it one that that might be satisfied by financial contributions by developed states as members of institutions such as the IBRD or the EU, which are then allocated by the institution to developing states? Or might it allow each developing state to claim aid from each developed state on a bilateral basis?

A related question is whether a developing state which is an ICESCR party that agrees to changes in its social funding (e.g. charging for primary education, reducing social security payments) as a condition of receiving a loan from the IBRD or the IMF is in breach of the ICESCR. Tooze[277] summarises the practice of the CESCR in the area as follows:

"... the CESCR has on some occasions been prepared to accept in general terms that some aspects of SAPs [structural adjustment programmes required of states as a condition for a loan] have 'impeded the implementation of the Covenant's provisions, particularly with regard to the most vulnerable groups' without referring to evidence that proves the point.[278] In one instance it went as far as to recognise that implementation of the SAP approved by the IMF and WB 'impacted negatively on the enjoyment of economic, social and cultural rights by increasing poverty and unemployment, worsening income distribution and causing the col-lapse of social services'.[279] ...

However, in other cases the CESCR ... has accepted that SAPs 'will frequently involve a major element of austerity' but may also be unavoidable if long term economic progress is to

---

[276] (2002) 2 H.R.L.R. 229 at 251–252.
[277] (2002) 2 H.R.L.R. 229. Some footnotes omitted. As to the human rights obligations of the lending institution, see Skogly, *The Human Rights Obligations of the World Bank and the International Monetary Fund* (2001).
[278] UN Doc. E/C.12/1/Add.44, at para. 10 (Egypt) ...
[279] UN Doc. E/C.12/1/Add.40, at para. 10 (Cameroon) ...

be achieved.[280] And it has sometimes welcomed States' implementation of SAPs as well as States' cooperation with IFIs with a view to eradicating poverty ... These examples suggest that the CESCR is prepared to take on board the positive effects and necessity of SAPs, although it does not appear to do so with any consistency."

6. Lessons as to the feasibility of international petition procedures for economic, social and cultural rights may be learnt from national court cases. A series of three South African Constitutional Court cases applying constitutional guarantees of the social rights to health and housing are particularly instructive.[281]

7. The first of these was *Soobramoney v Minister of Health, KwaZulu-Natal*.[282] The appellant was in the final stages of chronic renal failure; his life could be prolonged by regular renal dialysis, but his condition was irreversible. Because of a shortage of kidney dialysis machines, the policy of the Department of Health was to give priority to patients whose condition was reversible. The appellant claimed that this was in breach of s.27 of the South African Constitution, which provides:

(1) Everyone has the right to have access to (a) health care services ...

(2) The state must take reasonable legislative and other measures, within its available resources, to achieve the progressive realisation of these rights.

(3) No one may be refused emergency treatment.

The Constitutional Court held that s.27 had not been infringed by refusing the applicant dialysis treatment:

"[22] The appellant's demand to receive dialysis treatment at a state hospital must be determined in accordance with the provisions of sections 27(1) and (2) and not section 27(3). These sections entitle everyone to have access to health care services provided by the state 'within its available resources' ...
[24] At present the Department of Health in KwaZulu-Natal does not have sufficient funds to cover the cost of the services which are being provided to the public. In 1996–1997 it overspent its budget by R152 million, and in the current year it is anticipated that the over-spending will be R700 million rand unless a serious cutback is made in the services which it provides ... Guidelines have therefore been established to assist the persons working in these clinics to make the agonizing choices which have to be made in deciding who should receive treatment, and who not ...
[25] By using the available dialysis machines in accordance with the guidelines more patients are benefited than would be the case if they were used to keep alive persons with chronic renal failure, and the outcome of the treatment is also likely to be more beneficial because it is directed to curing patients, and not simply to maintaining them in a chronically ill condition. It has not been suggested that these guidelines are unreasonable or that they were

---

[280] CESCR, General Comment 2, ...
[281] The case law of the Indian Supreme Court is also very helpful. For examples, see Craven, above, at n.271. See also at the regional level, *Autism-Europe v France*, European Committee of Social Rights (2004) 11 I.H.R.R. 843; and *The Social and Economic Rights Action Centre and the Centre for Economic and Social Rights*, African Commission on Human and Peoples' Rights (2003) 10 I.H.R.R. 282.
[282] (1998) 1 S.A. 965.

not applied fairly and rationally when the decision was taken by the Addington Hospital that the appellant did not qualify for dialysis ...

[30] ... The dilemma confronting health authorities faced with such cases was described by Sir Thomas Bingham MR in *R v. Cambridge Health Authority, ex parte B*:[283]

'... health authorities of all kinds are constantly pressed to make ends meet ... Difficult and agonising judgments have to be made as to how a limited budget is best allocated to the maximum advantage of the maximum number of patients. That is not a judgment which the Court can make.'

[31] One cannot but have sympathy for the appellant and his family, who face the cruel dilemma of having to impoverish themselves in order to secure the treatment that the appellant seeks in order to prolong his life. The hard and unpalatable facts is that is the appellant were a wealthy man he would be able to procure such treatment from private sources; he is not and has to look to the state to provide him with treatment. But the state's resources are limited and the appellant does not meet the criteria for admission to the renal dialysis programme. Unfortunately, this is true not only of the appellant but of many others who need access to renal dialysis units or to other health services. There are also those who need access to housing, food and water, employment opportunities, and social security."

8. The second case was *Government of the Republic of South Africa v Grootboom*.[284] The respondents had lived in grossly overcrowded shacks in a squatter settlement outside Cape Town in "lamentable" conditions, in which they had no water, sewerage, refuse collection or, in nearly all cases, electricity. The site was partly waterlogged and dangerously close to a main road. Faced with no forseeable prospect of public housing, the respondents moved their shacks to adjacent vacant land without consent. The owner obtained an eviction order, whereupon the respondents were forcibly removed at the municipality's expense to a sports field, there to face the winter under plastic sheeting. The Constitutional Court upheld their claim that their eviction was in breach of s.26 of the Constitution, which provides:

(1) Everyone has a right to have access to adequate housing.

(2) The state must take reasonable legislative and other measures, within its available resources, to achieve the progressive realisation of the right.[285]

The Court accepted that the Government had a good programme for the gradual provision of permanent housing for those in need and that what had been done so far in execution of the programme was "a major achievement." However, the programme made no provision "for temporary relief for ... people in desperate need", such as the respondents. Since a "programme that excludes a significant segment of society cannot be said to be reasonable", there was a breach of s.26.

9. The third case was *Minister of Health v Treatment Action Campaign*.[286] The respondents were associations and others concerned with the treatment of persons with HIV/AIDS who challenged the constitutionality of the appellants' programme for the provision of the antiretroviral drug

---

[283] [1995] 2 All ER 129 (CA) at 137d-f.
[284] (2001) 1 S.A. 46.
[285] The respondents also relied on s.28 on children's rights.
[286] (2002) 5 S.A. 721; 13 B.H.R.C. 1.

nevirapine to HIV positive mothers to prevent the transmission of the disease to their babies at birth. The Government programme provided for the supply of nevirapine only to mothers at two research and training sites, one rural and one urban, in each of the provinces in South Africa. Aftercare was provided for the infants concerned, who were monitored for two years. This was a test programme, that might lead to more general provision later once the efficacy and safety of the drug and the capacity of the public authorities to provide a full programme had been gauged. In financial terms, the reason for this limited approach was not the cost of the drug itself, which had been made available free by the manufacturer for five years, but the cost of providing the infrastructure for counselling and testing at public hospitals and clinics generally. The Constitutional Court upheld the respondents' allegation that the programme infringed s.27 of the Constitution (above).[287] Drawing on the approach it had taken in the *Soobramoney* and *Grootboom* cases, the Court stated:

"[25] The question on the present case... is not whether socio- economic rights are justiciable. Clearly they are. The question is whether the applicants have shown that the measures adopted by the government to provide access to health care services for HIV-positive mothers and their newborn babies fall short of its obligations under the Constitution ...

[26] ... It was contended that section 27(1) of the Constitution establishes an individual right vested in everyone. This right, so the contention went, has a minimum core to which every person in need is entitled. The concept of 'minimum core' was developed by the United Nations Committee on Economic, Social and Cultural Rights which is charged with monitoring the obligations undertaken by state parties to the International Covenant on Economic, Social and Cultural Rights.[288] ...

[34] Although Yacoob J indicated that evidence in a particular case may show that there is a minimum core of a particular service that should be taken into account in determining whether measures adopted by the state are reasonable, the socio-economic rights of the Constitution should not be construed as entitling everyone to demand that the minimum core be provided to them. Minimum core was thus treated as possibly being relevant to reason-ableness under section 26(2), and not as a self-standing right conferred on everyone under section 26(1).

[35] A purposive reading of sections 26 and 27 does not lead to any other conclusion. It is impossible to give everyone access even to a "core" service immediately. All that is possible, and all that can be expected of the state, is that it act reasonably to provide access to the socio-economic rights identified in sections 26 and 27 on a progressive basis. ...

[37] It should be borne in mind that in dealing with such matters the Courts are not institutionally equipped to make the wide-ranging factual and political enquiries necessary for determining what the minimum-core standards called for by the first and second amici should be, nor for deciding how public revenues should most effectively be spent. There are many pressing demands on the public purse. As was said in *Soobramoney*:

'The State has to manage its limited resources in order to address all these claims. There will be times when this requires it to adopt a holistic approach to the larger needs of society rather than to focus on the specific needs of particular individuals within society.'

[38] Courts are ill-suited to adjudicate upon issues where court orders could have multiple

---

[287] The Court also relied on s.28 on children's rights.
[288] CESCR General Comment 3 para 10, above, p.614.

social and economic consequences for the community. The Constitution contemplates rather a restrained and focused social role for the Courts, namely, to require the state to take measures to meet its constitutional obligations and to subject the reasonableness of these measures to evaluation. Such determinations of reasonableness may in fact have budgetary implications, but are not in themselves directed at rearranging budgets. In this way the judicial, legislative and executive functions achieve appropriate constitutional balance. ...

[67] The policy of confining nevirapine to research and training sites fails to address the needs of mother and their newborn children who do not have access to these sites. It fails to distinguish between the evaluation of programmes for reducing mother-to-child transmission and the need to provide access to health care services required by those who do not have access to the sites. ...

The fact that the research and training sites will provide crucial data on which a comprehensive programme for mother-to-child transmission can be developed and, if financially feasible, implemented is clearly of importance to government and to the country. So too is ongoing research into safety, efficacy and resistance. This does not mean, however, that until the best programme has been formulated and the necessary funds and infrastructure provided for the implementation of that programme, nevirapine must be withheld from mothers and children who do not have access to the research and training sites. Nor can it reasonably be withheld until medical research has been completed. A programme for the realisation of socio-economic rights must [as stated in *Grootboom*]

"be balanced and flexible and make appropriate provision for attention to ... crises and to short, medium and long term needs. A programme that excludes a significant segment of society cannot be said to be reasonable.'"

DECLARATION ON THE RIGHT TO DEVELOPMENT 1986

G.A. Resolution 41/128, G.A.O.R., 41st Sess., Supp. 53, p. 186 (1986)

Article 1

1. The right to development is an inalienable human right by virtue of which every human person and all peoples are entitled to participate in, contribute to and enjoy economic, social, cultural and political development, in which all human rights and fundamental freedoms can be fully realised.

2. The human right to development also implies the full realisation of the right of peoples to self-determination, which includes, subject to relevant provisions of both International Covenants on Human Rights, the exercise of their inalienable right to full sovereignty over all their natural wealth and resources.

Article 2

1. The human person is the central subject of development and should be the active participant and beneficiary of the right to development.

2. All human beings have a responsibility for development, individually and collectively, taking into account the need for full respect of their human rights and fundamental freedoms as well as their duties to the community, which alone can ensure the free and complete fulfilment of the human being, and they should therefore promote and protect an appropriate political, social and economic order for development.

3. States have the right and the duty to formulate appropriate national development policies that aim at the constant improvement of the well-being of the entire population and of all individuals, on the basis of their

active, free and meaningful participation in development and in the fair distribution of the benefits resulting therefrom.

Article 3

1. States have the primary responsibility for the creation of national and international conditions favourable to the realisation of the right to development.

2. The realisation of the right to development requires full respect for the principles of international law concerning friendly relations and co-operation among States in accordance with the Charter of the United Nations.

3. States have the duty to co-operate with each other in ensuring development and eliminating obstacles to development. States should fulfil their rights and duties in such a manner as to promote a new international economic order based on sovereign equality, interdependence, mutual interest and co-operation among all States, as well as to encourage the observance and realisation of human rights.

Article 4

1. States have the duty to take steps, individually and collectively, to formulate international development policies with a view to facilitating the full realisation of the right to development.

2. Sustained action is required to promote more rapid development of developing countries. As a complement to the efforts of developing countries effective international co-operation is essential in providing these countries with appropriate means and facilities to foster their comprehensive development.

Article 5

States shall take resolute steps to eliminate the massive and flagrant violations of the human rights of peoples and human beings affected by situations such as those resulting from *apartheid*, all forms of racism and racial discrimination, colonialism, foreign domination and occupation, aggression, foreign interference and threats against national sovereignty, national unity and territorial integrity, threats of war and refusal to recognise the fundamental right of peoples to self-determination.

Article 6

1. All States should co-operate with a view to promoting, encouraging and strengthening universal respect for and observance of all human rights and fundamental freedoms for all without any distinction as to race, sex, language and religion.

2. All human rights and fundamental freedoms are indivisible and interdependent; equal attention and urgent consideration should be given to the implementation, promotion and protection of civil, political, economic, social and cultural rights.

3. States should take steps to eliminate obstacles to development resulting from failure to observe civil and political rights as well as economic, social and cultural rights.

Article 7

All States should promote the establishment, maintenance and strengthening of international peace and security and, to that end, should do their utmost to achieve general and complete disarmament under effective international control as well as to ensure that the resources released by effective disarmament measures are used for comprehensive development, in particular that of the developing countries.

Article 8

1. States should undertake, at the national level, all necessary measures for the realisation of the right to development and shall ensure, inter alia, equality of opportunity for all in their access to basic resources, education, health services, food, housing, employment and the fair distribution of income. Effective measures should be undertaken to ensure that women have an active role in the development process. Appropriate economic and social reforms should be made with a view to eradicating all social injustices.

2. States should encourage popular participation in all spheres as an important factor in development and in the full realisation of all human rights.

Article 9

1. All the aspects of the right to development set forth in this Declaration are indivisible and interdependent and each of them should be considered in the context of the whole.

2. Nothing in this Declaration shall be construed as being contrary to the purposes and principles of the United Nations, or as implying that any State, group or person has a right to engage in any activity or to perform any act aimed at the violation of the rights set forth in the Universal Declaration of Human Rights and in the International Covenants on Human Rights.

Article 10

Steps should be taken to ensure the full exercise and progressive enhancement of the right to development, including the formulation, adoption and implementation of policy, legislative and other measures at the national and international levels.

Notes

1. The right to development is a controversial but important example of a claimed "third generation" or "solidarity" human right. Such rights, the theory of which dates only from the 1970s, are collective, group rights, in contrast with the individual rights of the first and second "generations".[289] The most well established example of such a right is the right to self-determination, above, p.104. Other candidates are the freedom of groups from genocide and the various peoples' rights, such as the right to peace and to the environment, found in the African Charter on Human Rights and Peoples' Rights[290]. Some Western states and commentators have been sceptical of such rights as human rights. Sieghart,[291] for example, states:

    "Apart from being new, what these rights have in common is that it is sometimes difficult to see how they can be vested in, or exercised by, individuals. According to the classical theory, only the rights of human individuals can be 'human' rights; any rights belonging to entities of some other kind (such as states, churches, corporations, trade unions, and so forth) may be highly desirable, accepted, valid, and even enforceable—but, whatever else they may be, they cannot be *human* rights."

    A balanced view is expressed by Crawford,[292] who concludes that "peoples' rights should be regarded as a sub-category of human rights":

    "One does not have to accept the view that international human rights are a closed category to regard some of the suggestions for the elaboration of 'solidarity rights' as mere novelties. . . . The excessive generality and the disregard for content demonstrated in some of the elaborations of new rights not only raise questions about individual proposals, but reflect badly on the notion of a 'third generation' of rights as such. Their relation to existing human rights is also problematic.

---

[289] On "third generation" human rights, see Alston (1982) 29 N.I.L.R. 307; Crawford, ed., *The Rights of Peoples* (1988); Marks (1981) 33 Rutgers L.R. 435; Sanders (1991) 13 H.R.Q. 368.

[290] Articles 23 and 24 respectively.

[291] *The Lawful Rights of Mankind* (1986), p.161.

[292] See above, n.288, pp.159–166 and (second extract) pp.65–66. Footnotes omitted.

Despite these difficulties, there is no doubt that the issues posed in the debate over peoples' rights are important ones. ... Can the legitimate interests of groups be sufficiently protected by recognition of the individual right to associate? Should individual rights, including the right to opt out of groups or communities, prevail over the interests of those groups or communities? Is development better thought of as a human right, and if so, should that right be treated as an individual or communal one?

... [In conclusion] there are good grounds for accepting the category of peoples' rights in international law. There is at least one incontrovertible case of a peoples' right, the right of self-determination. A second example, the principle of permanent sovereignty over natural resources, is also widely recognised. There may be other examples, although most are in the course of development rather than fully fledged rights. In view of the increasingly widespread reference to peoples' rights, in the African Charter of Human and Peoples Rights, in General Assembly resolutions, and also in the literature, the category should be regarded as an established one.

To say this does not imply that the category 'peoples' rights' requires that the term 'peoples' should have the same meaning for the purposes of all rights accepted as falling within the category, that peoples as distinct from individuals are necessarily the bearers of the rights in question, or that peoples are 'subjects' of international law in the orthodox sense, any more than human beings are subjects of international law notwithstanding the recognition that the category 'human rights' is an international law category with a distinct content. But recognition of the category does imply, first, that peoples' rights are distinct from the rights of States or governments ... and secondly, that the peoples in whom a particular right is vested are not inherently or necessarily represented by States or by the governments of States for that purpose. In particular cases, governments may be agents through which rights can be vindicated. But they will be acting in a secondary capacity, rather than as the holders of the right. ..."

With regard to the right to development in particular, Crawford states:

"Notwithstanding its scanty recognition in international human rights treaties, the notion of a right to development as a human or peoples' right is very much at the centre of the debate about peoples' rights ... The right to development is, outside specific contexts and specific instruments (e.g. relating to development aid, or the distribution of benefits in the law of the sea regime), less well integrated into the body of international practice than the notion of permanent sovereignty. So far as other States are concerned, the notion that 'peoples' have a right to development does not appear to differ from the proposition that States have such a right. So far, the assessment of one leading African international lawyer seems accurate [Umozurike, (1983) 77 A.J.I.L. 902 at 907]:

The right to development ... appears not to have attained the definitive status of a rule of law despite its powerful advocates. Its inclusion in the African Charter will be as effective as the Charter itself. The negative duty not to impede the development of States may go down well; the positive duty to aid such development, in the absence of specific accords, is a higher level of commitment that still rests on non legal considerations."

2. As the 1970s plan for a New International Economic Order, see above, p.475, lost momentum, efforts to alleviate third world economic problems turned to the idea of "development" as a human right,[293] resulting ultimately in the 1986 Declaration. Unfortunately, attempts to attract the support of developed states generally for the Declaration were both unsuccessful and the cause of a puzzling, compromise text. The resulting uncertainty as to both the meaning of the Declaration and whether it was intended to state rules of law, argues against regarding the Declaration as evidence that the right to development is a part of present customary international law.[294]

3. Does the Declaration see the right as an individual or a peoples' right, or both? What obligations does it impose upon a state to realise the right? Must it, in particular, ensure that a state's assets are used to achieve economic or social justice, as opposed, for example, to the vainglory of its leaders? Does the Declaration require that developed states give economic assistance to developing states, or does it just call for co-operation between states? May a state restrict civil or individual human rights (e.g. freedom of speech, the right to vote or freedom to join a trade union) in order to further economic progress and hence the implementation of the right to development? Is realisation of the right to development different from realisation of all of an individual's first and second generation rights?

4. A Working Group on the Right to Development was established by the UN Commission on Human Rights[295] to try to revitalise the idea of the right to development, which had failed to make progress beyond the adoption of the 1986 Declaration. The Working Group is focusing on the preparation of "a revised list of right-to-development criteria" and "operational sub-criteria" for the implementation of the right to development and on "aspects of international cooperation".[296]

5. *Millenium Development Goals ("MDGs")*. These derive from the UN Millennium Declaration[297] adopted by consensus by the General Assembly in 2000. The Declaration identifies and seeks to address the challenges confronting humanity in the new millennium. In 2001, eight MDGs were agreed upon as the international community's response to these challenges, with accompanying targets to be attained by 2015. The eight goals are to eradicate extreme poverty and hunger; to achieve universal primary education; to promote gender equality and empower women; to reduce child mortality; to improve maternal health; to combat HIV/AIDs, malaria and other diseases; to ensure environmental sustainability; and to develop a global partnership for

---

[293] The idea had first been suggested by M'Baye (1972) 5 H.R.J. 528. On the right to development, see Aguirre, *The Human Right to Development in a Globalized World* (2008); Alston and Robinson, *Human Rights and Development: Towards Mutual Reinforcement* (2005); Alston (1988) 1 H.H.R.Y. 4; id. (2005) 27 H.R.Q. 755; Andreasson and Marks, eds, *Development as a Human Right: Legal, Political and Economic Dimensions* (2007); Barsh (1991) 13 H.R.Q. 322; Brownlie, *The Human Right to Development,* Commonwealth Secretariat Study (1989); Chowdhury et al, eds, *The Right to Development in International Law* (1992); Hamm (2001) 23 H.R.Q. 1005; Iqbal (2007) 1 Pol. Perspectives 10; Kirchmeier, *The Right to Development—Where Do We stand?,* Dialogue on Globalisation Occasional Paper 23 (2006); Marks (2004) 17 H.H.R.YJ. 137; Rich, in Crawford, above at n.288, p.39; Koojimans (1990) 27 N.I.L.R. 315; Sen, *Development as Freedom* (2001); Sengupta (2002) 24 H.R.Q. 837; Sengupta, Negi and Basu, eds, *Reflections on the Right to Development* (2005); *The Legal Nature of the Right to Development and its Binding Nature,* E/CN.4/Sub 2/2004/16.

[294] The Declaration was not adopted by consensus, but by a vote of 146 to one (the US), with eight abstentions (including the FRG, Japan and the UK).

[295] Commission Resn 1998/7. See now HRC Resn 9/3 (2009). See most recently the Report of the 10th Session of the Working Group, A/HRC/12/28 (2009). The Working Group is assisted by a high level task force on the implementation of the right to development, established by Commission Resn 2004/7: see the Report of the Task Force 5th Session, A/HRC/12/WG.2/TF/2 (2009). See also the reports of the Independent Expert on the Right to Development (Sengupta): 6th and final Report, E/CN.4/04/WG.18/2.

[296] See the Report of the Working Group's 10th Session, above, n.294, para.44.

[297] A/RES/55/2.

development. The Working Group on the Right to Development has focused on Goal 8 (global partnership) in its work. Although the goals are not expressed in terms of human rights, they can readily be related to human rights, mostly in the ICESCR.[298]

----

3. CUSTOMARY INTERNATIONAL LAW[299]

RESTATEMENT OF THE LAW: THIRD RESTATEMENT OF U.S. FOREIGN RELATIONS LAW[300]

Vol.2 (1987), p.165

§ 702. Customary international law of human rights

A state violates international law if, as a matter of state policy, it practices, encourages, or condones

(a) genocide,

(b) slavery or slave trade,

(c) the murder or causing the disappearance of individuals,

(d) torture or other cruel, inhuman, or degrading treatment or punishment,

(e) prolonged arbitrary detention,

(f) systematic racial discrimination, or

(g) a consistent pattern of gross violations of internationally recognised human rights.

Comment: ...

f. Murder as state policy and capital punishment. Under this section, it is a violation of international law for a state to kill an individual other than as lawful punishment pursuant to conviction in accordance with due process of law, or as necessary under exigent circumstances, for example by police officials in line of duty in defence of themselves or of other innocent persons, or to prevent serious crime.

Capital punishment, imposed pursuant to conviction in accordance with due process of law, has not been recognised as a violation of the customary law of human rights. It may, however, constitute cruel or inhuman punishment under clause (d) if grossly disproportionate to the crime. Compare Article 6 of the Covenant on Civil and Political Rights. ...

j. Systematic religious discrimination. The United Nations Charter (Articles 1, 13, 55) links religious discrimination with racial discrimination and treats them alike; to the extent that racial discrimination violates the Charter religious discrimination does also. Religious discrimination is also treated identically with racial discrimination in the principal covenants and in the constitutions and laws of many states. There is as yet no convention on the elimination of religious discrimination, and there has been no concerted attack on such discrimination comparable to that on *apartheid*, but there is a strong case that systematic discrimination on grounds of religion as a matter of state policy is also a violation of customary law. ...

k. Right to property. The Universal Declaration of Human Rights includes the right to own and not to be arbitrarily deprived of property. ... There is, however, wide disagreement among states as to the scope and content of that right, which weighs against the conclusion that a human right to property generally has become a principle of customary law. ...

l. Gender discrimination. The United Nations Charter (Article 1(3)) and the Universal Declaration of Human

---

[298] See the Report of the Special Rapporteur on the Right to Health, A/59/422, pp.54 et seq. and Annex...See also Alston (2005) 27 H.R.Q. 755.

[299] See the excellent Colloquium papers in (1995–96) 25 Ga. J.I.C.L. 1.

[300] The *Restatement* is a private document prepared by a team of US international lawyers; it does not necessarily represent US Government views.

Rights (Article 2) prohibit discrimination in respect of human rights on various grounds, including sex. Discrimination on the basis of sex in respect of recognised rights is prohibited by a number of international agreements, including the Covenant on Civil and Political Rights, the Covenant on Economic, Social and Cultural Rights, and more generally by the Convention on the Elimination of All Forms of Discrimination Against Women. ... Gender-based discrimination is still practised in many states in varying degrees, but freedom from gender discrimination as state policy, in many matters, may already be a principle of customary international law. ...

   m. Consistent pattern of gross violations of human rights. The acts enumerated in clauses (a) to (f) are violations of customary law even if the practice is not consistent, or not part of a "pattern," and those acts are inherently "gross" violations of human rights. Clause (g) includes other infringements of recognised human rights that are not violations of customary law when committed singly or sporadically ...: they become violations of customary law if the state is guilty of a "consistent pattern of gross violations" as state policy. A violation is gross if it is particularly shocking because of the importance of the right or the gravity of the violation. All the rights proclaimed in the Universal Declaration and protected by the principal International Covenants are internationally recognised human rights, but some rights are fundamental and intrinsic to human dignity. Consistent patterns of violation of such rights as state policy may be deemed "gross" *ipso facto*. These include, for example, systematic harassment, invasions of the privacy of the home, arbitrary arrest and detention (even if not prolonged); denial of fair trial in criminal cases; grossly disproportionate punishment; denial of freedom to leave a country; denial of the right to return to one's country; mass uprooting of a country's population; denial of freedom of conscience and religion; denial of personality before the law; denial of basic privacy such as the right to marry and raise a family; and invidious racial or religious discrimination. ...

   n. Customary law of human rights and jus cogens. Not all human rights norms are peremptory norms (*jus cogens*), but those in clauses (a) to (f) of this section are, and an international agreement that violates them is void. ...

   o. Responsibility to all states (erga omnes). Violations of the rules stated in this section are violations of obligations to all other states and any state may invoke the ordinary remedies available to a state when its rights under customary law are violated. ...

Reporters' Notes

   1. *Customary law of human rights.* This section adopts the view that customary international law prohibits the particular human rights violations indicated, if the violations are state policy. This view is accepted by virtually all states; with the exception of the Republic of South Africa in respect of *apartheid*, no state claims the right to commit the practices set forth in this section as state policy, and few, if any, would deny that they are violations of international law. Other rights may already have become customary law and international law may develop to include additional rights. It has been argued that customary international law is already more comprehensive than here indicated and forbids violation of any of the rights set forth in the Universal Declaration. See ... McDougal, Lasswell, and Chen, Human Rights and World Public Order 273–74, 325–27 (1980); ...

   The practice of states has established the principles of this section in customary law, as indicated in the following notes. Clauses (a) through (e) (and perhaps (f)) also reflect general principles common to the major legal systems that may have been absorbed into international law.

   2. *State responsibility for private violations of rights.* Under customary law, the state is responsible for the acts enumerated in this section when committed by its officials as state policy, or, when committed by private persons, if they were encouraged or condoned as state policy. By contrast, under the Covenant on Civil and Political Rights, a state is required not only to respect but also to "ensure" the rights recognised by the Covenant, suggesting an obligation to act to prevent their violation whether by officials or by private persons. See art. 2. ...

   3. *Genocide.* The term was not coined until later, but genocide was in fact considered a "crime against humanity" in the indictments brought under the Nuremberg Charter, the principles of which were affirmed by the United Nations General Assembly in a resolution ... In another resolution adopted at the same time, the General Assembly declared genocide an international crime. G.A. Res. 96, 1. G.A.O.R. UN Doc. A/64/Add 1, at 188. The Convention on the Prevention and Punishment of the Crime of Genocide was the first human rights agreement concluded under United Nations auspices. ...

   Draft articles on state responsibility provisionally adopted by the International Law Commission would (in Article 19) declare "a serious breach on a widespread scale of an international obligation of essential importance for safeguarding the human being, such as ... genocide," to be an international crime. ...

   4. *Slavery and slave trade.* Slavery and slave trade are forbidden by international law, both as a matter of customary law and as general principles common to major legal systems. Slavery is outlawed by the con-

stitutions or laws of virtually all states. ... A convention to outlaw slavery was concluded ... in 1926,[301] and one on forced labour in 1930.[302] The Universal Declaration of Human Rights declares that slavery and the slave trade shall be prohibited in all their forms. art. 4. Slavery has been condemned and declared illegal by unanimous resolutions of the United Nations and other international bodies. ... The report of the International Law Commission, ... cites slavery as example of an international crime. Slavery and slave trade are also offences subject to universal jurisdiction to prescribe and adjudicate. ...

5. *Torture or other cruel, inhuman or degrading treatment or punishment.* Torture as well as other cruel, inhuman, or degrading treatment or punishment, when practiced as state policy, are violations of customary international law. The prohibition on torture at least, may also have been absorbed into international law as a general principle common to major legal systems. The prohibition is included in all comprehensive international instruments. ... Universal Declaration of Human Rights, art. 5 ... the International Covenant on Civil and Political Rights, art. 7; the European Convention on Human Rights, art. 3; the American Convention on Human Rights, art. 5; the African Charter of Human and Peoples' Rights, art. 5. ... Official torture is also barred by the constitutions or laws of states generally. ... The difference between torture and cruel, inhuman, or degrading treatment or punishment "derives principally from a difference in the intensity of the suffering inflicted." Ireland v. United Kingdom, 25 Pub. Eur. Ct. Hum. Rts., ser. A. para. 167 (1978).

6. *Prolonged arbitrary detention.* Arbitrary detention is cited as a violation of international law in all comprehensive international human rights instruments, e.g., the Universal Declaration, art. 9; the International Covenant on Civil and Political Rights, art. 9; the European Convention, art. 5; the American Convention, art. 7; the African Convention, art. 6. ...

7. *Systematic racial discrimination.* Numerous United Nations resolutions have declared *apartheid* to be a violation of international law. The General Assembly has adopted the International Convention on the Suppression and Punishment of the Crime of *Apartheid*. ... The International Court of Justice has declared *apartheid* to be "a flagrant violation of the purposes and principles of the Charter." See the advisory opinion, Legal Consequences for States of the Continued Presence of South Africa in Namibia, [1971] I.C.J. Rep. 3, 57. *Apartheid* is listed as an example of an international crime in the draft articles provisionally approved by the International Law Commission. ...

§ 703. Remedies for violation of human rights obligations

...

(2) Any state may pursue international remedies against any other state for a violation of the customary international law of human rights. ...

(3) An individual victim of a violation of a human rights agreement may pursue any remedy provided by that agreement or by other applicable international agreements.

Comment:

a. Remedies for violation of international human rights obligations. Under international law, a breach of an international obligation, whether deriving from customary law or from international agreement, gives rise to international remedies against the violating state. These remedies include the right to make an international claim; to resort to the International Court of Justice or other international tribunal to whose jurisdiction the complaining and responding states have submitted; and in some circumstances to some measures of self-help. ...

b. Remedies for violation of customary law of human rights. Since the obligations of the customary law of human rights are *erga omnes* (obligations to all states), any state may pursue remedies for their violation, even if the individual victims were not nationals of the complaining state and the violation did not affect any other particular interest of that state. ...

c. Remedies of individual victims. In general, individuals do not have direct international remedies against a state violating their human rights except where such remedies are provided by international agreement. ... Whether they have a remedy under the law of a state depends on that state's law. ... International human rights agreements generally require a state party to provide such remedies. See, e.g., International Covenant on Civil and Political Rights, Article 2(3). ...

---

[301] Ed. Slavery Convention 1926, (1927) U.K.T.S. 16, Cmd 2910; 60 L.N.T.S. 253. In force 1927. 99 parties, including the UK.
[302] Ed. Forced Labour Convention 1930, Cmd. 3693; 39 U.N.T.S. 55. In force 1932. 174 parties, including the UK.

Reporters' Notes ...

3. ... In the *Barcelona Traction* case, [above, p. 515] ... the International Court of Justice seemed to distinguish diplomatic protection in general, including protection for ordinary violations of human rights, which is available only for nationals of the complaining state ... from protection against violations of the "basic rights of the human person" set forth in this section, as to which "all States can be held to have a legal interest in their protection."

Notes

1. Commenting on the *U.S. Restatement*, Meron states[303]:

    > "... I believe that it is, perhaps, somewhat too cautious ... The right of self-determination, which the ICJ has recognised as customary, could safely have been added.[304] Among other customary human rights, or general principles of law, I would include the right to humane treatment of detainees, stated in Article 10 of the Political Covenant. There is little doubt that the prohibition of retroactive penal measures (which is non-derogable in the Political Covenant and in both the American and the European Conventions on Human Rights) stated in Article 15 of the Political Covenant is a norm of customary international law. I believe that at least the core of a number of the due process guarantees stated in Article 14 of the Covenant have a strong claim to customary law status.
    >
    > ... A somewhat different enumeration of customary rights prepared by Professor Lillich mentions the right to equality before the law and to non-discrimination, as stated in Article 7 of the Universal Declaration, as probably customary law, as well as the right of the individual to leave any country and to return to his own country.[305]
    >
    > Other scholars would list as customary the principle of non-refoulement in the context of Article 3 of the [UN Torture] Convention ... some economic, social and cultural or 'second generation' rights, and possibly even some solidarity or 'third generation' rights.[306] Such economic rights as have been recognised by the internal laws of most states (e.g. as a result of ratifications of ILO's international labour conventions) may have matured into general international law as general principles of law recognised by civilised nations."

2. Who are the right holders in the customary international law of human rights? States are subject to the resulting legal obligation, but who is the holder of the substantive right and who has the procedural right to enforce it? Does the Restatement or the Court in the *Barcelona Traction* case, paras 33–34, judgment, above, p.515, suppose that the individual is a subject of international law so that he or she has these legal rights, although enforceable perhaps only by states for them?[307] Or is he or she just the third party beneficiary of an obligation which each state owes to all other states (*erga omnes*), for example, not to torture individuals?

---

[303] *Human Rights and Humanitarian Norms as Customary Law* (1989), pp.95–8. Some footnotes omitted.
[304] ... Perhaps this right has not been included because of its "collective" or "group"—rather than individual—character. (However, the prohibition of genocide, which is listed in the Restatement, is also a "collective" right.) ...
[305] Lillich, "Civil Rights", in 1 Human Rights in International Law 115, 133, 151 (T. Meron ed. 1984).
[306] ... The General Assembly has declared that the right to development is "an inalienable human right." Declaration on the Right to Development, art. 1, ...
[307] See Crawford, above, p.623.

FILARTIGA v PENA-IRALA[308]

630 F. 2d 876 (1980); (1980) 19 I.L.M. 966. US Circuit Court of Appeals, 2nd Circuit

The plaintiffs, a father and daughter, were Paraguayan citizens who entered the United States in 1978 and applied for political asylum there. Shortly after their arrival, they learnt of the illegal presence in the United States of the defendant, who was a Paraguayan citizen and the former head of police in Asuncion, Paraguay. The plaintiffs brought civil proceedings for damages in a United States federal district court alleging that he had wrongfully caused the death of their son and brother (also a Paraguayan citizen) in Paraguay in 1976 by torture in retaliation for the father's political opposition to the Paraguayan Government. The cause of action was stated as arising under "wrongful death statutes; the United Nations Charter; the Universal Declaration of Human Rights; the United Nations Declaration against Torture; the American Declaration of the Rights and Duties of Man; and other pertinent declarations, documents and practices constituting the customary international law of human rights and the law of nations." It was claimed that the Court had jurisdiction under the United States Alien Tort Claims Act 1889 ("ATCA").[309] (28 U.S.C. § 1350) which establishes original federal district court jurisdiction over "all causes where an alien sues for a tort only, committed in violation of the law of nations." In this judgment for the Court of Appeals, the plaintiffs appeal against the District Court ruling that it did not have jurisdiction to hear the case was considered.

KAUFMAN, CIRCUIT JUDGE ...

A threshold question on the jurisdictional issue is whether the conduct alleged violates the law of nations. In light of the universal condemnation of torture in numerous international agreements, and the renunciation of torture as an instrument of official policy by virtually all of the nations of the world (in principle if not in practice), we find that an act of torture committed by a state official against one held in detention violates established norms of the international law of human rights. and hence the law of nations. ...

The United Nations Charter ... [Preamble, and Articles 55 and 56] makes it clear that in this modern age a state's treatment of its own citizens is a matter of international concern.

... although there is no universal agreement as to the precise extent of the "human rights and fundamental freedoms" guaranteed to all by the Charter, there is at present no dissent from the view that the guarantees include, at a bare minimum, the right to be free from torture. This prohibition has become part of customary international law, as evidenced and defined by the Universal Declaration of Human Rights ... which states, in plainest of terms, "no one shall be subjected to torture." The General Assembly has declared that the Charter precepts embodied in this Universal Declaration "constitute basic principles of international law." G.A. Res. 2635 (XXV) (Oct. 24, 1970).[310]

Particularly relevant is the [1975] Declaration on the Protection of All Persons from Being Subjected to Torture.[311] ... This Declaration, like the Declaration of Human Rights before it, was adopted without dissent by the General Assembly. ...

These UN declarations are significant because they specify with great precision the obligations of member nations under the Charter. ... it has been observed that the Universal Declaration of Human Rights "no longer fits into the dichotomy of 'binding treaty' against 'non-binding pronouncement,' but is rather an authoritative statement of the international community." E. Schwelb, *Human Rights and the International Community* 70 (1964). Thus a Declaration creates an expectation of adherence, and "insofar as the expectation is gradually justified by State practice, a declaration may by custom become recognised as laying down rules binding upon the States." 34 UN ESCOR, *supra*. Indeed, several commentators have concluded that the Universal Declaration

---

[308] See Blum and Steinhardt (1981) 22 H.I.L.J. 53; D'Zurilla (1981) 56 Tul. L.R. 186; Holt (1990) 20 Ga.J.I.C.L. 543; Ratner and Abrams, *Accountability for Human Rights Atrocities in International Law* (2nd edn. 2001); Simon (1993) 11 B.U.I.L.J. 1; the articles in (1981) 10 Ga.J.I.C.L. 305 et seq.; and the case notes in (1981) 75 A.J.I.L. 149, and (1981) 67 Virg. L.R. 1379.

[309] The ATCA, also known as the Alien Tort Statute ("ATS"), was enacted as a part of the Judiciary Act 1789.

[310] Ed. Below App.III. Does Resolution 2625 really declare this?

[311] Ed. G.A. Res. 3452, G.A.D.R., 30th Sess., Supp. 34, p.91 (1975).

has become, *in toto*, a part of binding, customary international law. Nayar, ... [19 Harv. Int. L.J. 813] at 816–17; Waldock, "Human Rights in Contemporary International Law and the Significance of the European Convention," *Int'l & Comp. L.Q.*, Supp. Publ. No. 11 at 15 (1965).

Turning to the act of torture, we have little difficulty discerning its universal renunciation in the modern usage and practice of nations. ... The international consensus surrounding torture has found expression in numerous international treaties and accords, *e.g. American Convention on Human Rights*, art. 5, ...; ... European Convention for the Protection of Human Rights and Fundamental Freedoms, art. 3. The substance of these international agreements is reflected in modern municipal—i.e. national—law as well. Although torture was once a routine concomitant of criminal interrogations in many nations, during the modern and hopefully more enlightened era it has been universally renounced. According to one survey, torture is prohibited, expressly or implicitly, by the constitutions of over fifty-five nations, including both the United States and Paraguay.

... United States diplomatic contacts confirm the universal abhorrence with which torture is viewed:

> In exchanges between United States embassies and all foreign states with which the United States maintains relations, it has been the Department of State's general experience that no government has asserted a right to torture its own nationals. Where reports of torture elicit some credence, a state usually responds by denial or, less frequently, by asserting that the conduct was unauthorised or constituted rough treatment short of torture.

Memorandum of the United States as *Amicus Curiae* at 16, n. 34.

Having examined the sources from which customary international law is derived—the usage of nations, judicial opinions and the works of jurists—we conclude that official torture is now prohibited by the law of nations. The prohibition is clear and unambiguous, and admits of no distinction between treatment of aliens and citizens.

The Court then held that the District Court did have jurisdiction under the 1789 Act to hear the case.

Notes

1. The Court of Appeals did not rule upon the question whether the claim should be dismissed on the ground of *forum non conveniens*. The defendant was allowed to return to Paraguay before the Court of Appeal's judgment. In later proceedings, the federal district court gave judgment against him in default. Each plaintiff was awarded $5 million punitive damages.[312]

2. The ATCA is invoked in cases where the violation of international law occurs abroad; violations that take place on United States territory may give rise to jurisdiction in tort, etc. under other more familiar rules.[313] The *Filartiga* case has been followed by others in which large amounts of damage have also been awarded.[314]

3. The *Filartiga* case concerned torture. In later cases prior to *Sosa v Alvarez Machain*,[315] US courts extended it to various other violations of international human rights law[316] and international humanitarian law.[317] In the *Sosa* case, the US Supreme Court cut back on the more expansive of these decisions, ruling that US courts should not recognise claims under the ATCA "for violations of any international law norm with less definite content and acceptance among civilized nations

---

[312] 577 F. Supp. 860 (1984).

[313] See, e.g. *Letellier v Chile*, 488 F. Supp. 665 D.D.C. (1980) (tort claim for the car bomb death in Washington D.C. of political opponents of the Chilean Government by its agents).

[314] Several cases have been brought successfully against former President Marcos for the torture and murder of Filipinos under his regime: see, *inter alia*, *Re Estate of Marcos*, 25 F. 3d 1467 (9th Cir. 1992). See also *Abebe-Jiri v Newego*, U.S.D.Ct.N.D.Ga. August 19, 1993 (Ethiopian Government torturer); and *Paul v Avril*, 812 F. Supp. 207 (S.D. Fla. 1993) (Haitian presidential adviser responsible for acts of torture).

[315] 542 U.S. 692 (2004).

[316] E.g. *Ralk v Lincoln County, GA*, 81 F. Supp. (2d) 1372 (Sd Ga (any ICCPR violation).

[317] E.g. *Tadic v Karadzic*, 70 F. (2d) 232 (2d Cir. 1995) (genocide, war crimes). See Posner (1996) 90 A.J.I.L. 655.

than the historical paradigms familiar when §1350 was enacted"[318] in 1789, these being "violations of safe conduct, infringement of the rights of ambassadors, and piracy".[319] Whereas the Court seemed to approve the *Filartiga* ruling on torture, and would probably allow ATCA jurisdiction in at least some of the violations of customary human rights law listed in the Restatement (above) and of international humanitarian law (genocide, war crimes and crimes against humanity), it does not extend to all violations of UN human rights treaty standards.

4.   The *Filartiga* case ruled that "official" torture, i.e. torture by persons acting for the state, was in violation of the "law of nations." In *Tadic v Karadizic*[320] it was held that genocide and war crimes committee by *private* individuals could give rise to ATCA liability as being contrary to the "law of nations" but that private acts of torture or summary execution could do so only if they were committed "in pursuit of genocide and war crimes". This is consistent with the rule that international human rights law generally only imposes (civil) liability on states, but that international humanitarian law imposes (criminal) liability on individuals. The public/private distinction is important for ATCA claims against companies.[321] In *Doe v Unocal Corpn*,[322] a claim concerning corporate complicity in state imposed forced labour in Myanmar, it was held that forced labour "is a modern variant of slavery that, like traditional variants of slave trading, does not require state action to give rise to liability under the ATCA", but that murder, rape and torture do.

5.   The ATCA gives jurisdiction only in cases brought by aliens. The Torture Victim Protection Act 1991 extends the jurisdiction of US courts to claims brought by US nationals of "torture and extrajudicial killings" committed "under actual or apparent authority or under colour of law of a foreign nation".

6.   Although a breakthrough, the *Filartiga* case has its limitations. It is dependent upon a defendant being within the jurisdiction[323] and having assets there against which a judgment may be enforced. The damages in the *Filartiga* case and similar cases have been paid in only a few cases.[324] State immunity has prevented these limitations from being sidestepped by bringing the claim against the state for which the human rights violator is acting, instead of the violator himself.[325] Nonetheless, *Filartiga* judgments meet the very real need of the victims of human rights violations and their families to have the truth objectively established and the responsibility of the violators publically pronounced. Such satisfaction and vindication may well be more important to them than any award of compensation. *Filartiga* judgments also may prevent the United States from being used as a place of refuge by human rights violators and may influence United States Government policies.

----

[318] 542 U.S. 692, 732 (2004).
[319] 542 U.S. 692, 715 (2004).
[320] See above at 316.
[321] See Joseph, *Corporations and Transnational Human Rights Litigation* (2004), Ch.2. The important question of the liability of corporations under the ATCA is the subject of current litigation.
[322] 395 F. (3d) 932 C.A.9 (Cal.).
[323] In the *Karadžić* case, a writ was served on the defendant in New York when he visited the United Nations. He then left the jurisdiction.
[324] See Coliver, Green and Hoffman (2005) 19 Emory I.L.R. 169.
[325] See the *Al Adsani* case, below, and the American cases quoted there.

AL-ADSANI v GOVERNMENT OF KUWAIT

Court of Appeal. March 12, 1995. Unreported

The facts of the case are summarised in the introductory note to the extract from the European Court of Human Rights judgment in *Al Adsani v UK*, above, p.284. In these proceedings, the plaintiff appealed against a judgment of Mantell J. holding that the Government of Kuwait was entitled to state immunity in respect of the plaintiff's claims in tort against it for the personal injuries caused by the beatings by the security guards in Kuwait and by the threats made in England.

STUART-SMITH L.J.

Jurisdiction of the English Courts in respect of foreign States is governed by the State Immunity Act 1978. Section 1(1) provides:

(1) A state is immune from the jurisdiction of the courts of the United Kingdom except as provided in the following provisions of this Part of this Act. ...
The only relevant exception is section 5, which provides:

A State is not immune as respects proceedings in respect of—

(a) death or personal injury; or
(b) damage or loss of tangible property,

caused by an act or omission in the United Kingdom.

It is plain that the events in Kuwait do not fall within the exception in section 5, and the express words of section 1 provide immunity to the First Defendant. Despite this, in what Mr. McDonald, Q.C. for the Plaintiff acknowledges is a bold submission, he contends that that section must be read subject to the implication that the State is only granted immunity if it is acting within the Law of Nations. So that the section reads: "A state *acting within the Law of Nations* is immune from jurisdiction except as provided ..."
In international law, torture is a violation of a fundamental human right, it is a crime and a tort for which the victim should be compensated. ...

Stuart-Smith L.J. cited the 1975 General Assembly Declaration on Torture, see above, n.310; the European Convention on Human Rights 1950, art.3; and the UN Torture Convention, arts 1, 2, 4.

The argument is ... that the international law against torture is so fundamental that it is a *jus cogens*, or compelling law, which overrides all other principles of international law, including the well-established principles of sovereign immunity. ...
It is inconceivable, it seems to me, that the draughtsman, who must have been well aware of the various international agreements about torture, intended section 1 to be subject to an overriding qualification.
Moreover, authority in the United States at the highest level is completely contrary to Mr. MacDonald's submission. In *Argentine Republic v. Amerada Hess Shipping Corporation* 488 U.S. 428 Supreme Court 1989, the United States Supreme Court had to consider the provisions of the Foreign State Immunities Act 1976, which in all material respects for present purposes is the same as State Immunity Act 1978. The action concerned a claim arising out of damage suffered by an oil tanker when attacked by Argentine military aircraft during the Falklands War. Jurisdiction was claimed in the United States District Court on the basis that the attack was in violation of the Law of Nations. In so claiming, the plaintiff was met with the provisions of the Act which provided no exceptions relevant to the facts of the case. A similar argument to that which is advanced by Mr. MacDonald was rejected by the Court. Rehnquist C.J., delivering the judgment of the court, said at page 7:

From Congress's decision to deny immunity to foreign states in the class of cases just mentioned, we draw the plain implication that immunity is granted in those cases involving alleged violations of international law that do not come within one of the FSIA's exceptions.

That reasoning was applied by the U.S. Court of Appeal for the 9th Circuit in *Siderman de Blake v. Republic of Argentina* 965 F (2d) 699 (1992). Jose Siderman claimed that he had been tortured by the Argentine Military Officials, for whom the State were responsible. ... Fletcher J., giving the judgment of the court, said:

> While we agree with the Sidermans that official acts of torture of the sort they allege Argentina to have committed constitute a *jus cogens* violation, we conclude that *Amerada Hess* forecloses their attempt to posit a basis for jurisdiction not expressly countenanced by the FSIA.

At page 56 he said this: ...

> Unfortunately, we do not write on a clean slate. We deal not only with customary international law, but with an affirmative Act of Congress, the FSIA. We must interpret the FSIA through the prism of *Amerada Hess*. Nothing in the text or legislative history of the FSIA explicitly addresses the effect violations of jus cogens might have on the FSIA's cloak of immunity.

Mr. MacDonald submits that we should not follow the highly persuasive judgments of the American Courts. I cannot agree.

A moment's reflection is enough to show that the practical consequences of the Plaintiff's submission would be dire. The Courts in the United Kingdom are open to all who seek their help, whether they are British citizens or not. A vast number of people come to this country each year seeking refuge and asylum, and many of these allege that they have been tortured in the country whence they came. Some of these claims are no doubt justified, others are more doubtful. Those who are presently charged with the responsibility for deciding whether applicants are genuine refugees have a difficult enough task, but at least they know much of the background and surrounding circumstances against which the claim is made. The Court would be in no such position. The foreign state would be unlikely to submit to the jurisdiction of the United Kingdom Court, and in its absence the Court would have no means of testing the claim or making a just determination.

I have no doubt the Judge was right to hold that the First Defendant is entitled to immunity in respect of the events alleged to have taken place in Kuwait.

Turning to the acts committed in England, the Judge said that he was satisfied that threats had been made, that they occurred within the United Kingdom and that personal injury had resulted from them. He added that this claim came as something of a postscript in the Plaintiff's main case and he entertained the suspicion, which I share, that this relatively minor head of claim may have been introduced simply to overcome problems of service and jurisdiction. But he was not satisfied that the threats emanated from a person or persons acting at the behest of the Government of Kuwait, or for whom the Government of Kuwait is otherwise vicariously responsible.

It is common ground that the onus is upon the Plaintiff to satisfy the Court on the balance of probability that the threats do so emanate ... While it is perfectly possible that those anonymous threats came from the First Defendant, it is equally likely, indeed I think more likely, that they came from the Second, Third or Fourth Defendants, who demonstrated without doubt their readiness to take the law into their own hands in Kuwait and subject the Plaintiff to extreme and life-threatening assaults.

It is accepted by the Plaintiff, as I understand it, that nothing said by the Ambassador amounted to a threat to the Plaintiff's life or limb. The warning that he gave was quite open. As the Judge commented, he did not "hide behind the cloak of anonymity". I do not think that any adverse inference can be drawn from those conversations. ...

For these reasons, I agree with the Judge that the Plaintiff does not establish jurisdiction against the First Defendant in relation to the threats in England. I would dismiss the appeal.

Ward L.J. delivered a concurring judgment. Buckley J. concurred.

Notes

1.   In deciding that no exception could be read into s.1 of the State Immunity Act 1978, the Court of Appeal adopted the same approach as the American courts in the *Hess* and *Siderman* cases quoted by Stuart-Smith L.J. In another American case, an argument that the doctrine of

sovereign immunity did not apply was also unsuccessful. In *Saudi Arabia v Nelson*,[326] when the plaintiff persisted in reporting safety defects at a state hospital in Saudi Arabia at which he was employed, he was detained and tortured by the police. His claim against Saudi Arabia in an American court for personal injuries was dismissed on grounds of state immunity. The plaintiff's argument that his claim was based upon his employment at a hospital and for that reason fell within the "commercial activity" exception in the Foreign State Immunities Act 1976 failed. Souter J., for the Supreme Court, stated that the "conduct boils down to abuse of the power of its police by the Saudi Government, and however monstrous such abuse undoubtedly may be, a foreign state's exercise of the power of its police has long been understood for the purpose of the restrictive theory as peculiarly sovereign in nature". Note that even if state immunity is not established, a state may still be immune from the execution of judgments against it: see 5th edn.

2. Are the policy arguments (see the refugee/asylum example) given by Stuart-Smith L.J. convincing?[327] Might another reason in the Court of Appeal's mind have been that it could be inappropriate for the British courts to act in cases where the executive is not inclined to do so internationally?

3. With the leave of the High Court[328] the plaintiff in *Al Adsani* served a writ in Kuwait on the Sheikh and two other members of the Kuwaiti royal family who were responsible for the ill treatment of the plaintiff in a claim in tort for personal injuries and obtained a default judgment in the High Court against them. In the absence of an equivalent to the Alien Tort Act 1790, the United Kingdom courts do not have *civil* jurisdiction over acts of torture committed entirely abroad, such as those in Kuwait in the *Al Adsani* case.

4. There is, however, *criminal* jurisdiction over individuals for official torture committed in the United Kingdom or elsewhere under s.134 of the Criminal Justice Act 1988.[329]

---

[326] (1993) 123 L. Ed. 47 at 61.

[327] See Marks (1997) 56 C.L.J. 8. Arguing that priority for sovereign immunity over human rights is out of date, see Bianchi, in Conforti and Francioni, eds, *Enforcing International Human Rights in Domestic Courts* (1997), Ch.17. On diplomatic immunity and human rights, see Vicuna (1991) 40 I.C.L.Q. 34.

[328] Leave to serve a writ out of the jurisdiction may be given by the High Court for a tort action where "the damage was sustained, or resulted from an act committed, within the jurisdiction": R.S.C., Ord.11, r.1(1)(f).

[329] See the *Pinochet* case, above, p.334.

10   THE LAW OF TREATIES

1. INTRODUCTORY NOTE[1]

The special importance of the law of treaties in international law scarcely needs emphasis. The treaty is the ubiquitous instrument through which all kinds of international transactions are conducted. It is also the closest analogy to legislation that international law has to offer. Although being challenged in some contexts in this latter role by the General Assembly resolution,[2] the multilateral treaty remains the best medium available at the moment for imposing binding rules of precision and details in the new areas into which international law is expanding[3] and for codifying, clarifying and supplementing the customary law already in existence in more traditional settings.

Given the extent to which treaties have long been woven into the fabric of international law, it is more than a little disappointing to find that the law governing them is in no happier a position than that of many other areas of customary international law. Whereas some rules are clear, others are not. In this situation, the adoption of the Vienna Convention on the Law of Treaties[4] in 1969 was particularly welcome. Like a number of other law-making treaties, it is based upon Draft Articles, supplemented by an invaluable Commentary, produced by the International Law Commission.[5] Like those treaties also, it is a compound of codification and of progressive development of customary international law.

Although the Convention does not have retroactive effect,[6] the materials in this chapter are

---

[1]   See Aust, *Modern Treaty Law and Practice* (2nd edn 2007); Elias, *The Modern Law of Treaties* (1974); Klabbers, *The Concept of Treaty in International Law* (1996); Reuter, *Introduction to the Law of Treaties* (2nd edn 1995, trans. and revisd by Mico and Haggenmacher); Sinclair, *The Vienna Convention on the Law of Treaties* (2nd edn 1984); and McNair, *Treaties*. The last of these is the classic work on the subject.

[2]   Insofar as it may state or generate custom.

[3]   e.g. human rights law and environmental law.

[4]   (1980), U.K.T.S. 58 Cmnd. 7964; 1155 U.N.T.S. 331; (1969) 8 I.L.M. 679; (1969) 63 A.J.I.L. 875. In force 1980. 108 parties, including the UK. The Convention was adopted on May 22, 1969, by the United Nations Conference on the Law of Treaties held at Vienna in two sessions in 1968 and 1969. See *UN Conference on the Law of Treaties, First and Second Session 1968 and 1969, Official Records*, UN Docs. A/Conf. 39/11 and Add 1. These are referred to in this chapter as *Treaty Conference Records*, 1968, 1969.

[5]   For the text of the Draft Articles and the Commentary, see Y.B.I.L.C., 1966, II, pp.177–274; (1967) 61 A.J.I.L. 263–463. Also of great value are the reports presented to the ILC by its four Special Rapporteurs, who were, in chronological order, Brierly, Lauterpacht, Fitzmaurice and Waldock. The reports are printed in the *Yearbooks* of the ILC on the Vienna Conference and Convention, see Kearney and Dalton (1970) 64 A.J.I.L. 495; Rosenne, *The Law of Treaties: A Guide to the Legislative History of the Vienna Convention* (1970); Sinclair (1970) 19 I.C.L.Q. 47. See also Rosenne (1966) 41 Wash. L.R. 261.

[6]   Article 4 of the Convention reads: "Without prejudice to the application of any rules set forth in the present Convention to which treaties would be subject under international law independently of the Convention, the Convention applies only to treaties which are concluded by States after the entry into force of the present Convention with regard to such States." But, as the text of art.4 indicates, those rules in the Vienna Convention that state custom apply as such to pre-"entry into force" treaties: *Iron Rhine Railway Arbitartion*, P.C.A. 2005, www.pca/cpa.org.On art.4, see McDade (1986) 35 I.C.L.Q. 499. On the law of treaties governing the relations between parties and non-parties to the Vienna Convention, see Vierdag (1982) 76 A.J.I.L. 779.

moulded around it. This is so because of the great impact that the Convention, which was adopted by 79 votes to 1, with 19 abstentions,[7] has had in reinforcing and advancing customary international law.[8] Most of the law of treaties is "lawyers' law" over which the political interests of states do not clash. In this situation, and although certain doctrinal legal disputes (e.g. that on treaty interpretation) exist and some difficult issues (e.g. in the law of reservations and material breach) are not resolved, the common interest of states in having a coherent, detailed and workable set of rules for their day-to-day international transactions has enhanced the attractiveness of the rules conveniently set out in the Convention. Less certain is the effect of the solutions offered by the Convention to the relatively few politically controversial questions concerning the substantive rules of the law of treaties (e.g. that concerning the doctrine of "unequal treaties"), although the idea of ius cogens has now taken root.

2. GENERAL CONSIDERATIONS

MCNAIR, THE FUNCTIONS AND DIFFERING LEGAL CHARACTER OF TREATIES

(1930) 11 B.Y.I.L. 100. Footnotes omitted

The internal laws of the modern state provide its members with a variety of legal instruments for the regulation of life within that community: the contract; the conveyance or assignment of immovable or movable property, which may be made for valuable consideration or may be a gift or an exchange; the gratuitous promise clothed in a particular form; the charter or private Act of Parliament creating a corporation; legislation, which may be constituent, such as a written constitution, fragmentary or complete, or may be declaratory of existing law, or create a new law, or codify existing law with comparatively unimportant changes. Further, though rarely, we may find a constitutional document which closely resembles the international treaty itself, for instance, Magna Carta.

It would not be suggested that all these differing private law transactions are governed by rules of universal or even of general application, and yet such is the underlying assumption of international lawyers in dealing with the only and sadly overworked instrument with which international society is equipped for the purpose of carrying out its multifarious transactions. Thus, if international society wishes to enact a fundamental, organic, constitutional law, such as the Covenant of the League of Nations was intended to be...it employs the treaty. If two states wish to put on record their adherence to the principle of the three-mile limit of territorial waters,...they use a treaty. If further they wish to enter into a bargain which derogates from that principle, again they use a treaty. If Denmark wishes to sell to the United States of America her West Indian possessions, as she did in 1916, or if Great Britain wishes to cede Heligoland to Germany in return for a recognition of certain British rights in Africa, as happened in 1890, they do so by treaty. Again, if the great European Powers are engaged upon one of their periodic resettlements and determine upon certain permanent dispositions to which they wish to give the force of "the public law of Europe," they must do it by treaty. And if it is desired to create an international organization such as the International Union for the Protection of Works of Art and Literature, which resembles the corporation of private law, it is done by treaty.

---

[7] *Treaty Conference Records*, 1969, pp.206–207. France dissented, and is still not a party. It objected to the provisions on ius cogens and the procedures providing for the settlement of disputes: p.203. A lot of the abstentions were by members of the Soviet bloc who objected to the failure of the Convention to adopt the principle of universality of participation in multilateral law-making treaties. They felt that all states should be entitled to participate in such treaties: pp.204–208. The Soviet bloc was concerned, for example, with the position of East Germany, Mainland China, North Korea and North Vietnam, which were not invited to Vienna. The Vienna Convention itself is open "for signature by all States, Members of the United Nations or of any of the specialised agencies or of the International Atomic Energy Agency or parties to the Statute of the International Court of Justice, and by any other state invited by the General Assembly of the United Nations to become a party to the Convention ..." (Convention, art.81). Some other abstentions were based on the inadequacy of the procedures providing for the settlement of disputes.

[8] Note the reliance placed upon the Convention by the ICJ in the *Legal Consequences* case, see below, p.703; the *Fisheries Jurisdiction* Cases, below, p.706; and the *Gabčíkovo-Nagymaros Project* case, below, p.708; and by the Law Officers of the Crown in 1971 in connection with the Simonstown Agreements. The law officers stated that the "rules of international law for the interpretation of treaties have recently been declared in the Vienna Convention ...": Cmnd. 4589, p.5.

Note

The above extract serves to illustrate the variety of purposes for which treaties are used and to raise the question, with which the author was concerned, of the problems that result for the law of treaties in having a single body of rules that covers all types of treaties. The question is one that needs to be borne in mind when reading the materials in the remainder of this chapter.

VIENNA CONVENTION ON THE LAW OF TREATIES 1969

See above p.637 n.4.

Article 1

The present Convention applies to treaties between States.

Article 2

1. For the purposes of the present Convention:

(a) "treaty" means an international agreement concluded between States in written form and governed by international law, whether embodied in a single instrument or in two or more related instruments and whatever its particular designation; ...

Article 3

The fact that the present Convention does not apply to international agreements concluded between States and other subjects of international law or between such other subjects of international law, or to international agreements not in written form, shall not affect:

(a) the legal force of such agreements;

(b) the application to them of any of the rules set forth in the present Convention to which they would be subject under international law independently of the Convention;

(c) the application of the Convention to the relations of States as between themselves under international agreements to which other subjects of international law are also parties.

Article 5

The present Convention applies to any treaty which is the constituent instrument of an international organization and to any treaty adopted within an international organization without prejudice to any relevant rules of the organization.

Article 6

Every State possesses capacity to conclude treaties.

Notes

1. *Capacity to make treaties.* The Convention reflects customary international law in providing that *states* may make treaties. Capacity to make treaties is, in fact, valuable evidence of statehood.[9]

---

[9] See above, pp.92 et seq.

According to the International Law Commission's Commentary, the term "state" is used in art.6 "with the same meaning as in the Charter of the United Nations, the Statute of the Court, the Geneva Convention on Diplomatic Relations; i.e. it means a State for the purposes of international law."[10]

The International Law Commission's Draft Articles contain a second paragraph to art.6 concerning *federal states* which reads as follows:

"States members of a federal union may possess a capacity to conclude treaties if such capacity is admitted by the federal constitution and within the limits there laid down."[11]

The Commentary to it reads:

"More frequently, the treaty-making capacity is vested exclusively in the federal government, but there is no rule of international law which precludes the component States from being invested with the power to conclude treaties with third States. Questions may arise in some cases as to whether the component State concludes the treaty as an organ of the federal State or in its own right. But on this point also the solution must be sought in the provisions of the federal constitution."[12]

An example of a federal state in which units within the federation have the power to make treaties is Germany.[13] The final text of the Vienna Convention omitted this paragraph in the Draft Articles. The difficulty it presented, which was mentioned by several delegations from federal states, was that the Vienna Convention had been limited to treaties made by "states" and had excluded those made by other subjects of international law. It was therefore, it was thought, inconsistent to include a provision concerning units within a federal state which "even if the law conferred upon them a certain capacity to conclude international agreements ... could not be assimilated in general to States. ..."[14]

Occasionally *colonial and similar territories* on their way to independence have been recognised as having treaty-making powers. Some former British colonies have been in this position.[15] Thus Australia, Canada, India, New Zealand and South Africa were invited to participate in the Peace Conference at Paris in 1919 and became parties to the Treaty of Versailles and founder members of the League of Nations.

The decision not to extend the Vienna Convention to treaties to which *public international organisations* are parties was explained by the International Law Commission in its Commentary as follows:

"Treaties concluded by international organisations have many special characteristics; and the

---

[10] Y.B.I.L.C., 1966, II, p.192.
[11] Y.B.I.L.C., 1966, II, p.191. See on federal states, Di Marzo (1978) 16 C.Y.I.L. 197. For an example of a "federal clause" in a treaty which limits the responsibility of the federal government for the action of units within the federation, see the 1969 American Convention on Human Rights, art.28.
[12] Y.B.I.L.C., 1966, II, p.192.
[13] Article 32(3) of the Bonn Constitution reads: "Insofar as the *Länder* have power to legislate, they may, with the consent of the Federal Government, conclude treaties with foreign states." Thus, for example the *Länder* of Baden-Wurttemberg and Bavaria became parties with Austria and Switzerland to a "Convention for the Protection of Lake Constance against Pollution of 27th October, 1960," printed as App.7 in *Fresh Water Pollution Control*, Council of Europe, 1966.
[14] Mr Groepper (West Germany), *Treaty Conference Records*, 1969, p.8. See the discussion generally, pp.6–15.
[15] See Fawcett, *The British Commonwealth in International Law* (1963), pp.144 et seq.

Commission considered that it would both unduly complicate and delay the drafting of the present articles if it were to attempt to include in them satisfactory provisions concerning treaties of international organisations."[16]

The 1986 Convention on the Law of Treaties between States and International Organisations or between International Organisations[17] confirms that international organisations have the capacity to enter into treaties in accordance with the rules of the organisation, i.e. the "constituent instruments, decisions and resolutions adopted in accordance with them, and established practice of the organisation" (art.6). In most cases, the capacity will derive from implied powers based upon "established practice."

Article 3 of the Vienna Convention, however, recognises that at customary international law entities other than states may have the international personality necessary to allow them to make treaties.

Individuals have never been recognised as having the capacity to make treaties, whether with states, or with other international persons with treaty-making capacity. The question has been discussed in the context of agreements between large municipal law companies and states, particularly agreements for the exploitation of oil. The nearest that the International Court of Justice has come to considering the question was in the *Anglo-Iranian Oil Company* case[18] in which it rejected an argument to the effect that a contract between Iran and the Anglo-Iranian Oil Company, a British company, was a treaty because of the part played by the United Kingdom Government in its negotiations. The Court stated:

"It is nothing more than a concessionary contract between a government and a foreign corporation."[19]

The Mandate for South West Africa was "an international agreement having the character of a treaty."[20] Are declarations accepting the compulsory jurisdiction of the International Court of Justice?[21]

2. *Intention to create legal relations.* This requirement, which is found in the law of contract in municipal law, is not mentioned in the Vienna Convention. The International Law Commission's Fourth Special Rapporteur stated that:

"in so far as this [requirement] may be relevant in any case, the element of intention is embraced in the phrase 'governed by international law.' "[22]

States not infrequently wish to reach an agreement without going to the extent of making it enforceable at law. The Final Act of the Helsinki Conference on Security and Co-operation in

---

[16] Y.B.I.L.C., 1966, II, p.187. See also Chiu, *The Capacity of International Organisations to Conclude Treaties* (1966). And see the *Reparation* Case, above, p.120.

[17] Misc. 11 (1987), Cm. 244; (1986) 25 I.L.M. 543. Not yet in force, 29 parties, including the UK; 35 required. The Convention contains a detailed legal régime modelled closely upon the 1969 Vienna Convention on the Law of Treaties. See Gaja (1987) 58 B.Y.I.L. 253; Isak and Loibl (1987) 38 O.Z.O.R.V. 49; Menon, *The Law of Treaties Between States and International Organisations* (1992).

[18] I.C.J. Rep. 1952, p.93.

[19] ibid. p.112. See further on such contracts, above, pp.497 et seq.

[20] *South Africa (Preliminary Objections)* cases, I.C.J. Rep. 1962 at p.330.

[21] See below, p.846.

[22] Fourth Report on the Law of Treaties, Y.B.I.L.C., 1965, II, p.12. On the law governing a treaty, see below, p.642.

Europe 1975[23] is an example.[24] The Act was stated to be "not eligible for registration under Article 102 of the Charter of the United Nations."[25] It was understood during the Conference that the Act would not be binding in law.[26]

In the *Oil Platforms (Preliminary Objections)* case,[27] the ICJ noted that, although the treaty is legally binding, a particular provision in it may be "drafted in terms so general that by itself it is not capable of generating legal rights and obligations." Thus the wording "there shall be firm and ensuring peace and sincere friendship between the United States and ... Iran" (art.1, 1955 Treaty of Friendship) did not generate legal rights and obligations, although it could be used to interpret the rest of the Treaty.

The minutes of a Tripartite Committee established by three states to negotiate the referral of a dispute to the ICJ were "diplomatic documents recording the state of progress of the negotiation", but "possessed no legally binding force".[28]

On the question whether intention to create legal relations is to be presumed when agreements are made between states, contrast the views of Fawcett[29] and Mann.[30]

3.   *"Governed by international law"*. The International Law Commission's Fourth Special Rapporteur stated in his First Report.[31]

> "... The Commission felt in 1959 that the element of subjection to international law is so essential a part of an international agreement that it should be expressly mentioned in the definition. There may be agreements between States, such as agreements for the acquisition of premises for a diplomatic mission or for some purely commercial transaction, the incidents of which are regulated by the local law of one of the parties or by a private law system determined by reference to conflict of laws principles. Whether in such cases the two States are internationally accountable to each other at all may be a nice question; but even if that were held to be so, it would not follow that the basis of their international accountability was a treaty obligation. At any rate, the Commission was clear that it ought to confine the notion of an 'international agreement' for the purposes of the law of treaties to one the whole formation and execution of which (as well as the obligation to execute) is governed by international law."

Article 2 of the Vienna Convention does not indicate the test to be used in determining whether an agreement between states is governed by international law. What should be the test? The intention of the parties? The subject matter of the agreement? Should there be a presumption

---

23   (1975) 14 I.L.M. 1292.

24   Note, however, the ICJ's reliance on the Final Act in the *Nicaragua* case *(Merits)*, para.189 below, p.729. Other examples are the 1977 Gleneagles Agreement on Sporting Contacts with South Africa, *Kessing's Archives*, p.28507 (text); and the 1978 Bonn Declaration on International Terrorism, above, p.57. See Aust (1986) 35 I.C.L.Q. 787; Busuttil (1982) 31 I.C.H.Q. 474; and Johnson (1959) 35 B.Y.I.L. 1. Such agreement form a part of "soft" international law, as to which see above, p.57. On treaties and soft law, see Boyle in Gowlland-Debbas, ed., *Multilateral Treaty Making* (2000), p.25.

25   Final (unnumbered) clauses.

26   Russell (1976) 70 A.J.I.L. 242 at 246. And see Schachter (1977) 71 A.J.I.L. p.296.

27   I.C.J. Rep. 1996, p.803 at p.820. A treaty provision that uses the term "should" instead of "must" may likewise not impose a *legal* obligation: see above, p.357.

28   *Maritime Delimitation and Territorial Questions between Qatar and Bahrain* case *(Jurisdiction and Admissibility No.2)*, I.C.J. Rep. 1995, p.6 at 16.

29   (1953) 30 B.Y.I.L. 381 at 385–400 (no presumption).

30   (1957) 33 B.Y.I.L. 20 at 30–32 (there is a presumption). See also Widdows (1979) 50 B.Y.I.L. 117.

31   Y.B.I.L.C., 1962, II, p.32.

that an inter-state agreement which is intended to create legal relations is governed by inter-national law?[32]

4. *Nomenclature.* The Vienna Convention adopts the term "treaty," not the term "agreement," as the generic term. In practice, a whole host of terms are used interchangeably with no legal significance turning upon the choice of one or another. The International Law Commission's Commentary reads:

> "Thus, in addition to 'treaty,' 'convention' and 'protocol,' one not infrequently finds titles such as 'declaration,' 'charter,' 'covenant,' 'pact,' "act," "statute," "agreement," "concordat," whilst names like 'declaration,' "agreement" and "modus vivendi" may well be found given both to formal and less formal types of agreements. As to the latter, their nomenclature is almost illimitable, even if some names such as "agreement," "exchange of notes," "exchange of letters," "memorandum of agreement," or "agreed minute" may be more common than others. It is true that some types of instruments are used more frequently for some purposes rather than others; it is also true that some titles are more frequently attached to some types of transaction rather than to others. But there is no exclusive or systematic use of nomen-clature for particular types of transaction."[33]

"Exchange of notes" and "Exchange of letters" take the form of an exchange of correspondence between States and often read not unlike the offer and acceptance letters familiar to any student of the law of contract. A treaty may also take the form of a joint communiqué issued by Government Ministers to the press at the end of a meeting, provided the necessary intention to enter into legal relations is present.[34]

5. *Oral treaties.* The Vienna Convention was limited to written treaties "in the interest of clarity and simplicity".[35] The International Law Commission's Commentary reads:

> "The restriction of the use of the term 'treaty' in the draft articles to international agreements expressed in writing is not intended to deny the legal force of oral agreements under inter-national law or to imply that some of the principles contained in later parts of the Com-mission's draft articles...may not have relevance in regard to oral agreements."[36]

6. *Consideration.* Treaties do not require consideration in the sense of the common law of contract. Territory, for example, can be ceded by treaty without consideration.

----

[32] See Mann (1944) 21 B.Y.I.L. 11 at 22–28; ibid. (1974) 68 A.J.I.L. 490; and Widdows, above, n.30.
[33] Y.B.I.L.C., 1966 II, 188. On the "memorandum of understanding", see McNeill (1994) 88 A.J.I.L. 821.
[34] *Aegean Sea* case, I.C.J. Rep. 1978, p.39. It does not matter that, as in that case, the communiqué is not signed or initialled.
[35] Y.B.I.L.C. p.10.
[36] Y.B.I.L.C. p.10. See also art.3, Vienna Convention.

3. THE MAKING OF TREATIES[37]

A. Note on the Treaty-Making Power in Municipal Law[38]

Each state is left free by international law to make its own constitutional arrangements for the exercise of its treaty-making power. In the United Kingdom, the making of treaties is a prerogative power of the Crown.[39] It is the Crown which issues full powers or other authority to negotiate and sign treaties and which ratifies treaties if this is called for. Approval by Parliament is not required.[40] British practice since 1890 concerning treaties of cession comes close to establishing an exception to this rule. McNair concludes from this practice that:

> "it is unlikely that the Crown will agree to cede any territory without being sure that Parliament would approve, or, if in doubt, without inserting a clause making the cession dependent upon Parliamentary approval."[41]

The Crown will occasionally, in its discretion, insert provisions in treaties making their entry into force conditional upon Parliamentary approval.[42] In 1924, the British Government announced the "Ponsonby Rule," as follows:

> "It is the intention of His Majesty's Government to lay on the Table of both Houses of Parliament every Treaty, when signed, for a period of 21 days, after which the Treaty will be ratified and published and circulated in the Treaty Series. In the case of important Treaties, the Government will, of course, take an opportunity of submitting them to the House for discussion within this period. ... But this means secret Treaties and secret clauses of Treaties will be rendered impossible. ... There are, of course, international conventions of a purely technical character which are not subject to ratification, and there is no reason to alter the procedure with regard to them."[43]

The rule does not affect the position in law. The laying of a treaty before Parliament before ratification is only "to enable Parliament to discuss treaties requiring ratification before ratification [occurs]," it is not legally required.[44]

The Rule has not been applied to the Declaration made by the United Kingdom accepting the compulsory jurisdiction of the International Court of Justice because there is no requirement of ratification.[45]

As of 1997, treaties laid before Parliament under the Ponsonby Rule have been accompanied by an explanatory memorandum which indicates the subject matter of the treaty, the reasons for becoming a party, the financial implications, any implementing legislation that will be required and what

---

[37] See generally, Blix, *Treaty-Making Power* (1960); Gowlland-Debbas, ed., *Multilateral Treaty Making* (2000); Holloway, *Modern Trends in Treaty Law* (1967); Jones, *Full Powers and Ratification* (1946). See also Leigh and Blakeslee, *National Treaty Law and Practice* (1995).

[38] On the status of treaties in municipal law, see above, Ch.3.

[39] See *R. v Secretary of State Ex p. Rees-Mogg* [1994] 1 All E.R. 457 CA.

[40] On the need, however, for parliamentary legislation if a treaty binding upon the UK in international law is to have effect in the municipal law of the UK, see above, pp.76 et seq.

[41] McNair, *Treaties*, p.97.

[42] See the examples given by McNair, pp.97–98.

[43] *Hansard*, HC, Vol.171, cols 2003–2004 (April 1, 1924).

[44] The UK Government is considering placing the Ponsonby Rule on a statutory footing: see the Ministry of Justice consultation paper, *The Governance of Britain—War Powers and Treaties: Limiting Executive Powers*, CP 26/07.

[45] *Hansard*, HC Vol.578, cols. 1145–1146 (November 27, 1957).

consultation has occurred and includes the text of any declarations and reservations made upon signature. Depending on their detail, explanatory memoranda may be relevant in the interpretation of a treaty.[46]

In 1996, a bill proposed by Lord Lester that would have required the approval of Parliament before the United Kingdom could become a party to a treaty was withdrawn.[47] Would such approval, which is required in many states and would be democratic, be desirable? Or might it slow down or prevent the United Kingdom becoming a party to some treaties?

The United States Constitution, art.II, s.2, states that the President "shall have power by and with the advice and consent of the Senate to make treaties, provided two-thirds of the Senators present concur. "The Senate has refused its consent for the ratification of some human rights treaties (e.g. the International Covenant on Economic, Social and Cultural Rights) submitted to it by the President. Distinct from "treaties" are "executive agreements." These are treaties in an international law sense but differ from "treaties" in United States constitutional law in that they are made by the President alone; they are not subject to approval by the United States Senate. There is no express provision for executive agreements in the Constitution; the power to make them is implied.[48]

B. The Treaty-Making Power in International Law[49]

MCNAIR, THE LAW OF TREATIES

2nd edn 1961, pp.15–21. Some footnotes omitted

The following are the forms in which treaties are usually cast . . .

(a) *Treaties in the form of agreements between states.* Instances of this practice can be found in . . . the Treaty of Versailles and other Peace Treaties which concluded the First World War . . .

(b) *Treaties in the form of agreements between heads of state,* which may perhaps be described as historically the oldest, and, in practice, the most orthodox, form in the case of treaties of an important character . . .

(c) *Agreements in the form of inter-governmental agreements.* This form is now becoming increasingly common, as a perusal of the United Nations Treaty Series will show. It is in keeping with the general tendency towards informality. For the United Kingdom it means that no intervention on the part of Her Majesty is required and no use of the Great Seal, and Full Powers are issued by the Secretary of State for Foreign Affairs under his own signature and seal of office. It has become the regular form for agreements made between the Commonwealth countries; its convenience in such cases is manifest. . . .

Most Exchanges of Notes, now very common, fall into the category of inter-governmental agreements. . . .

(d) *Agreements expressed as made between Departments, or ministers, or other subordinate organs or agencies of Governments.*

. . . These agreements are, generally speaking, arrangements which concern matters of private law rather than matters of an international legal character (e.g. arrangements for, or in connection with, the purchase of goods, or for the sale on a commercial basis of materials or supplies) and are not such as would be normally registrable under Article 102 of the Charter of the United Nations. . . .

It is. . .necessary in view of the complexity and variety of organs, central or local, through which functions of government (including sometimes commercial activities) are discharged in the modern State, to be alert to the difference between an organ or agency of the central Government and capable of binding it, on the one hand, and, on the other, an organ, whether local or not, which possesses a legal personality distinct from the State itself and has no such capacity. It is believed that it is true only of an organ or agency of the central Government to say that its agreements bind the State; but the precise relation of certain departments to the central Government varies greatly in different States, and every case requires separate consideration upon its facts.

---

[46] Dr Fox, Minister of State, F.C.O., *Hansard*, HL Vol.XX, W.A. 430 (December 16, 1996).

[47] For later bills introduced by Lord Lester, see above, 44, p.77.

[48] On the definition of executive agreements, see [1973] U.S. D.I.L. 185.

[49] See Parry (1950) 36 Trans.Grot.Soc. 149.

VIENNA CONVENTION ON THE LAW OF TREATIES 1969

See above, p.637, n.4

Article 7

1. A person is considered as representing a State for the purpose of adopting or authenticating the text of a treaty or for the purpose of expressing the consent of the State to be bound by a treaty if:

(a) he produces appropriate full powers[50]; or

(b) it appears from the practice of the States concerned or from other circumstances that their intention was to consider that person as representing the State for such purposes and to dispense with full powers.

2. In virtue of their functions and without having to produce full powers, the following are considered as representing their State:

(a) Heads of States, Heads of Government and Ministers for Foreign Affairs,[51] for the purpose of performing all acts relating to the conclusion of a treaty;

(b) heads of diplomatic missions, for the purpose of adopting the text of a treaty between the accrediting State and the State to which they are accredited;

(c) representatives accredited by States to an international conference or to an international organisation or one of its organs, for the purpose of adopting the text of a treaty in that conference, organisation or organ.

Note

The International Law Commission's Commentary reads:

"... the production of full powers is the fundamental safeguard to the representatives of the States concerned of each other's qualifications to represent their State for the purpose of performing the particular act in question;

... it is for the States to decide whether they may safely dispense with the production of full powers. In earlier times the production of full powers was almost invariably requested; and it is still common in the conclusion of more formal types of treaty. But a considerable proportion of modern treaties are concluded in simplified form, when more often than not the production of full powers is not required."[52]

Article 8

An act relating to the conclusion of a treaty performed by a person who cannot be considered under Article 7 as authorised to represent a State for that purpose is without legal effect unless afterwards confirmed by that State.

---

[50] Ed. The term "full powers" is defined in art.2(1)(c) of the Convention as "a document emanating from the competent authority of a State designating a person or persons to represent the State for negotiating, adopting or authenticating the text of a treaty, for expressing the consent of the State to be bound by a treaty, or for accomplishing any other act with respect to a treaty." Referring to art.7(1)(a), the ICJ stated that "(e)very head of state is presumed to be able to act on behalf of the he state in its international relations": *Genocide Convention (Bosnia and Herzegovina v Yugoslavia)* case *(Preliminary Objections)*, I.C.J. Rep. 1996, p.595 at 622.

[51] Ed. See the *Eastern Greenland* case, above p.746; *Land and Maritime Boundary between Cameroon and Nigeria*, I.C.J. Rep. 2002, p.303; and the *Armed Activities (New Application: 2002)* case, I.C.J. Rep. 2006, p.6.

[52] Y.B.I.L.C., 1966. II, p.193.

Note

The International Law Commissions's Commentary reads:

"Such cases [of acting without authority] are not, of course, likely to happen frequently, but instances have occurred. ... In 1951 a convention concerning the naming of cheeses concluded at Stresa was signed by a delegate on behalf of Norway and Sweden, whereas it appears that he had authority to do so only from the former country. In both these instances the treaty was subject to ratification and was in fact ratified. A further case, in which the same question may arise, and one more likely to occur in practice, is where an agent has authority to enter into a particular treaty, but goes beyond his full powers by accepting unauthorised extensions or modifications of it. An instance of such a case was Persia's attempt, in discussions in the Council of the League, to disavow the Treaty of Erzerum of 1847 on the ground that the Persian representative had gone beyond his authority in accepting a certain explanatory note when exchanging ratifications.
    ... Where there is no authority to enter into a treaty, it seems clear, on principle, that the State must be entitled to disavow the act of its representative, and the article so provides. On the other hand, it seems equally clear that, notwithstanding the representative's original lack of authority, the State may afterwards endorse his act and thereby establish its consent to be bound by the treaty. It will also be held to have done so by implication if it invokes the provisions of the treaty or otherwise acts in such a way as to appear to treat the act of its representative as effective."[53]

Article 9

1. The adoption of the text of a treaty takes place by the consent of all the States participating in its drawing up except as provided in paragraph 2.
2. The adoption of the text of a treaty at an international conference takes place by the vote of two-thirds of the States present and voting, unless by the same majority they shall decide to apply a different rule.

Note

The International Law Commission's Commentary reads:

"In former times the adoption of the text of a treaty almost always took place by the agreement of all the States participating in the negotiations and unanimity could be said to be the general rule. The growth of the practice of drawing up treaties in large international conferences or within international organisations has, however, led to so normal a use of the procedure of majority vote that, in the opinion of the Commission, it would be unrealistic to lay down unanimity as the general rule for the adoption of the texts of treaties drawn up at conferences or within organisations. Unanimity remains the general rule for bilateral treaties and for treaties drawn up between few States. But for other multilateral treaties a different general rule must be specified, although, of course, it will always be open to the States concerned to apply the rule of unanimity in a particular case if they should so decide. ...
    The Commission considered the further case of treaties like the Genocide Convention or the Convention on the Political Rights of Women, which are actually drawn up within an international organisation. Here, the voting rule for adopting the text of the treaty must clearly be the voting rule

---

[53] Y.B.I.L.C., 1966. II, p.194. See also art.46, below, p.687.

applicable in the particular organ in which the treaty is adopted. This case is, however, covered by the general provision in ... [art.5, Vienna Convention] regarding the application of the rules of an international organisation, and need not receive mention in the present article."[54]

On the attempt to adopt the 1982 Law of the Sea Convention by consensus, see above, p.323.

Article 11

The consent of a State to be bound by a treaty may be expressed by signature, exchange of instruments constituting a treaty, ratification, acceptance, approval or accession, or by any other means if so agreed.[55]

Article 12

1. The consent of a State to be bound by a treaty is expressed by the signature of its representative when:

(*a*) the treaty provides that signature shall have that effect;

(*b*) it is otherwise established that the negotiating States[56] were agreed that signature should have that effect[57]; or

(*c*) the intention of the State to give that effect to the signature appears from the full powers of its representative or was expressed during the negotiation.

2. For the purposes of paragraph 1:

(*a*) the initialling of a text constitutes a signature of the treaty when it is established that the negotiating States so agreed;

(*b*) the signature *ad referendum* of a treaty by a representative, if confirmed by his State, constitutes a full signature of the treaty.

Article 13

The consent of States to be bound by a treaty constituted by instruments exchanged between them is expressed by that exchange when:

(*a*) the instruments provide that their exchange shall have that effect; or

(*b*) it is otherwise established that those States were agreed that the exchange of instruments should have that effect.[58]

Article 14

1. The consent of a State to be bound by the treaty is expressed by ratification when:

(*a*) the treaty provides for such consent to be expressed by means of ratification;

(*b*) it is otherwise established that the negotiating States were agreed that ratification should be required;

---

[54] Y.B.I.L.C., 1966. II,

[55] Ed. art.2(1)(*b*) reads: "'ratification,' 'acceptance,' 'approval' and 'accession' mean in each case the international act so named whereby a State establishes on the international plane its consent to be bound by a treaty."

[56] Ed. art.2(1)(*e*) reads: "'negotiating State' means a State which took part in the drawing up and adoption of the text of the treaty."

[57] Ed. As in the *Land and Maritime Boundary between Cameroon and Nigeria* case, para.264, I.C.J. Rep. 2002, p.303.

[58] Ed. See Weinstein (1952) 29 B.Y.I.L. 205.

(c) the representative of the State has signed the treaty subject to ratification; or

(d) the intention of the State to sign the treaty subject to ratification appears from the full powers of its representative or was expressed during the negotiation.

2. The consent of a State to be bound by a treaty is expressed by acceptance or approval under conditions similar to those which apply to ratification.

Note

The International Law Commission's Commentary reads:

"The modern institution of ratification[59] in international law developed in the course of the nineteenth century. Earlier, ratification had been an essentially formal and limited act by which, after a treaty had been drawn up, a sovereign confirmed, or finally verified, the full powers previously issued to his representative to negotiate the treaty. It was then not an approval of the treaty itself but a confirmation that the representative had been invested with authority to negotiate it and, that being so, there was an obligation upon the sovereign to ratify his representative's full powers, if these had been in order. Ratification came, however, to be used in the majority of cases as the means of submitting the treaty-making power of the executive to parliamentary control, and ultimately the doctrine of ratification underwent a fundamental change. It was established that the treaty itself was subject to subsequent ratification by the State before it became binding. Furthermore, this development took place at a time when the great majority of international agreements were formal treaties. Not unnaturally, therefore, it came to be the opinion that the general rule is that ratification is necessary to render a treaty binding.

... Meanwhile, however, the expansion of intercourse between States, especially in economic and technical fields, led to an ever-increasing use of less formal types of international agreements, amongst which were exchanges of notes, and these agreements are usually intended by the parties to become binding by signature alone. On the other hand, an exchange of notes or other informal agreement, though employed for its ease and convenience, has sometimes expressly been made subject to ratification because of constitutional requirements in one or the other of the contracting States.

... The general result of these developments had been to complicate the law concerning the conditions under which treaties need ratification in order to make them binding. The controversy which surrounds the subject is, however, largely theoretical. The more formal types of instrument include, almost without exception, express provisions on the subject of ratification, and occasionally this is so even in the case of exchanges of notes or other instruments in simplified form. Moreover, whether they are of a formal or informal type, treaties normally either provide that the instrument shall be ratified or, by laying down that the treaty shall enter into force upon signature or upon a specified date or event, dispense with ratification. Total silence on the subject is exceptional, and the number of cases that remain to be covered by a general rule is very small. But, if the general rule is taken to be that ratification is necessary unless it is expressly or impliedly excluded, large exceptions qualifying a rule have to be inserted in order to bring it into accord with modern practice, with the result that the number of cases calling for the operation of the general rule is small. Indeed, the practical effect of choosing either that version of the general rule, or the opposite rule that ratification is unnecessary unless expressly agreed upon by the parties, is not very substantial ...

---

[59] Ed. On ratification, see Blix (1953) 30 B.Y.I.L. 352.

... Acceptance has become established in treaty practice during the past twenty years as a new procedure for becoming a party to treaties[60] ... on the international plane, 'acceptance' is an innovation which is more one of terminology than of method. If a treaty provides that it shall be open for signature 'subject to acceptance,' the process on the international plane is like 'signature subject to ratification' ...

... 'Signature subject to acceptance' was introduced into treaty practice principally in order to provide a simplified form of 'ratification' which would allow the government a further opportunity to examine the treaty when it is not necessarily obliged to submit it to a State's constitutional procedure for obtaining ratification. ...

... The observations in the preceding paragraph apply *mutatis mutandis* to 'approval,' whose introduction into the terminology of treaty-making is even more recent than that of 'acceptance.' "[61]

Article 15

The consent of a State to be bound by a treaty is expressed by accession when:

(*a*) the treaty provides that such consent may be expressed by that State by means of accession;

(*b*) it is otherwise established that the negotiating States were agreed that such consent may be expressed by that State by means of accession; or

(*c*) all the parties have subsequently agreed that such consent may be expressed by that State by means of accession.

Note

The International Law Commission's Commentary reads:

"Accession is the traditional method by which a State, in certain circumstances, becomes a party to a treaty of which it is not a signatory ...

Divergent opinions have been expressed in the past as to whether it is legally possible to accede to a treaty which is not yet in force and there is some support for the view that it is not possible. However, an examination of the most recent treaty practice shows that in practically all modern treaties which contain accession clauses the right to accede is made independent of the entry into force of the treaty, either expressly by allowing accession to take place before the date fixed for the entry into force of the treaty, or impliedly by making the entry into force of the treaty conditional on the deposit, inter alia, of instruments of accession."[62]

Article 16

Unless the treaty otherwise provides, instruments of ratification, acceptance, approval or accession establish the consent of a State to be bound by a treaty upon:

------

[60] Ed. See Liang (1950) 44 A.J.I.L. 333.
[61] Y.B.I.L.C., 1966, II, pp.197–198.
[62] Y.B.I.L.C., 1966, II, p.199.

(*a*) their exchange between the contracting States;

(*b*) their deposit with the depositary; or

(*c*) their notification to the contracting States or to the depositary, if so agreed.

Note

The International Law Commission's Commentary reads:

"The point of importance is the moment at which the consent to be bound is established and in operation with respect to contracting States. In the case of exchange of instruments there is no problem; it is the moment of exchange. In the case of the deposit of an instrument with a depositary, the problem arises whether the deposit by itself establishes the legal nexus between the depositing State and other contracting States or whether the legal nexus arises only upon their being informed by the depositary. The Commission considered that the existing general rule clearly is that the act of deposit by itself establishes the legal nexus."[63]

Article 18

A State is obliged to refrain from acts which would defeat the object and purpose of a treaty when:

(*a*) it has signed the treaty or has exchanged instruments constituting the treaty subject to ratification, acceptance or approval, until it shall have made its intention clear not to become a party to the treaty; or

(*b*) it has expressed its consent to be bound by the treaty, pending the entry into force of the treaty and provided that such entry into force is not unduly delayed.

Notes

1.   The International Law Commission's Commentary reads:

"That an obligation of good faith to refrain from acts calculated to frustrate the object of the treaty attaches to a State which has signed a treaty subject to ratification appears to be generally accepted."[64]

2.   The obligation under art.18 as a signatory to the Statute of the International Criminal Court ceased to exist for the US when it wrote to the UN Secretary General, as depositary, as follows[65]:

"This is to inform you ... that the United States does not intend to become a party to the ICC Statute. .... Accordingly, the United States has no legal obligations arising from its signature on December 31 2000. The United States requests that its intention not to become a party ... be reflected in the depositary's status lists relating to this treaty."

---

[63] Y.B.I.L.C., 1966, II, p.201.
[64] Y.B.I.L.C., 1966, II, p.202. On art.18, see Charme (1991) 25 Geo. Wash. J.I.L.E. 71; and Rogoff (1980) 32 Maine L.R. 263.
[65] US Department of State Press Statement, May 6, 2002.

C. Reservations[66]

VIENNA CONVENTION ON THE LAW OF TREATIES 1969

See above, p.637, n.4

Article 2

1. ... (d) "Reservation" means a unilateral statement, however phrased or named, made by a State, when signing, ratifying, accepting, approving or acceding to a treaty, where it purports to exclude or to modify the legal effect of certain provisions of the treaty in their application to that State.

Article 19

A State may, when signing, ratifying, accepting, approving, or acceding to a treaty, formulate a reservation unless:

(a) the reservation is prohibited by the treaty;

(b) the treaty provides that only specified reservations, which do not include the reservation in question, may be made; or

(c) in cases not falling under sub-paragraphs (a) and (b), the reservation is incompatible with the object and purpose of the treaty.

Article 20

1. A reservation expressly authorised by a treaty does not require any subsequent acceptance by the other contracting States unless the treaty so provides.

2. When it appears from the limited number of the negotiating States and the object and purpose of a treaty that the application of the treaty in its entirety between all the parties is an essential condition of the consent of each one to be bound by the treaty, a reservation requires acceptance by all the parties.

3. When a treaty is a constituent instrument of an international organisation and unless it otherwise provides, a reservation requires the acceptance of the competent organ of that organisation.

4. In cases not falling under the preceding paragraphs and unless the treaty otherwise provides:

(a) acceptance by another contracting State of a reservation constitutes the reserving State a party to the treaty in relation to that other State if or when the treaty is in force for those States;

(b) an objection by another contracting State to a reservation does not preclude the entry into force of the treaty as between the objecting and reserving States unless a contrary intention is definitely expressed by the objecting State;

(c) an act expressing a State's consent to be bound by the treaty and containing a reservation is effective as soon as at least one other contracting State has accepted the reservation.

5. For the purposes of paragraphs 2 and 4 and unless the treaty otherwise provides, a reservation is considered to have been accepted by a State if it shall have raised no objection to the reservation by the end of a period of

---

[66] See Bowett (1976–7) 48 B.Y.I.L. 67; Gaja in *Le droit international a l'heure de sa codification: etudes en l'honneur de Robert Ago*, Vol.I (1987), p.310; Greig (1995) 16 A.Y.I.L. 21; Horn, *Reservations and Interpretative Declarations to Multilateral Treaties* (1988); Piper (1985) 71 Iowa L.R. 295; Redgwell (1993) 64 B.Y.I.L. 245; Ruda (1975–III) 146 Hague Recueil 95; Tomuschat (1967) 27 Z.A.O.R.V. 463; Ziemele, ed., *Reservations to Human Rights Treaties and the Vienna Convention Regime* (2004).The ILC is preparing a set of draft guidelines on reservations to treaties with commentaries which is intended to assist states and international organisations in their practice. The guidelines are not intended to replace the reservations provisions of the Vienna Convention. For the fourteen Reports of the Special Rapporteur (M. Pellet) and the draft guidelines provisionally adopted to date, see the ILC annual reports, G.A.O.R., A/50/10 onwards.

twelve months after it was notified of the reservation or by the date on which it expressed its consent to be bound by the treaty, whichever is later.

Article 21

1. A reservation established with regard to another party in accordance with articles 19, 20 and 23:

(a) modifies for the reserving State in its relations with that other party the provisions of the treaty to which the reservation relates to the extent of the reservation; and

(b) modifies those provisions to the same extent for that other party in its relations with the reserving State.

2. The reservation does not modify the provisions of the treaty for the other parties to the treaty inter se.

3. When a State objecting to a reservation has not opposed the entry into force of the treaty between itself and the reserving State, the provisions to which the reservation relates do not apply as between the two States to the extent of the reservation.

Article 22

1. Unless the treaty otherwise provides, a reservation may be withdrawn at any time and the consent of a State which has accepted the reservation is not required for its withdrawal.

2. Unless the treaty otherwise provides, an objection to a reservation may be withdrawn at any time.

3. Unless the treaty otherwise provides, or it is otherwise agreed:

(a) the withdrawal of a reservation becomes operative in relation to another contracting State only when notice of it has been received by that State;[67]

(b) the withdrawal of an objection to a reservation becomes operative only when notice of it has been received by the State which formulated the reservation.

Article 23

1. A reservation, an express acceptance of a reservation and an objection to a reservation must be formulated in writing and communicated to the contracting States and other States entitled to become parties to the treaty.

2. If formulated when signing the treaty subject to ratification, acceptance or approval, a reservation must be formally confirmed by the reserving State when expressing its consent to be bound by the treaty. In such a case the reservation shall be considered as having been made on the date of its confirmation.

3. An express acceptance of, or an objection to, a reservation made previously to confirmation of the reservation does not itself require confirmation.

4. The withdrawal of a reservation or of an objection to a reservation must be formulated in writing.

Notes

1. The problems tackled in arts 19–23, Vienna Convention, concern only multilateral treaties. In the case of a bilateral treaty, a proposed reservation is, in effect, a counter offer which the other party can accept or reject. With regard to multilateral treaties, problems mainly arise where, as is often the case, the treaty does not have a reservations clause indicating what kinds of reservations are permitted or prohibited. In the absence of such a clause under art.19(c) the reservation is valid unless it is "incompatible with the object and purpose of the treaty". The "object and purpose" test is a very vague one which has proved very difficult to apply. Other questions that have become more important as the size of the international community has increased are whether a

---

[67] In the *Armed Activities (New Application: 2002)* case, I.C.J. Rep. 2006, p.6, although Rwanda had enacted a law that seemingly withdrew its reservations to all treaties, the withdrawal had not become operative as no action had been taken, particularly through the UN depository, to notify other states, as art.22(3) required.

reservation has to be accepted by all of the parties to be valid and, if not, what is the treaty relationship between a party that makes a reservation and one that objects to it. On these questions, in the inter-war years the League of Nations, holding to the classical doctrine, maintained that acceptance by all of the parties was required,[68] thus emphasising the integrity of the treaty, but the Pan American Union maintained that it was not.[69]

In a case that addressed these questions, in the *Reservations to the Convention on Genocide* case,[70] the ICJ advised as follows:

"the Court is of opinion,

in so far as concerns the Convention on the Prevention and Punishment of the Crime of Genocide,[71] in the event of a State ratifying or acceding to the Convention subject to a reservation made either on ratification or on accession, or on signature followed by ratification,

On Question I:

by seven votes to five,

that a State which has made and maintained a reservation which has been objected to by one or more of the parties to the Convention but not by others, can be regarded as being a party to the Convention if the reservation is compatible with the object and purpose of the Convention; otherwise, that State cannot be regarded as being a party to the Convention.

On Question II:

by seven votes to five,

(*a*) that if a party to the Convention objects to a reservation which it considers to be incompatible with the object and purpose of the Convention, it can in fact consider that the reserving State is not a party to the Convention;

(*b*) that if, on the other hand, a party accepts the reservation as being compatible with the object and purpose of the Convention, it can in fact consider that the reserving State is a party to the Convention.

On Question III:

by seven votes to five,

(*a*) that an objection to a reservation made by a signatory State which has not yet ratified the Convention can have the legal effect indicated in the reply to Question I only upon ratification. Until that moment it merely serves as a notice to the other State of the eventual attitude of the signatory State;

(*b*) that an objection to a reservation made by a State which is entitled to sign or accede but which has not yet done so, is without legal effect."

Clearly the Court preferred the Pan-American Union approach. In a joint dissenting judgment, Judges Guerrero, Sir Arnold McNair, Read and Hsu Mo considered that the League of Nations approach was consistent with customary international law.

2.   Basically, the Vienna Convention follows the Pan-American Union approach too. It substantially incorporates the International Law Commission's Draft Articles, except for art.20(4)(b), Vienna Convention. The Commission had proposed, partly to discourage reservations, that an objection

---

[68]   Report of the L.N. Committee of Experts for the Progressive Codification of International Law (1927) 8 L.N.O.J. 880 at 881.

[69]   *Reservations to Multilateral Conventions*, UN Doc. A/1372, p.11. The 1932 PAU approach has been changed by a new set of O.A.S. standards in line with the Vienna Convention on the Law of Treaties: [1973] U.S. D.I.L. 179.

[70]   I.C.J. Rep. 1951, p.15. Advisory Opinion.

[71]   Ed. Note that the Genocide Convention has no reservation clause.

would preclude entry into force of a treaty between the two states concerned unless a contrary intention were expressed by the objecting state.[72] At the suggestion of the USSR, which argued for complete freedom for states to make reservations, the contrary approach was adopted at Vienna.[73] The United Kingdom Government regards the Convention rules as stating custom.[74]

3. In its Commentary to its Draft Articles, the International Law Commission stated:

> "What is essential to ensure both the effectiveness and the integrity of the treaty is that a sufficient number of States should become parties to it, accepting the great bulk of its provisions. ... But when today the number of the negotiating States may be upwards of one hundred States with very diverse cultural, economic and political conditions, it seems necessary to assume that the power to make reservations without the risk of being totally excluded by the objection of one or even of a few States may be a factor in promoting a more general acceptance of multilateral treaties. Moreover, the failure of negotiating States to take the necessary steps to become parties to multilateral treaties appears a greater obstacle to the development of international law through the medium of treaties than the possibility that the integrity of such treaties may be unduly weakened by the liberal admission of reserving States as parties to them. The Commission also considered that, in the present era of change and of challenge to traditional concepts, the rule calculated to promote the widest possible acceptance of whatever measure of common agreement can be achieved and expressed in a multilateral treaty may be the one most suited to the immediate needs of the international community."[75]

4. The reservations to the Genocide Convention that led to the *Reservations* case were those made by a number of states not accepting art.9 of the Convention which provides for the compulsory jurisdiction of the ICJ in disputes arising under the Convention.[76] In the *Armed Activities (New Application: 2002)* case,[77] the DRC made an application to the ICJ against Rwanda alleging genocide in breach of the Genocide Convention, to which both states were parties, arising out of acts of armed aggression by Rwandan forces on DRC territory. Faced with an art.9 reservation by Rwanda, the DRC argued, inter alia, that the reservation was invalid because it prevented the ICJ from ruling on an alleged breach of a rule of ius cogens. The ICJ rejected this argument:

> "64. The Court will begin by reaffirming that 'the principles underlying the [Genocide] Convention are principles which are recognized by civilized nations as binding on States, even without any conventional obligation' and that a consequence of that conception is 'the universal character both of the condemnation of genocide and of the co-operation required "in order to liberate mankind from such an odious scourge" (Preamble to the Convention)' [*Reservations* case, p.23]. ... It follows that 'the rights and obligations enshrined by the Convention are rights[78] and obligations erga omnes' [*Genocide Convention ... (Bosnia and*

---

[72] Draft Articles. Art.17(4)(*b*).

[73] See *Treaty Conference Records*, 1969, pp.30–35.

[74] Dept. of Trade Memorandum to the House of Commons Select Committee on European Legislation 1978, printed in 1978 U.K.M.I.L., (1978) 49 B.Y.I.L. 378. The European Commission on Human Rights took the same view: *Temeltasch* case (1983) 5 E.H.R.R. 417 at 432.

[75] Y.B.I.L.C., 1966, II, pp.205–206. See Boyle (1980) 29 I.C.L.Q. 498.

[76] For the texts of these reservations and objections to them, see UN Doc ST/LEG/SER.E/15.

[77] I.C.J. Rep. 2006, p.6, at pp.26–28. On the *ius cogens* aspect of the case, see below, p.696.

[78] Ed. As Thirlway, in Evans, *International Law* (2nd edn 2006), at p.138, notes "rights *era omnes*" is inaccurate; obligations *erga omnes* gives rise to rights *omnium* (of all).

Herzegovina v. Yugoslavia case*), Preliminary Objections, Judgment, I.C.J. Rep. 1996 (II)*, p.616, para.31]. . .

The Court observes, however,. . .that 'the erga omnes character of a norm and the rule of consent to jurisdiction are two different things' (*East Timor (Portugal v. Australia, Judgment, I.C.J. Rep. 1995*, p.102, para.29), and that the mere fact that rights and obligations erga omnes may be at issue in a dispute would not give the Court jurisdiction to entertain that dispute.

The same applies to the relationship between peremptory norms of general international law *(jus cogens)* and the establishment of the Court's jurisdiction: the fact that a dispute relates to compliance with a norm having such a character, which is assuredly the case with regard to the prohibition of genocide, cannot of itself provide a basis for the jurisdiction of the Court to entertain that dispute. Under the Court's Statute that jurisdiction is always based on the consent of the parties. . . .

66. The Court notes. . .that it has already found that reservations are not prohibited under the Genocide Convention [*Reservations* case]. . .Thus, in the view of the Court, a reservation under the Genocide Convention would be permissible to the extent that such reservation is not incompatible with the object and purpose of the Convention.

67. Rwanda's reservation to Article IX of the Genocide Convention bears on the jurisdiction of the Court, and does not affect substantive obligations relating to acts of genocide them-selves under that Convention. In the circumstances of the present case, the Court cannot conclude that the reservation of Rwanda in question, which is meant to exclude a particular method of settling a dispute relating to the interpretation, application or fulfilment of the Convention, is to be regarded as being incompatible with the object and purpose of the Convention.

68. In fact, the Court has already had occasion in the past to give effect to such reservations to Article IX of the Convention (see *Legality of Use of Force (Yugoslavia v. Spain), Provisional Measures Order of 2 June 1999, I.C.J. Reports 1999*, p.772, paras.32–33 . . .). The Court further notes that, as a matter of the law of treaties, when Rwanda acceded to the Genocide Con-vention and made the reservation in question, the DRC made no objection to it.

69. In so far as the DRC contended further that Rwanda's reservation is in conflict with a peremptory norm of general international law, it suffices for the Court to note that no such norm presently exists requiring a State to consent to the jurisdiction of the Court in order to settle a dispute relating to the Genocide Convention. Rwanda's reservation cannot therefore, on such grounds, be regarded as lacking legal effect."

While not dissenting from the Court's ruling, Judges Higgins, Kooijmans, Elaraby, Owada and Simma suggested in their Joint Separate Opinion that the validity of reservations to art.9 was a matter that the Court should revisit:

"25. It is a matter for serious concern that at the beginning of the twenty-first century it is still for States to choose whether they consent to the Court adjudicating claims that they have committed genocide. It must be regarded as a very grave matter that a State should be in a position to shield from international judicial scrutiny any claim that might be made against it concerning genocide. . ., one of the greatest crimes known.

26. Judicial settlement of claims relating to genocide is highly desirable. At the same time, it cannot be said that the entire scheme of the Genocide Convention would necessarily collapse if some States make reservations to Article IX. Were is so, adherence to the jur-isdiction of the Court could have been made compulsory, as is now the case as regards the

European Convention on Human Rights in relation to the European Court of Human Rights. The International Court in 1951 held that no prohibition against reservations was to be inferred from the silence in the Genocide Convention itself. Further, it did so fully aware that the reservations in question in fact related to Article IX. In that context it may be recalled that the Convention defines Genocide (Article II), and identifies acts that 'shall be punishable' (Article III). Articles IV to VII concern measures to be undertaken by States to punish persons charged with genocide, primarily by enacting legislation within their own territory. There is also reference to trial by 'such international penal tribunal as may have jurisdiction with respect to those Contracting Parties which shall have accepted its jurisdiction'. The International Court of Justice is clearly not the penal tribunal envisaged to try and punish individuals.

27. No doubt these are the considerations that the Court has had in mind in it findings, thus far, that a reservation to Article IX is not incompatible with the objects and purposes of the Convention.

28. There are other elements, however, that continue to concern us. While the Court is not a monitoring body under a treaty in the normal sense of that term (that is to say, it does not receive obligatory reports from States upon which it examines them for compliance), it nonetheless does have an important role under the Genocide Convention. Under that Convention it is States who are the monitors of each other's compliance with prohibition on genocide. Article IX then gives a State who believes another State is committing genocide the chance to come to the Court. Article IX speaks not only of disputes over the interpretation and application of the Convention, but over the 'fulfilment of the Convention'. Further, the disputes that may be referred to the Court under Article IX 'include those relating to the responsibility of a State for genocide'.

29. It is thus not self-evident that a reservation to Article IX could not be regarded as incompatible with the object and purpose of the Convention and we believe that this is a matter that the Court should revisit for further consideration."

Are the arguments in the Separate Opinion persuasive? Why did the five judges not dissent?

5. For an example of a treaty provision prohibiting a certain kind of reservation, see art.64 of the European Convention on Human Rights 1950.[79] An unusual example of a treaty provision that expressly authorises a certain kind of reservation (art.20(1)) is art.75, American Convention on Human Rights 1969, which provides that the Convention "shall be subject to reservations only in conformity with" the Vienna Convention on the Law of Treaties. In the *Effect of Reservations* case,[80] the Inter-American Court of Human Rights concluded that art.75 incorporated by reference art.19(c), Vienna Convention and thereby expressly permitted reservations that are not "incompatible with the object and purpose" of the American Convention. Note also the "mathematical" test used in art.20 of the Racial Discrimination Convention for determining whether a reservation is incompatible with its "object and purpose."[81]

6. In the *Restrictions to the Death Penalty* case,[82] Guatemala had made a reservation to the guarantee of the right to life in the American Convention on Human Rights 1969, art.4, by which

---

[79] See the *Belilos* case, below, p.659.

[80] (1981) 22 I.L.M. 37 at 44.

[81] Article 20 states that a reservation is "incompatible" if at least two-thirds of the contracting parties object to it. This is a requirement that is unlikely to be met. It was not met in the *Armed Activities (New Application: 2002)* case, I.C.J. Rep. 2006, p.6, at p.35, para.77.

[82] (1984) 23 I.L.M. 320 at 341. See also *Boyce v Barbados* (2007) I.H.R.R. 435. The American Convention art.75, states that reservations to it are permitted if they are "in conformity" with the Vienna Convention.

it did not accept that guarantee's prohibition of the death penalty for "common crimes" (e.g. robbery) related to political offences. This raised the question whether a reservation to a non-derogable human rights treaty provision was permissible. On the question whether such a reservation was impermissible as being contrary to the "object and purpose" of the Convention, the American Court of Human Rights stated:

"Article 27 of the Convention allows the States Parties to suspend, in time of war, public danger, or other emergency that threatens their independence or security, the obligations they assumed by ratifying the Convention, provided that in doing so they do not suspend or derogate from certain basic or essential rights, among them the right to life guaranteed by Article 4. It would follow therefrom that a reservation which was designed to enable a State to suspend any of the non-derogable fundamental rights must be deemed to be incompatible with the object and purpose of the Convention and, consequently, not permitted by it. The situation would be different if the reservation sought merely to restrict certain aspects of a non-derogable right without depriving the right as a whole of its basic purpose. Since the reservation referred to by the Commission in its submission does not appear to be of a type that is designed to deny the right to life as such, the Court concludes that to that extent it can be considered, in principle, as not being incompatible with the object and purpose of the Convention."

On the rules governing the interpretation of reservations, the Court stated that since reservations became "an integral part" of a treaty by modifying or excluding its effect, they "must of necessity therefore also be interpreted by reference to relevant principles of general international law and the special rules set out in the Convention itself."[83]

7.   In the *English Channel Arbitration*,[84] France had made reservations to art.6, Continental Shelf Convention 1958 to which the United Kingdom had objected. As to the effect of these reservations and objections on the treaty relations under the Convention between the two parties, the Court of Arbitration stated:

"61. . . . the effect of the rejection [by the U.K.] may properly, in the view of the Court, be said to render the reservations non-opposable to the United Kingdom. Just as the effect of the French reservations is to prevent the United Kingdom from invoking the provisions of Article 6 except on the basis of the conditions stated in the reservations, so the effect of their rejection is to prevent the French Republic from imposing the reservations on the United Kingdom for the purpose of invoking against it as binding a delimitation made on the basis of the conditions contained in the reservations. Thus, the combined effect of the French reservations and their rejection by the United Kingdom is neither to render Article 6 inapplicable *in toto*, as the French Republic contends, nor to render it applicable *in toto*, as the United Kingdom primarily contends. It is to render the Article inapplicable as between the two countries to the extent, but only to the extent, of the reservations; and this is precisely the effect envisaged in such cases by Article 21, paragraph 3 of the Vienna Convention on the Law of Treaties and the effect indicated by the principle of mutuality of consent.

62. The fact that Article 6 is not applicable as between the Parties to the extent that it is

---

83   (1984) 23 I.L.M. 320 at p.341.
84   (1979) 18 I.L.M. 397 at 419. See also the *Legality of Use of Force (Yugoslavia v US)* case, Provisional Measures, June 2, 1999, I.C.J. Rep. 1999, p.916 at 924.

excluded by the French reservations does not mean that there are no legal rules to govern the delimitation of the boundary in areas where the reservation operates. On the contrary, as the International Court of Justice observed in the *North Sea Continental Shelf* cases, 'there are still rules and principles of law to be applied' (I.C.J. Rep. 1969, paragraph 83); and these are the rules and principles governing delimitation of the continental shelf in general international law."

8. An example of the operation of the principle of reciprocity in art.21(1), Vienna Convention is found in the facts of the *Libyan People's Bureau Incident*[85] in respect of the Libyan reservation to the Vienna Convention on Diplomatic Relations permitting it to open a diplomatic bag if it entertained strong doubts as to the legitimacy of its contents. In accordance with art.21(1)(*b*), Vienna Convention, the obligation in that Convention not to open another state's diplomatic bag was modified to the extent of the reservation and would not have prevented the United Kingdom opening the Libyan bag. Thus Sir John Freeland explained to the Foreign Affairs Committee[86]:

    "The fact of the matter is that the Law of Treaties Convention, which in this respect reflects customary international law, provides that where a State has established a reservation against another party, and that was the case with Libya as against the United Kingdom since we did not object, that reservation qualifies the obligation to which it is addressed for both of them. So, without more ado, we would have had the ability to respond."

9. Suppose that states A, B and C make a treaty by which they undertake to develop a new aeroplane and the treaty provides that "development costs will be shared by the contracting parties equally." The treaty has no provision on reservations. D accedes to the treaty but makes its accession subject to the reservation that it will not regard itself as bound if its share of the costs of the venture rises above a stated level. A objects to this reservation but does not say that the treaty has no effect between A and D; B expressly accepts the reservation; C makes no response. Is D a party to the treaty according to the Vienna Convention? If so, what are its relations with A, B and C? Who decides these questions?

BELILOS v SWITZERLAND[87]

E. ct. H.R., Series A, Vol.132; 10 EHRR 466. Judgment of April 20, 1988

The applicant claimed that she had not been given a fair trial in accordance with art.6, European Convention on Human Rights when she was convicted of a criminal offence by a municipal Police Board in Switzerland. Switzerland entered a preliminary objection to the effect that the case fell within the scope of an "interpretative declaration" concerning art.6 which it had made upon ratification and which, in its view, was a valid reservation under art.64 of the Convention. On ratification,

---

[85] Above, p.307.
[86] Foreign Affairs Committee Report, above, p.358, n.92, p.xxxi.
[87] See Bourguignon (1989) 29 Virg. J.I.L. 347; Cameron and Horn (1990) 33 G.Y.I.L. 69; McDonald (1988) 21 R.B.D.I. 429; Marks (1990) 39 I.C.L.Q. 300. See also the *Temeltasch* case above, p.655.

Switzerland had made what it described as two "interpretative declarations," including the one in issue, and two "reservations." In the following extract, the Court considered whether the art.6 "interpretative declaration"[88] was, despite its title, a reservation to which art.64 could apply.[89]

Judgment of the Court

41. The Commission ... reached the conclusion that the declaration was a mere interpretative declaration which did not have the effect of a reservation; it based its view both on the wording of the declaration and on the preparatory work. ... More generally, the Commission considered that if a State made both reservations and interpretative declarations at the same time, the latter could only exceptionally be equated with the former.

42. In the Government's submission, on the other hand, the declaration was a "qualified" interpretative declaration. It consequently was in the nature of a reservation within the meaning of Article 2(1)(d) of the Vienna Convention on the Law of Treaties ...

The Court considered a number of Government arguments in support of this submission, including the following:

44. Another factor, in the Government's submission, was the wording used in the declaration which clearly had a restrictive character.

The Court acknowledges that the wording of the original French text of the declaration, though not altogether clear, can be understood as constituting a reservation. ...

47. The Government derived an additional argument from the fact that there had been no reaction from the Secretary General of the Council of Europe or from the States Parties to the Convention. ... The Swiss Government inferred that it could in good faith take the declaration as having been tacitly accepted for the purposes of Article 64.

The Court does not agree with that analysis. The silence of the depository and the Contracting States does not deprive the Convention institutions of the power to make their own assessment. ...

48. ... Like the Commission and the Government, the Court recognises that it is necessary to ascertain the original intention of those who drafted the declaration. In its view, the documents show that Switzerland originally contemplated making a formal reservation but subsequently opted for the term "declaration." Although the documents do not make the reasons for the change of nomenclature entirely clear, they do show that the Federal Council has always been concerned to avoid the consequences which a broad view of the right of access to the courts ... would have for the system of public administration and of justice in the cantons and consequently to put forward the declaration as qualifying Switzerland's consent to be bound by the Convention.

49. The question whether a declaration described as "interpretative" must be regarded as a "reservation" is a difficult one, particularly—in the instant case—because the Swiss Government has made both "reservations" and "interpretative declarations" in the same instrument of ratification. More generally, the Court recognises the great importance, rightly emphasised by the Government, of the legal rules applicable to reservations and interpretative declarations made by States Parties to the Convention. Only reservations are mentioned in the Convention, but several States have also (or only) made interpretative declarations, without always making a clear distinction between the two.

In order to establish the legal character of such a declaration, one must look behind the title given to it and seek to determine the substantive content. In the present case, it appears that Switzerland meant to remove certain categories of proceedings from the ambit of Article 6(1) and to secure itself against an interpretation of that Article which it considered to be too broad. However, the court must see to it that the obligations arising under the Convention are not subject to restrictions which would not satisfy the requirements of Article 64 as regards reservations. Accordingly, it will examine the validity of the interpretative declaration in question, as in the case of a reservation, in the context of this provision.

---

[88] The "interpretative declaration" read: "The Swiss Federal Council considers that the guarantee of fair trial in Article 6(1) of the Convention, in the determination of civil rights and obligations or any criminal charge against the person in question is intended solely to ensure ultimate control by the judiciary over the acts or decisions of the public authorities relating to such rights or obligations or the determination of such a charge."

[89] Article 64(1) permits reservations other than those "of a general character."

The Court then held that the Swiss reservation was invalid because (i) it was a reservation of a "general character" (i.e. one that was "couched in terms that are too vague or broad for it to be possible to determine their exact scope or meaning") and so prohibited by art.64(1) and (ii) it had not been accompanied by a "brief statement of the laws concerned" (i.e. those that were incompatible with the Convention necessitating the reservation) as required by art.64(2), this being "not a purely formal requirement but a condition of substance."

60. In short, the declaration in question does not satisfy two of the requirements of Article 64 of the Convention, with the result that it must be held to be invalid. At the same time, it is beyond doubt that Switzerland is, and regards itself as, bound by the Convention irrespective of the validity of the declaration. Moreover, the Swiss Government recognised the Court's competence to determine the latter issue, which it argued before it. The Government's preliminary objection must therefore be rejected.

The Court upheld the applicant's claim that art.6 had been infringed on the facts of the case.

Notes

1.   The *Belilos* case mainly concerned the distinction between reservations and interpretative declarations. As to the latter, the Court adopted McRae's classification of "mere interpretative declarations" and "qualified interpretative declarations." McRae states[90]:

> "The legal effect of an interpretative declaration depends initially upon whether the declarant seeks only to offer an interpretation of the treaty that may be found subsequently to be incorrect (a "mere interpretative declaration"), or whether the declarant purports to make its acceptance of the provision in question conditional upon acquiescence in that interpretation (a "qualified interpretative declaration"). The significance of the former lies in the effect it may have in subsequent proceedings to interpret the treaty, and this significance will vary according to whether the declaration has been accepted, ignored or objected to by other contracting parties. The latter type of interpretative declaration, on the other hand, must be assimilated to a reservation, for by asserting that its interpretation overrides any contrary interpretation the declarant has purported to exclude or to modify the terms of the treaty. Hence the legal consequences that attach to reservations ought to apply to "qualified interpretative declarations. . . .
>
> The safest course for a state that is opposed to an interpretative declaration attached to another contracting party's instrument of acceptance is formally to object to it. The objecting state is protected should the declaration turn out to be a "qualified interpretative declaration", and the objection serves to diminish the effect the declaration might have, as a "mere interpretative declaration", upon the interpretation of the treaty."

The Court's approach underlines the wisdom of McRae's suggestion that a state opposed to an "interpretative declaration" should object to it in case it proves to be a reservation. Is it consistent with the need for certainty in international relations that a state may submit at the same time texts described as "interpretative declarations" and "reservations" and later be able to claim that one of the former is really a "reservation" after all? Note that under art.2(1)(d), a statement may

---

[90] (1978) 49 B.Y.I.L. 155 at 172–173. See also Nelson (2001) 50 I.C.L.Q. 767. And see the *Maritime Delimitation in the Black Sea* case, above, p.405, para.42.

be a reservation "however phrased or named", but that for an "interpretative declaration" to qualify as a reservation it must be made on one of the occasions specified in art.2(1)(d).

2.   *Effect of invalidity.* Another aspect of the case was the legal effect of the Court's determination that the Swiss reservation was inconsistent with art.64 and hence invalid. The Court took the view that Switzerland was fully bound by the Convention without the benefit of the reservation. It did not draw an analogy with the situation where a valid reservation is subject to an objection and art.21(3), Vienna Convention, above, p.653 applies, so that Switzerland would not have been bound by art.6 to the extent of its reservation. Another approach might have been prompted by Judge Lauterpacht's opinion in the *Norwegian Loans* case, below, p.856, in respect of invalid reservations to optional clause declarations. The Court might, that is, have considered whether the reservation was fundamental to Switzerland's acceptance of the Convention: if it was, the reservation would not have been severed and Switzerland's ratification of the Convention as a whole would have been invalid. Is the Court's judgment consistent with the ICJ's response to Question I in the *Reservations* case, above, p.811?[91] Is the Court's decision limited to the situation where, as on the facts (see judgment, para.60), the state concerned does not question the continued application of the treaty in the absence of the reservation?

GENERAL COMMENT 24 ON RESERVATIONS TO THE INTERNATIONAL COVENANT ON CIVIL AND POLITICAL RIGHTS[92]

Human Rights Committee, 1994. (1995) 15 H.R.L.J. 464; (1995) 2 I.H.R.R. 10

1. As of 1 November 1994, 46 of the 127 States parties to the International Covenant on Civil and Political Rights had, between them, entered 150 reservations of varying significance to their acceptance of the obligations of the Covenant. ... The number of reservations, their content and their scope may undermine the effective implementation of the Covenant and tend to weaken respect for the obligations of States parties. It is important for States parties to know exactly what obligations they, and other States parties, have in fact undertaken. ... This will require a determination as to whether a unilateral statement is a reservation or an interpretative declaration and a determination of its acceptability and effects. ...

4. The possibility of entering reservations may encourage States which consider that they have difficulties in guaranteeing all the rights in the Covenant nonetheless to accept the generality of obligations in that instrument. Reservations may serve a useful function to enable States to adapt specific elements in their laws to the inherent rights of each person as articulated in the Covenant. However, it is desirable in principle that States accept the full range of obligations, because the human rights norms are the legal expression of the essential rights that every person is entitled to as a human being.

5. The Covenant neither prohibits reservations nor mentions any type of permitted reservation. The same is true of the first Optional Protocol. ...

6. The absence of a prohibition on reservations does not mean that any reservation is permitted. ... Article 19(c) of the Vienna Convention on the Law of Treaties provides relevant guidance.[93] ...

7. In an instrument which articulates very many civil and political rights, each of the many articles, and indeed their interplay, secures the objectives of the Covenant. The object and purpose of the Covenant is to create legally binding standards for human rights by defining certain civil and political rights and placing them in a

---

[91]   On this and the effect of invalidity generally, see Marks, above, p.8, n.87. In *Loizidou v Turkey*, E. Ct. H.R.Rep. A310 (1995) a reservation to a declaration accepting jurisdiction was severed. For the HRC approach, see the *Kennedy* case, below, p.667.

[92]   See Redgwell (1997) 46 I.C.L.Q. 390.

[93]   Ed. See above, p.652. Although the Vienna Convention on the Law of Treaties was concluded in 1969 and entered into force in 1980—i.e. after the entry into force of the Covenant—its terms reflect the general international law on this matter as had already been affirmed by the International Court of Justice in *The Reservations to the Genocide Convention* case of 1951.

framework of obligations which are legally binding for those States which ratify; and to provide an efficacious supervisory machinery for the obligations undertaken.

8. Reservations that offend peremptory norms would not be compatible with the object and purpose of the Covenant. Although treaties that are mere exchanges of obligations between States allow them to reserve inter se application of rules of general international law, it is otherwise in human rights treaties, which are for the benefit of persons within their jurisdiction. Accordingly, provisions in the Covenant that represent customary international law (and *a fortiori* when they have the character of peremptory norms) may not be the subject of reservations. Accordingly, a State may not reserve the right to engage in slavery, to torture, to subject persons to cruel, inhuman or degrading treatment or punishment, to arbitrarily deprive persons of their lives, to arbitrarily arrest and detain persons, to deny freedom of thought, conscience and religion, to presume a person guilty unless he proves his innocence, to execute pregnant women or children, to permit the advocacy of national, racial or religious hatred, to deny to persons of marriageable age the right to marry, or to deny to minorities the right to enjoy their own culture, profess their own religion, or use their own language. And while reservations to particular clauses of Article 14 may be acceptable, a general reservation to the right to a fair trial would not be.

9. Applying more generally the object and purpose test to the Covenant, the Committee notes that, for example, a reservation to Article 1 denying peoples the right to determine their own political status and to pursue their economic, social and cultural development, would be incompatible with the object and purpose of the Covenant. Equally, a reservation to the obligation to respect and ensure the rights, and to do so on a non-discriminatory basis (Article 2(1)) would not be acceptable. Nor may a State reserve an entitlement not to take the necessary steps at the domestic level to give effect to the rights of the Covenant (Article 2(2)).

10. ... it falls for consideration as to whether reservations to the non-derogable provisions of the Covenant are compatible with its object and purpose. While there is no hierarchy of importance of rights under the Covenant, the operation of certain rights may not be suspended, even in times of national emergency. This underlines the great importance of non-derogable rights. But not all rights of profound importance, such as Articles 9 and 27 of the Covenant, have in fact been made non-derogable. One reason for certain rights being made non-derogable is because their suspension is irrelevant to the legitimate control of the state of national emergency (for example, no imprisonment for debt, in Article 11). Another reason is that derogation may indeed be impossible (as, for example, freedom of conscience). At the same time, some provisions are non-derogable exactly because without them there would be no rule of law. A reservation to the provisions of Article 4 itself, which precisely stipulates the balance to be struck between the interests of the State and the rights of the individual in times of emergency, would fall in this category. And some non-derogable rights, which in any event cannot be reserved because of their status as peremptory norms, are also of this character—the prohibition of torture and arbitrary deprivation of life are examples.[94] While there is no automatic correlation between reservations to non-derogable provisions, and reservations which offend against the object and purpose of the Covenant, a State has a heavy onus to justify such a reservation.

11. The Covenant consists not just of the specified rights, but of important supportive guarantees. These guarantees provide the necessary framework for securing the rights in the Covenant and are thus essential to its object and purpose. ... Reservations designed to remove these guarantees are thus not acceptable. Thus, a State could not make a reservation to Article 2, paragraph 3, of the Covenant, indicating that it intends to provide no remedies for human rights violations. ... A State may not reserve the right not to present a report and have it considered by the Committee. The Committee's role under the Covenant, whether under Article 40 or under the Optional Protocols, necessarily entails interpreting the provisions of the Covenant and the development of a jurisprudence. Accordingly, a reservation that rejects the Committee's competence to interpret the requirements of any provisions of the Covenant would also be contrary to the object and purpose of that treaty.

12. ... Domestic laws may need to be altered properly to reflect the requirements of the Covenant; and mechanisms at the domestic level will be needed to allow the Covenant rights to be enforceable at the local level. Reservations often reveal a tendency of States not to want to change a particular law. ... Of particular concern are widely formulated reservations which essentially render ineffective all Covenant rights which would require any change in national law to ensure compliance with Covenant obligations. No real international rights or obligations have thus been accepted. And when there is an absence of provisions to ensure that Covenant rights may be sued on in domestic courts, and, further, a failure to allow individual complaints to be brought to the Committee under the first Optional Protocol, all the essential elements of the Covenant guarantees have been removed.

---

[94] Reservations have been entered to both art.6 and art.7, but not in terms which reserve a right to torture or arbitrarily to deprive of life.

13. . . . The function of the first Optional Protocol is to allow claims in respect of [Covenant] . . . rights to be tested before the Committee. Accordingly, a reservation to an obligation of a State to respect and ensure a right contained in the Covenant, made under the first Optional Protocol when it has not previously been made in respect of the same rights under the Covenant, does not affect the State's duty to comply with its substantive obligation. A reservation cannot be made to the Covenant through the vehicle of the Optional Protocol but such a reservation would operate to ensure that the State's compliance with that obligation may not be tested by the Committee under the first Optional Protocol. And because the object and purpose of the first Optional Protocol is to allow the rights obligatory for a State under the Covenant to be tested before the Committee, a reservation that seeks to preclude this would be contrary to the object and purpose of the first Optional Protocol, even if not of the Covenant. A reservation to a substantive obligation made for the first time under the first Optional Protocol would seem to reflect an intention by the State concerned to prevent the Committee from expressing its views relating to a particular article of the Covenant in an individual case.

14. The Committee considers that reservations relating to the required procedures under the first Optional Protocol would not be compatible with its object and purpose. The Committee must control its own procedures as specified by the Optional Protocol and its rules of procedure. . . .

16. The Committee finds it important to address which body has the legal authority to make determinations as to whether specific reservations are compatible with the object and purpose of the Covenant. As for international treaties in general, the International Court of Justice has indicated in the *Reservations to the Genocide Convention* case (1951) that a State which objected to a reservation on the grounds of incompatibility with the object and purpose of a treaty could, through objecting, regard the treaty as not in effect as between itself and the reserving State. Article 20, paragraph 4, of the Vienna Convention on the Law of Treaties 1969 contains provisions most relevant to the present case on acceptance of and objection to reservations. This provides for the possibility of a State to object to a reservation made by another State. Article 21 deals with the legal effects of objections by States to reservations made by other States. Essentially, a reservation precludes the operation, as between the reserving and other States, of the provision reserved; and an objection thereto leads to the reservation being in operation as between the reserving and objecting State only to the extent that it has not been objected to.

17. . . . the Committee believes that . . . [the Vienna Convention's] provisions on the role of State objections in relation to reservations are inappropriate to address the problem of reservations to human rights treaties. Such treaties, and the Covenant specifically, are not a web of inter-State exchanges of mutual obligations. They concern the endowment of individuals with rights. The principle of inter-State reciprocity has no place, save perhaps in the limited context of reservations to declarations on the Committee's competence under Article 41. And because the operation of the classic rules on reservations is so inadequate for the Covenant, States have often not seen any legal interest in or need to object to reservations. The absence of protest by States cannot imply that a reservation is either compatible or incompatible with the object and purpose of the Covenant. Objections have been occasional, made by some States but not others, and on grounds not always specified; when an objection is made, it often does not specify a legal consequence, or sometimes even indicates that the objecting party nonetheless does not regard the Covenant as not in effect as between the parties concerned. In short, the pattern is so unclear that it is not safe to assume that a non-objecting State thinks that a particular reservation is acceptable. In the view of the Committee, because of the special characteristics of the Covenant as a human rights treaty, it is open to question what effect objections have between States inter se. However, an objection to a reservation made by States may provide some guidance to the Committee in its interpretation as to its compatibility with the object and purpose of the Covenant.

18. It necessarily falls to the Committee to determine whether a specific reservation is compatible with the object and purpose of the Covenant. This is in part because, as indicated above, it is an inappropriate task for States parties in relation to human rights treaties, and in part because it is a task that the Committee cannot avoid in the performance of its functions. In order to know the scope of its duty to examine a State's compliance under Article 40 or a communication under the first Optional Protocol, the Committee has necessarily to take a view on the compatibility of a reservation with the object and purpose of the Covenant and with general international law. Because of the special character of a human rights treaty, the compatibility of a reservation with the object and purpose of the Covenant must be established objectively, by reference to legal principles, and the Committee is particularly well placed to perform this task. The normal consequence of an unacceptable reservation is not that the Covenant will not be in effect at all for a reserving party. Rather, such a reservation will generally be severable, in the sense that the Covenant will be operative for the reserving party without benefit of the reservation.

19. Reservations must be specific and transparent, so that the Committee, those under the jurisdiction of the reserving State and other States parties may be clear as to what obligations of human rights compliance have or

have not been undertaken. Reservations may thus not be general, but must refer to a particular provision of the Covenant and indicate in precise terms its scope in relation thereto. When considering the compatibility of possible reservations with the object and purpose of the Covenant, States should also take into consideration the overall effect of a group of reservations, as well as the effect of each reservation on the integrity of the Covenant, which remains an essential consideration. States should not enter so many reservations that they are in effect accepting a limited number of human rights obligations, and not the Covenant as such. So that reservations do not lead to a perpetual non-attainment of international human rights standards, reservations should not systematically reduce the obligations undertaken only to the presently existing in less demanding standards of domestic law. Nor should interpretive declarations or reservations seek to remove an autonomous meaning to Covenant obligations, by pronouncing them to be identical, or to be accepted only insofar as they are identical, with existing provisions of domestic law. States should not seek through reservations or interpretative declarations to determine that the meaning of a provision of the Covenant is the same as that given by an organ of any other international treaty body.

Notes

1. As the Human Rights Committee indicates (para.18), it had no choice but to take a stand on the matter of reservations in order to assess whether a state was complying with its international obligations. Unfortunately, as a result of the strict limits on the powers of states that it suggests, the Committee finds itself at odds with some contracting parties[95] on certain key points. Thus, the United Kingdom Observations on the General Comment read in part:

   "4. The modern law of reservations to multilateral treaties ... owes it origin to the Advisory Opinion of the International Court of Justice of 28 May 1951 on Reservations to the Genocide Convention. The Genocide Convention is itself (in the Committee's phrase) a human rights treaty concluded for the benefit of persons within the jurisdiction of the States Parties to it. As the International Court observed, the Genocide Convention is of a type in which 'the Contracting States do not have any interests of their own; they merely have, one and all, a common interest, namely the accomplishment of those high purposes which are the *raison d'être* of the Convention'. It was in the light precisely of those characteristics of the Genocide Convention, and in the light of the desirability of widespread adherence to it, that the Court set out its approach towards reservations. The United Kingdom does not accordingly believe that rules different from those foreshadowed by the International Court and in due course embodied in the Vienna Convention on the Law of Treaties are required to enable the international community to cope with reservations to human rights treaties. The correct approach is rather to apply the general rules relating to reservations laid down in the Vienna Convention in a manner which takes full account of the particular characteristics of the treaty in question.[96] ...

   13. The Committee correctly identifies Articles 20 and 21 of the Vienna Convention on the Law of Treaties as containing the rules which, taken together, regulate the legal effect of reservations to multilateral treaties. The United Kingdom wonders however whether the Committee is right to assume their applicability to incompatible reservations. The rules cited clearly do apply to reservations which are fully compatible with the object and purpose but remain open for acceptance or objection (see paragraph 9 above). It is questionable however

---

[95] See the Observations on General Comment 24 by France, the UK and the US: (1997) 4 I.H.R.R. 6; (1996) 3 I.H.R.R. 261, (1996) 16 H.R.L.J. 424; and (1996) 3 I.H.R.R. 265, (1996) 16 H.R.L.J. 422, respectively.

[96] Ed. The ILC similarly takes the view that the Vienna Convention reservations provisions apply to human rights treaties as well as others: see G.A.O.R.. A/52/10, para.157 (1997). This contradicts the HRC position in General Comment 24, para.17. See also Hampson, Rapporteur, Final Working Paper on the Reservations to Human Rights Treaties, UN Sub Commission on Promotion and Protection of Human Rights, E/CN.4/Sub.2/2004/42.

whether they were intended also to cover reservations which are inadmissible *in limine*. For example, it seems highly improbable that a reservation expressly *prohibited* by the treaty (the case in Article 19(a) of the Vienna Convention) is open to acceptance by another Contracting State. And if so, there is no clear reason why the same should not apply to the other cases enumerated in Article 19, including incompatibility with the object and purpose under 19(c). The *Genocide Convention* Advisory Opinion did indeed deal directly with the matter, by stating that acceptance of a reservation as being *compatible* with the object and purpose entitles a party to consider the reserving State to be party to the treaty. In the converse case (i.e. the case where the reservation is *not* compatible with the object and purpose) the Court states plainly, 'that State cannot be regarded as being a party to the Convention'.[97] This is the approach which the United Kingdom has consistently followed in its own treaty practice.

14. The General Comment suggests, *per contra*, that an 'unacceptable' reservation will generally be severable, in the sense that the Covenant will be operative for the reserving party as if the reservation had not been entered. ...

15. The United Kingdom believes that the only sound approach is ... that adopted by the International Court of Justice: a State which purports to ratify a human rights treaty subject to a reservation which is fundamentally incompatible with participation in the treaty régime cannot be regarded as having become a party at all—unless it withdraws the reservation. The test of incompatibility is and should be an objective one, in which the views of competent third parties would carry weight. Ultimately however it is a matter for the treaty Parties themselves and, while the presence or absence of individual State 'objections' should not be decisive in relation to an objective standard, it would be surprising to find a reservation validly stigmatised as incompatible, with the object and purpose of the Covenant if none of the Parties had taken exception to it on that ground. For all other reservations the rules laid down in the Vienna Convention do and should apply—except to the extent that the treaty regulates such matters by its own terms."

The US observations on the General Comment read in part:

"It is clear that a State cannot exempt itself from a peremptory norm of international law by making a reservation to the Covenant. It is not at all clear that a State cannot choose to exclude one means of enforcement of particular norms by reserving against inclusion of those norms in its Covenant obligations.

The proposition that any reservation which contravenes a norm of customary international law is *per se* incompatible with the object and purpose of this or any other convention, however, is a much more significant and sweeping premise. It is, moreover, wholly unsupported by and is in fact contrary to international law. As recognized in the paragraph 10 analysis of non-derogable rights, an 'object and purpose' analysis by its nature requires consideration of the particular treaty, right, and reservation in question. ...

The precise specification of what is contrary to customary international law, moreover, is a much more substantial question than indicated by the Comment. Even where a rule is generally established in customary international law, the exact contours and meaning of the customary law principle may need to be considered.

Paragraph 8, however, asserts in a wholly conclusory fashion that a number of propositions are customary international law which, to speak plainly, are not. It cannot be established on

---
[97] I.C.J. Rep. 1951, p.29.

the basis of practice or other authority, for example, that the mere expression (albeit deplorable) of national, racial or religious hatred (unaccompanied by any overt action or preparation) is prohibited by customary international law. The Committee seems to be suggesting here that the reservations which a large number of States Parties have submitted to Article 20 are *per se* invalid. Similarly, while many are opposed to the death penalty in general and the juvenile death penalty in particular, the practice of States demonstrates that there is currently no blanket prohibition in customary international law. Such a cavalier approach to international law by itself would raise serious concerns about the methodology of the Committee as well as its authority.

Another point worthy of clarification is whether the Committee really intends that, in the many areas which it mentions in paragraphs 8–11, any reservation whatsoever is impermissible, or only those which wholly vitiate the right in question. At the end of paragraph 8, for example, it is suggested that while reservations to particular clauses of Article 14 may be acceptable, a general reservation could not be taken to the article as a whole. Presumably, the same must also be true for many of the other subjects mentioned. For example, even where there is a reservation to Article 20, one would not expect such a reservation to apply to advocacy of racial hatred which constitutes incitement to murder or other crime. ...

The reservations contained in the United States' instrument of ratification are integral parts of its consent to be bound by the Covenant and are not severable. If it were to be determined that any one or more of them were ineffective, the ratification as a whole could thereby be nullified.

The general view of the academic literature is that reservations are an essential part of the State's consent to be bound. They cannot simply be erased. This reflects the fundamental principle of the law of treaties: obligation is based on consent. A State which does not consent to a treaty is not bound by that treaty. A State which expressly withholds its consent from a provision cannot be presumed, on the basis of some legal fiction, to be bound by it. It is regrettable that General Comment 24 appears to suggest to the contrary."

2. Which view of the rules on reservations to human rights treaties is preferable? That of the Human Rights Committee or that of the United Kingdom and the United States indicated above? Is the Committee ambitious in its listing of the categories of derogations that would be contrary to the Covenant's object and purpose? Where should the balance be struck between the integrity of the treaty and the need to get as many states as possible on board? Is the Committee's view on the severance of invalid reservations comparable to that in the *Belilos* case, above, p.659, or was that case different because Switzerland did not appear to object to remaining bound by the ECHR without its reservation?[98]

3. The Human Rights Committee applied its approach to severance in *Kennedy v Trinidad and Tobago*.[99] In that case, Trinidad and Tobago first withdrew from the First Optional Protocol (by which a party accepts the right of individual petition), and then re-acceded with a new reservation excluding cases concerning "any prisoner who is under sentence of death in respect of any matter relating to his prosecution, his detention, his trial, his conviction, his sentence or the carrying out of the death sentence on him and any matter connected therewith". It did so

---

[98] See Gardner, ed., *Human Rights as General Norms and a State's Right to Opt Out* (1997); and Tyagi (2000) 71 B.Y.I.L. 181. See also Clark (1991) 85 A.J.I.L. 281.

[99] (2000) 7 I.H.R.R. 315.

because it was required by its Constitution not to keep persons on death row for longer than five years[100] and the registration of a petition under the Optional Protocol might well cause death row detention to be longer than that. The Committee found that the reservation was invalid and should be severed:

"6.7 The present reservation, which was entered after the publication of General Comment No.24, does not purport to exclude the competence of the Committee under the Optional Protocol with regard to any specific provision of the Covenant, but rather to the entire Covenant for one particular group of complainants, namely prisoners under sentence of death. This does not, however, make it compatible with the object and purpose of the Optional Protocol. On the contrary, the Committee cannot accept a reservation which singles out a certain group of individuals for lesser procedural protection than that which is enjoyed by the rest of the population. In the view of the Committee, this constitutes a discrimination which runs counter to some of the basic principles embodied in the Covenant and its Protocols, and for this reason the reservation cannot be deemed compatible with the object and purpose of the Optional Protocol. The consequence is that the Committee is not precluded from considering the present communication under the Optional Protocol."

Messrs Ando, Prafulachandra, Bhagwati, Klein and Kretzmer dissented:

"11. It must be stressed that if the constitutional constraints faced by the State party had placed it in a situation in which it was violating substantive Covenant rights, denunciation of the Optional Protocol, and subsequent reaccession, would not have been a legitimate step, as its object would have been to allow the State party to continue violating the Covenant with impunity. Fortunately, that is not the situation here [as the imposition of the death penalty is not *per se* a breach of the Covenant]. While the Committee has taken a different view from that taken by the Privy Council [in the *Pratt and Morgan* case] . . . on the question of whether the mere time on death row makes delay in implementation of a death sentence cruel and inhuman punishment, a State party which adheres to the Privy Council view does not violate its obligations under the Covenant.

12. In the light of the above, we see no reason to consider the State party's reservation incompatible with the object and purpose of the Optional Protocol. . . .

15. . . . It is no secret that this approach of the Committee [as to severance in General Comment No.24] has met with serious criticism. Many experts in international law consider the approach to be inconsistent with the basic premises of any treaty regime, which are that the treaty obligations of a state are a function of its consent to assume those obligations. If a reservation is incompatible with the object and purpose of a treaty, the critics argue, the reserving state does not become a party to the treaty unless it withdraws that reservation. According to the critics' view there is no good reason to depart from general principles of treaty law when dealing with reservations to the Covenant.

16. . . . even in dealing with reservations to the Covenant itself the Committee did not take the view that in every case an unacceptable reservation will fall aside, leaving the reserving state to become a party to the Covenant without benefit of the reservation. As can be see from [para.18]. . . of General Comment no. 24 . . . the Committee merely stated that this would

---

[100] *Pratt v Att-Gen. of Jamaica* [1994] 2 A.C. 1 PC.

normally be the case. The normal assumption will be that the ratification or accession is not dependent on the acceptability of the reservation and that the unacceptability of the reservation will not vitiate the reserving state's agreement to be a party to the Covenant. However, this assumption cannot apply when it is abundantly clear that the reserving state's agreement to becoming a party to the Covenant is *dependent* on the acceptability of the reservation. The same applies with reservations to the Optional Protocol.

17. ... the State Party ... explained why it could not accept the Committee's competence to deal with communications from persons under sentence of death. In these particular circumstances it is quite clear that Trinidad and Tobago was not prepared to be a party to the Optional Protocol without the particular reservation, and that its reaccession was dependent on acceptability of that reservation. It follows that if we had accepted the Committee's view that the reservation is invalid we would have had to hold that Trinidad and Tobago is not a party to the Optional Protocol. This would, of course, also have made the communication inadmissible."

D. Entry into Force

VIENNA CONVENTION ON THE LAW OF TREATIES 1969

See above, p.637, n.4

Article 24

1. A treaty enters into force in such a manner and upon such date as it may provide or as the negotiating States may agree.

2. Failing any such provision or agreement, a treaty enters into force as soon as consent to be bound by the treaty has been established for all the negotiating States.

3. When the consent of a State to be bound by a treaty is established on a date after the treaty has come into force, the treaty enters into force for that State on that date, unless the treaty otherwise provides.

4. The provisions of a treaty regulating the authentication of its text, the establishment of the consent of States to be bound by the treaty, the manner or date of its entry into force, reservations, the functions of the depositary and other matters arising necessarily before the entry into force of the treaty apply from the time of the adoption of its text.

Note

The Vienna Convention provides that for its purposes "contracting State" means "a State which has consented to be bound by the treaty, whether or not the treaty has entered into force" (art.2(1)(*f*)) and that "party" means "a State which has consented to be bound by the treaty and for which the treaty is in force" (art.2(1)(*g*)).

----

4. OBSERVANCE AND APPLICATION OF TREATIES

A. Pacta Sunt Servanda

VIENNA CONVENTION ON THE LAW OF TREATIES 1969

See above, p.637, n.4

Article 26

Every treaty in force is binding upon the parties to it and must be performed by them in good faith.

Note

The International Law Commission's Commentary reads:

"*Pacta sunt servanda*—the rule that treaties are binding on the parties and must be performed in good faith—is the fundamental principle of the law of treaties. There is much authority in the jurisprudence of international tribunals for the proposition that in the present context the principle of good faith is a legal principle which forms an integral part of the rule *pacta sunt servanda*. Thus, speaking of certain valuations to be made under Articles 95 and 96 of the Act of Algeciras, the Court said in the case concerning *Rights of Nationals of the United States of America in Morocco* (Judgment of August 27 1952)[101]: 'The power of making the valuation rests with the Customs authorities, but it is a power which must be exercised reasonably and in good faith.' Similarly, the Permanent Court of International Justice, in applying treaty clauses prohibiting discrimination against minorities, insisted in a number of cases, that the clauses must be so applied as to ensure the absence of discrimination in fact as well as in law; in other words, the obligation must not be evaded by a merely literal application of the clauses. Numerous precedents could also be found in the jurisprudence of arbitral tribunals. To give only one example, in the *North Atlantic Coast Fisheries Arbitration* the Tribunal, dealing with Great Britain's right to regulate fisheries in Canadian waters in which she had granted certain fishing rights to United States nationals by the Treaty of Ghent, said[102]: '... from the Treaty results an obligatory relation whereby the right of Great Britain to exercise its right of sovereignty by making regulations is limited to such regulations as are made in good faith, and are not in violation of the Treaty.'"[103]

----

[101] Ed. I.C.J. Rep. 1952, p.212.
[102] (1910) Reports of International Arbitral Awards, Vol.XI, p.188.
[103] Y.B.I.L.C., 1966, II, p.211.

B. *Relation with Internal Law*

VIENNA CONVENTION ON THE LAW OF TREATIES 1969

See above, p.637, n.4

Article 27

A party may not invoke the provisions of its internal law as justification for its failure to perform a treaty. This rule is without prejudice to Article 46.[104]

Note

See to the same effect the 1949 Draft Declaration on Rights and Duties of States, above, p.63.

C. *Non-retroactivity*

VIENNA CONVENTION ON THE LAW OF TREATIES 1969

See above, p.637, n.4

Article 28

Unless a different intention appears from the treaty or is otherwise established, its provisions do not bind a party in relation to any act or fact which took place or any situation which ceased to exist before the date of the entry into force of the treaty with respect to that party.

Notes

In the *De Becker* case,[105] the applicant alleged a violation by Belgium of art.10 of the European Convention on Human Rights. He had been convicted in 1947 of a criminal offence and sentenced to life imprisonment and to the forfeiture for life of certain civil rights in accordance with the Belgian Penal Code (art.123 *sexies*) including the right to participate in the running of a newspaper. The European Commission of Human Rights rejected the argument put by Belgium that the application was inadmissible *ratione temporis* because the sentence had been imposed before Belgium became a party to the Convention. It stated:

"whereas it should be pointed out in the first place that the judgment of the Brussels Military Court ... was delivered prior to 14th June, 1955, on which date the Convention came into force in respect of Belgium; whereas, moreover, the subsequent entry into force of the Convention cannot have invalidated retrospectively the forfeiture of rights complained of for all the preceding period, since the Convention, according to the generally recognised rules of international law, did not take effect retrospectively; whereas it follows that the Applicant cannot legally claim, for the period in question, to have been the victim of a violation of the rights guaranteed by the Convention, even if the state of affairs complained of is of a permanent nature; whereas it should nevertheless be noted that any person to whom the provisions of Article 123 sexies of the Belgian Penal Code are

---

[104] See below, p.687.
[105] (1958–59) 2 Y.B.E.C.H.R. 214.

applied, is, in accordance with the very terms of that Article, deprived *ipso facto* and for life of the rights in question; that De Becker thus finds himself permanently deprived of the rights enumerated in Article 123 sexies and, in the event of an infringement of the provisions of the said Article, he may at any time be convicted under Article 123 nonies; ... Whereas it therefore appears that the Applicant finds himself in a continuing situation in respect of which he claims to be the victim of a violation of the right to freedom of expression guaranteed by Article 10 of the Convention and that the Application, insofar as it concerns this continuing situation extending after June 14, 1955, is consequently not inadmissible *ratione temporis*[106];"

Article 28 of the Vienna Convention is consistent with such a ruling since the applicant's "situation" continued to exist after 1955.

What if a national of State A has his property confiscated by State B the day before a treaty between A and B comes into effect which makes such a confiscation illegal? Is State B liable under the treaty?

D. Territorial Application

VIENNA CONVENTION ON THE LAW OF TREATIES 1969

See above, p.637, n.4

Article 29

Unless a different intention appears from the treaty or is otherwise established, a treaty is binding upon each party in respect of its entire territory.

Note

A question arises as to the territorial application of treaties made by a state with overseas possessions and other territories for whose international affairs it is responsible. The International Law Commission's Fourth Special Rapporteur on the Law of Treaties reported that "the general understanding today clearly is that, in the absence of any territorial clause or other indication of a contrary intention, a treaty is presumed to apply to all the territories for which the contracting States are internationally responsible."[107] Thus treaties made by the British Government apply to overseas territories for which the United Kingdom is internationally responsible unless the treaty indicates otherwise. For an example of a "territorial clause," see art.56, European Convention on Human Rights 1950.[108]

As to the question of the extra-territorial application of human rights treaties, see above, pp.560, 601.

---

[106] (1958–59) 2 Y.B.E.C.H.R. pp.233–234.
[107] Third Report, Y.B.I.L.C., 1964, II, p.15.
[108] As to units within a federal state, see above, p.640.

E. Inconsistent Treaties

VIENNA CONVENTION ON THE LAW OF TREATIES 1969

See above, p.637, n.4

Article 30[109]

1. Subject to Article 103 of the Charter of the United Nations,[110] the rights and obligations of States parties to successive treaties relating to the same subject-matter shall be determined in accordance with the following paragraphs.

2. When a treaty specifies that it is subject to, or that it is not to be considered as incompatible with, an earlier or later treaty, the provisions of that other treaty prevail.

3. When all the parties to the earlier treaty are parties also to the later treaty but the earlier treaty is not terminated or suspended in operation under Article 59,[111] the earlier treaty applies only to the extent that its provisions are compatible with those of the later treaty.

4. When the parties to the later treaty do not include all the parties to the earlier one:

(a) as between States parties to both treaties the same rule applies as in paragraph 3;

(b) as between a State party to both treaties and a State party to only one of the treaties, the treaty to which both States are parties governs their mutual rights and obligations.

5. Paragraph 4 is without prejudice to Article 41,[112] or to any question of the termination or suspension of the operation of a treaty under Article 60[113] or to any question of responsibility which may arise for a State from the conclusion or application of a treaty the provisions of which are incompatible with its obligations towards another State under another treaty.

Notes

1.   Imagine that States A and B make a treaty in which each undertakes not to allow any foreign military bases on its territory. States B and C make a treaty the following year in which B agrees that C shall establish a foreign base on B's territory. A learns of the treaty between B and C and protests, whereupon B refuses to allow C to establish the promised base. Has C a good claim against B to reparation under art.30 of the Vienna Convention? What if B had ignored the protest? Would A then have had a good claim for reparation against B? Could either A or C insist upon specific performance?[114]

2.   Suppose that States D, E, and F agree by treaty to apply certain conservation measures when fishing for halibut and cod on the high seas. Later, D and E, but not F, become parties with a large number of other states, including G, to a halibut treaty by which fishing practices aimed at the conservation of halibut are agreed upon which are less strict than those in the earlier treaty between D, E, and F. Which rules as to the conservation of halibut and cod apply in the relations between D and E and D and F under art.30? Which rules concerning halibut apply in the relations between D and G under art.30?

---

[109] See Vierdag (1988) 59 B.Y.I.L. 75.
[110] Ed. Below, App.I.
[111] Ed. See below, p.699.
[112] Ed. This permits some of the parties to a multilateral treaty to modify it inter se.
[113] Ed. See below, p.700.
[114] It seems likely that specific performance is a "general principle of law" in the sense of art.38(1)(c), Statute of the ICJ, below, App I. On its extensive use in civil law systems, see Schlesinger, *Comparative Law* (7th edn 2009).

3. Imagine that the Security Council, acting under arts 41 and 25 of the United Nations Charter,[115] imposed in 1990 upon the members of the United Nations a legally binding obligation to refrain from supplying military weapons to State B, a United Nations member. State A, a United Nations member, has a treaty with State B that entered into force in 1975 that requires each state to supply the other with military weapons on request. State B now makes a request under the treaty. What is State A's legal position under the Vienna Convention? Would it matter if the treaty had entered into force in 1995? Or if State B was not a member of the United Nations? Note that, as acknowledged by art.30(1), Vienna Convention, obligations under the United Nations Charter prevail over treaty obligations regardless of date and the identity of the parties: art.103 of the Charter.

----

5. TREATY INTERPRETATION[116]

FITZMAURICE, THE LAW AND PROCEDURE OF THE INTERNATIONAL COURT OF JUSTICE: TREATY INTERPRETATION AND CERTAIN OTHER TREATY POINTS

(1951) 28 B.Y.I.L. 1. Some footnotes omitted

... There are today three main schools of thought on the subject, which could conveniently be called the "intentions of the parties" or "founding fathers" school; the "textual" or "ordinary meaning of the words" school; and the "teleological" or "aims and objects" school. The ideas of these three schools are not necessarily exclusive of one another, and theories of treaty interpretation can be constructed (and are indeed normally held) compounded of all three. However, each tends to confer the primacy on one particular aspect of treaty interpretation, if not to the exclusion, certainly to the subordination of the others. ... For the "intentions" school, the prime, indeed the only legitimate, object is to ascertain and give effect to the intentions, or presumed intentions, of the parties. ... For the "meaning of the text" school, the prime object is to establish what the text means according to the ordinary or apparent signification of its terms: the approach is therefore through the study and analysis of the text. For the "aims and objects" school, it is the general purpose of the treaty itself that counts, considered to some extent as having, or as having come to have, an existence of its own, independent of the original intentions of the framers. The main object is to establish this general purpose, and construe the particular clauses in the light of it: hence it is such matters as the general tenor and atmosphere of the treaty, the circumstances in which it was made, the place it has come to have in international life, which for this school indicate the approach to interpretation. It should be added that this last, the teleological, approach has its sphere of operation almost entirely in the field of general multilateral conventions, particularly those of the social, humanitarian, and law-making type.[117] All three approaches are capable, in a given case, of producing the same result in practice; but

---

115 Below, App I.
116 See Bos (1980) 27 N.I.L.R. 3; Fitzmaurice (1957) 33 B.Y.I.L. 203; Lauterpacht (1949) 26 B.Y.I.L. 48; McDougal (1967) 61 A.J.I.L. 992; McDougal, Lasswell and Miller, *The Interpretation of Agreements and World Public Order* (1967; reprinted with additions, 1994); Maluwa (1990) 37 N.I.L.R. 330; Merrills (1968–69) A.Y.I.L. 55; Rosenne (1966) 5 C.J.T.L. 205; Stone (1953–55) 1 Sydney L.R. 344; Vagts (1993) 4 E.J.I.L. 472; and Yambrusic, *Treaty Interpretation: Theory and Reality* (1987).
117 It may be useful to state briefly the main drawback of each method, if employed in isolation or pushed to an extreme. In the case of the "intentions" method, it is the element of unreality or fictitiousness frequently involved. There are so many cases in which the dispute has arisen precisely because the parties had no intentions on the point, or none that were genuinely common. To make the issue dependent on them involves either an abortive search or an artificial construction that does *not* in fact represent their intentions. The "textual" method suffers from the subjective elements involved in the notions of "clear" or "ordinary" meaning, which may be differently understood and applied according to the point of view of the individual judge. There may also be cases where the parties intended a term to be understood in a specialised sense, different from its ordinary one, but failed to make this clear on the face of the text. The teleological method, finally, is always in danger of "spilling over" into judicial legislation; it may amount, not to interpreting but, in effect, to amending an instrument in order to make it conform better with what the judge regards as its true purposes.

equally (even though the differences may, on analysis, prove to be more of emphasis and methodology than principle) they are capable of leading to radically divergent results.

INTERPRETATION OF PEACE TREATIES CASE (SECOND PHASE)

Advisory Opinion. I.C.J. Reports 1950, p.221

The three 1947 Peace Treaties between the Allied Powers, on the one hand, and Bulgaria, Hungary and Romania, on the other, provided for commissions to hear disputes concerning the "interpretation or execution of the treaty" where they could not be resolved by negotiation. The commissions were to consist of three members. The two parties to the dispute were to appoint a member each; the parties were then to agree upon a third. If they could not agree, the third member was to be appointed by the Secretary-General of the United Nations. Disputes arose over the human rights guarantees in the treaties which could not, the United Kingdom and the United States claimed, be settled by negotiation. Bulgaria, Hungary and Romania refused to appoint members to the commissions. The General Assembly asked the Court whether the Secretary-General could appoint the third member of a commission when one party had failed to appoint its member and, if so, whether a commission consisting of the third member and the appointee of the other party could hear a dispute. The Court answered the first question in the negative, so that the second question did not arise. In the course of its opinion, the Court made the following comments on treaty interpretation.

Opinion of the Court

... the Governments of Bulgaria, Hungary and Romania are under an obligation to appoint their representatives to the Treaty Commissions, and it is clear that refusal to fulfil a treaty obligation involves international responsibility. Nevertheless, such a refusal cannot alter the conditions contemplated in the Treaties for the exercise by the Secretary-General of his power of appointment. These conditions are not present in this case, and their absence is not made good by the fact that it is due to the breach of a treaty obligation. The failure of machinery for settling disputes by reason of the practical impossibility of creating the Commission provided for in the Treaties is one thing[118]; international responsibility is another. The breach of a treaty obligation cannot be remedied by creating a Commission which is not the kind of Commission contemplated by the Treaties. It is the duty of the Court to interpret the Treaties, not to revise them.

The principle of interpretation expressed in the maxim: *Ut res magis valeat quam pereat*, often referred to as the rule of effectiveness, cannot justify the Court in attributing to the provisions for the settlement of disputes in the Peace Treaties a meaning which, as stated above, would be contrary to their letter and spirit.

Notes

1. The Court thus refused to apply the principle of effectiveness, according to which a treaty should be interpreted to give effect to its object and purpose, in such a way as to override the clear meaning of the text. At this point it parted company from the teleological approach.

2. The principle has been applied by the Court in a less extreme form in several cases. In the *Ambatielos* case,[119] Greece and the United Kingdom had replaced one bilateral commercial treaty between them by another. A Declaration accompanying the new treaty provided for the arbitration of "claims based upon the provisions of the [old treaty]." The question arose whether, as argued by Greece, the Declaration applied to claims arising during the currency of the old

---

[118] Ed. For an example of a procedure for establishing a commission that would have avoided the difficulty in this case, see the Annex to the Vienna Convention on the Law of Treaties, below, p.716.

[119] I.C.J. Rep. 1952, p.28. Cf. the *Iron Rhine Railway Arbitration*, P.C.A. 2005, www.pca/cpa.org.

treaty which were brought after the new treaty had been made as well as to such claims brought before it had been made. The Court ruled in favour of Greece:

> "If the United Kingdom Government's interpretation were accepted, claims based on the Treaty of 1886, but brought after the conclusion of the Treaty of 1926 would be left without solution. They would not be subject to arbitration under either Treaty, although the provision on whose breach the claim was based might appear in both and might thus have been in force without a break since 1886. The Court cannot accept an interpretation which would have a result obviously contrary to the language of the Declaration and to the continuous will of both Parties to submit all differences to arbitration of one kind or another."[120]

The principle has also been used where the meaning of the text is unclear to prefer an interpretation that gives some effect to a provision over one that does not. In the *Corfu Channel* case,[121] the Special Agreement by which the case was referred to the Court asked, inter alia, "is there any duty to pay compensation?" Albania argued that this question required only an answer "yes" or "no"; it did not require the Court to assess the amount of compensation due. The Court rejected this argument. It noted that it had, in any event, in answer to another question in the Special Agreement, to say whether international responsibility existed. Since international responsibility carried with it under customary international law an obligation to compensate and since there was no obligation to compensate in the absence of international responsibility, on Albania's interpretation of the question, the answer to it would add nothing to what the parties would otherwise know. The British argument, that the question required the Court to assess compensation, was preferred in order to give the question meaning. The Court said:

> "It would indeed be incompatible with the generally accepted rules of interpretation to admit that a provision of this sort occurring in a special agreement should be devoid of purport or effect."[122]

The principle has been most strikingly applied by the Court in the specialised field of the constitutional law of international organisations to infer powers which are not expressly given to the organisation concerned but which are consistent with its purposes. See, in particular, the *Reparation*[123] and *Certain Expenses*[124] cases. See also the *South-West Africa* cases.[125]

VIENNA CONVENTION ON THE LAW OF TREATIES 1969

See above, p.637, n.4

Article 31

1. A treaty shall be interpreted in good faith in accordance with the ordinary meaning to be given to the terms of the treaty in their context and in the light of its object and purpose.

---

[120] I.C.J. Rep. 1952, p.45.
[121] I.C.J. Rep. 1949, p.4.
[122] I.C.J. Rep. 1949, p.24.
[123] See above, p.120.
[124] See below, p.831.
[125] I.C.J. Rep. 1966, p.6.

2. The context for the purpose of the interpretation of a treaty shall comprise in addition to the text, including its preamble and annexes:

(a) any agreement relating to the treaty which was made between all the parties in connexion with the conclusion of the treaty;

(b) any instrument which was made by one or more parties in connexion with the conclusion of the treaty and accepted by the other parties as an instrument related to the treaty;

3. There shall be taken into account, together with the context:

(a) any subsequent agreement between the parties regarding the interpretation of the treaty or the application of its provisions;

(b) any subsequent practice in the application of the treaty which establishes the agreement of the parties regarding its interpretation;

(c) any relevant rules of international law applicable in the relations between the parties.

4. A special meaning shall be given to a term if it is established that the parties so intended.

Notes

1. The Vienna Convention rules on treaty interpretation are accepted by states as custom[126] and are regularly applied by international courts as such.[127] Which of the three approaches discussed by Fitzmaurice[128] is adopted in the Vienna Convention? Note that the "object and purpose" of a treaty is to be referred to in determining the meaning of the "terms of the treaty" and not as an independent basis for interpretation.

2. On the *principle of effectiveness*, the International Law Commission's Commentary reads:

    "The Commission, however, took the view that, in so far as the maxim *ut res magis valeat quam pereat* reflects a true general rule of interpretation, it is embodied in [art.31, Vienna Convention] ... When a treaty is open to two interpretations one of which does and the other does not enable the treaty to have appropriate effects, good faith and the objects and purposes of the treaty demand that the former interpretation should be adopted."[129]

    The Commission clearly thought that the text as it stands permits the use of the principle in the way it has been used by the World Court.[130]

3. *The Textual or "plain meaning" approach*. As stated by the International Law Commission in its Commentary, "the jurisprudence of the International Court contains many pronouncements from which it is permissible to conclude that the textual approach to treaty interpretation is regarded by it as established law."[131] See, for example, the *Admissions* case[132] and the *Competence* case.[133]

---

[126] See, e.g. the British Law Officers' opinion, above, n.8.
[127] See, e.g. the *Maritime Delimitation and Territorial Questions between Qatar and Bahrain* case (*Jurisdiction and Admissibility No.2*), I.C.J. Rep. 1995, p.6 at p.18 and the *Restrictions to the Death Penalty* case, above, p.657. They are followed by the UK courts: see the *Fothergill* case, above, p.83.
[128] See above, p.832.
[129] Y.B.I.L.C., 1966, II, p.219.
[130] See above, pp.675–676.
[131] Y.B.I.L.C., 1966, II, p.220.
[132] I.C.J. Rep. 1948, p.57.
[133] I.C.J. Rep. 1950, p.4.

On the limits to a "purely grammatical" approach, see the *Aegean Sea Continental Shelf* case.[134]

4. Would the Optional Protocol of Signature concerning the Compulsory Settlement of Disputes[135] adopted at the 1958 Geneva Conference on the Law of the Sea relating to disputes arising under the four Conventions adopted at the Conference constitute part of the "context" that could be used in interpreting any of those Conventions under art.31(2)? Would the Resolution on Nuclear Tests on the High Seas[136] adopted at the same Conference? Could the definition of "warship" in the High Seas Convention be used to interpret the same term in the Territorial Sea Convention?[137]

5. *Subsequent Practice.* Fitzmaurice[138] states that:

> "... recourse to the subsequent conduct and practice of the parties in relation to the treaty is permissible, and may be desirable, as affording the best and most reliable evidence ... as to what its correct interpretation is."

The role of such practice is demonstrated by the following extract from the *Competence of the I.L.O. with respect to Agricultural Labour* case[139]:

> "If there were any ambiguity, the Court might, for the purpose of arriving at the true meaning, consider the action which has been taken under the Treaty. The Treaty was signed in June 1919, and it was not until October 1921, that any of the Contracting Parties raised the question whether agricultural labour fell within the competence of the International Labour Organisation. During the intervening period the subject of agriculture had repeatedly been discussed and had been dealt with in one form and another."

What if both or all of the parties to a treaty act upon it in a way that is contrary to the clear meaning of the text over a lengthy period of time before such action is challenged by one of their number? Has the treaty, in effect, been revised informally?[140]

There would seem to be no reason to distinguish between subsequent practice by both or all of the parties jointly and such practice by both or all of them separately that is to the same effect. The value of practice showing the interpretation of just one or some of the parties, however, is less certain. The International Law Commission thought that only practice establishing the understanding of "the parties as a whole"[141] should be used. The phrase "agreement of the parties" in art.31(3)(*b*) can probably be taken as reinforcing this view. Presumably, however, acquiescence is relevant so that the practice of one party of which the other parties have or can be deemed to have knowledge can, through lack of protest, establish the common interpretation of the parties. In the *Anglo-Iranian Oil Co.* case,[142] the International Court of Justice relied, in

---

[134] I.C.J. Rep. 1978, p.23.
[135] (1963) U.K.T.S. 60, Cmnd. 2112; 450 U.N.T.S. 169.
[136] See above, p.365, n.199.
[137] The definition originated in the I.L.C. Draft Articles, from which both Conventions derive.
[138] See above, n.116, p.210.
[139] P.C.I.J. Rep., Series B, No.2, pp.39–40 (1922). Subsequent practice was also relied upon in the *Land, Island and Maritime Frontier Dispute* case, I.C.J. Rep. 1992, p.351 at 586; and the *Jan Mayen* case, I.C.J. Rep.1993, p.38 at 51. See also *Tadic v Prosecutor (Jurisdiction)* (1996) 35 I.L.M. 35, ICTY; (1996) 3 I.H.R.R. 578; and *Eritrea-Ethiopia Boundary (Merits)* case, PCA, www. pca-cpa.org, para.3.6.
[140] See Fitzmaurice (1957) 33 B.Y.I.L. 203 at 225.
[141] Commentary, Y.B.I.L.C., 1966, II, p.222.
[142] I.C.J. Rep. 1952, p.92.

interpreting the Iranian declaration accepting the compulsory jurisdiction of the Court, upon an Iranian law approving the declaration some months after it was signed and some months before it was ratified. The Court said:

> "This clause . . . is . . . a decisive confirmation of the intention of the Government of Iran at the time when it accepted the compulsory jurisdiction of the Court. . . . It is contended that this evidence as to the intention of the Government of Iran should be rejected as inadmissible and that this Iranian law is a purely domestic instrument, unknown to other governments. The law is described as 'a private document written only in the Persian language which was not communicated to the League or to any of the other States which had made declarations.' The Court is unable to see why it should be prevented from taking this piece of evidence into consideration. The law was published in the Corpus of Iranian law voted and ratified during the period from January 15, 1931, to January 15, 1933. It has thus been available for the examination of other governments during a period of about twenty years. The law was filed for the sole purpose of throwing light on a disputed question of fact, namely, the intention of the Government of Iran at the time when it signed the Declaration."[143]

Clearly, the burden of watchfulness placed by the Court's approach upon other parties to a treaty, particularly as their numbers grow, is a very great one.[144]

When France acceded to the Geneva Convention on the Continental Shelf 1958, it declared its understanding of the meaning of arts 1 and 2 of the Convention,[145] to which no reservations are permitted. Such an "understanding" may qualify as an "instrument" in the sense of art.31(2)(b), Vienna Convention. As such it would be a factor to be taken into account when interpreting the Convention but would not by itself be conclusive.[146]

There may be a difference between action by a party accepting an obligation and other action. Referring to declarations made by South Africa on its obligations under the Mandate for South-West Africa, the International Court of Justice in the *South West Africa* case (1950)[147] said:

> "Interpretations placed upon legal instruments by the parties to them, though not conclusive as to their meaning, have considerable probative value when they contain recognition by a party of its own obligations under an instrument."

6. In the *Land and Maritime Boundary between Cameroon and Nigeria* case,[148] the ICJ stated that a term in a treaty must be interpreted in accordance "with the intention of the parties at the time." Thus, in that case, the location of the "mouth" of a river was at the place that the parties understood in 1931.

7. As to the establishment of a *"special meaning"* of a term (art.31(4)), Norway unsuccessfully

---

[143] I.C.J. Rep. 1952, p.107. On the juridical nature of declarations accepting the compulsory jurisdiction of the Court, see below, p.850.
[144] cf. above, p.32.
[145] See above, p.404, on the Declaration concerning art.2. The US noted the declarations "without prejudice": UN Doc. ST.LEG/SER.D/15, p.817.
[146] On "interpretative declarations" generally, see above, p.661.
[147] I.C.J. Rep. 1950, p.135.
[148] I.C.J. Rep. 2002, p.303, para.59. cf. *Eritrea-Ethiopia Boundary (Merits)* case, PCA, www.pca-cpa.org, para.3.5, in which the "principle of contemporality" was applied, meaning that "a treaty should be interpreted by reference to the circumstances prevailing at the time when the treaty was concluded". This meant "giving expressions (including names) used in the treaty the meaning that they would have possessed at that time". See Grieg, *Intertemporality and the Law of Treaties* (2001).

argued in the *Eastern Greenland* case[149] that "in the legislative and administrative acts of the XVIIIth century on which Denmark relies. . . the word 'Greenland' is used not in the geographical sense, but means only the colonies of the colonised area on the West coast." The Court stated:

"The geographical meaning of the word 'Greenland' . . . must be regarded as the ordinary meaning of the word. If it is alleged by one of the Parties that some unusual or exceptional meaning is to be attributed to it, it lies on that Party to establish its contention."

8.   *Particular rules and maxims.* McNair[150] states:

"From the time of Grotius onwards, if not before, successive generations of writers and, more recently, of arbitrators and judges, have elaborated rules for the interpretation of treaties, borrowing mainly from the private law of contract. One result . . . is that today for many of the so-called rules of interpretation that one party may invoke before a tribunal the adverse party can often . . . find another. . . . The many maxims and phrases . . . are merely prima facie guides to the intention of the parties and must always give way to contrary evidence of the intention of the parties in a particular case."

The Vienna Convention, adopting the scepticism voiced by McNair, refrains from attempting to codify the numerous rules and maxims of interpretation, many of which are familiar from municipal law, that undoubtedly exist. It remains true, however, that some of the rules and maxims thus frowned upon will be of help in many cases. This is true, for example, of the maxim *inclusio unius est exclusio alterius*, which was stated in the *Life Insurance Claims*[151] to be "a rule of both law and logic and applicable to the construction of treaties as well as municipal statutes and contracts." The comment on it by Lopes L.J. in *Colquhoun v Brooks*[152] is, however, worth noting:

"The exclusion is often the result of inadvertence or accident, and the maxim ought not to be applied, when its application, having regard to the subject matter to which it is to be applied, leads to inconsistency or injustice."

An example of a somewhat questionable principle is the principle of restrictive interpretation, whereby limitations upon a state's sovereignty are not to be presumed, which was relied on by the PCIJ in the *Wimbledon* case.[153] McNair states:

"It is believed to be now of declining importance and the time may not be far distant when it will disappear from the books. It dates from an age in which treaties were interpreted not by legal tribunals, and not even much by lawyers but by statesmen and diplomats. . . .
    It is difficult to defend the rule on a basis of logic. Every treaty obligation limits the sovereign powers of a State. With rare exceptions a treaty imposes obligations on both parties . . . if a so-called rule of interpretation is applied to restrict the obligations of one party, a

---

[149] P.C.I.J. Rep., Series A, No.53, p.49.
[150] *Treaties*, pp.364–366.
[151] *U.S. v Germany* (1924) 7 R.I.A.A. 91 at 111.
[152] (1888) 21 Q.B.D. 52 at 65. See McNair, *Treaties*, p.400.
[153] See above, p.222.

sovereign State, it reduces the reciprocal benefit or 'consideration' due to the other party, also a sovereign State, which seems to me to be absurd."[154]

It may, on occasions, contradict the principle of effectiveness.[155] It could have been used, for example, in opposition to the Greek contention in the *Ambatielos* case.[156]

The principle was also questioned in the *Iron Rhine Railway Arbitration* case,[157] where it was commented that "some authors note that the principle has not been relied upon in any recent jurisprudence of international courts and tribunals and that its contemporary relevance is to be doubted." But a restrictive interpretation is applied to unilateral acts.[158]

VIENNA CONVENTION ON THE LAW OF TREATIES 1969

See above, p.637, n.4

Article 32

Recourse may be had to supplementary means of interpretation, including the preparatory work of the treaty and the circumstances of its conclusion, in order to confirm the meaning resulting from the application of Article 31, or to determine the meaning when the interpretation according to Article 31:

(a) leaves the meaning ambiguous or obscure; or

(b) leads to a result which is manifestly absurd or unreasonable.

Notes

1. The preparatory work, or *travaux préparatoires*, of a treaty is purposely not defined in the Vienna Convention. The International Law Commission thought that "to do so might only lead to the possible exclusion of relevant evidence."[159] In general terms, it is the record of the drafting of a treaty. It includes records of negotiations between the states that participate in the drafting and, in some cases, records of the work of independent bodies of experts, such as the International Law Commission.[160] On a wide interpretation, it also includes such materials as unilateral statements by government spokesmen made prior to or at the time of the negotiations but not as a part of them. McNair[161] argues however, that evidence coming within this wider interpretation should not be admitted before international courts and tribunals: "Surely whatever value there may be in preparatory work is that it may afford evidence of the common intention of the parties."

   At the Vienna Conference, the United States argued forcefully, but unsuccessfully, for a rule

---

[154] *Symbolae Verzijl*, p.222 at 235–236; reprinted in McNair, *Treaties* App.A, p.754 at 765.
[155] See above, p.675.
[156] See above, p.529, n.470.
[157] P.C.A. 2005, p.26, www.pca-cpa.org. The tribunal noted that it is not applied in the interpretation of human rights treaties, in which the object and purpose, of protecting human rights, is dominant.
[158] See the I.L.C. Guiding Principles, Principle 7, above, p.51.
[159] Commentary, Y.B.I.L.C., 1966, II, p.223.
[160] In *Read v Secretary of State for the Home Dept.* [1989] A.C. 1014, HL, the explanatory report published with a Council of Europe convention was treated as a part of the *travaux*.
[161] *Treaties*, p.421.

permitting the use of the preparatory work equally with the text in determining the parties' intention and not just as the supplementary aid proposed by the International Law Commission.

Is it a good argument for the Convention approach by which the preparatory work is only a "supplementary aid" that "[t]he text adopted by the signatories is, with rare exceptions, the only and the most recent expression of their common intent?"[162] Is it a good argument in favour of allowing recourse to preparatory work in all cases to say that it does no harm to look at whatever evidence is available, and that, occasionally, it may help? It will be evident that much use is made of preparatory work in this case book. What impression do you have of its value for treaty interpretation from its use here? Is it helpful, for example, in deciding whether warships have a right of innocent passage through a foreign territorial sea under the 1982 Convention?[163] Or whether the conduct of nuclear tests on the high seas is permitted by art.87, 1982 Convention?[164]

In the *Employment of Women* case,[165] the Court referred to the preparatory work of a treaty to confirm the clear meaning of its text. Could it do this under the Vienna Convention? What would a court do if the preparatory work, resorted to for purposes of confirmation, contradicts the clear meaning of the text?

In the *Territorial Jurisdiction of the International Commission of the River Oder* case,[166] the Permanent Court of International Justice ruled that part of the preparatory work of the Treaty of Versailles 1919—the minutes of the Conference Committee on Ports, Waterways and Railways—could not be admitted in evidence before it for the purpose of interpreting the Treaty because not all of the parties to the case had participated in the drafting of the Treaty. The Vienna Convention contains no express limitation upon the use of the preparatory work in the sense of the ruling in the *Oder* case and the International Law Commission's Commentary shows that none was intended:

"The Commission doubted, however, whether this ruling reflected ... actual practice ... in the case of multilateral treaties. ... Moreover, ... [a] State acceding to a treaty ... is perfectly entitled to request to see the *travaux préparatoires*, if it wishes, before acceding."[167]

How acceptable would the rule in the *Oder* case be in interpreting the United Nations Charter, the number of parties to which is more than twice the original fifty who participated in its drafting?

2.   Note that "the circumstances of" the "conclusion" of a treaty (art.32) are, like the preparatory work, only a "supplementary means of interpretation." They were understood by the International Law Commission's Fourth Special Rapporteur as being "both the contemporary circumstances and the historical context in which the treaty was concluded."[168] An example of reliance upon background circumstances is found in the *Anglo-Iranian Oil Co.* case[169] where the International Court of Justice had to decide whether "treaties and conventions" in the Iranian declaration accepting the compulsory jurisdiction of the Court referred to treaties and conventions made before the declaration came into force as well as to those made afterwards. The Court noted:

---

[162] Huber, *Annuaire de l'Institut de Droit International* (1952), I, p.199, Translation.

[163] See above, p.351.

[164] See above, p.365.

[165] P.C.I.J. Rep., Series A/B, No.50 (1932). cf. the *Maritime Delimitation and Territorial Questions between Qatar and Bahrain* case *(Jurisdiction No.2)*, I.C.J. Rep. 1995, p.6 at 21.

[166] P.C.I.J. Rep., Series A, No.23 (1929).

[167] Y.B.I.L.C., 1966, II, p.223. See also Lauterpacht, *The Development of International Law by the International Court* (1958), p.137; and Rosenne (1963) 12 I.C.L.Q. 1378.

[168] Y.B.I.L.C., 1966, II, p.59.

[169] I.C.J. Rep. 1952, p.93.

"At the time when the Declaration was signed in October 1930 the Government of Iran considered all capitulatory treaties[170] as no longer binding, but was uncertain as to the legal effect of its unilateral denunciations. It is unlikely that the Government of Iran in such circumstances, should have been willing, on its own initiative, to agree that disputes relating to such treaties might be submitted for adjudication ... by virtue of a general clause in the Declaration."[171]

VIENNA CONVENTION ON THE LAW OF TREATIES 1969

See above, p.637, n.4

Article 33

1. When a treaty has been authenticated in two or more languages, the text is equally authoritative in each language, unless the treaty provides or the parties agree that, in case of divergence, a particular text shall prevail.

2. A version of the treaty in a language other than one of those in which the text was authenticated shall be considered an authentic text if the treaty so provides or the parties so agree.

3. The terms of the Treaty are presumed to have the same meaning in each authentic text.

4. Except where a particular text prevails in accordance with paragraph 1, when a comparison of the authentic texts discloses a difference of meaning which the application of Articles 31 and 32 does not remove, the meaning which best reconciles the texts, having regard to the object and purpose of the treaty, shall be adopted.

Notes[172]

1.   The International Law Commission's Commentary reads:

"The phenomenon of treaties drawn up in two or more languages has become extremely common and, with the advent of the United Nations, general multilateral treaties drawn up, or finally expressed, in five different languages have become quite numerous. When a treaty is plurilingual, there may or may not be a difference in the status of the different language versions for the purpose of interpretation. Each of the versions may have the status of an authentic text of the treaty; or one or more of them may be merely an 'official text', that is text which has been signed by the negotiating states but not accepted as authoritative; or one or more of them may be merely an 'official translation', that is a translation prepared by the parties or an individual government or by an organ of an international organisation. Today the majority of more formal treaties contain an express provision determining the status of the different language versions. If there is no such provision, it seems to be generally accepted that each of the versions in which the text of the treaty was 'drawn' up is to be considered authentic, and therefore authoritative for purpose of interpretation. Few plurilingual treaties containing more than one or two articles are without some discrepancy between the texts. The different genius of the languages, the absence of a complete consensus *ad idem*, or lack of sufficient time to co-ordinate the texts may result in minor or even major discrepancies in the meaning of the texts. In that event the plurality of the texts may be a serious additional source

---

[170] Ed. On capitulatory regimes, see above, p.10, n.46.
[171] I.C.J. Rep. 1952, p.105.
[172] See Hardy (1961) 37 B.Y.I.L. 72; Kuner (1991) 40 I.C.L.Q. 953; and Shelton (1997) 20 Hastings I.C.L.R. 611.

of ambiguity or obscurity in the terms of the treaty. On the other hand, when the meaning of terms is ambiguous or obscure in one language but it is clear and convincing as to the intentions of the parties in another, the plurilingual character of the treaty facilitates interpretations of the text the meaning of which is doubtful."[173]

2. The ICJ applied art.33(4), which it regarded as stating custom, in the *LeGrand* case.[174]

In the *Standard Oil Company Tankers* case,[175] the tribunal stated in interpreting a provision of the Treaty of Versailles 1919, of which the English and French texts are equally authentic, "... there is a notable discrepancy in these texts, for while the English stipulates that due regard shall be had to any 'legal or equitable interests,' which corresponds to very clear and well-known conceptions of English and American law, of which equity is a form, the French employs the infinitely vaguer phrase of 'droits et intérêts légitimes,' which corresponds to no definite legal idea ... therefore everything points to the conclusion that the French phrase is merely the translation of the English, in which alone the expression employed has legal sense, and which makes clear the general tenor of the articles." The tribunal then applied the English text.[176]

----

6. THIRD STATES[177]

FREE ZONES OF UPPER SAVOY AND THE DISTRICT OF GEX CASE

France v Switzerland (1932)

P.C.I.J. Reports, Series A/B, No.46

The facts of this case were nothing if not complicated. One of the many territorial problems that had to be dealt with at the Congress of Vienna in 1815 after the defeat of Napoleon was the future of Switzerland. On March 20, 1815, the powers participating in the Congress, who included France but not Switzerland, made a Declaration stating that if Switzerland "acceded to the stipulations contained in the present instrument, an Act shall be prepared containing the acknowledgment and the guarantee, on the part of all the Powers, of the perpetual neutrality of Switzerland in her new frontiers." One of the "stipulations" was that territory in the District of Gex on the French side of the proposed border between France and Switzerland and in the immediate vicinity of Geneva, which was to be just on the Swiss side of the border, should be linked with Geneva as a single economic unit. This was thought necessary partly because of the dependence of Geneva upon the District of Gex for food and other supplies. To this end, the Declaration stated, France would not levy customs duties upon goods crossing into Switzerland from the District of Gex. Switzerland acceded to the Declaration, whereupon a second Declaration was made by the same Powers at Vienna on November 20, 1815, acknowledging the "perpetual neutrality of Switzerland". Somewhat similar arrangements were also made concerning territory in the District of Savoy, which was then in the State of Sardinia

---

[173] Y.B.I.L.C., 1966, II, p.224–225.

[174] Below, p.870. cf. the *Wemhoff* case, E. Ct. H.R.Rep. A7 (1968); 1 E.H.R.R. 55 (the text that better achieved the purpose of a law-making treaty preferred).

[175] *U.S. v Reparation Commission* (1926) 2 R.I.A.A. 777 at 792. See also the *Mavrommatis Palestine Concessions* case, P.C.I.J. Rep., Series A, No.2 (1926), p.19.

[176] See also the *German Reparations* case (1924) 1 R.I.A.A. 429 at 439.

[177] See Chinkin, *Third Parties in International Law* (1993); Jiménez de Aréchaga (1956) 50 A.J.I.L. 338; Rosakis (1975) 35 Z.A.Ö.R.V. 1; and Schweisfurth (1985) 45 ibid. 653.

and later in France. The areas on the French and, originally, the Sardinian sides of the border with Switzerland in which these arrangements applied were known as the free zones.

As a result of changed circumstances, the justification for the zones had, arguably, disappeared by the time of the First World War. France wanted to end them and, on its initiative, art.435 of the Treaty of Versailles 1919 provided that the parties to the Treaty, who included France, but not Switzerland, agreed that the zones were "no longer consistent with present conditions, and that it is for France and Switzerland to come to an agreement together with a view to settling between themselves the status of these territories ...." Subsequently, the two states negotiated a treaty on the question which, although approved by the Swiss Diet, failed because it was rejected by a plebiscite of the Swiss people. Thereupon, France purported to abolish the zones unilaterally. In the present case, the Court was asked to decide whether art.435 had abrogated the zones or had created for Switzerland an obligation to abrogate them. The Court by six votes to five ruled, as a matter of construction of art.435, that it had done neither. It also made the following comments on the question of third state rights and duties. The zones are still in existence.

Judgment of the Court

It follows from the foregoing that Article 435, paragraph 2, as such, does not involve the abolition of the free zones. But, even were it otherwise, it is certain that in any case, Article 435 of the Treaty of Versailles is not binding upon Switzerland, who is not a Party to that Treaty, except to the extent to which that country accepted it. The extent is determined by the note of the Federal Council of May 5, 1919, an extract from which constitutes Annex I of the said Article. It is by that instrument, and by it alone, that Switzerland has acquiesced in the provision of Article 435; and she did so under certain conditions and reservations, set out in the said note, which state, inter alia: "The Federal Council would not wish that its acceptance of the above wording [*scil*. art.435, para.2, of the Treaty of Versailles] should lead to the conclusion that it would agree to the suppression of a system intended to give neighbouring territory the benefit of a special régime which is appropriate to the geographical and economical situation and which has been well tested" ...

On the question of the legal effect of the two Declarations of 1815 the Court stated:

It follows from all the foregoing that the creation of the Gex zone forms part of a territorial arrangement in favour of Switzerland, made as a result of an agreement between that country and the Powers, including France, which agreement confers on this zone the character of a contract to which Switzerland is a Party.

It also follows that no accession by Switzerland to the Declaration of November 20th was necessary and, in fact, no such accession was sought: it has never been contended that this Declaration is not binding owing to the absence of any accession by Switzerland.

The Court, having reached this conclusion simply on the basis of an examination of the situation of fact in regard to this case, need not consider the legal nature of the Gex zone from the point of view of whether it constitutes a stipulation in favour of a third Party.

But were the matter also to be envisaged from this aspect, the following observations should be made:

It cannot be lightly presumed that stipulations favourable to a third State have been adopted with the object of creating an actual right in its favour. There is however nothing to prevent the will of sovereign States from having this object and this effect. The question of the existence of a right acquired under an instrument drawn between other States is therefore one to be decided in each particular case: it must be ascertained whether the States which have stipulated in favour of a third State meant to create for that State an actual right which the latter has accepted as such.

VIENNA CONVENTION ON THE LAW OF TREATIES 1969

See above, p.637, n.4

Article 34

A treaty does not create either obligations or rights for a third State without its consent.

Article 35

An obligation arises for a third State from a provision of a treaty if the parties to the treaty intend the provision to be the means of establishing the obligation and the third State expressly accepts that obligation in writing.

Article 36

1. A right arises for a third State from a provision of a treaty if the parties to the treaty intend the provision to accord that right either to the third State, or to a group of States to which it belongs, or to all States, and the third State assents thereto. Its assent shall be presumed so long as the contrary is not indicated, unless the treaty otherwise provides.

2. A State exercising a right in accordance with paragraph 1 shall comply with the conditions for its exercise provided for in the treaty or established in conformity with the treaty.

Article 37

1. When an obligation has arisen for a third State in conformity with Article 35, the obligation may be revoked or modified only with the consent of the parties to the treaty and of the third State, unless it is established that they had otherwise agreed.

2. When a right has arisen for a third State in conformity with Article 36, the right may not be revoked or modified by the parties if it is established that the right was intended not to be revocable or subject to modification without the consent of the third State.

Article 38

Nothing in Articles 34 to 37 precludes a rule set forth in a treaty from becoming binding upon a third State as a customary rule of international law, recognised as such.

Notes

1. The general rule in art.34 of the Vienna Convention, which is known by the maxim *pacta tertiis nec nocent nec prosunt*, undoubtedly reflects customary international law.

2. Commenting upon its Draft Article concerning *obligations* that, in substance, became art.35 of the Vienna Convention, the International Law Commission acknowledged that the requirements in it are so strict that when they are met "there is, in effect, a second collateral agreement between the parties to the treaty, on the one hand, and the third state on the other; and that the juridical basis of the latter's obligation is not the treaty itself but the collateral agreement."[178]

3. Examples of third party rights are in the treaty provisions guaranteeing freedom of passage for ships through the Suez and Kiel Canals.[179] Note that in the case of the Hay-Pauncefote Treaty 1901 concerning the Panama Canal, in 1924 the United States Secretary of State took the position that "other nations ... not being parties to the treaty have no rights under it."[180]

---

[178] Y.B.I.L.C., 1966, II, p.227.
[179] See above, pp.222–225.
[180] 5 Hackworth 222.

4. Some writers have suggested that certain types of treaties affecting third parties, including the international canal treaties referred to in the previous note, should be seen not as contracts having effect for third parties but rather as instruments intending to establish, and accepted by the international community as being able to establish, legal changes valid *erga omnes*. Thus McNair[181] distinguishes "the predominantly contractual type of treaty whose main object is to create obligations (both rights and duties) *in personam*," on the one hand, from "dispositive or 'real' treaties" and "constitutive or semi-legislative treaties," on the other. "Dispositive" treaties are "treaties creating or affecting territorial rights, and resembling the conveyance of English and American private law. ..." McNair gives as examples treaties of cession, boundary treaties and mandate. As to "constitutive" treaties, he has in mind international settlements or arrangements such as those neutralising Switzerland and guaranteeing passage through the Suez Canal, as well as treaties creating states, e.g. Belgium, or other entities, e.g. the United Nations, and endowing them with legal personality valid *erga omnes*. McNair suggests that the effect of "dispositive" and "constitutive" treaties is best explained not in terms of contract but of "some inherent and distinctive juridical element in those treaties."[182] The International Law Commission decided against adopting such a distinction:

> "It considered that the provision in ... [art.36, Vienna Convention], regarding treaties intended to create rights in favour of States generally, together with the process mentioned in the present article, furnish a legal basis for the establishment of treaty obligations and rights valid *erga omnes*, which goes as far as is at present possible. Accordingly, it decided not to propose any special provision on treaties creating so-called objective régimes."[183]

5. What is the effect of art.2(6) of the United Nations Charter[184] for states not members of the United Nations?[185]

----

7. VALIDITY OF TREATIES[186]

A. Non-Compliance with Municipal Law Requirements

VIENNA CONVENTION ON THE LAW OF TREATIES 1969

See above, p.637, n.4

Article 46

1. A state may not invoke the fact that its consent to be bound by a treaty has been expressed in violation of a provision of its internal law regarding competence to conclude treaties as invalidating its consent unless that violation was manifest and concerned a rule of its internal law of fundamental importance.

2. A violation is manifest if it would be objectively evident to any State conducting itself in the matter in accordance with normal practice and in good faith.

---

[181] *Treaties*, p.256.
[182] *Treaties*, p.255.
[183] Y.B.I.L.C., 1966, II, p.231.
[184] Below, App.I.
[185] Contrast the views of Kelsen, *The Law of the United Nations* (1950), pp.106–110; and Kunz (1947) 41 A.J.I.L. 119.
[186] See Nahlik (1971) 65 A.J.I.L. 736. Note that art.42(1) of the Vienna Convention reads: "The validity of a treaty or of the consent of a State to be bound by a treaty may be impeached only through the application of the present Convention."

Article 47

If the authority of a representative to express the consent of a State to be bound by a particular treaty has been made subject to a specific restriction, his omission to observe that restriction may not be invoked as invalidating the consent expressed by him unless the restriction was notified to the other negotiating States prior to his expressing such consent.

Notes[187]

1. In the *Eastern Greenland* case,[188] Norway argued[189] that M. Ihlen was not competent under Norway's constitution to bind it on a matter such as that covered by the Ihlen declaration. Clearly the Court thought this to be irrelevant as far as international law was concerned. Similarly, in his report in the *Spanish Zones of Morocco Claims*,[190] M. Huber rejected a Spanish contention in respect of one of the claims—the *Rio-Martin* claim—that a treaty was not binding upon Spain because it had not been approved in a manner required by Moroccan law:

    "The *Rapporteur* finds it unnecessary to elucidate this point of Moroccan constitutional law. It is enough to point out that the aforementioned exchange of letters between the authorised agents of the two Governments manifestly establishes their shared desire to transfer to a house at Tetuan rights that the British Government held in respect of the house at Martin by the terms of a treaty still valid for the point at issue."

2. In the *Land and Maritime Boundary between Cameroon and Nigeria* case,[191] the ICJ rejected an argument by Nigeria that an agreement with Cameroon that was signed by the Nigerian Head of State was invalid because it had not been ratified by its Supreme Military Council, as the Nigerian constitution required. Applying art.46, the Court indicated that although "the rules concerning the authority to sign treaties for a state are constitutional rules of fundamental importance...a limitation of a Head of State's capacity in this respect is not manifest...unless it is properly publicized", particularly in view of the fact that Heads of State are recognised as representing their states for the purpose of concluding a treaty in art.7, Vienna Convention on the Law of Treaties, above, p.646. The Court added that "there is no general legal obligation for states to keep themselves informed of legislative and constitutional developments in other states which are or may become important for the international relations of these states."

3. The Government of the Isle of Man has no treaty-making power; treaties affecting the Isle of Man are made by the United Kingdom Government. Imagine that the Government of the Isle of Man were to purport to make a treaty with state A for the purchase of wheat. Could the United Kingdom avoid the treaty under art.46? Could State A?

4. The International Law Commission's Commentary reads:

    "... [Article 47] is confined to cases in which the defect of authority relates to the execution of an act by which a representative purports *finally* to establish his state's consent to be bound."[192]

---

[187] See Meron (1978) 49 B.Y.I.L 772.
[188] P.C.I.J. Rep., Ser.A/B, No.53 (1933). For the facts of the case and the Ihlen Declaration, see above, p.46.
[189] P.C.I.J. Rep., Ser.C, No.62, pp.566–568.
[190] *Great Britain v Spain* (1925) 2 R.I.A.A. 615 at 724. Translation.
[191] I.C.J. Rep. 2002, p.303 at p.430.
[192] Y.B.I.L.C., 1966, II, p.243.

Where a treaty signed by a representative in excess of his authority requires ratification, if the state ratifies it "it will necessarily be held to have endorsed the unauthorised act of its representative and, by doing so, to have cured the original defect of authority."[193]

B. Error

VIENNA CONVENTION ON THE LAW OF TREATIES 1969

See above, p.637, n.4

Article 48

1. A State may invoke an error in a treaty as invalidating its consent to be bound by the treaty if the error relates to a fact or situation which was assumed by that State to exist at the time when the treaty was concluded and formed an essential basis of its consent to be bound by the treaty.

2. Paragraph 1 shall not apply if the State in question contributed by its own conduct to the error or if the circumstances were such as to put that State on notice of a possible error.

3. An error relating only to the wording of the text of a treaty does not affect its validity; Article 79 then applies.

Notes

1. Error, or mistake, plays a much less important part in the law of treaties in international law than it does in the law of contract in municipal law. The considerable care generally attendant upon the conclusion of treaties, together with, in some cases, the publicity and political scrutiny afforded to their drafting help to make this so. In practice, the International Law Commission points out, almost all the recorded instances in which errors of substance have been alleged, "concern geographical errors, and most of them concern errors in maps."[194]

2. Does art.45 distinguish between mutual and unilateral error? Or between error of fact and of law?

3. In the *Temple* case,[195] the International Court of Justice was asked to rule that Cambodia, and not Thailand, had sovereignty over the Temple of Preah Vihear and that Thailand should both remove the armed guards and other persons it had placed in the Temple since 1954 and return sculptures and other objects it had taken therefrom. In 1904, the boundary between Cambodia (then a protectorate of France) and Thailand (then Siam) in the wild, remote and sparsely populated area of Preah Vihear was determined by a treaty between France and Siam. The treaty stated that it was to follow the watershed line and provided for the details to be worked out by a Mixed Franco-Siamese Commission. Surveys were conducted by technical experts for the Commission on the basis of which a map [the Annex I map] was prepared. This clearly placed the Temple in Cambodia. The map was never approved by the Commission which did not meet again after the map had been made. Cambodia relied upon the map. Thailand argued, inter alia, that the map embodied a material error because it did not follow the watershed line as required by the treaty. It argued this even though, as the Court found, the Siamese had received and accepted the map. The Court rejected Thailand's argument as follows:

---

[193] Y.B.I.L.C., 1966, II, p.243.
[194] Y.B.I.L.C., 1966, II, p.243.
[195] I.C.J. Rep. 1962, p.6.

"It is an established rule of law that the plea of error cannot be allowed as an element vitiating consent if the party advancing it contributed by its own conduct to the error, or could have avoided it, or if the circumstances were such as to put that party on notice of a possible error. The Court considers that the character and qualifications of the persons who saw the Annex I map on the Siamese side would alone make it difficult for Thailand to plead error in law. These persons included the members of the very Commission of Delimitation within whose competence this sector of the frontier had lain. . . ."[196]

C. Fraud and Corruption

VIENNA CONVENTION ON THE LAW OF TREATIES 1969

See above, p.637, n.4

Article 49

If a State has been induced to conclude a treaty by the fraudulent conduct of another negotiating State, the State may invoke fraud as invalidating its consent to be bound by the treaty.

Article 50

If the expression of a State's consent to be bound by a treaty has been procured through the corruption of its representative directly or indirectly by another negotiating State, the State may invoke such corruption as invalidating its consent to be bound by the treaty.

Note

Fraud and corruption, like error, are not very important in practice in the law of treaties. As to *fraud*, the International Law Commission stated:

"Fraud is a concept found in most systems of law, but the scope of the concept is not the same in all systems. In International law, the paucity of precedents means that there is little guidance to be found either in practice or in the jurisprudence of international tribunals as to the scope to be given to the concept. In these circumstances, the Commission considered whether it should attempt to define fraud in the law of treaties. The Commission concluded, however, that it would suffice to formulate the general concept of fraud applicable in the law of treaties and to leave its precise scope to be worked out in practice and in the decisions of international tribunals."[197]

As to *corruption of a representative*, it stated:

"The strong term 'corruption' is used expressly in order to indicate that only acts calculated to exercise a substantial influence on the disposition of the representative to conclude the treaty may be invoked as invalidating the expression of consent which he has purported to give on behalf of his state. The Commission did not mean to imply that under the present article a small courtesy or

---

[196] I.C.J. Rep. 1962, p.26.
[197] Y.B.I.L.C., 1966, II, p.244.

favour shown to a representative in connection with the conclusion of a treaty may be invoked as a pretext for invalidating the treaty."[198]

D. Coercion[199]

VIENNA CONVENTION ON THE LAW OF TREATIES 1969

See above, p.637, n.4

Article 51

The expression of a State's consent to be bound by a treaty which has been procured by the coercion of its representative through acts or threats directed against him shall be without any legal effect.

Article 52

A treaty is void if its conclusion has been procured by the threat or use of force in violation of the principles of international law embodied in the Charter of the United Nations.

Notes

1. Coercion of a representative of a state is rare. Article 51 is directed at coercion of a representative personally and not at coercion of him through a threat of action against his state. An example of the exercise of both is reported to have occurred when President Hacha of Czechoslovakia signed a treaty with Germany establishing a German protectorate over Bohemia and Moravia in Berlin at 2 am on March 15, 1939. According to one report:

    "The German ministers [Goering and Ribbentrop] were pitiless. ... They literally hunted Dr. Hacha and M. Chvalkovsky round the table on which the documents were lying, thrusting them continually before them, pushing pens into their hands, incessantly repeating that if they continued in their refusal, half of Prague would lie in ruins from bombing within two hours, and that this would be only the beginning."[200]

    Consent obtained contrary to art.51 is of no legal effect; the state whose representative has been coerced cannot regard it as otherwise. The International Law Commission thought:

    "that the use of coercion against the representative of a state for the purpose of procuring the conclusion of a treaty would be a matter of such gravity that the article should provide for the absolute nullity of a consent to a treaty so obtained."[201]

2. As to coercion of a state, the International Law Commission's Commentary reads:

    "The traditional doctrine prior to the Covenant of the League of Nations was that the validity of

---

[198] Y.B.I.L.C., 1966, II, p.245.
[199] See De Jong (1984) 15 N.Y.I.L. 209.
[200] Dispatch by M. Coulondre, the French Ambassador to Berlin, quoted in Shirer, *The Rise and Fall of the Third Reich* (Simon & Schuster, 1959), p.446.
[201] Y.B.I.L.C., 1966, II, p.246.

a treaty was not affected by the fact that it had been brought about by the threat or use of force. However, this doctrine was simply a reflection of the general attitude of international law during that era towards the legality of the use of force for the settlement of international disputes. With the Covenant and the Pact of Paris there began to develop a strong body of opinion which held that such treaties should no longer be recognised as legally valid. The endorsement of the criminality of aggressive war in the Charters of Allied Military Tribunals for the trial of the Axis war criminals, the clear-cut prohibition of the threat or use of force in Article 2(4) of the Charter of the United Nations, together with the practice of the United Nations itself, have reinforced and consolidated this development in the law. The Commission considers that these developments justify the conclusion that the invalidity of a treaty pro-cured by the illegal threat or use of force is a principle which is *lex lata* in the international law of today. ... Some members of the Commission expressed the view that any other forms of pressure, such as a threat to strangle the economy of a country, ought to be stated in the article as falling within the concept of coercion. The Commission, however, decided to define coercion in terms of a 'threat or use of force in violation of the principles of the Charter,'[202] and considered that the precise scope of the acts covered by this definition should be left to be determined in practice by interpretation of the relevant provisions of the Charter ... the phrase 'violation of the principles of the Charter' has been chosen rather than 'violation of the Charter,' in order that the article should not appear to be confined in its application to Members of the United Nations. The Commission further considered that a treaty procured by a threat or use of force in violation of the principles of the Charter must be characterised as void, rather than as voidable at the instance of the injured party. Even if it were conceivable that after being liberated from the influence of a threat or of a use of force a state might wish to allow a treaty procured from it by such means, the Commission considered it essential that the treaty should be regarded in law as void *ab initio*. This would enable the state concerned to take its decision in regard to the maintenance of the treaty in a position of full legal equality with the other state. If, therefore, the treaty were maintained in force, it would in effect be by the conclusion of a new treaty and not by the recognition of the validity of a treaty procured by means contrary to the most fundamental principles of the Charter of the United Nations."[203]

3.   In the *Fisheries Jurisdiction* (*Jurisdiction*) case,[204] the International Court of Justice stated:

"The letter of May 29, 1972 addressed to the Registrar by the Minister for Foreign Affairs of Iceland contains the following statement: 'The 1961 Exchange of Notes took place under extremely difficult circumstances, when the British Royal Navy had been using force to oppose the 12-mile fishery limit established by the Icelandic Government in 1958.'
    This statement could be interpreted as a veiled charge of duress purportedly rendering the Exchange of Notes void *ab initio*, and it was dealt with as such by the United Kingdom in its Memorial. There can be little doubt, as is implied in the Charter of the United Nations and recognised in Article 52 of the Vienna Convention on the Law of Treaties, that under con-temporary international law an agreement concluded under the threat or use of force is void. It is equally clear that a court cannot consider an accusation of this serious nature on the basis of

---

[202] Ed. Note that in art.52 this wording was changed to "in violation of the principles of *international law embodied* in the Charter. ..." Italics added.
[203] Y.B.I.L.C., 1966, II, pp.246–247.
[204] *U.K. v Iceland* I.C.J. Rep. 1973, p.14. On the claim of duress in respect of the U.S.-Iranian Hostages Settlement, see Redwine (1981) 14 Vand. J.T.L. 847.

a vague general charge unfortified by evidence in its support. The history of the negotiations which led up to the 1961 Exchange of Notes reveals that these instruments were freely negotiated by the interested parties on the basis of perfect equality and freedom of decision on both sides. No fact has been brought to the attention of the Court from any quarter suggesting the slightest doubt on this matter."

4. If State A were to attack State B and to be utterly defeated by it, would a peace treaty between the two states by which A agreed (i) to cede to B territory belonging to A and (ii) to pay compensation for injuries suffered by the population of B during the fighting be void because of coercion? Is art.75 of the Vienna Convention applicable? This reads:

"The provisions of the present Convention are without prejudice to any obligation in relation to a treaty which may arise for an aggressor State in consequence of measures taken in conformity with the Charter of the United Nations with reference to that State's aggression."

On the present validity of title to territory based upon treaties that were made before the rule stated in art.52 was established, see above, p.196. Note that it is the acceptance of the treaty that must be coerced. A treaty, such as the 1979 Egyptian-Israeli Treaty of Peace, see above, p.192, that is signed as a matter of choice is not invalid under art.52, even though its terms may have been dictated or influenced by a prior use of force.

5. During the time of the USSR, Soviet writers used to support a doctrine of "unequal treaties".[205] The Soviet International Law textbook[206] stated:

"The principle that international treaties must be observed does not extend to treaties which are imposed by force,[207] and which are unequal in character ...
    Equal treaties are treaties concluded on the basis of the equality of the parties; unequal treaties are those which do not fulfil this elementary requirement. Unequal treaties are not legally binding; ...
    Treaties must be based upon the sovereign equality of the contracting parties."

Krylov[208] cites as examples of "unequal treaties" those establishing capitulatory regimes "by which an imperialist power imposes its will upon a weaker state ..."[209] and the Munich Agreement of 1938,[210] by which France, Italy and the United Kingdom agreed to the cession to Germany of Sudeten German territory in Czechoslovakia. The Soviet International Law textbook gave the Anglo-Egyptian Treaty of Alliance of 1936[211] as a further example because it "violated the elementary sovereign rights of the Egyptian people."[212] Article 52 does not incorporate the Soviet doctrine. The "fundamental change of circumstances" rule[213] or the "clean slate" approach to state succession to treaties[214] might, however, be applicable in some cases. The

---

[205] On "unequal treaties", see Caflisch (1992) 35 G.Y.I.L. 52.
[206] Kozhevnikov, ed., *International Law* (1961), p.248.
[207] On the meaning of "force" in art.2(4) of the UN Charter, see below, p.723.
[208] (1947–I) 70 Hague Recueil 407.
[209] (1947–I) Hague Recueil p.434. Translation. On capitulatory regimes, see above, p.10, n.46.
[210] Misc. No. 8 (1938), Cmd. 5848.
[211] (1937) U.K.T.S. 6, Cmd. 5360.
[212] See above, n.200, p.28.
[213] See below, p.704.
[214] By this, a new state is not bound by the treaties made by its predecessor.

Soviet doctrine received support from some other writers.[215] At the Vienna Treaty Conference a Declaration on the Prohibition of Military, Political or Economic Coercion in the Conclusion of Treaties[216] was adopted by which the Conference:

"*Solemnly condemns* the threat or use of pressure in any form, whether military, political, or economic, by any state in order to coerce another State to perform any act relating to the conclusion of a treaty in violation of the principles of the sovereign equality of States and freedom of consent."

6.   Debtor states may agree to "belt tightening" conditions in World Bank loan agreements over which they have no choice. Are the treaty terms involved coerced?[217]

E. Ius Cogens[218]

VIENNA CONVENTION ON THE LAW OF TREATIES 1969

See above, p.637, n.4

Article 53

A treaty is void, if, at the time of its conclusion, it conflicts with a peremptory norm of general international law. For the purposes of the present Convention, a peremptory norm of general international law is a norm accepted and recognised by the international community of States as a whole as a norm from which no derogation is permitted and which can be modified only by a subsequent norm of general international law having the same character.

Article 64[219]

If a new peremptory norm of general international law emerges, any existing treaty which is in conflict with that norm becomes void and terminates.

Notes

1.   The International Law Commission's Commentary reads:

"The view that in the last analysis there is no rule of international law from which states cannot at their own free will contract out has become increasingly difficult to sustain, although some jurists deny the existence of any rules of ius cogens in international law, since in their view even the most general rules still fall short of being universal. The Commission pointed out that the law of the Charter concerning the prohibition of the use of force in itself constitutes a con-

---

[215] For a statement typical of several made by Asian writers, see Sinha (1965) 14 I.C.L.Q. 121.
[216] *Treaty Conference Records*, 1969, p.168.
[217] See Tooze (2002) 2 H.R.L.R. 229 at 255.
[218] See Gaja (1981–III) 172 Hague Recueil 271; Hannikainen, *Peremptory Norms: (Jus Cogens), in International Law* (1988); Mangallona (1976) 51 Phil. L.J. 521; Rozakis, *The Concept of Ius Cogens in the Law of Treaties* (1976); Scheuner (1967) 27 Z.A.O.R.V. 520; and (1969) 29 Z.A.O.R.V. 28; Schwarzenberger (1965) 43 Texas L.R. 456, a shorter version of which is printed in (1965) 18 C.L.P. 191; Schwelb (1967) 61 A.J.I.L. 946; Shelton (2006) 100 A.J.I.L. 291; Sztucki, *Ius Cogens and the Vienna Convention of the Law of Treaties* (1974); Verdross (1966) 60 A.J.I.L. 55.
[219] Article 64, which really contains a rule on termination, is included here for convenience.

spicuous example of a rule in international law having the character of ius cogens. Moreover, if some governments in their comments have expressed doubts as to the advisability of this article unless it is accompanied by provision for independent adjudication, only one questioned the existence of rules of ius cogens in the international law of today. Accordingly the Commission concluded that in codifying the law of treaties it must start from the basis that today there are certain rules from which states are not competent to derogate at all by a treaty arrangement, and which may be changed only by another rule of the same character. ... The emergence of rules having the character of ius cogens is comparatively recent, while international law is in process of rapid development. The Commission considered the right course to be to provide in general terms that a treaty is void if it conflicts with a rule of ius cogens and to leave the full content of this rule to be worked out in state practice and in the jurisprudence of international tribunals. Some members of the Commission felt that there might be advantage in specifying, by way of illustration, some of the most obvious and best settled rules of ius cogens in order to indicate by these examples the general nature and scope of the rule contained in the article. Examples suggested included (a) a treaty contemplating an unlawful use of force contrary to the principles of the Charter,[220] (b) a treaty contemplating the performance of any other act criminal under international law, and (c) a treaty contemplating or conniving at the commission of acts, such as trade in slaves,[221] piracy or genocide, in the suppression of which every state is called upon to co-operate. Other members expressed the view that, if examples were given, it would be undesirable to appear to limit the scope of the articles to cases involving acts which constitute crimes under international law; treaties violating human rights, the equality of states or the principle of self determination were mentioned as other possible examples."[222]

The Commission eventually decided against including any examples of rules of ius cogens in art.63 partly because "the mention of some cases ... might, even with the most careful drafting, lead to misunderstanding as to the position concerning other cases. ..."[223]

2.   Commenting upon the Vienna Conference, Sinclair states:

"Even before the Conference began, ... it was clear that the vast majority of international lawyers from the developing countries and from the Eastern European countries attached the highest importance to the concept that a treaty concluded in violation of an existing or new rule of ius cogens should be regarded as void and of no effect. ... On the other hand, the majority of Western European governments had, in their written and other comments on the Commission's proposals, expressed considerable doubts about the desirability of introducing de lege ferenda such a vague, indeterminate and undefined ground of invalidity; and some, including the United Kingdom Government, had stressed in addition that the application of the ius cogens articles must be made subject to independent adjudication."[224]

---

[220] Ed. See in the *Nicaragua* case, below, p.727.

[221] Ed. In the *Aloeboetoe* case (1994) 1–2 I.H.R.R. 208, the Inter-American Court of Human Rights ruled that a 1762 treaty that imposed an obligation to sell prisoners as slaves "would today be null and void because it contradicts the norms of *ius cogens superveniens.*"

[222] Y.B.I.L.C., 1966, II, pp.247–248.

[223] Y.B.I.L.C. 1966, II, p.248.

[224] See above, n.1, p.66.

It was partly because of doubt about the provisions on ius cogens that France voted against the adoption of the Convention:

> "It was no doubt a lofty concept but it was liable to jeopardise the stability of treaty law, which was a necessary safeguard in inter-State relations. On that point, even ... recourse to the International Court of Justice, could not make up for the lack of precision in the drafting of the texts. In consequence, the judge would be given such wide discretion that he would become an international legislature and that was not his proper function."[225]

3.   The International Law Commission returned to the question of the content of ius cogens in the Commentary to its Draft Articles on States Responsibility (2001).[226] What emerges from this more recent Commission Commentary and from other official and doctrinal sources is that there are just a small number of generally agreed rules of *ius cogens,* namely the prohibition of armed force contrary to art.2(4), slavery and the slave trade, genocide,[227] racial discrimination[228] and *apartheid*, torture, the basic rules of international humanitarian law, and the principle of self determination.[229]

4.   The ICJ recognised the concept of *ius cogens* as a part of customary international law in the *Armed Activities (New Application: 2002)* case, when considering the DRC argument that the Court had jurisdiction to adjudicate on its claim that Rwanda had committed genocide despite the latter's treaty reservation by which it did not accept the Court's jurisdiction in disputes arising under the Genocide Convention. The DRC argued (unsuccessfully) that the reservation was invalid because, as the Court agreed, genocide was *ius cogens*.[230] In his separate opinion, Judge ad hoc Dugard commented on the Court's approach to *ius cogens*:

> "4. This is the first occasion on which the International Court of Justice has given its support to the notion of *jus cogens*. It is strange that the Court has taken so long to reach this point because it has shown no hesitation in recognizing the notion of obligation *erga omnes*, which together with *jus cogens* affirms the normative hierarchy of international law. Indeed, the Court itself initiated the notion of obligation *erga omnes* in the *Barcelona Traction* case [above, p.515]...Until the present Judgment the Court carefully and deliberately avoided endorsing the notion of *jus cogens* despite the many opportunities it had to do so. In 1969 it refrained from pronouncing 'on any question of *jus cogens*' (*North Sea Continental Shelf* [above, p.22]...; in 1986 it acknowledged that the International Law Commission had found the prohibition on the use of force to have the character of *jus cogens*, but declined to align itself with this position (*Military and Paramilitary Activities in and against Nicaragua (Nicaragua v. United States of America), Merits, Judgment, I.C.J. Reports 1986, p.258, para.83*); and in 2002 it failed

---

[225] M. Hubert (France), *Treaty Conference Records* 1969, p.203.

[226] See Commentary to art.40, printed above, p.451.

[227] Cf. the *Armed Activities (New Application: 2002)* case, above p.656.

[228] Cf. *Juridical Condition and Rights of the Undocumented Migrants*, Inter-Am.Ct.H.R., Ser A No 18 (2003).

[229] Piracy is mentioned in the ILC Law of Treaties Commentary (and in academic literature), but not in its State Responsibility Commentary. Some other candidates mentioned in the Law of Treaties Commentary (treaties violating human rights and the equality of states) now lack support, and the concept of state "acts criminal under international law" has been abandoned by the ILC: see above, p.450. For other possible rules suggested in doctrine, see the lists compiled by Shelton, at p.303 (including a "duty to assassinate dictators") and Koskeniemmi, ILC Study Group Report on Fragmentation of International Law, 2006, at p.189. See also UN Human Rights Committee, General Comment No.24, para.8, above, p.662.

[230] See the extract from the Court's judgment, above, p.616.

to respond to an argument that the granting of immunity to a Foreign Minister for crimes against humanity violated a norm of *jus cogens* (*Arrest Warrant of 11 April 2000 (Democratic Republic of the Congo v. Belgium), Judgment, I.C.J. Reports 2002*, pp.23–26). ...

5. The failure of the International Court to endorse or pronounce on the subject of *jus cogens* has not gone unnoticed. Its silence has been aggravated by the fact that both other international tribunals (*Al-Adsani v. United Kingom*, 123 *International Law Reports* 24 (European Court of Human Rights); *Prosecutor v. Furundzija*, IT-95-17/1-T, paras.153–156, 121 *International Law Reports* 214, 260 (International Criminal Tribunal for the former Yugoslavia)) and national courts (see, for example, *R. v. Bow Street Metropolitan Stipendiary Magistrate: Ex Parte Pinochet Ugarte* (No.3) [1999] 2 All ER 97 (HL); *Ferrini v. Federal Republic of Germany* (Italian Court of Cassation) 11 March 2004; (2005) 99 *American Journal of International Law* 242) have invoked the term *jus cogens* to portray higher norms of international law.

6. The approval given to *jus cogens* by the Court in the present Judgment is to be welcomed. However, the Judgment stresses that the scope of *jus cogens* is not unlimited and that the concept is not to be used as an instrument to overthrow accepted doctrines of international law.

7. The Court's endorsement of *jus cogens* raises the question of the future role of *jus cogens* and the legal consequences to be attached to a violation of *jus cogens* for, as Ian Brownlie states, 'many problems of application remain' in respect of *jus cogens* (*Principles of Public International Law*, 6th ed. (2003), p.490).

8. It is today accepted that a treaty will be void if at the time of its conclusion, it conflicts with 'a peremptory norm of general international law' (art.53 of the Vienna Convention on the Law of Treaties of 1969); and that States must deny recognition to a situation created by the serious breach of a peremptory norm (Arts. 40 and 41 of the Draft Articles on the Responsibility of States for Internationally Wrongful Acts [above, pp.451–452], ...Moreover, it has been suggested that a Security Council resolution will be void if it conflicts with a norm of *jus cogens* (see the separate opinion of Judge *ad hoc* Sir Elihu Lauterpacht in the case concerning the *Application of the Convention on the Prevention and Punishment of the Crime of Genocide, (Bosnia and Herzegovina v. Yugoslavia (Serbia and Montenegro), Provisional Measures, Order of 13 September 1993, I.C.J. Reports 1993*, p.440, para.100). *Jus cogens* does, however, have a less spectacular role to play in the judicial process and it is this role that becomes important now that the Court has finally recognized the existence of peremptory norms. ...

12. In [earlier] ...cases the Court was faced with competing principles, State practice and precedents and preferred not to choose that solution which gave effect to a norm of *jus cogens*. ...

13. In the present case the Court is...not asked, in the exercise of its legitimate judicial function, to exercise its choice between competing sources in a manner which gives effect to a norm of *jus cogens*. On the contrary, it is asked to overthrow an established principle—that the basis of the Court's jurisdiction is consent—which is founded in its Statute (art.36), endorsed by unqualified State practice and backed by *opinio juris*. It is, in effect, asked to invoke a peremptory norm to trump a norm of general international law accepted and recognized by the international community of States as a whole, and which has guided the Court for over 80 years. This is a bridge too far. The Court cannot be expected to accept the arguments raised by the DRC for by so doing it would not engage in molecular law-making, but molar law-making that goes beyond the legitimate judicial function. Only States can amend Article 36 of the Court's Statute."

5.   The concept of *ius cogens* has similarities with that of obligations *erga omnes* that was spelt out in the *Barcelona Traction* case.[231] The two concepts are now recognised as customary international law. To a large extent, they proscribe much the same kind of conduct, namely conduct that is fundamentally unacceptable to the international community of states. Thus a treaty to commit genocide would be invalid as contrary to *ius cogens*, and acts of genocide by a state would be in breach of an obligation owed to all other states *erga omnes*.[232] Similar coincidences exist in cases of resort to armed force and acts of aggression; slavery and the slave trade; and apartheid.

----

8. TERMINATION OF, SUSPENSION OF AND WITHDRAWAL FROM TREATIES[233]

A. In Accordance with the Treaty or Otherwise by Consent

VIENNA CONVENTION ON THE LAW OF TREATIES 1969

See above, p.637, n.4

Article 54

The termination of a treaty or the withdrawal of a party may take place:

(a)   in conformity with the provisions of the treaty; or

(b)   at any time by consent of all the parties after consultation with the other contracting States.

Article 55

Unless the treaty otherwise provides, a multilateral treaty does not terminate by reason only of the fact that the number of the parties falls below the number necessary for its entry into force.

Article 56[234]

1. A treaty which contains no provision regarding its termination and which does not provide for denunciation or withdrawal is not subject to denunciation or withdrawal unless:

(a)   it is established that the parties intended to admit the possibility of denunciation or withdrawal; or

(b)   a right of denunciation or withdrawal may be implied by the nature of the treaty.

2. A party shall not give less than twelve months' notice of its intention to denounce or withdraw from a treaty under paragraph 1.[235]

---

[231]   See above, p.515. See also the *Wall* case, I.C.J. Rep.2004, p.136, para.155. See generally Ragazzi, *The Concept of International Obligations Erga Omnes* (1997). See Ganji, in Weiler, Cassese and Spinedi, eds, *International Crimes of State: A Critical Analysis of the I.L.C.'s Draft Article on State Responsibility* (1989), p.151.

[232]   *Armed Activities* (*New Application: 2002*) case, above, p.655.

[233]   See Kontou, *The Termination and Revision of Treaties in the Light of New Customary International Law* (1994). Note generally that art.42(2) of the Vienna Convention reads: "The termination of a treaty, its denunciation or the withdrawal of a party, may take place only as a result of the application of the provisions of the treaty or of the present Convention. The same rule applies to suspension of the operation of a treaty."

[234]   See Widdows (1982) 53 B.Y.I.L 83.

[235]   Ed. art.56(2) is based on "an obligation to act in good faith and have reasonable regard to the interests of the other party": *Agreement between WHO and Egypt case*, I.C.J. Rep. 1980, p.73 at p.95. Advisory Opinion.

Article 57

The operation of a treaty in regard to all the parties or to a particular party may be suspended:

(a) in conformity with the provisions of the treaty; or

(b) at any time by consent of all the parties after consultation with the other contracting States.

Article 58

1. Two or more parties to a multilateral treaty may conclude an agreement to suspend the operation of provisions of the treaty, temporarily and as between themselves alone, if:

(a) the possibility of such a suspension is provided for by the treaty; or

(b) the suspension in question is not prohibited by the treaty and:

   (i) does not affect the enjoyment by the other parties of their rights under the treaty or the performance of their obligations;
   (ii) is not incompatible with the object and purpose of the treaty.

2. Unless in a case falling under paragraph 1(a) the treaty otherwise provides, the parties in question shall notify the other parties of their intention to conclude the agreement and of those provisions of the treaty the operation of which they intend to suspend.

Article 59

A treaty shall be considered as terminated if all the parties to it conclude a later treaty relating to the same subject-matter and:

(a) it appears from the later treaty or is otherwise established that the parties intended that the matter should be governed by that treaty; or

(b) the provisions of the later treaty are so far incompatible with those of the earlier one that the two treaties are not capable of being applied at the same time.

2. The earlier treaty shall be considered as only suspended in operation if it appears from the later treaty or is otherwise established that such was the intention of the parties.

Note

The United Nations Charter is probably a treaty that allows the possibility of withdrawal under art.56(1)(a).[236] A treaty of political alliance would, probably be a treaty covered by art.56(1)(b).

---

[236] See 7 U.N.C.I.O., *Documents*, p.324.

B. Material Breach[237]

VIENNA CONVENTION ON THE LAW OF TREATIES 1969

See above, p.637, n.4

Article 60

1. A material breach of a bilateral treaty by one of the parties entitles the other to invoke the breach as a ground for terminating the treaty or suspending its operation in whole or in part.
2. A material breach of a multilateral treaty by one of the parties entitles:

(a) the other parties by unanimous agreement to suspend the operation of the treaty in whole or in part or to terminate it either:

(i) in the relations between themselves and the defaulting State or
(ii) as between all parties;

(b) a party specially affected by the breach to invoke it as a ground for suspending the operation of the treaty in whole or in part in the relations between itself and the defaulting State;

(c) any party other than the defaulting State to invoke the breach as a ground for suspending the operation of the treaty in whole or in part with respect to itself if the treaty is of such a character that a material breach of its provisions by one party radically changes the position of every party with respect to the further performance of its obligations under the treaty.

3. A material breach of a treaty, for the purposes of this article, consists in:

(a) a repudiation of the treaty not sanctioned by the present Convention; or

(b) the violation of a provision essential to the accomplishment of the object or purpose of the treaty.

4. The foregoing paragraphs are without prejudice to any provision in the treaty applicable in the event of a breach.
5. Paragraphs 1 to 3 do not apply to provisions relating to the protection of the human person contained in treaties of a humanitarian character, in particular to provisions prohibiting any form of reprisals against persons protected by such treaties.

Notes

1.   The International Law Commission's Commentary reads:

"The great majority of jurists recognise that a violation of a treaty by one party may give rise to a right in the other party to abrogate the treaty or to suspend the performance of its own obligations under the treaty. ... Opinion differs, however, as to the extent of the right to abrogate the treaty and the conditions under which it may be exercised. ... State practice does not give great assistance in determining the true extent of this right or the proper conditions for its exercise. In many cases, the denouncing State has decided for quite other reasons to put an end to the treaty and, having alleged the violation primarily to provide a pretext for its action, has not been prepared to enter into a serious discussion of the legal principles involved.

---

[237] See Chinkin (1982) 17 T.I.L.J. 387; Gomaa, *Suspension or Termination of Treaties on Grounds of Breach* (1996); Hutchinson (1988) 59 B.Y.I.L. 151; Kirgis (1989) 22 Cornell I.L.J. 549; Rosenne, *Breach of Treaty* (1985); Schwelb (1967) 7 Ind. J.I.L 309; Simma (1970) 20 O.Z.O.R.V.5. Sinha, *Unilateral Denunciation of Treaty because of Prior Violations of Obligations by Other Party* (1966).

The other party has usually contested the denunciation primarily on the basis of the facts; and, if it has sometimes used language appearing to deny that unilateral denunciation is ever justified, this has usually appeared rather to be a protest against the one-sided and arbitrary pronouncements of the denouncing State than a rejection of the right to denounce when serious violations are established. ... The Commission was agreed that a breach of a treaty, however serious, does not *ipso facto* put an end to the treaty, and also that it is not open to a State simply to allege a violation of the treaty and pronounce that treaty at an end. On the other hand, it considered that within certain limits and subject to certain safeguards the right of a party to invoke the breach of a treaty as a ground for terminating it or suspending its operation must be recognised. ... Some authorities have in the past seemed to assume that any breach of any provision would suffice to justify the denunciation of the treaty. The Commission, however, was unanimous that the right to terminate or suspend must be limited to cases where the breach is of a serious character. It preferred the term 'material' to 'fundamental' to express the kind of breach which is required. The word 'fundamental' might be understood as meaning that only the violation of a provision directly touching the central purposes of the treaty can ever justify the other party in terminating the treaty. But other provisions considered by a party to be essential to the effective execution of the treaty may have been very material in inducing it to enter into the treaty at all, even although these provisions may be of an ancillary character."[238]

Note, however, that although art.60 is available only in the case of a material breach, the general customary international law of countermeasures permits proportionate retaliation in the case of minor breaches of a treaty, as of any international law obligation.[239]

2. Support for the view that only a material, as opposed to any, breach justifies the termination or suspension of a treaty under the law of treaties is found in the *Tacna-Arica Arbitration*.[240] By art.3 of the 1883 Treaty of Ancon between Chile and Peru it was provided that the Peruvian provinces of Tacna and Arica, sovereignty over which was sought by both parties, were to remain in the possession of Chile, which had obtained possession of them by armed force, for ten years and that after that time a plebiscite would be held to determine their future. In 1922, after the parties had been unable to agree upon arrangements for the plebiscite, the question whether the plebiscite had still to be held was referred to arbitration. Peru alleged, inter alia, that "Chile by preventing the performance of Article 3 has discharged Peru from her obligations thereunder, and hence that a plebiscite should not now be held and that Chile should be regarded as a trespasser in the territory now in question since the year 1894."[241] Chile had prevented the holding of the plebiscite as envisaged in art.3, Peru argued, by her policy of "Chileanization" of the provinces by the introduction of Chilean nationals and by measures discriminating against Peruvians. The Arbitrator (President Coolidge, US) rejected this argument on the facts:

    "The Arbitrator is far from approving the course of Chilean administration and condoning the acts committed against Peruvians to which reference has been made, but finds no reason to conclude that a fair plebiscite in the present circumstances cannot be held under proper conditions or that a plebiscite should not be had. ... It is manifest that if abuses of admin-

---

[238] Y.B.I.L.C., 1966, II, pp.253–255.
[239] See above, p.455.
[240] *Chile v Peru* (1925) 2 R.I.A.A. 921.
[241] *Chile v Peru* (1925) 2 R.I.A.A. 921 at p.929.

istration could have the effect of terminating such an agreement, it would be necessary to establish such serious conditions as the consequence of administrative wrongs as would operate to frustrate the purpose of the agreement, and, in the opinion of the Arbitrator, a situation of such gravity has not been shown."[242]

3.   When is there a material breach under art.60(3)(b) in the case of a law-making treaty with a number of provisions of roughly equal importance? Would, for example, a breach of art.97 of the 1982 Law of the Sea Convention concerning criminal jurisdiction in respect of collisions on the high seas[243] be one?

4.   In the case of some treaties, the International Law Commission stated in its Commentary, "a breach by one party tends to undermine the whole regime of the treaty as between all the parties."[244] The Commission gave disarmament treaties as examples of such treaties and explained:

> "In the case of a material breach of such a treaty the interests of an individual party may not be adequately protected by the rules contained in paragraphs 2(a) and (b). It could not suspend the performance of its own obligations under the treaty *vis-à-vis* the defaulting State without at the same time violating its obligations to the other parties. Yet, unless it does so, it may be unable to protect itself against the threat resulting from the arming of the defaulting State. In these cases, where a material breach of the treaty by one party radically changes the position of every party with respect to the further performance of its obligations, the Commission considered that any party must be permitted without first obtaining the agreement of the other parties to suspend the operation of the treaty with respect to itself generally in its relations with all the other parties. Paragraph 2(c) accordingly so provides."[245]

Would the Nuclear Test Ban Treaty 1963,[246] or a treaty limiting the number of whales that may be caught annually be other examples of such treaties? Would art.60(2)(c) be available in respect of a material breach of the 1948 Genocide Convention?[247] (Would art.60(2)(b) be available in the same case?) What is the effect for the other innocent parties if one innocent party acts under art.60(2)(c)? On the question of suspension of the Vienna Convention on Diplomatic Relations in the context of the *Libyan People's Bureau Incident*, see above, p.306.

5.   Paragraph 5 of art.60 was added at Vienna. The provisions in the 1949 Geneva Red Cross Conventions[248] prohibiting reprisals against the persons protected by the Conventions were mentioned as coming within it.[249] Reference was also made to conventions concerning refugees, slavery, genocide, and human rights generally, although these do not contain provisions prohibiting reprisals in cases of breach.[250]

---

[242] *Chile v Peru* (1925) 2 R.I.A.A. 921 at pp.943–944.
[243] See above, p.377.
[244] Y.B.I.L.C., 1966, II, p.255.
[245] Y.B.I.L.C., 1966, II, p.255.
[246] See above, p.365. See on this question, Schwelb (1964) 58 A.J.I.L. 642 at 663–669.
[247] U.K.T.S. 58 (1970) Cmnd. 4421; 78 U.N.T.S.
[248] See, e.g. art.46 of the Geneva Convention for the Amelioration of the Condition of the Wounded and Sick in Armed Forces in the Field (1958) U.K.T.S. 39, Cmnd. 550; 75 U.N.T.S. 3: "Reprisals against the wounded, sick, personnel, buildings, or equipment protected by the Convention are prohibited."
[249] Mr Ruegger (Switzerland), introducing the amendment: *Treaty Conference Records*, 1969, p.112.
[250] Ibid.

LEGAL CONSEQUENCES FOR STATES OF THE CONTINUED PRESENCE OF SOUTH AFRICA IN NAMIBIA (SOUTH WEST AFRICA) NOTWITHSTANDING SECURITY COUNCIL RESOLUTION 276 (1970)

Advisory Opinion. I.C.J. Reports 1971, p.16

By Resolution 2145, the United Nations General Assembly, exercising the supervisory functions which the United Nations had taken over from the League of Nations, terminated the mandate in respect of Namibia/South West Africa conferred by the League on the United Kingdom and exercised on its behalf by South Africa. It did so because South Africa had "failed to fulfil its obligations" under the mandate and had, "in fact, disavowed the mandate." In the following extract, the Court, when it considered the legal consequences of South Africa's continued presence in Namibia/South West Africa despite the General Assembly's action, considered and applied the rules as to "material breach" of a treaty, which the mandate was. The Court was of the opinion that the mandate had been validly terminated.

Opinion of the Court

91. One of the fundamental principles governing the international relationship thus established is that a party which disowns or does not fulfil its own obligations cannot be recognised as retaining the rights which it claims to derive from the relationship.

94. In examining this action [resolution 2145] of the General Assembly it is appropriate to have regard to the general principles of international law regulating termination of a treaty relationship on account of breach. ... The rules laid down by the Vienna Convention on the Law of Treaties concerning termination of a treaty relationship on account of breach (adopted without a dissenting vote) may in many respects be considered as a codification of existing customary law on the subject. In the light of these rules [see art.60(3)], only a material breach of a treaty justifies termination. ...

95. General Assembly resolution 2145 (XXI) determines that both forms of material breach [in art.60(3)] had occurred in this case. By stressing that South Africa "has in fact, disavowed the Mandate," the General Assembly declared in fact that it had repudiated it. The resolution in question is therefore to be viewed as the exercise of the right to terminate a relationship in case of a deliberate and persistent violation of obligations which destroys the very object and purpose of that relationship.

96. It has been contended that the Covenant of the League of Nations did not confer on the Council of the League power to terminate a mandate for misconduct of the mandatory and that no such power could therefore be exercised by the United Nations, since it could not derive from the League greater powers than the latter itself had. For this objection to prevail it would be necessary to show that the mandates system, as established under the League, excluded the application of the general principle of law that a right of termination on account of breach must be presumed to exist in respect of all treaties, except as regards provisions relating to the protection of the human person contained in treaties of a humanitarian character (as indicated in art.60, para.5, of the Vienna Convention). The silence of a treaty as to the existence of such a right cannot be interpreted as implying the exclusion of a right which has its source outside of the treaty, in general international law, and is dependent on the occurrence of circumstances which are not normally envisaged when a treaty is concluded.

Note

The Court treated art.60 as stating customary international law "in many [unidentified] respects".[251] Article 60 was applied in the *Gabčíkovo-Nagymaros* below, p.708.

---

[251] See also the reference to art.60 in the *Appeal relating to the Jurisdiction of the I.C.A.O. Council* case, I.C.J. Rep. 1972, p.46 at 67. For commentary see Briggs (1974) 68 A.J.I.L. 51.

C. Supervening Impossibility of Performance

VIENNA CONVENTION ON THE LAW OF TREATIES 1969

See above, p.637, n.4

Article 61

1. A party may invoke the impossibility of performing a treaty as a ground for terminating or withdrawing from it if the impossibility results from the permanent disappearance or destruction of an object indispensible for the execution of the treaty. If the impossibility is temporary, it may be invoked only as a ground for suspending the operation of the treaty.

2. Impossibility of performance may not be invoked by a party as a ground for terminating, withdrawing from or suspending the operation of a treaty if the impossibility is the result of a breach by that party either of an obligation under the treaty or of any other international obligation owed to any other party to the treaty.

Notes

1.   The International Law Commission's Commentary reads:

"State practice furnishes few examples of the termination of a treaty on this ground. But the types of cases envisaged ... [include] the submergence of an island, the drying up of a river or the destruction of a dam or hydro-electric installation indispensable for the execution of a treaty."[252]

The law of state succession applies where a state party to a treaty ceases to exist: see above, p.117.

2.   Article 61 was applied in the *Gabčíkovo-Nagymaros* case, below, p.708.

D. Fundamental Change of Circumstances[253]

VIENNA CONVENTION ON THE LAW OF TREATIES 1969

See above, p.637, n.4

Article 62

1. A fundamental change of circumstances which has occurred with regard to those existing at the time of the conclusion of a treaty, and which was not foreseen by the parties, may not be invoked as a ground for terminating or withdrawing from the treaty unless:

   (a) the existence of those circumstances constituted an essential basis of the consent of the parties to be bound by the treaty; and

---

[252] Y.B.I.L.C., 1966, II, p.256.
[253] See Haraszti (1975–III) 146 Hague Recueil 1; Lissitzyn (1967) 61 A.J.I.L. 895; Schwelb (1969) 29 Z.A.O.R.V. 39; Toth 1974 Jur. Rev. 56, 147, 263.

(b) the effect of the change is radically to transform the extent of obligations still to be performed under the treaty.

2. A fundamental change of circumstances may not be invoked as a ground for terminating or withdrawing from a treaty:

(a) if the treaty establishes a boundary; or

(b) if the fundamental change is the result of a breach by the party invoking it either of an obligation under the treaty or of any other international obligation owed to any other party to the treaty.

3. If, under the foregoing paragraphs, a party may invoke a fundamental change of circumstances as a ground for terminating or withdrawing from a treaty it may also invoke the change as a ground for suspending the operation of the treaty.

Notes

1.   The International Law Commission's Commentary reads:

"Almost all modern jurists, however reluctantly, admit the existence in international law of the principle with which this article is concerned and which is commonly spoken of as the doctrine of *rebus sic stantibus*.[254] Just as many systems of municipal law recognise that, quite apart from any actual impossibility of performance, contracts may become inapplicable through a fundamental change of circumstances, so also treaties may become inapplicable for the same reason. Most jurists, however, at the same time enter a strong caveat as to the need to confine the scope of the doctrine within narrow limits and to regulate strictly the conditions under which it may be invoked; for the risks to the security of treaties which this doctrine presents in the absence of any general system of compulsory jurisdiction are obvious. The circumstances of international life are always changing and it is easy to allege that the changes render the treaty inapplicable. The evidence of the principle in customary law is considerable, but the International Court has not yet committed itself on the point. ... The principle of *rebus sic stantibus* has not infrequently been invoked in State practice either *eo nomine* or in the form of a reference to a general principle claimed to justify the termination or modification of treaty obligations by reason of changed circumstances. Broadly speaking, it shows a wide acceptance of the view that a fundamental change of circumstances may justify a demand for the termination or revision of a treaty, but also shows a strong disposition to question the right of a party to denounce a treaty unilaterally on this ground."[255]

The Commission rejected the view that the rule should be limited to "so-called perpetual treaties", i.e. "treaties not making any provision for their termination."[256] Although cases of "supervening impossibility of performance," dealt with under art.61, could be brought within art.62, the International Law Commission "considered that juridically 'impossibility of performance' and 'fundamental change of circumstances' are distinct grounds for regarding a treaty as having been terminated, and should be kept separate."[257]

---

[254] Ed. The term *rebus sic stantibus* means literally "things remaining as they are." Reference is often made to the *clausula rebus sic stantibus*, i.e. to an express or implied clause in a treaty conditioning its validity upon the continuance of the circumstances existing at the time when it is made.

[255] Y.B.I.L.C., 1966, II, pp.257 et seq.

[256] Y.B.I.L.C., 1966, II, p.259.

[257] Y.B.I.L.C., 1966, II, p.256.

2.   On the juridical basis of the rule, the International Law Commission's Commentary reads:

> "In the past the principle has almost always been presented in the guise of a tacit condition implied in every 'perpetual' treaty that would dissolve it in the event of a fundamental change of circumstances. The Commission noted, however, that the tendency today was to regard the implied term as only a fiction by which it was attempted to reconcile the principle of the dissolution of treaties in consequence of a fundamental change of circumstances with the rule *pacta sunt servanda*. In most cases the parties gave no thought to the possibility of a change of circumstances and, if they had done so, would probably have provided for it in a different manner. Furthermore, the Commission considered the fiction to be an undesirable one since it increased the risk of subjective interpretations and abuse. For this reason, the Commission was agreed that the theory of an implied term must be rejected and the doctrine formulated as an objective rule of law by which, on grounds of equity and justice, a fundamental change of circumstances may, under certain conditions, be invoked by a party as a ground for terminating the treaty."[258]

How does the rule compare with that of frustration in the common law of contract? What does the Commission mean when it refers to an "objective rule of law?" Is the test in art.62 one of reasonable foreseeability, or what was actually forseen? Is it the foresight of *all* of the parties?

FISHERIES JURISDICTION CASE (JURISDICTION)

United Kingdom v Iceland

I.C.J. Reports 1974, p.3

For the facts, see above, p.391. The treaty which Iceland sought to have terminated *rebus sic stantibus* was the 1961 exchange of notes with the United Kingdom by which either party could refer a dispute concerning Iceland's extension of its fishing zone to the ICJ, as the United Kingdom had done in this case.

Judgment of the Court

35. In his letter of May 29, 1972, to the Registrar, the Minister of Foreign Affairs of Iceland refers to "the changed circumstances resulting from the ever-increasing exploitation of the fishery resources in the seas surrounding Iceland."

36. ... the Government of Iceland is basing itself on the principle of termination of a treaty by reason of change of circumstances. International law admits that a fundamental change in the circumstances which determined the parties to accept a treaty, if it has resulted in a radical transformation of the extent of the obligations imposed by it, may, under certain conditions, afford the party affected a ground for invoking the termination or suspension of the treaty. This principle, and the conditions and exceptions to which it is subject, have been embodied in Article 62 of the Vienna Convention on the Law of Treaties, which may in many respects be considered as a codification of existing customary law on the subject of the termination of a treaty relationship on account of change of circumstances.

37. One of the basic requirements embodied in that Article is that the change of circumstances must have been a fundamental one. In this respect the Government of Iceland has, with regard to developments in fishing techniques, referred. .. to the increased exploitation of the fishery resources in the seas surrounding Iceland and

---

[258] Y.B.I.L.C., 1966, II, p.258.

to the danger of still further exploitation because of an increase in the catching capacity of fishing fleets. The Icelandic statements recall the exceptional dependence of that country on its fishing for its existence and economic development ...

38. The invocation by Iceland of its "vital interests," which were not made the subject of an express reservation to the acceptance of the jurisdictional obligation under the 1961 Exchange of Notes, must be interpreted, in the context of the assertion of changed circumstances, as an indication by Iceland of the reason why it regards as fundamental the changes which in its view have taken place in previously existing fishing techniques. This interpretation would correspond to the traditional view that the changes of circumstances which must be regarded as fundamental or vital are those which imperil the existence of vital development of one of the parties. ...

If, as contended by Iceland, there have been any fundamental changes in fishing techniques in the waters around Iceland, those changes might be relevant for the decision on the merits of the dispute. ... But the alleged changes could not affect in the least the obligation to submit to the Court's jurisdiction, which is the only issue at the present stage of the proceedings. It follows that the apprehended dangers for the vital interests of Iceland, resulting from changes in fishing techniques, cannot constitute a fundamental change with respect to the lapse or subsistence of the compromissory clause establishing the Court's jurisdiction. ...

43. Moreover, in order that a change of circumstances may give rise to a ground for invoking the termination of a treaty it is also necessary that it should have resulted in a radical transformation of the extent of the obligations still to be performed. The change must have increased the burden of the obligations to be executed to the extent of rendering the performance something essentially different from that originally undertaken. In respect of the obligation with which the Court is here concerned, this condition is wholly unsatisfied; the change of circumstances alleged by Iceland cannot be said to have transformed radically the extent of the jurisdictional obligation which is imposed in the 1961 Exchange of Notes. ... The present dispute is exactly of the character anticipated in the compromissory clause of the Exchange of Notes. Not only has the jurisdictional obligation not been radically transformed in its extent; it has remained precisely what it was in 1961.

44. In the United Kingdom Memorial it is asserted that there is a flaw in the Icelandic contention of circumstances: that the doctrine never operates so as to extinguish a treaty automatically or to allow an unchallengeable unilateral denunciation by one party; it only operates to confer a right to call for termination and, if that call is disputed, to submit the dispute to some organ or body with power to determine whether the conditions for the operation of the doctrine are present. In this connection the Applicant alludes to Articles 65 and 66 of the Vienna Convention on the Law of Treaties.

45. In the present case, the procedural complement to the doctrine of changed circumstances is already provided for in the 1961 Exchange of Notes, which specifically calls upon the parties to have recourse to the Court in the event of a dispute relating to Iceland's extension of fisheries jurisdiction. ...

SEPARATE OPINION OF JUDGE SIR GERALD FITZMAURICE.

With regard to the question of "changed circumstances" I have nothing to add to what is stated in paragraphs 35–43 of the Court's Judgment, except to emphasise that in my opinion the only change that could possibly be relevant (if at all) would be some change relating directly to the, so to speak, operability of the jurisdictional clause itself[259]—not to such things as developments in fishery techniques or in Iceland's situation relative to fisheries. These would indeed be matters that would militate for, not against, adjudication. But as regards the jurisdictional clause itself, the only "change" that has occurred is the purported extension of Icelandic fishery limits. This however is the absolute *reverse* of the type of change to which the doctrine of "changed circumstances" relates, namely one never contemplated by the Parties: it is in fact the actual change they did contemplate, and specified as the one that would give rise to the obligation to have recourse to adjudication.

Note

See also the *Free Zones* case, above, p.684.

---

[259] For instance if the character of the International Court itself had changed in the meantime so that it was no longer the entity the parties had had in mind, e.g. if owing to developments in the United Nations, the Court had been converted into a tribunal of mixed law and conciliation, proceeding on a basis other than a purely juridical one.

GABČÍKOVO-NAGYMAROS PROJECT CASE[260]

Hungary v Slovakia

I.C.J. Reports 1997, p.7

By a 1977 bilateral treaty, Hungary and Czechoslovakia agreed to construct a system of locks diverting a stretch of the Danube along a new channel on their territories to produce hydroelectricity, improve navigation[261] and protect against flooding. In 1989, Hungary unilaterally suspended and then abandoned work on the project because of strong public protest against its environmental impact. Thereupon, Czechoslovakia devised a plan (Variant C) that deviated from the treaty and involved the unilateral diversion of the Danube into a bypass canal on its territory. In November 1991, it commenced construction of the bypass canal, but did not take irreversible steps until October 1992, when it dammed the river. Meanwhile, in May 1992 Hungary had notified its termination of the 1977 treaty, citing Variant C as being in breach of it. In 1993, Hungary and Slovakia[262] referred the case to the ICJ by special agreement, asking the Court to rule on the legality of Hungary's suspension and abandonment of work on the project; Czechoslovakia's adoption and implementation of Variant C; and Hungary's termination of the treaty. The following extracts from the Court's judgment concern its application of the law of treaties to the dispute and of the rules allowing countermeasures.

Judgment of the Court

72. ... the Court wishes to make clear that it is aware of the serious problems with which Czechoslovakia was confronted as a result of Hungary's decision to relinquish most of the construction of the System of Locks for which it was responsible by virtue of the 1977 Treaty. Vast investments had been made, the construction at Gabčíkovo was all but finished, the bypass canal was completed ...

73. Czechoslovakia repeatedly denounced Hungary's suspension and abandonment of works as a fundamental breach of the 1977 Treaty and consequently could have invoked this breach as a ground for terminating the Treaty; but this would not have brought the Project any nearer to completion. It therefore chose to insist on the implementation of the Treaty by Hungary ...

When Hungary steadfastly refused to do so — although it had expressed its willingness to pay compensation for damage incurred by Czechoslovakia — and when negotiations stalled ... Czechoslovakia decided to put the Gabčíkovo system into operation unilaterally, exclusively under its own control and for its own benefit [by Variant C]. ...

77. ... the basic characteristic of the 1977 Treaty is, according to Article 1, to provide for the construction of the Gabčíkovo-Nagymaros System of Locks as a joint investment constituting a single and indivisible operational system of works. ... By definition all this could not be carried out by unilateral action. ... Variant C thus differed sharply from it in its legal characteristics.

78. Moreover, in practice, the operation of Variant C led Czechoslovakia to appropriate, essentially for its use and benefit, between 80 and 90 per cent of the waters of the Danube before returning them to the main bed of the river, despite the fact that the Danube is not only a shared international watercourse but also an international boundary river ...

The Court accordingly concludes [by ten votes to five] that Czechoslovakia, in putting Variant C into operation, was not applying the 1977 Treaty but, on the contrary, violated certain of its express provisions, and, in so doing, committed an internationally wrongful act.

79. The Court noted that between November 1991 and October 1992, Czechoslovakia confined itself to the execution, on its own territory, of the works which were necessary for the implementation of Variant C, but which could have been abandoned if an agreement had been reached between the parties and did not therefore

---

[260] See A-Khavari and Rothwell (1998) 22 Mel.U.L.R. 507; Bekker (1998) 92 A.J.I.L. 273.

[261] The USSR sought to improve navigation for its navy.

[262] The Court held that Slovakia had succeeded to the treaty obligations of Czechoslovakia, following the latter's division into two states in 1993.

predetermine the final decision to be taken. For as long as the Danube had not been unilaterally dammed, Variant C had not in fact been applied ...

82. ... The Court has ... to determine whether such wrongfulness may be precluded on the ground that the measure so adopted was in response to Hungary's prior failure to comply with its obligations under international law.

83. In order to be justifiable, a countermeasure must meet certain conditions ...

In the first place it must be taken in response to a previous international wrongful act of another State and must be directed against that State. Although not primarily presented as a countermeasure, it is clear that Variant C was a response to Hungary's suspension and abandonment of works and that it was directed against that State; and it is equally clear, in the Court's view [by fourteen votes to one], that Hungary's actions were internationally wrongful.

84. Secondly, the injured State must have called upon the State committing the wrongful act to discontinue its wrongful conduct or to make reparation for it. It is clear from the facts of the case ... that Czechoslovakia requested Hungary to resume the performance of its treaty obligations on many occasions.

85. In the view of the Court, an important consideration is that the effects of a countermeasure must be commensurate with the injury suffered, taking account of the rights in question. ...

The Court considers that Czechoslovakia, by unilaterally assuming control of a shared resource, and thereby depriving Hungary of its right to an equitable and reasonable share of the natural resources of the Danube — with the continuing effects of the diversion of these waters on the ecology of the riparian area of the Szigetköz — failed to respect the proportionality which is required by international law. ...

87. The Court ... is therefore not required to pass upon one other condition for the lawfulness of a countermeasure, namely that its purpose must be to induce the wrongdoing State to comply with its obligations under international law, and that the measure must therefore be reversible.

88. In the light of the conclusions reached above, the Court, in reply to the question put to it in Article 2, paragraph 1 (b), of the Special Agreement ..., finds [by nine votes to six] that Czechoslovakia was entitled to proceed, in November 1991, to Variant C in so far as it then confined itself to undertaking works which did not predetermine the final decision to be taken by it. On the other hand, Czechoslovakia was not entitled to put that Variant into operation from October 1992 ...

98. The question, as formulated in Article 2, paragraph 1 (c), of the Special Agreement, deals with treaty law since the Court is asked to determine what the legal effects are of the notification of termination of the Treaty ...

99. ... The Vienna Convention is not directly applicable to the 1977 Treaty inasmuch as both States ratified that Convention only after the Treaty's conclusion. Consequently only those rules which are declaratory of customary law are applicable to the 1977 Treaty ... this is the case, in many respects, with Articles 60 to 62 of the Vienna Convention, relating to termination or suspension of the operation of a treaty. On this, the Parties, too, were broadly in agreement.

100. The 1977 Treaty does not contain any provision regarding its termination. Nor is there any indication that the parties intended to admit the possibility of denunciation or withdrawal. ... Consequently, the parties not having agreed otherwise, the Treaty could be terminated only on the limited grounds enumerated in the Vienna Convention ...

102. Hungary ... relied on the principle of the impossibility of performance as reflected in Article 61 of the Vienna Convention on the Law of Treaties. Hungary's interpretation of the wording of Article 61 is, however, not in conformity with the terms of that Article, nor with the intentions of the Diplomatic Conference which adopted the Convention. Article 61, paragraph 1, requires the "permanent disappearance or destruction of an object indispensable for the execution" of the treaty to justify the termination of a treaty on grounds of impossibility of performance. During the conference, a proposal was made to extend the scope of the article by including in it cases such as the impossibility to make certain payments because of serious financial difficulties. ... Although it was recognized that such situations could lead to a preclusion of the wrongfulness of non-performance by a party of its treaty obligations, the participating States were not prepared to consider such situations to be a ground for terminating or suspending a treaty, and preferred to limit themselves to a narrower concept.

103. Hungary contended that the essential object of the Treaty — an economic joint investment which was consistent with environmental protection and which was operated by the two contracting parties jointly — had permanently disappeared and that the Treaty had thus become impossible to perform. It is not necessary for the Court to determine whether the term "object" in Article 61 can also be understood to embrace a legal régime as in any event, even if that were the case, it would have to conclude that in this instance that régime had not definitively ceased to exist. The 1977 Treaty — and in particular its Articles 15, 19 and 20 — actually made available to the parties the necessary means to proceed at any time, by negotiation, to the required readjust-

ments between economic imperatives and ecological imperatives. The Court would add that, if the joint exploitation of the investment was no longer possible, this was originally because Hungary did not carry out most of the works for which it was responsible under the 1977 Treaty; Article 61, paragraph 2, of the Vienna Convention expressly provides that impossibility of performance may not be invoked for the termination of a treaty by a party to that treaty when it results from the party's own breach of an obligation flowing from that treaty.

104. Hungary further argued that it was entitled to invoke a number of events which, cumulatively, would have constituted a fundamental change of circumstances. In this respect it specified profound changes of a political nature, the Project's diminishing economic viability, the progress of environmental knowledge and the development of new norms and prescriptions of international environmental law (see paragraph 95 above[263]).

The Court recalls that, in the *Fisheries Jurisdiction* case, it stated that

"Article 62 of the Vienna Convention on the Law of Treaties ... may in many respects be considered as a codification of existing customary law on the subject of the termination of a treaty relationship on account of change of circumstances" *(I.C.J. Reports 1973,* p.63, para.36).

The prevailing political situation was certainly relevant for the conclusion of the 1977 Treaty. But the Court will recall that the Treaty provided for a joint investment programme for the production of energy, the control of floods and the improvement of navigation on the Danube. In the Court's view, the prevalent political conditions were thus not so closely linked to the object and purpose of the Treaty that they constituted an essential basis of the consent of the parties and, in changing, radically altered the extent of the obligations still to be performed. The same holds good for the economic system in force at the time of the conclusion of the 1977 Treaty. Besides, even though the estimated profitability of the Project might have appeared less in 1992 than in 1977, it does not appear from the record before the Court that it was bound to diminish to such an extent that the treaty obligations of the parties would have been radically transformed as a result.

The Court does not consider that new developments in the state of environmental knowledge and of environmental law can be said to have been completely unforeseen. What is more, the formulation of Articles 15, 19 and 20, designed to accommodate change, made it possible for the parties to take account of such developments and to apply them when implementing those treaty provisions.

The changed circumstances advanced by Hungary are, in the Court's view, not of such a nature, either individually or collectively, that their effect would radically transform the extent of the obligations still to be performed in order to accomplish the Project. A fundamental change of circumstances must have been unforeseen; the existence of the circumstances at the time of the Treaty's conclusion must have constituted an essential basis of the consent of the parties to be bound by the Treaty. The negative and conditional wording of Article 62 of the Vienna Convention on the Law of Treaties is a clear indication moreover that the stability of treaty relations requires that the plea of fundamental change or circumstances be applied only in exceptional cases. ...

108. Hungary's main argument for invoking a material breach of the Treaty[264] was the construction and putting into operation of Variant C. As the Court has found in paragraph 79 above, Czechoslovakia violated the Treaty only when it diverted the waters of the Danube into the bypass canal in October 1992. In constructing the works which would lead to the putting into operation of Variant C, Czechoslovakia did not act unlawfully.

In the Court's view, therefore, the notification of termination by Hungary on 19 May 1992 was premature. No breach of the Treaty by Czechoslovakia had yet taken place and consequently Hungary was not entitled to invoke any such breach of the Treaty as a ground for terminating it when it did.

109. In this regard, it should be noted that, according to Hungary's Declaration on 19 May 1992, the termination of the 1977 Treaty was to take effect from 25 May 1992, that is only six days later. Both Parties agree that Articles 65 to 67 of the Vienna Convention on the Law of Treaties, if not codifying customary law, at least generally reflect customary international law and contain certain procedural principles which are based on an obligation to act in good faith. ...

---

[263] Ed. These changes concerned (para.95): "the notion of 'socialist integration', for which the Treaty had originally been a 'vehicle', but which subsequently disappeared; the 'single and indivisible operational system', which was to be replaced by a unilateral scheme; the fact that the basis of the planned joint investment had been overturned by the sudden emergence of both States into a market economy; the attitude of Czechoslovakia which had turned the 'framework treaty' into an 'immutable norm'; and, finally, the transformation of a treaty consistent with environmental protection into 'a prescription for environmental disaster'." Note that with the 1989 fall of the Berlin Wall, Hungary and Czechoslovakia began to pursue their own national interests free of USSR dominance, introducing market economies in the place of socialist ones.

[264] Ed. On material breach, see art.69, Vienna Convention on the Law of Treaties, below, p.712.

The termination of the Treaty by Hungary was to take effect six days after its notification. On neither of these dates had Hungary suffered injury resulting from acts of Czechoslovakia. The Court must therefore confirm its conclusion that Hungary's termination of the Treaty was premature.[265]

110. Nor can the Court overlook that Czechoslovakia committed the internationally wrongful act of putting into operation Variant C as a result of Hungary's own prior wrongful conduct. As was stated by the Permanent Court of International Justice:

> "It is, moreover, a principle generally accepted in the jurisprudence of international arbitration, as well as by municipal courts, that one Party cannot avail himself of the fact that the other has not fulfilled some obligation or has not had recourse to some means of redress, if the former Party has, by some illegal act, prevented the latter from fulfilling the obligation in question, or from having recourse to the tribunal which would have been open to him." (*Factory at Chorzów, Jurisdiction, Judgment No. 8, 1927, P.C.I.J., Series A, No. 9,* p.31.)

Hungary, by its own conduct, had prejudiced its right to terminate the Treaty; this would still have been the case even if Czechoslovakia, by the time of the purported termination, had violated a provision essential to the accomplishment of the object or purpose of the Treaty. ...

The Court also considered and rejected Hungarian claims that it could terminate the treaty on grounds of necessity and of the requirements of international environmental law.

Notes

1. In the *Gabčíkovo-Nagymaros* case, the Court applies the rules concerning the termination and suspension of treaties in arts 60–61 of the Vienna Convention, treating them as "in many respects" declaratory of custom. The Court rejected Hungary's fundamental change of circumstances argument. Having found that both Hungary and Slovakia had infringed their international law obligations, by suspending and abandoning work on the project and by unilaterally implementing Variant C respectively, the Court, by 13 votes to 2, required each of them to compensate the other for the damage caused by their illegal acts.

2. On the rules governing countermeasures, see above, p.455. When in 1991 EU member states suspended treaty obligations owed to the SFRY in response to the resumption of fighting in that state, they relied upon *rebus sic stantibus* not countermeasures: see above, p.461.

E. Severance of Diplomatic or Consular Relations

VIENNA CONVENTION ON THE LAW OF TREATIES 1969

See above, p.637, n.4

Article 63

The severence of diplomatic or consular relations between parties to a treaty does not affect the legal relations established between them by the treaty except in so far as the existence of diplomatic or consular relations is indispensable for the application of the treaty.

---

[265] Ed. The Court ruled, by 11 votes to 5, that the notice of termination had no legal effect.

Note

The International Law Commission noted in its Commentary that:

"the use of third states and even of direct channels as means for making necessary communications in case of severance of diplomatic relations are so common that the absence of the normal channels ought not to be recognised as a disappearance of a 'means' or of an 'object' indispensable for the execution of a treaty."[266]

Article 63 of the Vienna Convention differs from the Commission's Draft Article by the inclusion of the words "except in so far as" onwards. The severance of consular relations by the two parties to a treaty providing for a right of consular access to a detained national would presumably come within the stated exception.

F. Ius Cogens

See Article 64 of the Vienna Convention.[267]

9. GENERAL PROVISIONS ON THE INVALIDITY, TERMINATION AND SUSPENSION OF TREATIES

A. Consequences of Invalidity, Termination or Suspension

VIENNA CONVENTION ON THE LAW OF TREATIES 1969

See above, p.637, n.4

Article 69

1. A treaty the invalidity of which is established under the present convention is void. The provisions of a void treaty have no legal force.
2. If acts have nevertheless been performed in reliance on such a treaty:

(a) each party may require any other party to establish as far as possible in their mutual relations the position that would have existed if the acts had not been performed;

(b) acts performed in good faith before the invalidity was invoked are not rendered unlawful by reason only of the invalidity of the treaty.

3. In cases falling under articles 49, 50, 51 or 52, paragraph 2 does not apply with respect to the party to which the fraud, the act of corruption or the coercion is imputable.
4. In the case of the invalidity of a particular State's consent to be bound by multilateral treaty, the foregoing rules apply in the relations between that State and the parties to the treaty.

Article 70

1. Unless the treaty otherwise provides or the parties otherwise agree, the termination of a treaty under its provisions or in accordance with the present Convention:

---
[266] Y.B.I.L.C. 1966, II, p.261.
[267] Above, p.694.

(a) releases the parties from any obligation further to perform the treaty;

(b) does not affect any right, obligation or legal situation of the parties created through the execution of the treaty prior to its termination.

2. If a State denounces or withdraws from a multilateral treaty, paragraph 1 applies in the relations between that state and each of the other parties to the treaty from the date when such denunciation or withdrawal takes effect.

Article 71

1. In the case of a treaty which is void under Article 53 the parties shall:

(a) eliminate as far as possible the consequences of any act performed in reliance on any provision which conflicts with the peremptory norm of general international law; and

(b) bring their mutual relations into conformity with the peremptory norm of general international law.

2. In the case of a treaty which becomes void and terminates under Article 64, the termination of the treaty:

(a) releases the parties from any obligation further to perform the treaty;

(b) does not affect any right, obligation or legal situation of the parties created through the execution of the treaty prior to its termination; provided that those rights, obligations or situations may thereafter be maintained only to the extent that their maintenance is not in itself in conflict with the new peremptory norm of general international law.

Article 72

1. Unless the treaty otherwise provides or the parties otherwise agree, the suspension of the operation of a treaty under its provisions or in accordance with the present Convention:

(a) releases the parties between which the operation of the treaty is suspended from the obligation to perform the treaty in their mutual relations during the period of the suspension;

(b) does not otherwise affect the legal relations between the parties established by the treaty.

2. During the period of the suspension the parties shall refrain from acts tending to obstruct the resumption of the operation of the treaty.

Note

The International Law Commission's Commentary reads:

"The Commission considered that the establishment of the nullity of a treaty on any of the grounds set forth in . . . [arts 46–53 of the Vienna Convention] would mean that the treaty was void *ab initio* and not merely from the date when the ground was invoked. Only in the case of the treaty's becoming void and terminating under . . . [art.64 of the Vienna Convention[268]] would the treaty not be invalid as from the very moment of its purported conclusion."[269]

This view is reflected in art.69 of the Vienna Convention, as is the Commission's view that:

---

[268] On ius cogens, see above, p.694.
[269] Y.B.I.L.C., 1966, II, pp.264–265.

"where neither party was to be regarded as a wrongdoer in relation to the cause of nullity (i.e. where no fraud, corruption or coercion was imputable to either party), the legal position should be determined on the basis of taking account both of the invalidity of the treaty *ab initio* and of the good faith of the parties."[270]

Invalidity because of a rule of ius cogens is treated separately in art.71.

B. Separability of Treaty Provisions

VIENNA CONVENTION ON THE LAW OF TREATIES 1969

See above, p.637, n.4

Article 44

1. A right of a party, provided for in a treaty or arising under Article 56, to denounce, withdraw from or suspend the operation of the treaty may be exercised only with respect to the whole treaty unless the treaty otherwise provides or the parties otherwise agree.

2. A ground for invalidating, terminating, withdrawing from or suspending the operation of a treaty recognised in the present Convention may be invoked only with respect to the whole treaty except as provided in the following paragraphs or in Article 60.

3. If the ground relates solely to particular clauses, it may be invoked only with respect to those clauses where:

   (a) the said clauses are separable from the remainder of the treaty with regard to their application;

   (b) it appears from the treaty or is otherwise established that acceptance of those clauses was not an essential basis of the consent of the other party or parties to be bound by the treaty as a whole; and

   (c) continued performance of the remainder of the treaty would not be unjust.

4. In cases falling under Articles 49 and 50 the State entitled to invoke the fraud or corruption may do so with respect either to the whole treaty or, subject to paragraph 3, to the particular clauses alone.

5. In cases falling under Articles 51, 52 and 53, no separation of the provision of the treaty is permitted.

Notes

1.   There would seem to be little evidence in state practice or in judicial or arbitral decisions to indicate whether in the application of the rules concerning the invalidity, termination and suspension of treaties, the treaty must be regarded as a whole, so that if one provision of the treaty is found to be invalid the treaty as a whole is invalid, or whether the provision in question may be separated from the remainder, so that the validity or continued operation of the latter is not affected. One of the few pronouncements upon the subject is that by Judge Lauterpacht in his individual opinion in the *Norwegian Loans* case.[271] The International Law Commission, whose view is reflected in art.44 of the Vienna Convention, thought it was desirable to permit severance in appropriate cases, but that it was:

   "inappropriate that treaties between sovereign states should be capable of being invalidated,

---

[270] See above, n.269, p.265.
[271] See below, p.856. On invalid reservations, see above, p.662.

terminated or suspended in operation in their entirety even in cases where the ground of invalidity, termination or suspension may relate to quite secondary provisions in the treaty."[272]

2.   Article 44(3)(c) was added at Vienna to "ensure that the rule of separability laid down in [art.44] ... would not create the very kind of international friction which the Commission sought to avoid"[273] by it.

C. Loss of the Right to Invoke a Ground for Invalidating, etc., a Treaty

VIENNA CONVENTION ON THE LAW OF TREATIES 1969

See above, p.637, n.4

Article 45

A State may no longer invoke a ground for invalidating, terminating, withdrawing from or suspending the operation of a treaty under Articles 46 to 50 or Articles 60 to 62 if, after becoming aware of the facts:

(a) it shall have expressly agreed that the treaty is valid or remains in force or continues in operation, as the case may be; or

(b) it must by reason of its conduct be considered as having acquiesced in the validity of the treaty or in its maintenance in force or in operation, as the case may be.

D. Settlement of Disputes[274]

VIENNA CONVENTION ON THE LAW OF TREATIES 1969

See above, p.637, n.4

Article 65

1. A party which, under the provisions of the present Convention, invokes either a defect in its consent to be bound by a treaty or a ground for impeaching the validity of a treaty, terminating it, withdrawing from it or suspending its operation, must notify the other parties of its claim. The notification shall indicate the measure proposed to be taken with respect to the treaty and the reasons therefor.

2. If, after the expiry of a period which, except in cases of special urgency, shall not be less than three months after the receipt of the notification, no party has raised any objection, the party making the notification may carry out in the manner provided in Article 67 the measure which it has proposed.

3. If, however, objection has been raised by any other party, the parties shall seek a solution through the means indicated in Article 33 of the Charter of the United Nations.[275]

4. Nothing in the foregoing paragraphs shall affect the rights or obligations of the parties under any provisions in force binding the parties with regard to the settlement of disputes.

5. Without prejudice to Article 45, the fact that a State has not previously made the notification prescribed in paragraph 1 shall not prevent it from making such notification in answer to another party claiming performance of the treaty or alleging its violation.

---

[272] Commentary, Y.B.I.L.C., 1966, II, p.238.
[273] Mr Kearney (US), introducing the amendment, *Treaty Conference Records*, 1968, p.230.
[274] See Sinclair, above, n.1, pp.226 et seq.
[275] Ed. Below, App.I.

Article 66[276]

If, under paragraph 3, of Article 65, no solution has been reached within a period of 12 months following the date on which the objection was raised, the following procedures shall be followed:

(a) any one of the parties to a dispute concerning the application or the interpretation of Article 53[277] or 64[278] may, by a written application, submit it to the International Court of Justice for a decision unless the parties by common consent agree to submit the dispute to arbitration;

(b) any one of the parties to a dispute concerning the application or the interpretation of any of the other articles in Part V[279] of the present Convention may set in motion the procedure specified in the Annex to the Convention by submitting a request to that effect to the Secretary-General of the United Nations.

Annex *to the Convention*

1. A list of conciliators consisting of qualified jurists shall be drawn up and maintained by the Secretary-General of the United Nations. To this end, every state which is a Member of the United Nations or a party to the present Convention shall be invited to nominate two conciliators, and the names of the persons so nominated shall constitute the list. . . .

2. When a request has been made to the Secretary-General under Article 66, the Secretary-General shall bring the dispute before a conciliation commission constituted as follows:

The state or states constituting one of the parties to the dispute shall appoint:

(a) one conciliator of the nationality of that state or of one of those states, who may or may not be chosen from the list referred to in paragraph 1; and

(b) one conciliator not of the nationality of that state or of any of those states, who shall be chosen from the list.

The state or states constituting the other party to the dispute shall appoint two conciliators in the same way. The four conciliators chosen by the parties shall be appointed within sixty days following the date on which the Secretary-General receives the request.

The four conciliators shall, within sixty days following the date of the last of their own appointments, appoint a fifth conciliator chosen from the list, who shall be chairman.

If the appointment of the chairman or of any of the other conciliators has not been made within the period prescribed above for such appointment, it shall be made by the Secretary-General within sixty days following the expiry of that period. . . .

3. . . . Decisions and recommendations of the Commission shall be made by a majority vote of the five members.

4. The Commission may draw the attention of the parties to the dispute to any measures which might facilitate an amicable settlement.

5. The Commission shall hear the parties, examine the claims and objections, and make proposals to the parties with a view to reaching an amicable settlement of the dispute.

6. The Commission shall report within twelve months of its constitution. Its report shall be deposited with the Secretary-General and transmitted to the parties to the dispute. The report of the Commission, including any conclusions stated therein regarding the facts or questions of law, shall not be binding upon the parties and it shall have no other character than that of recommendations submitted for the consideration of the parties in order to facilitate an amicable settlement of the dispute . . .

---

[276] Article 66 is not declaratory of custom: *Armed Activities (New Application: 2002)* case, I.C.J. Rep. 2006, p.6 at p.45.
[277] Ed. Above, p.694.
[278] Ed. Above, p.694.
[279] Ed. arts 42–72.

Note

There was considerable debate at the Vienna Conference on the question of the procedure to be established for the settlement of disputes arising under the Convention. Certain states, including the United Kingdom, wanted provision for compulsory judicial settlement. It was felt that the rules in the Convention on invalidity, termination and suspension could easily be abused in the absence of compulsory and binding settlement procedures. This feeling was particularly strong with regard to the questions of ius cogens and fraud. Other states, including the USSR, with its then fundamental opposition to binding international settlement procedures independent of the control of the disputing parties, disagreed.[280] Eventually, "at the eleventh hour and in circumstances of high drama not fully revealed in the drab official records of the Conference,"[281] the compromise in arts 65 and 66 and the Annex to the Convention was adopted. How satisfactory a guarantee against abuse of the Convention is it?[282] What if, in cases other than ones concerning ius cogens, the parties cannot agree upon a solution after exhausting the procedure provided for in arts 65(3) and 66 and in the Annex? Has the claim invoking a defect in the claimant's consent, etc. failed?

----

10. REGISTRATION OF TREATIES[283]

See art.102, United Nations Charter.[284]

VIENNA CONVENTION ON THE LAW OF TREATIES 1969

See above, p.637, n.4

Article 80

1. Treaties shall, after their entry into force, be transmitted to the Secretariat of the United Nations for registration or filing and recording, as the case may be, and for publication. ...

Notes

1. By virtue of art.102, only treaties registered with the UN may be invoked before the ICJ. An unregistered treaty nonetheless remains legally binding between the parties.[285] The purpose of art.102 of the United Nations Charter, like that of its predecessor, art.18 of the League of Nations Covenant, is to give publicity to treaty relations and avoid secret treaties. This has, to a large

---

[280] See, e.g. Mr Khlestov (USSR), in *Treaty Conference Records*, 1969, pp.302–303. For a statement of the case for compulsory and binding settlement procedures, see Briggs (1967) 64 A.J.I.L. 976 at 983–988.

[281] Sinclair, above, n.1 pp.68–69.

[282] Note that France and Australia were influenced by the inadequacy—in their view—of the procedures for settlement when voting against the adoption of the Convention and abstaining respectively: *Treaty Conference Records*, 1969, pp.203–209.

[283] See Brandon (1952) 29 B.Y.I.L. 186; Brandon (1953) 47 A.J.I.L. 49; Higgins, *The Development of International Law by the Political Organs of the United Nations* (1963), pp.328–336; Lillich (1971) 65 A.J.I.L. 771; Hutchinson (1993) 46 C.L.P. 257; Tabory (1982) 76 A.J.I.L. 350.

[284] See below, App.I.

[285] *Maritime Delimitation and Territorial Questions between Qatar and Bahrain* case *(Jurisdiction and Admissibility No.1)*, I.C.J. Rep. 1994, p.112 at p.122.

extent,[286] been achieved. Treaties registered under art.102 are published in the United Nations Treaty Series, of which there are well over 2,000 volumes.

2.   The terms "treaty" and "international agreement" in art.102 have purposely been left undefined, "it being recognised that experience and practice will in themselves aid in giving definition to the terms of the Charter."[287] The Final Act of the Helsinki Conference on Security and Co-operation in Europe 1975, for example, was understood as not being eligible for registration since it was not binding in law.[288] At San Francisco it was thought that the word "agreement" must be understood as including "unilateral engagements of an international character which have been accepted by the state in whose favour such an engagement has been entered into."[289] On the basis of this interpretation, the Secretariat has, on its own initiative and with the approval of the General Assembly Sixth Committee, arranged[290] for the registration, inter alia, of declarations by new members of the United Nations accepting membership and declarations made under the "Optional Clause."[291] In respect of instruments submitted to it by Members, the Secretariat has taken the following position:

> "... the Secretariat ... follows the principle that it acts in accordance with the position of the Member State submitting an instrument for registration that so far as that party is concerned the instrument is a treaty or an international agreement within the meaning of Article 102. Registration of an instrument submitted by a Member State, therefore, does not imply a judgment by the Secretariat on the nature of the instrument, the status of a party, or any similar question. It is the understanding of the Secretariat that its action does not confer on the instrument the status of a treaty or an international agreement if it does not already have that status and does not confer on a party a status which it would not otherwise have."[292]

Thus, when, in 1957, Egypt submitted for registration a unilateral "Declaration on the Suez Canal and Agreements for its Operation,"[293] the Secretary-General replied that it would be registered on the understanding that Egypt thought that it came within art.102. The Secretariat has, however, had occasion to indicate its views with regard to certain types of instrument and has suggested, for example, that "postal agreements (even though concluded for example, between the respective postmaster-general)" are within art.102, but that agreements to which non-governmental international organisations (e.g. the International Patents Institute) are parties are not.[294] Clearly treaties between United Nations Members, on the one hand, and non-member states or public international organisations with treaty-making capacity, on the other, are covered. The International Law Commission's Commentary reads:

> "Although the Charter obligation is limited to Member States, non-member States have in practice 'registered' their treaties habitually with the Secretariat of the United Nations. Under Article 10 of the Regulations concerning the Registration and Publication of Treaties and

---

[286] It is known, however, that some treaties are not registered. This was true, for example, of a Franco-United States Agreement of September 6, 1960, on NATO Nuclear Weapons.
[287] G.A.O.R., 1st Sess., Part II, Plenary, Annex 91, p.1586.
[288] See Russell, above, n.26, p.246.
[289] 13 U.N.C.I.O., *Documents*, p.705.
[290] 5 *U.N. Repertory of Practice* 293.
[291] 5 *U.N. Repertory of Practice* 293.
[292] UN Doc. ST/LEG/SER./A/105, November 1955, Prefatory Note.
[293] 265 U.N.T.S. 299.
[294] 5 *U.N. Repertory of Practice* 295–296.

International Agreements adopted by the General Assembly, the term used instead of 'registration' when no Member of the United Nations is party to the agreement is 'filing and recording,' but in substance this is a form of voluntary registration."[295]

3. Could an unregistered treaty to which a member of the United Nations was a party be invoked by another party not a member of the United Nations before the International Court of Justice or an ad hoc arbitral tribunal?

---

[295] Y.B.I.L.C., 1966, II, p.273.

11 THE USE OF FORCE

1. INTRODUCTORY NOTE

This Chapter is concerned with the rules of international law (*ius ad bellum*) that prohibit the unilateral use of force by states and provide for collective measures through the United Nations to maintain or restore international peace and security. It does not consider the international law of armed conflict or international humanitarian law[1] (*ius in bello*) which governs conduct in armed conflict and in post conflict military occupation.[2]

2. THE UNILATERAL USE OF FORCE BY STATES[3]

A. The Prohibition of the Use of Force

GENERAL TREATY FOR THE RENUNCIATION OF WAR 1928[4]

U.K.T.S. 29 (1929), Cmnd. 3410; 94 L.N.T.S. 57

The Signatory States . . .

Persuaded that the time has come when a frank renunciation of war as an instrument of national policy should be made to the end that the peaceful and friendly relations now existing between their peoples may be perpetuated;

Convinced that all changes in their relations with one another should be sought only by pacific means and be the result of a peaceful and orderly process, and that any signatory Power which shall hereafter seek to promote its national interests by resort to war should be denied the benefits furnished by this Treaty. . . .

Have decided to conclude a Treaty. . . .

---

[1]   These terms are now commonly used instead of the "law of war" or the "law of warfare".

[2]   See mainly the Hague Conventions of 1899 and 1907, printed in Roberts and Guelff, eds, *Documents on the Law of War* (3rd edn 2000) (on the conduct of hostilities generally); the four 1949 Geneva Red Cross Conventions, ibid. (on the treatment of the injured, prisoners of war and civilians); and the two 1977 Protocols to the 1949 Conventions, (supplementing and revising the 1949 Conventions in their application to international conflicts (Protocol I) and extending the protection afforded to victims in non-international conflicts (Protocol II)). See generally, Byers, *War Law* (2005); Dinstein, *The Conduct of Hostilities under the Law of Armed Conflicts* (2004); Fleck, *The Handbook of Humanitarian Law in Armed Conflicts* (2nd edn 2008); Gazzini, *The Changing Rules on the Use of Force International Law* (2005); Green, *The Contemporary Law of Armed Conflict* (3rd edn 2008); Henckaerts and Doswald-Beck, *Customary International Humanitarian Law* (2005); Rogers, *Law on the Battlefield* (2nd edn 2004).

[3]   See Arend and Beck, *International Law and the Use of Force* (1993); Brownlie, *International Law and the Use of Force by States* (1963); Byers, *War Law* (2005); Dinstein, *War, Aggression and Self-Defence* (4th edn 2005); Franck, *Recourse to Force* (2002); Gray, *International Law and the Use of Force* (2nd edn 2004); Higgins, *The Development of International Law through the Political Organs of the UN* (1963), pp.167–239.

[4]   The Treaty is sometimes known as the Pact of Paris or the Briand-Kellogg Pact (after the French Foreign Minister and US Secretary of State respectively).

Article I

The High Contracting Parties solemnly declare in the names of their respective peoples that they condemn recourse to war for the solution of international controversies, and renounce it as an instrument of national policy in their relations with one another.

Article II

The High Contracting Parties agree that the settlement or solution of all disputes or conflicts of whatever nature or of whatever origin they may be, which may arise among them, shall never be sought except by pacific means.

Notes

1. Prior to the First World War, international law condoned the resort to war by states. The position was explained by Brierly[5] as follows:

    "The relation of war to the international system was stated by W. E. Hall in a well-known passage of his treatise in these words: 'International law has no alternative but to accept war, independently of the justice of its origin, as a relation which the parties to it may set up if they choose, and to busy itself only in regulating the effects of the relation'.[6] This view, which came to be more or less generally accepted by international lawyers in the course of the nineteenth century, marked the definite abandonment of the claim of the classical jurists to distinguish between *bellum iustum* and *bellum iniustum*.

2. After the First World War, the League of Nations Covenant[7] imposed some limitations upon "resort to war." It was not until the General Treaty of 1928, however, that a comprehensive prohibition of war as an instrument of national policy was achieved. Somewhat ironically, 63 states, i.e. virtually the whole of the international community at that time, were parties to the Treaty when the Second World War started in 1939. The Treaty has never been terminated.[8] For practical purposes, it has been superseded by art.2(4) of the United Nations Charter.

3. It has never been clear whether the Treaty prohibits armed force short of war as well as war. Thus, on the one hand, Bowett[9] states that the Pact only prohibits war "for under accepted terminology of international law (and without defending that terminology) measures involving the use of force but falling short of war are characterised as pacific; in this case Article 2 cannot be invoked as a reason for departing from the plain meaning of the terms of Article 1." Brownlie,[10] on the other hand, suggests that "the best guide to the meaning of the Pact is to be found by recourse to the subsequent practice of the parties" and concludes that this "leaves little room for doubt that it was understood to prohibit any substantial use of armed force."

4. It is now exceptional for the parties to hostilities to regard themselves as legally at war.[11] The importance of the question has been reduced by the fact that (i) the United Nations Charter rule

---

5   (1932) 4 Cam.L.J. 308.
6   *International Law* (8th edn), p.82.
7   See arts 15 and 16, (1919) U.K.T.S. 4, Cmd. 153.
8   There are now 67 parties.
9   See below, n.105, p.136.
10   See above, n.2, p.87.
11   See Greenwood (1987) 36 I.C.L.Q. 283. But see the 1971 Indo-Pakistani War, below, p.745. In the Falkland Islands "War," the UK studiously avoided any statement indicating that it regarded the conflict as war, and Argentina made no formal proclamation of war. cf. *Hansard*, HL Vol.459, col.646 (January 30, 1985).

on the use of force (art.2(4)), draws no distinction between war and armed force short of war and (ii) the 1949 Geneva Red Cross Conventions and the 1977 Protocols[12] apply to "all cases of declared war or of any other armed conflict which may arise between two or more of the High Contracting Parties, even if the state of war is not recognised by one of them."[13]

5.   Whatever the scope of the General Treaty, before 1945 the use of armed force was permitted in international law as a reprisal for an illegal act. [14] A countermeasures (a term that has replaced reprisal) involving the use of armed force is now prohibited by art.2(4), UN Charter.[15]

ARTICLE 2(4) UNITED NATIONS CHARTER

4. All Members shall refrain in their international relations from the threat or use of force against the territorial integrity or political independence of any state, or in any other manner inconsistent with the purposes of the United Nations.

Notes

1.   Although phrased in terms of "members" of the United Nations, art.2(4) is, as confirmed in the *Nicaragua (Merits)* case, below, p.727, a rule of customary international law applying to all states.

2.   The extent of the prohibition in art.2(4) is not clear from the text. The Security Council and the General Assembly, being political rather than judicial bodies, have not spent much time debating the niceties of international law in particular cases so that, with some exceptions, there is not a great deal to be found in their practice on the meaning of art.2(4). This is particularly so since the attention of representatives has usually been focused on questions of jurisdiction under art.39 (Is there a breach of the peace, etc.?) and not upon questions of compliance with art.2(4). Some more precise meaning has been given to art.2(4) by the Section on the Principle of the Use of Force of the 1970 General Assembly Declaration on Principles of International Laws concerning Friendly Relations and Co-operation among States, below, App.III, although that too is vaguely worded in places,[16] and by the *Nicaragua (Merits)* case. The Declaration can be taken to reflect the views of the United Nations membership as a whole on the legal meaning of the principles in the Charter upon which it elaborates.[17]

3.   *Force.* Article 2(4) prohibits the use of armed force, whether amounting to war or not. It does not prohibit political pressure (e.g. the refusal to ratify a treaty or the severance of diplomatic relations) or economic pressure (e.g. a trade boycott or the blocking of a bank account). As far as the latter is concerned, a proposal by Brazil during the drafting of art.2(4) that states should be

---

[12]   See above, n.2.
[13]   See art.2, common to the four 1949 Conventions. See also art.1, Protocols I and II.
[14]   See the *Naulilaa* case (1928) 2 R.I.A.A. 1012.
[15]   On countermeasures, see above, p.455.
[16]   On the Declaration generally, see Arangio-Ruiz, *The UN Declaration on Friendly Relations and the System of Sources of International Law* (1979); and Rosenstock (1971) 65 A.J.I.L. 713. On its drafting, see Hazard (1964) 58 A.J.I.L. 952; Houben (1967) 61 ibid. 703; Lee (1965) 14 I.C.L.Q. 1296; and McWhinney (1966) 60 A.J.I.L. 1. The Section on the Principle on the Use of Force is reinforced by the 1987 UN Declaration on the Enhancement of the Effectiveness of the Principle of Refraining from the Threat or Use of Force in International Relations, G.A. Resn. 42/22, G.A.O.R., 42nd Sess., Supp. 49, p.287 (1987). Both Declarations were adopted by consensus.
[17]   cf. the *Nicaragua (Merits)* case, judgment, para.188, below, p.729.

required to refrain from "economic measures" was rejected.[18] It is not wholly clear, however, whether this was because it was intended not to prohibit economic force or because the term "force" in art.2(4) was thought sufficient to cover it without specific mention. In the opinion of Goodrich, Hambro and Simons[19]:

"It seems reasonable to conclude that while various forms of economic and political coercion may be treated as threats to the peace, as contrary to certain of the declared purposes and principles of the Organisation, or as violating agreements entered into or recognised principles of international law, they are not to be regarded as coming necessarily under the prohibition of Article 2(4), which is to be understood as directed against the use of armed force."

The matter was purposely not clarified in the 1970 Declaration. This just refers to "force" in the Section on the Principle of the Use of Force because of disagreement between mainly Western states, who argued that only armed force was prohibited, and Soviet bloc and most (but not all) developing states, who claimed that "all forms of pressure, including those of a political and economic character, which have the effect of threatening the territorial integrity or political independence of any state" were prohibited.[20] The Western states were, however, prepared to admit, presciently in the light of the Arab oil boycott of 1973/74,[21] "that this was not to say that all forms of economic and political pressure which threatened the territorial integrity and poli-tical independence of another state were permissible; they might well constitute illegal inter-vention."[22] The Section of the 1970 Declaration on Principles of International Law on the Principle of Non-Intervention, which is distinct from the Section on the Principle of the Use of Force, prohibits economic coercion (but without defining it). In the *Nicaragua* (*Merits*) case (judgment, para.245, below, p.735), the ICJ found that the United States economic sanctions complained of by Nicaragua were not in breach of the principle of non-intervention.[23]

A use of armed force by State A against State D is clearly a breach of art.2(4). If State T intervenes by armed force to assist State A, it too is directly in breach of art.2(4). If it intervenes in the same way to assist State D, the right of collective self defence, below, p.748, may justify its conduct. If State T assists State A in its attack upon State D by providing it with military or other equipment, training facilities, land bases, etc. then State T is probably indirectly engaged in the "use of force" contrary to art.2(4).[24]

---

[18]   6 U.N.C.I.O., *Documents* 335.

[19]   *Charter of the United Nations* (3rd edn 1969), p.49.

[20]   UN Doc. A/AC.125/SR.114 (1970).

[21]   In late 1973 (just after the *Yom Kippur War*) and early 1974, the Arab oil-producing states, led by Saudi Arabia, imposed an embargo on the supply of oil to the US and other states (including all of the EEC countries) which they claimed were supporting Israel. The purpose was to cause those states to change their Middle East policies. For differing views on the legality of the embargo, which had a devastating economic effect, see the essays in Lillich, ed., *Economic Coercion and the New International Economic Order* (1976); and Paust and Blaustein, ed., *The Arab Oil Weapon* (1977).

[22]   UK representative (Mr Sinclair), UN Doc. A/AC.125/SR.25 (1966).

[23]   On the legality of US economic sanctions against Nicaragua, see Henderson (1986) 43 Wash. Lee L.R. 167. On the legality of economic sanctions generally, see Acevedo (1984) 78 A.J.I.L. 323; Barrie (1988) 82 A.J.I.L. 311; Delanis (1979) 12 Vand. J.T.L. 101; Farer (1985) 79 A.J.I.L. 405; Neff (1988) 59 B.Y.I.L. 113; and Parry, Blum, Lillich and Bilder (1977) 12 T.I.L.J. 1, 5, 17 and 41 respectively.

[24]   This last situation is not specifically mentioned in the 1970 Declaration. The Section in the Declaration on the Principle on the Use of Force, paras 8 and 9, prohibits intervention in a *civil war* to assist rebels, by such "indirect aggression"; it would seem that assistance of the same sort to state A using armed force against State D is as much the "use of force" as this and is otherwise a breach of art.2(4). In any event, such assistance to State A is contrary to the Principle of Non-Intervention in the 1970 Declaration. On the limited UN practice concerning aid to a state using armed force against another state, see Higgins, above, n.3, p.189.

4. *Threat of force.*[25] The ultimatum issued by France and the United Kingdom to Egypt and Israel in 1956 demanding a ceasefire within 12 hours would be a "threat of force". On the question whether a "signalled intention to use" nuclear weapons (or other kinds of force) or the possession of nuclear weapons is a threat of force contrary to art.2(4), see the *Legality of Nuclear Weapons* case, opinion, paras 47–48, below, p.789. Would another be the threat made by the Soviet Premier, Mr Khruschchev, in 1960 after the *U-2 Incident*, when he reportedly stated:

> "Those countries that have bases on their territories should note most carefully the following: if they allow others to fly from their base to our territory we shall hit at those bases."[26]

United States military manoeuvres near the Nicaraguan border were held not to be a "threat to force" in the *Nicaragua (Merits)* case.[27] But when, in 1994, "Iraqi artillery and tanks were deployed in positions pointing towards and within range of Kuwait, with ammunition at the ready" on the Iraqi side of the border, this was stated by the United Kingdom to be a "threat to Kuwait and a breach of the provisions of the Charter".[28] In *Guyana v Suriname,*[29] Suriname patrol boats ordered an oil rig and its service vessels, operating under a concession to a Canadian company granted by Guyana in a continental shelf area disputed by the two states, to leave the area within 12 hours or "the consequences would be theirs". The tribunal viewed this as a "threat of the use of force" in breach of art. 2(4), presumably as being "inconsistent with the purposes of the United Nations", which include the settlement of disputes by peaceful means.

5. *Against the territorial integrity or political independence of any state or in any manner, etc.* Article 2(4) prohibits the use of armed force by State A against State D that *either* deprives State D of the whole or a part of its territory (see, e.g. the invasion of Poland by Germany in 1939 and of Manchuria (a part of China) by Japan in 1931, p.188, above, respectively) *or* brings State D under State A's political control (see e.g. the *Afghanistan* case, below, p.744).[30]

The words "territorial integrity" (and "political independence") could be read as words of limitation, with a distinction being drawn between "integrity" (to do with annexation or permanent occupation or control) and "inviolability" (to do with trespass). Bowett[31] supports this limited reading on the basis in part that "the phrase having been included, it must be given its plain meaning." It was relied upon in the *Corfu Channel* case by the United Kingdom when it argued that *Operation Retail*, in which the Corfu Channel in Albanian territorial waters was mineswept by the United Kingdom after British ships had been damaged by mines in it, was not contrary to art.2(4):

> "But our action . . . threatened neither the territorial integrity nor the political independence of

---

[25] See Roscini (2007) N.I.L.R. 229; Sadurska (1988) 82 A.J.I.L. 239; Sturchler, *The Threat of Force in International Law* (2007); White and Cryer (1999) 29 Cal. West. I.L.J. 243.

[26] 5 Whiteman 714. On the *U-2 Incident*, see above, p.207. See also on "threats of force," UN Secretary-General *Report on the Question of Defining Aggression*, UN Doc. A/2211, p.52: ". . . the threat to use force is not always made in so crude and open a form [as an ultimatum]. There are sometimes veiled threats which may be very effective, but are difficult to detect."

[27] Judgment, para.227, below, p.331.

[28] Sir David Hannay, Security Council debate, October 16, 1994, S/PV. 3431, pp.11–12.

[29] (2007) *www.pca-cpa.org.*

[30] On the use of force by State A to obtain possession of territory to which it claims legal title but which is occupied by State B, see below, p.750.

[31] See below, n.105, p.152. The same author also points out (pp.150–151) that art.2(4) can be interpreted as requiring *either* a "specific intent," so that "the use or threat of force contravenes this obligation only where intended to jeopardise the political independence or territorial integrity of another state," *or* only that armed force must not be intentionally used with this result. The latter interpretation is the one that would appear to be followed in practice.

Albania. Albania suffered thereby neither territorial loss nor [loss to] any part of its political independence."[32]

Although this argument was not specifically considered in the judgment, the Court's condemnation of *Operation Retail* is not in sympathy with it.[33] Brownlie[34] argues convincingly against such a limited interpretation as follows:

"The conclusion warranted by the *travaux préparatoires* is that the phrase under discussion was not intended to be restrictive but, on the contrary, to give more specific guarantees to small states and that it cannot be interpreted as having a qualifying effect.

... The phrase 'political independence and territorial integrity' has been used on many occasions to epitomize the *total* of legal rights which a state has. Moreover, it is difficult to accept a 'plain meaning' which permits evasion of obligations by means of a verbal profession that there is no intention to infringe territorial integrity and which was not intended by the many delegations which approved the text. Lastly, if there is an ambiguity the principle of effectiveness should be applied."

See also the 1970 Declaration, 4th and 5th paragraphs of the Section on the Principle on the Use of Force, which support this wider interpretation. Even if the words "territorial integrity" were to be read restrictively, the final phrase of art.2(4) ("or in any manner inconsistent with the purposes of the United Nations"), nonetheless indicates that the paragraph, taken as a whole, contains a general prohibition on the use of armed force as "an instrument of national policy" (in the words of the Briand-Kellogg Pact), given that one of the "purposes of the United Nations" is to "maintain international peace and security" (Charter, art.1(1)). The use of armed force in international relations by way of reprisal is prohibited.[35] This is so whether the armed force is used in the territory of another state or not (e.g. the use of force against a ship or aircraft[36] outside the state of registration). The only justification for the use of armed force by one state against another under the legal regime of the Charter is self-defence, see below, p.746; participation in United Nations enforcement action, see below, pp.796 et seq.; or, seemingly, in some cases of humanitarian intervention with UN authorisation.[37] Otherwise the interest in international peace and security prevails.[38]

---

[32] *Corfu Channel* case, Pleadings, Vol.III, p.296.
[33] See the passage from the judgment, above, p.341.
[34] See above, n.3, pp.268–287.
[35] On reprisals, or countermeasures, see above, p.455.
[36] These would presumably not be "territory" for the purposes of art.2(4). cf. the facts of the *Gulf of Tonkin Incident*, below, p.754. In that case, the retaliation was justified as self-defence.
[37] See below, p.777.
[38] On the question whether armed force may be used to realise the right to self-determination, see below, p.739. It may not be used by states unilaterally to restore democracy: see Gray, above, at n.2, pp.49 et seq. However, the Security Council did authorise or approve multilateral force to restore democratically elected governments in Haiti and Sierra Leone respectively. Gray states: "It seems to go too far to argue that these instances of UN and regional [ECOWAS] action show a right for states unilaterally to use force to restore democratic government." p.52.

NICARAGUA CASE (MERITS)[39]

Nicaragua v United States

ICJ Reports 1986, p.14

In 1979, the right-wing Somoza Government in Nicaragua was overthrown by revolution by the left-wing Sandinista Government. In 1981, President Reagan terminated economic aid to Nicaragua on the ground that it had aided guerrillas fighting against the El Salvador Government, which enjoyed good relations with the United States, by allowing USSR arms to pass through its ports and territory en route for El Salvador. In this case, Nicaragua claimed that the United States had also acted against Nicaragua in other ways that were in violation of customary international law. It claimed, inter alia, that the United States had (i) used direct armed force against it by laying mines in Nicaraguan internal and territorial waters, causing damage to Nicaraguan and foreign merchant ships, and attacking and damaging Nicaraguan ports, oil installations and a naval base and (ii) given assistance to the *contras*, Nicaraguan guerrillas fighting to overthrow the Sandinista Government. Nicaragua also claimed that the United States had acted in breach of the bilateral 1956 US-Nicaraguan Treaty of Friendship, Commerce and Navigation.[40] In the following extracts, the Court considered first whether it had jurisdiction in respect of the claims by Nicaragua based on customary international law that had the same content as provisions rules in the UN Charter even though the United States had made a reservation to its acceptance of the Court's jurisdiction under art.36(2), ICJ Statute excluding "disputes arising under a multilateral treaty". Having found that it did, the Court went on to consider whether the United States had infringed customary international law. However, it found itself unable to decide whether the United States had infringed art.2(4), UN Charter or any other multilateral treaty provisions because of the United States reservation to its jurisdiction.

Judgment of the Court

175. The Court does not consider that, in the areas of law relevant to the present dispute, it can be claimed that all the customary rules which may be invoked have a content exactly identical to that of the rules contained in the treaties which cannot be applied by virtue of the United States reservation. On a number of points, the areas governed by the two sources of law do not exactly overlap, and the substantive rules in which they are framed are not identical in content. But in addition, even if a treaty norm and a customary norm relevant to the present dispute were to have exactly the same content, this would not be a reason for the Court to take the view that the operation of the treaty process must necessarily deprive the customary norm of its separate applicability. Nor can the multilateral treaty reservation be interpreted as meaning that, once applicable to a given dispute, it would exclude the application of any rule of customary international law the content of which was the same as, or analogous to, that of the treaty-law rule which had caused the reservation to become effective.

176. As regards the suggestion that the areas covered by the two sources of law are identical, the Court observes that the United Nations Charter, the convention to which most of the United States argument is directed, by no means covers the whole area of the regulation of the use of force in international relations. On one essential point, this treaty itself refers to pre-existing customary international law; this reference to customary law is contained in the actual text of Article 51, which mentions the "inherent right" (in the French text the "droit naturel") of individual or collective self-defence, which "nothing in the present Charter shall impair" and which applies in the event of an armed attack. The Court therefore finds that Article 51 of the Charter is only meaningful on the basis that there is a "natural" or "inherent" right of self-defence, and it is hard to see how this

---

[39] The full name of the case is *Case Concerning Military and Paramilitary Activities in and against Nicaragua.* See Bernheim (1985) 11 Yale J.I.L. 104; Briggs *et al.* (1987) 81 A.J.I.L. 78–183; Gill (1988) 1 Hague Y.I.L. 30; Hohmann and de Waart (1987) 34 N.I.L.R. 162; McDonald (1986) 24 C.Y.I.L. 127; Modabber (1988) 10 Loyola L.A.I.C.L.J. 449; Turner (1987) 20 Vand. J.T.L. 53; White (1989) 9 Int. Rel. 535.

[40] 9 U.S.T. 449.

can be other than of a customary nature, even if its present content has been confirmed and influenced by the Charter. Moreover the Charter, having itself recognized the existence of this right, does not go on to regulate directly all aspects of its content. For example, it does not contain any specific rule whereby self-defence would warrant only measures which are proportional to the armed attack and necessary to respond to it,[41] a rule well established in customary international law. Moreover, a definition of the "armed attack" which, if found to exist, authorizes the exercise of the "inherent right" of self-defence, is not provided in the Charter, and is not part of treaty law. It cannot therefore be held that Article 51 is a provision which "subsumes and supervenes" customary international law. It rather demonstrates that in the field in question, the importance of which for the present dispute need hardly be stressed, customary international law continues to exist alongside treaty law. The areas governed by the two sources of law thus do not overlap exactly, and the rules do not have the same content. This could also be demonstrated for other subjects, in particular for the principle of non-intervention.

177. But as observed above (paragraph 175), even if the customary norm and the treaty norm were to have exactly the same content, this would not be a reason for the Court to hold that the incorporation of the customary norm into treaty-law must deprive the customary norm of its applicability as distinct from that of the treaty norm. The existence of identical rules in international treaty law and customary law has been clearly recognized by the Court in the *North Sea Continental Shelf* cases. To a large extent, those cases turned on the question whether a rule enshrined in a treaty also existed as a customary rule, either because the treaty had merely codified the custom, or caused it to "crystallize", or because it had influenced its subsequent adoption. The Court found that this identity of content in treaty law and in customary international law did not exist in the case of the rule invoked, which appeared in one article of the treaty, but did not suggest that such identity was debarred as a matter of principle: on the contrary, it considered it to be clear that certain other articles of the treaty in question "were ... regarded as reflecting, or as crystallizing, received or at least emergent rules of customary international law" (*I.C.J. Reports 1969*, p.39, para.63). More generally, there are no grounds for holding that when customary international law is comprised of rules identical to those of treaty law, the latter "supervenes" the former, so that the customary international law has no further existence of its own.

178. There are a number of reasons for considering that, even if two norms belonging to two sources of international law appear identical in content, and even if the States in question are bound by these rules both on the level of treaty-law and on that of customary international law, these norms retain a separate existence. This is so from the standpoint of their applicability. In a legal dispute affecting two States, one of them may argue that the applicability of a treaty rule to its own conduct depends on the other State's conduct in respect of the application of other rules, on other subjects, also included in the same treaty. For example, if a State exercises its right to terminate or suspend the operation of a treaty on the ground of the violation by the other party of a "provision essential to the accomplishment of the object or purpose of the treaty" (in the words of art.60, para.3 *(b)*, of the Vienna Convention on the Law of Treaties), it is exempted, vis-à-vis the other State, from a rule of treaty-law because of the breach by that other State of a different rule of treaty-law. But if the two rules in question also exist as rules of customary international law, the failure of the one State to apply the one rule does not justify the other State in declining to apply the other rule. Rules which are identical in treaty law and in customary international law are also distinguishable by reference to the methods of interpretation and application. A State may accept a rule contained in a treaty not simply because it favours the application of the rule itself, but also because the treaty establishes what that State regards as desirable institutions or mechanisms to ensure implementation of the rule. Thus, if that rule parallels a rule of customary international law, two rules of the same content are subject to separate treatment as regards the organs competent to verify their implementation, depending on whether they are customary rules or treaty rules. The present dispute illustrates this point.

183. ... the Court has next to consider what are the rules of customary international law applicable to the present dispute. For this purpose, it has to direct its attention to the practice and *opinio juris* of States; as the Court recently observed,

It is of course axiomatic that the material of customary international law is to be looked for primarily in the actual practice and *opinio juris* of States, even though multilateral conventions may have an important role to play in recording and defining rules deriving from custom, or indeed in developing them. (*Continental Shelf (Libyan Arab Jamahiriya/Malta), I.C.J. Reports 1985*, pp.29–30, para.27.)

---

[41] Ed. As Judge Higgins pointed out in her opinion, para.5, in the *Legality of Nuclear Weapons* case, the Court here understands proportionality as referring to "what is proportionate to repelling the attack, not a requirement of symmetry between the mode of the initial attack and the mode of response".

In this respect the Court must not lose sight of the Charter of the United Nations and that of the Organization of American States, notwithstanding the operation of the multilateral treaty reservation. Although the Court has no jurisdiction to determine whether the conduct of the United States constitutes a breach of those conventions, it can and must take them into account in ascertaining the content of the customary international law which the United States is also alleged to have infringed.

184. The Court notes that there is in fact evidence, to be examined below, of a considerable degree of agreement between the Parties as to the content of the customary international law relating to the non-use of force and non-intervention. This concurrence of their views does not however dispense the Court from having itself to ascertain what rules of customary international law are applicable. The mere fact that States declare their recognition of certain rules is not sufficient for the Court to consider these as being part of customary international law, and as applicable as such to those States. Bound as it is by Article 38 of its Statute to apply, inter alia, international custom "as evidence of a general practice accepted as law", the Court may not disregard the essential role played by general practice. Where two States agree to incorporate a particular rule in a treaty, their agreement suffices to make that rule a legal one, binding upon them; but in the field of customary international law, the shared view of the Parties as to the content of what they regard as the rule is not enough. The Court must satisfy itself that the existence of the rule in the *opinio juris* of States is confirmed by practice.

185. In the present dispute, the Court, while exercising its jurisdiction only in respect of the application of the customary rules of non-use of force and non-intervention, cannot disregard the fact that the Parties are bound by these rules as a matter of treaty law and of customary international law. Furthermore, in the present case, apart from the treaty commitments binding the Parties to the rules in question, there are various instances of their having expressed recognition of the validity thereof as customary international law in other ways. It is therefore in the light of this "subjective element"—the expression used by the Court in its 1969 Judgment in the *North Sea Continental Shelf* cases (*I.C.J. Reports 1969*, p.44)—that the Court has to appraise the relevant practice.

186. It is not to be expected that in the practice of States the application of the rules in question should have been perfect, in the sense that States should have refrained, with complete consistency, from the use of force or from intervention in each other's internal affairs. The Court does not consider that, for a rule to be established as customary, the corresponding practice must be in absolutely rigorous conformity with the rule. In order to deduce the existence of customary rules, the Court deems it sufficient that the conduct of States should, in general, be consistent with such rules, and that instances of State conduct inconsistent with a given rule should generally have been treated as breaches of that rule, not as indications of the recognition of a new rule. If a State acts in a way prima facie incompatible with a recognized rule, but defends its conduct by appealing to exceptions or justifications contained within the rule itself, then whether or not the State's conduct is in fact justifiable on that basis, the significance of that attitude is to confirm rather than to weaken the rule. ...

188. The Court thus finds that both Parties [in their pleadings] take the view that the principles as to the use of force incorporated in the United Nations Charter correspond, in essentials, to those found in customary international law. ... The Court has however to be satisfied that there exists in customary international law an *opinio juris* [as to the binding character of these principles] ... This *opinio juris* may, though with all due caution, be deduced from, inter alia, the attitude of the Parties and the attitude of States towards certain General Assembly resolutions, and particularly resolution 2625 (XXV).[42] ... The effect of consent to the text of such resolutions ... may be understood as an acceptance of the validity of the rule or set of rules declared by the resolution by themselves. The principle of non-use of force, for example, may thus be regarded as a principle of customary international law, not as such conditioned by provisions relating to collective security, or to the facilities or armed contingents to be provided under Article 43 of the Charter. It would therefore seem apparent that the attitude referred to expresses an *opinio juris* respecting such rule (or set of rules), to be thenceforth treated separately from the provisions, especially those of an institutional kind, to which it is subject on the treaty-law plane of the Charter.

189. As regards the United States in particular, the weight of an expression of *opinio juris* can similarly be attached to its support of the resolution of the Sixth International Conference of American States condemning aggression (18 February 1928) and ratification of the Montevideo Convention on Rights and Duties of States (26 December 1933), Article 11 of which imposes the obligation not to recognize territorial acquisitions or special advantages which have been obtained by force. Also significant is United States acceptance of the principle of the prohibition of the use of force which is contained in the declaration on principles governing the mutual relations of States participating in the Conference on Security and Co-operation in Europe (Helsinki, 1 August 1975), whereby the participating States undertake to "refrain in their mutual relations, *as well as in their*

---

[42] Ed. Below, App.III.

international relations in general," (emphasis added) from the threat or use of force. Acceptance of a text in these terms confirms the existence of an *opinio juris* of the participating States prohibiting the use of force in international relations.

190. A further confirmation of the validity as customary international law of the principle of the prohibition of the use of force expressed in Article 2, paragraph 4, of the Charter of the United Nations may be found in the fact that it is frequently referred to in statements by State representatives as being not only a principle of customary international law but also a fundamental or cardinal principle of such law. The International Law Commission, in the course of its work on the codification of the law of treaties, expressed the view that "the law of the Charter concerning the prohibition of the use of force in itself constitutes a conspicuous example of a rule in international law having the character of *jus cogens*."[43] Nicaragua in its Memorial on the Merits submitted in the present case states that the principle prohibiting the use of force embodied in Article 2, paragraph 4, of the Charter of the United Nations "has come to be recognized as *jus cogens*". The United States, in its Counter-Memorial on the questions of jurisdiction and admissibility, found it material to quote the views of scholars that this principle is a "universal norm", a "universal international law", a "universally recognized principle of international law", and a "principle of *jus cogens*".

191. As regards certain particular aspects of the principle in question it will be necessary to distinguish the most grave forms of the use of force (those constituting an armed attack) from other less grave forms. In determining the legal rule which applies to these latter forms, the Court can again draw on the formulations contained in ... General Assembly resolution 2625 (XXV). ...

193. The general rule prohibiting force allows for certain exceptions. In view of the arguments advanced by the United States to justify the acts of which it is accused by Nicaragua the Court must express a view on the content of the right of self-defence, and more particularly the right of collective self-defence. First, with regard to the existence of this right, it notes that in the language of Article 51 of the United Nations Charter, the inherent right (or "droit naturel") which any State possesses in the event of an armed attack, covers both collective and individual self-defence. Thus, the Charter itself testifies to the existence of the right of collective self-defence in customary international law. Moreover ... [in resolution 2625 (XXV)] the reference to the prohibition of force is followed by a paragraph stating that:

> nothing in the foregoing paragraphs shall be construed as enlarging or diminishing in any way the scope of the provisions of the Charter concerning cases in which the use of force is lawful.

This resolution demonstrates that the States represented in the General Assembly regard the exception to the prohibition of force constituted by the right of individual or collective self-defence as already a matter of customary international law.

194. With regard to the characteristics governing the right of self-defence, ... reliance is placed by the Parties only on the right of self-defence in the case of an armed attack which has already occurred, and the issue of the lawfulness of a response to the imminent threat of armed attack has not been raised. Accordingly the Court expresses no view on that issue. The Parties also agree in holding that whether the response to the attack is lawful depends on observance of the criteria of the necessity and the proportionality of the measures taken in self-defence. ...

195. In the case of individual self-defence, the exercise of this right is subject to the State concerned having been the victim of an armed attack. Reliance on collective self-defence of course does not remove the need for this. There appears now to be general agreement on the nature of the acts which can be treated as constituting armed attacks. In particular, it may be considered to be agreed that an armed attack must be understood as including not merely action by regular armed forces across an international border, but also "the sending by or on behalf of a State of armed bands, groups, irregulars or mercenaries, which carry out acts of armed force against another State of such gravity as to amount to" (inter alia) an actual armed attack conducted by regular forces, "or its substantial involvement therein." This description, contained in Article 3, paragraph (*g*), of the Definition of Aggression annexed to General Assembly resolution 3314 (XXIX),[44] may be taken to reflect customary international law. The Court sees no reason to deny that, in customary law, the prohibition of armed attacks may apply to the sending by a State of armed bands to the territory of another State, if such an operation, because of its scale and effects, would have been classified as an armed attack rather than as a mere frontier incident had it been carried out by regular armed forces. But the Court does not believe that the concept

---

[43]   Ed. Y.B.I.L.C. 1966, II, p.247.
[44]   Ed. below, p.799.

of "armed attack" includes not only acts by armed bands where such acts occur on a significant scale but also assistance to rebels in the form of the provision of weapons or logistical or other support. Such assistance may be regarded as a threat or use of force, or amount to intervention in the internal or external affairs of other States. It is also clear that it is the State which is the victim of an armed attack which must form and declare the view that it has been so attacked. There is no rule in customary international law permitting its own assessment of the situation. ...

199. ... the Court [also] finds that in customary international law, whether of a general kind or that particular to the inter-American legal system,[45] there is no rule permitting the exercise of collective self-defence in the absence of a request by the State which regards itself as the victim of an armed attack. The Court concludes that the requirement of a request by the State which is the victim of the alleged attack is additional to the requirement that such a State should have declared itself to have been attacked.

200. ... Article 51 of the United Nations Charter requires that measures taken by States in exercise of this right of self-defence must be "immediately reported" to the Security Council. As the Court has observed above (paragraph ... 188), a principle enshrined in a treaty, if reflected in customary international law, may well be so unencumbered with the conditions and modalities surrounding it in the treaty. Whatever influence the Charter may have had on customary international law in these matters, it is clear that in customary international law it is not a condition of the lawfulness of the use of force in self-defence that a procedure so closely dependent on the content of a treaty commitment and of the institutions established by it, should have been followed. On the other hand, if self-defence is advanced as a justification for measures which would otherwise be in breach both of the principle of customary international law and of that contained in the Charter, it is to be expected that the conditions of the Charter should be respected. Thus for the purpose of enquiry into the customary law position, the absence of a report may be one of the factors indicating whether the State in question was itself convinced that it was acting in self-defence. ...

202. The principle of non-intervention involves the right of every sovereign State to conduct its affairs without outside interference; though examples of trespass against this principle are not infrequent, the Court considers that it is part and parcel of customary international law. As the Court has observed [in the *Corfu Channel case*]: "Between independent States, respect for territorial sovereignty is an essential foundation of international relations" (*I.C.J. Reports 1949*, p.35), and international law requires political integrity also to be respected. ... This principle [of non-intervention] is not, as such, spelt out in the Charter. But it was never intended that the Charter should embody written confirmation of every essential principle of international law in force. The existence in the *opinio juris* of States of the principle of non-intervention is backed by established and substantial practice. It has moreover been presented as a corollary of the principle of the sovereign equality of States. ...

203. The principle has since been reflected in numerous declarations adopted by international organisations and conferences in which the United States and Nicaragua have participated, e.g., General Assembly resolution 2131 (XX).[46] It is true that the United States, while it voted in favour of General Assembly resolution 2131 (XX), also declared at the time of its adoption in the First Committee that it considered the declaration in that resolution to be "only a statement of political intention and not a formulation of law." ... However, the essentials of resolution 2131 (XX) are repeated in the Declaration approved by resolution 2625 (XXV), which set out principles which the General Assembly declared to be "basic principles" of international law, and on the adoption of which no analogous statement was made by the United States representative.

204. ... In a different context, the United States expressly accepted the principles set forth in the declaration, to which reference has already been made, appearing in the Final Act of the Conference on Security and Co-operation in Europe (Helsinki, 1 August 1975),[47] including an elaborate statement of the principle of non-intervention; while these principles were presented as applying to the mutual relations among the participating States, it can be inferred that the text testifies to the existence, and the acceptance by the United States, of a customary principle which has universal application.

205. Notwithstanding the multiplicity of declarations by States accepting the principle of non-intervention, there remain two questions: first, what is the exact content of the principle so accepted, and secondly, is the practice sufficiently in conformity with it for this to be a rule of customary international law? As regards the first problem—that of the content of the principle of non-intervention—the Court will define only those aspects of the principle which appear to be relevant to the resolution of the dispute. In this respect it notes that, in view of the

---

[45] Ed. The Court relied on the request requirement in the regional 1947 Rio Treaty, 21 U.N.T.S. 77. In force 1948, 23 parties. It cited no evidence in support of a request requirement in *general* custom.
[46] Ed. Below, p.742.
[47] Ed. See above, p.536.

generally accepted formulations, the principle forbids all States or groups of States to intervene directly or indirectly in internal or external affairs of other States. A prohibited intervention must accordingly be one bearing on matters in which each State is permitted, by the principle of State sovereignty, to decide freely. One of these is the choice of a political, economic, social and cultural system, and the formulation of foreign policy. Intervention is wrongful when it uses methods of coercion in regard to such choices, which must remain free ones. The element of coercion, which defines, and indeed forms the very essence of, prohibited intervention, is particularly obvious in the case of an intervention which uses force, either in the direct form of military action, or in the indirect form of support for subversive or terrorist armed activities within another State. ... General Assembly resolution 2625 (XXV) equates assistance of this kind with the use of force by the assisting State when the acts committed in another State "involve a threat or use of force." These forms of action are therefore wrongful in the light of both the principle of non-use of force, and that of non-intervention ... .

206. However, before reaching a conclusion on the nature of prohibited intervention, the Court must be satisfied that State practice justifies it. There have been in recent years a number of instances of foreign intervention for the benefit of forces opposed to the government of another State. The Court is not here concerned with the process of decolonisation; this question is not in issue in the present case. It has to consider whether there might be indications of a practice illustrative of belief in a kind of general right for States to intervene, directly or indirectly, with or without armed force, in support of an internal opposition in another State, whose cause appeared particularly worthy by reason of the political and moral values with which it was identified. For such a general right to come into existence would involve a fundamental modification of the customary law principle of non-intervention.

207. In considering the instances of the conduct above described, the Court has to emphasise that, as was observed in the *North Sea Continental Shelf* cases, for a new customary rule to be formed, not only must the acts concerned "amount to a settled practice," but they must be accompanied by the *opinio juris sive necessitatis*. Either the States taking such action or other States in a position to react to it, must have behaved so that their conduct is

> "evidence of a belief that this practice is rendered obligatory by the existence of a rule of law requiring it. The need for such a belief, i.e., the existence of a subjective element, is implicit in the very notion of the *opinio juris sive necessitatis*." (*I.C.J. Reports 1969*, p.44, para.77.) ...

The significance for the Court of cases of State conduct prima facie inconsistent with the principle of non-intervention lies in the nature of the ground offered as justification. Reliance by a State on a novel right or any unprecedented exception to the principle might, if shared in principle by other States, tend towards a modification of customary international law. In fact however, the Court finds that States have not justified their conduct by reference to a new right of intervention or a new exception to the principle of its prohibition. The United States authorities have on some occasions clearly stated their grounds for intervening in the affairs of a foreign State for reasons connected with, for example, the domestic policies of that country, its ideology, the level of its armaments, or the direction of its foreign policy. But these were statements of international policy, and not an assertion of rules of existing international law.

209. The Court therefore finds that no such general right of intervention in support of an opposition within another State, exists in contemporary international law. The Court concludes that acts constituting a breach of the customary principle of non-intervention will also, if they directly or indirectly involve the use of force, constitute a breach of the principle of non-use of force in international relations.

210. When dealing with the rule of the prohibition of the use of force, the Court considered the exception to it constituted by the exercise of the right of collective self-defence in the event of armed attack. Similarly, it must now consider the following question: if one State acts towards another State in breach of the principle of non-intervention, may a third State lawfully take such action by way of counter-measures against the first State as would otherwise constitute an intervention in its internal affairs? A right to act in this way in the case of intervention would be analogous to the right of collective self-defence in the case of an armed attack, but both the act which gives rise to the reaction, and that reaction itself, would in principle be less grave. Since the Court is here dealing with a dispute in which a wrongful use of force is alleged, it has primarily to consider whether a State has a right to respond to intervention with intervention going so far as to justify a use of force in reaction to measures which do not constitute an armed attack but may nevertheless involve a use of force. The question is itself undeniably relevant from the theoretical viewpoint. However, since the Court is bound to confine its decision to those points of law which are essential to the settlement of the dispute before it, it is not for the Court here to determine what direct reactions are lawfully open to a State which considers itself the victim of another State's

act of intervention, possibly involving the use of force. Hence it has not to determine whether, in the event of Nicaragua's having committed any such acts against El Salvador, the latter was lawfully entitled to take any particular counter-measure. It might however be suggested that, in such a situation, the United States might have been permitted to intervene in Nicaragua in the exercise of some right analogous to the right of collective self-defence, one which might be resorted to in a case of intervention short of armed attack.

211. The Court has recalled above (paragraphs 193 to 195) that for one State to use force against another, on the ground that that State has committed a wrongful act of force against a third State, is regarded as lawful, by way of exception, only when the wrongful act provoking the response was an armed attack. Thus the lawfulness of the use of force by a State in response to a wrongful act of which it has not itself been the victim is not admitted when this wrongful act is not an armed attack. In the view of the Court, under international law in force today—whether customary international law or that of the United Nations system—States do not have a right of "collective" armed response to acts which do not constitute an "armed attack." ...

The Court considered the principles of state sovereignty, freedom of commerce and navigation and international humanitarian law and concluded that they were all infringed by a state that mines another state's ports. It then began to apply the customary international law that it had stated to the facts of the case.

227. The Court will first appraise the facts in the light of the principle of the non-use of force. ... For the most part, the complaints by Nicaragua are of the actual use of force against it by the United States. Of the acts which the Court has found imputable to the Government of the United States, the following are relevant in this respect:

— the laying of mines in Nicaraguan internal or territorial waters in early 1984 ...;
— certain attacks in Nicaraguan ports, oil installations and a naval base.[48] ...

These activities constitute infringements of the principle of the prohibition of the use of force, defined earlier, unless they are justified by circumstances which exclude their unlawfulness, a question now to be examined. The Court has also found ... the existence of military manoeuvres held by the United States near the Nicaraguan borders; and Nicaragua has made some suggestion that this constituted a "threat of force," which is equally forbidden by the principle of non-use of force. The Court is however not satisfied that the manoeuvres complained of, in the circumstances in which they were held, constituted on the part of the United States a breach, as against Nicaragua, of the principle forbidding recourse to the threat or use of force. ...

228. As to the claim that United States activities in relation to the *contras* constitute a breach of the customary international law principle of the non-use of force, the Court finds that ... the United States has committed a prima facie violation of that principle by its assistance to the *contras* in Nicaragua, by "organising or encouraging the organisation of irregular forces or armed bands ... for incursion into the territory of another State," and "participating in acts of civil strife ... in another State," in the terms of General Assembly resolution 2625 (XXV). According to that resolution, participation of this kind is contrary to the principle of the prohibition of the use of force when the facts of civil strife referred to "involve a threat or use of force." In the view of the Court, while the arming and training of the *contras* can certainly be said to involve the threat or use of force against Nicaragua, this is not necessarily so in respect of all the assistance given by the United States Government.[49] In particular the Court considers that the mere supply of funds to the *contras*, while undoubtedly an act of intervention in the internal affairs of Nicaragua, as will be explained below, does not in itself amount to a use of force."

---

[48] Ed. The Court found that the mining was effected not by the *contras* but by persons, probably "UCLAs" ["Unilaterally Controlled Latino Assets" in CIA vocabulary], "in the pay and acting on the instructions of ... [the CIA], under the supervision and with the logistic support of United States agents;" the attacks on ports, etc. were similarly executed by "'UCLAs,' while United States nationals participated in the planning, direction and support": I.C.J. Rep. 1986, pp.48–51.

[49] Ed. On the nature and extent of US involvement in *contra* activities, the Court stated (I.C.J. Rep. 1986, pp.61–62): "... the financial support given by the United States to ... the *contras* ... is a fully established fact. ... [However], the Court has not been able to satisfy itself that the respondent State 'created' the *contra* force ... Nor does the evidence warrant a finding that the United States gave 'direct and critical combat support,' at least if that form of words is taken to mean that this support was tantamount to direct intervention by the United States combat forces, or that all *contra* operations reflected strategy and tactics wholly devised by the United States. On the other hand, the Court holds it established that the United States authorities largely financed, trained, equipped, armed and organized the FDN".

229. The Court must thus consider whether ... the acts in question of the United States are justified by the exercise of its right of collective self-defence against an armed attack. ... For the Court to conclude that the United States was lawfully exercising its right of collective self-defence, it must first find that Nicaragua engaged in an armed attack against El Salvador, Honduras or Costa Rica.

230. As regards El Salvador, the Court has found ... that it is satisfied that between July 1979 and the early months of 1981, an intermittent flow of arms was routed via the territory of Nicaragua to the armed opposition in that country. The Court was not however satisfied that assistance has reached the Salvadorian armed opposition, on a scale of any significance, since the early months of 1981, or that the Government of Nicaragua was responsible for any flow of arms at either period. Even assuming that the supply of arms to the opposition in El Salvador could be treated as imputable to the Government of Nicaragua, to justify invocation of the right of collective self-defence in customary international law, it would have to be equated with an armed attack by Nicaragua on El Salvador. As stated above [para.195], the Court is unable to consider that, in customary international law, the provision of arms to the opposition in another State constitutes an armed attack on that State. Even at a time when the arms flow was at its peak, and again assuming the participation of the Nicaraguan Government, that would not constitute such armed attack.

231. Turning to Honduras and Costa Rica, the Court has also stated ... that it should find established that certain trans-border incursions into the territory of those two States, in 1982, 1983 and 1984, were imputable to the Government of Nicaragua. Very little information is however available to the Court as to the circumstances of these incursions or their possible motivations, which renders it difficult to decide whether they may be treated for legal purposes as amounting, singly or collectively, to an "armed attack" by Nicaragua on either or both States. ... There are however other considerations which justify the Court in finding that neither these incursions, nor the alleged supply of arms to the opposition in El Salvador, may be relied on as justifying the exercise of the right of collective self-defence.

232. The exercise of the right of collective self-defence presupposes that an armed attack has occurred; and it is evident that it is the victim State, being the most directly aware of that fact, which is likely to draw general attention to its plight. It is also evident that if the victim State wishes another State to come to its help in the exercise of the right of collective self-defence, it will normally make an express request to that effect. Thus in the present instance, the Court is entitled to take account, in judging the asserted justification of the exercise of collective self-defence by the United States, of the actual conduct of El Salvador, Honduras and Costa Rica at the relevant time, as indicative of a belief by the State in question that it was the victim of an armed attack by Nicaragua, and of the making of a request by the victim State to the United States for help in the exercise of collective self-defence.

233. The Court has seen no evidence that the conduct of those States was consistent with such a situation, either at the time when the United States first embarked on the activities which were allegedly justified by self-defence, or indeed for a long period subsequently. ...

235. There is also an aspect of the conduct of the United States which the Court is entitled to take into account. ... At no time, up to the present, has the United States Government addressed to the Security Council ... the report which is required by Article 51 of the United Nations Charter in respect of measures which a State believes itself bound to take when it exercises the right of individual or collective self-defence. The Court, whose decision has to be made on the basis of customary international law, has already observed that in the context of that law, the reporting obligation enshrined in Article 51 of the Charter of the United Nations does not exist. ... But the Court is justified in observing that this conduct of the United States hardly conforms with the latter's avowed conviction that it was acting in the context of collective self-defence as consecrated by Article 51 of the Charter. This fact is all the more noteworthy because, in the Security Council, the United States has itself taken the view that failure to observe the requirement to make a report contradicted a State's claim to be acting on the basis of collective self-defence (S/PV.2187).

236. Similarly, while no strict legal conclusion may be drawn from the date of El Salvador's announcement that it was the victim of an armed attack, and the date of its official request addressed to the United States concerning the exercise of collective self-defence, those dates have a significance as evidence of El Salvador's view of the situation. The declaration and the request of El Salvador, made publicly for the first time in August 1984, do not support the contention that in 1981 there was an armed attack capable of serving as a legal foundation for United States activities which began in the second half of that year. ...

237. Since the Court has found that the condition *sine qua non* required for the exercise of the right of collective self-defence by the United States is not fulfilled in this case ... even if the United States activities in question had been carried on in strict compliance with the canons of necessity and proportionality, they would not thereby become lawful. If however they were not, this may constitute an additional ground of wrongfulness.

On the question of necessity, the Court observes that the United States measures taken in December 1981 . . . cannot be said to correspond to a "necessity" justifying the United States action against Nicaragua on the basis of assistance given by Nicaragua to the armed opposition in El Salvador. First, these measures were only taken, and began to produce their effects, several months after the major offensive of the armed opposition against the Government of El Salvador had been completely repulsed (January 1981), and the actions of the opposition considerably reduced in consequence. Thus it was possible to eliminate the main danger to the Salvadorian Government without the United States embarking on activities in and against Nicaragua. . . . Whether or not the assistance to the *contras* might meet the criterion of proportionality, the Court cannot regard the United States activities . . . relating to the mining of the Nicaraguan ports and the attacks on ports, oil installations, etc., as satisfying that criterion. Whatever uncertainty may exist as to the exact scale of the aid received by the Salvadorian armed opposition from Nicaragua, it is clear that these latter United States activities in question could not have been proportionate to that aid. Finally on this point, the Court must also observe that the reaction of the United States in the context of what it regarded as self-defence was continued long after the period in which any presumed armed attack by Nicaragua could reasonably be contemplated.

238. Accordingly, the Court concludes that the plea of collective self-defence against an alleged armed attack on El Salvador, Honduras or Costa Rica, advanced by the United States to justify its conduct toward Nicaragua, cannot be upheld; and accordingly that the United States has violated the principle prohibiting recourse to the threat or use of force by the acts listed in paragraph 227 above, and by its assistance to the *contras* to the extent that this assistance "involve[s] a threat or use of force" . . .

239. The Court comes now to the application in this case of the principle of non-intervention in the internal affairs of States . . .

241. The Court . . . does not consider it necessary to seek to establish whether the intention of the United States to secure a change of governmental policies in Nicaragua went so far as to be equated with an endeavour to overthrow the Nicaraguan Government. It appears to the Court to be clearly established first, that the United States intended, by its support of the *contras*, to coerce the Government of Nicaragua in respect of matters in which each State is permitted, by the principle of State sovereignty, to decide freely (see paragraph 205 above); and secondly that the intention of the *contras* themselves was to overthrow the present Government of Nicaragua. . . . The Court considers that in international law, if one State, with a view to the coercion of another State, supports and assists armed bands in that State whose purpose is to overthrow the government of that State, that amounts to an intervention by the one State in the internal affairs of the other, whether or not the political objective of the State giving such support and assistance is equally far-reaching. It is for this reason that the Court has only examined the intentions of the United States Government so far as they bear on the question of self-defence.

242. The Court therefore finds that the support given by the United States, up to the end of September 1984, to the military and paramilitary activities of the *contras* in Nicaragua, by financial support, training, supply of weapons, intelligence and logistic support, constitutes a clear breach of the principle of non-intervention. The Court has however taken note that, with effect from the beginning of the United States governmental financial year 1985, namely 1 October 1984, the United States Congress has restricted the use of the funds appropriated for assistance to the *contras* to "humanitarian assistance." . . . There can be no doubt that the provision of strictly humanitarian aid to persons or forces in another country, whatever their political affiliations or objectives, cannot be regarded as unlawful intervention, or as in any other way contrary to international law. . . .

243. An essential feature of truly humanitarian aid is that it is given "without discrimination" of any kind. In the view of the Court, if the provision of "humanitarian assistance" is to escape condemnation as an intervention in the internal affairs of Nicaragua, not only must it be limited to the purposes hallowed in the practice of the Red Cross, namely "to prevent and alleviate human suffering," and "to protect life and health and to ensure respect for the human being"; it must also, and above all, be given without discrimination to all in need in Nicaragua, not merely to the *contras* and their dependents.

244. As already noted, Nicaragua has also asserted that the United States is responsible for an "indirect" form of intervention in its internal affairs inasmuch as it has taken, to Nicaragua's disadvantage, certain action of an economic nature. The Court's attention has been drawn in particular to the cessation of economic aid in April 1981; the 90 per cent reduction in the sugar quota for United States imports from Nicaragua in April 1981; and the trade embargo adopted on 1 May 1985. While admitting in principle that some of these actions were not unlawful in themselves, counsel for Nicaragua argued that these measures of economic constraint add up to a systematic violation of the principle of non-intervention.

245. The Court . . . is unable to regard such action on the economic plane as is here complained of as a breach of the customary-law principle of non-intervention.

246. Having concluded that the activities of the United States in relation to the activities of the *contras* in Nicaragua constitute prima facie acts of intervention, the Court must next consider whether they may nevertheless be justified on some legal ground. As the Court has stated, the principle of non-intervention derives from customary international law. It would certainly lose its effectiveness as a principle of law if intervention were to be justified by a mere request for assistance made by an opposition group in another State—supposing such a request to have actually been made by an opposition to the régime in Nicaragua in this instance. Indeed, it is difficult to see what would remain of the principle of non-intervention in international law if intervention, which is already allowable at the request of the government of a State, were also to be allowed at the request of the opposition. This would permit any State to intervene at any moment in the internal affairs of another State, whether at the request of the government or at the request of its opposition. Such a situation does not in the Court's view correspond to the present state of international law.

247. The Court has already indicated (paragraph 238) its conclusion that the conduct of the United States towards Nicaragua cannot be justified by the right of collective self-defence in response to an alleged armed attack on one or other of Nicaragua's neighbours. So far as regards the allegations of supply of arms by Nicaragua to the armed opposition in El Salvador, the Court has indicated that while the concept of an armed attack includes the despatch by one State of armed bands into the territory of another State, the supply of arms and other support to such bands cannot be equated with armed attack. Nevertheless, such activities may well constitute a breach of the principle of the non-use of force and an intervention in the internal affairs of a State, that is, a form of conduct which is certainly wrongful, but is of lesser gravity than an armed attack. The Court must therefore enquire now whether the activities of the United States towards Nicaragua might be justified as a response to an intervention by that State in the internal affairs of another State in Central America. ...

249. On the legal level the Court cannot regard response to an intervention by Nicaragua as such a justification. While an armed attack would give rise to an entitlement to collective self-defence, a use of force of a lesser degree of gravity cannot, as the Court has already observed ..., produce any entitlement to take collective counter-measures involving the use of force. The acts of which Nicaragua is accused, even assuming them to have been established and imputable to that State, could only have justified proportionate counter-measures on the part of the State which had been the victim of these acts, namely El Salvador, Honduras or Costa Rica. They could not justify counter-measures taken by a third State, the United States, and particularly could not justify intervention involving the use of force.

267. The Court also notes that Nicaragua is accused by the 1985 finding of the United States Congress of violating human rights. ...

268. ... while the United States might form its own appraisal of the situation as to respect for human rights in Nicaragua, the use of force could not be the appropriate method to monitor or ensure such respect. With regard to the steps actually taken, the protection of human rights, a strictly humanitarian objective, cannot be compatible with the mining of ports, the destruction of oil installations, or again with the training, arming and equipping of the *contras*. The Court concludes that the argument derived from the preservation of human rights in Nicaragua cannot afford a legal justification for the conduct of the United States, and cannot in any event be reconciled with the legal strategy of the respondent State, which is based on the right of collective self-defence.

Continuing to apply custom, the Court also found that the United States had infringed Nicaragua's sovereignty and freedom of maritime commerce and international humanitarian law by the conduct indicated in paras (5) and (6) of the *dispositif* (below). The Court also found breaches of the 1956 Treaty of Friendship.

292. For these reasons

THE COURT ...

(2) By twelve votes to three,[50]

---

[50] Ed. The judges in the majority were President Nagendra Singh; Vice-President de Lacharrière; Judges Lachs, Ruda, Elia, Ago, Sette-Camara, Mbaye, Bedjaoui, Ni and Evensen; Judge ad hoc Colliard. Judges Oda, Schwebel and Sir Robert Jennings dissented.

Rejects the justification of collective self-defence maintained by the United States of America in connection with the military and paramilitary activities in and against Nicaragua the subject of this case;

(3) By twelve votes to three,[51]

Decides that the United States of America, by training, arming, equipping, financing and supplying the *contra* forces or otherwise encouraging, supporting and aiding military and paramilitary activities in and against Nicaragua, has acted, against the Republic of Nicaragua, in breach of its obligation under customary international law not to *intervene* in the affairs of another State;

(4) By twelve votes to three,[52]

Decides that the United States of America, by certain attacks in Nicaraguan territory in 1983–1984 ... and further by those acts of intervention referred to in subparagraph (3) hereof which involve the use of force, has acted, against the Republic of Nicaragua, in breach of its obligation under customary international law not to use force against another State;

(5) By twelve votes to three,[53]

Decides that the United States of America, by directing or authorising overflights of Nicaraguan territory, and by the acts imputable to the United States referred to in subparagraph (4) hereof, has acted, against the Republic of Nicaragua, in breach of its obligation under customary international law not to violate the sovereignty of another State;

(6) By twelve votes to three,[54]

Decides that, by laying mines in the internal or territorial waters of the Republic of Nicaragua during the first months of 1984, the United States of America has acted, against the Republic of Nicaragua, in breach of its obligations under customary international law not to use force against another State, not to intervene in its affairs, not to violate its sovereignty and not to interrupt peaceful maritime commerce;

(7) By fourteen votes to one,[55]

Decides that, by the acts referred to in subparagraph (6) hereof, the United States of America has acted, against the Republic of Nicaragua, in breach of its obligations under Article XIX of the [1956] Treaty of Friendship, Commerce and Navigation ...;

(8) By fourteen votes to one,[56]

Decides that the United States of America, by failing to make known the existence and location of the mines laid by it, referred to in subparagraph (6) hereof, has acted in breach of its obligations under customary international law in this respect;

(9) By fourteen votes to one,[57]

Finds that the United States of America, by producing in 1983 a manual entitled *Operaciones sicológicas en*

---

[51] Ed. Judges Oda, Schwebel and Sir Robert Jennings dissented.
[52] See above, n.51.
[53] See above, n.51.
[54] See above, n.51.
[55] Ed. Judge Schwebel dissented.
[56] Ed. Judge Oda dissented.
[57] Ed. Judge Oda dissented.

guerra de guerrillas, and disseminating it to *contra* forces, has encouraged the commission by them of acts contrary to general principles of humanitarian law; but does not find a basis for concluding that any such acts which may have been committed are imputable to the United States of America as acts of the United States of America;

(10) By twelve votes to three,[58]

Decides that the United States of America, by the attacks on Nicaraguan territory referred to in subparagraph (4) hereof, and by declaring a general embargo on trade with Nicaragua on 1 May 1985, has committed acts calculated to deprive of its object and purpose the [1956] Treaty of Friendship, Commerce and Navigation . . .;

(11) By twelve votes to three,[59]

Decides that the United States of America, by the attacks on Nicaraguan territory referred to in subparagraph (4) hereof, and by declaring a general embargo on trade with Nicaragua on 1 May 1985, has acted in breach of its obligations under Article XIX of the [1956] Treaty of Friendship, Commerce and Navigation. . . .

Notes

1.   The *Nicaragua* (*Merits*) case gave the ICJ an unprecedented opportunity to explore the law governing the use of armed force and intervention by states and to do so in the area in which it was most in need of clarification, namely that in which State A gives assistance to rebels seeking to overthrow the government of State D or, conversely, to the government of State D to defeat rebels against it.

2.   *Indirect Use of Force.* The *Nicaragua* (*Merits*) case confirms that the giving of assistance to rebels may be an indirect use of force contrary to customary international law. Everything turns upon the kind of assistance. The Court held that the US had infringed the rule prohibiting the threat or use of force by "the arming and training of the *contras*," but that it had not done so by "the mere supply of funds."[60] Since the whole of the Section on the Principle on the Use of Force in the 1970 Declaration was accepted by the Court as amplifying the customary rule, other forms of assistance within that Section's very general language[61] can probably be taken to have been understood by it as involving the illegal use of force too. Thus the establishment, organisation or control[62] of a rebel force or the giving of material support (e.g. logistic support, bases) would also qualify. Whereas financial assistance is not an indirect use of force, it is nonetheless contrary to international law as intervention in another state's affairs.[63] Humanitarian assistance, how-

---

[58]   Ed. Judges Oda, Schwebel and Sir Robert Jennings dissented.

[59]   See above, n.58.

[60]   Judgment, para.228. See also the *Armed Activities* case, para.164, below, p.759. The distinction between these two forms of assistance, which is supportable on the basis that financial assistance, for example, to buy arms is more indirect or remote than giving the arms themselves, echoes the different wording of the 1965 Non-Intervention Declaration, below, p.742, which expressly prohibits financial assistance, and the section on the Principle of the Use of Force of the 1970 Declaration, App.III, below, which does not.

[61]   See paras 8 and 9.

[62]   There comes a point where the intervening state's control over a rebel force is so complete that the latter becomes an arm of the former so that its acts are imputable to that state. On this aspect of the *Nicaragua* (*Merits*) case, see above.

[63]   On intervention, see below, p.742.

ever, whether financial or otherwise (blankets, food, etc.) is perfectly lawful—provided that it is given equally to rebels and others in the community in need.[64]

There is disagreement on the question whether, exceptionally, a state may to assist a "people" fighting a war of national liberation, i.e. one to realise their right to self-determination.[65] Developing states take the view that the use of force by a colonial power to repress such action by a "people" is a breach of the rule prohibiting the use of force so that a state may intervene to give "material" (troops, equipment, etc.) as well as "moral" assistance to the rebels.[66] Western states deny that the prohibition of the use of force applies to action taken by a colonial (or other) state to repress an internal rebellion and argue that the Principle of Non-Intervention prohibits "material assistance". The Section on the Principle of Self-Determination in the 1970 Declaration intentionally avoids the issue by simply stating (para.6) that "such peoples are entitled to seek and receive support" (undefined). cf. the similarly equivocal wording of the 1974 General Assembly Resolution on the Definition of Aggression, art.7, below p.800. The question was purposely not considered in the *Nicaragua* (*Merits*) case (judgment, para.206). Gray[67] states:

> "Now that the decolonization process is almost complete, and now that South Africa has given up apartheid and its occupation of Namibia, the debate over the right of a people to seek self-determination through the use of force, with the help of third states, has lost much of its significance. The issue is still important in the context of the Palestinian struggle for self-determination in the territories of the West Bank and Gaza occupied by Israel since 1967, but the states which support the Palestinian claim to statehood generally prefer to make their case in terms of the violations by Israel of the law of belligerent occupation; they are reluctant openly to argue for a legal right to use force for self determination. ... The extension of the right of self-determination outside the colonial context in the break-up of the USSR, Yugoslavia, and Czechoslovakia has not brought with it any state support for the use of force for this end.[68] There is no support for the right to use force to attain self-determination outside the context of decolonization or illegal occupation. Still less is there any support by states for the right of ethnic groups to use force to secede from existing states. But when claims to secession, or even to more limited autonomy, are met with forcible repression, as in the cases of Kosovo, the Chechens, and the Kurds, the use of force against a people may strengthen its case for self-determination."[69]

In the *Nicaragua* (*Merits*) case, the Court did consider and reject (judgment, para.206) the idea

---

[64] *Nicaragua* (*Merits*) case, judgment, paras 242–243. The Court refrained from ruling on the legality of the humanitarian assistance given by the US for lack of information as to its use. On the *Invasion of Goa* case, in which India's self-determination justification was not supported in the Security Council, see above, p.189.

[65] See Wilson, *International Law and the Use of Force by National Liberation Movements* (1988).

[66] A number of General Assembly resolutions support the latter part of this view. See, e.g. G.A. Resn 2908, G.A.O.R., 27th Sess., Supp.30, p.2 (1972), which "urges all states ... to provide moral and material assistance to all peoples struggling for their freedom and independence in the colonial Territories and to those living under alien domination—in particular to the national liberation movements of the Territories of Africa ..." The resolution was adopted by 99 votes to five (France, Portugal, South Africa, UK, and the US), with 23 abstentions.

[67] See above, n.2, p.57. Some footnotes omitted.

[68] The Yugoslavia Arbitration Commission in Opinion 2 [see above, p.110] ... affirmed the right of self determination of the Bosnian Serbs, but denied that this gave them the right to use force to alter existing boundaries.

[69] See Supreme Court of Canada, *Reference re Secession of Quebec*, 37 ILM (1998) 1340 at 1372....

that there was a right of intervention (to the level of the use of force) to support the "political or moral values" of a rebellion. The prohibition of intervention is ideologically neutral; in particular, intervention is not permitted to assist a rebellion to protect democracy or human rights.[70]

3. *Assistance to governments.*[71] Like assistance by a state to rebels seeking to overthrow the government of another state, assistance to a government attempting to suppress a rebellion has been a common feature of international relations since the Second World War. The legality of assistance to a government *where the rebels are assisted by another state* was considered by the ICJ in the *Nicaragua* (*Merits*) case in the light of the US claim that its challenged action would be justified as assistance to the governments of El Salvador, Honduras and Costa Rica in the form of collective self defence against Nicaragua which was assisting rebels against them. The Court held that the right of self defence,[72] whether individual or collective, is only available in response to an "armed attack" and that the Nicaraguan assistance to rebels complained of did not constitute such an attack. The Court's definition of an "armed attack" (judgment, para.195), with its requirement of the sending of armed bands "by or on behalf of" the aggressor state to conduct an operation that meets the Court's "scale and effects" test, must mean that most cases of the indirect use of force contrary to customary international law by another state by the giving of assistance to rebels will not generate the right of self defence against that other state.[73] A less restrictive meaning of "armed attack" was suggested by Judge Sir Robert Jennings in his dissenting opinion[74]:

> "It may readily be agreed that the mere provision of arms cannot be said to amount to an armed attack. But the provision of arms may, nevertheless, be a very important element in what might be thought to amount to armed attack, where it is coupled with other kinds of involvement. Accordingly, it seems to me that to say that the provision of arms, coupled with 'logistical or other support' is not armed attack is going much too far. Logistical support may itself be crucial. ... If there is added to all this 'other support,' it becomes difficult to understand what it is, short of direct attack by a State's own forces, that may not be done apparently without a lawful response in the form of collective self-defence. ...
>   This looks to me neither realistic nor just in the world where power struggles are in every continent carried on by destabilisation, interference in civil strife, comfort, aid and encouragement to rebels, and the like. The original scheme of the United Nations Charter, whereby force would be deployed by the United Nations itself, ... has never come into effect. ... In this situation it seems dangerous to define unnecessarily strictly the conditions for lawful self-defence, so as to leave a large area where both a forcible response to force is forbidden. ..."

The approach suggested by Judge Sir Robert Jennings is in line with that of Western states. The text of the 1974 Resolution on the Definition of Aggression[75] which the Court relied upon for its

---

[70] cf. Schachter (1984) 78 A.J.I.L. 645 who argues against Reisman's claim, p.642, of a right to intervene "to increase the probability of the free choice of peoples' about their government." But, on another view, there may come a point where humanitarian intervention is permitted, in respect of human rights violations: see below, pp.777 et seq.

[71] See Doswald-Beck (1985) 56 B.Y.I.L. 189.

[72] On the right of self-defence generally, see below, p.746.

[73] But see, exceptionally, Renamo, the Mozambique rebel force, which conducted guerrilla warfare against the Mozambique Government in the 1980s: see White, above, n.39, p.549. Renamo was controlled by South Africa and could be said to have been "sent by or on behalf of it"—not just assisted by South Africa—and conducted operations that probably met the Court's "scale and effects" requirement, thus justifying individual and collective self-defence against South Africa.

[74] I.C.J. Rep. 1986, p.543.

[75] See art.3(*g*), below, p.800.

definition of an "armed attack", was a compromise between the views of Western and developing states.

The Court indicated that, although it has no right of self-defence (that would permit the use of armed force), a state faced with intervention by another state assisting rebels against it at a level not amounting to an "armed attack" may take "proportionate countermeasures" against the intervening state. These would include economic and political sanctions; the Court left unanswered (see judgment, paras 210, 249) the question whether armed force (e.g. by cross border raids to pursue guerrillas or to destroy their supply routes or bases) is also permitted. The Court was emphatic, however, that intervention below the level of an "armed attack" "could not justify countermeasures taken by a third state" (judgment, para.249) against a state assisting rebels. Thus, El Salvador, but not the US, could have taken them against Nicaragua. Intervention by a third state is "allowable at the request of the government of a state" (judgment, para.246), but only, by inference, against the rebels themselves and within the limits imposed by territorial sovereignty. El Salvador, for example, could have invited the US to send troops or provide arms to help it fight against the rebels on El Salvadoran territory, but the US could not have effected countermeasures against Nicaragua. Note that if the Court were, in an appropriate case, to decide that a victim state may react to unlawful intervention below the level of an armed attack by way of forcible countermeasures, it would be supposing a second and surprising exception (additional to self defence) to the rule that armed force is illegal in international relations—an exception that would significantly limit the present clear rule that reprisals are illegal. Might a better approach have been a wider definition of an "armed attack" (justifying self defence) along the lines suggested by Judge Sir Robert Jennings?

On the legality of assistance to the constitutional government to suppress *a rebellion that is not externally supported*, Wright[76] wrote in 1960 that international law:

"does not permit the use of force in the territory of another state on invitation either of the recognised or the insurgent government in times of rebellion, insurrection, or civil war. Since international law recognises the right of revolution, it cannot permit other states to intervene to prevent it."

This statement is consistent with the "broad principle" in the 1965 and 1970 Declarations "that internal conflicts within the state are the concern of that State alone"[77] and with the wish underlying the *Nicaragua* judgment to minimalise the internationalisation of conflict in the interest of international peace and security.[78] The United Kingdom supports a rule of non-intervention, save in the case of "temporary difficulties":

"Nevertheless, the United Kingdom did not consider that that rule in any way prejudiced the right of a legally constituted and internationally recognised Government to seek and receive from a friendly State assistance in preserving or restoring internal law and order. Of course, any Government which responded to such a request for assistance would have to satisfy itself that the response was proper, and it would have to expect its actions to come under the closest scrutiny of the international community. His Government believed, however, that it

---

[76] (1960) 54 A.J.I.L. 521 at 529.
[77] Bowett, in Moore, ed., below, n.80, at p.41.
[78] See White, above, n.39, at p.536. The lawfulness of intervention not involving the use of armed force to assist a government was recognised in the *Nicaragua* case, judgment, para.246, above, p.736.

would be wrong to suggest by an unduly broad definition of 'civil strife' that there were no circumstances in which a Government in temporary difficulties could seek and receive assistance from a friendly State which it trusted to render aid with full respect for the territorial integrity and political independence of the recipient State."[79]

B. Intervention in Civil Wars[80]

DECLARATION ON THE INADMISSIBILITY OF INTERVENTION IN THE DOMESTIC AFFAIRS OF STATES AND THE PROTECTION OF THEIR INDEPENDENCE AND SOVEREIGNTY 1965[81]

G.A. Resolution. 2131 (XX). December 21, 1965. G.A.O.R., 20th Sess., Supp. 14, p.11; (1966) 60 A.J.I.L. 662

The General Assembly . . . solemnly declares: . . .

1. No state has the right to intervene, directly or indirectly, for any reason whatever, in the internal or external affairs of any other state. Consequently, armed intervention and all other forms of interference or attempted threats against the personality of the state or against its political, economic and cultural elements, are condemned.

2. No state may use or encourage the use of economic, political or any other type of measures to coerce another state in order to obtain from it the subordination of the exercise of its sovereign rights or to secure from it advantages of any kind. Also, no state shall organise, assist, foment, finance, incite or tolerate subversive, terrorist or armed activities directed towards the violent overthrow of the régime of another state, or interfere in civil strife in another state.

3. The use of force to deprive peoples of their national identity constitutes a violation of their inalienable rights and of the principle of non-intervention.

4. The strict observance of these obligations is an essential condition to ensure that nations live together in peace with one another, since the practice of any form of intervention not only violates the spirit and letter of the Charter of the United Nations but also leads to the creation of situations which threaten international peace and security.

5. Every state has an inalienable right to choose its political, economic, social and cultural systems, without interference in any form by another State.

Notes

1. Paragraphs 1, 2, 3, and 5 of the 1965 Declaration were incorporated almost verbatim into the Section on the Principle of Non-Intervention in the 1970 Declaration on Principles of International Law, below, App.III. Both were regarded as stating the customary international law on intervention in the *Nicaragua* case (judgment, para.203).

[79] UK representative (Mr Sinclair) in the 1967 Special Committee on Principles of International Law, etc. UN Doc. A/AC.125/ SR.57, p.5; 1967 B.P.I.L. 36. cf. the 1986 Foreign Office Policy Document No.148, paras II.6–9, reprinted in U.K.M.I.L. 1986, (1986) 57 B.Y.I.L. 614.

[80] On the international law on intervention in civil wars generally, see Falk, ed., *The International Law of Civil War* (1971); Farer (1974–III) 142 Hague Recueil 291 (1974–II); Little, *Intervention* (1975); Luard, ed., *The International Regulation of Civil War* (1972); Moore, ed., *Law and Civil War in the Modern World* (1974); Tanca, *Foreign Armed Intervention in Internal Conflict* (1993).

[81] The Resolution was adopted by 109 to 0, with one abstention. The one abstaining state was the UK, which accepted the "fundamental propositions set out in the resolution" but objected to "the manner in which that resolution had been evolved and the imprecision of some of its language": 1967 B.P.I.L. 35, 36.

2. Although a state's interference in another state's affairs may not amount to the use of force, it may nonetheless be contrary to international law as intervention. Thus, in the *Nicaragua* case, the funding of the *contras*, although not an unlawful use of force, was illegal intervention (judgment, para.228). The prohibition upon intervention in civil wars (the sole subject of this section) is just one aspect of a more general prohibition the limits of which have always been uncertain and are not well defined in the vague language of the 1965 and 1970 Declarations. Intervention is defined by Oppenheim as "forcible or dictatorial interference by a State in the affairs of another State, calculated to impose certain conduct or consequences on that other State."[82] In the nineteenth century, it was often darkly associated with the armed intervention, on humanitarian or other grounds, by powerful European states in the affairs of their weaker brethren.[83] As the 1965 Declaration indicates, it also includes other, more subtle, forms of influence or control.[84] For example, intervention in the "external affairs" of another state (para.1) may include a case in which "State A sought to persuade State B by threats or by other measures amounting to economic coercion not to enter an association with other States."[85] The Principle of Non-Intervention in the 1965 and 1970 Declarations overlaps with that on the use of force in art.2(4) and the 1970 Declaration. An armed attack upon another State annexing its territory is the ultimate form of intervention. Certain kinds of assistance to rebels in a civil war is within both principles also: see the *Nicaragua* (*Merits*) case (judgment, para.205).

    The following notes contain accounts of instances of intervention by force in the affairs of other states. The justifications given by the intervening state vary from the request of the constitutional government, to the maintenance or exclusion of socialism or communism within or from a region, to the defence of nationals, to the existence of a treaty right of intervention. Are any of these cases ones in which the intervention can properly be justified on these grounds or otherwise in accordance with the rules as to the use of force and intervention?

3. *The Hungarian Uprising.*[86] On October 23, 1956, demonstrations took place in Budapest against the Hungarian Government calling, inter alia, for Mr Nagy to be brought into the Government. Fighting broke out and, at 2am on October 24, Russian tanks appeared in Budapest. Nonetheless, at 8.13am, it was announced that a new Government was to be formed under Mr Nagy. At 9am, it was announced that "the Government had applied for help to the Soviet formations stationed in Hungary [under the Warsaw Pact]." It is not clear when and by whom the application was made.[87] On November 1, Hungary denounced the Warsaw Pact after Mr Nagy had unsuccessfully demanded the withdrawal of new Soviet troops known to be entering Hungary. On the same day, Mr Nagy broadcast a declaration of Hungarian neutrality and called for the assistance of other states to defend it. On November 4, Soviet troops again entered Budapest and overcame resistance in a few days. On the same day, Mr Kadar announced that he had formed a Government in place of that of Mr Nagy and that he had requested the second intervention of Soviet troops. Thereafter the uprising petered out. The United Nations Special Committee on the Problem of Hungary, which was not allowed into Hungary to investigate, found it impossible to reach any conclusion on the question whether any request for aid had

---

[82] Oppenheim, Vol.I, p.430.
[83] cf. the passage in the *Corfu Channel* case judgment, I.C.J. Rep. 1949, p.4.
[84] See Damrosch (1989) 83 A.J.I.L. 1.
[85] UK representative (Mr Sinclair) in the 1967 Special Committee on Principles of International Law, etc. UN Doc. A/AC.125/SR.73, p.22; 1967 B.P.I.L. 39.
[86] The following summary is based on the Report of the UN Special Committee on the Problem of Hungary, G.A.O.R., 11th Sess., Supp. 18 (1957).
[87] It is not known when Mr Nagy's Government actually took office.

been made at the beginning; it rejected the Soviet argument[88] that what the committee called a "spontaneous national uprising" had been fomented by ex-Nazi leaders and Western powers who had sent in arms. The case demonstrates one of the weaknesses of allowing intervention at the request of the constitutional government, namely that of determining which is the constitutional government (if any can be found in the middle of a revolution) and whether it in fact made a request.

4.   *The Czechoslovak* case. In 1968, with the arrival of Mr Dubcek and other new leaders in power by lawful means, the still communist Government of Czechoslovakia introduced certain reforms resulting, inter alia, in increased freedom of speech, that were significantly at variance with Czechoslovakia's previous policies. In August 1968, troops from the USSR and other East European communist states entered Czechoslovakia. With the assistance of Soviet advisers, the policies and composition of the Czech Government thereafter gradually changed, with the movement towards liberalisation being reversed. The USSR first claimed that the Czech Government had requested the intervention, but this was strenuously denied by that Government. Later the intervention was explained by Mr Brezhnev, in a speech in Poland, as follows:

> "... It is well known, comrades, that there are common natural laws of socialist construction, deviation from which could lead from socialism as such. And when external and internal forces hostile to socialism try to turn the development of a given socialist country in the direction of restoration of the capitalist system ... this is no longer merely a problem for the country's people, but a common problem, the concern of all socialist countries.
>
>   It is quite clear that an action such as military assistance to a fraternal country to end a threat to the socialist system is an extraordinary measure, dictated by necessity; it can be called forth only by the overt actions of enemies of socialism within the country and beyond its boundaries, actions that create a threat to the common interests of the socialist camp."[89]

This doctrine of limited sovereignty, now abandoned, became known as the "Brezhnev Doctrine."[90]

5.   *The Afghanistan* case.[91] In 1978, the non-aligned Daud Government was ousted by force, leading ultimately in 1979 to a new USSR backed communist Government led by President Karmal, an Afghanistan politician flown to Afghanistan to take office by the USSR from virtual exile in Eastern Europe. The change of government was accompanied by an airlift into Kabul of 4,000 USSR troops. The USSR claimed that the Afghanistan Government had requested USSR intervention under a 1978 bilateral treaty of friendship[92] to protect Afghanistan from "armed incursions and provocations from outside." USSR troops, thought to number 100,000, were then brought into Afghanistan, assisting the Afghan army in fighting guerilla opponents of the Karmal (and later Najibullah) Government. A Security Council draft resolution which deplored the USSR intervention and called for the withdrawal of USSR troops was vetoed by the USSR.[93] A General

---

[88]   G.A.O.R., 11th Sess., Special Political Committee, 41st Meeting, p.189 (1957).
[89]   20 *Current Digest of the Soviet Press*, No.46, pp.3–4; December 4, 1968.
[90]   See Moore and Turner, *International Law and the Brezhnev Doctrine* (1987).
[91]   See *Keesing's Archives*, p.30229. On the current position in Afghanistan, see below, p.773.
[92]   For the terms of this treaty see, Bilateral Treaty of Friendship 1978, p.29459. It provides for the parties to "consult each other and take by agreement appropriate measures to ensure the security, independence and territorial integrity of their countries."
[93]   The vote, on January 7, 1980, was by 13 to 2 (GDR, USSR).

Assembly resolution of January 14, 1980[94] re-affirmed that "respect for the sovereignty, territorial integrity and political independence of every state is a fundamental principle of the Charter" and strongly deplored "the recent armed intervention in Afghanistan which is inconsistent with that principle." The resolution appealed to all states "to refrain from any interference in the internal affairs of that country" and called for the "immediate, unconditional and total withdrawal of the foreign troops from Afghanistan." The General Assembly resolution was phrased in the terms of both the Use of Force and Non-Intervention Principles in the 1970 Declaration. Under the 1988 Geneva Accords[95] between Afghanistan, Pakistan, the US and the USSR, the USSR withdrew its troops in 1989. Was the USSR intervention lawful?

6. *Bangladesh*. Until 1971, Pakistan consisted of East and West Pakistan, with India between the two parts. On March 26, 1971, East Pakistan declared itself independent under the name of Bangladesh. The Pakistan army was initially successful in suppressing the rebellion, but in November 1971 rebel guerrilla forces launched a general offensive with considerable success. There was evidence to suggest that India, which by then had taken into its territory about one million refugees from East Pakistan, had given the guerrillas military assistance and Pakistani and Indian troops clashed in the border area. On December 3, 1971, Pakistan attacked India in the west. This was regarded as a declaration of war by India and fighting began in earnest in east and west. By December 17, 1971, Pakistan had surrendered on both fronts. Bangladesh has since received general recognition (including that of Pakistan) as an independent state. Was India entitled in law to give military assistance to the Bangladeshi guerrillas? Was its refugee problem relevant? Was Pakistan entitled to attack India on December 3?[96]

7. *The Grenada* case.[97] In 1979, Maurice Bishop became Prime Minister of a new revolutionary Government of Grenada, a small Caribbean state, formerly a UK colony. The new Government, which, unlike its elected predecessor, had communist leanings, established links with Cuba and the USSR. In October 1983, disagreement within Bishop's party led to his Government being ousted by a more radical left-wing Government. On October 19, Bishop and some of his supporters were executed and 17 civilians, on some accounts possibly many more, were killed when government forces fired on the crowd. A curfew was ordered, with forces empowered to shoot on sight. On October 23, the US sent troops to Grenada, supported by troops from several other Caribbean states, who quickly took control of the island after fighting with Grenada forces. US troops were evacuated in December 1983 and a centre right Government was democratically elected in 1984. The US justified its intervention on three grounds: the protection of US nationals; a request to intervene from the Organisation of Eastern Caribbean States (OECS), of which Grenada was a member; and a request from the Governor-General of Grenada. These justifications have been doubted. Although there were US nationals in Grenada, all accounts suggest that they were not at risk. The competence of the OECS to request a non-member state to intervene in the absence of external aggression and by the procedure followed is questionable, and the Governor-General was probably not constitutionally competent to request assistance. A

---

[94]   G.A. Resn. ES–6/2; G.A.O.R., 6th Emerg. Sp. Sess., Supp. 1, p.2 (1980). The vote was by 104 votes to 18, with 18 abstentions.
[95]   (1988) 27 I.L.M. 577.
[96]   On self defence, see below, p.746.
[97]   See Beck (1993) 33 Virg. J.I.L. 765; Davidson, *Grenada* (1987); Doswald-Beck (1984) 31 N.I.L.R. 355; Gilmore, The *Grenada Intervention* (1984); Joyner (1984) 78 A.J.I.L. 131; Moore, ibid., 145; Quigley (1986–7) 18 Inter-American L.R. 271; Vagts (1984) 78 A.J.I.L. 169. As in other intervention cases, the existence and timing of the claimed requests for assistance are difficult to establish.

draft Security Council resolution condemning the US intervention as illegal was vetoed by the US.[98] A General Assembly resolution deploring the US action was adopted.[99]

8. *The Cyprus* case.[100] Cyprus has a population which is four-fifths Greek Cypriot and one-fifth Turkish Cypriot. The United Nations Force in Cyprus (UNFICYP) was established there in 1964[101] to help keep the peace between the two communities. Following the overthrow of the Makarios Government in 1974 by a coup supported by Greece and resulting in the establishment of a Greek Cypriot junta, Turkey invaded the island in the same month. The Security Council called upon "all states to respect the sovereignty, independence and territorial integrity of Cyprus" and demanded "an immediate end to foreign military intervention" in Cyprus that was contrary to such respect.[102] In 1983, an independent state called the Turkish Republic of Northern Cyprus was declared to have been established.[103] Turkey claimed that its intervention in 1974 was justified under the Treaty of Guarantee[104] made between Cyprus, Greece, Turkey, and the United Kingdom in 1960 when Cypriot independence was agreed. By this treaty, Cyprus undertook to "ensure the maintenance of its independence, territorial integrity and security, as well as respect for its constitution." (art.1). The three guaranteeing powers, who undertook to recognise and guarantee the independence, territorial integrity and security of Cyprus (art.2), agreed in the event of a breach of the treaty to consult to determine what representations or measures were necessary. Insofar as concerted action proved impossible, each of them reserved "the right to take action with the sole aim of establishing the state of affairs created" by the treaty (art.4). Could Turkey rely upon the treaty (supposing "action" includes the use of force and that tripartite consultation occurred (it had not)) to justify its intervention in the face of art.2(4) of the Charter or the Principle of Non-Intervention in the 1970 Declaration? Would art.103 of the United Nations Charter, below, App.I, be relevant?

C. *The Right of Self-Defence*[105]

THE CAROLINE CASE[106]

29 B.F.S.P. 1137–1138; 30 B.F.S.P. 195–196

The case arose out of the Canadian Rebellion of 1837. The rebel leaders, despite steps taken by United States authorities to prevent assistance being given to them, managed on December 13, 1837, to enlist at Buffalo in the United States the support of a large number of American nationals. The resulting force established itself on Navy Island in Canadian waters from which it raided the Canadian

---

[98] S.C.O.R., 2491st Meeting. October 27, 1983. Adopted by 108 votes to 9, with 27 abstentions.

[99] G.A. Resn. 38/7, G.A.O.R., 38th Sess., Supp. 47, p.19 (1983).

[100] See Polyviou, *Cyprus: The Tragedy and the Challenge* (1975); and Necatigil, *The Cyprus Question and the Turkish Position in International Law* (2nd edn 1993).

[101] On peacekeeping operations, see below, p.827.

[102] S.C. Resn. 353 (1974), S.C.O.R., 29th Year, *Resolutions and Decisions*, p.7. See, most recently, S.C. Resn. 440 (1978), S.C.O.R., 29th Year, p.11.

[103] See above, p.103.

[104] Cmnd. 1093.

[105] See Alexandrov, *Self-Defense Against the Use of Force*; Bowett, *Self-Defence in International Law* (1958); Mullerson, in Damrosch and Scheffer, *Law and Force in the New International Order* (1991), p.13; Salamanca-Aguado (2005) 16 E.J.I.L. 499. See also the Chatham House Principles on International Law on the Use of Force in Self-Defence, (2006) 55 I.C.L.Q. 963.

[106] See Jennings (1938) 32 A.J.I.L. 82; and Rogoff and Collins (1990) 16 Brooklyn J.I.L. 493.

shore and attacked passing British ships. The force was supplied from the United States shore by an American ship, the *Caroline*. On the night of December 29–30, the British seized the *Caroline*, which was then in the American port of Schlosser, fired her and sent her over Niagara Falls. Two United States nationals were killed. The legality of the British acts was discussed in detail in correspondence in 1841–1842 when Great Britain sought the release of a British subject, McLeod, who had been arrested in the United States on charges of murder and arson arising out of the incident.

MR. WEBSTER TO MR. FOX (APRIL 24, 1841).

It will be for … [Her Majesty's] Government to show a necessity of self-defence, instant, overwhelming, leaving no choice of means, and no moment for deliberation. It will be for it to show, also, that the local authorities of Canada, even supposing the necessity of the moment authorised them to enter the territories of The United States at all, did nothing unreasonable or excessive; since the act, justified by the necessity of self-defence, must be limited by that necessity, and kept clearly within it. It must be shown that admonition or remonstrance to the person on board the *Caroline* was impracticable, or would have been unavailing; it must be shown that day-light could not be waited for; that there could be no attempt at discrimination between the innocent and the guilty; that it would not have been enough to seize and detain the vessel; but that there was a necessity, present and inevitable, for attacking her in the darkness of the night, while moored to the shore, and while unarmed men were asleep on board, killing some and wounding others, and then drawing her into the current, above the cataract, setting her on fire, and, careless to know whether there might not be in her the innocent with the guilty, or the living with the dead, committing her to a fate which fills the imagination with horror. A necessity for all this, the Government of The United States cannot believe to have existed.

LORD ASHBURTON TO MR. WEBSTER (JULY 28, 1842)

It is so far satisfactory to perceive that we are perfectly agreed as to the general principles of international law applicable to this unfortunate case. Respect for the inviolable character of the territory of independent nations is the most essential foundation of civilisation. …

Notes

1. In his reply, Lord Ashburton sought to justify the British action in accordance with the test formulated by Webster, which has commonly been accepted as indicating when the pre-UN Charter, customary international law right of self-defence could be exercised.

2. *Anticipatory self-defence*. It was not doubted in the *Caroline* case that the British Government was entitled to anticipate further attacks. It was argued before the International Military Tribunal at Nuremberg that the German invasion of Norway in 1940 was an act of self-defence in the face of an imminent Allied landing there. The Tribunal recalled that preventive action in foreign territory is justified only in the circumstances cited by Webster in the *Caroline* case and found on the facts that there was no imminent threat of an Allied landing in Norway.[107]

ARTICLE 51 UNITED NATIONS CHARTER

Nothing in the present Charter shall impair the inherent right of individual or collective self-defence if an armed attack occurs against a Member of the United Nations, until the Security Council has taken measures necessary to maintain international peace and security. Measures taken by Members in the exercise of this right of self-defence shall be immediately reported to the Security Council and shall not in any way affect the authority and responsibility of the Security Council under the present Charter to take at any time such action as it deems necessary in order to maintain or restore international peace and security.

---

[107] (1947) 41 A.J.I.L. 205. cf. the I.M.T. for the Far East, judgment, pp.994–995, quoted in Horwitz, *The Tokyo Trial*, Int.Conc. No. 465 (1950), p.560.

Notes

1. By virtue of art.51, a state's "inherent" right of self-defence is an exception to the prohibition of the use of force in art.2(4), UN Charter. This "inherent" right is the right of self-defence in customary international law,[108] originally as it existed before 1945 and now as it has subsequently developed. This customary right of self-defence co-exists with the treaty-based right in art.51, and the indications are that the two rights have come to have the same meaning.[109]

2. As to the meaning, it is clear that the right of self-defence exists only where there is an "armed attack" against a state[110]; that it is a right of individual and collective self-defence[111]; and that the armed force used in self-defence must be both necessary and proportionate.[112] Less clear is whether the pre-1945 rights of anticipatory (now pre-emptive) self-defence and to protect nationals abroad still exist. Whereas, post 9/11, a consensus has emerged favouring the existence of the former, at least in response to some terrorist acts,[113] this is not true in the case of the latter.[114] The use of force in self-defence does not give rise to state reponsibility.[115]

3. The law and practice on self-defence has historically mostly concerned three different kinds of situation: large scale attacks by one state upon another of the classical sort (e.g. recently, the *Falkland Islands* case, below, p.749); lower scale cross border raids by guerrilla forces and others (e.g. the *Nicaragua* case, above, p.727); and government or terrorist activities injuring the nationals of another state abroad (the *US air raids on Libya* and *Entebbe Incident* cases, below, pp.770, 768). Recently, the focus has moved to Al-Qaida terrorist activity of the 9/11 kind, taken against individuals and property on the victim state's own territory. Most of this section of this chapter concerns the law that has been developed in the context of the first three of these situations. The final part considers the impact of 9/11 kinds of activity on that law.

4. *Armed attack*. The meaning of "armed attack" was considered in the *Nicaragua* case, para.195, above, p.730. Insofar as the cross border use of force by "regular armed forces" is concerned, the Court in that case supposes that not every such use of force is an "armed attack": its "scale and effects" must be sufficient. The Court's narrow definition of an "armed attack" also excludes "assistance to rebels in the form of the provision of weapons or logistical or other support". However, state practice concerning 9/11 accepts that terrorist action on the scale and with the effects of 9/11 may be an "armed attack", justifying self-defence against the state giving the terrorists a base or haven: see Gray, below, p.772. See also on "armed attack", the *Oil Platforms* case, below, p.750, and the *Partial Award: Ius ad Bellum: Ethiopia's Claims 1–8*, below, p.765.

5. *Collective Self-defence*. The customary international law right of collective self-defence was examined in the *Nicaragua (Merits)* case (judgment, paras 199–200, 232–8 above, pp.731, 734).

---

[108] See the *Nicaragua* case *(Merits)*, para.176, above, p.727. On the relationship between the pre-1945 customary rule and art.51, see the different views of Bowett, above, n.1, p.185, and Kelsen, *The Law of the United Nations* (1950), p.914.

[109] There is, however, a reporting obligation in art.51 which only applies to UN members. In practice, differences between the customary and treaty-based rights would only be significant for the very few non-UN member state, and in a case such as the *Nicaragua* case, above, p.727, in which the ICJ had only customary law jurisdiction.

[110] As to whether the attack may come from non-state actors as well as states, see the notes to the *Armed Activities* case, paras 146–147, below, p.758.

[111] *Nicaragua* case *(Merits)*, para.193, above, p.730.

[112] *Nicaragua* case *(Merits)*, para.176.

[113] See below, p.772.

[114] See below, p.770.

[115] See art.21, Draft Articles on Responsibility of States for Internationally Wrongful Acts, above, p.436.

Before State T may embark upon collective self-defence, State D must declare itself a victim of an armed attack and request State T's assistance.[116] There need not, however, be any threat to State T's security for it to be entitled to respond. In his dissenting opinion, Judge Sir Robert Jennings criticised this last aspect of the Court's judgment as follows[117]:

"The assisting State surely must, by going to the victim State's assistance, be also, and in *addition* to other requirements, in some measure defending itself. There should even in 'collective self-defence' be some real element of self involved with the notion of defence. This is presumably also the philosophy which underlies mutual security arrangements, such as the system of the Organisation of American States, for which indeed Article 51 was specifically designed."

The United Kingdom relied on the right of collective (as well as individual) self defence as a basis for its missile attacks on Afghanistan following 9/11. See below, p.772. See also the reference in Security Council Resolution 661 to collective self-defence in the *Invasion of Kuwait* case.[118]

6. *The Role of the Security Council.* The right of self-defence is a temporary one in the scheme of art.51, existing only until the Security Council acts. In practice, such is the power of the "veto," the Security Council may never act and the right of self-defence will be of unlimited duration. Who is to judge when the Council "has taken the measures necessary ... [etc.]"? The British Commentary on the Charter reads:

"It will be for the Security Council to decide whether these measures have been taken and whether they are adequate for the purpose. In the event of the Security Council failing to take any action, or if such action as it does take is clearly inadequate, the right of self-defence could be invoked by any Member or group of Members as justifying any action they thought fit to take."[119]

As to the obligation in art.51 to report "immediately" to the Security Council action taken in self-defence, note the Court's reliance, in the *Nicaragua* case *(Merits)*, para.235, above, p.734, on the absence of any report at all by the United States to the Security Council on the steps taken against Nicaragua when assessing whether the United States was, as it claimed, acting by way of (collective) self-defence. See also the *Armed Activities* case, para.145, below, p.758; the *Oil Platforms* case *(Merits)*, below, p.750; and the *Partial Award: Ius ad Bellum* case, below, p.765.

7. *The Falkland Islands War.*[120] On April 2, 1982, Argentine forces invaded the Falkland Islands in reliance upon Argentina's claim to sovereignty over them, as to which see above, p.183. On April 3, the Security Council adopted Resolution 502,[121] which read in part:

---

[116] Does the Court suppose in the *Nicaragua* case that state D has to request or approve the particular form that the assistance takes?

[117] I.C.J. Rep. 1986, p.545. Footnote omitted. Judge Sir Robert Jennings also questioned whether the requirements of "some sort of formal declaration and request might sometimes be unrealistic".

[118] See below, p.810.

[119] Misc. 9 (1945), Cmd. 6666, p.9.

[120] See Coll and Arend, *The Falklands War* (1985); and Franck (1983) 77 A.J.I.L. 109. On the background and for accounts of the invasion, see Calvert, *The Falkland Islands Crisis: the Rights and Wrongs* (1982); Hastings and Jenkins, *The Battle for The Falklands* (1983); Honeywell and Pearce, *Falkland Islands/Malvinas: Whose Crisis?* (1982); Sunday Times Insight Team, *The Falklands War* (1982).

[121] UN Doc. S/PV2346, p.6. The resolution was adopted by 10 votes (France, Guyana, Ireland, Japan, Jordan, Togo, Uganda, UK, US, Zaire) to one (Panama), with four abstentions (China, Poland, Spain, USSR). The resolution was adopted under art.40, UN Charter.

"The Security Council . . .

Determining that there exists a breach of the peace in the region of the Falkland Islands (Islas Malvinas),

1. Demands an immediate cessation of hostilities;

2. Demands an immediate withdrawal of all Argentine forces from the Falkland Islands (Islas Malvinas);

3. Calls on the governments of Argentina and the United Kingdom to seek a diplomatic solution to their differences and to respect fully the purposes and principles of the Charter of the United Nations.

On April 5, a British military expedition (the Task Force) sailed for the South Atlantic. Economic sanctions were imposed against Argentina by the United Kingdom and the European Communities. The United States gave the United Kingdom logistical assistance. The Organisation of American States resolved that its members should support Argentina. After diplomatic efforts to achieve a peaceful solution had failed, the Task Force landed on the Falklands on May 21. The Argentine garrison surrendered on June 14, 1982.

Argentina's reliance upon its claim to title as the legal basis for the invasion was not accepted by the Security Council. The United Kingdom justified its use of force to recover the Falklands as an "exercise of its inherent right of self-defence, recognised by Article 51 of the Charter."[122]

OIL PLATFORMS CASE (MERITS)[123]

Iran v United States

I.C.J. Reports 2003, p.161

During the Iran-Iraq War, a number of attacks on merchant shipping occurred in the Persian Gulf, causing the US and other states to provide naval escorts for ships flying their flags. In October 1987, the *Sea Isle City*, a Kuwaiti tanker that had been re-flagged to the US for escort purposes, was hit by a missile in Kuwaiti territorial waters. In April 1988, the warship USS *Samuel B. Roberts* was damaged by a mine in international waters while on escort duty. Claiming self defence, some three and four days after these incidents respectively, the US attacked Iranian oil platforms.

In this case, Iran claimed that the attacks on its platforms were in breach of the 1955 US-Iran Treaty of Amity, Economic Relations and Consular Rights. The Court accepted the US argument that, if they could be shown to be acts of self-defence at customary international law, the attacks could be justified under art.20(1)(d) of the Treaty, which permitted measures by a party "necessary to protect its essential security interests".

Judgment

51. . . .in order to establish that it was legally justified in attacking the Iranian platforms in exercise of the right of individual self-defence, the United States has to show that attacks had been made upon it for which Iran was responsible; and that those attacks were of such a nature as to be qualified as "armed attacks" within the

---

[122] UN Doc. 5/PV 2360, p.38.
[123] See Foster (2003) 7 Singapore J.I.C.L. 579; Garwood-Gowers (2004) 5 Mel.J.L. 241; Green (2004) 9 J.C.S.L. 357; Murphy (2004) A.J.I.L. 597; Raab (2004) 17 L.J.I.L. 719.

meaning of that expression in Article 51 of the United Nations Charter, and as understood in customary law on the use of force. As the Court observed in the case concerning *Military and Paramilitary Activities in and against Nicaragua*, it is necessary to distinguish "the most grave forms of the use of force (those constituting an armed attack) from other less grave forms" (*I.C.J. Reports 1986*, p.101, para.191), since "In the case of individual self-defence, the exercise of this right is subject to the State concerned having been the victim of an armed attack" (*ibid.*, p.103, para.195). The United States must also show that its actions were necessary and proportional to the armed attack made on it, and that the platforms were a legitimate military target open to attack in the exercise of self-defence. ...

61. ... the Court has examined with great care the evidence and arguments presented on each side, and finds that the evidence indicative of Iranian responsibility for the attack on the *Sea Isle City* is not sufficient to support the contentions of the United States. The conclusion to which the Court has come on this aspect of the case is thus that the burden of proof of the existence of an armed attack by Iran on the United States, in the form of the missile attack on the *Sea Isle City*, has not been discharged.

62. In its notification to the Security Council, and before the Court, the United States has however not relied solely on the *Sea Isle City* incident as constituting the "armed attack" to which the United States claimed to be responding. It asserted that that incident was "the latest in a series of such missile attacks against United States flag and other non-belligerent vessels in Kuwaiti waters in pursuit of peaceful commerce" ...

64. On the hypothesis that all the incidents complained of are to be attributed to Iran, and thus setting aside the question, examined above, of attribution to Iran of the specific attack on the *Sea Isle City*, the question is whether that attack, either in itself or in combination with the rest of the "series of ... attacks" cited by the United States can be categorized as an "armed attack" on the United States justifying self-defence. The Court notes first that the *Sea Isle City* was in Kuwaiti waters at the time of the attack on it, and that a Silkworm missile fired from (it is alleged) more than 100 km away could not have been aimed at the specific vessel, but simply programmed to hit some target in Kuwaiti waters. Secondly, the *Texaco Caribbean*, whatever its ownership [United States], was not flying a United States flag, so that an attack on the vessel is not in itself to be equated with an attack on that State. As regards the alleged firing on United States helicopters from Iranian gunboats and from the Reshadat oil platform, no persuasive evidence has been supplied to support this allegation. There is no evidence that the minelaying alleged to have been carried out by the *Iran Ajr*, at a time when Iran was at war with Iraq, was aimed specifically at the United States; and similarly it has not been established that the mine struck by the *Bridgeton* was laid with the specific intention of harming that ship, or other United States vessels. Even taken cumulatively, and reserving, as already noted, the question of Iranian responsibility, these incidents do not seem to the Court to constitute an armed attack on the United States, of the kind that the Court, in the case concerning Military and Paramilitary Activities in and against Nicaragua, qualified as a "most grave" form of the use of force ...

71. As in the case of the attack on the *Sea Isle City*, the first question is whether the United States has discharged the burden of proof that the USS *Samuel B. Roberts* was the victim of a mine laid by Iran. The Court notes that mines were being laid at the time by both belligerents in the Iran-Iraq war, so that evidence of other minelaying operations by Iran is not conclusive as to responsibility of Iran for this particular mine ... The main evidence that the mine struck by the USS *Samuel B. Roberts* was laid by Iran was the discovery of moored mines in the same area, bearing serial numbers matching other Iranian mines, in particular those found aboard the vessel *Iran Ajr* ... This evidence is highly suggestive, but not conclusive.

72. ... The Court does not exclude the possibility that the mining of a single military vessel might be sufficient to bring into play the "inherent right of self-defence"; but in view of all the circumstances, including the inconclusiveness of the evidence of Iran's responsibility for the mining of the USS *Samuel B. Roberts*, the Court is unable to hold that the attacks on the Salman and Nasr platforms have been shown to have been justifiably made in response to an "armed attack" on the United States by Iran, in the form of the mining of the USS *Samuel B. Roberts*.

73. [The Court next considered the question of "necessity" and "proportionality".] The United States claims that it considered in good faith that the attacks on the platforms were necessary to protect its essential security interests, and suggests that "A measure of discretion should be afforded to a party's good faith application of measures to protect its essential security interests". ... The Court does not however have to decide whether the United States interpretation of Article XX, paragraph 1 (*d*), on this point is correct, since the requirement of international law that measures taken avowedly in self-defence must have been necessary for that purpose is strict and objective, leaving no room for any "measure of discretion".[124] ...

---

[124] Ed. The fact the the US gave notice to the Security Council of the attacks on the platforms, as required under art.51 of acts of self-defence, did not thereby make them such: see judgment, para.40.

74. ... One aspect of these criteria [necessity and proportionality] is the nature of the target of the force used avowedly in self-defence ... the United States has ... presented evidence directed to showing that the platforms collected and reported intelligence concerning passing vessels, acted as a military communication link co-ordinating Iranian naval forces and served as actual staging bases to launch helicopter and small boat attacks on neutral commercial shipping ...

76. The Court is not sufficiently convinced that the evidence available supports the contentions of the United States as to the significance of the military presence and activity on the Reshadat oil platforms [*Sea Isle City* case]; and it notes that no such evidence is offered in respect of the Salman and Nasr complexes [*Roberts* case]. However, even accepting those contentions, for the purposes of discussion, the Court is unable to hold that the attacks made on the platforms could have been justified as acts of self-defence. The conditions for the exercise of the right of self-defence are well settled: as the Court observed in its Advisory Opinion on *Legality of the Threat or Use of Nuclear Weapons*, "The submission of the exercise of the right of self-defence to the conditions of necessity and proportionality is a rule of customary international law" (*I.C.J. Reports 1996 (I)*, p.245, para.41); and in the case concerning *Military and Paramilitary Activities in and against Nicaragua*, the Court referred to a specific rule "whereby self-defence would warrant only measures which are proportional to the armed attack and necessary to respond to it" as "a rule well established in customary international law" (*I.C.J. Reports 1986*, p.94, para.176). In the case both of the attack on the *Sea Isle City* and the mining of the USS *Samuel B. Roberts*, the Court is not satisfied that the attacks on the platforms were necessary to respond to these incidents. In this connection, the Court notes that there is no evidence that the United States complained to Iran of the military activities of the platforms, in the same way as it complained repeatedly of minelaying and attacks on neutral shipping, which does not suggest that the targeting of the platforms was seen as a necessary act. The Court would also observe that in the case of the attack of 19 October 1987, the United States forces attacked the R-4 platform as a "target of opportunity", not one previously identified as an appropriate military target ...

77. As to the requirement of proportionality, the attack of 19 October 1987 might, had the Court found that it was necessary in response to the *Sea Isle City* incident as an armed attack committed by Iran, have been considered proportionate. In the case of the attacks of 18 April 1988, however, they were conceived and executed as part of a more extensive operation entitled "Operation Praying Mantis". ... The question of the lawfulness of other aspects of that operation is not before the Court, since it is solely the action against the Salman and Nasr complexes that is presented as a breach of the 1955 Treaty; but the Court cannot assess in isolation the proportionality of that action to the attack to which it was said to be a response; it cannot close its eyes to the scale of the whole operation, which involved, inter alia, the destruction of two Iranian frigates and a number of other naval vessels and aircraft. As a response to the mining, by an unidentified agency, of a single United States warship, which was severely damaged but not sunk, and without loss of life, neither "Operation Praying Mantis" as a whole, nor even that part of it that destroyed the Salman and Nasr platforms, can be regarded, in the circumstances of this case, as a proportionate use of force in self-defence.

78. The Court thus concludes [by 14 votes to 2] from the foregoing that the actions carried out by United States forces against Iranian oil installations on 19 October 1987 and 18 April 1988 cannot be justified, under Article XX, paragraph 1 (*d*), of the 1955 Treaty, as being measures necessary to protect the essential security interests of the United States, since those actions constituted recourse to armed force not qualifying, under international law on the question, as acts of self-defence, and thus did not fall within the category of measures contemplated, upon its correct interpretation, by that provision of the Treaty.

Notes

1. The *Oil Platforms* case addresses a number of issues concerning the right to self defence in customary international law, including the requirements of necessity and proportionality.

2. *Armed attack.* Does the Court accept that an attack on (i) merchant or (ii) naval vessels flying a state's flag may be an "armed attack" to which it may respond by self defence involving armed force? See paras 64, 72 judgment. Note in this connection the references to self-defence in the *Korean Airline Flight 007 Incident*, above, p.208, the *Gulf of Tonkin Incident*, below, p.754, and the *Libyan People's Bureau Incident*, above, p.305. See further on the meaning of "armed attack", above p.748.

3. *Interference with vessels beyond the territorial sea.* There is a long-established right on the part of a state engaged in armed conflict to stop and search a vessel flying another's state flag on the

high seas where it is reasonably suspected of carrying weapons to another party to the conflict.[125] Following the Iranian searching of the *Barber Perseus*, a United Kingdom merchant vessel, in the Persian Gulf during the Iran-Iraq War, a Foreign Office Minister stated[126]:

"The U.K. upholds the general principle of freedom of navigation of the high seas. However, under Article 51 of the UN Charter, a State such as Iran actively engaged in an armed conflict, is entitled to exercise its inherent right of self-defence to stop and search a foreign merchant ship on the high seas if there are reasonable grounds for suspecting that the ship is taking arms to the other side for use in the conflict. This is an exceptional right: if the suspicions prove to be unfounded and if the ship has not committed acts calculated to give rise to suspicion, then the ship's owners have a good claim for compensation for loss caused by the delay."

In the Algerian emergency 1956–62, France stopped and searched several thousand foreign vessels on the high seas for weapons destined for rebel forces, claiming the right of self-defence.[127]

The Cuban Quarantine concerned the shipment of equipment that threatened the United States in the future, not in the context of existing hostilities. On October 22, 1962, President Kennedy announced the United States intention to impose a "strict quarantine on all offensive military equipment under shipment to Cuba".[128] The United States decided upon this policy after discovering that the USSR was sending to Cuba missiles and other weapons and materials which could be seen as a threat to United States security. On October 23, at the suggestion of the United States, the Security Council met and discussed the proposed quarantine but took no action.[129] On the same day, the Council of the Organisation of American States adopted a resolution[130] recommending that:

"member states, in accordance with Articles 6 and 8 of the Inter-American Treaty of Reciprocal Assistance[131] take all measures, individually and collectively, including the use of armed force, which they may deem necessary to ensure that the Government of Cuba cannot continue to receive from the Sino-Soviet powers military material and related supplies which may threaten the peace and security of the Continent and to prevent the missiles in Cuba with offensive capability from ever becoming an active threat to the peace and security of the Continent."

Following this, also on October 23, the United States President issued a Proclamation which in part gave the following authorisation:

---

[125] See the correspondence respecting the capture of the *Virginius*, Parl. Papers, LXXVI, 1874, p.85, Spain No.3 (1874), p.85. Some of the crew members were British subjects.

[126] *Hansard*, HC, Vol.90, col.428, (January 28, 1986) U.K.M.I.L. 1986; (1986) 57 B.Y.I.L. 583. In contrast, when Iran fired on the *Gentle Breeze*, a UK merchant ship, in the Gulf in 1987, the UK protested at a "flagrant violation of international law": U.K.M.I.L. 1987; (1987) 58 B.Y.I.L. 603. The Foreign Office chose to treat the *Barber Perseus* case under the law of peace; if the Iran-Iraq War came within the law of war, Iran was exercising a belligerent's right to stop and search neutral shipping: see Lowe (1986) 10 Mar. Pol. 171 at 183.

[127] 4 Whiteman 513–5. See Van Zwanenberg (1961) 10 I.C.L.Q. 785.

[128] *Keesings Archives*, p.19061.

[129] S.C.O.R., 17th Year, 1022nd–1025th Meetings.

[130] 47 *US Dept. of State Bull.* 723.

[131] Ed. The "Rio Treaty," signed at Rio de Janeiro on September 2, 1947: 21 U.N.T.S. 77.

"Any vessel or craft which may be proceeding toward Cuba may be intercepted and may be directed to identify itself, its cargo, equipment and stores and its ports of call, to stop, to lie to, to submit to visit and search, or to proceed as directed. Any vessel which fails or refuses to respond to or to comply with directions shall be subject to being taken into custody."

It was intended that these powers would be exercised "within a reasonable distance of Cuba".[132] During the course of the "quarantine", a Lebanese ship under charter to the USSR was boarded but allowed to proceed and a Soviet tanker was cleared after visual checking from alongside. Both incidents occurred on the high seas. Other ships heading for Cuba changed course of their own accord.[133] The operation was ended on November 21, 1962. Meeker (United States Deputy Legal Adviser) justified the United States action as follows:

"The quarantine was based on a collective judgment and recommendation of the American Republics made under the Rio Treaty. It was considered not to contravene Article 2, paragraph 4, because it was a measure adopted by a regional organisation in conformity with the provisions of Chapter VIII of the Charter.[134] The purposes of the Organisation and its activities were considered to be consistent with the purposes and principles of the United Nations as provided in Article 52. This being the case, the quarantine would no more violate Article 2, paragraph 4, than measures voted for by the Council under Chapter VII, by the General Assembly under Articles 10 and 11, or taken by United Nations members in conformity with Article 51."[135]

Did the United States have a good case on this ground?[136] Note that Meeker does not justify the quarantine on the basis of "self-defence".[137] Could he have done so? Note also the following comment by Dean Acheson, a former United States Secretary of State for Foreign Affairs:

"I must conclude that the propriety of the Cuban quarantine is not a legal issue. The power, position and prestige of the United States has been challenged by another state; and law simply does not deal with such questions of ultimate power—power that comes close to the source of sovereignty. I cannot believe that there are principles of law that say we must accept destruction of our way of life. ... The survival of states is not a matter of law."[138]

The 1982 Law of the Sea Convention, art.110(1), makes no provision for jurisdiction over vessels on the high seas on the basis of self-defence.[139]

4. *Gulf of Tonkin Incident.* On August 2 and 4, 1964, in the context of the Vietnam war, North Vietnamese torpedo-boats attacked United States warships in the Gulf of Tonkin, but were beaten off. The attacks occurred on the high seas. In retaliation, on August 5, the United States

---

[132] Proclamation 3504 (1963) 57 A.J.I.L. 512.
[133] See Christol and Davis (1963) 57 A.J.I.L. 525 at 530.
[134] Ed. Below, App.I.
[135] (1963) 57 A.J.I.L. 515.
[136] See the article cited in n.133 above; and Wright (1963) 57 A.J.I.L. 546.
[137] Note, however, the following passage in the President's broadcast on October 22: "We no longer live in a world where only the actual firing of weapons represents a sufficient challenge to a nation's security to constitute a maximum peril. Nuclear weapons are so destructive, and ballistic missiles so swift, that any substantially increased possibility of their use or any sudden change in their deployment may well be regarded as a threat to the peace". *Keesing's Archives,* p.19060.
[138] (1963) 57 Proc. A.S.I.L. 14.
[139] See above, p.380.

bombed the base from which the torpedo-boats operated and an oil storage depot to great effect. The retaliatory measures were justified by the United States in terms of freedom of the high seas and the right of self-defence. The British representative to the Security Council supported this view:

"The latest attacks on the United States ships took place, according to the information we have been given, some sixty-five miles from land. It seems to my delegation in these circumstances that, having regard to the repeated nature of these attacks and their mounting scale, the United States Government has a right in accordance with international law, to take action directed to prevent the recurrence of such attacks on its ships. Preventive action in accordance with that aim is an essential right which is embraced by any definition of that principle of self-defence. It therefore seems to my delegation that the action taken by the United States Government is fully consistent with Article 51 of the Charter."[140]

The USSR representative characterised the measures as an "act of aggression". No resolution was voted upon or adopted.

5. *The right of anticipatory self defence.* The question whether there is a right of anticipatory self-defence is hotly contested by writers and in state practice. The Court left the question open in the *Nicaragua* case, para.194, and did not refer to it in the *Oil Platforms* case. In the latter case, the US relied upon the "cumulation of events" theory, see below, p.756.

A right of anticipatory self-defence was understood to exist prior to 1945. If art.51 is understood by states as indicating the full extent of the current right of self-defence,[141] there must be doubt as to whether the right of anticipatory self-defence survives in view of the use of the phrase "an armed attack occurs" in its text. Brownlie[142] states, for example, that "the ordinary meaning of the phrase precludes action which is preventative in character." In contrast, Bowett[143] argues:

"The history of art.51 suggests ... that the article should safeguard the right of self-defence, not restrict it ... furthermore, it is a restriction [no right of anticipatory self-defence] which bears no relation to the realities of a situation which may arise prior to an actual attack and call for self-defence immediately if it is to be of any avail at all. No state can be expected to await an initial attack which, in the present state of armaments, may well destroy that state's capacity for further resistance and so jeopardise its very existence."

Henkin[144] argues against a right of anticipatory self-defence as follows:

"Nothing in ... its drafting ... suggests that the framers of the Charter intended something broader than the language implied ... It was that mild, old-fashioned Second World War which persuaded all nations that for the future national interests will have to be vindicated, or necessary change achieved, as well as can be by political means, but not by war and military self-help. They recognised the exception of self-defence in emergency, but limited to actual armed attack, which is clear, unambiguous, subject to proof, and not easily open to mis-

---

[140] 1964 B.P.I.L. 268.
[141] See above, p.748.
[142] See above, n.3, p.275.
[143] See above, n.105, pp.188–192. cf. Greenwood (1987) 89 W.Virg. L.R. 933 at 943.
[144] *How Nations Behave* (2nd edn 1979), pp.141–142. cf. Brownlie (1989) Coexistence 17.

interpretation or fabrication ... It is precisely in the age of the major deterrent that nations should not be encouraged to strike first under pretext of prevention of pre-emption."

When does an armed attack begin to "occur"? Before soldiers, aircraft or missiles cross the border? From the time that troops are massed or ships set sail? The wider the meaning, the less the divergence between the two views.

The difference between the two views would also be diminished if the "cumulation of events" theory of self-defence were adopted. According to this theory, which is followed in their practice by such states as Israel,[145] the US,[146] the United Kingdom[147] and South Africa[148] and which has great attractions for states faced with constant cross-border guerilla raids and other ongoing threats, such as those in the *Oil Platforms* and *Armed Activities* cases, now that reprisals are prohibited by art.2(4), a series of attacks should be viewed as a whole, so that action taken to prevent predictable future attacks in the series can be seen not as anticipatory self-defence but as self-defence against one attack that continues to occur. However, the Security Council has consistently rejected such an approach, regarding such action, despite its primary purpose (defence, not retaliation), as reprisals.[149] Pre-emptive strikes, therefore, can only be justified on the basis of a right of anticipatory self-defence, which, prior to 9/11 at least, has supposed a reasonable belief that a particular attack, or raid, is imminent. Note, however, that the limited definition of an "armed attack" (justifying self-defence) in the *Nicaragua* case considerably limits any self defence claim.

As to the requirement of imminence,[150] In 1981, Israel attacked and destroyed a nuclear reactor nearing completion in Iraq, justifying its conduct on the ground of anticipatory self-defence: the reactor would be used to manufacture weapons that would be used against Israel.[151] The Israeli action was unanimously condemned by the Security Council as a "clear violation" of art.2(4). Could the threat posed by the reactor have been regarded as sufficiently "imminent" for the purposes of any right of anticipatory self-defence?

For the post 9/11 position concerning anticipatory, or pre-emptive, self-defence in the "war on terrorism", see below, pp.772 et seq.

---

[145] See, e.g. the Israeli raid on Beirut airport, 13 civil aeroplanes valued at over $40 million were destroyed while on the ground at Beirut airport by Israeli commandos. There was no loss of life. The raid was in retaliation for an attack on December 26 on an El Al aeroplane at Athens airport by Palestinian guerillas. The aeroplane was damaged and a passenger–an Israeli– killed. The Security Council condemned Israel "for its premeditated military action in violation of its obligations under the Charter" and considered that Lebanon was entitled to "appropriate redress for the destruction it has suffered": S.C. Resn. 262 (1968), S.C.O.R., 23rd Year, *Resolutions and Decisions*, p.12. Adopted unanimously. See Falk (1969) 63 A.J.I.L. 415; and Blum (1970) 64 ibid., 73. cf. the Israeli bombing of the PLO headquarters in Tunisia, killing between 45 and 70 people, following the killing of Israeli tourists in Cyprus by Palestinian guerillas. The bombing was condemned by the Security Council as "an act of armed aggression ... in flagrant violation of ... international law": S.C. Resn. 573 (1985), S.C.O.R., 40th Year, *Resolutions and Decisions*, p.23. The resolution was adopted by 14 votes to 0, with the US abstaining.

[146] See, e.g. the *Libyan Air raid* case, below, p.770.

[147] ibid.

[148] During *apartheid*, South Africa regularly made cross-border raids into neighbouring African states to attack ANC bases on a "cumulation of events" basis, the ANC being perceived as posing a security threat to South Africa by it terrorist attacks: see Kwakwa (1987) Yale J.I.L. 421. South Africa was consistently condemned by the Security Council for such incursions: see, e.g. S.C. Resn. 568 (1984), S.C.O.R., 40th Year, *Resolutions and Decisions*, p.20 (attack on Botswana "an act of aggression").

[149] See Bowett (1972) 66 A.J.I.L. 1.

[150] For the US challenge to this requirement post 9/11, see below, p.774.

[151] S.C. Resn. (1981) S.C.O.R., 36th Year, *Resolutions and Decisions*, p.10. For the Security Council debate, see S/PV.2280, June 12, 1981, reprinted in (1981) 20 I.L.M. 965. See D'Amato (1983) 77 A.J.I.L. 584; and Mallinson and Mallinson (1982) 15 Vand. J.T.L. 417.

THE ARMED ACTIVITIES CASE[152]

Democratic Republic of the Congo v Uganda

I.C.J. Rep. 2005, p.168

In May 1997, President Mobutu's Government of the DRC (then Zaire) was overthrown by force by a Congolese rebel force, the "AFDL", which had the support of Uganda and Rwanda. On taking office, President Kabila, the former "AFDL" leader, consented to the presence of Ugandan military forces in Eastern DRC territory in the border area between the two states, to prevent cross-border raids into Uganda by anti-Ugandan Government Congolese rebel forces. The ICJ found that, relations between the Kabila Government and Uganda and Rwanda having deteriorated, this consent had been withdrawn so that all foreign troops, particularly those of Rwanda and Uganda, no longer had permission to remain on DRC territory—in the case of Ugandan troops as of August 8, 1998 at the latest. But instead of leaving, in operation "Safe Haven" Ugandan military forces advanced further into DRC territory, occupying several towns and airports and a substantial part of Eastern DRC. Ugandan forces remained in the DRC until June 2003. Uganda justified the continued presence of its forces on grounds of self-defence. In particular, Uganda was concerned that fighting by rebel groups against the Kabila Government had led to a civil war situation in which that government had lost control of parts of its territory, exacerbating the problem of cross-border raids into Uganda, and also had obtained the assistance of Sudan, a long-term enemy of Uganda, in support of Ugandan rebels.

In this application under the "optional clause", the DRC claimed that Uganda had, inter alia, violated the prohibition on the use of force in international law and committed breaches of international humanitarian law and international human rights law.

On Uganda's failure to comply with the Court's provisional measures order, see below p.874.

Judgment of the Court

118. ...The Court will...examine whether,...when its forces were rapidly advancing across the DRC, Uganda was entitled to engage in military action in self-defence against the DRC...in the period from August 1998 till June 2003. ...

143. The Court recalls that Uganda has insisted in this case that operation "Safe Haven" was not a use of force against an anticipated attack. As was the case also in the *Military and Paramilitary Activities in and against Nicaragua (Nicaragua v. United States of America)* case, "reliance is placed by the Parties only on the right of self-defence in the case of an armed attack which has already occurred, and the issue of the lawfulness of a response to the imminent threat of armed attack has not been raised" (*I.C.J. Reports 1986*, p. 103, para. 194). The Court there found that "[a]ccordingly [it] expresses no view on that issue". So it is in the present case. The Court feels constrained, however, to observe that the wording of the Ugandan High Command document on the position regarding the presence of the UPDF [Uganda armed forces] in the DRC makes no reference whatever to armed attacks that have already occurred against Uganda at the hands of the DRC (or indeed by persons for whose action the DRC is claimed to be responsible). Rather, the position of the High Command is that it is necessary "to secure Uganda's legitimate security interests". The specified security needs are essentially preventative . to ensure that the political vacuum does not adversely affect Uganda, to prevent attacks from "genocidal elements", to be in a position to safeguard Uganda from irresponsible threats of invasion, to "deny the Sudan the opportunity to use the territory of the DRC to destabilize Uganda". Only one of the five listed objectives refers to a response to acts that had already taken place—the neutralization of "Uganda dissident groups which have been receiving assistance from the Government of the DRC and the Sudan". ...

---

[152] See Barbour (2007) 40 N.Y.J.I.L.P. 13; Dufresne (2007) 40 N.Y.J.I.L.P. 171; Halink (2007) 40 N.Y.J.I.L.P. 13; Kingsbury and Weiler (2007) 40 N.Y.J.I.L.P. 1; Lang (2007) 40 N.Y.J.I.L.P. 107; Okowa (2006) 77 B.Y.I.L. 203; id. (2006) 55 I.C.L.Q. 742.

145. The Court would first observe that in August and early September 1998 Uganda did not report to the Security Council events that it had regarded as requiring it to act in self-defence.

146. It is further to be noted that, while Uganda claimed to have acted in self-defence, it did not ever claim that it had been subjected to an armed attack by the armed forces of the DRC. The "armed attacks" to which reference was made came rather from the ADF [the Allied Democratic Force, consisting of Ugandan forces opposed to the Ugandan Government]. The Court has found above (paragraphs 131-135) that there is no satisfactory proof of the involvement in these attacks, direct or indirect, of the Government of the DRC. The attacks did not emanate from armed bands or irregulars sent by the DRC or on behalf of the DRC, within the sense of Article 3 *(g)* of General Assembly resolution 3314 (XXIX) on the definition of aggression [below, p.800] .... The Court is of the view that, on the evidence before it, even if this series of deplorable attacks could be regarded as cumulative in character, they still remained non-attributable to the DRC.

147. For all these reasons, the Court finds that the legal and factual circumstances for the exercise of a right of self-defence by Uganda against the DRC were not present. Accordingly, the Court has no need to respond to the contentions of the Parties as to whether and under what conditions contemporary international law provides for a right of self-defence against large-scale attacks by irregular forces. Equally, since the preconditions for the exercise of self-defence do not exist in the circumstances of the present case, the Court has no need to enquire whether such an entitlement to self-defence was in fact exercised in circumstances of necessity and in a manner that was proportionate. The Court cannot fail to observe, however, that the taking of airports and towns many hundreds of kilometres from Uganda's border would not seem proportionate to the series of transborder attacks it claimed had given rise to the right of self-defence, nor to be necessary to that end.

148. The prohibition against the use of force [in art.2(4)] is a cornerstone of the United Nations Charter....Article 51 of the Charter may justify a use of force in self-defence only within the strict confines there laid down. It does not allow the use of force by a State to protect perceived security interests beyond these parameters. Other means are available to a concerned State, including, in particular, recourse to the Security Council.

149. The Court has found that, from 7 August 1998 onwards, Uganda engaged in the use of force for purposes and in locations for which it had no consent whatever. ...

153. The evidence has shown that the UPDF traversed vast areas of the DRC, violating the sovereignty of that country. It engaged in military operations in a multitude of locations, including Bunia, Kisangani, Gbadolite and Ituri, and many others. These were grave violations of Article 2, paragraph 4, of the Charter.

154. The Court notes that the Security Council, on 16 June 2000, expressed "outrage at renewed fighting between Ugandan and Rwandan forces in Kisangani", and condemned it as a "violation of the sovereignty and territorial integrity of the Democratic Republic of the Congo" (United Nations doc. S/RES/1304 (2000)).

155. The Court further observes that Uganda...decided in early August 1998 to launch an offensive together with various factions which sought to overthrow the Government of the DRC. The DRC has in particular claimed that, from September 1998 onwards, Uganda both created and controlled the MLC rebel group led by Mr. Bemba. ...

160. The Court concludes that there is no credible evidence to suggest that Uganda created the MLC. Uganda has acknowledged giving training and military support and there is evidence to that effect. The Court has not received probative evidence that Uganda controlled, or could control, the manner in which Mr. Bemba put such assistance to use. In the view of the Court, the conduct of the MLC was not that of "an organ" of Uganda (Article 4, International Law Commission Draft Articles on Responsibility of States for internationally wrongful acts, 2001), nor that of an entity exercising elements of governmental authority on its behalf (Article 5). The Court has considered whether the MLC's conduct was "on the instructions of, or under the direction or control of" Uganda (Article 8) and finds that there is no probative evidence by reference to which it has been persuaded that this was the case. Accordingly, no issue arises in the present case as to whether the requisite tests are met for sufficiency of control of paramilitaries (see *Military and Paramilitary Activities in and against Nicaragua (Nicaragua* v. *United States of America), Merits, Judgment, I.C.J. Reports 1986*, pp. 62-65, paras. 109-115).

161. The Court would comment, however, that, even if the evidence does not suggest that the MLC's conduct is attributable to Uganda, the training and military support given by Uganda to the ALC, the military wing of the MLC, violates certain obligations of international law.

162. Thus the Declaration on Principles of International Law Concerning Friendly Relations and Co-operation Among States in accordance with the Charter of the United Nations (hereinafter "the Declaration on Friendly Relations") provides that:

"Every State has the duty to refrain from organizing, instigating, assisting or participating in acts of civil strife or terrorist acts in another State or acquiescing in organized activities within its territory directed towards the commission of such acts, when the acts referred to in the present paragraph involve a threat or use of force." (General Assembly resolution 2625 (XXV), 24 October 1970.)

The Declaration further provides that,

"no State shall organize, assist, foment, finance, incite or tolerate subversive, terrorist or armed activities directed towards the violent overthrow of the regime of another State, or interfere in civil strife in another State" *(ibid.)*.

These provisions are declaratory of customary international law.

163. The Court considers that the obligations arising under the principles of non-use of force and non-intervention were violated by Uganda even if the objectives of Uganda were not to overthrow President Kabila, and were directed to securing towns and airports for reason of its perceived security needs, and in support of the parallel activity of those engaged in civil war.

164. In the case concerning *Military and Paramilitary Activities in and against Nicaragua (Nicaragua* v. *United States of America)* case, the Court made it clear that the principle of non-intervention prohibits a State "to intervene, directly or indirectly, with or without armed force, in support of an internal opposition in another State" *(I.C.J. Reports 1986*, p. 108, para. 206). The Court notes that in the present case it has been presented with probative evidence as to military intervention. The Court further affirms that acts which breach the principle of non-intervention "will also, if they directly or indirectly involve the use of force, constitute a breach of the principle of non-use of force in international relations"(ibid., pp. 109-110, para. 209).

165. In relation to the first of the DRC's final submissions, the Court accordingly concludes that Uganda has violated the sovereignty and also the territorial integrity of the DRC. Uganda's actions equally constituted an interference in the internal affairs of the DRC and in the civil war there raging. The unlawful military intervention by Uganda was of such a magnitude and duration that the Court considers it to be a grave violation of the prohibition on the use of force expressed in Article 2, paragraph 4, of the Charter. ...

[The Court then held that Uganda was an occupying power under the 1907 Hague Regulations in those parts of DRC territory in which its troops were present.]

179. The Court, having concluded that Uganda was an occupying Power in Ituri [a DRC province] at the relevant time, finds that Uganda's responsibility is engaged both for any acts of its military that violated its international obligations and for any lack of vigilance in preventing violations of human rights and international humanitarian law by other actors present in the occupied territory, including rebel groups acting on their own account. ...

205. The Court will now examine the allegations by the DRC concerning violations by Uganda of its obligations under international human rights law and international humanitarian law during its military intervention in the DRC.. . . .

In order to rule on the DRC's claim, it is not necessary for the Court to make findings of fact with regard to each individual incident alleged.

206. The Court first turns to the DRC's claims that the Ugandan armed forces caused loss of life to the civilian population, committed acts of torture and other forms of inhumane treatment, and destroyed villages and dwellings of civilians. The Court observes that the report of the Special Rapporteur of the Commission on Human Rights of 18 January 2000 (E/CN/4/2000/42, para. 112) refers to massacres carried out by Ugandan troops in Beni on 14 November 1999. The Secretary-General in his Third report on MONUC [the UN Mission in the DRC] concluded that Rwandan and Ugandan armed forces "should be held accountable for the loss of life and the property damage they inflicted on the civilian population of Kisangani" (doc. S/2000/566 of 12 June 2000, para. 79). Security Council resolution 1304 (2000) of 16 June 2000 deplored "the loss of civilian lives, the threat to the civilian population and the damage to property inflicted by the forces of Uganda and Rwanda on the Congolese population". Several incidents of atrocities committed by Ugandan troops against the civilian population, including torture and killings, are referred to in the report of the Special Rapporteur of the Commission on Human Rights of 1 February 2001 (E/CN/4/2001/40, paras. 112, 148-151). MONUC's special report on the events in Ituri, January 2002-December 2003 (doc. S/2004/573 of 16 July 2004, paras. 19, 42-43, 62) contains much

evidence of direct involvement by UPDF troops, in the context of the Hema-Lendu ethnic conflict in Ituri, in the killings of civilians and the destruction of their houses. In addition to particular incidents, it is stated that "[h]undreds of localities were destroyed by UPDF and the Hema South militias" (para. 21); "UPDF also carried out widespread bombing and destruction of hundreds of villages from 2000 to 2002" (para. 27).

207. The Court therefore finds the coincidence of reports from credible sources sufficient to convince it that massive human rights violations and grave breaches of international humanitarian law were committed by the UPDF on the territory of the DRC.

208. The Court further finds that there is sufficient evidence of a reliable quality to support the DRC's allegation that the UPDF failed to protect the civilian population and to distinguish between combatants and non-combatants in the course of fighting against other troops . . .

[In making this finding, and that in para.209, the Court relied upon evidence from UN reports similar to those relied upon in para.206.]

209. The Court considers that there is also persuasive evidence that the UPDF incited ethnic conflicts and took no action to prevent such conflicts in Ituri district. . . .

210. The Court finds that there is convincing evidence of the training in UPDF training camps of child soldiers and of the UPDF's failure to prevent the recruitment of child soldiers in areas under its control. . . .

213. The Court turns now to the question as to whether acts and omissions of the UPDF and its officers and soldiers are attributable to Uganda. The conduct of the UPDF as a whole is clearly attributable to Uganda, being the conduct of a State organ. According to a well-established rule of international law, which is of customary character, "the conduct of any organ of a State must be regarded as an act of that State" (*Difference Relating to Immunity from Legal Process of a Special Rapporteur of the Commission on Human Rights, Advisory Opinion, I.C.J. Reports 1999 (I)*, p. 87, para. 62). The conduct of individual soldiers and officers of the UPDF is to be considered as the conduct of a State organ. In the Court's view, by virtue of the military status and function of Ugandan soldiers in the DRC, their conduct is attributable to Uganda. . . .

214. It is furthermore irrelevant for the attribution of their conduct to Uganda whether the UPDF personnel acted contrary to the instructions given or exceeded their authority. According to a well-established rule of a customary nature, as reflected in Article 3 of the Fourth Hague Convention respecting the Laws and Customs of War on Land of 1907 as well as in Article 91 of Protocol I additional to the Geneva Conventions of 1949, a party to an armed conflict shall be responsible for all acts by persons forming part of its armed forces.

215. The Court, having established that the conduct of the UPDF and of the officers and soldiers of the UPDF is attributable to Uganda, must now examine whether this conduct constitutes a breach of Uganda's international obligations. In this regard, the Court needs to determine the rules and principles of international human rights law and international humanitarian law which are relevant for this purpose.

216. The Court first recalls that it had occasion to address the issues of the relationship between international humanitarian law and international human rights law and of the applicability of international human rights law instruments outside national territory in its Advisory Opinion of 9 July 2004 on the *Legal Consequences of the Construction of a Wall in the Occupied Palestinian Territory*. In this Advisory Opinion the Court. . .concluded that both branches of international law, namely international human rights law and international humanitarian law, would have to be taken into consideration. The Court further concluded that international human rights instruments are applicable "in respect of acts done by a State in the exercise of its jurisdiction outside its own territory", particularly in occupied territories (ibid., pp. 178-181, paras. 107-113 [below, pp.601-602]). . . .

219. In view of the foregoing, the Court finds that the acts committed by the UPDF and officers and soldiers of the UPDF . . . are in clear violation of the obligations under the Hague Regulations of 1907, Articles 25, 27 and 28, as well as Articles 43, 46 and 47 with regard to obligations of an occupying Power. These obligations are binding on the Parties as customary international law. Uganda also violated the following provisions of the international humanitarian law and international human rights law instruments, to which both Uganda and the DRC are parties: [the Court listed the Fourth Geneva Red Cross Convention, arts 27, 32 and 53; the International Covenant on Civil and Political Rights, art 6(1) and 7; the First Additional Protocol to the Geneva Red Cross Conventions, arts 48, 51, 52, 57, 58 and 75(1) (2); the African Charter on Human and Peoples' Rights, arts 4 and 5; the Convention on the Rights of the Child ("CRC"), art.38 (2) (3); and the Optional Protocol to the CRC on Children in Armed Conflict, arts 1, 2, 3 (3) (4), 5 and 6.] . . .

220. The Court thus concludes that Uganda is internationally responsible for violations of international human rights law and international humanitarian law committed by the UPDF and by its members in the territory of the DRC and for failing to comply with its obligations as an occupying Power in Ituri in respect of violations of international human rights law and international humanitarian law in the occupied territory.

221. The Court finally would point out that, while it has pronounced on the violations of international human

rights law and international humanitarian law committed by Ugandan military forces on the territory of the DRC, it nonetheless observes that the actions of the various parties in the complex conflict in the DRC have contributed to the immense suffering faced by the Congolese population. The Court is painfully aware that many atrocities have been committed in the course of the conflict. It is incumbent on all those involved in the conflict to support the peace process in the DRC and other peace processes in the Great Lakes area, in order to ensure respect for human rights in the region.

[The Court finally examined claims by the DRC that Uganda had exploited its natural resources in violation in international law.]

242. Having examined the case file, the Court finds that it does not have at its disposal credible evidence to prove that there was a governmental policy of Uganda directed at the exploitation of natural resources of the DRC or that Uganda's military intervention was carried out in order to obtain access to Congolese resources. At the same time, the Court considers that it has ample credible and persuasive evidence to conclude that officers and soldiers of the UPDF, including the most high-ranking officers, were involved in the looting, plundering and exploitation of the DRC's natural resources and that the military authorities did not take any measures to put an end to these acts. . . .

244. The Court finds that it cannot uphold the contention of the DRC that Uganda violated the principle of the DRC's sovereignty over its natural resources. . .The Court recalls that the principle of permanent sovereignty over natural resources is expressed in General Assembly resolution 1803 (XVII) of 14 December 1962 and further elaborated in the Declaration on the Establishment of a New International Economic Order (General Assembly resolution 3201 (S.VI) of 1 May 1974) and the Charter of Economic Rights and Duties of States (General Assembly resolution 3281 (XXIX) of 12 December 1974). While recognizing the importance of this principle, which is a principle of customary international law, the Court notes that there is nothing in these General Assembly resolutions which suggests that they are applicable to the specific situation of looting, pillage and exploitation of certain natural resources by members of the army of a State militarily intervening in another State, which is the subject-matter of the DRC's third submission. . . .

245. As the Court has already stated. . ., the acts and omissions of members of Uganda's military forces in the DRC engage Uganda's international responsibility in all circumstances, whether it was an occupying Power in particular regions or not. Thus, whenever members of the UPDF were involved in the looting, plundering and exploitation of natural resources in the territory of the DRC, they acted in violation of the *jus in bello*, which prohibits the commission of such acts by a foreign army in the territory where it is present. The Court notes in this regard that both Article 47 of the Hague Regulations of 1907 and Article 33 of the Fourth Geneva Convention of 1949 prohibit pillage.

The Court further observes that both the DRC and Uganda are parties to the African Charter on Human and Peoples' Rights of 27 June 1981, which in paragraph 2 of Article 21, states that "[i]n case of spoliation the dispossessed people shall have the right to the lawful recovery of its property as well as to an adequate compensation".

246. The Court finds that there is sufficient evidence to support the DRC's claim that Uganda violated its duty of vigilance by not taking adequate measures to ensure that its military forces did not engage in the looting, plundering and exploitation of the DRC's natural resources. . . .

247. As for the claim that Uganda also failed to prevent the looting, plundering and illegal exploitation of the DRC's natural resources by rebel groups, the Court has already found that the latter were not under the control of Uganda. . . . Thus, with regard to the illegal activities of such groups outside of Ituri, it cannot conclude that Uganda was in breach of its duty of vigilance.

248. The Court further observes that the fact that Uganda was the occupying Power in Ituri district. . .extends Uganda's obligation to take appropriate measures to prevent the looting, plundering and exploitation of natural resources in the occupied territory to cover private persons in this district and not only members of Ugandan military forces. It is apparent from various findings of the Porter Commission that rather than preventing the illegal traffic in natural resources, including diamonds, high-ranking members of the UPDF facilitated such activities by commercial entities. . . .

250. The Court concludes that it is in possession of sufficient credible evidence to find that Uganda is internationally responsible for acts of looting, plundering and exploitation of the DRC's natural resources committed by members of the UPDF in the territory of the DRC, for violating its obligation of vigilance in regard to these acts and for failing to comply with its obligations under Article 43 of the Hague Regulations of 1907 as

an occupying Power in Ituri in respect of all acts of looting, plundering and exploitation of natural resources in the occupied territory. ...

345. For these reasons,

THE COURT,

(1) By sixteen votes to one,

Finds that the Republic of Uganda, by engaging in military activities against the Democratic Republic of the Congo on the latter's territory, by occupying Ituri and by actively extending military, logistic, economic and financial support to irregular forces having operated on the territory of the DRC, violated the principle of non-use of force in international relations and the principle of non-intervention; ...

(3) By sixteen votes to one,

Finds that the Republic of Uganda, by the conduct of its armed forces, which committed acts of killing, torture and other forms of inhumane treatment of the Congolese civilian population, destroyed villages and civilian buildings, failed to distinguish between civilian and military targets and to protect the civilian population in fighting with other combatants, trained child soldiers, incited ethnic conflict and failed to take measures to put an end to such conflict; as well as by its failure, as an occupying Power, to take measures to respect and ensure respect for human rights and international humanitarian law in Ituri district, violated its obligations under international human rights law and international humanitarian law; ...

(4) By sixteen votes to one,

Finds that the Republic of Uganda, by acts of looting, plundering and exploitation of Congolese natural resources committed by members of the Ugandan armed forces in the territory of the Democratic Republic of the Congo and by its failure to comply with its obligations as an occupying Power in Ituri district to prevent acts of looting, plundering and exploitation of Congolese natural resources, violated obligations owed to the Democratic Republic of the Congo under international law;

(5) Unanimously,

Finds that the Republic of Uganda is under obligation to make reparation to the Democratic Republic of the Congo for the injury caused;

(6) Unanimously,

Decides that, failing agreement between the Parties, the question of reparation due to the Democratic Republic of the Congo shall be settled by the Court, and reserves for this purpose the subsequent procedure in the case; ...

Separate Opinion of Judge Simma

1. Let me emphasize at the outset that I agree with everything the Court is saying in its judgment. Rather, what I am concerned about are certain issues on which the Court decided to say nothing. ...

2. One deliberate omission characterizing the Judgment will strike any politically alert reader: it is the way in which the Court has avoided dealing with the explicit request of the DRC to find that Uganda, by its massive use of force against the Applicant has committed an act of aggression. In this regard I associate myself with the criticism expressed in the separate opinion of Judge Elaraby. After all, Uganda invaded a part of the territory of the DRC of the size of Germany and kept it under her own control, or that of the various Congolese warlords she befriended, for several years, helping herself to the immense natural riches of these tormented regions. In its Judgment the Court cannot but acknowledge of course that by engaging in these "military activities" Uganda "violated the principle of non-use of force in international relations and the principle of non-intervention" (Judgment paragraph 345(1). The Judgment gets toughest in paragraph 165 of its reasoning where it states that "[t]he unlawful military intervention by Uganda was of such a magnitude and duration that the Court considers it to be a grave violation of the prohibition of the use of force expressed in Article 2, paragraph 4, of the Charter". So, why not call a spade a spade? If there ever was a military activity before the Court that deserves to be qualified as an act of aggression, it is the Ugandan invasion of the DRC. Compared to its scale and impact, the military adventures the Court had to deal with in earlier cases, as in *Corfu Channel, Nicaragua,* or *Oil Platforms,* border on the insignificant.

3. It is true that the United Nations Security Council, despite adopting a whole series of resolutions on the situation in the Great Lakes region...has never gone as far as expressly qualifying the Ugandan invasion as an act of aggression, even though it must appear as a textbook example of the first one of the definitions of "this most serious and dangerous form of the illegal use of force" laid down in General Assembly resolution 3314 (XXIX). The Council will have had its own—political—reasons for refraining from such a determination. But the Court, as the principal *judicial* organ of the United Nations, does not have to follow that course. Its very raison

d'être is to arrive at decisions based on law and nothing but the law, keeping the political context of the cases before it in mind, of course, but not desisting from stating what is manifest out of regard for such non-legal considerations. This is the division of labour between the Court and the political organs of the United Nations envisaged by the Charter!

4. I am in agreement with the Court's finding in paragraph 146 of the judgment that the "armed attacks" to which Uganda referred when claiming to have acted in self-defence against the DRC, were perpetrated not by the Congolese armed forces but rather by the Allied Democratic Forces (ADF), that is, from a rebel group operating against Uganda from Congolese territory. The Court stated that Uganda could provide no satisfactory proof that would have sustained its allegation that these attacks emanated from armed bands or regulars sent by or on behalf of the DRC. Thus these attacks are not attributable to the DRC.

5. The Court, however, then finds, that for these reasons, the legal and factual circumstances for the exercise of a right to self-defence by Uganda against the DRC were not present (judgment, paragraph 147). Accordingly, the Court continues, it has no need to respond to the contentions of the Parties as to whether and under what conditions contemporary international law provides for a right of self-defence against large-scale attacks by irregular forces (ibid.).

6. Thus, the reasoning on which the Judgment relies in its findings on the first submission by the DRC appears to be as follows:

— since the submission of the DRC requests the Court (only) to find that it was Uganda's use of force against the DRC which constituted an act of aggression, and

— since the Court does not consider that the military activities carried out from Congolese territory onto the territory of the Respondent by anti-Uganda rebel forces are attributable to the DRC,

— and since therefore Uganda's claim that its use of force against the DRC was justified as an exercise of self-defence, cannot be upheld,

it suffices for the Court to find Uganda in breach of the prohibition of the use of force enshrined in the United Nations Charter and in general international law. The Applicant, the Court appears to say, has not asked for anything beyond that. Therefore, it is not necessary for the Court to deal with the legal qualification of either the cross-boundary military activities of the anti-Ugandan groups as such, or of the Ugandan countermeasures against these hostile acts.

7. What thus remains unanswered by the Court is the question whether, even if not attributable to the DRC, such activities could have been repelled by Uganda through engaging these groups also on Congolese territory, if necessary, provided that the rebel attacks were of a scale sufficient to reach the threshold of an "armed attack" within the meaning of Article 51 of the United Nations Charter.

8. Like Judge Kooijmans in... his separate opinion, I submit that the Court should have taken the opportunity presented by the present case to clarify the state of the law on a highly controversial matter which is marked by great controversy and confusion—not the least because it was the Court itself that has substantially contributed to this confusion by its *Nicaragua* Judgment of two decades ago ...

9. From the *Nicaragua* case onwards the Court has made several pronouncements on questions of use of force and self-defence which are problematic less for the things they say than for the questions they leave open, prominently among them the issue of self-defence against armed attacks by non-State actors.

10. The most recent—and most pertinent—statement in this context is to be found in the (extremely succinct) discussion by the Court in its *Wall* Opinion of the Israeli argument that the separation barrier under construction was a measure wholly consistent with the right of States to self-defence enshrined in Article 51 of the Charter (*Legal Consequences of the Construction of a Wall in the Occupied Palestinian Territory, Advisory Opinion, I.C.J. Reports 2004*, p.194, para.138) To this argument the Court replied that Article 51 recognizes the existence of an inherent right of self-defence in the case of an armed attack by one State against another. Since Israel did not claim that the attacks against it were imputable to a foreign State, however, Article 51 of the Charter had no relevance in the case of the wall (*ibid.*, para.139 [above, p.604]).

11. Such a restrictive reading of Article 51 might well have reflected the state, or rather the prevailing interpretation, of the international law on self-defence for a long time. However, in the light of more recent developments not only in State practice but also with regard to accompanying *opinio juris*, it ought urgently to be reconsidered, also by the Court. As is well known, these developments were triggered by the terrorist attacks of September 11, in the wake of which claims that Article 51 also covers defensive measures against terrorist groups have been received far more favourably by the international community than other extensive re-readings of the

relevant Charter provisions, particularly the "Bush doctrine" justifying the pre-emptive use of force.[153] Security Council resolutions 1368 (2001) and 1373 (2001) cannot but be read as affirmations of the view that large-scale attacks by non-State actors can qualify as "armed attacks" within the meaning of Article 51.

12. In his separate opinion, Judge Kooijmans points to the fact that the almost complete absence of governmental authority in the whole or part of the territory of certain States has unfortunately become a phenomenon as familiar as international terrorism (separate opinion of Judge Kooijmans, para.30). I fully agree with his conclusions that, if armed attacks are carried out by irregular forces from such territory against a neighbouring State, these activities are still armed attacks even if they cannot be attributed to the territorial State, and, further, that it "would be unreasonable to deny the attacked State the right to self-defence merely because there is no attacker State and the Charter does not so require so"(*ibid.*).[154]

13. I also subscribe to Judge Kooijmans' opinion that the lawfulness of the conduct of the attacked State in the face of such an armed attack by a non-State group must be put to the same test as that applied in the case of a claim of self-defence against a State, namely, does the scale of the armed action by the irregulars amount to an armed attack and, if so, is the defensive action by the attacked State in conformity with the requirements of necessity and proportionality? (*Ibid.*, para.31).

14. In applying this test to the military activities of Uganda on Congolese territory from August 1998 onwards, Judge Kooijmans concludes—and I agree—that, while the activities that Uganda conducted in August in an area contiguous to the border may still be regarded as keeping within these limits, the stepping up of Ugandan military operations starting with the occupation of the Kisangani airport and continuing thereafter, leading the Ugandan forces far into the interior of the DRC, assumed a magnitude and duration that could not possibly be justified any longer by reliance on any right of self-defence. Thus, at this point, our view meets with, and shares, the Court's final conclusion that Uganda's military intervention constitutes "a grave violation of the prohibition on the use of force expressed in Article 2, paragraph 4, of the Charter" (Judgment, paragraph 165).

Notes

1. This was one of three cases brought in 1999 by the DRC against Burundi, Rwanda and Uganda alleging the illegal use of force by the latter states in DRC territory. The cases against Burundi and Rwanda were withdrawn by the DRC[155] and the Court held that it had no jurisdiction to consider a later application by the DRC against Rwanda.[156]

2. *Self-defence.* Having found that the cross-border attacks from DRC territory into Uganda by non-state actors could not be attributed to the DRC, the Court found no need to consider whether Uganda could resort to armed force in DRC territory by way of self-defence in response to them without DRC consent, seemingly for the reasons given by Judge Simma in his separate opinion, para.6. Judges Kooijmans and Simma, paras 9 et seq., did tackle this question and, in line with post-9/11 state practice and contrary to the Court's view in the *Wall* case, suggest that the right to self-defence may now extend to "armed attacks" by non-state actors where they emanate from territory where there is an "almost complete absence of governmental authority" being exercised by the government of the state concerned (in this case the DRC government). See further, below, pp.772 et seq, on post-9/11 terrorist attacks.

    The Court also found (para.143), that, as in the *Nicaragua* case, there was no need for it to consider whether there is a right of anticipatory self-defence in international law. Here too, post-9/11 state practice suggests that such a right may exist in some circumstances: see below, p.775. The Court did, however, comment that in any event Uganda's military operations deep into DRC territory did not meet the self-defence requirements of necessity and proportionality (para.147).

---

[153] Th.Bruha/Ch. Tams, "Self-Defence Against Terrorist Attacks. Considerations in the Light of the ICJ's "Israeli Wall" Opinion, in: K. Dicke *et al* (eds), *Weltinnenrecht. Liber Amicorum Jost Delbrück*, Berlin 2005, pp.84–112, at p.97.

[154] Referring to Y. Dinstein, *War, Aggression, and Self-Defence* (3rd edn 2002) p.216.

[155] I.C.J. Rep. 2001, p.3

[156] I.C.J. Rep. 2006. See Orakhelashvili (2006) 55 I.C.L.Q. 753.

3. *Article 2(4) and aggression,* Having rejected Uganda's self-defence argument, the Court (para.153) had no difficulty in finding that Uganda had committed "grave violations" of art.2(4) of the Charter. Judges Simma and Elaraby considered that it was also responsible for an act of aggression, and criticised the Court for not ruling on this claim by the DRC. Kingsbury and Weiler[157] suggest that the Court may have declined to make such a ruling because it "could have had implications for the ongoing attempts to define aggression" as a crime within the jurisdiction of the ICC and the "political tensions within that lawmaking process." Was this a good reason?

4. The Court maintained the position it had taken in its advisory opinion in the *Legality of Nuclear Weapons* case to the effect that *international human rights law* continues to apply in time of armed conflict, in company with *international humanitarian law*: it is not replaced by the latter as *lex specialis*. In finding that there had been "massive human rights violations" and "grave breaches of international humanitarian law", the Court relied upon UN reports; it did not make its own findings of fact (para.205). Is this a satisfactory approach for a court of law?[158]

5. On Uganda's successful counterclaim for occupation of its embassy, etc., see above, p.134.

PARTIAL AWARD: IUS AD BELLUM: ETHIOPIA'S CLAIMS 1–8

Eritrea Ethiopia Claims Commission 2005. Some footnotes omitted

This award arose out of the Eritrean-Ethiopian War 1998–2000, in which the two states fought over disputed territory in the border region between them. On May 12, 1998, Eritrean forces attacked and took possession of the area surrounding the town of Badme that was then peacefully administered by Ethiopia, but to which Eritrea claimed title by treaty. By the time of the ceasefire, Ethiopia had regained control of this territory and other territory that Eritrea had taken, and advanced further into Eritrean territory. Following the ceasefire, the two states agreed upon a Boundary Commission, which in 2002 upheld Eritrea's claim to title by treaty of the area around Badme. Ethiopia did not accept the Commission's decision and continues to occupy this area. In this partial award, the Claims Commission ruled upon the legality of Eritrea's resort to armed force.

Partial Award

6. Ethiopia claimed that Eritrea carried out a series of unlawful armed attacks against it, beginning on May 12, 1998, in violation of the *jus ad bellum* ...

8. In essence. Ethiopia contended that Eritrea planned and carried out these attacks against Ethiopia in violation of its obligations under international law, including notably the requirement of Article 2, paragraph 4, of the Charter of the United Nations...Ethiopia alleged that, between May 12 and June 11, 1998, Eritrea launched a "full scale" invasion of Ethiopia at many points along their mutual border from Badme in the west to Bure in the east.

9. ...Eritrea made the following...defensive assertions: (a) that Ethiopia was unlawfully occupying Eritrean territory in the area around Badme, which was the area of much of the initial hostilities in May 1998, citing the decision of the Eritrea-Ethiopia Boundary Commission of April 13, 2002[159]; (b) that Ethiopian armed militia near Badme carried out forcible incursions into Eritrea in early May 1998 and fired on Eritrean forces on May 6 and 7, killing eight Eritrean soldiers and setting off fighting between small units in the area during the next several days...Eritrea argued that its actions in taking Badme and adjacent areas on May 12, 1998 were lawful measures of self-defense, consistent with Article 51 of the UN Charter, taken in response to the fighting near Badme that

---
[157] See above at n.152, p.11.
[158] For criticism of the Court's approach, see Halink, above at n.152.
[159] ... *reprinted in* 41 I.L.M. p.1057 (2002).

began on May 6 and 7, 1998. While Eritrea asserted that these incidents occurred within Eritrean territory, Ethiopia asserted that they occurred within Ethiopian territory.

10.The Commission cannot accept the legal position that seems to underlie the first of these Eritrean contentions—that recourse to force by Eritrea would have been lawful because some of the territory concerned was territory to which Eritrea had a valid claim. ...the practice of States and the writings of eminent publicists show that self-defense cannot be invoked to settle territorial disputes.[160] In that connection, the Commission notes that border disputes between States are so frequent that any exception to the prohibition of the threat or use of force for territory that is allegedly occupied unlawfully would create a large and dangerous hole in a fundamental rule of international law.

11. ...In general, recourse to the use of armed force by one State against another is unlawful unless it is used in self-defense or occurs with the sanction of the Security Council pursuant to Chapter VII of the UN Charter. As the text of Article 51 of the Charter makes clear, the predicate for a valid claim of self-defense under the Charter is that the party resorting to force has been subjected to an armed attack. Localized border encounters between small infantry units, even those involving the loss of life, do not constitute an armed attack for purposes of the Charter. In that connection, the Commission notes that Eritrea did not report its use of armed force against Ethiopia on May 12, 1998 to the Security Council as measures taken in self-defense, as it would be obligated to do by Article 51 of the Charter in case of self-defense against armed attack,

12.With respect to the events in the vicinity of Badme that occurred during the period from May 6–12, 1998, the Commission...is satisfied that these relatively minor incidents were not of a magnitude to constitute an armed attack by either State against the other within the meaning of Article 51 of the UN Charter. ...

14. ...on May 12, 1998, Eritrean armed forces, comprised of at least two brigades of regular soldiers, supported by tanks and artillery, attacked the town of Badme and several other border areas in Ethiopia's Tahtay Adiabo Wereda, as well as at least two places in its neighboring Laelay Adiabo Wereda. On that day and in the days immediately following, Eritrean armed forces then pushed across the flat Badme plain to higher ground in the east....the Ethiopian defenders were composed merely of militia and some police, who were quickly forced to retreat by the invading Eritrean forces. Given the absence of an armed attack against Eritrea, the attack that began on May 12 cannot be justified as lawful self-defense under the UN Charter.

15.The areas initially invaded by Eritrean forces on that day were all either within undisputed Ethiopian territory or within territory that was peacefully administered by Ethiopia and that later would be on the Ethiopian side of the line to which Ethiopian armed forces were obligated to withdraw in 2000 under the Cease-Fire Agreement of June 18, 2000. ...

16.Consequently, the Commission holds that Eritrea violated Article 2, paragraph 4, of the Charter of the United Nations by resorting to armed force to attack and occupy Badme, then under peaceful administration by Ethiopia, as well as other territory in the Tahtay Adiabo and Laelay Adiabo Weredas of Ethiopia, in an attack that began on May 12, 1998, and is liable to compensate Ethiopia, for the damages caused by that violation of international law.

Notes

1.   Rejecting Eritrea's argument based on self-defence, the Commission found that it had violated art.2(4) by its recourse to force against Ethiopia.

2.   Gray[161] criticises the Commission's treatment (para 10) of the question whether a state may use force to obtain possession of territory to which it has a claim to title:

---

[160] See, e.g., Declaration on Principles of International Law Concerning Friendly Relations and Cooperation Among States in Accordance with the Charter of the United Nations (the "Friendly Relations Declaration"), UN General Assembly Resolution 2625 (XXV) of Oct. 24, 1970, G.A. Res. 2625, U.N. GAOR, 25th Sess., Supp. No.28, U.N. Doc. A/8028, reprinted in 9 I.L.M. p.1292 (1970 ("[E]very State has the duty to refrain from the threat or use of force...as a means of solving international disputes, including territorial disputes"); Gaetano Arangio-Ruiz, The United Nations Declaration On Friendly Relations and the System of the Sources of International Law pp.104–105 (Sijthoff & Noordhoff 1979); Alfred Verdross & Bruno Simma, Universelles Volkerrecht p.905 (Duncker und Humblot 1984); Michel Virally, Article 2: Paragraphe 4, in La Charte Des Nations Unies pp.119–125 Economica, 2d ed. 1991); Oscar Schachter, International Law in Theory and Practice p.116 (Nijhoff 1991); Peter Malanczuk, Akehurst's Modern Introduction to International Law pp.314–315 (Routledge, 7th rev., ed. 1997).

[161] (2006) 17 E.J.I.L. 699 at pp.711–712.

"It is true that the use of force in self-defence does not give title to territory, and in that sense [as the Commission states] 'self-defence cannot be invoked to settle territorial disputes'. Thus the UN does not accept Israel's legal title to the West Bank and Gaza,[162] even if it was acting in self-defence in 1967. But Eritrea was not arguing that its use of force gave title to the disputed territory. Its position was that it had title on the basis of colonial treaties and that it was using force to defend its territory against Ethiopian occupation/attack.

The Claims Commission's view was in fact based on a selective reading of the Declaration, for this says not only that '[e]very State has the duty to refrain from the threat or use of force...as a means of solving international disputes, including territorial disputes', but also that

[e]very State has the duty to refrain from the threat or use of force to violate the *existing* international boundaries of another State...Every State likewise has the duty to refrain from the threat or use of force to violate international lines of demarcation, such as armistice lines, established by or pursuant to an international agreement to which it is a party or which it is otherwise bound to respect.

Eritrea was required by the Claims Commission to *respect a line which was not an international boundary*, nor even a ceasefire line at the time of the use of force, but was merely based on the presence of Ethiopia's (illegal) administration in what turned out to be Eritrean territory.[163] Ethiopia's acts of administration had not been enough to give Ethiopia title to Badme but did, according to the Commission, give it the right to use force. The Commission focused on Ethiopian allegations about the use of force on 12 May and did not adequately consider whether it was in fact Ethiopia which was illegally using force to occupy Eritrea's territory."

In the Eritrea-Ethiopia case it was only after Eritrea had used force, in 1998, that Eritrea's title to Badme was confirmed by the Boundary Commission, in 2002; in the meantime Eritrea and Ethiopia disputed title. Jennings[164] suggests that in such a case the state in Eritrea's position should, unless its claim to title is very clear, refer its claim to title to the ICJ before resorting to armed force:

"...since the establishment of a valid title is, as is easily appreciated from the cases, by no means a simple matter, it is not to be expected that a particular issue of title will usually be so very clear as to justify forcible action by a claimant State on the mere strength of its own case.....it would seem reasonable to suggest that where a State does believe that it has a good legal title to territory presently in the possession of another State, it ought to challenge the latter State by making a unilateral application to the Court, before it can feel justified in taking forcible action even though, *if* its case is justified, the action may be domestic action and no breach of the Charter. And certainly also it ought, if it has repossessed the territory by force, to be willing even thereafter to submit the question of title to the Court at the suit of the newly dispossessed State...where force is alleged to be justified on the ground of an existing legal

---

[162] Ed. See above, pp.191 et seq.
[163] The situation is thus different from Argentina's invasion of the Falklands (1982) and Iraq's invasion of Kuwait (1990) where the use of force was condemned by the UN Security Council because it violated an international boundary, even if that boundary was contested. A comparison might be made between Ethiopia's occupation of Eritrean territory and South Africa's illegal occupation of Namibia: South Africa's claim to use force in self-defence against frontline states was rejected by many on the basis that it had no title to the Namibian territory it was defending.
[164] See above, at p.164, n.1, pp.72–73.

title, and can in the nature of things only be justified on that ground, there must be a strong presumption against the validity of such an alleged title where the claimant is not willing to have that claim properly determined in a court of law."

In contrast with the factual situation in the Eritrea-Ethiopia case, the use of force by State A to recover territory to which it claims title that has been taken from it by force by State B (also claiming title) *immediately after* the territory has been taken by State B may be justified on a basis of self-defence, as in the case of the United Kingdom's use of force to recover the Falkland Islands.[165]

THE ENTEBBE INCIDENT[166]

UN Doc. S/PV. 1939, pp.27, 51–59, 92 and UN Doc. S/PV. 1941, pp.31–32. Reprinted in (1976) 15 I.L.M. 1224

On June 27, 1976, an Air France airliner bound for Paris from Tel Aviv was hijacked over Greece after leaving Athens airport. Two of the hijackers appear to have been West German nationals; the other two held Arab passports. The airliner was diverted to Entebbe airport in Uganda where the Jewish passengers (about 100) were separated from the others and the latter released. The hijackers demanded the release of about 50 Palestinian terrorists imprisoned in various countries. The evidence seems to suggest that Uganda did not take such steps as it might have done against the hijackers and, indeed, helped them, although Uganda denied this. On July 3, 1976, Israel flew transport aircraft and soldiers to Entebbe and rescued the hostages by force. The hijackers were killed during the operation, as were some Ugandan and Israeli soldiers. There was also extensive damage to Ugandan aircraft and the airport. The following is an extract from the Security Council debate on the matter in July 1976.

LT. COL. JUMA ORIS ABDULLAH (UGANDA).

Uganda gave all the help and hospitality it was capable of giving to all the hostages. The response to this humanitarian gesture by Zionist Israel—the vehicle of imperialism—was to invade Uganda, once again living up to its record of barbarism and banditry. ...

We call upon this Council unreservedly to condemn in the strongest possible terms Israel's barbaric, unprovoked and unwarranted aggression against the sovereign Republic of Uganda. Uganda demands full compensation from Israel for the damage to life and property caused during its invasion. ...

MR. HERZOG (ISRAEL).

Uganda violated a basic tenet of international law in failing to protect foreign nationals on its territory. Furthermore, it behaved in a manner which constituted a gross violation of the 1970 Hague Convention on the Suppression of Unlawful Seizure of Aircraft. This Convention had been ratified by both Israel and Uganda. ...

The right of a State to take military action to protect its nationals in mortal danger is recognised by all legal authorities in international law. In *Self Defence in International Law*, Professor Bowett states, on page 87, that the right of the State to intervene by the use or threat of force for the protection of its nationals suffering injuries within the territory of another State is generally admitted, both in the writings of jurists and in the practice of

---

[165] See above, p.749.
[166] See Akehurst (1977) 5 Int. Rel. 3; Boyle (1982) 29 N.I.L.R. 32; Green (1976) 6 Is. Y.N.R. 312; Krift (1977) 4 Brooklyn J.I.L. 43; and Margo (1977) 94 S.A.L.J. 306. For a full account of the incident, see Stevenson, *90 Minutes at Entebbe* (1976).

States. In the arbitration between Great Britain and Spain in 1925, one of the series known as the Spanish Moroccan claims[167] Judge Huber, as Rapporteur of the Commission, stated:

> However, it cannot be denied that at a certain point the interest of a State in exercising protection over its nationals and their property can take precedence over territorial sovereignty, despite the absence of any conventional provisions. ... It presupposes the inadequacy of any other means of protection against some injury, actual or imminent, to the persons or property of nationals and, moreover, an injury which results either from the acts of the territorial State and its authorities or from the acts of individuals or groups of individuals which the territorial State is unable, or unwilling, to prevent.

In the *Law of Nations*, 6th edition, p.427, Brierly states as follows:

> Every effort must be made to get the United Nations to act. But, if the United Nations is not in a position to move in time and the need for instant action is manifest, it would be difficult to deny the legitimacy of action in defence of nationals which every responsible Government would feel bound to take if it had the means to do so; this is, of course, on the basis that the action was strictly limited to securing the safe removal of the threatened nationals.[168] ...

The right of self-defence is enshrined in international law and in the Charter of the United Nations and can be applied on the basis of the classic formulation, as was done in the well-known Caroline Case, permitting such action where there is a

> necessity of self-defence, instant, overwhelming, leaving no choice of means and no moment for deliberation.

That was exactly the situation which faced the Government of Israel.

MR. OYONO (CAMEROON).

The Security Council, which is responsible for international peace and security, must vigorously condemn this barbaric act which constitutes a flagrant violation of the norms of international law and flouts the spirit and letter of the United Nations Charter, Article 2, paragraph 4. ...

In the spirit of the Charter, that prohibition means that Member States have an obligation to settle their international disputes by peaceful means in order to maintain international peace and security. I need hardly remind you that our Organisation is not dedicated to anarchy or to the notion that might makes right, but is an organised community whose mutually accepted principles and rules must be scrupulously respected, and their violation adequately punished.

It is the corner-stone of our Organisation that there can be no justification for the use of force against the sovereignty, independence or territorial integrity of a State, unless we wish to imperil international co-operation in its present form and indeed the very existence of States that do not yet possess modern, sophisticated systems of detection and deterrence.

Notes

1. The *Entebbe Incident* concerned the use of armed force by a state to defend its nationals in the territory of another state. No resolution was adopted at the end of the debate. A United Kingdom/United States draft resolution[169] which limited itself to condemning hijacking and did not comment on the conduct of the parties did not receive the necessary votes for adoption and a draft resolution[170] proposed by Benin/Libya/Tanzania condemning Israel was not put to the vote.

---

[167] Ed. *GB v Spain* (1925) 2 R.I.A.A. 615.
[168] Ed. O'Connell, *International Law* (2nd edn) Vol.I, p.303 is quoted to the same effect.
[169] UN Doc. S/12138; (1976) 15 I.L.M. 1226.
[170] UN Doc. S/12139; (1976) 15 I.L.M. 1227.

2. By no means all writers agree with those quoted by the Israeli representative in the debate on a post-1945[171] right to defend nationals abroad. Brownlie, for example, states:

    "... it is very doubtful if the present form of intervention has any basis in the modern law. The instances in which states have purported to exercise it, and the terms in which it is delimited, show that it provides infinite opportunities for abuse.[172] Forcible intervention is now unlawful. It is true that the protection of nationals presents particular difficulties and that a government faced with a deliberate massacre of a considerable number of nationals in a foreign state would have cogent reasons of humanity for acting, and would also be under very great political pressure. The possible risks of denying the legality of action in a case of such urgency, an exceptional circumstance, must be weighed against the more calculable dangers of providing legal pretexts for the commission of breaches of the peace in the pursuit of national rather than humanitarian interests."[173]

3. Does the part of the Court's judgment in the *Corfu Channel* case on intervention (above, p.341), support Brownlie? If there is a right to protect nationals abroad, how serious does the threat to their person have to be for it to arise? Is there any support for a right to intervene to protect the property of nationals abroad?[174] On humanitarian intervention, see below, p.777.

4. On the United States attempt to rescue the hostages in Iran, see the *U.S. Diplomatic and Consular Staff* case, above, p.312. The United States justified its action, in a report to the Security Council pursuant to art.51, Charter, as being "in exercise of its inherent right of self-defence with the aim of extricating American nationals who are and remain the victims of the Iranian armed attack on our Embassy."[175] The Court did not rule upon legality of the rescue attempt.[176]

5. The *Nicaragua* case does not support Israel's contention. The facts of that case may both explain why the Court did not in that case address the question of the forcible protection of nationals abroad and why the wording of the judgment could be read by implication as excluding it. It is noticeable, however, that the Court did not *expressly* reserve this question (contrast its treatment of anticipatory self-defence) and that the thrust of the *Nicaragua* judgment is to minimise the opportunities for the lawful use of force in international relations.

6. *United States air raid on Libya*.[177] On April 15, 1986 United States military aircraft based in the United Kingdom and on United States aircraft carriers in the Mediterranean bombed military targets in Libya, hitting most of the targets successfully but killing, it was estimated, approximately 100 civilians as well. The air strike was in response to what the United States was sure was a series of Libyan conducted or supported terrorist acts against United States nationals and property, including the April 9 bombing of a Berlin nightclub in which a United States soldier was killed and 50 other soldiers were injured.[178] President Reagan characterised the mission as being

---

[171] For state practice evidencing the right before then, see Bowett, above, n.105, pp.96–105.

[172] Ed. Might the *Hungarian* case, above, p.743, and the *Grenada* case, above, p.745 support this view?

[173] See above, n.2, p.301. See generally Ronzitti, *Rescuing Nationals Abroad through Military Coercion and Intervention on Grounds of Humanity* (1985). On the 1990 Liberian Incident, see Lillich (1992) 35 G.Y.I.L. 205.

[174] See the Lord Chancellor's statement justifying the 1956 Anglo-French invasion of Suez to protect Suez Canal installations: *Hansard*, HL Vol.199, cols 1348 et seq., (November 1, 1956).

[175] I.C.J. Rep. 1979, at p.18. See D'Angelo (1981) 21 Virg.J.I.L. 485. cf. the *Mayaguez* case (rescue by US troops by force of a US merchant ship and its crew captured by Cambodia; justified as self-defence of nationals): [1975] U.S.D.I.L. 777. See Paust (1975–1976) 85 Yale L.J. 774.

[176] Judges Morozov and Tarazi concluded that it was not justified by art.51, Charter: I.C.J. Rep. 1980, at pp.57, 64, respectively.

[177] See Greenwood (1987) 89 W.Virg.L.R. 933.

[178] 23 US nationals died in terrorist attacks in 1985: Greenwood, above, citing Falk, in Thompson, ed., *Mad Dogs* (1986), p.124.

"fully consistent with Article 51 of the UN Charter"; it was "pre-emptive action" that would "not only diminish Col. Kadhafi's capacity to export terror" but also "provide him with incentives and reasons to change his criminal behaviour." A draft Security Council resolution condemning the air strike received the required majority (11 to four votes), but was vetoed by the United States and the United Kingdom.[179] Speaking in support of the legality of the United States action, and of the United Kingdom participation in it, the British representative on the Security Council stated[180]:

"The United States has, as any of us do, the inherent right of self-defence, as reaffirmed in Article 51 of the Charter.

... the right of self-defence is not an entirely passive right. It plainly includes the right to destroy or weaken the capacity of one's assailant, to reduce his resources, and to weaken his will so as to discourage and prevent further violence.

At the same time, the right of self-defence should be used in a proportionate way. That is why when President Reagan told Mrs Thatcher last week that the United States intended to take action, she concentrated on the principle of self-defence and the consequent need to limit the action and to relate the selection of targets clearly to terrorism."

7. A somewhat similar incident occurred on June 26, 1993 when the United States destroyed the Iraqi intelligence headquarters in Baghdad by missiles fired from United States aircraft carriers. The attack caused the loss of six or more civilian lives as some missiles went astray. The attack followed the uncovering of an unexecuted Iraqi plan to kill President Bush in Kuwait in April 1993. The United States justified its attack under art.51 and reported it to the Security Council, as that provision required. The United States stated[181]:

"Our response has been proportionate and aimed at a target directly linked to the operation against President Bush. It was designed to damage the terrorist infrastructure of the Iraqi regime, reduce its ability to promote terrorism and deter further acts of aggression against the United States."

The United Kingdom supported the United States attack ("proper and proportionate"), as did the Russian Federation; France "fully understands" the reason for the attack; China and other states indicated their concern.[182] Was this a case of self defence or a reprisal?[183]

----

[179] S/PV. 2682, April 21, 1986, France, UK and US vetoes.
[180] S/PV. 2679, pp.27–28, U.K.M.I.L. 1986; (1986) 57 B.Y.I.L. 641.
[181] UN Doc. S/PV. 3245, p.6. On the incident, see Baker (1994) 24 Ga.J.I.C.L. 99; Quigley (1994) 17 Hastings I.C.L.R. 241; Kritsiotis (1996) 45 I.C.L.Q. 162; Reisman (1994) 5 E.J.I.L. 120.
[182] UN Doc. S/PV. 3245, pp.13 et seq. *Keesings Archives*, p.39531.
[183] See Gray (1994) 65 B.Y.I.L. 135 at 170.

GRAY, SELF-DEFENCE AGAINST TERRORISM

Extract from Evans, ed., *International Law* (2nd edn 2004), pp.602–604

The attacks on the World Trade Center and the Pentagon on 11 September 2001 brought a revolutionary challenge to the doctrine of self-defence and a reassessment of the law in this area.[184] Before 11 September 2001 the use of force in response to terrorist attacks on nationals abroad had been controversial; only Israel and the USA had expressly claimed to exercise such a right. In some cases this was against a State asserted to be directly responsible for terrorist attacks on US or Israeli nationals. The USA took action against Libya in 1986 in response to Libyan-sponsored terrorist attacks on US nationals abroad; it also mounted missile attacks against Iraq in 1993 in response to a failed assassination attempt against ex-President Bush.[185] In 1998 the USA went further in its attacks on terrorist training camps in Afghanistan and an alleged chemical weapons factory in Sudan in response to terrorist attacks on US embassies in Africa. In 1985 Israel had taken action against headquarters of the PLO in Tunis, in response to an attack on an Israeli secret service agent in Cyprus; this was unanimously condemned by the Security Council and not accepted as lawful self-defence. In contrast, response to the United States actions was ambivalent. Russia moved from support to doubt; most developed States expressed sympathy but not clear acceptance of such a wide legal doctrine of self-defence.

In response to the attacks of 11 September 2001 on the World Trade Center and the Pentagon, the USA began *Operation Enduring Freedom* on 7 October 2001 with the aim of disrupting the use of Afghanistan as a terrorist base. It relied on self-defence as the basis for its use of force against Afghanistan; in its report to the Security Council under Article 51 the USA claimed to be acting in self-defence. The UK which was involved in the first day of missile attacks on Afghanistan also invoked individual and collective self-defence.[186] These claims may seem controversial in the light of the previous doubts as to whether the right to self-defence could extend to action against past terrorist attacks, but *Operation Enduring Freedom* received massive support and the action was almost universally accepted as self-defence. NATO invoked Article 5 of the NATO Treaty for the first time;[187] this provides that an attack on one member State is an attack on all. Other collective self-defence organizations also took the view that the attack was an armed attack for the purposes of collective self-defence; the OAS and ANZUS followed the approach of NATO. The EU, China, Russia, Japan, and Pakistan also supported this view. Many states have played a supporting role in the military campaign. Only Iran and Iraq expressly challenged the legality of the operation. In Resolution 1368 passed on 12 September 2001 to condemn the attacks the Security Council had expressly recognized the right of self-defence. Subsequently Resolution 1373 on measures against international terrorism, passed on 14 November 2001, also included express reference to individual and collective self-defence. This was the first time that the Security Council had recognized the right to use force in self-defence against terrorist action.

This use of force goes beyond the traditional model of self-defence in many ways. It seems that the massive State support for the legality of the US claim to self-defence could constitute instant customary international law and an authoritative reinterpretation of the UN Charter, however radical the alteration from many States' prior conception of the right to self-defence. First, it widens the concept of armed attack. Article 51 originally envisaged self-defence against an attack by a State and those invoking the right generally took care to attribute responsibility to a State. Now it is arguable that a terrorist attack on a State's territory by a non-State actor may be an armed attack which justifies a response against the State which harboured those responsible. Some uncertainty remains as to the degree of State involvement required.

The right to self-defence claimed by the USA and the UK in response to the terrorist attacks is also pre-emptive. Both the USA and the UK in their letters to the Security Council say that their action is in response to the attack on the World Trade Center; for the USA the aim is to deter further attacks on the United States, for the UK 'to avert the continuing threat of attacks from the same source'. That is, although the initial attack had ended and thus it would be difficult to invoke self-defence against that attack, the USA and UK clearly felt the need to avoid the appearance of punitive (and unlawful) reprisals. Many States in the past have rejected the legality of pre-emptive self-defence, but they accepted this wide right to self-defence by the USA, at least in regard to *Operation Enduring Freedom*. However, there is still controversy as to the scope of this right; it is not clear how far

---

[184] See the account of the facts in (2002) 96 AJIL 237, and editorial comments in (2001) 95 AJIL 833. Ed. See also Byers (2002) 51 I.C.L.Q. 401.

[185] Ed. see above, pp.770–771.

[186] Ed. UK letter to the President of the Security Council, U.K.M.I.L. 2001, (2001) 72 B.Y.I.L. 682.

[187] Ed. Statement by the NATO Secretary-General, October 2, 2001 (2001) 40 I.L.M. 1268.

the international response should be construed as a general acceptance of anticipatory or pre-emptive use of force outside the context of terrorism.

Another possible restriction on this apparently very wide and, for many States, new doctrine of self-defence is that the right of self-defence against terrorism may exist only in cases where the right has been asserted by the Security Council, as here in Resolutions 1368 and 1373. Several States regarded this Security Council backing as crucial to the US claim to self-defence.

Also questions arise as to necessity and proportionality. The bombing campaign against Al Qaida and the Taliban regime continued for several months; the USA at the start of *Operation Enduring Freedom* warned that the war against terrorism could take years. In a campaign to prevent future terrorist attacks it is difficult to identify an appropriate end to the action, but the longer it continues and the more destruction it involves the more difficult it is to argue that it is proportionate. If the use of force proves ineffective in deterring terrorist attacks it is also difficult to argue that it is necessary.

Notes

1. *September 11 2001.*[188] On 9/11, 19 Al-Qaida activists (15 Saudi Arabian nationals, two United Arab Emirates nationals, one Egyptian national and one Lebanese national) boarded and hijacked four passenger jets owned by US airline companies on scheduled flights within the US. They flew two of the jets into the twin towers of the World Trade Center in New York and one into the Pentagon in Washington; the fourth crashed in a field in Pennsylvania.

    Nearly 3,000 persons, nationals of 70 or so states, were killed.

    On September 12, the Security Council unanimously adopted Resolution 1368 (2001), which stated:

    > "The Security Council . . .
    >   *Recognizing* the inherent right of individual or collective self-defence in accordance with the Charter,
    >   1. *Unequivocally condemns* in the strongest terms the horrifying terrorist attacks which took place on 11 September 2001 in New York, Washington, D.C. and Pennsylvania and regards such acts, like any act of international terrorism, as a threat to international peace and security; . . ."

2. *The invasion of Afghanistan.* Following 9/11, on September 20, 2001, in an Address to a joint session of Congress,[189] President Bush stated that "enemies of freedom have committed an act of war against our country" and declared a "war on terrorism" that "begins with Al Quaeda". He called upon the Taliban Government[190] to hand over to the US "all of the leaders of Al Quaeda who hide in your land" and "close immediately and permanently every terrorist training camp in Afghanistan". The Taliban Government rejected these demands, in the absence of proof linking Bin Laden to 9/11.

    Relying upon the right to self-defence, on October 7, 2001, the US, joined initially by the UK, began a programme of air strikes against Afghanistan. In addition, US and UK special forces supported a ground offensive by the Northern Alliance, composed of Afghanistan opponents of the Taliban regime. In November 2001, US marines were deployed on the ground, as were a

---

[188] See Byers (2002) 51 I.C.L.Q. 401; Cassese (2001) 12 E.J.I.L. 993; Delbruck (2001) 44 G.Y.I.L. 9; Katselli and Shah (2003) 52 I.C.L.Q. 245; Murphy (2002) 43 Harv. I.L.J. 41; id. (2002) 96 A.J.I.L. 237; Myjer and White (2002) 7 J.C. & S.L. 5; Paust (2002) 35 Cornell I.L.J. 533; Ratner (2002) 96 A.J.I.L. 905;
[189] For text see *www.whitehouse.gov/news/releases*.
[190] This was not recognised by the US as the Government of Afghanistan.

small number of Russian and UK forces. In early December 2001, the Northern Alliance, supported by US and UK special forces and US air bombing, completed the defeat of the Taliban army.

3. The 2001 Bonn Conference on the political future of Afghanistan resulted in a new Afghan constitution, and the election of President Karzai and the Afghan National Assembly. In 2001, the Security Council established the International Security Assistance Force ("ISAF"),[191] with the current mandate of supporting the Afghan Government "in the maintenance of security" in the whole of Afghanistan so that the Government, "as well as the personnel of the UN and other civilian personnel engaged, in particular, in reconstruction and humanitarian efforts, can operate in a secure environment" and of providing "security assistance for the performance of other tasks in support of the Bonn Agreement".[192] In 2003, NATO took command of ISAF at the request of the UN and the Afghan Government. In 2009, ISAF had over 55,000 troops from 26 NATO partners or other states. The United Nations Assistance Mission in Afghanistan ("UNAMA")[193] also functions, with a broad civil assistance role.

4. As Gray notes, the legality of the invasion of Afghanistan was not called into question by states generally, and the Security Council, by its reference to self-defence in Resolution 1368 (2001), would appear to recognise that the right to anticipatory self-defence does extend to the very exceptional circumstances of that case. Does, or should, this recognition go beyond factual situations of the extreme character of 9/11? Note the dangers pointed to by Gray inherent in any extensive reading of a right to anticipatory, or pre-emptive, self-defence. See also the claims made by the United States in its *National Security Strategy*, below.

US NATIONAL SECURITY STRATEGY

(2002) 41 I.L.M 1478

For centuries, international law recognized that nations need not suffer an attack before they can lawfully take action to defend themselves against forces that present an imminent danger of attack. Legal scholars and international jurists often conditioned the legitimacy of pre-emption on the existence of an imminent threat – most often a visible mobilization of armies, navies, and air forces preparing to attack.

We must adapt the concept of imminent threat to the capabilities and objectives of today's adversaries. Rogue states and terrorists do not seek to attack us using conventional means. They know such attacks would fail. Instead, they rely on acts of terror and, potentially, the use of weapons of mass destruction-weapons that can easily be concealed, delivered covertly, and used without warning.

The targets of these attacks are our military forces and our civilian population, in direct violation of one of the principal norms of the law of warfare. As was demonstrated by the losses on September 11, 2001, mass civilian casualties is the specific objective of terrorists and these losses would be exponentially more severe if terrorists acquired and used weapons of mass destruction.

The United States has long maintained the option of pre-emptive actions to counter a sufficient threat to our national security. The greater the threat, the greater is the risk of inaction-and the more compelling the case for taking anticipatory action to defend ourselves, even if uncertainty remains as to the time and place of the enemy's attack. To forestall or prevent such hostile acts by our adversaries the United States will, if necessary, act pre-emptively.

---

[191] Security Council Resolution 1386 (2001), adopted under Ch.VII, Charter, there being a "threat to the peace". ISAF's mandate has been renewed and developed in later Security Council resolutions, most recently resolution 1833 (2008).
[192] Security Council Resolution 1510 (2003).
[193] Established by Security Council Resolution 1401 (2002).

Notes

1.   In September 2002, the United States adopted its *National Security Strategy* in which it set out its approach to the threat posed by 9/11 and other possible security threats from rogue states, such as Iran, Iraq and North Korea, and terrorist sources such as Al-Qaida.[194] The above extract concerns the right to self-defence. It makes an ambitious claim to the certain existence of the right to anticipatory, or pre-emptive[195] self-defence and proposes its adaptation in the light of the new situation so as to exclude the requirement of "imminence". Examples of what this might entail are the Sudan and Yemen cases summarised in the following notes, as well as the Afghanistan case. Whereas states generally supported the action taken against Afghanistan on the basis of self-defence following 9/11 with the implied approval of the Security Council (see the reference to self-defence in Security Council Resolution 1368, above, and the general lack of criticism in later debates), the position taken by the US on self-defence in its *National Security Strategy* has not met with approval. Even the United Kingdom has not given its support. Responding to a suggestion that the Government might "reconsider the notion of imminence in the light of the new threats to international peace and security",[196] the British Foreign Secretary, who assumed the existence of a right of anticipatory self-defence, supposed the continued existence of the requirement:

> "There is already scope under international law to take into account all of the circumstances, including likelihood, nature and seriousness of any attack, in determining whether any threat is imminent ... We would therefore not wish to attempt to reach consensus internationally on the precise circumstances in which military action in anticipatory self-defence may be taken by states."[197]

This lack of support from other states suggests that the United States is not leading a move towards a new rule of customary international law (for this process, see above, p.32). Although many states might in appropriate circumstances welcome a broad right of pre-emptive self-defence, it carries with it the potential for abuse, particularly by a powerful state or a state that has the backing of such a state.

Gray[198] comments on response to the United States position as follows:

> "Other States have not shown themselves willing to go so far in stretching the boundaries of self-defence, but there have been some indications that there is now a more open acceptance of anticipatory self-defence than previously. A UN High Level Panel was set up to respond to the new challenges to the collective security system after 11 September 2001; in its Report of December 2004 it accepted a right of anticipatory self-defence.[199] The UN Secretary-General in his response to the High Level Panel, 'In Larger Freedom' (March 2005), also accepted this previously controversial doctrine, although in more cautious terms, saying that 'imminent

---

[194] See Bothe (2003) 14 E.J.I.L. 227; Glennon (2001–2) 25 H.J.L. & Pub. Pol. 539; Gray (2002) 1 Chinese J.I.L. 437; Henderson (2004) 9 J.C. & S.L. 3; Sofaer (2003) 14 E.J.I.L. 209.

[195] The term "pre-emptive" is now commonly used in place of "anticipatory", sometimes signalling a more expansive understanding of the right.

[196] Foreign Affairs Committee, Second Report 2002-3, HC 196, para.150.

[197] Response to the Foreign Affairs Committee's Second Report, Cm.5793, p.8.

[198] Evans, ed., *International Law* (2nd edn 2004), p.604.

[199] Report of the Secretary General's High Level Panel on Threats, Challenges and Change, UN Doc A/59/565.

threats are fully covered by Article 51.'[200] Several states now appear willing to accept this position, but they do not go far as to accept a right of purely pre-emptive action in the absence of an imminent threat. That is, there is little sign of support for a more fundamental transformation of self-defence along the lines suggested in the US National Security Strategy. As the High Level Panel said, there is no right to self-defence if the threat of armed attack is not imminent. If there are good arguments for preventive military action, with good evidence to support them, they should be put to the Security Council which can authorize action if it chooses to. 'For those impatient with such a response, the answer must be that in a world full of potential threats the right to the global order and the norm of non-intervention is simply too great for the legality of unilateral preventive action.'"

2. On August 7, 1998, the United States embassies in Kenya and Tanzania were bombed by local members of the Al-Qaida network. 211 persons were killed in Nairobi, and 13 in Dar Es Salem. Most of these were African nationals, either local embassy employees or civilians; 12 United States nationals working in the Nairobi embassy were killed. Both buildings were severely damaged.

    On August 21, 1998, American cruise missiles attacked six Al-Qaida training sites in Afghanistan and a factory in Sudan that was (mistakenly) believed to be linked to Osama Bin Laden and in production of chemicals for use in nerve gas, causing injuries to seven persons. The attacks were designed to prevent further terrorist attacks for which there was "very specific information" that the Al-Qaida network was planning. Could these United States attacks be justified as an exercise of the right to anticipatory self-defence, as claimed before the *National Security Strategy*?

3. In November, 2002, a US missile launched from a CIA-operated unmanned aerial vehicle, or drone, killed Qaed Salim Sinan al-Harethi, Al-Qaida's leader in Yemen, and five other persons as they travelled in a car in Yemen. Al-Harethi was believed to have planned the 2000 suicide attack in which a small boat rammed the *USS Cole* in Aden, Yemen, killing 17 US crew members. Could these United States attacks be justified as an exercise of the right to anticipatory or pre-emptive self-defence, as claimed before or under the *National Security Strategy*? Or should the US have tracked and sought to arrest the suspected terrorist? The Swedish Foreign Minister, Anna Lindh, stated that the killings were "a summary execution that violates human rights. Even terrorists must be treated according to international law. Otherwise any country can start executing those they consider terrorists."[201]

---

[200] UN Doc A/59/2005.
[201] Quoted in *National Catholic Report*, November 15, 2002. For Human Rights Committee condemnation of similar targeted killings by Israel of alleged Palestinian terrorists, see above, p.566. Following CIA attempts to assassinate various foreign leaders, President Ford's Executive Order 11905, s.5(g), prohibited US government employees from engaging in "political assassinations". The 2002 Yemen killings were considered by the US government not to fall within the Order.

D. Humanitarian Intervention[202]

UK FOREIGN OFFICE POLICY DOCUMENT NO.148

U.K.M.I.L. 1986; (1986) 57 B.Y.I.L. 614

II.18. The final, and by far the most controversial, category of exceptions to the general prohibition on intervention is that on humanitarian grounds. This should be distinguished from action to protect a state's own nationals abroad ... The vast literature on this subject in the past and present century has wrestled with the difficulty of reconciling a state's supposedly absolute sovereignty with even more fundamental human rights which may be held to justify intervention on behalf of oppressed nationals of another state.

II.20. ... Lauterpacht's rationale for humanitarian intervention is that 'ultimately, peace is more endangered by tyrannical contempt for human rights than by attempts to assert, through intervention, the sanctity of human personality.'[203] A substantial body of opinion and of practice has thus supported the view that when a state commits cruelties against and persecution of its nationals in such a way as to deny their fundamental human rights and to shock the conscience of mankind, intervention in the interest of humanity is legally permissible.

II.21. The state practice to which advocates of the right of humanitarian intervention have appealed provides an uncertain basis on which to rest such a right. Not least this is because history has shown that humanitarian ends are almost always mixed with other less laudable motives for intervening, and because often the 'humanitarian' benefits of an intervention are either not claimed by the intervening state or are only put forward as an *ex post facto* justification of the intervention. In the nineteenth century, interventions by the Western Powers to protect the Christian and other minorities in the Ottoman Empire, such as the Maronites on Mount Lebanon,[204] are those most often said to have been for humanitarian ends. The two most discussed instances of alleged humanitarian intervention since 1945 are the Indian invasion of Bangladesh in 1971[205] and Tanzania's 'humanitarian' invasion of Uganda in 1979.[206] But, although both did result in unquestionable benefits for, respectively, the peoples of East Bengal and Uganda, India and Tanzania were reluctant to use humanitarian ends to justify their invasion of a neighbour's territory. Both preferred to quote the right to self-defence under Article 51. And in each case the self-interest of the invading state was clearly involved.

II.22. In fact, the best case that can be made in support of humanitarian intervention is that it cannot be said to be unambiguously illegal. ... But the overwhelming majority of contemporary legal opinion comes down against the existence of a right of humanitarian intervention, for three main reasons: first, the UN Charter and the corpus of modern international law do not seem specifically to incorporate such a right; secondly, state practice in the past two centuries, and especially since 1945, at best provides only a handful of genuine cases of humanitarian intervention, and, on most assessments, none at all; and finally, on prudential grounds, that the scope for abusing such a right argues strongly against its creation. ... In essence, therefore, the case against making

---

[202] On the question whether there is a right of humanitarian intervention, see the contrasting views in Lillich, ed., *Humanitarian Intervention and the United Nations* (1973); and Moore, ed., *Law and Civil War in the Modern World* (1974) (articles by Brownlie and Lillich). See also on humanitarian intervention in international law, Chesterman, *Just War or Just Peace?: Humanitarian Intervention and International Law* (2001); Franck and Rodley (1973) 67 A.J.I.L. 275; Goodman (2006) 100 A.J.I.L. 107; Holzgrefe and Keohane, eds, *Humanitarian Intervention* (2003); Kritsiotis (1998) 19 Mich. J.I.L. 1005; Murphy, *Humanitarian Intervention* (1996); Orford, *Reading Humanitarian Intervention* (2003); Rodley, ed., *To Loose the Bands of Wickedness* (1992); Ronzitti, above, n.173; Sarooshi, *Humanitarian Intervention and International Humanitarian Assistance* (1994); Teson, *Humanitarian Intervention* (2nd edn 1997); Tsagourias, *Jurisprudence of International Law: the Humanitarian Dimension* (2000); Tyagi (1995) 16 Mich. J.I.L. 883; Verwey (1985) 32 N.I.L.R. 357; Welsh, *Humanitarian Intervention and International Relations* (2004); Wheeler, *Saving Strangers: Humanitarian Intervention in International Society* (2000).

[203] *International Law and Human Rights*, p.32.

[204] Ed. In 1860, in events erupting from the same religious tension that affected Lebanon during the 1975–1990 civil war, some 5,000 Christians were killed by Moslems. By treaty, Turkey, which then held the Lebanon as a part of its Empire, agreed with the major Western powers that action should be taken to end the killings and a French force was sent on behalf of the European powers. See Pogany (1986) 35 I.C.L.Q. 182.

[205] Ed. See above, p.745.

[206] Ed. After Uganda had illegally occupied a part of Tanzania by armed force, Tanzania used armed force to eject the Ugandan troops and continued on into Uganda. Together with Ugandan rebels, Tanzanian forces defeated President Amin's forces, causing President Amin to flee and the replacement of his government, which had been responsible for atrocious human rights violations, with an estimated 300,000 deaths. Although Tanzania did not unequivocally justify its invasion of Uganda on grounds of humanitarian intervention, commentators have suggested that this was the only possible legal basis: see, e.g. Teson, above, n.202, pp.179–195.

humanitarian intervention an exception to the principle of non-intervention is that its doubtful benefits would be heavily outweighed by its costs in terms of respect for international law.

Note

Humanitarian intervention is claimed by some writers to be a second implied limitation on the prohibition on the use of armed force by states[207] in art.2(4), UN Charter (the first being self defence). After reviewing academic opinion and state practice on the subject, the above UK Policy Document concluded that such a limitation on art.2(4) was neither proven nor desirable. Although the UK has since modified its position in the context of Iraq and Kosovo (see below), the Document is reprinted because it probably still reflects the position of most states and hence customary international law.

SECURITY COUNCIL RESOLUTION 688 (1991)

April 3, 1991. S.C.O.R., 46th Year, Resolutions and Decisions, p.31

The Security Council ...
Recalling Article 2, paragraph 7, of the Charter of the United Nations,
Gravely concerned by the repression of the Iraqi civilian population in many parts of Iraq, including most recently in Kurdish populated areas which led to a massive flow of refugees towards and across international frontiers and to cross border incursions, which threaten international peace and security in the region,
Deeply disturbed by the magnitude of the human suffering involved ...
Reaffirming the commitment of all Member States to the sovereignty, territorial integrity and political independence of Iraq and of all States in the area ...
1. *Condemns* the repression of the Iraqi civilian population in many parts of Iraq, including most recently in Kurdish populated areas, the consequences of which threaten international peace and security in the region;
2. *Demands* that Iraq, as a contribution to removing the threat to international peace and security in the region, immediately end this repression and expresses the hope in the same context that an open dialogue will take place to ensure that the human and political rights of all Iraqi citizens are respected;
3. *Insists* that Iraq allow immediate access by international humanitarian organizations to all those in need of assistance in all parts of Iraq and to make available all necessary facilities for their operations; ...
5. *Requests further* the Secretary-General to use all the resources at his disposal, including those of the relevant United Nations agencies, to address urgently the critical needs of the refugees and displaced Iraqi population;
6. *Appeals* to all Member States and to all humanitarian organizations to contribute to these humanitarian relief efforts ...

Notes

1.   After the Iraqi army occupying Kuwait was defeated,[208] rebellions against President Saddam Hussein's rule occurred in both northern and southern Iraq. These were put down with brutal ferocity by the still strong Iraqi army causing a flood of refugees. In northern Iraq well over 1 million Kurdish refugees fled to the Turkish and Iranian borders where they received some Western aid, although many died.[209] Resolution 688 was a response to this situation.[210] It was adopted by 10 votes to three (Cuba, Yemen, Zimbabwe), with two absentions (China and India). The resolution was heavily criticised by those states voting against and abstaining as being

---

[207] Teson, above, n.202, pp.179–195.
[208] On the Kuwait war, see below, p.809.
[209] See the Report of the Secretary-General, UN Doc. S/22454, March 28, 1991.
[210] On Resolution 688, see Gallant (1991) 7 Am. U.J.I.L.P.881.

concerned with a domestic jurisdiction issue within art.2(7), UN Charter.[211] The reference to art.2(7) in its preamble suggests that Resolution 688 was not made under Ch.VII so that art.2(7) applies.[212]

2. Following the adoption of Resolution 688 in April 1991 United States, United Kingdom and French land forces established, despite initial Iraqi objections, "safe havens" in northern Iraq for the Kurds, providing them with a secure place in which to live and receive food and other humanitarian assistance.[213] The coalition forces left in July 1991 and were replaced, with Iraqi consent, by UN guards. The coalition states also established "no fly zones", from which Iraqi aircraft were excluded, in Iraq north of the 38th parallel and south of the 32nd parallel in order to protect the Kurds and the Shiite/Marsh Arab population respectively from Iraqi attack. This initiative was taken further by the United States and the United Kingdom in 1999 to include pre-emptive strikes by their aircraft against Iraqi missile sites and military facilities on self defence grounds.[214]

3. Although not authorised by the Security Council, these initiatives, while criticised by Iraq and some other states as illegal, were not formally condemned by the UN. To some extent, they might be considered to fall within the "humanitarian aid" dicta in the *Nicaragua* case.[215] To the extent that they involved the presence of foreign armed forces in Iraq without the consent of its government for the protection of lives from government killings, they raise the question of humanitarian intervention in the sense understood in the above UK Policy Document. The United Kingdom was clear that they were not taken under Resolution 688, and certainly its terms do not provide for them. The United Kingdom, which had been doubtful about the legality and merits of humanitarian intervention by individual states in Foreign Office Policy Document No.148, above p.777, was prepared to recognise an evolution in the law in a case such as Iraq, by states acting through the UN or by themselves. In the course of questioning before the House of Commons Foreign Affairs Committee in 1992, Mr Aust, FCO, Legal Counsellor, gave the following answers that relate to humanitarian intervention generally and the Iraqi case in particular[216]:

"... Resolution 688, which applies not only to northern Iraq but to the whole of Iraq, was not made under Chapter VII. Resolution 688 recognized that there was a severe human rights and humanitarian situation in Iraq and, in particular, northern Iraq; but the intervention in northern Iraq 'Provide Comfort' was in fact, not specifically mandated by the United Nations, but the states taking action in northern Iraq did so in exercise of the customary international law principle of humanitarian intervention.

... the practice of states does show over a long period that it is generally accepted that in extreme circumstances a state can intervene in another state for humanitarian reasons. I think before doing so though a state would have to ask itself several questions. First of all, whether

---

[211] See e.g. China, UN Doc. S/PV 2982, p.56.

[212] On art.2(7), see below, p.827. By its terms, see Appendix I below, the domestic jurisdiction limitation in art.2(7) does not apply to Ch.VII enforcement action.

[213] On the "safe havens", see Freedman and Boren, in Rodley, ed., *To Loose the Bands of Wickedness* (1992), Ch.3; and Malanczuk (1991) 2 E.J.I.L. 114.

[214] Russia condemned these strikes as illegal: Security Council 4008th Meeting, May 21, 1999, S/PV.4008 p.2. See also China, p.4.

[215] Judgment, para.242, above, p.735. This concerned assistance to the *contras* who were fighting against the Nicaraguan Government; insofar as assistance to them by the US was not such aid, it might in the Court's view amount to the indirect use of force by the US against Nicaragua contrary to art.2(4).

[216] Parliamentary Papers, 1992–1993, HC, Paper 235–iii, pp.85, 92. See also the FCO Memorandum to the HC Foreign Affairs Committee, U.K.M.I.L. 1992, (1992) 63 B.Y.I.L. 825.

there was a compelling and an urgent situation of extreme humanitarian distress which demanded immediate relief. It would have to ask itself whether the other state was itself able or willing to meet that distress and deal with it. Also whether there was any other practical alternative to intervening in order to relieve the stress, and also whether the action could be limited in time and scope. ...

... Resolution 688 did not actually authorize it but it did recognize there was a very serious situation in Iraq, particularly in North Iraq. Most of the precedents before that relate perhaps more to intervention in order to protect one's own nationals who are being mistreated or neglected by the territorial state. But international law in this field develops to meet new situations and that is what we are seeing now in the case of Iraq."

Is the development being referred to in the above extract one that covers intervention to provide humanitarian assistance to persons who lack food, shelter, etc., only? Or does it extend also to the more familiar situation historically of large scale killings by the territorial state? Consider whether the UN actions in Bosnia and Herzegovina, Somalia and Rwanda, below, suppose UN competence to act under Chapter VII in both of the above situations too?

4. *Bosnia and Herzegovina.* Following the humanitarian action taken in Iraq, the Security Council, in the post–Cold War era, found itself able to act, despite the doubts of some of its members, for at least partly humanitarian reasons in a number of situations of internal conflict.[217] Although the facts of these situations vary, in all of them, in contrast with the Iraqi situation, the action was (i) clearly UN action, at least in the sense that named UN forces were used,[218] and (ii) taken under Chapter VII, on a generous reading of a "threat to the peace" basis for jurisdiction in art.39.[219]

The first of these cases was Bosnia and Herzegovina. Here the Security Council acted through a number of resolutions to secure the provision of humanitarian assistance and the protection of civilians during the civil war in that state and to exclude intervention in the war by Serbia and Montenegro. By Resolution 770,[220] which was adopted in August 1992, the Council:

"Recognising that the situation in Bosnia and Herzegovina constitutes a threat to international peace and security and that the provision of humanitarian assistance in Bosnia and Herze-govina is an important element in the Council's efforts to restore international peace and security. ...

Acting under Chapter VII ...

2. Calls upon states to take nationally or through regional agencies or arrangements all measures necessary to facilitate in coordination with the United Nations the delivery by relevant United Nations humanitarian organisations and others of humanitarian assistance to Sarajevo and wherever needed in other parts of Bosnia and Herzegovina ..."

By Resolution 776,[221] para.2 of Resolution 770 was eventually implemented through UNPRO-

---

[217] See Farer, in Damrosch, ed., *Enforcing Restraint: Collective Intervention in Internal Conflicts* (1993), Ch.8; and Freudenschuss (1994) 5 E.J.I.L. 492.
[218] The Somalian and Rwandan operations were dominated by the US and France respectively.
[219] See below, p.796.
[220] S.C.O.R., *Resolutions and Decisions*, 1992, p.24. Adopted by 12 votes to 0, with three abstentions (China, India, Zimbabwe).
[221] S.C.O.R., *Resolutions and Decisions*, 1992, p.33.

FOR.[222] Later Security Council resolutions, again made under Chapter VII, took matters further by authorising the United States to intercept shipping to enforce UN sanctions against the FRY[223]; establishing a no-fly zone over Bosnia and Herzegovina[224]; and establishing safe havens in Bosnia and Herzegovina for Muslims which UNPROFOR would protect.[225]

5. *Somalia*.[226] In December 1992, the UN Security Council authorised intervention to provide humanitarian assistance in the context of the civil war in Somalia.[227] By then, the fighting between the warring factions had developed to such a point that the relief agencies were being prevented from providing the humanitarian assistance urgently needed by one million or so persons facing starvation. Resolution 794 read in part[228]:

> "The Security Council ...
> Recognising the unique character of the present situation in Somalia ... Determining that the magnitude of the human tragedy caused by the conflict in Somalia, further exacerbated by the obstacles being created to the distribution of humanitarian assistance, constitutes a threat to international peace and security ...
> 10. Acting under Chapter VII[229] of the Charter of the United Nations, authorises the Secretary-General and Member states ... to use all necessary means to establish as soon as possible a secure environment for humanitarian relief operations in Somalia."

The resolution called on "all Member States which are in a position to do so to provide military forces" under the unified command of the United States. The result was the establishment of UNITAF, a multi-national force, consisting mostly of United States troops. However, although the distribution of humanitarian relief was improved, matters did not go well. In the face of armed opposition against UNITAF from the warring factions, the Security Council decided by Resolution 814[230] to establish UNOSOM II with a mandate to take enforcement action involving the forcible disarmament of all local factions, including General Aidid's forces. UNOSOM II was not under United States command, the United States withdrawing most of its forces. Following attacks by General Aidid's forces resulting in serious UNOSOM II casualties, the Security Council adopted Resolution 837[231] authorising "all necessary measures against all those responsible for the armed attacks ... to establish the effective authority of UNOSOM II throughout Somalia", including their arrest, trial and punishment. General Aidid evaded capture and, with the political situation not improving, UNOSOM II military operations were gradually scaled down, with all troops having left by the end of 1995. The Somalia case is an important precedent for UN action

---

[222] As to which, see above, p.135.

[223] Resolution 787, p.29. In 1991, an arms embargo was imposed in the territory of the former Yugoslavia generally, S.C. Resolution 713, 1991, p.42; and in 1992 sanctions were imposed against Serbia and Montenegro, S.C. Resolution 757, 1992, p.13.

[224] S.C. Resolution 816, 1993, p.4.

[225] S.C. Resolution 819, 824, 836, 844, S.C.O.R., *Resolutions and Decisions* 1993, pp.6, 8, 13, 15. Unfortunately, the safe havens were not properly protected, resulting most tragically in the massacre of nearly 8,000 Muslims by Bosnian Serbs in Srebrenica. See the Secretary General's Srebrenica Report pursuant to G.A. Resn. 53/35, UN Doc. A/54/549 (1999).

[226] See Hutchinson (1993) 34 Harv. I.L.J. 624; and Makinda, *Seeking Peace from Chaos: Humanitarian Intervention in Somalia* (1993).

[227] See further on the civil war, above, pp.93–94.

[228] S.C.O.R., *Resolutions and Decisions*, 1992, p.63. Adopted unanimously.

[229] Ed. By finding a threat to the peace and hence being able to act under Ch.VII, the Security Council avoided any limitation that might be argued for under art.2(7), Charter.

[230] S.C.O.R., *Resolutions and Decisions*, 1993, p.80.

[231] S.C.O.R., *Resolutions and Decisions*, 1993, p.83. Adopted unanimously.

under Chapter VII for the provision of humanitarian aid in a purely civil war situation in the absence of government consent, although the operation itself is generally deemed to have been largely a failure in the face of opposition by the competing warlords.

6. *Rwanda*. The Rwandan population is composed largely of members of the Hutu (85 per cent) and Tutsi tribes. Between April and July 1994, approximately half a million Tutsis were killed in genocidal acts organised by an interim government of extremist Hutus, and over a million other Tutsis fled into neighbouring states. In June 1994, the Security Council, acting under Chapter VII, adopted Resolution 929.[232] This authorised member states in co-operation with the Secretary-General and using "all necessary means" to conduct an operation with the object of (i) contributing, impartially, to the security and protection of displaced persons, refugees and civilians at risk, inter alia, by establishing secure humanitarian areas and (ii) supporting the distribution of relief supplies. To this end, UNAMIR II was established under French command and with mostly French and African personnel. UNAMIR II remained in being until 1996. The UN has been severely criticised for not acting quickly and effectively enough to prevent many of the killings.[233]

NATO INTERVENTION IN KOSOVO

Security Council, 3988th Meeting. UN Doc S/PV.3988. March, 24 1999

MR. LAVROV (RUSSIAN FEDERATION)

... Those who are involved in this unilateral use of force against the sovereign Federal Republic of Yugoslavia – carried out in violation of the Charter of the United Nations and without the authorization of the Security Council – must realize the heavy responsibility they bear for subverting the Charter and other norms of international law and for attempting to establish in the world, de facto, the primacy of force and unilateral diktat ...

Attempts to justify the NATO strikes with arguments about preventing a humanitarian catastrophe in Kosovo are completely untenable ... These attempts [are] in no way based on the Charter or other generally recognized rules of international law ... Moreover, by the terms of the definition of aggression adopted by the General Assembly in 1974,

"No consideration of whatever nature, whether political, economic, military or otherwise, may serve as a justification for aggression". (*General Assembly resolution 3314 (XXIX), annex, article 5, para.1*) ...

MR. BURLEIGH (UNITED STATES OF AMERICA)

... We and our allies... believe that such action is necessary to respond to Belgrade's brutal persecution of Kosovar Albanians, violations of international law, excessive and indiscriminate use of force, refusal to negotiate to resolve the issue peacefully and recent military build-up in Kosovo – all of which foreshadow a humanitarian catastrophe of immense proportions ...

We have begun today's action to avert this humanitarian catastrophe and to deter further aggression and repression in Kosovo ...

In this context we believe that action by NATO is justified and necessary to stop the violence and prevent an even greater humanitarian disaster ...

---

[232] S.C.O.R., *Resolutions and Decisions*, 1994, p.62. Adopted by 10 votes to 0, with five abstentions (New Zealand, China, Brazil, Pakistan and Nigeria).

[233] See Gray, above, at n.3, p.229, who suggests that "states' reluctance to play a major role in Rwanda was strongly influenced by the experience of Yugoslavia and Somalia.".

SIR JEREMY GREENSTOCK (UNITED KINGDOM):

... The action being taken is legal. It is justified as an exceptional measure to prevent an overwhelming humanitarian catastrophe. Under present circumstances in Kosovo, there is convincing evidence that such a catastrophe is imminent. Renewed acts of repression by the authorities of the Federal Republic of Yugoslavia would cause further loss of civilian life and would lead to displacement of the civilian population on a large scale and in hostile conditions.

Every means short of force has been tried to avert this situation. In these circumstances, and as an exceptional measure on grounds of overwhelming humanitarian necessity, military intervention is legally justifiable. The force now proposed is directed exclusively to averting a humanitarian catastrophe, and is the minimum judged necessary for that purpose ...

MR. DEJAMMET (FRANCE)

... In resolutions 1199 (1998) and 1203 (1998), the Security Council affirmed that the deterioration of the situation in Kosovo posed a threat to peace and security in the region. In resolution 1199 (1998), the Council demanded in particular that the Belgrade authorities immediately cease hostilities and maintain a cease-fire in Kosovo; that they take immediate steps to avert the impending humanitarian catastrophe; that they cease all action by the security forces affecting the civilian population and order the withdrawal of security units used for repression of civilians; and that they make rapid progress, in the framework of a dialogue with the Albanian community of Kosovo, towards a political solution to the problems of Kosovo ...

The [nato] actions that have been decided upon are a response to the violation by Belgrade of its international obligations, which stem in particular from the Security Council resolutions adopted under Chapter VII of the United Nations Charter. The Belgrade authorities must be persuaded that the only way to settle the crisis in Kosovo is for them to halt their military offensives in Kosovo and to accept the framework defined by the Rambouillet agreements ...

THE PRESIDENT:

I shall now make a statement in my capacity as the representative of China. Today, 24 March, the North Atlantic Treaty Organisation (NATO), with the United States in the lead, mobilized its airborne military forces and launched military strikes against the Federal Republic of Yugoslavia, seriously exacerbating the situation in the Balkan region. This act amounts to a blatant violation of the United Nations Charter and of the accepted norms of international law ...

The question of Kosovo, as an internal matter of the Federal Republic of Yugoslavia, should be resolved among the parties concerned in the Federal Republic of Yugoslavia themselves ...

It has always been our position that under the Charter it is the Security Council that bears primary responsibility for the maintenance of international peace and security. And it is only the Security Council that can determine whether a given situation threatens international peace and security and can take appropriate action. We are firmly opposed to any act that violates this principle and that challenges the authority of the Security Council.

MR. SHARMA (INDIA):

... Kosovo is recognized as part of the sovereign territory of the Federal Republic of Yugoslavia. Under the application of Article 2, paragraph 7 [UN Charter, below, App.I], the United Nations has no role in the settlement of the domestic political problems of the Federal Republic. The only exception laid down by Article 2, Paragraph 7, would be the "application of enforcement measures under Chapter VII". The attacks now taking place against the Federal Republic of Yugoslavia have not been authorized by the Council, acting under Chapter VII, and are therefore completely illegal ...

Notes

1. *NATO intervention in Kosovo.*[234] NATO military intervention in Kosovo (Operation Allied Force) was in reaction to the ill-treatment by the FRY authorities of the Albanian majority (over 90 per cent) population of Kosovo, an autonomous province within the predominantly Serbian state of the FRY.[235] This escalated with the killing of 45 civilians in the town of Racak in January 1999.[236]

    Agreements promoted by NATO for FRY withdrawal from Kosovo were negotiated at Rambouillet following this incident. When these were rejected by President Milosevic, NATO began a 78 day period of aerial bombing of targets in Belgrade and other parts of the FRY, causing extensive damage and loss of life and leading to surrender by the FRY and the withdrawal of its forces from Kosovo. NATO did not clearly state the legal basis for its military action.[237] The Security Council debated the NATO aerial bombing campaign in the FRY on March 24, 1999, the day that it began. In the above extracts, state representatives comment upon its legality. The statements above by the UK and US in the Security Council suggest that the basis was humanitarian intervention; that by France suggests that it was non-compliance with Security Council Resolutions and failure to accept the Rambouillet agreements. The NATO action was considered illegal by Russia and China, as well as by India and other members of the non-aligned movement. On March 26, 1999, a draft resolution to condemn the NATO action as a breach of art.2(4) was defeated by a large majority (12 votes to three (China, Russia and Namibia)).

2. *The Legality of Use of Force cases before the ICJ.* These were brought by the FRY (later Serbia and Montenegro) against 10 NATO members, challenging the legality of the NATO aerial bombing campaign. The FRY contested both the legality of the intervention in its domestic affairs and the proportionality of the aerial bombing that occurred. The Court held that it had no jurisdiction to hear the cases.[238]

    In the course of oral argument on the FRY's unsuccessful request for provisional measures in these cases, few arguments as to the merits were presented by the NATO states. The fullest argument was that of Belgium:

    "As regards the intervention, the Kingdom of Belgium takes the view that the Security Council's resolutions which I have just cited [resolutions 1160, 1199, 1203] provide an unchallengeable basis for the armed intervention ... But we need to go further and develop

---

[234] See Brownlie and Apperley (2000) 49 I.C.L.Q. 878; Chinkin (2000) 49 I.C.L.Q. 910; Greenwood (2000) 49 I.C.L.Q. 926; Lowe (2000) 49 I.C.L.Q. 934; Cassese (1999) 10 E.J.I.L. 23; Duursma (1999) 12 L.J.I.L. 287; Glennon, *Limits of Law, Prerogatives of Power: Intervention after Kosovo* (2001); Hippold (2001) 12 E.J.I.L. 437; Krisch (2002) 13 E.J.I.L. 323; Kritsiotis (2000) 49 I.C.L.Q. 330; Roberts (1999) 41 Survival 102; Rodley and Cali (2007) 7 H.R.L.R. 275; Simma (1999) 10 E.J.I.L. 1; and the editorial comments in (1999) 93 A.J.I.L. 824 et seq.

[235] On the background of the fighting between NLA and FRY forces, see above, p.95.

[236] The US described the situation as follows (Security Council, S/PV.3988, p.4, March 26, 1999):
"We have received disturbing reports that Federal Republic of Yugoslavia forces are using human shields, that non-combatants are being rounded up in large groups and that some are being summarily executed ...
Even today Federal Republic of Yugoslavia forces are pressing their offensive against civilians, burning and looting, and attacking Kosovar Albanian political leaders. Some 60,000 people have been forced to flee their homes since the last round of peace talks began in France, and that number is increasing daily. It stands now at more than 250,000 displaced persons – one in 10 of Kosovo's population. This is a human catastrophe."

[237] See the articles by Simma and Kritsiotis, above, at n.234. The justification would appear to have been a combination of the UK and French justifications in the Security Council, above. On NATO's perception of its changed role after the end of the Cold War, see Simma, above, pp.14–21.

[238] See, e.g. *Legality of Use of Force (Serbia and Montenegro v UK)*, I.C.J. Rep. 2004, p.1307.

the idea of armed humanitarian intervention. NATO, and the Kingdom of Belgium in parti-cular, felt obliged to intervene to forestall an ongoing humanitarian catastrophe, acknowl-edged in Security Council resolutions, [to] safeguard ... essential values which also rank as *jus cogens* ... the right to life, physical integrity, the prohibition of torture ...

Thus this is not an intervention against the territorial integrity or independence of the former Republic of Yugoslavia. The purpose of NATO's intervention is to rescue a people in peril, in deep distress. For this reason the Kingdom of Belgium takes the view that this is an armed humanitarian intervention, compatible with Article 2, paragraph 4, of the Charter, which covers only intervention against the territorial integrity or political independence of a State."

3.   From the state practice in the *NATO Intervention in Kosovo* case, it has to be deduced that it is *not* generally accepted by states that unilateral or collective humanitarian intervention that is not authorised by the UN is lawful. In the absence of consensus, such humanitarian intervention is not an exception to the prohibition of the use of armed force by states in art.2(4), UN Charter and in customary international law.[239]

4.   Note, however, that the Constitutive Act of the African Union 2002, art.4(h) provides:

"The Union shall function in accordance with the following principles...

h.   The right of the Union to intervene in a Member State pursuant to a decision of the Assembly in respect of grave circumstances, namely war crimes, genocide and crimes against humanity; ...

UNITED KINGDOM GUIDELINES ON HUMANITARIAN INTERVENTION

Speech by Mr Robin Cook, Secretary of State for Foreign and Commonwealth Affairs, 19 July 2002, U.K.M.I.L. 2000, (2000) 71 B.Y.I.L. 646

No-one can claim any longer that massive violations of humanitarian law or crimes against humanity fall solely within a state's domestic jurisdiction ...

And there is now a well-established body of international law on genocide, crimes against humanity and war crimes. The Tribunals for War Crimes in Rwanda and Yugoslavia operate in this context. So will the new International Criminal Court. They illustrate the growing international determination not to allow state sover-eignty to act as a shield for war criminals.

But it is not enough to react after the event. It is far better to prevent genocide than to punish the perpetrators after the grisly evidence and mass graves are discovered. It is not good enough to have UN Blue Helmets standing aside while acts of unspeakable cruelty are carried out. We cannot accept another Srebrenica.

Exceptional circumstances demand an exceptional response. Just such circumstances arose in Kosovo. Regrettably, the threat of veto by two of the Permanent Members made Security Council action impossible despite majority support for our cause. But, under these exceptional circumstances, we were still justified, in every respect, in intervening as we did through NATO ...

The international community is more likely to act if there are clear principles to guide us when to act. Britain has submitted to the UN Secretary–General a framework to guide intervention by the international community. Today, I want to share with you six of the principles on which we can build such a framework.

First, any intervention, by definition, is an admission of failure of prevention. We need a strengthened culture of

---

[239] Judging by the continued stand—after the failure of the draft Security Council Resolution of March 26, 1999—taken by the Non-Aligned Movement, as well as China and Russia, to the effect that *Operation Allied Force* was contrary to art.2(4), that failure would appear to have been a political decision not to condemn the NATO action, not a recognition of its legality: see Byers and Chesterman, in Holzgrefe and Keohane, above, at n.202, p.177.

conflict prevention ... We need to stop the trade in small arms, and the illicit trade in diamonds which often fuels conflict ... We need to use development policies to eliminate the causes of conflict – poverty above all. And we need to end the use of children as soldiers.

Second, we should maintain the principle that armed force should only be used as a last resort. Intervention may take many forms, including mediation, as in Cyprus, sanctions, as in Angola, observer missions, as in Georgia, and international condemnation, as in more countries than I care to mention.

Third, the immediate responsibility for halting violence rests with the state in which it occurs. Sometimes a state would like to act but cannot. Then the international community should be ready to help if asked, as we were in Sierra Leone. But other states refuse to halt the violence, or are themselves the cause of the violence – as with Milosevic's Serbia.

Fourth, when faced with an overwhelming humanitarian catastrophe, which a government has shown it is unwilling or unable to prevent or is actively promoting, the international community should intervene. Intervention in internal affairs is a sensitive issue. So there must be convincing evidence of extreme humanitarian distress on a large scale, requiring urgent relief. It must be objectively clear that there is no practicable alternative to the use of force to save lives. But we should act on the principle that a UN member state should not be able to plead its sovereign rights to shield conduct which is inconsistent with its obligations as a member of the UN. We need to strike the correct balance between the sovereign rights of states and the humanitarian right of the international community to intervene where necessary, as it was in Kosovo.

Fifth, any use of force should be proportionate to achieving the humanitarian purpose and carried out in accordance with international law. We should be sure that the scale of potential or actual human suffering justifies the dangers of military action. And it must be likely to achieve its objectives.

Sixth, any use of force should be collective. No individual country can reserve to itself the right to act on behalf of the international community. Our intervention in Kosovo was a collective decision, backed by the 19 members of NATO and unanimously by the 42 European nations which attended the Washington NATO Summit in April 1999. Our own preference would be that, wherever possible, the authority of the Security Council should be secured.

Notes

1. These guidelines[240] were triggered by the Iraq case considered above, p.778, and, particularly, by the NATO bombing of the FRY in 1999. They mark a departure in United Kingdom practice from the position taken earlier by it in the FCO Policy Document No.148, above, p.777, and go as far as any state would appear to have gone in accepting that humanitarian intervention may be lawful. Among NATO states, it is noticeable that the US and Germany are both on record as regarding the Kosovo case as exceptional[241] and no other state, except for Belgium,[242] has formulated a general right of humanitarian intervention.

2. For humanitarian intervention to be lawful in accordance with the *Guidelines*, the six principles listed in them must be respected. As these principles indicate, the claimed right is limited to collective action by more than one state, though not necessarily subject to UN authorisation, express or implied.

----

[240] See also the statement by Lord Malloch-Brown, FCO Minister, *Hansard*, HL, Vol.696, col.626–630 (November 15, 2007); (2007) 68 B.Y.I.L. 843.

[241] See Simma, above, at n.234, at p.13 (Germany); and Byers and Chesterman, above, at n.239, p.99.

[242] See the Belgian position in the *Legality of Use of Force case*, above, p.784.

E. Responsibility to Protect[243]

The concept of "responsibility to protect" has recently been formulated as a response to the problem of "humanitarian catastrophes". In their 2004 Report, the Secretary General's High Level Panel[244] stated:

"201. The successive humanitarian disasters in Somalia, Bosnia and Herzegovina, Rwanda, Kosovo and now Darfur, Sudan have concentrated attention not on the immunities of sovereign Governments but their responsibilities, both to their own people and to the wider international community. There is a growing recognition that the issue is not the 'right to intervene' of any State, but the 'responsibility to protect' of *every* State when it comes to people suffering from avoidable catastrophe—mass murder and rape, ethnic cleansing by forcible expulsion and terror, and deliberate starvation and exposure to disease. And there is a growing acceptance that while sovereign Governments have the primary responsibility to protect their own citizens from such catastrophes, when they are unable to unwilling to do so that responsibility should be taken up by the wider international community—with it spanning a continuum involving prevention, response to violence, if necessary, rebuilding shattered societies. The primary focus should be on assisting the cessation of violence through mediation and other tools and the protection of people through such measures as the dispatch of humanitarian, human rights and police missions. Force, if it needs to be used, should be deployed as a last resort.

202. The Security Council. . .and the wider international community have come to accept that, under Chapter VII and in pursuit of the emerging norm of a collective international responsibility to protect, it can always authorize military action to redress catastrophic internal wrongs if it is prepared to declare that the situation is a 'threat to international peace and security', not especially difficult when breaches of international law are involved."

The concept of "responsibility to protect" was then inserted in General Assembly Resolution 61/1 (2005): World Summit Outcome as follows:

"138. Each individual State has the responsibility to protect its populations from genocide, war crimes, ethnic cleansing and crimes against humanity. This responsibility entails the prevention of such crimes, including their incitement, through appropriate and necessary means. . . .

139. The international community, through the United Nations, also has the responsibility to use appropriate diplomatic, humanitarian and other peaceful means, in accordance with Chapters VI and VIII of the Charter, to help to protect populations from genocide, war crimes, ethnic cleansing and crimes against humanity. In this context we are prepared to take collective action, in a timely and decisive manner, through the Security Council, in accordance with the Charter, including Chapter VII, on a case-by-case basis and in cooperation with relevant regional organizations as appropriate, should peaceful means be inadequate and national authorities are manifestly failing to protect their populations from genocide, war crimes, ethnic cleansing and crimes against humanity . . ."

---

[243] See Amerasinghe (2006) 3 Int. Org. L.R. 7; Evans (2004) 98 A.S.I.L. Proc. 37; Molier (2006) 53 N.I.L.R. 37; Stahn (2007) 101 A.J.I.L. 99.

[244] *A More Secure World: Our Shared Responsibility*, Report of the Secretary General's High Level Panel on Threats, Challenges and Change (2004). The concept originated in *The Responsibility to Protect* (2001), a report by the International Commission on Intervention and State Sovereignty (a private group) and later taken up in the UN Secretary General's Report, *In Larger Freedom: Towards Development, Security and Human Rights for All*, A/59/.2005. None of these documents are state practice.

The High Level Panel's Report refers to "an emerging norm of a collective responsibility to protect", but General Assembly Resolution 60/1 contains no comparable wording that might be indicative of any intention by states to formulate customary international law. As yet at least, it would seem that the "responsibility to protect" involves a political rather than a legal undertaking. How does it compare with "humanitarian intervention"? Is it limited to collective intervention by force under Chapters VI or VII of the UN Charter, or does it also envisage unilateral or collective use of force without UN authorisation? Is there a duty, not a power, to act? How does the "responsibility to protect" differ from the duty in art.41 of the I.L.C. Draft Articles on the Responsibility of States for Internationally Wrongful Act "to co-operate" to bring to an end a "serious breach" of a peremptory norm?[245]

F. Legality of Nuclear Weapons[246]

LEGALITY OF THE THREAT OR USE OF NUCLEAR WEAPONS CASE

Advisory Opinion. I.C.J. Rep. 1996, p.226

By G.A. Resolution 49/75K, the UN General Assembly requested an opinion on the following question: "Is the threat or use of nuclear weapons in any circumstances permitted under international law?" After ruling that it had jurisdiction to give the opinion, see below, p.875, the Court responded as follows:

Opinion of the Court

36. ... in order correctly to apply to the present case the Charter law on the use of force and the law applicable in armed conflict, in particular humanitarian law, it is imperative for the Court to take account of the unique characteristics of nuclear weapons, and in particular their destructive capacity, their capacity to cause untold human suffering, and their ability to cause damage to generations to come.

38. The ... prohibition of the use of force [in Article 2(4)] is to be considered in the light of other relevant provisions of the Charter. In Article 51, the Charter recognizes the inherent right of individual or collective self-defence if an armed attack occurs. A further lawful use of force is envisaged in Article 42, whereby the Security Council may take military enforcement measures in conformity with Chapter VII of the Charter.

39. These provisions do not refer to specific weapons. They apply to any use of force, regardless of the weapons employed. The Charter neither expressly prohibits, nor permits, the use of any specific weapon, including nuclear weapons. A weapon that is already unlawful per se, whether by treaty or custom, does not become lawful by reason of its being used for a legitimate purpose under the Charter.

40. The entitlement to resort to self-defence under Article 51 is subject to certain constraints. Some of these constraints are inherent in the very concept of self defence. Other requirements are specified in Article 51.

41. The submission of the exercise of the right of self-defence to the conditions of necessity and proportionality is a rule of customary international law. As the Court stated in the [Nicaragua case, para.176, above, p.727] ...: "there is a specific rule whereby self-defence would warrant only measures which are proportional to the armed attack and necessary to respond to it, a rule well established in customary international law". This dual condition applies equally to Article 51 of the Charter, whatever the means of force employed.

42. The proportionality principle may thus not in itself exclude the use of nuclear weapons in self-defence in all circumstances. But at the same time, a use of force that is proportionate under the law of self-defence, must, in order to be lawful, also meet the requirements of the law applicable in armed conflict which comprise in particular the principles and rules of humanitarian law.

43. Certain States have in their written and oral pleadings suggested that ... the very nature of nuclear weapons, and the high probability of an escalation of nuclear exchanges, mean that there is an extremely strong

[245] See above, p.452.
[246] On the Advisory Opinion, see Bekker (1997) 91 A.J.I.L. 126; Clark (1996) 7 Crim. L.F. 265; Falk (1997) 91 A.J.I.L. 64. See earlier, Green (1988–1989) 17 Den. J.I.L.P.1; Pogany, ed., Nuclear Weapons and International Law (1987); Schwarzenberger, The Legality of Nuclear Weapons (1958); Weston (1983) 28 McGill L.J. 542.

risk of devastation. The risk factor is said to negate the possibility of the condition of proportionality being complied with. The Court does not find it necessary to embark upon the quantification of such risks; nor does it need to enquire into the question whether tactical nuclear weapons exist which are sufficiently precise to limit those risks: it suffices for the Court to note that the very nature of all nuclear weapons and the profound risks associated therewith are further considerations to be borne in mind by States believing they can exercise a nuclear response in self-defence in accordance with the requirements of proportionality. . . .

46. Certain States asserted that the use of nuclear weapons in the conduct of reprisals would be lawful. The Court does not have to examine, in this context, the question of armed reprisals in time of peace, which are considered to be unlawful. Nor does it have to pronounce on the question of belligerent reprisals save to observe that in any case any right of recourse to such reprisals would, like self-defence, be governed inter alia by the principle of proportionality.

47. In order to lessen or eliminate the risk of unlawful attack, States sometimes signal that they possess certain weapons to use in self-defence against any State violating their territorial integrity or political independence. Whether a signalled intention to use force if certain events occur is or is not a "threat" within Article 2, paragraph 4, of the Charter depends upon various factors. If the envisaged use of force is itself unlawful, the stated readiness to use it would be a threat prohibited under Article 2, paragraph 4. Thus it would be illegal for a State to threaten force to secure territory from another State, or to cause it to follow or not follow certain political or economic paths. The notions of "threat" and "use" of force under Article 2, paragraph 4, of the Charter stand together in the sense that if the use of force itself in a given case is illegal—for whatever reason—the threat to use such force will likewise be illegal. In short, if it is to be lawful, the declared readiness of a State to use force must be a use of force that is in conformity with the Charter. For the rest, no State—whether or not it defended the policy of deterrence—suggested to the Court that it would be lawful to threaten to use force if the use of force contemplated would be illegal.

48. Some States put forward the argument that possession of nuclear weapons is itself an unlawful threat to use force. Possession of nuclear weapons may indeed justify an inference of preparedness to use them. In order to be effective, the policy of deterrence, by which those States possessing or under the umbrella of nuclear weapons seek to discourage military aggression by demonstrating that it will serve no purpose, necessitates that the intention to use nuclear weapons be credible. Whether this is a "threat" contrary to Article 2, paragraph 4, depends upon whether the particular use of force envisaged would be directed against the territorial integrity or political independence of a State, or against the Purposes of the United Nations or whether, in the event that it were intended as a means of defence, it would necessarily violate the principles of necessity and proportionality. In any of these circumstances the use of force, and the threat to use it, would be unlawful under the law of the Charter.

49. Moreover, the Security Council may take enforcement measures under Chapter VII of the Charter. From the statements presented to it the Court does not consider it necessary to address questions which might, in a given case, arise from the application of Chapter VII.

50. The terms of the question put to the Court by the General Assembly in resolution 49/75K could in principle also cover a threat or use of nuclear weapons by a State within its own boundaries. However, this particular aspect has not been dealt with by any of the States which addressed the Court orally or in writing in these proceedings. The Court finds that it is not called upon to deal with an internal use of nuclear weapons.

51. Having dealt with the Charter provisions relating to the threat or use of force, the Court will now turn to the law applicable in situations of armed conflict. It will first address the question whether there are specific rules in international law regulating the legality or illegality of recourse to nuclear weapons per se; it will then examine the question put to it in the light of the law applicable in armed conflict proper, i.e. the principles and rules of humanitarian law applicable in armed conflict, and the law of neutrality.

52. The Court notes by way of introduction that international customary and treaty law does not contain any specific prescription authorizing the threat or use of nuclear weapons or any other weapon in general or in certain circumstances, in particular those of the exercise of legitimate self-defence. Nor, however, is there any principle or rule of international law which would make the legality of the threat or use of nuclear weapons or of any other weapons dependent on a specific authorization. State practice shows that the illegality of the use of certain weapons as such does not result from an absence of authorization but, on the contrary, is formulated in terms of prohibition.

53. The Court must therefore now examine whether there is any prohibition of recourse to nuclear weapons as such; it will first ascertain whether there is a conventional prescription to this effect . . .

57. The pattern until now has been for weapons of mass destruction to be declared illegal by specific instruments. The most recent such instruments are the Convention of 10 April 1972 on the Prohibition of the

Development, Production and Stockpiling of Bacteriological (Biological) and Toxic Weapons and on their Destruction[247]—which prohibits the possession of bacteriological and toxic weapons and reinforces the prohibition of their use—and the Convention of 13 January 1993 on the Prohibition of the Development, Production, Stockpiling and Use of Chemical Weapons and on Their Destruction[248]—which prohibits all use of chemical weapons and requires the destruction of existing stocks. Each of these instruments has been negotiated and adopted in its own context and for its own reasons. The Court does not find any specific prohibition of recourse to nuclear weapons in treaties expressly prohibiting the use of certain weapons of mass destruction.

58. In the last two decades, a great many negotiations have been conducted regarding nuclear weapons; they have not resulted in a treaty of general prohibition of the same kind as for bacteriological and chemical weapons. However, a number of specific treaties have been concluded in order to limit:

(a) the acquisition, manufacture and possession of nuclear weapons.[249] ...

(b) the deployment of nuclear weapons.[250] ...

(c) the testing of nuclear weapons.[251] ...

59. Recourse to nuclear weapons is directly addressed by two of these Conventions [the Tlatelolco and Rarotonga Treaties] and also in connection with the indefinite extension of the Treaty on the Non-Proliferation of Nuclear Weapons of 1968[252] ...

62. The Court notes that the treaties dealing exclusively with acquisition, manufacture, possession, deployment and testing of nuclear weapons, without specifically addressing their threat or use, certainly point to an increasing concern in the international community with these weapons; the Court concludes from this that these treaties could therefore be seen as foreshadowing a future general prohibition of the use of such weapons, but they do not constitute such a prohibition by themselves. As to the treaties of Tlatelolco and Rarotonga and their Protocols, and also the declarations made in connection with the indefinite extension of the Treaty on the Non-Proliferation of Nuclear Weapons, it emerges from these instruments that:

(a) a number of States have undertaken not to use nuclear weapons in specific zones (Latin America; the South Pacific) or against certain other States (non-nuclear-weapon States which are parties to the Treaty on the Non-Proliferation of Nuclear Weapons);

(b) nevertheless, even within this framework, the nuclear-weapon States have reserved the right to use nuclear weapons in certain circumstances; and

(c) these reservations met with no objection from the parties to the Tlatelolco or Rarotonga Treaties or from the Security Council.

63. These two treaties, the security assurances given in 1995 by the nuclear-weapon States and the fact that the Security Council took note of them with satisfaction, testify to a growing awareness of the need to liberate the community of States and the international public from the dangers resulting from the existence of nuclear weapons. The Court moreover notes the signing, even more recently, on 15 December 1995, at Bangkok, of a Treaty on the Southeast Asia Nuclear-Weapon-Free Zone, and on 11 April 1996, at Cairo, of a treaty on the creation of a nuclear-weapons-free zone in Africa. It does not, however, view these elements as amounting to a comprehensive and universal conventional prohibition on the use, or the threat of use, of those weapons as such.

64. The Court will now turn to an examination of customary international law to determine whether a prohibition of the threat or use of nuclear weapons as such flows from that source of law. As the Court has stated, the substance of that law must be "looked for primarily in the actual practice and *opinio juris* of States" (*Continental Shelf (Libyan Arab Jamahiriya/Malta), Judgment, I.C.J. Reports 1985*, p.29, para.27).

---

[247] Ed. 1015 U.N.T.S. 163; (1976) U.K.T.S. 11, Cmnd. 6397.

[248] Ed. Misc. 21 (1993), Cm. 2331; (1993) 32 I.L.M. 800.

[249] Ed. The Court cited, inter alia, the Tlatelolco Treaty, 634 U.N.T.S. 326; (1970) U.K.T.S. 54, Cmnd. 4409; the Rarotonga Treaty (1985) 24 I.L.M. 1442; and the 1990 German Settlement Treaty, (1991) U.K.T.S. 88, Cm. 1756; (1990) 29 I.L.M. 1186. The first two of these made Latin America and the South Pacific respectively nuclear free zones.

[250] Ed. The Court cited, inter alia, the Tlatelolco and Rarotonga Treaties, above, and the Antarctica Treaty, above, p.198.

[251] Ed. The Court cited, inter alia, the Tlatelolco and Rarotonga Treaties, above, and the Nuclear Test Ban Treaty, U.K.T.S. 3 (1964), Cmnd. 2245; 480 U.N.T.S. 43.

[252] Ed. 788 U.N.T.S. 169; (1970) U.K.T.S. 96, Cmnd. 4503.

65. States which hold the view that the use of nuclear weapons is illegal ... refer to a consistent practice of non-utilization of nuclear weapons by States since 1945 and they would see in that practice the expression of an *opinio juris* on the part of those who possess such weapons.

66. Some other States, which assert the legality of the threat and use of nuclear weapons in certain circumstances, invoked the doctrine and practice of deterrence in support of their argument. They recall that they have always, in concert with certain other States, reserved the right to use those weapons in the exercise of the right to self-defence against an armed attack threatening their vital security interests. In their view, if nuclear weapons have not been used since 1945, it is not on account of an existing or nascent custom but merely because circumstances that might justify their use have fortunately not arisen.

67. The Court does not intend to pronounce here upon the practice known as the "policy of deterrence". It notes that it is a fact that a number of States adhered to that practice during the greater part of the Cold War and continue to adhere to it. Furthermore, the Members of the international community are profoundly divided on the matter of whether non-recourse to nuclear weapons over the past fifty years constitutes the expression of an *opinio juris*. Under these circumstances the Court does not consider itself able to find that there is such an *opinio juris* ...

70. The Court notes that General Assembly resolutions, even if they are not binding, may sometimes have normative value. They can, in certain circumstances, provide evidence important for establishing the existence of a rule or the emergence of an *opinio juris*. To establish whether this is true of a given General Assembly resolution, it is necessary to look at its content and the conditions of its adoption; it is also necessary to see whether an *opinio juris* exists as to its normative character. Or a series of resolutions may show the gradual evolution of the *opinio juris* required for the establishment of a new rule.

71. Examined in their totality, the General Assembly resolutions put before the Court declare that the use of nuclear weapons would be "a direct violation of the Charter of the United Nations"; and in certain formulations that such use "should be prohibited". The focus of these resolutions has sometimes shifted to diverse related matters; however, several of the resolutions under consideration in the present case have been adopted with substantial numbers of negative votes and abstentions; thus, although those resolutions are a clear sign of deep concern regarding the problem of nuclear weapons, they still fall short of establishing the existence of an *opinio juris* on the illegality of the use of such weapons.

72. The Court further notes that the first of the resolutions of the General Assembly expressly proclaiming the illegality of the use of nuclear weapons, resolution 1653 (XVI) of 24 November 1961 (mentioned in subsequent resolutions), after referring to certain international declarations and binding agreements, from the Declaration of St. Petersburg of 1868 to the Geneva Protocol of 1925, proceeded to qualify the legal nature of nuclear weapons, determine their effects, and apply general rules of customary international law to nuclear weapons in particular. That application by the General Assembly of general rules of customary law to the particular case of nuclear weapons indicates that, in its view, there was no specific rule of customary law which prohibited the use of nuclear weapons; if such a rule had existed, the General Assembly could simply have referred to it and would not have needed to undertake such an exercise of legal qualification.

73. Having said this, the Court points out that the adoption each year by the General Assembly, by a large majority, of resolutions recalling the content of resolution 1653 (XVI), and requesting the member States to conclude a convention prohibiting the use of nuclear weapons in any circumstance, reveals the desire of a very large section of the international community to take, by a specific and express prohibition of the use of nuclear weapons, a significant step forward along the road to complete nuclear disarmament. The emergence, as *lex lata*, of a customary rule specifically prohibiting the use of nuclear weapons as such is hampered by the continuing tensions between the nascent *opinio juris* on the one hand, and the still strong adherence to the practice of deterrence on the other.

The Court then considered whether the use of nuclear weapons was consistent with international humanitarian law and the law of neutrality.

90. Although the applicability of the principles and rules of humanitarian law and of the principle of neutrality to nuclear weapons is hardly disputed, the conclusions to be drawn from this applicability are, on the other hand, controversial.

91. According to one point of view, the fact that recourse to nuclear weapons is subject to and regulated by the law of armed conflict does not necessarily mean that such recourse is as such prohibited. As one State put it to the Court: ...

the legality of the use of nuclear weapons must therefore be assessed in the light of the applicable principles of international law regarding the use of force and the conduct of hostilities, as is the case with other methods and means of warfare (United Kingdom, Written Statement, p.75, para.4.2(3)); and

The reality ... is that nuclear weapons might be used in a wide variety of circumstances with very different results in terms of likely civilian casualties. In some cases, such as the use of a low yield nuclear weapon against warships on the High Seas or troops in sparsely populated areas, it is possible to envisage a nuclear attack which caused comparatively few civilian casualties. It is by no means the case that every use of nuclear weapons against a military objective would inevitably cause very great collateral civilian casualties. (United Kingdom, Written Statement, p.53, para.3.70; see also United States of America, Oral Statement, CR 95/34, pp.89–90.)

92. Another view holds that recourse to nuclear weapons could never be compatible with the principles and rules of humanitarian law and is therefore prohibited. In the event of their use, nuclear weapons would in all circumstances be unable to draw any distinction between the civilian population and combatants, or between civilian objects and military objectives, and their effects, largely uncontrollable, could not be restricted, either in time or in space, to lawful military targets. Such weapons would kill and destroy in a necessarily indiscriminate manner, on account of the blast, heat and radiation occasioned by the nuclear explosion and the effects induced; and the number of casualties which would ensue would be enormous. The use of nuclear weapons would therefore be prohibited in any circumstance, notwithstanding the absence of any explicit conventional prohibition. That view lay at the basis of the assertions by certain States before the Court that nuclear weapons are by their nature illegal under customary international law, by virtue of the fundamental principle of humanity. ...

94. The Court would observe that none of the States advocating the legality of the use of nuclear weapons under certain circumstances, including the "clean" use of smaller, low yield, tactical nuclear weapons, has indicated what, supposing such limited use were feasible, would be the precise circumstances justifying such use; nor whether such limited use would not tend to escalate into the all-out use of high yield nuclear weapons. This being so, the Court does not consider that it has a sufficient basis for a determination on the validity of this view.

95. Nor can the Court make a determination on the validity of the view that the recourse to nuclear weapons would be illegal in any circumstance owing to their inherent and total incompatibility with the law applicable in armed conflict. Certainly, as the Court has already indicated, the principles and rules of law applicable in armed conflict—at the heart of which is the overriding consideration of humanity—make the conduct of armed hostilities subject to a number of strict requirements. Thus, methods and means of warfare, which would preclude any distinction between civilian and military targets, or which would result in unnecessary suffering to combatants are prohibited. In view of the unique characteristics of nuclear weapons, to which the Court has referred above, the use of such weapons in fact seems scarcely reconcilable with respect for such requirements. Nevertheless, the Court considers that it does not have sufficient elements to enable it to conclude with certainty that the use of nuclear weapons would necessarily be at variance with the principles and rules of law applicable in armed conflict in any circumstance.

96. Furthermore, the Court cannot lose sight of the fundamental right of every State to survival, and thus its right to resort to self-defence, in accordance with Article 51 of the Charter, when its survival is at stake.

Nor can it ignore the practice referred to as "policy of deterrence", to which an appreciable section of the international community adhered for many years. The Court also notes the reservations which certain nuclear-weapon States have appended to the undertakings they have given, notably under the Protocols to the Treaties of Tlatelolco and Rarotonga, and also under the declarations made by them in connection with the extension of the Treaty on the Non-Proliferation of Nuclear Weapons, not to resort to such weapons.

97. Accordingly, in view of the present state of international law viewed as a whole, as examined above by the Court, and of the elements of fact at its disposal, the Court is led to observe that it cannot reach a definitive conclusion as to the legality or illegality of the use of nuclear weapons by a State in an extreme circumstance of self-defence, in which its very survival would be at stake.

98. ... international law, and with it the stability of the international order which it is intended to govern, are bound to suffer from the continuing difference of views with regard to the legal status of weapons as deadly as nuclear weapons. It is consequently important to put an end to this state of affairs: the long-promised complete nuclear disarmament appears to be the most appropriate means of achieving that result. ...

99. In these circumstances, the Court appreciates the full importance of the recognition by Article VI of the Treaty on the Non-Proliferation of Nuclear Weapons of an obligation to negotiate in good faith a nuclear disarmament. The legal import of that obligation goes beyond that of a mere obligation of conduct; the

obligation involved here is an obligation to achieve a precise result—nuclear disarmament in all its aspects—by adopting a particular course of conduct, namely, the pursuit of negotiations on the matter in good faith.

100. ... In the view of the Court, [its fulfilment] remains without any doubt an objective of vital importance to the whole of the international community today. ...

105. For these reasons,

THE COURT ...

(2) *Replies* in the following manner to the question put by the General Assembly:

A. Unanimously,

There is in neither customary nor conventional international law any specific authorization of the threat or use of nuclear weapons;

B. By eleven votes to three,[253]

There is in neither customary nor conventional international law any comprehensive and universal prohibition of the threat or use of nuclear weapons as such; ...

C. Unanimously,

A threat or use of force by means of nuclear weapons that is contrary to Article 2, paragraph 4, of the United Nations Charter and that fails to meet all the requirements of Article 51 is unlawful;

D. Unanimously,

A threat or use of nuclear weapons should also be compatible with the requirements of the international law applicable in armed conflict, particularly those of the principles and rules of international humanitarian law, as well as with specific obligations under treaties and other undertakings which expressly deal with nuclear weapons;

E. By seven votes to seven, by the President's casting vote,[254]

It follows from the above-mentioned requirements that the threat or use of nuclear weapons would generally be contrary to the rules of international law applicable in armed conflict, and in particular the principles and rules of humanitarian law;

However, in view of the current state of international law, and of the elements of fact at its disposal, the Court cannot conclude definitively whether the threat or use of nuclear weapons would be lawful or unlawful in an extreme circumstance of self-defence, in which the very survival of a State would be at stake;

F. Unanimously,

There exists an obligation to pursue in good faith and bring to a conclusion negotiations leading to nuclear disarmament in all its aspects under strict and effective international control.

Dissenting Opinion of Judge Higgins

7. I have not been able to vote for these findings [in para.2E of the *dispositif*] for several reasons. It is an essential requirement of the judicial process that a court should show the steps by which it reaches its conclusions. I believe the Court has not done so in respect of the first part of paragraph 2E. The findings in a judicial *dispositif* should be clear. I believe paragraph 2E is unclear in its meaning (and one may suspect that this lack of

---

[253] Judges Shahabuddeen, Weeramantry and Koroma dissented.

[254] In favour: President Bedjaoui; Judges Ranjeva, Herczegh, Shi, Fleischhauer, Vereschetin, Ferrari Bravo. Against: Vice-President Schwebel; Judges Oda, Guillaume, Shahabuddeen, Weeramantry, Koroma, Higgins.

clarity is perhaps regarded as a virtue). I greatly regret the *non liquet* offered in the second part of paragraph 2E. ...

8. After finding that the threat or use of nuclear weapons is not prohibited *per se* by reference to the Charter or treaty law, the Court moves to see if it is prohibited *per se* by reference to the law of armed conflict (and especially humanitarian law).

9. It is not sufficient, to answer the question put to it, for the Court merely briefly to state the requirements of the law of armed conflict (including humanitarian law) and then simply to move to the conclusion that the threat or use of nuclear weapons is generally unlawful by reference to these principles and norms. The Court limits itself to affirming that the principles and rules of humanitarian law apply to nuclear weapons. It finds in paragraph 95, by reference to "the unique characteristics of nuclear weapons", that their use is "scarcely reconcilable" with the requirements of humanitarian law and "would generally be contrary" to humanitarian law (*dispositif*, para.2E). At no point in its Opinion does the Court engage in the task that is surely at the heart of the question asked: the systematic application of the relevant law to the use or threat of nuclear weapons. It reaches its conclusions without the benefit of detailed analysis. An essential step in the judicial process–that of legal reasoning—has been omitted. ...

25. I do not consider it juridically meaningful to say that the use of nuclear weapons is "generally contrary to the rules of international law applicable in armed conflict, and in particular the principles and rules of humanitarian law". What does the term "generally" mean? Is it a numerical allusion, or is it a reference to different types of nuclear weapons, or is it a suggestion that the rules of humanitarian law cannot be met save for exceptions? If so, where is the Court's analysis of these rules, properly understood, and their application to nuclear weapons? And what are any exceptions to be read into the term "generally"? Are they to be linked to an exceptional ability to comply with humanitarian law? Or does the term "generally", especially in the light of paragraph 96, suggest that if a use of nuclear weapons in extreme circumstances of self-defence were lawful, that might *of itself* exceptionally make such a use compatible with the humanitarian law? The phraseology of paragraph 2E of the *dispositif* raises all these questions and answers none of them. ...

27. The meaning of the second sentence of paragraph 2E of the *dispositif*, and thus what the two sentences of paragraph 2E of the *dispositif* mean when taken together, is unclear. The second sentence is presumably not referring to self-defence in those exceptional circumstances, implied by the word "generally", that might allow a threat or use of nuclear weapons to be compatible with humanitarian law. If, as the Court has indicated in paragraph 42 (and operative paragraph 2C), the Charter law does not *per se* make a use of nuclear weapons illegal, and if a specific use complied with the provisions of Article 51 *and* was also compatible with humanitarian law, the Court can hardly be saying in the second sentence of paragraph 2E that it knows not whether such a use would be lawful or unlawful.

28. Therefore it seems the Court is addressing the "general" circumstances that it envisages—namely that a threat or use of nuclear weapons violates humanitarian law—and that it is addressing whether in *those* circumstances a use of force *in extremis* and in conformity with Article 51 of the Charter, might nonetheless be regarded as be lawful, or not. The Court answers that it does not know.

29. What the Court has done is reach a conclusion of "incompatibility in general" with humanitarian law; and then effectively pronounce a *non liquet* on whether a use of nuclear weapons in self-defence when the survival of a State is at issue might still be lawful, even were the particular use to be contrary to humanitarian law. Through this formula of non-pronouncement the Court necessarily leaves open the possibility that a use of nuclear weapons contrary to humanitarian law might nonetheless be lawful. This goes beyond anything that was claimed by the nuclear weapons States appearing before the Court, who fully accepted that any lawful threat or use of nuclear weapons would have to comply with both the *jus ad bellum* and the *jus in bello* (see para.86). ...

32. Can the reference to "the current state of international law" [in para.2E] possibly refer to humanitarian law? ... [H]umanitarian law ... is very well-developed. The fact that its principles are broadly stated and often raise further questions that require a response can be no ground for a *non liquet*. It is exactly the judicial function to take principles of general application, to elaborate their meaning and to apply them to specific situations. This is precisely the role of the International Court, whether in contentious proceedings or in its advisory function.

33. Perhaps the reference to "the current state of international law" is a reference to perceived tensions between the widespread acceptance of the possession of nuclear weapons (and thus, it may be presumed, of the legality of their use in certain circumstances) as mentioned by the Court in paragraphs 67 and 96 on the one hand, and the requirements of humanitarian law on the other. If so, I believe this to be a false dichotomy. The pursuit of deterrence, the shielding under the nuclear umbrella, the silent acceptance of reservations and declarations by the nuclear powers to treaties prohibiting the use of nuclear weapons in certain regions, the seeking of possible security assurances—all this points to a significant international practice which is surely

relevant not only to the law of self-defence but also to humanitarian law. If a substantial number of States in the international community believe that the use of nuclear weapons might *in extremis* be compatible with their duties under the Charter (whether as nuclear powers or as beneficiaries of "the umbrella" or security assurances) they presumably *also* believe that they would not be violating their duties under humanitarian law.

34. Nothing in relevant statements made suggests that those States giving nuclear assurances or receiving them believed that they would be violating humanitarian law,—but decided nonetheless to act in disregard of such violation. In sum, such weight as may be given to the State practice just referred to has a relevance for our understanding of the complex provisions of humanitarian law as much as for the provisions of the Charter law of self-defence.

35. For all of these reasons, I am unable to see why the Court resorts to the answer it does in the second part of paragraph 2E of the *dispositif*.

36. It is also, I think, an important and well-established principle that the concept of *non liquet*—for that is what we have here—is no part of the Court's jurisprudence. . . .

38. This unwelcome formulation ignores sixty-five years of proud judicial history and also the convictions of those who went before us. Former President of the International Court, Judge Elias, reminds us that there are what he terms "useful devices" to assist if there are difficulties in applying the usual sources of international law. In his view these "preclude the Court from pleading *non liquet* in any given case" (Elias, *The International Court of Justice and Some Contemporary Problems*. 1983, p.14).

39. The learned editors of the 9th Edition of *Oppenheim's International Law* remind us:

> there is [not] always a clear and specific legal rule readily applicable to every international situation, but that every international situation is capable of being determined *as a matter of law* (Jennings and Watts, Vol.1, p.13). . . .

41 . . . The judicial lodestar, whether in difficult questions of interpretation of humanitarian law, or in resolving claimed tensions between competing norms, must be those values that international law seeks to promote and protect. In the present case, it is the physical survival of peoples that we must constantly have in view. We live in a decentralized world order, in which some States are known to possess nuclear weapons but choose to remain outside of the non-proliferation treaty system; while other such non-parties have declared their intention to obtain nuclear weapons; and yet other States are believed clandestinely to possess, or to be working shortly to possess nuclear weapons (some of whom indeed may be party to the NPT). It is not clear to me that either a pronouncement of illegality in all circumstances of the use of nuclear weapons or the answers formulated by the Court in paragraph 2E best serve to protect mankind against that unimaginable suffering that we all fear.

Notes

1. Was it an abdication of responsibility for the Court not to express an opinion (see para.2E, *dispositif*) on the question whether the threat or use of nuclear weapons "would be lawful or unlawful in an extreme circumstance of self-defence"? If the leading world powers take the view, as they do, that they may lawfully use nuclear weapons in self-defence as a last resort, can this be contrary to customary international law? Nuclear weapons were used at Hiroshima, inter alia, to bring the Second World War with Japan to an end without the loss of military lives that further conventional armed force would entail. Would such a use now be illegal?

2. The request for the above advisory opinion by the UN General Assembly had been preceded by a similar request for an advisory opinion by the General Assembly of the World Health Organi-sation (WHO). The Court declined to give an opinion in respect of the WHO request for jur-isdictional reasons: see below, p.877.

3. COLLECTIVE MEASURES THROUGH THE UNITED NATIONS[255]

A. Introductory Note

Under art.2(4), United Nations Charter, states renounced their unilateral right to resort to armed force by way of reprisal against other states who used illegal armed force against them. In place of such unilateral action, provision was made for collective action through the United Nations. This may occur through the Security Council under Chapters VI and VII, United Nationals Charter, which provide for the investigation of disputes or situations and recommendations for the settlement of disputes, etc. (Chapter VI) and for enforcement action (Chapter VII) respectively.

B. Action Under Chapter VI

See Chapter VI, arts 33–38, United Nations Charter, below Appendix I.

Note

Under Chapter VI of the Charter, the Security Council may investigate any dispute or situation that may endanger international peace and security (art.34). It may, under art.36, recommend appropriate procedures or methods of adjustment of disputes, particularly those listed in art.33 (e.g. conciliation or resort to the ICJ). It may also make its own recommendations for the settlement of a dispute in accordance with arts 37 or 38. The Security Council may make recommendations only when acting under Chapter VI; legally binding decisions may only be made under Chapter VII. Action taken under Chapter VI is subject to the domestic jurisdiction limitation in art.2(7), UN Charter, see below, p.826; enforcement measures under Chapter VII are not. Disputes or situations may be referred to the Council under Chapter VI by a state or states in accordance with the terms of arts 35 and 37.[256]

C. Security Council Action under Chapter VII: Jurisdiction[257]

See Article 39, United Nations Charter, below, Appendix I.

SIMMA, THE CHARTER OF THE UNITED NATIONS: A COMMENTARY

2nd edn 2002, Vol.1, pp.722–726. Some footnotes omitted

The broadest and most indistinct concept in art.39, although certainly crucial for the maintenance of peace, is that of threat to the peace. In practice, it is almost the only one used by the SC, whereas the existence of breaches of the peace or acts of aggression is usually not specifically determined, even if obvious ...

While the concept of threat to the peace in art.39 may have originally referred mainly to threats of inter-state conflicts ..., the SC soon abandoned such a strict reading. Already the Palestine Conflict in 1948 was no clear-cut inter-state war, but the SC did not hesitate to regard it as a threat to the peace ... Likewise, in 1961, the SC determined a threat to the peace with respect to the conflict in Congo, which was predominantly internal in character.[258] After the end of the Cold War, however, the SC significantly reinforced such a broader inter-pretation and it seems by now widely accepted that extreme violence within a state can give rise to Chapter VII

---

[255] See Bailey and Daws, *The Procedure of the United Nations Security Council* (3rd edn 1998); Sarooshi, *The United Nations and the Development of Collective Security* (1999); White, *Keeping the Peace* (2nd edn 1997).

[256] For commentaries on arts 33–38 Charter, see Simma, ed., *The Charter of the United Nations* (2nd edn 2002), Vol.I., Ch.VI.

[257] See Kirgis (1995) 89 A.J.I.L. 506.

[258] SC Res. 161, Feb 21, 1961.

enforcement action. Thus, in the Yugoslav war, long before the seceding States were recognised as independent, the SC determined the existence of a threat to the peace, apparently implying that fighting on a considerable scale with the possibility of outside intervention suffices to reach the threshold of art.39.[259] While in this case some members of the SC initially emphasized the role of the consent of the Yugoslav government,[260] they were less reluctant in later instances. In 1992, for example, the SC determined that the situation in Somalia, characterized by heavy fighting between different factions within the country, constituted a threat to international peace and security ...[261] Since then, the SC has established a consistent practice in dealing with internal conflicts through its measures in the cases of Liberia, Angola, Rwanda, Burundi, Zaire, Albania, the Central African Republic, Sierra Leone, and East Timor.[262] While in some of these cases, the SC still made reference to transborder consequences of the conflicts and their effect on regional stability, in a number of others, both the text of the resolutions and the debates preceding their adoption show that the threat to peace, in the view of the SC, consisted in the internal situations as such.[263] With regard to this practice, it appears now safe to assume that any internal conflict of a considerable scale can constitute a threat to international peace and security ...

A similar evolution has taken place with respect to violations of human rights and humanitarian law ... In 1991, without expressly mentioning Chapter VII, the SC determined that the 'consequences' of the repression of the Kurdish population of Northern Iraq, in particular the refugee flows and cross-border incursions, constituted a threat to the peace.[264] In later instances, there was less emphasis on trans-border effects, and the suffering of the population as such became increasingly decisive. Thus, in the case of Somalia, the SC determined that 'the magnitude of the human tragedy ... constitutes a threat to international peace and security', and with respect to both Rwanda and Eastern Zaire, it found the threat to the peace in the 'magnitude of the humanitarian crisis'.[265] Since this development did not lead to principled opposition among states, one may conclude that the severe and widespread suffering of the civilian population in armed conflicts can give rise to a threat to international peace and security. This has been reaffirmed by unanimously adopted statements of the SC to the effect that 'the deliberate targeting of civilian populations or other protected persons and the committing of widespread violations of international humanitarian and human rights law in situations of armed conflict may constitute a threat to international peace and security'.[266]

This evolution of the concept of a threat to the peace reflects the increased importance of the individual in the international legal order, but it does not warrant the conclusion that any severe violation of human rights could give rise to SC action under Chapter VII. The SC enjoys its far-reaching powers only for matters of peace and security; it is not set up to enforce all overarching values of the international community. This functional limitation thus necessitates that any threat to the peace be in some way linked to a present or impending armed conflict or other destabilization of the security of a country or region ...

Less legal change has occurred with respect to violations of democratic principles, although the SC in two instances specifically took action with a view to enforcing these principles.[267] In 1993 and 1994, the SC determined the existence of a threat to international peace in Haiti as the overthrown government was not reinstated.[268] Similarly, after 1997, the SC took measures to force the Sierra Leonean military junta to return to constitutional, democratic order and to accept the return of the government in exile.[269] These instances, however, do not justify the conclusion that the violation of democratic standards as such constitutes a threat to the peace. In both cases, the undemocratic change was part of a dangerous overall situation, in particular a

---

[259] SC Res. 713, Sept. 25, 1991; confirmed in Sc res. 724, Dec. 15, 1991, and later resolutions.

[260] Cf. Weller,M ... AJIL 86 (1992), pp.577–81.

[261] SC Res. 733, Jan. 23, 1992.

[262] See, e.g., on Liberia, SC Res. 788, Nov. 19, 1993; on Angola SC Res. 864, Sept. 15, 1993; 1127, Aug. 28, 2000; on Rwanda, SC Res. 918, May 17, 1994; 929, June 22, 1994; on Burundi, SC Res. 1072, Aug. 30, 1996; on Zaire, SC. Res. 1078, Nov. 9, 1996; on Albania, SC Res. 1101, Mar. 28, 1997; 1114, June 19 1997; on the Central African Republic, SC Res. 1125, Aug.6, 1997; 1136, Nov. 6, 1997; on Sierre Leone, SC Res. 1132, Oct. 8, 1997; 1289, Feb. 7, 2000; 1306, Jul.5, 2000; on East Timor, SC Res. 1264, Sept. 15, 1999; 1272, Oct. 25, 1999.

[263] See, e.g., SC Res. 864, Sept. 15, 1993, on Angola; 929, June 22, 1994, on Rwanda; 1101, Mar. 28, 1997, on Albania.

[264] SC Res. 688, Apr. 5, 1991.

[265] SC Res. 794, Dec. 3, 1992, on Somalia; 929, June 22, 1994, on Rwanda; 1078, Nov. 9, 1996, on Zaire ... Ed. In S.C. Resn.1816 (2008), the Security Council acted under Chapter VII to authorise states to act against piracy off the coast of Somalia, having determined that it "exacerbates' the threat to the peace" that continued in Somalia. See above, p.383.

[266] SC Res. 1296, Apr. 19, 2000; 1314, Aug. 11, 2000.

[267] See Byers, M./Chesterman, S., ... in Democratic Governance and International Law (Fox, G./Roth, B. eds., 2000) pp.281–92.

[268] SC Res. 841, June 16, 1993; 917, May 6, 1994; 940, July 31, 1994; cf. Corten, O., ... EJIL 6 (1995), pp.116–33.

[269] SC Res. 1132, Oct. 8 1997; 1270, Oct. 22, 1999; 1289, Feb. 7, 2000; 1306, July 5, 2000 ...

severe destabilization of the countries, a degradation of the humanitarian situation, and refugee flows. The case of Sierra Leone was characterized, in addition, by the outbreak of civil strife, which in itself could be considered as a threat to the peace. Moreover, regarding an undemocratic internal order per se as a threat to the peace would conflict with the 'police' function of the SC under Chapter VII: the SC is, in principle, limited to short-term crisis management, but may not take binding measures with a view to establishing a peaceful international order in general. Thus, although democratic government might be conducive to international peace, and although a right to such government may be emerging,[270] it cannot be imposed by the SC, but must be achieved through other mechanisms. However, if coupled with a crisis which itself constitutes a threat to the peace, undemocratic change might justify Chapter VII enforcement action ...

During the 1990s, the SC came to take part in the increasing efforts of the international community to combat terrorism, through both general statements and concrete action.[271] In particular, in a number of cases, the SC considered insufficient action of States against terrorism as threats to the peace. In 1992, Libya rejected a request by the United States and the United Kingdom to hand over two Libyans who had allegedly acted as agents for Libya and had placed a bomb on Pan American flight 103, destroying it over Lockerbie, Scotland. The SC first supported this request through a non-binding resolution, and upon Libya's non-compliance determined 'that the failure by the Libyan government to demonstrate by concrete actions its renunciation of terrorism and in particular its continued failure to respond fully and effectively to the requests in Resolution 731 (1992) constitute a threat to international peace and security.[272] The ICJ declared that prima facie the obligation to carry out decisions of the SC under art.25 applied to this resolution, thereby implying that it could not be treated as prima facie ultra vires and therefore null and void.[273] In the cases of Sudan and Afghanistan, the SC adopted a very similar approach. It subjected both States to enforcement measures because they had not complied with earlier requests by the SC to extradite suspects for trial.[274] These measures, unlike those against Libya, were not the object of significant criticism. Principled objection against this practice also seems to be unjustified as international terrorism, in general, creates severe destabilizing effects on the international order.[275] Accordingly, the Council has taken the step to declare that 'any act of international terrorism' constitutes a threat to international peace and security (SC Res. 1371, Sept. 28, 2001; see also the declaration on terrorism in SC Res. 1377, Nov 12, 2001) ...

As the examples indicate, the notion of a threat to the peace has undergone considerable change, notably with respect to internal situations. This does not mean, however, that it has become limitless. On the contrary, the above considerations may lead to the conclusion that a threat to the peace exists when, in a particular situation, a danger of the use of force on a considerable scale arises. This definition would encompass internal conflicts, but would exclude situations of concern that are either unconnected to a particular crisis or do not involve the danger of forcible action. In any case, though, the SC enjoys broad discretion in the assessment of the situation and the gravity of the danger.

Notes

1.   As the above extract from Simma indicates, the Security Council usually relies upon the concept of a "threat to the peace", generously interpreted, as the basis for its jurisdiction under art.39. Only exceptionally has it found an "act of aggression" or a "breach of the peace". Often the Security Council acts under Chapter VII without discussing the question of jurisdiction under art.39 at all, let alone deciding upon which part of art.39—"breach of the peace," etc.—its jurisdiction is founded. In so far as the Security Council does discuss or decide these questions, it is difficult to rationalise its practice because of the influence of political considerations.

    On the question of the competence of the ICJ to review decisions of the Security Council, which

---

[270] See Franck, T.M., ... AJIL 86 (1992), pp.46–91; but see also Roth, B., Governmental Illegitimacy in International Law (1999); Marks, S., The Riddle of All Constitutions: International Law, Democracy, and the Critique of Ideology (2000).
[271] For general statements, see, e.g., SC Res. 1189, Aug. 13, 1998; SC Res. 1269, Oct. 19, 1999; SC Res. 1373, Sept. 28, 2001.
[272] SC Res. 731, Jan. 21, 1992; SC res. 748, Mar. 31, 1992.
[273] Lockerbie, I.C.J. Reports (1992), pp.114, 126.
[274] SC Res. 1054, Apr. 26, 1996; 1070, Aug. 16, 1996, on Sudan; SC Res. 1267, Oct. 15, 1999; 1333, Dec. 19, 2000, on Afghanistan.
[275] See, in general, SC Res. 1269, Oct. 19, 1999; S/PRST/1999/29, Oct. 22, 1999.

was raised by the *Lockerbie* case, in which the Security Council had found that Libya was responsible for a "threat to the peace," see below, p.878.

2. *Breach of the peace*. A breach of the peace, which would seem to include any use of armed force, has, despite the evidence of much world conflict since 1945, rarely been found to have occurred. The only cases are the *Korean* case, below, p.806; the *Falkland Islands War*, above, p.749; the *Iran–Iraq War*[276] and the *Invasion of Kuwait* case, below, p.809.

RESOLUTION ON THE DEFINITION OF AGGRESSION 1974

G.A.Resolution. 3314 (XXIX). December 14, 1974. G.A.O.R. 29th Sess., Supp. 31, p.142; (1975) 69 A.J.I.L. 480

The General Assembly adopts the following definition of Aggression:

Article 1

Aggression is the use of armed force by a State against the sovereignty, territorial integrity or political independence of another State, or in any other manner inconsistent with the Charter of the United Nations, as set out in this Definition.

Explanatory note: In this Definition the term "State":

(*a*) Is used without prejudice to questions of recognition or to whether a State is a Member of the United Nations;

(*b*) includes the concept of a "group of States" where appropriate.

Article 2

The first use of armed force by a State in contravention of the Charter shall constitute *prima facie* evidence of an act of aggression although the Security Council may, in conformity with the Charter, conclude that a determination that an act of aggression has been committed would not be justified in the light of other relevant circumstances, including the fact that the acts concerned or their consequences are not of sufficient gravity.

Article 3

Any of the following acts, regardless of a declaration of war, shall, subject to and in accordance with the provisions of Article 2, qualify as an act of aggression:

(*a*) The invasion or attack by the armed forces of a State of the territory of another State, or any military occupation, however temporary, resulting from such invasion or attack, or an annexation by the use of force of the territory of another State or part thereof;

(*b*) Bombardment by the armed forces of a State against the territory of another State or the use of any weapons by a State against the territory of another State;

(*c*) The blockade of the ports or coasts of a State by the armed forces of another State; ...

(*e*) The use of armed forces of one State which are within the territory of another State with the agreement of the receiving State, in contravention of the conditions provided for in the agreement or any extension of their presence in such territory beyond the termination of the agreement;

---

[276] S.C. Resn 598 (1987), S.C.O.R., 42nd Year., *Resolutions and Decisions*, p.5; (1987) 26 I.L.M. 1479.

(f) The action of a State in allowing its territory, which it has placed at the disposal of another State, to be used by that other State for perpetrating an act of aggression against a third State[277]

(g) The sending by or on behalf of a State of armed bands, groups, irregulars or mercenaries, which carry out acts of armed force against another State of such gravity as to amount to the acts listed above, or its substantial involvement therein.

Article 4

The acts enumerated above are not exhaustive and the Security Council may determine that other acts constitute aggression under the provisions of the Charter.

Article 5

1. No consideration of whatever nature, whether political, economic, military or otherwise, may serve as a justification for aggression.

2. A war of aggression is a crime against international peace. Aggression gives rise to international responsibility.

3. No territorial acquisition or special advantage resulting from aggression is or shall be recognized as lawful.

Article 6

Nothing in this Definition shall be construed as in any way enlarging or diminishing the scope of the Charter including its provisions concerning cases in which the use of force is lawful.

Article 7

Nothing in this Definition, and in particular Article 3, could in any way prejudice the right to self-determination, freedom and independence, as derived from the Charter, of peoples forcibly deprived of that right and referred to in the Declaration on Principles of International Law concerning Friendly Relations and Co-operation among States in accordance with the Charter of the United Nations, particularly peoples under colonial and racist régimes or other forms of alien domination; nor the right of these peoples to struggle to that end and to seek and receive support, in accordance with the principles of the Charter and in conformity with the above-mentioned Declaration.

Notes

1. Resolution 3314 provides a definition of aggression for the purpose of UN action under the Charter.[278] The Resolution refers to the following explanatory notes in the Report of the Special Committee on the Question of Defining Aggression[279]:

    "1. With reference to Article 3, paragraph (b), the Special Committee agreed that the expression 'any weapons' is used without making a distinction between conventional weapons, weapons of mass destruction and any other kind of weapon.

    2. With reference to Article 5, paragraph 1, the Committee had in mind, in particular, the principle contained in the Declaration on Principles of International Law concerning Friendly Relations and Co-operation among States in accordance with the Charter of the United Nations according to which 'No State or group of States has the right to intervene, directly, for any reason whatever, in the internal or external affairs of any other State.'

---

[277] Ed. See the UK assistance to the US in the *Libyan Air Raid* case: above, p.770.

[278] The International Criminal Court will have jurisdiction over the crime of aggression, once it has been defined for this purpose: art.5(2), ICC Statute.

[279] G.A.O.R., 29th Sess., Supp. 19 (1974).

3. With reference to Article 5, paragraph 2, the words 'international responsibility' are used without prejudice to the scope of this term.

4. With reference to Article 5, paragraph 3, the Committee states that this paragraph should not be construed so as to prejudice the established principles of international law relating to the inadmissibility of territorial acquisition resulting from the threat or use of force."

2. The question of the definition of aggression was the subject of debate within the United Nations for over 20 years. After a long period during which the Special Committee on the Question of Defining Aggression seemed to be doing no more than going through the motions, the spirit of détente of the early 1970s led to the adoption of the present definition by the Committee and then by the General Assembly. In both cases adoption was by consensus, i.e. without a vote.[280] The definition has had a mixed reception.[281] It glosses over or avoids many disputed points in the interest of agreement.

3. The 1974 text contains elements of each of the two approaches to the definition of aggression that had been championed over the years of debate: the enumerative approach, by which all of the acts that constitute aggression are listed, and the general definition approach. The general definition in art.1 follows the pattern of art.2(4), Charter. Like art.2(4), it is limited to armed force; despite the doubts of a number of states, it excludes economic aggression.[282] "The economic, ideological and other modes of aggression were carefully considered ... but the result was an interpretation that they did not fall within the term 'aggression' as it had been used in the Charter."[283] Article 1 differs from art.2(4) in that it does not control the *threat* of armed force. It seems unlikely that "sovereignty" adds anything to "political independence" in the definition. The reference to "recognition" in the explanatory note to art.1 is intended to protect entities such as Kosovo whose status is disputed. Article 2 is a compromise between the priority principle preferred by some states (e.g. the USSR) and an approach emphasising the intent and purpose of the alleged aggressor supported by others (e.g. the United Kingdom). "Other relevant circumstances" in art.2 would include the intention of the state resorting to force, which might be to engage in individual or collective self-defence. To safeguard the interests of landlocked states, it was agreed that nothing in art.3(c) "shall be construed as justification for a State to block, contrary to international law, the routes of free access of a landlocked country to and from the sea.[284] It was also agreed that nothing in art.3(d) "shall be construed as in any way prejudicing or diminishing the authority of a coastal state to enforce its national legislation in maritime zones within the limits of its national jurisdiction provided such exercise is not inconsistent with the Charter of the United Nations."[285] This makes it clear that a coastal state is not committing aggression when, for example, it takes action in the enforcement of its maritime rights.[286] Article 3(f)(g) covers indirect aggression, but is not as extensive as the equivalent provision in the 1970

---

[280] On consensus, see above, p.12.
[281] See Broms (1977–I) 154 Hague Recueil 299; Brown-John (1977) 15 C.Y.I.L. 301; Cassin et al., (1975) 16 H.I.L.J. 589; Ferencz, *Defining International Aggression* (1975) 2 Vols.; Garvey (1977) 17 Virg. J.J.I.L. 177; Stone (1977) 71 A.J.I.L. 224; ibid., *Conflict through Consensus: UN Approaches to Aggression*, (1977).
[282] See, however, Stone, above, n.281, p.230.
[283] Broms, above, n.281, p.386.
[284] Report of the Sixth Committee of the General Assembly on the Question of Defining Aggression, December 6, 1974, UN Doc. A/9890, para.9.
[285] Ibid., para.10.
[286] See above, p.390.

Declaration on Principles of International Law.[287] However, art.4 indicates that the list in art.3 is not exhaustive. Article 5(2) distinguishes between a "*war* of aggression" and "aggression" generally and characterises only the former as criminal. The understanding would seem to have been that a war of aggression results in individual criminal responsibility under international law (as at Nuremberg) but that other, lesser forms of aggression give rise only to state responsibility of a civil kind, with an obligation only to make reparation.[288] Article 6 has in mind, but carefully avoids defining, the right to self-defence.

4.   The Resolution is intended to assist the General Assembly and the Security Council by clarifying a key concept (see its use in arts 1 and 39, Charter) in the United Nations scheme for the maintenance of international peace and security and which (like many others) is left undefined in the text of the Charter. Although a General Assembly resolution is not binding upon the Security Council, the definition has had an effect upon Security Council practice; the concept has since been referred to frequently in draft resolutions and debate and has generally "gained more substance than before."[289]

5.   The first finding by the Security Council that "aggression" had occurred was made in 1976, after the adoption of the 1974 definition, when South Africa was condemned for its "aggression" against Angola.[290] Apart from South Africa, such findings have only been made against Israel,[291] the "illegal racist or minority regime" of Southern Rhodesia[292] and Iraq.[293] The General Assembly has not been so reticent.[294] See also the finding of aggression in the Separate Opinions of Judges Kooijimans and Simma in the *Armed Activities* case, above p.763.

D. Security Council Action Under Chapter vii: Powers

See arts 40–50, United Nations Charter, below, App.I.

i. Armed force under Article 42: generally

Note

It was originally intended that enforcement action under Chapter VII involving armed force, i.e. under art.42, would be effected by the United Nations using armed forces provided by Member States in accordance with bilateral agreements between each of them and the Security Council under art.43. Because of the Cold War and the power of the veto, no such agreements were ever made and before 1990 the Korean and Southern Rhodesia cases were the only clear cases in which the Security Council

---

[287] See below, App.III. There is no equivalent to para.9 of the Section on the Principle on the Use of Force. In the *Nicaragua* case, para.195, above, p.730, art.3(g) was understood to state custom.

[288] See Ferencz, above, n.281, n.70, Vol.II, p.43.

[289] Broms, above, n.281, p.383. The Resolution (para.4) "calls the attention of the Security Council to the definition it contains and recommends its use under Article 39." The possibility of formally adopting the definition was considered within the Security Council but not pursued: p.397, n.137.

[290] S.C. Resn. 387 (1976), S.C.O.R., 20th year, *Resolutions and Decisions*, p.11. Several findings of aggression have since been made against South Africa (see, e.g. S.C.Resn 568 (1984).

[291] See S.C. Resn. 573 (1985) (air strike on PLO headquarters in Tunis).

[292] See S.C. Resn. 411 (1977)(attacks on Mozambique).

[293] See S.C. Resn. 667 (1990), below, n.350.

[294] An early example was G.A. Resn. 498, G.A.O.R., 5th sess., Supp.20A, p.1 (1951) (aggression by China by assistance to North Korea).

proved able to take any initiative involving the use of armed force.[295] In the post-Cold War climate, art.42 has been revivified, with the Security Council acting under it on a number of occasions on the basis of an interpretation of art.42 by which it may authorise, though not require, a state or states (a "coalition of the willing") to use armed force to maintain or restore international peace and security. Such action is not United Nations action,[296] but authorised state action that would otherwise be in breach of art.2(4). Following cases such as Kosovo and Iraq, a controversial question is whether such action may be based upon implied authorisation, to be read into a Security Council resolution that does not expressly authorise force: see the Iraq War, below, p.819. The following extract from Simma gives an account of the evolution of practice under art.42 and the current state of play, taking a strong stand against implied powers.

SIMMA, THE CHARTER OF THE UNITED NATIONS: A COMMENTARY

2nd edn 2002, Vol.1, pp.751–758. Some footnotes omitted

During the Cold War, the innovative character of art.42 had almost no impact. Before 1991, the only case in which large-scale military operations followed a decision of the SC did not fall under art.42. In the case of Korea, the SC merely recommended that States provide assistance to South Korea in repelling the North Korean attack on the basis of collective self-defence under art.51 ... In contrast, the authorization of the peace-keeping operation in the Congo in 1960–4 contained elements which arguably fell under art.42.[297] Article 42 also provided the legal basis for the authorization of the United Kingdom to apply force against tankers approaching the harbour of Beira in order to discharge oil for Rhodesia ...

Since 1990, however, the SC has made use of art.42 in a significant number of cases. Most prominent among them was, of course, the authorization of member States to repel the Iraqi invasion of Kuwait, which followed an earlier decision to enforce economic sanctions against Iraq by a naval blockade. Another large-scale operation was mounted in 1992 when the SC empowered member States to take military action in support of the peace-keeping force in Somalia, and, in the following year, conferred enforcement powers on the peace-keeping force itself.[298] During the Bosnian War, the SC first confined its authorization of the use of force to the facilitation of the delivery of humanitarian assistance, and then expanded it to the enforcement of economic sanctions and of a no-fly zone. Later it included the use of force in defence of 'certain safe areas', which led to significant air strikes in 1995.[299]

In 1994, another large-scale use of force was authorized in order to ensure the return of the elected president to Haiti after economic sanctions and a maritime blockade had proved unsuccessful.[300] In contrast, the genocide in Rwanda in the same year met with a much less forceful reaction by the SC, mainly due to the lack of readiness by States to provide sufficient troops. Only after a significant lapse of time did the SC authorize an expansion of the mandate of the UN peace-keeping force and an intervention by particular member States.[301]

The Rwandan Case was evidence of a significant change in the practice of the SC. Severe setbacks encountered in the course of some of the earlier operations, in particular those in Somalia and Bosnia, had led

---

[295] However, the UN's peacekeeping role did develop during this period; see below, p.1015.

[296] As to whether there was UN action in Korea, see below, p.980. UN peacekeeping forces may now have an enforcement dimension in their mandate, and are clearly UN forces.

[297] See SC Res. 161, Feb. 21, 1961; SC Res. 169, Nov.24, 1961; and the reference to Arts. 25 and 49 in SC Res. 146, Aug 9, 1960. cf. Abi-Saab, G., *The United Nations Operation in the Congo, 1960–64* (1978), pp.103-6, 165; but see also Bowett, pp.175–80; Schachter, O. (Miller, E.M.) ... AJIL 55 (1961), pp.3–9, who regard Arts. 39 and 40 as the appropriate legal bases. See also *Certain Expenses*, I.C.J. Reports (1962), pp.164–5.

[298] SC Res 794, Dec. 3, 1992; SC Res. 814, Mar. 26, 1993 ...

[299] SC Res. 770, Aug. 13, 1992; SC Res. 787, Nov. 16, 1992; SC Res. 816, Mar. 31, 1993; SC Res. 836, June 4, 1993; see Weller M., ZaöRV56 (1996), pp.70–177.

[300] SC Res. 875, Oct. 16, 1993; SC Res. 917, May 6, 1994; SC Res. 940, Jul. 31, 1994; see Malone, D., *Decision-making in the UN Security Council: the Case of Haiti, 1990–1997* (1998) ...

[301] SC Res. 918, May 17, 1994; SC Res. 925, June 8, 1994; SC Res. 929, June 22, 1994; the expansion of the mandate of UNAMIR by the two former resolutions was, however, not effected under Chapter VII, but was framed as self-defence ...

the SC to adopt an increasingly restrictive approach from 1994 onwards ... Only towards the end of the 1990s, the SC again came to authorize larger operations on the basis of art.42. In 1997, it endorsed the intervention of ECOWAS in Sierra Leone and, under art.53, empowered the organization to ensure the implementation of the economic embargo imposed on the country. When ECOWAS decided to withdraw its forces from Sierra Leone in 1999, the SC established a large peace-keeping operation, endowed with powers to use force that reached far beyond self-defence.[302] In the same year, it authorized an international civil and security presence in Kosovo, likewise empowered to take forceful action on the basis of Chapter VII of the Charter and consisting of both multinational forces and a UN peace-keeping operation.[303] For East Timor, the SC established a similar transitional authority, this time entirely run by the UN, after a multinational force operating on the basis of a Chapter VII mandate had provisionally restored peace and security in the territory.[304] In 2000, the SC endowed the UN observer mission in the Democratic Republic of Congo with the right to use force in order to protect not only itself, but also civilians under imminent threat and, in the end of 2001, it used Chapter VII to authorize an international force for the assistance of the Afghan Interim Authority in the maintenance of security in Kabul.[305] Thus, after some caution of the SC in the middle of the 1990s, art.42 has regained significance as a basis for enforcement action, though in a more limited way than some had expected after its revitalization in the Second Gulf War, and with mixed success ...

As the wording of art.42 indicates, it is up to the SC to decide whether to take military action and to which degree. For member States to be able to take military measures on behalf of the UN, it is thus not sufficient that the SC merely determines a threat to the peace without specifying the means and extent of the action designed to remove this threat. The same conclusion is to be drawn from art.39, which clearly separates the determination of a situation allowing for enforcement action and the decision on the kind of action. Otherwise, the enhanced centralization of the use of force, as sought by the Charter in contrast to the Covenant of the League, would be severely put into question.[306]

This implies that, in the absence of a specific decision in this regard, the use of force by States to implement SC Resolutions is unlawful, unless it can be based on independent legal grounds ...

Thus, in the case of Kosovo, NATO's claim to enforce previous SC Resolutions through the use of force against Yugoslavia was untenable, and the attacks could have been justified only on the basis of a unilateral right to act. The same holds true for the establishment and defence of the no-fly zones in Iraq, which had not been authorized by the resolution the acting States claimed to enforce. For the air strikes against Iraq, however, the United States and the United Kingdom relied on a SC Resolution, dating back to 1990 which indeed contained an authorization to use force, but could hardly be interpreted as allowing for such action after the Second Gulf War had been terminated. Similarly, the Council did not authorize military action of the United States in response to the terrorist attacks of September 2001; however, in reaffirming the right to self-defence it made clear that its resolutions were not intended to bar action otherwise lawful under art.51 of the Charter (SC Res. 1368, Sept. 12, 2001; SC Res. 1373, Sept. 28, 2001).

In practice, the deployment of peace-keeping forces has come closest to the original conception of the Charter. These forces operate under UN command, mainly responsible to the SG, and therefore constitute a mode of centralized implementation on the basis of ad hoc agreements with member States ... Until recently, however, they did not take part in enforcement measures, but were confined to action with the consent of the parties, perhaps with the exception of the [1960–64] Congo operation ... To some degree, this changed in the 1990s, when peace-keeping units were authorized to use force not only in self-defence, but also in pursuance of such goals as the delivery of humanitarian assistance or the protection of the civilian population. While this was sometimes incorrectly considered as merely an expansion of the option of self-defence not necessitating specific

---

[302] cf. UN Doc. S/PRST/1997/36, Jul. 11, 1997; SC Res. 1132, Oct. 8, 1997; SC Res. 1270, Oct. 22, 1999; SC Res. 1289, Feb. 7, 2000 ...

[303] SC Res. 1244, June 10, 1999 ...

[304] SC Res. 1264, Sept. 15, 1999; SC Res. 1272, Oct 25, 1999.

[305] SC Res. 1291, Feb. 24, 2000; SC Res. 1386, Dec. 20, 2001 ...

[306] cf. Krisch, N. ... Max Planck *UNYB* 3 (1999), pp.86–94; Lobel, J./Ratner, M. ... *AJIL* 93 (1999), pp.128–9; Gowland-Debbas, V. ... *EJIL* 11 (2000), pp.366–83.

authorization,[307] the SC has in a number of cases based its respective resolutions on Chapter VII, creating operations with mixed legal bases.[308] In practice, this has sometimes led to severe operational problems, in particular with respect to the neutrality of UN troops and their capacity to engage in combat.[309] Legally, however, this expansion of peace-keeping tasks does not create serious difficulties ...

The Charter does not state clearly whether, in the absence of agreements under art.43, the SC should be able to act under art.42 at all, and this question has accordingly been much debated ... it seems more in line with the concept of the Charter to permit action by the SC under art.42 even though the conditions as set out originally, have not been met. In this vein, the ICJ, in its Advisory Opinion in the *Certain Expenses* Case, rejected the view that the SC was barred from taking action by military means, stating that the Charter could not be read as leaving the SC 'impotent in the face of an emergency situation when agreements under art.43 have not been concluded'.[310] Although the ICJ was solely concerned with peace-keeping and did not specifically mention action under art.42, the same line of reasoning applies in the latter context. Accordingly, the predominant view in legal literature now subscribes to the view that in the absence of agreements under art.43, the SC is able to take measures under art.42, in particular through the authorization of member States to use force.

This interpretation is confirmed by the practice of the SC. While its action on Korea, constituting a mere recommendation to act in collective self-defence ..., is inconclusive in this respect ... the absence of agreements under art.43 ... was not regarded as an obstacle to action under art.42 in the Rhodesian Case ...

After that, the question as to whether the SC could authorize member States to use force arose again in the Second Gulf War in 1990–1. Here, the SC called upon States to use force first in order to enforce the economic embargo, and later to drive Iraq out of Kuwait, without, however, pronouncing itself on the legal nature of these authorizations.[311] Some commentators, therefore, opined that the SC merely endorsed the exercise of collective self-defence, but did not replace it with international enforcement action.[312] It seems more convincing, however, to see art.42 as the basis of both resolutions,[313] since their stated aim was to enforce previous decisions of the SC, not to assist in self-defence. In addition, the scope of action authorized by Res. 678 (Nov. 29, 1990) included the restoration of 'international peace and security in the area' and thus reached well beyond that allowed under art.51. Moreover, both Resolutions were mainly intended to provide greater legitimacy to the use of force by making it an action of the international community rather than one of individual States. This is confirmed by the attitude of the acting States, which justified their operation primarily with reference to UN authority and only in rare instances through reliance on self-defence.[314] ...

Later State practice confirms the view that the SC can authorize member States, in groups or individually, to use force despite the lack of agreements under art.43. The SC followed this path in the cases of Somalia, Bosnia, Haiti, Rwanda, Eastern Zaire, Albania, the Central African Republic, Kosovo (KFOR) and East Timor ... Moreover, in some of these cases, in particular in Somalia and Rwanda, no other legal basis for the use of force, such as self-defence or consent of the State concerned, was available. Thus, by accepting the legality of the operations as such, States implicitly accepted the legality of the authorization practice of the SC.

This approach of the SC was not always free from criticism. Especially in the beginning of the 1990s, some States raised concern over the deviation from the original Charter conception by simply authorizing member States to use force.[315] Most of them, however, did not object to the authorizations as such, but rather to the lack of SC control over the actual execution ... Therefore, State practice, in principle, has accepted that art.42 allows for the mere authorization of the use of force by member States in the absence of agreements under art.43.

---

[307] cf. e.g., SC Res. 918, May 17, 1994, on the extension of the mandate of UNAMIR in Rwanda, recognizing 'that UNAMIR may be required to take action in self-defence against persons or groups who threaten protected sites and populations, United Nations and other humanitarian personnel or the means of delivery and distribution of humanitarian relief' ...

[308] cf. SC Res. 814, Mar. 26, 1993, and SC Res. 837, June 6, 1993, on Somalia; SC Res. 836, June 4, 1993, on Bosnia; SC Res. 1270, Oct. 22, 1999 and SC Res. 1289, Feb. 7, 2000, on Sierra Leone; SC Res. 1291, Feb. 24, 2000, on the Democratic Republic of Congo ...

[309] cf. the SG's *Supplement to an Agenda for Peace*, UN Doc. A/50/60-S/1995/1, Jan. 3, 1995, para.35.

[310] *Certain Expenses*, I.C.J. Reports (1962), p.167.

[311] SC Res. 665, Aug. 25, 1990, and SC Res. 678, Nov. 29, 1990.

[312] See, e.g. Fleischhauer, C.A., ... *ASIL Proc.* 85 (1991), 431 ... The SG seems to have taken the same view, see UN Press Release SG/SM.1200, Apr. 24, 1991.

[313] cf., e.g., Franck, T./Patel, F. ... *AJIL* 85 (1991), pp.63–4; Greenwood, C., ... *MLR* 55 (1992), p.169; Weller, M. ... *AfJICL* 3 (1991), p.26 ...

[314] cf. UN Doc. S/22090, S/22097, S/22100, Jan. 17, 1991; and the discussion in the SC in UN Doc. S/PV.2977, Feb. 14, 1991 ...

[315] See the statements of Iraq, Yemen and Cuba on SC Res. 665, UN Doc. S/PV.2938, Aug. 25, 1990, pp.8–11, 12–15, 71. Most criticism by other States remained on a rather political level ...

ii. The Korean Case[316]

Note

Korea became part of Japan in 1910. In 1943, the Allied Powers agreed that it would become an independent state when the Second World War ended. In 1945, Japanese troops in Korea surrendered to the USSR north of the 38th Parallel and to the United States south of it. As agreed at the Moscow Conference of December 1945, a Joint Commission composed of USSR and United States representatives was then established to assist in the formation of a provisional Korean Government and, ultimately, of a single Korean state. The Joint Commission soon found itself at loggerheads, and in September 1947, the question of Korea was submitted to the General Assembly by the United States. The USSR denied the United Nations' competence to act on the ground that arrangements for Korea's future had been set in train by other means. Despite this, the General Assembly discussed the question and resolved that elections for a Korean national assembly should be held under supervision of the United Nations Temporary Commission on Korea which was established for this purpose. The Commission was not allowed into North Korea (i.e. north of the 38th Parallel) but it supervised and approved elections held in the South. A South Korean Government was established and, on December 12, 1948, approved by the General Assembly.

On June 25, 1950, North Korean armed forces crossed the 38th Parallel into South Korea and fighting broke out. The resulting crisis was immediately debated by the Security Council.

SECURITY COUNCIL RESOLUTION OF JULY 7, 1950

S.C.O.R., 5th Year, Resolutions and Decisions, p.5

The Security Council ...

1. Welcomes the prompt and vigorous support which governments and peoples of the United Nations have given to its Resolutions of 25 and 27 June 1950 to assist the Republic of Korea in defending itself against armed attack and thus to restore international peace and security in the area;

2. Notes that Members of the United Nations have transmitted to the United Nations offers of assistance for the Republic of Korea;

3. Recommends that all Members providing military forces and other assistance pursuant to the aforesaid Security Council resolutions make such forces and other assistance available to a unified command under the United States;

4. Requests the United States to designate the commander of such forces;

5. Authorizes the unified command at its discretion to use the United Nations flag in the course of operations against North Korean forces concurrently with flags of the various nations participating;

6. Requests the United States to provide the Security Council with reports as appropriate on the course of action taken under the unified command.[317]

Notes

1.   Taking advantage of the (voluntary) absence of the USSR from its meetings, in 1950 the Security Council first determined on June 25, 1950 that the Northern invasion of South Korea was a

---

[316] See Bowett, *United Nations Forces* (1964), Ch.3; Kelsen, *Recent Trends in the Law of the United Nations* (1950), a supplement to the same author's *The Law of the United Nations*, Ch.2; Kunz (1951) 45 A.J.I.L. 137; Stone, *Legal Controls of International Conflict* (2nd edn 1959), pp.228–237.

[317] Adopted by seven votes (China, Cuba, Ecuador, France, Norway, UK, US) to 0 with three abstentions (Egypt, India, Yugoslavia). The USSR was absent.

"breach of the peace."[318] This was followed on June 27 by a resolution[319] in which the Council "recommends that the Members of the United Nations furnish such assistance to the Republic of Korea as may be necessary to repel the armed attack and to restore international peace and security." Many states responded to this call. "By the end of 1950, personnel, transport, commodities, supplies, funds, facilities and other assistance had been offered ... by 39 Member States of the United Nations in accordance with the Security Council's resolution of 27 June 1950, by one non-member State [Italy] and by nine organisations."[320] Sixteen member states finally sent armed forces to Korea.[321]

2. The Security Council ceased to play an active part in the conduct of the war after the representative of the USSR resumed his seat on August 1, 1950. By early October the United Nations force had pushed North Korean forces back to the 38th Parallel and the question was whether it should cross it. On October 7, the General Assembly, acting on a report from the UN Commission in Korea, passed a resolution[322] which, by implication, authorised it to do so. By late October, troops from mainland China had entered the war and in mid-November they achieved considerable success against the United Nations force. After the USSR had vetoed a draft resolution condemning the Chinese action on November 30[323] the General Assembly became the organ effectively seised of the question. On February 1, 1951, the General Assembly adopted a resolution[324] finding that Communist China "by giving direct aid and assistance to those who were already committing aggression in Korea and by engaging in hostilities against United Nations forces" was "itself engaged in aggression" in Korea and calling upon it to "cause its forces and nationals in Korea to cease hostilities against the United Nations forces and to withdraw from Korea." Truce negotiations between the United Nations Command and a Chinese-North Korean delegation were begun in July 1951. Neither the General Assembly nor the Security Council were involved except that on December 3, 1952, the Assembly adopted a resolution[325] relating to the repatriation of war prisoners when that question had brought negotiations almost to a halt. "In actual fact, the armistice negotiations were conducted by the United Nations Command under instructions which in the final analysis were given by the United States government in Washington."[326] An armistice in Korea come into effect on July 27, 1953. Attempts at a political settlement of the Korean Question at the Geneva Conference in 1954 were unsuccessful.

3. In proposing the Security Council resolution of July 7, 1950, the representative of the United Kingdom said:

"It is clear to all concerned that unified command is essential if confusion is to be avoided ... Had the Charter come fully into force and had the agreement provided for in Article 43 of the Charter been concluded, we should, of course, have proceeded differently, and the action to be taken by the Security Council to repel the armed attack would no doubt have been founded on

---

[318] Resolution adopted by nine votes (China, Cuba, Ecuador, Egypt, France, India, Norway, UK, US) to 0 with one abstention (Yugoslavia). The USSR was absent.

[319] Adopted by seven votes (China, Cuba, Ecuador, France, Norway, UK, US) to one (Yugoslavia), with two members abstaining (Egypt, India). The USSR was absent. India later accepted the resolution.

[320] Yearbook of the United Nations (1950), p.226.

[321] Australia, Belgium, Canada, Colombia, Ethiopia, France, Greece, Luxembourg, the Netherlands, New Zealand, Philippines, Thailand, Turkey, South Africa, UK and US.

[322] Resn 376, G.A.O.R., 5th Sess., Supp. 20, pp.9–10 (1950).

[323] See S.C.O.R., 5th Year, 530th Meeting, p.25 (1950).

[324] Resn 498, G.A.O.R., 5th Sess., Supp. 20A, p.1 (1951).

[325] Resn 610 G.A.O.R., 7th Sess., Supp. No. 20, p.3 (1953).

[326] Goodrich, Collective Measures against Aggression, (1953) Int. Conc. No. 494, p.178.

Article 42. As it is, however, the Council can naturally act only under Article 39, which enables the Security Council to recommend what measures should be taken to restore international peace and security. The necessary recommendations were duly made in the resolutions of 25 and 27 June, but in the nature of things they could only be recommendations to individual Members of the United Nations. It could not therefore be the United Nations or the Security Council which themselves appointed a United Nations commander. All the Security Council can do is to recommend that one of its members should designate the commander of the forces which individual members have now made available."[327]

4. The constitutionality of the Security Council resolutions of June-July 1950 is uncertain.[328] Is it relevant that neither North nor South Korea were members of the United Nations or that, arguably, neither were states? Does it matter that the USSR was absent when they were adopted? On this last question, note that whereas there is a well established practice accepted by all the permanent members of the Security Council by which abstention by a permanent member does not "veto" a resolution[329] there is no such practice with regard to absence and the USSR has consistently maintained that the Korean resolutions were invalid because of its absence. Although the USSR was in violation of art.28 in absenting itself from the Council, this would not justify the Security Council in acting in the USSR's absence even if the violation were regarded as a "material breach."[330] The "veto" power was given to permanent members because of their primary responsibility in fact to maintain international peace and security.[331] Could it have been intended that the Security Council should adopt resolutions such as the Korean ones without the participation of all the permanent members? Arguing from the text of the Charter, if art.27 meant *all* the permanent members, should it not have said so, like the art.108? On the other hand, if it meant all the permanent members *present*, should it not have said that (compare art.18(3))?[332] Would the Council be able to act in the absence of all the permanent members?

5. On the question whether the force in Korea was a United Nations force, note the conclusion of Bowett.[333]

    "There can be no doubt that, in practice, the overwhelming majority of States involved in the Korean action were fully prepared to regard it as a United Nations action involving United Nations Forces."

Bowett refers to a number of facts indicating acceptance of this view of the nature of the force, including the use of the United Nations flag and the adoption of General Assembly Resolution 483(V)[334] authorising the award of a "distinguishing ribbon or other insignia for personnel which had participated in Korea in the defence of the principles of the Charter of the United Nations." An alternative view, which avoids the problem of the constitutionality of the Security Council

---

[327] S.C.O.R., 5th Year, 476th Meeting, pp.3–4 (1950).
[328] See the literature above, n.316.
[329] The ICJ stated in the *Legal Consequences* case, I.C.J. Rep. 1971, p.22, that the practice "has been generally accepted by Members of the United Nations and evidences a general practice of that Organisation."
[330] On "material breach" in the law of treaties, see above, p.700.
[331] See the Four Power Statement, June 7, 1945, 11 U.N.C.I.O., *Documents* 711.
[332] See Kelsen, *Law of the United Nations* (1950), pp.240–244.
[333] See above, n.316, p.47.
[334] G.A.O.R., 5th Sess., Supp. No.20, p.76 (1950).

resolutions, is that the force was an exercise of the customary international law right of collective self-defence, recommended by the Security Council under art.39.[335]

6. *Southern Rhodesia case.* The only occasion[336] on which the Security Council authorised the use of force under art.42 prior to the *Invasion of Kuwait* case was in the very different *Southern Rhodesia* case. There the United Kingdom was authorised to use force in support of Security Council economic sanctions against Southern Rhodesia. Having determined that the continued existence of the illegal racist regime in Southern Rhodesia was a "threat to the peace" in Resolution 221 (1969),[337] the Council "calls upon the Government of the United Kingdom to prevent by the use of force if necessary the arrival at Beira of vessels reasonably believed to be carrying oil destined for Rhodesia, and empowers the United Kingdom to arrest and detain the tanker known as the *Joanna V* upon her departure from Beira in the event her oil cargo is discharged there." A British armed naval party did board a Greek tanker, the *Manuela*, on the high seas off Beira under these powers and British warships maintained a Beira patrol until 1975. The *Joanna V* did not discharge oil. Authorisation of states to use force in support of art.41 sanctions, of which this was the first, have since been made in a number of later cases, including Iraq, see below, p.824.

---

iii. The Invasion of Kuwait[338]

SECURITY COUNCIL RESOLUTION 660 (1990)

August 2, 1990. S.C.O.R., 45th Year, Resolutions and Decisions, p.19; (1990) 29 I.L.M. 1325

The Security Council ...
Determining that there exists a breach of international peace and security as regards the Iraqi invasion of Kuwait,
Acting under Articles 39 and 40 of the Charter of the United Nations,
1. Condemns the Iraqi invasion of Kuwait;
2. Demands that Iraq withdraw immediately and unconditionally all its forces to the positions in which they were located on 1 August 1990;
3. Calls upon Iraq and Kuwait to begin immediately intensive negotiations for the resolution of their differences and supports all efforts in this regard, and especially those of the League of Arab States ...[339]

Note

Iraqi armed forces invaded Kuwait on August 2, 1990. Resolution 660 placed the Security Council within the confines of Ch.VII within hours of the Iraqi invasion, following which Iraqi forces quickly obtained control over all Kuwait's territory. All of the permanent members voted for the resolution. The Security Council preferred to use the more neutral term "breach of the peace," rather than "act of

---

[335] See Simma, above, p.824. See also Stone, above, n.316, pp.234–237.
[336] On the *Congo* case 1960–64, see Simma above, p.716.
[337] S.C.O.R., 21st year, *Resolutions and Decisions*, p.5. Adopted by 10 votes to 0, with 5 abstentions, including France.
[338] See Franck and Patel (1991) 85 A.J.I.L. 63; Gray (1994) 65 B.Y.I.L. 135; Greenwood (1992) 55 M.L.R. 153; Joyner (1991) 32 Virg. J.I.L. 1; Kaikobad (1992) 63 B.Y.I.L. 299; Khan (1993) 45 Stan.L.R. 425; Lavalle (1992) 23 N.Y.I.L. 3; Moore, *Crisis in the Gulf: Enforcing the Rule of Law* (1992); Roberts (1993) 25 N.Y.U.J.I.L.P. 687; Rostow (1991) 85 A.J.I.L. 506; Rowe, *The Gulf War 1990–1 in International Law and English Law* (1993); Schachter (1991) 85 A.J.I.L. 452; Warbrick (1991) 40 I.C.L.Q. 482; Weller (1991) 3 A.J.I.C.L. 1; White and McCoubrey (1991) 10 Int. Rel. 347. For documents, see Lauterpacht, Greenwood, Weller and Bethlehem, *The Kuwait Crisis: Basic Documents* (1991), Vol.1. See also *The United Nations and the Iraq–Kuwait Conflict 1990–6, UN Blue Book Series No. 9* (1996).
[339] Adopted by 14 votes to 0, with no abstentions. Yemen did not participate in the vote.

aggression," although it is clear that Iraq had committed large scale armed aggression without legal justification.[340] Iraq initially justified its invasion by stating that its troops had been invited into Kuwait by an opposition group to restore order to the country[341] but it soon became clear that Iraq's intention was to incorporate Kuwait into Iraq by force. Iraq appears to have no claim to Kuwait in the light of the 1963 agreement between Iraq and Kuwait whereby the boundary between the two countries was formally recognised.[342] Annexation by force is declared to be unlawful in the General Assembly's 1970 Declaration on Principles of International Law.

SECURITY COUNCIL RESOLUTION 661 (1990)

August 6, 1990. S.C.O.R., 45th Year, Resolutions and Decisions, p.19; (1990) 29 I.L.M. 1325

The Security Council . . .
Deeply concerned that . . . resolution [660] has not been implemented . . .
Affirming the inherent right of individual or collective self-defence, in response to the armed attack by Iraq against Kuwait, in accordance with Article 51 of the Charter,
Acting, under Chapter VII of the Charter . . .
2. Decides . . . to take the following measures to secure compliance of Iraq with paragraph 2 of resolution 660 . . . and to restore the authority of the legitimate government of Kuwait;
3. Decides that all States shall prevent:

(a) The import into their territories of all commodities and products originating in Iraq or Kuwait or exported therefrom after the date of the present resolution;

(b) Any activities by their nationals or in their territories which would promote . . . the export . . . of any commodities or products from Iraq or Kuwait; . . .

(c) The sale or supply by their nationals or from their territories . . . of any commodities or products, including weapons or any other military equipment . . . but not including supplies intended strictly for medical purposes, and, in humanitarian circumstances, foodstuffs, to any person or body in Iraq or Kuwait . . .

4. Decides that all States shall not make available to the Government of Iraq . . . any funds . . .
5. Calls upon all States, including States non-members of the United Nations, to act strictly in accordance with the provisions of the present resolution notwithstanding any contract entered into or licence granted before the present resolution;
6. Decides to establish . . . a Committee of the Security Council consisting of all the members of the Council, to undertake the following tasks . . .

(a) To examine the reports on the progress of the implementation of the present resolution which will be submitted by the Secretary General;

(b) To seek from all States further information regarding the action taken by them concerning the effective implementation of the provisions laid down in the present resolution . . .[343]

Notes

1.   As with most of the resolutions adopted in the Gulf crisis, the discussion leading up to the adoption of Resolution 661 was very brief, agreement having been hammered out before the

---
[340] "Invasion" is the principal type of armed aggression listed in the General Assembly's Definition of Aggression, see above, p.799.
[341] UN Doc. S/PV. 2932, p.11.
[342] 485 U.N.T.S. 321.
[343] Adopted by 13 votes to 0, with two abstentions (Cuba and Yemen).

public meeting. One result of this was that some ambiguities in the resolution were not clarified by any of the representatives' statements. One problem that arose regarding Resolution 661, in which the Security Council impliedly acted under art.41 to impose sanctions, concerned the mechanism by which foodstuffs would be allowed into Iraq and Kuwait. This was clarified to a certain extent by Security Council Resolution 666[344] adopted on September 13, 1990, which authorised the Secretary General to report to the Sanctions Committee on the food needs of the people of Iraq and Kuwait with particular attention to children, expectant mothers, the sick and the elderly and to report on how those needs would best be met.[345] Resolution 661 contained Security Council "decisions" that were legally binding under art.25, Charter. It applies to "all states", including non-UN members.

2. As well as resolutions fine tuning the embargo,[346] the Security Council also adopted a series of resolutions in the period prior to the authorisation of full scale force against Iraq which were more in the nature of declarations or judgments on certain Iraqi actions.[347] On August 9, 1990, the Security Council unanimously adopted Resolution 662[348] which decided that the Iraqi "merger" of Kuwait into Iraq was "null and void" and called upon states not to recognise the annexation. Resolution 664,[349] unanimously adopted on August 18, 1990, demanded that Iraq release foreign nationals held hostage in Iraq and Kuwait. Resolution 667[350] of September 16, 1990, unanimously condemned Iraq for its "aggressive acts" against diplomatic premises and personnel in Kuwait and demanded that Iraq comply with the Vienna Conventions on Diplomatic and Consular Relations. Resolution 674,[351] of October 29, 1990 reminded Iraq "that under international law it is liable for any loss, damage or injury arising in regard to Kuwait and third States, and their nationals and corporations, as a result of the invasion and illegal occupation of Kuwait by Iraq" and invited those States, etc. to compile information regarding claims to be made against Iraq. Resolution 677,[352] adopted unanimously on November 28, 1990, condemned Iraqi attempts to alter the demographic composition of Kuwait by deporting thousands of Kuwaiti citizens to Iraq.[353] All but Resolution 662 were expressly adopted under ChapterVII of the Charter.[354] As now common in its practice, the Council did not specify which Article of Chapter VII it was relying on.

----

[344] S.C.O.R. 45th Year, *Resolutions and Decisions*, p.22; (1990) 29 I.L.M. 1330. Adopted by 13 votes to 2 (Cuba, Yemen).
[345] See also S.C. Resn. 670, September 25, 1990, ibid. p.24; (1990) 29 I.L.M. 1334. Adopted by 14 votes to one (Cuba). This made it clear that the sanctions extended to air traffic.
[346] See also S.C. Resn. 669, September 24, 1990, ibid. p.24; (1990) 29 I.L.M. 1333, which entrusted the Sanctions Committee established under Resn. 661 to examine requests for economic assistance under the provisions of art.50, Charter, made by states other than Iraq suffering loss as a result of the imposition of the sanctions.
[347] On the judicial role of the Security Council see Schachter (1964) 58 A.J.I.L. 960; and Higgins (1970) 64 A.J.I.L. 1.
[348] S.C.O.R., 45th Year, *Resolutions and Decisions*, p.20; (1990) 29 I.L.M. 1327.
[349] Ibid. (1990) 29 I.L.M. 1328.
[350] Ibid. (1990) 29 I.L.M. 1332.
[351] Ibid. Adopted by 13 votes to 0, with two abstentions (Cuba and Yemen).
[352] Ibid. Adopted unanimously.
[353] The Security Council also discussed the atrocities carried out by Iraqi forces in Kuwait at the meeting at which this resolution was adopted: UN Doc. S/PV. 2962.
[354] Resn. 662 appeared to be treated as a binding decision of the Security Council by the members of the Council voting for it: UN Doc. S/PV. 2934. The resolution referred to S.C. Resns 660 and 661 which were expressly adopted under Ch.VII.

SECURITY COUNCIL RESOLUTION 665 (1990)

August 25, 1990. S.C.O.R., 45th Year, Resolutions and Decisions, p.21; (1990) 29 I.L.M. 1329

The Security Council . . .

Having decided to impose economic sanctions under Chapter VII of the Charter . . .

Gravely alarmed that Iraq continues to refuse to comply with resolutions [660, 661, 662, and 664] and in particular at the conduct of the government of Iraq in using Iraqi flag vessels to export oil,

1. Calls upon those Member States co-operating with the Government of Kuwait which are deploying maritime forces to the area to use such measures commensurate to the specific circumstances as may be necessary under the authority of the Security Council to halt all inward and outward maritime shipping in order to inspect and verify their cargoes and destinations and to ensure strict implementation of . . . resolution 661 . . .

4. Further requests the States concerned to co-ordinate their actions . . . using as appropriate mechanisms of the Military Staff Committee . . [355]

Notes

1. This resolution allowed the predominantly Western naval forces in the Gulf to stop and search vessels suspected of trading with Iraq or sailing from Iraq and to use minimum force for this purpose. The exact power upon which such an authorisation is based is unclear,[356] although there is a "precedent" for it in the authorisation to the United Kingdom to use force to stop oil reaching the port of Beira in 1966.[357] Some members felt uneasy that force was being authorised without the agreements necessary under art.43.[358] This was perhaps the reason why the resolution referred to the Military Staff Committee although there was no evidence of any formal control of the operation by this Committee.[359]

2. In the period before the Security Council authorised the use of force against Iraq by Resolution 678, below, the United States and the United Kingdom asserted that the growing military presence in the Gulf was both at the request of the Saudi government to protect Saudi Arabia from further Iraqi expansion and a form of collective self-defence of Kuwait at the request of the deposed Kuwaiti government if Iraq failed to withdraw.[360] In voting for Resolution 665, both states reserved the right to act in collective self-defence of Kuwait without the need for Security Council authorisation, and stated that authorisation was sought on this occasion for political rather than legal reasons.[361]

3. The Prime Minister, Mrs Thatcher, in her House of Commons speech of September 6, 1990 made clear the British position:

    "Resolution 661, which called for comprehensive economic sanctions expressly affirms the inherent right of individual or collective self-defence, in response to an armed attack by Iraq against Kuwait, in accordance with article 51 of the United Nations Charter. We hope that economic sanctions will prove to be sufficient. That is why they must be strictly enforced. But

---

[355] Adopted by 13 votes to 0, with two abstentions (Cuba and Yemen).

[356] See Simma, above, pp.796 and 803.

[357] See above, p.809.

[358] See UN Doc. S/PV. 2938, p.11 (Cuba) and p.21 (Colombia). See also the objections by Iraq: p.66.

[359] For this Committee, see art.47, UN Charter.

[360] See Keesing's Archives, p.37638.

[361] See UN Doc. S/PV. 2938, p.26 (US) and p.47 (UK). No such reservations were expressed at the adoption of Resn. 678, below, which authorised the full scale use of force against Iraq on November 29, 1990, S/PV. 2963, p.78 (UK) and p.101 (US). No other member made such a reservation. Indeed, some expressed the view that the use of force could only be authorised by the Security Council: see, e.g. p.74 (Malaysia).

we are not precluded by reason of any Security Council resolution from exercising the inherent right of collective self-defence in accordance with the rules of international law."[362]

Resolution 661 refers to art.51 which preserves the inherent right of self-defence "until the Security Council has taken measures necessary to maintain international peace and security". Could it be argued that comprehensive mandatory sanctions are such measures and that once the Council has adopted them any right to use force outside the framework of the United Nations is lost or suspended until the Security Council terminates the sanctions? In the Falklands War debate, Sir Anthony Parsons, the British representative, suggested that the measures must be effective before they can impair the right of self-defence.[363]

SECURITY COUNCIL RESOLUTION 678 (1990)

November 29, 1990. S.C.O.R., 45th Year, Resolutions and Decisions, p.27; (1990) 29 I.L.M. 1565

The Security Council,
Recalling and reaffirming [all its previous resolutions on the Gulf] ...
Acting under Chapter VII of the Charter ...
1. Demands that Iraq comply fully with resolution 660 (1990) and all subsequent resolutions and decides, while maintaining all its decisions, to allow Iraq one final opportunity, as a pause of goodwill, to do so;
2. Authorises Member States co-operating with the Government of Kuwait, unless Iraq on or before January 15, 1991 fully implements, as set forth in paragraph 1 above, the foregoing resolutions, to use all necessary means to uphold and implement Security Council resolution 660 (1990) and all subsequent relevant resolutions and to restore international peace and security in the area;
3. Requests all States to provide appropriate support for the actions undertaken in pursuance of paragraph 2 of this resolution;
4. Requests the States concerned to keep the Council regularly informed on the progress of actions undertaken pursuant to paragraphs 2 and 3 of this resolution.[364]

Notes

1. By this Resolution, the Security Council decided that sanctions alone were insufficient to make Iraq withdraw from Kuwait, and so authorised Member States, which in practice meant the coalition forces already gathered in the Gulf, commanded by the United States, to use "all necessary means" including armed force to enforce the decisions of the Security Council. Iraq objected to the Resolution, stating, inter alia, that it was only under arts 42 and 43 of the Charter that force could be sanctioned by the Security Council.[365] However, in the post Cold War period the Security Council has clearly established that, despite the absence of art.43 agreements, it may act under art.42 by authorising states to use force, which is what happened in this case.[366] The only obligation imposed on the states contributing to the coalition forces was to report periodically to the Security Council (para.4).

    Another interpretation is that the action of the coalition states throughout was not action authorised under Chapter VII but an exercise of the right of collective self defence, with the

---

[362] *Hansard*, HC Vol.177, col.737.
[363] UN Doc. S/PV 2362, p.104.
[364] Adopted by 12 votes to two (Cuba and Yemen), with one abstention (China).
[365] UN Doc. S/PV. 2963, pp.19–20.
[366] See Simma, above, p.805; and Schachter, above, n.338, p.464.

coalition defending Kuwait, and the "authorisation" in Resolution 678 being of political rather than legal significance.[367]

2. It was upon the basis of Resolution 678 that the coalition forces gathered in the Gulf[368] started their air campaign on January 16, 1991 soon after the deadline had run out without any concrete signs of an Iraqi withdrawal. The ground offensive for the liberation of Kuwait started on February 24, 1991 and was successful in its objective of removing the Iraqi army from Kuwait within five days. As with the resolution authorising the use of force in Korea,[369] Resolution 678 included the phrase authorising the use of force "to restore international peace and security in the region". In 1991, the coalition, appeared to interpret Resolution 678 as only authorising the enforcement of the previous Security Council resolutions directed at removing Iraq from Kuwait, rather than interpreting the resolution in a wider sense. Coalition forces did enter Iraq and forcefully occupied parts of southern Iraq for several weeks following the cease-fire, and the coalition air forces did mount continuous attacks on military targets throughout Iraq as well as Kuwait, but the coalition did not attempt to remove the Iraqi regime of Saddam Hussein. The phrase "to restore international peace and security in the region" was central to the UK argument justifying the 2003 invasion of Iraq, see below, p.819.

3. A temporary ceasefire was detailed in Security Council Resolution 686 of March 2, 1991[370] by which Iraq, inter alia, accepted liability for any damage caused by the invasion and agreed to rescind its annexation of Kuwait. A formal cease-fire was established by Security Council Resolution 687 of April 3, 1991, below.

4. On the humanitarian intervention by the coalition in Iraq after the cease fire (safe havens, no-fly zones, etc.), see above, p.809.

----

iv. The Invasion of Iraq 2003[371]

SECURITY COUNCIL RESOLUTION 687 (1991)

April 3, 1991 S.C.O.R., 46th Year, Resolutions and Decisions, p.11. (1991) 30 I.L.M. 846

The Security Council,
Recalling its resolutions 660 (1990) of 2 August 1990, 661 (1990) of 6 August 1990, 662 (1990) of 9 August 1990, 664 (1990) of 18 August 1990, 665 (1990) of 25 August 1990, 666 (1990) of 13 September 1990, 667 (1990)

---

[367] Schachter, above, n.338, p.460, n.24, notes that Resolution 678 was "probably of decisive importance in obtaining U.S. congressional approval." He also quotes, p.461, n.28, Mr Fleischhauer, a Legal Counsel to the UN Secretary-General, stating that *Resolution 678* was not adopted under art.42 because it did not provide for "a collective enforcement action by the United Nations, let alone under its command." In contrast with Korea, there was no provision for a UN command structure, force title or flag: pp.459–60.

[368] By the end of 1990, 29 countries had contributed to the US inspired response to the Iraqi invasion: Argentina, Australia, Bahrain, Bangladesh, Belgium, Canada, Czechoslovakia, Denmark, Egypt, France, Germany, Greece, Italy, Kuwait, Morocco, the Netherlands, New Zealand, Niger, Norway, Oman, Pakistan, Qatar, Saudi Arabia, Senegal, Spain, Syria, the United Arab Emirates, the UK and the US. At this time 750,000 "allied" or "coalition" troops faced 500,000 Iraqi troops. The US commanded the coalition forces and contributed 500,000 troops. *Keesing's Archives*, pp.37935–36.

[369] S.C. Resn. of June 27, 1950, S.C.O.R., 5th Year, *Resolutions and Decisions*, p.5.

[370] S.C.O.R., 46th Year, *Resolutions and Decisions*, p.8 Adopted by 11 votes to one (Cuba), with three abstentions (China, India, Yemen).

[371] See Bellamy (2003) 4 M.J.I.L. 497; the notes by Damrosch and Oxman, Yoo, Wedgwood, Gardiner, Falk, Sapiro, Franck, Farer and Stromseth in (2003) 97 A.J.I.L. 553 et seq.; Lowe (2003) 52 I.C.L.Q. 859; McGoldrick, *From 9–11 to the Iraq War 2003* (2004); White and Myjer (2003) 8 J.C. & S.L.1.

of 16 September 1990, 669 (1990) of 24 September 1990, 670 (1990) of 25 September 1990, 674 (1990) of 29 October 1990, 677 (1990) of 28 November 1990, 678 (1990) of 29 November 1990 and 686 (1991) of 2 March 1991 ...

Affirming the commitment of all Member States to the sovereignty, territorial integrity and political independence of Kuwait and Iraq, and noting the intention expressed by the Member States cooperating with Kuwait under paragraph 2 of resolution 678 (1990) to bring their military presence in Iraq to an end as soon as possible consistent with paragraph 8 of resolution 686 (1991) ...

Conscious also of the statements by Iraq threatening to use weapons in violation of its obligations under the Geneva Protocol for the Prohibition of the Use in War of Asphyxiating, Poisonous or Other Gases, and of Bacteriological Methods of Warfare, signed at Geneva on 17 June 1925, and of its prior use of chemical weapons and affirming that grave consequences would follow any further use by Iraq of such weapons,

Recalling that Iraq has subscribed to the Declaration adopted by all States participating in the Conference of States Parties to the 1925 Geneva Protocol and Other Interested States, held in Paris from 7 to 11 January 1989, establishing the objective of universal elimination of chemical and biological weapons,

Recalling also that Iraq has signed the Convention on the Prohibition of the Development, Production and Stockpiling of Bacteriological (Biological) and Toxin Weapons and on Their Destruction, of 10 April 1972,

Noting the importance of Iraq ratifying this Convention ...

Aware of the use by Iraq of ballistic missiles in unprovoked attacks and therefore of the need to take specific measures in regard to such missiles located in Iraq,

Concerned by the reports in the hands of Member States that Iraq has attempted to acquire materials for a nuclear-weapons programme contrary to its obligations under the Treaty on the Non-Proliferation of Nuclear Weapons of 1 July 1968 ...

Conscious of the need to take the following measures acting under Chapter VII of the Charter.

1. Affirms all thirteen resolutions noted above, except as expressly changed below to achieve the goals of this resolution, including a formal cease-fire; ...

8. Decides that Iraq shall unconditionally accept the destruction, removal, or rendering harmless, under international supervision, of:

(a) All chemical and biological weapons and all stocks of agents and all related subsystems and components and all research, development, support and manufacturing facilities.

(b) All ballistic missiles with a range greater than 150 kilometres and related major parts and repair and production facilities;

9. Decides for the implementation of paragraph 8 above, the following:

(a) Iraq shall submit to the Secretary-General, within fifteen days of the adoption of the present resolution, a declaration of the locations, amounts and types of all items specified in paragraph 8 and agree to urgent, on-site inspection as specified below;

(b) The Secretary-General, in consultation with the appropriate Governments and, where appropriate, with the Director-General of the World Health Organization, within forty-five days of the passage of the present resolution, shall develop, and submit to the Council for approval, a plan calling for the completion of the following acts within forty-five days of such approval:

  (i)   The forming of a Special Commission, which shall carry out immediate on-site inspection of Iraq's biological, chemical and missile capabilities, based on Iraq's declaration and the designation of any additional locations by the Special Commission itself;

  (ii) The yielding by Iraq of possession to the Special Commission for destruction, removal or rendering harmless, taking into account the requirements of public safety, of all items specified under paragraph 8(a) above, including items at the additional locations designated by the Special Commission under paragraph 9(b) (i) above and the destruction by Iraq, under the supervision of the Special Commission, of all its missile capabilities, including launchers, as specified under paragraph 8(b) above;

  (iii) The provision by the Special Commission of the assistance and cooperation to the Director-General of the International Atomic Energy Agency required in paragraphs 12 and 13 below;

10. Decides that Iraq shall unconditionally undertake not to use, develop, construct or acquire any of the items specified in paragraphs 8 and 9 above and requests the Secretary-General, in consultation with the Special Commission, to develop a plan for the future ongoing monitoring and verification of Iraq's compliance with this paragraph, to be submitted to the Security Council for approval within one hundred and twenty days of the passage of this resolution; ...

12. Decides that Iraq shall unconditionally agree not to acquire or develop nuclear weapons or nuclear-weapons-usable material or any subsystems or components or any research, development, support or manufacturing facilities related to the above; to submit to the Secretary-General and the Director-General of the International Atomic Energy Agency within fifteen days of the adoption of the present resolution a declaration of the locations, amounts, and types of all items specified above; to place all of its nuclear-weapons-usable materials under the exclusive control, for custody and removal, of the International Atomic Energy Agency, with the assistance and cooperation of the Special Commission as provided for in the plan of the Secretary-General discussed in paragraph 9(b) above; to accept, in accordance with the arrangements provided for in paragraph 13 below, urgent on-site inspection and the destruction, removal or rendering harmless as appropriate of all items specified above; and to accept the plan discussed in paragraph 13 below for the future ongoing monitoring and verification of its compliance with these undertakings.

13. Requests the Director-General of the International Atomic Energy Agency, through the Secretary-General, with the assistance and cooperation of the Special Commission as provided for in the plan of the Secretary-General in paragraph 9(b) above, to carry out immediate on-site inspection of Iraq's nuclear capabilities based on Iraq's declarations and the designation of any additional locations by the Special Commission; to develop a plan for submission to the Security Council within forty-five days calling for the destruction, removal, or rendering harmless as appropriate of all items listed in paragraph 12 above, to carry out the plan within forty-five days following approval by the Security Council; and to develop a plan, taking into account the rights and obligations of Iraq under the Treaty on the Non-Proliferation of Nuclear Weapons of 1 July 1968, for the future ongoing monitoring and verification of Iraq's compliance with paragraph 12 above, including an inventory of all nuclear material in Iraq subject to the Agency's verification and inspections to confirm that Agency safeguards cover all relevant nuclear activities in Iraq, to be submitted to the Security Council for approval within one hundred and twenty days of the passage of the present resolution...

33. Declares that, upon official notification by Iraq to the Secretary-General and to the Security Council of its acceptance of the provisions above, a formal cease-fire is effective between Iraq and Kuwait and the Member States cooperating with Kuwait in accordance with resolution 678 (1990); ...

Notes

1. Resolution 687 was adopted unanimously under Ch.VII and accepted unconditionally by Iraq.

2. In addition to establishing a ceasefire (para.1), Resolution 687 contained many provisions requiring action by Iraq. It required Iraq to return all Kuwaiti property that had been seized during the invasion and to compensate those who had suffered loss or injury. With regard to the duty to compensate, a Compensation Commission and a Compensation Fund, to be financed out of Iraqi oil sales, were established by the Security Council.[372] The Commission made recommendations for payment. The resolution did not immediately lift the sanctions imposed against Iraq by Resolution 661, and in particular a strict arms embargo was maintained. In 1996, however, a "food for oil" deal was agreed, by which Iraq was permitted to sell a limited amount of oil to buy food, medicines and other humanitarian goods.[373]

3. Crucially, Resolution 687 also imposed obligations upon Iraq, contained in paras 8–13 printed above, requiring the destruction, etc. under international supervision of Iraq's weapons of mass destruction (WMD). Iraq was to provide a list of WMD and "on site" inspections by UN weapons inspectors were to be facilitated, leading to the destruction, etc. of all of Iraq's WMD. To this end,

---

[372] S.C. Resn. 692 (1991), S.C.O.R., 46th Year, *Resolutions and Decisions*, p.18.
[373] See *Keesing's Archives*, p.41424.

a UN appointed Special Commission (UNSCOM, later UNMOVIC) was established to work with the International Atomic Agency.

SECURITY COUNCIL RESOLUTION 1441 (2002)

20 December 2002. S/RES/1441 (2002)

The Security Council...

Recognizing the threat Iraq's non-compliance with Council resolutions and proliferation of weapons of mass destruction and long-range missiles poses to international peace and security,

Recalling that its resolution 678 (1990) authorized Member States to use all necessary means to uphold and implement its resolution 660 (1990) of 2 August 1990 and all relevant resolutions subsequent to Resolution 660 (1990) and to restore international peace and security in the area,

Further recalling that its resolution 687 (1991) imposed obligations on Iraq as a necessary step for achievement of its stated objective of restoring international peace and security in the area,

Deploring the fact that Iraq has not provided an accurate, full, final, and complete disclosure as required by resolution 687 (1991), of all aspects of its programmes to develop weapons of mass destruction and ballistic missiles with a range greater than one hundred and fifty kilometres, and of all holdings of such weapons, their components and production facilities and locations, as well as all other nuclear programmes, including any which it claims are for purposes not related to nuclear-weapons-usable material,

Deploring further that Iraq repeatedly obstructed immediate, unconditional, and unrestricted access to sites designated by the United Nations Special Commission (UNSCOM) and the International Atomic Energy Agency (IAEA), failed to cooperate fully and unconditionally with UNSCOM and IAEA weapons inspectors, as required by resolution 687 (1991), and ultimately ceased all cooperation with UNSCOM and the IAEA in 1998,

Deploring the absence, since December 1998, in Iraq of international monitoring, inspection, and verification, as required by relevant resolutions, of weapons of mass destruction and ballistic missiles, in spite of the Council's repeated demands that Iraq provide immediate, unconditional and unrestricted access to the United Nations Monitoring, Verification and Inspection Commission (UNMOVIC), established in resolution 1284 (1999) as the successor organization to UNSCOM, and the IAEA, and regretting the consequent prolonging of the crisis in the region and the suffering of the Iraqi people,

Deploring also that the Government of Iraq has failed to comply with its commitments pursuant to resolution 687 (1991) with regard to terrorism, pursuant to resolution 688 (1991) to end repression of its civilian population and to provide access by international humanitarian organisation to all those in need of assistance in Iraq, and pursuant to resolutions 686 (1991), 687 (1991), and 1284 (1999) to return or cooperate in accounting for Kuwaiti and third country nationals wrongfully detailed by Iraq, or to return Kuwaiti property wrongfully seized by Iraq.

Recalling that in its resolution 687 (1991) the Council declared that a ceasefire would be based on acceptance by Iraq of the provisions of that resolution, including the obligations on Iraq contained therein,

Determined to ensure full and immediate compliance by Iraq without conditions or restrictions with its obligations under resolution 687 (1991) and other relevant resolutions and recalling that the resolutions of the Council constitute the governing standard of Iraqi compliance...

Acting under Chapter VII of the Charter of the United Nations,

1. Decides that Iraq has been and remains in material breach of its obligations under relevant resolutions, including resolution 687 (1991), in particular through Iraq's failure to cooperate with United Nations inspectors and the IAEA, and to complete the actions required under paragraphs 8 to 13 of resolution 687 (1991);

2. Decides, while acknowledging paragraph 1 above, to afford Iraq, by this resolution, a final opportunity to comply with its disarmament obligations under relevant resolutions of the Council; and accordingly decides to set up an enhanced inspection regime with the aim of bringing to full and verified completion the disarmament process established by resolution 687 (1991) and subsequent resolutions of the Council;

3. Decides that, in order to begin to comply with its disarmament obligations, in addition to submitting the required biannual declarations, the Government of Iraq shall provide to UNMOVIC, the IAEA, and the Council, not later than 30 days from the date of this resolution, a currently accurate, full, and complete declaration of all aspects of its programmes to develop chemical, biological, and nuclear weapons, ballistic missiles, and other delivery systems such as unmanned aerial vehicles and dispersal systems designed for use on aircraft, including

any holdings and precise locations of such weapons, components, sub-components, stocks of agents, and related material and equipment, the locations and work of its research, development and production facilities, as well as all other chemical, biological, and nuclear programmes, including any which it claims are for purposes not related to weapon production or material;

4. Decides that false statements or omissions in the declarations submitted by Iraq pursuant to this resolution and failure by Iraq at any time to comply with, and cooperate fully in the implementation of this resolution shall constitute a further material breach of Iraq's obligations and will be reported to the Council for assessment in accordance with paras 11 and 12 below;

5. Decides that Iraq shall provide UNMOVIC, and the IAEA immediate, unimpeded, unconditional, and unrestricted access to any and all, including underground, areas, facilities, buildings, equipment, records, and means of transport which they wish to inspect as well as immediate, unimpeded, unrestricted, and private access to all officials and other persons whom UNMOVIC or the IAEA wish to interview in the mode or location of UNMOVIC's or the IAEA's choice pursuant to any aspect of their mandates; further decides that UNMOVIC and the IAEA may at their discretion conduct interviews inside or outside of Iraq, may facilitate the travel of those interviewed and family members outside of Iraq, and that, at the sole discretion of UNMOVIC and the IAEA, such interviews may occur without the presence of observers from the Iraqi government; and instructs UNMOVIC and requests the IAEA to resume inspections no later than 45 days following adoption of this resolution and to update the Council 60 days thereafter; . . .

11. Directs the Executive Chairman of UNMOVIC and the Director-General of the IAEA to report immediately to the Council any interference by Iraq with inspection activities, as well as any failure by Iraq to comply with its disarmament obligations, including its obligations regarding inspections under this resolution;

12. Decides to convene immediately upon receipt of a report in accordance with paragraphs 4 or 11 above, in order to consider the situation and the need for full compliance with all of the relevant Council resolutions in order to secure international peace and security;

Notes

1. For more than a decade, Iraq failed to comply with its disarmament obligations in paras 8–13 of Resolution 687, by obstructing the work of UN weapons inspectors who were looking for WMD and in other ways. In January 1993, when Iraq acted so as to prevent further UNSCOM short notice inspections, the President of the Security Council, declared this to be a "material breach" of Resolution 687 and warned of the "serious consequences" that might result from "continued defiance".[374] In response, on January 13, 1993, the United States, France and the United Kingdom made air raids on sites in Iraq.[375] In 1998, in Resolution 1205, acting under Chapter VII, the Council "condemns the decision by Iraq . . . to cease co-operation with the Special Commission as a flagrant violation of resolution 687."[376] Following UNSCOM reports of continued obstruction subsequent to this resolution, in December 1998 the United States and the United Kingdom conducted four days of missile strikes against Iraqi sites. Even so, Iraq continued in its policy of non-co-operation with UN inspectors, to the point where they were withdrawn for a time.

2. It was with this background that, in December 2002, in Resolution 1441 above, the Security Council, after deciding that Iraq "has been and remains in material breach" (para.1) of Resolution 687 and other resolutions, decided to give Iraq "a final opportunity to comply with its disarmament obligations" (para.2).

3. On March 19, 2003, after much Security Council debate and effort to cause Iraq to co-operate

---

[374] Presidential Statement, January 7, 2003, UN Doc. S/25081 (1993); presidential note, January 11, 2003, UN Doc. 25091 (1993).

[375] See Kritsiotis (1996) 45 I.C.L.Q. 162; Lobel and Ratner (1999) 93 A.J.I.L. 124; Wedgwood (1998) 92 A.J.I.L. 724. For the UN Secretary General's statement supporting the legality of this action, see the FCO Memorandum, below, p.819.

[376] See also, inter alia, S.C. Resn. 1134 (1997) (repeated refusals to allow inspectors access to sites a "flagrant violation of resolution 687"); and S.C. Resn. 1154 (1998) ("any violation" of Resolution 687 "would have severest consequences for Iraq").

fully in the implementation of Resolution 687, United States and United Kingdom forces,[377] under United States command, invaded Iraq. On May 1, 2003, following the fall of Baghdad to coalition forces, President Bush announced the "end of major combat operations." The invasion had taken place after attempts to have the Security Council adopt a "second resolution" (additional to Resolution 1441), a draft of which was promoted by the United States, the United Kingdom and Spain, were unsuccessful. It was generally understood that the purpose of the second resolution, whatever its precise wording, would have been to authorise an invasion of Iraq for the continued material breach of Resolution 1441.

IRAQ: LEGAL BASIS FOR THE USE OF FORCE

United Kingdom Foreign and Commonwealth Office Memorandum March 17, 2003; (2002) 52 I.C.L.Q. 812

1. The legal basis for any military action against Iraq would be the authorisation which the Security Council, by its resolution 678 (1990), gave to Member States to use all necessary, means to restore international peace and security in the area. That authorisation was suspended but not terminated by Security Council resolution (SCR) 687 (1991), and revived by SCR, 1441 (2002). In SCR 1441, the Security Council has determined—

(1) that Iraq's possession of weapons of mass destruction (WMD) constitutes a threat to international peace and security;

(2) that Iraq has failed—in clear violation of its legal obligations—to disarm; and

(3) that, in consequence, Iraq is in material breach of the conditions for the ceasefire laid down by the Council in SCR 687 at the end of the hostilities in 1991, thus reviving the authorisation in SCR 678 ...

2. Chapter VII of the United Nations Charter gives the Security Council the power to authorise States to take such military action as may be necessary to maintain or restore international peace and security.

3. In the case of Iraq, the Security Council took such a step following the Iraqi invasion of Kuwait. Paragraph 2 of SCR 678 authorised 'Member States co-operating with the Government of Kuwait ... to use all necessary means to uphold and implement resolution 660 (1990) and all subsequent relevant resolutions and to restore international peace and security in the area.' The phrase 'all necessary means' was understood then (as it is now) as including the use of force.

4. Following the liberation of Kuwait, the Security Council adopted SCR 687. This resolution set out steps which the Council required Iraq to take in order to restore international peace and security in the area. Iraq's acceptance of those requirements was the condition for the declaration of a formal ceasefire. Those steps included the destruction of all WMD under international supervision and the requirement that Iraq should not attempt to acquire such weapons or the means of their manufacture. As a means to achieving the disarmament required by the Security Council, SCR 687 also required Iraq to submit to extensive weapons inspection by UNSCOM (now UNMOVIC) and the IAEA. The Security Council was quite clear that these steps were essential to the restoration of international peace and security in the area.

5. SCR 687 did not repeal the authorisation to use force in paragraph 2 of SCR 678. On the contrary, it confirmed that SCR 678 remained in force. The authorisation was suspended for so long as Iraq complied with the conditions of the ceasefire. But the authorisation could be revived if the Council determined that Iraq was acting in material breach of the requirements of SCR 687. Although almost twelve years have elapsed since SCR 687 was adopted, Iraq has never taken the steps required of it by the Council. Throughout that period the Council has repeatedly condemned Iraq for violations of SCR 687 and has adopted numerous resolutions on the subject. In 1993 and again in 1998 the coalition took military action under the revived authority of SCR 678 to deal with the threat to international peace and security posed by those violations.

6. In relation to the action in 1993, the Minister of State at the Foreign and Commonwealth Office wrote: 'The

---

[377] Ground forces from Australia and Poland, and naval forces from Denmark and Spain also took part.

Security Council determined in its statements of 8 and 11 January that Iraq was in material breach of resolutions 687 and its related resolutions, and warned Iraq that serious consequences would ensue from continued failure to comply with its obligations. Resolution 687 lays down the terms for the formal ceasefire between the coalition states and Iraq at the end of the hostilities mandated by the Security Council in resolution 678. These terms are binding in themselves but have also been specifically accepted by Iraq as a condition for the formal ceasefire to come into effect. In the light of Iraq's continued breaches of Security Council resolution 687 and thus of the ceasefire terms, and the repeated warnings given by the Security Council and members of the coalition, their forces were entitled to take necessary and proportionate action in order to ensure that Iraq complies with those terms.'

7. On 14 January 1993, in relation to the UK/US military action the previous day, the then UN Secretary-General said: 'The raid yesterday, and the forces which carried out the raid, have received a mandate from the Security Council according to resolution 678, and the cause of the raid was the violation by Iraq of resolution 687 concerning the ceasefire. So, as Secretary-General of the United Nations, I can say that this action was taken and conforms to the resolutions of the Security Council and conforms to the Charter of the United Nations.'

8. In relation to the military action undertaken in 1998, the then Parliamentary Under-Secretary of State (now Minister of State) at the Foreign and Commonwealth Office, Baroness Symons of Vernham Dean stated: 'In our previous discussions in this House some of your Lordships asked about the legality of our action. Any action involving UK forces would be based on international law. The Charter of the United Nations allows for the use of force under the authority of the Security Council. The Security Council resolution adopted before the Gulf conflict authorised the use of force in order to restore international peace and security in the region. Iraq is in clear breach of Security Council resolution 687 which laid down the conditions for the ceasefire at the end of the conflict. Those conditions included a requirement on Iraq to eliminate its weapons of mass destruction under international supervision. Those conditions have been broken.' . . .

9. It is against that legal background that United Kingdom and the United States brought to the Council the draft resolution which was eventually adopted unanimously as SCR 1441 on 8 November 2002. The preamble to that resolution again expressly referred to SCR 678, confirming once more that that resolution was still in force. It also recognised the threat that Iraq's non-compliance with Council resolutions posed to international peace and security; and it recalled that SCR 687 imposed obligations on Iraq as a necessary step for the achievement of its objective of restoring international peace and security. In paragraph 1 the Council went on to decide that Iraq 'has been and remains in material breach' of its obligations under SCR 687 and other relevant resolutions. The use of the term 'material breach' is of the utmost importance because the practice of the Security Council during the 1990's shows that it was just such a finding of material breach by Iraq which served to revive the authorisation of force in SCR 678.

10. On this occasion, however, the Council decided (in paragraph 2 of SCR 1441) to offer Iraq 'a final opportunity to comply with its disarmament obligations.' Iraq was required to produce an accurate, full and complete declaration of all aspects of its prohibited programmes (paragraph 3), and to provide immediate and unrestricted access to UNMOVIC and IAEA (paragraph 5). Failure by Iraq to comply with the requirements of SCR 1441 was declared to be a further material breach of Iraq's obligations (paragraph 4), in addition to the continuing breach already identified in paragraph 1. In the event of a further breach (paragraph 4), or interference by Iraq with the inspectors or failure to comply with any of the disarmament obligations under any of the relevant resolutions (paragraph 11), the matter was to be reported to the Security Council. The Security Council was then to convene 'to consider the situation and the need for full compliance with all of the relevant Council resolutions in order to secure international peace and security' (paragraph 12). The Council warned Iraq (paragraph 13) that 'it will face serious consequences as a result of its continued violations of its obligations'.

11. It is important to stress that SCR 1441 did not revive the 678 authorisation immediately on its adoption. There was no 'automaticity'. The resolution afforded Iraq a final opportunity to comply and it provided for any failure by Iraq to be 'considered' by the Security Council (under paragraph 12 of the resolution). That paragraph does not, however, mean that no further action can be taken without a new resolution of the Council. Had that been the intention, it would have provided that the Council would decide what needed to be done to restore international peace and security, not that it would consider the matter. The choice of words was deliberate: a proposal that there should be a requirement for a decision by the Council, a position maintained by several Council members, was not adopted. Instead the members of the Council opted for the formula that the Council must consider the matter before any action is taken.

12. That consideration has taken place regularly since the adoption of SCR 1441. It is plain, including from UNMOVIC's statements to the Security Council, its Twelfth Quarterly Report and the so-called 'Clusters Document', that Iraq has not complied as required with its disarmament obligations. Whatever other differences

there may have been in the Security Council, no member of the Council has questioned this conclusion. It therefore follows that Iraq has not taken the final opportunity offered to it and remains in material breach of the disarmament obligations which, for twelve years, the Council has insisted are essential for the restoration of peace and security. In these circumstances, the authorisation to use force contained in SCR 678 revives.

Notes

1. The United Kingdom's legal justification for the invasion of Iraq is most fully stated in the above FCO Memorandum.[378] The invasion is justified on the basis of Security Council resolutions; no suggestion is made that it could be justified as self defence or humanitarian intervention. The United States relied upon Security Council resolutions, but also invoked the right of pre-emptive self-defence, as that right is claimed by the United States in its *National Security Strategy*, above, p.774.[379]

2. In September 2002, the United Kingdom published *Iraq's Weapons of Mass Destruction: The Assessment of the British Government*.[380] In this dossier, it was concluded, inter alia, that:

    "Iraq possesses extended-range versions of the SCUD ballistic missile in breach of UNSCR 687 which are capable of reaching Cyprus [and hence British forces based there] ...
    Iraq's military forces are able to use chemical and biological weapons, with command, control and logistical arrangements in place. The Iraqi military are able to deploy these weapons within 45 minutes of a decision to do so."

    The FCO Memorandum does not rely upon these conclusions to provide an argument based upon anticipatory self defence. Could it have done so?

MCGOLDRICK, FROM 9–11 TO THE IRAQ WAR

2004 pp.78–86. Some footnotes omitted.

THE LEGAL ARGUMENT AGAINST THE WAR IN IRAQ

... On the evidence there was no justification under self-defence or humanitarian intervention. Moreover, it is quite clear that most of the members of the SC were not agreed that the relevant SC resolutions could be interpreted in the way put forward by the UK and the US. For example, Russia argued that the:

[R]esolutions considered in their entirety and in combination with other resolutions on Iraq, official statements of States on their interpretation and provisions of the UN Charter which were the basis for their adoption, show that the Security Council did not authorise Member States in this case to use force against Iraq.[381]

The argument against the legality interpretation is that the authority of Resolution 678 had effectively lapsed altogether or, at best, could only be resuscitated by the SC itself, as it remained actively 'seized' of the matter.[382]

---

[378] See also the UK Attorney General's Advice, *Hansard*, HL Vol.646, cols WA 2–3 (March 17, 2003); (2003) 52 I.C.L.Q. 811; and see the UK letter to the President of the Security Council, UN Doc. S/2003/350. cf. the Australian letter to the President of the Security Council, UN Doc. S/2003/352, which also relies only on Security Council resolutions.

[379] See Taft and Buchwald (2003) 97 A.J.I.L. 557. Taft was the Legal Adviser to the US Department of State. See also the US letter to the President of the Security Council, UN Doc. 2/2003/351.

[380] p.17. *www.number10.gov.uk/output/*

[381] See the Russian legal assessment [(2003) 52 I.C.L.Q. 1059].

[382] See, eg, UNSC Res 1154. See T Franck, 'What Happens Now? The United Nations after Iraq' (2003) 97 *AJIL* 607 at 612–14.

The authority of Resolution 678 could not be resuscitated by the individual members of the 1991 coalition (the states that cooperated with Kuwait).[383] Indeed, one could tenably argue that the coalition no longer existed. Adam Roberts expressed the argument as follows:

[T]he post-charter legal order creates a presumption against the use of force by states; that the decision to resume hostilities should be in the hands of the Security Council, especially in circumstances where the legitimacy of the use of force before the cease-fire depended significantly on the authorization by the Security Council; and that, although the cease-fire was between Iraq and the coalition which had fought against it, the Security Council had defined the terms of the cease-fire, was itself a party to it, and should determine how to respond to violations.[384] ...

There was no subsequent resolution and no 'second Resolution' following Resolution 1441, which included the expression 'all necessary means'. The SC had used this expression in a number of resolutions since Resolution 678.[385] Given that recent SC practice, there was no room for a doctrine of implied authorisation.[386] The intention of Resolution 1441 was that the SC alone would determine whether the 'serious consequences' that Iraq would face would include the use of force. That there was no 'automaticity' in Resolution 1441 had been made clear by the members of the SC, including the US and the UK, in the debate when Resolution 1441 was adopted. The UK's Foreign Affairs Committee considered that Resolution 1441, 'would not provide unambiguous authorisation for military action'.[387] The reference to Resolution 678 in the preamble to Resolution 1441 was not a revival of the authorisation of member states to use force. It was only a warning to Iraq that the decision on the revival of such an authorisation could be taken by the Security Council.

Vaughan Lowe has described the revival doctrine as follows:

There is the fact that Resolution 1441, on its face, patently does not authorize the use of force against Iraq and does not indicate that the authorization to the 1991 States acting in coalition with Kuwait could possibly be revived. There is the fact that there is no known doctrine of the revival of authorisations in Security Council resolutions, on which some implied revival could be based. There is the wording of later resolutions, such as the much-overlooked Resolution 686, and Resolution 687, which suggest that the authorisation to use force was given only for the duration of the operation to expel Iraq from Kuwait and that it is for the Security Council to decide what, if any, further action is to be taken against Iraq. There is the fact that, far from having abandoned interest in the matter the Security Council was itself actively seized of the matter at all critical times. And there are the express views of the Security Council members set out in the debates on Resolution 1441 which make it clear that, in contrast to the view of the United States, some Members required a second resolution explicitly granting an authorisation to use force, before force could be used against Iraq.

Furthermore, for the 'revival' argument to succeed it would have to be explained what the limits were upon the 1991 authorisation to states acting in coalition with Kuwait ...[388]

On 24 February 2003, the US, the UK and Spain had presented a draft SC resolution (regularly referred to as the 'second resolution') that would have made a Chapter VII *decision* that Iraq has 'failed to take the final opportunity afforded it in Resolution 1441 (2002)' ... on 17 March 2003, when it became clear that the resolution might not attract the support of a majority of the SC, and that in any event France would veto it, the draft resolution was withdrawn. As a consequence, there was no express or implied authorisation for the use of force against Iraq ...

Even though the second resolution did not contain any reference to force or to 'all necessary measures' a number of states made clear in advance that they would oppose it because of a perception that almost any second resolution would be misinterpreted as authorising force to be used against Iraq. 'France will not allow any

---

[383] This would imply that they considered the uses of force by the US and the UK in 1993 and 1998 to be illegal as well. ...

[384] Memorandum by A Roberts to FAC, 'International Law and the Iraq War' 24 June 2003, written evidence to the Tenth Report of FAC, Session 2003–03. . See also A Roberts, 'Counter-Terrorism, Armed Force And The Laws Of War' (2002) 44 *Survival* 7 ...

[385] See UNSC Res 770 (Bosnia), 794 (Somalia), 940 (Haiti), 929 (Rwanda).

[386] See J Lobel and M Ratner, 'Bypassing the Security Council: Ambiguous Authorizations to Use Force, Cease-Fires and the Iraqi Inspection Regime' (1999) 93 *AJIL* 124.

[387] [Second Report, FCA, session 2003–3, HC 96 (2002), para.172].

[388] Lowe [(2003) 52 I.C.L.Q. 859] at 865–66 (notes omitted) ...

resolution to be adopted that authorises the automatic use of force'.[389] ... Russia also committed itself to vetoing any second resolution for the same reasons ... Germany, a non-permanent member of the SC, was also opposed.[390] ...

... it was to open to those three states, and to the majority of the members of the SC, to take the view that, even though Iraq was in material breach, it did not pose an immediate threat, that the inspections regime was producing results and needed to be continued and that the risks of action were greater than those of inaction.[391] ...

When the SC discussions finally broke down in March 2003, France, Russia and Germany remained strongly opposed to the use of force.[392] ...

Asked whether an attack on Iraq without Security Council authorisation would violate the UN Charter, the UN Secretary-General, in an unusual intervention, stated that, 'If the US and others were to go outside the Council and take military action, it would not be in conformity with the Charter'.[393] ... The comments of the Secretary-General in 2003 suggest that he takes a different view on legality of the use of force against Iraq than his predecessor did on 1993.[394] In any event, the use of force in 1993 had a much more plausible connection with the purposes of resolution 678. ...

It has been submitted above that the legality argument of the US and the UK based on SC resolutions is a tenable and defensible one. However the US and the UK could not persuade the other members of the SC that the relevant SC resolutions could be interpreted in this way. Similarly, a majority [of] member states of the UN have rejected their interpretation. The coalition of over 40 states that the US cited in support of its action did not express support for the legal views of the US and the UK in public (although many of them may have done so in private). Unless we have an international legal system in which all states ultimately, rather than merely initially, exercise a right of auto-interpretation, then one is forced to the conclusion that the better view of international law in 2003 is that the US and the UK acted illegally.[395] One suspects that this would be the view of the International Court of Justice if the issue ever came before it. If there were a right of auto-interpretation for states then, presumably it would have been open to Iraq as well ...

There is also a more general legitimacy argument related to the idea of international law as a discipline of law. After considering the legality arguments Vaughan Lowe made what he describes as a 'more basic point' about the discussions of the legality of the Iraq War:

> It is simply unacceptable that a step as serious and important as a massive military attack upon a State should be launched on the basis of a legal argument dependent upon dubious inferences drawn from silences in Resolution 1441 and the muffled echoes of earlier resolutions, unsupported by any contemporary authorisation to use force. No domestic court or authority in the United States or the United Kingdom would tolerate governmental action based upon such flimsy arguments.[396]

Note

Whose arguments are the more convincing? Those in the FCO Memorandum, above, p.1003, or those presented by McGoldrick? In the absence of a "second resolution", the FCO Memorandum relies heavily upon the concept of implied authorisation by the Security Council. Can the authority given by

---

[389] UN Doc S/PV/4714, p.19 (representative of France).

[390] See UN Doc S/PV/4707, pp.29–30 (Fischer, Vice Chancellor and Minister for Foreign Affairs of Germany).

[391] See eg, UN Doc S/PV/4714 (7 March 2003) (representatives of Syria, Russia, France, China). Richard Falk has argued that the SC's witholding of the mandate 'represented a responsible exercise of constitutional restraint'. R Falk, 'What Future for the UN Charter System of War Prevention?' (2003) 97 AJIL 590 at 598 ...

[392] See UN Doc S/PV/4721 (19 March 2003). See also the earliest Memorandum to the SC from France, Russia and Germany, 24 February 2003.

[393] Press Conference, Monday 10 March 2003 (UN).

[394] [See FCO Memorandum, above, p.20, para.7].

[395] ... R Sifris, 'Operation Iraqi Freedom: The Legality of the War' (2003) 4(2) Melbourne Journal of International Law 521 (concluding that the use of force against Iraq was probably not legal, but also contending that the combined threat of weapons of mass destruction and terrorism, as well as the changing values of the international community, are precipating a paradigm shift in international law): 'Whilst the use of force against Iraq was probably illegal according to the traditional understanding of international law, the law is in the process of changing. What remains undetermined is whether, ultimately, change will be propelled by US might or by a global consensus on what is right', ibid. 560.

[396] Lowe [n.388] above, 866.

Resolution 678 to Member States generally in 1990 to use force against Iraq to "restore international peace and security in the area" (para.2) in the context of the invasion of Kuwait really be said to have been revived so as to authorise its force in the different context of non-compliance with Iraq's disarmament obligations (unconnected with Kuwait) in Resolution 1441? Even if so, is it open just to a small number of the original coalition to act? Can the argument for revival, and for implied Security Council authority, succeed when it is clear that most of the current members of the Security Council in 2003, including three permanent members, did not support it? And, as suggested by Lowe, should not a decision on such an important issue as the invasion of a state with the authority of the international community not require clear, express and generally supported authority from the Security Council?

----

v. Measures Short of Armed Force

See art.41, United Nations Charter, below, App.I.

SIMMA, THE CHARTER OF THE UNITED NATIONS: A COMMENTARY

2nd edn 2002, Vol.1, pp.738–740

Although regarded as a cornerstone of the new system of collective security of the UN, art.41 remained a dead letter for more than two decades. Only in 1966 could the SC agree on a mandatory embargo in order to force the racist minority regime of Southern Rhodesia to resign. Despite the authorization to use force for its implementation and a significant extension two years later, this embargo suffered from a lack of observance by member States, and it took 13 years until it could be lifted.[397] During the Cold War, art.41 was applied in only one more case, that of South Africa. After long years of recommendations on trade restrictions, the SC enacted a mandatory arms embargo against South Africa in 1977, which produced limited results and remained in place until 1994.[398]

In contrast, since the end of the Cold War, enforcement action under art.41 has become a common instrument of peace maintenance. Starting with the reaction to the Iraqi invasion of Kuwait, economic sanctions were used in 14 cases between 1990 and mid–1992, and art.41 has also been the basis for a range of other measures. During this time, however, the way in which non-military enforcement action was used varied considerably. In the beginning, and notably in the cases of Iraq, the Former Yugoslavia, and Haiti, comprehensive economic embargoes, backed by military enforcement appeared to be the most effective tool to force reluctant governments to bow to the will of the international community.[399] But while this policy generated some, albeit limited, success the unintended side-effects on the civilian population became more and more evident. Particularly the disastrous humanitarian situation of the Iraqi people, aggravated by the obstructive behaviour of the Iraqi government, raised concerns about the appropriateness of economic sanctions in general, and led the UNSG to call sanctions 'a blunt instrument'.[400]

Thus, since the mid–1990's, economic embargoes were used much more cautiously and in a more limited way, and attempts were made to develop 'targeted', 'smart' sanctions, which should hit those responsible for the breach of the peace and leave innocent bystanders unaffected. New embargoes were often limited to arms and selected crucial goods such as diamonds. Moreover, air traffic was restricted, and specific individuals were hit by the freezing of foreign accounts as well as prohibitions on international travel ... While these measures indeed had a lesser adverse impact on the civilian population, their effectiveness was limited too. Arms embargoes,

---

[397] cf. Gowlland-Debbas, Collective Responses, pp.423–663 ... :

[398] For a detailed account of the measures and their effects, see *How Sanctions Work: Lessons from South Africa* (Crawford, N.C./Klotz,A.,eds.,1999).

[399] See, inter alia, SC Res. 661, Aug. 6, 1990 and SC Res. 687, Apr. 3, 1991, on Iraq; SC Res. 757, May 30, 1992, on the former Yugoslavia; SC Res. 841, June 16, 1993, and SC Res. 917, May 6, 1994, on Haiti ...

[400] cf. the *Supplement to An Agenda for Peace*, UN Doc. A/50/60-s/1995/1, Jan. 3, 1995, para.70; similarly the *Millenium Report*, UN Doc. A/54/2000, Apr. 3, 2000 p.50 ...

though frequently imposed, proved vulnerable to evasion since effectiveness mechanisms to monitor and enforce compliance were lacking. Thus, at the end of the 1990s, the focus shifted towards effective enforcement mechanisms, such as investigative bodies, market regulation for certain goods, technical assistance to neighbouring States, and the criminal prosecution of sanctions violators. ... Apart from these sanctions in the classical sense, art.41 provided the legal basis for a number of atypical measures as well. These included the creation of international criminal tribunals for the Former Yugoslavia and Rwanda in 1993 and 1994, and the establishment of international administrations for territories such as Kosovo and East Timor in 1999 ...

More than other measures, non-military enforcement action under art.41 often severely affects third States, in particular when trade relations with the targeted State are restricted. Such consequences do not free the States concerned from their obligations to implement the SC measures, but they allow them to address a request to the SC under art.50 ....

While measures under art.41 are typically addressed to member States, the SC has in several cases taken action against non-state entities [e.g. Southern Rhodesia] and individuals and has even created legal obligations for them.

E. The powers of the General Assembly

GRAY, INTERNATIONAL LAW AND THE USE OF FORCE

2nd edn 2004, pp.200–201

The inaction of the Security Council during the Cold War led the General Assembly to assume a role greater than originally envisaged. The Charter provides for a division of functions between the two organs. Article 11(2) says that the General Assembly may discuss questions relating to the maintenance of international peace and security and make recommendations (except as provided in Article 12); but any such question on which action is necessary shall be referred to the Security Council. Article 12 is designed to prevent clashes between the two bodies; it provides that, while the Security Council is exercising its functions with regard to a particular dispute or situation, the General Assembly shall not make any recommendation unless the Security Council so requests. But these two provisions have been flexibly interpreted in such a way that there is no strict division of functions.[401]

The General Assembly, concerned at the inaction of the Security Council and its failure to play the role provided in the Charter, passed the *Uniting for Peace Resolution* in 1950. This allowed it to call emergency meetings in the event of Security Council failure because of lack of unanimity of the permanent members to exercise its primary responsibility for the maintenance of peace and security in any case where there appears to be a threat to the peace, breach of the peace or act of aggression. The General Assembly may then recommend collective measures, including the use of armed force if necessary.[402] Using this procedure it recommended the establishment of peacekeeping forces in the Middle East. The legality of this was upheld by the International Court of Justice in the *Certain Expenses* case; it explained away the provision of Article 11(2) that questions on which action was necessary should be referred to the Security Council on the basis that the Security Council has a primary but not an exclusive responsibility for the maintenance of international peace and security. The Court also relied on the less convincing argument that it is only enforcement action and not peacekeeping action that must be referred to the Security Council.[403]

Article 12 has also been gradually eroded. The General Assembly has made recommendations even when the Security Council was dealing actively with an issue. If the Security Council was not actually exercising its functions at that moment, or if a resolution was blocked by a veto, the General Assembly has assumed it is free to make recommendations, provided that these did not directly contradict a Security Council Resolution.[404] The General Assembly has accordingly passed a series of resolutions condemning certain behaviour when the Security Council could not agree on a resolution or could not take measures against a wrongdoing state. Some

---

[401] On the drafting history, see Franck, *Recourse to Force* (2002) at 31.

[402] GA Res 377(V).

[403] *Certain Expenses* case, I.C.J. Reports (1962) 151. Since UNEF it has been the Security Council rather than the General Assembly which has established peacekeeping forces.

[404] Simma (ed.), *The Charter of the United Nations: A Commentary* (2nd edn 2002) at 288; Blum, *Eroding the United Nations Charter* (1993), 103; Gray, "Bosnia and Herzegovina: Civil War or Inter-State Conflict: Characterisation and Consequences", 67 BYIL (1996) 155.

western states were unhappy at this; they said that the repetition of resolutions condemning states was a pointless rhetorical exercise. This was the response when the General Assembly called for the imposition of sanctions on South Africa after the USA and the UK had blocked this in the Security Council. Recently the General Assembly regarded itself as free to call on the Security Council to lift the arms embargo on Bosnia-Herzegovina when the Security Council had been divided as to whether to do so. Technically it may be possible to make out a case on the basis of the practice of the two bodies that this did not contravene Article 12, but it seems to be precisely the type of situation that Article 12 was designed to prevent.[405]

F. The Domestic Jurisdiction Limitation[406]

See art.2(7), United Nations Charter, below, Appendix I.

Notes

1.   The provision equivalent to art.2(7) in the League of Nations Covenant was art.15(8) which read:

"If the dispute between the parties is claimed by one of them, and is found by the Council, to arise out of a matter which by international law is solely within the domestic jurisdiction of that party, the Council shall so report, and shall make no recommendations as to its settlement."

In its Advisory Opinion in the *Nationality Decrees issued in Tunis and Morocco* case[407] the PCIJ was asked whether questions concerning the application to British subjects of nationality decrees made in Tunis and Morocco by France were matters of domestic jurisdiction in the sense of art.15(8). The Court replied in the negative. It stated:

"The question whether a certain matter is or is not solely within the jurisdiction of a state is an essentially relative question; it depends upon the development of international relations. Thus, in the present state of international law, questions of nationality are, in the opinion of the Court, in principle within this reserved domain.
      For the purpose of the present opinion, it is enough to observe that it may well happen that, in a matter which, like that of nationality, is not, in principle, regulated by international law, the right of a state to use its discretion is nevertheless restricted by obligations which it may have undertaken towards other states. In such a case, jurisdiction which, in principle, belongs solely to the state, is limited by rules of international law. Article 15, paragraph 8, then ceases to apply as regards those states which are entitled to invoke such rules, and the dispute as to the question whether a state has or has not the right to take certain measures becomes in these circumstances a dispute of an international character and falls outside the scope of the exception contained in this paragraph."[408]

2.   Objections to United Nations jurisdiction based upon art.2(7) have been raised in connection with such subjects as the character or internal activities of national governments (including respect for human rights) and the administration and future of non-self-governing territories. When the General Assembly has decided to take jurisdiction in respect of a question despite the protests of the state concerned, that state has, on occasions, walked out. South Africa walked out during

---

[405] Gray, ibid.
[406] See Gilmour (1967) 16 I.C.L.Q. 330; Goodrich, Hambro and Simons, Charter of the United Nations (3rd edn 1969) pp.60–73; Higgins, above, p.886, n.1, pp.58–130.
[407] P.C.I.J. Rep., Ser. B, No.4 (1923).
[408] P.C.I.J. Rep., Ser.B, No.4 (1923).

discussion of *apartheid*; France did so when Algeria was discussed; and the United Kingdom was not present when voting on a matter concerning Southern Rhodesia occurred (before 1965). On the narrow reading of art.2(7) in a humanitarian context, see the *Iraqi Safe Havens* case, above, p.779.

3.   Article 2(7) has had little impact in recent years. Simma's Commentary states:

"Article 2(7) was intended to strengthen the protection of States against incursions into their domestic affairs. In practice, however, art.2(7) has been increasingly eroded and emptied of substance. This is not so much because the term 'intervention' has been narrowly inter- preted. . .but rather because more and more matters are no longer recognized as belonging to the domestic jurisdiction of States. . .This development raises the question whether art.2(7) has become largely obsolete or whether a new interpretation is necessary. It is true that there are not many matters left which a majority of States continues to insist are essentially within domestic jurisdiction. . .The most important field is perhaps the question of election monitoring . . ."[409]

G. Peacekeeping Operations[410]

GRAY, INTERNATIONAL LAW AND THE USE OF FORCE

2nd edn, 2004, pp.201–227. Some footnotes omitted.

In response to the inability of the Security Council to take enforcement action under Chapter VII, the institution of peacekeeping evolved during the Cold War. There was no express basis for this in the Charter, but the institution has evolved through the practice of the United Nations and its legality is no longer challenged by any state. Commentators have speculated that a legal basis may be found in the power of the General Assembly to establish subsidiary organs, or under Chapter VI on peaceful settlement, or under Article 40 on provisional measures.[411] All of these may be theoretical possibilities, but in practice, there has been no express reference to any of these in the resolutions establishing peacekeeping forces and the debate seems to be without practical significance . . .

There was a wide variety of types of operation which came to share the name of peacekeeping. Most of the Cold War peacekeeping operations were interposed between states; very few were established to play a role in ending civil conflict.

The earliest were limited observation forces; the first major forces were UNEF, established by the General Assembly in the Middle East from 1956 to 1967, and ONUC, established by the Secretary-General with Security Council authorization in the Congo[412] from 1960 to 1964 . . .

After UNEF was terminated the UN Secretary-General produced a report examining the 'new and unique experiment' and setting out guidelines for future operations.[413] The mandate of UNEF under General Assembly Resolutions 998 and 1000 had been 'to secure and supervise' the cease-fire and withdrawal of foreign forces from Egypt, and later to maintain peaceful conditions in the area by its deployment along the armistice line

---

[409] *The Charter of the United Nations: A Commentary* (2nd edn), Vol.1, p.171.

[410] See Cassese, ed., *United Nations Peace-Keeping: Legal Essays* (1978); Higgins, *United Nations Peace-Keeping: Documents and Commentary*, 4 vols (1969–81); McCoubrey and White, *The Blue Helmets: Legal Regulation of United Nations Military Operations* (1996); Morphet, "UN Peacekeeping and Election Monitoring" in *United Nations, Divided World* (Roberts and Kingsbury eds., 2nd edn 1993); Hill and Malik, *Peacekeeping and the United Nations* (1996); Ratner, *The New UN Peace- keeping* (1995); UN Publications, *The Blue Helmets: A Review of United Nations Peacekeeping* (3rd edn 1996).

[411] Simma (ed.) *The Charter of the United Nations: A Commentary* (2nd edn 2002) at 648.

[412] Subsequently Zaire, and now the Democratic Republic of the Congo.

[413] Report of the Secretary-General, *Summary study of the experience derived from the establishment and operation of the Force*, A/3943.

between Egypt and Israel. It had been agreed that the force should not include troops from the permanent members of the Security Council or of any other country which for geographical or other reasons might have a special interest in the conflict. It operated with the consent of the host state and was withdrawn when Egypt terminated its consent in 1967 ... It operated under a Status of Forces Agreement (SOFA), with the host state establishing the rights and privileges of the UN forces ... It should use force only in self-defence. A wide interpretation of this right was not acceptable because it would blur the distinction between these operations and those under Chapter VII.

Most of the UN operations, which later became known as peacekeeping operations, followed these principles. But ONUC departed from them and showed the dangers of so doing. It was originally created to assist the government of the Congo in the chaotic aftermath of independence in 1960. Its mandate was to give the government military and technical assistance after the collapse of essential services until national security forces were able fully to meet their tasks, but it became embroiled in the conflict when its original mandate was expanded. Resolution 161, although not formally passed under Chapter VII, used the language of Article 39 in its concern that the danger of civil war constituted a threat to international peace and security. It authorized ONUC to use force going beyond self-defence in order to prevent civil war; the resolution urged ONUC 'to take all appropriate measures to prevent the occurrence of civil war in the Congo ... including the use of force, if necessary, in the last resort'. Later Resolution 169 went further and not only affirmed the territorial integrity of the Congo but authorized the Secretary-General to use force to end the attempted secession of the province of Katanga and to expel foreign mercenaries. This led ONUC to assume responsibilities that went beyond normal peacekeeping. Its numbers were increased to 20,000 to respond to the expansion of its mandate and it was involved in fighting against those seeking secession.[414] The type of controversy that arose over the extension of peacekeeping in the Congo has recurred with regard to the operations in Yugoslavia and Somalia ...

The Security Council vastly increased its peacekeeping activities after the Cold War ... In the forty years from 1945 to 1988 there were fifteen operations; in the ten years from 1988 to 1998 over twenty-five new forces were established; and seven more in the last five years.[415] The majority of these new forces were deployed within states involved in civil wars rather than between states.... Because most peacekeeping after the Cold War had been within states, challenges had arisen that had not been encountered since the Congo operation in the 1960s. UN forces were faced by irregular forces rather than regular armies, civilians were the main victims of the conflicts, civil conflict brought humanitarian emergencies and refugees, state institutions collapsed. All these factors meant that international intervention had to go beyond military and humanitarian operations to bringing about national reconciliation and re-establishing effective government. Peacekeeping in such contexts was more complex and more expensive than more limited operations such as monitoring a cease-fire or controlling a buffer zone. This was to be a second generation of peacekeeping[416] ...

The forces established in 1999 in Kosovo and East Timor marked a further development:

[T]hey are qualitatively different from almost any other the Organisation has ever undertaken. In each place the United Nations is the administration, responsible for fulfilling all the functions of a state—from fiscal management and judicial affairs to everyday municipal services, such as cleaning the streets and conducting customs formalities at the borders. This is a new order of magnitude for an organization that more customarily provides States with technical assistance in such areas, rather than assuming complete responsibility for them. And it is a new order of magnitude for peacekeeping operations as well, making them extraordinarily complex and almost as dependent on civilian experts as on military personnel.[417]

Accordingly UNMIK and UNTAET could be seen as the third generation of peacekeeping ...

UN peacekeeping forces played a major role in the settlement of long-standing conflicts that had been fuelled by the Cold War ...

The following peacekeeping operations are then surveyed: UNGOMAP (Afghanistan), UNTAG

---

[414] See Higgins, *United Nations Peacekeeping 1946–1967*, Vol III, 5; Abi-Saab, *The United Nations Operations in the Congo 1960–1964* (1978); Virally, 'Les Nations Unies et L'affaire du Congo', 1960 AFDI 557.
[415] See list of peacekeeping forces on UN website, *www.un.org/Depts/dpko/dpko/list*.
[416] [UN Secretary-General, *Supplement to an Agenda for Peace*], S/1995/1;1995 UNYB 175. Ed. See Ratner, *The New UN Peacekeeping* (1995).
[417] Address of Deputy-Secretary-General, Press Release DSG/SM/91.

(Namibia), UNAVEM II (Angola), UNOMOZ (Mozambique), UNTAC (Cambodia), UNUCA (Central America) and ONUSAL (El Salvador)

This brief survey of UN peacekeeping operations in those conflicts where the end of the Cold War facilitated settlement shows that the forces played an extensive role involving a very wide range of activities. Only UNGOMAP in Afghanistan was a limited force of a traditional kind; the others were large and complex operations with functions including disarmament, election monitoring, human rights, and re-establishment of civil society. They involved significant civilian participation as well as more traditional military functions such as monitoring cease-fires. In the terms of the *Agenda for Peace*, these were peace-building as well as peace-keeping operations . . .

But the end of the Cold War also contributed to the outbreak of new conflicts. The break-up of Yugoslavia and the competing claims of Croats, Bosnians, and Serbs led to conflict; the UN undertook several operations in the former Yugoslavia. The break-up of the USSR into its fifteen constituent republics also brought with it pressures for further subdivision on ethnic lines and the first UN peacekeeping force in the former USSR was established in Georgia in 1993 . . .

Also, when the USSR and the USA and other powers withdrew support from governments which they had helped to keep in power during the Cold War, those governments were weakened and in many cases civil war resulted. UN peacekeeping operations played a role in some of these conflicts. Thus, for example, the UN became involved in peacekeeping operations in Somalia when civil war broke out after the overthrow of the Siad Barre regime, which had long been supported by Western states. In Liberia, when the government of the Western-backed President Doe was overthrown, the UN sent a peacekeeping force to supplement the work of a regional force . . .

In other African states it was internal conflict as much as Cold War factors which contributed to the outbreak of conflict.[418] . . .The DRC plunged into conflict after the overthrow of President Mobutu who had been supported in power by France during the Cold War; conflicts in neighbouring Rwanda, Uganda, and Angola spilled over into the DRC. The Security Council provided for the establishment of a UN force in the DRC, but its deployment was delayed. Here and in Sierra Leone the parties struggled for power and control of the rich resources of the state; internal conflicts spilled over into regional instability involving other states in the region. In Sierra Leone a UN peacekeeping force was established in 1999 but ran into difficulty. UN forces were also established in response to civil conflict in the neighbouring states of Côte d'Ivoire and Liberia.. . .

Optimism about the role that peacekeeping forces would be able to play after the end of the Cold War was one of the factors that led to an expansion of their mandates. They not only took on wider roles in the re-creation of civil society as described above; there was also a blurring of the differences between peacekeeping and enforcement action. The Secretary-General, in his 1992 *Agenda for Peace*, had envisaged a more ambitious role for peacekeeping forces. He wrote of a new concept of peacemaking; this would involve UN forces operating under Article 40, of the UN Charter to enforce rather merely monitor cease-fires.[419] The expansion of the traditional model of peacekeeping and blurring of the distinction between peacekeeping and enforcement was most marked in Yugoslavia and Somalia; UN experience in these conflicts led to a rethinking of the relationship and a much more cautious attitude, by both the Secretary-General in his 1995 *Supplement to An Agenda for Peace* and the Security Council.. . .In Yugoslavia and Somalia peacekeeping and enforcement action blurred together when peacekeeping forces were given functions that went beyond traditional peacekeeping. In Yugoslavia UNPROFOR was set-up in 1991 as a traditional peacekeeping force. . . . From February 1993 the Security Council began to use Chapter VII . . . Resolution 807 expressed concern. . .at the cease-fire violations; it determined that the situation constituted a threat to peace and security in the region and then went on: 'determined to ensure the security of UNPROFOR, and to this end acting under Chapter VII' they demanded that the parties comply fully with the UN peacekeeping plan in Croatia, observe Security Council resolutions and respect fully UNPROFOR's unimpeded freedom of movement.[420] . . . France said that the reference to Chapter VII did not imply any automatic authority to resort to force other than in self-defence, but gave UNPROFOR the authority it needed to surmount the obstacles in the way of the execution of its mandate.[421]

UNPROFOR was later also authorized to use force in protection of the safe havens. The Security Council, faced

---

[418] See Report of the Secretary-General, *The causes of conflict and the promotion of durable peace and sustainable development in Africa*, S/1998/318, 37 ILM (1998) 913.
[419] *Agenda for Peace* para 44, 31 ILM (1992) 953.
[420] *SC* 3174th meeting (1993).
[421] *SC* 3344th meeting (1994); 3527th meeting (1995).

with calls to act in response to ethnic cleansing, especially that by the Bosnian Serbs, proclaimed several 'safe areas' in 1993; it followed this by extending the mandate of UNPROFOR in Resolution 836 to enable it not only to monitor the cease-fire and to participate in the delivery of humanitarian relief in the safe areas, but also 'acting in self-defence to take the necessary measures including the use of force' in reply to bombardments and armed incursions into the safe areas. But member states were not willing to provide the 30,000 troops estimated by the UN Secretary-General to be necessary for the performance of this mandate. The 7,000 troops actually provided were militarily incapable of protecting the safe areas against attack by the Bosnian Serbs and the protection for one ethnic group was seen as undermining the impartiality of UNPROFOR.[422] ...

Thus the use of Chapter VII in the resolutions on UNPROFOR [and its successors] LUNCRO and UNTAES increased expectations as to what they might achieve, but did not in itself give these forces enforcement powers in the absence of further express provision. The lack of realistic mandates and of adequate resources meant that the forces were not able to fulfil the expectations raised ...

The experience in Somalia of UNOSOM I, UNITAF and UNOSOM II is reviewed, revealing the same blurring of functions and resulting problems.

As in Bosnia, there was no real cease-fire in place [in Somalia] and the peacekeeping force [UNOSOM I] was sent in even though there was no peace to keep ... Its purpose was to deter attacks on humanitarian relief operations and it was to use force only in self-defence. But UNOSOM I proved unable to operate beyond Mogadishu or to carry out its mandate in the absence of cooperation of the warring parties.

The Security Council responded to this by sending a different type of force. In December 1992 it authorized the deployment of member states in a multi-national non-UN force, UNITAF, to 'use all necessary means to establish a secure environment' for humanitarian relief operations. Operational command was assumed by the USA and it contributed more than two-thirds of the troops. The authorization of this operation was another new departure for the UN. It was the first time that Chapter VII was used, not to authorize force against a wrongdoing state such as Iraq, but for humanitarian aims in a civil war ... It achieved limited success in securing the delivery of humanitarian relief, but it was not able to operate throughout Somalia and it did not secure the disarmament of the warring factions ...

The Security Council in Resolution 814 (adopted unanimously) replaced both UNOSOM I and UNITAF by UNOSOM II, the first peace enforcement operation under the command of the UN, created under Chapter VII, with functions that went beyond traditional peacekeeping.[423] UNOSOM II was mandated in Resolution 814 to operate throughout Somalia: to monitor the cessation of hostilities and compliance with the cease-fire agreements; to prevent any resumption of violence and, if necessary, to take appropriate action against any faction violating the cease-fire; to secure disarmament of the organized factions; to maintain security at ports, airports and lines of communication needed for deliveries of humanitarian assistance; to protect the UN civilian staff; to clear mines; and to assist refugees to return home. This innovative combination of peacekeeping and Chapter VII proved only partially successful ... Resolution 837 was passed in response to the murder of UN peacekeepers by one of the factions led by General Aidid ... This resolution authorized the UN forces to arrest and try those responsible for the killings. Under this mandate US troops suffered losses when their operation in pursuit of General Aidid went wrong. After this the USA was no longer willing to continue the operation and announced complete withdrawal of its forces by March 1994 ... In the continued absence of cooperation from the warring parties and the reluctance of contributing states to maintain their troops in Somalia, the operation was terminated in March 1995 ...

[Another] way in which the Security Council blurred the traditional distinctions between peacekeeping and

---

[422] Akashi, 'The Use of Force in a UN Peacekeeping Operation: Lessons Learnt from the Safe Areas Mandate', 19 Fordham ILJ (1995) 312; 1994 UNYB 522; Report of the Secretary-General pursuant to GA Resolution 53/35 (1998), *Srebrenica report*.

[423] For the first time the USA contributed troops to serve under UN command; this led to serious problems in securing unity of command. The USA tended to operate outside the UN command structure. The Secretary-General, in the *Supplement to an Agenda for Peace* (S/1995/1 at para 41), said that the experience in Somalia underlined again the necessity for a peacekeeping force to act as an integrated whole. That necessity is all the more imperative when the mission is operating in dangerous conditions. There must be no attempt by troop-contributing governments to provide guidance, let alone give orders, to their contingents on operational matters. To do so creates divisions within the force. It can also create the impression that the operation is serving the policy objectives of the contributing governments rather than the collective will of the UN as formulated by the Security Council. Such impressions inevitably undermine an operation's legitimacy and effectiveness.

enforcement action in Yugoslavia and Somalia was through the establishment of both peacekeeping and enforcement forces to operate at the same time ... This happened first in Yugoslavia, where UNPROFOR was operating on the ground as a peacekeeping force; the Security Council subsequently authorized NATO member states to use force under Chapter VII.

Thus the combination of two different types of operations at the same time during on-going armed conflict led to serious problems in Yugoslavia and in Somalia ... Peacekeeping operations were endangered by forcible intervention and the states authorized to use force were hampered by the presence on the ground of vulnerable peacekeeping forces. There were fundamental problems as to who could authorize operations and of coordination between the two forces. The combination of the two types of operation has proved more successful after the conclusion of conflict[424] ...

The lessons of Yugoslavia and Somalia are now widely accepted. Peacekeeping and enforcement forces may not be compatible. ... it is not possible gradually to increase the functions of peacekeeping forces to include elements of enforcement without endangering the impartiality of the force. If a peacekeeping force is to be given Chapter VII enforcement functions, it must be given commensurate forces, equipment, and logistical support. The Secretary-General, in his 1995 *Supplement to An Agenda for Peace*, abandoned the expansive optimism of the earlier *Agenda for Peace* and retreated to the more traditional concept of peacekeeping. He stressed the basic principles of consent of the parties, impartiality, and the non-use of force except in self-defence. Three aspects of recent mandates had led peacekeeping operations to undermine these basic principles: the tasks of protecting humanitarian operations during continuing warfare, protecting civilian populations in safe areas, and pressing the parties to achieve national reconciliation at a pace faster than they were ready to accept. It has repeatedly been asserted that peacekeeping forces must never again be deployed into an environment in which there is no cease-fire or peace agreement.

The Security Council in a Statement welcomed the Secretary-General's analysis in the *Supplement to An Agenda for Peace* and also reiterated the practical requirements of successful peacekeeping: the need for a clear mandate, a fixed time frame, an effective command structure, and secure financing[425] ... The UN Special Committee on Peacekeeping report on the undertaking of a comprehensive review of the whole question of peacekeeping also stressed the importance of respect for the principles of consent, impartiality, and non-use of force, except in self-defence; the need for clear mandates, objectives, and command structures.[426]

Notes

1. As indicated by Gray, there is no article in the UN Charter that provides for peacekeeping forces. Their constitutionality was confirmed in the *Certain Expenses* case.[427] In this case, certain UN members had fallen badly behind in paying their UN dues because they refused to accept the assessments against them so far as they related to the financing of UNEF and ONUC. Advising that the financing was constitutional, the Court stated:

    "... such expenditures must be tested by their relationship to the purposes of the United Nations in the sense that if an expenditure were made for a purpose which is not one of the purposes of the United Nations [stated in art.1], it could not be considered an 'expense of the Organisation' [art.17 UN Charter].

    ... When the Organisation takes action which warrants the assertion that it was appropriate for the fulfilment of one of the stated purposes of the United Nations, the presumption is that such an action is not ultra vires the Organisation.

    ... it is apparent that the operations [of UNEF and ONUC] were undertaken to fulfil a prime purpose of the United Nations, that is, to promote and to maintain a peaceful settlement of the situation. This being true, the Secretary-General properly exercised the authority given to him to incur financial obligations of the Organisation."

---

[424] This may also be seen in Kosovo and East Timor ...
[425] S/PRST/1995/9; see also Special Peacekeeping Committee Press Release GA/PK/163.
[426] Report of the Special Committee on Peacekeeping, A/54/839; see also UN Press Release GA/SPD/179 (May 2000).
[427] I.C.J. Rep. 1962, p.151. Advisory Opinion.

2. The experience of involving UN peacekeeping forces in Yugoslavia and Somalia in the use of force beyond the traditional self-defence limit provided a salutary lesson, echoing that of ONUC, particularly in respect of the tragic events in the safe haven of Srebrenica and as UNOSOM II found itself caught up in conflict with Somalia warlords. One consequence of this lesson was the delay in UN intervention in Rwanda in 1994, with states being reluctant to commit their troops. Despite knowledge by the world of the genocidal massacres of Tutsis by Hutus that began in April 1994, with over half a million people being killed, it was not for some months that UNAMIR, the UN force that had existed in the area since 1993, was given the necessary troops to act in any way effectively.[428]

3. For an account of Security Council practice authorising enforcement action by UN peacekeeping forces under art.42, see Simma, above, p.804.

4. Another result of the lessons of Yugoslavia and Somalia was that peacekeeping forces were not established under Chapter VII again for several years.[429] However, there has been a reversion to earlier practice: UNMIK (Kosovo) and UNTEAT (East Timor) were established under Chapter VII in 1999, as was UNMIL (Liberia) in 2003.[430]

5. Proposals for the reform of peacekeeping operations were made in the Brahimi Report.[431] The proposals have been favourably received by the Secretary-General and by states and are being implemented.[432]

---

[428] See UN Dept of Peacekeeping, *Comprehensive Report on Lessons Learnt from UNAMIR*; and UN blue book series, Vol.10, *The United Nations and Rwanda 1993–1996*.

[429] See Gray, above, n.2, pp.230–232, who notes that the peacekeeping operations in Georgia, Liberia (before 2003), Tajikstan, Central African Republic and Sierra Leone were not established under Ch.VII.

[430] Although the peacekeeping forces in Sierra Leone (UNAMSIL, 1999–2005) and the Democratic Republic of the Congo (MONUC, 1999–) were not established under Ch.VII, the Security Council acted under it to empower them to act as necessary for security purposes: see Gray, above, at n.2, pp.244 et seq.

[431] *Report of the Panel on UN Peace Operations* (2000), *www.un.org/peace/reports/*. For a critique of the Report, see Durch, Holt, Earle, Shanahan, *The Brahimi Report and the Future of UN Peace Operations* (2003, Henry L. Stimson Center).

[432] See the *Report of Special Committee on Peacekeeping Operations*, UN Doc. A/57/767 (2001); and the Reports by the Secretary-General, UN Docs. A/55/502 and A/57/711; and S.C. Resns 1318 (2000), 1327 (2000) and 1353 (2001) and G.A. Resns 57/129 and 57/767.

12 ARBITRATION AND JUDICIAL SETTLEMENT OF DISPUTES[1]

1. INTRODUCTORY NOTE

It is a principle of international law that states "shall settle their international disputes by peaceful means"[2] and not by resort to force. This principle is reinforced by art.33, UN Charter[3] and the 1982 Manila Declaration on the Peaceful Settlement of International Disputes.[4] In practice, most disputes are settled through negotiation between the parties or by third-party assistance in the form of good offices, mediation, conciliation or the conduct of fact-finding inquiries.[5] As in municipal law, in international law litigation is very much a matter of last resort. The possible worsening of relations by unilateral recourse to law, the uncertainty of the outcome of legal proceedings,[6] and the embarrassment and finality of an adverse ruling by a body beyond one's control are considerations common to both systems which conspire to make this so.[7] If the cost of legal proceedings sometimes deters the plaintiff at the national level, the absence in most cases of compulsory jurisdiction is an even greater weapon for the defendant in international law.

This chapter is limited to the machinery for the settlement of disputes upon a basis of law, whether by arbitration or judicial settlement. This is so for reasons of space and because arbitral tribunals and courts apply international law so that their functioning is of particular interest to lawyers.

---

[1] See Collier and Lowe, *The Settlement of Disputes in International Law* (1999); Evans, ed., *Remedies in International Law* (1999); Lauterpacht, *Aspects of the Administration of International Justice* (1991); Merrills, *International Dispute Settlement* (4th edn 2005); and Oellers-Frahm and Zimmerman, *Dispute Settlement in Public International Law* (2001).

[2] Article 2(3), UN Charter, below, App.I. See Hutchinson (1992) 14 A.Y.I.L. 1. Although Article 2(3) is expressed in terms of UN "members," it can be taken to state customary international law.

[3] App.I, below.

[4] GA Resn.37/10, G.A.O.R., 37th Sess., Supp. 51, p.261 (1982); and (1982) 21 I.L.M. 449 (final draft).

[5] See Bar-Yaacov, *The Handling of International Disputes by Means of Inquiry* (1974); Cot, *International Conciliation* (1968), Eng. trans. (by Myers) (1972); David Davies Memorial Institute of International Studies, *Report of a Study Group on the Peaceful Settlement of International Disputes* (1966); Lall, ed., *Multilateral Negotiation and Mediation* (1985); Northedge and Donelan, *International Disputes* (1971); UN Office of Legal Affairs, *Handbook on the Peaceful Settlement of Disputes between States* (1992); Vallat, in *Cambridge Essays in International Law* (1965), p.155. On the important WTO dispute settlement procedures, see Van Den Bossche, *The Law and Practice of the WTO* (2nd edn 2008), pp.168 et seq. On UNCLOS procedures, see above pp.414 et seq. For an example of a fact-finding commission of inquiry, see the *Red Crusader case*, above, p.390. For an example of conciliation, see the *Jan Mayen case*, above, p.338.

[6] Paradoxically, some of the uncertainty of international law is, as Gross points out (in Gross, ed., *The Future of the International Court of Justice* (1976) Vol.II, p.727 at p.746), because so few cases are taken to court.

[7] cf. Fitzmaurice in *The Future of the International Court*, below, n.23, pp.463–470.

2. ARBITRATION[8]

INTERPRETATION OF ARTICLE 3, PARAGRAPH 2, OF THE TREATY OF LAUSANNE

Advisory Opinion, P.C.I.J. Reports, Series B, No.12, at p.26 (1925)

Opinion of the Court

If the word "arbitration" is taken in a wide sense, characterised simply by the binding force of the pronouncement made by a third Party to whom the interested Parties have had recourse, it may well be said that the decision in question is an "arbitral award."

This term, on the other hand, would hardly be the right one, if the intention were to convey a common and more limited conception of arbitration, namely, that which has for its object the settlement of differences between States by *judges* of their own choice and *on the basis of respect for law* (Hague Convention for the pacific settlement of international disputes, dated October 18th, 1907, Article 37). It appears, in fact, that according to the arguments put forward on both sides before the Council, the settlement of the dispute in question depends, at all events for the most part, on consideration not of a legal character; moreover, it is impossible, properly speaking, to regard the Council, acting in its capacity of an organ of the League of Nations ... as a tribunal of arbitrators.

Notes

1. The definition of arbitration adopted in the *Treaty of Lausanne* case was followed by the ICJ in the *Maritime Delimitation and Territorial Questions (Bahrain v Qatar)* case.[9] Arbitration was similarly defined by the International Law Commission as "a procedure for the settlement of disputes between States by a binding award on the basis of law and as a result of an undertaking voluntarily accepted."[10] Schwarzenberger states:

    "The only difference between arbitration and *judicial settlement* lies in the method of selecting the members of these judicial organs. While, in arbitration proceedings, this is done by agreement between the parties, judicial settlement presupposes the existence of a standing tribunal with its own bench of judges and its own rules of procedure which parties to a dispute must accept."[11]

2. In origin, international arbitration was a vehicle for the resolution of *inter-state* disputes, and it is still regularly used for this purpose.[12] In recent years provision has also been made for mixed international arbitrations in which claims are brought by individuals or corporate entities against states.[13] The arbitration of foreign investment disputes under the ICSID Convention is the most important ongoing example.[14] Such procedures now commonly take the place of inter-state

---

8   See Merrills, above, n.1, Ch.5.
9   I.C.J. Rep. 2001, p.40.
10 Y.B.I.L.C., 1953, II, p.202.
11 *Manual of International Law* (6th edn 1976), p.195.
12 See, e.g. *Eritrea v Yemen*, above, p.219. On the provision for inter-state arbitration in the WTO and UNCLOS, see Van Den Bossche, above, n.5, and above, pp.414 et seq, respectively.
13 See Toope, *Mixed International Arbitrations* (1990).
14 See above, p.503. See also the Iran-US Claims Tribunal, which continues in operation for large claims. It was established in 1981 to consider inter-state claims and claims by US nationals against Iran and vice versa arising out of the Iranian hostages crisis. In the case of small claims by US or Iranian nationals, the national state was authorised to bring the claims on their behalf; in the case of large claims nationals, usually companies, were permitted to bring their own claims. See Merrills, above, n.1, pp.119 et seq. As to private investment claims against states under the 1992 North American Free Trade Agreement (NAFTA), 32 I.L.M. 289 (1993), see Collier and Lowe, above, at n.1, pp.111 et seq.

claims in which the claimant state acts by way of diplomatic protection of a national against another state. Where there are large numbers of claims against a state by non-nationals (e.g. following the state's nationalisation of foreign property), an alternative to international arbitration is the "lump sum settlement agreement".[15]

3. Arbitration tribunals may consist of a single arbitrator or they may be collegiate bodies.[16] In the *Rainbow Warrior* case[17] the UN Secretary-General was called upon to arbitrate for the first time. If the tribunal is a collegiate body, it will usually be a mixed commission,[18] i.e. one upon which sit two or more arbitrators (commissioners, etc.) appointed in equal numbers by each of the parties separately plus an Umpire (or Presiding Commissioner, etc.) appointed jointly by the parties or by the arbitrators appointed by them.

4. *The Permanent Court of Arbitration* ("PCA").[19] This was established in 1900 in accordance with the 1899 Hague Convention for the Pacific Settlement of International Disputes[20] and, later, the 1907 Convention of the same name.[21] The PCA is based at The Hague, in the same building as the ICJ. It is not in fact a "court". Operating through its Bureau, the PCA offers procedures, a courtroom and registry facilities and other assistance for the conduct of both inter-state and mixed international arbitrations for the parties to arbitration cases that agree to use them. The Conventions themselves provide arbitration procedures, though the Court has devised its own modern sets of rules of procedure for different kinds of disputes. Arbitrators may be selected from the Court's panel of arbitrators nominated by Convention parties, but this is not required. Under UNCITRAL Arbitration Rules, the PCA Secretary-General provides the "default" mechanism for the appointment of arbitrators where the parties cannot agree. After a period when the PCA had little or no arbitration work and appeared to be on its way out, it is now a very active body, with a caseload of over 20 cases in 2008. In that year it served as the registry for the two Eritrea-Ethiopia Boundary and Claims Commissions, two tribunals established under UNCLOS and many mixed arbitrations under investment treaties or contracts.

---

[15] See above, p.504. Cf. the UN Compensation Commission which had jurisdiction to award compensation out of Iraqi oil revenues for damage caused by the 1990 Iraq invasion and occupation of Kuwait: see Caron and Morris (2002) 13 E.J.I.L. 183; Gattini (2002) 13 E.J.I.L. 161; Heiskanen, 296 Hague Recueil 255 (2000); Lillich, ed., *The UN Compensation Commission* (1995).

[16] See Johnson (1953) 30 B.Y.I.L. 53.

[17] (1987) 26 I.L.M. 1346.

[18] See, e.g. the Mexican Claims Commission by which several of the cases in Ch.8 were decided.

[19] On the Court, see Hamilton, Requena and Van Scheltinga, eds, *The Permanent Court of Arbitration* (1999) and Jonkman, 279 Hague Recueil 9 (1999).

[20] (1901) U.K.T.S. 9, Cd. 798. The Convention entered into force in 1900.

[21] (1971) U.K.T.S. 6, Cmnd. 4575. In force 1910. 108 parties, including the UK, to one or both Conventions. The 1907 Convention revised the 1899 Convention in the light of the experience of the Court in its early cases.

3. THE WORLD COURT[22]

The state of health of the World Court has improved remarkably in recent times. Whereas there were years in the 1960s to the 1980s when the Court had very little to do, the Court's list in the 1990s and since has been much healthier. If there used to be concern over its uncertain future,[23] the need now is to ensure it can cope with all of the cases referred to it.[24] One reason[25] for this change is an increase in confidence in the Court. In the years after the *South-West Africa* cases,[26] the Court's reputation plummeted among developing states, who saw the Court as wedded to western attitudes and approaches to international law.[27] The *Nicaragua* case marked a change of perception on their part and the Court now has cases to which states from many regions of the world are parties.

In several cases in the 1970s and 1980s, the Court experienced the phenomenon of the "non-appearing" defendant.[28] Iceland boycotted the proceedings in the *Fisheries Jurisdiction* cases and in five later cases the defendant state did not appear.[29] This can, as in the *Nicaragua* case, present difficulties in ensuring that the Court has all of the evidence it needs in order to decide a case. It has not been a problem recently.

However, a persisting problem is part of the general weakness of effectiveness that international law faces. Whereas the judgments and orders of the PCIJ in contentious litigation were all complied with, the record of the ICJ since the Second World War has been less satisfactory. The judgments in the *Corfu Channel* case, the *Fisheries Jurisdiction* cases, the *U.S. Diplomatic and Consular Staff in Tehran* case, and the *Nicaragua* case were not respected,[30] and most orders for provisional measures have not been followed.[31] The judgment in the *Right of Passage* case, above, p.220, was soon negated by the Indian invasion of Goa. On the power, as yet unexercised, of the Security Council to enforce decisions of the Court, see art.94(2) of the Charter.[32] In 1986, the US vetoed a draft Security

---

[22] See Amr, *The Role of the International Court of Justice as the Principal Judicial Organ of the United Nations* (2003); Bowett et al, *The International Court of Justice: Process, Practice and Procedure* (1997); Damrosch, ed., *The International Court of Justice at a Crossroads* (1987); Gardner and Wickremasinghe, eds, *The International Court of Justice: Process, Practice and Procedure* (1997); Lowe and Fitzmaurice, eds, *Fifty Years of the International Court of Justice* (1996); Muller, Raic and Thuransky, eds, *The International Court of Justice: its Future Role after 50 years* (1997); Peck and Lee, eds, *Increasing the Effectiveness of the International Court of Justice* (1997); Rosenne, *The Law and Practice of the International Court 1920–2005* (4th edn 2006) 4 Vols; Thirlway, in Evans, ed., International Law (2003), Ch.18; Zimmermann, Tomuschat, Oellers-Fram, Tams and Thienel, eds, *The Statute of the International Court of Justice* (2006).

[23] See Gross, ed., *The Future of the International Court of Justice* (3 vols, 1976).

[24] See the Study Group Report, below, n.62. In early 2009, the Court has 14 pending cases.

[25] There has also been a large increase in the 1990s in the number of states who are the Court's potential clients in contentious litigation.

[26] I.C.J. Rep. 1966, p.6. Having earlier held that it had jurisdiction in the cases, the Court in effect reversed this decision by ruling that Liberia and Ethiopia, the claimant states, lacked the necessary "legal right or interest" to bring these cases alleging that South Africa had not complied with its obligations under the mandate for South-West Africa/Namibia. The Court's judgment angered a majority of the General Assembly to the point where its Fourth Committee refused to approve a financial appropriation for the Court.

[27] One reason for the establishment of a new International Tribunal for the Law of the Sea, see above, p.503, by UNCLOS III was a lack of confidence in the ICJ.

[28] See Elkind, *Non-Appearance before the International Court of Justice* (1984); Fitzmaurice (1980) 51 B.Y.I.L. 89; Sinclair (1981) 31 I.C.L.Q. 338; and Thirlway, *Non-Appearance before the International Court of Justice* (1985).

[29] The *Nuclear Test* cases above, p.365; the *Pakistani Prisoners of War Case*, I.C.J. Rep. 1973, pp.328, 347; the *Aegean Sea Continental Shelf* case, I.C.J. Rep. 1978, p.3; the *U.S. Diplomatic and Consular Staff* case, above, p.312; the *Nicaragua* case, above, p.727. For the *Fisheries Jurisdiction* cases, see above, p.391.

[30] But, after many years of stalemate, in 1992, as a part of a general settlement of claims between the two states, the UK approved the delivery to Albania of the gold that had been the subject matter of the *Monetary Gold* case, see below, p.845; and Albania paid the U.K. £2 million in respect of all British claims against it. Following this, the Corfu Channel Incident was regarded as closed; (1992) 63 B.Y.I.L. 781.

[31] On provisional measures, see below, p.870.

[32] Below, App.II. See Kerley, in *The Future of the International Court of Justice*, above, n.23, p.276.

Council resolution calling for "full and immediate compliance" with the *Nicaragua* case judgment,[33] and in 2008 a Mexican national was executed by the state of Texas contrary to the judgment in the *Avena* case.[34] More encouragingly, Nigeria returned to Cameroon territory in the area of Lake Chad and, despite considerable opposition in Nigeria, the Bakassi Peninsula, as required by the *Land and Maritime Boundary between Cameroon and Nigeria* case[35].

5. *The ICJ and other international courts and tribunals*. Recent years have seen an increase in the number of specialised and regional courts and tribunals. The most important of these are the International Tribunal of the Law of the Sea ("ITLOS") and the International Criminal Court.[36] There are also various other international criminal tribunals[37] and regional human rights and other courts.[38]

Precipitated by the establishment of the ITLOS, there has been much discussion of the consequences of a "proliferation" of courts and tribunals, with the pre-eminent position of the ICJ as a lawmaker[39] being the main subject of debate.[40] Concern was expressed by President Guillaume of the ICJ as follows[41]:

"No new international court should be created without first questioning whether the duties which the international legislator intends to confer on it could not be better performed by an existing court. International courts should be aware of the dangers involved in the fragmentation of the law and take efforts to avoid such dangers. However, those measures may not be enough, and the International Court of Justice, the only judicial body vested with universal and general jurisdiction, has a role to play in this area. For the purpose of maintaining the unity of the law, the various existing courts or those yet to be created could, in my opinion, be empowered in certain cases— indeed encouraged—to request advisory opinions from the International Court of Justice through the intermediary of the Security Council or through the General Assembly."

In contrast, Judge Higgins[42] stated:

"We thus today have a certain decentralisation of some of the topics with which the ICJ *can* in principle deal to new, highly specialised bodies, whose members are experts in a subject matter which becomes ever more complex, which are more open to non-State actors and which can respond rapidly. I think this is an inevitable consequence of the busy and complex world in which we live and is not a cause of regret. I do not agree with the call of successive Presidents, made at

---

[33] UN Inf. Centre London *Newsletter* November 6, 1986.

[34] I.C.J. Rep. 2004, p.12.

[35] I.C.J. Rep. 2002, p.303. On recent compliance, see Paulson, 98 A.J.I.L. 434 (2004) and Llamzon, 18 E.J.I.L. 815 (2007).

[36] On the role of the panels and appellate body within the WTO dispute settlement procedures, see Merrills, above, at n.1, Ch.9.

[37] The main ones are the International Criminal Tribunals for the Former Yugoslavia ("ICTY") and Rwanda ("ICTR"); the Special Court for Sierra Leone; and the Special Tribunal for Cambodia.

[38] The European Court of Human Rights, the Inter-American Court of Human Rights, the African Court of Justice and Human Rights; and the European Court of Justice. There are also several sub-regional courts and tribunals, mostly in Africa, including the East African Community ("EAC") Court of Justice; the Economic Community of West African States ("ECO-WAS") Court of Justice; and the Southern African Development Community ("SADC") Tribunal.

[39] In most cases there is no problem of overlapping access, as only states may be parties to cases before the ICJ; many of the above bodies have individuals as applicants or defendants.

[40] See, e.g. Buergenthal (2001) 14 L.J.I.L. 267; Charney, 271 Hague Receuil 101 (1998); Kingsbury (1999) N.Y.U.J.I.L.P. 679; the ILC Study Group Report, finalised by Koskenniemi, *Fragmentation of International Law*, 2006, UN Doc. A/CN.4/L.682; and Shany, *The Competing Jurisdictions of International Courts and Tribunals* (2003). On the relationship between the ICJ and ITLOS, see above, p.419. A high proportion of the ICJ's cases have concerned the law of the sea.

[41] UN Doc. A/56/PV.32, p.9, quoted in Rosenne (2001) 291 Hague Receuil 13 at 133.

[42] (2001) 50 I.C.L.Q. 121 at 122–123.

the UN General Assembly, for the ICJ to provide advisory opinions to other tribunals on points of international law. This seeks to re-establish the old order of things and ignores the very reasons that have occasioned the new decentralisation. ....

The International Court, while *de facto* shedding some of the more specialised subject matter over which it has competence in principle, nonetheless retains a central importance. It is the body where the great legal-political issues of the day between States are litigated. These issues—title to territory, treaty matters, issues relating to the use of force, everything to do with the UN—are critical in their implications. They also necessarily take a certain time to handle. The Court remains the primary judicial organ of the United Nations and the only court which can give advisory opinions to the UN and its specialised agencies, and the only court which can deal with the interface of the various fields of international law. Further, it is striking that even as new judicial bodies spring up, the Court is busier than at any time in its history, with cases of great weight and importance from every corner of the world. Even as this judicial decentralisation occurs, the Court's docket gets larger and larger.

The important task for the Court is not to reinvent itself—even were it able to—in the image of more recent tribunals, but rather to ensure that it can respond as efficaciously as possible to its clientele—sovereign States and international organisations—who seem to find ever more work for it to do."

Issues that arise concern "forum shopping" and possibly contradictory decisions for the same litigant or litigants before different courts or tribunals[43] in essentially the same case and inconsistent development of international law in the absence of any established hierarchy of courts or tribunals. A notable example of the latter is the different tests adopted by the ICJ and ICTY for a state's responsibility for para-military units not part of its armed forces.[44]

A. Organisation

See arts 2–33, Statute of the International Court of Justice.[45]

Notes

1.   The World Court, which is by far the most important international court, is the name commonly given to the Permanent Court of International Justice and the present International Court of Justice. The Permanent Court of International Justice was established in 1920 under the auspices of the League of Nations. In 1946, it was replaced by the International Court of Justice, which was made "the principal judicial organ of the United Nations" by art.92 of the United Nations Charter. The International Court of Justice is organised in accordance with the Statute of the International Court of Justice which is a part of the United Nations Charter and which in most respects is identical with the Statute of its predecessor. The World Court has always had its seat at The Hague.

2.   The 15 members of the Court, with the states of which they are nationals,[46] are: President Owada

---

[43] See, e.g. the Ireland-UK Mox Plant litigation, involving ITLOS and PCA arbitrations and an ECJ case: see ILC Study Group Report, above, at n.40, p.12.

[44] In the *Tadic* case, 38 I.L.M. 1540 (1999), the ICTY adopted an "effective control" test, rejecting the "overall control" test adopted by the ICJ in the *Nicaragua* case, I.C.J. Rep. 1986, p.14, and confirmed by the ICJ in the post-*Tadic Genocide (Bosnia v Yugoslavia)* case, I.C.J. Rep. 2007, p.1 at p.144.

[45] See App.I, below. The Statute is supplemented by the ICJ Rules of Court and Practice Directions, available at *www.icj-cij.org*.

[46] A state may have only one national on the Court. An ad hoc judge may have the same nationality as an elected judge.

(Japan); Vice-President Tomka (Slovakia); Judges Shi (China); Koroma (Sierra Leone); Al-Kha-sawneh (Jordan); Buergenthal (US); Simma (Germany); Abraham (France); Keith (New Zealand); Sepúlveda-Amor (Mexico); Bennouna (Morocco); Skotnikov (Russia); Cançado Trindade (Brazil); Yusuf (Somalia); and Greenwood (UK). There has only ever been one woman elected to the Court (Judge Higgins, former President); none at present. Judge Bastid was an ad hoc judge.

3. Judges are elected by the Security Council and the General Assembly according to a complicated procedure (Statute, arts 4–14) in which a lot of political and other competition occurs. In recent years, the balance of nationalities represented on the Court has changed with the nature of the international community.[47] The understanding now is that the 15 seats on the Court are dis-tributed (in terms of nationalities and power blocs) as follows: nationals of five western (Eur-opean and other) states; three African states (usually one francophonic civil law, one anglophonic common law and one Arab); three Asian states; two East European states[48]; and two Latin American and Caribbean states. It is also the convention that there should be a national of each of the five permanent members of the Security Council. This has been the case since 1945 save that there was no Chinese judge (nationalist or communist) between 1967 and 1985 when no candidate was put forward by Beijing.

4. The Court normally sits as a full court of 15 judges, although cases may be referred to an ad hoc chamber of three or more judges.[49] There is no appeal from a chamber decision to the full Court.

5. The Court gives a single, collegiate judgment. Individual judges in the majority may add their own separate opinions. Individual dissenting judges may give dissenting opinions.[50] The Court's judgments are in English and French, with the authentic text printed on the left hand page. On the ICJ's reliance on precedent, see above, p.43.

6. *Recusal.*[51] Provision is made in arts 17 and 24, Statute of the Court, below, Appendix I, for the recusal of judges, i.e. their non-participation in particular cases. This usually occurs because a judge has, before election to the Court, been involved in a case, e.g. as a state party adviser. Generally, the judge takes the initiative to recuse him or herself and there is no objection by the

---

[47] In 1920, there were 10 Judges from western Europe; two from Asia; two from South America; and one from the US. In the period immediately after the Second World War, Latin American representation rose to four; it has since fallen as Afro-Asian representation has increased. The number of western European judges has also declined, although it is still sub-stantial. See Schwarzenberger (1982) 36 Y.B.W.A. 241. See on the election process generally, Rosenne, in the *The Future of the International Court of Justice*, above, n.23. On the "cultural" balance of the Court; see McWhinney (1987) 65 Wash. U.L.R. 873; and Prott, *The Latent Power of Culture and the International Judge* (1979).

[48] Although there are, in a Cold War sense, still two East European judges, this category is out of date.

[49] The *Gulf of Maine* case, I.C.J. Rep. 1984, p.146, was the first such case. See most recently the *Frontier Dispute* case (*Benin v Niger*), I.C.J. Rep. 2005, p.90. The composition of the *Gulf of Maine* Chamber, which consisted wholly of North American and West European judges, was "entirely in accordance with the latent wishes of the parties": Judge Oda, *Gulf of Maine* (*Order*) case, I.C.J. Rep. 1982, p.10. Judge Oda was one of several judges who were critical of the litigants' influence in the *Gulf of Maine* case as being inconsistent with the Court's sovereignty and prejudicing the universal quality of its jur-isprudence. But he later conceded that this influence was "inevitable if a chamber is to be viable": *Land, Island and Frontier Dispute* case, I.C.J. Rep. 1987, p.10. The Court also has an Environmental Chamber for environmental cases and a Chamber of Summary Procedure (neither used so far). See Schwebel (1986) 61 Wash L.R. 1061 at 1070. On chambers, see art.26, Statute, below, App.III. See generally, Mosler, in Dinstein, ed., *International Law in a Time of Perplexity: Essays in Honour of Shabtai Rosenne* (1989); Oda (1988) 82 A.J.I.L. 556; Ostrihansky (1988) 37 I.C.L.Q. 30; Schwebel (1987) 81 A.J.I.L. 831; and Valencia-Ospina in Lowe and Fitzmaurice, above, n.22.

[50] See Hussain, *Dissenting and Separate Opinions at the World Court* (1984).

[51] See Couvreur, in Zimmerman et al, above, n.22, p.337.

Court.[52] There was an unsuccessful challenge by South Africa to the participation of ICJ President Sir Zafrulla Khan and Judges Padilla Nervo and Morozov in the *Legal Consequences* case[53] because they had been members of their states' delegations during UN discussion of the Southwest Africa situation.

GROSS, THE INTERNATIONAL COURT OF JUSTICE: CONSIDERATION OF REQUIREMENTS FOR ENHANCING ITS ROLE IN THE INTERNATIONAL LEGAL ORDER

in The Future of the International Court of Justice, above, n.23, Vol.I, pp.61–64.
Some footnotes omitted

The institution of judges ad hoc in contentious cases [under art.31, Statute of the Court] and in advisory proceedings under Articles 68 of the Statute and ... [art.102(3)] of the [revised] Rules of the Court has been a matter of controversy between those who would suppress it for the sake of enhancing the impartiality of the Court[54] and those who, for a variety of reasons, would maintain it.[55] There are also those who, occupying a middle ground, assert that the abolition of judges ad hoc should be combined with the exclusion of "national" judges from the bench, that is, judges who are [members of the Court and] nationals of one or both parties before the Court.[56] In this view, the essential objective is equality between the parties; this can be achieved either by adding to the bench a judge ad hoc or by excluding the "national judge." ...

Fitzmaurice [has] attacked the system ... arguing in particular two points: First, those who advocate its retention on the ground that it increases confidence in the Court argue from an impermissible premises that judges, particularly ad hoc judges, will necessarily espouse the view of their government. Secondly, once a case is terminated, a judge ad hoc may feel himself free of every obligation of confidence and may reveal to his government what had been said in the deliberations of the Court. This could have harmful consequences for the independence of judges, particularly if such revelations occurred shortly before elections to the Court.[57] ...

The fact of the matter is that in every case where the majority of the Court gave a favourable judgment for the appointing state, the judge ad hoc concurred, and he dissented in nearly every case where the judgment went against it.[58] Such voting alignments, even if the ad hoc judge is the only dissenting judge, as was the case in the recent *Barcelona Traction*[59] judgment, do not necessarily reflect on the independence of the judges concerned. Even the majority of 14 in that case could be wrong, and, despite concurrence in the result, there was wide disparity in the actual reasoning of the various judges. ...

It has often been observed that where two parties appoint judges ad hoc, their votes cancel each other out. In litigation where only one party appoints a judge ad hoc, the other party having a national as a titular judge, his vote could make a difference in marginal cases, but there have been no such cases. ...

It is recognised on all sides that diplomatic susceptibilities and politico-psychological considerations are involved, and if one takes them seriously, then the system of judges ad hoc should be left alone. To the purist it will remain objectionable as a survival of the basic idea of arbitration in the system of international adjudication. ...

---

[52] E.g. Judge Higgins recused herself in the *Genocide Convention* case, I.C.J. Rep. 1996, p.595, having been a member of the Human Rights Committee when aspects of the case arose under the Covenant on Civil and Political Right.

[53] I.C.J. Rep. 1971, p.16. On the recusal issue in this case, see Rosenne, in *The Future of the International Court of Justice,* above, at n.3, Vol.1, p.389. Israel unsuccessfully challenged Judge Elaraby's participation in the *Wall* case: his earlier activities as an Egyptian diplomatic representative had not involved "participation" in the case: I.C.J. Rep. 2004, p.3.

[54] For a recent view, see F. L. Grieves, *Supranationalism and International Adjudication*, (1969), p.180.

[55] [Rosenne, *The Law and Practice of the International Court* (1965), pp.202–205.]

[56] Erik Castrén, "Revision de la Charte des Nations Unies," 7 Revue Hellénique de Droit International 20–34, at 32 (1954).

[57] Ed. 45 *Annuaire de l'Institute de droit international*, II, p.444 (1954).

[58] Ed. Exceptionally, Judge ad hoc Bastid joined a unanimous court in a judgment against Tunisia, which had appointed her, in the *Continental Shelf* case (*Tunisia v Libya*) (*Application for Revision and Interpretation of the Judgment*), I.C.J. Rep. 1985, p.192 at p.247.

[59] Ed. above, p.515. National judges "not infrequently" vote against their national state: Thirlway, in Evans, ed., *International Law* (2nd edn 2006), p.564.

Notes

1. *National and ad hoc judges.* A judge of the nationality of a state party to a case "retains the right to sit in the case" (art.31(1), Statute of the Court). A party that does not have a national on the Court may choose an ad hoc judge to sit in the case (art.31(2) (3)).

2. In the *Application of the Genocide Convention* case *(Provisional Measures)*,[60] Judge ad hoc Lauterpacht explained the role of the ad hoc judge as follows:

    > "He has, I believe, the special obligation to endeavour to ensure that, so far as is reasonable, every relevant argument in favour of the party that has appointed him has been fully appreciated in the course of collegial consideration and, ultimately, is reflected—though not necessarily accepted—in any separate or dissenting opinion that he may write."

B. Access in Contentious Litigation

See arts 34–35, Statute of the International Court of Justice and art.93 of the United Nations Charter.[61]

Notes

1. Article 34, Statute of the Court provides that only states may be parties to cases before the Court. On the question whether access should be opened to public international organisations or to individuals or companies, a study group on the Court reported[62]:

    > "80 The principle reflected in Article 34 of the Court's Statute—that only States may appear before the Court in contentious cases—is long established and it has not been a main focus of criticism. Yet, since neither international personality nor the capacity to bring claims is restricted to States, as the Court itself affirmed in the *Reparations* case, the logic of excluding the United Nations and specialised agencies from using the Court as parties is not self-evident. These organisations are compelled to use arbitration in their disputes with States, or else use the device of the 'binding' advisory opinion.[63] From the perspective of the rules of law, this device is evidently inadequate. It is a significant gap in institutional arrangements that public international organisations cannot be held legally accountable to States in the principal judicial organ of the international community, nor can States be held legally accountable to such organisations. This is the more odd in that, in substance, public international organisations are nothing other than States acting collectively.
    >
    > 81 On the other hand, there seems to be little demand for direct standing from the organisations themselves, and there is the difficulty that such a change would require an amendment of Article 34 of the Statute. If disputes between States and international orga-

---

[60] Order of September 13, 1999, I.C.J. Rep. 1993, p.325 at 409. See also the dissenting opinion of Judge ad hoc Franck in the *Pulau Litigan* case, I.C.J. Rep. 2002, p.625, paras 9–12. On ad hoc and national judges, see Schwebel (1998) 48 I.C.L.Q. 889.

[61] See below, App.I.

[62] Report of the Study Group on the International Court of Justice established by the British Institute of International and Comparative Law (1996) 45 I.C.L.Q. Supp. pp.24–25.

[63] Ed. See below, p.874.

nisations were to go to the ICJ, they would, of course, add to the pressure on the Court's list, and so make it all the more important that the 'core' problem identified above [i.e. the pressure of work of the Court] be effectively addressed. ...

84 Although, in the past, academic criticism of the 'only States' provision in Article 34 has sometimes ventured to suggest that individuals should be given *locus standi*,[64] there is no strong support for this idea in current thinking. Indeed, if the contemporary concern is over how the Court can cope with inter-State disputes, it would be counterproductive to compound the problem by opening up the Court to individuals—and there are in any case other fora in which human rights cases by individuals can be pursued."

2. Article 35(1) provides that the Court "shall be open to the states parties to the present Statute". All UN members are parties to the Statute: art.93, UN Charter. In the *Legality of Use of Force* cases,[65] the ICJ held that it had no jurisdiction in cases brought by Serbia and Montenegro as that state was not an UN member, and hence not a party to the Statute on that basis, at the relevant time. Non-UN member states may become parties to the Statute by complying with the conditions set by the General Assembly on the recommendation of the Security Council.[66] No state is a party on this basis at present.[67] A state not a party to the Statute may have access to the Court by making a declaration accepting its jurisdiction.[68]

C. Jurisdiction In Contentious Litigation

See arts 36–37, Statute of the International Court of Justice.[69]

i. Jurisdiction under Article 36(1)

ROSENNE, THE LAW AND PRACTICE OF THE INTERNATIONAL COURT 1920 –2005

4th edn 2006, Vol.II, pp.643–865. Footnotes omitted

The classic method by which the parties refer a case to the Court [by agreement between them] is by a *special agreement* (*compromis*). ... It is an agreement by which by two or more States agree to refer a particular and defined case or matter to the Court for decision. The distinguishing feature of the special agreement as a title of jurisdiction is that jurisdiction is conferred on the Court and the Court is seised of the concrete case by the single act of notification of this agreement to the Court. Only if an agreement has this double effect is it a true special agreement. ...

---

[64] Ed. See further Rosenne above, n.25, Ch.10.
[65] E.g. *Legality of Use of Force (Serbia and Montenegro v UK)* case (Preliminary Objections), I.C.J. Rep. 2004, p.1307. But see the *Genocide Convention* case, I.C.J. Rep. 2007, paras 88 et seq.
[66] Article 93(2), UN Charter. For these conditions, see G.A. Res. 91(1), December 11, 1946.
[67] Liechtenstein, Nauru, San Marino and Switzerland were before becoming UN members.
[68] Article 35(2), ICJ Statute and SC Resn.9 (1946), October 15, 1946.
[69] See below, App.I.

In the Permanent Court, eleven cases were instituted by special agreement. Between 1946 and 2004 ... thirteen cases have been instituted in this way.[70]

The second method of conferring jurisdiction [by agreement under a treaty in force] is by a compromissory clause in a multilateral or bilateral treaty.[71]

CERTAIN QUESTIONS OF MUTUAL ASSISTANCE IN CRIMINAL MATTERS

Djibouti v France (2008)

I.C.J. Reports 2008

In this case, France failed to respond to a request by Djibouti asking that the French authorities send it their judicial investigation file into a case involving the death of a French judge on secondment in Djibouti for the purposes of a judicial investigation in Djibouti. The Court upheld Djibouti's claim that this failure was in breach of a bilateral treaty of mutual assistance in criminal matters between the two states insofar as France had failed to comply with its obligation under the treaty to inform Djibouti of the reason why it had refused to execute an international letter rogatory containing the request.

Djibouti had commenced proceedings in the case by filing an unilateral application against France under art.40(1), Statute of the Court. In response, in a letter to the Court, France expressly agreed, under art.38(5), Rules of the Court, to the Court's jurisdiction in the case. In the following passage, in the first case in which the Court applied art.38(5), the Court explores the nature of its *forum prorogatum* jurisdiction.

Judgment of the Court

60. The jurisdiction of the Court is based on the consent of States, under the conditions expressed therein. However, neither the Statute of the Court nor its Rules require that the consent of the parties which thus confers jurisdiction on the Court be expressed in any particular form (*Corfu Channel (United Kingdom* v. *Albania), Preliminary Objection, Judgment, 1948, I.C.J. Reports 1947-1948*, p. 27). ... Thus, in accordance with Article 36, paragraph 1, of the Statute, such consent may result from an explicit agreement of the parties, that agreement being able to be manifested in a variety of ways. Further, States may recognize the jurisdiction of the Court by making declarations to this effect under Article 36, paragraph 2, of the Statute.

61. The Court has also interpreted Article 36, paragraph 1, of the Statute as enabling consent to be deduced from certain acts, thus accepting the possibility of *forum prorogatum*. This modality is applied when a respondent State has, through its conduct before the Court or in relation to the applicant party, acted in such a way as to have consented to the jurisdiction of the Court ...

62. The consent allowing for the Court to assume jurisdiction must be certain. That is so, no more and no less, for jurisdiction based on *forum prorogatum*. As the Court has recently explained, whatever the basis of consent, the attitude of the respondent State must "be capable of being regarded as 'an unequivocal indication' of the desire of that State to accept the Court's jurisdiction in a 'voluntary and indisputable' manner" (*Armed Activities on the Territory of the Congo (New Application: 2002) (Democratic Republic of the Congo* v. *Rwanda), Jurisdiction and Admissibility, Judgment, I.C.J. Reports 2006*, p. 18; .... For the Court to exercise jurisdiction on the basis of *forum prorogatum*, the element of consent must be either explicit or clearly to be deduced from the relevant conduct of a State (*Anglo-Iranian Oil Co. (United Kingdom* v. *Iran), Preliminary Objection, Judgment, I.C.J. Reports 1952*, pp. 113-114; .... .

63. The Court observes that this is the first time it falls to the Court to decide on the merits of a dispute

---

[70] Ed. more recent special agreement cases include the *Land, Island and Maritime Frontier Dispute* case I.C.J. Rep. 1990, p.92; and the *Gabčíkovo-Nagymaros Project* case above, p.708. On compromissory clauses, see Charney (1987) 81 A.J.I.L. 855.

[71] Ed. See, e.g. the *U.S. Diplomatic and Consular Staff in Tehran* case, above, p.312; and the *Application of the Genocide Convention* case, I.C.J. Rep. 2007. On the current status of the 1928 General Act of Arbitration, as a basis for jurisdiction, see the *Aerial Incident of 10 August 1999* case (*Pakistan v India*), I.C.J. Rep. 2000, p.12, paras 26 et seq. And see Merrills (1980) 39 C.L.J. 137.

brought before it by an application based on Article 38, paragraph 5,[72] of the Rules of Court. This provision was introduced by the Court into its Rules in 1978. The purpose of this amendment was to allow a State which proposes to found the jurisdiction of the Court to entertain a case upon a consent thereto yet to be given or manifested by another State to file an application setting out its claims and inviting the latter to consent to the Court dealing with them, without prejudice to the rules governing the sound administration of justice. Before this revision, the Court treated this type of application in the same way as any other application submitted to it: the Registry would issue the usual notifications and the "case" was entered in the General List of the Court. It could only be removed from the List if the respondent State explicitly rejected the Court's jurisdiction to entertain it. The Court was therefore obliged to enter in its General List "cases" for which it plainly did not have jurisdiction and in which, therefore, no further action could be taken; it was consequently obliged to issue orders so as to remove them from its List (see *Treatment in Hungary of Aircraft and Crew of United States of America (United States of America v. Hungary), Order of 12 July 1954, I.C.J. Reports 1954*, p. 99; ... Article 38, paragraph 5, now provides, firstly, that no entry is made in the General List unless and until the State against which such application is made consents to the Court's jurisdiction to entertain the case and, secondly, that, except for the transmission of the application to that State, no action is to be taken in the proceedings. The State which is thus asked to consent to the Court's jurisdiction to settle a dispute is completely free to respond as it sees fit; if it consents to the Court's jurisdiction, it is for it to specify, if necessary, the aspects of the dispute which it agrees to submit to the judgment of the Court. The deferred and *ad hoc* nature of the Respondent's consent, as contemplated by Article 38, paragraph 5, of the Rules of Court, makes the procedure set out there a means of establishing *forum prorogatum*.

64. Article 38, paragraph 5, of the Rules of Court must also be read and interpreted in the light of paragraph 2 of that Article, which reads as follows: "The application shall specify as far as possible the legal grounds upon which the jurisdiction of the Court is said to be based; it shall also specify the precise nature of the claim, together with a succinct statement of the facts and grounds on which the claim is based." The expression "as far as possible" used in this provision was inserted in the Rules of Court of the Permanent Court of International Justice in 1936, precisely in order to preserve the possibility for the Court to found its jurisdiction on *forum prorogatum* ... This expression was used in the original Rules of Court of the International Court of Justice in 1946 and has remained there ever since. Obviously, the jurisdiction of the Court can be founded on *forum prorogatum* in a variety of ways, by no means all of which fall under Article 38, paragraph 5.

Notes

1. A case may be referred to the Court by the parties under art.36(1) not only by special agreement or under a compromissory clause in a treaty, but also *forum prorogatum*.[73] This was the doctrine relied upon by the Court to establish its jurisdiction in the *Mutual Assistance* case. By this the Court has jurisdiction where the parties give their consent by separate acts expressly or impliedly accepting it, one of those acts being the making of an unilateral application under art.40(1) of the Statute of the Court.

2. In the *Mutual Assistance* case, France gave *express* consent by a letter to the Court in response to Djibouti's unilateral application under art.40(1) which was transmitted to it under art.38(5) of the Rules of the Court.[74] Similarly, in the pre-art.38(5) *Corfu Channel* case,[75] the Court held that it has jurisdiction when Albania responded to a unilateral application by the United Kingdom under art.40(1), which was communicated to it by the Court, by a letter to the Court *expressly* accepting the Court's jurisdiction. When Albania later objected to the Court's jurisdiction, the Court held

---

[72] Article 38 (5) reads: "When the applicant State proposes to found the jurisdiction of the Court upon a consent thereto yet to be given or manifested by the State against which such application is made, the application shall be transmitted to that State. It shall not however be entered in the General List, nor any action be taken in the proceedings, unless and until the State against which such application is made consents to the Court's jurisdiction for the purposes of the case."

[73] On *forum prorogatum*, see Yee (1992) 42 G.Y.I.L. 147.

[74] Cf. the *Certain Criminal Proceedings in France* case (*Provisional Measures*), I.C.J. Rep. 2003, p.102 (express acceptance by France of jurisdiction by letter to the Court in response to unilateral application). See Yee, 16 L.J.I.L. 701 (2003).

[75] I.C.J. Rep. 1948, p.15.

that Albania had waived its right to challenge the admissibility of the claim. In other cases, the Court has *inferred* jurisdiction *forum prorogatum* from the participation of a state in the proceedings in the case. In the *Mavrommatis* (*Merits*) case, brought by Greece against the United Kingdom, the United Kingdom replied in its written argument to an issue raised by Greece that was not within the jurisdiction of the Court under the mandate for Palestine under which the case had been brought, thus impliedly accepting the Court's jurisdiction on the issue. The Court decided that it had jurisdiction in respect of the issue "in consequence of an agreement between the parties resulting from the written proceedings ..."[76] In the *Rights of Minorities in Polish Upper Silesia* case, in which Poland had first raised objections to jurisdiction in its second written pleadings (its rejoinder) after having argued the case on its merits in its first written pleadings (its counter-memorial), the Court said:

"And there seems to be no doubt that the consent of a State to the submission of a dispute to the Court may not only result from an express declaration, but may also be inferred from acts conclusively establishing it. It seems hard to deny that the submission of arguments on the merits, without making reservations in regard to the question of jurisdiction, must be regarded as an unequivocal indication of the desire of a State to obtain a decision on the merits of a suit. ... If, in a special case, the Respondent has, by an express declaration, indicated his desire to obtain a decision on the merits and his intention to abstain from raising the question of jurisdiction, it seems clear that he cannot, later on in the proceedings, go back upon that declaration."[77]

In contrast, in the *Armed Activities* case (*New Application: 2002*),[78] the Court held that it did not have jurisdiction *forum prorogatum* in the case even though the DRC had pleaded and appeared in the case, for the reason that it had done so "solely for the purpose of challenging that jurisdiction".

3. As the Court indicates in the *Mutual Assistance* case, art.38(5) was introduced to deal with the kind of "fishing" for jurisdiction that used to happen in cases in which a state would make an art.40(1) application when no basis for jurisdiction was available other than *forum prorogatum* and see how the other potential party to the case reacted.[79] Even though the chances of establishing jurisdiction in these cases were slight, they were entered on the Court's list, eventually being removed when the other state did not respond. Now under art.38(5) such a case is not entered on the Court's list unless the other state responds positively. For example, in 1992, an unilateral application by Hungary concerning the Gabčíkovo-Nagymaros Project was transmitted to Slovakia but not entered on the Court's list when Slovakia did not respond at all. Later, jurisdiction was established in the case of that name[80] by special agreement between the two states.

4. It is possible for the respondent state/s to take the initiative to establish jurisdiction *forum prorogatum*. In the *Monetary Gold* case, the respondent states—France, the United Kingdom and the United States—indicated their willingness in the Washington Statement of April 25, 1951, to

[76] P.C.I.J. Rep., Ser. A, No.5, p.27 (1925).
[77] P.C.I.J. Rep., Ser. A, No.15, pp.24–25 (1928). See also the *Chorzów Factory* (*Indemnity*) (*Merits*) case, P.C.I.J. Rep., Ser. A, No.17, p.37 (1928).
[78] I.C.J. Rep. 2006, p.6, para.22.
[79] See, e.g. the *Treatment in Hungary of Aircraft* case referred to by the Court in para.63.
[80] I.C.J. Rep. 1997, p.7. See also the *Genocide Convention* case (*Preliminary Objections*), I.C.J. Rep. 1996, p.595 at p.621, in which Bosnia and Herzegovina sought unsuccessfully to rely upon *forum prorogatum* as an additional basis for jurisdiction.

be brought before the Court by either Albania or Italy. In response, Italy filed an application with the Court but then challenged the Court's jurisdiction. Rejecting Italy's objections, the Court stated, inter alia:

"The Governments of France, the United Kingdom and the United States of America, and the Government of Italy, by their separate and successive acts—the adoption of the Washington Statement, in the one case, and in the other case, the deposit on May 19, 1953, of the Declaration of acceptance of the jurisdiction of the Court and the filing of the Application— have referred a case to the Court within the meaning of Article 36(1) of its Statute. They have thus conferred jurisdiction on the Court to deal with the questions submitted in the Application of the Italian Government."[81]

5.   Article 36 (1) of the Statute also refers to the Court having jurisdiction in respect of "all matters specially provided for in the Charter of the United Nations". This wording was included at a time when it was hoped that the Charter would provide for the Court to have compulsory jurisdiction. There is no provision in the Charter as it was finally drafted to which the wording could be taken to refer. A Security Council recommendation under art.36(3), Charter, recommending that a dispute be referred to the Court does not qualify: see the Separate Opinion of Judges Basdevant, Alvarez, Winiasrski, Zoricic, De Visscher, Badawi and Krylov in the *Corfu Channel* case *Preliminary Objections*).[82]

----

ii. Jurisdiction under Article 36(2)[83]

UNITED KINGDOM DECLARATION ACCEPTING THE COMPULSORY JURISDICTION OF THE COURT

http://untreaty.un.org

1. The Government of the United Kingdom of Great Britain and Northern Ireland accept as compulsory *ipso facto* and without special convention, on condition of reciprocity, the jurisdiction of the International Court of Justice, in conformity with paragraph 2 of Article 36 of the Statute of the Court, until such time as notice may be given to terminate the acceptance, over all disputes arising after 1 January 1974, with regard to situations or facts subsequent to the same date, other than:

  (i)   any dispute which the United Kingdom has agreed with the other Party or Parties thereto to settle by some other method of peaceful settlement;

  (ii) any dispute with the government of any other country which is or has been a Member of the Commonwealth;

  (iii) any dispute in respect of which any other Party to the dispute has accepted the compulsory jurisdiction of the International Court of Justice only in relation to or for the purpose of the dispute; or where the acceptance of the Court's compulsory jurisdiction on behalf of any other Party to the dispute was

---

[81] I.C.J. Rep. 1954, p.19, at 31. The Court declined to hear the case because it lacked jurisdiction on another ground (Albania was not a party to the proceedings): see below, p.869.

[82] I.C.J. Rep. 1948, p.15.

[83] See Alexandrov (2001) 14 L.J.I.L. 89; Briggs, (1958–I) 93 *Hague Recueil* 224; Gross, in Damrosch, above, n.22, p.19; Fitzmaurice (1999) 20 A.Y.I.L. 127; Kelly (1987) 12 Yale J.I.L. 342; Merrills (1979) 50 B.Y.I.L. 87; and ibid. (1993) 64 B.Y.I.L. 197; Oda (1988) 59 B.Y.I.L. 1; Szafarz, *The Compulsory Jurisdiction of the International Court of Justice* (1993), Ch.3; Waldock (1955–56) 32 B.Y.I.L. 244.

deposited or ratified less than twelve months prior to the filing of the application bringing the dispute before the Court.

2. The Government of the United Kingdom also reserve the right at any time, by means of a notification addressed to the Secretary-General of the United Nations, and with effect as from the moment of such notification, either to add to, amend or withdraw any of the foregoing reservations, or any that may hereafter be added.

Notes

1. Under art.36(2) of the Statute of the Court, which is known as the "optional clause", a state may make an unilateral declaration by which it accepts the Court's jurisdiction in all "legal disputes" vis-à-vis all other states that make such declarations. If States A and B have made such declarations, State A may seize the Court of a case against State B. This "compulsory jurisdiction" is subject to certain limitations, particularly limitations that follow from any reservations to the Court's jurisdiction that a state has attached to its declaration or from the principle of reciprocity (see below).

2. There are 65 declarations under the "optional clause" in force.[84] France terminated its declaration in 1974 as a result of the *Nuclear Tests* cases.[85] The US terminated its declaration in 1985 because of the *Nicaragua* case.[86] The UK is now the only Security Council permanent member that is bound by the optional clause. Many declarations are terminable upon notice[87]; some others are terminable upon a specific period of notice[88]; others are valid for five-year periods which are automatically renewed in the absence of notice to the contrary before their expiry.[89] A number contain no time limit (and no provision for notice).[90] In the *Nicaragua* (*Jurisdiction and Admissibility*) case, judgment, para.63, p.864, below, the Court stated that a declaration (e.g. the Nicaraguan one: text below, n.131) for an indefinite period of time was terminable on "reasonable" notice. A declaration terminable upon notice is one that is made for a "certain time" (Statute, art.36(3)).[91] The value for the state making it of a declaration terminable upon notice was demonstrated in 1954 when Australia withdrew its declaration of 1940, which had been valid for five years and then became terminable upon notice, and made a new one adding a reservation in respect of disputes concerning pearl fishing off the Australian coast. At the time it seemed likely that Japan might bring a claim against Australia with this subject matter before the Court under the "optional clause." Note also the reservation made by Canada in 1970 (and since withdrawn). In view of its 1970 legislation on arctic waters, which controversially extended its jurisdiction to control pollution in those waters and which brought an immediate protest from the United States, Canada terminated its declaration and made a new

---

[84] They are those of Australia, Austria, Barbados, Belgium, Botswana, Bulgaria, Cambodia, Cameroon, Canada, Costa Rica, Cote d'Ivoire, Cyprus, Denmark, DRC, Djibouti, Dominica, Dominican Republic, Egypt, Estonia, Finland, Gambia, Georgia, Greece, Guinea, Guinea-Bissau, Haiti, Honduras, Hungary, India, Japan, Kenya, Lesotho, Liberia, Liechtenstein, Luxembourg, Madagascar, Malawi, Malta, Mauritius, Mexico, Netherlands, New Zealand, Nicaragua, Nigeria, Norway, Pakistan, Panama, Paraguay, Peru, Philippines, Poland, Portugal, Senegal, Slovakia, Somalia, Spain, Sudan, Suriname, Swaziland, Sweden, Switzerland, Togo, Uganda, U.K., Uruguay. Is there any discernible pattern of states?

[85] As to which see above, p.365.

[86] Above, p.727.

[87] See e.g. the UK declaration. Some of these (e.g. the Austrian declaration) had originally been valid for a certain number of years after which they were stated to be terminable upon notice.

[88] e.g. Norway.

[89] e.g. Sweden.

[90] e.g. Uganda.

[91] *Right of Passage case (Preliminary Objections)*, I.C.J. Rep. 1957, p.125.

one with a new reservation excluding disputes about the legislation. Canada explained that its "new reservation ... does not in any way reflect lack of confidence in the Court but takes into account the limitations within which the Court must operate and the deficiencies of the law which it must interpret and apply."[92]

3. The current United Kingdom Declaration under art.36(2) was deposited on July 5, 2004.[93] It contains several reservations. Reservations (i)–(iii) are not expressly permitted by art.36. In practice, however, the Court has accepted that states may attach reservations to their declarations in addition to the conditions which they may attach in accordance with art.36(3).[94] Reservation (ii) in the British declaration, excluding disputes with "a Member [or former member] of the Commonwealth", is found also in the Indian declaration and was pleaded successfully to prevent the Court taking jurisdiction in the *Aerial Incident of 10 August 1999* case (*Pakistan v India*).[95]

4. Reservation (iii) in the United Kingdom declaration applies to the Egyptian declaration, by which the jurisdiction of the Court is accepted by Egypt solely in connection with certain disputes concerning the Suez Canal.[96] Note also that the same reservation would have prevented Portugal bringing a case against the United Kingdom in the way that it brought the *Right of Passage* case[97] against India. Portugal made its declaration, which was valid for one year and then became terminable upon notice (which has not yet been given), on December 19, 1955. It brought its application on December 22, 1955. Reservation (iii) did prevent the Court having jurisdiction under art.36(2) in the *Legality of Use of Force* case (*Yugoslavia v UK*),[98] in which Yugoslavia had deposited its declaration only three days before making its application to the Court.

Reservation (iii) would also have come into play in the *Land and Maritime Boundary between Cameroon and Nigeria* case.[99] There Cameroon deposited its art.36(2) declaration[100] on March 3, 1994. The UN Secretary-General, as depositary, did not transmit copies of the Cameroonian declaration to the parties to the Statute until 11 months later, by which time, on March 29, 1994, Cameroon had filed its application against Nigeria. Applying the *Right of Passage* case, the Court held that it had jurisdiction despite the speed with which the application was brought. The Court also rejected an argument based upon the *Nicaragua* case:

> "32. Nigeria maintains however that, in any event, Cameroon could not file an application before the Court without allowing a reasonable period to elapse 'as would ... have enabled the Secretary-General to take the action required of him in relation to Cameroon's Declaration of 3 March 1994'. Compliance with that time period is essential, the more so because, according to Nigeria, the Court, in its Judgment of 26 November 1984 in the case concerning

---

[92] (1970) 9 I.L.M. 612. See McDonald 1970) 8 C.Y.I.L. 3.

[93] The 2004 Declaration replaces the UK's 1969 Declaration, Misc No.4 (1969), Cmnd. 3872.

[94] On reservations generally, see Alexandrov, *Reservations in Unilateral Declarations accepting the Compulsory Jurisdiction of the International Court of Justice* (1995).

[95] I.C.J. Rep. 2000, p.12. The wording "has been a member" was added when it thought that Mauritius might leave the Commonwealth to avoid reservation (ii) in order to bring a case against the UK concerning the Chagos Islands: see Aust, *Handbook of International Law* (2005), p.454.

[96] See above, p.784.

[97] I.C.J. Rep. 1957, p.125.

[98] Provisional Measures, Order of June 2, 1999, I.C.J. Rep. 1999, p.826.

[99] Preliminary Objections, I.C.J. Rep. 1998, p.275.

[100] Valid for five years and thereafter until notice given to terminate it. Following the case, Nigeria deposited a new optional clause declaration with a "twelve months" reservation like that in UK reservation (iii).

Military and Paramilitary Activities in and against Nicaragua, required a reasonable time for the withdrawal of declarations under the Optional Clause. ...

34. The Court considers that the foregoing conclusion in respect of the withdrawal of declarations under the Optional Clause is not applicable to the deposit of those declarations. Withdrawal ends existing consensual bonds, while deposit establishes such bonds. The effect of withdrawal is therefore purely and simply to deprive other States which have already accepted the jurisdiction of the Court of the right they had to bring proceedings before it against the withdrawing State. In contrast, the deposit of a declaration does not deprive those States of any accrued right. Accordingly no time period is required for the establishment of a consensual bond following such a deposit.

35. The Court notes moreover that to require a reasonable time to elapse before a declaration can take effect would be to introduce an element of uncertainty into the operation of the Optional Clause system. In the case concerning *Right of Passage over Indian Territory*, the Court had considered that it could not create such uncertainty. The conclusions it had reached then remain valid and apply all the more since the growth in the number of States party to the Statute and the intensification of inter-State relations since 1957 have increased the possibilities of legal disputes capable of being submitted to the Court. The Court cannot introduce into the Optional Clause an additional time requirement which is not there."

5. "On condition of reciprocity" in the United Kingdom declaration refers to the *principle of reciprocity* which follows from the wording "in relation to any other state accepting the same obligation" in art.36(2).[101] According to this principle, a state accepts the Court's jurisdiction vis-à-vis any other state only in so far as that state has accepted it also. If State A makes a declaration subject to reservation X and State B makes one subject to reservation Y, the Court has jurisdiction to hear disputes between these two states only insofar as they are not covered by reservations X or Y. In other words, "jurisdiction is conferred on the Court only to the extent to which the two declarations coincide in conferring it."[102] See further on the principle of reciprocity, the extracts from the three cases immediately below these notes.[103] The "reciprocity" condition in art.36(3) is quite distinct from the principle of reciprocity in art.36(2) and was introduced to cover the case where a state might only want to be bound by the Court's jurisdiction if a worthwhile number of other states were bound or if a state whose acceptance was particularly important to it was bound.

In the *Nicaragua* case (*Jurisdiction and Admissibility*, judgment, para.62 (below p.864), the Court held that the principle of reciprocity only applies to "the scope and substance of the commitments entered into"; it does not extend to the "formal conditions of their creation, duration or extinction". Accordingly, in that case, the US was not permitted to rely upon the "terminable upon notice" limitation in the Nicaraguan declaration. The 1990 Spanish "Optional Clause" declaration provides:

"The withdrawal of [this] ... Declaration shall become effective after a period of six months has elapsed from the date of receipt by the Secretary-General of the United Nations of the relevant notification by the Spanish Government. However, in respect of States which have established

---

[101] See Weiss, in Damrosch, ed., above, n.22, p.82.
[102] *Anglo-Iranian Oil Co.* case, I.C.J. Rep. 1952, p.93, at 103.
[103] The principle was also invoked successfully as it applied under the 1928 General Act in the *Aegean Sea Continental Shelf* case, I.C.J. Rep. 1978, p.37. Turkey was allowed to rely upon a Greek reservation to the Act to exclude the Court's jurisdiction.

a period of less than six months between notification of the withdrawal of their Declaration and in becoming effective, the withdrawal of the Spanish Declaration shall become effective after such shorter period has elapsed."

Would this achieve the result that the US unsuccessfully sought to achieve on the basis of the principle of reciprocity in the *Nicaragua* case?

6. *Juridical character of a declaration*. In the *Nicaragua* case (*Jurisdiction and Admissibility*),[104] the Court referred to optional clause declarations as "unilateral acts" establishing "a series of bilateral engagements." In the *Fisheries Jurisdiction (Spain v Canada)* case,[105] the Court expounded more fully on the juridical nature of optional clause declarations and the law that governs their interpretation:

"44. The Court recalls that the interpretation of declarations made under Article 36, paragraph 2, of the Statute, and of any reservations they contain, is directed to establishing whether mutual consent has been given to the jurisdiction of the Court.

It is for each State, in formulating its declaration, to decide upon the limits it places upon its acceptance of the jurisdiction of the Court. ... Conditions or reservations thus do not by their terms derogate from a wider acceptance already given. ... There is thus no reason to interpret them restrictively. All elements in a declaration under Article 36, paragraph 2, of the Statute which, read together, comprise the acceptance by the declarant State of the Court's jurisdiction, are to be interpreted as a unity, applying the same legal principles of interpretation throughout. ...

46. A declaration of acceptance of the compulsory jurisdiction of the Court, whether there are specified limits set to that acceptance or not, is a unilateral act of State sovereignty. At the same time, it establishes a consensual bond and the potential for a jurisdictional link with the other States which have made declarations pursuant to Article 36, paragraph 2, of the Statute, and 'makes a standing offer to the other States party to the Statute which have not yet deposited a declaration of acceptance' (*Land and Maritime Boundary between Cameroon and Nigeria (Cameroon v. Nigeria), Preliminary Objections, I.C.J. Reports 1998*, para. 25). The régime relating to the interpretation of declarations made under Article 36 of the Statute is not identical with that established for the interpretation of treaties by the Vienna Convention on the Law of Treaties (*ibid.*, para. 30) ... the provisions of that Convention may only apply analogously to the extent compatible with the *sui generis* character of the unilateral acceptance of the Court's jurisdiction.

47. In the event, the Court has in earlier cases elaborated the appropriate rules for the interpretation of declarations and reservations. Every declaration 'must be interpreted as it stands, having regard to the words actually used' (*Anglo-Iranian Oil Co., Preliminary Objection, Judgment, I.C.J. Reports 1952*, p. 105). ... Therefore, declarations and reservations are to be read as a whole. ...

48. At the same time, since a declaration under Article 36, paragraph 2, of the Statute, is a unilaterally drafted instrument, the Court has not hesitated to place a certain emphasis on the intention of the depositing State. Indeed, in the case concerning the *Anglo-Iranian Oil Co.*, the Court found that the limiting words chosen in Iran's declaration were 'a decisive confirmation

---

[104] Judgment, para.60, below, p.863.

[105] I.C.J. Rep. 1998, p.432. See also the *Land and Maritime Boundary (Preliminary Objections)* case (*Cameroon v Nigeria*), I.C.J. Rep. 1998, p.275, paras 25 et seq.

of the intention of the Government of Iran at the time when it accepted the compulsory jurisdiction of the Court' (ibid., p.107).

49. The Court will thus interpret the relevant words of a declaration including a reservation contained therein in a natural and reasonable way, having due regard to the intention of the State concerned at the time when it accepted the compulsory jurisdiction of the Court. The intention of a reserving State may be deduced not only from the text of the relevant clause, but also from the context in which the clause is to be read, and an examination of evidence regarding the circumstances of its preparation and the purposes intended to be served. ...

In the present case the Court has such explanations in the form of Canadian ministerial statements, parliamentary debates, legislative proposals and press communiqués.

50. Where, moreover, an existing declaration has been replaced by a new declaration which contains a reservation, as in this case, the intentions of the Government may also be ascertained by comparing the terms of the two instruments.

51. The *contra proferentem* rule may have a role to play in the interpretation of contractual provisions. However, it follows from the foregoing analysis that the rule has no role to play in this case in interpreting the reservation contained in the unilateral declaration made by Canada under Article 36, paragraph 2, of the Statute.

52. The Court was addressed by both parties on the principle of effectiveness. Certainly, this principle has an important role in the law of treaties and in the jurisprudence of this Court; however, what is required in the first place for a reservation to a declaration made under Article 36, paragraph 2, of the Statute, is that it should be interpreted in a manner compatible with the effect sought by the reserving State.

53. Spain has contended that, in case of doubt, reservations contained in declarations are to be interpreted consistently with legality and that any interpretation which is inconsistent with the Statute of the Court, the Charter of the United Nations or with general international law is inadmissible. ...

54. ... In point of fact, reservations from the Court's jurisdiction may be made by States for a variety of reasons; sometimes precisely because they feel vulnerable about the legality of their position or policy. Nowhere in the Court's case-law has it been suggested that interpretation in accordance with the legality under international law of the matters exempted from the jurisdiction of the Court is a rule that governs the interpretation of such reservations ...

55. There is a fundamental distinction between the acceptance by a State of the Court's jurisdiction and the compatibility of particular acts with international law. The former requires consent. The latter question can only be reached when the Court deals with the merits, after having established its jurisdiction and having heard full legal argument by both parties."

7.   The fact that a case comes within a reservation to an "optional clause" declaration so that the Court lacks jurisdiction under art.36(2) does not affect the possibility of the Court having jurisdiction on some other basis (e.g. a jurisdiction clause in a treaty between the parties): *Appeal Relating to the Jurisdiction of the I.C.A.O. Council* case.[106]

---

[106] I.C.J. Rep. 1972, p.46, p.53.

8.   Although preliminary objections to jurisdiction have been upheld in most ICJ cases in which "optional clause" applications have been made,[107] the ICJ has held that it has jurisdiction on the basis of art.36(2) in a significant number of other cases.[108]

INTERHANDEL CASE

Switzerland v U.S.

I.C.J. Reports 1959, p.6

Switzerland brought this claim against the United States for the restitution of the assets of Inter-handel, a Swiss company, in the United States. The property had been taken by the United States in 1942 on the ground that Interhandel was German, and so enemy, controlled. Switzerland disputed this and, after several years of negotiation, etc. in 1948 asked the United States to return Inter-handel's property. On July 26, 1948, the United States refused to do so. After unsuccessful court proceedings in the United States, in 1957 Switzerland instituted proceedings under the "optional clause".

Judgment of the Court

According to [the United States Second Preliminary Objection to the Court's jurisdiction] ... the present dispute, even if it is subsequent to the date of the Declaration of the United States, arose before July 28, 1948, the date of the entry into force of the Swiss Declaration. The argument set out in the Preliminary Objections is as follows:

The United States Declaration, which was effective August 26th, 1946, contained the clause limiting the Court's jurisdiction to disputes "hereafter arising," while no such qualifying clause is contained in the Swiss Declaration which was effective July 28th, 1948. But the reciprocity principle ... requires that as between the United States and Switzerland the Court's jurisdiction be limited to disputes arising after July 28th, 1948. ... Otherwise, retroactive effect would be given to the compulsory jurisdiction of the Court.

In particular, it was contended with regard to disputes arising after August 26th, 1946, but before July 28th, 1948, that "Switzerland, as a Respondent, could have invoked the principle of reciprocity and claimed that, in the same way as the United States is not bound to accept the Court's jurisdiction with respect to disputes arising before its acceptance, Switzerland, too, could not be required to accept the Court's jurisdiction in relation to disputes arising before its acceptance."

Reciprocity in the case of Declarations accepting the compulsory jurisdiction of the Court enables a Party to invoke a reservation to that acceptance which it has not expressed in its own Declaration but which the other Party has expressed in its Declaration. For example, Switzerland, which has not expressed in its Declaration any reservation *ratione temporis*, while the United States has accepted the compulsory jurisdiction of the Court only in respect of disputes to August 26th, 1946, might, if in the position of Respondent, invoke by virtue of reciprocity against the United States the American reservation if the United States attempted to refer to the Court a dispute with Switzerland which had arisen before August 26th, 1946. This is the effect of reciprocity in this connection. Reciprocity enables the State which has made the wider acceptance of the jurisdiction of the Court to rely upon

---

[107]   See, e.g. the *Aerial Incident of 10 August 1999* case (*Pakistan v India*), I.C.J. Rep. 2000, p.12; and the *Fisheries Jurisdiction* case (*Spain v Canada*), I.C.J. Rep. 1998, p.432.

[108]   These include the *Anglo-Norwegian Fisheries* case, above, p.327; the *U.S. Nationals in Morocco* case, I.C.J. Rep., p.176; the *Right of Passage* case, above, p.220; the *Temple* case, I.C.J. Rep. 1962, p.6; the *Nicaragua* case, below; p.860; the *Arbitral Award of 1989* case, I.C.J. Rep. 1991, p.53; the *Jan Mayen* case, I.C.J. Rep. 1993, p.38; the *Land and Maritime Boundary between Cameroon and Nigeria* case (*Preliminary Objections*), I.C.J. Rep. 1998, p.275; and the *Arrest Warrant of 11 April 2000* case (*DRC v Belgium*), I.C.J. Rep. 2002, p.3.

the reservations to the acceptance laid down by the other Party. There the effect of reciprocity ends. It cannot justify a State in this instance, the United States in relying upon a restriction which the other Party, Switzerland, has not included in its own Declaration.

The Second Preliminary Objection must therefore be rejected. ...

Notes

1. A reservation of the sort in issue here is a reservation *ratione temporis*. What if the declaration made by Switzerland had contained a reservation limiting that state's acceptance of the Court's jurisdiction to disputes arising after its declaration came into force on July 28, 1948? Assuming that the dispute in the case arose subsequent to the date of the United States declaration but before July 28, 1948, could the United States then have relied on the principle of reciprocity to better effect than it was able to do on the facts of the case as they actually were?

2. The United States also objected unsuccessfully to jurisdiction on the ground that the dispute had arisen before the United States acceptance of the Court's jurisdiction in 1946 in respect of "disputes arising hereafter." Although the United States had taken Interhandel's assets in 1942 and although the United States and Switzerland had disagreed over the enemy or non-enemy character of Interhandel before 1946, in the Court's opinion the dispute itself only arose when the United States refused Switzerland's request to return Interhandel's assets on July 26, 1948. Applying the United States *ratione temporis* reservation, the Court noted that "the facts and situation which have led to a dispute must not be confused with the dispute itself."[109] The United Kingdom declaration, above, p.104, applies to disputes arising as of 1945, "with regard to situations or facts subsequent to the same date." Would such a formula have helped the United States in the *Interhandel* case.[110]

3. A limitation to subsequent "situations or facts", which can be difficult to apply, was in issue in the *Right of Passage (Merits)* case.[111] There the Indian declaration extended to "all disputes arising after February 5th, 1930, with regard to situations or facts subsequent to the same date." The Court held that the "dispute" in the case arose in 1954, when India contested the exercise of a right of passage over Indian territory. As to the date of the "situation or facts", the Court stated:

    "The facts or situations to which regard must be had in this connection are those with regard to which the dispute has arisen or, in other words, as was said by the Permanent Court in the case concerning the *Electricity Company of Sofia and Bulgaria*, only 'those which must be considered as being the source of the dispute', those which are its 'real cause'. The Permanent Court, in this connection, was unwilling to regard as such an earlier arbitral award which was the source of the rights claimed by one of the Parties, but which had given rise to no difficulty prior to the facts constituting the subject of the dispute. 'It is true', it said, 'that a dispute may presuppose the existence of some prior situation or fact, but it does not follow that the dispute arises in regard to that situation or fact.' (Series A/B, No. 77, p. 82.) The Permanent Court thus drew a distinction between the situations or facts which constitute the source of the rights claimed by one of the Parties and the situations or facts which are the source of the dispute. Only the latter are to be taken into account for the purpose of applying the Declaration accepting the jurisdiction of the Court.

    The dispute submitted to the Court is one with regard to a situation and, at the same time,

---

[109] I.C.J. Rep. 1959, p.22.
[110] See Greig, *International Law* (2nd edn 1976), pp.657–61.
[111] I.C.J. Rep. 1960, p.6 at 35. For the facts of this case, see above, p.220.

with regard to certain facts: on the one hand there is the situation of the Portuguese enclaves within the territory of India, which gave rise to the need for a right of passage for Portugal and to its claim to such a right; on the other hand there are the facts of 1954 which Portugal advances as showing the failure of India to comply with its obligations, infringements of that right.

Up to 1954 the situation of those territories may have given rise to a few minor incidents, but passage had been effected without any controversy as to the title under which it was effected. It was only in 1954 that such a controversy arose and the dispute relates both to the existence of a right of passage to go into the enclaved territories and to India's failure to comply with obligations which, according to Portugal, were binding upon it in this connection. It was from all of this that the dispute referred to the Court arose; it is with regard to all of this that the dispute exists. This whole, whatever may have been the earlier origin of one of its parts, came into existence only after 5 February 1930. The time-condition to which acceptance of the jurisdiction of the Court was made subject by the Declaration of India is therefore complied with."

4.   In the *Certain Property* case,[112] Czechoslovakia had in 1945 confiscated a painting owned by Prince Franz Josef II of Liechtenstein under the Benes Decree, which authorised the confiscation of property of persons belonging to the "German and Hungarian people". When in 1991 the painting was sent to Cologne for an exhibition, Prince Hans-Adam II of Liechtenstein claimed its return in the German courts, but his claim was dismissed because of a 1952 post-war settlement treaty which barred claims in these courts concerning German external assets. In this case, Liechtenstein brought proceedings in the ICJ against Germany, arguing that the latter had not respected the property rights of Liechtenstein nationals. The Court had jurisdiction in the case under the European Convention for the Peaceful Settlement of Disputes 1957, except in respect of "disputes relating to facts and situations prior to the entry into force of this Convention as between the parties to the dispute", which occurred in 1980. The Court held that it lacked jurisdiction *ratione temporis*. Citing the *Right of Passage* and earlier cases, the Court concluded that, although the proceedings before it were initiated by Liechtenstein following the decisions in the German courts in the 1990s, the "source or real cause" of the dispute between the two states was to be found in the 1945 Benes Decree and the 1952 treaty, which pre-dated the "critical" date of 1980.

5.   On the "self-judging" or "automatic" reservation aspect of the *Interhandel* case, see below, p.857. The Court finally declined jurisdiction in the case because local remedies had not been fully exhausted.

-----

[112] I.C.J. Rep. 2005, p.6.

NORWEGIAN LOANS CASE[113]

France v Norway

I.C.J. Reports 1957, p.9

France brought this claim against Norway under the "optional clause" on behalf of French holders of Norwegian bonds. Norway objected to the Court's jurisdiction on several grounds, including that discussed in the following extract from its judgment. Judge Lauterpacht reached the same decision as the Court, but for different reasons.

Judgment of the Court

The Court will at the outset direct its attention to the Preliminary Objections of the Norwegian Government. ...

It will be recalled that the French Declaration accepting the compulsory jurisdiction of the Court contains the following reservation:

This declaration does not apply to differences relating to matters which are essentially within the national jurisdiction as understood by the Government of the French Republic.

In the Preliminary Objections filed by the Norwegian Government it is stated:

The Norwegian Government did not insert any such reservation in its own Declaration. But is has the right to rely upon the restrictions placed by France upon her own undertakings.

Convinced that the dispute which has been brought before the Court by the Application of July 6, 1955, is within the domestic jurisdiction, the Norwegian Government considers itself fully entitled to rely on this right. Accordingly, it requests the Court to decline, on grounds that it lacks jurisdiction, the function which the French Government would have it assume.

... in the present case the jurisdiction of the Court depends upon the Declarations made by the Parties in accordance with Article 36, paragraph 2, of the Statute on condition of reciprocity; and that, since two unilateral declarations are involved, such jurisdiction is conferred upon the Court only to the extent to which the Declarations coincide in conferring it. A comparison between the two Declarations shows that the French Declaration accepts the Court's jurisdiction within narrower limits than the Norwegian Declaration; consequently the common will of the Parties, which is the basis of the Court's jurisdiction, exists within these narrower limits indicated by the French reservation. ...

In accordance with the condition of reciprocity to which acceptance of the compulsory jurisdiction is made subject in both Declarations and which is provided for in Article 36, paragraph 3, of the Statute, Norway, equally with France, is entitled to except from the compulsory jurisdiction of the Court disputes understood by Norway to be essentially within its national jurisdiction. ...

The Court does not consider that it should examine whether the French reservation is consistent with the undertaking of a legal obligation and is compatible with Article 36, paragraph 6, of the Statute which provides. ...

The validity of the reservation has not been questioned by the Parties. It is clear that France fully maintains its Declarations, including the reservation, and that Norway relies upon the reservation. ...

The Court considers that the Norwegian Government is entitled, by virtue of the condition of reciprocity, to invoke the reservation contained in the French Declaration of March 1, 1949; that this reservation excludes from the jurisdiction of the Court the dispute which has been referred to it by the Application of the French Government; that consequently the Court is without jurisdiction to entertain the Application. ...

For these reasons, the Court, by 12 votes to three,[114] finds that it is without jurisdiction to adjudicate upon the

---

[113] See Jennings (1958) 7 I.C.L.Q. 349. On "automatic" reservations, see Crawford (1979) 50 B.Y.I.L. 63.

[114] The judges in the majority were President Hackworth; Vice-President Badawi; Judges Winiarski, Zoričić, Klaestad, Armand-Ugon, Kojevnikov, Sir Muhammad Zafrulla Khan, Sir Hersch Lauterpacht, Moreno Quintana, Córdova and Wellington Koo. Judges Guerrero, Basdevant and Read dissented.

dispute which has been brought before it by the Application of the Government of the French Republic of July 6, 1955.

INDIVIDUAL OPINION OF JUDGE LAUTERPACHT

.... I consider that as the French Declaration of Acceptance excludes from the jurisdiction of the Court, "matters which are essentially within the national jurisdiction as understood by the Government of the French Republic"— it is for the reason of that latter qualification an instrument incapable of producing legal effects before this Court and of establishing its jurisdiction. This is so for the double reason that: (a) it is contrary to the Statute of the Court; (b) the existence of the obligation being dependent upon the determination by the Government accepting the Optional Clause, the Acceptance does not constitute a legal obligation. That Declaration of Acceptance cannot, accordingly, provide a basis for the jurisdiction of the Court. ...

If that type of reservation is valid, then the Court is not in the position to exercise the power conferred upon it— in fact, the duty imposed upon it—under paragraph 6 of Article 36 of its Statute. ... The French reservation lays down that if, with regard to that particular question, there is a dispute between the Parties as to whether the Court has jurisdiction, the matter shall be settled by a decision of the French Government. The French reservation is thus not only contrary to one of the most fundamental principles of international—and national— jurisprudence according to which it is within the inherent power of a tribunal to interpret the text establishing its jurisdiction. It is also contrary to a clear specific provision of the Statute of the Court as well as to the general Articles I and 92 of the Statute and of the Charter, respectively, which require the Court to function in accordance with its Statute.

Now what is the result of the fact that a reservation or part of it are contrary to the provisions of the Statute of the Court? The result is that that reservation or that part of it is invalid. Some examples may usefully illustrate that aspect of the question: What would be the position if in accepting—or purporting to accept—the obligations of Article 36 of the Statute, a State were to exclude the operation of paragraph 6 of that Article not only with regard to one reservation but with regard to all reservations or, generally, with regard to any disputed question of the jurisdiction of the Court?

What would be the position if the Declaration were to make it a condition that the oral proceedings of the Court shall be secret; or that its Judgment shall not be binding unless given by unanimity; or that it should contain no reasons; or that Dissenting Opinion shall be attached; or that Judges of certain nationality or nationalities shall be excluded; or that, contrary to what is said in Article 38 of its Statute, the Court shall apply only treaties and custom in the sense that it shall not be authorised to apply general principles of law as recognised by civilised States and that if it is unable to base its decision on treaty or custom it shall pronounce a *non liquet*? ...

In accepting the jurisdiction of the Court Governments are free to limit its jurisdiction in a drastic manner. As a result there may be little left in the Acceptance which is subject to the jurisdiction of the Court. This the Governments, as trustees of the interests entrusted to them, are fully entitled to do. Their right to append reservations which are not inconsistent with the Statute is no longer in question. But the question whether that little that is left is or is not subject to the jurisdiction of the Court must be determined by the Court itself. ...

I arrive at the same conclusion on the second—and different—ground, namely, that having regard to the formulation of the reservation of national jurisdiction on the part of the French Government the Acceptance embodying the "automatic reservation" is invalid as lacking in an essential condition of validity of a legal instrument. ... An instrument in which a party is entitled to determine the existence of its obligation is not a valid and enforceable legal instrument of which a court of law can take cognizance. It is not a legal instrument. It is a declaration of a political principle and purpose. ...

If the clause of the Acceptance reserving to the declaring Government the right of unilateral determination is invalid, then there are only two alternatives open to the Court: it may either treat as invalid that particular part of the reservation or it may consider the entire Acceptance to be tainted with invalidity. (There is a third possibility— which has only to be mentioned in order to be dismissed—namely, that the clause in question invalidates not the Acceptance as a whole but the particular reservation. This would mean that the entire reservation of matters of national jurisdiction would be treated as invalid while the Declaration of Acceptance as such would be treated as fully in force).

International practice on the subject is not sufficiently abundant to permit a confident attempt at general-isation and some help may justifiably be sought in applicable general principles of law as developed in municipal law. That general principle of law is that it is legitimate—and perhaps obligatory—to sever an invalid condition from the rest of the [contract or other legal] instrument and to treat the latter as valid provided that having regard to the intention of the parties and the nature of the instrument the condition in question does not constitute an essential part of the instrument. *Utile non debet per inutile vitiari*. The same applies also to provisions and reservations relating to the jurisdiction of the Court. It would be consistent with the previous practice of the Court that it should, if only possible, uphold its jurisdiction when such a course is compatible with the intention of the parties and that it should not allow its jurisdiction to be defeated as the result of remediable defects of expression which are not of an essential character. If that principle were applied to the case now before the Court this would mean that, while the French acceptance as a whole would remain valid, the limitation expressed in the words "as understood by the Government of the French Republic" would be treated as invalid and non-existent with the further result that Norway could not rely on it. The outcome of the interpretation thus adopted would be somewhat startling inasmuch as it would, in the present case, favour the very State which originally made that reservation and defeat the objection of the defendant State—an aspect of the question commented upon in another part of this Opinion. That fact need not necessarily be a decisive reason against the adoption of any such interpretation.

However, I consider that it is not open to the Court in the present case to sever the invalid condition from the Acceptance as a whole. For the principle of severance applies only to provisions and conditions which are not of the essence of the undertaking. Now an examination of the history of this particular form of the reservation of national jurisdiction shows that the unilateral right of determining whether the dispute is essentially within domestic jurisdiction has been regarded by the declaring State as one of the crucial limitations—perhaps the crucial limitation—of the obligation undertaken by the acceptance of the Optional Clause of Article 36 of the Statute. As is well known, that particular limitation is, substantially, a repetition of the formula adopted, after considerable discussion, by the Senate of the United States of America in giving its consent and advice to the acceptance, in 1946, of the Optional Clause by that country. That instrument is not before the Court and it would not be proper for me to comment upon it except to the extent of noting that the reservation in question was included therein having regard to the decisive importance attached to it and notwithstanding the doubts, expressed in various quarters, as to its consistency with the Statute. It will also be noted that some governments, such as those of India and the Union of South Africa, have attributed so much importance to that particular formation of the reservation that they cancelled their previous acceptance of the Optional Clause in order to insert, in a substituted Declaration of Acceptance, a clause reserving for themselves the right of unilateral determination. To ignore that clause and to maintain the binding force of the Declaration as a whole would be to ignore an essential and deliberate condition of the Acceptance.

Notes

1. Note that Norway was entitled to rely on France's reservation as if it read "as understood by the *Norwegian* Government." Since France had excluded cases concerning *its* domestic jurisdiction, Norway could do likewise. How did the Court manage to avoid ruling on the validity of the reservation? Could the Court have done so if France had been relying on it?

2. Judge Guerrero, who was the only other judge in the *Norwegian Loans* case to express an opinion on the validity of the French Declaration, stated in his dissenting opinion:

    "By the fact that France reserves her right to determine herself the limit between her own national jurisdiction and the jurisdiction of the Court, France renders void her main undertaking, for the latter ceases to be compulsory if it is France and not the Court that holds the power to determine the limit between their respective jurisdictions. The reservation conflicts also with paragraph 6 of Article 36. ...."[115]

    He did not "agree that the Court is without jurisdiction when its lack of jurisdiction is founded on the terms of a unilateral instrument which I consider to be contrary to the spirit and to the letter of the Statute and which, in my view, is, for that reason, null and void."[116]

3. In the *Interhandel* case, brought by Switzerland against the United States, the Court was con-

---

[115] I.C.J. Rep. 1957, p.68. See Shihata, *The Power of the International Court to Determine its own Jurisdiction* (1965).
[116] I.C.J. Rep. 1957, p.70.

fronted with the same form of "domestic jurisdiction" reservation in the United States Declaration.[117] It did not, however, either when deciding not to order certain interim measures[118] or when upholding the United States objections to its jurisdiction,[119] find it necessary to comment on the validity of the reservation or the Declaration containing it even though the reservation was invoked by the United States at both stages. In deciding that it lacked jurisdiction, the Court ruled instead that Switzerland had not exhausted local remedies, thus making it unnecessary for the Court to consider the objection to its jurisdiction presented by the United States (and challenged by Switzerland) relying upon the reservation.

Several judges in their separate opinions at the Preliminary Objection stage did, however, consider the questions that the objection raised. In his opinion, Judge Lauterpacht elaborated upon the position he had taken in the *Norwegian Loans* case.[120] Judge Spender reached the same conclusions as Judge Lauterpacht. Judge Klaestad, the President of the Court, agreed that the reservation was contrary to art.36(6). As to the effect of this, he stated:

"It appears from the debate in the United States Senate concerning the acceptance of the compulsory jurisdiction of the Court ... that fear was expressed lest the Court might assume jurisdiction in matters which are essentially within the domestic jurisdiction of the United States, particularly in matters of immigration and the regulation of tariffs and duties and similar matters. The navigation of the Panama Canal was also referred to. Such were the considerations underlying the acceptance of Reservation (b). It may be doubted whether the Senate was fully aware of the possibility that this Reservation might entail the nullity of the whole Declaration of Acceptance, leaving the United States in the same legal situation with regard to the Court as States which have filed no such Declarations. Would the Senate have accepted this Reservation if it had been thought that the United States would thereby place themselves in such a situation, taking back by means of the Reservation what was otherwise given by the acceptance of the Declaration? The debate in the Senate does not appear to afford sufficient ground for such a supposition.

For my part, I am satisfied that it was the true intention of the competent authorities of the United States to issue a real and effective Declaration accepting the compulsory jurisdiction of the Court, though—it is true—with far-reaching exceptions. That this view is not unfounded appears to be shown by the subsequent attitude of the United States Government. ...

These considerations have led me to the conclusion that the Court, both by its Statute and by the Charter, is prevented from acting upon that part of the Reservation which is in conflict with Article 36, paragraph 6, of the Statute, but that this circumstance does not necessarily imply that it is impossible for the Court to give effect to the other parts of the Declaration of Acceptance which are in conformity with the Statute. Part (a) of the Fourth Preliminary Objection should therefore in my view be rejected."[121]

Judge ad hoc Carry stated that he agreed "generally" with Judge Klaestad's Opinion; he did not give a full judgment of his own. Judge Armand-Ugon reached the same conclusion as Judge

---

[117] See on the case, Briggs (1959) 53 A.J.I.L. 301 and at 547.
[118] I.C.J. Rep. 1957, p.105.
[119] I.C.J. Rep. 1959, p.6.
[120] In the *Nicaragua* case, Judge Schwebel saw "great force" in Judge Lauterpacht's argument, although "since declarations incorporating self-judging provisions apparently have been treated as valid, certainly by the declarants, for many years, the passage of time may have rendered Judge Lauterpacht's analysis less compelling today ...": I.C.J. Rep. 1984, pp.601–602.
[121] I.C.J. Rep. 1959, pp.77–78.

Klaestad. As to the effect of the reservation's invalidity, he was of the opinion that it "does not imply that the acceptance of the Court's jurisdiction, given in the American Declaration, is altogether without value and to be considered as null and void in its entirety. ... The way in which this Declaration was employed by the Government of the United States in ... cases [which the US has submitted to the Court] shows that the reservation ... was not a determining factor at the time of its formulation and submission."[122] In his judgment with respect to interim measures, Judge Wellington Koo considered that the reservation was applicable at that stage and was valid.[123]

4. In the *Aerial Incident of July 27, 1955*, case,[124] which was brought by the United States against Bulgaria, Bulgaria invoked the United States domestic jurisdiction reservation. The United States withdrew the case before the Court made any ruling on its jurisdiction.

5. There are five declarations in force with "domestic jurisdiction" reservations of the "self-judging" or "automatic" kind: those of Liberia, Malawi, Mexico, Philippines and Sudan.[125] A number of declarations[126] have reservations excluding "disputes with regard to questions which by international law fall exclusively within the jurisdiction of [the state making it]" or differently worded reservations to that effect. Some of them omit any reference to international law but, at the same time, do not add "self-judging" words. Are such reservations open to challenge too? Do they serve any purpose? The 1957 Declaration made by the United Kingdom, contained a reservation in respect of " ... any question which, in the opinion of the Government of the United Kingdom, affects the national security of the United Kingdom or any of its dependent territories."[127] Was this open to the same objections as those raised against the French and United States domestic jurisdiction reservations?

Might reliance by a state upon a "self judging" reservation in a case to which no state acting in good faith or reasonably would have concluded it did apply founder on the "principle of good faith" to which the Court refers in the *Nicaragua* case (judgment, para.60, below, p.863) or the administrative law doctrine of "abuse of power," which might claim to be a general principle of law?[128]

---

[122] I.C.J. Rep. p.93.
[123] I.C.J. Rep. 1957, pp.113–114.
[124] I.C.J. Rep. 1960, p.146.
[125] The French and US declarations containing such reservations have been withdrawn. The Philippines reservation was added in 1972.
[126] e.g. the Canadian declaration.
[127] The reservation was omitted in a revised declaration in 1958.
[128] Note that the US, quite properly, did not rely upon its self-judging reservation in the *Nicaragua* case. Had it done so, would the Court have had occasion to consider its validity? See the *Norwegian Loans* case, where neither side challenged the validity of the comparable French reservation.

NICARAGUA CASE (JURISDICTION AND ADMISSIBILITY)[129]

Nicaragua v U.S.

I.C.J. Reports 1984, p.392

Nicaragua made a unilateral application under art.40, ICJ Statute claiming that the US had acted in breach of its international law obligations by the use of force against Nicaragua and otherwise intervening in Nicaraguan affairs in support of guerrillas fighting to overthrow the Nicaraguan Government.[130] Nicaragua argued that the Court had jurisdiction to hear the case under the "optional clause" and under the 1956 US-Nicaraguan Treaty of Friendship. With regard to the optional clause, Nicaragua relied upon its 1929 Declaration[131] and the US 1946 Declaration accepting the Court's compulsory jurisdiction. There was, however, a problem with the Nicaraguan 1929 Declaration. Although a signatory to the PCIJ Statute, and hence competent to make an optional clause declaration under it, Nicaragua had never completed the ratification process.[132] Consequently, the Statute, and so the Declaration made under it, were never in force for Nicaragua. Under art.36(5), ICJ Statute, provision is made for optional clause declarations under the PCIJ Statute "which are still in force" to remain in force, giving the ICJ compulsory jurisdiction under them. In this case, the US argued that, not having been in force, the Nicaraguan Declaration could not be "still in force" so that it did not come within art.36(5). In the present judgment, the Court disagreed.

Judgment of the Court

26. The Court notes that Nicaragua, having failed to deposit its instrument of ratification of the Protocol of Signature of the Statute of the Permanent Court, was not a party to that treaty. Consequently the Declaration made by Nicaragua in 1929 had not acquired binding force prior to such effect as Article 36, paragraph 5, of the Statute of the International Court of Justice might produce.

27. However, while the declaration had not acquired binding force, it is not disputed that it could have done so ... at any time between the making of Nicaragua's declaration and the day on which the new Court came into existence, if not later, ratification of the Protocol of Signature would have sufficed to transform the content of the 1929 Declaration into a binding commitment; no one would have asked Nicaragua to make a new declaration. ... In sum, Nicaragua's 1929 Declaration was valid at the moment when Nicaragua became a party to the Statute of the new Court; it had retained its potential effect. ...

28. The characteristics of Nicaragua's declaration have now to be compared with the conditions of applicability of Article 36, paragraph 5, as laid down in that provision. ... [one] condition which declarations have to fulfil is that they should be "still in force" (in English) or "faites pour une durée qui n'est pas encore expirée" (in French).

30. ... it does not appear possible to reconcile the two [language] versions of Article 36, paragraph 5, by considering that both versions refer to binding declarations. ... According to the *travaux préparatoires* the word "binding" was never suggested; and if it had been suggested for the English text, there is no doubt that the drafters would never have let the French text stand as finally worded. Furthermore, the Court does not consider the French text to imply that *la durée non expirée* (the unexpired period) is that of a commitment of a binding character. It may be granted that, for a period to continue or expire, it is necessary for some legal effect to have

---

[129] See Briggs (1979) 85 A.J.I.L. 373; Cutler (1985) 25 Virg.J.I.L. 437; Franck (1979) 85 A.J.I.L. 379; Greig (1991) 62 B.Y.I.L. 119; Highet (1987) 21 Int. Lawyer 1083; Kirgis (1979) 85 A.J.I.L. 652; Ostrihansky (1988) 1 Hague.Y.I.L. 3; Reisman (1980) 86 A.J.I.L. 128.

[130] See further the *Nicaragua* (*Merits*) case, above, p.727.

[131] The Nicaraguan Declaration reads: "On behalf of the Republic of Nicaragua I recognise as compulsory unconditionally the jurisdiction of the Permanent Court of International Justice." There are no reservations.

[132] In 1939 the Nicaraguan Foreign Minister sent a telegram to the League of Nations as depository, saying that the Statute had been ratified according to Nicaraguan consitutional law and that the instrument of ratification would be deposited. In 1942, the League wrote to Nicaragua noting that the instrument had not been received. During proceedings in the *Nicaragua* case, Nicaragua acknowledged that the process of ratification had not been completed and raised the possibility that the instrument might have been lost in wartime transit at sea.

come into existence. But this effect does not necessarily have to be of a binding nature. A declaration validly made under Article 36 of the Statute of the Permanent Court had a certain validity which could be preserved or destroyed, and it is perfectly possible to read the French text as implying only this validity.

31. ... the Court cannot but be struck by the fact that the French Delegation at the San Francisco Conference called for the expression "still in force" to be translated, not by "encore en vigueur" but by the term: "pour une durée qui n'est pas encore expirée." In view of the excellent equivalence of the expressions "encore en vigueur" and "still in force," the deliberate choice of the expression "pour une durée qui n'est pas encore expirée" seems to denote an intention to widen the scope of Article 36, paragraph 5, so as to cover declarations which have not acquired binding force. ... It is therefore the Court's opinion that the English version in no way expressly excludes a valid declaration of unexpired duration, made by a State not party to the Protocol of Signature of the Statute of the Permanent Court, and therefore not of a binding character. ...

36. This finding as regards the interpretation of Article 36, paragraph 5, must, finally, be compared to the conduct of States and international organisations in regard to this interpretation. In that respect, particular weight must be ascribed to certain official publications, namely the *I.C.J. Yearbook* (since 1946–1947), the *Reports* of the Court to the General Assembly of the United Nations (since 1968) and the annually published collection of *Signatures, Ratifications, Acceptances, Accessions, etc.*, concerning the Multilateral Conventions and Agreements in respect of which the Secretary-General acts as Depositary. The Court notes that, ever since they first appeared, all these publications have regularly placed Nicaragua on the list of those States that have recognised the compulsory jurisdiction of the Court by virtue of Article 36, paragraph 5, of the Statute. Even if the *I.C.J. Yearbook* has, in the issue for 1946–1947 and as from the issue for 1955–1956 onwards, contained a note[133] recalling certain facts concerning Nicaragua's ratification of the Protocol of Signature of the Statute of the Permanent Court of International Justice, this publication has never modified the classification of Nicaragua or the binding character attributed to its 1929 Declaration—indeed the *Yearbooks* list Nicaragua among the States "still bound by" their declarations under Article 36 of the Statute of the Permanent Court. ...

37. The Court has no intention of assigning these publications any role that would be contrary to their nature but will content itself with noting that they attest a certain interpretation of Article 36, paragraph 5 (whereby that provision would cover the declaration of Nicaragua), and the rejection of an opposite interpretation (which would refuse to classify Nicaragua among the States covered by that Article). ... the inclusion of Nicaragua in the "List of States which have recognised the compulsory jurisdiction of the International Court of Justice, or which are still bound by their acceptance of the Optional Clause of the Statute of the Permanent Court of International Justice," as from the appearance of the first *I.C.J. Yearbook* (1946–1947), contrasts with its exclusion from the list in the last Report of the Permanent Court of International Justice of "States bound by the [optional] clause." It is therefore difficult to escape the conclusion that the basis of this innovation was to be found in the possibility that a declaration which, though not of binding character, was still valid, and was so for a period that had not yet expired, permitted the application of Article 36, paragraph 5, so long as the State in question, by ratifying the Statute of the International Court of Justice, provided it with the institutional foundation that it had hitherto lacked. From that moment on, Nicaragua would have become "bound" by its 1929 Declaration, and could, for practical purposes, appropriately be included in the same *Yearbook* list as the States which have been bound even prior to the coming into force of the post-war Statute.

38. The importance of this lies in the significance to be attached to the conduct of the States concerned, which is dependent on the testimony thus furnished by these publications. The point is not that the Court in its administrative capacity took a decision as to Nicaragua's status which would be binding upon it in its judicial capacity, since this clearly could not be so. It is that the listing found appropriate for Nicaragua amounted over the years to a series of attestations which were entirely official and public, and extremely numerous, and ranged over a period of nearly 40 years; and that hence the States concerned—first and foremost, Nicaragua—had every opportunity of accepting or rejecting the thus-proclaimed applicability of Article 36, paragraph 5, to the Nicaraguan Declaration of 1929.

39. ... Having regard to the public and unchanging nature of the official statements concerning Nicaragua's commitment under the Optional-Clause system, the silence of its Government can only be interpreted as an acceptance of the classification thus assigned to it. It cannot be supposed that that Government could have believed that its silence could be tantamount to anything other than acquiescence. Besides, the Court would remark that if proceedings had been instituted against Nicaragua at any time in these recent years, and it had sought to deny that, by the operation of Article 36, paragraph 5, it had recognised the compulsory jurisdiction of the Court, the Court would probably have rejected that argument. ... If the Court considers that it would have

---

[133] Ed. The note recalled, inter alia that no instrument of ratification had been received

decided that Nicaragua would have been bound in a case in which it was the Respondent, it must conclude that its jurisdiction is identically established in a case where Nicaragua is the Applicant.

40. As for States other than Nicaragua, including those which could be supposed to have the closest interest in that State's legal situation in regard to the Court's jurisdiction, they have never challenged the interpretation to which the publications of the United Nations bear witness and whereby the case of Nicaragua is covered by Article 36, paragraph 5. Such States as themselves publish lists of States bound by the compulsory jurisdiction of the Court have placed Nicaragua on their lists. Of course, the Court is well aware that such national publications simply reproduce those of the United Nations, where that particular point is concerned. Nevertheless, it would be difficult to interpret the fact of such reproduction as signifying an objection to the interpretation thus given; on the contrary, this reproduction contributes to the generality of the opinion which appears to have been cherished by States parties to the Statute as regards the applicability to Nicaragua of Article 36, paragraph 5.

41. Finally, what States believe regarding the legal situation of Nicaragua so far as the compulsory jurisdiction of the Court is concerned may emerge from the conclusions drawn by certain governments as regards the possibility of obliging Nicaragua to appear before the Court or of escaping any proceedings it may institute. The Court would therefore recall that in the case concerning the *Arbitral Award Made by the King of Spain on December 23 1906*[134] Honduras founded its application both on a special agreement, the Washington Agreement, and on Nicaragua's Optional-Clause declaration. It is also difficult for the Court not to consider that the United States letter of April 6, 1984[135] implies that at that date the United States, like other States, believed that Nicaragua was bound by the Court's jurisdiction in accordance with the terms of its 1929 Declaration.

42. The Court thus finds that the interpretation whereby the provisions of Article 36, paragraph 5, cover the case of Nicaragua has been confirmed by the subsequent conduct of the parties to the treaty in question, the Statute of the Court. However, the conduct of States which has been considered has been in relation to publications of the Court and of the United Nations Secretariat which ... do not indicate the legal reasoning leading to the conclusion that Nicaragua fell within the category of States to whose declarations Article 36, paragraph 5, applied. The view might have been taken that that paragraph applied because the Nicaraguan telegram of November 29, 1939 in itself constituted ratification of the Protocol of Signature. It should therefore be observed that the conduct of Nicaragua in relation to the publications in question also supports a finding of jurisdiction under Article 36, paragraph 2, of the Statute independently of the interpretation and effect of paragraph 5 of that Article.

43. Nicaragua has in fact also contended that the validity of Nicaragua's recognition of the compulsory jurisdiction of the Court finds an independent basis in the conduct of the Parties. ...

44. The United States however objects that this contention of Nicaragua is flatly inconsistent with the Statute of the Court, which provides only for consent to jurisdiction to be manifested in specified ways; an "independent title of jurisdiction, as Nicaragua calls it, is an impossibility." ...

46. ... The question is therefore whether, even if the consent of Nicaragua is real, the Court can decide that it has been given valid expression even on the hypothesis that the 1929 Declaration was without validity, and given that no other declaration has been deposited by Nicaragua since it became a party to the Statute of the International Court of Justice. In this connection the Court notes that Nicaragua's situation has been wholly unique, in that it was the publications of the Court itself ... which affirmed (and still affirm today, for that matter) that Nicaragua had accomplished the formality in question. Hence, if the Court were to object that Nicaragua ought to have made a declaration under Article 36, paragraph 2, it would be penalising Nicaragua for having attached undue weight to the information given on that point by the Court and the Secretary-General of the United Nations and, in sum, having (on account of the authority of their sponsors) regarded them as more reliable than they really were.

47. ... The Court finds that this exceptional situation cannot be without effect on the requirements obtaining as regards the formalities that are indispensable for the consent of a State to its compulsory jurisdiction to have been validly given. It considers therefore that, having regard to the origin and generality of the statements to the effect that Nicaragua was bound by its 1929 Declaration, it is right to conclude that the constant acquiescence of that State in those affirmations constitutes a valid mode of manifestation of its intent to recognise the compulsory jurisdiction of the Court under Article 36, paragraph 2, of the Statute, and that accordingly Nicaragua is, vis-à-vis the United States, a State accepting "the same obligation" under that Article.

48. The United States, however, further contends that even if Nicaragua is otherwise entitled to invoke against the United States the jurisdiction of the Court under Article 36, paragraphs 2 and 5, of the Statute, Nicaragua's

---

[134] Ed. I.C.J. Rep. 1960, p.192.
[135] Ed. The Schultz letter. See below, p.863.

conduct in relation to the United States over the course of many years estops Nicaragua from doing so. The United States asserts that since 1943 Nicaragua has consistently represented to the United States of America that Nicaragua was not bound by the Optional Clause, and when the occasion arose that this was material to the United States diplomatic activities, the United States relied upon those Nicaraguan representations. ...

49. In 1943, the United States ambassador to Nicaragua consulted the Nicaraguan Foreign Minister on the question whether the Protocol of Signature of the Statute of the Permanent Court had been ratified by Nicaragua. According to a despatch from the Ambassador to Washington, a decree of July 1935 signed by the President of Nicaragua, mentioning the approval of the ratification by the Senate and Chamber of Deputies, was traced, as was a copy of the telegram to the Secretariat of the League of Nations dated 29 November 1939 ... The decree stated that it was to become effective on the date of its publication in *La Gaceta*. The Ambassador informed his Government that:

"The Foreign Minister informs me that the decree was never published in *La Gaceta*. He also declared that there is no record to the instrument of ratification having been transmitted to Geneva. It would appear that, while appropriate legislative action was taken in Nicaragua to approve adherence to the Protocol, Nicaragua is not legally bound thereby, in as much as it did not deposit its official document of ratification with the League of Nations." ...

According to the United States, the United States and Nicaragua could only have understood at that point in time that Nicaragua was not bound by the Optional Clause, and that understanding never changed.

50. ... in 1955–1958 there was diplomatic contact between Honduras, Nicaragua and the United States over the dispute which was eventually determined by the Court as the case of the *Arbitral Award Made by the King of Spain on 23 December 1906* (I.C.J. Reports 1960, p. 192). One of the questions then under examination was whether Honduras would be entitled to institute proceedings against Nicaragua in reliance upon the 1929 Declaration and Article 36, paragraph 5, of the Statute, and in this connection ... the [Nicaraguan] Ambassador is alleged to have observed [to U.S. officials] that there was

"some doubt as to whether Nicaragua would be officially obligated to submit to the International Court because an instrument of ratification of the Court's jurisdiction was never sent" ...

51. ... the Court does not need to deal at length with the contention based on estoppel. The Court has found that the conduct of Nicaragua, having regard to the very particular circumstances in which it was placed, was such as to evince its consent to be bound in such a way as to constitute a valid mode of acceptance of jurisdiction (paragraph 47, above). It is thus evident that the Court cannot regard the information obtained by the United States in 1943, or the doubts expressed in diplomatic contacts in 1955, as sufficient to overturn that conclusion, let alone to support an estoppel. Nicaragua's contention that since 1946 it has consistently maintained that it is subject to the jurisdiction of the Court, is supported by substantial evidence.

Having established that the Nicaraguan Optional Clause Declaration could give it jurisdiction, the Court then considered the effect of the 1984 Schultz letter sent by the US to the UN purporting to modify its 1946 Declaration by excluding for two years "disputes with any Central American state or arising out of or related to events in Central America." The letter stated that "notwithstanding the terms of the ... [1946] declaration, this proviso shall take effect immediately."

59. Declarations of acceptance of the compulsory jurisdiction of the Court are facultative, unilateral engagements, that States are absolutely free to make or not to make. In making the declaration a State is equally free either to do so unconditionally and without limit of time for its duration, or to qualify it with conditions or reservations. In particular, it may limit its effect to disputes arising after a certain date; or it may specify how long the declaration itself shall remain in force, or what notice (if any) will be required to terminate it. However, the unilateral nature of declarations does not signify that the State making the declaration is free to amend the scope and the contents of its solemn commitments as it pleases.[136] ...

60. ... the declarations, even though they are unilateral acts, establish a series of bilateral engagements with

---

[136] Ed. The Court quoted the *Nuclear Tests* case, judgment, para.43, above, p.47.

other States accepting the same obligation of compulsory jurisdiction, in which the conditions, reservations and time-limit clauses are taken into consideration. In the establishment of this network of engagements, which constitutes the Optional-Clause system, the principle of good faith plays an important role. . . .

61. The most important question relating to the effect of the 1984 notification is whether the United States was free to disregard the clause of six months' notice which, freely and by its own choice it had appended to its 1946 Declaration. In so doing the United States entered into an obligation which is binding upon it *vis-à-vis* other States parties to the Optional-Clause system. Although the United States retained the right to modify the contents of the 1946 Declaration or to terminate it, a power which is inherent in any unilateral act of a State, it has, nevertheless assumed an inescapable obligation towards other States accepting the Optional Clause, by stating formally and solemnly that any such change should take effect only after six months have elapsed as from the date of notice.

62. The United States has argued that the Nicaraguan 1929 Declaration, being of undefined duration, is liable to immediate termination, without previous notice, and that therefore Nicaragua has not accepted "the same obligation" as itself for the purposes of Article 36, paragraph 2, and consequently may not rely on the six months' notice proviso against the United States. The Court does not however consider that this argument entitles the United States validly to act in non-application of the time-limit proviso included in the 1946 Declaration. The notion of reciprocity is concerned with the scope and substance of the commitments entered into, including reservations, and not with the formal conditions of their creation, duration or extinction. It appears clearly that reciprocity cannot be invoked in order to excuse departure from the terms of a State's own declaration, whatever its scope, limitations or conditions. . . .

63. Moreover, since the United States purported to act on April 6, 1984 in such a way as to modify its 1946 Declaration with sufficiently immediate effect to bar an Application filed on April 9, 1984, it would be necessary, if reciprocity is to be relied on, for the Nicaraguan Declaration to be terminable with immediate effect. But the right of immediate termination of declarations with indefinite duration is far from established. It appears from the requirements of good faith that they should be treated, by analogy, according to the law of treaties, which requires a reasonable time for withdrawal from or termination of treaties that contain no provision regarding the duration of their validity. Since Nicaragua has in fact not manifested any intention to withdraw its own declaration, the question of what reasonable period of notice would legally be required does not need to be further examined: it need only be observed that from 6 to 9 April would not amount to a "reasonable time."

64. The Court would also recall that in previous cases in which it has had to examine the reciprocal effect of declarations made under the Optional Clause, it has determined whether or not the "same obligation" was in existence at the moment of seising of the Court, by comparing the effect of the provisions, in particular the reservations, of the two declarations at that moment. The Court is not convinced that it would be appropriate, or possible, to try to determine whether a State against which proceedings had not yet been instituted could rely on a provision in another State's declaration to terminate or modify its obligations before the Court was seised. . . .

65. In sum, the six months' notice clause forms an important integral part of the United States Declaration and it is a condition that must be complied with in case of either termination or modification. Consequently, the 1984 notification, in the present case, cannot override the obligation of the United States to submit to the compulsory jurisdiction of the Court *vis-à-vis* Nicaragua, a State accepting the same obligation.

67. The question remains to be resolved whether the United States Declaration of 1946, though not suspended in its effects vis-à-vis Nicaragua by the 1984 notification, constitutes the necessary consent of the United States to the jurisdiction of the Court in the present case, taking into account the reservations which were attached to the declaration. Specifically, the United States has invoked proviso (c) to that declaration, which provides that the United States acceptance of the Court's compulsory jurisdiction shall not extend to "disputes arising under a multilateral treaty, unless (1) all parties to the treaty affected by the decision are also parties to the case before the Court, or (2) the United States of America specially agrees to jurisdiction." . . .

73. It may first be noted that the multilateral treaty reservation could not bar adjudication by the Court of all Nicaragua's claims, because Nicaragua, in its Application, does not confine those claims only to violations of the four multilateral conventions referred to.[137] . . . On the contrary, Nicaragua invokes a number of principles of customary and general international law that, according to the Application, have been violated by the United States. The Court cannot dismiss the claims of Nicaragua under principles of customary and general international law, simply because such principles have been enshrined in the texts of the conventions relied upon by Nicaragua. The fact that the above-mentioned principles, recognised as such, have been codified or embodied in multilateral conventions does not mean that they cease to exist and to apply as principles of customary law, even

---

[137] Ed. These were the UN Charter and three Inter-American treaties.

as regards countries that are parties to such conventions. Principles such as those of the non-use of force, non-intervention, respect for the independence and territorial integrity of States, and the freedom of navigation, continue to be binding as part of customary international law, despite the operation of provisions of conventional law in which they have been incorporated. Therefore, since the claim before the Court in this case is not confined to violation of the multilateral conventional provisions invoked, it would not in any event be barred by the multilateral treaty reservation in the United States 1946 Declaration.

The Court then held that it also had jurisdiction under the dispute settlement provision of the 1956 US-Nicaraguan Treaty of Friendship, there being a dispute arising in respect of the treaty's provisions guaranteeing freedom of commerce and navigation.

113. For these reasons,

THE COURT,

(1)(a) *finds*, by 11 votes to five,[138] that it has jurisdiction to entertain the Application filed by the Republic of Nicaragua on April 9, 1984, on the basis of Article 36, paragraphs 2 and 5, of the Statute of the Court;

(b) *finds*, by 14 votes to two,[139] that it has jurisdiction to entertain the Application filed by the Republic of Nicaragua on April 9, 1984, in so far as that Application relates to a dispute concerning the interpretation or application of the Treaty of Friendship, Commerce and Navigation between the United States of America and the Republic of Nicaragua signed at Managua on January 21, 1956, on the basis of Article XXIV of that Treaty;

(c) *finds*, by 15 votes to one,[140] that it has jurisdiction to entertain the case.

Separate Opinion of Judge Sir Robert Jennings

The question ... is whether Article 36, paragraph 5, of the present Court's Statute had the effect of trans-ferring to the new Court, Nicaragua's subscription to the Optional Clause of the Protocol of Signature and the Statute of the Permanent Court, which entire instrument required ratification; but which was never ratified, with the admitted consequence that Nicaragua never became obligated by the compulsory jurisdiction of the Permanent Court?

The answer would seem to be placed beyond doubt according to the English text of Article 36, paragraph 5, ...

One can do no more than speculate on the purpose of the change in the French text [from *en vigueur*], for the records are sparse. So one is left with the rule that if there be, which I doubt, material difference between the meaning of the texts, the one which best reconciles the different language versions, all five of them that is to say, is to be preferred. For the present case at least there is no great difficulty in doing that. A declaration of acceptance of compulsory jurisdiction, which declaration never came into operation under the old Statute, certainly cannot be said, under the new Statute, to be "still in force," which is the language used in four of the versions of the Statute; and is the meaning consonant with what was said to be the purpose of the provision, namely the carry over to the new Court of obligations created in respect of the old Court.

There is no difficulty in collecting the same meaning in the French formula: *pour une durée qui n'est pas encore expirée*. What is referred to by that formula is surely a declaration by which the compulsory jurisdiction of the Permanent Court was actually established. A declaration to which, owing to failure to ratify the Protocol, no date of commencement of the obligation in respect of the Permanent Court could be assigned, cannot be said to be *pour une durée qui n'est pas encore expirée*. That which never began cannot be said to have had a duration at all.

... The judgment of the Court ... regards the *Yearbooks* and other publications as a factor confirming its interpretation of the effect of Article 36, paragraph 5; if not an independent source of jurisdiction for the Court. In my view, thus to allow considerable, and even decisive, effect, to statements in the Court's *Yearbook* is mistaken in general principle; ...

... the Court should always distinguish between its administrative functions—including the compilation of the *Yearbook* by the Registrar on the Court's instructions—and its judicial functions. When there is a dispute between States as to the Court's jurisdiction, that dispute may be, as in the present case, submitted to the Court for

---

[138] Judges Mosler, Oda, Ago, Schwebel and Sir Robert Jennings dissented.
[139] Judges Ruda and Schwebel dissented.
[140] Judges Schwebel dissented.

determination in its judicial capacity. To hold, after the exchange of voluminous written pleadings and after two rounds of oral proceedings, that the matter was, before all this, virtually settled as a result of the action of the Registrar acting on behalf of the Court in its administrative capacity, and without benefit of judicial argument and procedure, is not free from an element of absurdity.

But even apart from the objections of principle, the *Yearbooks* do not at all yield any certain message on the status of the Nicaraguan declaration; on the contrary they consistently—each one of them—alert the attentive reader to the existence of doubts.

Notes

1. Finding that the Court's decision that it had jurisdiction in the case to be "contrary to law and fact,"[141] the US decided not to participate further in the case and did not present evidence or arguments on the merits.[142] In 1985, the US terminated its optional clause declaration.[143] Having read the Court's judgment as to jurisdiction, would you agree with the US Government's position that the Court was "determined to find in favour of Nicaragua,"[144] or with Franck, who, although critical of the Court's reasoning, suggests that "it would be hard for a fair-minded reader of the majority's reasoned opinion to conclude that this result could not be reached by a dedicated and impartial judge?"[145]

2. As well as finding that it had jurisdiction, the Court also rejected, unanimously, US objections as to admissibility,[146] including objections to the effect that the dispute concerned a matter that should be resolved by the political organs of the United Nations rather than its Court and that the Court should not involve itself in a situation that concerned an ongoing armed conflict.[147] On the propriety of Nicaragua's reference of the case to the Court, the 1982 Manila Declaration on the Peaceful Settlement of International Disputes,[148] reads:

    "Recourse to judicial settlement of legal disputes, particularly referral to the International Court of Justice, should not be considered an unfriendly act between States."

---

[141] (1985) 24 I.L.M. 246.

[142] For criticism of this action, see Franck, above, n.129. Supporting it, see Almond (1987) 17 Cal. W.I.L.J. 146.

[143] For criticism of the US termination, see Gardner (1985) 24 Col J.T.L 421. See generally, Arend, ed., *The U.S. and the Compulsory Jurisdiction of the International Court of Justice* (1986).

[144] (1985) 24 I.L.M. 248.

[145] See above, n.129, p.382.

[146] The distinction between objections as to jurisdiction and as to admissibility is explained by Fitzmaurice (1958) 34 B.Y.I.L 12–13, as follows: "The latter is a plea that the tribunal should rule the claim to be inadmissible on some ground other than its ultimate merits: the former is a plea that the tribunal itself is incompetent to give any rulings at all as to the merits or the admissibility of the claim." Examples of objections as to admissibility are objections based on the rules on the nationality of claims or the exhaustion of local remedies.

[147] On this aspect of the case and the related question of the distinction between "legal" and "political" disputes (see the text of art.36(2)), see Almond, above, p.142, Gordon, in Damrosch, above; n.22, Merrills (1987) 24 Coexistence 169. See also on the Court and the Security Council below, p.878. The fact that negotiations are being actively pursued is also not a bar to recourse to judicial settlement or arbitration: *Aegean Sea Continental Shelf* case I.C.J. Rep. 1978, p.13.

[148] See above, n.4.

D. Third States in Contentious Litigation[149]

EAST TIMOR CASE

Portugal v Australia

I.C.J. Reports 1995, p.90

Portugal brought an application instituting proceedings against Australia under art.36(2), ICJ Statute. Portugal claimed that Australia had failed to respect the rights of Portugal as the administering power of East Timor, and the right of the people of East Timor to self-determination, by entering into a 1989 treaty with Indonesia, which had occupied by force and illegally claimed title to East Timor. The treaty delimited the continental shelf between East Timor and Australia. In the following extract, the Court considered Australia's objection to the Court's jurisdiction in the case on the ground that it would be required to determine Indonesia's rights and duties without that state's consent. On the legality of Indonesia's claim to East Timor, see above, p.109.

Judgment of the Court

26. The Court recalls in this respect that one of the fundamental principles of its Statute is that it cannot decide a dispute between States without the consent of those States to its jurisdiction. This principle was reaffirmed in the Judgment given by the Court in the case concerning *Monetary Gold Removed from Rome in 1943* and confirmed in several of its subsequent decisions . . .

27. The Court notes that Portugal's claim . . . is based on the assertion that Portugal alone in its capacity as administering Power, had the power to enter into the Treaty on behalf of East Timor, that Australia disregarded this exclusive power, and, in so doing, violated its obligations to respect the status of Portugal and that of East Timor.

The Court also observes that Australia, for its part, rejects Portugal's claim to the exclusive power to conclude treaties on behalf of East Timor, and the very fact that it entered into the 1989 Treaty with Indonesia shows that it considered that Indonesia had that power. Australia in substance argues that even if Portugal had retained that power, on whatever basis, after withdrawing from East Timor, the possibility existed that the power could later pass to another State under general international law, and that it did so pass to Indonesia; Australia affirms moreover that, if the power in question did pass to Indonesia, it was acting in conformity with international law in entering into the 1989 Treaty with that State, and could not have violated any of the obligations Portugal attributes to it. Thus, for Australia, the fundamental question in the present case is ultimately whether, in 1989, the power to conclude a treaty on behalf of East Timor in relation to its continental shelf lay with Portugal or with Indonesia.

28. The Court has carefully considered the argument advanced by Portugal which seeks to separate Australia's behaviour from that of Indonesia. However, in the view of the Court, Australia's behaviour cannot be assessed without first entering into the question why it is that Indonesia could not lawfully have concluded the 1989 Treaty, while Portugal allegedly could have done so; the very subject-matter of the Court's decision would necessarily be a determination whether, having regard to the circumstances in which Indonesia entered and remained in East Timor, it could or could not have acquired the power to enter into treaties on behalf of East Timor relating to the resources of its continental shelf. The Court could not make such a determination in the absence of the consent of Indonesia.

29. However, Portugal puts forward an additional argument aiming to show that the principle formulated by the Court in the case concerning *Monetary Gold Removed from Rome in 1943* is not applicable in the present case. It maintains, in effect, that the rights which Australia allegedly breached were rights *erga omnes* and that accordingly Portugal could require it, individually, to respect them regardless of whether or not another State had conducted itself in a similarly unlawful manner.

In the Court's view, Portugal's assertion that the right of peoples to self-determination, as it evolved from the Charter and from United Nations practice, has an *erga omnes* character, is irreproachable. The principle of self-

---

[149] See Chinkin, *Third Parties in International Law* (1993), Chs 7 and 8.

determination of peoples has been recognized by the United Nations Charter and in the jurisprudence of the Court (see *Legal Consequences for States of the Continued Presence of South Africa in Namibia (South West Africa) notwithstanding Security Council Resolution 276 (1970), Advisory Opinion, I.C.J. Reports 1971*, pp. 31–32, paras. 52–53; *Western Sahara, Advisory Opinion, I.C.J. Reports 1975*, pp. 31–33, paras. 54–59); it is one of the essential principles of contemporary international law. However, the Court considers that the *erga omnes* character of a norm and the rule of consent to jurisdiction are two different things. Whatever the nature of the obligations invoked, the Court could not rule on the lawfulness of the conduct of a State when its judgment would imply an evaluation of the lawfulness of the conduct of another State which is not a party to the case. Where this is so, the Court cannot act, even if the right in question is a right *erga omnes*.

The Court then rejected an argument by Portugal that the Court would not have to decide who had the capacity to act for East Timor because the General Assembly and the Security Council had determined that Portugal was the administering power, see the resolutions cited above, p.109, which determinations the Court would accept as "givens". In the Court's view, the resolutions did not establish that third states should deal exclusively with Portugal in respect of East Timor's continental shelf.

34. The Court emphasizes that it is not necessarily prevented from adjudicating when the judgment it is asked to give might affect the legal interests of a State which is not a party to the case. Thus, in the case concerning *Certain Phosphate Lands in Nauru (Nauru v. Australia)*, it stated, inter alia, as follows:

> In the present case, the interests of New Zealand and the United Kingdom do not constitute the very subject-matter of the judgment to be rendered on the merits of Nauru's Application ... In the present case, the determination of the responsibility of New Zealand or the United Kingdom is not a prerequisite for the determination of the responsibility of Australia, the only object of Nauru's claim ... In the present case, a finding by the Court regarding the existence or the content of the responsibility attributed to Australia by Nauru might well have implications for the legal situation of the two other States concerned, but no finding in respect of that legal situation will be needed as a basis for the Court's decision on Nauru's claims against Australia. Accordingly, the Court cannot decline to exercise its jurisdiction. (*I.C.J. Reports 1992*, pp.261–261, para. 55).

However, in this case, the effects of the judgment requested by Portugal would amount to a determination that Indonesia's entry into and continued presence in East Timor are unlawful and that, as a consequence, it does not have the treaty-making power in matters relating to the continental shelf resources of East Timor. Indonesia's rights and obligations would thus constitute the very subject-matter of such a judgment made in the absence of that State's consent. Such a judgment would run directly counter to the "well-established principle of international law embodied in the Court's Statute, namely, that the Court can only exercise jurisdiction over a State with its consent" (*Monetary Gold Removed from Rome in 1943, Judgment, I.C.J. Reports 1954*, p. 32).

38. For these reasons,

THE COURT,

By fourteen votes to two,[150]

Finds that it cannot in the present case exercise the jurisdiction conferred upon it by the declarations made by the Parties under Article 36, paragraph 2, of its Statute to adjudicate upon the dispute referred to it by the Application of the Portuguese Republic.

---

[150] In favour: President Bedjaoui; Vice-President Schwebel; Judges Oda, Sir Robert Jennings, Guillaume, Shahabuddeen, Aguilar-Mawdsley, Ranjeva, Herczegh, Shi, Fleischhauer, Koroma, Vereshchetin; Judge ad hoc Sir Ninian Stephen. Judge Weeramantry and Judge ad hoc Skubiszewski dissented.

Notes

1. *No jurisdiction to rule on the rights and obligations of third states.* In this case the Court applied its ruling in the *Monetary Gold* case that it may not give judgment on a case between States A and B that would require it to rule upon the international law rights and obligations of State C where that third state had not given its consent to this happening by becoming a party to the case. In the *East Timor* case, Indonesia had no wish to become a party to the case and, unlike Australia, could not be brought before the Court under art.36(2), as it had not made an "optional clause" declaration.

2. The *Monetary Gold* case[151] concerned gold belonging to the National Bank of Albania that had been seized by Germany from a bank in Rome during the Second World War. It had since fallen into the hands of the allied forces and was to be distributed by a Tripartite Commission, consisting of France, the United Kingdom and the United States. Following an arbitral decision against it, and acting under an agreement that gave the Court jurisdiction in the matter, Italy instituted proceedings before the Court, against the three allied powers claiming the gold, but Albania, in whose favour the arbitrator had decided, declined to be a party to the case before the ICJ. The Court decided that it did not have jurisdiction because "Albania's legal interests would not only be affected by a decision, but would form the very subject-matter of the decision."

3. In the *Land and Maritime Boundary between Cameroon and Nigeria* case,[152] the Court ruled that it was able to rule on the maritime boundary between the two parties, but only to the extent that it was not called upon to "decide upon the legal rights of third States not parties to the proceedings". In that case, the third parties "whose rights might be affected" were Equatorial Guinea (which was permitted to intervene, see below) and Sao Tomé (which had not requested such permission).

4. *Requests by third states to participate in proceedings.* A different situation from that in the *East Timor* case is that in which a third state wishes to participate in a case without becoming a party to it.[153] It may become a party with the consent of the other party or parties, which may have been given earlier by treaty[154] or under art.36(2), or may be given ad hoc by special agreement. Otherwise, there is the possibility of intervention, as a third party, under arts 62 or 63, ICJ Statute, below, App.III.

5. A Chamber of the Court gave Nicaragua permission to intervene under art.62 in the *Land, Island and Maritime Frontier Dispute* case (*El Salvador v Honduras*),[155] although only in respect of the legal regime of the Gulf of Fonseca; the application was refused in respect of other matters before the Court. The Court stated:

    "72. ... the fact is that El Salvador now claims that the waters of the Gulf are subject to a condominium of the coastal States, and has indeed suggested that that régime 'would in any case have been applicable to the Gulf under customary international law'. Nicaragua has referred to the fact that Nicaragua plainly has rights in the Gulf of Fonseca, the existence of which is undisputed, and contends that 'The condominium, if it is declared to be applicable, would by its very nature involve three riparians, and not only the parties to the Special

---

[151] I.C.J. Rep. 1954, p.19 at p.32.

[152] I.C.J. rep. 2002, p.303, para.238.

[153] On intervention by a third state, see Grieg (1992) 32 Virg.J.I.L. 285; Macdonald and Hughes (1993) 5 A.J.I.C.L. 1; Ruda, in Lowe and Fitzmaurice, above, Ch.26; Rosenne, *Intervention in the International Court of Justice* (1993).

[154] In the *Monetary Gold* case, Albania could have seized the Court under the agreement on the basis of which Italy did so.

[155] I.C.J. Rep. 1990, p.92 at 121.

Agreement.' In the opinion of the Chamber, this is a sufficient demonstration by Nicaragua that it has an interest of a legal nature in the determination whether or not this is the régime governing the waters of the Gulf: the very definition of a condominium points to this conclusion. Furthermore, a decision in favour of some of the Honduran theses would equally be such as may affect legal interests of Nicaragua."

In the same case, the chamber held that there was no need for a state to have a "jurisdiction link" (i.e. the capacity to be a party to the case itself) to be granted permission to intervene in a case. This was confirmed by the full court in the *Land and Maritime Boundary between Cameroon and Nigeria* case,[156] which is the only other case in which an application to intervene under art.62 (by Equatorial Guinea) has been successful. Intervention under art.62 is a matter for the Court; there is no right to intervene and the parties to the case may only seek to persuade the Court to adopt any view that they have. The burden of proof is on the state seeking to intervene.[157] A state may be permitted to intervene even though there is no "jurisdictional link" between the intervening state and the parties to the case.[158] Since it is not a party to the case, an intervening state is not bound by the Court's judgment: see art.59, ICJ Statute.

6.   Intervention under art.63, which applies in cases where a state is a party to a treaty that is being interpreted by the Court, has been permitted in two cases: the *Wimbledon* case[159] and the *Haya de la Torre* case.[160] Although a third state may have a right to intervene under art.63, the Court must first decide whether it qualifies.[161]

E. Provisional Measures in Contentious Litigation[162]

See art.41, Statute of the International Court of Justice.[163]

LAGRAND CASE

Germany v United States

I.C.J. Reports 2001, p.466

Walter and Carl LaGrand were German citizens who had been born in Germany but, aged four and five, had moved with their German mother to the United States where they had been permanent residents ever since. They were arrested in 1982, convicted of murder in 1984 and sentenced to death. Under art.36(1)(a) of the Vienna Convention on Consular Relations 1963, to which Germany and the United States were parties, they had a right to consular access and to be informed of this right.

---

[156] I.C.J. Rep. 1999, p.1029. Permission was refused in the *Pulau Ligitan and Pulau Sipadan* case, I.C.J. Rep. 2001, p.575 at n.603, the Philippines not showing the required "interest of a legal nature". On the Court's historically restrictive approach, see Chinkin (1986) 80 A.J.I.L. 495; and McGinley (1985) 34 I.C.L.Q. 671.

[157] *Land, Island and Maritime Frontier Dispute* case, I.C.J. Rep. 1990, p.117.

[158] Ibid.

[159] See above, p.222 (Poland intervened).

[160] I.C.J. Rep. 1951, p.71.

[161] On the Court's refusal to permit El Salvador to intervene under art.63 in the *Nicaragua* case, see Damrosch, above, n.22, p.376.

[162] See Rosenne, *Provisional Measures in International Law* (2005), Palchetti, 21 L.J.I.L. 623 (2008); Merrills (1995) 44 I.C.L.Q. 90; Oda, in Lowe and Fitzmaurice, above, n.22, Ch.29; Sztucki, *Interim Measures in the Hague Court* (1983).

[163] See below, App.I. See also r.66 of Rules of Court.

Having heard of this right from other sources, the brothers contacted the German consulate in 1992, while appeal proceedings in their cases were still pending. They were not officially informed of the right by the United States until December 1998. German Government representations to halt the executions were unsuccessful, and Carl LaGrand was executed in February 1999.

On March 2, 1999, the day before the scheduled execution of Walter LaGrand, Germany filed an application instituting proceedings against the United States under art.36(1), ICJ Statute and the Optional Protocol concerning the Settlement of Disputes to the Vienna Convention on Consular Relations 1963. The application alleged a breach of art.36(1)(a), Vienna Convention and requested provisional measures. On March 3, 1999, the Court indicated provisional measures aimed at ensuring that Walter LaGrand was not executed while the case was pending. However, he was executed on the same day.

In argument, the United States conceded that it had infringed art.36(1)(a), Vienna Convention. The following extracts from the Court's judgment concern the question whether the indication of provisional measures was legally binding and whether the United States had complied with it.

Judgment of the Court

99. ... The Court will therefore now proceed to the interpretation of Article 41 of the Statute. It will do so in accordance with customary international law, reflected in Article 31 of the 1969 Vienna Convention on the Law of Treaties. According to paragraph 1 of Article 31, a treaty must be interpreted in good faith in accordance with the ordinary meaning to be given to its terms in their context and in light of the treaty's object and purpose.

100. The French text of Article 41 reads as follows:

"1. La Cour a le pouvoir d'*indiquer*, si elle estime que les circonstances l'exigent, quelles mesures conservatoires du droit de chacun *doivent* être prises à titre provisoire.

2. En attendant l'arrêt définitif, l'*indication* de ces mesures est immédiatement notifiée aux parties et au Conseil de sécurité." (Emphasis added.)

In this text, the terms "indiquer" and "l'indication" may be deemed to be neutral as to the mandatory character of the measure concerned; by contrast the words "doivent être prises" have an imperative character.

For its part, the English version of Article 41 reads as follows:

"1. The Court shall have the power to *indicate*, if it considers that circumstances so require, any provisional measures which *ought* to be taken to preserve the respective rights of either party.

2. Pending the final decision, notice of the measures *suggested* shall forthwith be given to the parties and to the Security Council." (Emphasis added.)

According to the United States, the use in the English version of "indicate" instead of "order", of "ought" instead of "must" or "shall", and of "suggested" instead of "ordered", is to be understood as implying that decisions under Article 41 lack mandatory effect. It might however be argued, having regard to the fact that in 1920 the French text was the original version, that such terms such as "indicate" and "ought" have a meaning equivalent to "order" and "must" or "shall".

101. Finding itself faced with two texts which are not in total harmony, the Court will first of all note that according to Article 92 of the Charter, the Statute "forms an integral part of the present Charter". Under Article 111 of the Charter, the French and English texts of the latter are "equally authentic". The same is equally true of the Statute.

In cases of divergence between the equally authentic versions of the Statute, neither it nor the Charter indicates how to proceed. In the absence of agreement between the parties in this respect, it is appropriate to refer to paragraph 4 of Article 33 of the Vienna Convention on the Law of Treaties, which in the view of the Court again reflects customary international law. This provision reads "when a comparison of the authentic texts discloses a difference of meaning which the application of Articles 31 and 32 does not remove the meaning which best reconciles the texts, having regard to the object and purpose of the treaty, shall be adopted".

The Court will therefore now consider the object and purpose of the Statute together with the context of Article 41.

102. The object and purpose of the Statute is to enable the Court to fulfil the functions provided therein, and, in particular, the basic function of judicial settlement of international disputes by binding decisions in accordance with Article 59 of the Statute. The context in which Article 41 has to be seen within the Statute is to prevent the Court from being hampered in the exercise of its functions because the respective rights of the parties to a dispute before the Court are not preserved. It follows from the object and purpose of the Statute, as well as from the terms of Article 41 when read in their context, that the power to indicate provisional measures entails that such measures should be binding, inasmuch as the power in question is based on the necessity, when the circumstances call for it, to safeguard, and to avoid prejudice to, the rights of the parties as determined by the final judgment of the Court. The contention that provisional measures indicated under Article 41 might not be binding would be contrary to the object and purpose of that Article.

103. A related reason which points to the binding character of orders made under Article 41 and to which the Court attaches importance is the existence of a principle which has already been recognized by the Permanent Court of International Justice when it spoke of

"the principle universally accepted by international tribunals and likewise laid down in many conventions . . . to the effect that the parties to a case must abstain from any measure capable of exercising a prejudicial effect in regard to the execution of the decision to be given, and, in general, not allow any step of any kind to be taken which might aggravate or extend the dispute" (*Electricity Company of Sofia and Bulgaria, Order of 5 December 1939, P.C.I.J, Series A/B, No. 79, p. 199*).

Furthermore measures designed to avoid aggravating or extending disputes have frequently been indicated by the Court. They were indicated with the purpose of being implemented. . . .

104. Given the conclusions reached by the Court above in interpreting the text of Article 41 of the Statute in the light of its object and purpose, it does not consider it necessary to resort to the preparatory work in order to determine the meaning of that Article. The Court would nevertheless point out that the preparatory work of the Statute does not preclude the conclusion that orders under Article 41 have binding force. . . .

108. The Court finally needs to consider whether Article 94 of the United Nations Charter[164] precludes attributing binding effect to orders indicating provisional measures. . . .

The question arises as to the meaning to be attributed to the words "the decision of the International Court of Justice" in paragraph 1 of this Article. This wording could be understood as referring not merely to the Court's judgments but to any decision rendered by it, thus including orders indicating provisional measures. It could also be interpreted to mean only judgments rendered by the Court as provided in paragraph 2 of Article 94. In this regard, the fact that in Articles 56 to 60 of the Court's Statute both the word "decision" and the word "judgment" are used does little to clarify the matter.

Under the first interpretation of paragraph 1 of Article 94, the text of the paragraph would confirm the binding nature of provisional measures; whereas the second interpretation would in no way preclude their being accorded binding force under Article 41 of the Statute. The Court accordingly concludes that Article 94 of the Charter does not prevent orders made under Article 41 from having a binding character.

109. In short, it is clear that none of the sources of interpretation referred to in the relevant Articles of the Vienna Convention on the Law of Treaties, including the preparatory work, contradict the conclusions drawn from the terms of Article 41 read in their context and in the light of the object and purpose of the Statute. Thus, the Court has reached the conclusion that orders on provisional measures under Article 41 have binding effect. . . .

111. As regards the question whether the United States has complied with the obligation incumbent upon it as a result of the Order of 3 March 1999, the Court observes that the Order indicated two provisional measures, the first of which states that

"[t]he United States of America should take all measures at its disposal to ensure that Walter LaGrand is not executed pending the final decision in these proceedings, and should inform the Court of all the measures which it has taken in implementation of this Order".

The second measure required the Government of the United States to "transmit this Order to the Governor of the State of Arizona". The information required on the measures taken in implementation of this Order was given to the Court by a letter of 8 March 1999 from the Legal Counsellor of the United States Embassy at The Hague.

---

[164] Ed. For the text, see below, App.III.

According to this letter, on 3 March 1999 the State Department had transmitted to the Governor of Arizona a copy of the Court's Order. "In view of the extremely late hour of the receipt of the Court Order", the letter of 8 March went on to say, "no further steps were feasible".

The United States authorities have thus limited themselves to the mere transmission of the text of the Order to the Governor of Arizona. This certainly met the requirement of the second of the two measures indicated. As to the first measure, the ... Court agrees that due to the extremely late presentation of the request for provisional measures, there was certainly very little time for the United States authorities to act.

112. The Court observes, nevertheless, that the mere transmission of its Order to the Governor of Arizona without any comment, particularly without even so much as a plea for a temporary stay and an explanation that there is no general agreement on the position of the United States that orders of the International Court of Justice on provisional measures are non-binding, was certainly less than could have been done even in the short time available.[165] ...

115. ... Under these circumstances the Court concludes [by 13 votes to 2] that the United States has not complied with the Order of 3 March 1999.

Notes

1. The Court's judgment in the *LaGrand* case resolves a question that had been "the subject of extensive controversy in the literature",[166] namely whether indications of provisional measures are legally binding.

2. Another question which has arisen in respect of the Court's power to indicate provisional (or interim) measures has concerned the circumstances in which they can be indicated before the Court's jurisdiction has been established to hear the merits of a case. The difficulty has been to find a rule that properly takes account both of the fact that the Court may ultimately decide that it lacks jurisdiction to hear the case and of the fact that the parties' rights may be irreparably damaged before a decision as to jurisdiction is taken. After some uncertainty in earlier cases,[167] the Court has now settled on a prima facie jurisdiction test. In the *Application of the Genocide Convention* case,[168] the Court stated:

    "14. Whereas on a request for provisional measures the Court need not, before deciding whether or not to indicate them, finally satisfy itself that it has jurisdiction on the merits of the case, yet it ought not to indicate such measures unless the provisions invoked by the Applicant or found in the Statute appear, *prima facie*, to afford a basis on which the jurisdiction of the Court might be established; whereas this consideration embraces both *rationae personae* and *rationae materiae*, even though, inasmuch as almost all States are today parties to the Statute of the Court, it is generally only the latter which requires to be considered; ..."

3. Commenting on the *LaGrand* case, Thirlway[169] suggests that "in light of the *travaux préparatoires* and of the general trend of interpretation of the text in practice", the Court's "view of Article 41 may be regarded as somewhat revolutionary". He also wonders whether it may have a "negative influence on advance acceptance of jurisdiction", increasing the temptation for states to "commence proceedings on shaky jurisdictional foundation in the hope of getting at least the short-term benefit" of a binding order for provisional measures. In 2005, following the ICJ judgments

---

[165] Ed. On the litigation before the US Supreme Court in these cases, see above, p.86.
[166] Judgment, para.99. For the differing views see the literature cited above, n.162.
[167] See the *Anglo-Iranian Oil Co.* case (*Interim Measures*), I.C.J. Rep. 1951, p.89; and *Nuclear Tests* cases (*Interim Protection*), I.C.J. Rep. 1973, p.99.
[168] Order for Provisional Measures, April 8, 1993, I.C.J. Rep.1993, p.3.
[169] See above, at n.22, pp.574, 587.

on the merits in the *LaGrand* and the similar *Avena*[170] cases, in both of which it was held that the US was in breach of art.36, Convention on Consular Relations, the US withdrew from the Optional Protocol to the Convention on Consular Relations on the Compulsory Settlement of Disputes, so that no further cases could be brought under it. The ICJ ruling on the binding force of provisional measures may also have contributed to this withdrawal.

4.   Generally, states have not respected provisional measures that are indicated against them. This was true in the *Anglo-Iranian Oil Co.* case, the *Fisheries Jurisdiction* cases, the *Nuclear Tests* cases and the *U.S. Diplomatic and Consular Staff in Tehran* case and there would not appear to have been full compliance in the *Nicaragua* case. In the *Armed Activities* case,[171] Uganda was held not to have complied with an order to refrain from any action, "in particular any armed action, which might prejudice the rights of the other party ... or which might aggravate or extend the dispute before the Court or make it more difficult to resolve". Oda has written[172]: "It is not going too far to state that the provisional measures indicated by the Court have had hardly any practical effect in most cases of a highly charged political nature."

F. Advisory Jurisdiction[173]

See art.96, United Nations Charter and arts 65–68, Statute of the International Court of Justice.[174]

Note

In addition to its jurisdiction to decide cases brought by states under art.36 of its Statute, the ICJ

"may give an advisory opinion on any legal question at the request of whatever body may be authorised by or in accordance with the Charter of the United Nations to make such a request."[175]

The General Assembly and the Security Council are authorised "by" the Charter[176] to request opinions. ECOSOC, the Trusteeship Council and the Interim Committee of the General Assembly have been authorised "in accordance with" the Charter,[177] as have most of the UN specialised agencies and the International Atomic Energy Authority.

States may not request advisory opinions, but they are permitted, along with international organisations, to participate in proceedings before the Court.[178] Individuals and other entities have no locus standi.

---

[170] I.C.J. Rep. 2004, p.12.
[171] I.C.J. Rep. 2000, p.113 and I.C.J. Rep. 2005, p.168. See Savadogo (2001) 72 B.Y.I.L. 357.
[172] Lowe and Fitzmaurice, above, n.22, p.557.
[173] See Keith, *The Extent of the Advisory Jurisdiction of the International Court of Justice* (1971); Pomerance, *The Advisory Function of the International Court in the League and UN Eras* (1973); Pratap, *The Advisory Jurisdiction of the International Court* (1972); Szasz, in *The Future of the International Court of Justice*, above, n.23, Vol.II, p.499.
[174] Below, App.I.
[175] Statute of the Court, art.65(1).
[176] UN Charter, art.96(1).
[177] UN Charter, art.96(2). The UN Secretary-General has proposed that he be allowed to request advisory opinions. For differing views on the matter, see Schwebel (1984) 78 A.J.I.L. 869; and Higgins, in Lowe and Fitzmaurice, above, n.22, Ch.31.
[178] Article 66, Statute of the Court. Over 20 states made written and/or oral statements to the Court in the *Nuclear Weapons* case, above, p.788. Palestine was allowed to participate in the *Wall* case in view of its General Assembly observer status and as co-sponsor of the resolution requesting the opinion.

Although advisory opinions are not binding in law upon the requesting body, they have over the years usually been accepted and acted upon by it and by any state concerned. Whereas the record of formal acceptance of opinions remains good, that of compliance in fact has not been perfect. Striking examples were the failure of the General Assembly to enforce the opinion given to it in the *Certain Expenses* case,[179] the steadfast refusal of the old South Africa over many years to fall in line with the opinions on South West Africa/Namibia[180] and Israel's negative response to the *Wall* opinion.[181]

Occasionally, provision is made in advance for an opinion to be binding. The 1946 General Convention on the Privileges and Immunities of the United Nations provides that if a difference arises between the United Nations and a member a request for an advisory opinion should be made by an organ of the United Nations and that the opinion rendered by the Court "shall be accepted as decisive by the parties."[182]

Recourse to the Court for advisory opinions has declined since 1945. Whereas the Permanent Court of International Justice gave 27 opinions in 18 years, the International Court of Justice has so far given only 24.[183] Requests have concerned constitutional questions about the functioning of the requesting body,[184] points of law relevant to a dispute between states[185] or abstract questions of law.[186]

LEGALITY OF THE THREAT OR USE OF NUCLEAR WEAPONS CASE

Advisory Opinion. I.C.J. Rep. 1996, p.226

For the question put to the Court by the UN General Assembly in this case, see the extract above, p.788. In the following extract, the Court considered whether it had jurisdiction to respond.

Opinion of the Court

13. The Court must furthermore satisfy itself that the advisory opinion requested does indeed relate to a "legal question" within the meaning of [Article 65 of] its Statute and the United Nations Charter. ...

The question put to the Court by the General Assembly is indeed a legal one, since the Court is asked to rule on the compatibility of the threat or use of nuclear weapons with the relevant principles and rules of international law. To do this, the Court must identify the existing principles and rules, interpret them and apply them to the threat or use of nuclear weapons, thus offering a reply to the question posed based on law.

The fact that this question also has political aspects, as, in the nature of things, is the case with so many questions which arise in international life, does not suffice to deprive it of its character as a "legal question" and to "deprive the Court of a competence expressly conferred on it by its Statute" (*Application for Review of Judgement No. 158 of the United Nations Administrative Tribunal, Advisory Opinion, I.C.J. Reports 1973*, p.172, para.14). Whatever its political aspects, the Court cannot refuse to admit the legal character of a question which invites it to discharge an essentially judicial task, namely, an assessment of the legality of the possible conduct of States with regard to the obligations imposed upon them by international law (cf. *Conditions of Admission of a*

---

[179] See above, p.831.
[180] See above, p.120.
[181] See above, p.600. General Assembly Resolution A/RES/ES-10/15 (2004), para.2 "demands that Israel ... comply with its legal obligations and mentioned in the advisory opinion" which included dismantling the wall.
[182] Article 30, (1950) U.K.T.S. 10, Cmnd. 7891. cf. art.XII, Statute of the I.L.O. Administrative Tribunal. See Ago (1991) 85 A.J.I.L. 439.
[183] A request for an advisory opinion on the status of Kosovo is pending: see above, p.95.
[184] e.g. the *Certain Expenses* case, above, p.831.
[185] e.g. the *Western Sahara* case, above, p.106 and the *Wall* case, above, p.600.
[186] e.g. the *Legality of Nuclear Weapons* case, above, p.788.

State to Membership in the United Nations (Article 4 of the Charter), Advisory Opinion, I.C.J. Reports 1947–1948, pp.61–62; ...

Furthermore, as the Court said in the Opinion it gave in 1980 concerning the *Interpretation of the Agreement of 25 March 1951 between the WHO and Egypt;*

Indeed, in situations in which political considerations are prominent it may be particularly necessary for an international organization to obtain an advisory opinion from the Court as to the legal principles applicable with respect to the matter under debate ... "(*Interpretation of the Agreement of 25 March 1951 between the WHO and Egypt, Advisory Opinion, I.C.J. Reports 1980,* p.87, para.33).

The Court moreover considers that the political nature of the motives which may be said to have inspired the request and the political implications that the opinion given might have are of no relevance in the establishment of its jurisdiction to give such an opinion.

14. Article 65, paragraph 1, of the Statute provides: "The Court *may* give an advisory opinion ..." (Emphasis added.) This is more than an enabling provision. As the Court has repeatedly emphasized, the Statute leaves a discretion as to whether or not it will give an advisory opinion that has been requested of it, once it has established its competence to do so. In this context, the Court has previously noted as follows:

The Court's Opinion is given not to the States, but to the organ which is entitled to request it; the reply of the Court, itself an 'organ of the United Nations', represents its participation in the activities of the Organization, and, in principle, should not be refused." (*Interpretation of Peace Treaties with Bulgaria, Hungary and Romania, First Phase, Advisory Opinion, I.C.J. Reports 1950,* p.71;

The Court has constantly been mindful of its responsibilities as "the principal judicial organ of the United Nations" (Charter, art.92). When considering each request, it is mindful that it should not, in principle refuse to give an advisory opinion. In accordance with the consistent jurisprudence of the Court, only "compelling reasons" could lead it to such a refusal (... *Western Sahara, Advisory Opinion, I.C.J. Reports 1975,* p.21 ...). There has been no refusal, based on the discretionary power of the Court, to act upon a request for advisory opinion in the history of the present Court; in the case concerning the *Legality of the Use by a State of Nuclear Weapons in Armed Conflict*, the refusal to give the World Health Organization the advisory opinion requested by it was justified by the Court's lack of jurisdiction in that case. The Permanent Court of International Justice took the view on only one occasion that it could not reply to a question put to it, having regard to the very particular circumstances of the case, among which were that the question directly concerned an already existing dispute, one of the States parties to which was neither a party to the Statute of the Permanent Court nor a Member of the League of Nations, objected to the proceedings, and refused to take part in any way (*Status of Eastern Carelia, P.C.I.J., Series B, No. 5*).

15. Most of the reasons adduced in these proceedings in order to persuade the Court that in the exercise of its discretionary power it should decline to render the opinion requested by General Assembly resolution 49/75K were summarized in the following statement made by one State in the written proceedings:

The question presented is vague and abstract, addressing complex issues which are the subject of consideration among interested States and within other bodies of the United Nations which have an express mandate to address these matters. An opinion by the Court in regard to the question presented would provide no practical assistance to the General Assembly in carrying out its functions under the Charter. Such an opinion has the potential of undermining progress already made or being made on this sensitive subject and, therefore, is contrary to the interest of the United Nations Organization." (United States of America, Written Statement, pp.1–2; ...)

In contending that the question put to the Court is vague and abstract, some States appeared to mean by this that there exists no specific dispute on the subject-matter of the question. In order to respond to this argument, it is necessary to distinguish between requirements governing contentious procedure and those applicable to advisory opinions. The purpose of the advisory function is not to settle—at least directly—disputes between States, but to offer legal advice to the organs and institutions requesting the opinion (cf. *Interpretation of Peace Treaties I.C.J. Reports 1950*, p.71). The fact that the question put to the Court does not relate to a specific dispute should consequently not lead the Court to decline to give the opinion requested.

Moreover, it is the clear position of the Court that to contend that it should not deal with a question couched in abstract terms is "a mere affirmation devoid of any justification", and that "the Court may give an advisory opinion on any legal question, abstract or otherwise" (*Conditions of Admission of a State to Membership in the United Nations (Article 4 of the Charter), Advisory Opinion, 1948, I.C.J. Reports 1947–1948*, p.61 ...).

Certain States have however expressed the fear that the abstract nature of the question might lead the Court to make hypothetical or speculative declarations outside the scope of its judicial function. The Court does not consider that, in giving an advisory opinion in the present case, it would necessarily have to write "scenarios", to study various types of nuclear weapons and to evaluate highly complex and controversial technological, strategic and scientific information. The Court will simply address the issues arising in all their aspects by applying the legal rules relevant to the situation.

16. Certain States have observed that the General Assembly has not explained to the Court for what precise purposes it seeks the advisory opinion. Nevertheless, it is not for the Court itself to purport to decide whether or not an advisory opinion is needed by the Assembly for the performance of its functions. The General Assembly has the right to decide for itself on the usefulness of an opinion in the light of its own needs.

Equally, once the Assembly has asked, by adopting a resolution, for an advisory opinion on a legal question, the Court, in determining whether there are any compelling reasons for it to refuse to give such an opinion, will not have regard to the origins or to the political history of the request or to the distribution of votes in respect of the adopted resolution.

17. It has also been submitted that a reply from the Court in this case might adversely affect disarmament negotiations and would, therefore, be contrary to the interest of the United Nations. The Court is aware that, no matter what might be its conclusions in any opinion it might give, they would have relevance for the continuing debate on the matter in the General Assembly and would present an additional element in the negotiations on the matter. Beyond that, the effect of the opinion is a matter of appreciation. The Court has heard contrary positions advanced and there are no evident criteria by which it can prefer one assessment to another. That being so, the Court cannot regard this factor as a compelling reason to decline to exercise its jurisdiction.

18. Finally, it has been contended by some States that in answering the question posed, the Court would be going beyond its judicial role and would be taking upon itself a law-making capacity. It is clear that the Court cannot legislate, and, in the circumstances of the present case, it is not called upon to do so. Rather its task is to engage in its normal judicial function of ascertaining the existence or otherwise of legal principles and rules applicable to the threat or use of nuclear weapons. The contention that the giving of an answer to the question posed would require the Court to legislate is based on a supposition that the present *corpus juris* is devoid of relevant rules in this matter. The Court could not accede to this argument; it states the existing law and does not legislate. This is so even if, in stating and applying the law, the Court necessarily has to specify its scope and sometimes note its general trend.

19. In view of what is stated above, the Court concludes that it has the authority to deliver an opinion on the question posed by the General Assembly, and that there exist no "compelling reasons" which would lead the Court to exercise its discretion not to do so.

An entirely different question is whether the Court, under the constraints placed upon its as a judicial organ, will be able to give a complete answer to the question asked of it. However, that is a different matter from a refusal to answer at all.

Notes

1. As the Court notes, Opinion, para.14, the *Eastern Carelia* case is the only one in which the World Court has declined, in the exercise of its discretion, to give an opinion that fell within its jurisdiction. In that case, Russia had refused to participate in the proceedings. The opinion sought concerned the interpretation of a peace treaty between Russia and Finland that bore upon a dispute between them on the status of Eastern Carelia. The Court was concerned that it would, in effect, be deciding the dispute without the consent of one of the parties and without its account of the facts.

2. The refusal to give an opinion in the *Legality of the Use by a State of Nuclear Weapons in Armed Conflict* case (the *WHO Nuclear Weapons* case), was different from the *Eastern Carelia* case in that it was based on jurisdictional grounds. The question put to the Court by the WHO General Assembly in that case, in a decision of September 3, 1993, was:

"In view of the health and environmental effects, would the use of nuclear weapons by a state in war or other armed conflict be a breach of its obligations under international law including the WHO Constitution?"

The Court held, by 11 votes to three, that the question did not fall within the scope of WHO's "activities", as is required by art.96(2), Charter, when a question is put to the Court by an authorised specialised agency.[187] The Court interpreted the WHO Constitution, art.2, as giving WHO the competence to deal with the effects on health of the use of nuclear weapons and to act preventively to protect people from these effects. But the question put to the Court concerned the legality, rather than the effects, of the use of nuclear weapons, which was a matter that did not fall within WHO's remit.

The above two cases are the only ones in which the World Court has not given a requested opinion. As stated by the Court in the *Nuclear Weapons* case, Opinion, para.14, only "compelling reasons" would justify it refusing a request.

G. *The World Court and the Security Council.*[188]

CASE CONCERNING QUESTIONS OF INTERPRETATION AND APPLICATION OF THE MONTREAL CONVENTION ARISING OUT OF THE AERIAL INCIDENT AT LOCKERBIE (PROVISIONAL MEASURES)

Libya v U.K.

I.C.J. Reports 1992, p.3

At the request of the US, the UK and France, on January 21, 1992, the Security Council adopted Resolution 731, which "urged" Libya, inter alia, to respond to the request of those three states to extradite two Libyan nationals for trial in Scotland for the Lockerbie bombing. On March 3, 1992, Libya instituted proceedings against the US[189] and the UK before the ICJ under art.14, Montreal Convention for the Suppression of Unlawful Acts Against the Safety of Civil Aviation.[190] Libya asked the Court to declare that: (i) it had complied with its obligations under the Montreal Convention by taking the required steps to investigate the case and prosecute the two Libyans[191]; and (ii) the UK had breached the Convention by seeking to force Libya to return the alleged offenders and by not providing assistance for the Libyan proceedings.

Also on March 3, 1993, Libya applied to the Court for provisional measures. After the oral hearing

---

[187] There is no such limit for the General Assembly or the Security Council which may seek an opinion on "any legal question" although the Court has sometimes looked for a link with their "activities": see the *Wall* case, I.C.J. Rep. 2004, p.136 at 145.

[188] See Akande (1997) 46 I.C.L.Q. 309; Alvarez (1996) 90 A.J.I.L. 1; Bedjaoui, *The New World Order and the Security Council* (1994); Brownlie, *Essays in Honour of Wang Tieya* (1994); Franck (1992) 86 A.J.I.L. 519; Gill (1995) 26 N.Y.I.L. 33; Gowlland-Debbas (1994) 88 A.J.I.L. 643; Macdonald (1993) 31 C.Y.I.L. 3; Reisman (1993) 87 A.J.I.L. 83; Skubiszewski, in Lowe and Fitzmaurice, above, n.22, Chs.33; Watson (1993) 34 Harv.I.L.J. 1.

[189] For the case brought by Libya against the US, see I.C.J. Rep. 1992, p.234.

[190] Article 14 provides that a Convention party may unilaterally request the reference of a dispute concerning the interpretation or application of the Convention to arbitration; if agreement on a tribunal is not possible within six months of the request, it may unilaterally refer the case to the ICJ. Libya did not wait six months.

[191] The Montreal Convention requires a party, in its discretion, to prosecute or extradite an alleged offender. Libya decided to prosecute. In any event there was also no extradition treaty between Libya and the UK and Libya, like many states, does not extradite its own nationals.

of this application, the Security Council, at the request of the same three states, adopted Resolution 748, under Chapter VII of the Charter, requiring Libya to return the alleged offenders and imposing sanctions against it for not doing so. The Council acted on the basis that Libya had been engaged in international terrorism, which was a "threat to the peace" under art.39, Charter.

The request for provisional measures was rejected because of Resolution 748. In 2003, the cases were discontinued at the request of the parties. On the criminal prosecution of two Libyans in connection with the hijacking, see above, p.238. Had the case gone forward before the Court, it might have been, depending upon the arguments put, that the Court would have been called upon to consider the legality of Security Council Resolutions 731 and 748, the latter of which imposes an obligation upon Libya to extradite the alleged offenders whereas the Montreal Convention allows Libya a choice. The Court found it unnecessary to consider this question when ruling on Libya's provisional measures request. However, several judges, including Judge Weeramantry, did reflect upon the Court's competence to review the legality of Security Council resolutions and related matters in their individual opinions.

Dissenting Opinion of Judge Weeramantry

This case has raised as perhaps no case has done in the past, certain questions of importance and interest concerning the respective functions of this Court and the Security Council. ...

In the United Nations system, the sphere of [the Security Council and the Court] ... is laid down in the Charter, as within a domestic jurisdiction it may be laid down in a constitution. However, unlike in many domestic systems where the judicial arm may sit in review over the actions of the executive arm, subjecting those acts to the test of legality under the Constitution, in the United Nations system the International Court of Justice is not vested with the review or appellate jurisdiction often given to the highest courts within a domestic framework (... *Legal Consequences* ... *I.C.J. Reports 1971*, p.16). At the same time, it is the principal judicial organ of the United Nations, charged with the task, inter alia, of deciding in accordance with international law such disputes as are submitted to it (art.38 of the Statute of the Court). ...

As a judicial organ, it will be the Court's duty from time to time to examine and determine from a strictly legal point of view matters which may at the same time be the subject of determination from an executive or political point of view by another principal organ of the United Nations. ... The concepts it uses are juridical concepts, its criteria are standards of legality, its method is that of legal proof. Its tests of validity and the bases of its decisions are naturally not the same as they would be before a political or executive organ of the United Nations.

Yet this much they have in common—that all organs alike exercise their authority under and in terms of the Charter. There can never truly be a question of opposition of one organ to another but rather a common subjection of all organs to the Charter. The interpretation of Charter provisions is primarily a matter of law, and such questions of law may in appropriate circumstances come before the Court for judicial determination. When this does occur, the Court acts as guardian of the Charter and of international law for, in the international arena, there is no higher body charged with judicial functions and with the determination of questions of interpretation and application of international law. Anchored to the Charter in particular and to international law in general, the Court considers such legal matters as are properly brought before it and the fact that its judicial decision based upon the law may have political consequences is not a factor that would deflect it from discharging its duties under the Charter of the United Nations and the Statute of the Court. ...

It is clear ... that the Court must at all times preserve its independence in performing the functions which the Charter has committed to it as the United Nations' principal judicial organ. It is clear also that in many an instance the performance of those independent functions will lead the Court to a result in total consonance with the conclusions of the Security Council. But it by no means follows from these propositions that the Court when properly seised of a legal dispute should co-operate with the Security Council to the extent of desisting from exercising its independent judgment on matters of law properly before it. ...

There have indeed been prior instances where the same matter has come up for consideration before both the Security Council and the Court. Mention may be made in this connection of the following cases where the jurisdiction of both the Court and the Security Council was invoked in one and the same matter: *Aegean Sea Continental Shelf, Interim Protection (I.C.J. Reports 1976*, p.3); *United States Diplomatic and Consular Staff in*

Tehran, Provisional Measures (I.C.J. Reports 1979, p.7); *Military and Paramilitary Activities in and against Nicaragua, Provisional Measures (I.C.J. Reports 1984*, p.169).

In all these cases, however, the Court and the Council were approached by the same party, seeking before these different organs the relief appropriate to the nature and function of each. ...

In the present case, the Court and the Council have been approached by opposite parties to the dispute, each claiming a form of relief consistent with its own position. It is this situation which gives special importance to the current case. ...

In the *United States Diplomatic and Consular Staff in Tehran* case, the Court observed that:

it does not seem to have occurred to any member of the Council that there was or could be anything irregular in the simultaneous exercise of their respective functions by the Court and the Security Council. Nor is there in this any cause for surprise. (*I.C.J. Reports 1980*, p.21, para.40.)

The role of the Court was made even clearer when the Court observed:

Whereas Article 12 of the Charter expressly forbids the General Assembly to make any recommendation with regard to a dispute or situation while the Security Council is exercising its functions in respect of that dispute or situation, no such restriction is placed on the functioning of the Court by any provision of either the Charter or the Statute of the Court. The reasons are clear. It is for the Court, the principal judicial organ of the United Nations, to resolve any legal questions that may be in issue between parties to the dispute; and the resolution of such legal questions by the Court may be an important and sometimes decisive, factor in promoting the peaceful settlement of the dispute. (*Ibid.*, p.22, para.40; see also *Military and Paramilitary Activities in and against Nicaragua, I.C.J. Reports 1984*, pp.433–434, para.93.) ...

The submission before us relating to the exercise of Security Council powers in adopting resolution 731 (1992) calls for a brief examination of those powers from a strictly legal point of view. ...

The Security Council] is charged under Article 24 with the primary responsibility for the maintenance of international peace and security and has a mandate from all Member States to act on their behalf in this regard. By Article 25, all Members agree to accept and carry out its decisions.

Chapter VI entrusts it with powers and responsibilities in regard to settlement of disputes, and Chapter VII gives it very special powers when it determines the existence of any threat to the peace, breach of the peace or act of aggression. Such determination is a matter entirely within its discretion.

With these provisions should be read Article 103 of the Charter which states that in the event of a conflict between the obligations of the Members of the United Nations under the Charter and their obligations under any international agreement, their obligations under the Charter shall prevail. Seeing that Security Council decisions are to be accepted and carried out by all Member States, the obligations thus created are given priority by Article 103 over obligations under any other agreement.

All this amounts to enormous power indeed and international law as embodied in the Charter requires all States to recognize this power and act according to the directions issuing from it.

But does this mean that the Security Council discharges its variegated functions free of all limitations, or is there a circumscribing boundary of norms of principles within which its responsibilities are to be discharged?

Article 24 itself offers us an immediate signpost to such a circumscribing boundary when it provides in Article 24(2) that the Security Council, in discharging its duties under Article 24(1), "*shall* act in accordance with the Purposes and Principles of the United Nations". The duty is imperative and the limits are categorically stated.

Judge Weeramantry then reviewed the *travaux préparatoires* of the UN Charter and continued:

The history of the United Nations Charter thus corroborates the view that a clear limitation on the plenitude of the Security Council's powers is that those powers must be exercised in accordance with the well-established principles of international law. It is true this limitation must be restrictively interpreted and is confined only to the principles and objects which appear in Chapter I of the Charter ... The restriction nevertheless exists and constitutes an important principle of law in the interpretation of the United Nations Charter.

The obligation of the Court, as one of the principal organs of the United Nations, to "co-operate in the attainment of the aims of the Organization and strive to give effect to the decisions of other principal organs, and not achieve results which would render them nugatory" (Rosenne, *The Law and Practice of the International Court*, p.70) should be read in the light of this clear limitation.

Notes

1. As Judge Weeramantry demonstrates, it is well understood that the Court and the Security Council may both exercise jurisdiction in a case or matter at the same time. What is also clear, is that the Court has no power of judicial review or appeal in respect of Security Council action: there is no remedy available before the ICJ that is comparable to those available before national courts, such as an application for *certiorari* before the UK courts, by which a state or other international legal person might challenge the legality of Security Council action directly.

2. At the same time, the Security Council does not have unlimited jurisdiction and if the extent of its powers or the legality of its acts are called in question in proceedings before the ICJ, the latter has competence, within as yet not wholly defined limits, to pronounce upon the questions raised. The occasions for doing so may occur in the exercise by the Court of its advisory jurisdiction, as in the *Certain Expenses* case, above, p.831 and the *Legal Consequences* case, see below, or in the course of contentious litigation, as on the facts of the *Lockerbie* case.

3. The limits to the powers of the Security Council and the legality of its acts were matters raised in argument before the Court in the *Legal Consequences* case.[192] In Resolution 2145 the General Assembly declared that South Africa had failed to fulfil its obligations under the mandate for South West Africa/Namibia and decided that the mandate had, as a result, been terminated. When South Africa failed to withdraw from South West Africa/Namibia, as called upon to do by Security Council Resolutions 264 and 269, the Council, in Resolution 276, declared the continued presence of South Africa in South West Africa/Namibia to be illegal. In the *Legal Consequences* case, the Council asked the Court: "What are the legal consequences for states of the continued presence of South Africa in Namibia?" A key issue was whether the Security Council resolutions, which were not adopted under Chapter VII, were decisions that were legally binding upon member states under art.25, Charter. The Court determined that they were. In his dissenting opinion, Judge Fitzmaurice considered the general question of the limits to the Security Council's powers as follows:

    "If the effect of [Article 24, Charter] were automatically to make *all* decisions of the Security Council binding, then the words 'in accordance with the present Charter' [in art.25] would be quite superfluous. They would add nothing to the preceding and only other phrase in the Article, namely 'The Members of the United Nations agree to accept and carry out the decisions of the Security Council', which they are clearly intended to qualify. They effectively do so only if the decisions referred to are those which *are* duly binding 'in accordance with the present Charter' ...

    115. There is more. *Even when acting under Chapter VII of the Charter itself*, the Security Council has no power to abrogate or alter territorial rights, whether of sovereignty or administration. Even a war-time occupation of a country or territory cannot operate to do that. It must await the peace settlement. This is a principle of international law that is as well-established as any there can be,—and the Security Council is as much subject to it (for the United Nations is itself a subject of international law) as any of its individual member States are. The Security Council might, after making the necessary determinations under Article 39 of the Charter, order the occupation of a country or piece of territory *in order to restore peace and*

---

[192] I.C.J. Rep. 1971, p.16. As the case demonstrated, many of the same considerations as apply to the Court's competence to review the powers and acts of the Security Council apply also to its competence vis-à-vis the General Assembly, although the powers and political sensitivity of the acts of the Council are clearly greater.

security, but it could not thereby, or as part of that operation, abrogate or alter territorial rights,—and the right to administer a mandated territory is a territorial right without which the territory could not be governed or the mandate be operated. It was to keep the peace, not to change the world order, that the Security Council was set up.

116. These limitations on the powers of the Security Council are necessary because of the all too great ease with which any acutely controversial international situation can be represented as involving a latent threat to peace and security, even where it is really too remote genuinely to constitute one. Without these limitations, the functions of the Security Council could be used for purposes never originally intended . . . . [where there was] no threat to peace and security other than such as might be artificially created as a pretext for the realization of ulterior purposes."

4. The question of the competence of the Court to decide whether the Security Council has exceeded the limits of its powers that are found to exist was also in issue in the *Legal Consequences* case.[193] Responding to French Government objections that the General Assembly Resolution 2145 terminating the mandate was ultra vires, the Court stated:

> "89. Undoubtedly, the Court does not possess powers of judicial review or appeal in respect of the decision taken by the United Nations organs concerned. The question of the validity or conformity with the Charter of General Assembly resolution 2145 (XXI) or of related Security Council resolutions does not form the subject of the request for advisory opinion. However, in the exercise of its judicial function and since objections have been advanced the Court, in the course of its reasoning, will consider these objections before determining any legal consequences arising from those resolutions."

Having then examined the constitutional basis for Resolution 2145 and the related Security Council resolutions, the Court concluded that they were valid. In so doing, as Judge ad hoc El-Kosheri stated in his dissenting opinion in the *Lockerbie* case,[194] "the Court implied that it was perfectly conceivable that it could reach a negative conclusion, were it to detect any violation of the Charter or departure from the Charter's purposes and principles." Such an approach is almost inevitable for a judicial body. As Judge Petrén stated in his separate opinion in the *Legal Consequences* case[195]:

> "So long as the validity of the resolutions upon which resolution 276 (1970) is based has not been established, it is clearly impossible for the Court to pronounce on the legal consequences of resolution 276 (1970), for there can be no such legal consequences if the basic resolutions are illegal, and to give a finding as though there were such would be incompatible with the role of a court. It seems to me that the majority should have expressed itself on this point more precisely and firmly, but I note that it likewise considered that the opinion must include an examination of the validity of the resolutions in question."

5. The question then is how broad is the Court's power of review. In particular, would it be open to the Court to rule that the Security Council's interpretation of what might constitute a threat to

---

[193] I.C.J. Rep. 1971, n.1 at p.45.
[194] I.C.J. Rep. 1992, pp.102–103.
[195] I.C.J. Rep. 1992, p.131.

the peace,[196] was incorrect as a matter of law?[197] Could it go further and exercise a power of judicial review over a decision on the facts in a particular case as to whether there was a threat to the peace or act of aggression? Or over a decision to adopt a particular response (economic sanctions, the establishment of a war crimes tribunal?[198]) to a threat to the peace? Later in his opinion, Judge Weeramantry suggested that the Court could not question Security Council action under Chapter VII:

"... once we enter the sphere of Chapter VII, the matter takes on a different complexion, for the determination under Article 39 of the existence of any threat to the peace, breach of the peace or act of aggression, is one entirely within the discretion of the Council. It would appear that the Council and no other is the judge of the existence of the state of affairs which brings Chapter VII into operation. That decision is taken by the Security Council in its own judgment and in the exercise of the full discretion given to it by Article 39. Once taken, the door is opened to the various decisions the Council may make under that Chapter."

---

[196] International terrorism? The likely reaction of other states to an internal conflict or humanitarian need? See on threats to the peace generally, above, pp.796 et seq.

[197] The doctrine of "subsequent practice" in the interpretation of treaties, above, p.678, suggests that the Security Council's interpretation of its powers should be respected if it is accepted and followed by UN members generally. cf. the Yugoslav Tribunal's judgment in the *Tadic* case 35 I.L.M. 35; (1996) 3 I.H.R.R. 578.

[198] See the Yugoslav Tribunal's judgment in the *Tadic* case on this point, above, n.197.

APPENDIX I

CHARTER OF THE UNITED NATIONS

WE THE PEOPLES OF THE UNITED NATIONS DETERMINED to save succeeding generations from the scourge of war, which twice in our lifetime has brought untold sorrow to mankind, and to reaffirm faith in fundamental human rights, in the dignity and worth of the human person, in the equal rights of men and women and of nations large and small, and to establish conditions under which justice and respect for the obligations arising from treaties and other sources of international law can be maintained, and to promote social progress and better standards of life in larger freedom,

AND FOR THESE ENDS to practise tolerance and live together in peace with one another as good neighbours, and to unite our strength to maintain international peace and security, and to ensure, by the acceptance of principles and the institution of methods, that armed force shall not be used, save in the common interest, and to employ international machinery for the promotion of the economic and social advancement of all peoples.

HAVE RESOLVED TO COMBINE OUR EFFORTS TO ACCOMPLISH THESE AIMS. Accordingly, our respective Governments, through representatives assembled in the city of San Francisco, who have exhibited their full powers found to be in good and due form, have agreed to the present Charter of the United Nations and do hereby establish an international organisation to be known as the United Nations.

Chapter I

PURPOSES AND PRINCIPLES

Article 1

The Purposes of the United Nations are:

1. To maintain international peace and security, and to that end: to take effective collective measures for the prevention and removal of threats to the peace, and for the suppression of acts of aggression or other breaches of the peace, and to bring about by peaceful means, and in conformity with the principles of justice and international law, adjustment or settlement of international disputes or situations which might lead to a breach of the peace;

2. To develop friendly relations among nations based on respect for the principles of equal rights and self-determination of peoples, and to take other appropriate measures to strengthen universal peace;

3. To achieve international co-operation in solving international problems of an economic, social, cultural, or humanitarian character, and in promoting and encouraging respect for human rights and for fundamental freedom for all without distinction as to race, sex, language, or religion; and

4. To be a centre for harmonising the actions in the attainment of these common ends.

Article 2

The Organisation and its Members, in pursuit of the Purposes stated in Article 1, shall act in accordance with the following Principles.

1. The Organisation is based on the principle of the sovereign equality of all its Members.

2. All Members, in order to ensure to all of them the rights and benefits resulting from membership, shall fulfil in good faith the obligations assumed by them in accordance with the present Charter.

3. All Members shall settle their international disputes by peaceful means in such a manner that international peace and security, and justice, are not endangered.

4. All Members shall refrain in their international relations from the threat or use of force against the territorial integrity or political independence of any state, or in any other manner inconsistent with the Purposes of the United Nations.

5. All Members shall give the United Nations every assistance in any action it takes in accordance with the present Charter, and shall refrain from giving assistance to any state against which the United Nations is taking preventive or enforcement action.

6. The Organisation shall ensure that states which are not Members of the United Nations act in accordance with these Principles so far as may be necessary for the maintenance of peace and security.

7. Nothing contained in the present Charter shall authorise the United Nations to intervene in matters which are essentially within the domestic jurisdiction of any state or shall require the Members to submit such matters to settlement under the present Charter; but this principle shall not prejudice the application of enforcement measures under Chapter VII.

Chapter II

MEMBERSHIP

Article 3

The original Members of the United Nations shall be the states which, having participated in the United Nations Conference on International Organisation at San Francisco, or having previously signed the Declaration by United Nations on January 1, 1942, sign the present Charter and ratify it in accordance with Article 110.

Article 4

1. Membership in the United Nations is open to all other peace-loving states which accept the obligations contained in the present Charter and, in the judgment of the Organisation, are able and willing to carry out these obligations.

2. The admission of any such state to membership in the United Nations will be effected by a decision of the General Assembly upon the recommendation of the Security Council.

Article 5

A Member of the United Nations against which preventive or enforcement action has been taken by the Security Council may be suspended from the exercise of the rights and privileges of membership by the General Assembly upon the recommendation of the Security Council. The exercise of these rights and privileges may be restored by the Security Council.

Article 6

A Member of the United Nations which has persistently violated the Principles contained in the present Charter may be expelled from the Organisation by the General Assembly upon the recommendation of the Security Council.

Chapter III

ORGANS

Article 7

1. There are established as the principal organs of the United Nations: a General Assembly, a Security Council, a Economic and Social Council, a Trusteeship Council, an International Court of Justice, and a Secretariat.

2. Such subsidiary organs as may be found necessary may be established in accordance with the present Charter.

Article 8

The United Nations shall place no restrictions on the eligibility of men and women to participate in any capacity and under conditions of equality in its principal and subsidiary organs.

Chapter IV

THE GENERAL ASSEMBLY

Composition

Article 9

1. The General Assembly shall consist of all the Members of the United Nations.

2. Each Member shall have not more than five representatives in the General Assembly.

Functions and Powers

Article 10

The General Assembly may discuss any questions or any matters within the scope of the present Charter or relating to the powers and functions of any organs provided for in the present Charter, and, except as provided in Article 12, may make recommendations to the Members of the United Nations or to the Security Council or to both on any such questions or matters.

Article 11

1. The General Assembly may consider the general principles of co-operation in the maintenance of inter-national peace and security, including the principles governing disarmament and the regulations of armaments, and may make recommendations with regard to such principles to the Members or to the Security Council or to both.

2. The General Assembly may discuss any questions relating to the maintenance of international peace and security brought before it by any Member of the United Nations, or by the Security Council, or by a state which is not a Member of the United Nations in accordance with Article 35, paragraph 2, and, except as provided in Article 12, may make recommendations with regard to any such questions to the state or states concerned or to the Security Council or to both. Any such question on which action is necessary shall be referred to the Security Council by the General Assembly either before or after discussion.

3. The General Assembly may call the attention of the Security Council to situations which are likely to endanger international peace and security.

4. The powers of the General Assembly set forth in this Article shall not limit the general scope of Article 10.

Article 12

1. While the Security Council is exercising in respect of any dispute or situation the functions assigned to it in the present Charter, the General Assembly shall not make any recommendation with regard to that dispute or situation unless the Security Council so requests.

2. The Secretary-General, with the consent of the Security Council, shall notify the General Assembly at each session of any matters relative to the maintenance of international peace and security which are being dealt with by the Security Council and shall similarly notify the General Assembly, or the Members of the United Nations if the General Assembly is not in session, immediately the Security Council ceases to deal with such matters.

Article 13

1. The General Assembly shall initiate studies and make recommendations for the purpose of:

a.   promoting international co-operation in the political field and encouraging the progressive development of international law and its codification;

b.   promoting international co-operation in the economic, social, cultural, educational, and health fields, and assisting in the realisation of human rights and fundamental freedoms for all without distinction as to race, sex, language, or religion.

2. The further responsibilities, functions and powers of the General Assembly with respect to matters mentioned in paragraph 1(b) above are set forth in Chapters IX and X.

Article 14

Subject to the provisions of Article 12, the General Assembly may recommend measures for the peaceful adjustment of any situation, regardless of origin, which it deems likely to impair the general welfare or friendly relations among nations, including situations resulting from the violation of the provisions of the present Charter setting forth the Purposes and Principles of the United Nations.

Article 15

1. The General Assembly shall receive and consider annual and special reports from the Security Council; these reports shall include an account of the measures that the Security Council has decided upon or taken to maintain international peace and security.

2. The General Assembly shall receive and consider reports from the other organs of the United Nations.

Article 16

The General Assembly shall perform such functions with respect to the international trusteeship system as are assigned to it under Chapter XII and XIII, including the approval of the trusteeship agreements for areas not designated as strategic.

Article 17

1. The General Assembly shall consider and approve the budget of the Organisation.

2. The expenses of the Organisation shall be borne by the Members as apportioned by the General Assembly.

3. The General Assembly shall consider and approve any financial and budgetary arrangements with specialised agencies referred to in Article 57 and shall examine the administrative budgets of such specialised agencies with a view to making recommendations to the agencies concerned.

Voting

Article 18

1. Each member of the General Assembly shall have one vote.

2. Decisions of the General Assembly on important questions shall be made by a two-thirds majority of the members present and voting. These questions shall include: recommendations with respect to the maintenance of international peace and security, the election of the non-permanent members of the Security Council, the election of the members of the Economic and Social Council, the election of members of the Trusteeship Council in accordance with paragraph 1(c) of Article 86, the admission of new Members to the United Nations, the suspension of the rights and privileges of membership, the expulsion of Members, questions relating to the operation of the trusteeship system, and budgetary questions.

3. Decisions on other questions, including the determination of additional categories of questions to be decided by a two-thirds majority, shall be made by a majority of the members present and voting.

Article 19

A Member of the United Nations which is in arrears in the payment of its financial contributions to the Organisation shall have no vote in the General Assembly if the amount of its arrears equals or exceeds the amount of the contributions due from it for the preceding two full years. The General Assembly may, nevertheless, permit such a Member to vote if it is satisfied that the failure to pay is due to conditions beyond the control of the Member.

Article 20

The General Assembly shall meet in regular annual sessions and in such special sessions as occasion may require. Special sessions shall be convoked by the Secretary-General at the request of the Security Council or of a majority of the Members of the United Nations.

Article 21

The General Assembly shall adopt its own rules of procedure. It shall elect its President for each session.

Article 22

The General Assembly may establish such subsidiary organs as it deems necessary for the performance of its functions.

Chapter V

THE SECURITY COUNCIL

Composition

Article 23[1]

1. The Security Council shall consist of fifteen[2] Members of the United Nations. The Republic of China, France, the Union of Soviet Socialist Republics, the United Kingdom of Great Britain and Northern Ireland, and the United States of America shall be permanent members of the Security Council. The General Assembly shall elect ten other Members of the United Nations to be non-permanent members of the Security Council, due regard being specially paid, in the first instance to the contribution of Members of the United Nations to the main-

---

[1]   As amended in 1965.
[2]   Formerly 11.

tenance of international peace and security and to the other purposes of the Organisation, and also to equitable geographical distribution.

2. The non-permanent members of the Security Council shall be elected for a term of two years. In the first election of the non-permanent members after the increase of the membership of the Security Council from eleven to fifteen, two of the four additional members shall be chosen for a term of one year. A retiring member shall not be eligible for immediate re-election.

3. Each member of the Security Council shall have one representative.

Functions and Powers

Article 24

1. In order to ensure prompt and effective action by the United Nations, its Members confer on the Security Council primary responsibility for the maintenance of international peace and security, and agree that in carrying out its duties under this responsibility the Security Council acts on their behalf.

2. In discharging these duties the Security Council shall act in accordance with the Purposes and Principles of the United Nations. The specific powers granted to the Security Council for the discharge of these duties are laid down in Chapters VI, VII, VIII and XII.

3. The Security Council shall submit annual and, when necessary, special reports to the General Assembly for its consideration.

Article 25

The Members of the United Nations agree to accept and carry out the decisions of the Security Council in accordance with the present Charter.

Article 26

In order to promote the establishment and maintenance of international peace and security with the least diversion for armaments of the world's human and economic resources, the Security Council shall be responsible for formulating, with the assistance of the Military Staff Committee referred to in Article 47, plans to be submitted to the Members of the United Nations for the establishment of a system for the regulation of armaments.

Voting

Article 27[3]

1. Each member of the Security Council shall have one vote.

2. Decisions of the Security Council on procedural matters shall be made by an affirmative vote of nine[4] members.

3. Decisions of the Security Council on all other matters shall be made by an affirmative vote of nine[5] members including the concurring votes of the permanent members; provided that, in decisions under Chapter VI, and under paragraph 3 of Article 52, a party to a dispute shall abstain from voting.

---

[3]   As amended in 1965.
[4]   Formerly seven.
[5]   Formerly seven.

Procedure

Article 28

1. The Security Council shall be so organised as to be able to function continuously. Each member of the Security Council shall for this purpose be represented at all times at the seat of the Organisation.

2. The Security Council shall hold periodical meetings at which each of its members may, if it so desires, be represented by a member of the government or by some other specially designated representative.

3. The Security Council may hold meetings at such places other than the seat of the Organisation as in its judgment will best facilitate its work.

Article 29

The Security Council may establish such subsidiary organs as it deems necessary for the performance of its functions.

Article 30

The Security Council shall adopt its own rules of procedure, including the method of selecting its President.

Article 31

Any Member of the United Nations which is not a member of the Security Council may participate, without vote, in the discussion of any question brought before the Security Council whenever the latter considers that the interests of that Member are specially affected.

Article 32

Any Member of the United Nations which is not a member of the Security Council or any state which is not a Member of the United Nations, if it is a party to a dispute under consideration by the Security Council, shall be invited to participate, without vote, in the discussion relating to the dispute. The Security Council shall lay down such conditions as it deems just for the participation of a state which is not a Member of the United Nations.

Chapter VI

PACIFIC SETTLEMENT OF DISPUTES

Article 33

1. The parties to any dispute, the continuance of which is likely to endanger the maintenance of international peace and security, shall, first of all, seek a solution by negotiation, enquiry, mediation, conciliation, arbitration, judicial settlement, resort to regional agencies or arrangements, or other peaceful means of their own choice.

2. The Security Council shall, when it deems necessary, call upon the parties to settle their dispute by such means.

Article 34

The Security Council may investigate any dispute, or any situation which might lead to international friction or give rise to a dispute, in order to determine whether the continuance of the dispute or situation is likely to endanger the maintenance of international peace and security.

Article 35

1. Any Member of the United Nations may bring any dispute, or any situation of the nature referred to in Article 34, to the attention of the Security Council or of the General Assembly.

2. A state which is not a Member of the United Nations may bring to the attention of the Security Council or of the General Assembly any dispute to which it is a party if it accepts in advance, for the purposes of the dispute, the obligations of pacific settlement provided in the present Charter.

3. The proceedings of the General Assembly in respect of matters brought to its attention under this Article will be subject to the provisions of Articles 11 and 12.

Article 36

1. The Security Council may, at any stage of a dispute of the nature referred to in Article 33 or of a situation of like nature, recommend appropriate procedures or methods of adjustment.

2. The Security Council should take into consideration any procedures for the settlement of the dispute which have already been adopted by the parties.

3. In making recommendations under this Article the Security Council should also take into consideration that legal disputes should as a general rule be referred by the parties to the International Court of Justice in accordance with the provisions of the Statute of the Court.

Article 37

1. Should the parties to a dispute of the nature referred to in Article 33 fail to settle it by the means indicated in that Article, they shall refer it to the Security Council.

2. If the Security Council deems that the continuance of the dispute is in fact likely to endanger the maintenance of international peace and security, it shall decide whether to take action under Article 36 or to recommend such terms of settlement as it may consider appropriate.

Article 38

Without prejudice to the provisions of Articles 33 to 37, the Security Council may, if all the parties to any dispute so request, make recommendations to the parties with a view to a pacific settlement of the dispute.

Chapter VII

ACTION WITH RESPECT TO THREATS TO THE PEACE, BREACHES OF THE PEACE, AND ACTS OF AGGRESSION

Article 39

The Security Council shall determine the existence of any threat to the peace, breach of the peace, or act of aggression and shall make recommendations, or decide what measures shall be taken in accordance with Article 41 and 42, to maintain or restore international peace and security.

Article 40

In order to prevent an aggravation of the situation, the Security Council may, before making the recommendations or deciding upon the measures provided for in Article 39, call upon the parties concerned to comply with such provisional measures as it deems necessary or desirable. Such provisional measures shall be without prejudice to the rights, claims, or position of the parties concerned. The Security Council shall duly take account of failure to comply with such provisional measures.

Article 41

The Security Council may decide what measures not involving the use of armed force are to be employed to give effect to its decisions, and it may call upon the Members of the United Nations to apply such measures. These may include complete or partial interruption of economic relations and of rail, sea, air, postal, telegraphic, radio, and other means of communication, and the severance of diplomatic relations.

Article 42

Should the Security Council consider that measures provided for in Article 41 would be inadequate or have proved to be inadequate, it may take such action by air, sea or land forces as may be necessary to maintain or restore international peace and security. Such action may include demonstrations, blockade, and other operations by air, sea, or land forces of Members of the United Nations.

Article 43

1. All Members of the United Nations, in order to contribute to the maintenance of international peace and security, undertake to make available to the Security Council, on its call and in accordance with a special agreement or agreements, armed forces, assistance, and facilities, including rights of passage, necessary for the purpose of maintaining international peace and security.

2. Such agreement or agreements shall govern the numbers and types of forces, their degree of readiness and general location, and the nature of the facilities and assistance to be provided.

3. The agreement or agreements shall be negotiated as soon as possible on the initiative of the Security Council. They shall be concluded between the Security Council and Members or between the Security Council and groups of Members and shall be subject to ratification by the signatory states in accordance with their respective constitutional processes.

Article 44

When the Security Council has decided to use force it shall, before calling upon a Member not represented on it to provide armed forces in fulfilment of the obligations assumed under Article 43, invite that Member, if the Member so desires, to participate in the decisions of the Security Council concerning the employment of contingents of that Member's armed forces.

Article 45

In order to enable the United Nations to take urgent military measures, Members shall hold immediately available national airforce contingents for combined international enforcement action. The strength and degree of readiness of these contingents and plans for their combined action shall be determined, within the limits laid down in the special agreement or agreements referred to in Article 43, by the Security Council with the assistance of the Military Staff Committee.

Article 46

Plans for the application of armed force shall be made by the Security Council with the assistance of the Military Staff Committee.

Article 47

1. There shall be established a Military Staff Committee to advise and assist the Security Council on all questions relating to the Security Council's military requirements for the maintenance of international peace and security, the employment and command of forces placed at its disposal, the regulation of armaments, and possible disarmament.

2. The Military Staff Committee shall consist of the Chiefs of Staff of the permanent members of the Security

Council or their representatives. Any Member of the United Nations not permanently represented on the Committee shall be invited by the Committee to be associated with it when the efficient discharge of the Committee's responsibilities requires the participation of that Member in its work.

3. The Military Staff Committee, shall be responsible under the Security Council for the strategic direction of any armed forces placed at the disposal of the Security Council. Questions relating to the command of such forces shall be worked out subsequently.

4. The Military Staff Committee with the authorisation of the Security Council and after consultation with appropriate regional agencies, may establish regional sub-committees.

Article 48

1. The action required to carry out the decisions of the Security Council for the maintenance of international peace and security shall be taken by all the Members of the United Nations or by some of them, as the Security Council may determine.

2. Such decisions shall be carried out by the Members of the United Nations directly and through their action in the appropriate international agencies of which they are members.

Article 49

The Members of the United Nations shall join in affording mutual assistance in carrying out the measures decided upon by the Security Council.

Article 50

If preventive or enforcement measures against any state are taken by the Security Council, any other state, whether a Member of the United Nations or not, which finds itself confronted with special economic problems arising from the carrying out of those measures shall have the right to consult the Security Council with regard to a solution of those problems.

Article 51

Nothing in the present Charter shall impair the inherent right of individual or collective self-defence if an armed attack occurs against a Member of the United Nations, until the Security Council has taken measures necessary to maintain international peace and security. Measures taken by Members in the exercise of this right of self-defence shall be immediately reported to the Security Council and shall not in any way affect the authority and responsibility of the Security Council under the present Charter to take at any time such action as it deems necessary in order to maintain or restore international peace and security.

Chapter VIII

REGIONAL ARRANGEMENTS

Article 52

1. Nothing in the present Charter precludes the existence of regional arrangements or agencies for dealing with such matters relating to the maintenance of international peace and security as are appropriate for regional action, provided that such arrangements or agencies and their activities are consistent with the Purposes and Principles of the United Nations.

2. The Members of the United Nations entering into such arrangements or constituting such agencies shall make every effort to achieve pacific settlement of local disputes through such regional arrangements or by such regional agencies before referring them to the Security Council.

3. The Security Council shall encourage the development of pacific settlement of local disputes through such

regional arrangements or by such regional agencies either on the initiative of the state concerned or by reference from the Security Council.

4. This Article in no way impairs the application of Articles 34 and 35.

Article 53

1. The Security Council shall, where appropriate, utilize such regional arrangements or agencies for enforcement action under its authority. But no enforcement action shall be taken under regional arrangements or by regional agencies without the authorisation of the Security Council, with the exception of measures against any enemy state, as defined in paragraph 2 of this Article, provided for pursuant to Article 107 or in regional arrangements directed against renewal of aggressive policy on the part of any such state, until such time as the Organisation may, on request of the Governments concerned, be charged with the responsibility for preventing further aggression by such a state.

2. The term enemy state as used in paragraph 1 of this Article applies to any state which during the Second World War has been an enemy of any signatory of the present Charter.

Article 54

The Security Council shall at all times be kept fully informed of activities undertaken or in contemplation under regional arrangements or by regional agencies for the maintenance of international peace and security.

Chapter IX

INTERNATIONAL ECONOMIC AND SOCIAL CO-OPERATION

Article 55

With a view to the creation of conditions of stability and well-being which are necessary for peaceful and friendly relations among nations based on respect for the principle of equal rights and self-determination of peoples, the United Nations shall promote:

a.   higher standards of living, full employment, and conditions of economic and social progress and development;

b.   solutions of international economic, social, health, and related problems; and international cultural and educational co-operation; and

c.   universal respect for, and observance of, human rights and fundamental freedoms for all without distinction as to race, sex, language, or religion.

Article 56

All Members pledge themselves to take joint and separate action in co-operation with the Organisation for the achievement of the purposes set forth in Article 55.

Chapter X

THE ECONOMIC AND SOCIAL COUNCIL

Composition

Article 61[6]

1. The Economic and Social Council shall consist of fifty-four[7] Members of the United Nations elected by the General Assembly.

2. Subject to the provisions of paragraph 3, eighteen[8] members of the Economic and Social Council shall be elected each year for a term for a three years. A retiring member shall be eligible for immediate re-election.

3. At the first election after the increase in the membership of the Economic and Social Council from twenty-seven to fifty-four members, in addition to the members elected in place of the nine[9] members whose term of office expires at the end of that year, twenty-seven additional members shall be elected. Of these twenty-seven additional members, the term of office of nine[10] members so elected shall expire at the end of one year, and of nine[11] other members at the end of two years, in accordance with arrangements made by the General Assembly.

4. Each member of the Economic and Social Council shall have one representative.

Functions and Powers

Article 62

1. The Economic and Social Council may make or initiate studies and reports with respect to international economic, social, cultural, educational, health, and related matters and may make recommendations with respect to any such matters to the General Assembly, to the Members of the United Nations, and to the specialized agencies concerned.

2. It may make recommendations for the purpose of promoting respect for, and observance of, human rights and fundamental freedoms for all.

3. It may prepare draft conversions for submission to the General Assembly, with respect to matters falling within its competence.

4. It may, call, in accordance with the rules prescribed by the United Nations, international conferences on matters falling within its competence.

Article 68

The Economic and Social Council shall set up commissions in economic and social fields and for the promotion of human rights, and such other commissions as may be required for the performance of its functions.

---

[6] As amended in 1973.
[7] Originally 18.
[8] Originally six.
[9] Originally six.
[10] Originally six.
[11] Originally six.

Chapter XIV

THE INTERNATIONAL COURT OF JUSTICE

Article 92

The International Court of Justice shall be the principal judicial organ of the United Nations. It shall function in accordance with the annexed Statute, which is based upon the Statute of the Permanent Court of International Justice and forms an integral part of the present Charter.

Article 93

1. All Members of the United Nations are *ipso facto* parties to the Statute of the International Court of Justice.

2. A state which is not a Member of the United Nations may become a party to the Statute of the International Court of Justice on conditions to be determined in each case by the General Assembly upon the recommendation of the Security Council.

Article 94

1. Each Member of the United Nations undertakes to comply with the decision of the International Court of Justice in any case to which it is a party.

2. If any party to a case fails to perform the obligations incumbent upon it under a judgment rendered by the Court, the other party may have recourse to the Security Council, which may, if it deems necessary, make recommendations or decide upon measures to be taken to give effect to the judgment.

Article 95

Nothing in the present Charter shall prevent Members of the United Nations from entrusting the solution of their differences to other tribunals by virtue of agreements already in existence or which may be concluded in the future.

Article 96

1. The General Assembly or the Security Council may request the International Court of Justice to give an advisory opinion on any legal question.

2. Other organs of the United Nations and specialized agencies, which may at any time be so authorized by the General Assembly, may also request advisory opinions of the Court on legal questions arising within the scope of their activities.

Chapter XV

THE SECRETARIAT

Article 97

The Secretariat shall comprise a Secretary-General and such staff as the Organization may require. The Secretary-General shall be appointed by the General Assembly upon the recommendation of the Security Council. He shall be the chief administrative officer of the Organization.

Article 98

The Secretary-General shall act in that capacity in all meetings of the General Assembly, of the Security Council, of the Economic and Social Council, and of the Trusteeship Council, and shall perform such other functions as are entrusted to him by these organs. The Secretary-General shall make an annual report to the General Assembly on the work of the Organisation.

Article 99

The Secretary-General may bring to the attention of the Security Council any matter which in his opinion may threaten the maintenance of international peace and security.

Article 100

1. In the performance of their duties the Secretary-General and the staff shall not seek or receive instructions from any government or from any other authority external to the Organization. They shall refrain from any action which might reflect on their position as international officials responsible only to the Organization.

2. Each Member of the United Nations undertakes to respect the exclusively international character of the responsibilities of the Secretary-General and the staff and not to seek to influence them in the discharge of their responsibilities.

Article 101

1. The staff shall be appointed by the Secretary-General under regulations established by the General Assembly.

Chapter XVI

MISCELLANEOUS PROVISIONS

Article 102

1. Every treaty and every international agreement entered into by any Member of the United Nations after the present Charter comes into force shall as soon as possible be registered with the Secretariat and published by it.

2. No party to any such treaty or international agreement which has not been registered in accordance with the provisions of paragraph 1 of this Article may invoke that treaty or agreement before any organ of the United Nations.

Article 103

In the event of a conflict between the obligations of the Members of the United Nations under the present Charter and their obligations under any other international agreement, their obligations under the present Charter shall prevail.

Article 104

The Organization shall enjoy in the territory of each of its Members such legal capacity as may be necessary for the exercise of its functions and the fulfilment of its purposes.

Article 105

1. The Organization shall enjoy in the territory of each of its Members such privileges and immunities as are necessary for the fulfilment of its purposes.

2. Representatives of the Members of the United Nations and officials of the Organization shall similarly enjoy such privileges and immunities as are necessary for the independent exercise of their functions in connexion with the Organization.

3. The General Assembly may make recommendations with a view to determining the details of the appli-

cation of paragraphs 1 and 2 of this Article or may propose conventions to the Members of the United Nations for this purpose.

Chapter XVIII

AMENDMENTS

Article 108

Amendments to the present Charter shall come into force for all Members of the United Nations when they have been adopted by a vote of two-thirds of the members of the General Assembly and ratified in accordance with their respective constitutional processes by two-thirds of the Members of the United Nations, including all the permanent members of the Security Council.

Article 109[12]

1. A General Conference of the Members of the United Nations for the purpose of reviewing the present Charter may be held at a date and place to be fixed by a two-thirds vote of the members of the General Assembly and by a vote of any ten[13] members of the Security Council. Each Member of the United Nations shall have one vote in the conference.

2. Any alteration of the present Charter recommended by a two-thirds vote of the conference shall take effect when ratified in accordance with their respective constitutional processes by two-thirds of the Members of the United Nations including all the permanent members of the Security Council.

3. If such a conference has not been held before the tenth annual session of the General Assembly following the coming into force of the present Charter, the proposal to call such a conference shall be placed on the agenda of that session of the General Assembly, and the conference shall be held if so decided by a majority vote of the members of the General Assembly and by a vote of any seven members of the Security Council.

Chapter XIX

RATIFICATION AND SIGNATURE

Article 111

The present Charter, of which the Chinese, French, Russian, English, and Spanish texts are equally authentic, shall remain deposited in the archives of the Government of the United States of America. ...

STATUTE OF THE INTERNATIONAL COURT OF JUSTICE

Article 1

The International Court of Justice established by the Charter of the United Nations as the principal judicial organ of the United Nations shall be constituted and shall function in accordance with the provisions of the present Statute.

---

[12]   As amended in 1968.
[13]   Formerly seven.

Chapter 1

ORGANIZATION OF THE COURT

Article 2

The Court shall be composed of a body of independent judges, elected regardless of their nationality from among persons of high moral character, who possess the qualifications required in their respective countries for appointment to the highest judicial offices, or are jurisconsults of recognized competence in international law.

Article 3

1. The Court shall consist of fifteen members, no two of whom may be nationals of the same state.

2. A person who for the purposes of membership in the Court could be regarded as a national of more than one state shall be deemed to be a national of the one in which he ordinarily exercises civil and political rights.

Article 4

1. The members of the Court shall be elected by the General Assembly and by the Security Council from a list of persons nominated by the national groups in the Permanent Court of Arbitration, in accordance with the following provisions.

2. In the case of Members of the United Nations not represented in the Permanent Court of Arbitration, candidates shall be nominated by the national groups appointed for this purpose by their governments under the same conditions as those prescribed for members of the Permanent Court of Arbitration by Article 44 of the Convention of The Hague of 1907 for the pacific settlement of international disputes.

3. The conditions under which a state which is a party to the present Statute but is not a Member of the United Nations may participate in electing the members of the Court shall, in the absence of a special agreement, be laid down by the General Assembly upon recommendation of the Security Council.

Article 5

1. At least three months before the date of the election, the Secretary-General of the United Nations shall address a written request to the members of the Permanent Court of Arbitration belonging to the states which are parties to the present Statute, and to the members of the national groups appointed under Article 4, paragraph 2, inviting them to undertake, within a given time, by national groups, the nomination of persons in a position to accept the duties of a member of the Court.

2. No group may nominate more than four persons, not more than two of whom shall be of their own nationality. In no case may the number of candidates nominated by a group be more than double the number of seats to be filled.

Article 6

Before making these nominations, each national group is recommended to consult its highest court of justice, its legal faculties and schools of law, and its national academies and national sections of international academies devoted to the study of law.

Article 8

The General Assembly and the Security Council shall proceed independently of one another to elect the members of the Court.

Article 9

At every election, the electors shall bear in mind not only that the persons to be elected should individually possess the qualifications required, but also that in the body as a whole the representation of the main forms of civilization and of the principal legal systems of the world should be assured.

Article 10

1. Those candidates who obtain an absolute majority of votes in the General Assembly and in the Security Council shall be considered as elected.

2. Any vote of the Security Council, whether for the election of judges or for the appointment of members of the conference envisaged in Article 12, shall be taken without any distinction between permanent and non-permanent members of the Security Council.

3. In the event of more than one national of the same state obtaining an absolute majority of the votes both of the General Assembly and of the Security Council, the eldest of these only shall be considered as elected.

Article 11

If, after the first meeting held for the purpose of the election, one or more seats remain to be filled, a second and, if necessary, a third meeting shall take place.

Article 12

1. If, after the third meeting, one or more seats still remain unfilled, a joint conference consisting of six members, three appointed by the General Assembly and three by the Security Council, may be formed at any time at the request of either the General Assembly or the Security Council, for the purpose of choosing by the vote of an absolute majority one name for each seat still vacant, to submit to the General Assembly and the Security Council for their respective acceptance.

2. If the joint conference is unanimously agreed upon any person who fulfills the required conditions, he may be included in its list, even though he was not included in the list of nominations referred to in Article 7.

3. If the joint conference is satisfied that it will not be successful in procuring an election, those members of the Court who have already been elected shall, within a period to be fixed by the Security Council, proceed to fill the vacant seats by selection from among those candidates who have obtained votes either in the General Assembly or in the Security Council.

4. In the event of an equality of votes among the judges, the eldest judge shall have a casting vote.

Article 13

1. The members of the Court shall be elected for nine years and may be re-elected; provided, however, that of the judges elected at the first election, the terms of five judges shall expire at the end of three years and the terms of five more judges shall expire at the end of six years.

2. The judges whose terms are to expire at the end of above-mentioned initial periods of three and six years shall be chosen by lot to be drawn by the Secretary-General immediately after the first election has been completed.

3. The members of the Court shall continue to discharge their duties until their places have been filled. Though replaced, they shall finish any cases which they may have begun.

4. In the case of the resignation of a member of the Court, the resignation shall be addressed to the President of the Court for transmission to the Secretary-General. This last notification makes the place vacant.

Article 14

Vacancies shall be filled by the same method as that laid down for the first election, subject to the following provision: the Secretary-General shall, within one month of the occurrence of the vacancy, proceed to issue the invitations provided for in Article 5, and the date of the election shall be fixed by the Security Council.

Article 15

A member of the Court elected to replace a member whose term of office has not expired shall hold office for the remainder of his predecessor's term.

Article 16

1. No member of the Court may exercise any political or administrative function, or engage in any other occupation of a professional nature.

2. Any doubt on this point shall be settled by the decision of the Court.

Article 17

1. No member of the Court may act as agent, counsel, or advocate in any case.

2. No member may participate in the decision of any case in which he has previously taken part as agent, counsel, or advocate for one of the parties, or as a member of a national or international court, or of a commission of enquiry, or in any other capacity.

3. Any doubt on this point shall be settled by the decision of the Court.

Article 18

1. No member of the Court can be dismissed unless, in the unanimous opinion of the other members, he has ceased to fulfil the required conditions.

2. Formal notification thereof shall be made to the Secretary-General by the Registrar.

3. This notification makes the place vacant.

Article 19

The members of the Court, when engaged on the business of the Court, shall enjoy diplomatic privileges and immunities.

Article 21

1. The Court shall elect its President and Vice-President for three years; they may be re-elected. ...

Article 22

1. The seat of the Court shall be established at The Hague. This, however, shall not prevent the Court from sitting and exercising its functions elsewhere whenever the Court considers it desirable. ...

Article 23

1. The Court shall remain permanently in session, except during the judicial vacations, the dates and duration of which shall be fixed by the Court. ...

3. Members of the Court shall be bound, unless they are on leave or prevented from attending by illness or other serious reasons duly explained to the President, to hold themselves permanently at the disposal of the Court.

Article 24

1. If, for some special reason, a member of the Court considers that he should not take part in the decision of a particular case, he shall so inform the President.

2. If the President considers that for some special reason one of the members of the Court should not sit in a particular case, he shall give him notice accordingly.

3. If in any such case the member of the Court and the President disagree, the matter shall be settled by the decision of the Court.

Article 25

1. The full Court shall sit except when it is expressly provided otherwise in the present Statute.

2. Subject to the condition that the number of judges available to constitute the Court is not thereby reduced below eleven, the Rules of the Court may provide for allowing one or more judges, according to circumstances and in rotation, to be dispensed from sitting.

3. A quorum of nine judges shall suffice to constitute the Court.

Article 26

1. The Court may from time to time form one or more chambers, composed of three or more judges as the Court may determine, for dealing with particular categories of cases; for example, labour cases and cases relating to transit and communications.

2. The Court may at any time form a chamber for dealing with a particular case. The number of judges to constitute such a chamber shall be determined by the Court with the approval of the parties.

3. Cases shall be heard and determined by the chambers provided for in this Article if the parties so request.

Article 27

A judgment given by any of the chambers provided for in Articles 26 and 29 shall be considered as rendered by the Court.

Article 29

With a view to the speedy dispatch of business, the Court shall form annually a chamber composed of five judges which, at the request of the parties, may hear and determine cases by summary procedure. In addition, two judges shall be selected for the purpose of replacing judges who find it impossible to sit.

Article 31

1. Judges of the nationality of each of the parties shall retain their right to sit in the case before the Court.

2. If the Court includes upon the Bench a judge of the nationality of one of the parties, any other party may choose a person to sit as judge. Such person shall be chosen preferably from among those persons who have been nominated as candidates as provided in Articles 4 and 5.

3. If the Court includes upon the Bench no judge of the nationality of the parties, each of these parties may proceed to choose a judge as provided in paragraph 2 of this Article.

4. The provisions of this Article shall apply to the case of Articles 26 and 29. In such cases, the President shall request one or, if necessary, two of the members of the Court forming the chamber to give place to the members of the Court of the nationality of the parties concerned, and, failing such, or if they are unable to be present, to the judges specially chosen by the parties.

5. Should there be several parties in the same interest, they shall, for the purpose of the preceding provisions, be reckoned as one party only. Any doubt upon this point shall be settled by the decision of the Court.

6. Judges chosen as laid down in paragraphs 2, 3, and 4 of this Article shall fulfil the conditions required by Articles 2, 17 (paragraph 2), 20, and 24 of the present Statute. They shall take part in the decision on terms of complete equality with their colleagues.

Article 33

The expenses of the Court shall be borne by the United Nations in such a manner as shall be decided by the General Assembly.

Chapter 2

COMPETENCE OF THE COURT

Article 34

1. Only states may be parties in cases before the Court.

2. The Court, subject to and in conformity with its Rules, may request of public international organisations information relevant to cases before it, and shall receive such information presented by such organisations on their own initiative.

3. Whenever the construction of the constituent instrument of a public international organisation or of an international convention adopted thereunder is in question in a case before the Court, the Registrar shall so notify the public international organisation concerned and shall communicate to it copies of all the written proceedings.

Article 35

1. The Court shall be open to the states parties to the present Statute.

2. The conditions under which the Court shall be open to other states shall, subject to the special provisions contained in treaties in force, be laid down by the Security Council, but in no case shall such conditions place the parties in a position of inequality before the Court.

3. When a state which is not a Member of the United Nations is a party to a case, the Court shall fix the amount which that party is to contribute towards the expenses of the Court. This provision shall not apply if such state is bearing a share of the expenses of the Court.

Article 36

1. The jurisdiction of the Court comprises all cases which the parties refer to it and all matters specially provided for in the Charter of the United Nations or in treaties and conventions in force.

2. The states parties to the present Statute may at any time declare that they recognise as compulsory *ipso facto* and without special agreement, in relation to any other states accepting the same obligation, the jurisdiction of the Court in all legal disputes concerning:

a.   the interpretation of a treaty;

b.   any question of international law;

c.   the existence of any fact which, if established, would constitute a breach of an international obligation;

d.   the nature or extent of the reparation to be made for the breach of an international obligation.

3. The declarations referred to above may be made unconditionally or on condition of reciprocity on the part of several or certain states, or for a certain time.

4. Such declarations shall be deposited with the Secretary-General of the United Nations, who shall transmit copies thereof to the parties to the Statute and to the Registrar of the Court.

5. Declarations made under Article 36 of the Statute of the Permanent Court of International Justice and which are still in force shall be deemed, as between the parties to the present Statute, to be acceptance of the compulsory jurisdiction of the International Court of Justice for the period which they still have to run and in accordance with their terms.

6. In the event of a dispute as to whether the Court has jurisdiction, the matter shall be settled by the decision of the Court.

Article 37

Whenever a treaty or convention in force provides for reference of a matter to a tribunal to have been instituted by the League of Nations, or to the Permanent Court of International Justice, the matter shall, as between the parties to the present Statute, be referred to the International Court of Justice.

Article 38

1. The Court, whose function is to decide in accordance with international law such disputes as are submitted to it, shall apply:

a. international conventions, whether general or particular, establishing rules expressly recognised by the contesting states;

b. international custom, as evidence of a general practice accepted as law;

c. the general principles of law recognised by civilised nations;

d. subject to the provisions of Article 59, judicial decisions and the teachings of the most highly qualified publicists of the various nations, as subsidiary means for the determination of rules of law.

2. This provision shall not prejudice the power of the Court to decide a case *ex aequo et bono*, if the parties agree thereon.

Chapter 3

PROCEDURE

Article 39

1. The official languages of the Court shall be French and English. If the parties agree that the case shall be conducted in French, the judgment shall be delivered in French. If the parties agree that the case shall be conducted in English, the judgment shall be delivered in English.

2. In the absence of an agreement as to which language shall be employed each party may, in the pleadings, use the language which it prefers; the decision of the Court shall be given in French and English. In this case the Court shall at the same time determine which of the two texts shall be considered as authoritative.

3. The Court shall, at the request of any party, authorise a language other than French or English to be used by that party.

Article 40

1. Cases are brought before the Court, as the case may be, either by the notification of the special agreement or by a written application addressed to the Registrar. In either case the subject of the dispute and the parties shall be indicated.

2. The Registrar shall forthwith communicate the application to all concerned.

3. He shall also notify the Members of the United Nations through the Secretary-General, and also any other states entitled to appear before the Court.

Article 41

1. The Court shall have the power to indicate, if it considers that circumstances so require, any provisional measures which ought to be taken to preserve the respective rights of either party.

2. Pending the final decision, notice of the measures suggested shall forthwith be given to the parties and to the Security Council.

Article 53

1. Whenever one of the parties does not appear before the Court, or fails to defend its case, the other party may call upon the Court to decide in favour of its claim.

2. The Court must, before doing so, satisfy itself, not only that it has jurisdiction in accordance with Articles 36 and 37, but also that the claim is well founded in fact and law.

Article 55

1. All questions shall be decided by a majority of the judges present.

2. In the event of an equality of votes, the President or the judge who acts in his place shall have a casting vote.

Article 56

1. The judgment shall state the reasons on which it is based.

2. It shall contain the names of the judges who have taken part in the decision.

Article 57

If the judgment does not represent in whole or in part the unanimous opinion of the judges, any judge shall be entitled to deliver a separate opinion.

Article 59

The decision of the Court has no binding force except between the parties and in respect of that particular case.

Article 60

The judgment is final and without appeal. In the event of dispute as to the meaning or scope of the judgment, the Court shall construe it upon the request of any party.

Article 61

1. An application for revision of a judgment may be made only when it is based upon the discovery of some fact of such a nature as to be a decisive factor, which fact was, when the judgment was given, unknown to the Court and also to the party claiming revision, always provided that such ignorance was not due to negligence. ...

Article 62

1. Should a state consider that it has an interest of a legal nature which may be affected by the decision in the case, it may submit a request to the Court to be permitted to intervene.

2. It shall be for the Court to decide upon this request.

Article 63

1. Whenever the construction of a convention to which states other than those concerned in the case are parties is in question, the Registrar shall notify all such states forthwith.

2. Every state so notified has the right to intervene in the proceedings; but if it uses this right, the construction given by the judgment will be equally binding upon it.

Article 64

Unless otherwise decided by the Court, each party shall bear its own costs.

Chapter 4

ADVISORY OPINIONS

Article 65

1. The Court may give an advisory opinion on any legal question at the request of whatever body may be authorised by or in accordance with the Charter of the United Nations to make such a request.

2. Questions upon which the advisory opinion of the Court is asked shall be laid before the Court by means of a written request containing an exact statement of the question upon which an opinion is required, and accompanied by all documents likely to throw light upon the question.

Article 66

1. The Registrar shall forthwith give notice of the request for an advisory opinion to all states entitled to appear before the Court.

2. The Registrar shall also, by means of a special and direct communication, notify any state entitled to appear before the Court or international organisation considered by the Court, or, should it not be sitting, by the President, as likely to be able to furnish information on the question, that the Court will be prepared to receive, within a time limit to be fixed by the President, written statements, or to hear, at a public sitting to be held for the purpose, oral statements relating to the question.

3. Should any such state entitled to appear before the Court have failed to receive the special communication referred to in paragraph 2 of this Article, such state may express a desire to submit a written statement or to be heard; and the Court will decide.

4. States and organisations having presented written or oral statement or both shall be permitted to comment on the statements made by other states or organisations in the form, to the extent, and within the time limits which the Court, or, should it not be sitting, the President, shall decide in each particular case. Accordingly, the Registrar shall in due time communicate any such written statements to states and organisations having submitted similar statements.

Article 67

The Court shall deliver its advisory opinion in open court, notice having been given to the Secretary-General and to the representatives of Members of the United Nations, of other states and of international organisations immediately concerned.

Article 68

In the exercise of its advisory functions the Court shall further be guided by the provisions of the present Statute which apply in contentious cases to the extent to which it recognises them to be applicable.

APPENDIX II

MEMBERS OF THE UNITED NATIONS

There are 192 members. The date indicates the year of admission; no date is given for the 51 original members.

Afghanistan (1946)
Albania (1955)
Algeria (1962)
Andorra (1993)
Angola (1976)
Antigua and Barbuda (1981)
Argentina
Armenia (1992)
Australia
Austria (1955)
Azerbaijan (1992)
Bahamas (1973)
Bahrain (1971)
Bangladesh (1974)
Barbados (1966)
Belarus (formerly Byelorussian
  SSR)
Belgium
Belize (1981)
Benin (formerly Dahomey) (1960)
Bhutan (1971)
Bolivia
Bosnia and Herzegovina (1992)
Botswana (1966)
Brazil
Brunei Darussalam (1984)
Bulgaria (1955)
Burkino Faso (formerly Upper
  Volta) (1960)
Burundi (1962)
Cambodia (1955)
Cameroon (1960)
Canada
Cape Verde (1975)
Central African Republic (1960)
Chad (1960)
Chile
China[1]
Colombia

Comoros (1975)
Congo (1960)
Congo, Democratic Republic of
  (formerly Zaire) (1960)
Costa Rica
Côte D'Ivoire (1960)
Croatia (1992)
Cuba
Cyprus (1960)
Czech Rep. (1993)[2]
Denmark
Djibouti (1977)
Dominica (1978)
Dominican Republic
Ecuador
Egypt[3]
El Salvador
Equatorial Guinea (1968)
Eritrea (1993)
Estonia (1991)
Ethiopia
Fiji (1970)
Finland (1955)
France
Gabon (1960)
Gambia (1965)
Georgia (1992)
Germany (1973)[4]
Ghana (1957)
Greece
Grenada (1974)
Guatemala
Guinea (1958)
Guinea-Bissau (1974)
Guyana (1966)
Haiti
Honduras
Hungary (1955)
Iceland (1946)

India
Indonesia (1950)
Iran
Iraq
Ireland (1955)
Israel (1949)
Italy (1955)
Jamaica (1962)
Japan (1956)
Jordan (1955)
Kazakhstan (1992)
Kenya (1963)
Kiribati (1999)
Korea, Democratic People's
  Republic (1991)
Korea, Republic of (1991)
Kuwait (1963)
Kyrgyzstan (1992)
Lao People's Democratic Republic
  (1955)
Latvia (1991)
Lebanon
Lesotho (1966)
Liberia
Libyan Arab Jamahiriya (1955)
Liechtenstein (1990)
Lithuania (1991)
Luxembourg
Macedonia, Former Yugoslav
  Republic of (1993)
Madagascar (1960)
Malawi (1964)
Malaysia (1957)[5]
Maldives (1965)
Mali (1960)
Malta (1964)
Marshall Islands (1990)
Mauritania (1961)
Mauritius (1968)

Mexico
Micronesia, Federated States of
    (1991)
Moldova, Rep. of (1992)
Monaco (1993)
Mongolia (1961)
Montenegro (2006)
Morocco (1956)
Mozambique (1975)
Myanmar (formerly Burma) (1948)
Namibia (1990)
Nauru (1999)
Nepal (1955)
Netherlands
New Zealand
Nicaragua
Niger (1960)
Nigeria (1960)
Norway
Oman (1971)
Pakistan (1947)
Palau (1994)
Panama
Papua New Guinea (1975)
Paraguay
Peru
Philippines
Poland

Portugal (1955)
Qatar (1971)
Romania (1955)
Russian Federation
Rwanda (1962)
Samoa (1976)
San Marino (1992)
Sao Tomé and Principe (1975)
Saudi Arabia
Senegal (1960)
Serbia (2000)[6]
Seychelles (1976)
Sierra Leone (1961)
Singapore (1965)[7]
Slovakia (1993)
Slovenia (1992)
Solomon Is (1978)
Somalia (1960)
South Africa
Spain (1955)
Sri Lanka (1955)
St Kitts and Nevis (1983)
St Lucia (1979)
St Vincent and the Grenadines
    (1980)
Sudan (1956)
Suriname (1975)
Swazilland (1963)

Sweden (1946)
Switzerland (2002)
Syria (1945)[8]
Tajikistan (1992)
Thailand (1946)
Timor-Leste (2002)
Togo (1960)
Tonga (1999)
Trinidad and Tobago (1962)
Tunisia (1956)
Turkey
Turkmenistan (1992)
Tuvalu (2000)
Uganda (1962)
Ukraine (formerly Ukranian SSR)
United Arab Emirates (1971)
United Kingdom
United Republic of Tanzania
    (1961)[9]
United States
Uruguay
Uzbekistan (1992)
Vanuatu (1981)
Venezuela
Viet Nam (1977)
Yemen (1947)[10]
Zambia (1964)
Zimbabwe (1980)

---

[1] Following the 1949 revolution in China, the defeated Chiang Kai-shek Government, which had withdrawn to Taiwan, continued to be recognised as the Government of China in the UN. By resolution 2758 (XXVI) of October 25, 1971, the General Assembly decided "to restore all its rights to the People's Republic of China and to recognize the representatives of its Government as the only legitimate representatives of China to the United Nations, and to expel forthwith the representatives of Chiang Kai-shek from the place they unlawfully occupy at the United Nations and in all the organizations related to it".

[2] Czechoslovakia was an original UN member. When the Czech Republic and Slovakia separated by mutual agreement in 1993, they were each admitted to the UN.

[3] In 1958, Egypt and Syria united as the one state of the United Arab Republic, which replaced its predecessors as a single UN member. In 1961, Egypt and Syria resumed their separate membership when the union was dissolved.

[4] In 1990, the German Democratic Republic, a UN member (1973), united with the Federal Republic of Germany.

[5] The Federation of Malaya (1957) changed its name to Malaysia in 1963, when Singapore and other territories joined. Singapore became an independent state and UN member, both in 1964.

[6] Yugoslavia was an original UN member. On its replacement by Bosnia and Herzegovina, Croatia, the Former Yugoslav Republic of Macedonia, Montenegro, Serbia and Slovenia, all now UN members, see above, p.117.

[7] See n.5 above.

[8] See n.3 above.

[9] Tanganyika (1961) and Zanzibar (1963) were UN members. They united as the United Republic of Tanzania and became a single UN member, both in 1964.

[10] Yemen (1947) and Democratic Yemen (1967) were UN members. They united to become the Republic of Yemen and a single UN member, both in 1990.

APPENDIX III

GENERAL ASSEMBLY DECLARATION ON PRINCIPLES OF INTERNATIONAL LAW CONCERNING FRIENDLY RELATIONS AND CO-OPERATION AMONG STATES IN ACCORDANCE WITH THE CHARTER OF THE UNITED NATIONS 1970[1]

The General Assembly ...

1. *Solemnly proclaims* the following principles:

The principle that States shall refrain in their international relations from the threat or use of force against the territorial integrity or political independence of any State, or in any other manner inconsistent with the purposes of the United Nations.

Every State has the duty to refrain in its international relations from the threat or use of force against the territorial integrity or political independence of any State, or in any other manner inconsistent with the purposes of the United Nations. Such a threat or use of force constitutes a violation of international law and the Charter of the United Nations and shall never be employed as a means of settling international issues.

A war of aggression constitutes a crime against the peace for which there is responsibility under international law.

In accordance with the purposes and principles of the United Nations, States have the duty to refrain from propaganda for wars of aggression.

Every State has the duty to refrain from the threat or use of force to violate the existing international boundaries of another State or as a means of solving international disputes, including territorial disputes and problems concerning frontiers of States.

Every State likewise has the duty to refrain from the threat or use of force to violate international lines of demarcation, such as armistice lines, established by or pursuant to an international agreement to which it is a party or which it is otherwise bound to respect. Nothing in the foregoing shall be construed as prejudicing the positions of the parties concerned with regard to the status and effects of such lines under their special régimes or as affecting their temporary character.

States have a duty to refrain from acts of reprisal involving the use of force.

Every State has the duty to refrain from any forcible action which deprives peoples referred to in the elaboration of the principle of equal rights and self-determination of their right to self-determination and freedom and independence.

Every State has the duty to refrain from organising or encouraging the organisation of irregular forces or armed bands, including mercenaries, for incursion into the territory of another State.

Every State has the duty to refrain from organising, instigating, assisting or participating in acts of civil strife or terrorist acts in another State or acquiescing in organised activities within its territory directed towards the commission of such acts, when the acts referred to in the present paragraph involve a threat or use of force.

The territory of a State shall not be the object of military occupation resulting from the use of force in contravention of the provisions of the Charter. The territory of a State shall not be the object of acquisition by

---

[1]   G.A. Resn 2625 (XXV), October 24, 1970. The resolution was adopted by the General Assembly without a vote.

another State resulting from the threat or use of force. No territorial acquisition resulting from the threat or use of force shall be recognised as legal. Nothing in the foregoing shall be construed as affecting:

(a) Provisions of the Charter or any international agreement prior to the Charter régime and valid under international law; or

(b) The powers of the Security Council under the Charter.

All States shall pursue in good faith negotiations for the early conclusion of a universal treaty on general and complete disarmament under effective international control and strive to adopt appropriate measures to reduce international tensions and strengthen confidence among States.

All States shall comply in good faith with their obligations under the generally recognised principles and rules of international law with respect to the maintenance of international peace and security, and shall endeavour to make the United Nations security system based upon the Charter more effective.

Nothing in the foregoing paragraphs shall be construed as enlarging or diminishing in any way the scope of the provisions of the Charter concerning cases in which the use of force is lawful.

The principle that States shall settle their international disputes by
peaceful means in such a manner that international peace
and security and justice are not endangered

Every State shall settle its international disputes with other States by peaceful means, in such a manner that international peace and security, and justice, are not endangered.

Every State shall accordingly seek early and just settlement of their international disputes by negotiation, inquiry, mediation, conciliation, arbitration, judicial settlement, resort to regional agencies or arrangements or other peaceful means of their choice. In seeking such a settlement, the parties shall agree upon such peaceful means as may be appropriate to the circumstances and nature of the dispute.

The parties to a dispute have the duty, in the event of failure to reach a solution by any one of the above peaceful means, to continue to seek a settlement of the dispute by other peaceful means agreed upon by them.

States parties to an international dispute, as well as other States, shall refrain from any action which may aggravate the situation so as to endanger the maintenance of international peace and security, and shall act in accordance with the purposes and principles of the United Nations.

International disputes shall be settled on the basis of the sovereign equality of States and in accordance with the principle of free choice of means. Recourse to, or acceptance of, a settlement procedure freely agreed to by States with regard to existing or future disputes to which they are parties shall not be regarded as incompatible with sovereign equality.

Nothing in the foregoing paragraphs prejudices or derogates from the applicable provisions of the Charter, in particular those relating to the pacific settlement of international disputes.

The principle concerning the duty not to intervene in matters within the domestic
jurisdiction of any State, in accordance with the Charter

No State or group of States has the right to intervene, directly or indirectly, for any reason whatever, in the internal or external affairs of any other State. Consequently, armed intervention and all other forms of interference or attempted threats against the personality of the State or against its political, economic and cultural elements, are in violation of international law.

No State may use or encourage the use of economic, political or any other type of measures to coerce another State in order to obtain from it the subordination of the exercise of its sovereign rights and to secure from it advantages of any kind. Also, no State shall organise, assist, foment, finance, incite or tolerate subversive, terrorist or armed activities directed towards the violent overthrow of the régime of another State, or interfere in civil strife in another State.

The use of force to deprive peoples of their national identity constitutes a violation of their inalienable rights and of the principle of non-intervention.

Every State has an inalienable right to choose its political, economic, social and cultural systems, without interference in any form by another State.

Nothing in the foregoing paragraphs shall be construed as affecting the relevant provisions of the Charter relating to the maintenance of international peace and security.

The duty of States to co-operate with one another in accordance
with the Charter

States have the duty to co-operate with one another, irrespective of the differences in their political, economic and social systems, in the various spheres of international relations, in order to maintain international peace and security and to promote international economic stability and progress, the general welfare of nations and international co-operation free from discrimination based on such differences.

To this end:

(a) States shall co-operate with other States in the maintenance of international peace and security;

(b) States shall co-operate in the promotion of universal respect for and observance of human rights and fundamental freedoms for all, and in the elimination of all forms of racial discrimination and all forms of religious intolerance;

(c) States shall conduct their international relations in the economic, social, cultural, technical and trade fields in accordance with the principles of sovereign equality and non-intervention;

(d) States Members of the United Nations have the duty to take joint and separate action in co-operation with the United Nations in accordance with the relevant provisions of the Charter.

States should co-operate in the economic, social and cultural fields as well as in the field of science and technology and for the promotion of international cultural and educational progress. States should co-operate in the promotion of economic growth throughout the world, especially that of the developing countries.

The principle of equal rights and self-determination of peoples

By virtue of the principle of equal rights and self-determination of peoples enshrined in the Charter, all peoples have the right freely to determine, without external interference, their political status and to pursue their economic, social and cultural development, and every State has the duty to respect this right in accordance with the provisions of the Charter.

Every State has the duty to promote, through joint and separate action, the realisation of the principle of equal rights and self-determination of peoples, in accordance with the provisions of the Charter, and to render assistance to the United Nations in carrying out the responsibilities entrusted to it by the Charter regarding the implementation of the principle in order:

(a) To promote friendly relations and co-operation among States; and

(b) To bring a speedy end to colonialism, having regard to the freely expressed will of the peoples concerned;

and bearing in mind that subjection of peoples to alien subjugation, domination and exploitation constitutes a violation of the principle, as well as a denial of fundamental human rights, and is contrary to the Charter of the United Nations.

Every State has the duty to promote through joint and separate action universal respect for the observance of human rights and fundamental freedoms in accordance with the Charter.

The establishment of a sovereign and independent State, the free association or integration with an independent State or the emergence into any other political status freely determined by a people constitute modes of implementing the right of self-determination by that people.

Every State has the duty to refrain from any forcible action which deprives peoples referred to above in the elaboration of the present principle of their right to self-determination and freedom and independence. In their actions against and resistance to such forcible action in pursuit of the exercise of their right to self-determination, such peoples are entitled to seek and to receive support in accordance with the purposes and principles of the Charter of the United Nations.

The territory of a colony or other non-governing territory has, under the Charter of the United Nations, a status separate and distinct from the territory of the State administering it; and such separate and distinct status under the Charter shall exist until the people of the colony or non-self-governing territory have exercised their right of self-determination in accordance with the Charter, and particularly its purposes and principles.

Nothing in the foregoing paragraphs shall be construed as authorizing or encouraging any action which would dismember or impair, totally or in part, the territorial integrity or political unity of sovereign and independent States conducting themselves in compliance with the principle of equal rights and self-determination of peoples as described above and thus possessed of a government representing the whole people belonging to the territory without distinction as to race, creed or colour.

Every State shall refrain from any action aimed at the partial or total disruption of the national unity and territorial integrity of any other State or country.

The principle of sovereign equality of States

All States enjoy sovereign equality. They have equal rights and duties and are equal members of the international community, notwithstanding differences of an economic, social political or other nature.

In particular, sovereign equality includes the following elements:

(a) States are juridically equal;

(b) Each State enjoys the rights inherent in full sovereignty;

(c) Each State has the duty to respect the personality of other States;

(d) The territorial integrity and political independence of the State are inviolable;

(e) Each State has the right freely to choose and develop its political, social, economic and cultural systems;

(f) Each State has the duty to comply fully and in good faith with its international obligations and to live in peace with other States.

The principle that States shall fulfil in good faith the obligations assumed by them in accordance with the Charter

Every State has the duty to fulfil in good faith the obligations assumed by it in accordance with the Charter of the United Nations.

Every State has the duty to fulfil in good faith its obligations under the generally recognized principles and rules of international law.

Every State has the duty to fulfil in good faith its obligations under international agreements valid under the generally recognized principles and rules of international law.

Where obligations arising under international agreements are in conflict with the obligations of Members of the United Nations under the Charter of the United Nations, the obligations under the Charter shall prevail.

2. *Declares* that:

In their interpretation and application the above principles are interrelated and each principle should be construed in the context of the other principles.

Nothing in this Declaration shall be construed as prejudicing in any manner the provisions of the Charter or the rights and duties of Member States under the Charter or the rights of peoples under the Charter taking into account the elaboration of these rights in this Declaration.

3. *Declares further* that:

The principles of the Charter which are embodied in this Declaration constitute basic principles of international law, and consequently appeals to all States to be guided by these principles in their international conduct and to develop their mutual relations on the basis of their strict observance.

INDEX